LET'S GO

■ PAGES PACKED WITH ESSENTIAL INFORMATION

"Value-packed, unbeatable, accurate, and comprehensive."

—*The Los Angeles Times*

"The guides are aimed not only at young budget travelers but at the independent traveler; a sort of streetwise cookbook for traveling alone."

—*The New York Times*

"Unbeatable; good sight-seeing advice; up-to-date info on restaurants, hotels, and inns; a commitment to money-saving travel; and a wry style that brightens nearly every page."

—*The Washington Post*

■ THE BEST TRAVEL BARGAINS IN YOUR BUDGET

"All the dirt, dirt cheap."

—*People*

"Let's Go follows the creed that you don't have to toss your life's savings to the wind to travel—unless you want to."

—*The Salt Lake Tribune*

■ REAL ADVICE FOR REAL EXPERIENCES

"The writers seem to have experienced every rooster-packed bus and lunar-surfaced mattress about which they write."

—*The New York Times*

"[Let's Go's] devoted updaters really walk the walk (and thumb the ride, and trek the trail). Learn how to fish, haggle, find work—anywhere."

—*Food & Wine*

"A world-wise traveling companion—always ready with friendly advice and helpful hints, all sprinkled with a bit of wit."

—*The Philadelphia Inquirer*

■ A GUIDE WITH A SPIRIT AND A SOCIAL CONSCIENCE

"Lighthearted and sophisticated, informative and fun to read. [Let's Go] helps the novice traveler navigate like a knowledgeable old hand."

—*Atlanta Journal-Constitution*

"The serious mission at the book's core reveals itself in exhortations to respect the culture and the environment—and, if possible, to visit as a volunteer, a student, or a teacher rather than a tourist."

—*San Francisco Chronicle*

LET'S GO PUBLICATIONS

TRAVEL GUIDES

Australia 9th edition
Austria & Switzerland 12th edition
Brazil 1st edition
Britain 2008
California 10th edition
Central America 9th edition
Chile 2nd edition
China 5th edition
Costa Rica 3rd edition
Eastern Europe 13th edition
Ecuador 1st edition
Egypt 2nd edition
Europe 2008
France 2008
Germany 13th edition
Greece 9th edition
Hawaii 4th edition
India & Nepal 8th edition
Ireland 13th edition
Israel 4th edition
Italy 2008
Japan 1st edition
Mexico 22nd edition
New Zealand 8th edition
Peru 1st edition
Puerto Rico 3rd edition
Southeast Asia 9th edition
Spain & Portugal 2008
Thailand 3rd edition
USA 24th edition
Vietnam 2nd edition
Western Europe 2008

ROADTRIP GUIDE

Roadtripping USA 2nd edition

ADVENTURE GUIDES

Alaska 1st edition
Pacific Northwest 1st edition
Southwest USA 3rd edition

CITY GUIDES

Amsterdam 5th edition
Barcelona 3rd edition
Boston 4th edition
London 16th edition
New York City 16th edition
Paris 14th edition
Rome 12th edition
San Francisco 4th edition
Washington, D.C. 13th edition

POCKET CITY GUIDES

Amsterdam
Berlin
Boston
Chicago
London
New York City
Paris
San Francisco
Venice
Washington, D.C.

LET'S GO

GREECE

MEGHAN C. JOYCE EDITOR
JAKE A. FOLEY ASSOCIATE EDITOR

RESEARCHER-WRITERS
MICHELLE BURFORD
DAN GURNEY
CHARLES FISHER-POST
ANDREA JONAS
JOANNE LEE
ANDRES SCHABELMAN

JOY DING MAP EDITOR
JULIE VODHANEL MANAGING EDITOR

ST. MARTIN'S PRESS ❧ NEW YORK

Maps by David Lindroth copyright © 2008 by St. Martin's Press.

Distributed outside the USA and Canada by Macmillan.

ISBN-13: 978-0-312-37450-1
ISBN-10: 0-312-37450-X
Ninth edition
10 9 8 7 6 5 4 3 2 1

Let's Go: Greece is written by Let's Go Publications, 67 Mount Auburn St., Cambridge, MA 02138, USA.

CONTENTS

HOW TO USE THIS BOOK

COVERAGE LAYOUT. *Let's Go: Greece* begins in **Athens,** the heart of the country and a natural jumping off point. From there, coverage extends into the **Peloponnese,** up through mountainous **Central Greece,** and into the remote expanse of **Northern Greece.** Departing from the mainland, we embark on a tour of Greece's legendary islands, starting with the **Saronic Gulf Islands, Evia,** and the **Sporades,** then continuing into the Aegean sea to the **Cyclades, Dodecanese,** and **Northeast Aegean Islands.** We then head west to the **Ionian Islands,** ending with a trip south to **Crete.** The **suggested itineraries** at the beginning of each chapter point to the best sports in each region and can help structure either a long or short trip.

TRANSPORTATION INFO. For connecting between destinations, info is listed under the Transportation section of the departure city. Parentheticals usually provide the trip duration, frequency, and price, which is for one-way trips unless otherwise stated. For general info on travel, consult the **Essentials** chapter (p. 8).

NON-COVERAGE SECTIONS. Before departing, consult the **Discover Greece** chapter (p. 1) for recommendations on when to go and check out country-wide suggested itineraries (p. 4). Logistical and practical questions are answered in the **Essentials** chapter (p. 8), and the **Life and Times** chapter (p. 50) gives an overview of Greek history, culture, and customs. **Beyond Tourism** (p. 76) suggests volunteer, study abroad, and temporary work opportunities to enrich your travel experience. The **Appendix** (p. 622) lists Greek phrases, pronunciations, and other quick and helpful reference info.

SCHOLARLY ARTICLES. At the end of Life and Times, **Gregory A. Maniatis** examines the presence of Greek culture outside of Greece, and then looks into its influence on the country itself (p. 3). After the Beyond Tourism chapter, Harvard Classics department graduate and former *Let's Go* editor **Leanna Boychenko** shares her experiences on an archaeological dig in Athens (p. 5).

PRICE DIVERSITY. Our researchers list establishments in order of value from best to worst, denoting their absolute favorites with the *Let's Go* thumbs-up (✍). Since the cheapest price does not always mean the best value, we have incorporated a system of price ranges for accommodations and food listings (p. XVI).

LANGUAGE AND OTHER QUIRKS. The Greek name of each city and town is printed after its English name. Transliterations give syllabic pronunciation, with the stressed syllables capitalized. For a guide to the Greek alphabet, see the **Appendix** (p. 622).

A NOTE TO OUR READERS. The information for this book was gathered by *Let's Go* researchers from May through August of 2007. Each listing is based on one researcher's opinion, formed during his or her visit at a particular time. Those traveling at other times may have different experiences since prices, dates, hours, and conditions are always subject to change. You are urged to check the facts presented in this book beforehand to avoid inconvenience and surprises.

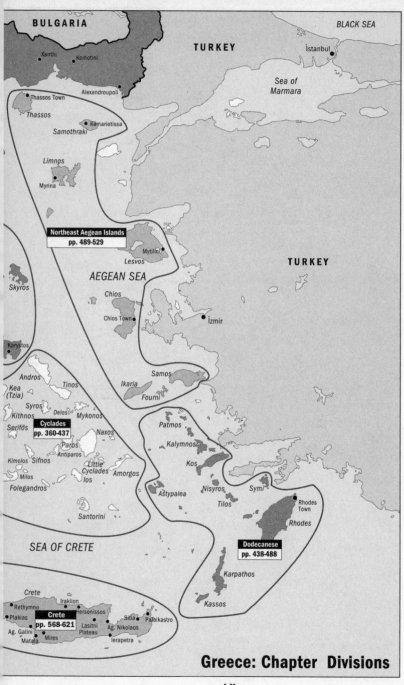

BULGARIA

BLACK SEA

Xanthi Komotini

TURKEY

İstanbul

Sea of
Marmara

Alexandroupoli

Thassos Town

Thassos

Kamariotissa

Samothraki

Limnos

Myrina

Northeast Aegean Islands
pp. 489-529

Mytilini

Lesvos

TURKEY

AEGEAN SEA

Skyros

Chios

Chios Town

İzmir

Karystos

Andros

Tinos

Samos

*Kea
(Tzia)*

Ikaria

Syros *Delos* Mykonos

Fourni

Kithnos

Patmos

Serifos

Cyclades
pp. 360-437

Naxos

Kalymnos

Paros

Antiparos

Kos

Kimolos *Sifnos*

*Little
Cyclades*

Amorgos

Milos

Ios

Nisyros *Symi*

Folegandros

Astypalea

Tilos

Rhodes
Town

Santorini

Rhodes

SEA OF CRETE

Dodecanese
pp. 438-488

Karpathos

Crete

Iraklion

Rethymno

Hersonissos

Kassos

Plakias

Crete
pp. 568-621

Sitia Palaikastro

Lasitni
Plateau

Ag. Nikolaos

Ag. Galini

Ierapetra

Matala Mires

Greece: Chapter Divisions

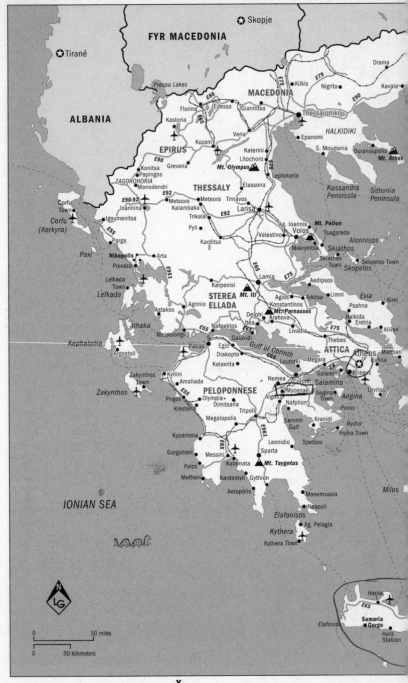

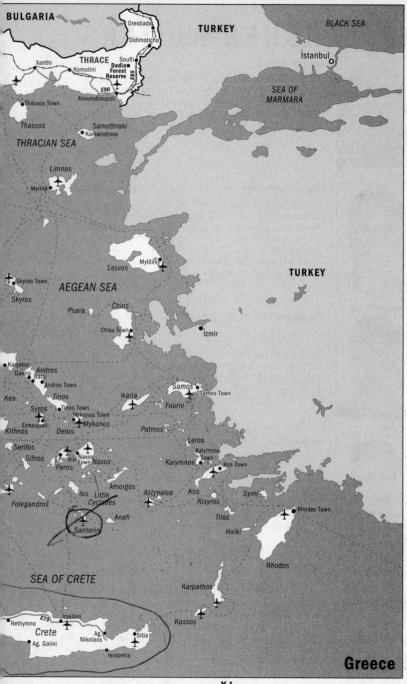

Greece

RESEARCHER-WRITERS

Michelle Burford *Athens and the Cyclades*

Hailing from Harlem, NY, Michelle traded one big city for another as she tore up the streets and sights of Athens. She never failed to sample cocktails at each nightlife hot spot, even if it meant sacrificing her braids to the humidity. A founding editor of *O*, the Oprah Magazine, Michelle used her experience to craft witty and honest reviews.

Charles Fisher-Post *The Peloponnese and the Ionian Islands*

Armed with a three-word Greek vocabulary (*dromos*, *efkaristo*, and *signome*) and three weeks of Boy Scout training, Charles faced the uncertainties of ferry transportation with uncommon patience. Creative and independent, he left no cave unexplored and no trail untrodden. Continuing his personal travel odyssey, he'll spend the 2007-2008 school year studying in Ghana and Granada, Spain.

Dan Gurney *Athens, Evia and the Sporades, Central Greece, the Peloponnese, and the Cyclades*

As if being the National Champion on the Button Accordion and Founder of the Harvard Foosball Club weren't enough, Dan added Intrepid Researcher to his list of well-earned titles. Aside from maintaining a photo blog and composing love songs for his devastatingly attractive editors, Dan managed to add new coverage to both the book and his face—he grew a serious beard.

Andrea Jonas *The Dodecanese, Northeast Aegean, and Saronic Gulf*

Andrea deftly traversed over 20 islands, sampling gyros and getting the lowdown on local life. A chemistry and physics major, she certainly was in her element (!) as she charmed domatia owners and travel agents, even scoring a free trip to Turkey. Andrea earned the title of Team Greece's resident ferry expert as she effortlessly powered through three island chains, leaving thumbpicks in her wake.

Joanne Lee *Crete and the Cyclades*

Having survived creepy advances from a one-toothed domatia neighbor and countless *raki* hangovers, Joanne came to consider Crete a second home. She earned a spot in her editors' hearts by showering them with gifts of *halvadopita* and a "Somebody who loves me sent me this shirt from Crete" T-shirt. She'll continue her philanthropy in Zambia working for the Clinton Foundation.

Andres Schabelman *Northern and Central Greece*

Unbearably good-looking and shamelessly flirtatious, Andres had no qualms about sacrificing his body for Let's Go. The only things he loves more than exploring the world are the number 12, spicy food, and vinegar. Andres brought the New Orleans flavor to Northern and Central Greece as he entertained his editors with uncensored anecdotes, loving nicknames, and a fresh perspective.

CONTRIBUTING WRITERS

Leanna Boychenko majored in Classics at Harvard College. She was the Associate Editor of *Let's Go: Greece 2005* and the Editor of *Let's Go: New Zealand 2006*.

Gregory A. Maniatis is the founder of *Odyssey Magazine*, an international magazine about Greece and Greeks around the world.

ACKNOWLEDGMENTS

LET'S GO

TEAM GREECE THANKS: Our RWs for gracefully conquering Greece for the gazillionth time. Julie for showering us with sweets and support. Joy for being a delight, and for writing us cute notes. Mon$y Pod for blazin' sweet jams, breaking for youtube, and providing a work environment completely devoid of productivity. Team Britain for a perpetual, puntastic pod-party. The countless Georges, Nicks, and Dimitris who helped our RWs along the way.

MEGHAN THANKS: My family for being wonderful and supportive, as always. Mon$y Pod for Grendel's Wednesdays and Mix 98.5. Jake for speaking Greek and being lovingly cynical. Pat for letting me borrow that top. Jen for being as ugly as a bear. Julie for teaching me so much. Joy for being a joy. Victoria for convincing me to apply for this job and for being my other big sister. All my girl friends for being constant sources of advice and love.

JAKE THANKS: All my family for a great summer and endless support. Meghan for being a terrific captain and putting up with my jokes and "irregular" hours. Julie for catching my misspellings and all your help. Joy for being the bomb Map Ed. Britain for not making it awkward when you were jealous of our L&T headers. Mon$y pod, I'm gonna miss you like a child misses their blanket.

JOY THANKS: Meghan for rock and Jake for roll, for always smiling, and for making these the best maps possible. All the RWs for their tireless work, and sending back anecdotes that make me laugh. Mapland for Starbucks, techno, and empathy. BW and AB for making it rain. Mom and Dad for lovingly and supportively putting up with an MIA daughter all summer. And LG love!

Editor
Meghan C. Joyce
Associate Editor
Jake A. Foley
Managing Editor
Julie Vodhanel
Map Editor
Joy Ding
Typesetter
Victoria Esquivel-Korsiak

Publishing Director
Jennifer Q. Wong
Editor-in-Chief
Silvia Gonzalez Killingsworth
Production Manager
Victoria Esquivel-Korsiak
Cartography Manager
Thomas MacDonald Barron
Editorial Managers
Anne Bensson, Calina Ciobanu, Rachel Nolan
Financial Manager
Sara Culver
Business and Marketing Manager
Julie Vodhanel
Personnel Manager
Victoria Norelid
Production Associate
Jansen A. S. Thurmer
Director of E-Commerce & IT
Patrick Carroll
Website Manager
Kathryne A. Bevilacqua
Office Coordinators
Juan L. Peña, Bradley J. Jones

Director of Advertising Sales
Hunter McDonald
Senior Advertising Associate
Daniel Lee

President
William Hauser
General Managers
Bob Rombauer, Jim McKellar

XIV

ABOUT LET'S GO

NOT YOUR PARENTS' TRAVEL GUIDE

At Let's Go, we see every trip as the chance of a lifetime. If your dream is to grab a machete and forge through the jungles of Costa Rica, we can take you there. If you'd rather bask in the Riviera sun at a beachside cafe, we'll set you a table. We write for readers who know that there's more to travel than sharing double deckers with tourists and who believe that travel can change both themselves and the world—whether they plan to spend six days in Mexico City or six months in Europe. We'll show you just how far your money can go, and prove that the greatest limitation on your adventures is not your wallet, but your imagination.

BEYOND THE TOURIST EXPERIENCE

To help you gain a deeper connection with the places you travel, our fearless researchers scour the globe to give you the heads-up on both world-renowned and off-the-beaten-track attractions, sights, and destinations. They engage with the local culture only to emerge with the freshest insights on everything from local festivals to regional cuisine. We've also opened our pages to respected writers and scholars to hear their takes on the countries and regions we cover, and asked travelers who have worked, studied, or volunteered abroad to contribute first-person accounts of their experiences. In addition, we increased our coverage of responsible travel and expanded each guide's Beyond Tourism chapter to share more ideas about how to give back while on the road.

FORTY-EIGHT YEARS OF WISDOM

Let's Go got its start in 1960, when a group of creative and well-traveled students compiled their experience and advice into a 20-page mimeographed pamphlet, which they gave to travelers on charter flights to Europe. Four and a half decades later, we've expanded to cover six continents and all kinds of travel—while retaining our founders' adventurous attitude toward the world. Laced with witty prose and total candor, our guides are still researched and written entirely by students on shoestring budgets, experienced travelers who know that train strikes, stolen luggage, food poisoning, and marriage proposals are all part of a day's work.

THE LET'S GO COMMUNITY

More than just a travel guide company, Let's Go is a community. Our small staff comes together because of our shared passion for travel and our desire to help other travelers see the world the way it was meant to be seen. We love it when our readers become part of the Let's Go community as well—when you travel, drop us a postcard (67 Mt. Auburn St., Cambridge, MA 02138, USA), send us an e-mail (feedback@letsgo.com), or post on our forum (http://www.letsgo.com/connect/forum) to tell us about your adventures and discoveries.

For more information, visit us online: www.letsgo.com.

PRICE RANGES
GREECE

Our researchers list establishments in order of value from best to worst; our favorites are denoted by the Let's Go thumbs-up (🖢). However, because the best value is not always the cheapest price, we have also incorporated a system of price ranges, based on a rough expectation of what you'll spend. For **accommodations,** we base our range on the cheapest price for which a single traveler can stay for one night. For **restaurants** and other dining establishments, we estimate the average amount a traveler will spend. The table tells you what you'll *typically* find in Greece at the corresponding price range; keep in mind that no system can allow for every individual establishment's quirks, and you'll typically get more for your money in larger cities. In other words: expect anything.

ACCOMMODATIONS	RANGE	WHAT YOU'RE *LIKELY* TO FIND
❶	under €17	Campgrounds and most dorm rooms. Expect bunk beds and a communal bath; you may have to provide or rent towels and sheets.
❷	€17-27	Domatia, high-end hostels, or small hotels. You may have a private bathroom, or there may be a sink in your room and a communal shower in the hall.
❸	€28-37	A small room with a private bath in a budget hotel or domatia. Decent amenities, such as phone, TV, and sometimes air-conditioning. Breakfast may be included in the price of the room.
❹	€38-72	Similar to 3, but may have more amenities, larger rooms, better views, or a better location.
❺	above €72	Large hotels or upscale chains. If it's a 5 and it doesn't have all the perks you want, you've paid too much.
FOOD	RANGE	WHAT YOU'RE *LIKELY* TO FIND
❶	under €5	Mostly street-corner stands, gyro and *souvlaki* huts, bakeries, or fast-food joints.
❷	€5-9	Sandwich shops, pizzerias, and low-priced entrees. May be takeout or sit-down, sometimes with a server.
❸	€10-15	Mid-priced entrees, seafood, and pasta dishes. More upscale ethnic eateries.
❹	€16-25	A somewhat fancy restaurant or taverna. Few restaurants in this price range have a dress code, but some may look down on T-shirts and jeans.
❺	above €25	Intricate, fancy entrees and a decent wine list. Slacks and dress shirts may be expected.

DISCOVER GREECE

Greece (Ελλάδα) is a land where sacred monasteries are mountainside fixtures, leisurely seaside siestas are standard issue, and circle-dancing and drinking until daybreak are summer rites. The ancient Greeks sprung to prominence with their philosophical, literary, artistic, and athletic mastery. Millennia later, visitors explore evidence of magnificent past civilizations, as well as Greece's island beaches, spectacular gorges, and famous hospitality. The all-encompassing Greek lifestyle is a deliciously frustrating mix of high-speed chaos and sun-inspired lounging, as old men hold lively debates in town plateias, teenagers zoom on mopeds around the clock, and unpredictable schedules force tourists to adopt the natives' go-with-the-flow take on life.

FACTS AND FIGURES

OFFICIAL NAME Hellenic Republic

POPULATION 10,706,290

CAPITAL Athens

LENGTH OF COASTLINE PER GREEK CITIZEN 1.37m

AVERAGE BAR CLOSING TIME Sunrise or when the ouzo runs out

YEARS OF CIVILIZATION About 5200

DAYS OF SUNSHINE PER YEAR 300

PERCENTAGE OF ISLANDS INHABITED 12%

RATIO OF FOREIGNERS TO LOCALS 9:10

NUMBER OF GODS IN THE ANCIENT GREEK PANTHEON 12

NUMBER OF GODS IN THE GREEK ORTHODOX CHURCH 1

NUMBER OF OLIVE TREES PER GREEK CITIZEN: 12

WHEN TO GO

June through August is **high season** in Greece. Bar-studded beaches set the scene for revelry and Dionysian indulgence, as the 38°C (100°F) sun blazes over ancient cities and modern-day sun-worshippers alike. Hotels, domatia, and sights are, like the nightlife, in full swing. If the crowds and frantic pace of summer travel are not your style, consider visiting with the lighter crowds of May, early June, or September, when avid hikers can take advantage of the pleasant weather to traverse the unsullied expanses of Northern and Central Greece. In ski areas like Mt. Parnassos (p. 204), Kalavrita (p. 158), and Karpenisi (p. 218), winter brings another high season. Accommodations and food are cheaper in the **low season,** but many sights, restaurants, and nightlife options have shorter hours or close altogether. At this time of year, Greece takes a break from farming, fishing, and tourism; ferries, buses, and trains run less frequently; and life is quieter.

THINGS TO DO

Mountain chains, bougainvillea-speckled islands, green olive groves, and the brilliantly blue Aegean comprise the refuge of mythological heroes and beasts. This varied land of isolated villages and majestic ruins satisfies even the pickiest visitor with its infinite diversions. Check out the **Suggested Itineraries** boxes that begin each chapter by outlining regional bests, but don't be afraid to plot out your own route: the famous Greek hospitality will make you feel welcome wherever you go.

TOP TEN PLACES TO MEET A GREEK GOD

The first god you should befriend is Hermes, the traveler god. Once he's on your side, you can concentrate on wooing the many other ancient deities whose legends live on in Greece.

1. Visit the volcanoes of **Nisyros** (p. 469) and **Santorini** (p. 416) to see the forge of Hephaestus, god of fire.

2. Explore the **Dadia Forest Reserve** (p. 314) or the **Prespa Lakes** (p. 297) in search of Artemis, protectress of the woods.

3. Partying on **Mykonos** (p. 370) or **Ios** (p. 409) will put you in the alcoholic stupor needed to bond with wine god Dionysus.

4. Seek the guidance of Athena, goddess of war and wisdom, at her patron city, **Athens** (p. 87).

5. Corfu's **Canal d'Amour** (p. 530) might help you find love goddess Aphrodite—or at least a mortal replacement.

6. A hike through Crete's **Valley of Death** (p. 619) might lead you to Hades.

7. You may run into Apollo at his oracle at **Delphi** (p. 207) or sanctuary at **Delos** (p. 378).

8. **Lesvos** (p. 503), home of the 10th Muse, Sappho, is a good place to seek the other nine.

9. Find Poseidon at his temple on **Cape Sounion** (p. 120), if you don't run into him on a ferry.

10. **Mt. Olympus** (p. 288). Duh.

THE ROAD TO RUINS

In Greece, it's harder to avoid ruins than to find them. Since they survive in a broad spectrum of importance, quality of preservation, and overall impressiveness, you may find yourself bored unless you're a Classicist or archaeologist. There are, of course, the not-to-be-missed famous sights, which never disappoint. The perfectly proportioned columns of the **Parthenon** (p. 110), combined with the sun's beating rays and the brilliant gleam of marble, conjure up the same awe they inspired in centuries of worshippers. At Cape Sounion, the seaside **Temple of Poseidon** (p. 120) sits on a 60m promontory overlooking the Aegean. If you can catch the floating island of **Delos** (p. 378), birthplace of Apollo and Artemis, you will find an island-wide archaeological site. A voyage through the **Peloponnese** will take you back to the era of nymphs, satyrs, and gods in disguise. Sprint across the well-preserved stadium on the way to the original Olympic fields at **Ancient Olympia** (p. 166), wander through watery, fresco-covered tunnels at **Corinth** (p. 134), peer into Agamemnon's tomb at **Mycenae** (p. 146), or cry over an ancient tragedy in the theater at **Epidavros** (p. 148). Byzantine times stand still at the site of **Mystras** (p. 190), the former center of Constantinople's rule in the Peloponnese. After traversing mountain roads, visitors can seek wisdom at the ancient **Oracle of Delphi** (p. 211), then wander up north to the ruins of **Pella** (p. 279) and **Vergina** (p. 278), once ruled by Philip II and his son Alexander the Great. **Samothraki** (p. 522), a pre-Hellenic cult-capital, will lead you out to the islands and even farther back in time. The Minoan palaces of **Knossos** (p. 595) and **Phaistos** (p. 600) come straight out of mythology, and Santorini's **Akrotiri** (p. 422) displays a Minoan world frozen in time by lava from a volcanic eruption.

ISLANDS IN THE SUN

The islands have long been a sun-worshipper's paradise, from those who follow Helios and Apollo to the disciples of tanning oil. Beachside days melt through spectacular sunsets into starry, disco-filled nights and back again, in a continuum of **hedonistic delight.** Besides the heavenly sands and turquoise waters, the islands offer ancient sites, intriguing museums, and peaceful small-town life. A favorite of international vacationers, **Skiathos** (p. 343), in the Sporades, harbors the piney Biotrope of Koukounaries beach and lovely Lalaria. In the Aegean Sea, **Santorini's** (p. 416) black-sand beaches soak up the sun's hot rays and stay warm long after the stunning sunsets over the Sea of Crete have faded. The wide variety of beaches and multi-colored rocks of **Milos** (p. 425) seem like a rainbow-splashed paradise. Sea caves once ransacked by pirates on the coast of **Skyros** (p. 356) now welcome swimmers. After basking on the shore of **Lesvos** (p. 507), visitors can stop to pay homage to **Sappho** or visit one of the only **petrified forests** in the world. Stumble out of all those pesky clothes at wild Paradise beach on **Mykonos** (p. 370), or seek solace on a secluded strip of sand. Snorkeling, water-skiing, or just loafing in the sun fill the days on **Ios** (p. 409) and **Naxos** (p. 383). Signs of Odysseus are hidden on his home island, **Ithaka** (p. 549), and on **Corfu** (p. 530), where he was shipwrecked. Paleohora in **Crete** (p. 579) and castle-crowned Haraki beach on **Rhodes** (p. 438) beg travelers to drop their packs in the languid sun.

▧ LET'S GO PICKS

BEST PLACE TO CONDUCT A CENSUS: The number of people in the village of **Agios Achillios** (p. 298) in Prespa can be counted on 1 person's fingers and toes. Counting the citizens of **Megalo Horio** (p. 221) in Evritania, however, would require 10 people's digits.

BEST PLACE TO THINK DEEP THOUGHTS: Take your most profound questions and ideas to Athens's **Agora** (p. 111), where master philosopher Socrates once taught. In **Vikos Gorge** (p. 262), any thought can be considered deep.

BEST PLACE TO RECREATE A BATTLE: Each October, a 1571 naval battle is recreated at **Nafpaktos'** Old Port, complete with pyrotechnics (p. 214).

BEST PLACE TO PRETEND YOU'RE AN OLYMPIC ATHLETE: At ancient **Olympia** (p. 166), you can take a lap around the stadium where Greek athletes competed 2300 years ago.

BEST PLACES TO GET DIRTY: The mud from Messolongi's **lagoon** (p. 216) is said to have healing properties. The small town of Galaxidi marks the start of Lent each year with a **flour fight** (p. 214).

BEST PLACE TO TAKE A BATH: You can bathe nude in the springs at **Therma** (p. 524), a daytrip from Kamariotissa. Relax in the naturally radioactive waters at **Agios Kirykos** (p. 497), renowned for their healing powers.

BEST OBJECTS M.I.A.: Greeks have been longing for their **Colossus of Rhodes** (p. 447) since it tumbled into the Aegean in 226 BC. The celebrated **Winged Victory of Samothrace** (p. 525) resides in the Louvre in Paris. Ever since Lord Elgin shipped its marble reliefs to the British Museum in London, the **Acropolis** (p. 108) in Athens has been missing some key parts.

BEST EVIDENCE OF INBREEDING: The Prespa Lakes' **dwarf cows** (p. 298) were bred small so that they wouldn't sink in the area's plentiful swamps. The **midget elephants** (p. 464) whose bones were found in Livadia on Tilos evolved to be small on their own.

MOST WELL-PRESERVED BODIES: Mary Magdalene's hand (p. 304) is kept in Simonos Petra monastery on Mt. Athos. The Osios Loukas monastery keeps its namesake **saint's body** (p. 206) in a Snow White-esque glass coffin. If you peek through the reliquary at Patras's Agio Andreas cathedral, you may see the top of **Saint Andrew's head** (p. 155).

BEST MULTI-PURPOSE BUILDINGS: The **San Marco Church** (p. 594) in Iraklion doubles as a venue for rotating art exhibits. Edessa's nighttime hot spot **Kanavourgeio** (p. 295) was once a hemp factory.

TAKE A HIKE

Take out your walking stick and rev up your engines. Hiking or motorbiking—or a combination of the two—lets you cruise among rural villages independent of sporadic bus schedules. On foot, you'll cross through graceful hills, passing mountain goats and wildflowers along the way. To the delight of climbers, 80% of the Greek landscape is mountainous. Clamber to the abode of the gods at Mount Olympus (p. 288), ascending over 2900 steep, stunning meters to one of its eight peaks. During the summer, Dionysus's old watering hole, Mount Parnassos (p. 204), makes a great hiking and mountain-biking trip. The traditional villages of the Zagorohoria (p. 261) and their surrounding wilderness turn mere walking into an enticing adventure. On Mount Athos (p. 301), trails verge on sublime, as the paths from monastery to monastery scramble over grass-carpeted crags and yield divine views of the sea below. Neighboring Vikos Gorge (p. 262), the world's steepest canyon, challenges hikers with a 6hr. trek. The easier 11km hike between drowsy Dimitsana (p. 171) and cobblestoned Stemnitsa (p. 174) will remove you from the tourist bustle of the rest of the Peloponnese and treat you to beautiful Arcadian vistas. Odysseus's kingdom of Ithaka (p. 549) is an untapped hiker's paradise, where the Cave of the Nymphs—the hiding place for Odysseus's treasure—will seduce you. Northern Thassos (p. 525) is full of secluded ruins, superior hikes, and village-to-village strolls. Alonnisos (p. 352), a largely uninhabited Sporadic island, is criss-crossed by trails and moped-friendly roads, each hugged by beaches ideal for refueling after a tiring hike. In Crete, Samaria Gorge (p. 577), Europe's longest gorge, and the quieter Valley of Death (p. 620) plunge you below eagles' nests and trees that cling to the steep canyon sides. The trails around Zaros wind up to Zeus's childhood hiding place, Kamares Cave (p. 599).

SUGGESTED ITINERARIES

RUINS, RAMBLES, AND RELICS (1 WEEK)

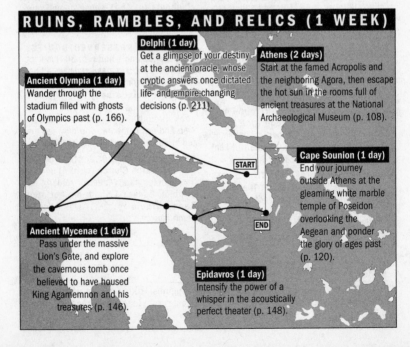

Delphi (1 day)
Get a glimpse of your destiny at the ancient oracle, whose cryptic answers once dictated life- and empire-changing decisions (p. 211).

Ancient Olympia (1 day)
Wander through the stadium filled with ghosts of Olympics past (p. 166).

Athens (2 days)
Start at the famed Acropolis and the neighboring Agora, then escape the hot sun in the rooms full of ancient treasures at the National Archaeological Museum (p. 108).

START

Cape Sounion (1 day)
End your journey outside Athens at the gleaming white marble temple of Poseidon overlooking the Aegean and ponder the glory of ages past (p. 120).

END

Ancient Mycenae (1 day)
Pass under the massive Lion's Gate, and explore the cavernous tomb once believed to have housed King Agamemnon and his treasures (p. 146).

Epidavros (1 day)
Intensify the power of a whisper in the acoustically perfect theater (p. 148).

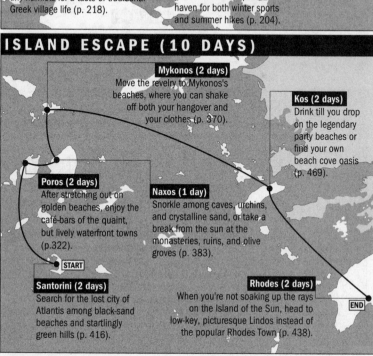

NORTHERN OUTDOORS (3 WEEKS)

Thessaloniki Area (4 days)
Trek through under-touristed mainland Greece, home of cliff-side monasteries, cobblestoned traditional villiages, and awe-inspiring mountainous landscapes (p. 266).

START

Dadia Forest Reserve (1 day)
Try to pick out each of the 36 raptor species that fly over these thickly wooded hills (p. 314).

Zagorohoria (3 days)
END Shirk modern trans-portation and enjoy walking from village to village through the stunning Vikos Gorge (p. 261).

Mount Olympus (3 days)
Choose among the eight breathtaking peaks of this divine mountain (p. 288).

Thassos (2 days)
Set out on one of the lush trails that gave this "Green Island" its nickname (p. 525).

Alonnisos (2 days)
Scale the precipitous coastal cliffs of the only inhabited island in Greece's National Marine Park (p. 352).

Karpenisi (4 days)
Make your way through the area's extraordinary foothills and stop at the tiny hamlets for a taste of traditional Greek village life (p. 218).

Mount Parnassos (2 days)
Strap on either your skis or your pack to hit the slopes of this haven for both winter sports and summer hikes (p. 204).

ISLAND ESCAPE (10 DAYS)

Mykonos (2 days)
Move the revelry to Mykonos's beaches, where you can shake off both your hangover and your clothes (p. 370).

Kos (2 days)
Drink till you drop on the legendary party beaches or find your own beach cove oasis (p. 469).

Poros (2 days)
After stretching out on golden beaches, enjoy the café-bars of the quaint, but lively waterfront towns (p.322).

Naxos (1 day)
Snorkle among caves, urchins, and crystalline sand, or take a break from the sun at the monasteries, ruins, and olive groves (p. 383).

START

Santorini (2 days)
Search for the lost city of Atlantis among black-sand beaches and startlingly green hills (p. 416).

Rhodes (2 days)
When you're not soaking up the rays on the Island of the Sun, head to low-key, picturesque Lindos instead of the popular Rhodes Town (p. 438).

END

GREEK TO ME (8 WEEKS)

Zagorohoria (2 days)
Ramble through petite towns that stick to traditional folkways (p. 261).

Thessaloniki (4 days)
Re-enter urban life in this culturally and historically diverse city filled with Byzantine- and Turkish-inspired sights (p. 266).

Corfu (3 days)
Explore beaches, hikes, ancient sites, and laid-back villages on this endlessly diverse island (p. 530).

Mount Olympus (1 day)
Challenge yourself to reach the cloud-top home of the gods (p. 288).

Skiathos (2 days)
Return to the beach and pop open a beer at this party hub (p. 343).

Karpenisi (2 days)
Wander through serene villages, enjoying rural life and the gorgeous Greek countryside (p. 218).

Ithaka (2 days)
Wander to the legendary island home of Odysseus (p. 549).

Delphi (1 day)
Seek the advice of the legendary oracle or get inspired by the mesmerizing panoramic views (p. 207).

START

Kephaolonia (2 days)
Catch the ferry from Patras to this nature lover's paradise with some of the Mediterranean's best beaches (p. 553).

Ancient Olympia (1 day)
Pay a visit to the home of international (or inter-city-state) athletic competition (p. 166).

Nafplion (3 days)
Use this quaint, Venetian-influenced town as a base to visit the neighboring Theater of Epidavros and ancient sites of Mycenae, Epidavros, and Corinth (p. 141).

Athens (5 days)
Live the big-city life in its many diverse neighborhoods and visit the National Archaeological Museum, the Acropolis, the Agora, and the many smaller museums for a refresher course in Greek history (p. 87).

Hania (2 days)
Stroll along the port then head south to hike the awe-inspiring Samaria Gorge (p. 577)–the longest in Europe.

Iraklion (3 days)
Spend a day in the city, then head to the nearby Minoan ruins of Knossos and Phaistos (p. 589).

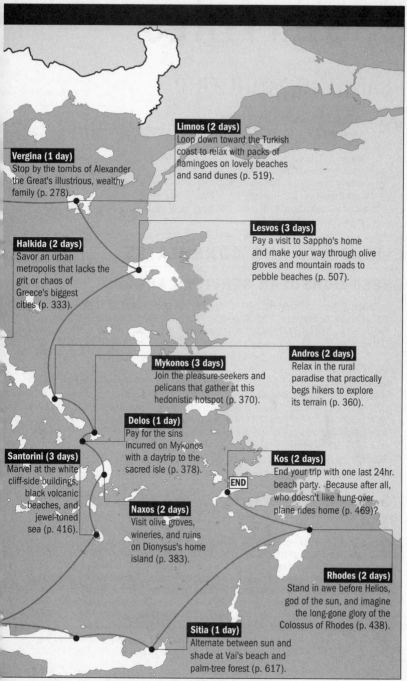

Limnos (2 days)
Loop down toward the Turkish coast to relax with packs of flamingoes on lovely beaches and sand dunes (p. 519).

Vergina (1 day)
Stop by the tombs of Alexander the Great's illustrious, wealthy family (p. 278).

Lesvos (3 days)
Pay a visit to Sappho's home and make your way through olive groves and mountain roads to pebble beaches (p. 507).

Halkida (2 days)
Savor an urban metropolis that lacks the grit or chaos of Greece's biggest cities (p. 333).

Mykonos (3 days)
Join the pleasure-seekers and pelicans that gather at this hedonistic hotspot (p. 370).

Andros (2 days)
Relax in the rural paradise that practically begs hikers to explore its terrain (p. 360).

Delos (1 day)
Pay for the sins incurred on Mykonos with a daytrip to the sacred isle (p. 378).

Kos (2 days)
End your trip with one last 24hr. beach party. Because after all, who doesn't like hung-over plane rides home (p. 469)?

Santorini (3 days)
Marvel at the white cliff-side buildings, black volcanic beaches, and jewel-toned sea (p. 416).

Naxos (2 days)
Visit olive groves, wineries, and ruins on Dionysus's home island (p. 383).

END

Rhodes (2 days)
Stand in awe before Helios, god of the sun, and imagine the long-gone glory of the Colossus of Rhodes (p. 438).

Sitia (1 day)
Alternate between sun and shade at Vai's beach and palm-tree forest (p. 617).

ESSENTIALS

PLANNING YOUR TRIP

ENTRANCE REQUIREMENTS
Passport (p. 9). Required for citizens of Australia, Canada, Ireland, New Zealand, the UK, and the US.
Visa (p. 11). Required only for stays over three months for citizens of Australia, Canada, Ireland, New Zealand, the UK, and the US.
Inoculations (p. 20). Not required.
Work Permit (p. 11). Required for all EU citizens planning to work in Greece for over three months and all other foreigners planning to work in Greece for any length of time.

EMBASSIES AND CONSULATES

GREEK CONSULAR SERVICES ABROAD

Australia: 9 Turrana St., Yarralumla, Canberra, ACT 2600 (☎02 6273 3011; fax 02 6273 2620). **Consulates:** 300 Flinders St., Adelaide, SA 5000 (☎08 8232 8049; fax 08 8232 3184); 37-39 Albert Rd., Melbourne, VIC 3004 (☎03 9866 4524; fax 03 9866 4933); 16 St. George's Terr., Perth, WA 6000 (☎08 9325 6608; fax 08 9325 2940); 219-223 Castlereagh St., Sydney, NSW 2000 (☎02 9264 9130; fax 02 9264 6135).

Canada: 80 MacLaren St., Ottawa, ON K2P 0K6 (☎613-238-6271; fax 613-238-5676; www.greekembassy.ca). **Consulates:** 1170 Pl. du Frère André, Ste. 300, Montreal, QC H3B 3C6 (☎514-875-2119; fax 514-875-8781; www.grconsulatemtl.net); 365 Bloor St. E., Ste. 1800, Toronto, ON M4W-3L4 (☎416-515-0133; fax 416-515-0209; www.grconsulate.com); 500-688 West Hastings St., Vancouver, BC V6B 1P1 (☎604-681-1381; fax 604-681-6656; www.vancouver.grconsulate.ca).

Ireland: 1 Upper Pembroke St., Dublin 2 (☎1 676 7254; fax 1 661 8892).

New Zealand: 5-7 Willeston St., Box 24066, Wellington (☎4 473 7775; fax 4 473 7441).

UK: 1a Holland Park, London W11 3TP (☎20 72 29 38 50; fax 20 72 29 72 21; www.greekembassy.org.uk). **Consulate:** 1a Holland Park, London W11 3TP (☎20 72 21 64 67; fax 20 72 43 32 02).

US: 2221 Massachusetts Ave. NW, Washington, D.C. 20008 (☎202-939-1306; fax 202-939-1324; www.greekembassy.org). **Consulates:** Tower Place, Ste. 1670 3340, Peachtree Rd. NE, Atlanta, GA 30326 (☎404-261-3313; fax 404-262-2798; www.greekembassy.org/atlanta); 86 Beacon St., Boston, MA 02108 (☎617-523-0100; fax 617-523-0511; www.greekembassy.org/boston); 650 N. St. Clair St., Chicago, IL 60611 (☎312-335-3915; fax 312-335-3958; www.greekembassy.org/chicago); 520 Post Oak Blvd., Ste. 450, Houston, TX 77027 (☎713-840-7522; fax 713-840-0614; www.greekembassy.org/houston); 12424 Wilshire Blvd., Ste. 800, Los Angeles, CA 90025 (☎310-826-5555; fax 310-826-8670; www.greekembassy.org/losangeles); 69 E. 79th St., New York, NY 10021 (☎212-988-5500; fax 212-734-

8492; www.greekembassy.org/newyork); 2441 Gough St., San Francisco, CA 94123 (☎415-775-2102; fax 415-776-6815; www.greekembassy.org/sanfrancisco).

CONSULAR SERVICES IN GREECE

Australia: Level 6, Thon Building, Kifisias and Alexandras Ave., Ambelokipi, Athens 115 23 (☎21087 04 000; fax 21087 04 111; www.ausemb.gr).

Canada: Ioannou Ghennadiou 4, Athens 115 21 (☎21072 73 400; fax 21072 73 480; www.dfait-maeci.gc.ca/canadaeuropa/greece). **Consulate:** Tsimiski 12, Thessaloniki 546 24 (☎23102 56 350; fax 23102 56 351).

European Community: Vas. Sofias 2, Athens 106 74 (☎21072 51 000; fax 21072 44 620).

Ireland: Vas. Konstantinou 7, Athens 106 74 (☎21072 32 771; fax 21072 93 383).

New Zealand: Kifissias76, Ambelokipi, Athens 115 26 (☎21069 24 136; fax 21069 24 821).

UK: Ploutarchou 1, Athens 106 75 (☎21072 72 600; fax 21072 72 720; www.british-embassy.gr).

US: Vas. Sofias 91, Athens 101 60 (☎21072 12 951; www.usembassy.gr). **Consulate:** Tsimiski 43, Thessaloniki 646 23 (☎23102 42 905; 23102 42 927; www.usconsulate.gr).

TOURIST OFFICES

Start early when trying to contact tourist offices—like most things Greek, they run on their own schedule. Polite persistence coupled with genuine excitement and interest works wonders. Two national organizations oversee tourism: the **Greek National Tourist Organization (GNTO),** known as the **"EOT"** in Greece, and the **tourist police.** The GNTO can supply general information about sights and accommodations throughout the country. The main office is in Athens at Tsoha 7 (☎21087 07 000; www.gnto.gr). Another information desk is located at El. Venizelos Airport (☎21035 30 445 or 21035 30 448). Tourist police deal with local travel issues like finding a room or bus schedules. Officers are often quite willing to help, though their English may be limited. *Let's Go* lists locations and contact information for tourist offices and the tourist police in the **Practical Information** section of each city or town. There are also official Greek tourism boards in several countries:

Australia and New Zealand: 37-49 Pitt St., Sydney, NSW 2000 (☎02 9241 1663; fax 02 9241 2499).

Canada: 1500 Don Mills Rd. Ste. 102, Toronto, ON M3B 3K4 (☎416-968-2220; fax 416-968-6533); 1170 Place du Frère André, Montreal, QC H3B C36 (☎514-871-1535; fax 514-871-1498).

UK and Ireland: 4 Conduit St., London W1S 2DJ (☎20 74 95 93 00; fax 20 72 87 13 69; www.gnto.co.uk).

US: Olympic Tower, 645 Fifth Ave., Ste. 903, New York, NY 10022 (☎212-421-5777; fax 212-826-6940; www.greektourism.com).

DOCUMENTS AND FORMALITIES

PASSPORTS

REQUIREMENTS

Foreign citizens, including those of Australia, Canada, Ireland, New Zealand, the UK, and the US, need valid passports to enter Greece and to re-enter their home countries. Greece does not allow entrance if the holder's passport expires three months after the period of intended stay; returning home with an expired passport is illegal and may result in a fine.

NEW PASSPORTS

Citizens of Australia, Canada, Ireland, New Zealand, the UK, and the US can apply for a passport at any passport office or at selected post offices and courts of law. Citizens of these countries also can download passport applications from the official website of their country's government or passport office. Any new passport or renewal applications must be filed well in advance of the departure date, though most passport offices offer rush services for a very steep fee. Note, however, that "rushed" passports still take up to two weeks to arrive.

ONE EUROPE. European unity has come a long way since 1958, when the European Economic Community (EEC) was created to promote European solidarity and cooperation. Since then, the EEC has become the European Union (EU), a mighty political, legal, and economic institution. On May 1, 2004, ten South, Central, and Eastern European countries—Cyprus, the Czech Republic, Estonia, Hungary, Latvia, Lithuania, Malta, Poland, Slovakia, and Slovenia—were admitted to the EU, joining 15 other member states: Austria, Belgium, Denmark, Finland, France, Germany, Greece, Ireland, Italy, Luxembourg, the Netherlands, Portugal, Spain, Sweden, and the UK. On January 1, 2007, Bulgaria and Romania became the two newest members of the EU.

What does this have to do with the average non-EU tourist? The EU's policy of **freedom of movement** means that border controls between the first 15 member states (minus Ireland and the UK, but plus Norway and Iceland) have been abolished, and visa policies harmonized. Under this treaty, formally known as the **Schengen Agreement,** you're still required to carry a passport (or government-issued ID card for EU citizens) when crossing an internal border, but once you've been admitted into one country, you're free to travel to other participating states. On June 5, 2005, Switzerland ratified the treaty but has yet to implement it. The 10 newest member states of the EU are anticipated to implement the policy in October of 2007. Britain and Ireland also have formed a **common travel area,** abolishing passport controls between the UK and the Republic of Ireland.

For more important consequences of the EU for travelers, see **The Euro** (p. 13).

PASSPORT MAINTENANCE

Photocopy the page of your passport with your photo, as well as your visas, traveler's check serial numbers, and any other important documents. Carry one set of copies in a safe place, apart from the originals, and leave another set at home. Consulates recommend that you also carry an expired passport or an official copy of your birth certificate in a part of your baggage separate from other documents.

If you lose your passport, immediately notify the local police and the nearest embassy or consulate of your home government. To expedite its replacement, you must show ID and proof of citizenship; it also helps to know all information previously recorded in the passport. In some cases, a replacement may take weeks to process, and it may be valid only for a limited time. Any visas stamped in your old passport will be irretrievably lost. In an emergency, ask for immediate temporary traveling papers that will permit you to re-enter your home country.

VISAS, INVITATIONS, AND WORK PERMITS

VISAS

EU citizens do not need a visa to stay in Greece. Citizens of Australia, Canada, New Zealand, and the US do not need a visa for stays of up to 90 days, though this three-month period begins upon entry into any of the countries in the EU's **freedom of movement** zone (see **One Europe,** above). Those staying longer than 90 days may purchase a visa from the Greek embassy or consulate in the area of your permanent residence. Visas allow the holder to spend six months in Greece. If you decide to stay in Greece longer than planned, make sure to apply for a visa extension well in advance—applications must be submitted at least 20 days before the three-month expiration date of normal non-visa travel.

Double-check entrance requirements at the nearest embassy or consulate of **Greece** (listed under **Greek Consular Services Abroad,** on p. 8) for up-to-date info before departure. US citizens can also consult http://travel.state.gov.

Entering **Greece** to study requires a student visa. For more information, see **Beyond Tourism** (p. 76).

WORK PERMITS
Admission as a visitor does not include the right to work, which is authorized only by a work permit. For more information, see the **Beyond Tourism** chapter (p. 76).

IDENTIFICATION
When you travel, always carry at least two forms of identification on your person, including a photo ID; a passport and a driver's license or birth certificate is usually an adequate combination. Never carry all your IDs together; split them up in case of theft or loss, and keep photocopies in your luggage and at home.

STUDENT, TEACHER, AND YOUTH IDENTIFICATION
The **International Student Identity Card (ISIC),** the most widely accepted form of student ID, provides discounts on some sights, accommodations, food, and transportation; access to a 24hr. emergency helpline; and insurance benefits for US cardholders (see **Insurance,** p. 20). Applicants must be full-time secondary or postsecondary school students at least 12 years of age. Because of the proliferation of fake ISICs, some services (particularly airlines) require additional proof of student identity. For travelers who are under 26 years old but are not students, the **International Youth Travel Card (IYTC)** also offers many of the same benefits as the ISIC.

The **International Teacher Identity Card (ITIC)** offers teachers the same insurance coverage as the ISIC and similar but limited discounts. To qualify for the card, teachers must currently be employed and have worked a minimum of 18hr. per week for at least one school year.

Each of these identity cards costs US$22. ISICs, ITICS, and IYTCs are valid for one year from the date of issue. To learn more about ISICs, ITICs, and IYTCs, try www.myisic.com. Many student travel agencies (p. 24) issue the cards; for a list of issuing agencies or more information, see the **International Student Travel Confederation (ISTC)** website (www.istc.org).

The **International Student Exchange Card (ISE Card)** is a similar identification card available to students, faculty, and youths aged 12 to 26. The card provides discounts, medical benefits, access to a 24hr. emergency helpline, and the ability to purchase student airfares. An ISE Card costs US$25; call ☎ 800-255-8000 (in North America) or ☎ 480-951-1177 (from all other continents) for more info, or visit www.isecard.com.

CUSTOMS
Upon entering Greece, you must declare certain items from abroad and pay a duty on the value of those articles if they exceed the allowance established by Greece's customs service. Note that goods and gifts purchased at **duty-free** shops abroad are not exempt from duty or sales tax; "duty-free" merely means that you need not pay a tax in the country of purchase. In 1999, duty-free allowances were abolished for travel among EU member states, but they still exist for those arriving from outside the EU. Upon returning home, you likewise must declare all articles acquired

abroad and pay a duty on the value of articles in excess of your home country's allowance. In order to expedite your return, make a list of any valuables brought from home and register them with customs before traveling abroad, and be sure to keep receipts for all goods acquired abroad.

 CUSTOMS IN THE EU. As well as freedom of movement of people within the EU (see p. 10), travelers in the 15 original EU member countries (Austria, Belgium, Denmark, Finland, France, Germany, Greece, Ireland, Italy, Luxembourg, the Netherlands, Portugal, Spain, Sweden, and the UK) also can take advantage of the freedom of movement of goods. This means that there are no customs controls at internal EU borders, and travelers are free to transport whatever legal substances they like as long as it is for their own personal (non-commercial) use—up to 800 cigarettes, 10L of spirits, 90L of wine (including up to 60L of sparkling wine), and 110L of beer. Duty-free allowances were abolished in 1999 for travel among the original 15 EU member states; this now also applies to Cyprus and Malta. However, travelers between the EU and the rest of the world still get a duty-free allowance when passing through customs.

Greece imposes a value added tax (VAT) on sales, which is included in the retail price—16% on purchases made on the mainland, 11.5% on purchases made in the Aegean islands. Travelers from non-EU countries who spend more than €120 in one shop in one day are entitled to claim some of their VAT on these items when leaving Greece, as long as they take the items out of Greece within three months of their purchase. Claiming your VAT refund can involve complicated paperwork; try to ask about VAT at any shops where you make substantial purchases, or contact **Global Refund** (☎21032 30 730; www.globalrefund.org) for more information.

MONEY

CURRENCY AND EXCHANGE

The currency chart below is based on August 2007 exchange rates between local currency and Australian dollars (AUS$), Canadian dollars (CDN$), European Union euro (EUR€), New Zealand dollars (NZ$), British pounds (UK£), and US dollars (US$). Check the currency converter on websites like www.xe.com or www.bloomberg.com, or look in a large newspaper for the latest exchange rates.

EURO (€)		
AUS$1 = €0.63	€1 = AUS$1.58	
CDN$1 = €0.70	€1 = CDN$1.44	
NZ$1 = €0.57	€1= NZ$1.76	
UK£1 = €1.49	€1 = UK£.067	
US$1 = €0.75	€1 = US$1.34	

As a general rule, it's cheaper to convert money in Greece than at home. While currency exchange probably will be available in your arrival airport, it's wise to bring enough foreign currency to last for the first 24 to 72 hours of your trip.

When changing money abroad, try to go only to a bank (τράπεζα, TRAH-peh-za) that has at most a 5% margin between the buy and sell prices. Since you lose money with every transaction, **convert large sums** (unless the currency is depreciating rapidly), but **no more than you'll need.**

If you use traveler's checks or bills, carry some in small denominations (the equivalent of US$50 or less) for times when you are forced to exchange money at disadvantageous rates, but bring a range of denominations since charges may be levied per check cashed. Store your money in a variety of forms; ideally, at any given time you will be carrying some cash, some traveler's checks, and an ATM and/or credit card.

THE EURO. The official currency of 13 members of the European Union—Austria, Belgium, Finland, France, Germany, Greece, Ireland, Italy, Luxembourg, the Netherlands, Portugal, Slovenia, and Spain—is now the euro.

The currency has some important—and positive—consequences for travelers hitting more than one euro-zone country. For one thing, money-changers across the euro-zone are obliged to exchange money at the official, fixed rate (see below), and at no commission (though they may still charge a small service fee). Secondly, euro-denominated traveler's checks allow you to pay for goods and services across the euro-zone, again at the official rate and commission-free.

At the time of printing, 1€=US$1.36=CDN$1.44=NZ$1.86= UK£.068=AUS$1.62. For more info, check a currency converter (such as www.xe.com) or www.europa.eu.int.

ESSENTIALS

TRAVELER'S CHECKS

Traveler's checks are one of the safest means of carrying funds. American Express and Visa are the most recognized brands. Many banks and agencies sell them for a small commission. Check issuers provide refunds if the checks are lost or stolen, and many provide additional services, such as toll-free refund hotlines abroad, emergency message services, and assistance with lost and stolen credit cards or passports. Traveler's checks are accepted all over Greece, and can be cashed in all Greek banks and exchange bureaus, though they are used less and less frequently. Ask about toll-free refund hotlines and the location of refund centers when purchasing checks, and always carry emergency cash.

American Express: Checks available with commission at select banks, at all AmEx offices, and online (www.americanexpress.com; US residents only). American Express cardholders also can purchase checks by phone (☎800-528-4800). Checks available in Australian, British, Canadian, European, Japanese, and US currencies, among others. American Express also offers the Travelers Cheque Card, a prepaid reloadable card. Checks for Two can be signed by either of two people traveling together. For purchase locations or more information, contact AmEx's service centers: in Greece ☎21032 62 626, Australia 61 29 271 8666, in New Zealand 649 367 4567, in the UK 441 273 696 933, in Canada and the US 800-221-7282; elsewhere, call the US collect at 1-336-393-1111.

Travelex: Visa TravelMoney prepaid cash card and Visa traveler's checks available. For information about Thomas Cook MasterCard in Canada and the US call ☎800-223-7373, in the UK 0800 622 101, in Greece 008 00441 31 409; elsewhere call the UK collect at +44 1733 318 950. For information about Interpayment Visa in the US and Canada call ☎800-732-1322, in the UK 0800 515 884, in Greece 008 00441 31 411; elsewhere call the UK collect at +44 1733 318 949. For more information, visit www.travelex.com.

Visa: Checks available (generally with commission) at banks worldwide. For the location of the nearest office, call the Visa Travelers Cheque Global Refund and Assistance Center: in the UK ☎0800 895 078, in the US 800-227-6811, in Greece 008 0049 31 410; elsewhere, call the UK collect at +44 2079 378 091. Checks available in British, Canadian, European, Japanese, and US currencies, among others. Visa also offers TravelMoney, a prepaid debit card that can be reloaded online or by phone. For more information on Visa travel services, see http://usa.visa.com/personal/using_visa/travel_with_visa.html.

ESSENTIALS

CREDIT, DEBIT, AND ATM CARDS

Where they are accepted, credit cards often offer superior exchange rates—up to 5% better than the retail rate used by banks and other currency exchange establishments. Credit cards may also offer services such as insurance or emergency help, and are sometimes required to reserve hotel rooms or rental cars. **MasterCard** and **Visa** are the most frequently accepted; **American Express** cards work at some ATMs, at AmEx offices, and at major airports.

The use of ATM cards is widespread in Greece. Depending on the system that your home bank uses, you most likely can access your personal bank account from abroad. ATMs get the same wholesale exchange rate as credit cards, but there is often a limit on the amount of money you can withdraw per day (usually around US$500). There is typically also a surcharge of US$1-5 per withdrawal.

Debit cards are as convenient as credit cards but withdraw money directly from the holder's checking account. A debit card can be used wherever its associated credit card company (usually MasterCard or Visa) is accepted. Debit cards often also function as ATM cards and can be used to withdraw cash from associated banks and ATMs throughout Greece.

The two major international money networks are **MasterCard/Maestro/Cirrus** (for ATM locations ☎800-424-7787 or www.mastercard.com) and **Visa/PLUS** (for ATM locations ☎800-847-2911 or www.visa.com). Most ATMs charge a transaction fee that is paid to the bank that owns the ATM.

PINS AND ATMS. To use a cash or credit card to withdraw money from a cash machine (ATM) in Europe, you must have a four-digit **Personal Identification Number (PIN).** If your PIN is longer than four digits, ask your bank whether you can just use the first four, or whether you'll need a new PIN. **Credit cards** usually don't come with PINs, so if you intend to hit up ATMs in Europe with a credit card to get cash advances, call your credit card company before leaving to request one.

Travelers with alphabetic, rather than numerical, PINs may also be thrown off by the lack of letters on European cash machines. The following are the corresponding numbers to use: 1=QZ; 2=ABC; 3=DEF; 4=GHI; 5=JKL; 6=MNO; 7=PRS; 8=TUV; and 9=WXY. Note that if you mistakenly punch the wrong code into the machine three times, it will swallow your card for good.

GETTING MONEY FROM HOME

If you run out of money while traveling, the easiest and cheapest solution is to have someone back home make a deposit to your bank account. If that is impossible, consider one of the following options.

WIRING MONEY

It is possible to arrange a **bank money transfer,** which means asking a bank back home to wire money to a bank in Greece. This is the cheapest way to transfer cash, but it's also the slowest, usually taking several days or more. Note that some banks may only release your funds in local currency, potentially sticking you with a poor exchange rate; inquire about this in advance. Money transfer services like **Western Union** are faster and more convenient than bank transfers, but also much pricier. Western Union has many locations worldwide. To find one, visit www.westernunion.com, or call in Australia ☎1800 173 833, in Canada and the US 800-325-6000, in the UK 0800 833 833, or in Greece 21090 05 000. To wire money using a credit card (Discover, MasterCard, Visa), call in Canada and the US 800-CALL-CASH, in the UK ☎0800 833 833. Money transfer services are also available to **American Express** cardholders and at selected **Thomas Cook** offices.

US STATE DEPARTMENT (US CITIZENS ONLY)
In serious emergencies only, the US State Department will forward money within hours to the nearest consular office, which then will disburse it according to instructions for a US$30 fee. If you wish to use this service, you must contact the Overseas Citizens Service division of the US State Department (☎202-647-5225, toll-free 888-407-4747).

COSTS
The cost of your trip will vary considerably depending on where you go, how you travel, and where you stay. The most significant expenses probably will be your round-trip (return) **airfare** to Greece (see **Getting to Greece: By Plane,** p. 23) and a **railpass** or **bus pass** (p. 28). Before you go, spend some time calculating a reasonable daily budget.

STAYING ON A BUDGET
In general, a bare-bones day in Greece (camping or sleeping in hostels, buying food at supermarkets) costs US$48-72 (€40-60); a slightly cushier day (sleeping in hostels, domatia, or a budget hotel, eating one meal at a restaurant, going out at night) costs US$65-90 (€55-75); and for a luxurious day, the sky's the limit. Remember emergency reserve funds (at least US$200) when planning how much money you'll need. That said, don't go overboard. Though staying within your budget is important, don't do so at the expense of your health or a great travel experience.

TIPS FOR SAVING MONEY
Some simple ways to save include searching out opportunities for free entertainment, splitting accommodation and food costs with trustworthy fellow travelers, and buying food in supermarkets rather than eating out. Bring a **sleepsack** (p. 16) to save on sheet charges in hostels, and do your **laundry** in the sink (unless you're explicitly prohibited from doing so). Museums often have certain days once a month or once a week when admission is free; plan accordingly. If you are eligible, consider getting an ISIC or an IYTC (p. 11); many sights and museums offer reduced admission to students and youths. For getting around quickly, bikes are the most economical option. Renting a bike is cheaper than renting a moped or scooter. Don't forget about walking, though; you can learn a lot about a city by seeing it on foot. Drinking at bars and clubs quickly becomes expensive. It's cheaper to buy alcohol at a supermarket and imbibe before going out.

TOP TEN WAYS TO SAV IN GREECE

Though Greece has become more expensive in the past few years it's still accessible to the budge traveler—provided you know a few tips, that is.

1. Buy food at outdoor markets grocery stores, or gyro stands instead of dining out at tavernas.

2. Try to stay in domatia—they're often cheaper than hotels and will give you a local experience.

3. Plan your route around wha you want to do, not where you want to go. For example, if you want to visit island beaches, the Dodecanese will be much cheaper than the Saronic Gulf.

4. Bargain (where appropriate).

5. Rent a moped, not a car. The can get you where you need to go for under €10 per day.

6. Watch for days when you car get into museums for free.

7. Build outdoors experiences into your itinerary. Hiking or lying on a beach won't cost a euro.

8. Instead of buying drinks a bars or clubs, get your buzz on before you go out at *ouzeria,* o with the free shots of ouzo or *tsi pouro* you get after many taverna meals.

9. Visit the free (or very cheap archaeological sites to get you ancient fix instead of going to the archaeological museums.

10. Bypass the waterfront estab lishments and head inland Everything—food, rooms, and sights—will be cheaper.

TIPPING AND BARGAINING

Greek law stipulates that restaurant and cafe prices include a 13% gratuity surcharge. You do not need to leave a tip unless you want to show your appreciation for a particularly good server (around 5%), but it is common to round up your check to the nearest euro. Similar rules apply to taxi rides.

Bargaining skills won't get you as far as they would have even five years ago, but you can try your luck when appropriate. Paying the asked price for street wares might leave the seller marveling at your naïveté, while bargaining at the shop of a master craftsman would be disrespectful. The price tends to be more flexible in informal venues. If it's unclear whether bargaining is appropriate in a situation, hang back and watch someone else buy. Also, if you seem unsure, merchants might start the negotiations themselves. Merchants with any pride in their wares will refuse to sell to someone who has offended them in the negotiations. **Domatia** (p. 39) prices rise in summer and drop in winter (unless you're visiting a mountain town known for winter activities). You'll likely have success bargaining in domatia and other small hotels. If your **taxi** trip won't be metered or ticketed—though you should generally seek out metered rides—bargain before you get going.

TAXES

Greece imposes a value added tax (VAT) on sales, for more information, see the **Customs** section (p. 11).

PACKING

Pack lightly: Lay out only what you absolutely need, then take half the clothes and twice the money. The Travelite FAQ (www.travelite.org) is a good resource for tips on traveling light. The online **Universal Packing List** (http://upl.codeq.info) will generate a customized list of suggested items based on your trip length, the expected climate, your planned activities, and other factors. If you plan to do a lot of hiking, also consult **The Great Outdoors,** p. 41. Some frequent travelers keep a bag packed with all the essentials: passport, money belt, hat, socks, etc. Then, when they decide to leave, they know they haven't forgotten anything.

Luggage: If you plan to cover most of your itinerary by foot, a sturdy **frame backpack** is unbeatable. (For the basics on buying a pack, see p. 43.) Toting a **suitcase** or **trunk** is fine if you plan to live in one or two cities and explore from there, but not a great idea if you plan to move around frequently. In addition to your main piece of luggage, a **daypack** (a small backpack or courier bag) is useful.

Clothing: If you are in Greece at the height of summer, you'll need little more than **comfortable shoes,** a few changes of **light clothes,** and a **jacket.** When Greece gets chilly in the winter months, rains come frequently, so bring a **rain jacket** (Gore-Tex® is both waterproof and breathable). **Flip-flops** or waterproof sandals are must-haves for grubby hostel showers. To visit monasteries or churches, men will need a lightweight pair of **pants** and women will need a **long skirt;** both will need clothes that cover the shoulders. If you plan on taking ferries you'll want a **windproof jacket,** and, if you want to hike, add sturdy shoes or **hiking boots** and **thick socks.** You may also want one outfit for going out at night, and maybe a nicer pair of shoes.

Sleepsack: Some hostels require that you either provide your own linen or rent sheets from them. Save cash by making your own sleepsack: fold a full-size sheet in half the long way, then sew it closed along the long side and one of the short sides.

Converters and Adapters: In Greece, electricity is 220 volts AC, enough to fry any 120V North American appliance. 220/240V electrical appliances won't work with a 120V current, either. Americans and Canadians should buy an adapter (which changes the shape of the plug; US$5) and a converter (which changes the voltage; US$20-$30). Don't make the mistake of using only an adapter (unless appliance instructions explicitly state otherwise). Australians and New Zealanders (who use 230V at home) won't need a converter, but will need a set of adapters to use anything electrical. For more on all things adaptable, check out http://kropla.com/electric.htm.

Toiletries: Deodorant, razors, tampons, condoms, and toothbrushes are often available, but it may be difficult to find your preferred brand; bring extras. Contact lenses are likely to be expensive and difficult to find, so bring enough extra pairs and solution for your entire trip. Also bring your glasses and a copy of your prescription in case you need emergency replacements. If you use heat-disinfection, either switch temporarily to a chemical disinfection system (check first to make sure it's safe with your brand of lenses), or buy a converter to 220/240V.

First-Aid Kit: For a basic first-aid kit, pack bandages, a pain reliever, antibiotic cream, a thermometer, a multifunction pocketknife, tweezers, moleskin, decongestant, motion-sickness remedy, diarrhea or upset-stomach medication (Pepto Bismol® or Imodium®), an antihistamine, sunscreen, insect repellent, and burn ointment.

Film: Film and developing in Greece are expensive (about US$11 for a roll of 24 color exposures), so consider bringing along enough film for your entire trip and developing it at home. If you don't want to bother with film, consider using a digital camera. Although it requires a steep initial investment, a digital camera means you never have to buy film again. Just be sure to bring along a large enough memory card and extra (or recharge-able) batteries. For more info on digital cameras, visit www.shortcourses.com/choos-ing/contents.htm. Less serious photographers may want to bring a disposable camera or two. Airport security X-rays can fog film, so buy a lead-lined pouch at a camera store or ask security to hand-inspect it. Always pack film in your carry-on luggage, since higher-intensity X-rays are used on checked luggage.

Other Useful Items: For safety purposes, you should bring a **money belt** and a small **pad-lock.** Basic **outdoors equipment** (plastic water bottle, compass, waterproof matches, pocketknife, sunglasses, sunscreen, hat) may also prove useful. **Quick repairs** of torn garments can be done on the road with a needle and thread; also consider bringing elec-trical tape for patching tears. If you want to do laundry by hand, bring detergent, a small rubber ball to stop up the sink, and string for a makeshift clothes line. Other things you're liable to forget include: an umbrella, sealable **plastic bags** (for damp clothes, soap, food, shampoo, and other spillables), an **alarm clock,** safety pins, rubber bands, a flashlight, earplugs, garbage bags, and a small calculator. A **cell phone** can be a lifesaver (literally) on the road; see p. 37 for information on acquiring one that will work in Greece.

Important Documents: Don't forget your passport, traveler's checks, ATM and/or credit cards, adequate ID, and photocopies of all of the aforementioned in case these docu-ments are lost or stolen. Also check that you have any of the following that might apply to you: a hosteling membership card (p. 40); driver's license (p. 11); travel insurance forms (p. 20); ISIC (p. 11); and/or rail or bus pass (p. 29).

SAFETY AND HEALTH

GENERAL ADVICE

In any type of crisis situation, the most important thing to do is **stay calm.** Your country's embassy abroad (p. 9) is usually your best resource when things go wrong; registering with that embassy upon arrival in the country is often a good idea. The government offices listed in the **Travel Advisories** box (p. 19) can provide information on the services they offer their citizens in case of emergencies abroad.

LOCAL LAWS AND POLICE

Greek police are used to having foreigners around, but that does not mean they allow them to break the law. Photographs and notes cannot be taken near military establishments (including docks). The purchase of pirated goods (including CDs) is illegal; keep your receipts for proof of purchase. Taking objects or rocks from ancient sites is forbidden and can incur fines or prison sentences. Drunk driving and indecent behavior also can result in arrest, fines, and imprisonment. A passport or photo ID should be carried with you at all times.

DRUGS AND ALCOHOL

Visitors of all ages generally have little difficulty obtaining alcohol in Greece. Drugs laws are very strict. Conviction for possession, use, or trafficking of drugs, including marijuana, will result in imprisonment and fines. If you use **prescription drugs,** have a copy of the prescriptions themselves and a note from a doctor available, especially at border crossings. Keep all medication with you in your carry-on luggage. Authorities are particularly vigilant at the Turkish and Albanian borders.

SPECIFIC CONCERNS

EARTHQUAKES

Greece experiences frequent and occasionally large earthquakes. Earthquakes cannot be predicted and can occur at any time of day. If an earthquake does occur, protect yourself by moving underneath a sturdy doorway, table, or desk. In mountainous regions, landslides may follow quakes.

DEMONSTRATIONS AND POLITICAL GATHERINGS

Strikes and demonstrations occur often in Greece and can be inconvenient, but more serious civil disorder is not generally a problem. Still, it is wise to pay attention to where demonstrations are, and try to avoid them as there is always the possibility of violence. Common areas for protest include Exarhia (especially by the Polytechnic University), Omonia, Pl. Syndagma and Pl. Mavili (near the US embassy) in Athens, and the area near Aristotle University in Thessaloniki.

TERRORISM

As in any other part of the world, the threat of terrorism exists in Greece. The best thing you can do is be aware of your surroundings, especially in crowded areas or tourist sites. Domestic terrorism in Greece is carried out mostly by anarchist groups, but it tends to be on a low scale and directed at the government. The box below on **travel advisories** lists offices to contact and webpages to visit to get the most updated list of your home country's government's advisories about travel.

PERSONAL SAFETY

EXPLORING AND TRAVELING

To avoid unwanted attention, try to blend in as much as possible. Respecting local customs (in many cases, dressing more conservatively than you would at home) may placate would-be hecklers. Familiarize yourself with your surroundings before setting out, and carry yourself with confidence. Check maps in shops and restaurants rather than on the street. If you are traveling alone, be sure someone at home knows your itinerary, and never tell anyone you meet that you're by yourself. When walking at night, stick to busy, well-lit streets and avoid dark alleyways. If you ever feel uncomfortable, leave the area as quickly and directly as you can.

TRAVEL ADVISORIES. The following government offices provide travel information and advisories by telephone, by fax, or via the web:

Australian Department of Foreign Affairs and Trade: ☎612 6261 1111; www.dfat.gov.au.

Canadian Department of Foreign Affairs and International Trade (DFAIT): ☎800-267-8376; www.dfait-maeci.gc.ca. Call for their free booklet, *Bon Voyage...But.*

New Zealand Ministry of Foreign Affairs: ☎044 398 000; www.mfat.govt.nz.

United Kingdom Foreign and Commonwealth Office: ☎20 70 08 15 00; www.fco.gov.uk.

US Department of State: ☎888-407-4747; http://travel.state.gov. Visit the website for the booklet *A Safe Trip Abroad.*

There is no sure-fire way to avoid all the threatening situations you might encounter while traveling, but a good **self-defense course** will give you concrete ways to react to unwanted advances. **Impact, Prepare,** and **Model Mugging** can refer you to local self-defense courses in Australia, Canada, Switzerland, and the US. Visit the website at www.modelmugging.org for a list of nearby chapters.

If you are using a **car,** learn local driving signals and wear a seatbelt. Study route maps before you hit the road, and if you plan on spending a lot of time driving, consider bringing spare parts. For long drives in desolate areas, invest in a cellular phone and a roadside assistance program (see p. 34). Park your vehicle in a garage or well-traveled area, and use a steering wheel locking device in larger cities. **Sleeping in your car** is the most dangerous way to get your rest, and it's also illegal in many countries. For info on the perils of **hitchhiking,** see p. 35.

POSSESSIONS AND VALUABLES

Never leave your belongings unattended; crime occurs in even the most safe-looking hostel or hotel. Bring your own padlock for hostel lockers, and don't ever store valuables in a locker. Be particularly careful on **buses** and **trains;** horror stories abound about determined thieves who wait for travelers to fall asleep. Carry your bag or purse in front of you where you can see it. When traveling with others, sleep in alternate shifts. When alone, use good judgment in selecting a train compartment: never stay in an empty one, and use a lock to secure your pack to the luggage rack. Use extra caution if traveling at night or on overnight trains. Try to sleep on top bunks with your luggage stored above you (if not in bed with you), and keep important documents and other valuables on you at all times.

There are a few steps you can take to minimize the financial risk associated with traveling. First, **bring as little with you as possible.** Second, buy a few combination **padlocks** to secure your belongings either in your pack or in a hostel or train station locker. Third, **carry as little cash as possible.** Keep your traveler's checks and ATM/credit cards in a **money belt**—not a "fanny pack"—along with your passport and ID cards. Fourth, **keep a small cash reserve separate from your primary stash.** This should be about US$50 (US$ or euro are best) sewn into or stored in the depths of your pack, along with your traveler's check numbers and photocopies of your passport, your birth certificate, and other important documents.

In large cities **con artists** often work in groups and may involve children. Beware of certain classics: sob stories that require money, rolls of bills "found" on the street, mustard spilled (or saliva spit) onto your shoulder to distract you while they snatch your bag. **Never let your passport and your bags out of your sight.** Hostel workers sometimes stand at bus and train station arrival points to recruit tired and disoriented travelers to their hostel; never believe strangers who tell you that theirs is the only hostel open. Beware of **pickpockets** in city crowds, especially on public transportation. Though Greece typically has very low petty crime rates, complaints of pickpockets, especially around Athens, have increased. Also, be alert in public telephone booths: If you must say your calling card number, do so very quietly; if you punch it in, make sure no one can look over your shoulder.

If you will be traveling with electronic devices, such as a laptop computer or a PDA, check whether your homeowner's insurance covers loss, theft, or damage when you travel. If not, consider purchasing a separate insurance policy. **Safeware** (☎ 800-800-1492; www.safeware.com) specializes in covering computers and charges $90 for 90-day comprehensive international travel coverage up to $4000.

PRE-DEPARTURE HEALTH

In your **passport,** write the names of any people you wish to be contacted in case of a medical emergency, and list any allergies or medical conditions. Matching a prescription to a foreign equivalent is not always easy, safe, or possible, so if you take prescription drugs, consider carrying up-to-date prescriptions or a statement from your doctor stating the medication's trade name, manufacturer, chemical name, and dosage. While traveling, be sure to keep all medication with you in your carry-on luggage. For tips on packing a **first-aid kit** and other health essentials, see p. 17. Greek doctors and pharmacists most likely will recognize the words "antibiotic," "penicillin," "acetaminophen," etc.

IMMUNIZATIONS AND PRECAUTIONS

Though no immunizations are needed to travel in Greece, travelers over two years old should be up-to-date with the following vaccines: MMR (for measles, mumps, and rubella); DTaP or Td (for diphtheria, tetanus, and pertussis); IPV (for polio); Hib (for *Haemophilus influenzae* B); and HepB (for Hepatitis B). For recommendations on immunizations and prophylaxis, consult the Centers for Disease Control and Prevention (CDC; see below) in the US or the equivalent in your home country, and check with a doctor for guidance.

USEFUL ORGANIZATIONS AND PUBLICATIONS

The American **Centers for Disease Control and Prevention** (**CDC;** ☎ 877-FYI-TRIP; www.cdc.gov/travel) maintains an international travelers' hotline and an informative website. Consult the appropriate government agency of your home country for consular information sheets on health, entry requirements, and other issues for various countries (see the listings in the box on **Travel Advisories,** p. 19). For quick information on health and other travel warnings, call the **Overseas Citizens Services** (M-F 8am-8pm from US ☎ 888-407-4747, from overseas 202-501-4444), or contact a passport agency, embassy, or consulate abroad. For information on medical evacuation services and travel insurance firms, see the US government's website at http://travel.state.gov/travel/abroad_health.html or the **British Foreign and Commonwealth Office** (www.fco.gov.uk). For general health information, contact the **American Red Cross** (☎ 202-303-4498; www.redcross.org).

STAYING HEALTHY

Common sense is the simplest prescription for good health while you travel. Drink lots of fluids to prevent dehydration and constipation, and wear sturdy, broken-in shoes and clean socks. The Greek sun can be especially brutal in the summer, so also be sure to bring a hat and sunscreen.

ONCE IN GREECE

ENVIRONMENTAL HAZARDS

Heat exhaustion and dehydration: Heat exhaustion leads to nausea, excessive thirst, headaches, and dizziness. Avoid it by drinking plenty of fluids, eating salty foods (e.g., crackers), abstaining from dehydrating beverages (e.g., alcohol and caffeinated beverages), and wearing sunscreen. Continuous heat stress eventually can lead to heatstroke, characterized by a rising temperature, severe headache, delirium and cessation of sweating. Victims should be cooled off with wet towels and taken to a doctor.

Sunburn: Always wear sunscreen (SPF 30 is good) when spending excessive amounts of time outdoors, or you may end up toasted like Icarus. If you do fall victim to Helios's wrath, drink more fluids than usual and apply an aloe-based lotion. Severe sunburns can lead to sun poisoning, a condition that affects the entire body, causing fever, chills, nausea, and vomiting. Sun poisoning always should be treated by a doctor.

High Altitude: It's not easy for mortals to scale Mt. Olympus. If you're visiting Greece's mountainous regions, allow your body a couple of days to adjust to less oxygen before exerting yourself. Note that alcohol is more potent and UV rays are stronger at high elevations.

INSECT-BORNE DISEASES

Many diseases are transmitted by insects—mainly mosquitoes, fleas, ticks, and lice. Be aware of insects in wet or forested areas, especially while hiking and camping; wear long pants and long sleeves, tuck your pants into your socks, and use a mosquito net. Use insect repellents such as DEET and soak or spray your gear with permethrin (licensed in the US only for use on clothing). **Mosquitoes**—responsible for diseases including malaria, dengue fever, and yellow fever—can be particularly dangerous in wet, swampy, or wooded areas. **Ticks**—which can carry Lyme and other diseases—can be dangerous in rural and forested regions, particularly in Northern and Central Greece.

Tick-borne encephalitis: A viral infection of the central nervous system transmitted during the summer by tick bites (primarily in wooded areas) or by consumption of unpasteurized dairy products. The risk of contracting the disease is relatively low, especially if precautions are taken against tick bites.

Lyme disease: A bacterial infection carried by ticks and marked by a circular bull's-eye rash of 2in. or more. Later symptoms include fever, headache, fatigue, and aches and pains. Antibiotics are effective if administered early. Left untreated, Lyme can cause problems in joints, the heart, and the nervous system. If you find a tick attached to your skin, grasp the head with tweezers as close to your skin as possible and apply slow, steady traction. Removing a tick within 24 hours greatly reduces the risk of infection. Do not try to remove ticks with petroleum jelly, nail polish remover, or a hot match. Ticks usually inhabit moist, shaded environments and heavily wooded areas. If you are going to be hiking in these areas, wear long clothes and DEET.

Other insect-borne diseases: Lymphatic filariasis is a roundworm infestation transmitted by mosquitoes. Infection causes enlargement of extremities and has no vaccine. **Leishmaniasis,** a parasite transmitted by sand flies, can occur on both the islands and the mainland. Common symptoms are fever, weakness, and swelling of the spleen, as well as skin sores weeks to months after the bite. There is a treatment, but no vaccine.

FOOD- AND WATER-BORNE DISEASES

Prevention is the best cure: be sure that your food is properly cooked and the water you drink is clean. Though Greece's tap water is very safe, it is generally a good idea to peel fruits and vegetables and drink bottled water in rural areas of the more remote islands. Watch out for food from markets or street vendors that may have been cooked in unhygienic conditions. Other culprits are raw shellfish, unpasteurized milk, and sauces containing raw eggs. Buy bottled water, or purify your own water by bringing it to a rolling boil or treating it with **iodine tablets;** note, however, that some parasites such as *giardia* have exteriors that resist iodine treatment, so boiling is more reliable. Always wash your hands before eating or bring a quick-drying purifying liquid hand cleaner.

 Due to the plumbing system in Greece, toilet paper should not be flushed. A trash can generally is provided for anything you might throw into the toilet.

Traveler's diarrhea: Results from drinking fecally contaminated water or eating uncooked and contaminated foods. Symptoms include nausea, bloating, and urgency. Try quick-energy, non-sugary foods with protein and carbohydrates to keep your strength up. Over-the-counter anti-diarrheals (e.g., Imodium®) may counteract the problem. The most dangerous side effect is dehydration; drink 8 oz. of water with ½ tsp. of sugar or honey and a pinch of salt, try uncaffeinated soft drinks, or eat salted crackers. If you develop a fever or your symptoms don't go away after 4-5 days, consult a doctor. Consult a doctor immediately for treatment of diarrhea in children.

OTHER INFECTIOUS DISEASES

The following diseases exist in every part of the world. Travelers should know how to recognize them and what to do if they suspect they have been infected.

Rabies: Transmitted through the saliva of infected animals; fatal if untreated. By the time symptoms (thirst and muscle spasms) appear, the disease is in its terminal stage. If you are bitten, wash the wound, seek immediate medical care, and try to have the animal located. A rabies vaccine, which consists of 3 shots given over a 21-day period, is available and recommended for developing world travel, but is only semi-effective.

Hepatitis B: A viral infection of the liver transmitted via blood or other bodily fluids. Symptoms, which may not surface until years after infection, include jaundice, appetite loss, fever, and joint pain. It is transmitted through unprotected sex and unclean needles. A 3-shot vaccination sequence is recommended for sexually active travelers and anyone planning to seek medical treatment abroad; it must begin 6 months before traveling.

Hepatitis C: Like Hepatitis B, but the mode of transmission differs. IV drug users, those with occupational exposure to blood, hemodialysis patients, and recipients of blood transfusions are at the highest risk, but the disease also can be spread through sexual contact or sharing items like razors and toothbrushes that may have traces of blood on them. No symptoms are exhibited. If untreated, Hepatitis C can lead to liver failure.

AIDS and HIV: For detailed information on Acquired Immune Deficiency Syndrome (AIDS) in Greece, call the US Centers for Disease Control's 24hr. hotline at ☎800-342-2437, or contact the Joint United Nations Programme on HIV/AIDS (UNAIDS), 20 Ave. Appia, CH-1211 Geneva 27, Switzerland (☎22 791 3666; fax 22 791 4187).

Sexually transmitted infections (STIs): Gonorrhea, chlamydia, genital warts, syphilis, herpes, HPV, and other STIs are easier to catch than HIV and can be just as serious. Though condoms may protect you from some STIs, oral or even tactile contact can lead to transmission. If you think you may have contracted an STI, see a doctor immediately.

OTHER HEALTH CONCERNS

MEDICAL CARE ON THE ROAD

All travelers from the EU receive free health care in Greece with the presentation of an **E111 form.** A doctor can be found on every inhabited island and in every town; emergency treatment is available to travelers of all nationalities in public hospitals. While Greece offers outstanding medical training, the healthcare system is vastly underfunded. Public hospitals are overcrowded; in some locations, their hygiene may be questionable. Private hospitals generally provide better care, but they cost more; to use them you will need good **health insurance.** If your regular policy does not cover travel abroad, you may wish to buy additional coverage.

Pharmacies (φαρμακία, far-mah-KEE-ah), labeled by green or red crosses, are common. In most towns and cities, at least one pharmacy is open at all hours—most post listings of available 24hr. pharmacies in their windows.

If you are concerned about obtaining medical assistance while traveling, you may wish to employ special support services. The *MedPass* from **GlobalCare, Inc.,** 6875 Shiloh Rd. East, Alpharetta, GA 30005, USA (☎800-860-1111; www.global-care.net), provides 24hr. international medical assistance, support, and medical evacuation resources. The **International Association for Medical Assistance to Travelers (IAMAT;** US ☎716-754-4883, Canada 519-836-0102; www.iamat.org) has free membership, lists English-speaking doctors worldwide, and offers detailed info on immunization requirements and sanitation. If your regular **insurance** policy does not cover travel abroad, you may wish to purchase additional coverage (see p. 20).

Those with medical conditions (such as diabetes, allergies to antibiotics, epilepsy, or heart conditions) may want to obtain a **MedicAlert** membership (US$40 per year), which includes among other things a stainless steel ID tag and a 24hr. collect-call number. Contact the MedicAlert Foundation International, 2323 Colorado Ave., Turlock, CA 95382, USA (☎888-633-4298, outside US ☎209-668-3333; www.medicalert.org).

WOMEN'S HEALTH

Women traveling in unsanitary conditions are vulnerable to **urinary tract, bladder, and kidney infections.** Over-the-counter medicines sometimes can alleviate symptoms, but if they persist, see a doctor. **Vaginal yeast infections** may flare up in hot and humid climates. Wearing loosely fitting pants or a skirt and cotton underwear will help, as will over-the-counter remedies like Monistat® or Gyne-Lotrimin®. Bring supplies from home if you are prone to infection, as they may be difficult to find on the road. And, since **tampons, pads,** and reliable **contraceptive devices** are sometimes hard to find when traveling, bring supplies with you. **Abortion** is legal in Greece. A useful resource for reproductive health is the **Family Planning Association of Greece** (☎21072 86 332), Alkaiou 10, Athens 115 28.

GETTING TO GREECE

BY PLANE

When it comes to airfare, a little effort can save you a bundle. Courier fares are the cheapest for those whose plans are flexible enough to deal with the restrictions. Tickets sold by consolidators and standby seating are also good deals, but last-minute specials, airfare wars, and charter flights often beat these fares. The key is to hunt around, be flexible, and ask about discounts. Students, seniors, and those under 26 never should pay full price for a ticket.

AIRFARES

Airfares to Greece peak between June and August; holidays also are expensive. The cheapest times to travel are October and late March. Midweek (M-Th morning) round-trip flights run US$40-50 cheaper than weekend flights, but they are generally more crowded and less likely to permit frequent-flier upgrades. Not fixing a return date ("open return") or arriving in and departing from different cities ("open-jaw") can be pricier than round-trip flights. Patching one-way flights together is the most expensive way to travel. Flights between Greece's capitals or regional hubs and islands will tend to be cheaper.

If Greece is only one stop on a more extensive globe-hop, consider a round-the-world (RTW) ticket. Tickets usually include at least five stops and are valid for about a year; prices range US$1200-5000. Try **Northwest Airlines/KLM** (☎800-225-2525; www.nwa.com) or **Star Alliance,** a consortium of 16 airlines including United Airlines (www.staralliance.com).

Fares for roundtrip flights to Athens from the US or Canadian east coast generally cost US$600-800 in low season (Oct.-Mar.) and US$1200-1600 in high season (June-Sept.); from the US or Canadian west coast US$800-1100 in low season and US$1400-1700 in high season; from the UK, £80-150 in low or high season; from Australia AUS$1500-1900 in low season and AUS$1800-2500 in high season; from New Zealand NZ$1900-2500 in low season and NZ$2100-3000 in high season.

BUDGET AND STUDENT TRAVEL AGENCIES

While knowledgeable agents specializing in flights to Greece can make your life easy and help you save, they may not spend the time to find you the lowest possible fare. Travelers holding **ISICs** and **IYTCs** (see p. 11) qualify for big discounts from student travel agencies. Most flights from budget agencies are on major airlines, but in peak season some may sell seats on less reliable chartered aircraft.

CTS Travel, 30 Rathbone Pl., London W1T 1GQ, UK (☎20 74 47 50 00; www.ctstravel.co.uk). A British student travel agent with offices in 39 countries including the US, Empire State Building, 350 Fifth Ave., Suite 7813, New York, NY 10118 (☎877-287-6665; www.ctstravelusa.com).

STA Travel, 5900 Wilshire Blvd., Ste. 900, Los Angeles, CA 90036, USA (24hr. reservations and info ☎800-781-4040; www.statravel.com). A student and youth travel organization with over 150 offices worldwide (check their website for a listing of all their offices), including US offices in Boston, Chicago, Los Angeles, New York, Seattle, San Francisco, and Washington, D.C. Ticket booking, travel insurance, railpasses, and more. Walk-in offices are located throughout Australia (☎03 9207 5900), New Zealand (☎09 309 9723), and the UK (☎08701 630 026).

Travel CUTS (Canadian Universities Travel Services Limited), 187 College St., Toronto, ON M5T 1P7, Canada (☎888-592-2887; www.travelcuts.com). Offices across Canada and the US including Los Angeles, New York, Seattle, and San Francisco.

USIT, 19-21 Aston Quay, Dublin 2, Ireland (☎01 602 1904; www.usit.ie), Ireland's leading student/budget travel agency has 20 offices throughout Northern Ireland and the Republic of Ireland. Offers programs to work, study, and volunteer worldwide.

Wasteels, Skoubogade 6, 1158 Copenhagen K., Denmark (☎3314 4633; www.wasteels.com). A huge chain with 180 locations across Europe. Sells Wasteels BIJ tickets discounted 30-45% off regular fare, 2nd-class international point-to-point train tickets with unlimited stopovers for those under 26 (sold only in Europe).

COMMERCIAL AIRLINES

The commercial airlines' lowest regular offer is the **APEX** (Advance Purchase Excursion) fare, which provides confirmed reservations and allows "open-jaw" tickets. Generally, reservations must be made seven to 21 days ahead of departure, with seven- to 14-day minimum-stay and up to 90-day maximum-stay restrictions. These fares carry hefty cancellation and change penalties (fees rise in summer). Book peak-season APEX fares early. Use **Expedia** (www.expedia.com) or **Travelocity** (www.travelocity.com) to get an idea of the lowest published fares, then use

FLIGHT PLANNING ON THE INTERNET. The Internet may be the budget traveler's dream when it comes to finding and booking bargain fares, but the array of options can be overwhelming. Many airline sites offer special last-minute deals on the Web. **Cheap-Flight-To** (www.cheap-flight-to.com/greece.htm) and **GreeceFlights** (www.greeceflights.com) specialize in booking discounted flights, and **easyJet** (www.easyjet.com) finds cheap flights from major European cities to Athens.

STA (www.statravel.com) and **StudentUniverse** (www.studentuniverse.com) provide quotes on student tickets, while **Orbitz** (www.orbitz.com), **Expedia** (www.expedia.com), and **Travelocity** (www.travelocity.com) offer full travel services. **Priceline** (www.priceline.com) lets you specify a price, and obligates you to buy any ticket that meets or beats it; **Hotwire** (www.hotwire.com) offers bargain fares, but won't reveal the airline or flight times until you buy. Other sites that compile deals include www.bestfares.com, www.flights.com, www.lowestfare.com, www.onetravel.com, and www.travelzoo.com.

SideStep (www.sidestep.com) and **Booking Buddy** (www.bookingbuddy.com) are online tools that can help sift through multiple offers; these two let you enter your trip information once and search multiple sites.

Air Traveler's Handbook (www.faqs.org/faqs/travel/air/handbook) is an indispensable resource on the Internet; it has a comprehensive listing of links to everything you need to know before you board a plane.

the resources outlined here to try to beat those fares. Low-season fares should be appreciably cheaper than the **high-season** (June-Sept.) ones listed here.

TRAVELING FROM NORTH AMERICA

Most direct flights from North America to Greece leave from New York, and there are no direct flights from the West Coast. Standard commercial carriers like **American** (☎800-433-7300; www.aa.com), **United** (☎800-538-2929; www.ual.com), and **Northwest** (☎800-447-4747; www.nwa.com) will probably offer the most convenient flights, but they may not be the cheapest, unless you grab a special promotion or airfare war ticket. You likely will find flying one of the following "discount" airlines a better deal, if their limited departure points are convenient for you.

Finnair: ☎800-950-5000; www.finnair.com. Cheap round-trips from San Francisco, New York, and Toronto to Helsinki; connections throughout Europe.

Icelandair: ☎800-223-5500; www.icelandair.com. Stopovers in Iceland for no extra cost on most transatlantic flights. For last-minute offers, subscribe to their email Lucky Fares.

SWISS: ☎877-359-7947; www.swiss.com. Inexpensive flights to Athens from New York and Boston; usually connects through Zurich.

TRAVELING FROM IRELAND AND THE UK

Because there are many carriers flying from the UK to the continent, *Let's Go* only includes discount airlines or those with cheap specials. The **Air Travel Advisory Bureau** in London (☎0870 737 0021; www.atab.co.uk) provides referrals to travel agencies and consolidators that offer discounted airfares out of the UK. **Cheapflights** (www.cheapflights.co.uk) publishes airfare bargains.

British Airways: UK ☎0870 850 9850; www.britishairways.com.

easyJet: UK ☎08712 442 366; www.easyjet.com. London to Athens, Barcelona, Madrid, Nice, Palma, and Zurich (UK£72-141).

KLM: UK ☎0870 507 4074; www.klmuk.com. Cheap round-trip tickets from London and elsewhere to Athens and other European cities.

TRAVELING FROM AUSTRALIA AND NEW ZEALAND

Qantas Air: Australia ☎13 13 13, New Zealand ☎0800 808 767; www.qantas.com.au. Flies from Australia and New Zealand to London. Then catch connections on other airlines to Greece from London.

Singapore Air: Australia ☎13 10 11, New Zealand ☎0800 808 909; www.singaporeair.com. Flies from Auckland, Sydney, Melbourne, and Perth to Athens.

Thai Airways: Australia ☎1300 65 19 60, New Zealand ☎09 377 38 86; www.thaiair.com. Flies from Auckland, Melbourne, Perth, and Sydney to Athens.

AIR COURIER FLIGHTS

Those who travel light should consider courier flights. Couriers help transport cargo on international flights by using their checked luggage space for freight. Generally, couriers are limited to carry-ons and must deal with complex flight restrictions. Most flights are round-trip only, with short fixed-length stays and a limit of a one ticket per issue. Most of these flights also operate only out of major gateway cities, mostly in North America. Round-trip courier fares from the US to Greece run about US$600. Most flights leave from Los Angeles, Miami, New York, or San Francisco in the US and from Montreal, Toronto, or Vancouver in Canada. Generally, you must be over 18 (in some cases 21). In summer, the most popular destinations usually require an advance reservation of about two weeks (you usually can book up to two months ahead). Super-discounted fares are common for "last-minute" flights (three to 14 days ahead). The organizations below provide members with lists of opportunities and courier brokers for an annual fee.

International Association of Air Travel Couriers (**IAATC;** www.courier.org). From 7 North American cities to European cities. One-year membership US$45.

Courier Travel (www.couriertravel.org). Searchable online database. Multiple departure points in the US to **various European destinations.**

STANDBY FLIGHTS

Traveling standby requires flexibility in arrival and departure dates. Companies dealing in standby flights sell vouchers rather than tickets, along with the promise to get you to your destination (or near your destination) within a certain window of time (typically 1-5 days). You call in before your specific window of time to hear your flight options and the probability that you will be able to board each flight. You then can decide which flights you want to try to catch, show up at the appropriate airport at the appropriate time, present your voucher, and board if space is available. Vouchers usually can be bought for both one-way and round-trip travel. You may receive a monetary refund only if every available flight within your date range is full; if you opt not to take an available (but perhaps less convenient) flight, you only can get credit toward future travel. Read agreements with any company offering standby flights with care, paying attention to fine print. To check on a company's service record in the US, contact the Better Business Bureau (☎703-276-0100; www.bbb.org). It is difficult to receive refunds, and clients' vouchers will not be honored when an airline fails to receive payment in time.

TICKET CONSOLIDATORS

Ticket consolidators, or **"bucket shops,"** buy unsold tickets in bulk from commercial airlines and sell them at discounted rates. The best place to look is in the Sunday travel section of any major newspaper (such as *The New York Times*), where many bucket shops place tiny ads. Call quickly, as availability is extremely limited. Not all bucket shops are reliable, so insist on a receipt that gives full details of restrictions, refunds, and tickets, and pay by credit card (in spite of the 2-5% fee) so you can stop payment if you never receive your tickets. For more info, see www.travel-library.com/air-travel/consolidators.html.

TRAVELING FROM CANADA AND THE US

Some consolidators worth trying are **Rebel** (☎ 800-732-3588; www.rebeltours.com), **Cheap Tickets** (www.cheaptickets.com), **Flights.com** (www.flights.com), and **TravelHUB** (www.travelhub.com). *Let's Go* does not endorse any of these agencies. As always, be cautious, and research companies before you hand over your credit card number.

CHARTER FLIGHTS

Tour operators contract charter flights with airlines in order to fly extra loads of passengers during peak season. These flights are far from hassle-free. They occur less frequently than major airlines, make refunds particularly difficult, and are almost always fully booked. Their scheduled times may change and they may be cancelled at the last moment (as late as 48 hours before the trip, and without a full refund). In addition, check-in, boarding, and baggage claim for them are often much slower. They can be, however, much cheaper.

Discount clubs and fare brokers offer members savings on last-minute charter and tour deals. Study contracts closely; you don't want to end up with an unwanted overnight layover. **Travelers Advantage** (☎ 800-835-8747; www.travelersadvantage.com; US$90 annual fee includes discounts and cheap flight directories) specializes in **European** travel and tour packages.

BY FERRY OR BUS

BY FERRY. Ferries are a popular way to get to and travel within Greece; finding a boat agency to facilitate your trip should not be difficult. Be warned that **ferries run on irregular schedules.** A few websites, such as **www.ferries.gr,** have tried to keep updated schedules online but often are incomplete. Try to look at a schedule as close to your departure date as possible; you usually can find one at a tourist office or posted at the dock. That said, you also should make reservations and **check in at least 2hr. in advance;** late boarders may find their seats gone. If you sleep on the deck, bring warm clothes and a sleeping bag. Bicycles travel free, but motorcycles cost extra. Bring food to avoid high prices onboard.

The major ports of departure from Italy to Greece are Ancona and Brindisi, in the southeast. Bari, Otranto, Trieste, and Venice also have a few connections. For Greece-Italy schedules, see Patras (p. 150), Kephalonia (p. 553), Corfu (p. 530), or Igoumenitsa (p. 246). Ferries also run from Samos, Chios, and Kos to various Turkish ports. Though no ferries run directly from Albania, several have connections to Bari and Brindisi, where you can switch ferries to catch one to Greece.

BY BUS. There are very few buses running directly from any European city to Greece. **Eurolines,** Via Mercadante 2/b, Firenze 50144, Italy (☎ 055 35 71 10; www.eurolines.it) and **Busabout,** 258 Vauxhall Bridge Road, London SW1V 1BS, UK (☎ 020 7950 1661; www.busabout.com), transport travelers to Italian ports including Ancona, Brindisi, and Venice on their own buses, then arrange ferry transport to locations in Greece. From there, travelers can catch connections to locations throughout Greece. Both Eurolines and Busabout offer **international bus passes,** which often are cheaper than railpasses and allow unlimited travel on a hop-on, hop-off basis between major European cities.

BY TRAIN

A number of international train routes connect Greece via Thessaloniki to most European cities. Eurail (www.eurail.com) passes are valid in Greece, and may be a useful purchase if you plan to visit other European countries in which they are valid. Unfortunately, the Greek rail system is one of Europe's most antiquated and least efficient. A trip from Vienna to Athens takes about three days. For routes and info on special offers, see the **OSE** website (www.osenet.gr).

SHOULD YOU BUY A RAILPASS? You either can buy a **railpass,** which allows you unlimited travel within a particular region for a given period of time, or rely on buying individual **point-to-point** tickets as you go. Railpasses were conceived to allow you to jump on any train in Europe, go wherever you want whenever you want, and change your plans at will. In practice, it's not so simple. You still must stand in line to validate your pass, pay for supplements, and fork over cash for seat reservations. More importantly, passes don't always pay off. Because of Greece's limited railway system, you may not be able to use the train enough to pay off the cost of a pass. In most cases, buses will be preferable.

MULTINATIONAL RAILPASSES. Eurail is **valid** in most of Western Europe: Austria, Belgium, Denmark, Finland, France, Germany, Greece, Hungary, Ireland, Italy, Luxembourg, the Netherlands, Norway, Portugal, Romania, Spain, Sweden, and Switzerland. It is **not valid** in the UK. Several plans are available to fit a variety of itineraries. Passholders receive a timetable for major routes and a map with details on possible ferry, steamer, bus, car rental, and hotel discounts. Passholders often also receive reduced fares or free passage on many bus and boat lines. Eurailpasses are designed by the EU, and can be bought only by non-Europeans, almost exclusively from non-European distributors. The passes are sold at uniform prices determined by the EU. Some travel agents tack on a US$10 handling fee, and others offer bonuses with purchase, so shop around. Keep in mind that prices usually go up each year, so you can save by purchasing before January 1 (you have 3 months from the purchase to validate your pass in Europe).

It is best to buy your Eurail before leaving; only a few places in major European cities sell them, and at a marked-up price. You can get a replacement for a lost pass only if you have purchased insurance on it under the Pass Protection Plan (US$14). Eurailpasses are available through travel agents, student travel agencies like STA and Council, and **Rail Europe** (Canada ☎ 800-361-7245, UK 08 708 371 371, US 877-257-2887; www.raileurope.com) or **DER Travel Services,** whose services are available at several outfits across the US (☎ 800-782-2424; www.der.com).

If your travels will include the Balkan countries bordering Greece, a regional pass often provides a good value. The **Balkan Flexipass,** which is valid for travel in Bulgaria, Greece, the Former Yugoslav Republic of Macedonia (FYROM), Romania, Serbia and Montenegro, and Turkey, allows the pass owner to travel five days out of one month in first class for only US$225.

One daily train connects Istanbul with Thessaloniki, Greece via Alexandroupoli (14 hrs., €14). To go to Athens, you must change trains in Thessaloniki; there are no direct Athens-Istanbul trains.

BORDER CROSSINGS

Greece shares its borders in the north with Albania, Bulgaria, FYROM, and Turkey. Overland transportation between Greece and its northern neighbors is limited to buses and some trains to all bordering countries except Albania. Thessaloniki is the main hub for transportation between Greece and its border countries.

GETTING AROUND GREECE

BY BOAT

If you spend any time on Greece's many islands, you will get to know their wide-spread, unpredictable system of ferries and other aquatic transport very, very well. Arrive at the dock 1-2hr. before departure for a decent seat, though ferries could depart at any point, from 5min. early to 3hr. late. Bring a **windbreaker** if you want to wander the deck when at sea. For short distances, indoor seats fill up quickly.

FERRIES

MAKING SENSE OF FERRIES. Ferries are absolutely essential for reaching the Greek islands, but with schedules that sometimes change week to week (or day to day), they can leave travelers baffled. The key to making good use of ferries is understanding ferry routes and planning your trip accordingly. The ferry service in Greece is sparse during low-season months, but begins to pick up as summer approaches and brings waves of island-seeking tourists. Most ferries, rather than shuttling back and forth between two destinations, trace a four- or five-port route. Many ferry companies will allow you to buy your round-trip ticket **"split,"** meaning that you can ride the Piraeus-Syros-Tinos-Mykonos ferry from Piraeus to Syros, get off, get back on when the same ferry passes Syros several days later, proceed to Tinos, and so on. Remember that geographic proximity is no guarantee that you'll be able to get to one island from another. Also note that there is very little service from the Cyclades to the Dodecanese. Understanding the routes also will help you make sense of discrepancies in ticket prices and travel times.

MAJOR PORTS AND SCHEDULES. As the millennia-old port of Athens, **Piraeus** is the heart of the ferry routes through the Aegean Sea. Routes run to most major islands in the Cyclades, as well as Crete, the Saronic Gulf Islands, several major islands in the Dodecanese and Northeast Aegean Islands, and Turkey. **Rafina,** Athens's smaller, eastern port, sends ferries to Evia, some of the northernmost Cyclades, and many of the Northeast Aegean Islands. Most ferries depart for the Ionian Islands from **Patras** or **Kyllini** on the Peloponnese or **Igoumenitsa** in Epirus. **Agios Konstantinos** and **Volos** handle most ferries to the Sporades and Evia.

Available from ferry companies or posted at the port police, regional schedules with the departure times, routes, and names of each departing ferry are published weekly. Make sure to look at the most updated version of the ferry schedules or call the agency on the island from which you want to leave. As particular ferries, even within companies, vary widely in quality, local travelers should pay close attention to the model of the ferry that they will be riding. Ask around or check on the web (www.ferries.gr) for tips, ferry schedules, and prices.

HYDROFOILS AND CATAMARANS

Hellas Flying Dolphins (☎21041 99 000; www.dolphins.gr or www.hellenicsea-ways.gr) runs most of the hydrofoils and catamarans.

DOLPHIN RIDES. Flying Dolphins, the standard name for hydrofoils in Greece, go twice as fast and look twice as cool, but cost twice as much. If you have cash to spare and want to minimize travel time, these crafts provide extensive, standardized, and sanitized transport between islands; offices and services are listed in the **Transportation** sections of all cities and towns.

Keep in mind that traveling by Dolphin is like traveling by seaborne airplane: passengers are assigned seats and are required to stay in the climate-controlled cabin for the duration of the trip, which may be less than ideal for the easily seasick. There's also something unfortunate about sailing the Aegean in a craft that won't let you get salt on your fingers and wind in your hair.

CATAMARANS. These high-speed double-hulled boats are similar to hydrofoils in speed and cost, but are generally more reliable. They are also very popular with tourists, so don't expect to be able to buy a same-day ticket.

BY PLANE

Olympic Airlines, Greece's national carrier, can be found at Syngrou 96-100, Athens 11741 (☎21092 69 111), and in many other cities. The Olympic Airways website (www.olympicairlines.com) lists information for every office around the globe. **Aegean Airlines** (☎80111 20 000 or 21062 61 000; www.aegeanair.com), a smaller Crete-based airline, also offers flights throughout the mainland and to many of the islands. For flight info within Greece, check regional **Practical Information** listings of airports, destinations, and prices, or get a brochure at any airline office. In recent years, Greece's domestic service has increased appreciably; from Athens a 1hr. flight (US$75-200) can get you to most islands. Even in low season, remote destinations are serviced several times weekly, while more developed areas can have several flights per day. Try to reserve tickets one week in advance.

No-frills airlines have made hopscotching around Europe by air increasingly affordable and convenient. Though these flights often feature inconvenient hours or serve less-popular regional airports, with one-way flights averaging about US$80, it's never been faster or easier to jet across the Continent. The airline with the most inexpensive flights from the UK to Greece is **easyJet** (UK ☎0871 244 2366; www.easyjet.com); it serves 74 key European airports across the UK, France, Spain, Switzerland, the Netherlands, Denmark, Italy, Czech Republic, Greece, Germany, and Portugal. The **Star Alliance European Airpass** (www.staralliance.com) offers economy-class fares as low as US$65 for travel within 41 European countries. The pass is available to transatlantic passengers on Star Alliance carriers, including Air Canada, Austrian Airlines, Lufthansa, Scandinavian Airlines System, Singapore Airlines, Thai Airways International, United Airlines, US Airways, and others. In addition, a number of European airlines offer discount coupon packets. Most are only available as tack-ons for transatlantic passengers, but some are stand-alone offers. Finally, check out the *FlightPass* offered by **Europe by Air** (☎ 888-321-4737; www.europebyair.com), which allows you to country-hop to over 150 European cities (US$99 per one-way flight).

BY BUS

Buses are an essential part of travel in Greece. Service is more extensive, more efficient, and often more comfortable than on trains, and fares are cheap. Unless you're sticking close to train routes, **KTEL** bus service should be sufficient for longer bus trips. Always check with an official source about scheduled departures. Posted schedules are often outdated and all services are curtailed significantly on Saturday and Sunday; bus schedules on major holidays run according to Sunday schedules. Unless they are going longer distances, buses rarely run at night. The English-language weekly newspaper *Athens News* prints Athens bus schedules; they are also available online (www.ktel.org). Try to arrive at least 10min. ahead of time, as Greek buses have a habit of leaving early. In major cities KTEL bus lines may have different stations for different destinations, and schedules generally refer to **endpoints** (e.g., "the bus leaves Kalloni at 3pm and arrives in Mytilini at 4pm") with no mention of the numerous stops in between.

Ask the **conductor** before entering the bus whether it's going to your destination (the signs on the front can be misleading), and ask to be warned when you get there. If you're stowing bags underneath, make sure they're in the compartment for your destination (conductors take great pride in packing the bus for easy unloading, and may refuse to open the "final destination" compartment at the "halfway" stop). If the bus passes your stop, stand up and yell **"STAH-see"** (στάση). On the road, stand near a sign reading στάση to pick up an intercity bus. KTEL buses are **green** or occasionally **orange** or **yellow,** while intercity buses are usually **blue.** For long-distance rides, **buy your ticket beforehand** in the office (otherwise, you may have to stand for the entire journey). For shorter trips, pay the conductor after you have boarded; reasonably close change is expected.

BY TRAIN

Although trains in Greece are cheap, they run less frequently than buses and don't cover as wide a geographic area. They are generally slower than other European trains and can get pretty gritty. If you're lucky, you may come across a new, air-conditioned, intercity train, which is worth the slightly more expensive price.

The **Hellenic Railways Association,** or **OSE (www.osenet.gr), connects Athens to major Greek cities (like Thessaloniki, Patras, and Volos).** Lines do not yet go to the mainland's west coast (although plans are in progress to extend the railway to Ioannina), and they are rarely useful for remote areas or archaeological sites. Bring food and water, because on-board cafes are pricey. Second-class compartments, which seat two to six, are great places to meet fellow travelers. However, it is wise to lock your compartment and keep valuables on your person; for safety tips, see p. 18. For long trips, make sure you are on the correct car, as trains sometimes split at crossroads. Towns listed in parentheses on European train schedules require a train switch at the town listed immediately before the parenthesis.

DOMESTIC RAILPASSES

If you are planning to spend much time within Greece, a national pass—valid on all rail lines in Greece—may be more cost-effective than a multinational pass.

NATIONAL RAILPASSES. The domestic analog of the Eurailpass, the **Greece Pass** offers from three to ten days of unlimited first-class travel in one month on railways throughout Greece, as well as discounts on ferry crossings from Patras to Brindisi (Italy), operated by Hellenic Mediterranean Lines, on the domestic lines of Minoan Lines between Patras and Corfu and between Piraeus and Heraklion, and on a one-day cruise from Athens to Aegina, Poros and Hydra, operated by Ionian Travel. This pass must be purchased from a travel agent or **Rail Europe** (p. 28) before you leave for Europe, and costs from US$132 (3-day pass) to US$416 (10-day pass) for adults, US$112/384 for the under-26 youth pass, and US$99/301 for children 12 and under. You need to get your pass validated before you use it on the train; just bring the pass and your passport to an official in the train station prior to use so that he or she can record the first and last day of the eligibility of the pass. The pass must be validated within six months of issue in order to remain effective. For more information, check out http://www.raileurope.com/us/rail/passes/greek_flexipass_rail_fly.htm.

INTERRAIL. InterRail offers passes that allow travel throughout 30 European countries (including Greece), as well as passes limited to one country. To be eligible, you must have been living in one of the 30 participating countries for at least six months. The Greece Pass includes from three to eight days of travel in one month and costs €74-148 for adults; the Greece Plus Pass also covers the ferry between Greece and Italy operated by Attica Group and costs €117-243. For more information, visit www.railpassshop.com.

BY CAR

Cars are a good choice in Greece, a country where public transportation is generally nonexistent in the night hours; they are especially useful in regions like Crete, where buses between nearby small towns often follow maddeningly indirect routes. Ferries will take you and your car island-hopping if you pay a transport fee for the car. Drivers in Greece must be comfortable with a **standard transmission,** winding mountain roads, and the Greek alphabet—signs in Greek appear roughly 100m before the transliterated versions. Driving is especially useful for exploring remote villages in northern Greece.

With a fatal accident rate that tops those of most countries in Europe, driving in Greece can be a dangerous enterprise. Drivers are notoriously reckless (especially in Athens), often driving on sidewalks and expecting pedestrians to move out of the way. Speed limits often go unposted and are utterly ignored. You must be 18 years old to drive, and both front-seat passengers are required by law to wear seatbelts; common sense says that all passengers should be strapped in. As in the US, cars drive on the right-hand side of the road. For an informal primer on European road signs and conventions, check out www.travlang.com/signs. The **Association for Safe International Road Travel (ASIRT),** 11769 Gainsborough Rd., Potomac, MD 20854, USA (US ☎301-983-5252; www.asirt.org), can provide more specific information about road conditions.

CAR ASSISTANCE. The **Automobile and Touring Club of Greece (ELPA),** Messogion 395, Athens 15343 (☎21060 68 800; www.elpa.gr), provides assistance and offers reciprocal membership to foreign auto club members. They also have 24hr. emergency road assistance (☎104) and a tourist information line (☎174 in Athens).

TAXIS. Taxis can be an invaluable means of transportation in areas where towns are close together but bus routes are sparse. Prices vary throughout Greece. When taking taxis, be aware that some drivers tinker with their meters, while others may not turn their meter on at all, taking you somewhere and then charging an exorbitant fee. Ask the cost of the fare in advance, and if you don't see the meter running yell "taxi-MEH-tro!" (meter). Also, if you ask for a hotel, your driver might have another one in mind—one that has paid him a commission to bring you there. Be firm about where you're going; don't trust a driver who says your hotel is closed.

RENTING

Agencies may quote low daily rates that exclude the 18% VAT and **Collision Damage Waiver (CDW)** insurance. Some places quote low rates and then hit you with hidden charges, such as refueling bills if you come back with less than a full tank, **or up to €300 drop-off charge.** Most companies won't let you drive the car outside Greece. Foreign drivers are required to have an **International Driving Permit (IDP; p. 34)** and an **International Insurance Certificate** to drive in Greece, but EU drivers only need their EU driver's license. Take note that smaller rental cars might have difficulty getting up some of Greece's mountainous roads with four or five people in the car.

RENTAL AGENCIES

Try checking with both the local office in your destination and the major international office in your home country to make sure you get the best price and accurate information. Local desk numbers are included in town listings; for home-country numbers, call your toll-free directory.

To rent a car in Greece, you need to be at least 21 years old. Some agencies require renters to be 23 or 25. Policies and prices vary from agency to agency. Small local operations occasionally rent to people under 21, but be sure to ask about the insurance coverage and deductible and always check the fine print. For more specific information about car rental in Greece, contact the **Panhellenic Federation of Offices for Car & Motorbike Rentals** (☎28102 80 914). Rental agencies with operations in Greece include:

Auto Europe, 39 Commercial St., P.O. Box 7006, Portland, ME 04112, USA (Canada and the US ☎888-223-5555 or 207-842-2000; www.autoeurope.com).

Avis (Greece ☎21032 24 951, Australia 1300 137 498, Canada 800-879-2847, New Zealand 09 526 2847, UK 08706 060 100, US 800-230-4898; www.avis.gr).

Europe by Car (US ☎800-223-1516 or 212-581-3040; www.europebycar.com).

Europcar (Canada and the US ☎877-940-6900; www.europcar.com).

Hertz, Vraniotioti 31, Kifisia 14564 (Greece ☎21062 64 000; www.hertz.gr).

COSTS AND INSURANCE

Rental car prices start at around €35 per day. Expect to pay more for larger cars and for 4WD. **Standard transmission** is usually your only option when renting cars in Greece. Most rental packages offer unlimited kilometers. Return the car with a full tank of petrol (gasoline) to avoid high fuel charges. Be sure to ask whether the price includes **insurance** against theft and collision. Remember that if you are driving a conventional rental vehicle on an **unpaved road,** you are almost never covered by insurance; ask before leaving the rental agency. Beware that cars rented on an **American Express** or **Visa/MasterCard Gold** or **Platinum** credit card in Greece might not carry the automatic insurance that they would in some other countries; check with your credit card company. Insurance plans almost always come with an **excess** (or deductible) of around €300. This means you pay for all damages up to that sum, unless they are the fault of another vehicle. The excess you will be quoted applies to collisions with other vehicles; collisions with non-vehicles such as trees (sometimes known as "single-vehicle collisions") will cost you even more. The excess often can be reduced or waived entirely if you pay an additional charge, around €15 per day. National car rental chains often allow **one-way rentals,** picking up in one city and dropping off in another. There is usually a minimum hire period and sometimes an extra drop-off charge of several hundred euro.

ESSENTIALS

ESSENTIALS

DRIVING PERMITS AND CAR INSURANCE

INTERNATIONAL DRIVING PERMIT (IDP)

If you plan to drive while in **Greece**, you must **be over 18 and** have an International Driving Permit (IDP), accompanied by a valid driver's license from your home country. Your IDP, valid for one year, must be issued in your home country before you leave. An IDP application usually requires one or two photos, a current local license, an additional form of identification, and a fee. To apply, contact your home country's automobile association. Be careful when purchasing an IDP online or anywhere other than your home automobile association; many vendors sell permits of questionable legitimacy for higher prices.

CAR INSURANCE

Most credit cards cover standard insurance. If you rent, lease, or borrow a car, you will need a **Green Card,** or **International Insurance Certificate,** to certify that you have liability insurance and that it applies abroad. Green cards can be obtained at car rental agencies, car dealers (for those leasing cars), some travel agents, and some border crossings. Rental agencies may require you to purchase theft insurance.

ON THE ROAD

Speed limits in Greece range from 50km in developed areas to 100-120km on highways. There are four major national highways in Greece: the E65 runs from Patras to Athens via Corinth; the new E65 runs from Corinth to Tripoli; the E75 runs from Athens to Thessaloniki via Larisa; the Egnatia Odos highway runs from Igoumenitsa to the Turkish border in Evros via Thessaloniki. **Petrol (gasoline)** prices vary but average about €1 per liter in Athens.

DRIVING PRECAUTIONS When traveling in the summer or in the desert, bring substantial amounts of water (a suggested 5 liters of **water** per person per day) for drinking and for the radiator. For long drives to unpopulated areas, register with police before beginning the trek and again upon arrival at the destination. Check with the local automobile club for details. When traveling for long distances, make sure tires are in good repair and have enough air, and get good maps. A **compass** and a **car manual** can also be very useful. You should always carry a **spare tire** and **jack, jumper cables, extra oil, flares,** a **flashlight,** and **heavy blankets** (in case your car breaks down at night or in the winter). If you don't know how to **change a tire,** learn before heading out, especially if you are planning on traveling in deserted areas. Blowouts on dirt roads are very common. If your car breaks down, **stay in your vehicle;** if you wander off, there's less likelihood trackers will find you.

DANGERS

Large sections of the highways in Greece have only one lane in each direction, so Greek drivers tend to use the hard shoulder as a second, slower lane. This means there is no emergency lane in these areas, so avoid driving in the slower lane when going around blind corners to avoid a collision with a stopped vehicle. Likewise, if you break down, don't pull over to the hard shoulder on roads where it could be used as an extra lane.

CAR ASSISTANCE

Ask at your rental agency for the best local roadside assistance option. The **Automobile and Touring Company of Greece (ELPA),** (☎21068 98 710 or 21068 98 711; www.elpaasfaleies.gr), which offers coverage to members of AAA, CAA and other similar assistance services. Check with your membership department for information on using the ELPA shared services in Greece.

BY MOPED

Motorbiking is a popular way of touring Greece's winding roads. Although renting wheels is the most cost-efficient way to avoid unreliable public transportation, they can be uncomfortable for long distances, dangerous in the rain, and unpredictable on rough roads. On many islands, roads suddenly turn into tiny trails that must be walked. Moped (μηχανάκι, mee-hah-NAH-kee) rental shop owners often loosen the front brakes on the bikes to discourage riders from using them (relying on the front brakes makes accidents more likely), so use the back brakes. If you've never driven a moped before, a cliffside road is not the place to learn.

 UNSAFE AT ANY SPEED. A word of caution: most tourist-related accidents occur on mopeds, and the majority of deaths of US tourists in Greece involve mopeds. Regardless of your level of experience, winding, poorly maintained roads and reckless drivers make using a moped hazardous. Always wear a helmet and never ride with a backpack.

RENTING. Shops renting mopeds are everywhere. Although a law passed in 2000 mandates that mopeds can only be rented to those licensed to operate such a vehicle, this is rarely, if ever, enforced. Bike quality, speed of service in case of breakdown, and prices for longer periods vary drastically, but expect to pay at least €10 per day for a 50cc scooter, the cheapest bike that still has the power to tackle mountain roads. More high-tech bikes cost 20-30% more and usually require a Greek motorcycle license. Ask before renting if the price quote includes tax, insurance, and a full tank of gas, or you may pay a few unexpected euro. Information on local moped rentals is in the Practical Information section for individual cities and towns.

BY THUMB

 Let's Go never recommends hitchhiking as a safe means of transportation, and none of the information presented here is intended to do so.

Let's Go strongly urges you to consider the risks before you choose to hitchhike. Hitching means entrusting your life to a stranger and risking assault, sexual harassment, theft, and unsafe driving. For women traveling alone (or even in pairs), hitching is just too dangerous to risk in Greece. A man and a woman are a less dangerous combination; two men will have a harder time getting a lift, while three men will go nowhere. Greeks are not eager to pick up foreigners and foreign cars are often filled with other travelers. Safety-minded hitchers do not get in the back of a two-door car and never let go of their backpacks. If they feel threatened, they insist on being let off, no matter where they are. They may also act as if they are going to open the car door or vomit on the upholstery to get a driver to stop.

KEEPING IN TOUCH

BY EMAIL AND INTERNET

The Internet becomes more accessible each year in Greece. **Internet cafes** are listed in the **Practical Information** sections of towns and cities. Expect to pay €2-6 per hour. Though in some places it's possible to forge a remote link with your home server, in most cases this is a much slower (and thus more expensive) option than taking advantage of free **web-based email accounts** (e.g., those offered at www.hotmail.com and www.yahoo.com).

ESSENTIALS

Increasingly, travelers find that taking their **laptop computers** on the road can be a convenient option for staying connected. Laptop users can call an Internet service provider via a modem using long-distance phone cards specifically intended for such calls. They may also find Internet cafes that allow them to connect their laptops to the Internet. Travelers with wireless-enabled computers may be able to take advantage of an increasing number of Internet "hotspots," where they can get online for free or for a small fee. Wireless is most easily found in Athens. Newer computers can detect these hotspots automatically; otherwise, websites like www.jiwire.com and www.locfinder.net can help you find them. For information on insuring your laptop while traveling, see p. 19.

 WARY WI-FI. Wireless hot spots make Internet access possible in public and remote places. Unfortunately, they also pose **security risks.** Hot spots are public, open networks that use unencrypted, unsecured connections. They are susceptible to hacks and "packet sniffing"—ways of stealing passwords and other private information. To prevent problems, disable ad hoc mode, turn off file sharing, turn off network discovery, encrypt your e-mail, turn on your firewall, beware of phony networks, and watch for over-the-shoulder creeps. Ask the establishment whose wireless you're using for the name of the network so you know you're on the right one. If you are in the vicinity and do not plan to access the Internet, turn off your wireless adapter completely.

BY TELEPHONE

CALLING HOME FROM GREECE

Your best bet for international calls from Greece is to buy a prepaid phone card from a company like **@bcard** or **OTE.** The cheapest kind comes with a PIN and a toll-free access number which you dial to make international as well as domestic calls. These cards are sold by euro amount rather than time limit; rates vary, so shop around. Phone rates typically tend to be highest in the morning, lower in the evening, and lowest on Sunday and late at night. You can buy prepaid cards throughout Greece at Internet cafes, kiosks, and OTEs

Another option is to purchase a **calling card,** linked to a major national telecommunications service in your home country. Calls are billed collect or to your account. To obtain a calling card, contact the appropriate company listed below. There are often advantages to purchasing calling cards online, including better rates and immediate access to your account. To call home with a calling card, contact the operator for your service provider in Greece by dialing the appropriate toll-free access number (listed below in the third column).

COMPANY	TO OBTAIN A CARD:	TO CALL ABROAD:
AT&T (US)	800-364-9292 or www.att.com	800-364-9292
Canada Direct	800-561-8868 or www.infocanadadirect.com	00 800 1611
MCI (US)	800-777-5000 or www.minutepass.com	00 800 1211
Telecom New Zealand Direct	www.telecom.co.nz	3 374 0253 (charges will apply)
Telstra Australia	www.telstra.com	612 9396 1193

Placing a **collect call** through an international operator can be expensive, but may be necessary in case of an emergency. You frequently can call collect without even possessing a company's calling card just by calling its access number and following the instructions.

PLACING INTERNATIONAL CALLS. To call Greece from home or to call home from Greece dial:

1. The **international dialing prefix.** To call from **Australia,** dial 0011; **Canada** or the **US,** 011; **Ireland, New Zealand,** the **UK,** or **Greece,** 00.
2. The **country code** of the place you're calling. To call **Australia,** dial 61; **Canada** or the **US,** 1; **Ireland,** 353; **New Zealand,** 64; the **UK,** 44; **Greece,** 30.
3. The **city/area code.** *Let's Go* lists the city/area codes in Greece opposite each city or town's name at the beginning of its listing, next to a ☎.
4. The local number. Note that in the text of this book, all phone numbers are listed with the full 10 digits, including both city/area code and local number.

CALLING WITHIN GREECE

The simplest way to call within the country is to use a **prepaid OTE phone card** available at kiosks and OTEs. There are local OTE offices in most towns and cardphones are often outside. Swipe your card in the payphone and the computerized phone will tell you how much time, in units, it has left. Another kind of prepaid telephone card comes with a PIN and a toll-free access number. Instead of inserting the card into the phone, you call the access number and follow the directions on the card. These cards can be used to make international as well as domestic calls. Phone rates typically tend to be highest in the morning, lower in the evening, and lowest on Sunday and late at night.

CELLULAR PHONES

Greece has very good cell phone coverage, and as all incoming calls are free, a cell phone might be a good investment. Buying an international cell phone that can be used in Greece, however, can be extremely expensive. Stick to a Greek cell phone; a bare-bones model will probably cost around €50. The international standard for cell phones is **Global System for Mobile Communication (GSM).** To make and receive calls in Greece you will need a **GSM-compatible phone** and a **SIM (Subscriber Identity Module) card,** a country-specific, thumbnail-sized chip that gives you a local phone number and plugs you into the local network. Many SIM cards are **prepaid,** meaning that they come with calling time included and you don't need to sign up for a monthly service plan. Incoming calls are frequently free. When you use up the prepaid time, you can buy additional cards or vouchers (usually available at convenience stores) to "top up" your phone. For more information on GSM phones, check out www.telestial.com, www.orange.co.uk, www.roadpost.com, or www.planetomni.com. Companies like **Cellular Abroad** (www.cellularabroad.com) rent cell phones that work in a variety of destinations around the world, providing a simpler option than picking up a phone in-country.

GSM PHONES. Just having a GSM phone doesn't mean you're necessarily good to go when you travel abroad. The majority of GSM phones sold in the United States operate on a different **frequency** (1900) than international phones (900/1800) and will not work abroad. Tri-band phones work on all three frequencies (900/1800/1900) and will operate through most of the world. Additionally, some GSM phones are **SIM-locked** and will only accept SIM cards from a single carrier. You'll need a **SIM-unlocked** phone to use a SIM card from a local carrier when you travel.

TIME DIFFERENCES

Greece is two hours ahead of **Greenwich Mean Time (GMT),** seven hours ahead of New York, ten hours ahead of San Francisco and Vancouver, and eight hours behind Sydney. Greece observes **daylight saving time,** though it may be at a different time than your home country. More info is at www.worldtimeserver.com.

The following table applies from late October to early April.

4AM	5AM	6AM	7AM	8AM	NOON	2PM	10PM
Vancouver Seattle San Francisco Los Angeles	Denver	Chicago	New York Toronto	New Brunswick	London	**ATHENS**	Sydney Canberra Melbourne

This table is applicable from early April to late October.

4AM	5AM	6AM	7AM	8AM	NOON	2PM	9PM
Vancouver Seattle San Francisco Los Angeles	Denver	Chicago	New York Toronto	New Brunswick	London	**ATHENS**	Sydney Canberra Melbourne

BY MAIL

SENDING MAIL HOME FROM GREECE

Airmail is the best way to send mail home from Greece. **Aerogrammes,** printed sheets that fold into envelopes and travel via airmail, are available at post offices. Write "airmail," and "par avion" on the front. Most post offices will charge exorbitant fees or simply refuse to send aerogrammes with enclosures. **Surface mail** is by far the cheapest and slowest way to send mail. It takes one to two months to cross the Atlantic and one to three to cross the Pacific—good for heavy items you won't need for a while, such as souvenirs or other articles you've acquired along the way that are weighing down your pack. The Greek Post has a website in both Greek and English (www.elta-net.gr), which provides basic information. Postcards and letters to international locations (up to 20g and 16.5cm by 24.5cm) cost €0.65 for standard mailing. Within Europe, they should take 3-4 days to arrive. Outside of Europe, they should take seven to 10 days.

SENDING MAIL TO GREECE

To ensure timely delivery, mark envelopes "airmail" and "par avion." In addition to the standard postage system whose rates are listed below, **Federal Express** (www.fedex.com; Australia ☎ 13 26 10, Canada and the US 800-463-3339, Ireland 1800 535 800, New Zealand 0800 733 339, the UK 0800 123 800) handles express mail services from most countries to Greece; for example, they can get a letter from New York to Greece in one to two days for US$40, and from London to Greece in three to four days for UK₤30. Sending a postcard or letter within Greece (up to 20g and 16.5cm by 24.5cm) costs €0.49.

Australia: Allow 5-7 days for regular airmail to Greece. Postcards cost AUS$1.10; letters 20-500g AUS$2-11; packages up to 2kg AUS$9.50-53. Express courier service can get a letter to Greece in 2-3 days for AUS$38.50. www.auspost.com.au/pac.

Canada: Allow 2 weeks for regular airmail to Greece. Postcards and letters up to 30g cost CDN$1.45; packages up to 0.5kg CDN$12; 2kg package CDN$17 by surface,

CDN$41 by air. Purolator International can get a letter to Greece in 2-4 days for CDN$45. www.canadapost.ca/personal/rates/default-e.asp.

Ireland: Allow 4-6 days for regular airmail to Greece. Postcards and letters up to 50g cost €0.55-1.20; packages up to 0.5kg €2-4, up to 2kg €6-13. Swiftpost International can get a letter to Greece quickly for €5.20. www.letterpost.ie.

New Zealand: Allow 1-2 weeks for regular airmail to Greece. Postcards and letters up to 200g cost NZ$1.50-5; packages up to 0.5kg NZ$6-15, up to 2kg NZ$15-47. International Express can get a letter under 0.5kg to Greece in 2-5 days for NZ$45. www.nzpost.co.nz/Cultures/en-NZ/OnlineTools/RateFinder.

UK: Allow 3 days for regular airmail to Greece. Letters up to 20g cost UK£0.42; packages up to 0.5kg UK£0.60-5, up to 2kg UK£5-18. UK Airsure delivers letters 1 day faster for UK£4 more. www.royalmail.co.uk.

US: Allow 4-10 days for regular airmail to Greece. Postcards cost US$0.70; letters up to 16oz. US$0.80-8.70; packages up to 5 lbs. US$22.75. Global Express Mail takes 2-3 days and costs from US$23. http://ircalc.usps.gov.

RECEIVING MAIL IN GREECE

There are several ways to arrange pick-up of letters sent to you by friends and relatives while you are abroad. Mail can be sent via **Poste Restante** (General Delivery) to almost any city or town in Greece with a post office, **and it is generally reliable.** Address *Poste Restante* letters like so:

Xena WARRIOR PRINCESS

Hania Post Office

Hania, Greece 73100

Poste Restante

The mail will go to the central post office, unless you specify a post office by street address or postal code. It's best to use the largest post office, since mail might be sent there regardless. Bring your passport (or other photo ID) for pick-up; occasionally there is a small fee. If the clerks insist that there is nothing for you, have them check under your first name as well. *Let's Go* lists post offices in the **Practical Information** section for each city and most towns.

ACCOMMODATIONS

DOMATIA (ROOMS TO LET)

Private homes all over Greece put up signs offering domatia (rooms to let). Domatia are perhaps the ideal accommodations: they are cheap and let you absorb some local culture by staying in a Greek home. Always negotiate with owners before settling on a price. You may be greeted by domatia owners as you step out at a bus stop or port; though this is illegal in many areas, it is still common. Many rooms offered at the bus stop or port are inexpensive; since proprietors are in direct competition with other owners, good deals abound. Make owners pinpoint the location of their house and don't pay until you've seen the room.

While domatia may be run like small hotels in tourist towns, in out-of-the-way places they can provide warm coffee at night and friendly conversation. Prices vary depending on region and season. You can expect to pay about €15-25 for a single in the more remote areas of Northern and Central Greece and €20-35 for a single (€25-45 for a double) on heavily traveled islands. Never pay more for a domatio than you would for a hotel in town, and remember that domatia owners often can be bargained down, especially when the house is not full. If in doubt, ask the tourist police: they may be able to set you up with a room and conduct the negotiations. Most private rooms operate only in high season and are the best option for those arriving without reservations.

HOSTELS

Many hostels are laid out dorm-style, often with large single-sex rooms and bunk beds, although private rooms that sleep two to four are becoming more common. They sometimes have kitchens and utensils for your use, bike or moped rentals, storage areas, transportation to airports, breakfast and other meals, laundry facilities, and Internet access. There can be drawbacks: some hostels close during certain daytime "lockout" hours, have a curfew, don't accept reservations, impose a maximum stay, or, less frequently, require that you do chores. In Greece, hostel beds average around €15-30.

A HOSTELER'S BILL OF RIGHTS. There are certain standard features that we do not include in our hostel listings. Unless we state otherwise, you can expect that every hostel has no lockout, no curfew, a kitchen, free hot showers, some system of secure luggage storage, and no key deposit.

Hostels are not as prevalent in Greece as they are throughout the rest of Europe. Those that exist (usually in the most popular tourist destinations) are almost never affiliated with an international hosteling organization, so a hosteling membership won't do you much good. Hostels are not regulated so don't be surprised if some are less than clean or don't offer sheets and towels. Some Greek hostels offer private rooms for families and couples, and others have a maximum stay of five days. Greek **youth hostels** generally have fewer restrictions than those farther north in Europe. Many are open year-round and few have early curfews (some curfews, however, are strictly enforced—you might be left in the streets if you come back too late). In summer they usually stay open 6-10am and 1pm-midnight (shorter hours in winter). It's advisable to book in advance in the summer at some of the more popular hostels in Athens, Santorini, Crete, or Nafplion.

HOTELS AND PENSIONS

Hotel singles in Greece start at €20 per night, doubles €30. You'll typically share a hall bath; a private bath will cost extra. Smaller **guesthouses** and **pensions** often are cheaper than hotels. If you make **reservations** in writing, indicate your night of arrival and the number of nights you plan to stay. The hotel will send you a confirmation and may request payment for the first night. Often it is easiest to make reservations over the phone with a credit card.

The government oversees the construction and classification of most hotels, which are grouped into six classes: "L," "luxury," is followed by "A" through "E," in descending order of amenities. Greece gradually is transitioning to the star-based classification system used by many other European nations. Assume hotels do not have amenities such as A/C and TV unless they are specified. More information is available from the **Hellenic Chamber of Hotels,** Stadiou 24, Athens 10564 (☎21033 10 022; www.grhotels.gr). Late at night, in low season, or in a large town, it's a buyer's market and bargaining is appropriate. Hotels often ask for your passport as a security deposit, but don't give it to them—suggest that they take down your passport number or offer to pay up front. Sleazy hotel owners might offer you only their most expensive rooms, compel you to buy breakfast, squeeze three people into a hostel-size triple and charge each for a single, or quote a price for a room that includes breakfast and private shower and then charge extra for both. Don't pay until you've seen the room. If a room seems unreasonably expensive, stress that you don't want luxuries and they might give you a cheaper option. If you think you've been exploited, threaten to file a report with the tourist police. The threat alone often resolves "misunderstandings."

HOME EXCHANGES

Home exchange offers travelers various types of homes, plus the opportunity to live like a native and cut down on accommodation fees. Contact HomeExchange.com, P.O. Box 787, Hermosa Beach, CA 90254, USA (☎800-877-8723; fax 310-798-3865; www.homeexchange.com), **or** Intervac International Home Exchange, Perikleous 34, Maroussi, Athens 15122 (☎21080 61 943; www.intervac.com).

LONG-TERM ACCOMMODATIONS

Travelers planning to stay in Greece for extended periods of time may find it most cost-effective to rent an **apartment.** A basic one-bedroom (or studio) apartment in Athens will range €600-1000 per month. Besides the rent itself, prospective tenants usually are also required to front a security deposit (frequently one month's rent) and the last month's rent. Newspapers like *Athens News* (www.athensnews.gr) and websites like www.expatriates.com and Craigslist (http://athens.craigslist.org/apa/) can be useful in finding an apartment or house.

CAMPING

Camping in Greece not only saves you money, but provides refuge from the regulations of hostels and the monotony of hotel rooms. The **Greek National Tourist Organization** (**GNTO;** p. 9) is primarily responsible for campgrounds; most GNTO campgrounds have drinking water, lavatories, and electricity. To find these, contact the Panhellenic Campings Association, Solonos 102, Athens 10673 (☎/fax 21036 21 560). Ask at local tourist offices for more info on the **Hellenic Touring Club,** which runs a number of campgrounds, especially in Northern Greece. Greece also has many private campgrounds, which may include pools, mini-marts, and tavernas. Prices depend on the facilities; you'll likely pay €4-8 per person and €2-3 per tent. See **The Great Outdoors,** below.

THE GREAT OUTDOORS

The **Great Outdoor Recreation Page** (www.gorp.com) provides excellent general information for travelers planning on camping or spending time in the outdoors.

LEAVE NO TRACE. Let's Go encourages travelers to embrace the "Leave No Trace" ethic, minimizing their impact on natural environments and protecting them for future generations. Trekkers and wilderness enthusiasts should set up camp on durable surfaces, use cookstoves instead of campfires, bury human waste away from water supplies, bag trash and carry it out with them, and respect wildlife and natural objects. For more detailed information, contact the **Leave No Trace Center for Outdoor Ethics,** P.O. Box 997, Boulder, CO 80306 (☎800-332-4100 or 303-442-8222; www.lnt.org).

ESSENTIALS

USEFUL RESOURCES

A variety of publishing companies offer hiking guidebooks to meet the educational needs of novice or expert. For information about camping, hiking, and biking, write or call the publishers listed below to receive a free catalog. Campers heading to Europe should consider buying an **International Camping Carnet.** Similar to a hostel membership card, it's required at a few campgrounds and sometimes provides discounts. It is available in North America from the **Family Campers and RVers Association** and in the UK from **The Caravan Club** (see below).

Automobile Association, Contact Centre, Lambert House, Stockport Road, Cheadle SK8 2DY, UK (☎08706 000 371; www.theAA.com).

The Caravan Club, East Grinstead House, East Grinstead, West Sussex, RH19 1UA, UK (☎01342 326 944; www.caravanclub.co.uk). For UK£34, members receive access to sites, insurance services, equipment discounts, maps, and a monthly magazine.

Family Campers and RVers, 4804 Transit Rd., Bldg. #2, Depew, NY 14043, USA (☎800-245-9755; www.fcrv.org). Membership (US$25) includes *Camping Today* magazine.

Sierra Club Books, 85 Second St., 2nd fl., San Francisco, CA 94105, USA (☎415-977-5500; www.sierraclub.org). Publishes general resource books on hiking and camping, as well as specific guides on Greece.

The Mountaineers Books, 1001 SW Klickitat Way, Ste. 201, Seattle, WA 98134, USA (☎206-223-6303; www.mountaineersbooks.org). Over 600 titles on hiking, biking, mountaineering, natural history, and conservation.

NATIONAL PARKS

Although the environment and wildlife in Greece were largely ignored in the past, the situation has been improving greatly. The EU required that Greece set up a managed wildlife preserve on Zakynthos in 2000, and designated 274 areas—which, combined, cover 18% of Greece—as protected.

In addition to protected sites, there are 10 National Parks in Greece, covering 169,709 acres. These are Mt. Aenos in Kephalonia, Vikos Gorge and the Aoos River canyon in Ioannina, Lefka Ori (Samaria Gorge) in Hania, Crete, Mt. Iti in Fthiotida, Mt. Olympos in Pieria, Mt. Parnassos in Fokida and Viotia, Mt. Parnitha in Attica, Cape Sounion in Attica, the Pindos Mountains in Ioannina, and the Prespa Lakes in northern Greece. There are two protected marine parks, around Alonissos and Zakynthos. Dolphins and monk seals make their home near Alonissos, while Zakynthos's Laganas Bay is home to the loggerhead turtle, an endangered species. Wetlands throughout Greece are also protected. There are various opportunities for people interested in volunteering to work for the environment (p. 77).

WILDERNESS SAFETY

Staying **warm, dry,** and **well hydrated** is key to a happy and safe wilderness experience. For any hike, prepare yourself for an emergency by packing a first-aid kit, a reflector, a whistle, high-energy food, extra water, raingear, a hat, mittens, and extra socks. For warmth, wear wool or insulating synthetic materials designed for the outdoors. Cotton is a bad choice as it dries painfully slowly.

Check **weather forecasts** often and pay attention to the skies when hiking, as weather patterns can change suddenly. Always let someone—a friend, your hostel, a park ranger, or a local hiking organization—know when and where you are going. Know your physical limits and do not attempt a hike beyond your ability. See **Safety and Health,** p. 17, for information on outdoor medical concerns.

While there are no particularly dangerous animals to avoid in Greece, some pests will annoy you if you don't take precaution. The particularly bothersome type of mosquito that thrives in Greece lives indoors and is active only after dark. Variations of this mosquito are found on all the islands, especially wetter islands, such as Zakynthos and Corfu. Wear long pants and arm yourself with deterrent spray or oil to ward off these pests. It is also helpful to spray the curtains and keep them closed, or drape mosquito netting around your bed.

CAMPING AND HIKING EQUIPMENT

WHAT TO BUY

Good camping equipment is both sturdy and light. North American suppliers tend to offer the most competitive prices.

Sleeping Bags: Most sleeping bags are rated by season; "summer" means 30-40°F (around 0°C) at night; "four-season" or "winter" often means below 0°F (-17°C). Bags are made of **down** (warm and light, but expensive, and miserable when wet) or of **synthetic** material (heavy, durable, and warm when wet). Prices range US$50-250 for a summer synthetic to US$200-300 for a good down winter bag. **Sleeping bag pads** include foam pads (US$10-30), air mattresses (US$15-50), and self-inflating mats (US$30-120). Bring a **stuff sack** to store your bag and keep it dry.

Tents: The best tents are free-standing (with their own frames and suspension systems), set up quickly, and only require staking in high winds. Low-profile dome tents are the best all-around. Worthy 2-person tents start at US$100, 4-person tents start at US$160. Make sure your tent has a rain fly and seal its seams with waterproofer. Other useful accessories include a **battery-operated lantern,** a plastic **groundcloth,** and a nylon **tarp.**

Backpacks: Internal-frame packs mold well to your back, keep a lower center of gravity, and flex adequately to allow you to hike difficult trails, while **external-frame packs** are more comfortable for long hikes over even terrain, as they carry weight higher and distribute it more evenly. Make sure your pack has a strong, padded hip-belt to transfer weight to your legs. There are models designed specifically for women. Any serious backpacking requires a pack of at least 4000 cu. in. (16,000cc), plus 500 cu. in. for sleeping bags in internal-frame packs. Sturdy backpacks cost anywhere from US$125 to 420—your pack is an area where it doesn't pay to economize. On your hunt for the perfect pack, fill up prospective models with something heavy, strap it on correctly, and walk around the store to get a sense of how the model distributes weight. Either buy a **rain cover** (US$10-20) or store all of your belongings in plastic bags inside your pack.

Boots: Be sure to wear hiking boots with good **ankle support.** They should fit snugly and comfortably over 1-2 pairs of **wool socks** and a pair of thin **liner socks.** Break in boots over several weeks before you go to spare yourself blisters.

Other Necessities: Synthetic layers, like those made of polypropylene or polyester, and a pile jacket will keep you warm even when wet. A **space blanket** (US$5-15) will help you to retain body heat and doubles as a groundcloth. Plastic **water bottles** are vital; look for shatter- and leak-resistant models. Carry **water-purification tablets** for when you can't boil water. Although most campgrounds provide campfire sites, you may want to bring a small **metal grate** or grill. For those places that forbid fires or the gathering of firewood, you'll need a **camp stove** (the classic Coleman starts at US$50) and a propane-filled **fuel bottle** to operate it. Also bring a **first-aid kit, pocketknife, insect repellent,** and **waterproof matches** or a **lighter.**

WHERE TO BUY IT

The online and mail-order companies listed below offer lower prices than many retail stores. A visit to a local camping or outdoors store will give you a good sense of the look and weight of certain items before you buy.

Campmor, 400 Corporate Dr., PO Box 680, Mahwah, NJ 07430, USA (☎800-525-4784; www.campmor.com).

Cotswold Outdoor, Unit 11 Kemble Business Park, Crudwell, Malmesbury Wiltshire, SN16 9SH, UK (☎08704 427 755; www.cotswoldoutdoor.com).

Discount Camping, 833 Main North Rd., Pooraka, South Australia 5095, Australia (☎618 8262 3399; www.discountcamping.com.au).

Eastern Mountain Sports (EMS), 1 Vose Farm Rd., Peterborough, NH 03458, USA (☎888-463-6367; www.ems.com).

Gear-Zone, 8 Burnet Rd., Sweetbriar Rd. Industrial Estate, Norwich, NR3 2BS, UK (☎1603 410 108; www.gear-zone.co.uk).

L.L. Bean, Freeport, ME 04033, USA (US and Canada ☎800-441-5713; UK 0800 891 297; www.llbean.com).

Mountain Designs, 443a Nudgee Rd., Hendra, Queensland 4011, Australia (☎+617 3114 4300; www.mountaindesigns.com).

Recreational Equipment, Inc. (REI), Sumner, WA 98352, USA (Canada and the US ☎800-426-4840, elsewhere 253-891-2500; www.rei.com).

ORGANIZED ADVENTURE TRIPS

Organized adventure tours offer another way of exploring the wild. Activities include hiking, biking, skiing, canoeing, kayaking, rafting, climbing, photo safaris, and archaeological digs. Tourism bureaus often can suggest parks, trails, and outfitters. Organizations that specialize in camping and outdoor equipment like REI and EMS (see above) also are good sources for information.

Specialty Travel Index, P.O. Box 458, San Anselmo, CA 94979, USA (US ☎888-624-4030, elsewhere 415-455-1643; www.specialtytravel.com).

SPECIFIC CONCERNS

SUSTAINABLE TRAVEL

As the number of travelers on the road continues to rise, the detrimental effect they can have on natural environments becomes an increasing concern. With this in mind, Let's Go promotes the philosophy of **sustainable travel.** Through a sensitivity to issues of ecology and sustainability, today's travelers can be a powerful force in preserving as well as restoring the places they visit.

Ecotourism, a rising trend in sustainable travel, focuses on the conservation of natural habitats and how to use them to build up the economy without exploitation or overdevelopment. Travelers can make a difference by supporting organizations and establishments that pay attention to their impact on their natural surroundings and that strive to be environmentally friendly.

In Greece, travelers have ample opportunity to put the sustainable travel ethos into practice. Because so much of the country is undeveloped, backpackers play an important role in keeping the environment pristine. Small actions, like packing up excess waste when leaving a campground, using environmentally-friendly shampoo when bathing in the outdoors, and picking up trash on a beach go a long way. You also can promote ecotourism by supporting organizations that synthesize tourism with conservation. The **Ecotourist Centre of Dadia** (http://ecoclub.com/dadia/lodge.html), for example, supports conservation efforts in the Dadia Forest. See this book's **Beyond Tourism** chapter (p. 76) for opportunities to volunteer for environmental causes in Greece

---

ECOTOURISM RESOURCES. For more information on environmentally responsible tourism, contact one of the organizations below:

Conservation International, 2011 Crystal Dr., Ste. 500, Arlington, VA 22202, USA (☎800-406-2306 or 703-341-2400; www.conservation.org).

Green Globe 21, Green Globe vof, Verbenalaan 1, 2111 ZL Aerdenhout, The Netherlands (☎31 23 544 0306; www.greenglobe.com).

International Ecotourism Society, 1333 H St. NW, Ste. 300E, Washington, D.C. 20005, USA (☎202-347-9203; www.ecotourism.org).

United Nations Environment Program (UNEP), 39-43 Quai André Citroën, 75739 Paris Cedex 15, France (☎33 1 44 37 14 50; www.uneptie.org/pc/tourism).

TRAVELING ALONE

There are many benefits to traveling alone, including independence and a greater opportunity to connect with locals. On the other hand, solo travelers are more vulnerable targets of harassment and street theft. If you are traveling alone, look confident, try not to stand out as a tourist, and be especially careful in deserted or very crowded areas. Stay away from areas that are not well lit. If questioned, never admit that you are traveling alone. Maintain regular contact with someone at home who knows your itinerary, and always research your destination before traveling. For more tips, pick up *Traveling Solo* by Eleanor Berman (Globe Pequot Press, US$18), visit www.travelaloneandloveit.com, or subscribe to **Connecting: Solo Travel Network,** 689 Park Rd., Unit 6, Gibsons, BC V0N 1V7, Canada (☎604-886-9099; www.cstn.org; membership US$30-48).

WOMEN TRAVELERS

Women exploring on their own inevitably face some additional safety concerns, but it's easy to be adventurous without taking undue risks. If you are concerned, consider staying in hostels that offer single rooms that lock from the inside or in religious organizations with single-sex rooms. Stick to centrally located accommodations and avoid solitary late-night treks or metro rides.

Always carry extra cash for a phone call, bus, or taxi. **Hitchhiking** is never safe for lone women, or even for two women traveling together. Look as if you know where you're going and approach older women or couples for directions if you're lost or uncomfortable.

Generally, the less you look like a tourist, the better off you'll be. Dress conservatively, especially in rural areas. Wearing a conspicuous **wedding band** sometimes helps to prevent unwanted advances.

Your best answer to verbal harassment is no answer at all; feigning deafness, sitting motionless, and staring straight ahead at nothing in particular will usually do the trick. The extremely persistent can sometimes be dissuaded by a firm, loud, and very public "Go away!" (FEE-ghe!). **Older Greek women** can help you in a bind; they're sharp, wise, fearless, and your best allies if you need information, advice, or a respite from persistent amorous attempts. If that fails, don't hesitate to seek a police officer or passerby if you're being harassed. Remember the word for police: αστυνομία (ah-stee-no-MEE-a). Memorize the emergency numbers in places you visit, and consider carrying a whistle on your keychain. A self-defense course will both prepare you for a potential attack and raise your level of awareness of your surroundings (see **Personal Safety**, p. 18). Also be sure you are aware of the health concerns (see p. 23) that women face when traveling.

GLBT TRAVELERS

Though legal in Greece since 1951, homosexuality still is frowned upon socially—especially in more conservative villages—and gay, lesbian, bisexual, and transgendered (GLBT) individuals are not legally protected from discrimination. That said, cosmopolitan regions like Athens and Thessaloniki offer some gay bars and clubs. The islands of **Hydra, Lesvos, Rhodes, Ios,** and **Mykonos** (arguably the most gay-friendly destination in Europe) offer gay and lesbian hotels, bars, and clubs.

To avoid hassles at airports and border crossings, **transgendered travelers** should make sure that all their travel documents consistently report the same gender. Many countries (including Australia, Canada, Ireland, New Zealand, the UK, and the US) will amend the passports of post-operative transsexuals to reflect their gender, although governments are generally less willing to amend documents for pre-operative transsexuals and other transgendered individuals. Listed below are contact organizations, mail-order catalogs, and publishers that offer materials addressing some specific concerns. **Out and About** (www.planetout.com) offers a weekly newsletter addressing travel concerns and a comprehensive site addressing gay travel concerns. The online newspaper **365gay.com** also has a travel section (www.365gay.com/travel/travelchannel.htm). The website **http://greekgayguide.net** provides information on the GLBT scene throughout Greece. Another helpful website, **www.purpleroofs.com,** provides an international gay and lesbian travel directory.

Gay's the Word, 66 Marchmont St., London WC1N 1AB, UK (☎44 020 7278 7654; http://freespace.virgin.net/gays.theword/). The largest gay and lesbian bookshop in the UK, with both fiction and non-fiction titles. Mail-order service available.

Giovanni's Room, 345 South 12th St., Philadelphia, PA 19107, USA (☎215-923-2960; www.queerbooks.com). An international lesbian and gay bookstore with mail-order service (carries many of the publications listed below).

International Lesbian and Gay Association (ILGA), Avenue des Villas 34, 1060 Brussels, Belgium (☎32 2 502 2471; www.ilga.org). Provides political information, such as homosexuality laws of individual countries.

ADDITIONAL RESOURCES: GLBT

Spartacus: International Gay Guide. Bruno Gmunder Verlag (US$33).

Damron Men's Travel Guide, Damron Accommodations Guide, Damron City Guide, and *Damron Women's Traveller.* Damron Travel Guides (US$18-24). For info, call ☎800-462-6654 or visit www.damron.com.

Ferrari Guides' Gay Travel A to Z, Ferrari Guides' Men's Travel in Your Pocket, Ferrari Guides' Women's Travel in Your Pocket, and *Ferrari Guides' Inn Places.* Ferrari Publications (US$16-20).

The Gay Vacation Guide: The Best Trips and How to Plan Them, Mark Chesnut. Kensington Books (US$15).

TRAVELERS WITH DISABILITIES

The **Paralympic Games,** which took place in Athens in September 2004, inspired Greece to begin improving its facilities for disabled people. Hotels, train stations, cruise ships, and airports increasingly are installing facilities for the disabled, and special air transportation to many of the larger islands is available aboard Olympic Airways. Still, Greece's mountainous terrain and winding, uneven streets can prove difficult for travelers with disabilities, and few of the archaeological sites or smaller towns are wheelchair-accessible. Those with disabilities should inform airlines and hotels when making reservations; time may be needed to prepare special accommodations. Call ahead to restaurants, museums, and other facilities to find out if they are handicapped-accessible. **Guide dog owners** should note that there is **no quarantine** for taking dogs in and out of Greece. While rail is probably the best form of travel for disabled travelers in Europe, the railway systems of Greece have limited wheelchair accessibility. For those who wish to rent cars, some major **car rental** agencies (e.g., Hertz) offer hand-controlled vehicles.

USEFUL ORGANIZATIONS

Accessible Journeys, 35 West Sellers Ave., Ridley Park, PA 19078, USA (☎800-846-4537; www.disabilitytravel.com). Designs tours for wheelchair users and slow walkers. The site has tips and forums for all travelers.

Flying Wheels Travel, 143 W. Bridge St., Owatonna, MN 55060, USA (☎507-451-5005; www.flyingwheelstravel.com). Specializes in escorted trips to Europe for people with physical disabilities; plans custom trips worldwide.

Mobility International USA (MIUSA), P.O. Box 10767, Eugene, OR 97440, USA (☎541-343-1284; www.miusa.org). Provides a variety of books and other publications containing information for travelers with disabilities.

Society for Accessible Travel and Hospitality (SATH), 347 Fifth Ave., Ste. 610, New York, NY 10016, USA (☎212-447-7284; www.sath.org). An advocacy group that publishes free online travel information. Annual membership US$49, students and seniors US$29.

MINORITY TRAVELERS

Greeks stare, point, and whisper as a daily pastime. If you're not obviously Greek, everyone will want to know who you are. While Greeks tend to hold stereotypes about every group of people imaginable, they place a great value on **individualism;** you may be asked (out of curiosity, not malice) all manner of questions or referred to continually as "the [insert your nationality here]," "the [insert religion here]," or simply "the foreigner." Greece presents two strong and entirely different views about foreigners, and travelers should expect to encounter both. On the one hand, the Greek tradition of **hospitality** is unmatched. Greeks consider it almost a sacred duty to help travelers, providing them with advice and homemade food. On the other hand, it's important to remember Greece's historical position: most European nations have at one time or another invaded, betrayed, or colonized part of Greece, forging an "us-versus-them" mentality. Greeks are proud of their heritage and nationality, and often tend to view racial, religious, and cultural diversity as detrimental to society. That said, it is rare that **minority travelers** ever face any overt discrimination or violence. Non-white travelers admittedly will have more trouble blending in and will be at the receiving end of more stares, questions, and comments. Once the locals' curiosity is satisfied, however, you should be welcomed.

DIETARY CONCERNS

Vegetarians can make do in Greece if they don't mind making a meal of appetizers—green beans (φασολάκια, fah-so-LAH-kia), Greek salad (χοριάτικη, ho-ree-AH-tee-kee), spinach pie (σπανοκόπιτα, spa-no-KO-pee-ta), and boiled greens (χόρτα, HOR-tah). **Ask before you order;** many seemingly vegetarian entrees (like stuffed vegetables) can contain meat. **Vegans** should be aware that it is virtually impossible to avoid all animal products in Greek food. One exception occurs during **Lent,** when meat and meat stock disappear from many dishes. There are almost no Greek vegetarians, so if questioned your best bet is to argue weather ("It's so hot I only want vegetables") or allergies ("I'm allergic to lamb and goat"), as opposed to ideology. This book has made an effort to list some of the few vegetarian restaurants in Greece. The travel section of the The Vegetarian Resource Group's website, at **www.vrg.org/travel,** has a comprehensive list of organizations and websites that are geared toward helping vegetarians and vegans traveling abroad. For more information, visit your local bookstore or health food store, and consult *The Vegetarian Traveler: Where to Stay if You're Vegetarian, Vegan, Environmentally Sensitive,* by Jed and Susan Civic (Larson Publications; US$16). Vegetarians will also find numerous resources on the web; try **www.vegdining.com** and **www.happycow.net,** for starters.

Travelers who keep kosher likely will run into difficulty in Greece. There are few kosher establishments. Observant travelers should contact synagogues in larger Greek cities where they still exist, such as Thessaloniki, for information on kosher restaurants. Your own synagogue should have access to lists of Jewish institutions across the nation. If you are strict in your observance, you might have to prepare your own food on the road. A good resource is the *Jewish Travel Guide,* edited by Michael Zaidner (Vallentine Mitchell; US$18). Travelers looking for halal restaurants likely will find them in areas with large Muslim populations in Northern Greece; in other regions you might have to make your own meals. The website **www.zabihah.com** is a useful resource for finding restaurants.

OTHER RESOURCES

Let's Go tries to cover all aspects of budget travel, but we can't put *everything* in our guides. Listed below are books and websites that can serve as jumping-off points for your own research.

USEFUL PUBLICATIONS

Greece: An Oxford Archaeological Guide, Tony Spawforth, Christopher Mee, and Anthony Spawforth. Oxford Press, 2001. Thorough and wide-ranging guide to visiting Greece's ancient sites.

A Literary Companion to Travel in Greece, Richard Stoneman. J. Paul Getty Museum Publications, 1994 (US$20; US$14 on www.amazon.com). A collection of writings and artwork inspired by the natural beauty of Greece, arranged topographically.

Odyssey: The World of Greece, www.odyssey.gr. Intelligent bi-monthly magazine about Greece written for people of the diaspora.

Hunter Publishing, P.O. Box 476, Walpole, MA 02081, USA (☎800-255-0343; www.hunterpublishing.com), has an extensive catalogue of travel guides and diving and adventure travel books.

Rand McNally, P.O. Box 7600, Chicago, IL 60680, USA (☎847-329-8100; www.rand-mcnally.com), publishes road atlases.

WORLD WIDE WEB

Almost every aspect of budget travel is accessible via the web. In 10 minutes at the keyboard, you can make a hostel reservation, get advice on travel hot spots from other travelers, or find out how much a train from Athens to Thessaloniki costs.

Listed here are some regional and travel-related sites to start off your surfing; other relevant websites are listed throughout the book. Because website turnover is high, use search engines (e.g., www.google.com) to strike out on your own.

 WWW.LETSGO.COM Our website features extensive content from our guides; a community forum where travelers can connect with each other, ask questions or advice, and share stories and tips; and expanded resources to help you plan your trip. Visit us to browse by destination and to find information about ordering our titles.

THE ART OF TRAVEL

Backpacker's Ultimate Guide: www.bugeurope.com. Tips on packing, transportation, and where to go. Also tons of country-specific travel information.

BootsnAll.com: www.bootsnall.com. Numerous resources for independent travelers, from planning your trip to reporting on it when you get back.

How to See the World: www.artoftravel.com. A compendium of great travel tips, from cheap flights to self defense to interacting with local culture.

Travel Intelligence: www.travelintelligence.net. A large collection of travel writing by distinguished travel writers.

Travel Library: www.travel-library.com. A fantastic set of links for general information and personal travelogues.

World Hum: www.worldhum.com. An independently produced collection of "travel dispatches from a shrinking planet."

INFORMATION ON GREECE

Atevo Travel: www.atevo.com/guides/destinations. Detailed introductions, travel tips, and suggested itineraries.

CIA World Factbook: www.odci.gov/cia/publications/factbook/index.html. Tons of vital statistics on Greece's geography, government, economy, and people.

Geographia: www.geographia.com. Highlights, culture, and people of Greece.

Greek Ferries: www.ferries.gr. Claims to maintain a complete and updated list of ferry schedules over all the Greek islands.

Kathimerini: www.ekathimerini.com. The online version of a prominent international English newspaper in Greece.

The Internet Guide to Greece: www.gogreece.com. Features maps, references, and discussions, and listings of Greek businesses, schools, news sources, and sports.

The Ministry of Culture: www.culture.gr. Events, history, "cultural maps of Greece," and other frills.

The New Greece Network: www.newgreece.8m.com. Unusual links to information about Greece and tourist advice.

TravelPage: www.travelpage.com. Links to official tourist office sites in Greece.

PlanetRider: www.planetrider.com. A subjective list of links to the "best" websites covering the culture and tourist attractions of Greece.

United Hellas: www.united-hellas.com. A database of all things Greek, from small businesses and folk art sources to places to buy a boat.

World Travel Guide: www.travel-guides.com. Helpful practical info.

LIFE AND TIMES

Greece is a tapestry of cultures and influences, its threads spun by east and west, ancient and modern times, proud emperors and freedom fighters. It's hardly surprising that this land, praised for its hospitality, has played host to a succession of towering civilizations: from the Egyptian and Babylonian influences evident in Crete's Minoan civilization, to the Orthodox Christian customs developed in Byzantine era, to the pointed arches and spices that linger after 400 years of Ottoman rule, each visiting power left its mark on Greece. In 1821, Greece declared its independence from the Turkish empire, and since then, the country has worked to build a modern democracy along the sparkling shores of the Mediterranean.

HISTORY AND POLITICS

ANCIENT GREECE (7000 BC-AD 324)

The **Neolithic** period in Greece began around 7000 BC with the birth of a farming culture. Over thousands of years and with the influence of Middle Eastern immigrants and traders, Greek culture grew from agricultural and fishing communities into the grand societies of the Minoan and Mycenaean civilizations, and later into the glorious apex of the Classical period. Over the period of just a few generations, Classical Greeks produced a dazzling, enduring body of literature and philosophy.

THE BRONZE AGE (3000-1100 BC)

2000 BC
Bronze-wielding Minoans rule the sea from their Cretan palaces, fearing no foe...

1500 BC
...except for the mysterious natural disasters that wipe out their whole civilization by the 15th century BC.

NICE MINOAN YOU! (3000-1500 BC)

Though the Greeks had long worked with copper, the advent of bronze metallurgy kicked off a rapid expansion of Greek influence. By 2000 BC, the Crete-based **Minoans** had constructed huge palaces as centers of government, religion, and trade like Knossos (p. 595), Malia (p. 610), and Phaistos (p. 600). Around 1500 BC, however, the Minoan civilization mysteriously was destroyed. One explanation is that a 1645 BC volcanic explosion on the island of Thera, now **Santorini,** caused a devastating tsunami. This disaster is thought to have had lasting cultural repercussions that reduced the Minoans' once magnificent empire to burnt-out ruins and broken pots. Their writing system, Linear A, which remains indecipherable, also faded into the debris.

1500-1100 BC
Archaic Greek Empires, round two: Mycenaeans from the mainland try their hand at imperial rule.

THE MIGHTY MYCENAEANS (1500-1100 BC)

After Minoan civilization went out with a bang, the Aegean fell under the sway of a mainland people called the Mycenaeans. Mycenaean rule extended throughout the southern mainland, Crete, the Cyclades, and the Dodecanese as far as Cyprus, but power was stratified, centering on grand palaces at Tiryns, Pylos, Thebes, and Mycenae. In Mycenae and Tiryns, inhabitants built citadels surrounded by "Cyclopean" walls, so-called because later Greeks thought only a Cyclops could lift such massive stones (and perhaps because the crooked structure implied the builders' lack of depth perception). The Linear B writing system inscribed on tablets found at these sites mystified linguists for years until Michael Ventris, an architect-turned-linguist, cracked the code in 1954. Ventris found that the scratched characters simply represented early phonetic syllables of Greek. The Mycenaeans' written legacy, however, extends far beyond those stone tablets into the pages of **Homer,** the 8th century BC poet—some hypothesize that Mycenaean military expeditions to Troy in Asia Minor ignited the **Trojan War,** described in Homer's **Iliad.** The war was ignited when Paris, prince of Troy and the most beautiful man in the world, abducted Helen from Menelaus, king of Sparta. Enraged, Menelaus launched a war on Troy and its supporting regions that lasted 10 years. Finally, Odysseus clinched a victory by using the much-famed Trojan Horse; thinking it was a gift of surrender, the Trojans let the huge wooden creature into their city walls, only to be attacked that night by the Greek soldiers hiding inside it.

1200 BC
Paris and Helen make love *and* war when the Trojan War erupts after their elopement.

A SHOT IN THE THE DARK AGE: (1100-800 BC)

Bronze Age Aegean civilizations met an abrupt end in the 12th century BC, when an invasion of **Dorians** from the Balkan highlands to the north scattered the Mycenaeans, relocating Greeks to Asia Minor and the coast of the Black Sea. This break-up marks the onset of the **Dark Age,** whose name reflects modern-day historians' relative lack of knowledge about it. Although seaborne trade flourished in Athens, the rest of what we now know as Greece suffered from a loss of trade. The desperate population emigrated in large numbers to the Dodecanese islands, Asia Minor, and Cyprus. By the end of the 8th century, however, the development of the city-state began to put the Greeks back on the map.

1100 BC
Dorian invaders bring iron and the remarkable ability to avoid making progress for the next 300 years.

WE BUILT THIS CITY-STATE ON ROCK AND ROLL: THE ARCHAIC PERIOD (800-500 BC)

The Archaic Period's advances forged a cohesive Greek identity. The **Greek alphabet,** the first coinage, the first Panathenaic festival, the beginning of colonial expansion, and the first **Olympic Games** all appeared during this time. Bonded by a shared language, the residents of city-states began to see themselves as Greeks, not just Athenians or Spartans, as they had in the past. In a testament to this rising communal identity, the **Eleusinian Mysteries,** the most sacred of religious celebrations in ancient Greece, were opened to anybody who spoke Greek. Foreigners, however, were scorned and ridiculed—they were called **barbaroi** (barbarians), a word intended to mock their non-Greek languages, which to Greek ears sounded like a nonsensical "bar-bar-bar."

During this time, the **polis,** or city-state, rose as the major Greek political unit. A typical *polis* was ruled in this period by an aristocracy and encompassed the city proper and surrounding areas. Within any town, the strategically placed **acropolis,** or

776 BC
Let the games begin! Greek pride swells with the first Olympics Games.

citadel, and **agora,** or marketplace, marked the two major cultural landmarks. Thinkers pondered philosophy and traders hawked their wares amid the agora's **stoas** (colonnaded administrative buildings). Outside the city center, **amphitheaters** and stadiums hosted major public events from dramatic and athletic exhibitions to political and religious gatherings.

ON TOP OF THE WORLD: CLASSICAL GREECE (500-399 BC)

The Classical Period began amid a series of attacks on the Greek city-states from the east. From roughly 500-477 BC, mighty king **Darius** and his son **Xerxes** sought to expand the **Persian** empire by force. Led by Athens and Sparta, the Greeks overcame overwhelming odds to defeat the Persians in legendary battles at Marathon, Plataea, and Salamis. The **hoplite phalanx,** a novel battle formation intended to intimidate and protect, clinched the Greek victory.

Prosperity ensued, and victorious Athens rose to prominence as the wealthiest and most influential *polis* in all of Greece. Equipped with a strong navy (built for use in the Persian Wars on the advice of famed statesman and general **Themistocles**), Athens made waves in the Mediterranean and established itself as the powerful head of the **Delian League,** an organization of city-states that, although formed to defend against Persian aggression, soon became the Athenian empire. Proudly adhering to its system of direct democracy, Athens ushered in an era of extraordinary achievement in art, literature, and philosophy. Its subject city-states, however, were growing frustrated with what they saw as Athens's greed.

Meanwhile, in the Peloponnese, Sparta devoted itself to an autocratic dual monarchy and a lifestyle that demonstrated the value of rigorous militarism above all else. Male Spartans spent their lives from age 7 to 60 in military training, conquest, or defense; women trained to become fit mothers and proper models for their military sons. Rising competition between Athens and Sparta eventually dragged the rest of Greece into the violent **Peloponnesian War** (431-404 BC), sparked in part by rapid Athenian expansion under **Pericles.** The war ended in defeat for Athens, as Spartan soldiers captured the city and established an oligarchic rule there. Athenians soon revolted, restoring their democracy in 403 BC, but the formerly dominant city-state soon plunged into unrest. It was this revived democracy that executed the great philosopher **Socrates** for questioning the sanctioned gods and corrupting the youth.

PHILIP AND HIS PHALANX (399-336 BC)

The period after the Peloponnesian War witnessed a gradual devolution of city-state power. First Sparta and later Thebes tried to lead and maintain a unified Greek alliance, but both ultimately succumbed to Persian political influence. A new force in **Macedonia** soon capitalized on the weakness of the rest

490 BC
Phiddipides runs 26 miles to deliver the news of victory at Marathon, inaugurating an athletic tradition for the ages. Luckily, Phidippides's immediate death after his run does not become an official part of the modern race.

431-404 BC
The Persian War's victors turn on each other in the Peloponnesian War.

399 BC
Socrates is sentenced to death by drinking hemlock, bringing his controversial philosophizing to a bitter end.

of Greece and seized control. **King Philip II,** with his improved phalanx (a closely formed group of infantry with overlapping spears and joined shields), conquered the Greek city-states in 338 BC at the Battle of Chaeronea. Though many Greeks saw him as a foreign barbarian, Philip did his best to prove that he wanted to unify Greek society—subject, of course, to his monarchy—and not to destroy it.

ALEXANDER THE AVERAGE (336-323 BC)

Alexander, who actually was pretty great, took the throne after his father, Philip, was assassinated in 336 BC. The charismatic 21-year-old had been tutored by the great Athenian thinker **Aristotle.** Greece's new lord was quite the fan of Homer's epics—he is said to have slept with a copy of the *Iliad* under his pillow—and, perhaps inspired by those mythic battles, he ruled with an iron fist. In 335 BC Alexander mercilessly razed Thebes, leaving only the house of the poet Pindar. Once in control of Greece, he expanded his dominion and ultimately would reach as far as India and Egypt. While taking control of the Persian capital of Persepolis, Alexander gained the loyalty and respect of his followers by leading and participating in the most dangerous battles himself. By the time of his sudden death at 33, Alexander's rule had spread Greek culture and language throughout the eastern Mediterranean. During the **Hellenistic Era** that followed, Classical learning continued to diffuse throughout the former empire, reaching distant realms.

The Macedonian Empire quickly crumbled after Alexander's death in 323 BC, restoring some independence to the Greek city-states. At that point, three Greek dynasties ruled simultaneously, each convinced of its right to sole power: the Antigonid in Macedonia, the Seleucid in Syria and Asia Minor, and the Ptolemaic in Egypt. Greek self-rule, however, would not last: the Romans began invading in 201 BC; by 146 BC Greece was conquered entirely and became part of the Roman Empire.

MAGNA GRAECIA TO MAGNA ROMA (201 BC-AD 324)

The Romans wanted desperately both to emulate and to control Greece. As they defeated the Seleucids of Asia Minor and conquered Macedonia in the **First and Second Macedonian Wars,** the Romans filled the power vacuum left by Alexander. At the end of the second war in 197 BC, Greece gained nominal "independence," but was still treated as a territory. Greek cities began to support their former enemies against Rome, and the Achaean League, a confederation made primarily of northern Peloponnese towns, openly rebelled in 146 BC. Rome flexed its muscles in response, destroying Corinth and imposing oppressive restrictions on Greece.

Though Roman treatment of its Greek province varied widely over the next centuries, Hellenic culture seeped steadily into Roman society. Roman authors modeled their work after Greek

336 BC
Alexander ascends to the throne and proceeds to conquer the known world before the age of 35.

LIFE AND TIMES

323 BC
Alexander the Great's death leaves Greece vulnerable to Roman conquest.

201-146 BC
Copycats! Rome absorbs Greek culture into its identity along with Greek territory.

classics, Greek sculpture was brought to Roman homes, and Roman architects used Greek styles. As the Roman poet Horace wrote, "*Graecia capta ferum victorem cepit*" ("Captive Greece captured its brutish conqueror"), and a Greco-Roman culture spread throughout the Roman Empire. Gradually, the Roman Empire declined; historians blame various causes from disease to overextension of the military.

BYZANTINE ERA (AD 324-1453)

Unlike other lands, which were ruined by the decline of the Roman Empire, Greece emerged into a period of cultural rebirth and prosperity. Power stretched from the Balkans through Greece to Asia Minor and Egypt, lands which soon would be referred to as **Byzantium.**

NEW ROME, NEW RELIGION: THE RISE OF CONSTANTINOPLE

As Rome slowly weakened, its empire split into lopsided halves. The stronger Eastern Empire was centered in Greece and the Mideast, and the destabilized Western Empire was based in Rome; each had its own set of rulers. This unusual political arrangement ended unsurprisingly in the two empires competing for power. Western **Emperor Constantine** converted to Christianity and plunged Greece into civil war, defeating Eastern **Emperor Licinius** in AD 324 and establishing himself as sole Roman Emperor. Constantine soon founded a **Nova Roma** (New Rome) on the site of Byzantium, a Greek colony at the northern tip of Asia Minor. The capital, dubbed **Constantinople** after the emperor's death and later renamed **Istanbul** by Ottoman rulers, gave Constantine's Christian empire a strategic location between the Black Sea and the Aegean Sea. Christianity flourished in Greece under Constantine and his successors: **Theodosius I** banned paganism in AD 391, and in AD 395 the Olympic Games were outlawed for their nudity. While foreign invaders overran its holdings in Western Europe, what came to be known as the Byzantine Empire made Greece a center of learning, trade, and influence unrivaled in its time.

During the 6th century, **Emperor Justinian's** battles against the Sassanians of Persia and the western Vandals (who had sacked Rome) overextended the empire's strength. Justinian's successes came in domestic politics as he codified Roman laws and undertook massive building projects, such as the awe-inspiring **Church of Agia Sophia**, an architectural masterpiece that still stands in Istanbul. However, the empire's strength waned under constant raids by Avars, Mongols, and Slavs.

IT'S NOT YOU, IT'S ME: THE GREAT SCHISM

Ensuing Arab conquests distracted imperial attention in the early 8th century, as did **iconoclasm**, an icon-smashing religious movement. Greek Christians then believed that visual

AD 324
Emperor Constantine defeats Emperor Licinius, creating a unified Christian Empire.

AD 395
Let the games be gone! Naked Greek athletes are deemed inappropriate in a Christian empire, and their Olympic games are outlawed.

representations of God violated the second commandment against idolatry, and some interpreted their defeat in battle against the Arabs as punishment for this violation. By the mid-700s, Church doctrine demanded that all images be demolished, but, to the benefit of modern-day art historians, iconoclasm itself eventually was crushed in 843.

The crowning of **Charlemagne,** King of the Franks, as Holy Roman Emperor by Pope Leo III in 800 fed growing tensions between East and West sections of the so-called **Byzantine Commonwealth;** the creation of a Holy Roman Empire in the West served only to further divide the two factions. The bitter **Great Schism** of 1054 resulted in a mutual excommunication of the Orthodox and Roman Catholic Churches' leaders—each church declared the other a false church, and the two factions developed into the distinct denominations they are today.

THE CURSE OF CRUSADERS

Even as they protected themselves from invaders, the Byzantine Greeks continued to spread Christianity. Missionaries reached out into the Slavic kingdoms and Russia, sowing the seeds of Orthodox Christianity throughout Eastern Europe. In 1071 the Byzantines lost control of eastern Anatolia to the **Selçuk Turks,** and Greek monasteries in the Aegean and Black Sea areas were transformed into armed fortresses to ward off Turkish pirates. From 1200 to 1400, the Byzantine Empire was invaded by **Norman** and **Venetian** crusaders, who looted and desecrated Constantinople in 1204 and tried to impose western Catholic culture on the city. Despite strong leaders, Byzantium needed to ally with Latin, Slavic, and even Turkish rulers through marriage to survive. Finally, the once-indomitable Byzantine Empire, the longest-lasting empire in history, was reduced to only Constantinople and its environs. On May 29, 1453 (a day still considered cursed by Greeks), the Ottoman Turks at last overran the fading city.

1054
Growing theological and political tensions lead to the Great Schism between the Roman Catholic and Orthodox Churches.

OTTOMAN RULE (1453-1821)

ISTANBUL, NOT CONSTANTINOPLE

As soon as the Turks moved in, they renamed Constantine's capital Istanbul, reinstating the city as the seat of an empire. The **Ottoman Empire** prospered at first, though eventually its diverse regions grew apart. The Muslim Turkish rulers treated their Greek subjects as a **millet**—a semi-autonomous community ruled by its own religious leaders—though Greeks could choose to integrate into Ottoman society. The head of the Orthodox millet, the Ecumenical Patriarch of Constantinople, was ultimately accountable to the Sultan, the empire's divine ruler. For centuries, Turkish dominance was threatened only by the hardy Venetian navy, which continued to make incursions on the Sultan's Greek territory. Meanwhile, the Orthodox Church's strong tradition became the foundation of Greek autonomy. Fueled by religious tension and the Ottoman government's harsh taxation system, anti-Turk nationalist sentiments began to build.

1453
A dark day in May: Constantinople falls to the Ottoman Sultan Mehmet II on May 29.

LIFE AND TIMES

THE GREAT IDEA (1821-1900)

UP IN ARMS: THE GREEK NATIONALIST REVOLT (1821-1829)

On March 25, 1821, Bishop Germanos of Patras raised a Greek flag at the monastery of Agia Lavra (p. 161), sparking an empire-wide **rebellion.** Middle-class rebels hoped the Orthodox Russian czar and Greek peasants would join the revolt; when they didn't, the rebels met a crushing defeat. Disorganized but devoted guerrillas in the Peloponnese waged sporadic war on the Turkish government for the next decade. Under the leadership of rebel heroes Botsaris, Koundouritis, Mavrokordatos, Miaoulis, and Ypsilanti, the Greeks slowly chipped away at Ottoman control. The Greek passion for independence stirred up a feeling of **philhellenism** in Europe, which eventually convinced Britain, France, and Russia to adopt the Greek cause. Finally, in 1829, with military support from other European powers, Greece won its independence. But to the Greeks' dismay, the narrow borders of the new monarchical state included only a fraction of the six million Greeks living under Ottoman rule. For the next century, Greek politics centered on achieving the *Megali Idea*—the **Great Idea:** freeing Istanbul from the Turks and uniting all Greeks, even those in Asia Minor, into one sovereign state. Although Greece gained back some territory over the next century, including **Thessaloniki** and the island of **Crete,** it never realized these ambitious goals.

NEW BEGINNINGS (1829-1900)

After the War of Independence, joy dissolved into disappointment. Puny and poor, the Greek state was divided by an agrarian problem that plagued it for the entire century: landowners clung to their traditional privileges while peasants demanded the land redistribution that they had been promised in exchange for fighting.

The first president of Greece, **Ioannis Kapodistrias,** was elected in 1827 and made an earnest—if autocratic—attempt to create a strong government. His assassination in 1831 thwarted plans to establish a democracy and prompted a European political intervention. Britain, France, and Germany declared Greece a **monarchy,** and in 1833 gave the crown to German **Prince Otto,** a rich, powerful teenager who angered Greeks by appointing his German cronies to high-ranking positions. He moved the capital from its provisional site in Nafplion to Athens, and created a parliamentary system. Though he embraced the *Megali Idea*, Otto's support for Austria in opposing Italian unification led to an upsurge in latent resentments against the leadership. In 1862, the Athens garrison staged a coup, removing Otto from power. In need of a leader, the Greeks accepted the British choice of the Danish prince, **George I,** as king, and regained control of the Ionian Islands in the deal. George's rule brought general stability, Greece's first railways, and a new constitution which played down the king's power and empha-

1821
A Greek flag over a monastery ignites rebellion against Turkish rulers.

1829
European powers, feeling obligation to thousands of years of Western civilization, step in to help the Greek cause.

1833
"Otto-cratic" German prince becomes king of Greece.

sized the importance of the elected Prime Minister. Problems of land distribution, however, remained unsolved.

TWENTIETH CENTURY

COHESION AND CATASTROPHE (1900-1932)

The Prime Minister elected in 1910, **Eleftherios Venizelos,** who has been immortalized in street names throughout modern Greece, made extensive progress in stabilizing the country. In the aftermath of the Balkan Wars, Venizelos successfully worked to reunify Crete with Greece. Later, savvy Balkan alliances nearly doubled Greek territory. With the momentum that followed the additions of Macedonia and Epirus to Greece, Venizelos set up an Allied revolutionary government in Thessaloniki. After WWI, Venizelos learned that Greece would not be receiving land in Asia Minor, so in 1919 he ordered an outright invasion of Turkey. However, the young Turkish general (and de facto leader of the country) Mustafa Kemal, later known as **Atatürk,** crushed the Greek army. As it retreated, Turkish forces ordered the slaughter of Greek and Armenian citizens along the Turkish coast. Putting an end to the violence, the 1923 **Treaty of Lausanne** enacted a massive **population exchange** that sent one million Greeks living in Asia Minor to Greece and 400,000 Turkish Muslims from Greece to Turkey. Called the *Katastrofí*, or Catastrophe, this exchange drew the curtain on Greece's *Megali Idea*.

THE EMERGING STATE AND THE SECOND WORLD WAR (1932-1945)

Political and economic turmoil rocked the 1930s, as Greeks lived through brief intervals of democracy, monarchy, and military rule. **King George II** lost power through a series of coups that reinstated a democracy; Venizelos, the former Prime Minister, headed the new government for five years, though royalists eventually forced his exile. When George II resumed the throne in 1936, he personally appointed extreme nationalist **General Ioannis Metaxas** as Prime Minister. Metaxas inaugurated an oppressive military state, but his leadership during the early stages of WWII earned him lasting respect. In 1940, Metaxas is said to have rejected Mussolini's request that Italy occupy Greece during WWII with a resounding "Οχι!" ("NO!"); the Greeks now celebrate **Ohi Day** as a national holiday. Although it held off the Italian forces, Greece fell to Germany in 1941 and endured four years of bloody and brutal Axis occupation. During this time, communist-led resistance received broad support from the Greek populace, but Western powers, wary of a Communist Greece, hesitated to fund anti-Nazi resistance forces that also opposed monarchy. Tragically, over one million Greek Jews perished in Nazi concentration camps during this time.

1862
A coup ousts the unpopular king.

1896
Let the games resume! The Olympics return to Greece with the inauguration of the modern Olympic Games in Athens.

1919
Venizelos unsuccessfully invades Turkey.

1923
In the Treaty of Lausanne, Greece and Turkey decide that the best way to end a war over territory is to exchange large groups of people, uprooting countless families.

LIFE AND TIMES

BREAK UP AND MAKE UP: CIVIL WAR AND RECONSTRUCTION (1944-75)

The devastating Greek Civil War, marked by purges and starvation, broke out in 1944 between Greek loyalists and communists. With economic support from the US under the **Truman Doctrine,** the anti-communist coalition government eventually defeated the Soviet-backed Democratic Army of Greece in 1949. Keeping a visible hand in Greek politics, the US helped place **General Papagos, Constantine Karamanlis,** and the right-wing **Greek Rally Party** in power. During this time, Greece began to find its place among Western democracies, becoming a member of **NATO** in 1952. When Karamanlis resigned after the assassination of a Communist official in 1963, left-wing **George Papandreou** came to power.

On April 21, 1967, a group of unknown colonels staged a coup which resulted in **military junta** rule for seven years. Making use of torture, censorship, and arbitrary arrests to repress Communist forces, the junta enjoyed official US support and investment at the height of the Cold War. Yet after helping provoke a Turkish invasion of Cyprus and a nationwide **student uprising,** which left 20 dead, the junta lost power in 1974. Former president Karamanlis returned to power with a newly-formed conservative party, **New Democracy (ND),** instituting parliamentary elections and organizing a referendum on the form of government. Monarchy was defeated by a two-thirds vote, and a new constitution was approved by Parliament on June 19, 1975.

DEMOCRACY REBORN: GIVE GREECE A CHANCE (1975–PRESENT)

The constitution of 1975 established Greece as a **presidential parliamentary republic,** generally modeled after the democracies of other Western European nations. The Parliament is elected based on a system of **proportional representation,** and the leader of the party with the majority in Parliament becomes the Prime Minister. Parliament in turn elects a ceremonial president to a five-year term, but the Prime Minister and the cabinet play the most influential roles in the political process. The Church of Greece is under protection of the state, which pays for maintenance of churches and for the clergy's salaries.

THE POWER PENDULUM

Guided by founder **Andreas Papandreou,** the leftist **Panhellenic Socialist Movement (PASOK)** won landslide electoral victories in 1981 and 1985. Appealing to voters with the simple slogan *"Allaghi"* ("Change"), Prime Minister Papandreou promised a radical break with the past. In office he steered Greece into the **European Community (EC),** now the EU, and pioneered women's rights legislation. Papandreou's refusal to conform to some geopolitical positions, however, angered many in the West. After three general elections in 10 months, **Constantine Mitsotakis** of the more conservative New Democracy party became Prime Minister by a slim majority.

Attempting to solve Greece's economic and diplomatic problems and align the country with mainstream European politics, Mitsotakis imposed an **austerity program,** limiting wage increases and authorizing the sale of state enterprises. This policy became vastly unpopular when it threatened many public sector jobs, and, in 1993, a resurgent Papandreou defeated Mitsotakis in an emergency election. Two years later, poor health forced Papandreou to leave his post.

Fellow socialist **Costas Simitis** took control of the party in 1996 and pursued aggressive economic reforms, privatizing banks and previously state-owned companies despite the opposition of perpetually striking labor unions. PASOK also made strides in international relations by becoming more NATO-friendly and opening talks with Turkey. The administration slashed Greece's budget deficit, brought inflation down, and cut the national debt.

1981-96
Left-wing Andreas Papandreou and conservative Constantine Mitsotakis take turns in the office of Prime Minister.

GREECE TODAY

In the 2004 elections, power went back to New Democracy, elevating **Kostas Karamanlis** to Prime Minister and returning former Foreign Minister **George Papandreou's** PASOK to the minority party. Karamanlis's administration has focused its efforts on the economic development of northern Greece, has promised to alleviate the strain on farmers, and hopes to reform Albanian immigration policy.

THE KKE

The **Greek Communist Party,** or **KKE,** is the third-strongest political party in Greece, but still far behind ND and PASOK. Suspicious of NATO and the West, KKE members resent American cultural dominance, and are responsible for much of the visible anti-American sentiment in Greece.

GREECE AND TURKEY: BREAKING THE ICE

One of Greece's continuing projects is normalizing relations with nearby Turkey. The two nations have been on less-than-friendly terms in the past (p. 56), but, in part through mutual displays of support after both countries suffered devastating earthquakes in 1999, they have begun to patch up their relationship. In January 2001, when he was Foreign Minister, George Papandreou traveled to Turkey, the first such visit in 37 years. There he signed cooperation agreements concerning tourism, the environment, the protection of investments, and terrorism.

A big obstacle straining Greece-Turkey relations is the little island of **Cyprus.** The Republic of Cyprus, internationally recognized by the UN and all foreign governments aside from Turkey, is a member of the EU. Turkish Cyprus, in the northern part of the Island, is recognized only by Turkey. A unification plan proposed by the United Nations came to a vote in April 2004, and though it passed in the Turkish half of Cyprus, it did not come close to gaining the votes necessary in the southern

2004
Let the games return! Prime Minister Costas Karamanlis brings the 28th modern Olympic Games to the nation of their ancient birth.

LIFE AND TIMES

Republic of Cyprus. In March 2007, the demolition of the wall on Ledra Street in Nicosa, Cyprus's capital, marked an important step in Greek-Turkish relations by facilitating crossing between the two sides of the divided city.

PEOPLE

DEMOGRAPHICS

About **11 million** people live in Greece. The extremely homogeneous population is 98% ethnically Greek and 98% Greek Orthodox (p. 61), but the large number of foreigners who travel in Greece each year makes the country seem more diverse.

MINORITIES

Greece is peppered with small but distinct ethnic and religious minorities. Currently about 500,000 to 1,000,000 **Albanians** make up the country's largest minority population. Despite the Greek government and people's general denial of racism, concerns remain about prejudice toward this expanding refugee and migrant population. In past years, reports of violence against illegal Albanian immigrants by the Greek border patrol have cropped up with increasing frequency.

The over 130,000 Slavic and Turkish **Muslims** in Thrace comprise the biggest religious minority group. Though the older generation of Muslims remains separate from Orthodox Greeks in language and culture, younger generations are integrated with mainstream Greek society. Gypsies, or **Roma,** make up another significant minority group. They have remained on the fringes of Greek society for centuries and now are concentrated in Athens and Thessaloniki. The status of the Roma population, plagued by devastating poverty, is viewed as one of the country's largest social problems. **Jewish** communities have been present in Greece since the AD first century, but about 90 percent of Jews were deported to concentration camps during the Nazi occupation in WWII (p. 57), despite the efforts of the Greek Orthodox Church and many individuals to shelter them. Only about 5500 Jews live in Greece today. Other official minorities include the **Vlachs** and the **Sarakatsanis,** both of which are groups of nomadic shepherds descended from Latin speakers who settled in Greece. The region of Macedonia is home to some 60,000 **Slavs,** who are still unrecognized as a minority by the Greek government.

LANGUAGE

Aside from being a medium for communication, the Greek language, Ellinika (Ελληνικά, eh-lee-nee-KAH) is a link to Greece's past and a key to its continued presence in the future. During the 5th-century BC Golden Age (p. 52), Greek flourished as the language of democracy, philosophy, and power; with Alexander the Great's expansion campaigns, it spread as the *lingua franca* through much of the Near East. Now, however, barely 12 million people speak Greek around the world, so each and every speaker is seen as essential to the continuation of the language.

To the non-Greek speaker, the nuanced levels of idiom, irony, and poetry in the language can present a seemingly impenetrable wall to understanding. Although mastering Greek is a daunting task, learning enough to order a meal or get to the airport is surprisingly easy. The Greek language is phonetic (though a cursory knowledge of the alphabet does not always help with the many double consonants and double vowels), and all multisyllabic Greek words come with a handy accent called a *tonos*, which marks the emphasized syllable. Most sentences are simple, and their structure is similar to that of English. Fortunately, many Greeks—and certainly most working in the tourist industry—will understand English.

MYTHOLOGY

Greek myths simmer with spicy, titillating scandal as they explain the origins of natural phenomena and the ways of the world. The adventures of the gods and their mortal counterparts have inspired artists, writers, musicians, and psychoanalysts for centuries. Moreover, Greek mythology is inextricably intertwined with the nation's religion, history, and literature.

Worship centered on prayer and offerings to the gods. Temples and rites were the heart of religious practice, and pilgrimages often were taken to consult oracles or to appease angered gods. Foreign deities were welcomed into the Greek pantheon, the canon of gods, to make sure no god was ignored or offended. There was even an altar to the unknown god, to keep the bases covered.

The Greek gods behaved like soap-opera characters who can't be written off the show—the immortal all-stars lacked morals and were slaves to lust, greed, and jealousy. The Greeks knew that these divine passions were not to be trifled with: mythology is full of ugly examples of what happens to mortals who challenge or disrespect gods. The weaver **Arachne** was turned into a spider because she dared to declare herself more skilled than Athena. **Tantalus,** after serving the gods human flesh at a feast, was condemned to stand in a pool in Hades, forever tormented by hunger and thirst with "tantalizing" food and water just beyond his grasp. When King Minos didn't make an expected sacrifice to Poseidon, the sea god struck Minos's wife, **Pasiphaë,** with an insatiable lust for a bull. Pasiphaë then conceived and bore the **Minotaur,** a cannibal bull-boy. Though the worship of Greek gods faded with the advent of Christianity, the pantheon's legacy is still visible in Greece's plentiful ancient ruins, not to mention the myths that survive today.

RELIGION

THE ORTHODOX CHURCH

Christianity in Greece dates to the AD first century. The **Apostle Paul** and other missionaries were the first to spread Christianity and establish Christian communities in cities in Greece and Asia Minor. Five of Paul's epistles (letters), which eventually formed part of the **New Testament,** were addressed to these new Christian communities. By the 4th century, the Christians had escaped persecution and the Church was well established throughout the Mediterranean. After the 11th-century Great Schism (p. 54), Greek churches became part of Eastern Christianity, centered at the **Patriarchate of Constantinople.** A member of the family of Orthodox Churches, the Church of Greece received **autocephalous** status in 1850, meaning that its head bishop no longer would be required to report to any higher-ranking official. The Church is still under the spiritual guidance of the Ecumenical Patriarch in Constantinople. The Church of Crete, the dioceses of some Greek islands, and the dioceses in Northern Greece remain a part of the Patriarchate of Constantinople, but the Church of Cyprus has been autocephalous since the 4th century.

The Orthodox Church of Greece is the preeminent religious body in the country today. Over 90% of the population of Greece is baptized. There are hundreds of monastic communities, the most prominent of which are located on the highly-regulated **Mount Athos Peninsula.** Orthodox doctrine in the Church of Greece centers on Jesus and his Gospel. Orthodox Christianity, which takes its name from the Greek "orthos" meaning "true" and "doxa" meaning "belief," affirms a loving God who entered into this life in the person of Jesus. Honored as Lord and Savior,

Christ revealed the one God as Father, Son, and Holy Spirit: the Holy Trinity. The Church celebrates these beliefs in worship during the service of the **Divine Liturgy.** Faith is also expressed in scripture and tradition, which includes the veneration of icons, prayers, a rich history of rituals and customs, and the **Ecumenical Councils.** Because of their religious example, the saints are greatly honored.

TURF WARS

For nearly two centuries, the structural arrangement between the Church of Greece and the Patriarchate of Constantinople has remained peaceful but tense. The Church of Greece's boundaries do not line up with those of the Greek state, and many believe that the Church of Greece should encompass the country's internationally recognized borders. Such sentiment crystallized in the spring of 2004, when territorial tension surfaced between the Archbishop of the Greek Church and the Ecumenical Patriarch. When three vacancies for sees (bishop seats) opened in northern Greece, an area under the Patriarchate's control, 35 bishops in the Hierarchy (the full body of the Church of Greece) affirmed the Archbishop's motion to elect new bishops for the sees. Such a violation of jurisdiction was not welcomed by the Ecumenical Patriarch, who threatened to break communion with the Archbishop. Though both sides eventually compromised, the significant eruption underscores the often uncomfortable relationship between the independent Greek Church and the central branch of Orthodox Christianity.

OTHER RELIGIOUS TRADITIONS

While Orthodox Christianity reigns in Greek society and the government grants certain advantages and support to the Church of Greece, the Greek Constitution guarantees freedom of religion and repudiates proselytizing. There are a few Armenian Orthodox and Roman Catholic communities, and some Muslim communities exist, mostly in Northern Greece. Before WWII, Greece had a thriving Jewish population, but only a few organized Jewish communities remain today.

FOOD AND DRINK

Greece's Mediterranean location lends its food a Middle Eastern flavor. Medical studies have highlighted the Greek diet as a good model for **healthful** eating; its reliance on unsaturated olive oil, fresh fish, and vegetables has prevented high rates of heart disease and obesity despite the populace's fairly sedentary lifestyle. Though the prevalence of cheap and greasy foods has caused some recent health concerns, penny-pinching carnivores will thank Zeus for lamb, chicken, or beef **souvlaki** and hot-off-the-spit **gyros**—pronounced "Ghee-ro"—stuffed into pitas. Vegetarians can eat their fill on the cheap, though this might mean putting together a meal of several **mezedes** (small snack dishes). **Toast** refers to a panini-like grilled sandwich, not to be confused with plain bread out of the toaster. **Tzatziki,** a garlicky cucumber yogurt dip served with bread, is a good way to start off a meal (or ripen your breath enough to ward off amorous overtures). Try the feta-piled **horiatiki** (Greek salad), savory pastries like **tiropita** (flaky, tissue-thin layers of pastry—called phyllo—full of feta), **spanikopita** (spinach and feta phyllo pastry), and the cheeses and fresh fruits and vegetables found at markets in cities. **Baklava,** a dessert made of phyllo, nuts, and honey, is a sweet way to round off your meal.

Caffeine cravers will find a few options, including the strong, sweet sludge that is **Greek coffee,** the instant coffee referred to as **"Nes"** (as in "Nescafé"), or the frothy, iced-coffee **frappés** that take an edge off the heat in the summer. Potent **raki** and **tsipouro,** moonshine born from the remnants of wine-making, are popular on the mainland and Crete. Wine, important enough in ancient Greece to monopolize the attention of principal god Dionysus, is plentiful and widely varied. **Ouzo,** a powerful, licorice-flavored Greek spirit, is served before meals with a glass of water—when you pour the ouzo into the water, the mixture turns white. Say, "Γεια μας!" (Yah mas), which is the Greek equivalent of "Cheers!" before drinking.

Breakfast, served only in the early morning, generally consists of coffee and a simple piece of toast with *marmelada* (jam), a pastry, or thick Greek yogurt with honey. Lunch, a hearty and leisurely meal, usually is eaten sometime between 2 and 5pm. Dinner, a drawn-out, relaxed affair, is served late, sometime between 10pm and midnight. A Greek restaurant is known as a **taverna** or **estiatorio** (often the more expensive of the two), and a grille is a **psistaria. Kafeneios** are traditional coffee shops frequented primarily by groups of older Greek men; women may feel uncomfortable in some of them. Many restaurants don't offer printed menus, so waiters will ask you if you want salad, appetizers, or the works. Be careful not to wind up with mountains of food—Greek portions tend to be large. Restaurants often put bread and water on the table; an added charge for the bread and sometimes the water may or may not be listed on the menu. Most Greeks pay with **cash** when they dine out, so don't expect to be able to eat your way through the country with a credit card. Service is always included in the check, but it is customary to round the bill up or leave some coins as an extra tip.

CUSTOMS AND ETIQUETTE

HOME HOSPITALITY

■**Greek hospitality** is legendary. From your first days in the country, you may be invited to drop by a stranger's home for coffee, share a meal at a local taverna, or attend an engagement party or baptism. The invitations are genuine; it's impossible to spend any length of time in the country and not have some friendly interaction with locals. Greet new acquaintances with *"kalimera"* ("good morning") or *"kalispera"* ("good evening"). Personal questions are ordinary and expected in Greece; people you've just met will ask about family, career, salary, and other information. Returning questions in kind is expected and appreciated, so don't be embarrassed to be friendly!

FOOD AND DRINK

Offering food and drink to guests is how the Greeks say hello. When offered, take it—it's almost always considered rude to refuse. Hosts usually will offer coffee upon a guest's arrival. Visiting and gossiping over coffee, either at a cafe or at someone's home, is how many Greeks spend their nights. Wine drinkers should note that glasses are filled only halfway but are constantly replenished; it's considered bad manners to empty your glass. When out to eat, the bill usually is paid by the host rather than split among the diners. Even though it's understood that the host will foot the bill, dramatic (but fruitless) attempts to throw in money are common. Never offer money in return for an invitation to dine at someone's home. A small gift, such as a toy for the host's children, is a welcome token of gratitude.

R-E-S-P-E-C-T!

It is customary to show deference to elders, which may mean offering a seat on a bus or helping someone cross the street. Visitors to churches are expected to dress conservatively; both men and women always should cover their shoulders and knees. Take signs forbidding photography seriously. Even if photography isn't specifically forbidden in a particular church or monastery, it remains extremely rude and offensive. Never photograph anything having to do with the military. Even if you're hoping that a tiny rock from Delphi will become your own personal oracle if you take it home with you, refrain from pocketing "souvenirs" from ancient sites, as it is considered disrespectful and is possible cause for arrest.

LIFE AND TIMES

ART AND ARCHITECTURE

Remnants of centuries of legendary craftsmanship abound in Greece. The number and quality of carefully crafted works that have survived to the present day attest to the importance of art in the ancient and modern Greek worlds. Classical Greeks used diverse materials to represent the faces of the mighty gods, the deeds of mythical heroes, and the natural beauty they saw in the human body. Although modern audiences admire ancient Greek statues and pottery in museums, it is important to remember that the Greeks produced art not just to marvel at its beauty but also for use in everyday life. Pottery was the Tupperware® of the time, used as daily dishware and for storage and trade. Architecture developed through the functional construction of stadiums, commercial buildings, and religious temples. Today, Greece's double legacy of form and function lives on: the styles developed by Greek painters and sculptors have continued to reverberate through centuries of art and architecture.

CYCLADIC/MINOAN PERIOD (3000-1500 BC)

"Less is more" was the motto for the Bronze Age **Cycladic civilizations** that produced a minimalist style of sculpture, surviving mostly as small marble statuettes. These miniature pieces gracefully simplified the human form; a nude goddess, arms folded straight across her body, is a typical figure. The **Minoans** of Crete also created scores of miniature votive statuettes, like the two earthenware snake goddesses, decorated with opaque colored glazes, which reside in Iraklion's Archaeological Museum (p. 591). It was architecture, however, that brought the Minoans glory, with formidable palaces like the one at Knossos (p. 594). The palaces were cities unto themselves, and their labyrinthine design echoed the complex administrative and religious roles of Minoan priest-kings. The massive pillars, ceremonial stairways, and decorative stucco reflect Near Eastern aesthetic and structural influences resulting from commercial contact with Egypt and Mesopotamia.

Minoan artists adorned plaster with bull-leaping ceremonies, gardens, and jumping dolphins in vibrant frescoes. Though a little dusty, several Minoan frescoes were preserved in the ash of the epic volcanic eruption that destroyed much of Fira (modern Santorini) around 1500 BC; this style of fresco can be seen at the National Archaeological Museum in Athens (p. 113), at Knossos, or in Iraklion's Archaeological Museum. The Minoans also were renowned throughout the Aegean for their multicolored **Kamares-style pottery,** which consist of red and white ornamentation on a dark background. Kamares-style designs include curvy abstract patterns and stylized ocean and plant motifs.

MYCENAEAN PERIOD (1500-1100 BC)

The Mycenaean palaces at Mycenae, Pylos, Thebes, and Tiryns followed a more symmetrical design than earlier architecture had and centered on the *megaron*, a Near East-inspired reception room. Decorative frescoes revamped the fanciful Minoan model according to Mycenaean warrior taste.

Trailblazers in their own right, the **Mycenaeans** were the first Europeans to produce monumental sculpture. By 1500 BC Mycenaean royal graves had evolved into *tholoi*, beehive-shaped stone structures covered in packed earth. While the relief work on these tombs shows Minoan influence, the larger-than-life masonry is distinctly Mycenaean. The royal tombs and triangular 13th-century BC **Lion's Gate** sculpture at Mycenae (p. 147) also display this aesthetic.

IT'S HIP TO BE SQUARE: GEOMETRIC PERIOD (1100-700 BC)

A new ceramics-based art form evolved out of the collapse of Mycenaean civilization and the Dark Age that followed. There to pick up the pieces were the **Athenians,** who stood at the center of the new movement. Their pottery of the Proto-Geometric period (1100-900 BC) was decorated with Mycenaean-inspired spirals, arcs, patterned lines, and concentric circles. These patterns became more intricate in the Geometric Period, as artists covered clay figurines and pottery with abstract angular motifs that resembled woven baskets. Identically posed stick-figure humans and grazing animals began to appear among the continuous, patterned bands and tight rows of thick black lines. Signs of Near Eastern contact with Greece showed up again in Orientalized pottery, as Syrian and Phoenician floral and animal designs adorned Greek cooking vessels. Architects of the Geometric Period focused on the development of one-room temples with columned porches. These temples were regarded as the houses of the gods or goddesses they honored, and each *oikos* (house) came complete with a sculpture of its inhabitant.

ARCHAIC PERIOD (700-480 BC)

During the Archaic Period, Greek art and architecture gradually traded stylized lines for the curving, human realism that would come to characterize the later Classical Period. It was in this period that structures such as the acropolis, agora, amphitheater, and gymnasium were perfected.

The **Doric** and **Ionic** orders—whose columns have lined many an art history student's nightmares—diverged during these years. The Doric order breathed new life into temples' one-room inner sanctums and outer colonnades with straight-arrow marble columns. Around the 6th century BC however, the Greek colonies along the coast of Asia Minor branched off into the exotic Ionic order. Austere Doric designs just wouldn't do for the Ionian architects, who conjured slender, fluted columns, often topping them with twin curlicued volutes. Ornate Ionic temples boasted forests of columns: the **Temple of Hera on Samos** (p. 493) had 134.

The depiction of the human body began to flourish during the Archaic period, with sculptors crafting large-scale male figures called *kouroi*. Each *kouros* was a naked young man in a rigid pose lifted from Egyptian statues—one leg forward with both feet planted firmly, hands clenched at sides—and grinning the famous Archaic smile. The female equivalent of the *kouros*, the *kore*, sported the latest fashions instead of her birthday suit; sculptors suggested the female form through folds and hemlines of the *kore's* clothing. By the 5th century BC, sculpture turned toward realistic depiction, reaching its height soon afterward in the Classical Period. The relaxed posture of the free-standing **Kritios Boy** (490 BC), now in the Acropolis Museum (p. 108), broke the stiff, symmetrical mold of its Archaic model: the Kritios Boy's weight is shifted onto one leg and his hips and torso tilt naturally.

Though sculptors focused on realism, two-dimensional art remained abstract. Athenian vase painters depicted humans using Corinth's black figure technique, drawing black silhouettes with carved features. Human figures appeared in the half-profile of Egyptian art: moving figures' chests faced forward, and each person stared straight out with both eyes. Figures conveyed emotion with gestures rather than facial expressions, pulling their hair in grief or flailing their limbs in joy.

ALBANIA

FYROM

BULG

PELLA
Philip II and his son, Alexander the Great, ruled an enormous Macedonian empire from the capital whose ruins lie here.

VERGINA
The final resting place of the Macedonian kings, complete with treasures from Philip II's tomb.

MACEDONIA

Edessa ●

Amphibolis ●

● Thessaloniki

DODONI
The site of Zeus's oak tree oracle, the second most important in ancient Greece.

GREECE

Thermaic Gulf

Mount▲ Olympus Litochoro

DION
Home to the sanctuary of Egyptian Isis and the famed mosaics of the villa of Dionysus.

THESSALY

Corfu Town ●

Corfu

EPIRUS

■ Meteora

Volos ●

SPORADES

Ioannina

Nekromentio

Nikopolis

Preveza ● ● Aktion

I O N I A N

Thermon

DELPHI
Apollo's oracle here was consulted by ancient Greeks on matters of the highest importance.

Livadia ●

Evia

Osios Loukas ●

I S L A N D S

Gulf of Corinth

Athens ★

ANCIENT CORINTH
The well-preserved site of one of ancient Greece's most famous cities, including fountains, temples, and a magnificent fortress.

PELOPONNESE

Corinth ● Isthmia

Eleusis ●

Aegina

Temple of Aphaia

● Olympia

Mantinia

Nemea ●

Tiryns ●

Epidavros ●

SARONIC GULF ISLAND

OLYMPIA
The temples, training grounds, and stadium of the original Olympic Games.

Argos ●

● Tripoli

Tegea ●

Saronic Gulf

SARONIC GULF ISLAND

Ancient Messini

Nestor's Palace

■ Sparta

EPIDAVROS
An ancient theater engineered to acoustic perfection

Kalamata

MYSTRAS
The ruins of a great Byzantine fortress perch above the olive groves of Laconia.

Ionian Sea

Monemvasia ●

MYCENAE
Legendary home of Agamemnon and the Atreid clan of Classical tragedy.

0   50 miles

0   50 kilometers

M E D I T E R R A N E A N   S E A

Hania ●

■ Byzantine Sights

⚔ Ancient Ruins

🏛 Temples and Sanctuaries

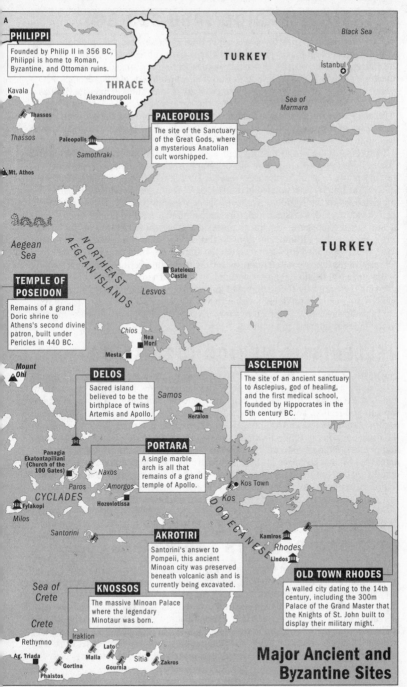

Black Sea

PHILIPPI

Founded by Philip II in 356 BC, Philippi is home to Roman, Byzantine, and Ottoman ruins.

TURKEY

İstanbul

Kavala

THRACE

Alexandroupoli

Sea of Marmara

Thassos

PALEOPOLIS

The site of the Sanctuary of the Great Gods, where a mysterious Anatolian cult worshipped.

Thassos

Paleopolis

Samothraki

Mt. Athos

Aegean Sea

NORTHEAST AEGEAN ISLANDS

TURKEY

Gatelouzi Castle

Lesvos

TEMPLE OF POSEIDON

Remains of a grand Doric shrine to Athens's second divine patron, built under Pericles in 440 BC.

Chios

Nea Moni

Mesta

Mount Ohi

DELOS

Sacred island believed to be the birthplace of twins Artemis and Apollo.

Samos

ASCLEPION

The site of an ancient sanctuary to Asclepius, god of healing, and the first medical school, founded by Hippocrates in the 5th century BC.

Heraion

Panagia Ekatontapiliani (Church of the 100 Gates)

PORTARA

A single marble arch is all that remains of a grand temple of Apollo.

Naxos

Paros

Amorgos

Kos Town

Kos

CYCLADES

Hozoviotissa

DODECANESE

Fylakopi

Milos

Santorini

AKROTIRI

Santorini's answer to Pompeii, this ancient Minoan city was preserved beneath volcanic ash and is currently being excavated.

Kamiros

Rhodes

Lindos

OLD TOWN RHODES

A walled city dating to the 14th century, including the 300m Palace of the Grand Master that the Knights of St. John built to display their military might.

Sea of Crete

KNOSSOS

The massive Minoan Palace where the legendary Minotaur was born.

Crete

Rethymno

Iraklion

Lato

Ag. Triada

Gortina

Malia

Gournia

Sitia

Zakros

Phaistos

Major Ancient and Byzantine Sites

CLASSICAL PERIOD (480-323 BC)

The arts flourished during the Classical Period, as Athens reached the peak of its political and economic power under **Pericles** and his successors (p. 55). Perfecting the Doric and Ionic orders, Classical temples were more spacious and fluid than the stocky temples of the Archaic Period. The majestic **Athenian Acropolis** (p. 106) gazed down over Athens, crowned by its star attraction, the ▓ **Parthenon.** Built as a temple for Athena, protectress of Athens, the Parthenon once held the huge statue of **Athena Parthenos.** Created by **Phidias**, the same sculptor who worked on the **Temple of Zeus at Olympia** (p. 169), this monumental work of perfect proportion was over 40 ft. tall and was chryselephantine (made of ivory and gold).

Sculptors mastered the natural representation of the human form during the Classical Period. The sculptures of the Temple of Zeus at Olympia reveal meticulous attention to detail. Sculptures from the Classical Period include the **Charioteer** (470 BC) at Delphi, now housed in the Delphi Museum, and **Poseidon** (465 BC) now immortalized in the National Archaeological Museum (p. 113). By the middle of the 5th century BC, Classical sculptors had adopted a detailed humanism that still lacked facial expression. Sculptors pursued a universal perfection of the human form, suppressing all imperfections in the service of the impersonal, idealized style, which remained in vogue through the start of the 4th century BC.

Classical potters swooned over the red figure technique that had been gaining steam since 540 BC. Red figure vase painting featured a black painted background, allowing the naturally reddish clay to show through as the drawn figures. Vasemakers then painted on details with a fine brush. Inspired by the new-found realism in sculpture, early Classical masters used this technique to indicate emotion on the faces of humans and animals.

HELLENISTIC PERIOD (323-46 BC)

The death of **Alexander the Great** marked the beginning of the Hellenistic Period, a prodigious era for art and architecture. During this time, two of the Seven Wonders of the Ancient World were created: the **Colossus of Rhodes,** a gigantic statue of the sun god Helios, and the **Pharos,** a monumental lighthouse on the Alexandria harbor. Architectural innovations, like the **Corinthian Order** of columns (based on the Ionic column but topped with a capital of acanthus leaves), enhanced temples and public buildings. Astoundingly precise acoustics graced the amphitheaters at **Argos** (p. 143) and **Epidavros** (p. 149); a coin dropped on stage is audible in the most distant seat in the theaters even 2200 years after their construction. Hellenistic sculpture exuded passion and tested the aesthetic value of ugliness, displaying all the technical mastery and twice the emotion of Classical works.

SEE YA, ZEUS!: BYZANTINE AND OTTOMAN PERIODS (AD 324-1829)

The art and architecture in Greece under Byzantine and Ottoman rule was limited by the often-strict expectations of these imperial cultures. Though Byzantine artistry developed within a set of religious conventions that discouraged creative experimentation, artists at the time still created magnificent mosaics, iconography, and church architecture. Early Byzantine churches were based on the Roman basilica layout, with long buildings featuring a semicircular apse at one end and windows lining a wooden ceiling. The floor and lower parts of the walls were usually covered in marble and the upper parts reserved for mosaics and frescoes.

Byzantine artists transformed almost any flat surface they found into glittering art by illuminating manuscripts, carving ivory panels, embossing bronze doors, and covering cloisonné enamels with jewels. **Byzantine iconography** aimed for religious authenticity; artists underwent years of spiritual and technical training before gaining permission to portray sacred subjects. Each figure stares out with a soul-searing gaze, and the determined frontal pose against a gold background in the church's dim light creates the illusion of the figure floating between the iconostasis (icon screen separating the altar from the people) and the viewer. In Byzantine **mosaics**, a unique shimmering effect adds to the brilliance, as contrasting gold and silver tesserae (the constituent small cubes of stone or ceramic covered in glass or metallic foil) reflect the light at sharp angles. Sparkling examples can be seen in churches in **Thessaloniki** (p. 276), at the **Monastery of Osios Loukas** (p. 211), on **Mount Athos** (p. 308), and at **Meteora** (p. 241).

MODERN ART (1829-PRESENT)

Nationalist sentiment after Greek independence led the government to subsidize local art. **King Otto** encouraged young artists to study their craft in Munich, and the Polytechneion, Greece's first modern art school, was established in 1838. The first wave of post-independence Greek painters showed strong German influence, while sculptors looked to Classical Greece for inspiration. Modern Greek painters have experimented with various European trends, including Impressionism, Expressionism, and Surrealism. Other painters rejected foreign influence, among them the much adored **Theophilos Chatzimichael** (1873-1934). The contemporary paintings of **Yiannis Psychopedis** (b. 1945) combine social and aesthetic criticism. Painter **Opy Zouni** (b. 1941) has won international renown for her geometric art.

LITERATURE

EARLY MASTERS

EPIC TALES

The Greek literary tradition began as rich oral poetry, long before written Greek appeared. The most famous tale-teller is **Homer**, who may or may not have composed the *Iliad* and the *Odyssey* in the 8th century BC. Details of the legendary poet's life range from sparse to nonexistent, and it remains unclear precisely who pulled folktales about the **Trojan War** and its aftermath into the two epics. Regardless of their author's true identity, the *Iliad's* mythic military struggle is a classic account of heroism's human costs, while the *Odyssey* has inspired many of the journeys, physical and otherwise, that have filled the ranks of Western literature.

SING IN ME, O MUSE

Homer's contemporary **Hesiod** chronicled the five Ages of Man in *Works and Days*, offering advice on farming, rural life, and other human experiences. In the *Theogony*, he gave an account of the creation of the world and the genealogy of the gods. **Archilochus of Paros** wrote biting satirical and erotic poetry; legend holds that an entire family hanged themselves after they were ridiculed in his verse.

On Lesvos in the 7th century BC, lyric poet **Sappho**, ancient Greece's only known female poet, earned herself the title of the 10th Muse. **Pindar** of Thebes (518-438 BC), acclaimed by the ancients as the greatest of poets, wrote odes commissioned by sports-nut nobles to commemorate athletic victories. **Callimachus** (305-240 BC), who lived in Alexandria, wrote elegies in Hellenistic Greek. His personal tone and wit greatly influenced Roman poetry. **Apollonius of Rhodes** also worked from Alexandria and invented the popular form of the mini-epic.

STORY BECOMES HISTORY

Herodotus (484-c. 425 BC) wrote up the epic battles and personalities of the Persian Wars—plus centuries' worth of melodramatic context and rumor—in his monumental (and rather sensationalist) *Histories*, earning him the title "Father of History." Herodotus's detailed account of the wars must have come from interviews with elderly men with sharp memories, as the battles in question took place during his childhood. Hardheaded **Thucydides** (c. 460-c. 400 BC) immortalized the Peloponnesian War, chronicling Athens's conflict with Sparta and examining the effects of war on nations and people. The genre of pseudo-historical romance took Greece by storm in the AD first century, generating personal love poems and erotic novels. **Plutarch,** writing around AD 100, constructed biographies of famous Greeks and Romans in *Parallel Lives*.

EMPERORS AND INTRIGUE: BYZANTINE LITERATURE

This era produced the most-read work of literature ever: the Greek-language New Testament of the **Bible.** After **Emperor Constantine** converted to Christianity in the AD 4th century (p. 58), most literature was written by monastery-bound theologians or court historians. In the 6th century, **Procopius,** one of **Emperor Justinian's** generals, reported on all aspects of his boss's reign. He wrote two conventional tracts for publication, Procopius's *History of His Own Time* and *On the Buildings*, and left behind a *Secret History*—an insider's account of the intrigues and debauchery common in the court of Justinian and his wife **Theodora. Photius** (820-893), twice appointed Patriarch of Constantinople, admired the "pagan" works of Homer and encouraged their study. This avid reader was a writer as well; his massive *Bibliotheca* chronicled Greek works in over 270 articles.

FACING THE PAST: MODERN LITERATURE

Greek independence in 1829 (p. 60) gave rise to the **Ionian School** of modern literature, which dealt with the political and personal issues of the Greek revolution. **Dionysios Solomos** (1798-1857), whose *Hymn to Liberty* became the Greek national anthem, is still referred to as the "national poet." **Constantine P. Cavafy** (1863-1933), whose famed poem "Ithaka" was read by John F. Kennedy Jr. at Jackie Onassis's funeral, played a key role in the revival and recognition of Greek poetry. Twentieth-century poets would infuse their own odes with **Modernism,** alternately denouncing and celebrating nationalism and politics. **George Seferis** (1900-1971), known for his symbolism- and mythology-imbued work, became the first Greek to win a Nobel Prize for Literature in 1963. In 1979 **Odysseas Elytis** (1911-1996), who looked at politics in a different light and incorporated French Surrealism into his work in an effort toward national redemption, was awarded the Nobel Prize for Literature as well. The many novels of **Nikos Kazantzakis** (1883-1957), perhaps the best known modern Greek author, include *Odyssey*, a modern sequel to the Homer's epic (1958), *Report to Greco* (1965), *Zorba the Greek* (1946), and *The Last Temptation of Christ* (1951); the last two were made into successful films. *Freedom or Death* (1956), his homage to Greek revolts against the Ottomans on his home island of Crete, analyzes the Greek-Turkish conflict and explores the concept of masculinity. More recently, social critic and author **Nikos**

Dimou has risen to fame as the acclaimed, but often controversial, Greek writer of *On the Misery of Being Greek* and numerous anthologies of poems.

SCIENCE AND PHILOSOPHY

The philosophical-scientific writings of the ancient Greeks awed even the practically minded Romans. According to Hellenic tradition, the first philosopher was the 6th-century BC thinker **Thales of Miletus,** who believed that the universe had an ordered structure and that everything moved toward a predetermined end. This teleology, or end-oriented world-view, contributed to every major Greek philosophy. **Pythagoras,** a math whiz and purported student of Thales, came up with theorems that still make regular appearances in high school math homework.

Early philosophical works, which survive on fragments of papyrus and in the reports of later writers, paved the road for **Socrates** (469-399 BC). Although Socrates refused to commit his words to untrustworthy paper, his legacy was preserved and carried on by his pupil **Plato** (428-348 BC). Socrates described himself as a gadfly, nipping at the ass of the horse that was Classical Athens. He brought philosophy down from the stars and into the agora, where he spent his days picking over the morals and beliefs of anyone who would stop for a chat. This style of asking questions is still called the **Socratic Method.** Socrates's radical lifestyle and constant questioning eventually angered influential Athenians, generally because he had proven them fools. In 399 BC, he was tried for impiety, introducing new gods, and corrupting the youth; he was sentenced to death by hemlock poisoning.

Plato became the new master philosopher of ancient Greece, primarily by writing up the sharp conversations that he and Socrates had had with other thinkers over bowls of wine. In *The Republic,* his most famous work, Plato muses about the components of an ideal state and the definition of a just individual. He believed that knowledge acquired through the senses is impure, and that only the soul can know the essence of things; the objects seen in life are only shadows of true Forms. Plato's pupil, **Aristotle** (384-322 BC), diverged from his mentor's teachings and took a more empirical approach to philosophy, placing value on knowledge gained from experience as well as from **abstract reason.** Aristotle's quest for knowledge reached into the realms of physics, biology, and mechanics. A few years later, **Euclid** wrote *The Elements,* the source of geometry even to the present. **Archimedes** created complex mathematical formulas with circles and cylinders, inventing the Archimedes screw, a device to move water, and conceiving of the principles of density and buoyancy during a particularly enlightening bath.

Greeks experimented in medicine as well. In the 5th century BC, before he became famous for his oath, **Hippocrates** suggested that disease might not be the result of divine punishment. A combination of speculation and observation yielded the idea of "four humors" flowing through the body (yellow bile, black bile, phlegm, and blood), which corresponded to personality traits and the four elements; an imbalance caused illness. Research in Alexandria, Egypt in the 3rd century BC pushed medical knowledge farther. Work on animal brains, hearts, and organs inspired **Galen of Pergamum** to try the art of human dissection, expanding knowledge about human anatomy.

Under Roman rule, Greek natural science wilted. The Romans were impressed by the body of knowledge the Greeks had acquired, but they were confused by the concept of "knowledge for knowledge's sake." During the Middle Ages, advancements in European medicine evaporated entirely. Fortunately, Greek scientists had written about their findings, which have thus survived throughout the ages.

LIFE AND TIMES

THE PERFORMING ARTS

THEATER

The precise origins of Greek theater are uncertain. Tragedy is sometimes said to have grown out of competitions in which the winner received a goat, thus earning the name *tragodoi* (goat songs). Comedy, on the other hand, probably developed out of songs and poetry written for the eternally appealing pastime of making fun of people. Greek drama played a major part in religious festivals in honor of **Dionysus,** where all attendants were performers in the chorus as well as audience members. Thespis, who was bold enough to step out of the chorus and deliver lines, is credited as the first actor (hence "thespian"). **Aeschylus** (525-456 BC) wrote the first dialogue between characters, and is best known for the *Oresteia,* his trilogy recounting an intergenerational revenge cycle. **Sophocles** (496-406 BC) followed with the cathartic **Oedipus** plays, which detail the ruinous tale of a man who becomes king of Thebes by unwittingly killing his father and marrying his mother. **Euripides** (485-406 BC), Sophocles's contemporary, added the biting observations of *Medea* and *The Bacchae* to the tradition. **Aristophanes** (450-385 BC) proved that puns and sexual innuendoes always get laughs. His smash-hit comedies poked fun at prominent citizens like Socrates or wartime policies: in the play *Lysistrata,* peace-loving Greek women withhold sex from their husbands until the end of the Peloponnesian War. **Menander** (342-291 BC), following in Aristophanes's footsteps, brought along **"New Comedy,"** which was loved and copied by the Romans.

Though the heyday of Greek theater ended with the fall of Classical Greece, theater in Crete flourished in the 15th and 16th centuries under Venetian control. A few contemporary playwrights, such as **Iakovos Kambanellis** (b. 1922), who incorporated his experiences in a WWII concentration camp into his socially conscious plays, have wooed audiences with portrayals of 20th-century Greek life. Classical Greek theater survives as an important influence, as most modern theater companies regularly remake the original masterpieces. The **Athens Festival,** held from May to October, features Classical drama at the ancient **Theater of Herod Atticus,** as well as concerts, opera, choruses, ballet, and modern dance. At the **Epidavros Theater Festival** (p. 149) every June to August, even a language barrier won't detract from the ominous chorus that, in Aeschylus's time, made "boys die of fright and women have miscarriages." Tickets for the festivals are available at the Athens Festival Box Office, 39 Panepistimiou St., inside the arcade. (☎21032 72 000. Open M-F 8:30am-4pm, Sa 9am-2:30pm.)

OPA!: MUSIC

Greek music reflects the Greek passion for life and tradition. Greeks have been making music since the Bronze Age, and early musical instruments from this period have been found on Crete. Although Greeks had no system of musical notation before the 5th century BC, they devised a theory of harmonics. It was necessary for early poets to remember musical formulas, since poems were sung or chanted. During the Classical Period, appreciation of music came to be considered an essential part of education, and the mark of a good musician became the ability to convey virtue through his music. An integral part of Greek drama, music also graced most other social gatherings and interactions. This tradition carried on through the ages in folk music, and in many areas today it is common to see a wide circle of locals and tourists, hands joined, dancing. The dance steps for the followers are comfortably repetitive, so don't hesitate to join in—enjoy yourself!

Though its earliest origins are disputed, a new musical style emerged from Turkey's western coast during the population exchange with Greece in the 1920s (p. 60) that unsettled established notions of poetic music. The Turkish influences merged with new types of music emanating from *tekedes* (hashish dens) and *amanedes* (Middle Eastern cafes). Gritty, urban *rembetika*, which may get its name from the Turkish word "rembet," meaning "outlaw," used traditional Greek instruments to sing about the stark side of modern life, focusing on drugs, prison, and alienation. *Rembetika* emerged as the cry of the lower class, as newly transplanted refugees living in urban shantytowns embraced its sorrowful expressiveness. Interest in traditional *rembetika* recently has resurfaced, and musicians strumming the ubiquitous *bouzouki* (a traditional Greek stringed instrument) can be found in restaurants, clubs, and cafes. Pop music in Greece combines traditional folk rhythms, Middle Eastern influences, and European club beats. Greece's hottest pop stars today, including **Anna Vissi, Sakis Rouvas,** and **Elena Paparizou,** mix traditional styles with contemporary sounds. Pop stars make the rounds at nightclubs where a dressed-to-the-nines audience lets loose. The trendiest venues' playlists are full of Europop and American hits from the 1970s and 80s.

HOLIDAYS AND FESTIVALS

Greece celebrates a host of religious and political holidays throughout the year. Major celebrations include the following:

DATE	NAME AND LOCATION	DESCRIPTION
January 1	Feast of St. Basil/New Year's Day	Commemorates the new year. Greeks traditionally cut a sweet bread (*vassilopita*) baked with a lucky coin inside.
January 6	Epiphany	Celebrates Jesus's baptism.
January 8	Gynecocracy, Thrace	Switches gender roles in Thracian villages; women sit in cafes and men do housework. Literally means "rule of women."
Late January or Early February	Carnival	Three weeks of feasting and dancing that precede Lenten fasting. Patras, Skyros, and Kephalonia host the best celebrations.
Early March	Clean Monday	Starts Lent (fasting period of about 40 days before Easter).
March 25	Greek Independence Day/ Feast of the Annunciation	Commemorates the 1821 struggle against the Ottoman Empire and celebrates Archangel Gabriel's visit to Mary.
Late April or early May	Easter	Celebrates Jesus's resurrection from the dead. The single holiest day in the Greek calendar is marked by countless traditions and all-day celebrations.
Late April or early May	St. George's Day	Honors the dragon-slaying knight with rowdy festivals.
May 1	Labor Day	Celebrates workers.
Early June	Ascension	Commemorates Jesus's ascension into heaven. Celebrated 40 days after Easter with different rituals in each region.
Mid June	Pentecost	The day of the Holy Spirit, celebrated 50 days after Easter.
August 15	Feast of the Assumption of the Virgin Mary	Honors Mary's ascent into heaven. Village and city celebrations abound.
September 8	The Virgin Mary's Birthday	Celebrates Mary's birthday; some villages finance a feast by auctioning off the honor of carrying the Virgin's icon.
October 26	Feast of St. Demetrius	Observed along with the opening of a new stock of wine. Celebrated enthusiastically in Thessaloniki.

LIFE AND TIMES

DATE	NAME AND LOCATION	DESCRIPTION
October 28	Ohi Day	Commemorates Metaxas's supposed response of "Όχι!" (OH-hee; "No!") to Mussolini's demand to occupy Greece in October of 1940
December 25	Christmas	Remembers Jesus's birth. Greeks celebrate both Christmas Eve and Christmas day, when children make the rounds singing *kalanda* (carols).

ADDITIONAL RESOURCES

BOOKS

Oxford History of Classical Art, by John Boardman. Oxford University Press. Details the history of Greek and Roman aesthetic innovation (2001).

Cambridge Illustrated History of Ancient Greece, by Paul Cartledge. Cambridge University Press (2002). A well-written, comprehensive look at all aspects of ancient Greece.

A Concise History of Greece, by Richard Clogg. Cambridge University Press (2002). An overview of modern Greek history from the 18th century through today.

▨ **Mythology,** by Edith Hamilton. Back Bay Books (1998). A standard introduction to Greek myths.

▨ **Colossus of Maroussi,** by Henry Miller. Minerva (1991). A zealous account of Miller's travels in Greece at the start of WWII.

Dinner with Persephone, by Patricia Storace. Granta Books (1998). Meditations on travel in Greece in the early 1990s with dry humor and gorgeous detail.

FILM

300, dir. Zack Snyder (2006). Based on Frank Miller's graphic novel, *300* chronicles the 480 BC Battle of Thermopylae against the Persians in this over-the-top Hollywood spectacle of guts and glory.

▨ **A Touch of Spice** or **Politiki Kouzina,** dir. Tassos Boulmetis (2003). The historical conflicts between the Greeks and Turks are illuminated by the story of Fanis, a Greek from Constantinople living in Athens who learns both culinary and life secrets from his grandfather.

Hercules, dirs. Ron Clements and John Musker (1997). Disney's version of the heroic demigod learns the importance of having a strong heart inside a strong body, through physical challenges, singing, and dancing.

Mediterraneo, dir. Gabriele Salvatores (1991). Eight soldiers find themselves stranded on an anonymous Greek island during WWII in this Italian comedy.

Z, dir. Costa-Gavras (1969). This thinly veiled depiction of a conspiracy to assassinate a liberal Greek politician won the Academy Award for Best Foreign Film.

Zorba The Greek, dir. Mihalis Kakogiannis (1964). An exuberant, sentimental film based on the novel by Nikos Kazantzakis. The most well-known movie about Greece.

the greek diaspora

The Greeks are everywhere: 1.5 million in America, over a half million in Germany, at least that many in the former USSR, and hundreds of thousands in Canada, South Africa, Asia, and Australia. All told, five million self-described Greeks live outside Greece, including a disproportionate number of the rich and famous: shipping mogul Aristotle Onassis (Turkey), film director Costa Gavras (France), and Spain's Queen Sophia come to mind, as do actress Jennifer Aniston, Pete Sampras (both California), and Nicholas Negroponte (UK), founder of the Media Lab at MIT.

But in leaving their home, Greeks always looked back—nostalgia, after all, is a Greek word. Rather than fade into their adopted cultures, they maintained *arriktoi desmoi*—unbreakable bonds—with their heritage. The very idea of modern Greece was imported by diaspora Greeks. Before the 1821 Revolution, most Ottoman subjects in the Greek peninsula were uneducated peasants. The Western-educated diaspora taught these Greeks about their history, explaining that they were the inheritors of ancient Greece.

The independence movement began in Paris and Vienna, where the first Greek newspapers were published in the 1700s. It was in Paris, too, where Adamantios Korais revived the Classical Greek language, *katharevousa*, which remained Greece's official tongue until the 1970s. In London, Alexandros Mavrokordatos financed the revolt against the Ottomans. In Odessa on the Black Sea in 1814, Greek merchants founded the society that became the revolution's nexus.

During the following decades, diaspora Greeks built the country's most prestigious schools, the National Library, the Archaeological Museum, and much of the infrastructure. And the diaspora elite's role in the Revolution was so profound that it sparked conflict with native Greeks—who, having suffered the Ottoman yoke, felt they had a greater claim to the new nation. But the historical vision of a Greece rooted in antiquity and Byzantium ulti-mately prevailed, expanding the notion of Greekness. Said one rousing orator in 1844 in the Greek parliament: "The Kingdom of Greece is not Greece. It constitutes only one part, the smallest and poorest. A Greek is not only a man who lives within the Kingdom, but also one who lives in Ioannina, Serrai, Adrianople, Constantinople, Smyrna, Trebizond, Crete and in any land associated with Greek history and the Greek race."

This notion of "cultural Greekness" was translated into the Great Idea, which guided Greek foreign policy for almost a century and sought to unite Greece with the capital of Byzantium, Constantinople (now Istanbul), and the Asia Minor coast. That dream ended in 1922, when Kemal Atatürk, the founder of Turkey, led an assault on Smyrna that killed tens of thousands of Greeks. The following year, the Treaty of Lausanne sent over one million Greeks from Asia Minor, their home for over 3000 years, to Greece, a homeland they had never known. A similar fate befell the 100,000 Greeks in Egypt, driven out by Nasser's 1952 revolution. The most recent flood of ethnic immigration came in the 1990s, when hundreds of thousands of Greeks liberated from communist rule in Albania and the former USSR made their way home.

Today's diaspora communities are largely the product of two great waves of economic emigration from Greece: the first at the turn of the 20th century, the second after World War II. The Greek-American community has grown vastly in size, influence, and economic might—they constitute the most prosperous ethnic group in the US. Similar success stories can be told of the communities in Australia, Canada, and in 70 other countries around the world.

"The very idea of modern Greece was imported by diaspora Greeks."

Gregory A. Maniatis is the founder of Odyssey Magazine, *the leading international magazine about Greece and Greeks around the world. He has also contributed to* New York Magazine, The Independent, The Washington Monthly, Time-Life Books, *and other publications.*

BEYOND TOURISM

A PHILOSOPHY FOR TRAVELERS

BEYOND TOURISM HIGHLIGHTS IN GREECE

STUDY classics, language, and theater at the Athens Centre (p. 83).

RESCUE endangered sea turtles on the beaches of Zakynthos (p. 77).

TEACH English to students of all ages in Crete (p. 79).

SCULPT like Phidias in the marble studio on Tinos (p. 83).

Let's Go believes that the connection between travelers and their destinations is an important one. We know that many travelers care passionately about the communities and environments they explore, but we also know that even conscientious tourists can inadvertently damage natural wonders and harm cultural environments. With this Beyond Tourism chapter, *Let's Go* hopes to promote a better understanding of Greece and enhance your experience there. You'll also find Beyond Tourism information throughout the book in the form of "Giving Back" features that highlight regional Beyond Tourism opportunities.

RESPONSIBLE TOURISM. In this chapter, you'll find many opportunities for those who want to do more than just travel. Responsible tourism in general, however, starts with a few simple guidelines. Be respectful of local religious and social customs. Staying aware of cultural expectations regarding dress and behavior is essential if you want to appreciate Greece's many sacred sites. Minimize environmental impact—Greece's natural beauty has lasted through thousands of years of civilizations, and we owe it to future generations not to litter or otherwise desecrate the land we visit. In general, try to be fair to the people you meet—don't be rude or inconsiderate, and don't take advantage of your hosts.

There are several options for those who seek to participate in Beyond Tourism activities in Greece. Opportunities for **volunteerism** abound, both with local and international organizations. As a volunteer in Greece, you can participate in projects from wildlife conservation to archaeological excavations, either on a short-term basis or as the main component of your trip. **Studying,** whether through direct enrollment in a local university or on an independent research project, can be an excellent way to visit and learn about Greece. Study programs often are coupled with travel opportunities and tours of the beautiful Greek countryside. **Working** is a good way to immerse yourself in the local culture and to finance your travels simultaneously. Many travelers structure their trips around the work that they can do along the way—either odd jobs as they go or full-time stints in cities where they stay for some time. Popular tourist destinations like Athens and many of the Cyclades and Ionian Islands are great places to look for jobs. It is important to note that you must get a work permit to work legally in Greece (p. 11).

VOLUNTEERING

Doing more than just sightseeing on a trip to Greece is easy. Though Greece is considered wealthy by international standards, there is no shortage of aid organizations that address the pertinent issues facing the country. From providing medical care to refugees to ensuring the survival of wildlife species for the future, Greece has plenty of opportunities to give back. Most people who volunteer in Greece do so on a short-term basis at organizations that make use of drop-in or summer volunteers. These are referenced both in this section and in the town and city listings. Short-term social services in Greece range from geriatric assistance, medical care, and work with refugees to wildlife and environmental conservation. The best way to find opportunities that match your interests and schedule may be to search online at websites like www.idealist.org and www.timebank.org.uk; most programs have contact information and many provide detailed descriptions and instructions on the Internet. Those looking for longer volunteer opportunities usually go through an organization that handles the logistical details and often provides a group environment and support system—for a fee. These costs can be hefty (although they frequently cover airfare and most living expenses).

WHY PAY MONEY TO VOLUNTEER? Many volunteers are surprised to learn that some organizations require large fees or "donations." While this may seem ridiculous at first, such fees usually keep the organization afloat, and often cover airfare, room, board, and administrative expenses for the volunteers. (Other organizations must rely on private donations and government subsidies.) If you're concerned about how a program spends its fees, request an annual report or finance account. A reputable organization won't refuse to inform you of how volunteer money is spent. Pay-to-volunteer programs might be a good idea for young travelers who are looking for more support and structure (such as pre-arranged transportation and housing) or anyone who would rather not deal with the uncertainty of creating a volunteer experience from scratch.

WILDLIFE CONSERVATION

SEA TURTLES

Archelon Sea Turtle Protection Society, 3h Marina Glyfadas, 166 75, Glyfada (☎210 89 82 600; www.archelon.gr). Non-profit group devoted to studying and protecting sea turtles on the beaches of Zakynthos, Crete, and the Peloponnese. Opportunities for seasonal field work and year-round work at the rehabilitation center. €150 participation fee for 6 weeks includes lodgings for those who work at the center. Field volunteers are put up at private campgrounds, but must provide their own camping equipment.

Earth, Sea, and Sky Ionian Nature Conservation, P.O. Box 1063, Saxilby, Lincoln LN1 2TN, UK (www.earthseasky.org). Promotes awareness of sustainable tourism and conservation. Although particularly concerned with sea turtles, they organize a variety of volunteer programs and preservation activities. Centered on Zakynthos.

The Katelios Group for the Research and Protection of Marine and Terrestrial Life, Kefalonia 280 86 (☎26710 81 009; www.kateliosgroup.org). Organizes volunteer efforts to protect hatchling sea turtles and promote sustainable development on Kefalonia. Volunteers pay €120 per month to participate in the summer, though the fee includes accommodations at their campsite.

The Mediterranean Association to Save the Sea Turtles (MEDASSET), Likavitou 1c, Athens 106 72 (☎21036 40 389; www.euroturtle.org/medasset). Assesses the condition of sea turtles throughout the Mediterranean, with sites at Zakynthos and Kephalonia. Volunteers can receive free lodging for at least 3 weeks of work at the Athens office.

OTHER FAUNA

Fiskardo's Nautical & Environmental Club (FNEC) and Ionian Sea Research Centre, Fiskardo, Kephalonia 280 84 (☎26740 41 081; www.fnec.gr). Conducts marine research, promotes environmental awareness, and engages volunteers in conservation efforts. Volunteers patrol the region on horseback to aid in forest fire protection, run an educational museum and radio station, participate in local community service projects, catalog marine mammals, and help with other environmental research.

Hellenic Ornithological Society, Vas. Irakleiou 24, Athens 106 82 (☎/fax 21082 27 937; www.ornithologiki.gr/en/enmain.htm) and Kastritsiou 8, Thessaloniki 54623 (☎/fax 23102 44 245). Organizes volunteer field work to protect endangered species of birds. Also seeks volunteers to help with office work and educational presentations.

Hellenic Society for the Study and Protection of the Monk Seal (MOm), 18 Solomou, Athens 106 82 (☎2105 22 2888; www.mom.gr). Runs a rehabilitation center on Alonnisos for the highly endangered Mediterranean monk seal. Also conducts information sessions for local fishermen and the general public about how to further conservation efforts. Volunteers should have a basic knowledge of Greek.

Lesbian Wildlife Hospital, O. Christofa I Chatzigianni, Agia Paraskevi, Lesvos 81102 (☎22530 32 006; www.wildlifeonlesvos.org). Provides medical aid for needy wildlife on the northeast Aegean island.

Rhodes Animal Welfare Society (RAWS), Tsairi, Rhodes 851 00 (☎/fax 22410 69 224; www.rhodesanimalwelfaresociety.gr). A non-profit organization that cares for stray animals and finds them new homes. Founded in 1990, RAWS has helped with nearly 5000 adoptions and has neutered 3000 animals.

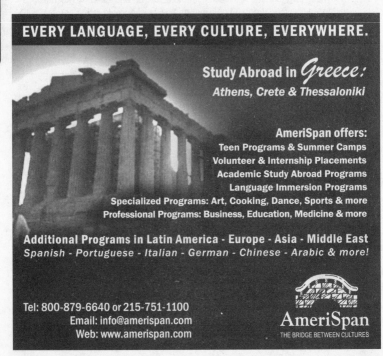

Tilos Park Association, Livadia, 850 02 (☎22460 70 892; www.tilos-park.org). Monitors seal, turtle, falcon, and orchid populations on Tilos and its 16 uninhabited islets. Volunteers can help with clean-up efforts on the beaches and paths, species monitoring, building a new nature appreciation trail, and island surveillance for illegal activities.

SOCIAL WELFARE

Global Volunteers, 375 E. Little Canada Rd., St. Paul, MN 551 17 (☎800-487-1074; www.globalvolunteers.org/1main/greece/volunteer_in_greece.htm). Sends volunteers to various locations in Crete to teach English to students or to provide care for and teach computer skills to physically and mentally handicapped individuals.

Medecins du Monde-Greece, Sapfous 12, Athens 105 53 (☎21032 13 150; www.mdmgreece.gr). A member of the international Medecins du Monde, the Greek branch brings together doctors, nurses, and non-medical personnel to provide medical care for refugees and victims of war, natural disasters, and other catastrophes in Greece and developing countries.

Multi-Functional Centre of Social Support and Integration of Refugees (www.redcross.gr). An initiative of the Hellenic Red Cross that provides social support to refugees and asylum seekers and helps integrate them into Greek society. The 1-week training program usually takes place in June.

OTHER OPPORTUNITIES

The American Farm School, Office of the Trustees and Greek Summer, 1133 Broadway, Ste. 1625, New York, NY 10010 (☎212-463-8434; www.afs.edu.gr) and P.O. Box 23, Thessaloniki 551 02 (☎23104 92 700). Runs community service projects in villages. The 6-week summer program for high school students in Thessaloniki is US$5500.

Conservation Volunteers Greece, Veranzerou 15, Athens 106 77 (☎21038 25 506; www.cvgpeep.gr). Volunteers ages 18-30 participate in 2- to 3-week community programs in various areas of Greece. Projects range from reforestation to preserving archaeological sites. Accommodations provided.

Service Civil International Voluntary Service (SCI-IVS), 5474 Walnut Level Rd., Crozet, VA 22932 (☎/fax 206-350-6585; www.sci-ivs.org). Arranges placement in a wide variety of volunteer work camps in Greece for those over 18. Registration fee US$195.

Volunteers for Peace, 1034 Tiffany Rd., Belmont, VT 05730 (☎802-259-2759; www.vfp.org). Arranges placement in work camps in many countries, including Greece. Membership (US$20) required for registration. Programs US$250 for 2-3 weeks.

Youth Action for Peace UK (YAP UK), P.O. Box 43670, London SE22 OXX, UK (☎08701 657 927; www.yap-uk.org). Offers opportunities such as volunteering at health institutions and renovating buildings in villages in Greece. Membership £25, students £10; work camp placement fee £110.

STUDYING

Study-abroad programs range from basic language and culture courses to college-level classes, often for credit. In order to choose a program that best fits your needs, research as much as you can before making your decision—determine costs and duration, as well as what kind of students participate in the program and what sort of accommodations are provided.

In programs that have large groups of students who speak the same language, you may feel more comfortable, but you will not have the same opportunity to

VISA INFORMATION. Passport-bearing citizens of Australia, Canada, the EU, New Zealand, Norway, Iceland, Switzerland, Japan, Israel, and the US are all allowed a 3-month stay in Greece without a visa, though they are not eligible for employment during that time. Apply for **visa extensions** at least 20 days prior to the 3-month expiration date. If you plan to study in Greece for longer than 3 months, a **student visa** is necessary. To get one, you must first obtain admission into an academic or language program in Greece. Then apply to your embassy for a student visa (US$20-45) for however long you want to study. Be sure to obtain a visa well before you leave.

practice a foreign language or to befriend other international students. Traditionally, Greek college students live in apartments as opposed to dorms, so you will be hard-pressed to experience dorm life studying abroad in Greece. A more likely scenario is that the study abroad program will place you in an apartment with other students in the program. If you live with a Greek family, there is a potential to build friendships with natives and to experience day-to-day life in more depth, but conditions can vary greatly from family to family and from region to region.

UNIVERSITIES

Most university-level study-abroad programs are conducted in Greek, although many programs offer classes in English and lower-level language courses. Those relatively fluent in Greek may find it cheaper to enroll directly in a university abroad, though getting college credit may be more difficult. You can search www.studyabroad.com for various semester-abroad programs that meet your criteria, including your desired location and focus of study. Most of the study programs based in Greece are located in highly traveled areas, especially in Athens, on Crete, and in the Cyclades. Programs vary tremendously in expense, academic quality, living conditions, and exposure to local culture and languages. The following is a sampling of organizations that can help place students in university programs abroad or that have their own branch in Greece.

AHA International, 221 NW 2nd Ave., Ste. 200, Portland, OR 97209 (☎800-654-2051; www.aha-intl.org). 12-week terms in the fall and spring or 4-week terms in the summer. Fees start at US$2920 for the summer term; US$7510 for the fall or spring terms.

American College of Thessaloniki (ACT), P.O. Box 21021, Pylea, Thessaloniki 555 10 (☎23103 98 238 or 23103 98 239; www.act.edu); study abroad admissions at Anatolia College Trustees Office, 130 Bowdoin, Ste. 1201-1202, Boston, MA 02108 (☎617 742 7992). ACT offers the opportunity to study in Greece in a predominately Greek student environment. Foreign students choose to enroll either for a term abroad or as an exchange student. Study abroad student fee starting at US$7950.

Arcadia University for Education Abroad, 450 S. Easton Rd., Glenside, PA 190 38 (☎866-927-2234; www.arcadia.edu/cea). Operates programs in Greece. Fall or spring term US$12,730; full year US$21,930.

The Athens Centre, Archimidous 48, Athens 116 36 (☎21070 12 268; www.athenscentre.gr). Offers language, classics, poetry, and theater classes. Many universities also are affiliated with the Athens Center. Semester courses €180-640; summer €1800-2200.

College Year in Athens, P.O. Box 390890, Cambridge, MA 02139 (US ☎617-868-8200, GRC 21075 60 749; www.cyathens.org). Runs semester-long, full-year, and summer programs that focus on ancient Greek civilization, East Mediterranean area studies, and modern Greek language for undergraduates. All courses taught in English. Summer programs include intensive modern Greek instruction on Paros and a 3-week archaeology program on Crete or Santorini. Fall or spring US$15950; full year US$28900; summer from US$2200.

Deree College, The American College of Greece, Gravias 6, Agia Paraskevi 153 42 (☎21060 09 800; www.acg.gr/deree). Bachelor's degrees granted in a wide variety of subjects. Classes taught in English. Open to students of all international backgrounds.

University of Indianapolis Athens Campus, Syntagma Square, Athens 105 57 (☎21032 37 077; www.uindy.gr). Offers fall and spring semesters at the University of Indianapolis's Athens branch. Provides students with residential hall housing in Plaka. Also organizes summer study programs.

Hellenic International Studies in the Arts (☎69460 87 430; www.hellenicinternational.org). Offers courses in painting and drawing, photography, writing, sculpture, and Cycladic culture, among other arts. Semester courses US$10850; summer US$2050.

Rutgers Study Abroad, 102 College Ave., New Brunswick, NJ 08901 (☎732-932-7787; studyabroad.rutgers.edu/program_greece.html). A 6-week program in Athens, the Peloponnese, Macedonia, and Crete focuses on material culture and history. NJ residents US$4200; non-NJ residents US$5200.

LANGUAGE SCHOOLS

Language schools can be independently run by international or local organizations or divisions of foreign universities. Though they rarely offer college credit, they can be a good alternative to university study if you desire either a deeper focus on the language or a slightly less rigorous courseload. These programs are also good for younger high school students who may not feel comfortable with older students in a university program.

Greek Language Institute, National Registration Center for Study Abroad, P.O. Box 1393, Milwaukee, WI 53201 (☎414 278 0631; www.nrcsa.com/country/greece.html). Branches in Athens, Thessaloniki, and Hania, Crete offer immersion-based classes. 2-week courses begin at US$1660; 4-week US$3205.

Kentro Ellinikou Politsmou (Hellenic Culture Center), Tilemahou 14, Athens 11472 (☎/fax 210 52 38 149; www.hcc.edu.gr) and Arethoussa, Ikaria 85302 (☎22750 61 140). Seminars in modern Greek language in Athens and on Ikaria. Courses from €440.

Lexis Centre of Greek Language and Culture, 48 Daskalogianni, Hania, Crete 73100 (☎2821 055673; www.lexis.edu.gr). 2- to 10-week courses, with extra activities and excursions available. Prices range €205-980.

Omilo, Tsaldari 13, Marousi 15122 (☎210 612 2896; www.omilo.com). Language courses for a range of proficiency levels offered in Athens, Nea Makri, Limni, and Nafplion. 1-week course €300; 2-week €550; 8-week €380-475.

School of Modern Greek Language at the Aristotle University of Thessaloniki, Thessaloniki 54124 (☎23109 97 576; www.auth.gr/smg). Year-long and seasonal intensive programs offered. Limited scholarships available; consult website. Courses from €300.

ART STUDY

Aegean Center for the Fine Arts, Paros 84400 (☎22840 23 287; www.aegeancenter.org). Offers a spring session in Paros and a fall session in both Paros and Tuscany, Italy. Singing, painting, drawing, photography, sculpture, print-making, literature, creative writing, and art history classes. Studio apartment housing in Greece; villa accommodations in Italy. University credit available. Financial aid available. Fall term €8800; spring term €7800.

Art Research Tours and International Studios, (☎800-232-6893; www.artistours.org/greece.html). A 24-day drawing program in Athens and the Peloponnese. US$3495, including airfare.

excavating in athens

Arriving in a new country alone, late at night, with no knowledge of the native language is a nerve-wracking experience. Things get even more complicated when the sites you're planning on

"A toothbrush is very useful when cleaning shards of pottery."

visiting haven't seen daylight in a couple thousand years. So needless to say, I was a little anxious when my plane landed in Athens. I had arrived just in time to get a few hours of sleep before starting a summer of volunteer work on an archaeological dig, and luckily the famous Greek hospitality helped me safely find my way to my apartment. For the next two months, I would be helping dig at the ancient Athenian Agora with the American School of Classical Studies.

At first, I was in awe. At 7am the morning after my arrival, we met at the site and got a tour of the ancient marketplace. I wondered how people could ever go on vacation to destinations that didn't have amazing artifacts like the Acropolis looming over them. Although I got accustomed to walking by the waterclock of the Roman Agora every day on my way to work and eating lunch under the shadow of the Hephaestion, the ruins never ceased to impress me.

Yet my digging summer wasn't all gawking at towering monuments. It became immediately apparent that the term "digging" would more accurately be described as "slowly scraping away." Excavating is far too delicate a process to just pull out a shovel and go—I never saw one the entire time I was there. We used the blunt end of miniature picks to steadily work away at the dirt, and our main instrument was a trowel, something I had once thought was only used for laying the mortar on bricks. I came to realize that a tiny speck of green in the dust can be incredibly exciting—it could be a coin,

you see—and that a toothbrush is very useful when cleaning shards of pottery.

There were disappointments, of course, like the time I watched as a potential tomb turned out to be maybe a latrine. The possibilities, however, were limitless. Working on a dig in which something fantastic could be discovered any second gave a constant adrenaline rush. One day, the entire site stopped work and watched as a large statue head was pulled out of the ground. Another time, I myself was lowered into the dark ground, sitting on a rope while two other workers cranked me down into a 2m deep well. It was there that I found a loom weight, one of my four personal discoveries of the summer (I also found three coins).

I had time on weekends to take short trips to other areas of Greece. I went to see the oracle of Delphi, the monasteries of Meteora, the sacred island of Delos, and Milos's volcanic sands. I also got to experience modern Athenian culture, sipping Nescafé, going to nightclubs where nobody was dancing, and visiting the city's museums.

A DIFFERENT PATH

"Working on a dig gave a constant adrenaline rush."

Living and working in Athens, I was able to see and do much more than the casual tourist. I touched and helped uncover ancient sites, and I got used to the cries of "*malaka*" by angry residents upset that archaeologists took down modern buildings. I became accustomed to the locals' perplexed looks when I walked through their ritzy neighborhoods covered in dirt. Now, at least, I can always introduce myself as an amateur archaeologist, as long as I don't get too specific—for all they know I spent my summer in Greece becoming a swashbuckling adventurer.

Leanna Boychenko majored in Classics at Harvard College. She was the Associate Editor of Let's Go: Greece 2005 *and the Editor of* Let's Go: New Zealand 2006.

Art School of the Aegean, P.O. Box 1375, Sarasota, FL 34230 (☎941-351-5597; www.greecetravel.com/schools/aegeanartschool). Offers 1- to 3-week summer programs in painting, ceramics, and writing on Samos. Must be 18+. US$950-2050.

Cycladic School, Folegandros 84011 (☎/fax 22860 41 472; cycladicschool.cndo.dk). 6- to 12-day classes on the history and culture of Greece, particularly of Folegandros. Features drawing and painting instruction.

Dellatolas Marble Sculpture Studio, Spitalia, Tinos 84200 (☎/fax 22830 23 664; www.tinosmarble.com). Offers artists' workshops in a functioning marble studio. Classes run May-Oct. 2-week course €980, each additional week €400.

Island Center for the Arts, Skopelos 37003 (☎24240 24 036; www.islandcenter.org). Runs painting and photography classes from Skopelos. 2-week courses from US$2835.

ARCHAEOLOGICAL DIGS

Students who find their way to Greece to study abroad often are those interested in classics and archaeology. The **Archaeologic Institute of America,** 656 Beacon St., Boston, MA 02215 (☎617 353 9361; www.archaeological.org), puts out the annual *Archaeological Fieldwork Opportunities Bulletin,* which lists sites in Greece and is available online at www.archaeological.org. Print editions of the bulletin cost US$20 and must be bought from the David Brown Book Co., P.O. Box 511, Oakville, CT 06779 (☎800 791 9354; www.oxbowbooks.com). The **Hellenic Ministry of Culture** (www.culture.gr) maintains a complete list of archaeological sites in Greece. Below is a list of organizations that can help you find an archaeological dig with participation opportunities.

The American School of Classical Studies at Athens, Souidias 54, Athens 10676 (US ☎609-683-0800, 21072 36 313; www.ascsa.edu.gr). Since 1881, American graduate students and professors have flocked here to participate in ongoing excavations of ancient sites, including Corinth and the ancient Athenian agora. A 6-week summer program (US$2950) allows undergraduates to work at its sites and others. Visit the website to find a list of publications and links to other archaeological programs.

Archaeology Abroad, 31-34 Gordon Sq., London WC1H OPY, UK (☎20 85 37 08 49; www.britarch.ac.uk/archabroad). A magazine about archaeology that contains biannual bulletins with fieldwork opportunities. Subscriptions £20-24.

British School in Athens, O. Souidias 52, Athens 10676 (GRC ☎21072 10 974 or 21072 92 146; UK 20 7862 8732; www.bsa.gla.ac.uk). Conducts fieldwork annually. Courses for undergraduates, postgraduates, and teachers also available. Recent work has been conducted at Athens, Delphi, and Pylos.

Canadian Institute in Greece, Dion. Aiginitou 7, Athens 11528 (☎21072 232 01; www.cig-icg.gr). Focuses on archaeological fieldwork and research at various sites throughout Greece.

German Archaeological Institute, Fidiou 1, Athens 10678 (☎21033 07 400; www.dainst.org). This research center offers an extensive archaeological library, publishes an annual journal, hosts lectures and forums, and assists in excavations.

OTHER INSTRUCTION

Athens Institute of Sailing, Alimos Marina, Athens (www.sailingcoursesingreece.com). Runs basic and intermediate sailing and yachting classes out of an Athens marina. Taught in English. Classes from €370.

Dora Stratou Dance, Scholiou 8, Plaka, Athens 10558 (☎21032 44 395; www.grdance.org). Offers folk dance and culture classes. 1-week workshop €120.

The Glorious Greek Kitchen, (☎21437 31 161; www.cuisineinternational.com; www.dianekochilas.com/glorious_1.asp). Cooking classes are held on Ikaria where instructor Diane Kochilas used to own a restaurant. 6-day class and housing US$1850.

Ionian Village, 83 St. Basil Rd., Garrison, NY 10524 (☎646-519-6190; www.ionianvillage.org). The Greek Orthodox Archdiocese of America runs this religious and cultural summer camp for teens and young adults up to the age of 30, most of whom are Greek Orthodox or of Greek descent. Programs are based at a resort-like facility west of Patras. Full registration including travel US$3950.

Skyros, 92 Prince of Wales Rd., London NW5 3NE, UK (☎20 72 67 44 24; www.skyros.com). Has 1- to 2-week sessions in the Sporades on various topics ranging from writing to yoga. Courses from £495.

Tasting Places, Unit 108, Buspace Studios, Conlan St., London W10 5AP, UK (☎20 74 60 00 77; www.tastingplaces.com). Offers a cooking class on Santorini with trips and tastings. 1-week course £1590.

WORKING

Some travelers want long-term jobs that allow them to get to know another part of the world as a member of the community, while others seek out short-term jobs to finance the next leg of their travels. Those who can teach English will find many job openings in Greece. Students can check with their university's foreign language departments, which may have connections to jobs abroad. Friends in Greece can expedite work permits or arrange work-for-accommodations deals.

 VISA INFORMATION. For legal employment in Greece, foreigners must apply for a **work permit** from the Ministry of Labor, Pireos 40, Athens 10182. Permits can be difficult to acquire, so apply well in advance. EU residents can work in Greece for up to 3 months without a work permit, but one is required for longer stays.

Many popular youth hostels have bulletin boards with both long- and short-term employment opportunities. City News (http://athens.citynews.com/Employment.html) lists updated opportunities for work in Athens. Websites www.jobs-in-europe.net and www.jobsabroad.com also can be helpful. EU citizens will have a much easier time finding work and will generally make better money than those from outside the EU.

LONG-TERM WORK

If you're planning on spending more than three months working in Greece, search for a job well in advance. Be aware that work permits can be hard to come by, and make sure that you will be employed by a company that will assist you in getting one. **International placement agencies** are often the easiest way to find employment abroad, especially for teaching English. **Internships,** usually for college students, are a good way to segue into working abroad. Though they are often unpaid or poorly paid, many say the experience is well worth it. Be wary of advertisements for companies who ask for fees to get you a job abroad—often the same listings are available for free online or in newspapers. One reputable organization is **AIESEC International,** which coordinates business jobs that aim to promote "peace and fulfillment of humankind's potential" in over 80 countries, including Greece. (☎21036 28 236; www.aiesec.org.) Another interesting opportunity is **Trekking Hellas,** Filellinon 7, Athens 10557, which hires experienced travelers to guide others on various expeditions throughout Greece, including mountain treks and sea kayaking. Applicants, who are generally between 22 and 35 and are fluent in more than one language, must go through extensive training to demonstrate their abilities in the outdoors. (☎21033 10 323; www.trekking.gr.)

TEACHING ENGLISH

Teaching jobs abroad are rarely well-paid, although some elite American schools offer competitive salaries. Volunteering as a teacher in lieu of getting paid is a popular option; volunteer teachers often receive a daily stipend to help with living expenses. In almost all cases, you must have at least a bachelor's degree to be a full-time teacher, although college undergraduates often can get summer positions teaching or tutoring. Those who wish to teach English in Greece should have a university degree (preferably in English literature or history) and a solid command of English. To obtain a teaching license in Greece, you must present your diploma and your passport translated into Greek, among other things; for current requirements contact the **Hellenic Ministry of Education,** Mitropoleos 15, Athens 10185. (www.ypepth.gr.) Greek schools rarely require teachers to have a **Teaching English as a Foreign Language (TEFL)** certificate, but certified teachers often find higher-paying jobs. Placement agencies or university fellowship programs are the best resources for finding teaching jobs in Greece. The alternative is to make contacts directly with schools or just to try your luck once you get there. If you are going with the latter, the best time to look is several weeks before the start of the school year in September. The following organizations are helpful in placing teachers in Greece.

GoAbroad.com, 8 E. First Ave., Ste. 102, Denver, CO 80203 (☎720-570-1702; www.goabroad.com or www.teachabroad.com). Its "Teach Abroad" section has useful listings for various teaching opportunities in a number of countries, including Greece.

International Schools Services (ISS), 15 Roszel Rd., P.O. Box 5910, Princeton, NJ 08543 (☎609 452 0990; www.iss.edu). Hires teachers for over 200 schools; applicants must have experience teaching or with international affairs. 2-year commitment expected.

Office of Overseas Schools, US Department of State, Room H328, SA-1, Washington, D.C. 20522 (☎202-261-8200; www.state.gov/m/a/os). Keeps a comprehensive list of both schools abroad and agencies that arrange for Americans to teach abroad.

AU PAIR WORK

Au pairs are typically women in their late teens or twenties who work as live-in nannies, caring for children and doing light housework in foreign countries in exchange for room, board, and a small spending allowance or stipend. One perk of the job is that it allows you to really get to know the country without the high expenses of traveling. Drawbacks, however, often include mediocre pay and long hours. Au pairs in Greece generally work 30-45 hr. per week, including a few evenings, for €45-70 per week, depending on the number of children, duties, and qualifications. Much of the au pair experience depends on the family with whom you're placed. The agencies below are a good starting point for looking for employment as an au pair.

Great Au Pair, 1329 Hwy. 395 North, Ste. 10-333, Gardnerville, NV 89410 (☎775 215 5770; www.greataupair.com). Places au pairs in over 140 countries, including Greece. 30-day membership US$60.

Lucy Locketts & Vanessa Bancroft Nanny and Domestic Agency, 400 Beacon Rd., Wibsey, Bradford, West Yorkshire BD6 3DJ, UK (☎/fax 12 74 40 28 22; www.lucylocketts.com). Places au pairs and experienced nannies in Greece.

Nine Muses, El. Venizelou 4B, P.O. Box 76080, Nea Smirni, Athens 17110 (www.ninemuses.gr). An agency with online applications that places au pairs who are EU nationals with families in Greece.

BEYOND TOURISM

SHORT-TERM WORK

Since traveling can get expensive, many travelers try their hand at odd jobs for a few weeks at a time to help finance another month or two of touring around. For citizens of Greece and of EU countries, getting a job in Greece is relatively simple. For all others, finding work in Greece can be difficult, as job opportunities are scarce, and the government tries to restrict employment to citizens and visitors from the EU. If your parents were born in an EU country, you may be able to claim dual citizenship or at least the right to a work permit. Arrive in the spring and early summer to search for **hotel jobs** (bartending, cleaning, etc.). Most nightspots don't require much paperwork, but offer meager pay. Check the bulletin boards of hostels and the classified ads of local newspapers, such as the *Athens News*.

Another popular option is to work at a hostel in exchange for free or discounted room and/or board. Most often, these short-term jobs are found by word of mouth, or simply by talking to the owner of a hostel or restaurant. Due to the high turn-over in the tourism industry, many places are eager for even temporary help.

Milos Beach Bar and Cafe, Skala, Kephalonia (May-Oct. ☎26710 83 188; Nov.-Apr. 83 231). Hires waitstaff, bartenders, and chefs for summer. Payment depends on qualifications and experience. Call in advance and ask for Joya Grouzi.

The Pink Palace, Agios Gordios, Corfu 490 84 (☎26610 53 103; www.thepinkpalace.com). Hires hotel staff, nightclub staff, and DJs. Send a letter of introduction, a resume, and a photo to Dr. George (georgegrammenos@yahoo.gr). Min. 2-month commitment required (p. 542).

FURTHER READING ON BEYOND TOURISM

Alternatives to the Peace Corps: A Directory of Global Volunteer Opportunities. Jennifer S. Willsea. Food First Books, 2003 (US$11).

Back Door Guide to Short-Term Job Adventures: Internships, Extraordinary Experiences, Seasonal Jobs, Volunteering, Working Abroad, by Michael Landes. Ten Speed Press, 2002 (US$21).

Green Volunteers: The World Guide to Voluntary Work in Nature. Fabio Ausenda. Universe, 2005 (US$15).

How to Get a Job in Europe. Robert Sanborn and Cheryl Matherly. Planning Communications, 2003 (US$23).

How to Live Your Dream of Volunteering Overseas, by Joseph Collins, Stefano DeZerega, and Zahara Heckscher. Penguin Books, 2002 (US$20).

International Directory of Voluntary Work, by Victoria Pybus. Peterson's Guides and Vacation Work, 2007 (US$20).

International Job Finder: Where the Jobs Are Worldwide, by Daniel Lauber and Kraig Rice. Planning Communications, 2002 (US$20).

Invest Yourself: The Catalogue of Volunteer Opportunities, published by the Commission on Voluntary Service and Action, 1997 (US$8).

Live and Work Abroad: A Guide for Modern Nomads, by Huw Francis and Michelyne Callan. Vacation-Work Publications, 2001 (US$16).

Summer Jobs Abroad 2007. Victoria Pybus and David Woodworth. Vacation Work Publications, 2004 (US$20).

Volunteer Vacations: Short-term Adventures That Will Benefit You and Others, by Doug Cutchins, Anne Geissinger, and Bill McMillon. Chicago Review Press, 2003 (US$18).

Work Abroad: The Complete Guide to Finding a Job Overseas, by Clayton A. Hubbs. Transitions Abroad Publishing, 2002 (US$16).

Work Your Way Around the World, by Susan Griffith. Vacation Work Publications, 2005 (US$22).

ATHENS Αθήνα AND ENVIRONS

During the construction of the Athenian metro 12 years ago, several unexpected obstacles obliged workers to pause abruptly. As they plunged their shovels into undisturbed earth, they stumbled upon dozens of ancient relics requiring immediate excavation. Today, these bits of sculpture and pottery rest behind a glass display case in the Pl. Syndagma station, which, like its sister stops, sparkles with efficiency. More than other ancient cities in Greece, Athens is tied to its illustrious past. Thousands of years' worth of ghosts gaze down from every hilltop and peek around each alleyway. Athens, however, is also a daring and modern place; its fiercely patriotic citizens pushed their capital into the 21st century with massive clean-up efforts and building projects before the 2004 Olympic Games. Contemporary art galleries flourish in the literal shadow of their older counterparts. Scores of outdoor theaters with views of the Acropolis play domestic and foreign films. Creatively international menus, hipster bars, and large warehouses converted into performance spaces crowd the streets among Byzantine churches, traditional tavernas, and toppled columns. Whether making your home here or passing through on your way to the islands, don't miss the chance to explore a city that, against all odds, is more energetic and exciting than ever.

 SUGGESTED ITINERARIES: ATHENS AND ENVIRONS

THREE DAYS Thank Athens's ancient builders for putting everything so close together, as you can check out the **Parthenon** (p. 110) and the surrounding sites of the **Acropolis** (p. 108) and **Agora** (p. 111) in one afternoon. Spend the rest of your time finding your way through Athens's **Byzantine churches** (p. 114) and varied **museums** (p. 116). Reserve one night for the hip restaurants and bars of **Exarhia** (p. 105) and **Plaka** (p. 107).

ONE WEEK First, find your bearings at **Mount Lycavittos** (p. 115), whose stunning 360° view will give you an idea of how far Athens sprawls. Tackle the classics around the **Acropolis** (p. 108) first, then make your way through the nearby neighborhoods. After getting your fill of the city, enjoy the beachside pleasures of **Glyfada** (p. 121) and its many nightclubs, then sprint over for an afternoon at **Marathon** (p. 122).

HISTORY

If you reach back far enough, Athens's history blurs into myth. In the first of what would be many epic struggles over this capital, **Poseidon** and **Athena** were said to have fought for the right to be the city's patron god. Poseidon struck the Acropolis with his trident and water gushed forth, but it was Athena's gift, an olive tree, that won the city's admiration and worship. Moving forward to the age of mortals, ancient Athenians believed that their *polis* had been united under the sword of **Theseus,** the Minotaur-slayer, as early as the 16th century BC. Capturing both the artistic and the political world by the 8th century BC, Athens's initial fame for Geo-

Athens

ACCOMMODATIONS

...ens International Hostel,	1	A2
...stel Aphrodite,	2	A1
...tel Dryades,	3	C2
...tel Orion,	4	C2
...e Exarcheion,	5	C2
...ngration Athens Youth Hostel	6	F6

FOOD

...:alos,	7	A4
...an,	8	C2
...okou Cook	9	C2
...epeXaria,	10	C2
...rlicious	11	D4
...tiatorio,	12	B3
...althy Food Vegetarian,	13	B3
...au'	14	B1
...llimarmaron,	15	D6
Barba Giannis	16	C2
...k Indian Restaurant	17	A3

Pasta Cafe,	18	C2
Posto Cafe,	19	D6
Savvas,	20	C2
Souvlaki Kavouras,	21	C2

NIGHTLIFE

Briki,	22	F2
Cafe 48,	23	E4
The Daily,	24	E3
Flower,	25	F2
Rock Underground,	26	C2
Train	27	C2
Wunderbar,	28	C2

MUSEUMS

Acropolis Museum,	29	B5
Agora Museum,	30	A5
Benaki Museum,	31	D4
Byzantine Museum,	32	D4
Frissiras Musuem,	33	C5

Goulandris Museum,	34	D4
Islamic Museum,	35	A4
Jewish Museum,	36	C5
Lalaounis Jewelry Museum,	37	B6
National Archaeolgical Museum,	38	C1
National Gallery,	39	E4
Popular Musical Instruments Museum,	40	B5
War Museum,	41	E4

SIGHTS

Acropolis,	42	B6
Hephaesteiou,	43	A6
Panathenaic Stadium,	44	D6
Parliament Building,	45	C5
Philopappos Monument,	46	A5
Socrates's Prison,	47	A6
Temple of Zeus,	48	C6

metric pottery foreshadowed a bright future. Two hundred years later, law-giver **Solon** ended the servitude of native citizens and established democratic law. Thus began Athens's long, often-tortured relationship with popular government.

Victory over Persia in the 5th century BC brought a **Golden Age** of democracy and art to the new Athenian empire. Philosophers like **Socrates, Plato,** and **Aristotle,** joined by playwrights like **Aeschylus, Aristophanes, Euripides,** and **Sophocles** gave Athens its legendary status as the birthplace of Western thought. Athens, however, didn't remain the center of the world for long. Militaristic Sparta crushed it in the bloody, drawn-out **Peloponnesian War** (431-404 BC), and power shifted northward when **Philip II** and **Alexander the Great** of Macedonia conquered Athens and the rest of the known world. By the AD 2nd century, the **Roman Empire** ruled the city, and in AD 324 **Constantine** simply ignored it, establishing his grand imperial capital in Constantinople. **Justinian** delivered a further blow to Athens in AD 529, banning the teaching of Classical philosophy and allowing the once-great city to fall into ruin.

Five hundred years later, Byzantine emperor **Basil II** ordered Athens's glory restored; in the coming centuries, it passed (along with much of Greece) through the hands of the **Franks,** the **Catalans,** and **Venetian** merchants. In 1456, the **Ottoman Turks** began their 400-year regime, leaving Athens a backwater. The success of the Greek independence effort in 1829 ushered in a new era of extensive restoration and passionate nationalism. Today, Athens's plateias, wide boulevards, and National Gardens follow the plan of architects hired by modern Greece's first king, the unpopular German prince **Otto**.

The 1923 **Treaty of Lausanne** and **population exchange** (p. 57) with Turkey brought Athens an influx of ethnic Greeks who had been living in Asia Minor. Rural workers then flocked to Athens, further swelling its ranks. In the past 100 years, the city's population has exploded from a paltry 169 families to almost half of Greece's 11 million residents. Preparations for the 2004 Olympic Games fueled another age of urban renewal in Athens; the transit authority fought the sinister *nefos* (smog) by banning cars from historic Plaka and by further restricting drivers' access to downtown areas. With its magnificent new public transportation system, Athens no longer suffers from the confounding urban sprawl produced by years of turnover. The new Eleftherios Venizelos Airport, which lies to the city's southeast, has been consistently rated among the world's best airports since its 2001 opening.

◼ INTERCITY TRANSPORTATION

Flights: Eleftherios Venizelos (☎21035 30 000; www.aia.gr). Greece's international airport has 1 massive but navigable terminal. Arrivals are on the ground fl., departures on the 2nd. The **Suburban Rail** runs along the new Attiki Odos highway and serves the airport from the city center (30min.). Since it is connected with Neratziotissa on green line 1 and Doukissis Plakentias on blue line 3, the most central stations are, respectively, Omonia and Syndagma. 4 **bus** lines run to and from the airport from Athens, Piraeus, and Rafina. To get from **Plateia Syndagma** in the city center to the airport, take the E95 (40-90min. depending on traffic, every 20min., €3), which runs 24hr. Pick it up on Amalias, near the top right corner of Pl. Syndagma. From the **Ethniki Amyna** metro station, take the E94 (every 10min. 7:30am-11:30pm, €3; wait by the exit) or the E95. From **Piraeus,** take the E96 (every 20-40min., €3), which runs 24hr. Catch the bus in Pl. Karaiskaki on the waterfront, on Akti Tzelepi, across from Philippis Tours. From **Rafina,** the bus (€3) leaves every 30min. from the stop midway up the ramp from the waterfront. Buses drop off at 1 of the 4 departure entrances and wait outside the 5 arrival exits. **Taxis** from the airport to Pl. Syndagma run €18-25, including the extra €0.29 charge for each piece of luggage over 10kg and a €3 surcharge from the airport. Watch drivers carefully; they often rig the meters.

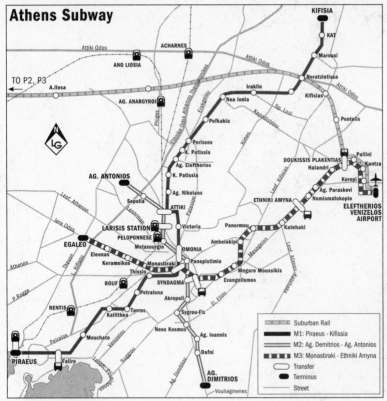

Athens Subway

KIFISIA

KAT

Marousi

Attiki Odos

ACHARNES

ANO LIOSIA

Neratziotissa

TO P2, P3

A.Ilosa

Iraklio

Kifisias

AG. ANARGYROI

Nea Ionia

Pentelis

Pefkakia

Pallini

Perissos

Kantza

A. Patissia

DOUKISSIS PLAKENTIAS

Ag. Eleftherios

Halandri

AG. ANTONIOS

Koropi

K. Patissia

Ag. Nikolaos

Ag. Paraskevi

Sepolia

ETHNIKI AMYNA

Nomismatokopio

ATTIKI

ELEFTHERIOS
VENIZELOS
AIRPORT

LARISIS STATION

Victoria

Panormou

Katehaki

PELOPONNESE

EGALEO

Metaxourgio

Ambelokipi

Eleonas

OMONIA

Kerameikos

Monastiraki

Panepistimio

Thissio

Megaro Moussikis

ROUF

SYNDAGMA

Evangelismos

Petralona

Akropoli

RENTIS

Tavros

Sygrou-Fix

Kallithea

Neos Kosmos

Ag. Ioannis

Moschato

Dafni

PIRAEUS

Faliro

AG.
DIMITRIOS

Vouliagmenes

Suburban Rail
M1: Piraeus - Kifissia
M2: Ag. Demitrios - Ag. Antonios
M3: Monastiraki - Ethniki Amyna
Transfer
Terminus
Street

Trains: Hellenic Railways (OSE), Sina 6 (☎21036 24 402, reservations 21052 97 777, timetables in Greek 1440; www.ose.gr). Contact the railway offices to confirm schedules before your trip.

Larisis Station: ☎21052 98 829. Ticket office open daily 5am-midnight. Trains go to Northern Greece. Take trolley #1 from El. Venizelou (Panepistimiou) in Pl. Syndagma (every 10min. 5am-midnight, €0.45) or take the metro to Sepolia. Trains depart for **Thessaloniki** (regular: 7hr., 5 per day, €14; express: 5½hr., 6 per day, €28). To get to **Bratislava, Bucharest, Budapest, Istanbul, Prague, Sofia,** and other international destinations, take a train from Larisis Station to Thessaloniki and change there.

Peloponnese Train Station: ☎21052 98 735 for buses to Albania, Bulgaria, and Turkey. Ticket office open daily 5:45am-9pm. From Diligani, easiest entry is through Larisis Station; exit to your right and go over the footbridge. From El. Venizelou (Panepistimiou) in Syndagma, take blue bus #057 (every 15min. 5am-11:30pm, €0.45). Serves **Kalamata** (6½hr., 3 per day, €7), **Nafplion** (3½hr., 2 per day, €5), and **Patras** (regular: 4¼hr., 3 per day, €5.30; express: 3½hr., 5 per day, €10). **Luggage storage** available (€2-3 per piece per day).

Buses: Athens has 4 bus terminals.

Terminal A: Kifissou 100 (☎21051 24 910 or 21051 32 601). Take blue bus #051 (every 15min. 5am-11:30pm, €0.45) from the corner of Zinonos and Menandrou near Pl. Omonia. Don't mistake the private travel agency at Terminal A for an information booth. Buses depart for: **Corfu** (10hr., 4 per day 7am-8:30pm, €30); **Corinth** (1½hr., every 30min. 5:45am-10pm, €7); **Igoumenitsa** (8hr., 5 per day 6:30am-9pm, €30); **Patras** (regular: 3hr., every 30min. 6am-10pm,

ATHENS

ATHENS

University

Ⓜ PANEPISTIMIOU

Koral

Sina

Akadimias

Omirou

Skoufa

Lykavitou

Anagnostopouliou

Hellenic
Railways
(OSE) ■

El. Venizelou (Panepistimiou)

Vissarionos

Dimokritou

Voukourestiou

Edouard Lo

Al. Soutsou

Pindarou

Milioni

Solonos

Skoufa

Athens
Festival
Office ■

Omirou

Amerikis

Valaoritou

Kanari

Solonos

Seferi

**FIL. ETERIAS
SQ.**

**National
Historical
Museum**

Voukourestiou

Kriezotou

Zalokosta

Akadimias

Merlin

Seferi

TO KOLONAKI
(50m)

PL.
KOLOKOTRONI

Stadiou

Smats

**Benaki
Museum**

Voulis

SYNDAGMA

Koumbari

Karageorgi Servias

Georgiou A

Ⓜ SYNDAGMA

Vasilisis Sophias

Irodou Attikou

Vasilis
Georgiou

Lekka

Niomas

Skopa

PL.
SYNDAGMA

**Parliament
Building**

Ⓜ SYNDAGMA

**Tomb of the
Unknown Soldier** ■

Mitropoleos

Othonos

Ⓜ SYNDAGMA

**Presidential
Residence**

Pendelis

**Olympic
Airways**

**Buses to El
Venizelou Airport**

Laundromat

mat

Voulis

Skoufou

Nikis

Filellinon

Amalias

Xenofontos

Entrance ■

Ipiti

**STA
Travel**

**Hellenic Railways
(OSE)** ■

Nikis

Lamahou

Souri

**National
Gardens**

Iperidou

Kodrou

Kydatheneon

**Jewish
Museum** 🏛

**Ag.
Triada**

Simonidi

ⓘ

Sotiros

**Folk Art
Museum**

Tsatsou K.

Nikis

**St. Paul's
Anglican Church**

**Zappeion Congress
and Exhibition Halls**

**Children's
Museum**

Pittakou

Monis Asteriou

Frissiras Museum

Dedalou

Amalias

**Outdoor
Cinema**

Laundromat

A. Geron

Dedalou

Tsangari

Peirandrou

■ **Fountain**

Thalou

Goura

Pittakou

Peirandrou

Vas. Olgas

Entrance to
**Temple of
Olympian Zeus**

**Hadrian's
Arch**

**Temple of
Olympian Zeus**

N

0   150 yards

0   150 meters

TO
PANATHENAIC
STADIUM
(15m)

PL.
STADIOU

Arditos
Hill

Central Athens

🏠 **ACCOMMODATIONS**

Acropolis House,	1	D4
Athens Backpackers	2	C6
Hotel Cecil,	3	B1
Hotel Kimon,	4	C4
Hotel Metropolis,	5	C3
Pella Inn,	6	C5
Phaedra Hotel,	7	A3
Student's &		
Traveler's Inn,	8	D5

🍴 **FOOD**

Amaltheia,	9	C5
Antonios Souvlaki,	10	C4
Artokopos,	11	D4
Attalos Restaurant,	12	B4
Cafe Voulis	13	D2
Chroma,	14	D3
Eat at Milton's,	15	C4
Furin Kazan,	16	D3
Gelatomania,	17	A2
Jackson Hall,	18	F2
Mandras,	19	A2
Matsoukas,	20	D3
Nikis Cafe,	21	D3
Noodle Bar,	22	D4
Pak Indian,	23	A1
Platanos,	24	B4
Savvas,	25	B3
T. Stamatopoulos,	26	C4

🍸 **NIGHTLIFE**

Bee,	27	A3
Bretto's,	28	C5
Revekka,	29	A2
Soul,	30	A1

€16; express: 2½hr., 20 per day 6am-7pm); **Thessaloniki** (6hr., 11 per day 7am-11:45pm, €32) via **Larisa; Zakynthos** (6hr.; 4 per day 6am-7pm; €25, includes ferry).

Terminal B: Liossion 260 (☎21083 17 153). Take blue bus #024 from Amalias near Pl. Syndagma outside the National Gardens or Panepistimiou (45min., every 20min. 5am-midnight, €0.45). Buses go to **Delphi** (3hr., 6 per day 7:30am-8pm, €13), **Halkida, Evia** (1¼hr.; every 30min. 5:30am-9pm, 9:45, 10:30pm; €7), and **Katerini** (5hr., 3 per day 9:45am-10pm, €27).

Mavromateon 29: ☎21082 10 872. In Exarhia. Walk up Patission from the National Archaeological Museum and turn right on Enianos; it's on the corner of Areos Park. Take trolley #2, 5, 9, 11 or 18. Buses to: **Agia Marina** (2½hr., M-Sa 5 per day 6am-4:30pm, €5) from which ferries depart for **Evia; Lavrio** (1¾hr., every 30min. 5:45am-9:30pm, €25); **Marathon** (2hr., every hr. 5:30am-10:30pm, €3.50); **Nea Makri** (1¼hr., every hr. 5:30am-10:30pm, €3.50); **Rafina** (1hr., every 30min. 5:40am-10:30pm, €3); **Sounion** (2hr., every hr. 6:30am-5:30pm, €5.60). Tickets are sold at 2 stands 50m apart.

Plateia Eleftherias: From Pl. Syndagma, go west on Ermou, turn right on Athinas, turn left on Evripidou, and walk to the end of the street. Buses A16 or B16 go to **Daphni monastery** and **Eleusis** (10-20min., 5am-11pm, €0.80).

Ferries: Check schedules at the tourist office, in the *Athens News,* with the Port Authority of Piraeus (☎21042 26 000), over the phone (☎1440), or at any travel agency. Most ferries dock at Piraeus, others at nearby Rafina. Those headed for the Sporades leave from Agios Konstantinos or Volos, and those going to the Ionian Islands leave from Patras, Kyllini, or Igoumenitsa.

Piraeus: Take M1 (green) south to its end or take bus #040 from Filellinon and Mitropoleos right off **Plateia Syndagma** (every 15min.). To nearly all Greek islands other than the Sporades and Ionians: **Iraklion, Hania,** and **Rethymno, Crete; Aegina, Hydra, Poros,** and **Spetses; Astypalea, Kalymnos, Kastelorizo, Kos, Leros, Patmos,** and **Rhodes; Amorgos, Anafi, Donousa, Folegandros, Iraklia, Ios, Kimolos, Kithnos, Koufonisia, Milos, Mykonos, Naxos, Paros, Santorini, Schinousa, Serifos, Sifnos, Sikinos, Syros,** and **Tinos; Chios, Ikaria, Lesvos, Limnos,** and **Samos.** See **Piraeus** (p. 126) for prices, frequencies, and durations.

Rafina: From Athens, buses leave for Rafina from Mavromateon 29, 2 blocks up along Areos Park or a 15min. walk from Pl. Syndagma (1hr., every 30min. 5:40am-10:30pm, €2). Ferries to: **Andros, Evia, Marmari, Mykonos, Naxos, Paros,** and **Tinos. Flying Dolphins** sail to: **Andros, Mykonos, Naxos, Paros, Syros,** and **Tinos.** See **Rafina** (p. 128) for prices, frequencies, and durations.

■ ORIENTATION

Athenian geography can mystify newcomers. When you're trying to figure out the city, check out the detailed free maps available at the tourist office (p. 98). While this information is available at several locations throughout the city, including the Rafina and Pireaus ports, the most convenient place to get a map (along with current ferry schedules) is in the arrivals hall at the airport terminal building (www.gnto.gr). The city map includes bus, trolley, and metro routes. *Now in Athens* magazine has a more detailed street plan. If you lose your bearings, ask for directions back to well-lit **Syndagma.** The **Acropolis,** which stands at the center of the city, is a good reference point. Athenian streets often have multiple spellings or names, so check the map again before you panic. Several English-language publications can help you navigate Athens. The weekly *Athens News* gives addresses, hours, and phone numbers for weekly happenings, as well as news and ferry information (€2.50; available at the airport and at kiosks around the city).

Athens and its suburbs occupy seven hills in southwestern Attica. **Syndagma,** the central plateia, is encircled by the other major neighborhoods. Clockwise, they are: **Plaka, Monastiraki, Psiri, Omonia, Exarhia, Kolonaki,** and **Pangrati.** The three major squares—Syndagma, Plaka, and Monistariki—are connected by three major streets: **Ermou, Athinas,** and **Stadio.**

A 30min. car, bus, or taxi ride south takes you to the seaside suburb of **Glyfada. Piraeus,** the primary port, lies to the southwest of central Athens. In a

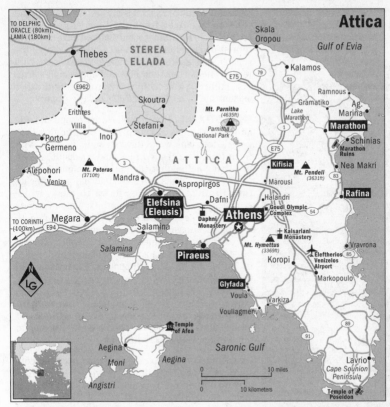

Attica

wider clockwise circle, **Kifisia** and **Marousi** outlie Athens to the north; the port of **Rafina** to the northeast; and **Lavrio** to the southeast. The new airport, **Eleftherios Venizelos,** is on the road to Lavrio.

SYNDAGMA. Plateia Syndagma (Σύνδαγμα) is the center of Athens. The stately, Neoclassical Parliament building and the Tomb of the Unknown Soldier rest at the foot of the National Gardens, looking down the long stretch of **Ermou,** populated with trend-seeking teenagers and street performers. Fast-food spots and elegant restaurants alternate with some of Athens's best museums and public transportation hubs. Airport-bound buses leave from in front of the Gardens, along **Amalias,** and the main metro entrance is across from the Parliament on Amalias. Banks, luxurious hotels, and enormous department stores crowd the square and its surrounding streets, **Georgiou, Filellinon,** and **Othonos. Nikis** and **Voulis,** behind Filellinon, are lined with inexpensive eateries, tourist offices, and stores. **Mitropoleos,** Ermou, and **Karageorgi Servias** (later becoming Perikleous, then Athinados) start here and extend far into Monastiraki and Psiri. Occasional public concerts, the changing of the guard at the Parliament building, and an abundance of unlicensed vendors add to Syndagma's status as an eventful and energetic center.

PLAKA. Plaka (Πλάκα), the busy maze of small roads on the hill beneath the Acropolis, is bounded by the **Temple of Olympian Zeus** and the plateia of the **Mitropoli**

THE LOCAL STORY

BELOVED BACKGAMMON

Walk down a side street or past a cafe in Athens, and chances are you'll see people playing backgammon. It's generally a solitary activity with the younger generation, but with elderly men it's a perfect opportunity for good-natured ribbing and unabashedly tense competition.

Although the unofficial national board game of Greece is quite similar to the American version of backgammon, there are a few differences. The patterned board is called the *tavli* and three variations of the game are played, often in succession: *portes* (the most similar to the American version of backgammon), *plakoto*, and *fevga*. Most Greeks learn all three games as children.

One of the reasons the game is so popular in Greece is that it has been played here for thousands of years. According to archaeological evidence of *tavli* boards, the Ancient Greeks played the game and might have learned it from the Persian Empire in Mesopotamia. *Tavli* variants are the oldest known games in history. It is no wonder, then, that backgammon is a beloved pastime in Greece. As with so many other elements of Greek life, the past has been flawlessly adopted into the present.

Cathedral. Many of its streets are pedestrian-only, and vendors take full advantage of the extra sidewalk space. While **Kydatheneon** and **Adrianou** have scores of tourist-oriented tavernas and souvenir shops, the smaller, quieter streets still have antique charm. With reasonable accommodations and appealing eateries just meters away from the Acropolis and other ancient sites, Plaka is an excellent place to stay.

MONASTIRAKI. Monastiraki (Μοναστηράκι; Little Monastery) hosts a fantastically frenetic flea market. Pedestrians wade through stalls heaping with fresh fruit, handcrafted rugs, and stacks of jewelry of varying authenticity and price. The pungent aromas of fish markets and souvlaki vendors permeate the vibrant square from dawn to dusk, while crowded tavernas and the nearby colony of trendy bars in Psiri keep pedestrian traffic flowing late into the night. Monastiraki's main plateia, which shares its name, has a large metro station as well as several fast-food joints; it is just off the main thoroughfare of **Ermou** and borders **Mitropoleos, Pandrossou,** and **Ifestou.** Many Byzantine churches and ancient ruins, including the **Roman Agora** and **Hadrian's Library,** crowd this area. The old buildings of **Psiri,** north of Ermou, and along the major thoroughfares of **Miaouli** and **Aristofanous** are bounded by **Evripidou** to the north and **Athinas** to the east.

OMONIA. Those who crave freedom from the constant rush of tourists in downtown Athens need to look no further than Omonia (Ομονία); it is predominantly locals who shop and relax at the indoor-outdoor cafes and snack bars in the busy melting pot of **Plateia Omonia.** That said, visitors should be wary of pickpockets and hustlers, especially in North Omonia. Due to its position outside the traditional tourist routes, this area defies Greece's reputation for homogeneity. The square bustles with ethnic and ideological diversity, and Greek is far from the only script you'll see on street signs. Between the parallel streets of **Agiou Konstantinou** and **Evripidou** is something of a "Little Asia," where the smell of curry wafts through the stalls and vendors sell goods from their homelands. Omonia is also a center of learning: **Polytechnic University** and the **National Library** are on **Panepistimiou** between the two plateias of Omonia and Syndagma. **Larisis Station,** serving northern Greece, and **Peloponnese Station,** serving the south, both are located on **Konstantinoupoleos,** northeast of **Plateia Karaiskaki,** and are accessible from **Deligiani.**

EXARHIA. In 1973, progressive Exarhia (Εξάρχια) was the site of a massive demonstration against the right-wing dictatorship. Today, students from the bordering university fill the same graffiti-covered streets as their former, more radical counterparts, though they gather now for a different cause. Their non-negotiable demand? Hip products, for sale at the thrift shops and record stores that pack this anarchist-enclave-turned-bohemian-mecca. The **Archaeological Museum** is here, among countless cafes pumping alternative music.

KOLONAKI. Athens may be the birthplace of Western democracy, but a modern-day plutocracy is alive and well in Kolonaki (Κολωνάκι). Euros flow like water in Athens's poshest district, nourishing the designer shops and upscale restaurants that crop up on its sidewalks almost as often as shady trees. Kolonaki lies uphill from Syndagma, at the foot of **Mount Lycavittos;** most of its commerce centers on glitzy **Patriarhi Ioakim,** while restaurants, bars, and cafes populate the smaller and more pedestrian-friendly **Plutarchou, Haritos,** and **Loukianou.** Kolonaki's **Benaki** and **Byzantine Museums** contain sizable collections of priceless artifacts, and with their reasonable entrance prices, they are far more palatable to the budget traveler than the nearby boutiques. Every Friday, **Xenokratous** is overtaken by the humbler pleasures of fresh fruits and vegetables, sold in the crowded **laiki** (farmer's market).

PANGRATI. Youths and yuppies chat over Fanta® or iced coffee and play backgammon in Pangrati (Παγγράτι), southeast of Kolonaki. Though close to the city center, Pangrati is quite intimate, with interesting shops less oriented toward tourists. The tree-lined streets allow for leisurely strolls, and the many cafes provide for casual evenings sipping mixed drinks or coffee. The area's major monuments are its Byzantine churches, the **Panathenaic Stadium,** and the **National Cemetery. Pangratiou Park,** however, is a reminder of the days before the area's gentrification.

⊟ LOCAL TRANSPORTATION

Buses: KTEL buses (the yellow ones) leave from Terminals A and B, Mavromateon 29, and Pl. Eleftherias, and travel all over the Attic peninsula. Unlike much of Greek transportation, they are punctual, so be on time. Buy KTEL bus tickets on board. The other buses frequently visible around Athens and its suburbs are blue, designated by 3-digit numbers. Both are good for travel throughout the city and ideal for daytrips to **Daphni** and **Kesariani,** the northern suburbs, **Glyfada** and the coast, and other destinations in the greater Athens area. Buy blue bus/trolley tickets (good for both) at any street kiosk and validate them yourself at the orange machine on board. A standard one-way ticket costs €0.45. Children under 6 ride free. There are several options for those who plan to use buses and trolleys frequently. You can buy many tickets at once, or opt for an "Airport 24hr." ticket (€3), which grants unlimited travel on city bus, trolley, and metro within 24hr. of its validation and, despite its name, need not be used solely to get to the airport. A weekly card (€10), valid on all forms of public transport, is also available. **Hold on to your ticket.** If you drop it or don't validate it—even when it seems like nobody is there to make you pay—you can be fined €18-30 on the spot by police. The metro stations' and tourist offices' maps of Athens label all of the most frequented routes. Buses run M-Sa 5am-11:30pm, Su and public holidays 5:30am-11:30pm. The **E95** from Syndagma to El. Venizelou airport, **E96** from Piraeus to El. Venizelou airport, and **#040** from Piraeus to Syndagma all run 24hr. Check KTEL bus schedules by calling Terminal A (☎21051 24 910) or B (☎21083 17 153).

Trolleys: Yellow and crowded, trolleys are distinguished from buses by their electrical antennae. Buy a bus/trolley ticket ahead of time at a kiosk (€0.45). Service is frequent and convenient for short hops within town. See the detailed metro and tourist office map for routes and stops. Trolleys operate M-Sa 5am-midnight, Su and public holidays 5:30am-midnight.

EASY RIDER. Unlimited weeklong passes for travel on any mode of public transportation are available for €10 where bus, metro, and tram tickets are sold. If you're in Athens for a week or more, it's a bargain: 7 daily round-trip journeys plus one more ride, and you break even.

Metro: Most of the Athens metro was rebuilt for the 2004 Olympics. It is now fast, convenient, and gleaming. The underground network consists of 3 lines. **M1,** the green line, runs from northern Kifisia to the port of Piraeus. A new station, Neratziotissa, between the stations of Eirini and Marousi, close to the northern end of the line, intersects with the Suburban Rail. **M2,** the red line, currently runs from Ag. Antonios to Ag. Dimitrios. It eventually will continue from Ag. Antonios to Anthoupoli and from Ag. Dimitrios to Helliniko toward the Saronic Gulf. **M3,** the blue line, which goes from Monastiraki in central Athens to Doukissis Plakentias (where it intersects the Suburban Rail) and the airport, will continue northwest from Monastiraki to Haidari, and ultimately may be extended to Port Zea in Piraeus. A €0.70 ticket allows for travel along any of the lines (transfer is permitted) in 1 direction for up to 1½hr. after its validation. For shorter jaunts around the city center, tickets range €0.30-0.60. Buy tickets at metro stations; tell the cashier your destination or buy a ticket from one of the many automatic machines. Trains run 5am-midnight. Remember to **hold on to your ticket** to avoid a fine.

Trams: Noiseless and electrically powered, 2 new tram lines opened in July 2004, right before the Olympic Games. **Line 1** runs from Pl. Syndagma, in the city center, down to the coast and continues south to Helliniko. It connects with the **M2** (red) in Neos Kosmos. **Line 2** begins in Neo Faliro, where it connects with the **M1** (green). From there it continues along the Apollo Coast to Glyfada.

Taxis: Meter rates start at €0.85, with an additional €0.30 per km within city limits and €0.56 outside city limits. Midnight-5am everything beyond the start price is €0.53 per km. There's a €3 surcharge for trips from the airport, and a €0.80 surcharge for trips from port, bus, and railway terminals; add €0.29 extra for each piece of luggage over 10kg. Pay what the meter shows, rounding it up to the next €0.20 as a **tip.** Hail your taxi by shouting your destination—not the street address, but the area (e.g., "Pangrati"). The driver will pick you up if he feels like heading that way. Get in the cab and tell the driver the exact address or site. Many drivers don't speak English, so write your destination down (in Greek if possible); include the area of the city, since streets in different parts of the city may share the same name. It's common to ride with other passengers going in the same direction. For an extra €1.50-2.50 you can schedule a pickup; call a radio taxi: **Ikaros** (☎21051 52 800); **Ermis** (☎21041 15 200); **Kosmos** (☎1300).

 If a cab already carrying passengers picks you up, be sure to check the meter when you get in. Don't get tricked into paying for more than the distance you traveled in the cab.

Car Rental: Try the places on **Syngrou.** €35-50 for a small car with 100km mileage (including tax and insurance); about €200-350 per week. Student discounts up to 50%. Prices rise in summer.

⑦ PRACTICAL INFORMATION

TOURIST AND FINANCIAL SERVICES

Tourist Office: Information Office, Amalias 26 (☎21033 10 392; www.gnto.gr). The staff is extremely friendly and offers brochures on travel throughout Greece and an indispensable Athens map (the same one is offered in larger metro stations). They can also give the most up-to-date bus, train, and ferry schedules and prices and lists of museums, embassies, and banks. Their website is also a good source of information. Going straight to a travel agency, however, is generally a quicker and easier way to make specific plans. Open M-F 10am-6pm, Sa-Su 10am-3pm.

Budget Travel: STA Travel, Voulis 43 (☎21032 11 188). Open M-F 9am-5pm, Sa 10am-2pm. **Consolas Travel,** Aiolou 100 (☎21032 19 228), on the 9th fl. above the post office. Open M and Sa 9am-2pm, Tu-F 9am-5pm. **Adrianos Travel, Ltd.,** Pandrossou 28 (☎21032 31 015; www.adrianostravel.gr), near Mitropoli Cathedral in Plaka, on the 2nd fl. Open M-F 9am-6pm, Sa 9am-1pm.

Embassies and Consulates: See **Embassies and Consulates,** p. 8.

Banks: National Bank, Karageorgi Servias 2 (☎21033 40 500), in Pl. Syndagma. Open M-Th 8am-2:30pm, F 8am-2pm; open for **currency exchange** M-F 3:30-5pm, Sa 9am-2pm, Su 9am-1pm. American Express, the post office, some hotels, and other banks (list available at tourist office) offer currency exchange. Commission about 5%. 24hr. currency exchange at the airport, but commissions there are usually exorbitant.

LOCAL SERVICES

Luggage Storage: Pacific Ltd. (☎21035 30 160; www.pacifictravel.gr), in El. Venizelos Airport's arrivals terminal across from the large cafe. Open 24hr. Main branch at Nikis 26 (☎21032 41 007) in Syndagma. €2 per day, €30 per month. Open M-Sa 8am-8pm, Su 9am-2pm. Many hotels have free or inexpensive luggage storage.

Bookstores: Around Syndagma, there are 2 **⬛Eleftheroudakis Book Stores,** Panepistimiou 17 (☎21032 58 440) and Nikis 20 (☎21032 29 388). The air-conditioned, 8-fl. Panepistimiou location has a Food Company cafe. It is a mecca for English-, French-, and German-speakers nostalgic for fiction, reference, and travel books in their native tongue. Open M-F 9am-9pm, Sa 9am-6pm. AmEx/MC/V. **Compendium Bookshop,** Nikodimou 5 (☎21032 21 248), just off Nikis on the left. Has new and used books, large fiction and poetry sections, poetry readings in winter, and a children's book room. Open M and W 9am-5pm, Tu and Th-F 9am-8pm, Sa 9:30am-3:30pm. **Zoodochou Pigis,** off Akademias in Omonia, is lined with bookstores frequented by students, selling old, new, and foreign books, magazines, and newspapers.

Libraries: The **British Council Library,** Pl. Kolonaki 17 (☎21036 71 300 or 21036 33 211). Offers books on English literature and language. Open July-Aug. M-F 9am-2pm; Sept.-June M-Sa 10am-7pm. **Hellenic American Union Library,** Massalias 22 (☎21036 80 000), on the 4th fl. of the Hellenic American Union behind Panepistimiou. Has a wide variety of English books on Greece. Open M and Th 10am-5pm, Tu 10am-8pm, W 10am-6pm, F 10am-4pm.

Laundromats: Most *plintirias* (launderers) have signs reading "Laundry." Be sure to specify if you don't mind mixing colors. **National,** Apollonos 17 (☎21032 32 226), in Syndagma. Wash, dry, and fold €4.50 per kg. Open M and W 8am-4pm, Tu and Th-F 8am-8pm. **Zenith,** Apollonos 12 and Pentelis 1 (☎21032 38 533). Wash and dry €4.50 per kg. Open M and W 8am-4pm, Tu and Th-F 8am-8pm. **Psaron 9** (☎21052 22 856), near the train stations. €9 per load. Open M-F 8am-8pm, Sa 8am-5pm, Su 8am-noon.

EMERGENCY AND COMMUNICATIONS

Emergency: Police ☎ 100 or 133. **Ambulance** ☎166. **Doctors** ☎105 or 21064 67 811; line available 2pm-7am. **Poison control** ☎21077 93 777. **AIDS Help Line** ☎21072 22 222. *Athens News* lists hospitals. Free emergency health care for tourists.

Tourist Police: Dimitrakopoulou 77 (☎171). Great for information, assistance, and emergencies. English spoken. Open 24hr.

ATHENS ADVENTURES

It's common for travelers to feel disoriented upon their arrival to Athens its labyrinthine street layout and immense size. Luckily, there's an easy, economical, and little-known solution: as a guest at the **Athens Backpackers Hostel,** you can take advantage of five guided trips, collectively known as "Athens Adventures." These trips explore the city and its surroundings on a backpacker's budget, acclimating visitors to both major attractions and lesser-known wonders.

1. Downtown walking tour (€5): Learn about Athens's history while visiting the best shopping and eating districts.

2. Athens by night (€5): See the hot spots that only locals know about.

3. Skiing/snowboarding (€49): Hit the slopes with transportation and lift ticket to Parnassos or Kalavrita (rentals extra).

4. Corinthian Experience (€45): See the Temple of Aphrodite and swim in the Gulf of Corinth (includes museum entrance fees, transportation, and lunch).

5. Medieval Nafplion (€45): Explore the town of Nafplion and the Nemea winery (includes museum entrance fees, transportation, and lunch).

To reserve a spot on a trip, email marketing@backpackers.gr or call ☎*21092 24 044.*

Pharmacies: Marked by a green cross. About 1 every 4 blocks is open 24hr.; they rotate. Once a pharmacy closes, it will list on its door the nearest ones that are open 24hr.; the "Useful Information" section of *Athens News* also lists the day's emergency pharmacies.

Hospitals: Emergency hospitals or clinics on duty can be reached at ☎106. **KAT,** Nikis 2 (☎21080 14 411), is located between Marousi and Kifisia. **Geniko Kratiko Nosokomio** (Y. Gennimatas; Public State Hospital), Mesogion 154 (☎21077 78 901). A state hospital, **Aeginitio,** Vas. Sofias 72 (☎21072 20 811) and Vas. Sofias 80 (☎21077 70 501), is closer to Athens's center. Near Kolonaki is the public hospital **Evangelismos,** Ypsilantou 45-47 (☎21072 01 000).

Telephones: OTE, Patission 85 (☎21082 14 449), Athinas 45 (☎21032 16 699), or Stadiou 15. Has phone books for most European and Anglophone countries. Overseas collect calls can only be made at Patission location. For information on **overseas calls,** dial ☎161 from any landline phone; for **directory assistance** in and outside of Athens, dial ☎131. Most phone booths in the city operate by **phone cards** (€3, €6, €12, or €24), available at OTE offices, kiosks, and tourist shops. For rates and general OTE info, call ☎134 (English spoken); for a domestic English-speaking operator, call ☎151. Open M-F 8am-2pm.

Internet Access: Athens teems with Internet cafes. Expect to pay €3-6 per hr.

Bits'n Bytes Internet, Kapnikareas 19 (☎21038 22 545; www.bnb.gr), in Plaka. This mother of new-age Internet cafes has fast connections in a spacious, blacklight-lit joint with A/C. 9am-midnight €5 per hr., midnight-9am €3 per hr. Vending machines sell coffee, juice (€1), and sandwiches (€1-2). Open 24hr. 2nd location in Exarhia, Akadamias 78 (☎21052 27 717).

Cafe 4U, 3 Septemvriou 24 (☎21052 01 564), in Omonia. A refuge off busy 3 Septemvriou, this cafe offers fast access. €2.50 per hr., min. €1.50.

Lobby Internet Cafe, Imittou 113 (☎21070 14 607), by Pl. Pangratiou, in Pangrati. Mainly a cafe with a few computers and a printer (€0.25 per page). €4 per hr., min. €2. Open daily 9am-1am.

Quicknet Cafe, Glathstonos 4 (☎21038 03 771), just off of Patission, in Exarhia. Extremely fancy with large, new flat-screen PCs, fast connections, A/C, and comfortable swivel chairs. €2.50 per hr., min. €1.50. Cappuccino €1.50. Open 24hr.

Rendez-Vous Cafe, Voulis 18 (☎21032 23 158), in Syndagma. Sip coffee or snack on fresh white chocolate chip cookies (€0.40). €3 per hr., min. €1. Open M-F 7:30am-9pm, Sa 7:30am-6pm.

Post Offices: For customer service inquiries call the Greek National Post Office (ELTA; ΕΛΤΑ) at ☎80011 82 000. For **shipping** abroad, try parcel post at the

Syndagma ELTA branch at Mitropoleos 60. (☎21032 42 489. Open M-F 7:30am-8pm.)

Acropolis/Plaka branch (☎21092 18 076). **Exchanges currency** and accepts **Poste Restante.** Sends packages up to 2kg abroad. Open M-F 7:30am-6pm. **Postal Code:** 11702.

Exarhia branch, at the corner of Zaimi and K. Deligiani. **Exchanges currency** and accepts **Poste Restante.** Open M-F 7:30am-2pm. **Postal Code:** 10022.

Omonia branch, Aiolou 100 (☎21032 53 586). Machine distributes stamps 24hr.; credit card required. **Poste Restante.** Accepts parcels up to 2kg abroad. Open M-F 7:30am-8pm, Sa 7:30am-2pm. **Postal Code:** 10200.

Syndagma branch (☎21062 26 253), on the corner of Mitropoleos. Sells stamps, **exchanges currency,** and accepts **Poste Restante. Postal Code:** 10300.

▐ ACCOMMODATIONS

The reception desk at **Youth Hostel #5,** Damareos 75, in Pangrati, also acts as the **Greek Youth Hostel Association** and lists 10 other affiliated hostels in Thessaloniki, Patras, and Olympia as well as on Santorini and Crete. (☎21075 19 530. Open M-F 9am-3pm.) The **Hellenic Chamber of Hotels,** Stadiou 24, provides info and reservations for hotels throughout Greece. Reservations require cash deposit, length of stay, and number of people; contact a month in advance. (☎21033 10 022; www.grhotels.gr. Open May-Nov. M-F 8:30am-1:30pm.)

ACCOMMODATIONS BY PRICE

UNDER €17 ❶		€27-37 ❸	
▧ Hostel Aphrodite (HI; p. 103)	OMN	▧ The Exarcheion (p. 103)	EXR
Athens International Hostel (HI; p. 103)	OMN	**€37-72 ❹**	
▧ Pangration Youth Hostel (p. 103)	PAN	Acropolis House (p. 102)	PLK
Pella Inn (p. 102)	MON	▧ Hotel Cecil (p. 102)	MON
Student's and Traveler's Inn (p. 102)	PLK	Hotel Dryades (p. 103)	EXR
		Hotel Kimon (p. 101)	SYN
€17-27 ❷		Hotel Metropolis (p. 101)	SYN
▧ Athens Backpackers (p. 102)	PLK	▧ Phaedra Hotel (p. 102)	PLK
▧ Hotel Orion (p. 103)	EXR		

EXR Exarhia **MON** Monastiraki **OMN** Omonia **PAN** Pangrati **PLK** Plaka **SYN** Syndagma

ACCOMMODATIONS BY AREA

SYNDAGMA

Tourist services are easy to find in the heart of Athens, but cheap, quality accommodations are difficult to track down. Though it can be noisy, Syndagma is a central location; just be wary of overpriced, underwhelming tourist traps.

Hotel Metropolis, Mitropoleos 46 (☎21032 17 469; www.hotelmetropolis.gr). Balconies with excellent views of the square or the Acropolis and the elevator make this otherwise simple hotel distinct. A/C, TV, and phone. Free luggage storage. Laundry €10 per load. Free Wi-Fi. Singles €55-70; doubles €60-80; triples €75-90. AmEx/MC/V. ❹

Hotel Kimon, Apollonos 27 (☎21033 14 658), near Patroöu and Apollonos. While the hotel's hallway carpet has seen brighter days, this 17-room hideaway boasts sizable rooms and an Acropolis view from the rooftop garden. The particularly spacious top-floor triple is a great group bargain. A marble staircase at the entrance, iron bedsteads, and brightly colored walls add a dash of verve to insipid decor. Rooms have TV, A/C, and bath; some have a balcony. Doubles €55-80; triples €80-100. Cash only. ❹

PLAKA

◪ **Athens Backpackers,** 12 Makri Street (☎21092 24 044; www.backpackers.gr). From the Acropolis metro stop, walk down Ath. Diakou for 30m, take the 1st left onto Makri; the hostel is on the corner. While its convenient location near a metro stop and most of the city's major sites are huge selling points, neither is as compelling as the Acropolis view from the rooftop, where cold beer (€2) and a terrace party are served nightly during summer. Generous space between bunks in tidy, spacious rooms. Free Wi-Fi and luggage storage, A/C, and a clean, communal kitchen facilities sweeten the deal. Some rooms have bath and patio. Laundry €5. 6- or 8-bed dorms €18-25. AmEx/MC/V. ❷

◪ **Phaedra Hotel,** Kodrou 3 (☎21032 49 737). The location is superb, the family owners couldn't be friendlier, and the plain rooms are spick and span. The enormous rooftop garden offers a view of the nearby Acropolis at a price that sets this 21-room hotel apart from its nearby competitors. Singles €50-60; doubles €60-70; triples €75-85. ❹

Student's and Traveler's Inn, Kydatheneon 16 (☎21032 44 808; www.studenttravelersinn.com). From the Syndagma metro stop, follow Filelinon in same direction as traffic. Take the 4th left and walk 300m. While rooms are unglamorous and bare, the hostel has A/C (except in dorms) and free Wi-Fi. The Inn courts backpackers with its balconies and a garden bar open until midnight daily. Breakfast (5:30-11:30am) €4-5.50. Storage €15 per month, €7 per week; free for 1 day. Reception 24hr. Co-ed dorms €25-27; doubles €55-65, with bath €60-70; triples €75-85; quads €88-100. For the cheapest digs, request the "dungeon" downstairs, a windowless co-ed dorm (€12). V. ❶

Acropolis House, 6-8 Koudro (☎21032 22 344). Across the street from Adonis Hotel. This 19th-century landmark building, a mansion-turned-guesthouse, has been run by the same family since 1965. While some of the rooms are a tad small and the interiors could use some refurbishing, the high ceilings and Neoclassical architectural detailing add charm. Breakfast included. A/C. Some rooms have bath. Doubles €67-87. ❹

MONASTIRAKI

With its nearby markets, Monastiraki is noisy at all hours, but the neighborhood's activity and central location make it an appealing place to set up camp. There is no shortage of cheap, high-quality accommodations, and ancient sights and buzzing nightlife are just a short walk away.

◪ **Hotel Cecil,** Athinas 39 (☎21032 17 079), on the border of Psiri, just a few blocks down from the Varvakia market and 4 blocks from the Monastiraki metro. Cecil has wood-floored, high-ceilinged rooms with spotless bath, A/C, and TV. Roof bar with Acropolis view. Breakfast included. Free luggage storage. Singles €50-70; doubles €79-99; triples €120-140; quads €145. AmEx/MC/V. ❹

Pella Inn, Karaiskaki 1 (☎21032 50 598). From the Monastiraki metro station, walk 2 blocks down Ermou, away from Pl. Syndagma. Tidy, well-equipped rooms overlook a street which, though bustling and often noisy, is particularly well-situated. On the dividing line between the old sights below the Acropolis and the newer, trendy nightlife of Psiri, Pella is minutes from many of Athens's best draws. From private balconies or the large rooftop seating area, guests enjoy beautiful, unobstructed views of the Acropolis. All rooms have fan, phone, and hot water. Breakfast included in room prices, €3 if you stay in dorms. Free luggage storage. Dorms €15; doubles €40-50; triples €60; quads €80. Prices are negotiable, especially during low season. ❶

OMONIA

Travelers will appreciate Omonia's location by the bus and train stations, and their wallets will appreciate its accommodations' low prices. The hostels here, though not glamorous, are some of the cheapest and friendliest in the city.

■ **Hostel Aphrodite (HI),** Einardou 12 (☎21088 10 589; www.hostelaphrodite.com). A welcoming environment with clean, simple rooms and a bar in the basement. Breakfast €3.50-5. Laundry €8. Free Internet. Safety deposit box. Free luggage storage. 8-bed-dorms €15; doubles €44; triples €57; quads €68. Prices subject to change and reduced in low season. Cash only. ●

Athens International Hostel (HI), Victor Hugo 16 (☎21052 32 540). Super-cheap lodgings in a gritty neighborhood. Some rooms have balcony and bath. Shared kitchen. Breakfast €2.50-5. Laundry €8 per 5kg. Free luggage storage; bring a padlock. Dorms €11; doubles €35. Cash only. ●

EXARHIA

Near the university bars and the Archaeological Museum, Exarhia is within walking distance of major public transportation. It's also brighter than nearby Omonia, making it a convenient and peaceful place to stay.

■ **The Exarcheion,** Themistokleous 55 (☎21038 00 731). Right at the center of the bustling neighborhood, near a string of restaurants and tavernas; 5min. by from the Omonia metro. Its rooms, though sparse and unadorned, retain a retro 1970s appeal. The 4-person apartments are a steal at €80 total. Rooms have A/C and balcony, and there is a rooftop garden bar. Breakfast €5. Internet access €3 per hr. Reservations recommended. Singles €35-40; doubles €45-50; triples €60-70; apartments €80. 10% discount for *Let's Go* readers. €10 discount for reserving online. ❸

■ **Hotel Orion,** Em. Benaki 105 (☎21038 27 362; fax 21038 05 193). From Pl. Omonia, walk up Em. Benaki, or take bus #230 from Pl. Syndagma. Filled with university students intent on experiencing Athens away from the tourist machine, Orion rents small rooms with A/C and TV; some have bath. You'll get a calf workout trekking up a hill and 2 sets of steep stairs to reach Orion, but the exquisite rooftop has an incredible Acropolis view. Listen to music on the terrace while you sunbathe, watch TV, or play board games. Breakfast €6. Internet access €2 per hr. Laundry €3. Singles €25-30; doubles €45-55; triples €60-65. ❷

Hotel Dryades, Dryadon 4 (☎21038 27 116). Next door to Hotel Orion. Orion's up-market sister is one of Athens's nicest mid-level accommodations, with large rooms and baths. Full kitchen and TV lounge. Breakfast €5. Internet access €2 per hr. Singles €40-45; doubles €50-60. ❹

PANGRATI

Kolonaki's high prices may scare off budget travelers, but Pangrati has a few affordable accommodations.

■ **Pagration Athens Youth Hostel,** Damareos 75 (☎21075 19 530). From Omonia or Pl. Syndagma take trolley #2 or 11 to Filolaou (past Imittou) or walk through the National Garden, down Eratosthenous, then 3 blocks down Efthidiou to Frinis, and down Frinis until you come to Damareos; it's on your right. There's no sign for this cheery, family-owned hostel—just the number 75 and a green door. The charming common spaces make this out-of-the-way hostel worth the 20-25min. walk to the city center. TV lounge and full kitchen. Hot showers €0.50. Laundry €4 to wash, with dryer €7; or line dry on the roof for free. Quiet hours 2:30-5pm and 11:30pm-7am. High season dorms €12. When the hostel fills up, the owner opens the roof (€10 per person) to travelers; bring a sleeping bag. Cash only. ●

▣ FOOD

FOOD BY PRICE

UNDER €5 ❶	
Artokopos (p. 105)	PLK
▣ Cafe Voulis (p. 104)	SYN
Coffee Right (p. 105)	MON
Cookou Cook (p. 107)	EXR
CrepeXaria (p. 107)	EXR
▣ Derlicious (p. 107)	KOL
Everest (p. 105)	MON
Gelatomania (p. 106)	MON
▣ Matsoukas (p. 104)	SYN
▣ Noodle Bar (p. 104)	SYN
Posto Cafe (p. 108)	PAN
Souvlaki Kavouras (p. 107)	EXR

€5-9 ❷	
Amaltheia (p. 105)	PLK
Antonis Souvlaki (p. 105)	PLK
Attalos (p. 105)	MON
▣ Bean (p. 107)	EXR
▣ Chroma (p. 104)	SYN

€5-9 ❷, CONTD.	
Estiatorio	OMN
Healthy Food Vegetarian (p. 106)	OMN
Işau' (p. 106)	OMN
▣ Kallimarmaron (p. 107)	PAN
▣ Mandras (p. 105)	MON
Nikis Cafe (p. 105)	SYN
▣ O Barba Giannis (p. 107)	EXR
Pasta Cafe (p. 107)	EXR
▣ Platanos (p. 105)	PLK
Savvas (p. 105)	MON
T. Stamatopoulos (p. 105)	PLK

€9-15 ❸	
Furin Kazan (p. 104)	SYN
Jackson Hall (p. 107)	KOL
Pak Indian (p. 106)	OMN

€15-25 ❹	
Eat at Milton's (p. 105)	PLK

EXR Exarhia **KOL** Kolonaki **MON** Monastiraki **OMN** Omonia **PAN** Pangrati **PLK** Plaka
SYN Syndagma

FOOD BY AREA

SYNDAGMA

Just beyond the main square's local chains, inexpensive eateries offer quick, delicious options for the budget traveler.

▣ **Chroma,** Lekka 8 (☎21033 17 793). Join trendy diners on the red and white leather couches at this upscale swankfest for grilled chicken and rice (€8.50), or enjoy a mixed drink when the cafe becomes a bar in the evening. Open M-F and Su 8am-2am, Sa 8am-10pm. ❷

▣ **Noodle Bar,** Apollonos 11 (☎21033 18 585). This bright, spotless cafe offers Greek salads to please even the feta-phobic. Light options, including the mango salad (€4.90) and Thai chicken coconut soup (€4.10), are served on glossy black tables. Takeout and delivery available. Open M-Sa 11am-midnight, Su 5:30pm-midnight. ❶

▣ **Matsoukas,** Karageorgi Servias 3 (☎21032 52 054), lines its walls with chocolates, cookies, and other traditional sweets. Try the especially decadent dark chocolate (€24 per kg). Open daily 8am-midnight. ❶

▣ **Cafe Voulis** (☎21032 34 33), on Voulis St., just off Ermou. This adorable cafe overflows with young locals in search of wine, espresso, and tasty pasta take-out selections. Chicken pasta €3. Open daily 10am-10pm. ❶

Furin Kazan, Apollonos 2 (☎21032 29 170). Follow Nikis to Apollonos, which is parallel to Mitropoleos and begins 1 block away from the square. Sushi, rice dishes, and noodles in an informal, cafe-like setting. Salmon avocado maki €10.50. Yakisoba noodles with shrimp and vegetables €8. Open M-Sa 11:30am-11pm. ❸

Nikis Cafe, Nikis 3 (☎21032 34 971), near Ermou. Nestled in a lively corner, Nikis is both a light cafe (caesar salad €7) and a bustling bar (strawberry or banana margaritas €8). Savory crepes €5-7. Kitchen open noon-midnight; bar open 7pm-2am. ❷

PLAKA

Plaka teems with lively dining options. During the day, ubiquitous **mini-marts** sell yogurt, spanakopita, and fresh fruit. **Vendors** roast souvlaki by the bushel, and **gelaterias** open their doors for icy treats. **Artokopos ❶,** Kydatheneon 1, across from Student and Travellers' Inn, has delicious warm bread. After nightfall, the old district's crowded streets fill with the glowing lights and live music that radiate from nearby tavernas. Wade through the small army of aggressive waiters vying for your attention and pick from one of the many spots with uninterrupted views of the Roman Agora, Mt. Lycavittos, or the Acropolis.

■ **Taverna Platanos,** Diogenous 4 (☎21032 20 666), near the Popular Musical Instruments Museum. Steps away from the touristy bustle of Adrianou and Kydatheneon, Platanos offers authentic fare in a secluded setting. Under a plant-draped trellis or inside the cozy taverna, diners choose from a wide-ranging menu. Tomato salad €3. Lamb with string beans €7. Open M-Sa noon-4:30pm and 7:30pm-midnight, Su noon-4:30pm. ❷

Antonis Souvlaki, Adrianou 118 (☎21032 46 838). The great deals at this tiny, unlabeled storefront would be easy to miss if not for the crowds of locals at its door. Pork or chicken gyros €6.80. Mythos beer €1.30. Open daily 10am-9:30pm. ❷

Amaltheia, Tripodon 16 (☎21032 24 635). Marble tables, antique mirrors, and delicate flower arrangements give a French feel to this welcoming spot, which serves sweet crepes (€5.20-€8.10), yogurt desserts (€4-5), and frappés (€2.80). At night, lights illuminate the buzzing cafe. Open M-Th and Su 10am-1am, F-Sa 10am-2am. ❷

T. Stamatopoulos, Lissiou 26 (☎21032 28 722). Family-owned since 1882, this popular restaurant has a bright outdoor terrace and lively Greek music 9:30-11pm. Veal in wine sauce €8.50. Open M and W-Su 7pm-3am. ❷

Eat at Milton's, Adrianou 91 (☎21032 49 129; eatatmiltons.gr). An oasis of modern hipsterdom among ancient ruins and traditional tavernas, Eat at Milton's serves classy-cool dishes like grilled salmon (€19). If that's too pricey for dinner, take a daytime dessert (lemon soufflé €6.50) or coffee (€2-3.50) break. Open daily 8am-1am. ❹

MONASTIRAKI

A group of inexpensive tavernas and fresh takeout options sits across from the metro, where Ermou meets Athinas. Nearby, **Everest ❶** serves baguette sandwiches and pastries (€1-4) and **CoffeeRight ❶,** a ubiquitous espresso bar, offers excellent frappés (€1-3) and pastries (€2-4).

■ **Mandras,** Ag. Anargiron 8 (☎21032 13 765), at Taki. Live, modern Greek music plays for a young, buzzing crowd of locals in this attractive brick building in the heart of Psiri. The *pleurotous* (mushrooms grilled with oil and vinegar; €6.20) makes a great light meal. Spicy grilled chicken €9.20. Open daily 8am-4am. Music 2pm-4am. ❷

Savvas, Mitropoleos 86 (☎21032 45 048). Cab drivers and kiosk vendors recommend this famous souvlaki joint as the best in town. Restaurant prices for gyros (€6-9) shrink to €1.70 for takeout orders. Open daily 10am-3am. ❷

Attalos Restaurant, Adrianou 9 (☎21032 19 520), near the Thisseon area. On the edge of the Agora and the Temple of Hephaestus, outdoor tables have excellent views. Large white umbrellas and yellow tablecloths make the restaurant bright and inviting. The menu ranges from mussels *saganaki* (€6.20) to a vegetarian's dream plate of zucchini, eggplant, and tomato croquettes (serves 2-4; €8). Open daily 10am-1am. ❷

ATHENS

ESPRESS-YO' SELF

Good coffee can be hard to come by in Greece. Those who don't know how to order will find themselves sucking down cup after tedious €2 cup of instant Nescafé, the unofficial national beverage. In reality, traditional Greek coffee is on par with Italian brews and comes in a surprising variety of preparation styles. Long before the invention of *sanka*, Greek men gathered at *kafeneios* for backgammon, gossip, and good Greek java. Pull up a chair at a traditional cafe and savor the local flavor.

Steely eyed, iron-jawed village men take their coffee *sketos*, straight from the pot and unadulterated by milk or sugar. Order just a *kafe* and it typically comes *metrios*, with one spoonful of sugar mixed in after boiling. Those with a sweet tooth should try *kafe glukus*, which has a subtle honey flavor produced by boiling the sugar with grounds *(katakathi)*. To get rid of the bitter surface foam, order sweet, double-boiled *kafe glukus vrastos*. Sip your coffee with some ice water, but don't swallow the sludge at the bottom. Hotels with kitchens almost always provide the small metal *briki* for boiling; the rule is one tablespoon per cup. Boil until a thick froth forms, then drink without stirring. Making your own *kafe* is cheaper, but you'll miss the socializing that goes with the laid-back buzz of the *kafenion*, which is always good to the last drop.

Gelatomania, Agatharho 21 (☎21032 30 001), at Taki. Ice cream is always cool, but Gelatomania makes it trendy. The enormous glass walls of this hip parlor fold away in warm weather, so the corner spot becomes a sheltered outdoor space in the middle of buzzing bars and restaurants. Red-cushioned couches and small black tables fill the cafe, where heaping displays of homemade ice cream tempt with creative flavors like wafer and gum. €2 per scoop. Iced chocolate €3.50. Waffle with ice cream €5.50. Open daily 10am-4am. ❶

OMONIA

Fast food chains and kiosks fill the frenetic square with quick, inexpensive fare. More interesting ethnic and vegetarian options are a bit farther from the metro. Those with kitchen access should consider the well-stocked **Galaxias Discount Market,** Peoniou 25. (Open M-F and Su 8am-9pm, Sa 8am-8pm.) At the marketplace on Athinas, between Monastiraki and Omonia, all-night restaurants satisfy stomach rumblings from 3pm-7am. If you're in northern Omonia on a Saturday, check out the farmer's market along Alkamenous, near Einardou.

Pak Indian Restaurant, Menandrou 13 (☎21032 19 412). Dark mirrors, Indian lanterns, and pungent scents may make you wonder if you've stepped into a land where generic souvlaki joints are just an idle dream. Veggie *samosa* €1.50. Lamb *rogan josh* (with ginger, tomato, onions, and spices) €10. Open daily 2pm-midnight. MC/V. ❸

Healthy Food Vegetarian Restaurant and Grocery Store, Panepistimiou 57-58 (☎21038 18 021). This meatless kitchen makes different specials every day (€5-7). In the past these have included tofu souvlaki, soy *pastitsio,* and freshly squeezed fruit juices (pear €3). Its adjacent sister store sells produce, herbal remedies, and books. Open M-F 8am-9:30pm, Sa 8am-8pm, Su 8am-4pm. ❷

Işau', Kapnokoptiriu 4 (☎21052 35 672). Directly across the street from Aharnon 17. Homestyle Romanian food, a rarity in Greece, is served at low prices in a pleasant atmosphere. A 2nd level of seating and a bar add to the restaurant's appeal at night. Try the Mititei (grilled Romanian hamburger, €4.80) with the *tzatziki* salad (cucumbers, yogurt, and garlic, €2.50). Entrees €4-6. Open daily 10am-1am. ❷

Estiatorio, Sokratous 33 (☎21052 44 726). The name simply means "restaurant" in Greek, and this unassuming joint doesn't aspire to anything fancy. But if you can make it within the unorthodox hours, you'll get a rare taste of local flavor. Veal with okra €6. Eggplant with minced meat €6. Entrees €4-6. Open M-Sa 5am-5pm. ❷

EXARHIA

Hungry 20-somethings demand cheap food around Exarhia, and many of the options are basic but tasty. Cheap, speedy souvlaki (€1-2) is available at **Souvlaki Kavouras ❶**, Themistokleous 64.

O Barba Giannis, Em. Benaki (☎21038 24 138). From Syndagma, walk up Stadiou and make a right on Em. Benaki; it's the yellow building on the corner with tall green doors. "Uncle John's" is informal, but that's how the locals like it—just ask the Athenian students, CEOs, and artists who count themselves among this taverna's regulars. Specials €5-10. Open M-Sa noon-1:30am. ❷

Bean, Em. Benaki 45 (☎21033 00 010), near Pasta Cafe. Modern decor belies the menu's taverna flavor. Hanging lamps and small white lights illuminate this simple indoor-outdoor space. Daily specials are listed on colorful placemats decorated with photos. Pastas €5-6. Italian-influenced salads €4-5.50. Open M-Sa 1pm-midnight. ❷

Cookou Cook, Themistokleous 66 (☎21038 31 955). Blue walls, mosaic tables, and eccentric decorations adorn this funky spot, which fuses creative gourmet with speed and informality. Greek salad €4.50. Salmon teriyaki €5. Open M-Sa 1pm-1am; summer M-Sa 7am-7pm. ❶

Pasta Cafe, Em. Benaki 58 (☎21038 38 186), 5min. from the Omonia metro. Glass walls and low brown booths make this small, square room feel spacious and welcoming. The chef cooks up fresh vegetable dishes (€3-6) and flavorful pastas (€4-6). Open M-F noon-midnight, Sa noon-8pm. ❷

CrepeXaria (☎21038 40 773), on the corner of Ikonomou and M. Themistokleous on Pl. Exarhia. Some takeout places throw your food in a styrofoam box before you dash off. Here, they wrap your concoction of choice in a warm, fresh crepe: just as fast and twice as tasty as the average doggie bag. Choose your own savory or sweet combinations— eggs, bacon, cheese, and onion (€5.50) or chocolate, strawberry, and hazelnut (€3.10) are particularly good. Open daily noon-5am. ❶

KOLONAKI

The *laiki* in Plateia Dexamani every Friday, with an array of vendors selling everything from souvlaki to fresh olives, is your best bet if you're on a budget. In general, though, Kolonaki caters to those who can splurge on fine dining.

Derlicious, Tsakalof 14 (☎21036 30 284), tucked between boutiques on the southernmost block of Tsakalof. The sign is written in Greek letters, so find this hole-in-the-wall fast food joint by looking for an array of tables in the shade. It's rare to find such low-priced fare in Kolonaki, and although Derlicious is part of a chain, the personal touch of the friendly staff is immediately evident. Try the *flaouto* (big tortilla) with chicken (€3.22). Open M-W and Su 1pm-4am, Th 1pm-5am, F-Sa 1pm-6am. ❶

Jackson Hall, Milioni 4 (☎21036 16 546). In Kolonaki, even the lowly hamburger can be elegant. This trendy steakhouse, which unabashedly caters to American tourists, will charge you €14 for a New York "Classic" Burger (lettuce, tomato, and onion), but the wood-paneled ambience makes it worth it. Chocolate souffle with ice cream €7. Open daily 10am-3am. MC/V. ❸

PANGRATI

Imitou, the main drag, is dotted with relaxing cafes and is close to the surprisingly big **Spar** supermarket, Formionos 23. (Open M-F 8am-9pm, Sa 8am-8pm).

Kallimarmaron, Eforionos 13 (☎21070 19 727). Walk east from the Panathenaic Stadium (away from the Acropolis) on Vas. Konstandinou, then turn right on Eratosthenous and left onto the alley-like Eforionos. This elegant taverna isn't much to look at from the outside, but inside, high ceilings and earthy colors accompany home-cooked special-ties. Although the menu changes nearly every day, try staples like the Kallimarmaron salad with vegetables and mustard sauce (€6) or fried pork (€8). Open M-Sa noon-3pm and 8pm-11pm, Su noon-3pm. DC/MC/V. ❷

Posto Cafe, Pl. Plastira 2 (☎21075 10 210). Just to the right once you reach Plastira Sq. from Eratosthenous. In a small storefront tucked behind a white awning, Posto is a relaxed place to enjoy an espresso (€1.80) or a fresh, quick bite to eat. Try the vegeta-ble pizza (€1.50) or spanakopita (€1.50). ❶

◉ SIGHTS

ACROPOLIS

Reach the entrance on the west side by walking north from Areopagitou, by following the signs from Plaka, or by exiting the Agora to the south and following the path uphill. The well-worn marble can be slippery, so wear shoes with good traction. ☎21032 10 219. Open daily in summer 8am-7:30 pm; in winter 8am-2:30pm. Admission includes entrance to the Acropolis, the Agora, the Roman Agora, the Olympian Temple of Zeus, and the Theater of Dionysos, within a 48hr. period. €12, students and EU citizens over 65 €6, under 19 free. Tickets can be purchased at any of the sights.

As the most well-known symbol of Athens, the profile of the Acropolis is a com-mon sight around the world. Upon climbing the steps up to the Propylaia, even the most jaded traveler will be awed by the majesty of the immense structures arrayed on the plateau. The Parthenon, built in the 5th century BC, towers over the Aegean, featuring a panoramic view of the city. Although a visit to the Acropolis seems to be de rigeur for those spending time in Athens, it really is the best way to gain a firsthand understanding of the majesty of ancient Greek civilization. Visit as early in the day as possible to avoid massive crowds and the intense midday sun.

HISTORY

BEGINNINGS. The area of the Acropolis was originally the tiny city of Athens, inhabited by **Mycenaeans** worshipping a nature goddess. As the fledgling polis grew into a sprawling military power, the strategic hilltop site was fortified into a refuge for Athenians in times of war. Wealthy **aristoi,** noblemen who considered themselves closer to God than commoners, took control of Athens in the 12th cen-tury BC, moving power downhill to the Agora and leaving the Acropolis as a purely religious site. A wooden shrine went up to Athena Polias, defender of crops and fertility, and her alter ego Pallas Athena, the city's virgin protectress.

PERICLEAN PROJECT. The Acropolis as it stands today owes much to the deter-mination of **Pericles** (C. 495-429 BC). After Athens's victory against Persia left it in control of a growing empire, this Classical leader commissioned a series of grand architectural displays. Basking in post-Marathon glory, Pericles convinced mem-bers of the Delian League to donate great sums to the polis's beautification cam-paign. This imperial fund raising footed the bill to secure legendary artists, including **Iktinos, Kallikrates,** and **Phidias,** for the site's new design. In 447 BC, only 10 years after construction commenced, they unveiled the completed **Parthenon,** dedicated to Athena. Work on the **Propylaea,** the **Temple of Athena Nike,** and the **Ere-chtheion** soon followed. Even in the Golden Age of Athens, however, citizens were quick to complain that Pericles's Acropolis project was too extravagant. Plutarch memorably blasted the leader for "gilding and bedizening" Athens like a "wanton woman adding precious stones to her wardrobe." Luckily for modern viewers, Per-icles persisted, commissioning more temples on the Acropolis, the **Hephaesteion** in the Agora, and the **Temple of Poseidon** at Sounion.

The Acropolis

TO ATHENS

TO ANCIENT AGORA (500m)

Theorias

Beulé Gate

Pedestal of Agrippa

Propylaia

Temple of Athena Nike

Entrance

Shrine of Aegeus

Altar of Artemis

Brauronion

TO PHILOPAPPOS HILL (150m)

Odeon of Herodes Atticus

Arrephoria

Statue of Athena Promachos

Sacred Olive Tree of Athena

Erechtheion (Caryatids)

Panathenaic Way

Chalcotheque

Parthenon

Sanctuary of Zeus Polieus

Altar of Rome and Augustus

Acropolis Museum

Prostyle Stoa

Asclepion

Stoa of Eumenes

Dionissiou Areopagitou

Theater of Dionysus

0   30 yards
0   30 meters

ATHENS

THE TEST OF TIME. Almost as soon as the Acropolis was completed, it fell to Sparta in 404 BC. Ever since, its function has shifted every time it has changed hands. Byzantine Christians renamed it the **"Church of Agia Sophia,"** worshipping there (and defacing the pagan sculptures) until **Frankish Crusaders** made the building a fortified palace for the Dukes de la Roche in 1205. Catholics came to use the space as a church again, dedicating it to **Notre Dame d'Athènes,** and by the 15th century **Ottoman** rulers had cast it as a mosque.

The Acropolis's buildings themselves remained remarkably intact until a Venetian siege in 1687, when the attackers' shells accidentally blew up a Turkish supply of gunpowder stored under the Parthenon's roof. Its structure has deteriorated since then. By the dawn of the 19th century, British Lord Elgin was chiseling the most stunning marble reliefs off of the Parthenon and carting them to London, where they remain, displayed in the British Museum despite pleas by the Greek government for their return. Large-scale restoration efforts on the Acropolis are still underway, and much of the Parthenon statuary that Elgin didn't make off with recently has been relocated to the Acropolis Museum to shelter it from acid rain.

RUINS

The first structure within the site's gate is the **Temple of Athena Nike,** on the upper right platform as you walk up the stairs. Along the path where a Classical ramp once lay, visitors walk through the Roman **Beulé Gate,** named for the French archaeologist who unearthed it, and past the imposing **Propylaea,** the unfinished entrance attributed to Mnesikles. Famous for its ambitious multi-story design, the Propylaea combines Ionic columns with a Doric exterior.

■**PARTHENON.** The ancient architect Iktinos overlooked no details in the design of the **Temple of Athena Parthenos,** more commonly known as the Parthenon. He placed eight columns instead of the typical six at the front of the temple. Fearing that perspective would make them look spindly from a low vantage point, Iktinos made each column bulge slightly to create an optical illusion of perfect symmetry. In plotting the temple's dimensions, he followed a meticulous four-to-nine ratio, a variation on the aesthetically ideal Golden Mean. Iktinos's obsession with proportion and order, traits that came to epitomize Classical architecture, pushed the Parthenon past traditional Doric boxiness into the sublime.

The **metopes** (scenes in the open spaces above the columns) that once bordered the sides of the Parthenon celebrated Athens's rise to such greatness. On the far right of the southern side, the Lapiths battled the Centaurs, while on the east the Olympian gods triumphed over the Titans. The north side depicted the victory of the Greeks over the Trojans, and the western facade reveled in Athens's triumph over the Amazons. The **pediments** at either end marked the zenith of Classical decorative sculpture. The east pediment once depicted Athena's birth, while the west pediment showed Athena and Poseidon's contest for the city's devotion. Many of these celebratory pieces, damaged over the centuries, are now in London's British Museum or in the Acropolis Museum.

Inside the temple, in front of a pool of water, stood Phidias's greatest sculptural feat: a 12m gold and ivory statue of Athena. Although the statue since has been destroyed, the National Museum houses an AD 2nd-century Roman copy, which is fearsomely grand even at its significantly reduced size.

TEMPLE OF ATHENA NIKE. This tiny temple, on the right as you first enter the Propylaia, is undergoing a renovation process that has involved rebuilding it from the ground up. It first was constructed in the middle of the Peloponnesian War, during a brief respite known as the "Peace of Nikias" (421-415 BC). Ringed by eight miniature Ionic columns, it housed a statue of winged Nike, the goddess of victory. When the Athenians were seized by a paranoid fear that

ATHENS FOR POCKET CHANGE. Budget travelers, rejoice: you're in Athens, where the wine is cheap, the food is cheaper, and the sights are (almost) free. Most of the ruins are outdoors, letting visitors ramble around the **Rock of Saint Paul** (p. 119), the **Philopappos Monument** (p. 113), and **Mount Lycavittos** (p. 115) without dropping a euro. After leaving your bags at the **Student's and Traveler's Inn** (p. 102), pick up local wine, beer, or juice (€1-3) from a corner kiosk and a gyro (€1-2) from **Savvas** (p. 105), and picnic at 1 of these ancient sights with great Acropolis views. Also note that the **Benaki Museum of Islamic Art** (p. 117) is free on Wednesday, the **Ilias Lalounis Jewelry Museum** (p. 118) is free on Wednesday after 3pm and on Saturday 9-11am, and the **War Museum** (p. 118) and **Popular Musical Instruments Museum** (p. 117) never have admission fees.

Nike would flee and take with her any chance of victory in the renewed war, they clipped the statue's wings. The remains of the 5m thick **Cyclopean wall** that once surrounded the entire Acropolis now lie below this temple.

ERECHTHEION. The Erechtheion, to the left of the Parthenon, contains the famous Caryatid sculptures, six women who support the roof on the south side. They're actually replicas; most of the originals can be found in the Acropolis Museum. The structure was built in 406 BC, just before Sparta defeated Athens in the Peloponnesian War. It is named after a snake-bodied hero whom Poseidon speared in a dispute over the city's patronage. When Poseidon struck a truce with Athena, he was allowed to share her temple—so the eastern half is devoted to the goddess of wisdom and the western part to the god of the sea. The eastern porch, with its six Ionic columns, contained an olive-wood statue of Athena; like the Temple of Athena Nike, it contrasts with the Parthenon's dignified Doric columns.

■ACROPOLIS MUSEUM. Although the Acropolis Museum currently is undergoing extensive renovations, it still is arguably the most striking part of the entire complex, with a collection composed exclusively of masterpieces. Five of the original Erechtheion **Caryatids** appear monumentally huge in their small glass casement. The carvings of a lion devouring a bull and of a wrestling match between Herakles and a sea monster display the Ancient Greeks' mastery of anatomical detail and emotional expression. Notice the empty space where room has been left for the British to return the missing Elgin marbles. (*Open daily 8am-7:30pm; hours are shortened in the low season. No flash photography or posing with the statues. English labels. Avoid going 10am-1pm, when it is most crowded.*)

OTHER SIGHTS ON THE ACROPOLIS. The southwestern corner of the Acropolis overlooks the reconstructed **Odeon of Herodes Atticus,** a functional theater dating from the Roman period (AD 160). (*M-Sa 8am-7pm. €2, students €1, visitors with an Acropolis ticket free. MC/V.*) For performance information head to the Odeon box office on Dionysiou Areopagitou. (*☎21032 32 771. Open daily 9am-2pm and 6-9pm.*) The **Athens Hellenic Festival** occurs every summer, with numerous performances in the Odeon; schedules are available at the booth across from the theater. (*Panepistimiou 39. Contact the Athens Festival Office for more information about summertime shows. ☎21032 72 000. Most shows start at 9pm and tickets cost around €30, but range €20-500. Open M-F 8:30am-4pm, Sa 9am-2:30pm.*) Nearby are the ruins of the **Classical Theater of Dionysus,** the **Asclepion,** and the **Stoa of Eumenes II.**

AGORA

Enter the Agora either off Pl. Thission, off Adrianou, or as you descend from the Acropolis. ☎21032 10 185. Map kiosks are plentiful throughout the park, but it might be helpful to bring extra material. Open daily 8am-7:30pm. €4, students and EU seniors €2, under 19 and visitors with an Acropolis ticket free.

If the Acropolis was the showpiece of the ancient capital, the Agora was its heart and soul, serving as the city's marketplace, administrative center, and focus of daily life from the 6th century BC through the AD 6th century. Many of the great debates of Athenian democracy were held here; Socrates, Aristotle, Demosthenes, Xenophon, and St. Paul all instructed in its stalls. Following its heyday, the Agora, like the Acropolis, passed through the hands of various conquerors. The ancient market emerged again in the 19th century, when a residential area built above it was razed for excavations. Today, the Agora is a peaceful respite from the bustling commerce that surrounds it. As you explore the ruins, you're likely to hear the sounds of nature overpowering the low buzz of traffic.

■**HEPHAESTEION.** The Hephaesteion, built in 415 BC on a hill in the northwestern corner of the Agora, is the best-preserved Classical temple in Greece. If you stand with your back to the rest of the Agora, you easily can make out the detailed original **friezes** that cover the top of the temple's inner chamber. They depict the battle between Athenian hero Theseus and the Pallantids.

ODEON OF AGRIPPA. This concert hall, built for Roman Emperor Augustus's son-in-law and right-hand man, now stands in ruins on the left of the Agora as you walk from the museum to the Hephaesteion. When the roof collapsed in AD 150, the Odeon was rebuilt at half its former size. From then on, it served as a lecture hall.

STOA OF ATTALOS. This multi-purpose building was filled with shops and was home to informal philosophers' gatherings. Attalos II, King of Pergamon, built the Stoa in the 2nd century BC as a gift to Athens. Reconstructed between 1953 and 1956, it now houses the **Agora Museum,** which contains relics from the site. The stars of the collection are the **black figure paintings** by Exekias and a **calyx krater** (a vase used to mix wine, with a form resembling the sepals of a flower), depicting Trojans and Greeks quarreling over the body of Patroclus, Achilles's closest companion and possible lover. *(☎21032 10 185. Open daily 8am-7:20pm.)*

MIDDLE STOA. Extending most of the way between the Stoa of Attalos and the Hephaesteion, the Middle Stoa was the largest building in the Agora and was used for a wide variety of organizational and religious purposes. Its red-tinted foundations make it easy to recognize. Although it was destroyed by a fire in AD 267, you can ascertain its immense size by the numerous column bases that remain.

OTHER ANCIENT SITES

ROMAN AGORA. The Roman Agora was built between 19 and 11 BC with donations from Julius and Octavian Caesar. The columns of the two surviving **prophylae** (halls), a nearly intact entrance gate, and the **gate of Athena Archgetis** stand as testaments to what was once a major meeting place for Athenians. Proving that people take interest in anything as long as it's old, the AD first-century **vespasianae,** or public toilets, are a popular site. A mosque dating from 1456 sits nearby. By far the Agora's most intriguing structure is the well-preserved (and restored) **Tower of the Winds.** This octagonal stone tower, built in the first century BC by the astronomer Andronikos, initially was crowned with a weathervane. The top of each side of the tower has a carving of the personification of each of the eight winds. On the walls are markings that allowed the structure to be used as a sundial from the outside and a water-clock from the inside. Since its construction, the tower also has functioned as a church and as a Dervish monastery. *(☎21032 45 220. Open daily 8am-7pm. €2; students €1; EU students, under 19, and visitors with an Acropolis ticket free.)*

TEMPLE OF ZEUS AND HADRIAN'S ARCH. Fifteen majestic Corinthian columns—the remnants of the largest temple ever built in Greece, dedicated to Zeus—stand on the edge of the National Gardens. Several shifts in power delayed the temple's completion until AD 131 under Hadrian's reign, six centuries after its first stones were set. To commemorate his monumental feat, Hadrian built an adjacent arch with two inscriptions. Facing the Acropolis, the arch reads "This is Athens, the ancient city of Theseus." On the other side, facing the emperor's addition, it proclaims, "This is the city of Hadrian and not of Theseus." Nearby, at Vas. Olgas and Amalias, is a memorial to a man whose ambitions were a bit less worldly, though no less grand: the English Romantic poet Lord Byron, who lost his life fighting for Greek independence. *(Entrance on Vas. Olgas at Amalias, across from the entrance to the National Garden. ☎21092 26 330. Open daily 8am-7pm. Temple admission €2, students €1, under 19 free. Arch free. A ticket gives access to the Acropolis, the theater of Dionysus, the Ancient Agora, the Roman Agora, and the Keramikos. €12, students €6.)*

KERAMIKOS. Most sites in the Agora are more dead than alive, but the Keramikos is especially so: it includes a large cemetery built around a segment of the **Sacred Way,** the road to Eleusis. The Sacred Gate arched over this road, lined with **public tombs** for state leaders, famous authors, and battle victims. Worshippers began the annual Panathenaic procession along its path. Also within the site is a section of the 40m wide boulevard that ran through the Agora and Diplyon Gate and ended at the sanctuary of Akademes, where **Plato** founded his Academy in the 4th century BC. The **Oberlaender Museum** displays finds from the burial sites; its pottery and sculpture are highlights. *(Northwest of the Agora; the archaeological site begins where Ermou and Pireos intersect. From Syndagma, walk toward Monastiraki on Ermou for 1km. ☎21034 63 552. Open M 11am-7:30pm, Tu-Su 8am-7:30pm. €2; non-EU students and EU seniors €1; EU students, under 19, and visitors with an Acropolis ticket free.)*

▧PHILOPAPPOS HILL. The Philopappos Hill, a lush respite from park-deprived Athens, is southwest of the Acropolis and is accessible from Apostolou Pavlou. Abundant trails, sheltered picnic areas, and a postcard-perfect view of the Parthenon make this a great place for afternoon exploration. A marble road weaves past **Agios Dimitrious,** where you're likely to stumble upon a church service in progress. According to legend, Dimitrious persuaded God to smite 17th-century Turkish invaders with lightning before they could harm the worshippers in this small, icon-filled church. Just before Ag. Dimitrious, a narrow path veers off to the left, toward a stone cave with iron bars. This nondescript opening was once, as a sign indicates, **Socrates's Prison;** a series of rooms was carved into the cliff face and later used to house treasures from the Acropolis during World War II. Farther up, toward the Acropolis, are the ruins of **Pnyx Hill,** where the Athenian Assembly once met, and the **Hill of the Nymphs,** which looks out on an ancient observatory.

The peak, where the marble **Monument of Philopappos** stands, has Athens's best view of the Acropolis. The angles and distance that render the view so breathtaking also made the Acropolis an easy target to the Venetians in 1687; it was from this peak that they shot the disastrous volley, accidentally detonating the Parthenon's gunpowder stores. The monument was erected between AD 114-116 in memory of Julius Antiochus Philopappos, a Roman dignitary who settled on the hill after being exiled from his home in the Near Eastern kingdom of Commagene.

HADRIAN'S LIBRARY. Just north of the Roman Agora, by the Monastiraki metro station, Hadrian's Library is situated around a large central courtyard. The library, originally built in AD 132, was damaged by a Herulian invasion in 267, then rebuilt from 407 to 412. The ruins of a 5th-century church, a 7th-century church, and a 12th-century cathedral sit on the same site. *(☎21032 49 350. Open M-F 8am-2pm. €2, students €1, EU students free.)*

ATHENS

XTENDED HAIR FAMILY

Before I left for Greece, my African-American beautician back in Manhattan promised me that the braids in my hair would last for "at least eight weeks." But since nearly everything falls apart when it's a record 41°C in Athens, my do suddenly became a don't in a mere 12.7 days. So I set out on a quest to find a black person in Greece who could re-braid my hair.

Though Greece is 98% Greek, I nonetheless spotted one black person during my first week in the country. But since she didn't speak English—and since her braids looked even more TLC-deprived than mine—I decided not to ask her for salon advice.

But then one morning when one of my braids completely unraveled, I got desperate: I marched out onto the main avenue, and I waited.

And waited.

And waited.

After 28 minutes, I actually saw another black person. I accosted her and cut straight to the point: "Where are all the black people in Greece?" In perfect English (halle-LOO-jah), the Senegalese woman explained that here were several black hair-braiding salons in a neighborhood called Kypseli—a central Athens neighborhood in which immigrant groups such as Poles, Albanians, and (bingo!) Africans have settled over the last several decades. She even sent me off with an extra hookup: She offered me the

BYZANTINE ATHENS

Hours vary. The best time to visit is 9-11am. Modest dress required.

Athens teems with places of worship. Sanctuaries pepper tiny streets, squeeze between modern buildings, and hide under porticos, their modest facades almost overwhelmed by modern architecture. Inside their doors, ornate, icon-filled rooms unfold, dimly lit and smelling of incense. If no service is in session (services usually Su morning and 6pm every evening), a recording of chanting may be playing.

Many historians see Constantine's establishment of a Christian empire in 324 BC as a death-knell for Classical culture. But the 11th- and 12th-century golden age of Byzantine art has left behind its own share of masterpieces—devotional mosaics, delicate icons, and cross-shaped domed buildings—many of which can be found on the streets of Athens. **Kapnikaria Church,** just below ground-level on Ermou and Kalamiotou, has typical Byzantine architecture; the frescoes inside are by a 20th-century painter, Photis Koruglou. Dedicated to the Virgin Mary, this church was built above the ruins of a temple to a female goddess, probably Athena or Demeter. (☎21032 24 462. Open M and W 8am-2pm, Tu and Th-F 8am-12:30pm and 5-7pm, Su 8-11:30am.) Down Mitropoleos from Syndagma, where the street intersects with Evangelistras and Pandrossou, are **Agios Eleftherios** and the **Mitropoli Cathedral,** still under construction after a recent earthquake. A frieze with the Attic calendar of feast days adorns the front facade. **Agia Apostoli,** which stands at the eastern edge of the Agora on Dioskouron and Polingnotou, dates from the early 11th century, making it one of Athens's oldest churches. White-walled **Metamorphosis,** on Theorias and Klepsidras, off Pritanou in Plaka, also was built in the 11th century, and was restored in 1956. Eleventh-century Russian Orthodox **Agia Triada,** a few blocks from Pl. Syndagma at Filellinon 21, is filled with silver angel icons. Farther on Filellinon is the **Sotira Lykodimou,** the largest medieval building in Athens, dating from 1031. Built as part of a Roman Catholic monastery, it is now a Russian Orthodox church. In **Ambelokipi,** north of Kolonaki next to Areos Park, Byzantine religiosity meets modern commercial development rather jarringly. Tiny **Panagitsa** (little Virgin) sits literally in the middle of Alexandros Hotel's driveway on T. Vassou, and 11th-century **Agioi Pantes** sleeps humbly at the back entrance of the Panathenaic stadium on A. Tsochas. The **Chapel of Saint George,** another small but elaborate structure, looms over Athens from the peak of Mt. Lycavittos, on top of a ruined temple to Zeus.

MODERN ATHENS

MOUNT LYCAVITTOS. From the peak of Mt. Lycavittos, the tallest of Athens's seven hills, visitors can see every inch of the city. A **funicular** rail (2min., every 10-30min. 9am-3pm, round-trip €5.50) travels to the top. The quaint **Chapel of Saint George,** with walls adorned with intricate religious murals, and a pricey restaurant crown the peak. Take your time appreciating the astounding 360° view that spans from the mountains over the Acropolis to the water. The colorful stadium seating of the Lycavittos Theater is 180° from the Acropolis. Using the Acropolis as a point of reference, the neighborhoods of Monastiraki, Omonia, and Exarhia are on your right. Continuing clockwise, you will see Areos Park behind the small circular patch of green that is Strefi, another of the seven hills. The eastern view gazes down onto more parks and Mt. Hymettus, and offers a glimpse of the Panathenaic Stadium, the National Garden, and the Temple of Olympian Zeus. *(A trail from the end of Loukianou in Kolonaki takes 15-20min. Hikers should bring water, watch out for cacti and slippery rocks, and not climb alone, especially at night.)*

PANATHENAIC STADIUM. Also known as the *Kallimarmaro* ("Pretty Marble"), the horseshoe-shaped Panathenaic Stadium is wedged between the National Gardens and the neighborhood of Pangrati, carved into a hill. The Byzantines destroyed the Classical stadium, but in 1895 its gleaming white marble was restored. The stadium was the site of the first modern Olympic Games in 1896 and was refurbished once again for 2004 games, where it served as the finish line for a marathon event that matched Phidippides's 490 BC route (see **Marathon,** p. 122). The stadium is known in the record books as the site of the most highly attended basketball game in history, with 60,000 spectators for a 1968 European League Final. Marble steles near the front honor Greece's gold and silver Olympic medalists. The stadium's history and sheer size make it worth a trip, but be warned that visitors no longer are permitted to walk past the fence that runs along its open end. *(On Vas. Konstantinou. From Syndagma, walk down Amalias 10min. to Vas Olgas and follow it to the left. Or take trolley #2, 4, or 11 from Syndagma. Free.)*

AROUND SYNDAGMA. Every hour on the hour around the clock, a small crowd of tourists assembles in front of the Parliament building to witness the ■**changing of the guard.** In precisely seven minutes, the *evzones* (guardsmen) on duty synchronize a series of jerky marionette moves that lead them away from their posts. Once new guards are in

phone number of a black beautician she called Lilly.

Moments later, I had Lilly on the phone. Within 48 hours, I was sashaying along the lively streets of Kypseli, marveling at the vibrant colors, animated conversations, and savory smells of ethnic cuisine in this enclave that reminded me of my own Harlem neighborhood.

As a longtime world traveler, I'd been in exactly such a hair dilemma before: several summers ago when I skedaddled over to Korea, I spent weeeeks trying to find the soul in Seoul. Back then, a gracious Nigerian woman rescued me from the frizzies. As it goes in Seoul, so it goes in Kypseli: the highly recommended Lilly actually outdid my regular Manhattan hair braider by a long shot. In less than two hours (and for a paltry €17), Lilly created 25 perfect rows of braids, which allowed some fresh (even if hot!) air to descend onto my scalp. For my remaining three weeks in the city, a whole new world of blacks—Kypseli braiders, mothers, sisters, and friends—became part of my extended hair family.

—Michelle Burford

place, an attendant hurriedly adjusts ruffled collars and stray hairs. Longer, more elaborate ceremonies take place on Sundays at 11am.

The ▨**National Gardens** sprawl serenely behind the Parliament building. Broad stripes of white gravel weave past patches of dense plant life, artificial ponds, and the occasional fallen column. A quiet refuge in the middle of Athens's busiest center, the gardens have shade and plenty of places to sit. Near the Zappeion, a building of exhibition and conference halls, are less natural diversions: an outdoor movie theater and a breezy patio restaurant. The park's dingy zoo is its least attractive (though perhaps most amusing) draw. A handful of ostriches wanders as peacocks flash their long wings at the stray dogs barking nearby.

OUTDOOR MARKETS. Athens's markets attract bargain-hunters, browsers, award-winning chefs, and a lot of *yiayias* (grandmothers dressed in widows' black). The ▨ **Flea Market,** adjacent to Pl. Monastiraki, is like a festive garage sale where old forks and teapots are sold alongside family heirlooms. Try to go on a Sunday, when the whole square is brought to life. *(Open M, W and Sa-Su 8am-8pm.)* **Varnakios,** the biggest outdoor food market in Athens, is on Athinas between Armodiou and Aristogeitonos. *(Open M-Th 6am-7pm, F-Sa 5am-8pm.)* Not for the faint of heart, the **meat market,** which closes at 3pm, overwhelms with the sights and smells of livers, kidneys, and skinned rabbits. Early risers can jostle with Athenian cooks for choice meats, fish, fruits, vegetables, breads, and cheeses. Roving farmers' markets, or *laikes,* pulsate throughout central Athens, stopping every morning to take over a *stenodthromos* (narrow street) in one particular neighborhood of the city. Other than following a trail of corn shucks and peanut shells, the best way to track them is to call the Athens office of **Laikes Agores,** Zoödochou Pigis 2-4 (☎ 21038 07 560).

NATIONAL CEMETERY. The National Cemetery in Pangrati is an impeccably maintained expanse of marble, cypress trees, and intricate tombs. Within its gates are the graves of politicians, actors, poets, and many others who died in Athens, from archaeologist **Heinrich Schliemann,** excavator of Troy and Mycenae, to **Melina Mercury,** the Greek film icon who starred in *Never on Sunday* before becoming the nation's Minister of Culture. There is a chapel on the main path where ceremonies are held. *(From Pl. Syndagma walk down Amalias for 15min. Turn left on Ath. Diakou, then walk across the intersection and down Anapavseos. ☎ 21092 36 118. Open daily in summer 8am-8pm; in winter 8am-6pm. Free. Modest dress required.)*

🏛 MUSEUMS

▨**NATIONAL ARCHAEOLOGICAL MUSEUM.** The National Archaeological Museum's collection consists almost exclusively of masterpieces. Countless spectacular objects trace the development of Greek art through its many periods. Heinrich Schliemann's golden Mask of Agamemnon (p. 146) shines brilliantly, though it actually belonged to a king who lived at least 300 years before the mythic Mycenaean leader. A female Cycladic statue stands as not only the most intact but the largest such sculpture to survive, topping 1.5m. Abundant *kouroi* from the 8th century BC onward lead toward the Classical bronze spear thrower who represents either Poseidon or Zeus. In the museum's lovely basement garden, mosaics and more sculptures line a cafe. *(Patission 44. Walk 20min. from Pl. Syndagma down Stadiou to Aiolou. Turn right onto Patission; or, take trolley #2, 4, 5, 9, 11, 15, or 18 from the uphill side of Syndagma or trolley #3 or 13 from the north side of Vas. Sofias. From the Victoria metro stop, walk straight to the 1st street, 28 Oktovriou; turn right and walk 5 blocks. ☎ 21082 17 717. Open Apr.-Oct. Tu-Su 8:30am-3pm; Nov.-Mar. M 10:30am-5pm, Tu-Su 8:30am-3pm. €7, students and EU seniors €3, EU students and under 19 free. No flash photography.)*

▨**BENAKI MUSEUM.** Over the course of his travels, philanthropist Antoine Benaki assembled a formidable collection of artwork and artifacts. They're now displayed (along with numerous additions) in his former home: a looming, white Neoclassical structure that is something of a masterpiece itself. Among the media represented are Neolithic, Classical, and Roman Period sculpture, Geometric pottery, traditional Greek costumes, and wonderfully recreated Byzantine period rooms. The museum also exhibits metalwork, jewelry, and paintings, which focus primarily on the Greek War of Independence. Check out the impressive and extensive gift shop before you leave. *(Vas. Sofias and Koumbari 1 in Kolonaki. ☎ 21036 71 000; www.benaki.gr. Open M, W, and F-Sa 9am-5pm, Th 9am-midnight, Su 9am-3pm. €6; seniors and adults with children €3; students with ISIC or university ID, teachers, and journalists free.)*

▨**BENAKI MUSEUM OF ISLAMIC ART.** Large glass windows, spotless marble staircases, and sparkling white walls give a newly minted sheen to this fabulous museum, which opened in 2005. Organized chronologically, brilliantly colored, well-preserved tiles, metalwork, and tapestries document the history of the Islamic world from the 12th to 18th centuries. The exhibit includes many examples of pottery and text with elegant Kufic inscriptions, as well as a marble reception room transported from a 17th-century Cairo mansion. The basement exhibits ruins as exciting as it is out of place: during the construction of the museum, builders discovered parts of the famed Themistoclean Wall, which the Greeks built in 478 BC to defend against Persian invaders. *(Ag. Asomaton 22 on Dipylou, in Psiri near the Thissiou metro. ☎ 21032 51 311; www.benaki.gr. Open Tu and Th-Su 9am-3pm, W 9am-9pm. €5, students and seniors €3. W free.)*

▨**BYZANTINE AND CHRISTIAN MUSEUM.** Within its newly renovated glass and marble interior, this well-organized museum documents the political, religious, and day-to-day aspects of life during the Byzantine Empire. Its collection of metalware, mosaics, sculpture, and painted icons presents Christianity in its earliest stages. One display describes the conversion of the Parthenon into the Church of Agia Sofia. Videos and photographs of the artifacts' original locations put them in context. *(Vas. Sofias 22. ☎ 21072 11 027. Open Tu-Su 8:30am-3pm. €4; students and seniors €2; EU students, under 18, disabled persons, families with 3 or more children, members of the Chamber of Fine Arts of Greece, military, and classicists free.)*

▨**POPULAR MUSICAL INSTRUMENTS MUSEUM.** This interactive museum is no place for silent contemplation. Audio headsets reproduce the music of the *kementzes* (bottle-shaped lyres) and *tsambouras* (goat-skin bagpipes) on display. Exhibits showcase antique instruments from the 18th, 19th, and 20th centuries. *(Diogenous 1-2 in Plaka. Going uphill on Pelopida, it's the door on your left just after you pass the Roman Agora. ☎ 21032 50 198. Open Tu and Th-Su 10am-2pm, W noon-6pm. Free.)*

GOULANDRIS MUSEUM OF CYCLADIC AND ANCIENT GREEK ART. This 19-year-old museum houses a collection of early Aegean art, ranging from 3000 BC to AD 300. Clay pots, painted amphoras, and pieces of jewelry fill the compact space. The celebrated marble Cycladic figurines, one of them almost life-size, are prized possessions. A glass corridor leads visitors to the extension, a recently renovated Neoclassical house that holds further information and temporary exhibitions. *(Neophytou Douka 4. Walk 10-15min. toward Kolonaki from Syndagma on Vas. Sofias; turn left on Neophytou Douka. ☎ 21072 28 321. Open M and W-F 10am-4pm, Su 10am-3pm. €5, seniors €2.50, ages 18-26 €1, archaeologists and archaeology students free with university pass.)*

NATIONAL GALLERY. The Gallery, also known as the "Alexander Soutzos Museum," traces Greek artists' experiments with Orientalism, Impressionism, Symbolism, Cubism, and more, from the 18th to the 21st centuries. Greece's War of Independence is memorialized in the ground floor's 19th-century portraits and other images. This floor also houses a handful of older paintings by masters from Italy, France, the Netherlands, and Spain, including several notable works by Domenikos Theotokopoulos, whose peers in late Renaissance Toledo found his Cretan origin notable enough to dub him "El Greco." The 2nd floor shows more conceptual contemporary works and has space for temporary exhibitions. *(Vas. Konstantinou 50, where Vas. Konstantinou meets Vas. Sofias by the Hilton. ☎ 21072 35 857 or 21072 35 937. Open M and W-Sa 9am-3pm, Su 10am-2pm; temporary exhibitions also open M and W 6-9pm. €6.50, students and seniors €3.50, under 12 free.)*

WAR MUSEUM. The War Museum, in a fittingly fortress-like building, documents Greece's martial history with weapons and uniforms from ancient times through the present. Newspaper clippings, letters from soldiers, flags, and photographs complement descriptions of battles. A small room contains artifacts from the extended conflict in Cyprus. The outside of the museum is guarded by tanks, cannons, and fighter jets that visitors can explore. *(Rizari 2, next to the Byzantine Museum, slightly off Vas. Sofias. ☎ 21072 52 974. Open Tu-Sa 9am-2pm, Su 9:30am-2pm. Free.)*

ILIAS LALAOUNIS JEWELRY MUSEUM. The site of this unusual museum was home to 20th-century Greek jeweler and goldsmith Lalaounis. He created masterpieces inspired by civilizations from the Byzantines to the Vikings, as well as by structures as basic as the web-like pattern formed by microscopic human cells. His designs are joined here by the gleaming adornments worn by people through the ages—"from prehistoric man to contemporary woman." Keep an eye out for handcrafters demonstrating ancient jewelry-making techniques. *(Kallisperi 12, south of the Acropolis. ☎ 21092 21 044. Open M and Th-Sa 9am-4pm, W 9am-9pm, Su 11am-4pm. €3, students and seniors €2.30. Free W 3-9pm, Sa 9-11am.)*

FOLK ART MUSEUM. For a crash course in Greek cultural history, visit this well-organized collection of traditional costumes, metalwork, ceramics, embroidery, and other art created outside the academy. One room, covered in murals by folk artist Theophilos Chatzimichael, has been transported intact from its original house. The informative, enchanting little museum also hosts temporary exhibitions. *(Kydatheneon 17, in Plaka. ☎ 21032 13 018. Open Tu-Su 10am-2pm. €2, students €1, EU students and children free.)*

FRISSIRAS MUSEUM OF CONTEMPORARY EUROPEAN PAINTING. This marvelously modern museum's location in the center of the Old City makes its white galleries and asymmetrical architecture still more striking. The collection rotates, and is comprised of contemporary painting that focuses on the human figure. The 2nd building, about 70m from the first, houses temporary exhibitions. *(Monis Asteriou 3 and 7, off Kydatheneon in Plaka. ☎ 21032 34 678; www.frissirasmuseum.com. Open W-F 10am-5pm, Sa-Su 11am-5pm. €6; AICA, groups of 4 or more, members of the Chamber of Arts, over 65, and under 25 €3; guides, members of ICOM, fine arts students, and disabled persons free.)*

JEWISH MUSEUM. This collection documents over two millennia of Jewish life in Greece with letters, costumes, photographs, religious items, and reconstructed spaces including the interior of Patras's old synagogue and a living room from the Ottoman period. The museum's fourth floor memorializes the tens of thousands of Greek Jews murdered by the Nazis and the resistance groups who fought to save them. An exhibit highlights the Jewish community of about 5000 living in Greece today. *(Nikis 39, in Plaka. ☎/fax 21032 25 582. Open M-F 9am-2:30pm, Su 10am-2pm. Library open Tu and Th 11am-1pm or by appointment. €5, students and seniors €3.)*

🄰 NIGHTLIFE

Many already exciting neighborhoods burst with life after dark. Quiet cafes become festive bars; restaurants vibrate with buzzing chatter and live music; outdoor theaters unlock their doors; people swarm around brilliantly illuminated ruins; and late-night clubgoers get the parties started. Athens offers an abundant array of unique entertainment, ranging from **movie screenings** in the National Gardens to live performances at the **Odeon of Herod Atticus** (☎21092 82 900; hellenicfestival.gr). The English-language monthly magazine *Inside Out* offers valuable information on events and festivals in Athens.

PLAKA

Locals avoid joining Acropolis-bound tourists during the day, but they flock to ancient sights at night. Enormous outdoor lights make most of the city's famous ruins visible from any modest hill. Before hitting the inviting bars below, join young Athenians wandering about the **Odeon** theater, hanging out in the **Acropolis,** or playing guitar and sharing beers on **Saint Paul's Rock.** You might catch the views from one of Athens's several outdoor rooftop movie theaters. **Cine Paris,** Kydatheneon 22 (☎21032 25 482), plays Hollywood films with Greek subtitles and sells movie posters. (Shows 8:45, 11:10pm. Tickets €7.30.) **Bretto's,** Kydatheneon 41 (☎21032 32 110), between Farmaki and Afroditis, serves almost exclusively local alcohol. Colorful bottles, giant barrels, and other ouzo paraphernalia line the walls of this one-room establishment, while mellow but upbeat crowds sample native drinks. (€2 per glass of sweet red wine; €5 per bottle. Open daily 10am-midnight.)

MONASTIRAKI AND PSIRI

The district's two neighborhoods follow opposite clocks. Just when the frenetic market roads of Monastiraki shut down for the day and silence finally reigns, the bar-heavy, club-speckled streets of Psiri awaken to prove their reputation as some of Athens's hippest and loudest.

🄰 **Soul,** Evripidou 65 (☎21033 10 907), in Psiri. Plays hip-hop, R&B, and dance music in a chic garden. Mixed drinks €7. Open May-Sept. M-Th and Su 9:30am-3:30am, F-Sa 9:30am-5am.

Bee, Miaouli 6 (☎21032 12 624), off Ermou at the corner of Miaouli and Themidos and a few blocks from the heart of Psiri. A hive of neon-colored plastic lights, Bee offers margaritas (€9.50) and other mixed drinks (€9) on a busy corner. Open M-Th 7pm-3am, F-Sa 7pm-6am.

Revekka, Miaouli 22 (☎21032 11 174), on Pl. Iroön, in the center of Psiri. This 2-fl. eclectic cafe-bar blossoms at night, when tables take over the sidewalk. Beer €2. Open daily 11am-3am.

EXARHIA

Exarhia is the student crowd's counterculture heaven. Energetic bars fill the streets, blasting music from jazz to death metal. *Athens News* has lists of movies played at the outdoor **Riviera Garden Art Cinema,** Valtetsiou 46 (€7, students €5).

🄰 **Wunderbar,** Themistokleous 80 (☎21038 18 577), on Pl. Exarhia. Local DJs spin pop and some electronic music. Star-shaped paper lanterns decorate the interior, while late-night revelers lounge under large umbrellas outside. Beer €5-6. Mixed drinks €8-9. Open M-Th 9am-3am, F-Su 9am-sunrise.

Rock Underground, Metaxa 21 (☎21038 22 019). Punky teenagers enjoy the immortal pairing of heavy-metal headbanging and backgammon in this smoky, brick-walled hangout. The sign out front mimics the logo of London's Tube system, hinting at the slightly British flavor of this cafe-bar. Beer €2-5. Mixed drinks €5. Open daily 10am-3am.

Train, Em. Benaki 72 (☎21038 44 355). High ceilings, bright walls, and scrumptious apple pie (€5) make this inviting cafe-bar a fave with the locals. Classic rock, pop, and reggae. Mixed drinks €7. Open daily 10am-2am.

KOLONAKI

Millioni and the eastern end of **Haritos** are the hottest spots for summertime action as long as you're prepared to shell out euro. At **City, Azul, Baila,** and **Le Souk,** all at Haritos 43, patrons drink beer (€5-6) and mixed drinks (€8-10) on tables that spill into the pedestrian-only street. Performances are staged in Lycavittos Theater as part of the **Athens Festival,** which has hosted acts from the Greek Orchestra to Pavarotti to the Talking Heads. In summer, open-air **Dexameni "CineFrame"** cinema, in the center of Pl. Dexameni at the foot of Mt. Lycavittos, plays Greek and American movies with surround sound. (☎21036 02 363. Shows daily 8:45, 11pm. €7, students €5, children under 5 free.) **Athinaia "Refresh"** cinemas, Haritos 50, is another nearby movie theater. (☎21072 15 717. Shows 9pm and 11pm. €6.50.)

Flower, Dorylaou 2 (☎21064 32 111), in Pl. Mavili. An intimate little dive, Flower offers drinks and snacks in a casual, mellow setting. Additional seating outside in the square. Shots €3. Mixed drinks €5. Open daily 7pm-late.

The Daily, Xenokratous 47 (☎21072 23 430), is under a trellis at the foot of Mt. Lycavittos. TVs show sports games at this cozy cafe-bar. Open-air seating in summer. Pints of Heineken €4, 0.5L €6. Mixed drinks €6-10. Open daily 8am-2am.

Cafe 48, Karneadou 48 (☎21072 52 434), 3 blocks down Ploutarchou from Haritos. Take a left on Karneadou and walk to the end of the block. This pink-walled, diner-like cafe-bar plays American music. Beer €3-4. Open daily 7am-midnight.

Briki, Dorylaou 6 (☎21064 52 380), in Pl. Mavili next to Flower, is a tiny bar with mod geometric-patterned lights and hanging decorations. Mixed drinks €8.50. Appetizers €3. Open daily 8am-4am, Sa-Su 8am-late.

PANGRATI

Where **Imitou** meets **Eftihidou,** clear plastic bungalow-like seating areas cluster in front of each cafe, offering pleasant spots for a coffee or mixed drink. **Village Cinemas,** Imitou 110, on the third floor of the Millennium Centre mall, shows the latest blockbusters in five state-of-the-art theaters. (☎21075 72 400. Call for listings and times.) **Ellas Espresso,** Pl. Plastira 8, which claims to be the oldest cafe in Athens, plays pop and Greek music in a shaded terrace and indoor bar with four TVs. (☎21075 62 565. Frappés €4. Open daily 9am-3am.)

■ DAYTRIPS FROM ATHENS

■ CAPE SOUNION PENINSULA Ακρωτήριο Σούνιο ☎22920

Orange-striped KTEL buses go to Cape Sounion from Athens. 1 leaves from the Mavroma-teon 14 bus stop (near Areos Park, on Alexandras and 28 Oktovriou-Patission) and stops at all points on the Apollo Coast (2hr., every hr. 6:30am-6pm, €5). The other follows a less scenic inland route that also stops at the port of Lavrio (2¼hr., every hr. 6am-6pm, €4). The last coastal bus leaves Sounion at 9pm, the last inland at 9:30pm.

A tiny tourist colony rests atop the sharp cliff of Cape Sounion, where in 600 BC ancient Greeks built the enormous ■ **Temple of Poseidon** in gleaming white marble. Legend holds that King Aegeus of Athens leapt to his death from these cliffs when he saw his son Theseus's ship sporting a black sail—a sign of his son's demise.

Unfortunately for Aegeus, Theseus was on board getting drunk with his sailing buddies and had forgotten to raise the victorious sail. Today, visitors flock to the area to see the 16 Doric temples that remain from Pericles's reconstruction in 440 BC. Hundreds of names are scribbled into the monumental structure; look closely for Lord Byron's on the square column as you face away from the cafeteria. Across the street 500m below is the somewhat deteriorated **Temple of Athena Sounias.** (Both temples ☎39 363. Open daily 10am-sunset except on Christmas, Easter, and May 1. €4, students and seniors over 65 €2, EU students and children under 18 free. Nov.-Mar. Su free.) The Cape has a handful of attractive beaches and hotels, down the inland side of the temple. Teeming with vacationing families, the beaches along the Apollo Coast between Piraeus and Cape Sounion have a carnival atmosphere on summer weekends. Towns often have free public beaches and, despite the area's crowds, some seaside stretches along the bus route remain uncrowded. Drivers will let you off almost anywhere if you ask. If you stay here, **Camping Bacchus ❶**, 50m toward Lavrio from Saron, is a decent option. Ask to stay by the entrance to avoid loud family caravans. The site has a bar, restaurant, laundry, and mini-mart. (☎39 572. €7.50 per person, €6.50 per tent. Tent rental €10.) Next to the bus station, **Cafe Naos ❶** more than redeems its unspectacular food with one of the best views in Attica. While eating, diners can gaze at the temple and over the Aegean. (Salami sandwich €2.80. Open daily 9am-after sunset.)

MOUNT PARNITHA

Bus #714 (Sa-Su 6:30am, 2:30pm; €0.65) leaves from Acharnon off Stounari, in a parking lot near Vathis Square. It's best to buy a ticket at a metro station or kiosk in advance; few places in the vicinity sell them, especially in the morning.

When the bus lets you off at the majestic peak of Mt. Parnitha, about 1hr. outside Athens, you will see, of all things, the tastelessly glitzy **Mont Parnes casino** (☎21024 69 111; open daily at 9am) and the **cable car** (every 30min. 8:30am-3pm, every 10min. after 3pm; €1.20) that takes you there. Luckily, this decidedly unnatural wonder is a lone intrusion, and there is still a vast national park to explore. Its many trails feel a world away from the city, though few are far from public transportation and well-equipped rest stops. The 19th Parnitha station, a few meters from Hotel-Chalet Kyklaminia and the **Tradia Chapel,** is a good place for hikers to begin; several trails start behind the kiosk. At the fork in the road toward Athens, a map with Greek labels marks paths uphill away from Mont Parnes. Hikes of varying levels of difficulty will lead you along paved roads, gravel paths, and narrow trails to **Skipiza Spring,** the **Caves of Pan,** and ▨ **Bafi Refuge ❶** (Μπάφι), a hostel and cafeteria with a beautiful lookout point and detailed trail maps. (☎21021 69 050. Beds €12.) To reach Bafi, turn uphill away from the casino at the fork in the road 0.5km below the casino. Follow signs to the white gravel path until trails diverge at a quarry-like ravine. From there, follow red markings past a small patch of steep rock after about 15min. and continue for another 10min. It's a fairly easy hike of about 3km. The bugs are particularly audacious, so insect repellent is a necessity.

GLYFADA AND THE COAST

Buses A2, A3, and B2 leave from Vas. Amalias and travel along the coastline on Poseidonos (30-40min., €0.90). The spotless, air-conditioned tram (€0.60) leaves from the same place every 8min. until midnight and is uninterrupted by traffic.

Stretching along the sea from Faliro to Sounion, Glyfada has become synonymous with swanky clubs and crowded beaches. Glyfada Town is a densely packed commercial center that teems with designer shops and a wide array of ethnic cuisine. Both ▨tram and bus hug the sea as they head from Athens to Glyfada, so you can scope out the **beaches** just beyond the stops named after them. The closest, **Edem,**

Batis, and **Kalamaki,** are less than pristine, but they charge no admission. Kalamaki in particular is known for its loud music and drunken, dancing masses. For a slightly quieter but still well-attended shore, head to Batis. Beyond Platas Glyfadas toward suburbs **Vouliagmeni** and **Varkiza,** beaches are cleaner and more secluded. Entrance fees of €5-10 often include use of pools and bungalows.

With beach views and hipster crowds, the clubs of Glyfada have earned their hot rep. They tend to be expensive, but cabs of trendy Athenians still flock here nightly. **Balux,** Vas. Georgiou B58 in Glyfada (☎21089 41 620), **Mao** (☎21089 44 048; pool open during the day €8), on Diadohou Paulou in Glyfada, and **Island** (☎21096 53 563), on Limanakia Vouliagmeni in Vouliagmeni, are three colorful, beachside options. Also look for **Prime** and **Envy.** Cover is usually €10-15, and club-wear is expected (i.e., no shorts). Drinks typically range €6-12 but can go as high as €100 for a bottle of vodka and mixers for your table. Envy and Mao are accessible by tram, but the best bet for most clubs is to call a **taxi** (☎21096 05 600). A cab to Glyfada should cost about €8, but traffic and nighttime charges can make rates swell to €10-15. Ask the price in advance; if your cab is packed with more than just your party, don't be swindled into a set price per individual.

Most daytime activity in Glyfada Town is on **Lazaraki** and **Metaxa,** both parallel to the nighttime strip that runs down the coast. Restaurants line Konstantinopoleos, including **Sushi Bar ❸,** Konstantinopoleos 15, on a breezy veranda. (☎21089 42 200. Sushi rolls €7-9. Open daily 12:30pm-12:30am. MC/V.) **San Marzano ❷,** Konstantinopoleos 13, serves Italian classics. (☎21096 81 124. Margherita pizza €6.60. Open daily 1pm-1am. AmEx/MC/V.) **Garden of Eden ❸,** Zerva 12, is a block from Hotel Ilion away from the center. Lebanese dishes like *makdous* (baby eggplant stuffed with walnuts and spices; €3.50) and *kas-kas* (meatballs in spicy tomato sauce; €8) are accented by stained-glass windows and hookahs. (Open daily 8:30pm-midnight. MC/V.)

On the Third Marina (toward the beach from tram stop Paleo Demarhio, opposite the church) is a **Sea Turtle Rescue Center,** where visitors can walk around pools that contain injured turtles rescued in Greece. Located inside old train cars, the center is Athens's only turtle hospital. The staff is eager to offer information and readily accepts volunteers. (☎21089 82 600. Open daily 5-8pm.)

MARATHON Μαραθώνας ☎22940

The bus from the Mavromateon 29 station in Athens goes to Marathon (1½hr., every hr. 5:30am-10:30pm, €4.10). Look for the "Marathon" label and remind the driver of your destination. When returning to Athens, look for an orange-striped bus among scores of tourist-tour ones, and flag it down. A car or taxi (☎66 277) is the best way to see the sights; they are spread out and there is often no public transportation.

Near the end of the Persian Wars in 490 BC, an overjoyed messenger ran 42km (26¼ mi.) from here to bring his fellow Athenians two words: "Νίκη ήμιν!" ("Victory to us!"). Though **Phidippides** collapsed and died of fatigue immediately afterward (this last 42km followed a grueling 450km the week before), his feat of endurance has made the town of Marathon's name a household word. In addition to the countless marathon races across the globe, runners today trace Phidippides's famous route twice annually here, where it all started. To tour Marathon and the surrounding area, most people find themselves taxis or cars; others go straight to Marathon beach and stay there. At **Ramnous,** 15km northeast, lie the ruins of the **Temple of Nemesis,** goddess of divine retribution, and **Thetis,** goddess of justice. (☎63 477. Open Tu-Su 8:30am-7pm. €3. Su free.) To reach the **Archaeological Museum of Marathonas** it's best to call a taxi, but if you're up for a walk, ask the bus driver to drop you at the "Mouseion and Marathonas" sign, after Marathon Town and the beach. Follow the signs through 2km of farms, bearing right at the fork, to the end of the paved Plateion road at #114. As you might expect, the museum highlights the pivotal battle against Persia that occurred here. An atrium displays the **Athenian trophy,** as well as gifts and slabs from tombs of the 192 Athenians who died in battle. The exhibits also include a collection of **Egyptian-style statues,** which wear Pharaoh costumes and symbols of control over Lower and Upper Egypt. Some 4th-century Greeks re-appropriated artistic traditions originally used for worshiping the Egyptian goddess Isis to create images for their cult of Demeter. Also on the museum grounds is a **burial site,** uncovered by archaeologist Spyros Marinatos in 1970. A wooden walkway surrounds the spooky mound of rocks, where visitors can peer through glass planks to see the remains of ancient skeletons buried there from 2000-1600 BC. The grassy **Tomb of the Fallen,** where the war victims from 490 BC are buried, is 15km from the town, behind the mountains and accessible only by private transport. (☎55 155. Open Tu-Su 8:30am-3pm. €3; students €2; EU students, children under 18, classicists, and archaeologists free.) Marathon beach also has an extensive, multi-building movie theater, **Village Cool Cinema,** 1-3 Tymbos, off Eleftherias. It plays mainstream English-language films with Greek subtitles nightly at 9 and 11:15pm. (☎55 603. Tickets €7.)

Marathon beach, a slightly hectic seaside town, is a nicer place to dine or stay than central Marathon. Some tavernas are set along the beach, and businesses center on the small plateia. **Marathon Hotel ❹,** Ag. Pantalimonos 25, 50m before the plateia on the road coming from Athens, has rooms with air-conditioning, TV, fridge, balcony, and bath. (☎55 222. Breakfast included. Singles €40; doubles €55; triples €65; quads €75.) Beachside taverna **O Vrahos ❷,** Chrisis Aktis 14, is a few buildings to the right of the plateia. (☎55 297. Calamari €8. Fresh fish €20-60 per kg. Open daily noon-1am.) **Avlaia ❷,** Poseidonos 7, on the beach, is a few doors down to the left of the plateia. (☎56 300. Spicy cheese dip €4. Fried fish €7.50.) A **supermarket** is inland from the plateia on Dimosthenous. (Open daily 8:30am-10pm.)

ELEUSIS Ελευσίνα ☎21055

Take bus A16 or B16 from Pl. Eleftherias in Athens (also called "Pl. Koumoundourou"); purchase tickets at adjacent kiosks. Buses take 45min.-1hr. and leave every 20min. ☎43 470. €3, students and seniors €2, EU students free. Open Tu-Su 8:30am-3pm. To find the ruins from the bus stop in Elefsina, follow signs, look for Odos and Dimitros streets, or walk toward the Greek flag on top of the Eleusinian acropolis.

Though the gritty industrial town Elefsina doesn't seem to have much in the way of secrets, revealing the details of the cult worship that took place here

MARATHON MADNESS

Lace up your Nikes for an event that draws thousands to Greece every winter: the Athens Classic Marathon. Circa 490 BC, messenger Phidippides cemented his place in posterity when he high-tailed it all the way from Marathon to Athens on foot—approximately 42.195 km, or 26¼ mi.—to proclaim the demise of the Persian forces with his last breath. The race, which includes everyone from schoolgirls to senior citizens, starts in Marathon and culminates in Athens' palatial Panathenaic Stadium—the place where the first modern Olympics were held. The stadium, which seats over 60,000, was built during Lykourgos's reign, around 330 BC. It was then thrice restored, most recently by Georgios Averof, who dished out 4 million drachmas in gold to renovate the grand area for the Olympic games on April 5, 1896.

Fear not, all ye faint of form: If your calves aren't quite up to the arduous 26 mi., you can join the hordes who gather to cheer contestants toward a triumphant finish. The event, held in October or November each year, is open to participants of all ages and fitness levels.

For information on entry fees, the date of this year's race, and online registration, call ☎21093 31 113 or 21093 15 886 or visit www.athensclassicmarathon.gr. Email info@athensclassicmarathon.

ATHENS

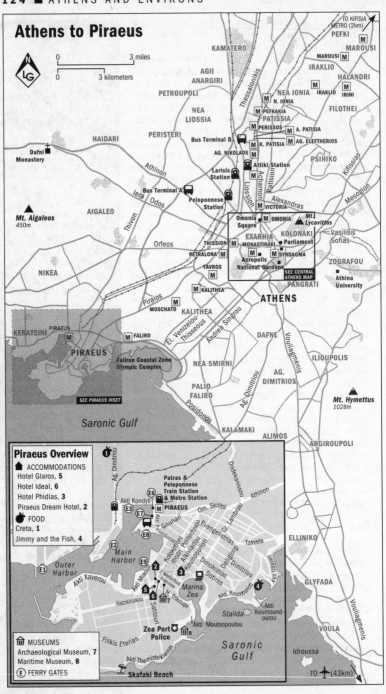

Athens to Piraeus

0 — 3 miles
0 — 3 kilometers

TO KIFISIA
METRO (2km)
PEFKI
MAROUSI Ⓜ
KAMATERO
MAROUSI Ⓜ
IRAKLIO
AGII
ANARGIRI
NEA IONIA Ⓜ
IRAKLIO Ⓜ IRINI
HALANDRI
PETROUPOLI
N. IONIA Ⓜ
NEA
LIOSSIA
PEFKAKIA
PATISSIA
FILOTHEI
PERISTERI
PERISSOS Ⓜ
A. PATISIA Ⓜ
HAIDARI
Bus Terminal B
AG. NIKOLAOS
K. PATISIA Ⓜ AG. ELEFTHERIOS
Dafni
Monastery
Larisis
Station
Attiki Station
PSIHIKO
Athinon
Bus Terminal A
 Peloponnese
Station
VICTORIA
Alexandras
Mt. Aigaleos
450m
AIGALEO
Iera Odos
Omonia
Square Ⓜ OMONIA
EXARHIA
Mt.
Lycavittos
Vasilisis
Sofias
Thivon
Orfeos
THISSION Ⓜ MONASTIRAKI
KOLONAKI
Parliament
SYNDAGMA
ZOGRAFOU
PETRALONA Ⓜ
Acropolis
TAVROS
National Gardens
SEE CENTRAL
ATHENS MAP
Athina
University
NIKEA
Piraios
MOSCHATO Ⓜ
KALITHEA Ⓜ
PANGRATI
ATHENS
KALITHEA
PIRAEUS
KERATSINI
Ⓜ
PIRAEUS Ⓜ FALIRO
DAFNE
Vouliagmenis
PIRAEUS
Faliron Coastal Zone
Olympic Complex
NEA SMIRNI
ILIOUPOLIS
SEE PIRAEUS INSET
PALIO
FALIRO
Posidonos
AG.
DIMITRIOS
Mt. Hymettus
1028m
Saronic Gulf
KALAMAKI
ALIMOS
ARGIROUPOLI

Piraeus Overview

🏠 ACCOMMODATIONS
Hotel Glaros, 5
Hotel Ideal, 6
Hotel Phidias, 3
Piraeus Dream Hotel, 2
🍎 FOOD
Creta, 1
Jimmy and the Fish, 4

🏛 MUSEUMS
Archaeological Museum, 7
Maritime Museum, 8
Ⓔ FERRY GATES

Patras &
Peloponnese
Train Station
& Metro Station
PIRAEUS
Akti Kondyli
Main
Harbor
Outer
Harbor
Marina
Zea
Akti Koundourou
Stalida
Akti
Koumoundourou
Zea Port
Police
Akti Moutsopoulou
Skafaki Beach
Saronic
Gulf
Idroussa
VOULA
TO ✈ (43km)

used to be punishable by death. When **Hades** abducted her daughter **Persephone,** harvest goddess **Demeter** was traumatized enough to begin inflicting the ravages of the four seasons on the earth. Here, myth holds, she found solace in the kindness of Eleusinians. In honor of the saga, countless ancients took part in a secretive nine-day ritual here each year, from Mycenaean times to AD 400. Initiates were rumored to have seen the darkest truths of life and death, and modern historians have speculated that gory sacrifices and powerful hallucinogens were involved in the rites. Ever since Roman Emperor Theodosius put an end to the pagan celebration, though, the precise components of the Eleusinian rites have remained unknown—just as Demeter's priests would have wanted it.

Today, fallen columns and crumbled arches mark the hill where the rituals took place. Brochures available at the ticket office provide a detailed blueprint of the original layout, and the **museum** houses two miniature plaster models. Despite the curators' best intentions, however, the ancient structures are unrecognizable. Years of erosion and attack have reduced the once-monumental acropolis to a sprawl of expansive, indistinguishable ruins; the intriguing history surrounding them can be appreciated without actually visiting the site itself.

KIFISIA Κηφισιά ☎ 21080

Things haven't changed much since the shady pine trees of this quiet, posh suburb drew Athenian aristocrats during Roman times. A large, manicured park and pristine marble streets lie 12km north of the city—just a few stops on the metro, but a wealthy world away from urban Athens.

⊟ ⚡ TRANSPORTATION AND PRACTICAL INFORMATION. Kifisia is best reached by rail but is also accessible by bus. Take **M1,** the **green line,** all the way to the last stop (30min., daily 5am-12:30am, €0.90). You also can take either the **A7** or **B7 bus** (30min., €0.60) from Akademias and Themistokleous in Omonia. **Taxis** (☎ 21062 33 100 or 21062 80 84 000) are available 24hr.

Kifisia has a large concentration of banks downtown. **Eurobank,** Kifisias 271, **exchanges currency** and traveler's checks. (Open M-Th 8am-2:30pm, F 8am-2pm.) **Citibank,** Levidou 16, also has a **24hr. ATM.** (Open M-Th 8:30am-2:30pm, F 8:30am-2pm). **Eleftheroudakis Bookstore,** Kifisias 268, offers a few English titles amid mostly Greek-language books. (Open M-F 9am-9pm, Sa 9am-5pm. AmEx/MC/V.) The **police,** Othonos 94, are near the Natural History Museum. (☎ 21062 34 450. 24hr. assistance ☎ 171. Open daily 8am-1:30pm.) Dial ☎ 166 for an **ambulance.** The **OTE** is at Papadiamanti 8. (☎ 21062 32 899. Open M and W 7:30am-3pm, Tu and Th-F 7:30am-8pm, Sa 8am-3pm.) The **post office,** Levidou 3a, set in a mini-square off the sidewalk, accepts **Poste Restante.** (☎ 17 665. Open M-F 7:30am-2pm.) **Postal Code:** 14503.

⌂ ⧉ ACCOMMODATIONS AND FOOD. If you're looking to slim down your wallet, Kifisia's hotels will be glad to help; otherwise, don't bother staying here. One comparatively modest option is **Hotel des Roses ❺,** Militiadou 4, just off Kyriazi. Rooms have air-conditioning, TV, fridge, bath, and a view of the hills. (☎ 19 952. Breakfast included. Singles €75-85; doubles €90-110.)

Food in Kifisia is more budget-friendly. At **Yo Sushi ❷,** Kifisias 238-240, sushi standbys such as salmon sashimi (€5.50), tuna maki (€6), and edamame (€3.50) are served on the outdoor terrace. (☎ 21062 32 346; http://yosushi.gr. Open daily 1pm-1am.) **Dos Hermanos ❸,** Kyriazi 24, serves excellent Mexican fare. (☎ 87 906. Mexican omelette €10. Chili con carne €14.50. Open Tu-Su 7pm-1am; in winter Tu-Sa 7pm-1am, Su 1pm-1am. MC/V.) **Pappa's Restaurant ❷,** Kifisias 222 and Drosini 3, makes spaghetti Neapolitana (€4), chicken with mustard sauce (€7.10), and a variety of pizzas (€6-9) in a huge, air-conditioned expanse. (☎ 18 463. Open daily noon-1am. AmEx/MC/V.) Kifisia also has many affordable take-out options, including the kiosks and cafes within or near the park. ☒ **Varsos ❶,** Kassaveti 5, is a factory-like dessert complex. Famous apricot-custard tarts (€3) and brioche (€1.20) have made this *patisserie* a classic. (☎12 472. Open M-F 7am-1am, Sa 7am-2am, Su 7am-midnight.) Another dessert option is **Crepes Kifisia ❶.** (☎21062 31 371. Most crepes under €4. Open M-Th and Su 11am-4am, F-Sa 11am-late.) **AB Supermarket,** on the corner of Levidou and Kassaveti, has an extensive selection for the picnic-bound. (☎82 812. Open M-F 8am-9pm, Sa 8am-6pm. AmEx/MC/V.)

◑ ♫ SIGHTS AND ENTERTAINMENT. The **Goulandris Museum of Natural History,** Levidou 13, has taxidermied birds and mammals native to Greece, as well as displays of insect, reptile, mollusk, and plant biology. A room dedicated to geology features a collection of minerals along with a few Jurassic bones and fossils. (☎15 870. Open M-Th and Sa-Su 9am-2pm. Closed Aug. 1-18. €4, students and children 5-18 €1.50, children under 5 free.) The **Gaia Center,** Othonos 100, is around the corner and filled with multimedia exhibits on ecological systems. Unfortunately, the lack of English labels reduces it to a soothing display of bells and whistles for a non-Greek speaker. (Open M-Th and Sa-Su 9am-2:30pm. €4.50, children €1.50.)

Cine Boubouniera, on the corner of Papadiamanti and Levidou, shows English-language movies in an outdoor garden during the summer. (Ticket office open daily 8:50am-noon. €7.) The **Bowling Center,** Kolokotroni 1, is a popular nighttime destination. (☎84 662. Game of bowling or 30min. billiards M-Th and Su €2-4, F-Sa €4-5.30. Beer €2. Mixed drinks €4-6. Open daily 10am-2am.) If you stay late you'll find some popular suburban bars including **Big Deals,** 50 H. Trikoupi. (☎21062 30 860. Mixed drinks €9-10. Open M-Th and Su 8pm-3:30am, F-Sa 8pm-later.)

PIRAEUS Πειραιάς   ☎21041

The natural harbor of Piraeus has been Athens's port since 493 BC, when Themistocles created a naval base for the growing Athenian fleet. A hilly peninsula studded with big apartment buildings, Piraeus is one of the busiest ports in the world. Though its charms may not be immediately obvious, Piraeus does have trendy shops, orange trees, and plenty of outdoor park space. Sprinkled among the fast-food joints and traffic are hip bars, coffee shops, and Internet cafes, where young people congregate in festive, noisy throngs.

▮ TRANSPORTATION

Most **ferries** circling Greece run from Piraeus. Unfortunately, the ferry schedule changes on a daily basis; the following listings are only approximate. Be flexible with your plans. Check *Athens News* and the back of the *Kathimerini* English edition or stop by a travel agency for updated schedules. Ferries sail directly to nearly all major Greek islands, except for the Sporades and Ionians. Until recently, there were five gates, organized by letter; now, gates are organized by number, all preceded by the prefix "E". Ferries for the Dodecanese leave from gate **E1.** For Chios and Lesvos, ferries depart from gate **E2.** For Crete, go to **E3.** Ferries for the Cyclades leave from **E7,** and ferries for the Saronic Gulf leave from **E8.** For Ikaria and Samos, ferries leave from **E9.** To: Aegina (1¼hr., every hr., €7.50); Amorgos (10hr., 5 per week, €24.50); Anafi (11hr., 3-4 per week, €26); Astypalea (10hr., 3 per week, €32); Chios (9hr., 1-2 per day, €22.30); Donousa (7hr., 2 per week, €20); Folegandros (9hr., 4 per week, €20); Hania, Crete (11hr., 1-2 per day, €22); Hydra (3¼hr., 2 per day, €9); Ikaria (8hr., 1-2 per day, €20); Ios (7½hr., 3 per day, €22); Iraklia (7hr., 3-4 per week, €22); Iraklion, Crete (11hr., 1-3 per day, €24); Kalymnos (12hr., 5 per day, €35.50); Kimolos (6½hr., daily, €19); Kithnos (3hr., 1-2 per day, €13); Kos (13½hr., 1-2 per day, €36); Koufonisia (8hr., 1 per week, €21); Leros (10hr., daily, €31); Lesvos (12hr., daily, €26); Limnos (18hr., 3 per week, €27); Milos (7hr., 1-2 per day, €20); Mykonos (6hr., 2-4 per day, €20); Naxos (6hr., 5-7 per day, €24); Paros (5hr., 4-7 per day, €24); Patmos (8hr., €30); Poros (2½hr., 5 per day, €10); Rethymno, Crete (11hr., 3 per week, €24); Rhodes (14hr., 2-5 per day, €43); Samos (10hr., €27); Santorini (9hr., 3-5 per day, €28); Schinousa (8hr., 2 per week, €23.10); Serifos (5hr., 1-2 per day, €15.20); Sifnos (6hr., 1-2 per day, €18); Sikinos (8hr., 4 per week, €26); Spetses (4hr., €12); Syros (4hr., 2-3 per day, €15); Tinos (5hr., 2 per day, €22.20). International ferries (2 per day, around €30) head to destinations in Turkey. **Hydrofoils** leave from the port of Zea and go to: Aegina (every hr.); Amorgos (1 per week); Hydra (6 per day); Ikaria (3 per week); Ios (6 per week); Kithnos (5 per day); Milos (1-2 per day); Mykonos (2-4 per day); Naxos (1-3 per day); Paros (1-4 per day); Poros (6 per day); Samos (2 per week); Santorini (daily); Serifos (6 per week); Sifnos (1-2 per day); Spetses (6 per day); Syros (2-4 per day); Tinos (2-4 per day). The **#96 bus** shuttles to and from the airport every 30min. (€3). Pick it up across from Fillipis Tours on Akti Tzelepi. The **#40** goes between Syndagma and Piraeus (every 15min. 5am-12:45am, €0.45). To get to Piraeus from Athens by **metro**, take the **M1** (green) line **Kifisia/Piraeus** to the last stop (20min., €0.70). The metro station is on Akti Poseidonos.

◢⁊ ORIENTATION AND PRACTICAL INFORMATION

Piraeus can seem chaotic and confusing, but there is a method to the madness. A free shuttle takes travelers from the metro to gate E1 every 15min. The large, busy street running alongside **Akti Miaouli** and **Akti Kondyli** is **Akti Poseidonos**. The hydrofoil port is on the other side of the peninsula, a 10min. walk along any of the streets running inland off Akti Miaouli.

Budget Travel: Most ticket agencies can be found on Akti Tzelepi and Akti Poseidonos. Bypass them for the extremely helpful ▧ **Fillipis Tours,** Akti Tzelepi 3 (☎21041 17 787 or 33 182). From the metro, go left and walk 200m until you come to Pl. Karaiskaki. Walk toward the water; it's on the left side of the cluster of offices, near ferry departure gate E8. They sell ferry and plane tickets, help with accommodations, store baggage for free, and rent cars. Open daily 5:30am-11pm.

Banks: Most banks along the waterfront **exchange currency. Citibank,** Akti Miaouli 47-49 (☎21092 93 000), has **ATMs.** Open M-Th 8am-2:30pm, F 8am-2pm.

Laundromat: Hionati Laundry, Bouboulinas 50 (☎21042 97 356), in Zea. €4 per kg. Open M-F 8am-2pm and 5-9pm, Sa 8am-3pm.

Emergency: Call the Athens **police** at ☎100 or an **ambulance** at ☎166. The **port police** (☎21042 26 000) are on Akti Tzelepi in the mirrored building. **Zea** has separate port police (☎21045 93 144) on the water. The **tourist police** can be reached at ☎171.

Telephones: OTE, Dimitriou 19. Open M, W, Sa 7:30am-3:30pm, Tu and Th-F 7:30am-7:30pm.

Internet Access: LaserNet (☎21041 29 905), in Kenari Square on Port Zea. A large dim room with a bar brimming with cyber junkies. €1 per hr. Open 24hr.

Post Office: The **main branch** (☎21041 71 5184) is on Tsamadou, a few blocks from Polytechniou. Open M-F 7:30am-8pm. **Postal Code:** 18501.

⎚ ◖ ACCOMMODATIONS AND FOOD

Inexpensive, quality accommodations are much more difficult to find in Piraeus than in Athens. **Pireaus Dream ❹,** on Notara Street a few blocks over from the E9 and E10 ferry gates, has stylishly decorated rooms, some of which overlook the bay. (☎21042 96 160. Breakfast included. Free Wi-Fi. Singles €55; doubles €65; triples €80.) Also on Notara St., **Hotel Ideal ❹** offers immaculate rooms with bath, TV, and air-conditioning. (Singles €50; doubles €65; triples €70.) Hotel Ideal's sister property, **Hotel Glaros ❹** (☎21042 94 050), just off Akti Miaouli, is a less glamorous but still adequate option for the same price. Pleasant, quiet **Hotel Phidias ❹**, Koundouriotou 189, between Bouboulinas and 2 Merarhias, offers spacious rooms with large bath, TV, and air-conditioning. (☎21042 96 160. Breakfast €7.50. Singles €50; doubles €60; triples €70; quads €80. MC/V.)

For a souvlaki spot still undiscovered by tourists, stop in at **Creta ❷** on Ag. Dimitrou. Walk left from the E3 ferry gates; after 200m, turn right at the church. The beef kebab (€7) and the meatless gyros (€2.50) are among the best choices. (☎21041 24 417. Open daily 10am-3am.) Inviting but pricey restaurants line the waterfront around Microlimano, the small bay to the south of the main port. If you're looking to splurge, join the swanky diners of **Jimmy and the Fish ❹**, Akti Koumoundorou 46. (☎21041 24 417. Mussels with tomato sauce and parmesan €13. Saffron risotto with porcini mushrooms €19. Strawberry soup with ice cream €7. Open daily 12:30pm-1am. AmEx/MC/V.) Bakeries and breadshops are a tasty, thrifty, and speedy dining alternative. Several **supermarkets** also are available, including one at 2 Merarhias and Karaiskou. (Open M-F 8am-9pm, Sa 8am-6pm.)

🔘 SIGHTS

The prized possession of the **Piraeus Archaeological Museum,** H. Trikoupi 31, is the second floor's **Piraeus Apollo,** a hulking hollow bronze figure with outstretched arms. A huge grave monument consisting of three statues—the deceased, his father, and his slave—dated to about 330 BC, is across the hall as you walk in. Found on the Black Sea coast, the monument once was painted in full color. Three other bronze statues of Athena and Artemis were found near the port in 1959; they had been shelved in a storeroom for safekeeping when Sulla besieged Piraeus in 86 BC. The strange spots of color in their eyes are precious stones. (☎21045 21 598. Open Tu-Su 8:30am-3pm. €4, students €2, children under 16 free.) Farther south at Zea, the ramp to the dock at Akti Themistokleous and Botassi leads to the **Hellenic Maritime Museum,** which traces naval history using detailed ship models. Inside its main entrance, the building includes part of the 5th-century Themistoclean wall, which protected the three ancient ports of Kantharos, Munychia, and Zea. Of particular note is a model of an Athenian *trireme* used in the Persian Wars; it is on display in Room B. The courtyard holds torpedo tubes, naval weapons, and part of a WWII submarine. (☎21045 16 264. Open Tu-Sa 9am-2pm. €3, children and students €1.50.)

RAFINA Ραφήνα ☎22940

Attica's second-most prominent port, Rafina can be thought of as a smaller, quieter version of Piraeus. Though ferry service from Rafina is not as frequent as service from Piraeus, departure frequency recently has increased, and prices can be as much as 10% cheaper. Compared to its larger counterpart, there's less to do in Rafina, but it's easier on the eyes, ears, and lungs.

Don't stay in Rafina unless you're stuck here, since it's boring and expensive. Down from the plateia overlooking the water, **Avra Hotel ❹** boasts decked-out rooms with air-conditioning, TV, phone, bath, and hair dryer. The hotel has both a restaurant and a bar. (☎22 780. Breakfast included. Singles, doubles, and triples €70-130.) **Hotel Corali ❹**, Pl. Plastira 11, rents standard rooms with bath, fridge, TV, air-conditioning, and phone. (☎22 477, owner's home 28 900. Singles €40-70; doubles €60-100; triples €70-120; quads €80-140.) For superb camping facilities, travel 2km to **Camping Kokkino Limanaki ❶**. (☎31 604; www.athenscamping.com. Tent rental €6.50. Huts €23-26.) Head right at the top of the ramp, right again at the end of the blue fence, then follow the coast to reach a waterfront lined with cafes, pizzerias, and tavernas. **O Vrahos ❸,** Vas. Pavlou 1, is toward the water on the left. The family that owns the taverna catches the fish they serve daily. (☎25 912. Mussels with rice €14.50. Open daily 11am-midnight.) Early ferry-catchers can try **Fournos tis Plateias ❶,** a bakery on the right side of the plateia facing the water. (☎26 083. Fresh bread €0.70. Various croissants from €1.40. Open daily 6:30am-11pm.) A **mini-mart** sells fruits, vegetables, and toiletries off Pl. Plastira, around the corner from the bakery. (Open daily 8am-2pm and 5-10pm.)

From Rafina, **ferries** go to: Andros (2hr., 5-6 per day, €10.50); Marmari, Evia (50min., 5-8 per day, €9); Mykonos (5hr., 4-6 per day, €16); Paros (1-2 per day, €21); Syros (2 per week, €14.10); Tinos (4hr., 5-6 per day, €15.50). **Flying Dolphins** zip daily to: Mykonos (1½hr., €30); Paros (€34); Syros (€23.40); Tinos (€27). The **port authority** (☎22 300) supplies info on ferry times, which fluctuate weekly and even daily, especially during high season. Along the waterfront, **Blue Star Ferries** (☎23 561), **Rafina Tours** (☎22 700), and **Hellas Flying Dolphins** (☎22 292) sell tickets for ferries and catamarans. (All open daily 6am-9pm.) **Taxis** (☎23 101) line up in front of the plateia. Both the **Commercial Bank,** two blocks inland from the plateia (☎25 184; open M-Th 8am-2:30pm, F 8am-2pm), and **Alpha Bank** (☎24 159; open M-Th 8am-2:30pm, F 8am-2pm), one block beyond the far left corner of the plateia, **exchange currency** and have **24hr. ATMs.** The waterfront also has 24hr. ATMs. Reach the **police** at ☎22 100 and the **port police** at ☎28 888. There is a **pharmacy** one block to the right of the plateia's right inland corner. (☎23 456. Open M-F 8:30am-2pm, Tu and Th-F 8:30am-2pm and 5:30-9pm.) For a **doctor,** call ☎22 633 or 28 428. In a **medical emergency,** dial ☎166. The **OTE** is in the unmarked building inland from the plateia, beside the church. (☎25 182. Open M-F 7:30am-3pm.) Facing inland at the dock, the **post office** is two streets to the right on El. Venizelou. **Postal Code:** 19009.

ATHENS

PELOPONNESE
Πελοπόννησος

Stretching its fingers into the Mediterranean, the Peloponnese transports its visitors to another time through its rich history and folklore. The achievements of ancient civilizations dot the peninsula's landscape, as most of Greece's significant archaeological sites—including Olympia, Mycenae, Messini, Corinth, Mystras, and Epidavros—rest in this former home of King Pelops. Breathtaking scenery, from the barren crags of Mani to the forested peaks and flower-blanketed pastures of Arcadia, imbues the land with astonishingly timeless natural beauty. Away from large, urban transportation hubs, the serene, sparsely populated mountain and seaside villages welcome visitors to traditional Greek living at its best.

 SUGGESTED ITINERARIES: PELOPONNESE

THREE DAYS Stay in picturesque **Nafplion** (p. 141), and take daytrips from there to the pre-Classical palace at **Mycenae** (p. 146) and the acoustically perfect theater at **Epidavros** (p. 148). On your last day, relax in the sleepy mountainside villages of **Dimitsana** (p. 171) or **Stemnitsa** (p. 174).

ONE WEEK After a couple of days at the ancient sites around **Nafplion**, swing westward through the idyllic towns of **Arcadia** (p. 169), then take a few laps around the stadium when you reach **Olympia** (p. 163). A final weekend in **Patras** (p. 150), a modern college town, will bring you back to the urban world.

CORINTHIA Κορινθία AND ARGOLIS Αργολίδα

Legend holds that Argos, a monster endowed with 100 unblinking eyes, once stalked the northern Peloponnese, subduing unruly satyrs and burly bulls. While these creatures have left no tangible evidence behind, the region's ruins of stone temples and fortresses reveal the spirit of the great cities of the ancient past—Mycenae, Corinth, and Argos—that once competed for control of land and sea. The bustling ports hearken back to a day when merchants peddled simpler wares, while in secluded mountainside villages a traditional, relaxed way of life survives. A new suburban line providing fast and cheap rail service from Argos and Corinth directly to Athens's international airport shows how the region has grown more connected to the Greek capital and the world beyond. Nafplion makes a good base for exploration, since this city, with its majestic Venetian architecture, allows for easy access to Epidavros, Mycenae, Corinth, and other destinations.

NEW CORINTH Κόρινθος   ☎27410

For the last few millennia, life in Corinth has been about location, location, location. The ancient city was a bustling commercial crossroads, doing business from its position on the isthmus separating the Peloponnese from the Greek mainland.

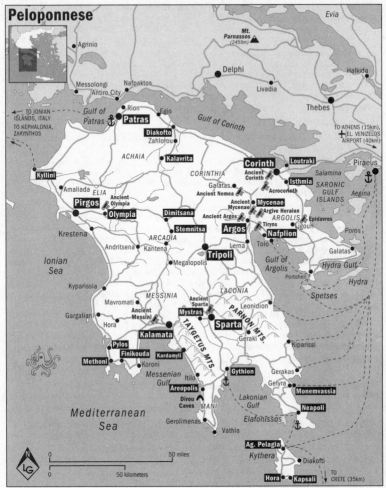

Peloponnese

Evia

Agrinio

Mt. Parnassos (2459m) ▲

Delphi

Halkida

Messolongi Nafpaktos
Antiro City *Livadia*

Rion Egio
Gulf of Patras **Patras** Thebes

TO IONIAN ISLANDS, ITALY
TO KEPHALONIA, ZAKYNTHOS

Diakofto
Zahlorou

Gulf of Corinth

TO ATHENS (15km),
✈ EL. VENIZELOS
AIRPORT (40km)

ACHAIA **Kalavrita**

Corinth **Loutraki**
Ancient Corinth Piraeus

Kyllini *CORINTHIA* Salamina ⚓

Galatas **Isthmia** SARONIC GULF ISLANDS

Amaliada *ELIA* Ancient Nemea Acrocorinth Aegina

Pirgos Ancient Olympia Ancient Mycenae **Mycenae** ARGOLIS
Argive Heraion **Epidavros**

Olympia **Dimitsana** Ancient Arges Ancient Tiryns Ligouri

Krestena **Stemnitsa** **Argos** Poros

ARCADIA **Nafplion** Galatas

Andritsena Karitena Lerna Tolo

Ionian Sea Megalopolis **Tripoli** Gulf of Argolis Hydra Gulf

Portoheli Hydra

Kyparissia *LACONIA* Spetses

MESSINIA Leonidion

Mavromati Ancient Sparta

Gargaliani Ancient Messini **Mystras** PARNON MTS.

Hora **Sparta**

Geraki Kiparissi

Kalamata TAYGETOS MTS.

Pylos

Finikouda **Kardamyli** Gerakas

Methoni Koroni Gefyra

Messenian Gulf Itilo **Gythion** ⚓

Areopolis **Monemvassia**

Dirou Caves *MANI* Lakonian Gulf **Neapoli**

Gerolimenas *Elafonissos*

Vathia

Mediterranean Sea

Ag. Pelagia

Kythera Diakofti

TO CRETE (35km)

Hora • **Kapsali**

0 ____ 50 miles
0 ____ 50 kilometers

The business of the modern city reflects how Corinth still exists as a gateway to southwestern Greece. Fast food, designer shops, and ATMs all cater to the crowds of people that flood the streets in the late morning and evening, making this small town feel as if it's bursting with activity. In the colder months, energy mostly centers in the downtown area, but in summer the focus shifts to Kalamia beach.

▣ TRANSPORTATION

Trains: There are 2 train stations in greater Corinth. The 1st is the older station right in town with service mainly to the larger towns of the Peloponnese. The 2nd can be reached by taxi (€3). It offers fast service to Athens, the airport, and Argos.

In-town station: ☎ 22 522 on Dimokratias, off Damaskinou. There are more expensive express trains to the most popular locations. One major train line heads along the northern coast to: **Dia-**

kofto (regular: 1¼hr., 5 per day 7:30am-7:30pm, €2.10. Express: 1hr.; 1:30, 5:30pm; €4.70); **Kyparissia** (regular: 5hr., 9:30am, €6.80. Express: 4hr.; 1:30, 5:30pm; €7.50); **Pirgos** (regular: 4½hr., 9:30am, €4.70. Express: 3½hr.; 1:30pm, 5:30pm; €5.60). Additionally, free trains take people from the in-town station to the new station (6 per day 8:00am-8:00pm).

Outside-town station: off Argous Ave. about 2km away from town. On foot, walk out the car exit of the parking lot and make a left on the highway, passing a stadium on your left and continuing straight until the road becomes Eth. Antistaseos, New Corinth's main street. A bus takes people into town as well. Trains go to: **Athens International Airport** (1¼hr., every 2hr. 7am-9pm, €8); **Athens** (1hr., every 2hr. 6am-10pm, €6); **Argos** and **Kalamata.**

Buses: There are 3 bus stations in town offering service to the surrounding regions and the Peloponnese.

Station A: ☎ 75 424, across the street from the train station on Dimokratias. Buses run to **Athens** (1½hr.; every 30min. 5am-9pm; €7, €12 round-trip).

Station B: ☎ 75 425. Walking inland on Eth. Antistasis, turn right on Koliatsou, halfway through the park; the station terminal is outside a bakery, on the corner of Koliatsou and Kolokotroni. Buy tickets on the bus. To **Ancient Corinth** (20min., every 30min. 6:10am-9:10pm, €1.20). Check the station for other destinations.

Argolis Station: Nafplion or Mycenae routes ☎ 24 403; Isthmia, Nemea, Loutraki routes ☎ 25 645, at the intersection of Eth. Antistaseois and Aratou, 1 block past the park. The station has two counters, each serving different destinations. The 1st counter on the right as you enter off Eth. Antistaseois serves: **Ag. Vasileio** (40min., 1:30pm, €2.40); **Athikia** (30min., 8 per day 9am-8pm, €1.80); **Hiliomodi** (20min., 11 per day 7:30am-9:20pm, €1.80); **Isthmia** (15min., 5 per day 9:40am-4:30pm, €1.20); **Katakali** (30min., 2pm, €2.30); **Klenia** (40min., 4 per day 9:30am-2:30pm, €2); **Korfos** (1hr.; 1:30pm, 5pm; €4.30); **Loutraki** (20min., every 30min. 5am-10pm, €1.60); **Nemea** (1hr., 7 per day 7:30am-9:20pm, €4.10); **Sofiko** (15min., 9 per day 7:15am-9:50pm, €3.20) via **Almiri** (€1.70), **Loutra** (€1.50), and **Xilokeriza** (€1.20); **Spathovouni** (30min., 12:20pm, €2.60). The counter in the back sells tickets to: **Argos** (1hr.; 7am, 2:30pm; €4), **Mycenae** (45min.; 7am, 2:30pm; €3.10) via **Fihtia,** and **Nafplion** (1½hr.; 7am, 2:30pm; €5). To get to Sparta or other points south, take the Loutraki bus to the stop 200m before the Corinth Canal and take the Athens bus to **Sparta, Kalamata, Koroni,** or **Tripoli.** These destinations also can be reached from the bus station southeast of town on the Circular Road, a.k.a Old Motorway. A taxi there costs €3.

Taxis: ☎ 73 000. Along Eth. Antistaseos, in front of the park and the Court of Justice.

✦ ? ORIENTATION AND PRACTICAL INFORMATION

The streets of New Corinth are organized in a grid. The main street, **Eth. Antistaseos,** runs from the marina inland. New Corinth hugs the curving coastline with **Ieratiki** and **Kalamia** beaches to the right as you look away from the water of the marina. **Ermou,** the central walkway, and **Kolokotroni** run parallel to Eth. Antistaseos, on the left and right respectively as you look away from the waterfront. All three intersect **Damaskinou,** which runs along the harbor. Most of the town's shops, restaurants, and hotels are found on these four streets. Two blocks inland from the shore, between Eth. Antistaseos and Ermou, is the city's central **park.** Opposite the park on Eth. Antistaseos stands the **Court of Justice,** where taxis line up. Bus station A and the train station are a few blocks southeast down Damaskinou from the marina. To find the harbor from the train station, turn left onto Dimokratias, then take the first right. Much of New Corinth's nightlife centers on **Kalamia beach.** To reach it, walk along downtown's other main street, **Koliatsou** (perpendicular to Eth. Antistaseos on either side of the park) from the left of the Court of Justice to **Ap. Pavlou,** the third street parallel and to the right of Eth. Antistaseos as you look inland. Take Ap. Pavlou inland, then make a right on **Notara** after the beautiful St. Paul Cathedral to reach the beach.

Tourist Office: Ermou 51 (☎ 23 282, emergencies 23 100). Serves mainly as the **tourist police,** and employees happily provide maps, brochures, and assistance. Some English spoken. Open daily 8am-2pm.

Banks: National Bank, Eth. Antistaseos 7 (☎23 934), 1 block up from the waterfront. Offers **currency exchange** and a **24hr. ATM.** Many banks with these services are within a few blocks of Eth. Antistaseos. Open M-Th 8am-2:30pm, F 8am-2pm.

Public Toilets: Across from the park on Eth. Antistaseos. Open daily 7am-10pm.

Police: Ermou 51 (☎81 100), across the park from the courthouse. Emergencies ☎100. Open 24hr.

Pharmacies: Many on Eth. Antistaseos, Koliatsou, and Ermou. Typically open M-F 8am-2pm and 5-8pm.

Hospital: ☎25 711, on Athinaion. Cross the train tracks and turn left; it's about 5-6 blocks from the train station. **Ambulance:** ☎166. Open 24hr.

Internet Access: Diadiktio (☎75 265), 20m down Damaskinou from Eth. Antistaseos with the water on your right. Internet €1.50 per hr. Coffee €2.30. Open daily 24hr. 8am-2am. **GNET,** 62 Ap. Pavlou (☎73 500), on the right side toward Notara and Kalamia beach. Offers modern machines and comfortable chairs. Internet €2 per hr. Coke €1.10. Coffee €2.50. Sandwiches €2.50-3. Open 24hr.

Post Office: Adimantou 35 (☎80 050 / 24 122), facing the park, between Eth. Antistaseos and Ermou. Open M-F 7:30am-5pm. **Postal Code:** 20100.

ACCOMMODATIONS

New Corinth's hotels, found mainly along Eth. Antistaseos and Damaskinou, offer generic, clean rooms for generally affordable prices. Campgrounds can be quite a distance from the city, making catching an early bus difficult.

Hotel Apollon, Damaskinou 2 (☎25 920). On the corner one block away from the in-town train station. Features TV, A/C, and Internet access (€1 per hr.) in modern, recently renovated rooms. Breakfast €7. Singles €35; doubles €45; triples €50; prices reduced in low season. Reservations recommended. ❹

Hotel Akti, Eth. Antistaseos 1 (☎23 337). Offers the best choice for the budget traveler downtown. Expect small and sparse, but clean rooms. The friendly owners, who are willing to bargain, make Hotel Akti a popular place for thrifty backpackers. Singles €20; doubles €35. Cash only. ❷

Hotel Ephira, Eth. Antistaseos 52 (☎22 434; www.ephirahotel.gr), between downtown and Kalamia Beach. Recently renovated, the hotel has a garden and a large dining room. Each room comes with TV, A/C, and phone and is neatly appointed, if small. Breakfast €5. Singles €55; doubles €65; triples €75; suites €150. MC/V. ❹

Blue Dolphin, on Lecheon beach (☎25 766; www.camping-blue-dolphin.gr), 6km outside downtown Corinth, 3.5km from Acrocorinth. The tourist-friendly campground offers both rooms and camping facilities. At the on-site restaurant and bar, the owners invite guests to wake up with bread and milk (€2) or relax with ice cream (€0.90-2). Buses leave for Lecheon beach every 30min. on weekdays (6am-10pm) and every hour on weekends (7am-10pm) from the Terminal A bus stop, though the campground's stop is on the main road, a short walk from the site. Kitchen and laundry facilities. Check-out 1pm. Camping €6.50 per person; singles €15; doubles €22. Tents also available to rent (€10 per person). Parking and electricity extra. Discounts available for cruise customers and large groups—call ahead. ❶

FOOD

After 9pm, the harbor perks up as residents flock to the waterfront to dine outdoors in the balmy evening air. Because fast, generic, and cheap food abounds in New Corinth, visitors often find themselves deciding where, not what, to eat. Stroll past the tavernas on Damaskinou by the waterfront plateia or down the pedestrian street Pilarinou for meat and fish specialties. For tavernas with beautiful oceanic views, walk down to Kalamia beach and meander along Meg. Alexandrou, the pedestrian path that parallels the breaking surf.

Arodo (☎71 500), on the corner of Meg. Alexandrou and Palama. Family-run establishment serves lunch and dinner on a spacious, comfortable deck inside and out. Try your hand at pronouncing and enjoying the *kolokithokeftedes* (cheese and zucchini croquettes; €3.50) or any of the day's fresh fish (€40-70 per kg). If you crave a specific type of fish or lobster not on the menu, call the day before and Arodo will buy and prepare it fresh for you—as long as you tell him to do so in Greek. Open daily 9am-1am. ❸

Verde (☎83 555), at the far end of the pedestrian walkway on the corner of Pigasou street. Serves fast food. In addition to low prices and instant gratification, there are burgers (€2.30-3.30) and a Greek take on a fried chicken platter (€5) among other selections. Open daily noon-1am. Delivery available. ❶

Allegro, Damaskinou 41 (☎28 361), on the corner. One of the few tavernas open for breakfast. Offers indoor and outdoor seating as well as a view of the waterfront. Hamburgers are served for €2.50, and the well-stocked bar will satisfy any thirst. Entrees €1.50-4. Beer and ouzo €2. Open daily 7am-2am. ❶

Neon Cafe (☎84 950), at the corner of Damaskinou and Eth. Antistaseos. Delights patrons with its prime real estate and giant glass windows that overlook the harbor. This modern cafeteria serves Greek coffee (€1.80) and mixed drinks, along with a selection of entrees (€5.50-9) and cheap snacks. Open daily 8am-1am. ❷

▮ NIGHTLIFE

Corinth can't boast much crazy clubbing after sunset, but for bars and late-night socializing, head to Kalamia Beach, where late-night crowds frequent the beachside establishments on the Mediterranean surf. Corinthians young and old are drawn to the pedestrian path of Meg. Alexandrou, which runs for about 300 restaurant-and-bar-lined yards paralleling the sea and offers views of the sparkling lights of the Corinthian coast all the way to Kiato. **Tango Bar,** at the far end of the beach, stays open far into the evening with an amicable staff, some of whom speak English fluently, and delicious drinks. Two or three times a month during the summer, the bar brings in "famous" DJs from Athens on Fridays or Sundays. Look for advertising posters in the window and around town. (Beer €3-5. Mixed drinks €6-7. Open M-F until 3:30am, F-Sa all night.) Other area bars include **XPose, Breeze,** and **Cafe-Bar Rescue. Freedom Music Bar** resides on the beach side of the walk, with a deck extending to the water's edge that sometimes tempts partiers into taking a moonlight swim. (Beer €5. Mixed drinks €6. Open until 3am.) For those seeking late-night dessert and a relaxed atmosphere, **Cafe Mon Ami,** midway down the path on the corner of Sina Street, offers many coffee drinks (Greek coffee €2, cappuccino €2.90) and desserts such as cheesecake, ice cream, and apple pie (€1.50-3.30). The scene quiets down near the cafes along Pilarinou, where you can enjoy an early evening drink in relative peace.

▮ DAYTRIPS FROM CORINTH

ANCIENT CORINTH Αρχαία Κόρινθος
Ancient Corinth is 7km southwest of New Corinth. Buses leave from Koliatsou and Kolokotroni (20min.; every 30min. 6:10am-9:10pm, return buses leave every hr. at half past; €1.20). ☎27410 31 207. Open daily 8:00am-7:30pm. Site map €2.50. Guidebooks €6. Site and museum €6, students €3, EU students and under 18 free. Every Su from Nov.-Mar., last weekends of Apr., May, June, and Sept., and major holidays free.

Ancient Corinth's opulent wealth and risqué delights were anything but old-fashioned. Prosperous merchants stopped by here to line their pockets and mingle with **hetairai,** famously clever courtesans in the service of Aphrodite. But don't go looking for their pleasure palaces: what remains of the Classical world's Sin City is buried beneath the ruins of the settlement the Romans built after sacking Corinth. Today, remnants of the Greek and Roman cities stand side by side.

ANCIENT SITE. The remains of the ancient Roman city stand with the older Greek ruins at the base of the Acrocorinth against a scenic mountain-and-ocean backdrop. As you enter, on the left you will notice the **Fountain of Glauke,** named after Jason the Argonaut's second wife, the daughter of Creon, King of Corinth. After Medea, Jason's seriously bitter ex, gave her a poisoned cloak, Glauke jumped into the fountain, trying in vain to stop the burning. Beyond you will notice the seven breathtaking original columns from the **Temple of Apollo** that defiantly have endured the trials of time since the 6th century BC. A walk around the side of the temple reveals that these remains are but a small portion of a long building that was supported by 38 columns. Standing on the other side of the temple, the **forum,** the center of Roman civil life, opens before you. Without a guidebook, it might be difficult to gain anything from these remains other than an impression of simply how skilled ancient Corinthian and Roman artisans and craftsmen were. A plaque in the forum indicates the **Julian Basilica,** which served as a courthouse and once held statues of the family of Julius Caesar.

To the left, near the exit at the edge of the site farthest from the museum, a broad stone stairway, unfortunately barred to visitors, descends into the **Peirene Fountain.** Once standing over 20 ft. tall, the fountain still has flowing water; the columns and fresco-covered tunnels inside the fountain survived the centuries unharmed. One creation myth claims that Peirene was the daughter of the river god Asopus. When Cenchrias, one of her sons with Poseidon, was killed by Artemis, she shed endless tears and became the spring. Just past the fountain is the **Perivolos of Apollo,** an open-air court surrounded by still more columns.

ARCHAEOLOGICAL MUSEUM. Accessible from within the site itself, the museum traces Corinth's history through Greek, Roman, and Byzantine rule. It proudly showcases an impressive collection of repaired statues, such as those from the Julian Basilica (27 BC-AD 4), statues of Augustus Caesar and his family, and tiny clay figurines dating back to the Neolithic Period. The expansive array of ancient works in the permanent exhibit ranges from a 6th-century BC marble statue of a sphinx to a series of restored mosaics from a nearby ancient Roman villa. Check out the Roman frescoes and mosaics and chart the changes in Greek pottery techniques from the Neolithic to Byzantine times. The museum's collections of sarcophagi and headless and limbless statues in the open-air courtyard are morbidly appealing. A guidebook might be worthwhile, as the museum's explanations are sparse.

▊FORTRESS AND ACROCORINTH. The Acrocorinth is located a steep 3.5km uphill from the museum. Emerging from the crags and ridges of the massif is the fortress built in the 10th century; its walls encircle the ruins of buildings from the 14th to 18th centuries. Those who want to experience the entire fortress should head past the first three gates and toward the summit. Here, where sacred *hetairai* once initiated disciples into the "mysteries of love" (read: ▊**crazy sex acts**) at Aphrodite's altar, and where Jason's flying horse, Pegasus, quenched its thirst, only a small chapel to St. Dimitrios remains. The dazzling view of Corinthia, however, makes a trip to the Acrocorinth wholly satisfying—even for the less historically inclined. Venture around the rest of the relatively empty fortress, which contains acres of towers, mosques, gates, and walls. Don't forget sturdy shoes, sunscreen, and water (bottles available at the cafe by the parking lot for €0.50); be careful on the rocks—they're slippery even when dry. *(The easiest way up the acro-*

THE FOURTH NEMEAD

Have you ever wanted to be an Olympic athlete, but couldn't fathom the hours of training and grueling devotion to a particular sport? If so, then maybe the Nemean Games are for you.

Nemeophytes—youthful lovers of Nemea—remember the city's ancient position as a host site of pan-Hellenic festivals held every four years regardless of intercity conflicts. However, the world chose to name the international games after one of Nemea's rival cities; Olympia also played host to the games, along with Delphi and Isthmia. In 1996, Nemea's dreams of recognition and historical significance came to fruition, and the Nemead was born.

Having successfully orchestrated the games in 2000 and 2004, the Society for the Revival of the Nemead (with over 12,200 members worldwide) would now like to invite you to come and participate in the festivities. Athletes enter the grounds through the ancient tunnel to the cheers of picnickers on the hillside and compete in barefoot races inside the ancient stadium. Winners receive the time-honored headband and palm frond symbolizing victory, as well as the prized celery crown.

The 2008 games are scheduled for June 21-22. For more information, call ☎ 510-642-5314 (US), or go online to www.nemeagames.gr or www.nemea.org.

corinth is by taxi from the center of the village of Ancient Corinth (€7); taxis will wait at the top of the acrocorinth to drive you back down (€15). The walk up the hill takes a little over an hour and can be confusing at times. Open daily 8:30am-7pm.)

ANCIENT NEMEA Αρχαία Νεμέα

The ancient site is 5km from modern Nemea. Take the bus from Corinth (45min.-1hr., 7 per day, €4.10) and ask to be let off at the ancient site. ☎ 27460 22 739. Museum, site, and stadium open daily 8:30am-7:30pm. Try to go earlier in the day, as catching a bus back can be difficult. Site and stadium €4, students and seniors €2, EU students and under 18 free.

Ancient Nemea might never have been excavated if a disastrous series of earthquakes in the 1880s hadn't led to construction and digging near the site. Today, the ruins are a refreshing silver lining for those feeling overwhelmed by the more commercialized ancient sites in Corinth. A spacious and well-maintained museum proudly displays the history of both the site and its excavation with a sizable collection of coins, tools, and statuettes, while at the same time putting it in context with the surrounding ancient sites. Excellent explanatory notes and videos in English help convey the historical significance of an area that once held the **Temple of Nemean Zeus**. Outside, seven massive columns stand starkly against the mountainous backdrop, though a few are not original. Visitors are greeted by an encased skeleton from an early Christian tomb, and can explore an ancient bathing chamber. Self-guided tours of the stadium, 200m up the road to the left, allow visitors to occupy the very track that once hosted Panhellenic contests linked with those at nearby Isthmia, Delphi, and Olympia.

ISTHMIA Ισθμία

The bus from New Corinth picks up from Terminal C at the station (15-20min., 5 per day 9:40am-4:30pm, €1.20). Ask to be let off at the museum, or get off at the Isthmia stop. Go straight 1km, turn right for 300m, and then turn left on the uphill road; the museum is on the right. Alternatively, take a taxi from Corinth (€6).

Held every other year during the springtime Festival of Poseidon, the Isthmian games attracted the best athletes from all of Hellas to compete in a series of contests. According to legend the games grew out of funeral rites hosted by Sisyphus for the child-hero Melikertes, in whose honor the champions donned pine and laurel crowns. Today little of the hillside site remains, save the foundation of the **Temple of Poseidon** and the **Later Stadium** used for the contests, both of which are open to the public. The adjacent **museum** (☎ 27410 37 244) holds a humble collection of artifacts like the glass opus sectile and 87 mosaic panels from the temple of Isis, which miraculously survived an earthquake at Kenchreai in AD 375.

LOUTRAKI Λουτράκι　　　　　　　　　　☎27440

In ancient times travelers came to Loutraki for its natural springs, which were said to have medicinal powers. Centuries later, while the springs still run a brisk business, the town's main draws are the Club Hotel Casino Loutraki and a gorgeous boardwalk along the pebbled-beach waterfront. With a relaxed atmosphere and crowded waterside bars, the town caters to locals and international visitors alike.

▐ TRANSPORTATION. The KTEL **bus station** is located at a triangular road island where Eleftheriou Venizelou, the main street, meets Periandrou and Iasonos. (☎83 000.) **Buses** leave the station for Athens (1½ hr., 8 per day 6am-9pm, €7.50) and Corinth (25min.; M-F every 30min. 5:30am-9:30pm, service reduced Sa-Su; €1.20). To reach Isthmia and the Corinth Canal, take the Corinth bus and get off just over the canal near the train station. **Boat excursions** are available at the dock past the park, including the **M/Y Alpha II** night cruise, which sails along the promenade. (☎21 937. Departs nightly at 8:30pm. €7.) **Taxis**, available 24hr., stop by the stand next to the tourist info kiosk on El. Venizelou. (☎61 000.) To rent a car, try the **Hertz** up the road at G. Lekka 12b. (☎62 950. Open M-Sa 9am-1pm and 6-9pm.) Or support the local **Ajax Rent-a-Car** nearby at G. Lekka 16. (☎22 062. Open daily 9am-9pm.)

▐▐ ORIENTATION AND PRACTICAL INFORMATION. Running parallel to the water, El. Venizelou curves away from Corinth at the northern end of the strip and becomes **Giorgiou Lekka**. The change from El. Venizelou to G. Lekka marks Loutraki's central square, but most of the tourist activity is located along the beach boardwalk and on El. Venizelou.

Loutraki has two **tourist information kiosks,** both of which provide maps for €3 and a helpful free guidebook. One is located on El. Venizelou, four blocks south of the bus station; the other is after the curve at the central plateia on G. Lekka, at the end of the town park. (Both open daily 9am-1pm and 5:30-9:30pm.) The friendly **Municipal Enterprise for Tourism** office, in the central square, can tell you about water parks, scuba diving, horseback riding, bike tours, and cruises. (☎26 001; www.loutraki.gr. Open M-F 8am-2pm.) To get to the **National Bank,** which has a **24hr. ATM,** follow El. Venizelou, with the water on your left, to the central plateia. (☎22 220. Open M-F 8am-2pm.) The fourth side street on the right coming from the bus inland (with the water on your left) is home to **SIC Laundry Service,** Lekka 3. (☎63 854. Wash and dry €12 per 4kg. Open M, W, Sa 8:30am-2pm, Tu, Th-F 8:30am-1:30pm and 5:30-8:30pm.) The **police** and the **tourist police** are in the same building, about 3km south of downtown Loutraki on El. Venizelou and the first left after the athletic stadium. (☎63 000. Open 24hr.) One of several **pharmacies** is at El. Venizelou 21. (☎22 334. Open daily 9am-2pm, Tu and Th-Su also 6pm-9pm.) The **hospital** is roughly a 30min. walk from the center of town; head five blocks up from El. Venizelou on Hatzopoulou, across from the information kiosk; follow the signs by turning right on Karaiskaki and continue straight for three blocks. (☎26 666. Open 24hr.) The **OTE**, which sells cell phones, is at El. Venizelou 10, on the left as you walk from the bus station with the water on your left. (☎61 999. Open M and W 7:30am-3pm, Tu and Th-F 7:30am-8pm, Sa 9am-3pm.) **Las Vegas Internet Cafe,** El. Venizelou 40, just past the information kiosk, offers **Internet access** as well as a pool table and bar. (☎69 397. €3 per hr., 15min. minimum. Open daily 8am-1:30am.) **Zoom,** just north of the bus station at El. Venizelou 18, is filled with vintage arcade machines and also has Internet access. (☎23 117. €2 per hr. Open daily 9am-midnight.) Walking down El. Venizelou with the water to your right, you'll find the **post office** about a block after the gas station on your right between El. Venizelou 46 and 48. (☎22 328. Open M-F 7:30am-2pm.) **Postal Code:** 20300.

⌂ 📷 ACCOMMODATIONS AND CAMPING. Loutraki boasts nearly 60 different hotel options. Those on a budget can try the hotels in the center of town, where El. Venizelou becomes G. Lekka, or down G. Lekka toward the waterfall; more expensive hotels sit closer to the waterfront. For **domatia**, call ☎22 456. To reach ▩**Le Petit France ❸**, M. Botsari 3, take the third right on El. Venizelou, walking from the bus station with the water on your left. Dina, the friendly, multilingual owner of this quaint, blue-shuttered hotel, extends her hospitality. Visitors can eat breakfast in the garden or in the lobby, which has a TV. Rooms come with balcony, ceiling fan, and bath. (☎22 401. Breakfast €4. Air-conditioning in most rooms. Singles €28-35; doubles €38. Family-style rooms available.) Nearly on the beach on the next street south of the bus station, **Hotel Marko ❹**, L. Katsoni 3, offers rooms with fridge, air-conditioning, bath, TV, phone, and balcony. Breakfast is served in the dining area which, later in the day,. doubles as a bar. (☎63 542. Breakfast included. High-season singles €40; doubles €55; 5-person suites €90. Low-season singles €30; doubles €35; 5-person suites €65.) **Hotel Possidonion ❸** is on the right side of the central plateia, coming from El. Venizelou. Spacious rooms with high ceilings and hardwood floors have phone, air-conditioning, TV, bath, and balcony with a view of the square. (☎22 273. Breakfast included. Singles €35; doubles €45.) **Camping** is available at **Isthmia beach ❶** on the Corinth Canal, where coin laundry machines are provided. (☎27410 37 447; www.isthmiacamping.gr. €5 per person, €3.70 per tent.) You also can camp 16km away at stunning **Lake Vouliagmeni**. To get there, travel north out of town on G. Lekka and follow the signs, or take a taxi, which will come back and pick you up in the afternoon, for €50.

🍴 FOOD. Loutraki's best dining options can be found in and around the hotels on El. Venizelou, or on the beachside boardwalk, Posidonos St. Several **supermarkets** are scattered along El. Venizelou. The **S.N.A.K.** at El. Venizelou 59, near the gas station, is the largest, and has a 24hr. Citibank ATM outside. (☎68 166. Open M-Sa 8am-9pm, Su 9am-2pm.) Locals flock to **Strougka ❸**, Posidonos 69, at the Corinth end of the waterfront, for its mouth-watering beef tenderloin (€14) and souvlaki (€7), served in plentiful portions. (☎65 747. Entrees €10-15. Open daily 10am-2am. Cash only.) At ▩**Grill House 71 ❶**, El. Venizelou 71, about an 8min. walk from the center of town, the chefs work furiously behind the searing grills to make inexpensive, scrumptious meals. Locals claim it serves the best pita souvlaki (€1.70) around. (☎61 776. Takeout and delivery available. Open daily 5:30pm-2am or later. Cash only.) At **Piazza di Giorgio ❶**, El. Venizelou 27, across from the bus station, try a lunch sandwich (€3-5) on delicious homemade bread. (☎64 300. Takeout and delivery available. Open daily 10am-2am or later.) Stylish **Pizza Ami ❷**, Posidonos 33, on the boardwalk past the bars, offers reasonably priced Italian cuisine and a wide selection of appetizing pizzas. (Entrees €5-10. Takeout and delivery available. Open M-F 5pm-late, Sa-Su 12am-late. MC/V.)

🎬 🍸 ENTERTAINMENT AND NIGHTLIFE. Loutraki is the birthplace of casinos in Greece, so if you're feeling lucky, stop by **Club Hotel Casino Loutraki,** Posidonos 48. It features 600 slot machines and 70 gambling tables with roulette, cards, and dice, as well as a swimming pool and hot tubs for its guests. (Casino ☎65 501, resort 60 300; www.club-hotel-loutraki.gr. Cover M-F €10, Sa-Su €15; includes free drinks at games. 23+. Open 24hr.) If you seek solace in Loutraki's famous healing waters, make an appointment at **Therma: Hydrotherapy Thermal Spa**, G. Lekka 14, across from the park. (☎22 215. Prices vary depending on treatment, €8-30. Open daily 8am-1pm.)

At night, as in the daytime, life in Loutraki revolves around the two main thoroughfares of El. Venizelou and the boardwalk. Couples stroll along the water's edge while teenagers hang out on the main street. Waterfront restaurants swell in summer, staying full well past midnight. Along the boardwalk, **Sax, Cafe Coral, Paul's, Jamaica, La Suerte, Essence,** and **El Niño** pump music for steady crowds of dancers and drinkers. (Mixed drinks €3-7.) The classy **Club Plori,** Posidonos 23, welcomes revelers into a large indoor-outdoor room filled with exposed brick, couches, and a vintage record collection. (☎28 211. Mixed drinks €7. Open M-F 8am-3:30am, Sa-Su 8am-late.) A few blocks north, **En Plo,** Psaron 2, mixes a nautical theme with red awnings and dark, glossy wood. (☎694 543. Beer €2.50-4.50. Mixed drinks €7. Open daily 8am-2:30am.) After midnight, taxis transport the party-hungry to discos on the city's edges. **Hype,** on Athinon Rd. toward Corinth, is filled with sweaty bodies pulsing past dawn. (☎66 996. Open F-Sa 11pm-7am.)

🄶 **SIGHTS.** The well-maintained **waterfalls,** a 12min. walk from the central plateia on G. Lekka, are even more enjoyable after dark; you can observe the colorful lighting and a series of pedestrian balconies from the charming **Katappaktes Cafe** on the patio below. (☎26 900. Open daily 10am-1am, later in summer.) **Lake Vouliagmeni,** 16km up the coast, is known for its blue water and tranquility. A bus runs from the station in Loutraki to the lake from mid-June to late August; for visits at other times of year, taxis (€50) are available. A 15min. taxi ride south of Loutraki will take you to **Water Fun,** a park with waterslides for all ages. (☎27410 81 400; www.water-fun.gr. Open daily 10:30am-6:30pm. €15, children €10.)

ARGOS Άργος ☎27510

According to Homer, Argos followed native hero Diomedes into war under the flag of Mycenae's mighty king, Agamemnon. Said to be the oldest continuously inhabited city in the western hemisphere, Argos remained the most powerful state in the Peloponnese through the 7th century BC. In a famous 494 BC battle, even formidable Sparta was unable to get past the city walls, defended mightily by Argive women. Later Argos stood with Corinth and Sparta as the pillars of the Peloponnesian League. But these events that shaped the city's illustrious legacy are obviously far in the past, leaving the modern traveler questioning what there is to see in Argos today. Although the main plateia and adjacent park, the archaeological museum, and the ancient theater are pleasant, it is hard to imagine the city's historical glory given its current state.

🄴 **TRANSPORTATION.** The Argolida station (☎67 324), on Kapodistriou, which runs parallel to and one block behind the side of the plateia with Hotel Morfeas, sends **buses** to: Athens (2½hr., 15 per day 5:30am-8:30pm, €10.20) via Corinth (€5); Mycenae (30min., 5 per day 7am-6:30pm, €2); Nafplion (30min.; every 30min. 6-8am and 9:30am-9:30pm; €1.20); Nemea (1hr.; 6:30am, 1pm; €3); Tripoli (1hr., 4 per day 8:45am-4:45pm, €5). Service is reduced on weekends.

🄴🄵 **ORIENTATION AND PRACTICAL INFORMATION.** Argos is a sprawling city with few landmarks, but most services are in or around the main plateia, marked by the large **Church of Saint Peter.** If you arrive by bus at the KTEL office, go right out of the station and turn left at the first intersection onto **Danaou.** If you're dropped off at the simple bus stop on the edge of a small park, the KTEL is straight ahead. Walking along Danaou, the plateia will be on your left and a small, taverna-lined park will be on your right.

There is a **National Bank** at Nikitara 2, off the plateia behind the small park. It has **currency exchange** and a **24hr. ATM.** The **police,** Ag. Artemiou 4 (☎67 222), are open 24hr. Head out from Vas. Sofias or follow the signs from the train station. The

hospital: (☎24 455) is 1km north of the plateia on Korinthou and is open 24hr. There is an **OTE** at Nikitara 8. From the plateia, walk 60m along the left side of the park past the ATM. (☎67 599. Open M and W 7:30am-3pm, Tu and Th-F 7:30am-9pm, Sa 9am-3pm.) For **Internet** access, try **NETP@RK.** Walk down Danaou past the plateia until Vas. Sofias, take a right, then take your first left onto Mustakopoulou. (☎24 096. €2 per hr. Water €0.50. Open daily 9am-4am.) The **post office,** which **exchanges currency,** is three blocks toward the plateia from the bus station at 32-34 Kapodistrou. (☎67 366. Open M-F 7:30am-2pm.) **Postal Code:** 21200.

▌▐ ACCOMMODATIONS AND FOOD. Argos's accommodations are disappointing, with a few mid-range hotels around the main plateia. The luxurious ▨**Hotel Morfeas ❸,** Danaou 2, has reasonable prices. The modern rooms come with air-conditioning, TV, fridge, phone, sleek bath, and balcony; many have unobstructed views of St. Peter's. There is a cafe in the lobby. (☎68 317; www.hotel-morfeas.gr. Free Internet. Breakfast €5. Singles €35-50; doubles €50-80; triples €60-90. MC/V.) Also in the main plateia behind St. Peter's is **Hotel Mycenas ❷,** an inexpensive, simple hotel that is well maintained, with a new paint job every year. Rooms come with air-conditioning, TV, bath, and fridge, and some have balcony. Ask for a room overlooking the plateia. (☎68 734. Breakfast €5. Singles €25-35; doubles €35-45; triples €45-55; quads €65-75. MC/V.) Don't be put off by the dark lobby at **Hotel Apollon ❷,** Papaflessa 13; the rooms themselves are spacious and well-lit, with balcony, air-conditioning, bath, and TV. Walking down Danaou into the plateia, take a right on Nikitara, then walk 50m to the small plaza. Head to the left, then take a right around its perimeter; the narrow alley is Papaflessa. (☎68 065. Singles €20-25; doubles €35-40; triples €38-50. AmEx/MC/V.)

Argos has the Peloponnese's largest ▨**open-air market,** in the empty lot 20m from the museum when walking away from the plateia. (Open W and Sa 7am-3pm.) Fast-food junkies can get their fix at the greasy gyro joints that clog the arteries of the plateia and the surrounding area. For a quick bite, **La Prima ❶,** Vas. Georgiou 8, is located in the park to the right off Danaou. This informal eatery serves Italian and grilled Greek fare; cramped seating makes take-out and delivery options appealing. (☎68 188. Salads €3-4.50. Extensive pasta options €4-5.) Those who prefer a more formal meal may be disappointed by the sit-down options, as there are few restaurants around the plateia. There are many supermarkets throughout the center of town, including gigantic **Atlantik Supermarket,** 30m to the right of the bus station facing the plateia. (Open M-F 8am-9pm, Sa 8am-8pm.)

◙ SIGHTS. Argos's superb **Archaeological Museum,** Kallergi and Vas. Olgas 1, has a large Mycenaean collection, Roman sculptures, several ancient weapons, and a garden courtyard with notable **Roman mosaics.** Follow Vas. Olgas from the plateia for 50m. to reach the museum. In the most striking of the mosaics, 12 figures personify the months of the year in their dress and expressions. Inside the museum, the Lerna Collection displays pottery from a prehistoric settlement, including pots imported from Troy. The statues on the second floor are mainly Roman copies of Classical designs, demonstrating Rome's admiration of its Greek territory. Though the explanations are in Greek and French, a small English pamphlet outlines the basic organization of the museum. (☎68 819. Open Tu-Su 8:30am-3pm.)

Though most of **ancient Argos** remains buried beneath the modern version, major ongoing excavations have taken place on the city's western fringe at the site of the ancient agora. From the museum, turn left and walk toward the open-air market. Turn left onto Phidonos and walk 5min. until the road ends. Make a right on Theatrou and walk to the end. Unfortunately, many of the potentially fascinating sights aren't in the best shape. With a seating capacity of 20,000, the 5th-century BC ▨**theater** was the largest of its time in the Greek world. Although it's not as well-preserved as its famous counterpart in Epidavros, its sheer size is still impressive. Nearby, what was once an extensive **Roman bath complex** is now little more than two red-brick walls, though many of the original floor mosaics are intricate, colorful, and intact. Similarly, the **Roman odeum**, 30m to the left of the baths with your back to the entrance, survives mostly as an outline. Across the street are the scattered remains of the **agora,** built in the 5th century BC and destroyed by Alaric's Visigoths in AD 39. (Open daily 8:30am-3pm. Free.)

Walk along Foroneos for about 1hr. or take the path from the ruins of the ancient theater to reach **The Castle of Larisa.** Franks, Venetians, and Ottomans all captured and ruled Argos in turn. As a result, the town's fortress is an architectural hodgepodge, combining disparate medieval and Turkish elements with Classical and Byzantine foundations. The Cyclopean walls are nearly 4000 years old. The ruins, about 4km above the city, provide stunning sunset views. The road to the castle is mostly unshaded, and it can get swelteringly hot in the summer, so bring water or take a taxi. (Open 24hr. Free.) The **Argive Heraion,** 10km northeast of Argos, dedicated to Hera, goddess of the Argives, was built in the 5th century BC. It prospered well into the AD 2nd century, hosting the celebrations that followed the official ending of the Heraia Games (archery contests held at Argos in the second year after each Olympics) and other annual festivals. Fifteen kilometers from Argos is the ruined city of **Dendra,** where tombs yielded the preserved suit of bronze armor now in the Nafplion Archaeological Museum.

NAFPLION Ναφπλιον ☎27520

Nafplion's Old Town fully earns its reputation as one of the most attractive getaways in Greece. The 15th-century Venetians' flawless urban design conveniently places everything within a few minutes' walk from the central square. With two breathtaking hilltop fortresses, romantic winding streets, and a buzzing waterfront to explore, visitors can spend days uncovering the secrets of Nafplion, one of the Argolid's most precious treasures.

▐ TRANSPORTATION

The **bus station,** Syngrou 8 (☎27 323), across from the park, has service to: Argos (20min., 2 per hr. 5:10am-10pm, €1.20); Athens (3hr., every hr. 5:10am-8pm, €11.30) via Corinth (2hr., €5.50); Epidavros (40min., 5 per day 10:15am-5:30pm, €2.50); Mycenae (45min., 3 per day 10am-2pm, €2.50); Tolo (20min., every hr. 7am-7.30pm, €1.20); Tripoli (1½hr.; 4 per day 8:30am-4:30pm, service reduced Sa-Su; €5). **Taxis** (☎24 120 or 24 72) congregate on Syngrou near the bus station. One block past the post office, **Rent-A-Moto,** Sidiras 15, rents mopeds. (☎22 702. €10-85 per day, depending on power of vehicle. Bicycles €10 per day; includes helmet and insurance. Open daily 8am-9pm.)

▟▓ ORIENTATION AND PRACTICAL INFORMATION

Bouboulinas is the waterfront promenade. To get there, turn left out of the bus station and follow **Syngrou,** which runs to the harbor, perpendicular to Bouboulinas. Three principal streets stretch west off Syngrou into the **Old Town.** Moving inland from Bouboulinas, the first is **Amalias,** the shopping street. **Vasileos Konstandinou,** the second, ends in **Plateia Syndagma,** the site of many tavernas, a bookstore, bank, and museum. The third is **Plapouta,** which becomes **Staikopoulou** in the vicinity of Pl. Syndagma. Across Syngrou, heading away from the Old Town, Plapouta becomes **25 Martiou,** Nafplion's largest avenue. Syngrou, behind the statue of Kapodistrias, marks the division between the Old Town and the modern **New Town.**

PELOPONNESE

Nafplion

▲ ACCOMMODATIONS
Dimitris Bekas's Domatia, **13**
Hotel Elena, **8**
Hotel Epidavros, **5**
Pension Marianna, **12**

● FOOD
Agora Music Cafe, **10**
Ekplous Cafe, **2**
Elatos, **3**
Elias, **9**
Mary's Corner, **6**
Pantheon Cafe, **4**
SandwichLand Canteen, **7**
Serio Cafe, **1**
Taverna Fanaria, **11**

Bourtzi
WI Bourtzi Castle

Gulf of Argos

TO LERNA (50km),
TRIPOLI (100km)

TO TIRYNS (4km),
ARGOS (12km)

TO TOLO (10km),
EPIDAVROS (27km)

TO KARATHONA BEACH

Agiou Adrianou
Vizandiou
Rue Marignas
Agiou Adrianou
Koutouna
Asklipiou
Kolokotroni
Nikitara
Kriou
25 Martiou
Vas. Georgiou
Bouboulinas
Argonaton
Charmanda
Eilou
Argous
Thisseos
Stadium
Irakleous
Kilkis
Navarinou
Vas. Pavlou
Swimming Pool
Atlantic Supermarket
National Gallery $
Sidiras Merarchias
Old Train Station LG
 V. Terzaki

NEW TOWN
New Train Station
Player V. Player
Polizoidhon
Breeze
Syngrou
Dhreve Nakion
Motor Traffic Rent-a-Moto
PL. KAPODISTRIAS
Statue of Kapodistrias
TAXI
Sofrani

Staikos Travel
Avis Rent A Car
Folklore Museum
Siokou
Vas. Alexandrou
Kotsonopoulou
Military Museum
Amalias
Vas. Konstandinou
OLD TOWN
Kokkinou
Ipsilandou
Vas. Olgas
Riga Fereou
Vas. Othonos
SYNTAGMA $
Archaeological Museum
Odyssey Bookstore
Ag. Spiridon
Komboloi Museum
Papanikolaou
Papanikolaou
Kapodistriou
Staikopoulou
Farmakopoulou
PL. TRION
Cathedral
Plapouta
Potomianou
Fotomara
Genadiou
Potamianou

ACRONAFPLIA
Nafplia Palace Elevator
Fortress
Aristidou
Zigomala
Polizoidhou
Avranitia Beach
Palamidi Fortress
TO KARATHONA (3km)

200 yards
200 meters

TO KARATHONA (3km)

Tourist Office: 25 Martiou (☎24 444), across from the OTE. Free maps and brochures of Nafplion and the surrounding area. Open daily 9am-1pm and 4-8pm.

Banks: There are 2 branches of the **National Bank of Greece,** both with **24hr. ATM.** One is in Pl. Syndagma (☎70 001); the other is on the corner across the street from the National Gallery on Sidiras Merarchias (☎21 355 or 21 354). Both are open M-Th 8am-2:30pm, F 8am-2pm. **Alpha Bank** (☎23 497), in Pl. Syndagma, has a **24hr. ATM** and **currency exchange.** Open M-Th 8am-2:30pm, F 8am-2pm.

Bookstore: Odyssey (☎23 430), in Pl. Syndagma, sells stamps, newspapers, maps, guidebooks, and paperback novels in English. Open daily 9am-2am.

Police: ☎21 100. Take Sidiras Merarchias east, turn left when you get to Asklipiou, go right on Rue Martignas, then left up Pavlou Kountourioti; it's on the right. Open 24hr. **Tourist police** (☎98 729) at the same address. Open daily 8am-2am.

Medical Services: Nafplion Hospital (☎27 309 or 24 235). Walk east on Sidiras Merarchias for 15min., then take a left onto Asklipiou. Hospital is on the right; the main entrance is on the opposite side of the block.

Telephones: OTE, Polizoidhou 2 (☎22 139). On the left side of 25 Martiou as you walk toward the New Town. Open M, W, Sa 7:30am-3pm, Tu and Th-F 7:30am-9pm, Su 8am-3pm. **Pay phones** are in front of the OTE and next to the National Bank in Pl. Syndagma.

Internet Access: Numerous options throughout Nafplion. **Breeze Games,** Bouboulinas 43 (☎26 141). €2 per hour. Open daily 9am-3am. **Player V. Player,** Bouboulinas 36 (☎21 418). €2 per hour. Open 24hr.

Post Office: ☎24 855. On the corner of Syngrou and Sidiras Merarchias. Western Union available. Open M-F 7:30am-2pm. **Postal Code:** 21100.

▛ ACCOMMODATIONS

If you choose wisely and bargain with owners, you can get good deals on accommodations in Nafplion. If you're looking for a luxurious experience, check out the hotels along the waterfront near the Acronafplia. Rooms in the Old Town are charming and beautifully situated, so they book quickly in summer. You can find **domatia** (called **"pensions"** here) all over town, especially higher uphill.

▨ **Dimitris Bekas's Domatia,** Efthimiopoulou 26 (☎24 256). This small pension exudes energy and offers a breathtaking view of Nafplion from the roof deck. Cozy rooms with shared bath and fridge offer the best value in Nafplion; some have a balcony and many have TV. Friendly manager Dimitris loves to chat, has a passion for American sports trivia, and steadfastly refuses to raise his prices during high season. Reservations recommended. Singles €22; doubles €28, with bath €30. ❷

▨ **Pension Marianna,** Potamianou 9 (☎24 256; www.pensionmarianna.gr). Tucked quietly into the mountainside, this gem has jaw-dropping views of the city and handsomely adorned rooms with A/C, TV, phone, minibar, and bath. Expensive but well worth it. Singles €65, with breakfast €75; doubles €75/80; triples €85/100. MC/V. ❹

Hotel Epidavros, Kokkinou 2 (☎27 541). Centrally located in the Old Town, mere steps from the Nafplion nightlife, this hotel has rooms with hardwood floors, A/C, TV, and bath. The owner also runs the **Tirins Hotel,** Othonos 41 (☎21 020), a block from the port, with slightly larger rooms. Singles from €40; doubles from €60. Bargain for lower prices on longer stays. ❸

Hotel Elena, Sidiras Merarchias 31 (☎23 888). 1 block behind Plaza Kapodistrias, away from the Old Town. Rooms come with A/C, TV, phone, bath, and balcony. Breakfast included. Singles €53; doubles €74. ❹

PELOPONNESE

FOOD

The Old Town's picturesque alleyways showcase countless romantic tavernas lit by soft lights amid flowers, balconies, and evening strollers. The early dinner crowd congregates around Pl. Syndagma; as the night goes on, many of the best dining options open on Staikopoulou. Meanwhile, the waterfront houses more expensive fish restaurants that exhibit their daily specials in translucent cold cases and may charge as much as €70 per entree. For those who would rather cook for themselves, **Atlantic Market,** Bouboulinas 4, is an excellent modern supermarket with a great selection. (☎26 626. Open daily 8am-9pm.)

▨ **Ellas,** in Pl. Syndagma (☎27 278). Refreshingly inexpensive considering its central location, with a cheerful staff and outdoor seating. The friendly owner, Costas, probably will draw you in as you stroll by. Chicken with rice €5. Salads €2.50. Entrees €5-7. Open daily noon-4pm and 7-11pm. MC/V. ❷

▨ **Mary's Corner,** Sidiras Mirarchias 11 (☎23 803). This neighborhood staple is a fresh, cheap alternative to the standard sit-down restaurant, with delicious souvlaki (€1.70), cheeseburgers (€3), and other entrees made in front of you. Open 24hr. 2 doors down is the **SandwichLand Canteen,** Sid. Mirarchias 6 (☎25 654), run by Mary's son and his wife. It serves a similar menu at slightly cheaper prices. Open daily noon-1am. ❶

Taverna Fanaria, Staikopoulou 13 (☎27 141). Provides a peaceful, intimate atmosphere in which to enjoy traditional Greek entrees or simply to people-watch. Salads €2.40-4. Lamb chops €8. Open daily noon-midnight. ❷

Elatos, Bouboulinas 71 (☎27 011). Those looking to treat themselves to a luxurious meal should look no further than Elatos to savor the wide array of fresh local seafood. Treat yourself to the fresh crawfish (€50 per kg). Entrees €11-17. Ask about the group rate, which often includes wine and beer. Open daily 10am-10pm. ❹

 NIGHTLIFE

Nightlife in Nafplion often involves enjoying a relaxing drink in one of the many bars on the waterfront near Pl. Syndagma or on Vas. Konstandinou or Staikopolou. International and Greek pop music floats out from **Agora Music Cafe,** Vas. Konstandinou 17, where you can drink an excellent frappé (€2.70) or espresso (€2) after dinner. (☎26 016. Open daily 8am-3am.) At night, the trendy cafe-bars along the waterfront, such as **Pantheon, Ekplous,** and **Serio,** surge with young heartthrobs and pounding beats. They offer beer (€3-5) and mixed drinks (€5.50-6.50). The search for alternative nightlife might land you in a taxi for the 15min. ride to **Tolo,** a tourist-packed beach resort. You also can take a **minicruise** of the harbor and get a close-up view of the **Bourtzi,** the castle on the harbor island. Small boats leave from the end of the dock. Call or visit the **Staikos Travel Agency,** Bouboulinas 50, for more information. (☎27 950. Open M-F 9am-2:30pm and 5:30-8:30pm, Sa 1-2:30pm.)

◉◗ **SIGHTS AND BEACHES**

Towering over the rooftops, the Palamidi Fortress and the Acronapflia immediately grab visitors' attention. But the Old Town itself, characterized by architectural diversity, is a display of living history. Pl. Syndagma boasts a Venetian mansion, a Turkish mosque, and a Byzantine church, while Ottoman fountains, cannons, monuments, and statues sit in the alleyways. After passing from the Venetians to the Ottomans and back again, in 1821 Nafplion served as headquarters for the Greek revolutionary government and as Greece's first capital (1821-

1834). President John Kapodistrias was assassinated here in Ag. Spiridon Church; the bullet hole is still visible in the church wall.

PALAMIDI FORTRESS. The supposed 999 steps (travelers attest that there are fewer—around 860) that once provided the only access to the 18th-century fort since have been supplemented by a 3km road (taxis €3.50-5). The steps begin from Polizoidhou past the park, marked by two cannonballs. The spectacular views from the fortress of the town, gulf, and much of the Argolid make the climb well worth it. The fortress itself is extensive, well preserved, and fun to explore (at your own risk if you leave the marked areas); be extremely cautious of drop-offs and ledges. Follow the signs to the "Prison of Kolokotrones," the tiny subterranean cell in which the famous Greek general was imprisoned by King Otto. For two weeks in June, coinciding with the full moon, there is a classical music festival with concerts every night. (Bring water and try to go in the morning, when the steps are shaded. ☎28 036. Open daily 8am-7pm; reduced hours in low season. €4, students and seniors €2, EU students and under 19 free.)

ACRONAFPLIA. The fortress walls of the Acronafplia, the acropolis of Nafplion, were fortified by three successive generations of conquerors—Byzantines, Franks, and Venetians. The views of the Palamidi Fortress, the gulf, and the Old Town are fantastic. (Take the tunnel that runs into the hill at the end of Zygomala to the Naf-plia Palace elevator, or follow the signs from the bus station.)

MUSEUMS. Nafplion has a wealth of modest but well-run museums. Opened in 2004, the **National Gallery-Nafplion Annex,** Sidiras Merarchias 23, is a must-see stop for the art lover or history buff. The museum houses a wide array of 19th-century oil paintings that depict the 1821 Greek Revolution, and has a section for temporary art exhibits. (Open M, Th, Sa 10am-3pm; W and F 10am-3pm and 5-8pm; Su 10am-2pm. €3, students and seniors €1.50, 12 and under free. M free.) The fascinating **Komboloi Museum,** Staikopoulou 25, allows visitors to explore all facets of the famous Greek komboloi (worry beads). The shop downstairs is run by museum founder Aris Evangelinos, a craftsman who has been featured in the New York Times and other newspapers. (☎/fax 21 618. Open M and W-Su 9:30am-9:30pm. €3, students and children free.) Nafplion's **Folklore Museum,** Vas. Alexandrou 1, is four blocks from the water at Sofrani. The award-winning collection features rotating themes based around Greek textiles, clothing, and furniture. (☎28 379. Open M and W-Sa 9am-3pm and 6-9pm, Su 9am-3pm. €4, students and children €2, groups €3.)

THE LOCAL STORY

DON'T WORRY, BEAD HAPPY

From the flashes of amber on the street to that whirring, clicking sound on the bus, you'll notice komboloi (come-boh-LOY), the fidget toy of the modern Greek, everywhere. Their name is rather self-explanatory, deriving from kombos, which means "knot," and loi, which refers to a group. Though almost always a loop of string filled with 16-20 beads, komboloi can range in shape and size, and the beads are made of materials ranging from amber and coral to bone and ivory. The komboli, the only secular beads of their type, are used primarily by men as a sort of stress reliever.

There are a number of theories as to komboloi's origin. Some claim they are an adaptation of the rosary-like komboskini used by the monks of Mt. Athos to count prayers. Others suggest that the strung beads, like so much else in Greece, were born out of resistance to the Ottoman occupation, as a mockery of the Turks' 40-bead prayer strings. Still others say that komboloi are a relatively recent fashion, imported from Asia Minor in the population exchange of the 1920s.

Learn more about the trend at Nafplion's Komboloi Museum, 25 Staikopoulou (☎27520 21 618). Open M and W-Su 9:30am-9:30pm. €3, students and children free.

The **Military/War Museum,** Amalias 22, toward the New Town from Pl. Syndagma, displays a collection of historic firearms. *(☎ 25 591. Open Tu-Su 9am-2pm. Free.)*

BEACHES. Arvanitia, Nafplion's secluded pebble beach, is on Polizoidhou past where the steps of Palamidi begin. On hot days, pop music blares over the noise of the sun-soaked crowd. For a cleaner, more serene alternative, take the footpath that runs along the water from the Arvanitia parking lot. The 45min. walk will reveal three quiet, rocky coves. If you're dying for a long, sandy beach, try the mostly undeveloped **Karathona** beach, a 3km hike along the coast from Arvanitia (taxi €3), or head to **Tolo,** where you can rent watersports equipment (€8-15). Buses (€1) head there from Nafplion every hour.

◪ DAYTRIPS FROM NAFPLION

◪ MYCENAE Μυκήνες

Buses go to Mycenae from Nafplion (45min.; 10am, noon, 2pm; €2.50). Take the bus to its final stop at the end of the asphalt road in the parking lot. Be careful not to get off at Argos, mistaking the fortress on the hill for Mycenae. The alternative is a shadeless 25min. walk uphill from town. Open daily June-Oct. 8am-7:30pm; Nov.-May 8am-3pm. Museum open M noon-7pm, Tu-Su 8am-7pm. Site, museum, and Agamemnon's Tomb €8, students and seniors €4, EU students and children free. Guidebooks €3.50-6.50. Bags larger than book-size are not allowed in the acropolis. Bring water, sturdy shoes, and a flashlight.

The spectacular remains of ancient Mycenae, which according to legend was founded by Perseus, are on a rocky knoll between Mt. Ag. Elia to the north and Mt. Zara to the south. Enough of the ancient citadel remains for visitors to imagine how magnificent it must have been in its heyday. Gargantuan **Cyclopean walls,** 13m high and 10m thick, surround the palace and its accompanying structures, which blanket most of the hill. Outside the central fortified city, down the road toward town, several impeccably preserved *tholoi* tombs—most notably the so-called **"Treasury of Atreus"**—clearly show the architectural expertise of the Mycenaeans. The bulk of the ruins dates from 1280 BC, when the city was the center of a vast Mycenaean Empire. The relics unearthed here number among the most celebrated archaeological discoveries in modern history, including countless jewels and the famous Mask of Agamemnon. As a result, many have been taken to the National Archaeological Museum in Athens (p. 116).

HISTORY. Mycenae's origins, interactions with other Near Eastern civilizations, and subsequent decline have long puzzled historians. Thought to have been settled as early as 2700 BC by a tribe from the Cyclades, Mycenae, along with other nearby cities, remained under the shadow of the Minoans for centuries. It wasn't until the collapse of the Minoan civilization in the mid-15th century BC that Mycenae rose to the top of the Greek world (p. 50). Mycenaean culture flourished for centuries until the 12th century BC, when the Dorians attacked from the north. The Dorians successfully conquered Greece, and Mycenae lost its grasp on the culture it had helped to create. The city remained inhabited through the Roman period, but by Byzantine times it had been swallowed by the earth and forgotten.

In 1874, German businessman, classicist, and amateur archaeologist **Heinrich Schliemann** arrived on the scene. Fresh from his lucrative dig at Troy and eager to further establish the historical validity of Homeric epics, he began a quest to uncover the city of Agamemnon, the king who, according to Homer, led the Greek forces in the Trojan War. It was impossible to overlook the probable connection between these finds and Homer's description of a "well-built citadel... rich in gold." Schliemann began his dig just inside the citadel walls at the spot where several

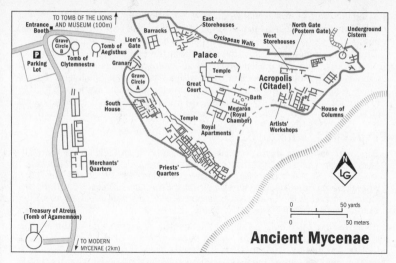

Ancient Mycenae

ancient authors described royal graves. He found massive walls that surrounded elaborate tombs laden with dazzling artifacts. Discovering 15 skeletons, which he believed to be those of Agamemnon and his cohorts, Schliemann sent a telegram to the Greek king that read, "Have gazed on face of Agamemnon." Moments after he removed its mask, however, the "face" underneath disintegrated. Modern archaeologists, who still cringe at the thought of such reckless excavation, date the tombs and mask to four centuries before the Trojan War.

RUINS. The two sights after the entrance booth are two impressive but oft-overlooked *tholoi*: the **Tomb of Aegisthus** and the **Tomb of Clytemnestra,** both with expansive burial chambers you can enter. When you return to the main path, you'll pass through the imposing **Lion's Gate,** the portal into the ancient city, with two lions carved in relief above the lintel (estimated to weigh 20 tons). On the right after the gate is **Grave Circle A,** where Schliemann found most of his artifacts. This area contains six 16th-century BC **shaft graves** that have yielded 14kg worth of gold.

The path winds back and forth up the hillside, passing remnants of homes, businesses, and shrines from the formerly bustling complex. The **palace** and **royal apartments** are at the highest part of the citadel on the right. The open spaces include guard rooms, private areas, and an impressive staircase; look for the **megaron,** or royal chamber, with its round hearth framed by the bases of four pillars. To the left of the citadel are the remaining stones of the ancient **temples,** thought to have been dedicated to Athena or Hera. The farthest end of the city, past the **Artisan Workshops,** is the best place to get a sense of the immensity of the complex's walls. For non-claustrophobics, the **underground cistern** offers a chance for exploration at your own risk. This tunnel, which bores 18m underground to what used to be a spring, guaranteed water during sieges. It's pitch black and the steps are uneven and slippery; use your flashlight, travel in a group, and watch your step.

Follow the asphalt 400m back toward the town of Mycenae to the **Tomb of Agamemnon** (a.k.a. the "Treasury of Atreus"), the largest and most impressive *tholos,* named by Schliemann for the king he so desperately wanted to discover here. The tomb is similar in design to the two *tholoi* near the entrance booth, but significantly larger and perfectly preserved. A 40m passage cut into the hillside leads through an immense doorway and into the grave itself; inside, glance up to see the

PELOPONNESE

120-ton lintel stones above you, arranged in concentric circles. The dim interior of the *tholos* conveys a ghostly majesty, but, to the dismay of both archaeologists and tourists, the tomb was found empty, having lost its valuables to robbers.

To reach the **museum,** follow the signs from the entrance booth, bearing left from the acropolis. The museum displays an extensive collection of pottery and ceramics, which show evidence of trade with areas as far as Spain and Afghanistan, as well as a detailed history of the ancient city and its excavations. While the most important artifacts found at the site are in the National Archaeological Museum in Athens, the museum offers gorgeous views of the neighboring hills.

EPIDAVROS Επίδαυρος

Buses run from Nafplion (45min.; 10:15am, noon, 2, 2:30, 5:30pm; €2.50). A snack bar and fancy restaurant serve the site but visitors may want to bring lunch. Museum and ticket office ☎27530 22 009. Site open in high season daily 8am-7:30pm; low season daily 8am-5pm; festival season F-Sa 8am-9pm. Museum closed M 8am-noon. Guidebook €2-10. Ticket includes entrance to the museum and archaeological site and a small map of the ruins. €6, students and seniors €3, EU students and under 18 free.

Epidavros was once both a town and a sanctuary, sacred first to the ancient deity Maleatas, then to Apollo, who assumed aspects of the former patron's identity. Eventually, the sanctuary's energies were directed toward Apollo's son, the medically gifted demigod Asclepius. When the good doctor got a little overzealous and began to raise people from the dead, Zeus laid the smack down with a thunderbolt. Asclepius, however, continued to guard over Epidavros, which became famous across the ancient world as a center of medicine. The prestige of the ancient health center reached its peak in the early 4th century BC, when people traveled across the Mediterranean for medical and mystical cures to a disastrous onslaught of plagues. Asclepius made diagnoses in dream visitations; recent finds indicate that surgeries took place here as well. Over the centuries, the complex grew to include temples dedicated to Aphrodite, Artemis, and Themis. The sanctuary complex was closed along with all other non-Christian sanctuaries by Emperor Theodosius II in AD 426. Today, with the notable exception of the theater, the ruins are not as well preserved as those at Mycenae. Restoration efforts have been underway for the past few years.

■ **THEATER.** Built into a hillside in the 3rd century BC, the **Theater of Epidavros** is without a doubt the site's most splendid structure. Initially constructed to accommodate 6000 people, its capacity was expanded to 12,300 in the next century. The theater's 55 tiers face half-forested, half-flaxen mountains so awe-striking they distract from the tragedies played out on the stage. However, the theater itself is just as spectacular. Attempt to grasp its vastness by standing on the top balcony and surveying the carefully constructed rows of seats below you. Though it often is said that the theater was designed by Polykleitos the Younger, architect of an even larger theater at Argos, it is not old enough to have been his work. The theater's acoustics defy belief, as yelling, singing, coin-dropping, whispering, and even match-lighting tourists from all nations enthusiastically demonstrate from the stage area—every sound made there can be heard even in the last row of seats. The secret to the theater's acoustic perfection is its symmetrical architecture; the entire amphitheater was built in proportion to the **Fibonacci sequence.**

The theater recently has come alive after centuries of silence: during July and August it hosts the ■**Epidavros Theater Festival.** During the festival, the National Theater of Greece and visiting companies perform Classical Greek plays translated into modern Greek. In recent years, the schedule has expanded to include eclectic musical and dance programs. *(☎21032 72 000. Performances begin at 9pm. Children under 6 prohibited from the front sections. Tickets can be purchased at the site's box* *office, in advance at the Athens Festival Box Office (☎ 21032 21 459), or at Nafplion's bus station. €10-100. On performance nights, KTEL buses make a round-trip trek from Nafplion (7:30pm, €4), leaving 20min. after the performance ends.)*

MUSEUM. The **Archaeological Museum** lies between the theater and the ruins. While much of the museum is closed to visitors because of restoration efforts, the three open rooms display a cramped but fascinating collection. The room closest to the entrance holds an array of ancient medical instruments, as well as a series of engraved stone tablets, some of which describe Asclepius's miraculous cures in detail. Make sure to check out the vast collection of marble statues in the middle room. The room farthest from the entrance is filled with intricate **entablatures** from the Temple of Asclepius and the *tholos.* Most impressive, however, is the perfectly preserved Corinthian capital, regarded as the architect's prototype for all the capitals of the Temple of Asclepius.

SANCTUARY OF ASCLEPIUS AND THOLOS. The extensive ruins of the sanctuary have undergone restoration efforts that use brand-new stone, rather than attempting to blend in with the past. Still, the ruins easily convey a sense of the massive size of the complex. Walking from the museum, you'll first pass the **Xenon,** an ancient hotel that now consists of little more than a maze of foundations. The **gymnasium** containing the remains of a **Roman odeon** is the first structure of the more concentrated complex of ruins. To the left is a **stadium,** of which only a few tiers of seats and the athletes' starting blocks survive. Two of the most important structures of the ancient sanctuary, the **Temple of Asclepius** and the famous **tholos,** are in front and to the left as you approach the ruins from the museum area. The *tholos,* thought to have been built by Polykleitos the Younger in the mid-4th century BC, contains a stone labyrinth that was intended to recreate trials in Hades—however, you must read about this on the information plaque, as visitors are not allowed to look into the vertical recesses of the *tholos.* Beside the *tholos* are the remains of the **abaton,** where ailing patients would wait for Asclepius to reveal the proper treatment. Farther along the path on the eastern edge of the site lie the ruins of 2nd-century **Roman baths.**

TIRYNS Τίρυνθα

Take the Argos bus from Nafplion (10min., 2 per hr. 5:10am-10pm, €1.20). You'll see the ruins on your right; get off just afterward and walk to the parking lot. When it's time to catch the bus back to Nafplion (every 30min. 5:15am-9:30pm), wait in the parking lot next to the cafes on the main road. ☎ 22 657. Guidebooks (€5) outline the history of the city. Open daily in high season 8am-7pm; low season 8am-3pm. €3, students and seniors €2, EU students and under 18 free. Su free.

About 4km northwest of Nafplion on the road to Argos lie the Mycenaean ruins of Tiryns, or **Tiryntha,** birthplace of Hercules. Heinrich Schliemann's excavation of the site began in 1875 and has been continued by the German Archaeological Institute (p. 83) ever since. Perched atop a 25m hill that provides a 360° view of the Argolid, Tiryns was nearly impregnable during ancient times—until its capture and destruction by the Argives in 468 BC. Parts of the stronghold date as far back as 2600 BC, but most of what remains (including the walls) was not built until a thousand years later in the Mycenaean Era.

At 8m tall, the massive walls surrounding the site reveal the immensity of the original fortifications; the walls on the eastern and southern slopes of the ancient acropolis reach a width of 20m. Vaulted galleries are concealed within these structures; go down the stairway at the far end from the entrance gate to see the best example. Many of the site's gems have been taken to the National Archaeological Museum in Athens (p. 116), rendering the site significantly less interesting. In fact, a general feeling of neglect pervades the complex; there is no museum, and the ruins themselves have no information plaques.

ELIA Ελεια **AND ACHAIA** Αχαία

In rural Elia and Achaia, pebble beaches near coastal plain port cities are as much a regional attraction as the jagged mountains rising dramatically inland. Summers bring locals and travelers alike to the inviting shores of the Mediterranean, while in winter Greeks and tourists head to higher ground to ski. The mountainous region was first settled by Achaians from the Argolid, and later ruled by Romans. Afterward, Franks, Ottomans, and Venetians all violently disputed this land, leaving a visible wake in the occasional ruins that crop up across the area's terrain.

PATRAS Πάτρας   ☎26106

Greece's third-largest city spreads from ancient hilltop ruins to a modern, heavily-trafficked harbor below in an eclectic mix of boutiques, businesses, and restaurants that quite literally rest on foundations of ancient times. Local Patrans, proud of their city, are quick to disparage the idea that most incoming tourists view the city as nothing more than a stopover on the way to Athens or an Italian or Ionian ferry destination. Stretching between storefronts throughout the city are stone pedestrian streets, picturesque alleys, and large, impressive plateias, perfect for exploring on foot. The populations of nearby universities, meanwhile, assure that Patras stays alive well into the late hours. Aside from festivals and shows held throughout the year, the city is well known for its Carnival celebrations. From mid-January to the start of Lent, Patras breaks out into Carnival madness—music, food, and all-night revelry.

▐▀ TRANSPORTATION

If you're coming from Athens by car, choose between the **New National Road,** which runs inland along the Gulf of Corinth, and the slower, scenic **Old National Road,** which hugs the coast. From central Greece, take the new **Rio Antirrio** bridge to Rio on the Peloponnese. From Rio, the #6 bus stops at **Kanakari** and **Aratou** (30min., €1.10), four blocks uphill from the main station.

Trains: Oth. Amalias 47 (☎39 108, info 39 109, for tickets abroad 39 110). **Ticket booth** open daily 5:30am-2:30am. MC/V. To: **Athens** (regular: 4hr., 8 per day, €9.40; express: 3¼hr., 5 per day 5:55am-5:55pm, €12.40), **Egio** (regular: 35min., 2:30am and noon, €1.20; express: 30min., 5 per day 5:55am-5:55pm, €3.60), and **Kalamata** (regular: 5½hr., 6am, €5; express: 4hr., 3 per day 11:40am-7:40pm, €10) via **Pirgos** (regular: €2.60; express: €5.40), where you can catch a train to **Olympia** (25min.). The trains to Athens are packed, so reserve seats even if you have a railpass.

Buses: KTEL (☎23 886, 23 887, or 23 888), on Oth. Amalias between Aratou and Zaïmi. Buses go to: **Athens** (3hr., 2:30am and every 30min. 5am-9:45pm, €16.20); **Egio** (every hr. 7am-9pm, €3.20); **Ioannina** (4hr.; M-Th and Sa 8:15am and 2:45pm, F and Su 8:15am, 12:30, 2:45, 5:30pm; €19.70); **Kalamata** (3hr.; 8am, 2:30pm; €19.30); **Kalavrita** (2hr.; M-F 4 per day 5:30am-4pm, Sa-Su 7:15am and 4pm; €6.80); **Pirgos** (2hr., 10 per day 5:30am-8:30pm, €8.40); **Thessaloniki** (7hr.; 8:30am, noon, 3:15, 9pm; €37.90); **Volos** (5hr., M-F and Su 3:30pm, €23). The **blue buses** around town are city buses. Buy tickets at one of the white kiosks; there's one in Pl. Giorgiou and another next to the bus station. Make sure to get a ticket for the return trip, as buying on the bus is not always possible.

Ferries: From Patras, boats go to **Kephalonia, Ithaka,** and **Corfu** in Greece, and **Brindisi, Bari, Ancona,** and **Venice** in Italy. Most ferries to Italy leave at night. Prices to Italy vary depending on type of passage and ferry line, so check the travel offices along Oth. Amalias and make sure to check prices for more than one line. **Superfast Ferries,** Oth. Amalias 12 (☎22 500; open 9am-9:30pm), which operates Blue Star lines, is the only

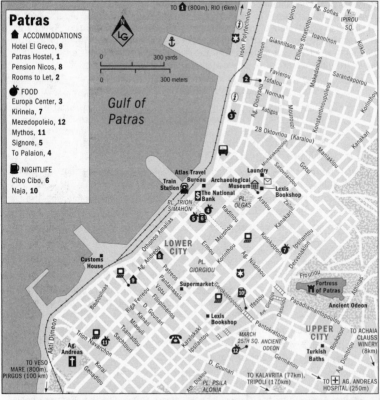

Patras

♠ ACCOMMODATIONS
Hotel El Greco, 9
Patras Hostel, 1
Pension Nicos, 8
Rooms to Let, 2

🍴 FOOD
Europa Center, 3
Kirineia, 7
Mezedopoleio, 12
Mythos, 11
Signore, 5
To Palaion, 4

🍷 NIGHTLIFE
Cibo Cibo, 6
Naja, 10

Gulf of Patras

company that accepts Eurail passes. Domestic ferries go to **Corfu** (7hr., M-W and F-Su midnight, €30-33) and **Vathy** on Ithaka (3½hr.; 12:30pm, also M-F and Su 8:30pm; €14.50) via **Sami** on Kephalonia (3hr., €14.50). For domestic and international departures and shipping concerns, head to **Atlas Travel Bureau,** (☎26102 24 439), opposite the train station. Open M-Th 9am-1pm and 3:30-6pm, F 9am-5pm, Sa 9am-1pm. For info on ferry departures, call the **Port Authority** (☎26103 41 002) or contact the Info Center or tourist police.

Car Rental: Many along Ag. Andreou. **Hertz Rent-A-Car,** Karalou 2 (☎26102 20 990). Turn right between the train station and the information center. Rates from €65 per day. Open M-Sa 8am-2pm and 4:40-8:30pm, Su 9:30am-1pm and 5:30-8pm. AmEx/MC/V.

Taxis: Line up in plateias and by the bus station. 24hr. **Radio Express** ☎26104 50 000 or 26104 18 300.

✳ 🛈 ORIENTATION AND PRACTICAL INFORMATION

Patras is divided into an upper and a lower city, both of which are arranged in a grid; most hotels, restaurants, and shops are in the heart of the lower city. **Othonas Amalias** (called **Iroön Polytechniou** past the new port) runs parallel to the waterfront. There are three main squares downtown. One block from the train station along Oth. Amalias is **Plateia Trion Simahon,** with palm trees, cafes, and kiosks.

Agios Nikolaou runs inland from the plateia and intersects the city's major east-west streets. From the corner of Ag. Nikolaou and **Mezonos,** walk three blocks south on Mezonos to find **Plateia Giorgiou,** with sculpted fountains. The heart of New Patras, lined with designer clothing shops, is between Pl. Giorgiou and **Plateia Olgas,** three blocks to the left with your back to the water. Access the upper city by walking away from the water on Ag. Nikolaou.

Tourist Office: The **Info Center,** Oth. Amalias 6 (☎26104 61 741; www.infocenter-patras.gr), between 28 Oktovriou and Astingos, provides festival schedules, transportation info, museum info, maps, brochures, **Internet** (20min.) and bicycles to explore the area (all free). It also offers information on Greece in English, French, German, Italian, and Spanish. The center displays artwork, regional products, and a diverse selection of local wines, along with directions to local wineries. Open daily 8am-10pm. There is also a smaller information kiosk in Pl. Trion Simahon.

Banks: National Bank (☎37 400), in Pl. Trion Simahon on the waterfront, has a **24hr. ATM** and **currency exchange.** Open M-F 8am-2:30pm.

Luggage Storage: Europa Center (p. 153) will store your bags for free. You also can store them at the port (€1.20; open 8am-10pm) and the train station (€1.60).

International Bookstore: Lexis Bookshop, Mezonos 38-40 (☎26102 20 919). By the Archaeology Museum. Has English and Greek books on Greek culture, history, and travel, as well as useful dictionaries. Open M-F 8:30am-2pm, Tu and Th-F also 5:30-9pm, Sa 8:30am-3pm. Their store at Patreos 90 (☎26102 74 831) only carries English-language books.

Laundromat: There are quite a few down Zaïmi. Try **All-Star Laundry** at 21 Zaïmi (☎26102 78 189), 3 blocks from the bus station. Wash and dry €7.50. Open M, W, Sa 9am-2pm, Tu and Th-F 9am-2pm and 5:30-9pm.

Police: ☎100. Ermou 95 on the corner of Karaiskaki, 6 blocks up from the waterfront.

Hospital: Ag. Andreas Hospital (☎26102 27 000), on Patron-Class past the church and on the left. For an **ambulance,** dial ☎166.

Telephones: OTE, at the corner of D. Gounari and Kanakari. Open M, W, Sa 7:30am-2:30pm, Tu and Th-F 7:30am-8:30pm.

Internet Access: There's no lack of Internet cafes in Patras. **The Web,** Gerokostopoulou 34, 1 block above Pl. Giorgiou on the right, bills itself as "the ultimate Internet and gaming experience." Midnight-2pm €1.50 per hr., 2pm-midnight €2.10 per hr. Soda €1; coffee €1.50; beer €3. **Ametron,** Korinthou 204 (☎26102 76 749), offers coffee and beer (€2.60) while you surf. €3 per hr. Open 8am-midnight. Another popular option is **Lanarena,** Ag. Andreou 149 (☎26102 73 063). €1.50 per hr. Coffee €1.50. Open 24hr. At 184 Riga Ferrou, on the corner of Trion Navarchon and across from Mythos is **Plug 'n Play** (☎26103 61 492). €1.50 per hr. Coffee €1.70. Beer €2. Printing €0.10 per sheet. Open daily 8am-4am.

Post Office: ☎26102 74 642. Zaimi 23 on the corner of Mezonos. Open M-F 7:30am-8pm, Sa (letters only) 7:30am-2pm. **Postal Code:** 26001.

ACCOMMODATIONS

Most hotels in Patras are on or near Ag. Andreou to the left of Pl. Trion Simahon facing inland, or on Ag. Nikolaou. While many are budget in appearance but not in price, some are diamonds in the rough.

■ **Pension Nicos,** Patreos 3 (☎23 757), 2 blocks off the waterfront. The best bet in Patras for price and location, 3 blocks from Pl. Trion Simahon. Rooms feature wood-paneling, high ceiling, balcony, A/C, and sink. Bar and roof terrace have excellent views of the harbor. From the lobby, ring the bell and pick up the phone to connect to the 3rd-fl. reception. Singles €20, with bath €25; doubles €30/35; triples €40/45. ❷

■ **Rooms to Let Spyros Vazouras,** Tofalou 2 (☎26104 52 152; www.patrasrooms.gr), 2 blocks up from the harbor, across from the new port entrance. These large, brightly tiled rooms are equipped with A/C, TV, and bath. Other perks include a communal fridge and a rooftop deck with ocean views. If the door is locked, press the intercom to contact Spyros's cell phone and he will be over quickly from his home next-door to take care of you, even at night. Singles €30; doubles €40. Additional bed €10. ❸

Hotel El Greco, Ag. Andreou 145 (☎26102 72 931; fax 26102 72 932). Walking along Andreou with the water on your right, it's 4 blocks past Pl. Trion Simahon on the left. Plants flourish in the modern lounge and lobby of this family-run establishment. Clean rooms have bath, TV, fridge, hairdryer, A/C, and some have a balcony. Breakfast €6. Check-out noon. Singles €40; doubles €55; triples €65-70. ❹

Patras Hostel, Iroön Polytechniou 62 (☎26104 27 278). From the port, walk away from town with the water on your left for about 1km. This creaky turn-of-the-century mansion sat empty for 43 years after being used by occupying Germans in WWII. Rooms are communal and unpretty and the bathrooms could probably never be completely clean without renovation. For those looking for a friendly place to crash and not much more, you certainly get what you pay for here. Leave valuables at reception desk. Sheets €0.50. Check-out 10:30am. Dorms €10. ❶

☐ FOOD

Walk along the waterfront and through any of the main plateias for options ranging from gyro stands to fancy Italian restaurants to quiet creperies. Better quality restaurants can be found by walking to the top of Kolokotroni from Pl. Olgas. Every square offers cafes with shaded outdoor seating where locals and tourists alike take time to cool down on hot summer afternoons with a cold drink and pastry. A walk through the Roman-ruin-lined streets of the upper old city, by the Odeion and Fortress, reveals tavernas where locals enjoy late dinners in relaxed old-world style. **Supermarkets** are scattered throughout town.

Europa Center (☎26104 37 006), on Oth. Amalias between the information center and bus station. This friendly cafeteria-style eatery is as much a support center for road-weary travelers as it is a restaurant, drawing visitors to its location near the city's transport hubs. The Greek-American owners are eager to introduce visitors to Patras and will happily assist tired backpackers. Europa Center provides useful services such as free luggage storage, Internet access (€2 per hr.), a few old-school arcade games, book exchange (without trade €3) and local tips. Appetizers €2.50. Salads €2.50-4. Entrees €5-9, including many vegetarian options. MC/V. ❷

Mezedopoleio, Germanou 2 (☎24 834), on the edge of March 25th Square down from the Odeion. Offering an array of salads (€3-5.50) and main dishes (€5-14), particularly of the off-the-grill variety, the extensive menu adds extra appeal to a restaurant whose main attraction is the outdoor seating in the square. The wide-branching trees of the plateia provide natural shade where patrons sample wine (€10-20) and cheese (€3-3.50; sampler €8) among friends. ❸

Mythos (☎26103 29 984), on the corner of Riga Fereou and Trion Navarhon near Agios Andreas. Choose between the outdoor seating or the cozy interior. In addition to salad options (€5-8), the cafe offers a wide variety of pastas and other entrees (€7-9). In a city where late-night eateries abound, the appealing setting is a major draw. English menus provided. Cover charge €1.50. Open daily 8pm-2am. ❸

Kirineia, Kolokotroni 63 (☎26102 74 340, delivery 26106 22 435). A Cyprian take on the traditional Greek taverna, Kirineia, just past the corner of Karaiskaki and

PATRAS PARADES

Every year on January 17, the figure of Dionysos, Greek god of debauchery, is installed on his throne in Patras. It is the first day of the triumphant celebration that marks the start of Carnival and the beginning of festivities that last two months.

Of primary importance are the numerous parades through the streets, made magnificent by majestic floats that are their centerpieces. Float-making is something that Patras and Carnival organizers take very seriously. The bright, funny, and marvelously crafted works of art are created by expert craftsmen employed by the Workshop of Carnival Artistic Constructions of Patras. These specially gifted artists work year-round in preparation for the festivities. (The workshop can be visited year-round; for more information contact the Information Center of Patras.)

The *bourboulia*, costumed balls that are held during the Carnival, add to the debauchery and fun. Held at the "Apollo" Municipal Theater, they feature women dressed in black robes from head to toe and black masks.

A favorite among many is the hidden treasure game that spreads over the entire city. Many thousands of costumed people, organized into teams, attempt to solve riddles and puzzles and navigate labyrinths testing memory and knowledge.

Children ages 6-12 flock to the

Kolokotroni, provides a comfortable atmosphere, quieter than the bustling restaurants lining Ag. Nikolaou below. Cypriot specialties such as grilled haloumi cheese (€3.50) and *seftalia* (Cyprus burger with spices and cheese; €5.80). Most tempting for those dining in large groups is the Cypriot "delicacy ritual" (€15 per person), where up to 22 different dishes are served. Entrees €5.80-7.50. English menus. ❷

Signore (☎26102 22 212), on Ag. Andreou across from Pl. Trion Simahon. In a central location, this fast-food pizza joint is busy round-the-clock, bustling with families grabbing pizza before a ferry ride to Italy and young hipsters looking for a bite to eat before a night of clubbing. Salads (€5-7), pizzas (€2.80 per slice) or crepes (€3.50-4.20) can be enjoyed in the airy dining room. Take-out and delivery available. Open daily 24hr. ❷

To Palaion, Ag. Nikolaou 13 (☎26102 26 435), between Agiou Andreou and Mihalakopoulou. With Mediterranean fare, a handsome, high-ceilinged dining hall, and umbrellas sheltering outdoor diners from the hottest of summer suns, this cafe attracts an older crowd with a variety of specialty dishes. Salads €5-8. Entrees €7.50-17. Desserts €3.50-8. Coffee €2-3. Open daily 8am-1am. MC/V. ❸

👁 SIGHTS

◾**ACHAIA CLAUSS WINERY.** A narrow road meanders uphill through grapevines and shaded countryside to this castle-like, internationally renowned winery, 8km southeast of Patras. Founded in 1861 by German-born Baron Gustav von Clauss, its weathered stone buildings have aged as well as its wine. Try a complimentary sample of its famous Mavrodaphne, a superb and sweet dessert wine reputedly named for the black eyes of Clauss's lost love, Daphne. Not only is the wine renowned in the international community—numerous awards, diplomas, and letters from grateful ambassadors adorn the walls—but the staff is friendly and incredibly knowledgeable. Be sure to take a tour of the old wine cellars to see the Imperial Cellar, where images of Dionysus rowing wine to shore grace the beautifully carved barrels. The oldest wine, a €1250 Mavrodaphne from 1873, is bottled for special occasions, most recently the 2004 Olympics in Athens. Visitors can buy other wines (€2.20-28) on the spot. Before you leave, wander around the main house to catch a breathtaking view of the ocean and Patras. *(Take bus #7 from the intersection of Gerokostopoulou and Kanakari towards Seravali; it stops at the main gate to the winery (30min., €1.15). The 10min. walk up the winding driveway is uphill and a bit tiring. ☎26103 68 276. Open daily 11am-3pm, with tours every hr. in English. Free.)*

AGIOS ANDREAS. The largest Orthodox cathedral in Greece, with a dome that soars to 46m and a capacity of 5500 people, is dedicated to St. Andrew. The saint was martyred here in the AD first century on an X-shaped crucifix (he felt unworthy of dying on a cross like Jesus's). A decade ago the Catholic Church returned St. Andrew's holy head to this place of martyrdom. The top of the head is visible through its reliquary, an ornate silver replica of the cathedral itself, in front of the remains of the crucifix on the right of the church. The cathedral's frescoes, gold mosaics, and delicately latticed windows are both religiously significant and artistic masterpieces. One highlight is the large, intricately carved wooden chandelier in the center. Behind the cathedral on Eth. Korai is the beautiful **Church of Saint Andrew,** the original church built between 1836 and 1843. This building has bright frescoes, chandeliers, and a small well allegedly built by the saint himself. Legend holds that anyone who drinks from the well will return to Patras. *(About 1.5km from the port. Walk along the waterfront or Ag. Andreou with the water to your right until you reach the cathedral; it will be on your left. Open daily 7am-9pm. Modest dress required.)*

THE FORTRESS OF PATRAS. Built over the ruins of an ancient acropolis using many of the same materials, Patras's fortress remains surprisingly intact considering its continuous, turbulent use from the AD 6th century to WWII. Controlled at times by the Byzantines, Franks, Turks, Venetians, and even the Vatican, the fortress serves as a tribute to the city below and the various influences that have helped shape it. More than just a monument to ages past, the fortress hosts occasional concerts in the courtyard. The castle's high location makes it a perfect spot to get a bird's-eye view of the city. *(Walk to the upper city from Ag. Nikolaou. Then walk about 10min., following the fortress wall on Papadiamandopoulou, to the main entrance at the opposite side of the castle along Athinas. ☎ 23 390. Open Tu-Sa 8:30am-3pm. Free.)*

ANCIENT ODEION. Southwest of the castle in the upper city, this Roman theater, built before AD 160 and used until the 3rd century, once held an audience of 2500. Ancient travel writer Pausanias described it as the second most impressive theater in Greece, after Athens's Theater of Herodes Atticus. Excavated in 1889, the theater was restored after WWII. Visitors now can make out the ancient *cavea*, where spectators sat, and *proskenion*, the wall at the back of the stage. *(☎ 26102 76 207. Open Tu-Su 8am-3pm. Free.)* The theater hosts the **Patras International Festival,** in which music groups play nightly. *(Mid-June to Sept. Check at Info Center for performance times and prices.)*

Carnival of the Kids, which has its own parade. Carnival's younger counterpart also puts together a mobile fun center where races, song contests, and shows are just some of the attractions.

Tsiknopempti is held on the Thursday two weeks prior to the final Sunday of Carnival. This party turns all of Patras into a taverna: from early morning until late at night, all open corners and squares in the city feature makeshift eateries serving grilled meats, while roving dance, music, and drama groups patrol the town performing.

On the last Sunday, the Grand Parade takes place. Though partiers are exhausted from the Poderati parade the night before, the Grand Parade is known to last up to 10 hours even in poor weather conditions. When all the festivities are finished, the great icon of Dionysos is set on fire in a brilliant flaming spectacle, while organizers set to work planning the following year's festivities.

For more information, contact the Patras Cultural Development Municipal Enterprise (☎ 26102 22 157; depap@otenet.gr) or check out the website (www.carnivalpatras.gr).

ARCHAEOLOGICAL MUSEUM. This two-room museum's most striking pieces are its Roman artifacts. Highlights include the mosaic floor of a Roman villa in Patras, a marble statue of Athena, and two cases containing amazingly intact gold jewelry, including a pair of earrings shaped like birds and a delicate gold-leaf necklace. *(Mezonos 42, next to Pl. Olgas at the corner of Mezonos and Aratou. ☎ 20 413. Open Tu-Su 8am-3pm. Guidebooks €3. Free.)*

TURKISH BATHS (HAMMAM). These baths in the old, upper part of Patras reputedly have been in continued use since 1500, although they received a renovation in 1987. *(29 Boukaouri St. ☎ 26102 74 267. M women: 9am-9pm; Tu men: 9am-2:30pm and 5:30-9pm, women: 2:30-5pm; W women: 9am-2:30pm and 5:30-9pm, men: 2:30-5pm; Th men: 9am-2:30pm and 5:30-9pm, women: 2:30-5pm; F women: 9am-9pm; Sa men: 9am-2:30pm and 5:30-9pm, women: 2:30-5pm.)*

🎵 🎭 ENTERTAINMENT AND NIGHTLIFE

For a relaxed night out, head along the waterfront with the water on your right. About 10min. past Ag. Andreas Cathedral, you'll come to the two-story **Veso Mare,** Akti Dymaion 17 (☎ 26103 65 500), an open-air outdoor mall complex that features a 16-lane bowling alley (€3-6 per game), eight movie theaters (€7), and many restaurants and cafes. (Open daily 9am-3am.)

At night, cafes and pubs downtown swell with patrons of all tastes. Teenagers from the suburbs hop out of taxis dressed to the nines, and cigarette smoke pervades the air while the crowd jabbers into cell phones. Ag. Nikolaou and Radinou (a pedestrian-only alley one block south of Pl. Olgas) generally cater to the trendy club crowd, while Pl. Olgas and Pl. Giorgiou host older couples and families—though not exclusively. For an intriguing late-night bar setting, head to ■**NAJA** at Gerokostopoulou 67, to the left of the stairs leading to the upper city and the odeion. Draping vines that accent a thatched roof and beams make this club seem like something out of a fairy tale. With occasional DJ or live music nights, NAJA fluctuates between a late-night jazz cafe and a pounding nightclub depending on the night and mood of the crowd. (Beer €3-6. Mixed drinks €5. Wine €5-6. Open daily 5pm-5am.) Consistently the most popular bar on Ag. Nikolaou, **Cibo Cibo** serves Italian food all day (salads €6-6.40; entrees €8.50) and mixed drinks (€6+) late into the night, when the thumping energy comes not from the noisy crowds outside but from the pounding bass within. (☎ 20 161. Open daily 7am-3am.) The party moves to the upper part of Gerokostopoulou (extending uphill from Pl. Giorgiou) at cafes underneath the romantic, dimly lit archways and along the steps to the upper city. Though Patras has much to offer in the way of bars and cafes, some of the wildest partiers head out of town. **Rio,** a beach area 6km to the northeast, accommodates Patras's club junkies. Some of the biggest clubs, like **H2O** or **Destino,** pass out flyers around town for their weekend pleasure-fests. Take bus #6 from Kanakari and Aratou (30min., €1) to the port, past the beach. Get off the bus just after the port before it turns left to head back to Patras; the strip is ahead as you walk with the water on your right. Buses to Rio only run until 11pm, so count on taking a cab home (€5-6). Along the strip, beer runs €3.50+. Mixed drinks are €5-7. An entire row of modern bars and clubs awaits, where you can pick the vibe you find most appealing, from the modern, sleek offerings of a club like **W,** to the Middle Eastern stylings of **Taj Mahal** (hookah €10). Most clubs are open in the afternoon and stay open late into the night. Across the water the expanse of the **Rio-Antirio Bridge,** the world's biggest cable bridge. For late-night relaxing by the shore away from the city and the throbbing pulse of nightclubs, head southwest to an area known as **Vrachneika,** where cafes stay open late into the night along the shore. Take the #5 bus (€1.20) from outside the Info Center. Buses stop running around 11pm; if you stay later you will need to take a cab back (€5).

DIAKOFTO Διακοφτό ☎ 26910

The village of Diakofto combines turquoise waters, picturesque houses, and mountains bursting with lush vegetation. Recently, the town has imported new trains from Switzerland to climb over the Vouraikos Gorge to Kalavrita. Diakofto, however, remains largely isolated from the tourists that have infested the more famous sights. It is only in July and August that the village comes alive, drawing visitors to its peaceful beaches, set before a dramatic backdrop of rock mountains.

▐ **TRANSPORTATION.** The station runs **trains** to Athens (regular: 3½hr., €8.60; express: 3hr., €10.70) via Corinth (regular: 1½hr., €2.10; express: 1hr., €4.70). The station offers **luggage storage** (free until 6pm for up to 2 bags). There is no bus station in Diakofto, but the **bus stop** (KTEL ☎ 62 388, schedules ☎ 22 424) is outside the train station on the inland side.

⚑▐ ORIENTATION AND PRACTICAL INFORMATION. Diakofto's small downtown and surrounding areas are fairly easy to navigate; residents are happy to help confused travelers. The train station (☎ 43 206) crosses Diakofto's two main roads. The main commercial street—sometimes called **Mihalakopoulou**—is perpendicular to the tracks on the inland side of the station and is flanked by bakeries, pharmacies, and cafes. On the side of the tracks closest to the beach, **Filippopoulou**, which is also perpendicular to the tracks, runs straight to the beach and harbor. Follow the road parallel to the tracks to the left for about 800m to reach the far end of the rocky beach. The road straight ahead reaches **Egkali beach** in a little over 1km.

Most of the town's services are on the main street; turn right as you exit the train station on the inland side, and take a left on the second street after the kiosk. Down on the right is the **National Bank,** which offers **currency exchange** and a **24hr. ATM.** (☎ 42 180. Open M-Th 8:45am-12:45pm, F 8:45am-12:15pm.) The **police station** is on the second floor of a building on the main street. (☎ 41 203, ☎ 22 100 on weekends. Open M-F 7am-2:30pm.) You'll find the **pharmacy** next to the bank. (☎ 42 885. Open M-Sa 8am-2pm and 5-9:30pm, Su 8am-2pm and 4pm-8:30pm.) The nearest **hospital** (☎ 22 222) is 15min. away in Egio and is accessible by bus or by **taxi** (☎ 41 402). For **emergencies,** call for an ambulance (☎ 166) or call the doctor at the local **clinic.** (☎ 41 260. Open M-F in the morning, W open later.) Another doctor operates out of a corner office near the Chris Paul Hotel (☎ 43 488) on the first street to the left as you exit the train station on the inland side. Past the police station, you will see **Club Alpha** on the right, which offers **Internet** access 24 hr. (9am-midnight €2 per hr.; midnight-9am €3 per hr.) as well as pool (€6 per hr.), snacks (beer €2-3, club sandwich €4.50), and videogames. The **post office** is farther down this side street just before it meets the second side street off the main road. (☎ 41 343. Open M-F 7:30am-2pm.) **Postal Code:** 25003.

▌ **ACCOMMODATIONS.** The town has few accommodations, and none are inexpensive. At the far end of the beach from the harbor on the corner of the street you'll find **Hotel Panorama ❸,** which features leather couches, an on-site restaurant, and warmly colored medium-size rooms with TV, fridge, air-conditioning, and decks with an ocean view. (☎ 41 614; www.greecepanorama.gr. Breakfast €5. Singles €30-40; doubles €40-50; family suites €55-70. Extra bed €5. MC/V.) **Chris Paul Hotel ❸,** one block inland from the train station and the first left off the main road, lies conveniently in the quaint downtown. It has an impressive marble lobby, private pool, dining room and full bar, as well as TV, deck, and air-conditioning in every room. (☎ 41 715; www.chrispaul-hotel.gr. Breakfast €5. Wheelchair accessible. Singles €30; doubles €55; triples €70. July-Aug. singles €35; doubles €65; triples €78. MC/V.) **Hotel Lemonies ❷,** halfway between the train station and the beach on Filippopoulou, offers rooms with bath, comfortable beds, air-conditioning, balcony, fridge, and TV, as well as two floors of well-lit indoor and outdoor seating areas for late-night socializing. (☎41 820; fax 43 710. Singles €30; doubles €40. Prices rise in July-Aug.) Though formal campgrounds along the beach have shut down, some travelers, mostly Greek, take their RVs to the shoreline and camp for the night. **Eleon Beach ❶**, 5km from Diakofto (follow the signs from the train station on Filippopoulou), has campsites.

◻ FOOD. Food options in Diakofto are limited to a few souvlaki joints and a couple of tavernas. The town's supermarket, **Market In**, is on the inland side of the tracks to the far right as you exit the train station. Offering mostly fruit and non-perishables, the market remains conveniently open while the town shuts down for an afternoon nap. (Open M-F 8am-9pm, Sa 8am-8pm.) The nicest place in town, **Kostas ❷**, on the main street a few stores past the pharmacy, is also one of the most affordable. Try the lamb *giouvetsi* (pasta dish; €6.50), or *pastitsio* (Greek lasagna; €5.50), as you enjoy the outdoor canopy and patio shaded by trees. At the harbor, **Kohili ❸** serves fresh seafood including gilthead, cod, and seabeam (€10-16), caught that morning by its own fishing boats. For those who enjoy harbor views but not sea fare, burgers (€6.50), pork fillet (€8.50), and other meat entrees off the grill are available. (☎41 844. Open Sept.-May F-Su 7:30pm-midnight; June-Aug. daily noon-5pm and 7:30pm-midnight. Call ahead to make group arrangements.) **Thrifonayoanides ❶**, the local bakery across from the train station on the beach side, offers filling spanakopita (€1.30). Bustling with locals, the small room has shelves lined with all types of freshly baked bread. (Open daily 8am-2pm.)

▨ NIGHTLIFE. After dinner, young people leave behind their espresso-sipping parents and head to the beach. **Egkali beach,** about 2km outside of town, attracts the region's trendiest. At the harbor, keep walking with the beach on your left. When the road ends at Hotel Panorama, continue walking on the beach or follow the road back toward the train tracks, and make a left when you reach them after 800m. The road ends at Egkali beach, where the gorgeous views and general trendiness of this short stretch of pebble beach make up for the hike from Diakofto. The first club on the beach, **Pili,** offers live Greek music with dancing and debauchery. (Mixed drinks €6-8. Open July-Aug. Th-Sa 10pm-7am.) Farther to the right is the **Blue Beach Club,** where padded couches and lounge chairs draw beach-goers by day, and loud American club beats and an extensive bar attract partiers all night. (Beer €3-5. Mixed drinks €6-7. Open M-Th and Su 10am-8pm, F-Sa 10am-5am; July-Aug. W-Sa 10am-5pm.) Pirate-themed **Koursaros,** with a wooden patio right by the water, serves coffee (€3) and *pastitsio* (€4.50) from the best spot on the beach. (☎43 100. Beer €3. Open June-Sept. M-Th 11am-7am, F-Su 24hr.)

KALAVRITA Καλάβρυτα ☎26920

Although most famous for its ski resort, which comes alive in the winter, the town of Kalavrita has much to offer year-round. Sitting in a valley amid the jagged, pine-covered peaks and ridges of the Xermos mountains, this close-knit village has access to dramatic hikes and religious and historical monuments.

▨ TRANSPORTATION

To reach the **bus station** (☎22 224), walk uphill on Eth. Antistasios and take the first right onto Kapota; it's on your left one block down at the intersection of three roads. **Buses** go to: Athens (3hr.; M-F 9am, 4:45pm; Sa-Su 4:45pm; €14.40), Egio (1¼hr.; M-F 9am, 4:45pm; Sa-Su 4:45pm; €4.50) via Diakopto, and Patras (2hr.; M-F 5 per day 6:15am-4:45pm, Sa-Su 8:30am, 4:45pm; €6.80). Call ahead as bus schedules can change unpredictably. At press time, renovations were under way on the **train** line from Kalavrita to Diakofto. **Taxis** (☎ 22 127) line up along the side of the plateia, as well as by the bus and train stations.

✦ ℹ ORIENTATION AND PRACTICAL INFORMATION

Finding your way around the village of Kalavrita mostly involves navigating three main roads, each running perpendicular to the train station and tracks on the uphill side. Facing uphill, the street to the left is **Konstantinou** (a few blocks later, its name changes to **Agios Alexiou**). The pedestrian walk to the center is **Syngrou** (which becomes **25 Martiou**), and the road to the right is **Kallimanti** (which becomes **Ethnikis Antistasios**). Uphill about 100m is the **central plateia.** Most of the town's accommodations, shops, and service centers are found on these three roads or connecting streets between.

The **National Bank,** 25 Martiou 4, 100m downhill from the central plateia, offers **currency exchange** and a **24hr. ATM.** (☎ 22 209. Open M-Th 8am-2:30pm, F 8am-2pm.) Walking from the train station, the **police,** Fotina 7 on the second floor, are to the right off Ag. Alexiou, four blocks beyond the central plateia. (☎ 23 333 or 22 213. Open 24hr.) Kalavrita's four **pharmacies** (☎ 22 097) are open during normal business hours (M-F 8am-2pm), and take turns staying open 24hr.; if one pharmacy is closed, it will post the phone number of an alternate place on its door. Find one across from the **hospital,** three blocks from the train station; follow the street parallel to the station on the uphill side to the right. (☎ 22 222. Open 24hr.) **Plug 'n Play,** across from Hotel Filoxenia on Eth Antistaseos, is a DVD shop that offers **Internet** access. (☎ 24 218. €2 per hr. Open daily 9am-midnight.) **Phones** can be found in the central plateia and by the train station. The **post office** is down the road at Ag. Alexiou 17. (☎ 22 225. Open M-F 7:30am-2pm.) **Postal Code:** 25001.

🛏 ACCOMMODATIONS

The few hotels in Kalavrita are a bit expensive for those traveling on a budget, even during the low season in the summer. Rooms are comfortable and clean, but prices sky-rocket during ski season. The best bet is to try any of the affordable, well-appointed **domatia;** numerous signs on the downhill side of the train station will lead you to them. **Hotel Maria ❹,** one block uphill from the train station on the right side of Syngrou, offers bright, clean rooms with TV, some with balcony, in a central location. (☎ 22 296; www.kalavrita.biz/maria.htm. Breakfast €5. Apr.-June and Sept.-Dec. 14 singles €25-30; doubles €40-50; triples €50-60. Dec. 15-Mar. doubles €70; triples €90; quads €110. July-Aug. 10% price increase.) On a side street to the right off Ag. Alexiou two blocks up from the plateia, **Sfaragoulia Inn ❸** offers about a dozen tiled rooms with air-conditioning, bath, and TV. Some rooms have a small deck. If no one is there, ask at Kynaitha on Eth. Antistasios, one block uphill from Hotel Filoxenia. (Call Kynaitha ☎ 22 609/22 044; www.kynaitha.gr. Singles €30; doubles €40; triples €50.) The 28 rooms at **Hotel Filoxenia ❺,** Eth. Antistasios 10, have undergone recent renovations, and a new small gymnasium and spa are available to guests for a fee. Though a bargain only in the summer, the rooms have air-conditioning, bath, HDTV, phone, and minibar. All rooms have a balcony and some have a jacuzzi. (☎ 22 422; www.hotelfiloxenia.gr. Singles €42 in summer, in winter €92; doubles €49/110. Prices may be discounted in the low season. Add 20% of double price for extra bed. Reservations recommended. MC/V.) On the left and behind the church heading toward the central plateia, **Anesis Hotel ❺** is lovely stone hotel which has the feel of a comfortable lodge. Its 14 well-furnished, warmly carpeted rooms have phone, TV, bath, and minibar. (☎ 23 070; www.anesishotel.gr. Breakfast included in winter, €6 in summer. Singles €40 in summer, in winter €75; doubles €45/95; triples €60/120. MC/V.)

PELOPONNESE

🗱 🏮 FOOD AND NIGHTLIFE

Indistinguishable tavernas and fast-food joints line Ag. Alexiou and Syngrou. Most serve Greek staples (€5-7). Across the street and uphill from the train station is a **"Super Market."** (Open M-Sa 8am-3:30pm and 5-10pm.) For better food in a less touristed area, head to 🖾**Spitiko ❷,** right across from the bus station. You may want to ask owner Dimitrios to pick your meal for you, then savor the delicious concoction that he brings out. The lamb *fricace* (€8-9) is one of his favorites. (☎24 260. Open most days 9am-1am.) The **Hotel Maria Cafe ❷,** right outside the hotel on Syngrou, serves scrumptious breakfast foods in large portions (omelettes €5.50). The traditional goat-milk yogurt with honey (€2.75) is too good to miss.

The most happening place in the winter is, unsurprisingly, the ski center, where people gather for evening drinks. On weekdays, nightlife centers around cafes on Syngrou and on the central plateia. **Portokali** dance club at the end of the train tracks plays Greek pop and light traditional music all night long. Catering to a younger crowd, **Diadromes** has a small bar and crowded dance space with rock tunes. Drinks here run €5. Those in the mood for classic rock from Greece and the US might prefer the vinyl stylings of **Skiniko,** a few blocks up from the plateia at 25 Martiou 59. (Mixed drinks €5. Open Sept.-May.) Next door to the church in the central plateia, **Slalom** serves drinks and snacks late into the night, and has some of the best outdoor seating in town under dim lamps strung through trees. (Coffee €1.50-3. Mixed drinks €5. Open daily 8am-1am.) **Bresler's Cafe,** Ag. Alexiou 1, plays mainly American club hits. (☎24 459. Snacks €1-1.70. Coffee €2-3. Beer €2.40. Mixed drinks €5-6. Open daily 6:30am-1am.)

👁 🏔 SIGHTS AND OUTDOOR ACTIVITIES

KALAVRITA SKI CENTER. 14km from downtown Kalavrita, the Kalavrita Ski Center operates eight lifts with 13 ski slopes of varying difficulty. With ski schools, restaurants, and Saturday-night skiing, the center caters to the needs of experts, beginners, and non-skiers. (☎24 241; www.kalavrita-ski.com. Taxis ☎22 127; €20. Buses run from the town to the mountain. Open Dec.-Apr. when there is snow 8:30am-4pm.)

SITE OF SACRIFICE. The site held most dear to the townspeople of Kalavrita is the Site of Sacrifice monument, a tribute to the Kalavritans who were massacred on December 13, 1943. After the murder of one of their troopers, the occupying Nazis gathered all the town's men and boys over age 13 on a hill outside of town under the pretext of a stern reprimand for the death. Instead, at 2:34pm, hidden troopers opened fire on the men and their sons. Immediately after, they locked Kalavrita's women and children in the town's school and set fire to the building and village. The school now is called the **Museum of Kalavritan Holocaust.** Today, one of the clocks of the town's reconstructed church is set permanently to 2:34, and an extensive memorial stands at the site itself. Heart-wrenching gravestones detail the names and ages of the victims, eternally commemorating them beneath a Greek flag and striking white cross. *(Walk up Ag. Alexiou from the train station and turn left at the signs near the square. The site is about 200m up the hill. Open Tu-Su 10am-5pm. €3, university students and over 65 €1.50. December 12-13 and May 18 Free.)*

🏛 DAYTRIPS FROM KALAVRITA

VOURAIKOS RIVER RAVINE. Perfect for summer hikes, the ravine is a celebration of Greece's mountainous beauty. Its wild cliff sides, waterfalls, caves, and untouched fauna and flora are so treasured by the town that, every May, Kalavrita's town hall organizes a communal ravine hike. Among the natural beauties is the River Styx, where the Olympian gods took their most sacred oaths. Explore the ravine by train or foot. *(A good starting point is Zachlorou, the halfway mark of the Diakopto-Kalavrita railroad; a taxi there costs €10. The railroad was under construction at press time.)*

AGIA LAVRA MONASTERY. Greece's revolutionary fighters were placed under oath at this site—it was the monks of Ag. Lavra who officially initiated the Revolution on March 25, 1821 (p. 56). The monastery was burned by both the Ottomans and Nazis, but some religious relics, including a 16th-century icon of the Virgin Mary, survived the flames. *(7km outside Kalavrita. Taxi €18. Open daily summer 10am-1pm and 4-5pm; winter 10am-1pm and 3-4pm.)*

CAVE OF THE LAKES. Alluded to in Greek mythology but only discovered by locals in 1964, this cave is graced with natural stalactites and stalagmites that pose in otherworldly rock formations. Unlike many of Greece's caves, this one has two levels of beautiful lakes and, as snow melts, waterfalls and flowing rivers emerge. *(17km outside of Kalavrita. ☎ 31 001 or 31 633. English signs point the way from the road behind the Site of Sacrifice. 20min taxi from Kalavrita, €35. A bus to the cave leaves from the Kalavrita bus station some days at 1pm. However, cabs don't wait, so get a cab for the return. Open Sept.-May M-F 9:30am-4:30pm, Sa-Su 9am-6pm; June-Aug. daily 9am-6pm. €8.)*

GREAT CAVE MONASTERY. Look for the signs reading Μόνη Μεγάλου Σπηλαιού. Sixteen centuries of religious history lie 950m above sea level, hidden in a monumental cave near Kalavrita. Built in AD 362, the Great Cave Monastery is the oldest monastery in Greece. It is home to a wax icon of the Virgin Mary, sculpted by St. Luke 2000 years ago. According to the friendly monks, the icon was discovered by a local saint, St. Efrosini, in the cave itself and has performed wondrous miracles ever since. Check out the church's ancient mosaic floors, frescoes, and bronze door. As you walk in, head toward the staircase that lies just right of the small gift shop—four cannons point the way to the museum (€2). Captions in both English and Greek describe the communion cups, clerical vestments, and religious manuscripts from the 11th-13th centuries. Especially noteworthy is the group of 400-year-old handmade crosses on the left wall. Follow a footpath uphill from the monastery and reach the "hole in the rock," rock formation with (surprise!) a hole in it, through which a mysterious whistle sometimes is heard. *(Unless you are driving, transportation is fairly difficult. Buses from Kalavrita to Egio run twice per day, 15min. Ask to be let off at the monastery. Taxis also are available; €22 round-trip. For a particularly scenic route, take the rail to Diakopto, get off at Zachlorou, and climb an ancient and well-marked footpath for 45min. Monastery open daily 7am-1pm and 2-7pm.)*

KYLLINI Κυλλήνη ☎ 26230

For a port town that handles almost all the tourist traffic to Zakynthos, Kyllini is surprisingly undeveloped; the town has almost no bus service, few accommodations, and a handful of cafes. This otherwise disappointing town's highlights are the ruins of a hilltop fortress (signs in town point the way) and its sandy, isolated beach. Since most travelers don't spend much time here, the beach is splendidly undisturbed but still features free lounge chairs under reed-woven umbrellas.

Sea Garden Domatia ❷, above the Sea Garden Restaurant two blocks inland from the port, offers nothing spectacular but is your best bet for an inexpensive night's rest. Rooms have TV, bath, balcony, fridge, and air-conditioning. (☎92 165. Breakfast €5-10. Rooms €20-35.) **Hotel Ionion ❸,** across from the Sea Garden Restaurant, may not seem like much at first but rents surprisingly large rooms with air-conditioning, TV, mini-fridge, and bath. A couple rooms share a bath—negotiate a lower price for these. (☎92 318. Singles €30-50; doubles €55-65.) **The Port of Tsampa ❷,** marked by a Greek sign, is the second restaurant past the Hotel Ionian facing the beach. Reasonable prices and a view of the sea ease patrons into a state of Greek relaxation. (☎92 585. Salads €2.70-4.20. Entrees €6-10 with numerous seafood options.)

Ferries sail from Kyllini to Argostoli, Kephalonia (2hr., 7:30pm, €12.50); Poros, Kephalonia (1½hr., 6-9 per day, €8.50); and Zakynthos (1hr., 5 per day 8am-9:45pm, €6.50). Buy tickets from one of the three kiosks on the dock; the kiosk on the right, facing the port entrance, sells tickets to Zakynthos, and the two on the left sell tickets to Kephalonia. Only Ionian Ferries sails to Argostoli. To leave Kyllini by land, take the **bus**, from the stop across from the port gate, to Pirgos (1½hr., 3 per day 7am-4:30pm, €4.60). Once in Pirgos, you can catch a bus to Olympia (35min., 7-16 per day, €1.90) or a train to Kyparissia or Patras. For all other bus connections you will have to spend €15 on a **taxi** (☎71 764) to Lehena, the nearest town on the main Patras-Pirgos highway. Taxis line up by the same shaded bench where the buses depart. There is no police station in Kyllini; the closest one is in Lehana (☎22 333). A **24hr. ATM** is on the dock next to the Killini Port Restaurant. To find the town's **pharmacy**, walk straight from the dock past the Sea Garden Restaurant and turn left. (Open daily 9am-1:30pm and 5:30-9:30pm.) The post office is a block past the pharmacy. (Open M-F 7:30am-2pm.) **Postal Code:** 27068.

PIRGOS Πύργος   ☎26210

Though Pirgos features regular and inexpensive connections by rail and by road to southwestern Greece and to Athens, it lacks sights and cheap accommodations. With more beautiful and intellectually stimulating cities nearby, it's hard to make a case for staying too long in relatively shabby Pirgos.

⊟ TRANSPORTATION. Pirgos has an extremely efficient and modern bus and train system that will get travelers around most of the Peloponnese and even up to Athens. The train station, Ypsilantou (Υψηλαντου) 12 (☎22 576), 450m downhill from the statue of Kolokotronis along Patron, has **trains** to: Patras (express: 1½hr., 4 per day 8:15am-4:20pm, €5.40; regular: 3 per day 12:28am-6:34pm, €2.80); Kyparissia (regular: 1hr., 3 per day 4:30am-3pm, €1.80; express: 3 per day 1:15pm-9:10pm, €4.40); Olympia (45min., 5 per day 7am-3:10pm, €0.70). The new KTEL bus station is downhill from the train station. Walk down Patron and turn left after the BP gas station onto Erithrou Stavrou. **Buses** run to: Amaliada (25min.; M-F 15 per day 5:30am-9:15pm, Sa 10 per day 7am-9:15pm, Su 7 per day 7:30am-9:15pm; €1.70); Kyllini (1½hr.; 10:30am, 2:15pm; €4.60); Olympia (35min.; M-F 16 per day 5:15am-9:45pm, Sa 11 per day 6:15am-9:45pm, Su 7 per day 7:15am-9:45pm; €1.90). **Taxis** (☎25 000) line up in the center of town by the OTE.

▨⊠ ORIENTATION AND PRACTICAL INFORMATION. The main road in Pirgos, **Mitropoliti Antoniou** (referred to by locals as **"Patron"**), runs from the bus station to the main square, **Plateia Kyprou.** The plateia and its side streets are the center of town life, with cafes and restaurants. The road that begins from the train station and continues upward to the plateia is **Themistokleous.** This road and Patron meet at the beginning of the plateia and intersect **Manolopoulou.** At the intersection of these three roads, you will see a large bronze statue of the Greek independence hero, Kolokotronis. From there, take any of the small pedestrian side streets on the right facing uphill to reach the plateia.

Banks can be found along Patron, next to the statue, and in the plateia. **Piraeus Bank**, next to the statue, has **24hr. ATMs** and **currency exchange.** (Open M-Th 8am-2:30pm, F 8am-2pm.) The **police station** is three blocks uphill from the train station. Walk up Patron and turn left on Karkarvitsa, next to Hotel Olympus. (☎81 734. Open daily 7:30am-10pm, for emergencies 24hr.) The local police also serve as the **tourist police.** (☎81 767. Open daily 8am-2pm.) **Pharmacies** cluster around the intersection of Patron and Manolopoulou. (Most open M-F 8am-2:30pm.) The **hospital** (☎ 22 222) is 2km west of town. **Internet Cafe** is in Pl. Kyprou on Letrinon, behind Goody's. (€2 per hr., min. €1. Open daily 9am-midnight.) The **post office** is at the corner of Manolopoulou and Grigoriou; facing uphill, take a right onto Manolopoulou at the statue. (☎ 33 117. Open M-F 7:30am-2pm.) **Postal Code:** 27100.

⚑☐ ACCOMMODATIONS AND FOOD. Backpackers who love the smell of hostel sheets and high-rollers who live for complimentary bathrobes will be disappointed by the accommodations in Pirgos. Options are limited to mediocre hotels along Patron and on the streets between the bus and train stations. Rates and amenities tend to be consistent. **Hotel Ilida ❹,** Patron 50 and Deligianni, to the right of the train station, is the classiest of the mediocre choices. The lobby shines with cushy leather chairs and leads upstairs to bright rooms with shell-shaped headboards, air-conditioning, TV, phone, and bath. (☎ 28 046. Breakfast €7. Singles €45; doubles €65. MC/V.) **Hotel Pantheon ❸,** Themistokleous 7, two blocks uphill from the train station, caters to those who need a little color to perk up a bland stay in Pirgos. Lime green doors and bright green carpeting adorn rooms with air-conditioning, fridge, hair dryer, spacious yellow beds, and blue-tiled bath. (☎ 29 746. Breakfast €6. Singles €35-50; doubles €45-80. MC/V.) One block uphill from the train station sits **Hotel Marily ❸,** at the intersection of Themistokleous and Deligianni. Its 30 rooms have air-conditioning, TV, phone, hair dryer, freezer, and bath. Hotel Marily's quiet location makes it a good place for a restful night. (☎ 28 133. Singles from €35; doubles from €45; triples from €60.)

It is difficult to find a good, full meal in Pirgos, since it is dominated by fast-food joints, cafes, and souvlaki stands. For something less on-the-go, **Restaurant Milano ❷,** on Themistokleous, is speedy, cheap, and very tasty. It's an especially a good choice for vegetarians and Italian-cuisine enthusiasts. (☎ 23 291. Salads €3-4. Pizza from brick oven €4.50-6.50. Pasta €4-5. Open daily 6pm-1:30am.) **O Vasilis ❶** (Ο Βασίλης), across from the Internet Cafe next to the main plateia, serves souvlaki and gyros in pitas (€1.40) and plates (€4) with fries. (☎ 31 104. Salads €2.50-4.)

OLYMPIA Ολυμπία   ☎ 26240

Set among quiet meadows of cypress and olive trees, modern Olympia bears little evidence of its cosmopolitan past. Though it is most famous as the home of the ancient Olympic Games, Olympia also boasts a pristine natural setting. The city teems with tourist shops and hotels but retains a relaxed pace of living that makes visiting its ancient sites and stunning surroundings a pleasure.

▦ TRANSPORTATION

Trains travel from Olympia to Pirgos (25min., 5 per day 7:20am-3:40pm, €0.70). Change in Pirgos for other destinations including Athens. Contact the train station (☎ 22 677) for updated information, as schedules and prices can change. The bus stop is about 100m down Kondili out of town, away from the ruins. The bus stops at a convenience store across from the sign, where tickets can be purchased. **Buses** go to Pirgos (35min.; M-F 17 per day 6:30am-10:15pm, Sa 11 per day 8:30am-10:15pm, Su 6 per day 8:30am-10:15pm; €1.90) and Tripoli (3½hr.; M-F 8:45am, 12:30, 5:30pm, Sa-Su 8:45am, 5:30pm; €10.60).

✴☑ ORIENTATION AND PRACTICAL INFORMATION

Olympia consists primarily of **Kondili,** the 1km main street. Maps of the town are pinned up on billboards at the street's ends, so it's difficult to get lost. At one end of Kondili, signs point to the museums and ancient sites. As you walk toward them, the main tourist office will be on your right next to the National Bank. The train station, a convenience store, and pricey tavernas sit on the side road that intersects Kondili across from the youth hostel.

Tourist Office: ☎23 173. On Kondili, near the ruins. Helpful staff provides bus schedules, information, and free maps. Open daily 9am-3pm.

Bank: National Bank (☎22 501), on Kondili next to the tourist office. Has **currency exchange** and a **24hr. ATM.** Open M-Th 8am-2:30pm, F 8am-2pm.

Police: Em. Kountsa 1 (☎22 100), 1 block up from Kondili, behind the tourist office. Open 24hr. Also serve as the **tourist police.**

Medical Services: ☎22 222. Olympia uses Pirgos's **hospital** but has its own 24hr. health center. Walk from the ruins to the other end of Kondili and turn left before the church. Continue straight as the road winds to the right, then turn right.

Telephones: Along Kondili across from the youth hostel.

Internet Access: Epathlon Cafe, Stephanopoulou 2 (☎23 894). Offers laptops and plays loud music. Turn off Kondili with the Youth Hostel on your right; it's on the left. €4 per hr. Open daily 9am-2am.

Taxis: Line up on the side street across from the youth hostel.

Post Office: ☎22 578. On Pierre de Coubertain, the side street past the tourist office on the right. Open M-F 7:30am-2pm. **Postal Code:** 27065.

♜ ACCOMMODATIONS AND CAMPING

The prices of Olympia's hotels are set according to amenities and location. Since tourist traffic doesn't fluctuate much with the seasons, prices stay stable.

Olympia Palace, Kondili 2 (☎23 101; www.olympia-palace.gr). Elegant rooms have A/C, satellite TV, safety deposit box, room service, bath with large tub, and balcony. Ask for rooms with large balcony facing the mountains. Breakfast included. Internet €5 per hr. Singles €40-55; doubles €65-75; triples €75-95; quads €90-120. MC/V. ❹

Hotel Kronion, Tsoureka 1 (22 188), on the road perpendicular to the train station. Kronio has large, bright rooms with A/C, TV, and bath. Free Internet in the lobby as well as free Wi-Fi for laptop users. Rooms recently redecorated. Breakfast included. Singles €40; doubles €48-50; triples €67. ❹

New Olympia (☎22 547), on the road that leads diagonally to the train station. The decor is a little behind the times—maybe "retro chic" if you stretch your imagination—but the rooms are spacious with A/C, TV, phone, balcony, and bath. Be prepared to bargain. Breakfast included. Singles €20-30; doubles €40-50; triples €70. ❷

Hotel Ilis (☎22 348), along Kondili next to the church. Offers not only the basic amenities (TV, A/C, and bath), but also a bright red lobby and orange doors, great views of the church, and use of the pool at Hotel Antonio. Breakfast included. Internet available. Singles €40; doubles €50; triples €60. Reservations recommended. ❹

Youth Hostel, Kondili 18 (☎22 580). A great place to get to know international backpackers, this hostel is in a good location and has the cheapest rooms in town. Helpful brochures introducing the ancient site and nature activities are posted up in the lobby. Hot showers available at limited times in early morning and afternoon. Sheets €1. Curfew 10:45pm. Check-out 10am-12:30pm. Dorms €10; doubles €25. ❶

Camping Diana (☎22 314), uphill on the road past the Museum of the Olympic Games (look for the small sign). Has hot water, helpful transportation info, a swimming pool,

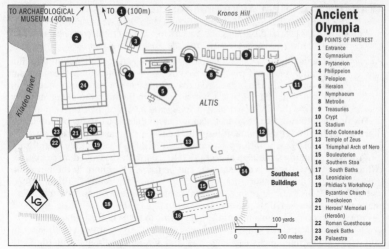

Ancient Olympia

● POINTS OF INTEREST
1 Entrance
2 Gymnasium
3 Prytaneion
4 Philippeion
5 Pelopion
6 Heraion
7 Nymphaeum
8 Metroôn
9 Treasuries
10 Crypt
11 Stadium
12 Echo Colonnade
13 Temple of Zeus
14 Triumphal Arch of Nero
15 Bouleuterion
16 Southern Stoa
17 South Baths
18 Leonidaion
19 Phidias's Workshop/
   Byzantine Church
20 Theokoleon
21 Heroes' Memorial
   (Heroôn)
22 Roman Guesthouse
23 Greek Baths
24 Palaestra

and a mini-mart. Shielded from the hot summer sun by trees and flowery bushes, it's cooler than other accommodations down the hill. Breakfast €6. €7 per person; €5 per small tent; €7 per large tent; €5 per car. ❶

FOOD

Along Kondili, **mini-marts, bakeries,** and **fast-food** joints compete for your attention and cash. Most are overpriced, but a short walk up the hill leads to solid, less expensive tavernas. The constant influx of crowds keeps most open 8am-1am. At night, locals and tourists mingle in the tavernas and bars along Kohili; around 1am, the younger crowd moves to the dance clubs in the middle of town.

Vasilakis (☎22 104), at the corner of Karamanli and Spiliopoulou. Take a right off Kondili before the Youth Hostel, or follow your nose to the delicious meat dishes whose aroma wafts through the entire block. A filling meal here is as Greek as it gets, from the souvlaki pita (€1.50) to the chicken with fries (€10). Open daily 11:30am-midnight. ❷

Aegean, on the side street to the train station next to New Olympia Hotel. Pick from the daily specials, or get one of the meals, which come with salad and soft drink or ouzo. All food homemade. Moussaka plate €4. Souvlaki plate €7. Open daily noon-11pm. ❷

Praxitelis Taverna, Spiliopouloy 3 (☎23 570), just past the police station walking toward the ruins. The multilingual menu offers pasta and meat from the grill as well as other options. Try one of the 7 "menu" options (€9-13), featuring combinations of Greek specialties and sides. Cover €0.50. Entrees €4-16. 10% discount to students with ID. Also lets rooms upstairs as Pension Leonideon. ❸

SIGHTS

Olympia has several museums that examine the town's ancient legacy and sur-roundings. Beyond these, the natural beauty of the area is a sight in itself. Orga-nized walks, river parties, rafting, and kayaking are just a few of the activities available through July and August. Participation is free, but early reservation is absolutely necessary. For more information visit the tourist office which can pro-vide both info and schedules.

PELOPONNESE

■ ANCIENT OLYMPIA ARCHAEOLOGICAL MUSEUM

☎ *22 742. Open Apr.-Oct. M 12:30-7:30pm, Tu-Su 8am-7:30pm; Nov.-Mar. daily 8:00am-3pm. €6, with ancient site €9; seniors and students with ID €3; EU students and under 18 free. Through the parking lot opposite the ancient site. Flash cameras prohibited.*

Many find ancient Olympia's gleaming new museum a greater attraction than the ancient site itself. A team of French archaeologists began unearthing the site from 1400 years of silt in 1829. The organized excavations that continue today started in 1875, and most of what has been extracted resides in the museum. Since military victors from across the Greek world sent spoils and pieces of their own equipment to Olympia as offerings to the gods, the museum doubles as a display of Greek military history, with entire rooms filled with helmets, cuirasses, greaves, swords, spear points, and other military paraphernalia. The most spectacular military offering is a common **Corinthian helmet** (490 BC), partially destroyed by oxidation. While richer, better preserved headgear can be found elsewhere in the museum, this helmet has a faint inscription on the chin guard that reads "Miltiades dedicated this to Zeus." Miltiades led the outnumbered Greeks to victory over the Persians at Marathon in 479 BC; he may have worn this helmet in the battle. Beside it is another headpiece, whose inscription reveals it to be from the Persian side.

The museum's array of sculpture includes some of the greatest extant pieces in the world. One stunning centerpiece is the large western pediment from the Temple of Zeus, depicting the myth about a group of centaurs who attended the wedding of the king of Lapiths. After having a few too many drinks, the horse-men made the mistake of trying to abduct the Lapith women, a move they surely regretted in the morning after the vicious battle that ensued. A 3m tall Apollo stands in the center of the scene, imposing peace and order on the group. The pediment's fragments have been reassembled along one wall of the main room. Even the overlooked objects here astound—every case holds pieces that would be highlights of a lesser collection. Don't miss the room dedicated to Phidias, including some of his tools and shards of a plain drinking cup that, when they were cleaned and mended, bore the inscription "I belong to Phidias."

■ ANCIENT OLYMPIA (SITE)

☎ *22 517. Open daily 8:30am-7:30pm. €6, seniors and students €3, EU students and children under 18 free; museum and site €9. The ruins are practically unmarked. Several guides are available at the museum shop—try those by A. and N. Yalouris (€8), Monolis Andronicos (€5.50), or the Ministry of Culture (€9).*

Before there were photo finishes, drug tests, and aerodymanic unisuits, there were the games of Olympia. A green tract between the rivers Kladeo and Alphios, the city was one of the ancient world's most important cultural centers for a millennium. Participants from Asia Minor, Greece, Macedonia, North Africa, and Sicily convened here to worship, compete, and learn among masterpieces of art and architecture and the most cultured poets and musicians. Every four years for 1169 years, warring city-states would call a sacred truce and travel to Olympia for the most splendid Panhellenic assembly of the ancient world.

HISTORICAL OVERVIEW. Olympia was settled in the 3rd millennium BC, when it was dedicated to **Gaia,** the Earth Mother, who had an oracle at the site. The first athletic contests commenced in Zeus's honor, only to be forgotten again until 884 BC. The first Olympic revival took place on the Oracle of Delphi's orders to Iphtos, King of Elia; prophecy told that the Games would save Greece from civil war and plague. The first recorded Olympiad was in 776 BC, which must have been a peaceful, disease-free year. Initially the most athletic men, naked as jaybirds, competed in a simple *stadion*, or foot-race, lasting 192m (the stadium's length). As the Games's popularity broadened, longer races, wrestling, boxing, the pentathlon (long jump, discus, javelin, running, and wrestling), the hoplite race (in full bronze armor), and equestrian events joined the slate of events. The Olympics were celebrated through the AD 4th century, until Emperor Theodosius concluded that the sanctuary (and thus the Games themselves) violated his anti-pagan laws. Soon thereafter earthquakes in AD 522 and 551 destroyed much of the Olympic site.

ARCHAEOLOGICAL SITE. The central sanctuary of the Olympic complex, eventually walled and dedicated to Zeus, was called the **Altis.** Over the centuries, it held temples, treasuries, and a number of monuments to the gods. The complex was surrounded by various facilities for participants and administrators, including the stadium on the far eastern side. **Pausanias,** a traveler-historian in the AD 2nd century, noted a whopping 69 monuments built by victors to thank the gods. A few sections are roped off, but you can climb up the steps of the Temple of Zeus and walk along its perimeter.

As you enter the site, facing south, veer slightly to the left to reach the **training grounds.** Here you'll find the remains of the 2nd-century BC **gymnasium.** This open-air quadrangle surrounded by Doric columns was reserved for athletes like runners and javelin throwers who needed space to practice. If you continue straight through the gymnasium, you will reach the re-erected columns of the square **Palaestra,** or wrestling school, built in the 3rd century BC. More than a mere athletic facility, the Palaestra ensured that competitors wouldn't become one-dimensional, uncivilized brutes. The young men wrestled one moment and studied metaphysics the next in nearby rooms.

As you continue south and slightly west, the next group of structures includes a reddish, surprisingly intact, walled-in building: the **workshop of Phidias,** the sculptor. For the **Temple of Olympian Zeus,** Phidias produced an ivory and gold statue of the god so magnificent that it became one of the **Seven Wonders of the Ancient World.** It stood 12.4m tall and portrayed the god seated on his throne with an expression revealing benevolence and glory. In tune with the themes of the Olympic Games, Zeus cupped a statue of Nike, the goddess of victory, in his right palm. When the Games were abolished in the 4th century, the statue was moved to Constantinople, where it was destroyed in a fire in AD 475. Adding insult to injury, the Byzantines built a **church** on top of the workshop in the AD 5th century, constructing new walls but leaving the foundation intact. As a result, the identity of the site was debated for years. The traditional sources were affirmed by recent excavations that have uncovered molds, sculpting tools, and the famous cup bearing the inscription "I belong to Phidias." These finds are currently in the museum. Just past the workshop and slightly to the left is the huge **Leonidaion,** built in 330 BC by a wealthy man from Naxos named Leonidas. Though the building officially was dedicated to Zeus some time after 350 BC, it served a primarily secular role, often hosting officials and other VIPs.

At the **Bouleuterion,** to the right as you face the entrance, lie the remains of the South Processional Gate to the Altis. The procession of athletes and trainers entered the sacred area on their way to the Bouleuterion (to the right of the gate), where the ancient Olympic council met. Each athlete was required to make a sacrifice to Zeus and take the sacred oath, swearing his eligibility and intent to abide by the rules of the Games.

North of the Bouleuterion (toward the entrance) are the ruins of the once-gigantic **Temple of Olympian Zeus,** the centerpiece of the Altis after its completion in 456 BC. Home to Phidias's awe-inspiring statue, the 27m long sanctuary was the largest temple completed on the Greek mainland before the Parthenon. The temple's elegant facade, impressive Doric columns, and accurately modeled pedimental sculpture exemplified the Classical design that evolved before the Persians invaded Greece. Today only a half-column stands, while the rest of these tremendous pillars, toppled in segments, lie as they fell after a 6th-century earthquake.

Past the temple, to the right as you face the entrance, lie the remains of the **Echo Stoa,** which was used for competitions between trumpeters and heralds. The musical prowess of the competitors no doubt was enhanced by the colonnade's rumored seven-fold echo. At the northern edge of the colonnade, stone blocks that once supported statues of victorious athletes lead to the **Crypt,** the official entrance to the **stadium** used by athletes and judges. This domed passageway (of which only one arch survives) and the stadium as it stands today are products of the Hellenistic period, built over the remains of the earlier, similarly positioned stadium. Having survived the effects of powerful earthquakes, the stadium appears much as it did 2300 years ago. The judges' stand and the start and finish lines are still in place, and the stadium's grassy banks still can seat nearly 40,000 spectators; you may feel inspired to take a lap or two to bond with Olympians of millennia past. As you leave the passageway to the stadium, the remains of **treasuries** erected by distant states to house votive offerings sit in a row on the northern hillside to your right. Continuing left as you face the hill, you'll see the space that once held the small-scale temples donated by individual cities. Beyond the treasuries are the remains of the **Nymphaeum** and the **Metroon,** an elegant 4th-century BC Doric temple dedicated to Zeus's mother, Rhea. Along the terrace of the treasuries stand the remains of the bases of 16 bronze statues of Zeus, built with money from fines collected from cheating athletes.

To the left facing the hill, past the Metroon and the Nymphaeum, are the dignified remains of the **Temple of Hera,** or **Heraion.** Erected around 600 BC, the temple is the oldest building at Olympia, the oldest Doric temple in Greece, and the best-preserved structure at the site. Originally built for both Zeus and Hera, it was devoted solely to the goddess when Zeus moved to his grander quarters (ironically now in far worse shape) in 457 BC. The *cella* of the temple is where the magnificent **Hermes of Praxiteles** was unearthed during excavations; the statue is now displayed in the site's museum. This temple figured prominently in the **Heraia,** a women's footrace as old, if not older, than the Olympic Games, also held every four years. Today's 🎫**Olympic flame** is lit every other year at the Altar of Hera, at the northeastern corner of the temple. From here, it is borne by a variety of means to the site of the modern Games. This trip can involve thousands of runners passing the torch hand-to-hand, also drawing on more current forms of transportation like boats, planes, and even laser beams (as in the unique case of the 1976 Montreal Games). The **Prytaneion** is northwest of the Temple of Hera and contains a hearth, the Altar of Hestia. The spirit of the Games reached its culmination here with feasts, held on behalf of the victors and official guests, expressing an appreciation for the virtues of discipline and honor embodied by the athletes.

OTHER SIGHTS

MUSEUM OF THE HISTORY OF THE OLYMPIC GAMES IN ANTIQUITY. This museum is jam-packed with info about the ancient **Olympic Games,** with multilingual explanations of the different events and antiquity's various other athletic festivals. Beyond a historical outline, specific artifacts dating back to the 9th century BC are arranged by event, from bronze **tripod cauldrons,** to portions of the original wreaths given as **prizes,** to intact **shields** and even a **wheel** from an iron chariot used in races. One highlight is a remarkably well-preserved mosaic floor from a Roman house in Patras that depicts Olympic events. Although the explanations of the Games are very thorough, many specific objects have little or no explanation; ask a friendly staff member for further information. *(At the end of Kondili, before the incline toward the ancient site; look for the signs. ☎ 29 119. Open Apr.-Oct. M 12:30-7:30pm, Tu-Su 8:30am-7:30pm; Nov.-Mar. M 12:30-3pm, Tu-Su 8:30am-3pm. Free.)*

MUSEUM OF THE HISTORY OF EXCAVATIONS IN OLYMPIA. The one small room that houses this museum—and bathrooms—presents a brief, nostalgic glance at the long process of excavation in Olympia, dating back to 1829. Beyond newspaper clippings from the 1800s and the official documents that allowed for excavations, the smaller objects on display—like a box filled with tickets to the old museum, inventory lists from the daily excavations, and pages from excavation diaries and manuscripts from 1908—add depth to the story of discovery. The museum also has a large collection of instruments used in the original excavation. Though small, this museum is valuable for understanding the practical side of the site's archaeology. (*Next door to the Museum of the History of the Olympic Games in Antiquity. If it is locked, ask a staff member at the Olympic Games museum to open it.*)

MUSEUM OF THE OLYMPIC GAMES. Tracing the modern Games from 1896 to 2004, this museum displays pins, stamps, photographs, posters from each Olympiad, and biographies of prominent athletes. Notice how the shape and style of the Olympic Torch has changed over the past century, and don't miss the silver medal from the 1996 Games in Atlanta, donated by Niki Bakoyianni, the women's high-jump medalist. (*☎ 22 544. 2 blocks from Kondili, on Avgerinou. Turn next to Hotel Ilis; it's the large white building at the end of the street. Open Tu-Su 8am-3:30pm. €2. Guidebook €6.*)

ARCADIA Αρκαδία

Beyond the noisy bustle of urban Tripoli, mountainous and heavily forested Arcadia is speckled with red-roofed villages and monasteries. Introduced into mythology and literature for its serene landscape, "Arcadia" became synonymous with pastoral paradise. Well past ancient times, an archetypal image lingered of a green idyll inhabited by Pan, Dionysus, nymphs, satyrs, and the lucky mortals who cavorted with them. While few foreign tourists venture as far as Arcadia's outer reaches, those who do can enjoy the rare company of mountain goats on the isolated slopes. A visit to one of the small villages like Dimitsana or Stemnitsa brings complete immersion into traditional Greek culture.

TRIPOLI Τρίπολη ☎ 27102

Visitors to Arcadia's capital, Tripoli, may find a trifecta of reasons to visit: a depth of nightlife options rarely found in Peloponnesean cities, a modern bus station serving a wide range of Greek towns, and... did we mention the nightlife already? While a visit to Tripoli is not likely to be the highlight of anyone's trip, the city does stay up late, and has no shortage of plateias to accommodate the night owls and youths who flock to the city on weekends for its bar and club scene.

▐ TRANSPORTATION

Buses: Tripoli has 2 bus stations; both are outside of town, 5min. taxi rides or 15-20min. walks from Pl. Kolokotronis. You also can take a blue bus from stops around town. Ask at the nearest kiosk.

KTEL Arcadias Station (☎ 22 560), Nafpliou 50. Walk along Venizelou (which becomes Nafpliou), the street across from the Arcadia Hotel with the arrow pointing down it toward the police station—it's on the right. Sends buses to: **Andritsena** (2hr.; 11:45am, 7:30pm; €6.80); **Athens** (2hr., 17 per day 5am-10pm, €12.80); **Patras** (3hr., 4 per day 8:30am-4pm, €15.60); **Dimitsana** (1½hr.; 1:30, 6:30pm; €5.60); **Megalopolis** (45min., 7 per day 10am-10:15pm, €2.90); **Nafplion** (1hr., 5 per day 7am-6:30pm, €5) via **Argos** (€5); **Pirgos** (3½hr., 6 per day 8:30am-8:30pm, €12.20). Blue buses leave for **Mantinea** and **Tegea** (1hr., every 15min., €1.40).

KTEL Messinia and Laconia depot (☎ 42 086), in a convenience store across from the train station. From Pl. Kolokotronis, take Venizelou then make your 1st right after 20m onto N. Lagopati and follow it to the end; it's on the left. Buses go to: **Kalamata** (1½hr., every hr. 8am-midnight, €6.90); **Patras**

(3hr., Sa 6:30am, €12.60); **Pylos** (3hr.; 11am, 5:30pm; €11.10); **Sparta** (1hr., 12 per day 9am-10:15pm, €4.70).

Trains: Facing the Messinia and Laconia bus depot across from the end of N Lagopati. Trains go to **Corinth** (2¼hr., 2:17am) via **Argos** (1hr.) and **Athens** (4½hr.; 9:54am, 5:54pm) via **Corinth** and **Argos.**

Taxis (☎33 010) line up in Pl. Ag. Vasiliou.

◼🛈 ORIENTATION AND PRACTICAL INFORMATION

Tripoli is a cross, with **Plateia Agiou Vasiliou,** marked by the **Church of Ag. Vasiliou,** at the central joint. Four other plateias form the ends of the cross, at the ends of the four roads that branch out from Ag. Vasiliou. From **Plateia Kolokotronis, Vasiliou Giorgiou,** to the left as you face the National Bank, takes you to Pl. Ag. Vasiliou. Facing the church in Pl. Ag. Vasiliou, turn left and head north onto **Ethnikis Antistasis** to reach **Plateia Petrinou,** recognizable by the large, Neoclassical Maliaropouli Theater. Continue on Eth. Antistasis past pedestrian-only **Deligianni,** which runs perpendicular to Eth. Antistasis. Farther up, the city **park** will be on your right. At the center of the park, to the left of Eth. Antistasis as you face Pl. Ag. Vasiliou, is **Plateia Areus,** with a 5m tall statue of war hero Kolokotronis.

Bank: National Bank, in Pl. Kolokotronis (☎27103 71 110). Another is on Eth. Antistasis (☎27103 71 156), 1 block from Pl. Ag. Vasiliou; take the 1st left as you head down Eth. Antistasis toward Pl. Petrinou. Both **exchange currency** and have a **24hr. ATM.** Both open M-Th 8am-2:30pm, F 8am-2pm.

Police: ☎24 847. About 1km from Pl. Kolokotronis. Walk toward the train station and go right at the traffic light; it's another 150m. Open 24hr.

Hospital: ☎38 542. On Panargadon. Walk straight ahead with your back to the church from Pl. Ag. Vasiliou; the road becomes E. Stavrou, which intersects with Panargadon after 500m. At the intersection, turn left. After 300m, look right, and you'll see the hospital. In an **emergency,** dial ☎166 or 100.

Telephones: OTE, 28 Oktovriou 29 (☎22 999). From Pl. Ag. Vasiliou, take Eth. Antistasis and go left on 28 Oktovriou at the National Bank branch. Offices are upstairs. Open M, W, Sa 7:30am-3pm, Tu and Th-F 7:30am-8:30pm.

Internet Access: Cinema Billiards Club, 45 Kennedy or 2 Deligianni (☎38 010), to the right off Eth. Antistasis walking from Kolokotronis. 10am-4pm €1 per hr., 4pm-midnight €2 per hr., midnight-2am €2.50 per hr.; min. €1. Open daily 10am-2am. **Memories Cafe** (☎35 600), on Dareioutou off Eth. Antistasis walking from Kolokotronis, before Deligianni. €2 per hr., min. €1. Coffee €2.50. Beer €4. Open daily 8am-3:30am.

Post Office: ☎22 565. Behind Galaxy Hotel in Pl. Ag. Vasiliou. Turn right 1 block past the war museum onto Nikitara. Open M-F 7:30am-8pm. **Postal Code:** 22100.

🛏 ACCOMMODATIONS

All of Tripoli's hotels are in or near the plateias. As a transportation hub with some of the best nightlife in the region, the city draws village youth looking for weekend clubs, businessmen attending conventions, and a diverse mix of international travelers stuck for the night, but it still lacks budget accommodations. ◪**Hotel Anaktorikon ❶,** Eth. Antistasis 48, between Deligiannis and the city park, offers old-world elegance and perks at decent prices. The plush red carpeting leads to sitting areas with artwork, luxurious red brocade couches, and a piano. Rooms have large bath with tub, air-conditioning, TV, phone, minibar, and balcony. Shrewd bargaining can lower prices by €20-30. (☎22 545. Breakfast €8. Singles €67; doubles €80; triples €96.) In Pl. Kolokotronis, travel into the past at **Arcadia Hotel ❸,** where the charmingly old-fashioned rooms come with leather-backed chairs and other classy furnishings. Each has bath, air-conditioning, TV, and a unique wallpaper pattern. (☎25 551. Singles €35; doubles €50; triples €60. V.) **Hotel Alex ❹**, Vas. Giorgiou 26, caters to those who prefer contemporary furnishings. Its leather and marble lobby and silver elevator give way to spotless white rooms with big bath, air-conditioning, TV, phone, and balcony. (☎23 465; www.alexhotel.gr. Breakfast €7. Singles €40; doubles €70; triples €85; quads €95; suites €100.)

⚑ FOOD

The restaurants in Tripoli generally aren't anything to write home about. There are a few good options bordering the park, though, and sandwich shops on Eth. Antistasis and Vas. Giorgiou pile baguettes with meat and cheese (around €2-3). The aptly named **Faces Bar and Restaurant ❸**, Deligianni 15, on the corner of Eth Antistasis, offers an extensive menu. The establishment's walls are decorated with the pictures of many famous 20th-century icons. Although the eatery is Chicago-themed—its owner is a former Windy City bookie—its food retains a Hellenic flair. The air-conditioned, wood-floored dining room upstairs rarely is used in summer, although diners in winter enjoy a view above the pedestrian street below. (☎27 750. 18 different salads €2.90-8.90 each. Vegetarian linguini €7.90. Main dishes €6-29. Open daily 9am-2am.) After a few hours exploring Tripoli's underwhelming eateries, you may answer the query posed by **Hungry? ❶**, on the corner of Deligianni and Tasou, with an emphatic "Ναι!" ("Yes!"). The large portions of delicious pizza (€2.80 per slice) leave no doubt as to why Tripoli's youth regularly stop at this eatery. (Burgers €2.20. Open 24hr.)

◉ 🖫 SIGHTS AND NIGHTLIFE

The **Archaeological Museum** is on Evangelistrias, in a pink building surrounded by rose bushes and sculpture. Walking from Pl. Kolokotronis to Pl. Ag. Vasiliou, take the first left, then turn left again. The museum has a large collection, with rooms of pottery and weaponry from the Neolithic to Roman periods. (☎42 148. Open Tu-Su 8am-3pm. €2, students and seniors €1, children free. Photography prohibited.) Walk to the left of the Galaxy Hotel in Pl. Ag. Vasiliou to find the **War Museum** on the left side of the street, marked by a large cannon in front. Look for the old photograph of Peristera Kraka, the female "Captain of West Macedonia." (Open Tu-Sa 9am-2pm, Su 9:30am-2pm. Free.)

Local high school students crowd the cafe-bars in the narrow pedestrian-only area around Deligianni and Eth. Antistasis. At **Cova,** pop music plays in a neo-19th-century bar, featuring high ceilings, tiles, stained glass, chandeliers, and lots of color. (Mixed drinks €6. Open daily 8am-3am. Beer €4.) Across the street from Hungry?, **Prince** is decorated in a modern Middle Eastern theme with bright paintings on the walls. (Beer €5. Mixed drinks €7. Open daily 9am-3am.) The side roads branching off of and parallel to Deligianni are home to some clubs (cover €10). In the summer, posters advertise dance groups, choirs, and plays performed in the city's main plateias and nearby villages. The **Tegea Panigyris** is a theater and dance festival in nearby Tegea, kicked off each year on August 14. During the festival, transportation shuttles Greeks out to the town, but for a regular schedule of local bus routes, check out the large sign in front of the Arcadia Hotel.

DIMITSANA Δημητσάνα ☎27950

A quintessential Arcadian village, Dimitsana clings to a steep, pine-covered mountainside about 65km from Tripoli. Built on the ruins of ancient Teuthis,

Dimitsana has been a center of Greek learning and revolutionary activity since the 16th century. Greek city-dwellers have been working to resettle Dimitsana, providing the money and energy to keep the town's historical buildings in good repair. Though relatively tiny, the town manages to feel more alive than one might expect, with locals flocking to cafes and tavernas that line the main road as it loops through town. With stunning views of endless mountains and the twinkling lights of Megalopolis, Dimitsana offers cozy hospitality in the winter and first-rate hikes along the Lousios River in the summer.

⚏ 🛈 TRANSPORTATION AND PRACTICAL INFORMATION. Getting around can be tricky in the mountains, where the villages are far apart and public transportation is almost non-existent. When planning trips, keep in mind that the town's two taxi drivers might siesta all afternoon. There is no Dimitsana bus station, only a bus kiosk by the health center, and buses pick up passengers at several different locations. Talk to the locals to find out approximate times and places to catch a bus, but don't be surprised if these estimates turn out to be off by an hour. You may want to try taking a bus from the nearby village of Karkalou if Dimitsana's options are too limited. The bus station in Tripoli (☎27102 22 560) will have the latest updates, especially for weekends and national holidays. **Buses** should run at 7:30am to Tripoli (1hr.) via Stemnitsa and at 7:30-8pm to Tripoli via Karkalou. Both fares are €5.60. A bus to Pyrgos meets the 7:30-8pm bus from Dimitsana in Karkalou. When you leave the bus kiosk, make sure to tell the driver where you want to go. The bus deposits those arriving on **Labardopoulou**, the main street, near the **taxi** stand (☎61 400), 30m downhill from the town center.

Walking uphill into the town center from Labardopoulou, you'll pass a string of cafes and stores to the left and a small grocery store (open daily 7:30am-10:30pm) just before a turn in the road. There you will find a **National Bank** with a **24hr. ATM** and **currency exchange.** (Open M-Th 8am-2:30pm, F 8am-2pm.) Opposite the grocery store is an alley leading to rooms and the Ecclesiastical Museum. The run-down **police station**, which has a flag hanging from its balcony, is just before the bank. To get upstairs, take the alley by the station and go around to the side of the building. (☎31 205. Open 24hr.) The **health center** (☎31 401 or 31 402; open 24hr.) is next to the bus kiosk, a 5min. walk down the road toward Karkalou; the closest **hospital** is in Tripoli. A small **pharmacy** is on your right, walking uphill from the bus stop. (☎31 477.) The **post office** is next to the bank, after the road turns. (Open M-F 7:30am-2pm.) **Postal Code:** 22007.

🛌 ACCOMMODATIONS. For its small size, Dimitsana has an impressive number of rooming options. Though **domatia** can be just as expensive as the hotels, there's no doubt that you get what you pay for. Most are beautifully furnished and built along the cliffside, yielding fantastic mountain views. High and low seasons are reversed here—the rooms get cheaper as it gets warmer. Off the main road but still close to the town center, **Vasilis Tsiapa ❹**, with a garden patio of colorful flowers, overlooks the mountains toward Megalopolis. Eight traditional stone rooms come with high wood ceilings, TV, bath, and fully-stocked kitchenette. Rooms have access to a common carpeted living room with a kitchen table, ship's wheel chandelier, and a balcony with a spectacular view. As you walk up the main road from the bus stop, turn right into the alley opposite the National Bank, pass the Ecclesiastical Museum and a parking lot, and the rooms will be down a stepped path on your left. (☎31 583. Breakfast included. Rooms €40-90. 2-person suite €50-100.) At the home of **Georgios Velissaropoulos ❸**, a short 3min. walk from the main road, the small gardens and magnificent valley views supplement rooms with kitchenette and access to a comfortable living room. To find the house, follow the road across from the police station and turn right after 25m; signs point the way another 75m down the winding stone street. (☎31 617. Singles €35-55; doubles €38-65; 2- to 4-person apartment €55-100.)

🏠🍴 **FOOD AND NIGHTLIFE.** Though Dimitsana's dining options are limited, your meal's mountain backdrop is worth every euro. In an elegant country house, **Drymonas ❷**, 200m past the post office on the road leading to Stemnitsa, has a rotating menu of classic Greek staples. Pork, lamb, and rabbit dishes (€7-10) come in large portions. (☎31 116. Salads €4.50-6. Rabbit with lemon sauce €8.20. Open daily 1-11:30pm.) **To Baroytadiko ❷**, on the patio across from the cab stand where the bus drops travelers, heaps plates with giant portions in a shaded outdoor dining area. Surrounded by evergreen trees, the space gives way to a disco in the winter, when patrons move across the street to the cozy, stone-walled dining room. (Boiled goat meat €7.50. Main dishes €6-10. Salads €3.50-6. Open daily 2pm-1am.) Have a snack or drink at relaxed **Cafe-Bar Brahos** at the turn onto the road to Stemnitsa after the bank. American pop plays inside Dimitsana's only steady semblance of nightlife, and the mountain views make the already lovely outdoor seating magnificent. At night the natural stone walls inside are lined with candles. (Beer €3. Mixed drinks €5. Coffee €2.50. Open daily noon-late.)

🔲 **SIGHTS.** Dimitsana has an impressive collection of museums that proudly commemorate its ecclesiastical, scholarly, and revolutionary heritage. The pride of the town, the **Historical Museum** was formerly the library of a ministry school that was established in 1764. Its collection of over 5000 books was decimated when the books were used as gunpowder during the War of Independence. The revamped and very much restocked library-museum now holds over 35,000 books. Some items from the original library are still on display, including a handful of Greek-Latin **incunabula**, 16th-century books from Venice and Basel that are among the first books ever printed. To find the library and museum, walk up the alley next to the police station and look for the courtyard with the statue and a large church; the entrance is on the wall farthest from the street. (Open Tu-Sa 9am-2pm.) The smaller but still fascinating **Ecclesiastical Museum** is in the alley opposite the National Bank. Located in the old mansion of Patriarch Gregory V, the museum contains the saint's church in its basement. The collection includes local icons and religious artifacts from the 17th century, including exceptionally well-preserved Bibles and the saint's own robes. (Open Apr.-Nov. M-Tu, Th, Sa-Su 10am-1:30pm and 5-7pm; Dec.-Mar. Sa-Su 10am-1:30pm and 4-6pm. Free.) Dimitsana is home to an **Open-Air Water Power Museum**, 1.6km from the village; take the main road as it turns past the bank and follow signs at the first fork downhill to the right. The exhibit brings back to life the tanneries and mills that were operated in the 16th through 20th centuries using the waters of the Lousios River.

If you have your own transportation, the old **Filosofou Monastery** (☎81 447) is worth visiting for its role in the Greek independence movement. Built in the Lousios Gorge in AD 963, the monastery was the location of the famous *krifto scholio* (secret school) where priests covertly maintained Greek education and the revolutionary spirit under Ottoman rule. To get there from Dimitsana, drive to the village of Markou, then take the road from that town, a total of 20km from Dimitsana. To reach the **Lousios River,** take the road to Stemnitsa and follow the signs at the fork. There is another entrance along the mountain road, 1km from Stemnitsa, 10km from the river. Summertime visitors seek adventure on the rapids, swim in the river, and gaze at the multicolored butterflies that migrate to the area. A hike through the gorge takes about 3½hr., but the best part of the trek starts after the Filosofou Monastery. Rafting and hiking tours are available. For more information or to arrange a tour, contact **Hellas Trekking** (☎21 912), based in the town of Maratha, a 1hr. drive from Dimitsana on the road through Stemnitsa.

PELOPONNESE

STEMNITSA Στεμνίτσα ☎ 27950

With its unspoiled mountain scenery and abundant flowers, greenery, and hidden courtyards, it is easy to see why Stemnitsa has been called one of the most beautiful towns in Greece. At the **Folk Art Museum,** 300m down the road leading away from Dimitsana, a series of rooms displays antiquated techniques once used by cobblers and candlemakers in an 18th-century mansion. (☎81 252. Open July-Sept. M and Su 11am-1pm, W-Th and Sa 11am-1pm and 6-8pm, F 6-8pm; Oct.-June M and W-F 11am-1pm, Sa-Su 11am-2pm. Free. No photography.) Between Dimitsana and Stemnitsa there are several monasteries, a few built right into the mountain face. Some of the roads and paths are unsuitable for cars and are best attempted on foot. A loop from Dimitsana to a monastery and then to Stemnitsa could be up to 30km, so plan accordingly. The 12th-century monastery of **Agios Ioannis Prodromos** is 7km from Stemnitsa and 13km from Dimitsana. During the War of Independence, it was a hospital and sanctuary for revolutionaries. Its icons are painted on the bare stone walls and gravity-defying monastic cells that seem to hang off the mountain. Take the road toward Dimitsana for 1km, turn left at the sign, and follow the road for another 7km. Once you hit the dirt path, the monastery is another 30min. by foot. (☎81 385. Open daily dawn-dusk. Modest dress required. Free.)

If you need to spend the night in the village, **Stemnitsa Domatia ❹,** a traditional stone building on the road from Dimitsana just outside the center of town and behind a colorful garden, has spacious rooms with bath. With balcony space and a cozy living room with a fireplace, the domatia offer characteristic Stemnitsan peace and quiet. (☎81 349. Breakfast included. Doubles and triples €50-60.) At the end of the plateia closer to the road away from Dimitsana is **Symposio ❷,** where traditional fare is prepared every day at the whim of the cook, eliminating the possibility of a menu. Instead walk into the kitchen to pick among the fresh dishes, which may include meatballs, stuffed tomatoes, or traditional beef stew. Expect to pay €6-9 for a plate, enjoyed either outside on the stone plateia or inside in a dining room with walls graced by personal photos. (☎81 500. Open daily 8am-10pm.) **Restaurant Stemnitsa ❷,** in the plateia across from the town hall, has a simple menu of tasty staple dishes. (☎81 371. Pork in tomato sauce €6. Main dishes €6-15. Open daily noon-11pm.) On the road out of town toward the art museum, there is a **bakery** and **supermarket,** among other small shops.

From Dimitsana, you can walk an easy, scenic 7km (1½hr.) along the winding road, catch the 7:30am bus, or pay for a **taxi** to Stemnitsa (€7). **Buses** come through Stemnitsa, but as with Dimitsana and other mountain villages, they are not necessarily regular or on time. On weekdays and some weekends, there are buses to Dimitsana at 2:15pm and to Tripoli at 7:30am. At the **town hall,** in the plateia, people are extremely friendly and helpful and speak English. (☎81 280. Open M-F 8am-3pm.) **Postal Code:** 22024.

MESSINIA Μεσσηνία

Messinia is a lush and largely tourist-free oasis in the arid Peloponnese. Renowned olives, figs, and grapes spring from the rich soil, and its dense forests hide the ruins of Venetian castles and Turkish fortresses. Most Messinians live at the head of the gulf around the sprawling labyrinth of Kalamata, though visitors may prefer to stay in the sleepy coastal towns with their clean beaches and quiet streets.

KALAMATA Καλαμάτα ☎ 27210

The Peloponnese's second-largest city, Kalamata does not offer the same ancient heritage as many of its sister cities. Nevertheless, it has a special place in the heart of any proud Greek: it was the first town to rise in successful revolt against Turkish rule on March 23, 1821, in the war that led to the formation of the Greek state. Hidden among the urban sprawl are museums, churches and theaters, while high above town the fortress ruins stand as a reminder of the region's past. Most visitors to the city mainly stick to the town's waterfront strip, hitting the beach by day and seaside clubs and restaurants by night.

⊏ TRANSPORTATION

Trains: ☎95 056. At the intersection of Sid. Stathmou and Frantzi. To: **Athens** (6½hr., 12:45pm, €11.60) via **Tripoli** (2½hr., €2.80) and **Corinth** (5¼hr., €5.60); **Pirgos** (3¼hr., 8 per day 5:53am-10pm, €2.80) via **Kyparissia** (2hr., 1.90); **Patras** (5½hr.; 5:53am, 9:57am; €5).

Buses: ☎22 851. Leave from the station on Artemidos, inland from Pl. Giorgiou and across the river from Aristomenous. Open daily 7am-10pm. To get to the waterfront from the bus station, take a taxi (€43) or walk down Artemidos and eventually cross to parallel Aristomenous, which leads to Pl. Giorgiou (40min.). Buses go to: **Areopolis** (2hr.; 4:45am, 7am, 1:15pm; €7.10); **Athens** (4hr., 13 per day 4:45am-10pm, €19); **Finikounda** (1½hr., 3 per day 5am-1pm, €6.30); **Itilo** (4 per day 4:45am-6:15pm) via Kardamyli (€3) and Stoupa (€3.70); **Koroni** (1½hr., 8 per day 5am-7pm, €4.10); **Mavromati** and **Ancient Messini** (1hr.; 5:40am, 2pm; €2.50); **Methoni** (1¾hr., 5 per day 5am-7:45pm, €5); **Patras** (3½hr.; 8:30am, 2:30pm; €19.30) via **Pirgos** (2½hr., €10.90); **Pylos** (1½hr., 7 per day 5am-7:45pm, €4.10); **Sparta** (2hr.; 9:15am, 2:30pm; €5); **Tripoli** (2hr., 8 per day 6am-10pm, €6.90). Local city buses (€0.90 per ride) are very limited. City buses depart from near Pl. 25 Martiou in the Old Town; look for the large street off Aristomenous. **Bus #1** and **5** go down Aristomenous to the water, then run along the water. Stops are on all main streets. Buy tickets on board.

Taxis: ☎26 565. Line up by the bus station and in Pl. Giorgiou.

Moped Rental: Alpha Rental (☎93 423; www.alphabike.gr), on Vyronos 1 block from the waterfront. Map, helmet, and insurance included. From €17 per day. Bicycle, from €6 per day. Open daily 8:30am-2pm and 4:30-8pm.

▮✴ ▮ ORIENTATION AND PRACTICAL INFORMATION

Kalamata is frustratingly spread out, so short-term visitors may want to stay by the waterfront's convenient grid. The city is divided into three sections. Closest to the water is a **residential section,** distinguished by the municipal park; most of the hotels and restaurants are here, along **Navarinou,** the waterfront street. Heading inland, you will reach **Plateia Giorgiou,** home to the train station, the post office, stores, and banks. The **Old Town,** with the castle, market, and bus station, is farthest from the ocean. Navigating your way across the city can be confusing, so pick up a map from the tourist office. The bus station is on **Artemidos.** From the station, follow Artemidos to the left for about 500m, and take the third river crossing on your left to **Aristomenous,** the main street. Eventually Aristomenous meets and runs along Pl. Giorgiou. Take the first river crossing and head directly away from the bus station to get to the Old Town and castle.

Tourist Office: A limited selection of pamphlets and free maps is available near Pl. Giorgiou at **DETAK,** Poliviou 6 (☎21 700), just off Aristomenous. Walk up Aristomenous from Pl. Giorgiou and signs will point the way. Open M-F 8am-2:30pm.

Banks: National Bank (☎28 047), in the southwest corner of Pl. Giorgiou. Other branches are 2 blocks to the north on Aristomenous and on Akrita on the waterfront. All have **24hr. ATMs** and **currency exchange.** Open M-Th 8am-2:30pm, F 8am-2pm.

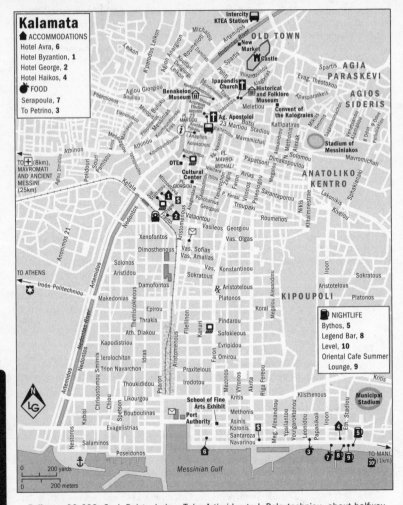

Kalamata

ACCOMMODATIONS
Hotel Avra, **6**
Hotel Byzantion, **1**
Hotel George, **2**
Hotel Haikos, **4**

FOOD
Serapoula, **7**
To Petrino, **3**

NIGHTLIFE
Bythos, **5**
Legend Bar, **8**
Level, **10**
Oriental Cafe Summer
Lounge, **9**

Police: ☎ 22 622. On I. Polytechniou. Take Artimidos to I. Poleytechniou, about halfway between the train station and the waterfront. Open 24hr.

Hospital: ☎ 46 000 or 27210 45 500. Near the town of Sperchogia, accessible by car or taxi. Call ☎ 166 in a medical **emergency**.

Telephones: OTE (☎ 26 099). In the northwestern corner of Pl. Giorgiou, opposite the National Bank. Open M and W 8am-3pm, Tu and Th-F 8am-9pm, Sa 9am-2:30pm.

Internet Access: The Web, Sid. Stathmou 19 (☎ 90 519), next to Hotel Byzantio, 1 block from Pl. Giorgiou. At the southern end of the plateia, turn right; it's across from the train station. Midnight-noon €2 per hr., noon-midnight €2.50 per hr. Open 24hr. **Matrix,** Faron 154, about 5 blocks up from the waterfront. Features a lively bar. €3 per hr., min. €1.50. Open daily 9am-2am. **Diktyo** (☎ 97 282), on Nedontos just past Vas. Georgiou. €1.80 per hr. €1.50 per hr. with membership. Open 24hr.

Post Office: (☎ 22 810), on Vas. Olgas. Turn left 1 block past the southern end of Pl. Giorgiou, toward the waterfront. Offers **Poste Restante.** Another branch is on the waterfront next to the tourist police. Open M-F 7:30am-2pm. **Postal Code:** 24100.

ACCOMMODATIONS AND FOOD

Hotels in Kalamata cluster around Pl. Giorgiou and the waterfront, but budget accommodations are few and far between. **Hotel George ❷,** on the corner of Dagre and Frantzi, has an intimate lobby that resembles a living room. Rooms have air-conditioning, TV, balcony and bath. As one of the cheapest places in town, it's often fully booked, so call ahead. (☎ 27 225. Singles €25-30; doubles €30-35.) Another good bet is nearby **Hotel Byzantion ❸,** Sid. Strethmou 13, one block from the train station. Simple rooms come with air-conditioning, TV, high ceilings, big bath, and balcony; those on the fifth floor are high enough to block out the city noise below. (☎ 86 824. Singles €35-40; doubles €45-50.) **Hotel Haikos ❸,** Navarinou 115, rents colorful, carpeted rooms with air-conditioning, TV, balcony, communal fridge, and hair dryer. (☎ 88 902; www.haikos.gr. Breakfast €6. Singles €40; doubles €55.) Beach bums who prefer to stay next to the lively waterfront may want to try **Hotel Avra ❶,** Santaroza 10, one block behind Navarinou between Kanari and Faron. The somewhat shabby exterior hides a somewhat shabby interior, though it is clean and the cheapest option in town. Large rooms have sink and balcony. (☎ 82 759. Singles €17-20; doubles €22-25; triples €29-32.)

With your back to the bus station, walk across the first bridge on your right to reach the massive **New Market.** The market contains countless meat, cheese, and fruit shops, alongside stands selling every imaginable type of household good. You can sample famous Kalamata olives and figs at the daily farmers' market, which opens around 8am. For a sit-down meal, family-owned **Serapoula ❷,** Navarino 14, serves standard Greek dishes. In a central location on the waterfront, but quieter than its showy neighbors, it is perfect for those who want to have a relaxing meal and still be able to afford after-dinner drinks. (☎ 20 985. Entrees €5-7.50. Salads €2.50-5. Open daily noon-1:30am.) **To Petrino ❸,** Navarinou 93, draws diners to the beachside under straw umbrellas. Try Greek specialties (€5.50-10) or meat from the grill (€6-15), with ostrich (€15) available as well as other occasional exotic meat selections. (☎ 29 097; www.petrino.8k.com. Open daily 10am-2am.)

SIGHTS

The 13th-century **castle,** built by Wilhelm Villehardouin, crowns a hill above the Old City. From Pl. 25 Martiou, walk up Ipapandis and turn right after the large church. Walk around to the back of the church and take your first left; you will see signs that point the way. Destroyed by Ottomans in 1685, the castle was rebuilt by Venetians a decade later. There are no written explanations, but feel free to ask any of the friendly staff for information. The castle encircles an open-air theater, which hosts the **Cultural Summer of Kalamata** from mid-July to the end of August, with jazz, rock, and Greek drama. Ask at the tourist office for details. (☎ 22 534. Open M-F 8am-7pm, Sa-Su 9am-3pm. Free.) Near the castle in the Old Town is one of Kalamata's most famous gems, the **Convent of the Kalograies** (known locally as **"Moni Kalograion"**). Founded in 1796, the convent houses nuns who spend their days hand-weaving silks used for the priests' robes. To get there, walk down the hill from the castle toward Ipapandi church and take a left onto Poukoupaprio before the church, or follow the signs. (Modest dress required.) Closer to the New Town, in a corner by Pl. 25 Martiou, is the 14th-century **Church of the Aghioi Apostoloi** (Holy Apostles). The church first gained recognition when a doe-eyed icon of the Virgin Mary was found there. The name of the city reflects the icon's appearance—*kala mata* means "good eyes."

After five years of restoration, the Old City's **Benakeion Archaeological Museum** proudly exhibits a small collection of statues, coins, and jewelry, with thorough captions in both English and Greek. The exceptionally preserved mosaic floor from Koroni, a ruined Roman villa nearby, is a particular highlight, along with the seals made from semi-precious stones on the second floor. (☎63 100. Open Tu-Su 8:30am-3pm.) The **Historical and Folklore Museum** (☎28 445), in the same square as Ipapandi church, in the past has exhibited everything from guns to icons to traditional costumes in its attempt to share Kalamata's rich historical traditions. Kalamata also proudly supports two professional **theaters.** Ask DETAK or the tourist police for info on events in the **Pantazopoulion Cultural Center** on Aristomenous. (☎94 819, or call the municipality at 28 000.) For information about and schedules of the widely known **Kalamata International Dance Festival** (☎83 086; www.kalamatadancefestival.gr), contact the Kalamata International Dance Center.

▐ NIGHTLIFE

At night in Kalamata, the youth shimmy into skin-tight garb and head to the cafes and bars on the waterfront or to the strip 1km east of the port. **Level,** Navarinou 302, two doors down from Balox towards Kalamata, is a neon-colored, psychedelic paradise for the huge crowds that dance late into the night. (Beer and mixed drinks €5-8. Open in summer daily midnight-7am.) Elsewhere on Navarinou, funky **Legend Bar's** large-screen TV broadcasts soccer matches for a rowdy clientele. (☎97 690. Mixed drinks and beer €5. Open daily 9am-late.) Next to Legend is **Oriental Cafe Summer Lounge,** Navarinou 121, a hookah bar that features belly dancer shows every night. (Hookah €5 per hr. Beer €5. Open daily 8am-3am.) Nearby, **Bythos Bar** sports blue and white decor in a large open-air space. (☎82 853. Beer €3. Mixed drinks €6. Open M-Th and Su 9am-4am, F-Sa 24hr.)

▐ DAYTRIPS FROM KALAMATA

MAVROMATI

The town is 25km from Kalamata and within walking distance of Ancient Messini. Buses leave from Kalamata (1hr.; 5:40am, 2pm; €2.50). Taxis €20-25.

The small town of Mavromati is charmingly impervious to the tour groups that file in and out of the nearby site. Visitors who stop into the mountain village itself are treated to incredible views of the site below. The main square contains the **Klepseydra fountain,** where clean, clear water runs from a dark hole in the rocks that resembles a black eye, or *mavro mati* in Greek. The 17th-century **Voulkanou Monastery,** 2.5km outside town, was a staging point for rebels in the War of Independence; its library holds priceless manuscripts.

ANCIENT MESSINI

The site is 300m downhill from Mavromati's main square. Take the bus to Valira and get off at Lambena. From there, take a taxi. ☎27240 51 046. Site open 8:30am-sunset. Free. Museum open Tu-Su 8am-3pm. €2, seniors €1, students free.

Pausanias wrote a detailed journal entry about his tour through thriving Messini in the AD 2nd century, and his account has been particularly useful for the excavations on **Mount Ithomi.** Over the last two decades, diggers have uncovered what quickly is becoming one of the most impressive ancient sites in Greece. Archaeologists believe the city dates back 2300 years, and there are signs of human settlement from thousands of years before. Fortunately, much of the city was buried by earth, preventing other cities from being built on top, and the artifacts have been protected from thieves and natural destruction. When the battle of Leuctra in 371 BC ended Spartan domination of the Peloponnese, Theban general and statesman **Epaminodas** built Messini, and named the new capital after the region's first queen. While the remains of a theater, stadium, gymnasium, public baths, and nine different temples have been uncovered, it is the city's **defensive walls** that receive the most attention. The 3m thick walls encircle 9km and represent the massive heft of 4th- and 3rd-century BC military architecture. The partitions were constructed so well that the city lay unharmed for 700 years. Originally, huge gates with towers and battlements interrupted the circuit. Of the four that survive, the **Arcadian gate** is in the best shape. Also impressive is the **fountain of Arsinoe,** whose waters flow through ancient tunnels from the Klepsydra fountain in the village of Mavromati. The temples of Demeter, Dioscuri, and Artemis Orthia are some of the best-preserved sacred monuments discovered in Messini. The **Ekklesiasterion,** a small theater used for political and cultural gatherings, also has been admirably restored. The site is unmarked, so purchasing a guidebook is a good idea. The **museum,** outside of Mavromati, is the artistic highlight of the site. Numerous marble statues found intact in the temples below, such as a 2m-tall statue of Hermes of Messini and a larger-than-life sandstone lion, still stand proudly.

KARDAMYLI Καρδαμύλη ☎ 27210

A small village community built up around the road from Kalamata to Areopolis and the southeastern Peloponnese, Kardamyli puts visitors in the delightful position of trying to figure out which view is more magnificent: the expansive sea stretching beyond the horizon, or the mountains that rise and fall, each one higher than the next. Hiking trails roaming through the Mt. Taygetus region and peaceful, uncrowded beaches make Kardamyli appealing for any type of traveler seeking an authentic Greek experience.

TRANSPORTATION AND PRACTICAL INFORMATION. Six **buses** run daily from Kalamata, dropping off near the *periptero* by the main plateia. There is no posted schedule, but the locals will tell you when the buses stop. If you're headed to Athens, take a bus to Kalamata (1hr.; M-F 5 per day 7:10-8pm, Sa 4 per day 7:10am-8pm, Su 3 per day 10:30am-8pm; €3). Buses also go to Itilo (1hr.; M-F 4 per day 6am-6pm, Sa-Su 3 per day 8:30am-6pm), where you can transfer to the Areopolis or Gytheio buses (20min.; M-F 6, 8:30am, 2:05pm, Sa-Su 8:30am; €1).

Most businesses are on the main road. The **bank,** with a **24hr. ATM,** is to the left away from the plateia, down the road on the other side of the grocery stores. (☎73 697. Open W 9:30am-1pm.) The **bookstore,** 100m to the right of the plateia on the left side of the street, has a large selection in English, along with maps (including hiking maps), tourbooks, and phone cards. (Open daily 9am-11:30pm.) To get to the **police station,** walk 5min. down the road to the left from the plateia and over the bridge; the station will be on a street to the left just before the large school. (☎73 209. Open 24hr.) The **pharmacy** is down the road to the right from the plateia about 75m. (☎73 270. Open M-F 8:30am-2pm and 6-9pm, Sa 10am-2pm and 6-8pm.) For **Internet** access, **Cafe Anna,** down the road to the right from the plateia, and **Cafe Aman,** next to Lela's Tavern, offer Wi-Fi. The **post office** is down the road to the right from the plateia. (Open M-F 7:30am-2pm.) **Postal Code:** 24022.

ACCOMMODATIONS AND FOOD. Travelers to tiny Kardamyli will be glad to discover that there's no shortage of reasonably priced rooms. **Olybia**

PELOPONNESIAN PLAYLIST

1. "Stairway to Heaven"—Led Zeppelin: **Monemvasia** (p. 195), where a steep staircase cut into the rock leads to Agia Sofia church, balanced on the cliff and begging to be photographed.

2. "Where the Streets Have No Name"—U2: The nameless cobbled streets and winding alleys of little **Dimitsana** (p. 171), up in the peaks of the Arcadian mountains, provide an atmosphere that could be the calming climax of your trip to Greece.

3. "Gimme Shelter"—The Rolling Stones: In **Tripoli** (p. 169), budget accommodations are indeed much more than just a shot away.

4. "I Can See For Miles"—The Who: The **Acrocorinth** (p. 134), a fortification on the top of a peak, has a panorama of the surrounding bodies of water and the mountains that rise inland.

5. "Renegade"—The Styx: **Kalamata** (p. 174) proudly boasts a history of civil disobedience—it was one of the leading towns in the early revolution movement that kicked off the Greek War of Independence.

6. "Destroyer"—The Kinks: Though the legendary armies of **Sparta** (p. 187) earned a reputation of invincibility by eliminating rival cities, little physical evidence remains of the city's former majesty.

Domatia ②, on the side street across from the post office, rents breezy, immaculate rooms with air-conditioning, fan, TV, and a shared kitchen. Olybia hands weary travelers a cold drink, a cup of coffee, and a map of hiking routes upon their arrival. (☎73 623. Singles €25-30; doubles €30-35.) Across from Olybia Domatia, energetic **Stratis Bravakos ②** lets spacious rooms that have kitchenette, fan, bath, wood-paneled furnishings, and balcony overlooking. (☎73 326. Singles €25-30; doubles €30-45; triples €35-50.) Closer to the ocean, you'll find **Pension Voula ③** a few doors down from the police station. It offers large, tiled rooms with TV, air-conditioning, balcony, sea view, fridge, and a large, newly appointed communal kitchen with an electric stove. (☎73 400. Rooms €35-50.) Travelers planning an extended stay in the area may want to consider **Hotel Anniska ④**, at the end of a side street to the right off the main road (turn at the large sign). It rents apartments for families (children must be under 16 years old) and studios. You can stay in either of its two buildings, both of which have lovely dining areas. All rooms include balcony, kitchen, TV, air-conditioning, phone, and bath. (☎73 600; www.anniska-liakoto.com. Studios €50-85; apartments €90-115. MC/V.)

Two large **supermarkets** are past the plateia on the road to Kalamata. **Spyreas,** with the yellow awning, has a better selection. (Open daily 9am-10pm.) As you walk past Olybia's rooms to the waterfront, turn right at the junction; after 50m you'll see ▓**Lela's Taverna ③**. The tree-covered patio juts onto the rocks, granting a waterfront view. The menu depends on whatever delicacies Lela decides to cook that day, but €15 will get you pleasantly stuffed, if not quite tipsy as well. (Open daily 12:30-4pm and 6-11pm.) **Koumaristria ③**, at the end of the downhill road by the bank, serves home-cooked specialties and uncommon dishes from across Greece. Jovial owner Grigoris recommends the Adrakla salad with onion and tomatoes (€6) and the lamb *kleftiko* with cheese, potatoes, and green peppers (€11). (☎73 250. Entrees €7-13. Open daily in summer noon-late; in winter 5pm-late.)

🎫🏖 **SIGHTS AND BEACHES.** Beyond its large pebble beach, Kardamyli is an excellent starting point for hikes. A short stroll up the road toward Kalamata will bring you to the small but worthwhile ruins of the **Old Town,** highlighted by the 17th-century Church of Ag. Spiridon and the Mourtzinos Tower. Though a bit vague and general in presentation, the site has detailed explanations in English and two refurbished rooms with modern exhibits detailing Mani's history. An information booth on the site sells a few books relating to local history for €15-25. (Open Tu-Su 8:30am-8pm. Free.) On an enormous natural bay encircled by lush mountains, the white-pebbled shore of the magnificent **Ritsa beach** is ideal for a leisurely early evening walk. From the main road to Kardamyli, take the small path to the beach after the bridge, then walk along the beach for 1km to reach Ritsa.

◢ HIKING. The hiking terrain surrounding the village competes with the enticing beaches as Kardamyli's main draw. Southeast of Kalamata, the limestone **Taygetus Mountains** divide Messinia and Laconia, running from Megalopolis down through the Taenarian promontory. Sacred to Apollo and Artemis, the mountains were named after Taygete, daughter of Atlas, mother of Lacedaemon, and lover of Zeus. Since those mythological origins, ancient and modern poets alike have glorified the range for its sheer size. Lampito declares in Aristophanes's *Lysistrata*, "I would climb as high as the peak of Taygetus, if thus I could find peace," while Nikiforos Vrettakos describes Mt. Taygetus as "the masculine child of [the Peloponnese]." With such a prestigious reputation, it is not hard to see why the mountain is a necessary stop for many travelers on their trips through southern Greece. Adventure-seekers are drawn to the challenging paths that lead to the mountain's peak at **Profitis Ilia** (elev. 2704m), and history buffs treasure the lower regions for their assortment of Byzantine churches, Venetian towers, Frankish forts, and Mycenaean tombs. Human hikers aside, 26 species of plants, 58 species of birds, and 35 species of reptiles (including the rare *Testudo marginata* turtle and a few varieties of snake) call the mountain home. The early morning reveals a hidden paradise of multicolored insects and a variety of reverberating animal sounds. Kardamyli is a good starting point for many day-hike trails with varying levels of difficulty. One popular 2hr. path begins at Kardamyli, goes through Old Kardamyli, up to Ag. Sophia (elev. 200m) and back to town via Petrovouni (elev. 180m). The trail is initially marked with yellow and black rectangles. Toward Petrovouni, follow the markers with red circles inside white squares. More experienced hikers may be interested in the 4hr. path that leads from Ag. Sophia to Kato Chora (elev. 450m), past the Vyros Gorge to Moni Satiros (elev. 150m), and finally to Kardamyli via a walk through a river bed. All the paths are narrow and rocky, and the area is filled with bugs, so it's a good idea to wear long pants.

7. "I'm Still Standing"—Elton John: After all these years—centuries, even—**Argos** (p. 139), reputedly the oldest continuously settled town in the Western world, remains (though its days of glory are a distant memory).

8. "Break on Through to the Otherside"—The Doors: With the creation of a new, record-length suspension bridge connecting the Peloponnese at Patras to northwestern Greece, the ever-expanding city hopes to become an even more important hub city in coming years.

9. "Turn to Stone"—ELO: In resource-deprived **Mani** (p. 191), famously tough Maniots knew not what other material to turn to in constructing their towered communities, historically preserved in **Areopolis's** (p. 193) historic Old Town.

10. "Shelter from the Storm"—Bob Dylan: In **Methoni** (p. 184), the impressive ruins of a once self-sufficient Venetian fortified town remain. Locals hid behind protective ramparts in the times of strife that are common throughout Peloponnesian history.

PYLOS Πύλος
☎ 27230

From the Odyssey's Telemachus to the builders of ancient fortifications, people have been drawn to Pylos for centuries. Pylos enjoys spectacular summer sunsets that paint the sky shades of orange and purple as the sun disappears behind Sfakteria island and Navarino bay. Despite its history, pleasant tavernas, nearby historical sites, and quaint narrow streets, the town at times seems mystifyingly absent of visitors even in the summer. Only an hour's drive from Kalamata, this seaside village is a shining example of authentic Peloponnesian living.

▐▌ ▐▌ TRANSPORTATION AND PRACTICAL INFORMATION. Buses (☎ 22 230) leave from the back of the plateia. Tickets are sold at the tiny KTEL office in the far right corner of the plateia facing inland. Buses go to: Athens (6½hr.; 9am, 4:30pm); Finikouda (20min., 4 per day 6am-7:15pm, €1.40); Kalamata (1½hr.; M-F 8 per day 6am-9:20pm, Sa 7 per day 6am-9:20pm, Su 4 per day 9am-9:20pm; €4.10); Kyparissia (1½hr.; M-F 5 per day 6:30am-4:30pm, Sa 4 per day 8:45am-4:30pm, Su 11am, 4:30pm) via Nestor's Palace (30min.) and Hora (45min.); Methoni (15min.; M-Sa 5 per day 6am-9pm, Su 8am, 2:15pm, 9pm; €1.20). To get to Koroni, take the bus to Finikouda and then to Horokorio, the stop nearest Koroni. Bus service is reduced on weekends. **Taxis** (☎ 22 555) line the left side of the plateia.

Most of the town's businesses line the plateia, the waterfront, and the roads leading to Methoni and Hora. Two tiny **beaches** lie to the right of the waterfront, as does the 16th-century Ottoman **Neocastro** on a forested hill. A **National Bank** with a **24hr. ATM** is in the plateia. (Open M-Th 8am-2:30pm, F 8am-2pm.) The **police** are in a building on the left side of the waterfront. (☎ 22 316. Open 24hr.) They double as the **tourist police.** To get to the **hospital,** take the road right from the plateia. (☎ 22 315. Open 24hr.) For the **OTE,** pass the post office, take the first left, then the second right at the top of the hill. (Open M-F 7:30am-3pm.) For **Internet** access, take the main uphill road to Kalamata to the near left of the plateia facing inland, and take the first right down the pedestrian road; **P@ndigit@l** will be on your left after two blocks. They sell access passwords to Wi-Fi networks in Pylos center and in Finikounda, and they plan to offer access to more networks in surrounding towns soon. (☎ 28 200; www.greecehotspot.com. Open M-Sa noon-10pm.) To find the **post office,** take the uphill road to the right at the far side of the plateia facing inland; it is on the left. (☎ 22 247. Open M-F 7:30am-2pm.) **Postal Code:** 24001.

▐▌ ▐▌ ACCOMMODATIONS AND CAMPING. You'll spot "rooms to let" signs as the bus descends into town from Kalamata. Open since 1945, ▨**Hotel Miremare ❹,** on the waterfront, has bright, colorful rooms with many posters and decorations, TV, fridge, bath, and balcony, all facing the sea. (☎ 22 751. Breakfast included. Singles €40-50; doubles €50-60; triples €60-70.) **Hotel Nilefs ❸,** Rene Pyot 4, behind the Archaeological Museum, has big rooms with colorful bath, air-conditioning, TV; some with balcony. It's on the road uphill from the waterfront on the right side of the plateia, facing inland. (☎ 22 518. Negotiate, especially during low season or if staying more than a night or two. Singles €30-40; doubles €40-60; triples €60-72.) **Navarino Beach Camping ❶,** 6km north of town at sandy, shallow Yialova beach, has a mini-mart, restaurant, communal kitchen, showers, public toilets, and laundry facilities. Look for signs pointing off the road between Kalamata and Pylos. (☎ 22 761. €6 per person, €3 per child 4-10, children under 4 free; €5 per small tent, €6 per large tent. Electricity €4. Internet access €3 per hr.)

▐▌ FOOD. Many waterfront restaurants serve taverna staples alongside fabulous sunset views. The road leading uphill from the left of the plateia is packed with excellent options. Sunset enthusiasts should catch a late dinner at ▨**0 Koykos ❷,**

up the road to Kalamata, to the left of the plateia. Inside is a modern homage to Greek interior design, with marble floors, rising brick columns, stone arches, and a wood-panel ceiling. The natural beauty of the setting sun, however, is best enjoyed from the wood-roofed, tiled front porch, while enjoying classic Greek tavern dishes. (☎22 950. Salads €2.50-4. Entrees €5-7.50. Vegetarian offerings €2.50-6. Souvlaki €1.10. Beer €2. Open daily noon-4pm and 8pm-1am.) Walking from the plateia with the water to the right, past the port police, **Ta Adelfia ❷** has good, cheap meals served quickly to tables right by the water. Tan tiles and wood accents provide the feel of a traditional taverna. Don't be confused by the "Navarino" sign on the above the restaurant; it's a vestige of a long-departed hotel on the second floor. (☎22 564. Salads €2.70-4.50. Entrees €4.50-12.50. Stuffed tomatoes and peppers €5.30. Fresh fish from €60 per kg. Open daily noon-4:30pm and 7pm-midnight.) Behind the back row of establishments lining the waterfront plateia, in Pl. Economidis, **La Piazza ❷** creates wonderful pastas and pizza. Try the "La Piazza" specials such as the Piazza pizza, bombarded with feta, bacon, peppers, and olives. (☎23 780. Pasta €4.50-5.50. Whole pizza €7-8. Open daily 6pm-midnight. Dec.-May closed Su.) **Four Seasons ❷,** the last taverna on the water to the right of town (facing inland), serves some of the freshest fish in town, with tables right on the water. Ask about the delicious, perpetually evolving dessert menu. (☎22 739. Fish €45-60 per kg. Entrees €5-7.50. Open daily noon-midnight.)

◪ ◪ **SIGHTS AND BEACHES.** Fortresses guard both sides of Navarino Bay. **Neocastro,** to the south, is easily accessible from the town; walk up the road to Methoni and turn right at the sign reading "Φρουριο" (Frourio). Built by the Turks in the 16th century, the fortress was won by the Greeks during the War of Independence. The well-preserved walls enclose 19 acres of land. Boasting a magnificent view of the bay, inside are a citadel and graceful church, which was originally a mosque. If you find the explanations lacking, ask a friendly staff member. The **Museum of the Rene Puaux Collection,** to the left as you enter the site, contains artistic works celebrating Greek triumph in the War of Independence from the personal collection of French journalist Rene Puaux. Prior to the museum's creation, the building was a maximum-security prison and occupied by Germans. (☎22 010. Site and museum open Tu-Su 8:30am-3pm. €3, seniors and students €2, EU students and children free.) At the **Archaeological Museum,** an unassuming white building on the uphill road to the right of the plateia facing inland, you'll find mostly pottery from Mycenaean palaces and jewelry from *tholos* tombs on display. The sophisticated Hellenistic glass vases in the back and the Mycenaean boar's tusk helmet are particularly eye-catching. (☎22 448. Open Tu-Su 8:30am-3pm. €2, seniors €1, students and children free.)

NAP TIME. From about 2-5pm in Greek summers, the heat peaks—and the crowds virtually disappear. Those intrepid travelers who wander through these blistering hours will find little to do: throughout the country, cafes will be empty, streets will be barren, and nearly every shop closed up for a lunch break. This siesta leaves you with one option: make like a native and head to the beach!

Just offshore is the island of **Sfakteria,** famed as the site of a rare Spartan defeat during the Peloponnesian War (p. 52) and home to the remains of a defensive wall built during that period. Sfakteria has a number of war memorials and a wooden church built by Russian soldiers without the use of a single nail. Aging aristocrats desperate for an heir may want to make use of the island's natural arch; legend has it that any pregnant woman who walks under it will bear a male child. To see the islands up close, you can take a **boat tour** from the port. Inquire at the small booth across from the port police. (☎ 23 115. 2hr., €8-10 per person. 11am-9pm.) The same booth also rents **motorboats.** (€40 for 6hr., €60 for 12hr. Gas not included.) If the tiny plots of sand that locals call "the beach" in Pylos don't do it for you, comparatively sizable **beaches** surround the town. Buses to Athens and Kyparissia pass by sandy, shallow, and much wider **Yialova beach,** 6km north of town, where sunken ships poke out from the waters. The **Navarino fortress** lies at the end of the beach, between Yialova and the more famous, seemingly never-ending **Xrisi Ammos** (Golden Sand) beach. Buses to Kyparissia can drop you off on a side road, and the beach is 3km away. Because of the infrequency of public transportation (especially on weekends), you may want to use private transportation. The motorboat tour booth will take tourists to the Golden beach for an extra €2 per person and stay for 3½hr. to allow for swimming.

❷ DAYTRIP FROM PYLOS: NESTOR'S PALACE. Pylos was second only to Mycenae in wealth and artistic development during Mycenaean times. The centerpiece of the archaeological site is the **palace** where, according to Homer, the horse-tamer Nestor met Telemachus, Odysseus's son. The palace is thought to have been built in the 13th century BC by Nestor's father Neleus, the founder of the Neleid Dynasty. It was destroyed by fire around 1200 BC. Under excavation since the early 20th century, the thigh-high remains of the site comprise three buildings. The main building, thought to be the king's residence, originally had a second floor with official and residential quarters and storerooms. The central throne room still contains a hearth. The ruins of a complex of isolated workshops and storerooms marked for oil and wine are to the northeast of the main palace, and scholars believe an older, smaller palace stood to the southeast. Archaeologists have discovered pottery, jewelry, various bronze and ivory objects, and a cache of over 600 **Linear B tablets** (p. 50) explaining some of the palace's administrative operations. Most finds are displayed at the National Archaeological Museum in Athens, though some pottery and surviving fragments of wall paintings are at the **museum** in Hora, 3km away. The chimney pipes that once were over the hearth and the gigantic *pithos* in the back room are particularly impressive.

A **Mycenaean tholos tomb** from around 1550 BC, thought to have held 17 graves, is across from the lower parking lot. Its size implies that there was a large settlement dating back to 1600 BC. Fortunately for archaeologists, hasty thieves left much of the tomb untouched during a gold-raiding escapade. Most of the artifacts are on display in Athens, but visitors still can explore underneath the dome of the *tholos*.

Buses from Pylos run to **Nestor's Palace** (30min., €1) via **Kyparissia** (1½hr., 2-5 per day, €4). Service tends to run late and is reduced on weekends. Check for the return times before getting off the bus—the last, and sometimes only, bus returns at 7pm. (Museum ☎ 27630 31 358; site ☎ 27230 31 437. Both open daily 8:30am-3pm. €3, seniors and students €2, EU students and children free.)

METHONI Μεθώνη ☎27230

Methoni is a beautiful seaside village made spectacular by its old castle, a remnant of Venetian and Turkish occupation of the region. Once a fortified town with tall battlements and a moat cutting it off from the mainland, Methoni is home to a peninsular tower where it is claimed that Miguel de Cervantes produced several romances while being held prisoner by Ottomons. The area is rich in natural beauty; in the *Iliad*, King Agamemnon lures Achilles back to fighting by offering him beautiful Methoni for his services. From the beautiful waterfront plateia, the sandy town beach stretches between the dock and the outer walls of the castles, with views of beautiful Sapientza island visible across the open water.

TRANSPORTATION AND PRACTICAL INFORMATION. There is no bus station in town, so your best bet is to ask locals for bus times. **Buses** go to Finikouda (30min.; 11am, 3:30pm; €1.40) and Pylos (15min., 4 per day 6am-9:30pm, €1.20); service is reduced on weekends. Buses also head daily to Athens (6hr., 8am, €25) via Pylos and Kalamata (2hr., €5).

The town's two main streets form a "Y" where the Pylos-Finikouda buses stop. Facing the fork, the upper road is lined with administrative offices and small businesses. The lower road on the left, **Mezonos**, leads to the castle and the **beach.** Turn left at **Plateia Syngrou**, recognizable by its waterless fountain, to reach the beachfront square, **Plateia Paralias.** A stroll along the beach road, **Poseidonos,** leads to the campgrounds and several bars. The **National Bank** with a **24hr. ATM** is 40m down the right fork. (☎31 295. Open M-Th 8am-2:30pm, F 8am-2pm.) Public **phones** can be found at the bus stop and in the beachfront plateia. Methoni has a small **police** force, open 1-2hr. per day next to the National Bank on the upper road, although it relies primarily on the **Pylos police.** (☎21 203. Open 24hr.) The **Trojan Horse,** on the left before the castle, offers **Internet** access. (€3 per hr., min. €1. Open daily 7:30am-3am.) The **post office** is two blocks down the lower street on the left side. (☎31 266. Open M-F 7:30am-2pm.) **Postal Code:** 24006.

ACCOMMODATIONS AND CAMPING. Since Methoni receives a fair amount of tourism, accommodations are pricey, especially in August. However, there is no shortage of rooms, and several "rooms to let" signs hang along the main road. Although they usually lack luxuries, domatia are a bit cheaper than many of the area's hotels. Near the end of the lower road, eight blocks from the bus stop, turn left at Pl. Syngrou to find **Hotel Alex ❸** in the beachfront plateia. Spacious, renovated rooms are superbly located and have air-conditioning, phone, minibar, bath, and balcony. (☎31 219. Singles €35-45; doubles €45-55; triples €50-65.) Next door at **Hotel Giota ❸,** Alex's owners rent smaller rooms for the same price. Reserve rooms by calling Hotel Alex. Walking down the lower road, the pink building before the first plateia is **Hotel Finikas ❸,** which has big rooms with colorful bath, TV, air-conditioning, and fridge. (☎31 390. Singles €30; doubles €40; triples €50.) **Seaside Camping Methoni ❶,** on Poseidonos, is a 5min. walk down the beach with the sea on your right. The public campground has a mini-mart, showers, hot water, toilets, and a nearby restaurant. (☎31 228. €4 per person, €2.50 per child; €3 per small tent, €3.50 per large tent; €2.50 per car. Electricity €3. 10% discount for stays over 14 nights or families with 3 or more children.)

FOOD. Several excellent tavernas and restaurants pepper Methoni. Head down the beachfront road to the left of the plateia two blocks to ▨**Klimataria ❷** for a Peloponnesean dining experience. Enjoy the atmosphere and Greek cuisine at its finest on the candle lit, vine-covered patio to the sounds of light Greek ballads. (☎31 544. Stuffed vine leaves with lemon sauce €4.30. Lamb *fricasse* €7.40. Salads €2.90-8.90. Cheese €2.80-4.20. Entrees €5-10. Open daily noon-4:30pm and 6-11:30pm. MC/V.) No-frills **Nontas ❶** serves high-quality food at cheap prices. Walking from the bus stop, turn left one block down the lower road. (☎31 791. *Tzatziki* €2. French fries €1.80. Souvlaki €1.50.) **Nikos ❷,** on Andromos Aftos, serves staples in a corner establishment where locals dine inside and out. It's the first left off the road left of the beachfront plateia, facing inland. Chicken in lemon sauce (€5) is a favorite, and vegetarian entrees are also available. (☎31 282. Salad €2.50-4.50. Entrees €5-7.50. Open daily noon-midnight.) In the waterfront plateia, the multilingual proprietor of **Meltemi ❷** serves varieties of traditional dishes in an outdoor setting. (☎31 187. Souvlaki €6-8. Open daily noon-4:30pm and 7pm-midnight.)

◨ **SIGHTS.** No visitor to the southwestern Peloponnese should miss Methoni's breathtaking ▧**Venetian fortress,** ruins of a mini-city with significant parts dating from as early as the 13th century. To get there, follow the lower street to its end. Walk to the right on the path outside the castle for a great view of the open sea and fortified back wall. Behind the fortress's fortified gate, paths ramble alongside towering arches, walls, and colorful wildflowers. Frankish foundations, Venetian battlements, and Turkish steam baths are testaments of the castle's unstable, multinational history. Walk to the far end of the fortification from the entrance to find the **bourtzi,** the picturesque guard tower annex built right on the water and the centerpiece of many Methoni postcards. (Open Sa-Su 8am-7pm. Free.) The town's sandy Methoni **beach** is a few blocks to the left of the end of the lower street.

FINIKOUNDA Φοινικούντα   ☎27230

Tiny Finikounda lies 10km from Methoni and 20km from Pylos, rounding out a trio of Messinian towns with available accommodations, worthy sites, and no evident signs of cookie-cutter tourist agencies. Finikounda unfolds along a narrow road paralleling a pleasant stretch of sandy beach, with waterfront establishments that manage to jive with the small village feel of the town without detracting from its natural allure. Some of the best **beaches** on the Peloponnesian coast are within easy walking distance of the town; locals will be able to provide directions. Those seeking energetic nightlife head to Pylos on weekends.

Should you opt to stay in Finikounda, find one of the many **domatia** along the waterfront or head to nearby campgrounds. At **Hotel Finikounda ❷,** next to the bus stop and a block from the water, large rooms with TV, air-conditioning, and fridge are comfortable and squeaky-clean, and the reception has a book exchange. (☎71 208. Breakfast €4. Singles €25-40; doubles €40-60; triples €45-60. MC/V.) ▧**Camping Anemomilos ❶** is on the beach just north of town. Situated among flowering shrubs and with easy beach access, the site has laundry, mail drop, restaurant, mini-mart, bar, showers, and Internet access (€2.50 per hr., €3 per 1½hr.). To reach the campsite, walk out of town on the road past Hotel Finikounda, then walk 300m toward Methoni and turn left toward the beach at the signs. (☎71 360. €4.70-5.30 per person, €2.70-3 per child. €3.30-4.50 per tent.) Restaurants are by no means hard to find, but if you want a view, walk to the left end of the waterfront (facing inland) to the enormous taverna **Elena ❷.** On the cliff side, Elena's terraced levels provide all diners with beautiful views of the harbor. Popular with families and tourists, it offers half-portions for kids and has a helpful pronunciation guide in the menu. (☎71 235. Salads €3.20-7.80. Vegetable dishes €5-6.50. Seafood €6.50-12.50. Open daily noon-1am.) A step up from its fast-food neighbors, **Apomera ❶** is a little farther to the right from the ATM, facing inland. Cheap, delicious food is served in a pretty, mellow beachside setting. (☎71 292. Entrees €4.50-8.50. Open daily 9am-midnight.) **Vinnitiko ❷,** between the ATM and Apomera, on a wooden plateau above the sand accented by flowers, is a good choice for seafood. (Salads €2.30-4.50. Fish €5.50-12. Open daily noon-midnight.) To find a **supermarket,** follow the signs from the bus stop away from the water for about 50m. (Open M-Sa 8am-3pm and 4-10pm, Su 8am-2pm and 4:30-9:30pm.)

Buses head to Kalamata (1½hr., 3-4 per day 7:15am-8:15pm) via Pylos (30min.), Methoni, and Harakopio. Service is reduced on weekends. The bus drops off and picks up at the small plateia one block up from the waterfront. Finikounda doesn't have a police station or post office, but there is a **24hr. ATM** at the end of the main road as you walk toward the waterfront from the bus stop.

LACONIA Λακωνία

Although known as the ancient dominion of Greece's formidable and minimalist city-state, visitors to Laconia will find the terrain surprisingly unspartan in its offerings. Home to some of the Peloponnese's highest peaks, the region features craggy mountains epically stabbing the surrounding skies. Ancient olive groves and ruins hint at the long history that has unfolded in Laconia over the centuries.

SPARTA Σπάρτη ☎27310

Built on top of the ancient city, modern Sparta's gritty urban sprawl barely hints at its namesake's historic past other than in the names of its streets. Still, it's by far the best base for exploring the ruins of Byzantine Mystras, 6km away. Sparta's role in shaping the fate and legends of ancient Greece was monumental. The bellicose state dominated the Peloponnese with its legendary discipline and nearly invincible armies. Its austere daily regimens can be traced back to 8th-century BC lawgiver Lycurgus, who demanded plain dress, simple food, and strict training for all citizens from a young age. Men and women were educated differently, but both were held to severely rigid standards. The Spartans produced almost no literature, art, or architecture, as they preferred to expend all their creative energy on the art of war. Finally capturing Athens in 404 BC to end the 28-year Peloponnesian War (p. 52), Sparta won its greatest victory and effectively began to rule Greece. Though it had earned its historical place as the military giant of Greece, Sparta's hold on power declined following challenges from the Thebans and the Macedonians in the fourth century BC. Earthquakes and slave revolts didn't help, and further losses in 222 and 195 BC to the Macedonians and the Romans, respectively, sapped the city's strength. Sparta slipped into obscurity until the modern city, whose citizens make olive oil, not war, was founded in 1843.

▐ TRANSPORTATION

To get to the **bus station** (☎26 441), walk downhill on Lykourgou toward the Archaeological Museum, continuing past a small forested area on your right. It will be on your right, 10 blocks from the town center. The bus station is often crowded and not particularly tourist-friendly, as there often are confusing transfers on the bus routes. **Buses** go to: Areopolis (1½hr., 4 per day 8am-6pm, €6); Athens (3½hr., 11 per day 5:45am-8pm, €16.80) via Tripoli (1hr., €4.70) and Corinth (2½hr., €11.10); Gerolimenas (2hr.; 6:45am, 2:30, 5:30pm; €8.90); Gythion (45min., 6 per day 7:30am-7pm, €3.70); Kalamata (1hr.; 9am, 2:30pm; €4); Monemvasia (2hr., 4 per day 5:45am-5:15pm, €8.70); Neapoli (3½hr., 4 per day 6am-5pm, €12.20); Molai (2hr., 6 per day 6:30am-6pm, €6.50); Pirgos Dirou (1½hr., 9am, €6.60). Buses to Mystras (20min., 10 per day 7:20am-8:20pm, €1.20) stop at the corner of Lykourgou and Leonidou, two blocks past the plateia away from the station.

▚ ▞ ORIENTATION AND PRACTICAL INFORMATION

Sparta is a grid. The main streets, **Paleologou** and **Lykourgou,** have most essentials and intersect in the center of town. From that intersection, the plateia is one block uphill along Lykourgou away from the bus station. Walking uphill toward the plateia along Paleologou, you will hit Ancient Sparta. To reach the center of town from the bus station, go about 10 blocks slightly uphill on Lykourgou.

Tourist Office: ☎26 771. On the 3rd fl. of the town hall, the glass building in the far left corner of the plateia facing away from Paleologou. English spoken. It is more a town administrative office than tourist center and is not particularly helpful. They offer info about Sparta only (not Mystras) and can direct you to a nearby photo shop to pick up a free map. Some hotel information also available. Open M-F 8am-2pm.

Bank: National Bank, Paleologou 106 (☎23 845), 3 blocks toward Ancient Sparta from Lykourgou and the town center. Has a **24hr. ATM, currency exchange,** and long lines. Open M-Th 8am-2:30pm, F 8am-2pm.

Police: ☎89 500. On Ep. Vresthenis, off Lykourgou, 1 block past the bus station toward the plateia. Open 24hr. The **tourist police** are in the same building. Open daily 8am-9pm. In an **emergency,** dial ☎100.

Hospital: ☎28 671. On Nosokomeio, 1km north of Sparta. 7 buses per day (€1) go there. Open 24hr.

Internet Access: Ladas Cafe (☎83 016, www.cafe-ladas.com). Visible from the plateia. 20m up on Lykourgou, on the right. The oldest cafe in town but with modern computers. €2 per hr. Open daily 7am-midnight. **Cosmos Internet Cafe,** Paleologou 34 (☎21 500), south of Lykourgou, away from Ancient Sparta. On the 2nd fl. of the video store. €3.50 per hr., min. €1. Open daily M-Su 8am-11pm.

Post Office: ☎26 565. Archidamou 84, off Lykourgou, halfway between the bus station and the center. Open M-F 7:30am-2pm. **Poste Restante. Postal Code:** 23100.

⌁ ACCOMMODATIONS

It's hard to find a bargain among the numerous mid-range hotels grouped on Paleologou. **Hotel Cecil ❷,** Paleologou 125, is five blocks north of Lykourgou toward Ancient Sparta, on the corner of Paleologou and Thermopilon. It may look scruffy on the outside, but the small intimate lobby gives way to pleasant, simple rooms with TV, air-conditioning, balcony, large bath, phone, and low beds. (☎24 980. Singles €25-35; doubles €45-55; triples €55-65. Reservations recommended.) **Hotel Lakonia ❸,** Paleologou 89, recently has undergone a dramatic renovation. The spiffy lobby and plushly carpeted hallways foreshadow comfortable rooms with wood floors, newly finished bath, air-conditioning, balcony, phone, hair dryer, fridge, and TV with cable. Internet is available for €5 per day. (☎28 951. www.lakoniahotel.gr. Breakfast included. Singles €35-45; doubles €55-70; triples €70-90.) **Hotel Apollon ❹,** Thermopilon 84, across Paleologou from Hotel Cecil, appeals to guests' playful side, with colorful rooms that have TV, air-conditioning, phone, balcony, large bath, and bright quilted bedspread. (☎22 491. Breakfast €7. Singles €38-40; doubles €54-60; triples €53. V.) To find **Camping Castle View ❶,** 2km from Mystras, take the Mystras bus and get off at the signs. The site has a brand-new pool, showers, bathrooms, laundry (€4), restaurant with a small mini-mart, and bar. (☎83 303. €5.50-6 per person, €4 per small tent, €5-6 per large tent, €4 per car. Electricity €4.)

⌁ FOOD

Sparta's restaurants serve standard menus at pretty reasonable prices. **Supermarkets** and **bakeries** fill the side streets of Paleologou, while cheap fast-food joints surround the main plateia. **Diethnes ❷,** on Paleologou, a few blocks to the right of the main intersection with Lykergous facing the plateia, offers tasty Greek food in an intimate garden with orange trees. Patrons may forget that they're in the midst of a busy city. Though it has a few vegetarian options (€4.50), the restaurant specializes in lamb entrees (€7), which come paired with all types of sides. (☎28 636. Entrees €5-8. Salads €2.50-4.50. Open daily 8am-midnight.) A large, fresh selection of local specialties and traditional Greek dishes keep **Elyssé Restaurant ❷,** Paleologou 113, across from the National Bank, busy at all times. The staff recommends one of the many vegetable entrees (€2.80-6) or the *bardouniobiko* (€6.90), a regional dish of chicken in tomato sauce, onions, and feta. (☎29 896. Open daily 11am-midnight.) **Parthenon ❶,** on Vrasida two blocks north of the intersection with Paleologou and one block east toward the bus station, offers Greek fast food in a classier-than-expected setting. (☎23767 23 767. Souvlaki €1.30-2.50. Gyros €1.70. Open daily 5pm-1:30am.) The elegant Menelaion Hotel may not be in the budget traveler's price range, but its popular **restaurant ❸** certainly is. Dishes from its huge menu are served either poolside or in a marble-floored dining room. The fabulous sourdough bread is an added plus. (Cover €0.50. Entrees €5-15. Salads €2.90-8. Fish €30 per kg. Open daily noon-4pm and 7:30pm-midnight.)

▣ NIGHTLIFE

At night, the side streets off Paleologou swell with young people, while the plateia draws families and an older crowd that drinks away the hours at outdoor cafes. Due to the literally Spartan laws, nightlife ends earlier on weekdays than in many other Greek cities (3:30am). Outside the plateia, **Ministry Music Hall,** on Paleologou one block north of the intersection with Lykourgou, is always packed. Brimming with energy and, of course, loud music, the Ministry is the place where Sparta's hipsters go to be seen. The interior is adorned with unicycles and mandolins, and the atmosphere is comfortable and welcoming. (Beer €2-3.50. Mixed drinks from €6. Open daily 8am-2am.) **Leghi Spartis,** a cafe in the beautiful Old Town Hall in the plateia, caters to those seeking a slightly calmer scene. Popular with families, it offers coffee (€2-3.50), mixed drinks (€5-6), snacks, desserts, and sandwiches. (Open daily 9am-3am.) **Caprice** is a deceptively large, popular club tucked behind neon green lights and small palm trees in the back of the plateia, with a large indoor space past the outdoor lounge. White leather-backed chairs support Sparta's most chic as they stiffly sip their drinks of choice. (Beer €3-5. Mixed drinks €6-7. Open daily 9pm-5am.)

◉ SIGHTS

What little remains of **Ancient Sparta** lies in an olive grove 1km north of town. An enormous statue of **Leonidas,** the famous warrior king who fell at the Battle of Thermopylae in 480 BC, looms over the northern end of Paleologou. The Spartans built a large tomb for their leader, but his body was never found. The tomb, therefore, still lays empty in a public park to the left of the road heading up to the ruins. To reach the ruins, turn left at the statue, then make your first right and follow the signs. The otherwise unimpressive site is highlighted by a few fragments of the acropolis and the remains of the **ancient theater.** To reach the theater, turn left at the sign to the first path branching off the main cobbled road.

Sparta's **Archaeological Museum,** on Lykourgou across from the OTE, is in a beautiful, well-kept park with a fountain and assorted ancient statuary. Headless statues usher visitors into the museum, which features a large collection of everything from beautiful mosaics to haunting votive masks used in ritual dances at the sanctuary of Artemis Orthia. The rooms to the right, facing inward, display various representations of the Dioscuri—the twins Castor and Pollux—locally revered as symbols of brotherly love and honor, as well as larger-than-life 3rd-century BC marble heads of Hercules and Hera. One room is devoted to prehistoric pottery, weaponry, and jewelry. English captions accompany all the artifacts. (☎28 575. Open Tu-Su 8am-7:30pm. €2, seniors and students €1, EU students and children free.) The **National Art Gallery,** Paleologou 123, next to Hotel Cecil, has a small permanent collection of 19th-century Dutch and French paintings, including one by Gustave Courbet. Upstairs, the gallery hosts temporary exhibits from the National

Gallery in Athens. (☎81 557. Open M-Sa 9am-3pm, Su 10am-2pm. Free.) For something refreshingly different, visit the **Museum of the Olive and Greek Olive Oil,** Othonos Amalias 129. If you walk three blocks to the left of Lykourgou facing the plateia and four blocks to the right, the museum will be on the left as the road ends. In this beautiful building that stands out among the ubiquitous concrete apartment complexes, three floors of exhibits explain the economic, technological, and cultural significance of the olive. (☎89 315. Open M and W-Su 10am-6pm. €3, students and seniors €1.50, EU students free.)

Many of the ruins surrounding Sparta are reachable by foot, though a few require a car. From the northeastern corner of town, near Hotel Apollon, a 10min. walk east along Odos Ton 118 toward Tripoli leads to the **Sanctuary of Artemis Orthia,** where Spartan youths proved their courage by enduring repeated floggings. Three remaining platforms of the **Shrine to Menelaus and Helen** are 5km away in the same direction. Take the road to Tripoli, past the bridge, and turn at the sign for "Menelaus Palace." The ruins of a **Shrine to Apollo** are 5km south on the road to Gythion in the town of Amiklai.

▓ DAYTRIP FROM SPARTA

▓ MYSTRAS

Buses leaving Sparta's main station and the corner of Lykourgou and Leonidou (20min., 9 per day 7:20am-8:20pm, €1.20) stop at the restaurant Xenia near the main entrance at the bottom of the hill. It gets hot and requires scrambling around, so go early, bring water, and wear comfortable shoes. Consider getting another resource like Guidebook Mystras, *by Manolis Chatzidakis (€6.50), to supplement your exploration. Free maps are available. ☎83 377. Open daily 8am-7:30pm. €5, students and children €3, EU students free.*

Once the religious center of all Byzantium and the locus of Constantinople's rule over the Peloponnese, Mystras lays dormant, a magnificent fortified city saturated with remains of Byzantine churches, chapels, and monasteries. Founded by French Crusader **Guillaume de Villehardouin** in 1249 with the building of a central castle at the top of the hill, the city first experienced a change of ownership in 1262 when it was captured by the Greeks. Under Greek rule, the town flourished; in the following centuries it grew to a city, draining Sparta of its inhabitants as they sought protection in Mystras's fortress. By the early 15th century, Mystras was an intellectual and cultural center with a thriving silk industry. But even the booming economy couldn't keep the lower classes at bay. Unhappy under the thumb of oppressive feudal lords and clergy, restless country folk eventually surged into town, set up schools, and created an early bourgeoisie. The glory days ended, however, when Turks invaded in 1460 and, over the next few centuries, the city crumbled to ruin. When King Otto founded modern Sparta in 1834, Mystras's fate was sealed with a table-turning exodus to its revived neighbor.

An intricate network of paths traces through three tiers of ruins, descending from royalty to nobility to commoners. Although not as well-preserved as many of the religious edifices that encircle it—they're almost completely intact, if a bit faded at the frescoes—the dramatic **castle** delivers a breathtaking view of the site and the surrounding countryside. Most people climb to the castle first and work their way down. The **palaces,** which date from the AD 13th to 15th centuries, are downhill from the castle, and feature a large throne-room among their pointed arches and dressed stone walls. Next to them is **Agia Sophia,** built by Manuel Katakouzenos, the first despot of Morea. This is where the city's royalty was buried, among the still-visible, striking frescoes. Farther downhill lies the magnificent **Pantanassa,** a convent with an elaborately ornamented facade, frescoes, and an icon of Mary said to work miracles. The ground floor displays many wall-paintings from the 17th and 18th centuries. On the lower tier you can find the **Metropolis of Agios Demetrios,** with its detailed frescoes, flowery courtyard, and small museum of architectural fragments, clothing, and jewelry. Its air-conditioned room holds everything from 14th-century manuscripts to marble sculptures to a reconstruction of a Byzantine woman's shoe. Also on the lower tier are the two churches that comprise the fortified monastery of **Brontochion.** The first, **Aphentiko** (a.k.a. **"Hodigitria"**), glows with two-story frescoes depicting saints; **Agios Theodoros** is its neighbor. In the far corner of the lower tier, every centimeter of the awe-inspiring **Church of Peribleptos** is bathed in colorful, exquisitely detailed religious paintings.

MANI Μάνη

Mani gets its name from the Greek word *manis*, which means "wrath" or "fury." Sparsely settled and encircling the intimidating Taygetus Mountains (p. 181), the region juts out vulnerably into the surrounding sea. During Roman times, Mani founded the league of Free Laconians and threw off Spartan domination. Ever since, Maniots have resisted foreign rule, boasting even today that not one Ottoman set foot on their soil. While historically fierce and proud of it, Maniots are warm hosts to those who visit their well-preserved villages and unique, gray stone tower houses. Home to Byzantine ruins, small fishing villages, world-class beaches, and the famous *Caretta caretta* sea turtle, Mani continues to surprise visitors with its diversity. The landscape follows suit: the lush north gives way to stark southern mountains, which stand out against the piercing blue oceans and endless stretches of sand and pebbles.

GYTHION Γύθειο ☎27330

Gythion unfolds along a long stretch of waterfront, spreading inland where the steep hill pressing against the sea turns away from the coast. It is the southern part of town that distinguishes this pleasant seaside village from its neighbors. Here, a narrow causeway connects the offshore island of Marathonisi to the mainland. From town, the sight of the wooded isle stretching out into the bay adds character to an already gorgeous view, while watching Gythion sparkle at night from Marathonisi is a not-to-be-missed experience.

⌐ TRANSPORTATION. Ferries go to Antikythera, Kissamos Kythera, and Pireus. Inquire at **Rozakis Travel** (☎22 207), on the waterfront by the police station. The bus station (☎22 228) is on the northern end of the waterfront, opposite a park. It sends **buses** to: Areopolis (30min., 4 per day 10:15am-6:45pm, €2.30) via the campgrounds (€1); Athens (4½hr., 6 per day 7:30am-7pm, €20.50) via Tripoli (2hr., €8.40) and Corinth (3½hr., €14.80); Gerolimenas (2hr.; 1, 6:45pm; €5.20); Kalamata (3hr.; M-Sa 7:30am, noon; €7); Pirgos Dirou (45min., 10:15am, €3.25); Sparta (40min., 6 per day 7:30am-7pm, €3.40). Departure and return times are posted outside the station. **Taxis** (☎23 400) line up outside the bus station and in the plateia and are available 24hr. **Moto Makis** (☎25 111), on the waterfront between the plateia and the causeway, rents mopeds. (Open daily 9am-1:30pm and 6-8:30pm.)

▓▐ ORIENTATION AND PRACTICAL INFORMATION. Going south from the bus station along the main harbor road, **Vasileos Pavlou,** you will find most hotels on your right. Stores and offices crowd around the inland plateia by the bus station. The small **Plateia Mavromichali** appears as the road curves and continues to the dock. Vas. Pavlou turns into Proth. Genataki after the plateia; Proth. Genataki ends at the causeway to Marathonissi.

To find the **tourist office,** go around the left corner of the bus station and bear left around the small plateia, following the road for 150m. (☎24 484. Open M-F 8am-2:30pm.) The **National Bank,** next to the bus station, has **currency exchange** and a **24hr. ATM.** (☎22 313. Open M-Th 8am-2pm, F 8am-1:30pm.) The **police station** is on Vas. Pavlou, halfway between the bus station and Pl. Mavromichali. (☎22 100. Open 24hr.) **Pharmacies** are scattered throughout town; one is across from the bus station. (☎22 036. Open M-F 8am-2pm and 5-9pm.) The nearest **hospital** is in Sparta, but a **health clinic** (☎22 001, 27330 22 002, or 27330 22 003) is on Proth. Genataki en route to the causeway. For an **ambulance,** dial ☎166. **Mystery Cafe,** on Kapsali, around the corner from the National Bank and down the street about 50m, has **Internet** access. (☎25 177. Beer €2.50. Coffee €2. €3 per hr., min. €1. Open daily 11am-1am.) Facing the bus station, go around the left corner and trace the plateia to Archaiou Theatrou; follow it to the right for two blocks to the **post office,** Ermou 18. (☎22 285. Open M-F 7:30am-2:30pm.) **Postal Code:** 23200.

ⓕ ACCOMMODATIONS. Gythion has an overabundance of seaside domatia and hotels, so prices are low and negotiable. With the same modern amenities and a cozy, at-home feel, the cheap domatia are a better option than the impersonal hotels that line the waterfront. Walk toward Marathonisi island causeway from the bus station with the water on your left to find the most budget-friendly accommodations. Gythion's campgrounds are located on Mavrovouni beach, an area popular with locals, 4km out of town toward Areopolis. They can be reached by bus (4 per day, €1) or taxi (€5). The charming Voulas family has been running **⊠Xenia Karlaftis Rooms ❷,** to the very left of the waterfront facing inland, for over 25 years. Now run by Xenia's daughter, who offers juice and homemade desserts to her guests upon arrival, the clean rooms have baths and views of Marathonissi. Most rooms have a balcony and TV. Each floor has a kitchen with free coffee and a fridge. In the summer, they also run **Zafeiro Apartments** with air-conditioning, TV, and balcony 3km from town, suitable for families with a car. (☎22 719. Singles €20-25; doubles €25-30; triples €30-40; quads €40; apartments €40-60.) **Matina Rooms ❷,** Vas. Pavlou 19, on the waterfront, rents spacious rooms with air-conditioning, TV, wood furniture, bath, and sea view in a central location near the police station. (☎22 518. Fridge on every floor. Singles €20-30; doubles €25-40; triples €30-50.) **Meltemi Camping ❶,** 4km south on the road to Areopolis, has an overwhelming number of amenities including showers, cooking area, washing machines (€4), market, restaurant, cinema, and pool. (☎22 833. €5 per person, €4 per child; €5 per tent, €4 per car; 2- to 5-person bungalows €30-55. Electricity €3.50.) **Gythion Bay Campgrounds ❶,** 5km south on the road toward Areopolis, has a large site shaded by orange, fig, and olive trees with laundry (€5), a mini-mart, restaurant, and showers. (☎22 522; www.gythio-camping.gr. €5-5.50 per person, €3.35 per child; €4.20 per tent, 2-person tent rental €8-9, 4-person €9-10. Electricity €3.60. Reserve rentals ahead.)

ⓕ FOOD. Walking along the waterfront, you can have your pick of reasonably priced seaside restaurants and tavernas. The food at **Masouleri Kokkalis ❶** is deliciously greasy and served on a pleasant patio in the back of Mavromichali plateia. (☎24 824. Souvlaki €1. Pita gyros and pita souvlaki €1.50. Other meat dishes €5-7. Open daily noon-1am.) **To Nisaki ❷,** on Marathonissi, provides an airy, calm setting for anyone looking to escape the waterfront tavernas' noisy crowds. It has a great view of the town during the day and at night, when the lights reflect of the gently rippling waters of the bay. During winter months when diners move inside, large windows keep the summer view intact for patrons. (☎23 830. Salad €2.50-4.80. *Tzatziki* €3.20. Fish from €46 per kg. Grilled entrees €5.50-12. Open daily 10am-1am.) **Saga ❸,** the classiest of the restaurants on Proth. Genataki between the causeway and the small plateia, prides itself on its fresh fare and excellent service. (☎21 358. Salads €3-7. Entrees €7.50-14. Fish from €15. Open daily 8am-1am. MC/V.) A **bakery** is across the street from Masouleri Kokkalis, and many **supermarkets** and **fruit stores** cluster around the bus station. (Most open 7:30am-2pm and 6-9pm.)

🖼️🏖️ **SIGHTS AND BEACHES. Marathonissi,** Gythion's must-see site, is a small wooded island laden with mythology and history. Here, Paris and Helen are said to have consummated their love. Lovebirds still flock to the island's small chapel for frequent weddings. Also on the island is the **Museum of Mani,** which features pictures and stories detailing the unique region. The masterfully built **ancient theater** of Gythion, spanning 240°, has endured the centuries remarkably well. Even its class distinctions remain—note the differences between the seats for dignitaries in front and the simpler seats farther back. Though the ruins themselves are very well-preserved, the current use of the surrounding field as a parking lot somewhat spoils the effect. The crumbling remains of ancient Roman walls that were destroyed by an earthquake lay scattered on the nearby hill. Heading away from the bus station, walk past the post office on Archaiou Theatrou until it ends at the theater entrance. The **Paliatzoures Antique Shop,** Vas. Pavlou 25, a few doors down from the police station, has furnished a number of museums in its day, as owner Costas will tell you. The store's specialty is 18th- and 19th-century weapons, with amazing pieces such as an intricately engraved silver sword from 1734. Beauty, status, and history don't come cheap, though: the sword is priced at €6000. Other items include everything from paintings to chandeliers to gongs. Ask Costas about his favorite items if you wish to get more of a background on some of the pieces you're looking at. (☎22 944. Open daily 11am-2pm and 6-9pm.) When traveling from Gythion to Areopolis, look for the Frankish **Castle of Pasava,** less than 5km from Gythion on the right (taxi €10). The road is dangerous, but domatia owners and the local consulate (☎22 210) can keep you posted on whether it's been improved. Farther along, another Frankish castle, the **Castle of Kelefa,** looks out to sea. To get there, take the bus to Areopolis and ask to be dropped off as close to the castle as possible; it's a 5km walk from the road. A taxi there runs about €18.

There is a disappointing **public beach** north of the bus station (walk with the water on your right); the better beaches are outside of town. **Mavrovouni,** home to the campgrounds, is 2km from Gythion toward Areopolis. Winds and deep waters make it a popular surfing spot. Plenty of beachgoers also hang out at one of the nearby bars along the 4.5km long beach, where beer runs €3-4 and mixed drinks are usually €5. Home to the **Caretta caretta,** an endangered sea turtle, Mavrovouni is also the site of a great deal of scientific research regarding the species. Visitors should ask the local tour agencies about precautions necessary to protect the turtles. From Gytheion, take one of the four daily buses, a taxi (€3.50), or walk 30-40min. Three kilometers north is rocky **Selinitsa,** known for its incredibly clear water and outstanding views of Gythion at night; to get there take a taxi (€5) or walk, following the signs that point the way. **Vathy,** a well-known and well-loved spot among locals, 10km along the road to Areopolis, has a mix of sun and shade that appeals to both the sun worshippers and the sunburned (taxi €11).

AREOPOLIS Αρεόπολη ☎27330

Situated at the foot of steep mountains and above the waters of the nearby Mediterranean, Areopolis has a natural beauty that makes it worth a visit. The cobbled, winding streets and traditionally designed stone buildings distinguish Areopolis. The town's plateia comes alive at night in summer; the stone street leading away from the highway beckons visitors to an old-world way of life.

☎ ⁊ TRANSPORTATION AND PRACTICAL INFORMATION. All services can be found in the plateia or off Kapetan Matapa, the main road running into the Old Town from the plateia. The bus station (☎51 229) is a corner counter in Xasero Taverna, across from the small chapel in the corner of the plateia. **Buses** from Areopolis go to Athens (5hr., 4 per day 8am-6pm, €22.70) via Gythion (35min., €2.30) and Sparta (1½hr., €6) and Itilo (20min.; M-Sa 6:30, 9am, 1:45pm; €1.20). From Itilo, you can catch a bus to Kalamata (4 per day). A bus running into Mani goes to the **Dirou Caves** (leaves 11am, returns 12:45pm; €1.20), Gerolimenas (40min., 3 per day 11:45am-7:30pm, €2.90), and Vatheia (1½hr.; M, W, F 1:45pm; €3.60), with limited service on Sunday and holidays.

To find the **National Bank,** with a **24hr. ATM,** walk on the main road away from Pirgos Dirou, making a left on the street closest to the gas station. (☎51 293. Open M-F 9am-1pm.) The **police** are 500m out of town on the main road toward Pirgos Dirou. (☎51 209. Open 24hr.) As you walk facing the sea, a **pharmacy** is two doors down from the post office. (☎29 510. Open M 8am-2pm, Tu-F 8am-2pm and 5-9pm.) A 24hr. **health center** (☎51 242 or 51 259) is 50m down a street that starts in the main plateia and runs away from the ocean, next to the first church; signs point the way. Opposite the health center is the **OTE.** (☎51 299. Open daily 8am-1pm.) The **post office** is on the street with the National Bank, across from Hotel Mani. It **exchanges currency** and traveler's checks, and offers **Poste Restante.** (☎51 230. Open M-F 7:30am-2pm.) **Postal Code:** 23062.

☎ ☐ ACCOMMODATIONS AND FOOD. Though you won't find much variety in price, Areopolis's rooms range from century-old tower houses to modern hotels. Follow Kapetan Matapa and turn left at the end to get to ☒**Tsimova's Rooms ❷,** behind the church in the Old Town. A haven for history buffs, this 300-year-old house supposedly once hosted Kolokotronis. A small garden sits between the reception room and the spacious, uniquely appointed rooms with air-conditioning, TV, mini-fridge, and bath. (☎51 301. Singles €25-60; doubles €35-60; triples €40-60.) On the same road as the National Bank, **Hotel Trapela ❹** combines the rustic beauty of its stone rooms and wood-paneled ceilings with elegant, modern furnishings. Each room comes with air-conditioning, TV, and minibar, and some have a view of the intimate backyard courtyard. Relax with a pleasant view on the top-floor lounge. (☎52 690; www.trapela.gr. Singles €50; doubles and triples €60-80; quads €120. Discounts for stays over 3 days. MC/V.) Across from Hotel Trapela, the family-run **Apelis rooms ❹** are in a quiet location close to the plateia within the family compound. The large doubles have marble floors, bath, TV, air-conditioning, pleasant wood furniture, and access to the family's garden. (☎51 474. Doubles €40-75; apartments with kitchen €60-90.)

Restaurants cluster in the plateia and around the Old Town, most offering traditional Greek cuisine. **Mparmpa Petros Taverna ❷** is along Kapetan Matapa on the left, walking from the small square toward the large church of the Old Town. The specialty dishes use pork raised on the owners' family farm. Before settling into the romantic garden seating area, you can take the friendly staff's tour of the kitchen. (☎51 205. Pork with wine sauce €8. Entrees €6.50-9. Open daily 1pm-late.) Across from the church in the Old Town, quiet **Lithostroto ❷** has an extensive menu and outdoor seating on the cobblestoned street right under a tree. (☎54 240. Stuffed vine leaves €6.50. Grilled meats €6-9. Salads €3-5. Cover €1.) In the plateia, **Nikola's Place ❷** serves Greek dishes in plentiful portions. Feel free to disregard the menu, as the waiters are happy to bring you into the kitchen to let you choose whatever looks good. (☎51 366. Entrees €6-10. Open daily 8am-1am.) You also can head to one of the area's **supermarkets.** There's one just off the plateia on the main road to Pirgos Dirou, and another on the road to the Old Town.

⚡ DAYTRIP FROM AREOPOLIS: DIROU CAVES. Part of a subterranean river, the unusual ⚡**Dirou Caves** (**Spilia Dirou** or **Vlihada Cave**) are cool and quiet. The caverns are strung with tiny crystalline stalactites, while vermillion stalagmites slice the 30m deep water's surface. Discovered at the end of the 19th century and opened to the public in 1971, the caves have yet to be fully explored. Experts speculate that they are 70km long and may extend all the way to Sparta. The 1.3km boat ride through the freshwater cave lasts about 30min., followed by a 10min. walk out of the caves. The tiny boats, guided only by a small oar, rock their way through the narrow, incredibly low channels. Passengers often have to duck and lean to avoid the stalactites, which change from brilliant orange to green in the various small enclosures. Floating lights illuminate the tour, but unlit recesses branch off on each side. On your way out, you can also visit the small **Neolithic Museum**, which displays findings from Alepotrypa Cave at Dirou. The unique olive leaves have remained relatively intact from Neolithic times, and the complete skeleton of a young woman is morbid but intriguing. A small pebble beach, popular with local children, sits to the side of the caves' exit.

MONEMVASIA Μονεμβασία ☎27320

Byzantine enthusiasts on their way to Monemvasia's sights may be puzzled when the bus drops them off in a modern town. The New Town of Monemvasia (a.k.a. "Gefyra") is a logical starting point for entry onto the island that contains the famed historical city. Below the monumental fortress built into precipitous cliffs, Old Town Monemvasia's winding cobblestoned paths, low archways, and narrow flights of stairs highlight the town's origins in the Middle Ages. A climb up the staircase uphill from the Old Town allows access to the top of the rock. Here, less-frequented ruins lie waiting to be appreciated and magnificent views of the rugged Peloponnesian coastline abound in all directions. Though it is home to hotels, quaint shops, and restaurants, the Old Town retains a distinctive medieval feel that isn't spoiled by its unabashed appeal to tourists.

▐ TRANSPORTATION. The bus station is located in the helpful Malvasia Travel Agency, on Spartis. All **buses** connect or stop in Molai. Daily buses at 7:15am, 2:15, and 5:15pm leave for: Athens (5½hr., €25.40) via Molai (30min., €2.20); Ithsmos (4½hr., €19.70); Sparta (2hr., €8.70); Tripoli (3hr., €13.30). An express bus to Athens switches in Sparta (daily 5:15am, M and F also 8:30am; €25.40). Athens buses also run to Piraeus (€25.40); check at Malvasia Travel for schedules. A local shuttle runs between Geyfra and the Old Town, stopping at the kiosk before the bridge in the New Town, and outside the main gate of the Old Town (daily, every 15min. 8am-midnight, €1) although the walk is an easy 15min. **Taxis** (☎61 274) drive around town, and a few can be found at the beginning of the bridge near the bus stop. The most reliable way to find one is to call.

▐▌ ORIENTATION AND PRACTICAL INFORMATION. Facing the causeway from the village, the harbor is to the right, and a pebbled beach is to the left. The main street, **23 Iouliou,** runs inland from the causeway before becoming **Spartis** and splitting off to the right at the fork. Most offices are on this street; smaller offshoots contain hotels and restaurants.

Malvasia Travel Agency is home to the bus station, **exchanges currency,** arranges moped rentals, and sells tickets for **ferries** and **Flying Dolphins.** (☎61 752. Open daily 7am-3pm and 5-8pm, hours reduced in low season.) Across from the bus station, the **National Bank** has a **24hr. ATM** and **currency exchange.** (☎61 201. Open M-Th 8am-1:30pm, F 8am-1pm.) The **police** are on Spartis, 50m to the right of Malvasia Travel. (☎61 210. Open 24hr.) **Internet** access is available at the **Baywatch Cafe,** on the left when facing the causeway 25m down the pebble beach. (€3 per hr., min. €1.50. Beer €1.50. Coffee €1.50. Open daily 11am-2am.) The **post office** is next to the National Bank. (☎61 231. Open M-F 7:30am-2pm.) **Postal Code:** 23070.

⌂⛺ ACCOMMODATIONS AND CAMPING. A room in one of the Old Town's traditional hotels will cost more than a room on the mainland (doubles from €60). An abundance of **domatia** options in the New Town keeps prices down (doubles €25-40). One of the New Town's better hotels is **⬛Hotel Belessis ❸**, a 20-room establishment of two picturesque stone buildings, about 250m from the causeway down Spartis to the right at the fork. The hard rock exterior belies cozy, comfortable rooms with air-conditioning, TV, bath, and lots of wood paneling. Rooms in the uphill building feel slightly more modern, though not more comfortable. (☎61 217. Singles and doubles €30-50; 4-person 2-fl. apartment with kitchenette and 2 baths €60-80.) **Petrino Domatia ❹**, another stone building along the harbor 150m down the left fork, rents clean rooms with air-conditioning, TV, fridge, and striking views. (☎61 136. Singles €40-50; doubles and triples €55-75.) **Hotel Akrogiali ❸**, across from Malvasia Travel on Spartis, has unspectacular rooms in a great location with air-conditioning, TV, small balcony, bath, and a common fridge. (☎61 360. Singles €30-35; doubles €40-45.) Those interested in camping should inquire about **Camping Paradise ❶** (☎61 123), 4km along the water on the mainland beach.

🍴 FOOD. ⬛Pipinellis Taverna ❷ is 2km from Monemvasia on the road to Camping Paradise. Take the left road at the fork in town, following the coast. This taverna serves fresh, homegrown produce in a pleasant setting; outside is a shaded garden patio surrounded by trees. Enjoy uncommon traditional dishes (rabbit casserole with lemon sauce, €7.50) at very reasonable prices. (☎61 044. Entrees €5-9. Open daily noon-1am.) If dining in Old Monemvasia seems attractive, try one of the first tavernas off the main road on the right. **Restaurant Matoula ❸**, whose outdoor garden gives diners a gorgeous view, is the oldest taverna in town. It justifies its €8 moussaka with friendly service and a traditional atmosphere. It might be hard to resist a bottle of regional wine (€7-23) and the nut cake with ice cream (€4) for dessert. (☎61 660. *Dolmades* €8. Entrees €8-14. Open daily noon-midnight. MC/V.) Bakeries and fast food are to the left off Spartis as the road forks by the harbor. To the left walking away from the causeway, on the water just after the dock landing, **Korali Grill House ❶** makes cheap and delicious pitas (souvlaki, gyros, and burger) for €1.70 each that threaten to run its more expensive neighbors out of business. It also doubles as **Paros ❷** restaurant, which serves seafood (€7-30) and nicely rounds out the options available to patrons. (☎61 134. Grilled entrees €6.50-12. Open daily 11am-2am.) Take a left two blocks down off of Spartis, across from Malvasia Travel, to find **Lekakis Supermarket.** (☎61 167. Open daily 7am-9pm.)

⬛ SIGHTS. ⬛Old Town Monemvasia deserves the constant attention it receives. An undeniable other-worldliness shrouds the city, adding an aura of medieval mystery to every tunnel and turn. The town's name, which means "one way," makes sense once you've passed through the single gate to Old Town Monemvasia, entering a city frozen in time. No cars or bikes are allowed through the gate, so packhorses bearing groceries and cases of beer are led back and forth to restaurants. Upon entering the gate, a cobbled street, lined with the surprisingly charming and whimsical decorations of tourist shops, winds through to the central plateia. There, the 1697 church of **Christos Elkomenos** (Christ in Chains) is on the left as you face the ocean, next to the bell tower. The **Archaeological Museum,** on the right of the plateia while facing the ocean, is an air-conditioned former mosque where Monemvasia's 13th-century prominence and strong commercial ties to the Western world are chronicled. (☎61 403. Open M noon-7:30pm, Tu-Su 8:30am-7:30pm. Free.) The Old

> **HANDICAPPED INACCESSIBLE.** Old Town Monemvasia's shortage of sidewalks, ramps, and elevators makes it nearly impossible for disabled travelers to explore the small island. The tourist office may be able to help make arrangements for visiting Monemvasia and other challenging areas nearby.

Town's greatest charm lies in the winding, nameless side streets to the fortified sea wall. To get to the oft-photographed 12th-century **Agia Sofia,** go up the stairs behind the Christos Elkomenos bell tower, to the left off the main road walking toward the plateia where a sign also points to the Hotel Byzantio and continue uphill until you reach the staircase. The walk from the plateia to the church takes about 20min. Although invading Turks defaced Agia Sofia's frescoes, its beauty is still breathtaking, as is the dramatic drop to the sea behind the church. It is balanced on the edge of the rock cliffs that also hold the remains of the city's **castle.** At the top of the staircase where signs point down one short path to Agia Sofia, an arrow points the way to the **cistern** that still provides the town's water. Rain was once Monemvasia's only source of water, and the complex network of cisterns have continued to collect and distribute water since their conception. The hike along it is full of slippery stones and uneven ground, so wear suitable shoes. From Agia Sofia, arrows pointing uphill indicate the path to the **citadel.** The arched ruins nearest to the New Town, a 10min. walk away, are visible from the mainland and offer a magnificent view over Gefyra and the surrounding coast.

NEAPOLI Νεάπολις   ☎27340

The most convenient gateway to Kythera from Peloponnesean Greece, Neapoli is a small seaside destination. The town's pebble and dark-sand **beaches** are accessible down a flight of steps from the waterfront road, lined by restaurants.

Because travelers flow through Neapoli on their way to summer vacations in Kythera, hotel prices skyrocket mid-July through August. A particularly colorful option is **Hotel Arsenakos ❷,** Akti Voion 198, whose bright yellow-and-red rooms have air-conditioning, TV, bath, phone, balcony, and fridge. A 5min. walk from the pier with the water on the left, the hotel is across the street from the beach. (☎22 991. Breakfast included in high season. Singles €25-55; doubles €30-60; triples €40-65; quads €45-80; 4-person suites €55-110. MC/V.) Also across the street from the beach, the rooms in bright white **Domatia Chrysoula ❷** are spacious and clean, with TV, air-conditioning, kitchenette, and lots of closet space; many have a balcony. (☎23 951. No English spoken. Singles €25-65; doubles €25-65; triples €35-65; 4-person apartments with full kitchen €50-65.) A bargain in high season, **Aivali ❸,** at the corner of the street to the post office next to the bridge, rents large rooms with lots of natural light, air-conditioning, TV, fridge, and balcony. (☎22 545. Singles €30-40; doubles €35-50.) The local cuisine is one of the first things travelers to Neapoli encounter as they stumble off the ferry; most restaurant owners grill octopi outside all day long. As you walk past the pier, with the water on your right, many of the restaurants are similar in both food and price. **Tzivaeri ❷** serves affordable seafood dishes (€6-14) as well as a variety of other entrees (€5-8.50) to patrons seated outdoors on the walk above the beach. (☎22 545. Stuffed peppers with cheese €4.50. Mixed meat dish €6.50. Open daily 6am-1am.) **Moreas ❷,** two blocks past Aivali with the water on the left, makes delectable meat and fish dishes for a mostly local clientele. Its outside tables are pulled as close to the beach as they can get, so you can watch the waves crash while you choose from the rotating menu. Indoors, the elegantly appointed dining room is set with non-paper tablecloths, a rarity on the taverna scene. (☎23 845. Salads €2.50-5. Entrees €5-8. Fish €40-45 per kg. Open daily 12:30-5pm and 8:30pm-midnight.)

Directly across from the pier, a few storefronts up an unnamed street, **Vatika Bay Travel** sells tickets for the Kythera ferries. (☎24 004. Open daily 8am-9pm.) Though hawkers may try to sell tickets by the pier, it is illegal to sell anywhere but in a travel shop. **Ferries** leave for Diakofti, Kythera (daily, €10). The **bus station** (☎23 222) is on an unmarked street off the right side of the waterfront facing inland, two blocks from the pier. **Buses** leave at 8:15am, 1:45, and 5pm for: Athens (6hr., €25) via Ag. Nikolaos (20min., €1.20); Molai (1½hr., €5.80); Sparta (3hr., €12.20); Tripoli (4hr., €16.80). Buses also run to Pounta, the port for Elafonissos (M-F 4 per day 7am-1:45pm, €1.20). A **National Bank** and **24hr. ATM** are on the waterfront across from the pier. (Open M-Th 8am-2:30pm, F 8am-2pm.) The **port police** (☎22 228) are one block from the National Bank in a small plateia behind the statue. The **post office** is one block inland on Dimokratias on the left of the waterfront as you face inland, past the bridge. (Open M-F 7:30am-2pm.) **Postal Code:** 23053.

KYTHERA Κύθηρα

According to myth, the island of Kythera rose from the waters where Zeus cast his father Cronus's severed head into the sea after castrating him. Springing from Cronus's foamy remains, Aphrodite washed up onto Kythera's shores and made it her homeland. In antiquity, the island held a large temple to the goddess, where she was worshipped as Aphrodite Urania, goddess of chaste love. Though one might not associate the island's barren, mountainous landscape with Aphrodite's famous worship-worthy fertility, its flowering shrubs, green valleys, and secluded villages hold a potent beauty. Today, the island remains blissfully untouched by mass tourism; its visitors are primarily Greek-Australians returning to visit family, not jetsetters looking for a year-round spring break. Kythera has a veritable laundry list of amazing things to see—whitewashed Cycladic houses, Byzantine churches, Venetian castles, widely varying beaches, deep canyons, and crystal-clear blue-green waters.

AGIA PELAGIA Άγια Πελαγία ☎27360

With the most hotels on the island and close proximity to six beautiful beaches, Agia Pelagia is a good place to set up camp. The town is less picturesque than southerly Hora or Kapsali, but accommodations and moped rentals are cheaper, and its waterfront tavernas offer some of the only nightlife on the tiny island. The ferry used to land here until the rough serf that makes the beach beautiful was deemed too intense for use as a viable port.

▐▌ TRANSPORTATION AND PRACTICAL INFORMATION. From Kapsali, **ferries** go to Gythion, Kalamata, Kasteli, Crete, and Neapoli. **Flying Dolphins** leave Kapsali for Piraeus. Be sure to check the schedules as soon as you arrive, as they frequently change. Ferry tickets are sold in a kiosk by the mini-mart at Diakofti's pier. The island's only **bus** runs mid-July through August once per day between Agia Pelagia and Kapsali in the south; it stops in small villages connected by subsidiary roads. The route travels down the island's main road, K. Dromos, and passes through Potamos (the largest town), Livadi, and Hora (Kythera). You can rent a **bicycle** (€6), **moped** (€20 per day), or **car** (from €30 per day) from **Active Rent-A-Car** along the waterfront. (☎33 207. Open daily 9am-7pm.) **Motorbike rentals** can be found in a field next to Taverna Faros, on the left side of the waterfront facing inland (from €15 per day, ask in the taverna).

The cottage 20m from Hotel Kythereia heading away from town is the **information office.** Though not an official tourist office, its staff has information about accommodations, sights, and flight and ferry schedules, as well as an infinite amount of patience for travelers trying to get their bearings. The nearest **bank** (☎33 209; open M-Th 8am-2pm, F 8am-1:30pm), **pharmacy** (☎34 220; open M-F 8:30am-2pm and 6-9pm), **hospital** (☎33 203), **Internet** facilities, and **post office** (☎33 225; open M-F 7:30am-2pm) are all in Potamos. The **port police** (☎33 280) are 50m to the right of the port facing inland, above Stella Restaurant. **Postal Code:** 80200.

⌂❑ ACCOMMODATIONS AND FOOD. You can find high-season bargains at the many domatia in town—doubles range €40-50, compared to hotels' €60-80. The tourist office has a list of domatia owners and can put you in contact with them. Blue and white **Hotel Kythereia ❷,** opposite the dock and the beach, is run by a spectacularly helpful and hospitable Greek-Australian family. The hotel's simple rooms have colorful bath, air-conditioning, TV, and shared fridge. It fills up quickly, so call ahead. (☎33 321. Singles €20-35; doubles €30-50. MC/V.)

Stella ❸, two doors from Hotel Kythereia, has a giant selection of menu options in a quieter area than the center-of-town tavernas. Outdoor seating puts you right next to the sandy beach with waves rolling in. Try the stuffed calamari with feta cheese (€8) and the "Special Veal" (€7.50) with cheese and eggplant—both delicious options. The bread never stops coming, and every meal ends with complimentary watermelon. (☎33 513. Entrees €6-13. Open daily noon-midnight.) To the right as you face inland on the waterfront, next to the town map, **Restaurant Kaleris ❷** serves mostly local cuisine to a mix of natives and visitors. A decent selection from the standard menu is augmented by daily specials that usually feature a local goat dish. (☎33 461. Kytheran noodles with beef fillet and sliced zucchini €8. Entrees €6.50-9. Open daily noon-1am.) Keep walking with the sea on the right to **Moustakias ❷,** which features live Greek music every Friday and Saturday night. Besides listing dish options such as the beef or rabbit *stifado* (€6.50), the menu also gives a little background on Kytheran history. (☎33 519. Entrees €6.50-10.) The town's **supermarket,** Kapsanis, is next door.

◧ BEACHES. Agia Pelagia boasts six beaches, all within a short distance of the town center. Starting from the main beach, continue south toward Potamos with the water on your left to five more beaches; bear left when the road forks. The road is paved as you pass the second beach, **Neo Kosmos,** about 300m from town, and turns to dirt after the Aphrodite Pelagia Hotel. Next is stunning **Fyriamo Beach** (500m from town), with its long stretch of red sand and dramatic cliffs in the background. About 1km farther is **Kalamitzi Beach;** the path there is difficult to find off the main road, so ask for directions at the information office. The gorgeous landscape, however, justifies the circuitous route. From there, the last beaches are easy to find. Isolated **Lorenzo Beach** is in a small cove that provides shade from the hot midday sun. **Lagatha** lies at the base of a dramatic ▨**canyon** at the end of the road, separating the ocean from the deep green waters of Lake Pekelagada.

❏ DAYTRIPS FROM KYTHERA. The island has enough sights to keep any visitor occupied. From the peaceful beach town of **Kapsali,** 2km east and downhill from Hora, a beautiful view unfurls, spanning two nearby lighthouses, the tall surrounding mountains, and the castle at Hora. The beach, with clear waters and a long sandy shore, is packed with waterfront tavernas and pedal boat rental agencies. At Paleohora, in the east opposite the canyon, are the ruins of the former fortified capital of the island, **Agios Dimitrios,** built during Byzantine rule. Despite the walls, the town was destroyed in 1537 by pirates led by the notorious Barbarossa. The modest but well-preserved remains of an over 1300-year-old **Venetian castle** sit steps from the center of town. Once in the castle, follow the signs to the church of Ag. Ioannis for a spectacular view of Kythera's mountains, valleys, and cliffs. The island's **beaches** are gorgeous as well, as the ocean's blue contrasts sharply with the bare, brown landscape. The best beaches are a bit difficult to reach, accessible only by dirt roads that can be perilous for mopeds or buses—a car is safer. On the eastern coast, a long staircase leads down to the often-empty ◪**Kaladi beach,** with sparkling coves and striking rock formations. Isolated **Halkos,** near Kalamos on the southern coast, shimmers with a quiet beauty.

The village of **Milopotamos** on the western side of the island is home to two of Kythera's most magnificent sites, including the **Milopotamos waterfall.** Its surrounding forest and sparkling waters provide a scenic, albeit cold, spot for a swim. Also near the village is the **Cave of Agia Sofia.** The most impressive of the island's several caves, Agia Sofia's walls are adorned with beautiful **frescoes** and are framed by eerie stalactites and stalagmites. The cave is a 30-40min. walk from Milopotamos.

HORA Χώρα   ☎27360

Hora (also called "Kythera"), the island's southern capital, is most famous for its large castle (open 7am-7pm; wheelchair-accessible; free) and whitewashed houses. Though usually a small, low-key community, it's often overwhelmed with visitors in high season.

The few accommodations that cater to visitors offer similar views and amenities, but domatia may have kitchens and lower prices. Hotels and domatia are mostly clustered around and along the main road. **Castello Apartments ❸** is up a few stairs to the left of the main road as you approach the fork from the plateia. Rooms come with air-conditioning, TV, kitchen, bath, and large balcony. Follow the path leading to the back of the building to find the reception. (☎31 069; www.castelloapts-kythera.gr. Doubles €30-45; triples and studios €45-55. MC/V.) Though a little more removed from the center of town, the unnamed **rooms ❸** above Salonikios include air-conditioning, TV, kitchenette, and balcony with views of the nearby mountains. Walk up the stairs to the right of the post office and turn right at the road; it's 20m down on the right. (☎31 922. Singles and doubles €30-60.) At family-run **Salonikios ❷,** the only taverna in town, diners are invited into the kitchen to choose their meals. Head up the stairs to the right of the post office and turn right. Sit inside or outside on the pleasant patio with a view down to Kapsali below. (☎31 705. Appetizers €2.50-5. Salads €4-5.50. Entrees €5-8.50.)

Flights depart Kythera for Athens (daily, €60). **Kithira Travel,** 50m uphill from the plateia, has ferry schedules and tickets for **Olympic Airways** flights and **Flying Dolphins.** (☎31 390. Open daily 8:30am-2pm and 6:30-9:30pm.) The **bus** (runs M-Sa) drops off outside town at the museum, then continues to Kapsali before returning to Ag. Pelagia. From the bus stop, walk downhill on the main road to get to the center of town. **Taxis** (☎31 720), which line up in the plateia, will take you to Diakofti (€25). Many taxi drivers take an all-afternoon siesta, though, so plan your ride in advance. There is a **National Bank** with a **24hr. ATM** in the plateia. (Open M-Th 8am-2:30pm, F 8am-2pm.) **Public toilets** are below the Agricultural Bank in the plateia; follow the steps outside the bank. Facing the water, Hora's main street begins in the plateia's lower left corner and runs downhill. Along it you'll find the **police,** 150m after you make a right at the fork in the road, on the street toward the castle. (☎31 206. Open 24hr.) The nearest **hospital** is in Potamos. **Internet** access is available at the one computer at **Typographics,** on the main road toward the police station. (☎39 016. €5 per hr., min. €2. Open daily in high season 8:30am-1pm; low season 8:30am-2pm and 5-10pm.) The **post office,** which has **Poste Restante,** is in the plateia. (☎31 274. Open M-F 7:30am-3pm.) **Postal Code:** 80100.

CENTRAL GREECE

Situated at the crossroads of the country, the expansive region of Central Greece is as diverse as its terrain is mountainous. Stretching from the foothills of Mt. Olympus in the north to the peaceful seaside villages that dot the shore of the Gulf of Corinth, Central Greece is charming, rugged, and authentic. Tiny villages cling to the cliff sides of the towering peaks surrounding Karpenisi, while the magnificent views from the lush terrain of the Mt. Pelion Peninsula let visitors gaze down at the twinkling lights of Volos. The region is home to the ruins of the ancient oracle at Delphi and the Byzantine monasteries atop immense stone pillars at Meteora, two must-see sights for any itinerary.

 SUGGESTED ITINERARIES: CENTRAL GREECE

THREE DAYS Take advantage of summer discounts and gorgeous hikes in **Arahova** (p. 204), a ski town where low and high seasons are reversed. Seek Apollo's guidance on how to spend the money you've saved at the **Delphic oracle** (p. 211). From there, go to **Galaxidi** (p. 212), where you will get an introduction to Greece's small-town countryside culture.

ONE WEEK Traverse some of Greece's best hiking country, starting with serene **Mount Parnassos** (p. 204). Next, hike among the small, charming towns in mountainous **Evritania** (p. 218), a region known as "the Switzerland of Greece." End your trip up north by climbing to the death-defying midair monasteries of **Meteora** (p. 240).

STEREA ELLADA

For centuries, advice-seeking pilgrims from across the ancient world gravitated to Sterea Ellada to inquire at the Oracle of Delphi. Many years later, 10th-century Orthodox saint Osios Loukas built a Byzantine monastery nearby, which ailing believers continue to visit today in search of a sacred cure. For more action-oriented visitors, the small mountain villages offer thrilling ski slopes, the western coast is covered in deep forest, and the monumental ruins shed light on tales of history. As it has over the course of history, Sterea Ellada caters to both the minds and the bodies of those that traverse its mountain paths and seaside villages.

THEBES (THIVA) Θήβα ☎ 22620

Buried beneath the low-rise apartment buildings and lazy tavernas of modern Thebes lies its claim to fame: an illustrious and notorious past. History has surfaced—literally—in spots throughout the city, as attempts at construction have revealed the edifices of ancient Thebes. Theban buildings grace the avenues of Cadmus (the city's legendary first king), Oedipus (exiled king and eponym of the Complex), and Epaminonda (the general who ended Spartan dominance). Rising to prominence during the height of the Greek city-state, 600-400 BC, Thebes capitalized on its fertile plains and strategic location between Northern Greece and the Peloponnese to become a cultural center and the inspiration for great works by Sophocles, Euripides, and Aeschylus. Alexander the Great's army cut this prosperity short around 335 BC by setting fire to the city, reducing it to rubble; only temples and Pindar's ancestral home were spared. Modern Thebes, a tiny, unremarkable city, doesn't quite live up to its vast reputation. To be fair, it's not really trying; instead, the city focuses on family and community, encouraging vibrant evenings on the main street. The unique combination of archaeological sites and inviting cafes makes Thebes an excellent daytrip.

⛏ TRANSPORTATION. The main **bus station** (☎27 512) is below Thebes at Estias 10. From there, buses depart for Athens (1½hr., every hr. 6am-8:15pm, €7). If you miss the direct bus between Thebes and Halkida (7:20, 10am; €3), take the Thebes-Athens bus and get off at the Skimatari stop (30min., €2.10). From there, cross under the highway overpass and wait at the sheltered bus stop on the far side, then catch the Athens-Halkida bus (10min., 30min., €1.70). Regular buses run to Livadia (45min., every hr. 7:40am-9:40pm, €3.20) from a stop about 2km out of town; walk all the way down Pindarou past the Archaeological Museum and go down the steps. Take the left fork then the right onto Laiou (Λαιου). Take a left onto St. Athanasiou and follow the blue signs to Livadia (Λειβαδια) to the small bus shelter before the gas station on your right. Buy your ticket on board. For **taxis** (☎27 077), visit Pindarou 45, where they wait in front of the garden 24hr.

▦ ORIENTATION. Two parallel main streets, **Epaminonda** and **Pindarou,** run from the top of the hill into the valley below. Epaminonda hosts a variety of cafes and shops; Pindarou is lined with small retail stores and businesses. From the bus station, with your back to the terminal and the dirt parking lot on your left, follow the road on your right and take the first right as it enters the roundabout. Follow **Eteokleous** up the hill to a plateia where first Pindarou and then Epaminonda veer to the right. Turn right onto Epaminonda to find hotels, tavernas, and other sights.

▨ PRACTICAL INFORMATION. There is a **National Bank,** Pindarou 94, with a **24hr. ATM.** (☎23 331. Open M-F 8am-2:30pm.) Just uphill on the other side of the street, there is an **Alpha Bank.** (Open M-Th 8am-2:30pm, F 8am-2pm.) Numerous **pharmacies** line Epaminonda and Pindarou; there is one just downhill from Hotel Meletiou. The **hospital** (☎24 444) is located out of town and is best reached by taxi (€3-5). The **OTE,** Vourdouba 20, is between Epaminonda and Pindarou. (☎27 799. Open M-F 7:30am-3pm, Sa 9am-2pm.) Turn left at the downhill end of Epaminonda's square to find **Central Internet Cafe,** Antigonis 39. It also has bowling, pool tables, foosball, and a bar. (☎24 111. €2 per hr. Open daily 10am-3am.) The **Post Office,** Drakou 17, is on a side street between Pindarou and Epaminonda. **Poste Restante** is available. (☎27 810. Open M-F 7:30am-2pm.) **Postal Code:** 32200.

▥ ACCOMMODATIONS. If you decide to spend the night in Thebes, there are only a few options in town, and they will all put a strain on your wallet. The friendly English-speaking staff at **Hotel Niovi ❸,** Epaminonda 63, offers rooms with air-conditioning, TV, and a beautifully tiled private bath. (☎29 888. Singles €35, with breakfast €38; doubles €40/45; triples €50/60. AmEx/MC/V.) Across the street, the rooms at **Hotel Meletiou ❹,** Epaminonda 58, have air-conditioning, TV, fridge, and bath in graceful, spacious surroundings. (☎27 333. Breakfast €7. Singles €50; doubles €100; triples €120. Cash only.) The most expensive option, **Hotel Dionysion ❹,** Dimokritou 5, is also the most luxurious, with gorgeous, ultra-modern baths. Walk downhill on Epaminonda and turn left. (☎89 253. Breakfast included. Singles €60; doubles €85; triples €110; quads €130.)

▨ FOOD. By evening, people fill the pedestrian-only sections of Thebes as cafes and tavernas move tables into the street. Bakeries, fruit stands, and gyro and souvlaki restaurants provide inexpensive options (€1-3). Most restaurants from Epaminonda to Pindarou offer similar fare at similar prices. A standout, however, is family-run **▧Pouros ❷,** Pl. Kadmias. Turn left on Antigonis from Epaminonda;

Central Greece

you'll see the large sign at the end of the street. The view of the plains beyond Thebes from the enchanting courtyard with a fountain is a picturesque backdrop for the generous portions of classic Greek food. (☎28 455. Meat sampler €4. Entrees €5-8. Open daily 8am-midnight.) **Dionysos ❷**, Epimanonda 88, just past the plateia, has been cooking traditional fare longer than the rest, first opening its doors in 1922. (☎24 445. Entrees €5-6.50. Veal with lemon €6.50. Open daily 8am-4:30pm and 6:30pm-2am. V.) If you prefer to make your own meals, try a supermarket like **Dia**, Epaminonda 63. It's directly underneath Hotel Niovi, across the street from Hotel Meletiou. (Open M-F 8:30am-9pm, Sa 8am-8pm.) There are two **Champion** markets, one on Pindarou 108 and another on Epaminonda 36, uphill from the hotels. (Both open M-F 8am-9pm, Sa 8am-4pm, Su 8am-2:30pm.)

◙⧉ SIGHTS AND NIGHTLIFE. Thebes's antiquities traditionally have been its main attraction, but the **Archaeological Museum**, Threpsiadou 1, at the end of Pindarou, closed for renovations in 2007. Even without access to its extensive collection of art and artifacts from roughly 45 centuries of history (3000 BC-AD 1500), you can peer into the open **excavation pits**—the source of the museum's collection—sprinkled among buildings throughout the city. Segments of a Mycenaean palace and acropolis (c. 1400 BC) are visible. The largest of these, the **House of Cadmus,** is on the left along the way to the museum, a block after the taxis, behind a green fence. Also nearby are the ancient **Mycenaean Chamber Tombs,** which are closed to the public, but whose entrances are still visible. Take Vourdouba down-hill from Pindarou, turn left on Avlidos, and then right up the stone stairs.

Chic **Cafe Theatro**, Epaminonda 79, is the square's most lively venue, with a DJ spinning pop for a young crowd that congregates outside on posh couches. (Tea and coffee €1.50-2.50. Mixed drinks €4. Open daily 8am-late.) Across the way, the **Athinaikou Cafe**, Epaminonda 72, serves drinks to a slightly older clientele.

PARNASSOS Παρνασσός AND
ARAHOVA Αράχωβα   ☎22670

The crowds at Mt. Parnassos (2457m) hit their peak in the winter, when ski and snowboard enthusiasts flock to the best slopes in all of Greece. By night, the frost-bitten masses thaw out in the mountainside village of Arahova, the country's larg-est ski resort, located a convenient 24km away. In the summer months, crowds desert both mountain and village, allowing the opportunistic traveler to hike the broad slopes undisturbed. Peaceful Arahova is especially magical after nightfall, when locals congregate on the cobblestoned sidewalks to enjoy local delights such as delicious unresinated red wine, Boeotian honey, and *tsipouro*, a pecu-liarly potent grape-seed brandy. Known for the pivotal role it played in Greece's War of Independence (see **Life and Times** p. p. 56), Arahova attracts quite a crowd each spring as residents don traditional garb and host a festival in honor of St. George, the renowned dragon-slayer and the town's patron saint.

⌨️ TRANSPORTATION AND PRACTICAL INFORMATION. Buses to Arahova stop at the end of town closest to Delphi, next to the kiosk in front of the main plateia. There is no bus station—ask the knowledgeable and friendly staff at the information office for bus schedules. **Buses** go to Amfissa (10min., 6 per day 10am-10:30pm, €1) via Delphi, Athens (2hr.; 6 per day M-Sa 5:45am-6:15pm, Su 7:45am-9:15pm; €12), and Livadia (35min.; M-F 7am, 4:15pm; Sa 12:50, 4:45pm; Su 4:15pm; €3.60). Getting from Arahova to Parnassos is slightly easier during ski season, when a bus runs there from Pl. Xenia (M-Th 8am, F-Su 3 per day 8:30am-2:30pm; €5). During the summer, go by **car** or **taxi** (☎31 566; round-trip €30) from Pl. Lakas. When negotiating the price, arrange for the driver to pick you up.

Arahova centers on **Delphon**, which points uphill toward Athens. **Plateia Xenia**, the main square, is followed by **Plateia Lakas** and **Plateia Pappaioannou** farther up the road. At the far end of Delphon, one side of the road becomes a scenic over-look. An **information office** is on the right before you enter town from Delphi, and the terrific staff can help with everything from bus times to discounted ski pack-ages. (☎31 630. Open M-F 9am-9pm, Sa-Su 9am-2pm and 5-8pm. Closed Su in sum-mer.) Just after Pl. Xenia on the left is the **National Bank**, with a **24hr. ATM.** (☎31 496. Open M-Th 8am-2:30pm, F 8am-2pm.) **Alpha Bank**, in Pl. Lakas on the right, **exchanges currency.** (☎32 561. Open M-Th 8am-2:30pm, F 8am-2pm.) A **laundry ser-vice** is on Delphon past Pl. Xenia toward Delphi. The **police** (☎31 333) are upstairs on the left side of Delphon past the town center. One of many **pharmacies** is just before the town center on the left. (☎31 252. Open M-Th 8:30am-2pm and 5:30-9:30pm.) The **OTE** is just before the town center on the right. (☎31 099. Open M-F 8am-3pm.) **Internet** access is at the **Royal Game Palace**, 20km down the road to the ski area after it branches off from the main road to Delphi. (☎69774 65 692. €3 per hr. Open daily 10am-late.) To find the **post office**, turn right in Pl. Xenia; it's uphill and on the right. (☎31 253. Open M-F 7:30am-2pm.) **Postal Code:** 32004.

📌 ACCOMMODATIONS AND FOOD. Hotels, pensions, and domatia cluster near Pl. Xenia and along Delphon toward Athens. High season here is winter and low season is summer; prices fluctuate accordingly. The larger hotels at the far end of town are closed during the summer, so pensions are the best bet for a summer traveler. ⬛**Pension Petrino ❹**, down the first alley on the right after Pl. Xenia, invites guests to unwind in cabin-style rooms with TV and bath, some with balcony. A second-story loft is perfect for families. (☎31 384. High-season singles €60-95; doubles €70-115. Low-season singles €20-30; doubles €40. Ask about discounts for longer stays. Prices drop for midweek stays in ski season.) Spend a hard day's night at **Pension Nostos ❹**, past the information office off Pl. Xenia. Its cozy, newly refurbished rooms with fridge, flat-screen TV, and balcony hosted the Beatles in 1967. (☎31 385. Breakfast included. Singles €50; doubles €60. Prices negotiable, and higher in winter. MC/V.)

Around dinnertime, wander through Arahova's lovely cobblestoned side streets to find tucked-away tavernas. Among them is ⬛**Panagiota ❷**, the best restaurant in town. Leave the main street and walk up the stairs near Pl. Pappaioannou to the upper church. Walk around the church and through the gateway on the far side. It's not cheap but upon savoring a bite of the locally grown chicken with white wine and tomato sauce (€7.60), you'll likely forget that such petty things as money even exist. (☎69445 05 068. Entrees €6-12. Open in winter daily noon-6pm and 8pm-midnight; in summer W-Su 6pm-midnight.) **Pizzeria Kellaria ❷**, on the right past Pl. Lakas, serves delicious pizzas (€5-10) and calzones (€5-8.50) from its brick oven, as well as savory and sweet crepes (€3-5). Taking your food to go knocks €1 off the price. (☎31 167. Open daily 8:30pm-late. Longer hours in the winter. Cash only.) The **bakeries** along the road to Delphi sell fresh bread and pastries (€0.50-2), and several small markets near Pl. Lakas offer self-service.

⬛⬛ **SKIING AND HIKING.** Winter activities are accessible at two main **ski centers: Kellaria** and **Parnassos**. Each has tavernas, equipment, and childcare services. Ski season is from December 15 to May 1. Fourteen lifts service 20 slopes, which have a combined length of 14,000m. (☎22340 22 693 for both. M-F €12 per day, Sa-Su €27 per day, students €8, children €5. Full week €80. Family discounts available.)

Though more goats than tourists frequent Parnassos in the summer, it's a peaceful spot for hiking and rock climbing, with literally breathtaking views—the air becomes noticeably thinner higher up. In summer, the only way to get to Parnassos from Arahova or Delphi is by taxi (€30); be sure to negotiate the price beforehand and ask the driver to return later at a set time. Because of the transportation issues, and because many of the mountain's trails are poorly marked, it's much more convenient and just as scenic to hike to the Corycian Cave near Delphi.

Those willing to make the trip to Parnassos can expect open air and the expansive vistas of the rocky mountainside. Before leaving, pick up a trail map and guide (€8) at the bookstore in Arahova, 20m along the road to the ski areas after it branches off from the main road to Delphi. The ski centers on the mountain provide free parking and a convenient base for most trips. An enjoyable hike that takes less than 3hr. each way begins at the **Hellenic Alpine Club Hut**, south of Kelaria, and ends at the peak of **Gerondovrachos.** Follow the line of ski pylons at first, then continue along the ridge line. A much longer hike (around 7hr. each way) to the highest peak, **Liakoura**, begins in the village of **Tithorea**, at the Church of Profitias Ilias. Follow the trail until you reach the Chapel of Aghios Georgios, where you should cross the riverbed and look for the Chapel of Aghios Ioannis. Take the trail that ascends the ridge and leads to the Tsares spring. Continue west past the Treis Tsoubes ridge, enter a ravine, and climb the slopes to the Tsarkos-Liakoura saddle, continuing to the summit. Consult the **Greek Alpine Club** in Athens (☎21032 12 429) or the **Skiing and Mountain Climbing Association of Amfissa** (☎28 577) about routes and refuges for climbers. If you don't speak Greek, ask the information office in Arahova to call for you. Trails can be poorly marked and usually are deserted (goats aside), so bring water and hike with a partner.

CENTRAL GREECE

The **E4** trail, one of the two main hiking routes in the area, begins in Delphi and runs south to north ranging in form from dirt roads to old mule paths. The more popular **22** trail sprawls across the mountain to the east, around the ski centers. Hiking these trails is a major undertaking and should be planned in detail beforehand; the conditions and difficulty can vary drastically depending on location and season, so be sure to inquire at the information office for details.

DAYTRIP FROM ARAHOVA: OSIOS LOUKAS (Οσιος Λουκάς).

Stunning Byzantine architecture, gold-laden mosaics, vibrant frescoes, and intricate brick and stonework adorn the monastery of ■**Osios Loukas.** Built in the 10th and 11th centuries and still in use today, this exquisite complex on the green slopes of Mt. Elikon, over 500m above sea level, overlooks the orchards and vineyards of Boeotia and Phokis. Christian Saint Osios Loukas was born in AD 896 in Delphi, a center formerly dedicated to the Olympian gods and polytheistic worship, and became a monk at the age of 14. In 946, Osios Loukas settled at the lush and enchanting site of the monastery that now bears his name, building a cell, a small church, and a garden. Rumors that his church's relic worked miracles brought believers, leading to an expansion of the grounds and the establishment of a monastery. With aid from fellow hermits and money from admirers, Osios Loukas began construction of two larger churches. The first, the **Church of the Panagia** (Church of the Virgin Mary), was finished soon after his death in 953. The larger and more ornate **Katholikon of Osios Loukas,** built in 1011, became the site of his reliquary. The monastery, which is undergoing minor exterior restoration, is scarred from 13th-century Frankish occupation and German bombing during WWII.

The complex consists of the two churches, a crypt, and monks' cells. The **Archaeology Museum,** on the right after the arched stone gate, sells guidebooks (€2.50-4) and tickets for entrance into the monastery. The one-room museum, formerly a workplace and refectory, has remnants and carvings from Osios Loukas's architectural past and merits only a glance. The Katholikon of Osios Loukas, past the museum on the right, is the monastery's most impressive area. Built on the "Greek cross" basilica plan, the church is resplendent with mosaics made of stone, enamel, and gold. Frescoes depict scenes from Christian lore, including an especially impressive one of Jesus on the upper dome.

A small passageway in the Katholikon's northwestern corner, at the front of the sanctuary on the left, links it to the Church of the Panagia. In this passageway is the monastery's most prized relic: the desiccated body of the saint himself, lying in a transparent glass coffin. Pilgrims come to pray at Osios Loukas's velvet-slippered feet, and thousands have said that his tomb cured them of various ailments. Some have even been bolder: Loukas's left hand, protruding from his habit, has lost a few fingers to relic-seekers. The crypt is between the museum and the churches, accessible by an entrance in the exterior of the Katholikon. Protected from the elements, its stunning frescoes have retained their original splendor. Past the crypt entrance is a small courtyard; walk in and to the left to peek at the luxurious digs enjoyed by medieval monks. Climbing the tower at the far end of the courtyard yields a stunning view. *(The lack of bus service from Arahova forces visitors to take a car or taxi. (☎31 566. 25min. each way.) When negotiating the price, ask the taxi driver either to wait an hour at the monastery (€40) or to return to town and pick you up later (€50). ☎22 797. Open daily May 3-Sept. 15 8am-2pm and 4-7pm; Sept. 16-May 2 8am-5pm. Modest dress required. €3, seniors and students €2, EU students and children free.)*

LIVADIA/KRYA SPRINGS   ☎22610

Renowned long ago as the site of the **Oracle of Zeus Trofonios,** the town of Livadia is now an urban jumble of small boutiques and plazas that cater mostly to businesspeople. The few hotels tend to be on the expensive side, and fast-food establishments clog the town center. Just beyond Livadia's streets and shops, however, is the peaceful brook of Krya Springs, lined with stone bridges, lush flora, and shaded cafes. To reach the springs from where the bus lets you off in the center of town, take Papaspirou until it branches into Boufidou. When Boufidou's pedestrian-only section ends, walk until you reach the brook, then follow the brook uphill to reach the springs. A shaded stone path leads upstream to Livadia's historical sights, past outdoor cafes and tavernas overlooking waterfalls. As you walk toward the spring, the city's **clock tower** looms to your right. The tower originally was used as a lighthouse during the French occupation, but was converted in 1803 when Lord Elgin donated the clock to gain favor with locals so he would be permitted to begin archaeological excavations. When you reach the tower marked as the **medieval castle,** turn right and follow the steep road uphill. Near the top, if you enter the castle and follow a footpath through overgrown greenery, you will find another crumbling tower, a **Byzantine church,** and a beautiful view. Continue following the brook, via the cobblestone path that runs past the bottom of the castle, to reach Krya's other sights. An **outdoor theater,** built into the side of a hill, is the site of the 20-day **cultural festival** of Trofonia held each September. Although it has been marred by graffiti, the theater still boasts spectacular acoustics and a seating capacity of 1500. Past the theater, near the end of the stone path, a series of just over 500 rock steps winds up the mountain past the former site of the Oracle of Zeus Trofonios, now marked by two small, spooky churches built in recesses in the cliff face. Make sure to bring water and be careful near the top where the steps become particularly steep as they lead to the upper church. For those seeking evening entertainment, a three-screen **cinema** (☎20 225) is located on Boufidou.

Hotels in Livadia are expensive and difficult to find. **Hotel Livadia ❹**, L. Papaspirou 4, across from the bus stop, offers tidy rooms with air-conditioning, phone, TV, and bath. (☎23 611. Singles €60; doubles €75.) Past the Byzantine church, you'll see the splendidly picturesque ◪**Xenia Cocktail Bar ❶**, situated directly over a series of waterfalls. Treat yourself to a cold drink or ice cream. (☎29 479. Beer €2.50-3.50. Open daily 9am-late.) After your hike, stop at **Krya Taverna ❷**, Trofonion 13, with the green awning at the base of the springs area, for a traditional Greek meal. (☎26 764. Souvlaki €1.20. Entrees €7-11.)

Take the **bus** to Livadia (35min.; M-F 7am, 4:15pm; Sa 12:50, 4:45pm; Su 4:15pm; €3.60.) The Athens-bound bus also stops in Livadia; ask the driver to let you off in the center of town, near Pl. L. Katsonis. Ask about returning buses before you get off or inquire at the Arahova tourist office before you leave for Livadia. The **National Bank,** which offers **currency exchange,** is at the end of Boufidou. (☎26 527. Open M-F 8am-2pm.) For **Internet** access, visit **NetCafe 1900,** directly across the street from the bus stop, on the second floor. (☎88 166. €2 per hr. Open daily 10am-2am.) There is a **post office** in the center of town that offers Western Union money transfers. (☎28 677. Open M-F 7:30am-3pm.) **Postal code:** 32100.

DELPHI Δελφοί   ☎22650

The sign along the road that marks the entrance to Delphi proclaims, "Every intellectual human being of free will deserves to be regarded as a citizen of the town of Delphi." Locals take this mentality to heart as they host the countless travelers who come to marvel at Delphi's wonders. This town of 2500 was once so significant that Greeks felt it was the *omphalos* (belly button) of the earth. Legend has it that Zeus simultaneously released two eagles, one toward the east and one toward the west. They collided directly over Delphi—now a sacred stone marks the spot. Nearby stood the impressive sanctuary of Apollo, home to the most important oracle of antiquity. Gaia (Mother Earth) was worshipped here until around 800 BC;

according to myth, Apollo defeated her snaky son Python at the site of the oracle, marking the advent of the Olympian gods. From then on, pilgrims from far and wide flocked to the oracle, seeking the cryptic guidance of Apollo's priestess. Delphi was also the site of the Pythian Games, held every four years in Apollo's honor. Athletes and poets would descend upon the theater and stadium to compete for the victor's laurel crown. Although the ancient oracle's temples and treasury have crumbled, largely due to an earthquake in the AD 7th century, Delphi remains a place of pilgrimage for tourists. Jewelry stores, expensive restaurants, trinket shops, and hotels now decorate the town that lies down the road from the ancient city. Beyond the tourist facade, however, are the magnificent ruins, hospitable residents, and stunning panoramic views that make Delphi a must-see.

⌐ TRANSPORTATION

The bus station is at the western end of town, on Pavlou, inside a cafe. (☎ 82 880. Open daily 8am-10:10pm.) From Delphi, **buses** go to: Amphissa (30min., 6 per day 6:30am-6.15pm, €1.80); Athens (3hr., 6 per day 5:30am-6pm, €13) via Livadia (50min., €3); Itea (30min., 4 per day 10:15am-8:15pm, €1.60); Lamia (2hr., 10:15am and 3pm, €7.80); Nafpaktos (2½hr., 3 per day 10:15am-3:45pm, €9.30) via Galaxidi (1hr., €3); Patras (3hr.; M-Sa 1:15pm, Su 3:45pm; €11.50); Thessaloniki (5hr.; M-Th and Sa 10:15am; F and Su 3pm; €29.90) via Katerini (€21), Larisa (€16), and Velestino (€13). **Taxis** (☎ 82 000) wait at the eastern end of Pavlou outside Cafe Delfikon.

▄✳ 🛈 ORIENTATION AND PRACTICAL INFORMATION

Delphi's main street, **Friderikis-Pavlou** (referred to here as "Pavlou"), runs east-west through town. Facing the city, **Apollonas** snakes uphill to the left, and Pavlou veers to the right, passing directly through the town. The oracle and museum are on Pavlou a few hundred meters past the town, toward Athens.

The **tourist office,** Pavlou 12 or Apollonas 11, is in the town hall. From Pavlou headed toward Athens, the office is up a flight of stairs on your left in a stucco courtyard. The friendly staff can assist with buses and accommodations or provide maps, information, and guidebooks. (☎ 82 900. Open M-F 8am-2:30pm.) If the office is closed, the bus station can help you out. The **National Bank,** Pavlou 16, has a **24hr. ATM.** (☎ 82 791. Open M-Th 8am-2:30pm, F 8am-2pm.) The **police** (☎ 82 222), available 24hr., are located at Sygrou 3, directly behind the church that sits at the peak of Apollonas. The **OTE,** Pavlou 10, is just past the steps to the information office. (Open M-Sa 7:30am-3:10pm.) The cafe on the ground level of **Hotel Parnassos,** on Pavlou across from the Down Town Club, has four computers with **Internet** access. (☎ 82 321. €4 per hr.; min. €2. Open daily 7:30am-midnight.) You also can find Internet at **Cafe Delfikon,** on Pavlou past Hotel Sibylla. (☎ 83 212. €4 per hr.; min. €2. Open daily 7:30am-1am.) The **post office,** Pavlou 25, provides **Poste Restante.** (☎ 82 376. Open M-F 7:30am-2pm.) **Postal Code:** 33054.

⌂ ⛺ ACCOMMODATIONS AND CAMPING

Delphi's expensive and homogenous hotel scene—with prices that peak during ski season, holidays, and festivals—contains a few budget diamonds in the rough. ▓**Hotel Sibylla ❷,** Pavlou 9, has comfortable rooms with TV, fan, bath, and a wonderful view. The kind owner Ioannis can help orient you in Delphi, provide restaurant recommendations, and exchange currency. (☎ 82 335; www.sibylla-hotel.gr. Singles €20-24; doubles €26-30; triples €35-40. Discount for *Let's Go* readers.) **Hotel Artemis ❷** and **Hotel Pan ❷** are across the street from each other at Pavlou 60 and 53, about 100m from the bus station. Both are managed by, coincidentally,

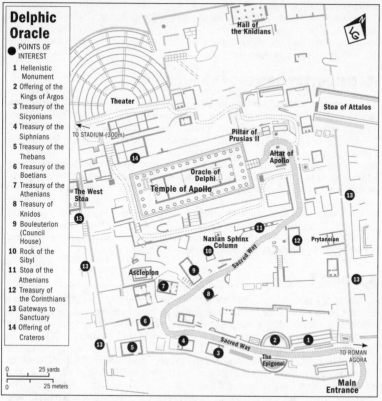

Delphic Oracle

● POINTS OF INTEREST

1 Hellenistic Monument
2 Offering of the Kings of Argos
3 Treasury of the Sicyonians
4 Treasury of the Siphnians
5 Treasury of the Thebans
6 Treasury of the Boetians
7 Treasury of the Athenians
8 Treasury of Knidos
9 Bouleuterion (Council House)
10 Rock of the Sibyl
11 Stoa of the Athenians
12 Treasury of the Corinthians
13 Gateways to Sanctuary
14 Offering of Crateros

Hall of the Knidians
Theater
Stoa of Attalos
TO STADIUM (300m)
Pillar of Prusias II
Altar of Apollo
Oracle of Delphi
Temple of Apollo
The West Stoa
Naxian Sphinx Column
Prytaneion
Asclepion
Sacred Way
Sacred Way
The Epigonoi
TO ROMAN AGORA
Main Entrance

0   25 yards
0   25 meters

another Ioannis—in this case, the hospitable and friendly Ioannis Lefas—and rent rooms with refreshing decor, air-conditioning, TV, and bath with a tub. Pan also offers gorgeous family-style rooms that can sleep up to five. (☎82 294; www.panartemis.gr. Breakfast included. Singles €20-35; doubles €30-45; triples €45-60; 5-person room €60-85. 10% discount for *Let's Go* readers. MC/V.) Buses heading west out of Delphi can drop you off at one of the nearby campsites. **Camping Apollon ❶** is the closest, only 1.5km out of town. It has a swimming pool, laundry (€5), mini-mart, restaurant, and great views. (☎82 762; www.apolloncamping.gr. €7 per person, €4 per tent. Tent rental €5.) You'll also find laundry (€5) and pools at **Delphi Camping ❶**, 4km out of town. (☎82 745. €6 per person, €4 per tent.)

⚑ FOOD

Several **mini-marts** and a **bakery** line Pavlou and Apollonas, and four pizza places are at the western end of Pavlou. While many tavernas are indistinguishable, local favorite ◪**Vakchos ❷**, Apollonas 31, just below the church, serves delicious local meats in imaginative settings. (☎83 186. Salad €3-6. Veal and onion stew €7.70. Open daily 8-10:30am, 11am-4pm, and 6:30-11pm.) You'll find locals mixed in with tourists at **Gargantuas ❷**, Dimou Fragkou 10, a few doors toward town from the bus station. The menu includes grilled lamb (€8), salad (€2.50), roast chicken (€5.50), and other Greek standbys. (☎82 488. Open daily noon-3pm and 7pm-1am.) For the best coffee in town, stop into **Melopoleio ❶**, Pavlou 14, near the town hall. Melopoleio's name means "honey shop," appropriately alluding to the delicious pastries they serve alongside their famous coffee. (☎83 247. Coffee €1.50-3. Pastries €2-3. Open daily 7am-midnight.)

♫ 🍷 ENTERTAINMENT AND NIGHTLIFE

The **European Cultural Center of Delphi** (☎82 731) hosts the **Festival of Greek Drama** with performances in the ancient theater in July. They also have temporary international art exhibitions. Contact their office in Athens (☎21033 12 781) for more information. Delphi is home to several other summer **festivals,** so ask around and keep an eye out for posters. Delphi's only two nightclubs are within stumbling distance of most hotels on Pavlou. Both open at 10pm and stay open until the customers leave. **Katoi Club** is about 75m up from the bus station on Pavlou. Moving lights suspended above the dance floor combined with a soft glow from the private tables create an electric atmosphere. The DJ plays a mix of American and international pop and is open to requests. (☎69325 26 578. Beer €3. Mixed drinks €5-8.) You'll hear **Down Town Club,** Pavlou 33, before you see it. Grab a drink at the bar or take advantage of the large dance floor. (☎69465 02 043. Beer €3. Mixed drinks €5. Cover €3-10.)

🥾 HIKING

Delphi is a perfect access point for some of the best hiking in the area; there are several trails with amazing views. At the steps on the eastern end of Apollonos where it meets Pavlou, you will find a detailed map of the trails that you can follow up Mt. Parnassos and the surrounding peaks. The **E4** trail, an easy day-hike up the side of the mountain, begins here. Climb the steps up to Sygrou and follow the road to the right, past the Museum of the Delphic Festivals, until it becomes dirt. Look for the metal pole on the left that marks the continuation of E4, and follow the trail markers (red squares and yellow lines) as you scramble up the hill. The trail is relatively well-marked but extremely rocky, so hikers should be careful and consider going in pairs. Past the initial hill on the edge of town, a 1hr. trek up the ancient footpath brings you to the top of the mountain, yielding magnificent views of Delphi town and the ancient stadium along the way.

For those interested in a more strenuous hike, an excursion to the magnificent 🎒**Corycian Cave** will take around 4-5hr. round-trip. Buy a trail map in advance, bring plenty of water, and hike with a partner. Have a taxi (20min., €25) drop you off next to the entrance of the trail that leads to the Corycian Cave. It is marked by a red triangle blaze. As you climb up, adjust your pace for the high altitude. The cave, at the top of the mountain, was an ancient sanctuary of Pan and the woodland nymphs. Its dusky, enormous interior certainly casts a spell; check out the impressive stalagmites in the back. Return back the way you came and take a right on the dirt road. Refill your water bottle at the fountain across from the forest ranger's hut, as it's the last you'll find before Delphi. When the road forks after 1km, take a left and head toward the "Delphi Panorama" and "Kroki." Walk for about 2km past fir trees and farmland, staying on the dirt road. Across from a cow pasture you'll see a pole that clearly marks an intersection with the E4. Take a left on the trail, marked by red squares and yellow lines, which will take you all the way back to Delphi. After a few kilometers of scrubby brush and the dry riverbed, a breathtaking view of the Delphi area gradually will unfold before you. Enjoy it all the way down the mountainside, likely with soaring birds as your only company.

SIGHTS

THE DELPHIC ORACLE

A sacred site from 1500 BC or earlier, the Oracle of Delphi was the most important source of sacred wisdom in the ancient world from around the 7th century BC until the advent of Orthodox Christianity. When the oracle answered a pilgrim's pressing question, usually with just a few pithily ambiguous words, its authority was accepted almost universally. After all, it was the Delphic oracle that foretold Cadmus's founding of Thebes and prophesied Oedipus's horrific fate. But the oracle held sway over more than religious matters and personal fortune-telling; Delphic approval sanctioned many political decisions, including the reforms that led to democracy in Athens. Hoping to make powerful friends and receive positive forecasts, city-states from all over the Greek world erected treasuries and donated immense sums to the oracle.

The Pythian Games, in which athletes, musicians, and poets were judged by Apollo's golden rule of harmony and balance, were held on the steps every four years from before the 5th century BC to the AD 4th century. Legend says that when the great Greek poet Homer participated in the Pythian Games, he lost because, although his poetic talent was unrivaled, his musicianship could not match it. From Delphi, head out of town on the road toward Athens and follow the highway to a paved path on the left, which leads to the ruins and museum.

ARCHAEOLOGICAL SITE. The inscription "Know thyself" has crumbled from the portal of the ancient temple, but it still governs the meditative atmosphere of peaceful, windswept Delphi. Cut into the steep mountainside, the ancient sanctuary reigns over the brush-dotted valley below. It more than lives up to its reputation as one of Greece's top archaeological sights; the sheer scale of the constructions will take your breath away. Now, as in the past, the **Temple of Apollo** is the centerpiece of the oracle site. A largely wooden incarnation of the temple was burned in 548 BC, was demolished again by an earthquake in 373 BC, and still lies in ruin today. Ancient proclamations etched along the stone base are still visible. To reach the Temple of Apollo, follow the **Sacred Way,** which winds up the site in the footsteps of ancient pilgrims. To the left are the treasuries of supplicant cities, including the reconstructed **Treasury of the Athenians,** excavated in the early 20th century. Past the Temple of Apollo, the theater, a picture of geometric perfection and amazing acoustics, is no less impressive. After one glance at the view, you will understand why performances held here never used backdrops. For a glimpse of ancient Delphi as an athletic arena, make your way up the winding trail to the **stadium** at the very top of the hill, and sit among the Greek and Roman ghosts in the stadium's seats. A sprint across the stadium while imagining the cheering crowd is a decidedly good use of time. Don't visit the site between 11am and 3pm unless you're armed with patience for an endless flow of tour groups. The site is staffed by knowledgeable guides who lead the groups from tour buses. They won't mind if you tag along and will be happy to answer your questions, especially if you give them a tip. *(Guidebooks and maps (€3-15) are sold at the entrance, but the tourist office in town can provide similar materials for free.)*

ARCHAEOLOGY MUSEUM. The museum, before the ruins on the left as you head out of town, houses artifacts exclusively from the ancient city. Don't let its modern exterior fool you; inside, the well-organized exhibitions are laid out in airy, gorgeous rooms. Among the notable collection are enormous 7th-century bronze shields, the frieze of the Siphnian Treasury, the altar from the temple of Athena Pronaia, a Naxian sphinx, the haunting bronze Charioteer of Delphi, and many of the impressive gifts presented as offerings to the oracle. The excavations that yielded these treasures began in 1892 and were completed in 1935 by the Ecole Française d'Athens. *(☎82 312. Open M noon-6:30pm, Tu-Su 7:30am-7:30pm. €6, students €3; site and museum €9/5.)*

OTHER SIGHTS

Before calling upon the oracle, pilgrims cleansed themselves both physically and spiritually in the **Kastalian Spring,** 200m past the main ruins along the road to Athens. Drinking from the spring is said to confer the gift of eloquence, but the danger of falling rocks has closed the spring to visitors, dooming them to a life of mumbling. Just past the spring, on the opposite side of the road, are the remains of an ancient **gymnasium** where athletes trained for the Pythian Games. All participants arrived one month before the competition to train here so that they would become accustomed to the thin mountain air. Another 200m down the road, the **Temple of Athena Pronaia** was the ancient entrance to Delphi and served as a lounge and campground for pilgrims bound for the sanctuary. Three remaining Doric columns of the original 20 of the stunning *tholos*, a round building used for an unknown purpose, are the sole evidence of its architectural mastery.

While in Delphi, consider visiting the small, fascinating **Museum of the Delphic Festivals,** which chronicles the celebrations held here in 1927 and 1930. The museum is in the former house of Eva Sikelianos (originally Eva Palmer of New York) and her husband Angelos, a Greek poet, who planned and staged recreations of the Pythian Games in the ancient theater and stadium. The productions were the first performances in an archaeological site and paved the way for other venues such as Epidavros. The museum displays a collection of the costumes that Eva designed from studying pictures on ancient vases and wove by hand on a loom, as well as the original sheet music and photographs from the two festivals. *(At the peak of Apollonos, walk uphill to the church. Turn right onto Sygrou, then walk uphill to the museum on the left. Open daily 8:30am-3pm. €1, students and groups €0.35.)*

GALAXIDI Γαλαξίδι   ☎ 22650

The quiet streets and pebble beaches of Galaxidi exude a laid-back charm. Built around a sheltered harbor, the town has a history of naval activity that scholars date back to as early as 3000 BC. Seafaring, in its modern incarnation, has evolved into pleasure boating, as locals lead tours for vacationing Europeans. Though quiet most of the year, Galaxidi erupts into glorious mayhem on *Kathari Dheftera* (Clean Monday), ushering in Orthodox Lent with a huge annual flour fight.

◪◪ TRANSPORTATION AND PRACTICAL INFORMATION. The two notable landmarks in town are the main plateia, marked by large palm trees, and the waterfront. The bus stop is in the plateia, by the start of the main street, **Nikolou Mama,** which leads to the harbor. **Buses** run to Itea (20min.; M-F 5 per day 7:15am-8pm, Sa-Su 4 per day 10am-8pm; €1.20), where you can transfer to Delphi (1hr., €3), and Nafpaktos (1½hr.; M-F 5 per day 6:15am-9:20pm, service reduced Sa-Su; €6.50). Buy tickets at **Kourdisto Portokali Cafe,** a few doors down Nik. Mama from the bus stop, on the right. Call ☎42 087 for schedules or ask at Hotel Poseidon. **Taxis** (☎41 243) are available 24hr.

The **National Bank** with a **24hr. ATM** is a few blocks farther down Nik. Mama, past Hotel Poseidon on the left. (☎42 312. Open M-F 8:30am-2pm.) The **police** station is in the main plateia across from the bus station. (☎41 222. Open daily 8am-2pm.) A **pharmacy,** Nik. Mama 17, is one block from the bus station. (☎41 122. Open M-Sa 8:30am-1:30pm and 6-9:30pm.) Galaxidi's **post office** is next to the bank on Nik. Mama and receives **Poste Restante.** (Open M-F 7:30am-2pm.) **Postal Code:** 33052.

◪◪ ACCOMMODATIONS AND FOOD. Look for **domatia** on side streets off Nik. Mama mixed in with expensive pensions and unremarkable hotels along the waterfront. Facing the bus stop from the main plateia, follow Nik. Mama to the right to reach ◩**Hotel Poseidon** ❸. This home-turned-hotel has a vivacious manager, Costas, who personifies Greek hospitality, and may greet you with a plate of fresh watermelon. The rooms' hardwood floors, high ceilings, air-conditioning, and TV make them as inviting as the welcome. (☎41 426. Delicious home-cooked breakfast included. Some rooms with bath. Singles €35; doubles €50; triples €58-78.) To reach **Hotel Galaxidi** ❹, Sigrou 11, turn right after the bank and continue down the street. Lovely rooms have air-conditioning, TV, a small balcony, and sailboat shower curtains. (☎41 850. Breakfast included. Singles €40; doubles €55.)

For an authentic Greek kitchen experience, take your appetite to **Taverna Albatross** ❷. Turn left on Kon. Satha before Hotel Poseidon; it's on the right side near the church. The cozy dining room and warmhearted staff make this restaurant seem more like a home. (☎42 233. Open daily 8am-3pm and 7pm-midnight. Entrees €5-7. Stuffed grape leaves €7. Cash only.) **To Perasma** ❶, Nik. Mama 40, across from the National Bank, has a carefully cooked, deliciously seasoned selection of traditional mainstays. (☎41 742. *Tzatziki* €2. Pita souvlaki €1.70. Open daily 5pm-midnight.) If you're willing to splurge for seafood, head to one of the tavernas along the harbor. Turning left at the bottom of Nik. Mama, you'll find a steady crowd vying for the blue-and-yellow tables at **O Tasos** ❷, which offers its own name-brand wine and serves giant, mouthwatering portions. (☎41 291. Grilled dishes €6-7. Fresh fish €44-60 per kg. Open daily 8am-midnight. MC/V.)

◪◩ **SIGHTS AND BEACHES.** On Kon. Satha, left off Nik. Mama, the immense **Church of Agios Nikolaos** houses fine mosaics and ornate wood carvings. (☎41 682. Open daily 8am-8pm. Modest dress required.) The 13th-century **Monastery of the Metamorphosis**, 6km from Galaxidi on the uphill road outside of town, has an amazing view of the town and harbor. Though the unshaded trip takes an hour by foot, the hike is enjoyable on a cool day, and the spectacular views are certainly worth it. Follow K. Papapetrou from the main plateia out of town past the school, beneath the highway, and follow the signs through the orange orchards. The **Nautical History Museum**, on the first street to your right off Kon. Satha, displays impressive artifacts from the town's past, including *amphorae* (jugs) recovered from the bottom of the gulf, proving that Galaxidi was a trading port even in prehistoric times. Other rooms show guns used during the War of Independence and nautical instru-

FLOUR POWER

While much of Greece is winding down from the pre-Lenten Carnival season on *Kathari Deftera* (Clean Monday), the real party is just getting underway for the citizens of Galaxidi—and it's definitely not very clean.

In accordance with an over 200-year-old annual tradition, the people of this otherwise serene seaside town bring in the first day of Orthodox Lent with a massive flour war. Residents and visitors of all ages throw on goggles, masks, and overalls, and scramble to chuck fistfuls of flour and ash at their closest neighbors, random townspeople, and the nearest hard surface. The flour is usually dyed a variety of bright colors, so both the people and the town end up blanketed in vivid, chaotic, Jackson Pollock-esque swirls and blobs.

After all of the flour has been thrown, the powdery people crowd into the center of their powdery town to continue the revelry with drinking, dancing, carousing, and eating. Some leap into the harbor to wash themselves off, while others take turns jumping over fire, a wild tradition that has somehow worked its way into the festivities' canon. In the end, everyone is happy and dirty, and the mess is left until morning to clean up.

ments. (☎41 795. Open daily July-Sept. 10:10am-1:30pm and 5:30-8:30pm; Oct.-May 10:10am-4:15pm. €5, seniors and students €2.50, under 12 free.)

Look for small, pebbly **beaches** scattered over the rocky shoreline that stretches out past the docks on the forest side of the harbor. Walk along Nik. Mama to the waterfront, then follow the harbor toward the forest to your left until you find a resting place that suits you. Several tiny islands are within swimming distance.

▓ FESTIVALS. While much of Greece is winding down from the pre-Lenten Carnival season on *Kathari Deftera* (Clean Monday), the real party is just getting underway for the citizens of Galaxidi—and it's definitely not very clean. In accordance with an over 200-year-old annual tradition, the people of this otherwise serene seaside town bring in the first day of Orthodox Lent with a massive flour war. Residents and visitors of all ages throw on goggles, masks, and overalls, and scramble to chuck fistfuls of flour and ash at their closest neighbors, random townspeople, and the nearest hard surface. The flour is usually dyed a variety of bright colors, so both the people and the town end up blanketed in vivid, chaotic, Jackson Pollock-esque swirls and blobs. After all the flour has been thrown, the celebration continues with drinking, dancing, carousing, and eating.

NAFPAKTOS Ναύπακτος ☎26340

Nafpaktos is a popular destination, but shows no signs of becoming a generic family resort town. The municipal government has worked hard to ensure that the area's history, which includes the famous Naval Battle of Nafpaktos, occupies a prominent place in daily life. Vacationing urbanites and Greek children sunbathe side by side on some of the most attractive pebble beaches in Central Greece, which extend from the picturesque Venetian fort in the Old Port. The tree-lined, pedestrian-only waterfront avenues are packed with cafes, tavernas, and playgrounds, creating the ideal atmosphere for bikeriding or an evening stroll.

⌷ TRANSPORTATION. Nafpaktos has two bus stations, one near Pl. Farmaki, the main plateia, the other east on Athinon by Pl. Kefalovrisou. The first station is located at Manassi 16 (☎27 224). Facing west on Athinon, turn left onto Manassi to find the station on the left, across from the back of the church. From here, **buses** serve Athens (3½hr.; 10am, 5pm; €15), Messolongi (1¼hr.; 6:30, 9:30am, 1pm; €4.20), and Thessaloniki (8hr.; 10:45am, 3:15pm; €28) via Lamia (3hr., €11). You also can take a bus to Antirrio (15min., 2 per hr. 5:50am-9:30pm, €1) to catch the hourly bus to Athens and the ferry that serves the Peloponnese. The second station, Asklipiou 1 (☎27 241), is six blocks east from the main plateia on Athinon, across from Pl. Kefalovrisou. Buses from here go to Amfissa (2hr.; 5 per day 5:45am-6:45pm, service reduced Sa-Su; €7.50) via Galaxidi (1½hr., €6.50) and Itea (1¾hr., €6.50), Delphi (2½hr.; 4 per day 5:30am-1:30pm, service reduced Sa-Su; €8), and Larisa (5hr., 8:30am, €22). **Taxis** (☎251 11) line up in front of the main plateia and near the harbor in the Old Port.

◰⊠ ORIENTATION AND PRACTICAL INFORMATION. Coming from the east, **Athinon** leads into the town's central plateia, where it becomes **Ilarchou Tzavela;** it then becomes **G. Ath. Nova** as it continues past the **Old Port.** One block toward the water from Athinon, **Noti Botsari** leads east. If you arrive on the bus from points eastward, such as Galaxidi, you'll likely be let off at the Asklipiou bus station. Walk in a general westerly direction—all roads lead to the Old Port.

There is a wonderfully helpful **tourist information office** on the southeastern corner of the Old Port's central plateia. The staff can orient you and provide a free tourist guide. Ask for the gregarious, English-speaking Stavroula Tsoukala. (☎38

533. Open daily 9am-2pm and 6-9pm.) The **National Bank,** Il. Tzavela 86 (☎20 184), and **Alpha Bank,** Il. Tzavela 81 (☎29 313), both just off the main plateia, **exchange currency** and have **24hr. ATMs.** (Both open M-Th 8am-2:30pm, F 8am-2pm.) The **police** (☎27 258) are located off G. Ath. Nova, about six blocks west of the Old Port. **Pharmacies,** all with varying hours, sit around the plateia and down Athinon. Call the police or a taxi to arrange transportation to the **hospital** (☎23 690) on the eastern end of town; otherwise, take the city bus east from any stop marked with "Stasi" (every 30min. 6am-10pm). The **library** has free **Internet** access. Walking from the central plateia, take a right at the National Bank and walk uphill; it's on your left. (☎27 288. Open M-F 8am-2:30pm.) **Hobby Club,** on Navmachias at the start of Psani beach, past the Old Port, also has **Internet** access. (☎22 288. €1.50 per hr., min. €1. Open daily 9am-2am.) The **post office,** Il. Tzavela 33, is a few blocks down from the banks, on the right. (☎27 232. Open M-F 7:30am-2pm.) **Postal Code:** 30300.

⚐⚑ ACCOMMODATIONS AND FOOD. Accommodations in Nafpaktos range from rather mediocre hotels along G. Ath. Nova to more expensive options by Gribovo beach; however, there are a few affordable gems in close proximity to the old town. In the heart of town, just past the Old Port plateia on G. Ath. Nova, dainty **▨Hotel Diethnes ❸** (Διεθνές) rents bright, colorful rooms with hardwood floors, air-conditioning, bath, TV, and balcony. English-speaking owner Spiros and his French-born wife are happy to answer questions about the city. (☎27 342. Singles €30-35; doubles €40. Extra bed €5.) **Hotel Akti ❸,** left on Gribovo from Pension Aphrodite and in front of the fountain, is a relatively new hotel whose vibrant, sizeable rooms have air-conditioning, fridge, TV, phone, balcony, and swanky bath. (☎28 464. Breakfast €5. Singles €30-50; doubles €45-70. MC/V.) At **Pension Aphrodite ❷,** just steps away from Club Cinema on Apokafkou, you'll find white rooms with air-conditioning, TV, and balcony. Head one block east from the main plateia on Athinon, then turn right on Arvanti and walk to the beach; the pension is on the right. Don't confuse it with Hotel Aphrodite, which is also in town. (☎27 230. Breakfast €5. Singles €25; doubles €40.) Follow G. Ath. Nova 4km out of town to **Platanitis Beach Camping ❶,** which has its own mini-mart, restaurant, and wooded campsites that extend to the pebbly beach. (☎31 555. €4.50 per person, €3.50-4 per tent. Tent rentals €6. Electricity €3.50.)

Bakeries, souvlaki stands, and fast-food restaurants clutter the central plateia area and Old Port. Luckily for anyone exhausted from a day at the beach or the castle, a few excellent restaurants are tucked away within easy walking distance. To reach the surprisingly affordable **▨Papoulis ❷,** which locals hail as the best taverna in the area, walk from the Old Port's central plateia toward the new town; hug the cobblestoned edge of the harbor and continue down the alley. The fact that the owner's mother grew up in the building adds a homey appeal to such flavorful dishes as the spicy country sausage with green peppers (€5) and other favorites. (☎21 578. Entrees €5-8. Open daily 11am-2am.) Head to the waterfront along Gribovo beach, just a few blocks down from the main plateia, for more tavernas. The first of the bunch, **O Stavros ❷** (Ο Σταυρος), Gribovo 7, serves succulent entrees ranging from rabbit with onions (€6.50) to pasta (€3-5) at tables on the beachfront. (☎27 473. Open daily 11am-1am.) On the other side of the Old Port near the middle of Psani beach and across from the playground, **Taverna Rotunda ❷,** Navmachias 2, has a wide selection of traditional Greek dishes. (☎23 553. Stuffed tomatoes €4.50. Fresh seafood €36-46 per kg. Open daily 9am-2am.)

◫⚐ SIGHTS AND BEACHES. The impressive **▨Venetian Castle,** one of the most important examples of fortress architecture in Greece, dominates the picturesque town from 200m above sea level. Besides having the best vista around, the citadel also contains the tiny **Church of the Prophet Elias,** the remains of a **Byzantine bath** and **church,** and a large **cistern** to help the fortress weather sieges. Its walls, which reach down to the port, formed five zones of fortification, and now are woven into the construction of modern houses on the hill. Footpaths wind around the walls, past fountains, and through century-old gates; one begins off Il. Tzavela just past the post office. Look for the cobblestoned steps and the sign that says "KASTRO/Castle" on the right. A leisurely walk up to the base of the fortress takes about 15min. When you hit the road just below the main fortifications, follow it uphill 1km to reach the castle. Alternatively, drive to the castle by following Athinon-Tzavela past the Old Port where it becomes G. Ath. Nova; veer right on Thermou and follow the signs. The **Old Port,** enclosed by low walls and watchtowers, is a romantic backdrop for the town's hottest cafes. Plaques on the walls commemorate the October 7, 1571 **Battle of Lepanto** in which the united Christian fleet defeated the Ottomans, bringing an end to their naval superiority. A statue also honors battle hero **Miguel de Cervantes Saavedra,** who wrote of his experiences in *Don Quixote.* Both the castle and the Old Port are lit up spectacularly at night.

Most leisure time around Nafpaktos is spent on the town's beaches, which form a large crescent with the Old Port at the center. Facing the water at the Old Port, **Gribovo beach** is to the left and **Psani beach,** the popular choice for sunbathers and families with its playgrounds and public showers, is to the right.

📋 🎷 **ENTERTAINMENT AND NIGHTLIFE.** Follow Psani beach away from the Old Port to its end to reach **Na Blue,** a waterpark with a pool, waterslides, bar, and free lounge chairs and umbrellas that line the beach. (Pool and waterslides €5-8, children €3. Open daily 11am-8pm.) Nafpaktos's week-long **Carnival,** held annually during the week before Lent, features music, dancing, and free wine and souvlaki. During the rest of the year, cafes and *ouzeria* along Psani beach and in the Old Port are filled with customers from around 8:30 to 11:30pm, when those who don't hit the hay hit the clubs. **Club Cinema,** Apokafkou 12, past Pension Aphrodite away from Gribovo, is one of the town's classiest nightlife destinations. An imposing front door conceals a large dance floor that spills out onto a beachfront patio. (☎ 26 026. Cover €5. Open F-Sa 11pm-late.)

MESSOLONGI Μεσολόγγι   ☎ 26310

In this compact, modern city, initial impressions can be deceiving. Look past the bleak apartment buildings and you'll find children riding bikes along intimate pedestrian-only streets and onto the inviting central plateia. As evening arrives, the sun sets lazily over the lagoon at the port, and sidewalk cafes near the town center fill up with locals. A sense of warm community spirit is evident all over Messolongi, making a city with relatively little to offer an attractive destination.

📧 **TRANSPORTATION. Buses** leave from the bus station, Mavrokordatou 5, just east of the central plateia, to: Agrinio (45min.; M-F 17 per day 6:15am-12:30am, Sa-Su 12 per day 7:45am-10pm; €3.30); Athens (4½hr., 10 per day 4:20am-10:30pm, €17); Nafpaktos (1¼hr.; M-F 5 per day 8:40am-3:40pm, Sa-Su 3 per day 10am-2:30pm; €3.50); Patras (45min.; M-F 8 per day 5:45am-7:40pm, Sa-Su 7 per day 7:20am-7:30pm; €4.10); Thessaloniki (10hr.; Sa-Su 10:10am, 2:30pm; €31.50). **Taxis** (☎ 22 623), available 24hr., wait in the central plateia.

📊 🔼 **ORIENTATION AND PRACTICAL INFORMATION.** The entrance to Messolongi is marked by a stone gate that once was part of its fortifications. The road running south through the city splits into **Spyrou Moustakli** to the left, which leads to the water, and **Eleftheron Poliorkimenon** to the right, which goes to the central plateia, **Plateia Markou Botsari**. From there, **Charilaou Trikoupi** runs east-west. Its many off-shoots are filled with cafes, bakeries, and tavernas. **Lord Byron** is the first street perpendicular to Charilaou Trikoupi west of the plateia, connecting it to **Pazekotsika,** which runs to the south.

Most necessities are in the central plateia or along Spirou Moustakli, a few blocks to the east. **Eurobank,** Deligiorgi 2 (☎24 220), on the northern side of the plateia, has a **24hr. ATM.** Go past Hotel Avra on Charilaou Trikoupi and turn right onto Lord Byron to find **Alpha Bank** and **National Bank,** which **exchange currency.** (All banks open M-Th 8am-2:30pm, F 8am-2pm.) There is a **laundromat** on Spirou Moustakli; take a left from the bus station and you'll see the colorful sign on the right after a few blocks. (☎27 660. Wash and dry €7. Open M-F 9am-2pm and 5:30-8pm, Sa 9am-2pm.) To reach the 24hr. **police station,** A. Damaskinou 11 (☎22 220) from the plateia, take the second right off Charilaou Trikoupi. One of several **pharmacies** is by the bus station. (☎24 311. Open M-F 8am-2pm and 5:30-9pm.) To get to the 24hr. **hospital** (☎57 100), turn right out of the stone gate and walk 3km. The **OTE,** Spirou Trikoupi 5, is across from the bus station. (☎51 425. Open M, W, Sa 7:20am-3pm; Tu and Th-F 7:20am-9pm.) Find **Internet** access at **Hackers.** Take the fifth right along Charilaou Trikoupi from the central plateia; you can see the sign from Ch. Trikoupi. (☎51 366. €2 per hr. Open 24hr.) The **post office** is on S. Moustakli, outside the central plateia. Take Spirou Trikoupi east and turn left on S. Moustakli; it's on your left. (☎22 605. Open M-F 7:30am-2pm.) **Postal Code:** 30200.

⌂◨ ACCOMMODATIONS AND FOOD. Messolongi's accommodations are limited and expensive. The cheapest hotel in town is also the oldest and one of the best. **Hotel Avra ❸,** Charilaou Trikoupi 1, in the main plateia, treats its guests to hallways painted with beautiful watercolor seascapes and rooms with tiled bath, air-conditioning, TV, and phone. (☎22 281. Singles €35; doubles €45; triples €55. Cash only.) For a comfortable stay at the water's edge, the modern **Hotel Theo Xenia ❹,** Tourlidos 2, 1km from the central plateia, rents carpeted rooms with air-conditioning, TV, phone, bath, hair dryer, minibar, and balcony. Follow S. Moustakli to the water and turn right, then continue along the water until you reach the hotel. (☎23 303. Breakfast €6. Singles €50; doubles €80; triples €96. AmEx/MC/V.)

Besides the cafes that line the main plateia, most of Messolongi's dining options lie in the pedestrian-only area behind Hotel Avra; walk down Charilaou Trikoupi and take any of the side streets on the left. **Pizza Remezzo ❷,** Pazikotzika 2, on the corner two blocks south of the square, makes delicious pizzas (€5-7) that utilize Greek cheeses and are sizable enough for leftovers. The mouthwatering Ripieno pizza (€6.50), with gouda, feta, parmesan, and fresh butter, is a dairy-lover's dream (and a vegan's nightmare), at nearly half the price you would pay anywhere else. (☎23 837. Pasta €3-6. Open daily 5:30pm-1am.) **Mezedopoleio ❷,** Pazikotzika 11, draws local regulars for its scrumptious appetizers (€2-5) like sliced potatoes with feta cheese. The Greek entrees (€3-9.50) and fresh fish are consistently good. (☎55 977. Cover €0.50. Open daily 9am-3am.) For those who prefer to prepare their own meals, there is an **Atlantic Supermarket** across from the post office on Spirou Moustakli. (☎26 851. Open M-F 8am-9pm, Sa 8am-8pm.)

◨◧ SIGHTS AND NIGHTLIFE. Naturally gorgeous and teeming with wildlife, the **lagoons** that surround the southern port of Messolongi attract visitors—but not swimmers—for the acclaimed therapeutic value and skin-rejuvenating properties of their mud. Near the stone gate that marks the entrance to town sits the **Garden of Heroes,** a collection of monuments honoring the nearly 10,000 citizens of Messolongi who died in the War of Independence trying to flee to freedom, an event known as the Exodus of 1826. The walls that enclose the garden, part of the city's original fortification, still have cannons mounted on them. (Open daily 9am-9pm. Free.) Outside the garden stands a statue honoring **Lord Byron,** who inspired the Messolongians to fight for independence. A memorial to his life and work is inside the town's **History Museum,** in the middle of the central plateia. The museum also has a large collection of paintings showcasing Messolongi's struggle for freedom. In the room to the left of the entrance, check out the fascinating early depictions of cities like Athens and Delphi, painted by European visitors. (☎22 134. Open daily 9am-1:30pm and 4-6pm. Free.) A short car or taxi ride will bring you to the ruins of **Ancient Pleuron,** 6km outside of town, where you can climb into the remains of Greek baths and admire the stonework of the former water reservoirs.

Nightfall brings the locals out into the main plateia and the side streets near Charilaou Trikoupi, as cafes turn up the music for a more bar-like atmosphere. Spend the evening in style at **Aperitto,** a popular cafe with an enormous semi-covered patio that blends in with bars on either side. From Charilaou Trikoupi, take a left on Eugenidou and a right on Ntolma. (☎71 754. Ice cream and drinks €2-8. Open daily 9am-1am.) Several clubs open for the summer; look for posters and ask at cafes for locations. By day, **Plaza Club,** next to Hotel Theo Xenia 1km from town, serves fresh Messolongi fish (€7-8) and grilled entrees (€5-12). Enjoy a poolside drink (€2-4) and admire the building's ebullient color scheme, or take a dip in the pool (€2). At night, traffic picks up at the **outdoor bar,** as the music gets louder and the crowds arrive. (☎25 122. Open in summer daily 9am-3am.)

EVRITANIA Ευριτάνια

With its towering alpine peaks, it is no surprise that Evritania often is referred to as the "Switzerland of Greece." Here, run-of-the-mill bus rides become epic adventures, passing heart-stopping ravines and lush river valleys on either side. This mountainous land was once a refuge for Greeks escaping Ottoman rule, but since then it has evolved into a wildlife sanctuary. Hikers and adventurers can explore green forests on trails that wander past tiny mountain villages to the highest peaks of the Louchi Mountains. Old churches and monasteries dot the mountains and overlook steep gorges where water enthusiasts hop in their rafts, canoes, and kayaks to try to tame the rushing Karpenisiotis, Krikelopotamos, and Tavropos rivers. The best way to explore Evritania is by foot. Take a stroll up and down the sunny streets of a hillside town, or hike to the peak of the closest mountain for a breathtaking change of perspective. A car, however, is the most sensible (and often the only) option for reaching the more remote villages. Rent one elsewhere before you come; no rental agencies exist and buses are sporadic.

KARPENISI Καρπενήσι   ☎22370

The alpine resort town of Karpenisi is Evritania's relaxed capital and the perfect base for exploring the nearby countryside and villages. Founded when five agrarian settlements in the foothills of Mt. Timfristos merged early in the era of Ottoman rule, Karpenisi suffered for years as an economic backwater, weakened by emigration and unemployment. In recent years, a thriving tourism industry has breathed new life into the city, bringing increased prosperity as outdoor enthusiasts discover the region's extraordinary beauty. Winter marks the peak tourist season, when Mt. Velouchi opens its six lifts to skiers and snowboarders. South of Karpenisi, streets give way to rolling pastures and the Karpenisiotis river gorge.

⌐ TRANSPORTATION. The bus station (☎80 013) is on Char. Trikoupi, a 10min. walk southeast of the plateia. Bus schedules change frequently, so be sure to confirm times. **Buses** run to: Agrinio (3½hr.; M-Th and Sa 9am; F 9am, 3:15pm; Su 1:15pm; €8); Athens (4½hr.; 9am, noon, 3:30pm; €18.20); Koryshades (10min.; Tu and Sa 6:30am, 1pm; €1); Lamia (1½hr., 5 per day 5am-3:30pm, €6); Megalo Horio and Mikro Horio (20min.; 6:50am, 1pm; €1.20); Proussos (1¼hr., 1 per week, €2.50). Ask at the station about service to smaller villages. In winter, buses to the Velouchi Ski Center (12km) can be arranged for large groups. **Taxis** (☎ 22 666), available 24hr., wait at the stand at the high end of the plateia.

◣ ▤ ORIENTATION AND PRACTICAL INFORMATION. Karpenisi is at the foot of Mt. Velouchi, about 75km west of Lamia. To get to the main plateia from the bus station, follow **Charilaou Trikoupi** downhill as it forks right, then make a right up steep **Karpenisioti,** which leads to the square. **Zinopoulou** borders the plateia's eastern side; Karpenisioti branches off from it as the two streets head downhill. The other main road, **Ethnikis Antistasis,** runs left, perpendicular to Zinopoulou at the top end of the plateia. As Eth. Antistasis passes the plateia, **Grigoriou Tsitsara** runs downhill to the left, between the church and the OTE, running roughly parallel to Zinopoulou and Karpenisioti. The largest **church** and the **town hall** are on the northern end of the plateia, near a **monument** to soldiers who died in 20th-century wars.

Directly across from the taxi stand, the **tourist office** is beneath a faded green sign labeled "Grafeio Tourismo." The staff downstairs, some of whom speak English, offer maps and brochures and can help with outdoor excursions. (☎/fax 21 016. Open M-F 9am-2pm and 5-8pm, Sa 10am-2pm and 5-8pm, Su 10am-2pm.) In winter, backpackers can contact the **Hellenic Alpine Club (EOS),** which runs several mountain refuge huts throughout Evritania (Karpenisi office ☎ 23 051, Lamia 26 786). **Trekking Hellas** (☎ 25 940), past the Karpenisi plateia down Karpenisioti on the right, offers kayak, rafting, and ski packages. Maps of the region are available at the information office in Karpenisi's main plateia. There are a number of **24hr. ATMs,** including one that also **exchanges currency,** at the **Alpha Bank,** Zinopoulou 7, in the plateia. (☎ 25 608. Open M-Th 8am-2:30pm, F 8am-2pm.) For **laundry,** visit **To Ariston** at Karpenisioti 30. (☎ 22 887. €3-10 per load. Open M-Sa 8am-2pm and 5-9pm.) The 24hr. **police,** Eth. Antistasis 9 (☎ 89 160), are down the street from the OTE, Eth. Antistasis 3 (open M-F 7:30am-1:30pm). The **hospital** (☎ 80 680), on P. Bakogianni, is a 10min. walk past the police station; signs point the way. Free, fast **Internet** access is available at the **library.** Take the first left after the police station; after the second intersection, it is up the hill about 200m on the left. (☎ 80 269. Open M and Th 4-9pm, Tu-W and F 10am-noon and 4-9pm.) The **post office,** Ag. Nikolaou 3, is off Karpenisioti to the left, and offers **Poste Restante.** (☎ 23 542. Open M-F 7:30am-2pm.) **Postal Code:** 36100.

▌ ACCOMMODATIONS. Hotels in Karpenisi aren't budget-friendly, particularly on weekends and during the winter high season. The cheapest option is a room at one of the local **domatia.** The tourist office lists rooms and prices. **◪Hotel Galini ❷** (Γαληινη), Riga Fereou 3, is set back on a nearby side street. To reach it, follow G. Tsitsara downhill and take the second right. True to its name, which means "serenity," the hotel offers quiet, comfortable rooms with balcony, fridge, TV, and bath. (☎ 22 914. Singles €20; doubles €30; triples €40. Longer stays may be discounted.) **Hotel Elvetia ❸,** Zinopoulou 17, has a comfy lounge and pleasant rooms with TV, large bath, phone, and balcony. (☎ 22 465; www.elvetiahotel.gr. Breakfast included. Prices fluctuate with season. Singles €36-80; doubles €45-100; triples €58-130.) Conveniently located just off the plateia, **City Hotel Apollonion ❹,** Karpenisioti 4, rents elegant, carpeted rooms with TV, balcony, phone, and gleaming tiled bath. (☎ 25 002. Breakfast included. Singles €55; doubles €65; triples €75.)

▐ FOOD. Karpenisi has a wide variety of excellent dining options, all within a short walk of the central plateia. Just beyond Hotel Galini away from the plateia,

SIT, SIT, SIT

It didn't take me long to realize that life moves more slowly in Greece. I noticed that nobody hustled or stressed or worried about a packed schedule that they could never keep. Afternoons were spent chatting over coffee instead of squeezing in a few extra hours at the gym.

My suspicions were confirmed one day when I met a New Jersey native now living in a small Evritanian mountain village. She said she was shocked at the Greek lifestyle when she first arrived, but soon realized that Americans "go, go, go! But why?" She posed a relevant question.

I decided to try the Greek philosophy for myself. That evening, I found a quiet bench in the main plateia and just...sat. I watched, observed, and thought. When I stood up much later, my life was clearer than it had been before, and I felt closer to the people around me.

Sitting and thinking has now become a habit, something I will take with me after my trip is over. If I had not tried it, I never would have seen the old man who picked his nose because he thought nobody was looking.

—Dan Gurney

the family-friendly **Taverna Panorama ❷**, Riga Fereou 18, serves meat dishes *tisoras* (charcoal-grilled; €6-8.50) under a thick canopy of leafy vines. (☎25 976. Veal with potatoes €7. Open daily 1-6pm and 7pm-midnight.) In a small alley to the left of the first street off Karpenisioti, **Folia ❷** (Φωλια) is a prime place to enjoy a Greek meal that won't break the bank. (☎24 405. Salads €2-2.50. Entrees €6-8. Open daily 3pm-midnight.) At **Posto ❶**, Karpenisioti 7, you can indulge late-night food cravings with souvlaki or a gyro. (☎21 241. Open M-Sa 11am-midnight.) Looking to upgrade your sweet tooth to saccharine? **Kitsios ❶**, Zinopoulou 13, directly off the plateia, serves fresh Greek pastries and ice cream. Slices of cake (€1.80 each) are cheap enough that you'll have to resist the temptation to try them all. (☎25 504. Cookies €7 per kg. Open daily 8:30am-10:30pm.) To put together your own meal, visit the **Paneboriki Supermarket,** Karpenisioti 38 (☎21 171; open M-F 8am-9pm, Sa 8am-8pm) on the right, or **Dia Discount Supermarket,** farther down on the left, at Karpenisioti 55 (☎22 272; open M-Sa 8am-8pm).

ENTERTAINMENT AND NIGHTLIFE. Saints' days are celebrated with religious services in the morning and revelry at night. Beginning at the end of July and continuing for about 25 days, Karpenisi hosts **Yiortes Dassous** (Celebrations of the Forest), replete with theatrical performances, dances, food, and music. When the snowflakes start to fall, the **Karpenisi Ski Center** (☎21 111), located 11km up Mt. Velouchi from the town, comes alive. The mountain has six lifts and 12 slopes that weave down 2000m of powdery bliss. The slopes at the top of the mountain are best reached by car; follow the signs to the ski center. Ask at the information office for any buses headed to the slopes. Ski season runs November to March.

The afternoon shifts into the evening as the small cafes where Karpenisians chat over iced coffee slowly evolve into crowded bars. Just down the street from the plateia, **Event**, Zinopoulou 10, is a popular late-night destination. (☎24 003. Mixed drinks €4-5. Open daily 9am-late.) A number of bars draw partiers out into the night just past the police station (so be on your best behavior!) on Eth. Antistasis. The most popular is breezy **Cinema Cafe,** which has an outdoor plateia and great mountain views. Take a left after the police station and it will be on the right. (☎69737 35 872. Coffee €2-3. Beer €3-5. Mixed drinks €5-6. Open daily 8am-3am.)

DAYTRIP FROM KARPENISI: PROSSOS. The area surrounding Karpenisi is like something out of a story book: old-fashioned stone houses rest on mountainsides while herds of goats snooze in nearby pastures. Actually getting to these places takes some initiative, though, as public transportation is sparse. The trip to the small village of Proussos is an adventure in itself; unless you catch the bus, which runs only once per week, enjoy the utterly spectacular roadside scenery and admire your taxi driver's uncanny ability to maintain control of his vehicle as it swerves alongside steep ravines and past intermittent, flimsy guardrails. The ▇**Monastery of the Virgin of Proussiotissa** here is well worth the trip. Inside is an icon of the Madonna said to have been painted by St. Luke the Evangelist and believed to work miracles. The monastery has an abundant stock of heavenly **loukoumi** (Turkish jellied candy covered in powdered sugar), offered to visitors by the hospitable monks. In the evenings, the monks' chanting mingles with the sound of rushing water from the Karpenisiotis River and echoes through the ravine. (Open daily dawn to dusk. Modest dress required. Free.) Proussos's **clock tower** belts out the hour from a precarious hilltop overlooking the monastery. The dark **Black Cave,** a rumored ancient oracle and a hideout for Greek women and children during the War of Independence, is along a trail that begins on the far side of the village near a bridge; bring a flashlight to explore. The village is a 20min. walk beyond the monastery on the main road. There are no hotels in Proussos, but as in most Evritanian villages, many homes offer fairly inexpensive **domatia,** marked by signs in the center of town. As for food, ▇**Ellinon Geuseis ❷,** just before the plateia on the left, is worth the trek from the monastery. The house specialty, *stamnas* (locally grown meat with feta cheese and tomato sauce; €7.50), is served on a porch with panoramic views of the gorge. (☎80 198. Open daily 8am-2am.)

Proussos is 15km beyond Megalo Horio and 32km beyond Karpenisi. Buses run sporadically, usually once per week, from Karpenisi; ask at the bus station for times. If there is a bus, you can catch it as it heads by Megalo or Mikro Horio; walk down to the main road or to the hamlet of Gavros. Ask to be let off at the monastery, on the left side of the road before you enter the village. Verify the return time as you exit the bus, but be prepared to take a taxi back to Karpenisi.

MIKRO Μικρό AND MEGALO HORIO Μεγάλο χωριό ☎22370

Fifteen kilometers down the road from Karpenisi are the "Big and Little Villages"—although objectively, neither merits much more than a "Tiny." Megalo Horio is the larger and more scenic of the two, and its bubbling brook, cobblestoned streets, and welcoming tavernas make it a great place to spend a day.

The original Mikro Horio was damaged in WWII when bombs scarred the village and occupying Nazis executed the town's 13 leading dignitaries. The town's bad luck continued when a 1963 landslide demolished the western section of the village. After the disaster, the population relocated down the hill to Neo Mikro Horio on the slopes of **Mount Helidona.** The route to the top of the mountain (3hr.) starts near the bus stop; a view of the river valleys and Kremaston Lake is the reward for the uphill trek. Lodgings range from simple, cheap domatia to expensive ski-lodge-style hotels. **To Horiatiko ❸** (Το Χοριάτικο), on the left as you enter the village from the main road, rents rooms during low season. Colorful flowers pave the way to beautifully furnished, spacious rooms with large balconies facing the mountains. (☎41 103. Doubles €30.) It also functions as a restaurant year-round, with entrees ranging €3-8. **Yonia ❸** (Γονια), a right-hand turn from the main road up past To Horiatiko, has white-walled, tiled rooms with bath and a small communal kitchen. (☎41 393. Singles and doubles €35.)

A few kilometers down the road from Mikro Horio toward Proussos, Megalo Horio is not so much a village as a handful of stone houses tossed haphazardly down a hillside. White-washed huts sit shoulder-to-shoulder with cafes above winding alleyways, creating an atmosphere of blissful relaxation. Midway up the hillside, the tables on the plateia overlook the breathtaking gorge of the Karpenisiotis River. An enormous, gnarled plane tree shades the plateia, and lime trees fill the air with the delicate scent of their blossoms. A few meters above the plateia, the main road in Megalo Horio splits in two. The left branch leads to the trailhead for the 3hr. climb up Mt. Kaliakouda, marked clearly to the top with red blazes. The right branch curves downhill and meanders past gorgeous homes on its way to the **Folklore Museum,** where displays of costumes and household objects shed light on life in this rural village. (☎41 502. Open F-Su 10am-2pm. Free.) Like the rest of Evritania, Megalo Horio has a number of rooms to let scattered throughout the village. The captivating rooms at **To Petrino** ❸ (Το Πετρινο), down from the plateia and up the road by the church, are extremely well furnished, each with TV, fridge, and bath; some have balcony and fireplace. (☎41 187. Singles €30; doubles €30-45.) Across the way, the **Avepada Inn** ❺ has an immaculately landscaped patio area and old-fashioned lanterns, creating a romantic atmosphere that may be worth the hefty bill. (☎41 479 or 69445 05 045. Breakfast included. Doubles €80-110. Suites €150.) For a sit-down meal, ⬛**Karveli** ❷ (Καρβελη), just past the plateia on the left, serves traditional Greek dishes all day. The local specialty, *galactobureco* (€3.50), one of the tastiest desserts around, can be described as custard on steroids. (☎41 339. Beer €2-3. Entrees €4-7. Open daily 8am-11pm.)

A **bus** runs from **Karpenisi** through Mikro Horio to Megalo Horio (25min.; 6:50am, 1pm; €1.20).

LAMIA Λαμία
☎22310

Sprawling Lamia is a jumping-off point for travelers bound for Northern or Central Greece. The city was important during the War of Independence and became the gateway for newly independent Greece in 1884. Currently, it serves as a decentralized and somewhat confusing transportation hub. Though most visitors only stay in Lamia long enough to see the inside of a bus station, don't judge it until you have explored the downtown area, which has more than enough excitement to entertain those looking to take a break from traveling. With its shop-lined streets, engaging Archaeological Museum, swinging nightlife, and bustling plateias, Lamia is a rich, eclectic city.

▣ TRANSPORTATION. There are two train stations in Lamia. The local train station, Konstantinopoulos 1 (☎44 883), is down the street from the local bus station. Two **trains** per day head to Athens (3hr.; 5:40am, 6:30pm; €6.20). Located about 10km west of Lamia, the Lionokladi train station (☎61 061) is the city's main rail stop and is along the Athens-Thessaloniki line. To reach the station, catch the bus marked "Stavros" (Σταυρος) either at the local bus station or the corner of Drosopolou and Hatzopolou at Pl. Parkou (10min., every hr. 6:05am-9:05pm, €0.70). You also can purchase train tickets at the **OSE office,** Averof 28 (☎23 201), the 3rd right down El. Venizelou from the southwestern corner of Pl. Parkou. From there, a bus will bring you to the station (2 per hr.), but beware of extra charges (€2-5). Intercity trains run to: Athens (3hr., 5 per day 9am-5pm, €7) via Livadia (1hr., €5), Thebes (1½hr., €4.20), and Thessaloniki (3¾hr., 5 per day 10:15am-10:50pm, €9.20). Express trains are available at higher prices; call the station for information.

There are four intercity bus stations. The first, Papakiriazi 27 (☎51 345), sends **buses** to Athens (3hr.; every hr. 5am-4pm and 5:30, 6:30, 9:15pm; €15). Take the Athens bus and ask to be let off at Agios Kostantinos (45min., €3.50) for ferries to the Sporades. The second station, Botsari 5 (☎28 955), serves Karpenisi (1½hr., 5 per day 7am-9pm, €5.20) and the Evritania region. Headed downhill from Pl. Parkou, walk down Satovriandou and turn right onto Botsari. The third is Nikopoleos 1 (☎22 802). Follow Thermopylon south away from the city. After the railroad tracks, Nikopoleos forks off to the left; the station is in a small shop on the left.

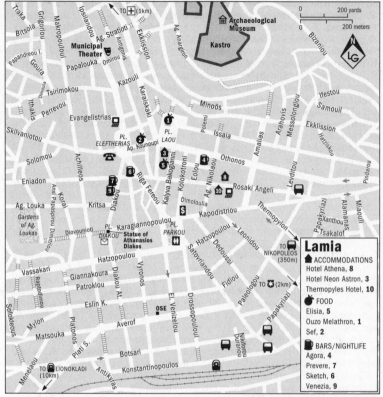

Lamia

⌂ ACCOMMODATIONS
Hotel Athena, **8**
Hotel Neon Astron, **3**
Thermopyles Hotel, **10**

🍎 FOOD
Elisia, **5**
Ouzo Melathron, **1**
Sef, **2**

🍺 BARS/NIGHTLIFE
Agora, **4**
Prevere, **7**
Sketch, **6**
Venezia, **9**

Buses run to: Agrinio (4hr.; 2:30, 6:45pm; €17); Delphi (2hr.; M-Sa 3 per day 10:40am-7pm; Su 12:45, 7pm; €6.50) via Amfissa (1½hr.; €5); Halkida (2½hr.; 1, 8pm; €11.30); Karditsa (M-Th and Sa 8 per day 10:45am-9:45pm, F and Su 7 per day 10:45am-9:45pm; €6.30); Patras (4hr.; M-F and Su 4 per day 12:30pm-1am, Sa 3 per day 12:30-7:15pm; €14); Thessaloniki (4hr.; M-Sa 11am, 6pm; Su 11am; €19) via Larisa (2hr., €10); Trikala (2½hr.; M-Th and Sa 7 per day 10:45am-7:45pm, F and Su 6 per day 10:45am-7:45pm; €7.10). The last intercity station is at Rosaki Angeli 69 (☎22 627), near the meeting point of Rosaki Angeli and Kapodistriou. It sends buses to Agia Marina (20min., 4 per day 6:20-9am, €1), Raches (50min., 5 per day 5:45am-8pm, €2.40), and Volos (2hr.; M-F and Su 9:15am, Sa 9am; €9.30).

The **local bus station** is at Konstantinopoulos 2 (☎51 348), below the city, near the railroad tracks where Satovriandou intersects Konstantinopoulos. Several buses per day go to small towns and villages around Lamia. A bus runs to Lionokladi train station (15min., every hr. 6am-9pm, €1). **Taxis** (☎34 555) wait 24hr. at stands in each of the four main plateias.

▣▣ **ORIENTATION AND PRACTICAL INFORMATION.** Inland off the Maliakos Gulf and 160km north of Athens, Lamia climbs gently to a northwesterly ridge, crowned by the **kastro**. The city extends outward from the roughly rectangular arrangement of its four central plateias. Southeastern **Plateia Parkou** is crowded and lined with banks. Maps are posted at its northern edge. From Pl. Parkou's northeastern corner, past the National Bank, **Kolokotroni** leads north to leafy **Plateia Laou.** West from Plateia Parkou up **Karagiannopolou** is sleepy **Plateia Diakou.** Head up **Riga Fereou** in the northwestern corner of Pl. Parkou to reach **Plateia Eleftherias,** home to Lamia's trendiest nightlife. Pl. Eleftherias connects with Pl. Diakou via **Diakou** on its southern side and with Pl. Laou via **Apostoli Kounoupi** on the eastern side. A network of small streets including **Rosaki Angeli** and **Karaiskaki** interlaces the squares and hosts small cafes, book stores, and boutiques.

Pl. Parkou teems with banks, including a **National Bank,** Kapodistriou 1, at the corner of Kolokotroni, with a **24hr. ATM.** (☎57 607. Open M-Th 8am-2:30pm, F 8am-2pm.) The **police** are about 2km out of town. To reach the station, take a taxi or follow Leonidou out of the city onto Athinon; it's on the right, about a block past Kavafi. (☎56 845. Limited English spoken. Open 24hr.) The 24hr. **hospital** (☎56 100 or 56 200) is just over 1km north of the city on Karaiskaki. The **OTE,** Skilvaniotou 1, is on the western side of Pl. Eleftherias. (Open M, W, Sa 7:30am-2pm, Tu and Th-F 7:30am-2pm and 5:30-9pm.) **Internet** access is available at **BattleNet,** Rosaki Angeli 40, across the street from Hotel Athena. The back room is lined with computers and comfortable chairs. (☎67 424. €2 per hr. Open 24hr.) You also can get connected at **Escape,** Ipsilandou 6, just north of Pl. Eleftherias. (☎20 240. €2 per hr. Open 24hr.) The **post office,** in Pl. Diakou, offers **Poste Restante.** (☎47 718. Open M-F 7:30am-2pm.) **Postal Code:** 35100.

▐▌▐▌ ACCOMMODATIONS AND FOOD. Those who choose to spend the night in Lamia can stay at any number of moderately priced hotels in the heart of the city, although the area is bustling and noisy all night long. At **Hotel Neon Astron ❷,** Pl. Laou 5, you'll find tastefully furnished rooms with TV, air-conditioning, phone, and bath. The hotel cat probably will greet you as you enter the small lounge on the second floor. (☎26 245. Singles €25; doubles €30; triples €40.) **Hotel Athena ❸,** Rosaki Angeli 41, two blocks east of Pl. Laou, has new, sparkling rooms fully equipped with bath, hair dryer, TV, air-conditioning, phone, and huge balcony. (☎20 700. Singles €30; doubles €40; triples €50.) **Thermopyles Hotel ❸,** Rosaki Angeli 36, has 15 tidy rooms with TV, phone, air-conditioning, small balcony, and bath. (☎21 366. Singles €30; doubles €40; triples €50.)

For fresh fruits and veggies, head to the markets along Rosaki Angeli and Othonos, both off Pl. Laou. **▨Ouzo Melathron ❷,** Aristoteli 3, off Pl. Laou (take the stairs on the northern side), has a 5ft. long menu that brims with creativity—and hilarious English translations—as it combines exotic and reinvented traditional dishes. Try not to laugh at choices like "transsexual lamb" (€4.40) or "bellymen's souvlaki" (€6.50). The food, beautifully presented in giant portions, is served in a lush courtyard under the glow of lanterns. (☎31 502; www.ouzomelathron.gr. Entrees €4-8.50. Open daily 11am-1am.) For a traditional Greek meal, visit **Elisia ❷** (Ηλυσια), Kalyva Bakogianni 10, just off Pl. Laou, around the corner to the left of Hotel Neon Astron. Try the delicious moussaka (€6), or roasted veal, pork, or lamb. (☎27 006. Entrees €4-8. Open daily 10am-midnight.) **Sef ❶** (Σεφ), Ap. Kounoupi 1, just off Pl. Laou, serves an arsenal of sweet and savory crepes (€1.50-3) to famished crowds well into the morning. (☎42 001. Open daily 9am-6am.)

◪ SIGHTS. The imposing remains of the **kastro** loom over the city. Built in the Classical period, it has undergone renovations under the Romans, Franks, Catalans, and Ottomans. Before Greece's 1884 annexation of Thessaly and Domokos, Lamia's kastro served as the core of the country's border defenses. The barracks building, built by King Otto in 1880, was used until WWII. It now serves as a well-organized **Archaeological Museum** that displays items from the Neolithic to Roman periods found in tombs outside Lamia. Aside from the numerous ceramic figurines and *amphorae*, highlights include the earliest preserved vase depicting a naval battle, a reconstructed floor mosaic, gold and bronze jewelry, and a fearsome collection of rusty weaponry. Head east out of Pl. Parkou on Kapodistriou and take the second left onto Amalias. Walk up the hill and cross Eklision when Amalias ends to go up a stone stairway. Turn right and follow the road at the top of the stairs, keeping the kastro on your left. After a 5min. walk, you'll see a marked path leading up to the museum entrance, inside the kastro's walls. (☎29 992. Museum and kastro open Tu-Su 8:30am-3pm. €2, students and under 18 free.) The way to the **Gardens of Agios Loukas**, a peaceful park on Ag. Loukas hill, begins at the top of Pl. Diakou behind a gloriously posed **Statue of Athanasios Diakos**. A War of Independence hero, Diakos was burned to death by the Turks in 1821. Take the steps up to the top, then go right to reach the gardens. For a fascinating look at local history, check out the **Folklore Museum**, Kalyva Bakogianni 6, just off Pl. Laou. Its small but well-displayed collection includes traditional clothing, farm equipment, and a vintage ouzo press. (☎37 832. Open M-Sa 8:30am-2:30pm. Free.)

🔲🔳 **ENTERTAINMENT AND NIGHTLIFE.** People congregate nightly in Pl. Eleftherias, filling the seats at the many cafes and nearby bars. **Sketch**, just off Pl. Eleftherias on Riga Fereou, with red awnings, serves drinks all day and night to a diverse clientele. (☎51 451. Open 7:30am-3am. Mixed drinks €7-8.) From May through September, **Agora**, Othonos 8, two blocks east of Pl. Laou on the right and down the steps, entertains crowds in its outdoor courtyard where the DJ plays fast-paced dance music. (☎ 51 350. Beer €4-6. Mixed drinks €6-7. Open daily 8pm-late.) Several cafes on Diakou, the street that runs between Pl. Eleftherias and Pl. Diakou, shed their daytime roles to cater to the nighttime bar crowd. Those like **Venezia**, Diakou 6 (☎46 525; open daily 8:30am-3am), and neighboring **Prevere** (☎23 422; open daily 9am-2am) cater to a young crowd.

🔳 **DAYTRIP FROM LAMIA: MT. ITI NATIONAL PARK.** Hiking and outdoor enthusiasts will enjoy the impressive gorges, scenic hiking trails, and small mountainside villages of **Mt. Iti** (Οίτι) **National Park**, located 35km to the southwest of Lamia. The boundaries of the national park extend to the base of the mountain, and the best points of access are the small villages at the mountain's base. **Ipati** is the most convenient base for a hike to the summit. A 6km trail begins on the western end of town, a block south of the main road. Hike with a partner and bring plenty of water, as there are no springs or fountains on the way up. At the summit, there is a refuge and an amazing view of the surrounding area. For those who prefer to stay closer to sea level, Ipati is home to a waterfall and the ruins of a kastro.

The village of **Loutra Ipatis** (Λουτρά Υπάτης), 5km closer to Lamia, has a beautiful public garden and an array of cafes and tavernas. To reach the 8km trail to the summit of Mt. Iti, walk south through town toward the mountain; at the southernmost end of town, you'll find a dirt road leading to the mountainside. The town's tree-shaded main intersection is populated with dining establishments, and the gardens are on the northeast side. Check out the mysterious covered pit in the gardens, with a bubbling hot spring barely visible at the bottom. For more hiking information, contact the **Hellenic Alpine Club of Lamia** (☎26 786), which can suggest routes and provide directions to mountain refuges. *(The mountain and its villages are best reached by car, but the local bus station in Lamia has service to many of the small villages. Twelve buses per day leave from Lamia's local station for Loutra Ipatis and nearby Ipati (20-25min., 5:30am-9pm, €1.50) and a return schedule is posted at the bus stops.)*

AGIOS KONSTANTINOS Άγιος Κονσταντίνος ☎22350

Directly at the foot of an imposing mountain range, Agios Konstantinos is the closest port to Athens with ferries to the Sporades; it thus functions as a busy portal between the mainland and the Aegean Sea. Most travelers will experience it as a layover during a longer journey; still, with a charming small-town feel and a grassy central plateia, Agios Konstantinos makes waiting for a ferry or bus easy to bear.

Due to its status as a transportation hub, Agios Konstantinos has a good variety of accommodations for a town of its size. **Hotel Poulia ❷,** 4 Thermopylon, is in the center of town off the right side of the plateia. Small rooms come with varying levels of amenities; some doubles have TV, air-conditioning, and bath. Helpful Dimitrios Ioannou and his wife serve a home-cooked breakfast at the bar downstairs for €5. (☎31 663. Singles €20; doubles €24, with bath €35-44; triples €30. Group rates available.) Friendly **Hotel Olga ❸,** 11 Evoikou, is the first in the strip of hotels along the highway to the right of the plateia. Spacious, white-tiled rooms have airconditioning, phone, fridge, TV, bath, and a balcony with a harbor view. (☎/fax 32 266. Breakfast €5. Singles €30; doubles €40; triples €50.) The main plateia is surrounded by inexpensive tavernas and bars; after dark, children play soccer on the grass while the rest of the community relaxes at the outdoor tables. Some of the best food in town can be found at ▇**To Parco ❷,** on the edge of the plateia farthest from the water. The fantastic *okta* (indigenous beans with a flavorful tomato sauce; €4), are not to be missed. If you play your cards right, you could score a complimentary piece of honey-drenched cake. (☎33 360. Open daily 8am-2am. Entrees €4-8.) **Kaltsas Grill House ❷,** on the right side of the plateia, serves generous portions of meat. (☎33 323. Pitas €1.80. Entrees €5-8. Open daily 9am-late.) For something sweet to tide you over until the next meal, **Artopoeia ❶,** 3 Thermopylon, by Hotel Poulia, sells bread and pastries (€0.50-2) heaping with powdered sugar. (☎31 684. Open daily 6am-9pm.)

Buses stop in front of the Galaxias Supermarket on the waterfront; the bus station is in a small cafe next door. (☎32 223.) **Buses** go to Athens (2½hr., 15 per day 6:45am-10pm, €11.50), Lamia (45min., every hr. 7:30am-11:30pm, €3.50), and Thessaloniki (4hr.; 7am, 2pm; €24.50). Ferries and Flying Dolphins (☎31 874) come to the pier, immediately seaward of the plateia. Buy your tickets from one of two offices on the right side of the plateia. **Ferries** leave for Alonnisos (4½hr; M 11am, 2pm; T-Th 11am; F 11am, 4:45, 6pm; Sa 9:30am, 3:30pm; €31.20), via Skiathos (3hr., €23) and Skopelos (4hr., €31.20). Check departure times posted outside the ticket offices; often it's best to call ahead to your destination to confirm times. (Alonnisos ticket office ☎24240 65 220; Skiathos 24270 22 204; Skopelos 24240 22 767.) **Flying Dolphins** go to Alonnisos (2hr.; M-F and Su 10:30am, 7:15pm; Sa 10:30am, 1:15pm; €32), via Skiathos (1½hr., €23.30), and Skopelos (1¾hr., €32). **Taxis** (☎31 850) line up behind the church. The **port police** (☎31 920), above the ticket offices, can help with ferry schedules. There are **24hr. ATMs** in front of the Galaxias supermarket and next to the OTE. The **OTE** is to the right of the plateia, around the corner and facing the highway. (☎31 699. Open M-F 7:30am-3pm.) A sign for the **post office,** 5 Riga Feraiou, 20m inland, is one block past the OTE toward Hotel Olga. (☎31 855. Open M-F 7:30am-2pm.) **Postal Code:** 35006.

THESSALY Θεσσαλ4α

From the urban bustle of Volos and Larisa to the peaceful villages of the Mt. Pelion Peninsula, Thessaly runs the gamut of lifestyles and attractions. The larger cities are home to some of the wildest nightlife on mainland Greece, while the otherworldly monasteries at Meteora define themselves by spiritual simplicity. Thessaly's plains are home to farmers who tend sheep and goats in the summer before returning home to fish from the waters of the Pinios River. In this out-of-the-way region, you'll find a wealth of genuine hospitality but very little English.

VOLOS Βόλος   ☎ 24210

Wayfaring Jason gave this city a permanent place in Greek mythology. It was from Volos that he and the Argonauts set sail on their quest for the Golden Fleece, a legend that the modern city has in no way forgotten: two main streets and half a dozen hotels are named in tribute to the ancient story. Much of contemporary Volos, however, has been shaped by historical rather than mythological events. In the 1923 population exchange (p. 57), many ethnic Greeks from Turkey arrived at the shores of the Pagasitic Gulf, significantly increasing the population of the city until it became one of Greece's largest. The Orthodox refugees brought their passion for carousing to Volos, establishing countless *tsipouradika* restaurants. The small bottles of distilled grape liquor served here are known as *tsipouro* and have brought the city national fame. Volos's orderly network of wide avenues contains a complete array of modern conveniences. Yet for a city of its size, Volos is refreshingly clean and safe. Come nightfall, strolling couples fill Volos's harborside, and dozens of cafes and seafood restaurants push tables up to the water.

▐▙ TRANSPORTATION

Trains: ☎ 24 056. Take Lambraki out of town and turn right at the flags at the end of the park. Walk 2-3min. down the road parallel to the track. Trains go to **Larisa** (intercity: 45min., 6:30am, €6. Regular: 1hr.; M-F 15 per day 5:53am-11:03pm, Sa-Su 7 per day 7:06am-9:28pm; €2.10). Change trains in Larisa for **Athens** and **Thessaloniki**.

Ferries: To: **Alonnisos** (4hr., 2 per week, €18), **Skiathos** (2¼hr., 2 per day, €15), and **Skopelos** (3½hr., 2 per day, €17). **Sporades Travel,** Argonafton 33 (☎ 23 400). English-speaking staff sells tickets. Open daily 6am-9pm.

Flying Dolphins: The agencies near the pier all sell tickets. Check with Falcon Tours, Argonafton 34 (☎ 21 626; www.hellenicseaways.gr). Open daily 7am-10pm. 3 per day go to Alonnisos (2hr.; 10am, 1, 7:30pm; €30) via Skiathos (1¼hr., €22), Glossa (1½hr., €24), and Skopelos (1¾hr., €28.20).

Buses: ☎ 33 254. In the Old Town, about a 10min. walk up Lambraki. To: **Agios Ioannis** (2½hr., 3 per day 5am-1:30pm, €5.50); **Athens** (4½hr., 12 per day 5:30am-1am, €20); **Larisa** (1hr., 12 per day 5:45am-1am, €4.10); **Makrynitsa** (45min., 10 per day 6:15am-9:30pm, €1.10) via **Portaria** (40min., €1); **Milies** (1hr., 6 per day 6am-7:30pm, €2); **Thessaloniki** (3hr., 9 per day 4:30am-8:30pm, €13.40); **Trikala** (2½hr., 4 per day 6:30am-7pm, €10.10); **Tsagarada** (1½hr., 4 per day 5am-3:30pm, €3.30). Service reduced Sa-Su and in winter.

Taxis: ☎ 27 777. Line up in front of Pl. Ag. Konstantinou 24hr.

Car Rental: Prices fluctuate depending on season and type of vehicle. **Avis,** Argonafton 41 (☎ 20 849). Mopeds from €15 per day. Cars from €30 per day. Open M-Sa 8:30am-9:30pm, Su 9:30am-1pm and 6-9pm. **European Car Rental,** Iasonos 83 (☎ 36 238). Mopeds from €25 per day. Cars from €45 per day. Open daily 9am-9pm.

✷▐ ORIENTATION AND PRACTICAL INFORMATION

Volos's bus station and tourist office are on **Lambraki,** main road, a 10min. walk west from the city and the waterfront. On its way into town, the road runs past the train station and **Riga Fereou Park** before coming to an end at a fountain. **Argonafton** is the waterfront walkway, home to lively tavernas and cafes. Moving inland, **Iasonos** and **Dimitriados** are the next streets parallel to the water; both are packed with banks, bakeries, and fast-food joints. After Dimitriados and also parallel to Argonafton, **Ermou,** a pedestrian-only street, contains boutiques that sell women's clothes and

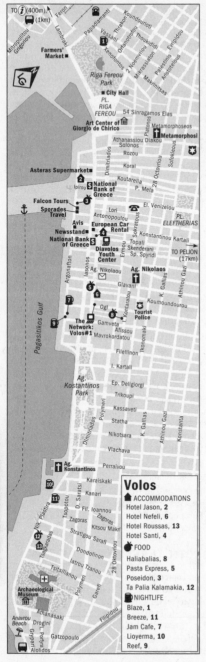

Volos

⌂ ACCOMMODATIONS
Hotel Jason, **2**
Hotel Nefeli, **6**
Hotel Roussas, **13**
Hotel Santi, **4**
♦ FOOD
Haliabalias, **8**
Pasta Express, **5**
Poseidon, **3**
Ta Palia Kalamakia, **12**
◗ NIGHTLIFE
Blaze, **1**
Breeze, **11**
Jam Cafe, **7**
Lioyerma, **10**
Reef, **9**

shoes. Near the center of the city, it leads into an open plateia with the **Church of Agios Nikolaos.** The point at which Ermou becomes **Polymeri** marks the start of the long seaside park. The **Church of Agios Konstantinos,** easily visible from the docks jutting out into the harbor, sits at the end of the park. Here, Argonafton and Dimitriados join to become **Nikolaou Plastira.** This quieter street heads past a few bars and *ouzeria* to the hospital and the Archaeological Museum before ending at Volos's popular **Anavrou beach** in the residential section of town.

Tourist Office: ☎20 273. Across the street from the bus station up Lambraki, in the large brick building with the fountain. Has maps, transportation timetables, and info about Volos and the Pelion Peninsula. Open daily 8am-10pm.

Banks: There are several major banks with **currency exchange** and **ATMs** on Iasonos and Dimitriados. **National Bank,** Iasonos 50 and 91 (☎90 800 and 34 811). Open M-Th 8am-2:30pm, F 8am-2pm. **Citibank,** Argonafton 27 (☎76 380), on the corner of El. Venizelou. Has a **24hr. ATM.** Open M-Th 8am-2:30pm, F 8am-2pm.

Bookstore: Newsstand, Iasonos 78 (☎23 200), 1 block inland from the meeting point of the port and Argonafton. Sells a small collection of English novels, magazines, history books, and travel guides, including *Let's Go* titles. Open daily 8am-10pm.

Police: ☎39 061. On the corner of Ath. Gazi and Ath. Diakou. Open 24hr. **Tourist police,** 28 Oktovriou 179 (☎39 065). Provide guides and free maps of the city. Open daily 8am-10pm.

Hospital: Polymeri 134 (☎94 200), next to the museum. Open 24hr.

Telephones: OTE, El. Venizelou 22 (☎95 936), on the corner of El. Venizelou and Sokratous. Open daily 7:30am-2pm.

Internet Access: Diavlos Youth Center, Topali 14 (☎25 363), off Dimitriados. The best rates in town and an atmosphere blessedly free of cigarette smoke. €1.20 per hr. Open M-F 10am-10pm.

The Network: Volos #1, Iasonos 141 (☎30 260). A gamer's paradise, lined with flat-screen computers. €2.50 per hr. Gaming €1.50 per hr. Open 24hr.

Post Office: Dimitriados 209 (☎90 602). At the intersection of Dimitriados and Ag. Nikolaou. **Poste Restante** available. Open M-F 7:30am-8pm. **Postal Code:** 38001.

ACCOMMODATIONS

Volos's hotels vary little in location and amenities and are almost never cheap. Most of the budget options are clustered in alleys along the waterfront or on the small streets leading away from the harbor. As usual, negotiating can slash prices.

Hotel Nefeli, Koumoundourou 10 (☎30 211). Named for the queen who sent her children away from danger aboard Hermes's magic flying ram, Hotel Nefeli has a staff that sees to its guests with comparable care. Elegant rooms come with TV, A/C, phone, balcony, and bath. Breakfast €8. Singles €52; doubles €65; triples €78. AmEx/MC/V. ❹

Hotel Jason, P. Mela 1 (☎26 075), on the waterfront across from the ferry dock. Some of the spare, pink and white rooms have A/C, and most have a balcony overlooking the water. All have phone, bath, fan, and TV. Singles €30; doubles €40; triples €60. ❸

Hotel Santi, Topali 13 (☎33 341), off Argonafton. Basic rooms with miraculously soft pillows include bath, TV, phone, A/C, small balcony, and an unbeatable location. Singles €30; doubles €40-45; triples €50-55. Bargain for lower prices for longer stays. ❸

Hotel Roussas (Ρουσσας), Iatrou Tzanou 1 (☎21 732), on the corner of Nik. Plastira and Iatrou Tzanou; look for the purple balconies. Though quite a bit removed from the main waterfront, Roussas, whose attractive rooms have bath, fridge, phone, A/C, TV, and balcony, is ideal for those looking to spend time relaxing on the beach. Singles €30; doubles €40; triples €50. Lower prices in winter. ❸

FOOD

Stock up on provisions for a beachside picnic at **Asteras Supermarket,** Iasonos 34-38. (☎31 524. Open M-F 8am-9pm, Sa 8am-8pm.) There's also a periodic **farmers' market** on Lambraki toward the bus station. Splurging on ouzo and *tsipouro* at one of Volos's signature waterfront *ouzeria* is a memorable experience. Each has a wide selection of *mezedes*, including seafood plates with prawns and octopus.

⊠ Haliabalias, Kontaratou 8 (☎20 234). Though this taverna is hidden in a niche, most locals will be able to help you find it. There is no set menu, but patrons can walk inside and choose from delicious home-style meals prepared for the day. Entrees €4-6. ❶

Ta Palia Kalamakia, N. Plastira 10 (☎24 048), near Hotel Roussas on the eastern edge of town. If you arrive by car, the house dog Hector will be sure to greet you heartily. Veal schnitzel €7. Entrees €5-8. Seafood €35-60 per kg. Open daily 11am-midnight. ❷

Poseidon, Argonafton 31 (☎36 629), opposite the ferry dock. This governing seafood presence on the waterfront offers the day's fresh catches, staying crowded well past midnight in the summer. 2-person seafood platter €20. Fish and seafood €35-60 per kg. Open daily 9am-3am. ❸

Pasta Express, Dimitriados 172 (☎21 888), opposite Hotel Nefeli at the intersection of Dimitriados and Koumoundourou. Forget about the overpriced Italian pizzerias that line the waterfront: if you don't mind ordering takeout, this is the place to go for a fast, tasty pizza or pasta. You can choose from a variety of ingredients and watch as they're cooked in front of you. Open daily 1pm-2am. Pizzas €6-7. Pastas €4-6. ❷

SIGHTS

The ⊠**Archaeological Museum,** Athanasaki 1, is a 20min. walk along the water from the ferry docks. It occupies a Neoclassical mansion and displays reconstructed tombs and *stelae* from Demetrias. The collection of miniature Neolithic objects includes seals, spindle whorls, tools of bone and stone, and a collection of hilariously obscene figurines. High ceilings and sleek exhibits make the museum a pleasure to visit. (☎25 285. Open Tu-Su 8:30am-3pm. €2, seniors €1, students free.) The museum can provide English pamphlets about the nearby archaeological sites at **Dimini** and **Sesklo.** Both are close to Volos; Dimini is 4km west of the city center and Sesklo is another 5.5km farther along the connecting road. Taxis there range €4-7. Dimini dates from 4000 BC and contains two major sites. The main site was constructed sometime at the end of the 5th millennium BC, and the more recent of the two, southwest of the main site, was built during the Mycenaean period. Both sites have ruins of houses and evidence of early city planning. Sesklo is the oldest known settlement in Thessaly and has the oldest acropolis in all of Greece, dating from 6500 BC. (☎85 960. Both open Tu-Su 8am-8pm. €2, seniors €1, students free. Tickets cover both sites.) The **Art Center of Giorgio de Chirico,** Metamorphoseos 3, next to the conservatory, showcases temporary exhibits of Greek modern art. The permanent collection upstairs is comprised of 19th- and 20th-century pieces. (☎31 701. Open M-F 10am-1pm and 6-9pm, Sa 10am-1pm, Su 6-9pm. Free.)

▣ NIGHTLIFE

The waterfront between the docks and Ag. Konstantinos becomes a hive of activity at night. Each of the cafes has its own character—there's enough variety to satisfy every taste. Young Greek couples congregate under soft yellow lighting at **Jam Cafe,** Argonafton 62 (☎76 156). The rowdier **Reef** (☎24 168), next door, has a blue phosphorescent glow that emanates from a full-sized fish tank in the middle of its floor. (Beer €3.50-5. Mixed drinks €6-7.50. Both open daily 9am-4am.) Cafe-bars by the museum and beach do their best to counteract the south's image as the quieter end of town. **Breeze,** Nik. Plastira 4B, plays house and pop. (☎35 420. Open daily 8am-3am.) Nearby **Lioyerma,** overlooking the harbor, rocks an outdoor bar and a sprawling network of couches and tables. (☎36 178. Beer €3.50-5. Mixed drinks €6.50-7. Open daily 9am-6am.) After getting drunk enough to let loose on the dance floor, locals head to **Blaze,** by the train station. (☎88 332. Cover €8; includes 1 drink. Mixed drinks €8. Open M-Th and Su until 3:30am, F-Sa until 6am.) For an even wilder time with a slightly heftier price tag, grab a cab (€4) to **Alykes.** This beach suburb hosts **Astra,** a popular traditional *bouzouki* haven. (☎62 182. Cover €10; includes 1 drink. Open F-Sa midnight-4am.) To dance to *rembetika* tunes, head to massive **Fengaria,** also in Alykes. (☎88 733. Cover €8-9; includes 1 drink. Open W-Sa midnight-4am.) The disco of choice in Alykes is **Noa,** a restaurant and bar that switches gears around 1am. (Mixed drinks €8-9. Open M-Th and Su until 3:30am, F-Sa until 6am.)

TSAGARADA ☎24260

In stunning Tsagarada, immaculate gardens cascade downhill into bluffs with the peaceful Sporades as a distant backdrop. Tsagarada has succumbed to some tourism of the particularly expensive variety, but its sprawling layout preserves the village's charm. Spread across a wide area on the slope just below the highway, Tsagarada is comprised of four hamlets: Ag. Kyriaki, Ag. Paraskevi, Ag. Stefanou, and Ag. Taxiarhon. In the main plateia, you will find the church of the hamlet's name and a massive, 1000-year-old plane tree. The tree's gnarled branches shade the cafe tables below and make it perfect for climbing. From the plateia, a well-marked path leads 1hr. down to the blue-green waters and pearlwhite stones of local favorite ▨**Milopotamos beach.**

Between Ag. Paraskevi and the main plateia, a stone path leads to the charming **Villa Ton Rodon ❹,** whose rooms have bath and TV. Shuttered doors open onto porches overlooking brilliant rose bushes and a panoramic view of the sea. (☎49 340. Breakfast included. Doubles €50-80, depending on season.) Just above the plateia, ▦**Anatoli ❷** serves delicious traditional Greek food. The covered outdoor patio offers a serene view of the Aegean over the treetops. (☎49 201. Chicken with spaghetti €6. Entrees €6-8. Open daily noon-midnight.)

Though Tsagarada is reachable from Ag. Ioannis by a 2hr. hike over difficult terrain, it's more convenient to take the **bus** from Volos (1½hr., 4 per day 8am-5pm, €3.30). Return schedules are posted in the bus stop, or you can ask at Anatoli Taverna. Most visitors will enter at Ag. Paraskevi, where a **tourist office** visible from the main road. (☎48 993. Open daily 9am-3pm). A **24hr. ATM,** the **post office** (☎49 215; open M-F 7:30am-2pm), and a covered bus stop are also near the main road.

MOUNT PELION Όρος Πήλιο

PENINSULA

The Mt. Pelion Peninsula once was home to a group of rowdy centaurs, who followed Chiron, their king, to the area. These mythical half-men, half-horses were well known for their insatiable sex drives, which drove them to have their way with whatever hot young nymphets they could find. Chiron, a healer and tutor to Achilles, was lured to Pelion by its abundant supply of over 1700 medicinal herbs. The cool, moist peninsula is a delicious anomaly in mostly sun-scorched Greece. Over the years, the mountains of Pelion have protected the area from invasion. While the rest of Greece groaned under Ottoman rule, the peninsula was an autonomous center of Greek nationalism.

MAKRYNITSA Μακρυνίτσα ☎24280

High in the Pelion mountain range, serene Makrynitsa soars over the Pagasitic Gulf. The town's breathtaking views of the Volos metropolitan area have earned it the apt nickname "balcony of Pelion." The small town extends only a few hundred meters in three directions from the main plateia, and cars are forbidden due to its designation as a protected traditional settlement. In the early evening, the setting sun illuminates the gulf with deep red and orange hues. Come nightfall, Makrynitsa looks down onto the indigo- and white-speckled valley like the best box seat in a giant opera house.

◪▨ TRANSPORTATION AND PRACTICAL INFORMATION. Makrynitsa is accessible by daily **buses** from Volos (45min., 10 per day 6:15am-9:30pm, €1.30) via the neighboring village of Portaria (40min., €1). From the bus turnaround, a short walk uphill hugging the mountainside takes you to the parking lot. Here, the leftmost road, **17 Martiou,** leads to the plateia. Don't get turned off as you pass shops selling tourist kitsch and medicinal herbs—the main plateia is gorgeous, shaded by immense oak trees and overlooking the mountainside below.

Portaria, 2km away, is a 20min. walk from Makrynitsa's parking lot. From there, you can catch buses to other Pelion destinations, including the beaches at Agios Yiannis and Milopotamos. **24hr. ATMs,** a **police station** (☎99 105; open 8am-2pm), and a **post office** (☎99 104; open M-F 8am-2pm) can be found in Portaria. There are pay phones and a mailbox in Makrynitsa's plateia. Postal Code: 37011.

◪◲ ACCOMMODATIONS AND FOOD. Because of its protected status, staying in Makrynitsa during the winter high season costs a fortune (singles around €65). Luckily, nearby Portaria has several exceptionally cheap **domatia** (singles around €20; doubles €30), and the upscale tourist hotels offer summer visitors cheaper prices and posh rooms. As nearly every building in Makrynitsa seems to be a hotel or domatia, there's plenty of selection. On 17 Martiou headed into Makrynitsa's plateia, you'll pass a series of domatia and hotels on the right. ◪**Hotel Theodora ❷** (Θεοδώρα) exudes luxury in its gorgeous, old-fashioned rooms, replete with wooden furniture, satin comforters, furry rugs, TV, bath, and amazing views of the Pagasitic Gulf. The warm proprietress and inexpensive prices seal the deal. (☎99 179. Breakfast €5. Singles €25; doubles €30; triples €35. Higher prices in winter. MC/V.) The domatia on the Volos side of the main parking lot, owned by the warm owner of **Leonidas Taverna ❸**, are another excellent option. (☎99 071. Singles €30; doubles €35-40. Prices negotiable.) Farther down 17 Martiou, just before the plateia, is **Hotel Kentavros ❸**, which has a garden and well-decorated rooms with TV, phone, and bath. (☎99 075. Singles €30-50; doubles €30-70.)

Several small restaurants have outdoor seating and spectacular views from elevated verandas. Most affordable is local *ouzeri* **A+B ❷**, past the plateia on the small trail that runs behind the church. From the porch, patrons have a superb view of Makrynitsa, Volos, and the gulf. (☎99 355. Entrees €5-6.50. Open daily 11am-midnight.) Right before A+B, near the end of the row of shops, is **Leonidas ❷**, just about the only other budget option in town. Try the flavorful *spetzofei* (sausage and peppers; €6.50), a local specialty. Top off your meal with homegrown figs drenched in honey. (☎99 533. Entrees €6-8. Open daily noon-6pm and 8pm-late.) In the plateia, **Pantheon ❸** monopolizes the spectacular vista of the Pagasitic Gulf, with tables that sit against the railing. The *moschari kokkonisto* (braised veal) and *kotopoulo fournou* (baked chicken) are both delicious. (☎99 143. Entrees €7-8. Open daily 8am-midnight.)

◪ **SIGHTS.** To reach the **Museum of Folk Art and the History of Pelion,** take the downhill path that begins to the left of the church in the plateia and follow the signs. On all three stories of a converted 1844 mansion, the museum highlights old stills used in making *tsipouro* and contains recreations of 18th-century Greek rooms. (☎99 505. Open Tu-Su 10am-5pm. €2, students free.) In the plateia, the building across from the church contains a wall mural painted by famed folk artist Theophilos Hadzimichali. The town's remarkable churches include the **Church of Agios Yiannis the Baptist** in the main plateia, where you can answer that burning question of what it's like to be inside a tree: the hollowed-out trunk of a tall, leafy tree looms by the entrance. The peaceful church of **Kimisi Theotokou** once housed a *krifto scholio*, a secret school that taught the forbidden Greek language during Ottoman rule. (Churches open at the whim of their caretakers; early to mid-morning and evening are the best times to visit.) From the main parking lot, a road leads steeply uphill to the **Monastery of Agios Gerasimos** (20min.), which grants a beautiful view. (Open daily 7am-noon and 4-6pm.) Makrynitsa's old houses are a sight in themselves. Stained-glass lanterns, false painted windows, and symbols to protect against evil spirits adorn the outer walls.

AGIOS IOANNIS Άγιος Ιωάννης ☎24260

Ideally, all the time you'll spend in Agios Ioannis is the 5min. it takes to turn from the bus stop and start walking up the coast. Heavy tourist traffic has sapped most of the charm from this small beachfront town. Nevertheless, it is within easy walking distance of areas with pristine natural beauty, and serves as a convenient starting point for exciting daytrips. Nearby Papa Nero beach has a few peaceful coves, and a 15min. walk farther will lead to the gorgeous, isolated village of Damouhari.

▣ ▨ **TRANSPORTATION AND PRACTICAL INFORMATION. Buses** leave daily for Volos from the parking lot (2½hr.; M-F 3 per day 7:15am-5pm, Sa-Su 3 per day 8:15am-5am; €5.50). **Taxis** (☎60946 08 968) are available by phone 24hr., but trips to nearby villages tend to be pricey.

The entire town sits along a beachfront main street, running from the parking lot past hotels, restaurants, and bakeries to the harbor at the far end. Near the parking lot, a bridge runs in the opposite direction from the main road, over the often-dry river, ending at the beach of **Papa Nero.** Detailed info, boats (from €55 per day), motorbikes (from €20 per day), and equipment are available at the **Les Hirondelles** office, just past Plazza restaurant. They specialize in helping to plan independent excursions and vacation packages. (☎31 181. Open daily 10am-2pm and 6-10pm.) The **police** in Tsagarada can be reached at ☎49 222. For **first aid,** call ☎31 950. A **hospital** (☎22 222) is 30km away in Zagora. **Internet** access is available at **Hotel Kentrikon,** in the alley between Plazza and Kyma Taverna (€5 per hr.).

▥▯ ACCOMMODATIONS AND FOOD. Many of the hotels in Ag. Ioannis are controlled by Les Hirondelles and are rather expensive for travelers who are not on one of their package tours. For an unforgettable experience away from the tourist hordes, walk 300m to the far edge of Papa Nero beach, and continue up the stone trail. There you'll find ▨**Pension Katerina ❸,** a family-run hotel with outstanding views of the Aegean. The comfortable rooms have bath, small kitchen, and fridge. The Fotopoulos family extends such warm hospitality that many customers come back year after year. (☎31 624 in summer, 56 806 in winter. Open May-Oct. Doubles and triples €35-55, depending on season.) The owner also rents a nearby house for up to a one-month stay. (Contact Pension Katerina. 2-4 people €50-80 per night. Lower prices for longer stays.) In town, **Hotel Martha ❹,** toward the parking lot end of the strip, has clean rooms with bath that practically bump up against the ocean. (☎31 406. Doubles €50; triples €60.) The **Papa Nero campground ❶,** near its namesake beach, is an oceanfront site with clean bathrooms and a small cafe. (☎31 319. €5 per person, €5 per tent. Laundry €5. Electricity €3. Tent rental €25.)

The strip is dominated by bakeries, cafes, and overpriced restaurants. Popular **Akrogiali ❷** is one exception to this rule, serving a variety of cooked and grilled entrees (€6-12) to sunbathers just back from the beach. (☎31 112. Fish and seafood €40-49 per kg. Open daily noon-11:30pm.)

▧ NIGHTLIFE. During the summer, several waterfront bars keep the town buzzing late into the night. **Kavos,** near the harbor, blares house, pop, and Greek music. (☎31 108. Beer €4. Mixed drinks €8. Open daily 11pm-late.) For a more intense clubbing experience, head to **Mamba,** 10km away in the Pelion beach village of Agia Saranta (taxi €7-9). A techno, house, and progressive haven for partiers looking to test their dancefloor stamina, Mamba shuts down for only 14hr. each week, officially "closing" at 8am and reopening at 10am for another day and night of hard-core partying. Enormous crowds fill the club on the weekends while international DJs spin the newest tracks. (Mixed drinks €8-9.)

▰ DAYTRIP FROM AGIOS IOANNIS: DAMOUHARI. The winding seaside lane at the end of Papa Nero will lead you to the town of ▨**Damouhari,** an easy 20min. walk. A visit to this tiny, breathtaking town (pop. 10-50, depending on whom you ask) makes the trip to Agios Ioannis worthwhile. Damouhari's few businesses line the main path. The vibrant blue waters of the protected cove are visible just to the left. Jutting out into the sea on the right hand side is a peninsula with the ruins of a castle, no more than a series of low stone walls, which are great fun to explore. The town largely forgoes souvenir shops, with no need to overtly emphasize the relaxed, intimate vibe that occurs naturally in a place of such beauty.

Next to the first small cluster of shops is **Victoria's Guest House ❹,** whose rooms have priceless views of the cove. (☎49 872. Singles €40; doubles €50; triples €55; 2-room apartments for up to 4 people €70.) Past Victoria's is **To Kastro ❷,** an excellent taverna owned by one of the town's two families, and often populated by energetic, inquisitive youngsters. (☎49 475. Entrees €5-7. Open daily 8am-1am.)

To get there, walk from Agios Ioannis along the length of Papa Nero beach until you reach a wooden boardwalk, which shortly turns into a *kalderimi* (laid stone path), passing a cove. Follow the yellow signs with a picture of a hiker. When you get to the road, head left for 10min. until you reach Damouhari. Follow the *kalderimi* downhill and alongside the cove to reach the center of town.

WESTERN THESSALY

LARISA Λάρισα

As the fifth-largest city in Greece, the capital of Thessaly, and the location of a regional NATO office, Larisa is certainly of national importance. As most Greeks know, however, it's no tourism hot spot. Lacking notable sights and inherent charm, Larisa, whose name means "stronghold" in Ancient Greek, likely will be no more than a stop en route to more exciting destinations. Those who do end up staying the night, though, will find a large university community that supports some of the best nightlife in mainland Greece. During the day, trendy boutiques, cheap shopping, and chic cafes might keep you busy for a couple of hours.

▐ TRANSPORTATION

To reach the train station (☎24102 36 250), head south on Panagouli and bear slightly left onto Paleologou at the 5-way intersection; it's on the southern side of the small park. Intercity express and regular **trains** run to Athens (4-5hr.; 12 per day 12:30am-11pm; regular €10.70, intercity €18), Volos (45min.; 17 per day 9:55am-10:50pm; regular €2.10, intercity €4.50) and Thessaloniki (1¾hr., 15 per day 12:20am-10:35pm, €5). **Buses** Leave from the main station (☎24105 37 777), 150m north of Pl. Laou at Olympou and Georgiadou. To: **Athens** (4¼hr., 9 per day 7am-1am, €24.20); **Ioannina** (4hr.; 9am, 3pm; €14); **Kastoria** (4hr., 3 per day 12:30pm-12:30am, €15.50); **Thessaloniki** (2hr.; M-F 14 per day 9am-9pm, Sa-Su 7 per day 10:30am-8pm; €13.10); **Volos** (1hr., 10 per day 7am-9:30pm, €4.20). There is a smaller branch station at Iroön Polytechniou 14 (☎24106 10 124). Walk south on Olympou to Pl. Laou, where Panagouli begins; continue south on Panagouli, turn right at the 5-way intersection, and walk about 600m to the gas station-bus stop on the left. Sends buses to: **Karditsa** (1hr., 9 per day 8am-8:30pm, €5) and **Trikala** (1hr., 7 per day 6:30am-7:30pm, €4). **Taxis** (☎24106 61 414) line up around the Pl. Tahydromiou 24hr.

✳ ▐ ORIENTATION AND PRACTICAL INFORMATION

Surrounded by fertile corn and wheat fields, Larisa is just southeast of the **Pineios River,** in the middle of eastern Thessaly. The bus station in the north and the train station in the south mark the boundaries of the city's main commercial district, which forms a grid of confusing, labyrinthine streets. A map is essential in Larisa for basic orientation, but asking around is still necessary because of constant construction and road closings. From the bus station, **Olympou** heads south to **Plateia Laou,** one of Larisa's three main squares. Here you will meet **Panagouli,** a broad avenue that runs perpendicular to **Kyprou** and heads to the bottom of the city, where it crosses **Iroön Polytechniou** at a **five-way intersection.** Panagouli marks the eastern border of **Plateia Ethnarhou Makariou,** the town center, often called **Plateia Tahydromiou** ("Post Office Square"). The northern edge of this plateia is formed by **Papakyriazi,** which can be taken west three blocks to **Papanastasiou.** From here, Papanastasiou runs north to **Plateia Mikhali Sagika,** and south past the post office and tourist office. You will hit **Mandilara,** which runs east-west, two blocks south from the post office.

Tourist Office: Ipirou 58 (☎24106 70 437). On Ipirou near the intersection with Botsari. Has maps, pamphlets, and advice. Limited English spoken. Open M-F 7am-2:30pm.

Police: Papanastasiou 86 (☎24106 83 137 or 24106 83 146), 7 blocks south of Papakiriazi and 1 block down from the tourist office. Open 24hr.

Hospital: ☎24105 34 471. On Georgiadou, east of the main bus station. Open 24hr.

Telephones: OTE (☎24109 95 376), across the street from the Folk Museum. Open M, W, F 8am-1:30pm and 5:30-8:30pm; Tu and Th 8am-1:30pm.

Internet Access: Traffic, Patroklou 14 (☎24102 50 210), at Rousvelt. This chic cafe has fast computers. €2 per hr. Frappés €2.50. Open 10am-3am.

Post Office: Papanastasiou 52 (☎24105 32 312). At Diakou. Open M-F 7:30am-8pm. **Poste Restante** and **currency exchange. Postal Code:** 41001.

ACCOMMODATIONS AND FOOD

Mid-range to upper-level hotels can be found along the side streets that connect the three main plateias. The cheapest options are near the train station and the smaller bus station, but they're a 1.5km hike south from the main bus station. In town, it's difficult to find a room for under €40. **Hotel Diethnes ❸,** Paleologou 8, on the left after exiting the train station, is a modern hotel with cool, nicely decorated rooms with bath, and a bar. (☎24102 34 210. Reception 24hr. Singles €33; doubles €40; triples €50.) One door down is **Hotel Pantheon ❸,** Paleologou 10. Its orange, yellow, and bright green rooms have TV, sink, air-conditioning, and phone; most have balcony and small bath. (☎24102 34 810. Singles €30-40; doubles €40-50.) **Hotel Doma ❸,** Skarlatou Soutsou 1, at the intersection with Kyprou, has spacious rooms with air-conditioning, TV, phone, balcony in a central location, and tiny bath. (☎24105 35 025. Breakfast €8. Singles €35; doubles €45; triples €55.)

Most of Larisa's cafes, bars, and tavernas are on Pl. Tahydromiou and its surrounding streets, where they blend into an uninterrupted river of chairs, tables, and blasting music. During the day, you'll perfect your pronunciation of *signomi* (excuse me) as you navigate this busy area. Tempting scents draw crowds into the *psistarias* (grills) on Panos, where lamb and whole chickens slowly turn on spits in the window of each establishment. On the southern side of Pl. Tahydromiou, **To Sidrivani ❷,** Protopapadaki 8, claims to be the oldest restaurant in Larisa. While many doubt this claim, it doesn't matter all that much because the bubbling pots are full of delicious homemade Greek cuisine. (☎24105 35 933. Lamb with vegetables €7. Vegetarian entrees available. Open noon-midnight.) **Frourio ❸** is located in the Byzantine fortress on the summit of Larisa's highest hill. Straw tables covered in white tablecloths dot the grass, and are surrounded by ancient stone walls, flowering trees, and a stork-topped cathedral. The view and the ambiance make up for the average food. (☎24109 37 173. Entrees €8-14. Open 6pm-1am.)

SIGHTS

Larisa's disappointing archaeological sites are clustered on the city's northern hill. Two ancient theaters have been uncovered in the last century but neither is open to the public; they have been undergoing continuous restoration for over 10 years. The theaters, called **Ancient Theater A** and **Ancient Theater B,** both date from the late 3rd century BC to the beginning of the Roman period and are located in Pl. Miteras, which begins at the corner of El. Venizelou and Papanastasiou and continues northward. In a field above Ancient Theater A are a couple of sections of columns from the ancient **acropolis,** which is no longer standing. The whole area is fenced off for construction, so all you can do is take a quick peek. Beyond the remnants of the acropolis is the **Byzantine fortress,** where an equally tiny section of the ruins is visible. (Open 24hr. Free.) Down the opposite side of the hill is the Peneios River. Crossing the river on Ag. Haralabous and turning right, you'll find shade-filled **Alkazar Park.** The park is without a doubt the most serene spot in the city—even the graffiti here seems decorative. The **Pinakothiki,** Mexali 28, on the corner of Patera and Mexali, about 5km from the center of town, has one of the best 20th-century art collections in Greece, with works by almost all of Greece's renowned modern artists. (☎24106 16 266. Open W-Su 10am-2:30pm and 6-8pm. €1, EU students free.) At the intersection of El. Venizelou and 31 Augustou is a small yellow mosque with a single minaret that now serves as the **Archaeological Museum.** (☎24102 88 515. Open Tu-Su 8:30am-3pm. Free.) Also showcasing Neolithic and Classical statues and ruins from the province, the collection's primary highlight is a mosaic floor that depicts Nike crowning Atton. The **Museum of Folk Art,** Mandilara 74, has rotating exhibits and a permanent display featuring material elements of Thessalian culture, such as traditional costumes, weapons, coins, and embroidery. The museum also houses a large photo collection and the town's historical archives. (☎24102 87 516. Open daily 8am-5pm. Free.)

■ NIGHTLIFE

At night, the area around Pl. Tahydromiou becomes one large outdoor cafe. Dense with students, the bars and clubs generally have reasonably priced drinks (beer €3-4) and the students take part in a wild club scene. Larisa's impressive discos generally have a €5-10 cover (includes 1 drink). Hip, young **Ermes,** Rousvelt 41, on Rousvelt and Mandilara in Pl. Trigoni, fills up before the other bars do. Though it's the least expensive of Larisa's bars, the red transparent stools and cushy white couches make cheap feel swanky. (☎24106 21 022. Mixed drinks €6.50. Open 9am-3am.) Everything in **De-Tox,** Asclepiou 23, on the northern side of Pl. Tahydromiou, points to getting intoxicated—the menus, chairs, and bar are all a beer-colored translucent yellow, and pop music plays for drunken and still-drinking crowds. (☎24102 57 838. Beer €4.50.) Its next-door neighbor, **Arco,** Papakiriazi 20, is another popular hangout, playing music late into the night. Tables spiral out into the plateia as English-speaking bartenders serve from the giant bar that dominates the middle of the cafe. (☎24105 36 798. Frappés €3. Beer €4. Mixed drinks €6. Open 9am-3:30am.) **Xilia Xeilia,** which means "a thousand lips," is a €4 taxi ride from Pl. Tahydromiou. An enormous open-air nightclub boasting a row of towering fountains and 10 bars, it plays live Greek music every night, often featuring performances by the best *bouzouki* players in Greece. (☎24102 88 845. Open M-Th and Su 10pm-3:30am, F-Sa 10pm-later.) **Red** is considered the hottest dance club in Larisa, about a €5-6 cab ride away. On especially wild nights, you may catch the bartenders diving into the indoor pool while the masses grind scandalously to Greek pop. (Beer €5. Mixed drinks €7. Open in summer 10pm-7am.)

TRIKALA Τρίκαλα   ☎24310

Many Greeks consider Trikala a provincial knock-off of Larisa, but it is more pleasant than its larger neighbor. The Letheos River, named for the underworld's river of forgetfulness, carves Trikala in half; acacias, chestnuts, plane trees, and pedestrian-friendly footbridges give the town charm. The remains of an Ottoman-era mosque and an *asclepion,* the labyrinthine old quarter, and the village-like hospitality will keep you from twiddling your thumbs at the bus station.

▐ **TRANSPORTATION.** The train station (☎27 214) is at the far southern end of Asklipiou, about 700m south of Pl. Riga Fereou. Continue straight along Asklipiou; 10 blocks from the river the yellow building will come into view. **Trains** go to: Athens (Regular: 5½hr., 9am, €15.80. Express: 4½hr.; 7:40am, 2:15, 5pm; €21.10), Kalambaka (20min., 5 per day 8am-8pm, €1.60), and Larisa (3 per day 9:30am-9pm, €4). The bus station (☎73 130) is on the river's southern bank about 150m downstream of Pl. Riga Fereou, at the corner of Othonos and Garivaldi. After crossing the bridge, make a left onto Othonos and continue one block down the river. It's on your right at the corner and has **buses** to: Athens (4½hr., 6 per day 7am-8pm, €24); Ioannina (3½hr., 3 per day 9am-3:10pm, €14.50); Kalambaka (30min., 16 per day 7am-10pm, €1.80); Larisa (1¼hr., 10 per day 6:30am-8:30pm, €4.80); Pyli (30min., 10 per day 6am-9:30pm, €1.70); Thessaloniki (3¼hr., 6 per day 7:30am-8:30pm, €16); Volos (2½hr., 5 per day 7:05am-7:05pm, €11:40). **Taxis** (☎22 022) wait in Pl. Iroön Polytechniou 24hr.

▓▐ **ORIENTATION AND PRACTICAL INFORMATION.** Trikala lies 58km west of Larisa. The Letheos River divides the town roughly northwest to southeast and the two main plateias lie directly across the river from each other: **Plateia Riga Fereou** in the south and **Plateia Polytechniou** in the north. The latter is home to a charming statue of a boy perpetually relieving himself into a small pond. **Asklipiou,** Trikala's main road, runs south from Pl. Riga Fereou, where it begins as a broad pedestrian arcade. It turns into a car-laden street after **Kapodistriou,** on its way to the train station south of town. **Vyronos** and **Garivaldi** cut diagonally across Asklipiou in succession. On the north bank, **Sarafi** leads west out of Pl. Polytechniou to **Varousi,** the old Turkish quarter, and the fortress in the northwest. **Martiou** runs parallel to Sarafi, two blocks away from the river.

A **National Bank** with an **ATM** is on the northern side of Pl. Polytechniou. (Open M-F 8am-2pm.) There's also a **24hr. ATM** on Asklipiou just south of Pl. Riga Fereou. The **police station** (☎27 303) is four blocks down Asklipiou at its intersection with Kapodistriou. The 24hr. **hospital** (☎22 222) is on the main road to Kardista. There is an **OTE** on 25 Martiou (☎95 328). For **Internet** access, walk one block past Hotel Dinas on Asklipou to **The Web.** Over 80 fast terminals keep Trikala's youth connected. (€2.20 per hr. Open 24hr.) The main **post office,** Sarafi 15, provides **currency exchange** and **Poste Restante.** Walk across the bridge from Pl. Riga Fereou and turn left on Sarafi. (☎27 415. Open M-F 7:30am-2pm.) **Postal Code:** 42100.

▐▐ **ACCOMMODATIONS AND FOOD.** Over the past couple of years, some high-end stores have come to Trikala in an attempt to cash in on the shopping craze started by nearby Larisa. This change has led to an increase in accommodation prices, but you still can find the most affordable digs in town at the **Hotel Palladion ❷,** Vyronos 4, one street west of Pl. Riga Fereou. The spacious, colorful rooms have phone, sink, TV, and marble floors. (☎28 091 or 37 260. Singles €25; doubles €33; triples €39.) **Hotel Dinas ❹,** two blocks down Asklipiou, is above one of the hippest cafes in town (the vertical sign says Hotel Ntina). The bright rooms have bath, TV, and air-conditioning. (☎74 777; fax 29 490. Singles €50; doubles €70; triples €80.) Easily spottable **Hotel Achilleion ❹** is south of the main bridge on Pl. Riga Fereou. Cozy rooms with large beds and wooden furniture have TV, phone, air-conditioning, and bath. (☎28 192; fax 74 858. Breakfast included. Singles €65; doubles €80; triples €100. V.)

Xatsiperou, one block west of Pl. Polytechniou off Martinou, is a lively spot for an evening meal. Join crowds of locals at **Taverna Thea Artemis ❷,** Ypsilandou 4, three blocks north of Martinou. Located in a quiet cafe-lined alley, this taverna serves heavenly dishes in huge portions. But don't expect the Greek staff to pamper you; this gritty place can make foreigners feel like they don't belong. (☎77 533. Entrees €5.50-11. Open 11:30am-1am.) A few blocks farther south, **To Dipylo ❷** serves no-nonsense Greek dishes. (☎72 722. Entrees €6-11. Open 11am-1:30am.)

🔲🔳 **SIGHTS AND NIGHTLIFE.** Looming above Varousi are the grand stone walls and bell tower of **Fort Trikkis**, first constructed in the 4th century BC and dedicated to Artemis. The fountain-decked park and cafe in the lower half of the fort has a great view and is an ideal setting for a frappé (€2.50). The upper half contains the bell tower and a small garden.

Pl. Riga Fereou and Asklipiou are packed with cafes blasting music and serving drinks until daybreak. In the afternoons and evenings, the chairs are lined up facing the pedestrian street—prime positioning for people-watching. Head to 🔲**Deal's** on Asklipiou where the menu is designed like a popular culture magazine. Try one of their dozen coffee drinks (€4) while you listen to American and British pop tunes at this hip cafe-bar. (☎22 902. Open daily 10am-1am.)

KALAMBAKA Καλαμπάκα ☎24320

East of the North Pindhos mountain range lies small, comfortable Kalambaka. Chances are you'll stay in Kalambaka if you plan on seeing Meteora in more than one day. The tourist-friendly town remains fairly inexpensive, despite the volume of people passing through. Kalambaka's fabulously slow pace, delicious food, and high-quality budget accommodations might make you think twice about leaving.

🔲 **TRANSPORTATION.** The distinctive yellow train station (☎22 451), on the corner of Pindou and Kondyli, is one block down from the bus station. **Trains** go to Athens (4½hr.; 6:30am, 5:35pm; €20.30) and Palaiofarsalos (1hr., 11 per day 6am-10pm, €3), where you can change trains to reach Thessaloniki (3hr., 6 per day 11:18am-8:55pm, €6.20). The main bus station, Averof 2, is downhill from Pl. Dimarhiou on Rodou. (☎22 432. Open 6:15am-9pm). **Buses** go to: Athens (5hr., 7 per day 7am-6:30pm, €24) via Lamia (3hr., €9); Ioannina (3hr.; 8:50am, 3:20pm; €10.20) via Metsovo (2hr., €5.10); Patras (5hr.; Tu 10am, F 5pm, Su 3pm; €24.40.); Thessaloniki (3½hr., 4 per day 7:30am-4:15pm, €10.90); Trikala (30min., every 30min. 6:15am-10:30pm, €2). Buses bound for Kastraki (5min., every hr. 7am-11pm, €0.80) and Meteora (15min.; M-F 9am, 1:30pm; Sa-Su 8:20am, 1pm; €1) leave from in front of Pl. Dimarhiou at the foot of the large fountain. The 9am bus to Meteora allows time to see the monasteries before taking the return bus back from Grand Meteoro at 1:30pm. Most visitors, however, walk back to Kalambaka (7km downhill), visiting monasteries along the way. **Taxis** (☎22 310) congregate 24hr. on Rodou, below the town hall square.

🔳🔲 **ORIENTATION AND PRACTICAL INFORMATION.** There are two squares in Kalambaka: **Plateia Dimarhiou** (Town Hall Square) and **Plateia Riga Fereou** (Central Square). Buses depart from Pl. Dimarhiou, which has a large fountain. Standing with your back to the fountain and the Meteora cliffs, you will see **Vlachava** to the left, **Rodou** in front, and **Ioanninon**, the road to Ioannina, downhill to the right. **Patriarchou Dimitriou** goes uphill to the right, while **Trikalon** heads slightly left to sunny Pl. Riga Fereou, home to various trees, banks, and restaurants. A horde of cafes and bars, open at all hours, congregates on the pedestrian street **Dimoula**, two blocks down Trikalon from Pl. Riga Fereou. With the cliffs on your left, **Kondyli** branches off to the right at the end of Pl. Riga Fereou.

Through a well-marked gate half a block down Kondyli on the right, the **tourist office**, Kondyli and Hatzipetrou 38, provides maps, hotel listings, and monastery hours. Helpful pamphlets are available after hours in a box on the door. (☎75 306.

Open M-F 8am-3:30pm.) The kiosk by the taxi stand below Pl. Dimarhiou also has maps of Kalambaka and Meteora. The **National Bank,** Sidirodromou 1 (☎77 178), in Pl. Riga Fereou, and the **Agricultural Bank,** Ioanninon 3, near Plateia Dimarhiou, have **24hr. ATMs.** (Both open M-Th 8am-2:30pm, F 8am-2pm.) The **police,** Ioanninon 17, are a 10min. walk from the center of town. (☎76 100. Open 24hr.) They share a building with the **tourist police.** A 24hr. **health center** (☎22 222) is 1km from town, on the road to Ioannina. The **OTE** is at Ioanninon 9; from the main plateia with your back to the cliffs, take a right. (☎22 121. Open M-F 7:30am-2:30pm.) **Arena,** Dimola 21, a block down Dimoula off Trikalon, has the cheapest **Internet** access in town on fast terminals. (☎77 999. €2 per hr. Open 10am-7am.) **Ouranio Toxo,** Trikalon 100, on the right at Trikalon's entrance to Pl. Riga Fereou, has five terminals and a bar. (☎24 688. €3 per hr. Frappés €1.80. Beer €2. Open 10am-2am.) The **post office,** Trikalon 23, between the two plateias, has **Poste Restante.** (☎22 467. Open M-F 7:30am-2pm.) **Postal Code:** 42200.

 ACCOMMODATIONS AND CAMPING. Hawks offering **domatia** here are infamous for luring travelers with promises of good prices, then hitting them with exorbitant surcharges; make sure you know the details before agreeing to anything. The accommodations with the best views, comfort, and hospitality are in the quiet, high-rise-free Old Town near the foot trail to Meteora. In the Old Town at the base of Meteora, ❧**Alsos House ❸,** Kanari 5, has spacious rooms with bath, air-conditioning, and a balcony with breathtaking views of Meteora. If you follow Vlachava from Plateia Dimarhiou until it ends, Alsos will be on your left. Amiable English-speaking proprietor Yiannis will pick guests up from the bus or train station, take them for walks on the hidden paths once used by monks, and enlighten them with deep conversation. (☎24 097; www.alsoshouse.gr. Shared kitchen. Breakfast included. Free Wi-Fi. Reservations recommended. Singles €30; doubles €40-50; triples €60; 2-room apartment with kitchen €70-80. Discounts for students. MC/V.) Farther up the road at the foot of the path that ascends the mountains, **Koka Roka ❷,** Kanari 21, rents large rooms and aims to satisfy a backpacker's every need. Always ready to chat and offer advice, Aussie-accented Arthur serves his guests and passersby a tasty meal every night. (☎24 554; kokaroka@yahoo.com. Breakfast €2. Laundry €10. Internet €3 per hr. Reception 24hr. Singles €20; doubles €35-40; triples €50-60.) If you're looking for a more luxurious option, go one house down from Alsos to **Elena Rooms ❹,** Kanari 3, which shares the same dazzling view. Recently renovated rooms have fireplace, air-conditioning, TV, free Internet access, and most importantly for weary backpackers, a shower equipped with a massage and sauna system. (☎77 789; www.elenaguest-house.gr. Breakfast €5. Reception 24hr. Singles €40; doubles €50; triples €60; quads €70.) A number of worthy campsites line the roads around Kalambaka and Kastraki. **Vrachos Camping ❶,** 1km out of town toward Kastraki and the monasteries, is the most popular and best maintained of the area's campsites, with a pool, restaurant, and great views. (☎22 293. Laundry €5. €6 per person, €3 per tent, €1 per car. Caravans with kitchen and bath €9. 10% discount for *Let's Go* readers.)

TIP **DOMATIA DILEMMA.** It's true that prices can be flexible when bargaining for domatia. Keep in mind, however, that if you're too stingy in negotiations, you may be trading away your host's hospitality for a few measly euro.

⊡ FOOD. Right in the center of town, ❧**Taverna Paramithy ❷** ("Fairy Tale Tavern"), Dimitriou 14, has cheap and delicious traditional cuisine. Meat and fish dishes are slow-cooked to perfection. (☎24 441. Entrees €4-8. Open daily 11am-midnight. Cash only.) Conversation is lively and constant at ❧ **Koka Roka Taverna ❷,** Kanari 21, inside its namesake hotel near the beginning of the Meteora footpath. The souvlaki and lamb chops have been described in the restaurant's guest book as a "religious experience." Koka Roka is also the cheapest place to enjoy a beer, with large €1.50 bottles. (☎24 554. Entrees €4-8. Open 8am-1am.) Diners at **Arhondariki ❷**, Trikalon 9, at the left end of Pl. Riga Fereou when facing the cliffs, are treated to dishes like the signature moussaka (€6), cooked with pure olive oil. Though the restaurant's yellow theme is banana-like, the food is fantastic and Sotiris, the owner, is a delight. (☎22 449. Entrees €4-8. Open noon-midnight.) To save some cash or to slap together a picnic for a day at the monasteries, visit the 24hr. **supermarket** just off Trikalon on Dimoula or the various **fruit stands** on Vlachava. Each Friday, Vlachava and its main cross street, Kondyli, turn into a full-scale **marketplace** (open 7am-3pm), selling fresh produce and household goods.

🎭🎟 **SIGHTS AND NIGHTLIFE.** Kalambaka's foremost attraction is the Byzantine **Church of the Assumption of the Virgin.** Follow signs in the plateia; after several blocks that wind up to the foot of the slopes, you'll spy its stone bell tower. The church was built in the 7th century atop a Classical temple whose pagan mosaics now are entombed beneath the floor. Though the main structure was remodeled in 1573, the original baptism basin remains at the entrance. (Open 8am-1pm and 4-9pm. €1.50. Modest dress required.) Visitors wondering about all those gorgeous yet rigidly standardized gilded icons can visit the operating **Workshop of Dimitris Zervopoulos,** across from Camping Kalambaka 1km down the road to Trikala. While sipping complimentary ouzo or lemonade, you can watch monks as they paint the world's next generation of icons in this heavenly—but heavily touristed—factory. During free tours, pleasant English-speaking guides explain production methods and even let you try applying 18-karat gold leaf to the unfinished icons. (☎75 466. Open daily 9am-8pm.) In late July, the town honors its patron saint with a celebration complete with music, dance, and food. Nearby Kastraki holds a three-day **wine festival** with free samples in late August.

Nightlife centers on Trikalon, a street south of Pl. Riga Fereou, plastered with neon signs and fast-food joints. At traditional *ouzeri* **Plaka**, on Trikalon just below Pl. Riga Fereou, the sound of live *bouzouki* and laughter carries to the nearby Meteora cliffs. (Mixed drinks €4-6. Open 6pm-3am.) The fountain-lined pedestrian walkway of Dimoula hosts a trendier scene, with lively bars that are virtually indistinguishable from one another. From Pl. Riga Fereou, continue on Trikalon toward Trikala; Dimoula is the second right leading downhill.

METEORA Μετέορα

The monastic community of Meteora (meh-TEH-o-rah), whose name means "hanging in the air" or "in suspense," rests atop awe-inspiring peaks that ascend to the sky. Believed to have been inhabited by hermits as early as the 11th century, the summits were chosen as the location of a series of 21 gravity-defying, frescoed Byzantine monasteries in the 14th century. Six of the monasteries are still in use and are open to the public; the largest and most popular are Grand Meteoro and Varlaam. The other four monasteries are less celebrated, meaning they are refreshingly more quiet, charming, and intimate. Still, Meteora is hardly an undiscovered treasure, and gift shops and tourists are as common as the frescoes.

🚌🛈 **TRANSPORTATION AND PRACTICAL INFORMATION**

Buses leave for Meteora from the Kalambaka fountain. (15min.; M-F 9am, 1:20pm; Sa-Su 8:30am, 1pm; €1.) Buy tickets on board. You also can take a **taxi** (around €5) from Kalambaka. Most monasteries close one day per week. Though most monasteries run on a 9am-5pm schedule, opening and closing hours vary from monastery to monastery and change often; consult the tourist office in Kalambaka for times. Even if a monastery is closed, it is still worth checking out, as the outside is often as spectacular as the interior. Photography is forbidden inside, and modest dress is required. Most of the monasteries close midday, so many people decide to pack picnics. (€2 per monastery, under 12 free.)

WALKING THE MONASTERIES

The origins of the settlements on the Meteora rocks are unknown: one story claims that the first recluse was **Barnabas,** a monk who founded the *skite* (a small, remote monastic cell) of the Holy Ghost in the mid-10th century. By the 11th century, hermits and ascetics followed his example, moving to the pinnacles and crevices of Meteora and worshipping in a church dedicated to the **Theotokos** (Mother of God), which still can be seen below the Ag. Nikolaos monastery. As persecution at the hands of Turkish and Frankish marauders increased in the 12th century, Orthodox Christians fled to the summits of these impregnable columns of rock. In 1344, the region's first monastic community was founded when the monk **Athanasios,** his spiritual father **Gregorios,** and 14 fellow monks began to build Grand Meteoro. Athanasios was a well-educated monk whose journeys brought him to Constantinople, Crete, and finally Mt. Athos, from which he fled to avoid Turkish invasions. He occupied his time weaving baskets in a nearby cave, and referred to women as "the sling" (that vault the stones of sin into men's hearts) or as "the affliction" (addicting men to the sinful pleasures of the flesh). He displayed this penchant for description slightly more constructively when he gave Meteora its name. Later, the Greek-Serbian king of Thessaly and Epirus, Ioannis Versis Angelos Komininos Palaeologos, traded regal comforts for Meteora's rugged rocks and built many of its later monasteries. When the Ottomans ruled most of Greece, Meteora served as an outpost of Christianity. In the 16th century, it grew into a community of 21 monasteries, which amassed large libraries of both religious and secular books and created dazzling icons and frescoes. However, when donations tapered off in the late 1700s and the popularity of monastic life waned, many of these manuscripts and books were sold for a fraction of their actual worth. Small brotherhoods still exist at Grand Meteoro, Varlaam, Agia Triada, and Agios Nikolaos, while Agios Stephanos and Roussanou are now convents.

The first ascetics scaled Meteora's cliffs by wedging timbers into the rock crevices to build small platforms; traces of these steps still can be seen in the walls. After the monasteries were completed, visitors arrived by means of extremely long rope ladders. Those who were too weak or too timid to climb were hoisted up in baskets. Once these devices were pulled up, though, the summits became inaccessible. Today, motorized winches have replaced the rope-spool cranes (though the old pulleys are still visible at each monastery), and only provisions are yanked up by rope. In 1922, in the ultimate facilitation of a quicker rise to heaven, bridges were built between the pillars, and steps were carved into the rocks.

Begin your tour of Meteora at Grand Meteoro, the largest and most famous monastery and the location of the bus stop. You then can work your way down through its neighbors, Varlaam, Roussanou, and Ag. Nikolaos. A sign on the highway between Varlaam and Roussanou marked "Ag. Triada" points into the bush to a short trail to Triada (20min.). The last monastery, Ag. Stephanos, is about 800m from Ag. Triada. Though it's probably a good idea to get a regional map before leaving Kalambaka, the monasteries are all within walking distance and are connected by a single road. To head back down to Kalambaka from Ag. Triada, walk as if you were to enter the monastery but instead take the right opening downhill. With Ag. Triada to your back, take the narrow, paved road on

THE TOOTH FAIRY'S NIGHTMARE

The Italians have their gelato, and the French their fancy cheeses, but when it comes to decadent, caloric goodness, they've got nothing on the rich *glykismata* (desserts) of Greek cuisine.

Greek pastries are traditionally comprised of some combination of fresh honey, chopped nuts, and phyllo dough—a light, flaky-thin crust made from layers of butter. *Kadaife*, resembling an overgrown Kellogg's® Mini-Wheat, is a fine example of this blessed union: shredded wheat and phyllo crammed with nuts, honey, and cinnamon. *Galactobourico* is a slight variation on the rule, as the honey-draped pastry is filled with a dense egg custard rather than a nut mixture. Coffee lovers should find a spot next to their *kafe* for *karidopeta*, a dark, moist nut cake similar in consistency to a coffee or carrot cake and topped with a syrup coating. *Loukou-mathes*, warm, deep-fried balls of dough, are the Greek equivalent of donuts, though they are usually eaten as an afternoon snack rather than a breakfast food. The celebrated granddaddy of all Greek *glykismata*, is, of course, baklava, comprising layer upon layer of phyllo filled with nuts, spices, and sticky honey syrup.

Most bakeries will offer to box your pastry to go, making it easy to enjoy it in a plateia whose public water fountains make cleaning up nice and convenient.

the left that curves around. Once Ag. Triada is on your left, you'll be able to pick up the main road.

Before heading out, stop by Alsos Rooms to speak with Yiannis; he is happy to provide his accurate, handwritten hiking map. The general advice given to tourists, however, is to stay on the roads at all times. If possible, split the Meteora hikes between two days, covering the eastern monasteries one day and the western ones another. Doing the entire circuit in a day will take 6-8 hr. All monasteries have water fountains, but always bring your own bottle.

GRAND METEORO. The **Monastery of the Transfiguration**, known as "Grand Meteoro" (Μεγάλου Μετέορου), is the site at which St. Athanasios began his imitation of the community at Mt. Athos in the 14th century. Looming 475m above Thessaly's plain, the complex, known in its entirety as **Platys Lithos**, reached its peak in the 16th century, when it was visited by the reigning patriarch and accorded the same privileges as the autonomous Mt. Athos. Around this time, the **Church of the Transfiguration** was built and was capped by an exalted dome with a *pantokrator* (a central image of Christ). The *katholikon* (nave) stands 24m high, and is constructed in Byzantine style with a 12-sided dome. Murals created by the mid-16th century Cretan painter Theophanes Bathas-Strelitzas cover the walls. If you manage to get past all of the tourists you will find a former carpenter's workshop, a small, haunting catacomb, the old kitchen, and a museum. The museum's collections of early printed texts by Plato and Aristotle and old gospel parchments attest to the monastery's past preeminence as an intellectual center. (☎22 278. Open M and W-Sa 9am-5pm. €2.)

VARLAAM. Varlaam, the second-largest monastery, is about 800m downhill from Grand Meteoro. The complex was founded in the 14th century by one of Athanasios's contemporaries who, in a display of true humility, named it after himself. The *katholikon*'s 16th-century frescoes depict hermits, martyrs, an apocalyptic sea serpent swallowing doomed sinners, and St. Sisoes looking pitifully upon Alexander the Great's skeleton. The monastery's **library** contains 290 manuscripts, including a miniature Bible from AD 959 that belonged to Emperor Constantine Porfyrogenitos. (☎22 277. Open M-W and F-Su 9am-2pm and 3:20-5pm. €2.)

ROUSSANOU. Bear right at the fork to reach Roussanou. Visible from most of the valley, it is one of Meteora's most spectacularly situated monasteries. With steep sides, three of which overlook the drop to the valley below, Roussanou seems to sprout from the steep cliff as a natural continuation of the boulders.

Its interior, which includes a portrait of Constantine the Great, can't match the heavenly exterior, accessible even to those with no ticket. Still, the *katholikon*, illuminated by light that streams through stained glass, is stunning. Roussanou proudly housed Greek refugees fleeing the Turks in 1757 and 1897; today it is home to an order of nuns. Though the crowds of tourists may make them difficult to see, the building contains fantastically strange frescoes of winged dragons, magical whales, and human-sized snakes. (☎ 22 649. Open daily 9am-6pm. €2.)

AGIOS NIKOLAOS. Farther down the road is the 16th-century monastery of Agios Nikolaos Anapafsas, only 2.5km from Kastraki. Built on the ruins of an older monastery, it is situated on the summit of a very narrow boulder. Construction constraints meant that Agios Nikolaos had to be built vertically rather than horizontally, making it the second-tallest monastery, next to Grand Meteoro. Standing at the top of the bell tower gives the impression that you're hanging in mid-air over mind-boggling depths. (☎ 22 375. Open M-Th and Sa-Su 9am-3:30pm. €2.)

AGIA TRIADA. On the metal bridge into Roussanou, face away from the monastery, and take the (mostly) paved path uphill on the right. When it hits the road, bear right and continue to find Agia Triada; movie buffs will recognize it from the James Bond flick *For Your Eyes Only*. As you head down the stairs that lead to the bathroom, enjoy the panoramic view of the Pindos Mountains in the distance with Kalambaka's traditional red-roofed houses immedietely below. Ambitious monk Dometius built the monastery in 1438, but many of the **wall paintings** weren't added until the 18th century. Unfortunately, most of the monastery's prized manuscripts and heirlooms were lost in WWII. (☎ 22 220. Open M-W and F-Su 9am-5pm. €2.)

AGIOS STEPHANOS. Originally a convent, Agios Stephanos became a monastery in the early 15th century. Today it is once again home to an active community of nuns. Of its two churches, the newer **Agios Haralambos,** built in 1798, is the more impressive. The older church, **Protomartia Stephanou,** built in 1350, is beginning to show the wear of its age, with faded frescoes and cracked walls. The **museum** displays icons, manuscripts, liturgical vestments, and crosses. Its intricate wooden *iconostasis* is carved into figures of birds, animals, and people. The gargoyle fountain at the top is a great place to fill up a water bottle, as the Ag. Stephanos's proximity to a spring makes the water here the purest and coldest on Meteora. (☎ 22 279. Open Tu-Su 9am-2pm and 3:30-6pm. €2.)

NORTHERN GREECE

Northern Greece does not experience the same mass tourism from which many other regions of the nation benefit. As you move inland, far from the cities and ever-popular beaches, the towns grow smaller, more self-contained, and more isolated from modern-day influences. Consisting of three provinces—Thrace, Macedonia, and Epirus—the region is starkly more Balkan than the remainder of Greece. With its proximity to and influence from the states of Albania, the Former Yugoslavian Republic Of Macedonia (FYROM), Bulgaria, and Turkey, tension from past disputes with both the Balkans and Turkey still hangs in the air. Thrace, the easternmost province, has a diverse population that includes a large number of Turkish Muslims and Eastern Orthodox immigrants whose influence is apparent in Thrace's architecture, markets, and cuisine. Macedonia is historically part of a much larger Greek province that extends into present-day Albania, FYROM, and Bulgaria, and has been a homeland of powerhouses ranging from antiquity's Alexander the Great to current urban giant Thessaloniki. Epirus, in the west, prospered under the imperial command of Ali Pasha in the early 19th century, but currently is best known as a hiker's haven with strikingly beautiful terrain. For travelers seeking distance from Athens and the islands, Northern Greece offers an idyllic escape, ripe with Byzantine heritage, countless traditional villages, and a landscape that soars from the depths of the Vikos Gorge up to the heights of Mt. Olympus, and back over the serenity of the Prespa Lakes. Connected ethnically and historically to its Balkan neighbors, the north is where the modern, multicultural Greek state surfaces.

SUGGESTED ITINERARIES: NORTHERN GREECE

FIVE DAYS Base your trip in vibrant, cosmopolitan **Thessaloniki** (p. 266), whose prominent minarets and fortresses recall centuries of Turkish rule. See what remains of the region's ancient past as the center of Alexander the Great's Macedonian empire at the sites of **Vergina** (p. 278), **Pella** (p. 279), and **Dion** (p. 287).

TWO WEEKS After getting to know Thessaloniki (p. 266), leave the city life behind for the chilly shores and sparsely populated villages of the **Prespa Lakes** (p. 297). As you travel southwest, take breaks to linger in the hamlets of **Zagorohoria** (p. 261) before hiking the super-steep **Vikos Gorge** (p. 262).

EPIRUS Ηπειρος

This mountainous region is world-famous for its beautiful trails, peaks, and reflecting lakes, and it draws international hikers for some of Greece's best outdoor treks. Those who enjoy exhilarating fresh air and quality trails will delight in the beauty of the Pindos Mountains region. The postcard-worthy towns and beaches of Parga see their share of tourism, but the Zagorohoria villages near the Vikos Gorge have retained a sense of timelessness, despite a recent influx of visitors. Epirus links itself to a living past—the old dialect of Vlach, branched off from

Northern Greece

Latin, still is spoken in some of the towns, and the preserved mosques of the dynamic 19th-century ruler Ali Pasha still grace the city of Ioannina.

IGOUMENITSA Ηγουμενίτσα ☎ 26650

A connection point between Italy and Greece, Igoumenitsa (ee-goo-men-IT-sa) is often a traveler's first or last glimpse of the Greek mainland. The town's enormous port, the third-largest in Greece, sends boats to four cities in Italy and to Corfu. Tourist agencies seem to outnumber people, harried backpackers scramble in search of their ships, and it appears as if life never stands still in this small, somewhat unsettling town.

⌁ TRANSPORTATION. Igoumenitsa's long **port** has 4 subdivisions from which **ferries** leave. The Old Port, on the waterfront's northern edge (follow the signs), mostly sends boats to Italy. Corfu Port is south of the Old Port. Beyond Corfu Port is the New Port, whose boats go to both Italy and Corfu. The Fourth Port, at the southernmost point of the harbor, sends ships to Italy. Tickets to Corfu (1¼hr.; 5 per day 4am-10pm; €6.50, students €3.20, children €2.60) can be purchased at Corfu Port in one of several white kiosks. They also can be bought on the ferries, but without discounts. For tickets to Italy, shop around at the waterfront agencies, as some have student rates and some accept Eurail and InterRail passes; bargain before you buy. Destinations include: Ancona (14hr., 11:30pm, €53-74); Bari (9hr.; 9pm, midnight; €27-40); Brindisi (7hr.; 1:30, 7:30am, €28-35); Venice (19hr., 10am, €54-74). Most boats depart before noon or late in the evening. Contact **Apeiros Travel,** Ethnikis Antistasis 20A, across from the entrance to the Old Port, for further information about ferry tickets. (☎ 26 944; www.aperios.gr. Open 8am-4pm and 6-11pm.) To reach the bus station, Kyprou 29 (☎ 22 309), from the ports, walk north along the waterfront to 23 Fevruariou, turn right, then take a left two blocks later on Kyprou. Open 5:30am-8:30pm. The ticket office is behind a cafe on the left, marked with a blue-and-white KTEL sign. **Buses** run to: Athens (7hr., 4 per day 7:30am-8:30pm, €37); Ioannina (2hr., 8 per day 6:30am-8pm, €8.20); Parga (1hr., 4 per day 6am-5:15pm, €4.50); Preveza (2hr.; 11:45am, 3:30pm; €8.60); Thessaloniki (8hr., 10:30am, €34). **Taxis** (☎ 25 000) wait on Eth. Antistasis, especially by Corfu Port, 24hr. For car rentals, try **Europcar,** Pargas 5, facing the police station between the Old Port and Corfu Port. (☎ 23 477. From €45 per day.)

⌁⌁ ORIENTATION AND PRACTICAL INFORMATION. Igoumenitsa is on the westernmost corner of mainland Greece, about 20km from the Albanian border. **Ethnikis Antistasis,** which becomes **Agion Apostolon** in front of Corfu Port, runs along the waterfront and overflows with travel agencies and banks. To the north, after it is divided by a lane barrier, the inland side of the street is bordered by an array of cafes and bars that mark it as the nightlife district. Igoumenitsa's main shopping area is on **Lamprari Grigariou,** the first pedestrian street parallel to the waterfront. To reach the central plateia, walk two blocks inland on **Eleftheriou Venizelou,** which begins across from the Old Port.

The **tourist office,** at the entrance to the Old Port, helps with transportation and accommodations and supplies free maps. (☎ 22 227. Open daily 8am-2pm.) A **National Bank,** Eth. Antistasis 20 (☎ 22 415; open M-Th 8am-2:30pm, F 8am-2pm), across the road from the Old Port, is in a string of banks that all **exchange currency** and have **ATMs.** The 24hr. **police station,** Ag. Apostolon 5 (☎ 22 100), on the continuation of Eth. Antistasis, is across from Corfu Port. The **tourist police** are in the same building. (☎ 29 647. Open 8:30am-1:30pm.) The **port police** are in a Corfu Port booth, near customs and passport control. The 24hr. **medical center,** Ag. Apostolon 7 (☎ 24 420), next door to the police station, offers basic care. They can help you reach the **hospital** (☎ 26640 22 203), 15min. away in Filiates. The **OTE,** Grigariou Labraki 35, is at pedestrian Grigariou's end. (☎ 23 499. Open M and W 7:30am-3pm, Tu and Th-F 7:30am-9pm, Sa 8am-2:30pm.) **All**

Time Cafe, Dagli 18, off Eth. Antistasis, about 300m from Alekos, has **Internet** access (€2.50 per hr.) and serves drinks and coffee (€2-5). (☎210 80. Open 9am-1am.) The **post office,** Tzavelenas 2, 1km north along the waterfront on the corner of a playground, accepts **Poste Restante.** (☎46 100. Open 7:30am-2pm.) **Postal Code:** 46100.

▐▌ ACCOMMODATIONS AND FOOD. Accommodations in Igoumenitsa are surprisingly underdeveloped given the volume of travelers that pass through the city. Overlooking the Old Port, **Jolly Hotel ❹,** Eth. Antistasis 14, has spacious, carpeted rooms and marble-tiled hallways. All of the mauve- and yellow-walled rooms have bath, air-conditioning, TV, and phone; some have a balcony with a view of the harbor. (☎23 971; www.jolly.50megs.com. Breakfast included. Reception 24hr. Singles €48; doubles €70; triples with fridge €85. MC/V.) With your back to Corfu Port, look left for the fluorescent lights of **Hotel Oscar ❸,** Ag. Apostolon 149. Though it is a bit run-down, Oscar is the best of the budget accommodations in the city. The rooms are simple, with marble floors and air-conditioning. (☎23 338. Reception 24hr. Singles €30; doubles €40; triples €50.) Look for **Hotel Egnatia ❸,** Eleftherias 2, in the central plateia's far right corner. Simple, small rooms have tile floor, balcony, bath, TV, phone, and air-conditioning. To avoid being woken up by morning traffic, ask for a room facing the quiet wooded area behind the hotel. Tell the receptionist what time you plan on returning if you don't want to be locked out. (☎23 455. Singles €31; doubles €44; triples €53; quads €61.)

The best of the city's restaurants are on the northern edge of the waterfront, past the ports. Dozens of **bakeries** and **markets** line the pedestrian street just inland from the harbor. **Alekos ❷,** Eth. Antistasis 84, north of the ports, specializes in fish caught in the harbor waters. The view of the port and large portions leave customers satisfied. (☎23 708. Entrees €4-7. Open 9am-12:30am.) **Mykonos ❷,** Eth. Antistasis 80, two blocks before Alekos toward the ports, has a vine-covered patio full of loquacious Greeks. Grilled octopus (€8.50) is the restaurant's specialty; the multilingual menu also includes pizza, pasta, Greek mainstays, and a few fish specialties. (☎27 567. Entrees €4-10. Open noon-midnight.) **Salonikios ❶,** Pargas 5, in front of the police station, is a simple bakery with a limited but delicious menu. (☎27 605. *Bougatsa* €1.80. Open daily 8am-9pm.

◨▐ ENTERTAINMENT AND NIGHTLIFE. Igoumenitsa's bland nightlife centers on a strip of bars along the waterfront. An open-air **cinema** next to Taverna Alekos shows American films in the summer. (shows 9:30, 11:15pm; €5). At **Privilege** (☎23 505) and **Envi,** a few doors down from Taverna Alekos, young tourists waiting for their ferries at cafe tables are entertained by American and Greek tunes on the weekends. After midnight, the crowd is almost entirely Greek. (Beer €2.50. Mixed drinks €4. Open until 5am.) A short distance from the city, dance clubs **Soho** and **Ostria** attract a trendy local crowd peppered with stranded tourists. (Beer €2. Mixed drinks €5-6. Cover €8; includes 1 drink.) Buses (€1) run every hour from the center of town until midnight. To return later, catch a taxi (€5).

PARGA Πάργα
☎ 26840

Parga's port on the Ionian Sea, currently the seat of a respectable tourism industry, was historically the source of great hardship for Pargians. The port was occupied almost continuously from the Mycenaean period until its absorption into the modern Greek state in 1913. Its brief stints of independence were aided by protection from the Venetians and, later, the French. The otherwise dreary 2000-person village springs to life in the summer, and though the tourist-centered nature of the town can be somewhat overwhelming, the long stretches of light beaches and narrow, hilly streets are nice enough to attract a sun-seeking traveler to Parga.

▐ TRANSPORTATION

The bus station (☎31 218) is a booth next to the Chinese (*Kineziko*) restaurant at the top of Sp. Livada. **Buses** run to: Athens (9hr., 3 per day 7am-5:30pm, €35); Igoumenitsa (1¼hr., 4 per day 7:15am-6:30pm, €4.40); Preveza (1½hr., 5 per day 7am-9:15pm, €6); Thessaloniki (9½hr., 7am, €39). **Ferries** head to Corfu Town (3hr., Th 8:30am, €35). **Taxis** (☎32 855) wait in front of the OTE and can be called 24hr.

▣ ▐ ORIENTATION AND PRACTICAL INFORMATION

The Norman Castle divides Parga's two beaches, **Valtos** and **Krioneri**, and most of the city is located on southern Krioneri's side. The main waterfront road has three names: from west to east, they are **Gregoriou Labraki, Anexartisias,** and **Agiou Athanassiou.** Walking toward Krioneri beach, which runs alongside Athanassiou, the road forks just before the sand begins; the uphill branch is **Riga Fereou.** With your back to the dock, the street heading inland is **Alex Baga,** which goes uphill to most of Parga's municipal buildings. Al. Baga meets **Spyrou Livada** at the town's main intersection, by the OTE. Turning right on Sp. Livada takes you up to the highway and bus stop. Parallel to the waterfront, **Vasila** leads to **Abensberg,** which ascends to the **Venetian castle** at the far southwestern corner of town. From here, a stone path goes down the other side to Valtos beach. Waterfront souvenir shops sell maps of Parga (€4) at the end of Anexartisias.

Tourist Office: There is no official tourist office in Parga, but private **tourist agencies** that pack the streets around the waterfront can help you find rooms, arrange daytrips, or rent a boat or car. **ITS,** Sp. Livada 4 (☎31 833), is 20m down the hill from the bus stop. The friendly, English-speaking staff has English newspapers, provides information about the area, arranges excursions, and **exchanges money.** Open daily 9am-10pm.

Budget Travel: Ephira Travel, Vassila 27 (☎31 525), in the heart of the old town. Helps with daily excursions and gives advice about the surrounding areas.

Bank: National Bank, Livada 9 (☎31 222). From the sea, walk 2 blocks left of the OTE on Sp. Livada. **24hr. ATM.** Open M-Th 8am-2:30pm, F 8am-2pm.

Police: Baga 18. With the OTE on your left and the shore behind you, it's straight ahead on your left. Has a helpful tourist bureau. Open 24hr. In **emergencies,** call the **port police,** Labraki 12 (☎31 227), in the harbor. Open 24hr.

Pharmacy: Lenas Dimitrious Pharmacy, Sp. Livada 6 (☎31 195), at the intersection of Sp. Livada and Baga, 2 doors down from ITS. Open M-F 8:30am-2pm and 6-9pm.

Medical Services: Livada 71 (☎31 233), about 600m down Livada. Open 24hr.

Telephones: OTE, Baga 7 (☎31 699), at the intersection of Sp. Livada and Baga. Open M-F 8am-1pm and 4-9pm.

Internet Access: Flamingo, Baga 12 (☎32 207), 2 doors down from the police station toward Sp. Livada. €3 per hr. Open daily 8am-2am. **Net Zone,** R. Fereou 6 (☎32 895), near the fork of Fereou and the waterfront walkway. €3 per hr. Open daily 11pm-1am.

Post Office: ☎31 295. On the first fl. of the police station building. Open M-F 7:30am-2pm. **Postal Code:** 48060.

▐ ▐ ACCOMMODATIONS AND CAMPING

Parga's hotels can be expensive, and prices spike in July and August by about 30%. **Domatia** (€25-35) cluster near the highway, around the southern end of the town, and at the top of the hill in the small street leading up to the castle. Some travelers on a tight budget choose to camp on nearby beaches, but those who want a shower stick to campsites.

San Nectarios Hotel, Ag. Marinas 2 (☎31 150). Walking toward the main road from the small bus kiosk, the hotel is straight ahead. The staff is helpful and willing to help you plan your stay. Rooms have TV, A/C, and bath. Wi-Fi €3 per hr. Reception 24hr. Singles €35-55; doubles €45-65, triples €55-75. ❸

Kostas and Martha Christou, Patatokou 6 (☎31 942), just below the entrance to the fortress, above a small bakery in a mustard-yellow building. A 5min. walk from the shores of Valtos beach, 6 clean, small, and simple rooms have wood furniture, bath, and balcony. The entire city and shoreline are visible from the balconies of the rooms that face the city. Shared kitchen. Reservations recommended at least 1 month in advance. Rooms for up to 3 €25. ❷

Hotel Galini (☎31 581). Walk down from the bus stop on Sp. Livada. After about 60m, an orchard with a walkway to will be to the right. Galini is at the end of the walkway. The proprietor, Mr. Drakos, who only speaks German and bits of English, rents quiet rooms with A/C, balcony, bath, and phone. Breakfast €4. Doubles €38-50; triples €46-60. ❹

Camping Valtos (☎31 287; www.campingvaltos.gr.). Close to both town and Valtos beach; follow the signs to Valtos and you will see it right behind the Tango Club. Covered with mulberry trees, the clean site features a restaurant, mini-mart, bar, laundry (wash €5 per load), and showers. Reception 24hr., but gates close to cars at midnight. €5 per person, €7 per large tent, €5 per small tent, €3 per car. Electricity €4.50. ❶

◖ FOOD

Even in high season when the port of Parga fills up with tourists, food isn't too pricey. Along the waterfront, some tavernas overcharge, but simply taking a look at the menu beforehand will prevent unnecessary splurges. Most waterfront tavernas, regardless of their price, serve high-quality, authentic food.

▨ Kastro Entasis, Abensberg 37 (☎31 119), just below the entrance to the fortress. From sweeping views and soft Greek music to palm trees, a fountain, and superb food, Kastro Entasis has it all. Achilles, the owner, swears by his pork fillet (€14), which comes stuffed with two kinds of cheese, mushrooms, and peppers. Entrees €8.50-15.50. ❸

Kontouni Tavern (☎32 715), in an alley beside Ag. Demetrius Square. Local delicacies such as meatballs with red sauce (€6) are served at this hidden gem. Open daily 11am-midnight. ❷

Rudis, Anexartisias 8-12 (☎31 693), across from the dock. This swanky, peach-colored restaurant serves creative Greek and Italian cuisine at tables on its balcony overlooking the island. Entrees €8.50-18. ❹

To Souli, Anexartisias 16 (☎31 658), a few doors beyond the ferry dock as you head toward Krioneri beach. The food served here is as Greek as it gets. Entrees €7-9. Fish €35 per kg. Open noon-midnight. ❷

♫ ◖ ENTERTAINMENT AND NIGHTLIFE

Despite the inordinate number of nightclubs and cafe-bars in this town, there aren't that many local partiers. At night, crowds of inebriated northern Europeans fill Parga's many waterfront bars and cafes. The population changes around midnight, when the older crowd heads to bed and the younger generation comes out to play. In the summer, clubs stay open until 4am on weekdays and at least 6am on weekends; in the winter, call in advance to find out.

🐾 **Blue Bar,** Abensberg 21 (☎32 067), on the road leading to the castle. This bar is aptly named: everything from the fans to the ash trays to the bartenders' hair is blue. This hip hangout with one of the best views of the port offers 120 mixed drinks, 42 of which were invented at the bar. The Happy Company (€24), serving 4-6 people, comes in a massive 5kg marble flower vase. Open daily 6pm-3am.

Tango Club (☎31 252), at the far end of Valtos beach. A student crowd frequents the bar and restaurant at this popular daytime party spot, while families with children fill the club's swimming pool. People still talk about the summer that owner Lefteris organized beach soccer games starring the Greek national team. Drinks €6. Open daily 9am-2am.

Factory, Themistokli 10 (☎32 625). This funky spot, splashed with bright colors, has been increasing in popularity for the past couple of years. The DJ spins Greek pop, house, and rock over furniture that was originally factory machinery. Beer €4. Mixed drinks €5. Open M-Th and Su midnight-4am, F-Sa midnight-8am.

Rendezvous (☎32 032), at the top of Kanali above Valtos beach. This locally popular, open-air *bouzouki* club opens July 10. Coffee €2. Drinks €4. Open daily 6pm-2am.

👁 ⚓ SIGHTS AND BEACHES

The **kastro** sits high on Parga's rocky headland. Built by the Normans, who later abandoned the city, the castle fell under the control of the Venetians from 1401 to 1797. In its glory days, the massive structure held 500 homes and 5000 Pargians. A surprising number of walls still stand, including the old barracks at the entrance, which are now the home of a small cafe. The cannons that lined the top, however, long since have fallen and are strewn about the enclosure. Sitting high above the town, the castle is a perfect spot to escape the sun and tourists and affords a stunning bird's eye view of Valtos beach. Have coffee at the romantic, newly renovated **Cafe Inside the Castle ❶.** Owner Gregoris will be happy to give you a history of the castle and might even have a drink with you in this quiet establishment. (☎31 150. Beer €2.50. Open 9am-1am.) Feel free to picnic on your own, as the shady pine and olive trees provide a break from the summer heat. Five minutes from the water, follow Abensberg up the hill to the castle spiked gates.

Krioneri, the closest beach to Parga's waterfront, just below Ag. Athanasiou, is also the most popular, attracting tons of daytime traffic. Paddleboats (€11 per hr.) or motorboats (€15 per hr.) are available for travelers who want to make the 100m journey to the **Island of Panagia.** From the island's small beach, a hike past the **spring** and the small **Church of the Panagia** takes you to remains of Napoleonic fortifications. One building has the telltale inscription "De la Patrie 1808." On the other side of the island is a quiet pinnacle with views of Paxi and Antipaxi. The beach at **Paleo Krioneri,** a 5min. walk around the rocks at the end of Krioneri, is a bit more secluded. At **Valtos beach,** on the other side of the castle, the crescent of sole-tickling pebbles turns to sand. From the end of Valtos, a trail leads past a *neromylos* (water mill) to **Ali Pasha's castle** on the top of the cliff, with views of the Ionians. Boats from the **Parga Mariners** that leave from the main dock in front of Caravel travel to smaller beaches, including cafe-lined **Lichnos** (2km), accessible by car or taxi boat (€4 round-trip). Though a boat no longer goes to secluded **Pogo,** ask the captain of the Lichnos boat to let you off there and make arrangements to have him or her pick you up on the way back.

Tour companies along the waterfront and on the ferry dock book **excursions.** The 2hr. trips to uninhabited Antipaxi (daily 10am, €15) are most popular, though others that end up at Antipaxi also stop at its occupied neighbor Paxi and several inner island caves (daily 10am, €25). Summer-only voyages sail to the swampy **River Acheron,** the mythical gateway to the Underworld, and to **Necromanteion** (the Oracle of the Dead). It's a 1hr. trip (€9) past cliffs, caves, and coves, then up the turtle- and snake-inhabited Acheron to the ancient swamp, now a corn field. A 30min. walk past fields with a constant sulfuric smell brings you to Necromanteion. The site is well-preserved with clay offerings, gigantic jugs, and a labyrinth meant to exclude sound from the windowless inner sanctum. A subterranean arched vault for communing with the dead can be accessed with caution by a set of steep, sometimes wet, metal steps. This supposed opening to Hades, where Odysseus conversed with the shades of his fallen comrades and relatives, is remarkably intact. Food is available in the nearby town of **Mesopotamo.** *(The site can be reached by taking the Preveza bus; 20min. Ask the driver to get off at Ammoydia and take a left on the dirt road; it's 2km away. To return, wait at the stop on the highway outside Mesopotamo for the Preveza-Parga bus. You also can call a taxi from Parga (€25) to come pick you up. ☎41 206. Open 10am-4pm. €2, students €1, EU students with ID free.)*

◪ DAYTRIP FROM PARGA: NIKOPOLIS

Former allies **Octavian Caesar** (later called Augustus) and **Mark Antony** faced off in the waters off Preveza in the naval battle of Actium in 31 BC, ultimately securing Octavian's rise to power as a sole ruler. Though Antony, working with his lover, Egyptian queen **Cleopatra,** brought with him the powerful Egyptian fleet, when many of his Roman friends abandoned him he lost the battle to Octavian. This civil war effectively ended the Roman Republic and jump-started the Roman Empire. In celebration of his victory, Octavian built ◪**Nikopolis,** meaning "City of Victory," at the point where he had camped on the eve of the battle. Surrounding cities were emptied as inhabitants and soldiers were resettled in this new capital. The well-preserved odeon, parts of fortification walls, baths, and the nymphaion (fountain pools at the end of the aqueduct) survive from this period and are within 10min. of the site's museum. The stadium, gymnasium, and Actium victory monument, above the city with a sweeping view of the waters, were built later outside the ancient city and are a 25min. walk away in modern Smyrntoula. When the Roman Empire declined, the city became an important early Christian center, and it is believed that St. Paul wrote his famous **Letter to Titus** here in the AD 1st century.

Raids from northern barbarians and the fall of the western empire in the 5th century led to a contraction of the city. **Emperor Justinian** surrounded the now-smaller city with a new Byzantine fortification; the impressive tower-studded wall is still visible. Look closely for pieces of friezes and reused Roman blocks in the wall that reveal the fate of many of the city's lost monuments. The remains of three basilicas, whose amazingly ornate mosaics now unfortunately are covered with sand, date from this time. As the site was once a sprawling city, it requires a good deal of walking, some through high grass and thistles, so long pants and closed-toed shoes are recommended. Though the flocks of sheep, reed-filled basilicas, ocean views, and olive-grove-shrouded ruins make for a fascinating day of exploration, it's nearly impossible to imagine how Nikopolis looked in its heyday. Since the lack of signs makes the details of the site even more difficult to discern, you may want to get an outside resource. The small two-room **museum** houses sarcophagi, friezes, and a marble bust of **Agrippa,** Octavian's victorious admiral. *(Take the bus to Preveza (1½hr., 5 per day 7am-9:15pm, €5) and ask the driver to let you off at Nikopolis. Specify that you are interested in the archaeological site, not the nearby club. To return, flag down the bus from Preveza to Parga (1½hr., 7 per day 7am-8pm, €6). The site is open Tu-Su 8am-7pm; museum Tu-Su 8am-3pm. €3, seniors €2, students and under 18 free.)*

IOANNINA Ιωάννινα   ☎26510

The eighth-largest city in Greece, Ioannina reached its political peak after it was captured in 1788 by Ali Pasha, an Albanian-born leader and visionary. Although a subject of the Ottoman Sultan, Ali intended to make this city the capital of his own Greek-Albanian empire. His fiery nature that earned him the title "Lion of Ioannina" eventually caused the Sultan to view him as a threat, leading to his execution in 1822. Present-day Ioannina is a charming, modern city whose delicious sweets alone make it worth a visit. With a bustling waterfront, the monumental Frourio, vibrant nightlife, and easy access to Dodoni, the Perama caves, and the Vikos Gorge, Ioannina deserves its status as the hub and capital of Epirus.

▐ TRANSPORTATION

Flights: From **Ioannina National Airport** (☎26 218). Flights go daily to **Athens** (1¼hr.; M-Th and Su 10:30am-7:40pm; F-Sa 10:30am, 1:40, 7:40pm; €80-100) and **Thessaloniki** (55min.; M 1:35pm, Tu 3:35pm, F and Su noon; €75-95). To reach the airport, take bus #2 or 7 (€0.80) from the stop in front of the clock in the central plateia, or get a taxi (€10). The **Olympic Airways office** (☎23 120) is at Pl. King Pirus where G. Averof splits into Napoleonda Zerva and Leoforos Dodonis. Open M-F 9am-3:30pm.

Buses: There are 3 terminals in town.

Main terminal, Zosimadon 4 (☎26 286). Call in advance, as some buses leave from the airport. To: **Athens** (6hr., 7 per day 7:15am-10:15pm, €33.30); **Igoumenitsa** (2hr., 8 per day 6:15am-8pm, €8.20); **Konitsa** (1hr., 7 per day 5am-7pm, €4.80); **Larisa** (3hr., 3 per day 10:45am-7pm, €14) via **Volos** (5hr., €17.50); **Metsovo** (1¼hr.; M-F 4 per day 5am-2pm; Sa 6:50am, 2pm; Su 4:30pm; €5); **Monodendri** (55min.; M and Th 6:15am, 2pm; €3); **Papingo** (1½hr.; M and Th 5am, 2pm; €4.10); **Parga** (1½hr., Aug.-Sept. 8:30am, €9.30); **Thessaloniki** (4½hr., 4 per day 10:30am-10:30pm, €27) via **Trikala** (2½hr., €11).

Preveza station, Bizaniou 28 (☎25 014). To: **Agrinio** (3hr., 6 per day 6am-7pm, €12); **Arta** (1½hr., 8 per day 5:45am-7:30pm, €5); **Dodoni** (30min.; M-F 7am, 2:45pm; €2.40) via **Mandio** (1hr., €3.50); **Patras** (4hr.; 9am, 2pm; €17.40); **Preveza** (1¾hr., M-F 8 per day 6am-8:15pm, €8:30).

KTEL Kastorias, G. Papandreou 58 (☎30 006). To **Kastoria** (3½hr.; 10am, 4pm; €16.30).

Ferries: Dock outside the Frourio and go to **Nisi** (every 30min. 7am-midnight, €2).

Taxis: ☎46 777. Wait 24hr. around the corner from the bus station and outside the Frourio, before the gates that lead to the Municipal Museum. Prices double after 1am. €1.50 charge for call.

◤ ⊡ ORIENTATION AND PRACTICAL INFORMATION

Ioannina is at the center of Epirus, at the edge of **Lake Pamvotis,** and surrounded by the peaks of Pindos. Not far into the lake is a small, hilly island called simply **"Nisi"** or **"Nissaki"** ("the island" or "the islet"). **Plateia King Pirus,** the city center, is across from **Litharitsia Park** and contains the Venetian **clock tower. Georgios Averof** is a broad avenue that runs from the main gate of the Old City to the city center. After the plateia, G. Averof becomes **Dodonis,** the city's primary artery, full of shops, restaurants, bars, and cafes. To reach the city center from the main bus station, turn left and walk uphill about 20m to an intersection with an Agricultural Bank. Facing the bank, walk uphill along the street on the left, which begins as **Dagli** and becomes **Markou Botsari** after a block. After three blocks, you'll emerge on G. Averof facing the park with the tall clock tower ahead of you. To your right, past the long building labeled "Prefecture of Ioannina" ("Νομαρχίον Ιωάννινων"), G. Averof turns into Dodonis. Bisecting Averof, with the kastro's walls on your right, **Karamanli** passes the main gate of the Frourio to the waterfront. Most of Ioannina's nightlife and a long line of outdoor cafes are located down Karamanli.

Tourist Office: EOT, Dodonis 39 (☎46 662), about 500m down Dodonis on the left, just past the playground. Friendly, English-speaking staff provides free maps, info, and a list of domatia in the province. Open M-F 7:30am-7:30pm.

Banks: Dodonis and Averof are full of banks with **24hr. ATMs. National Bank,** G. Averof 4 (☎26 434). On the right just after Pl. King Pirus, walking toward the waterfront. Open M-Th 8am-2pm, F 8am-1:30pm.

Police: 28 Oktovriou 11 (☎38 600). Across Botsari from the post office. Open 24hr. **Tourist police** (☎65 922; www.uoi.gr/tourist_police), in the same building. Have free maps and other info. Open daily 8am-10pm.

Hospital: 2 hospitals, each about 5km from the center of town. **Hatzikosta** (☎80 111), on Makriani on the way to Igoumenitsa, handles **emergencies** on even dates. **University Hospital** (☎99 111), on Universal, 5km from the end of Dodonis toward Dodoni, does so on odd dates.

Telephones: OTE, 28 Oktovriou 2-4 (☎29 999). Open M and W 7am-2pm.

Internet Access: Online i-cafe, Pirsinella 4 (☎72 512; www.onlinecafe.gr). On the 1st street on the right walking along Dodonis away from the waterfront. Has 75 terminals and even more overly enthusiastic gamers. €2 per hr. Open 24hr.

Post Office: 28 Oktovriou 1 (☎25 498), at the intersection of 28 Oktovriou and Botsari. Open M-F 7am-7pm. **Postal Code:** 45110.

ACCOMMODATIONS AND CAMPING

Expect to get what you pay for in Ioannina. This isn't a bad place to consider **camping.** Otherwise, hotels range from cheap, noisy, and slightly uncomfortable to expensive and luxurious.

Hotel Dioni, Tsirigoti 10 (☎27 032; www.epirus.com/dioni). At one of Ioannina's brightest, friendliest, quasi-budget options, rooms have A/C, TV, phone, free Wi-Fi, bath, and balcony. Bathroom hair dryers are equipped with 120V outlets. Breakfast €8. Singles €52; doubles €70; triples 90. AmEx/MC/V. ➍

Hotel Tourist, Kolleti 18 (☎25 070). Though it's in an unsettlingly dark area, the quiet, well-decorated rooms are far from G. Averof's incessant racket. Rooms have A/C, bath, phone, and TV. Reception 24hr. Singles €30; doubles €45; triples €70. ➌

Hotel Bretania, Pl. King Pirus 11a (☎29 396), at G. Averof and Dodonis, opposite the clock tower in the city center. An excellent location, with easy access to the sweets shop downstairs. Clean rooms have bathtub, A/C, TV, fridge, and lots of street noise. Breakfast €6. Singles €50; doubles €60; triples €80; quads €90. MC/V. ➍

Limnopoula, Kanari 10 (☎25 265). This unspectacular but well-priced campsite, near the town exit en route to Perama, has a lake, kitchen, phones, and a mini-mart. Despite the lack of English, the friendly staff is patient and accommodating. Reception 7am-midnight. €8 per person, €4 per tent, €5 per car. ➊

FOOD

G. Averof is saturated with souvlaki, gyro, and hamburger joints. Some inviting tavernas on Papagou by the waterfront combine sit-down meals, lake views, and live music. Follow G. Averof to the Frourio, and take a left on Karamanli; cafes soon give way to scenic tavernas. At almost any of the ubiquitous sweet shops, you can sample the delicious local baklava. Be sure to try Ioannina's speciality, *kaimaki*, a tasty Turkish ice cream made from sheep's milk.

Limni, Papagou 26 (☎78 988). This restaurant, whose name means "lake," is unsurprisingly located on the lakefront, with a charming patio and views of the mosque and mountains. The portions are huge and the prices are reasonable. Entrees €5-8. Open 10am-3am. AmEx/MC/V. ➋

Filippas, Pamvotidos 5 (☎31 170). Look for the yellow signs on the waterfront. The menu is an eclectic combination of different cultural cuisines, all prepared with a distinctly Greek spin. Entrees €7.50-12. ❸

 Diethnes (☎26 690), in Pl. King Pirus across from the clock tower. This shop has been keeping local dentists in business since 1950 by carrying every sugary food imaginable, including top-notch *kaimaki* (€1 per scoop). 6 other locations are spread around Ioannina, but this one is where it all began. Open 7am-2:30am. ❶

Brettania Cafe (☎30 600), in Pl. King Pirus before Diethnes and below Hotel Brettania. This classy patisserie with French decor and style offers 10 different kinds of local baklava (€12 per kg). Open 9am-11:30pm. ❶

👁 SIGHTS

🏛THE FROURIO

Ioannina's signature landmark, the Frourio (a.k.a. the **kastro** or the **"Old City"**) presides regally over the shore, with a slender minaret at each end. Most of the castle was built in the 13th century by Thomas Preljubovic, the Serbian ruler of Ioannina who also was known as **"Albanitoktonos"** ("Albanian-killer"). In order to secure a bloodless surrender in their conquest of 1430, the Turks assured Ioanninans that they could remain in their houses within the fortress walls. After a failed 1611 Greek insurrection led by the fanatical Bishop of Trikala, however, the Turks cracked down. One Sunday, when all the Greeks were in church, the Turks seized their houses. Nicknaming the bishop **"Skilosofos"** ("he who has the wisdom of a dog"), they captured him and skinned him alive. At many points throughout the kastro's history, however, Jews, Turkish Muslims, and Christians lived peacefully side by side; even when the great Ali Pasha came to power and rebuilt the walls in 1795, the communities flourished together in peace. The approximately 4000 Jews dwindled to the present day 100 when the Nazis sent the Jewish community to death camps, and the fortress hasn't seen the same level of cohabitation since then. The Frourio now is home to placid neighborhoods with narrow streets, old Turkish-style homes, several museums, and all Ioannina's major sights. Though its several entrances are all open 24hr, the main entrance, like that of any self-respecting fortress, has several sharp turns to make invasion slow and tricky. Just outside this entrance is an unmarked shrine to **Saint George the Neomartyr.** Ioannina's patron saint, he was tortured and hanged in 1838 by Turkish overlords for marrying a Christian.

THE ITŞ KALE. To reach the Itş Kale (the inner citadel) from the Frourio's main entrance, take a right and then the first left; continue until you reach the long ramp that heads up to the site. This strategic high place was made the city's primary fortress in 1205 and later became Ali Pasha's headquarters, where he lived, built a mosque, and was buried. Though it once was enveloped in turmoil, the Itş Kale is now a peaceful area, surrounded by the Pindos Mountains and Pamvotis Lake. The small ruined buildings on both sides as you enter the walls were guard posts, and the cafe on the left was originally a kitchen. To the immediate right along the wall are the remnants of Ali Pasha's *hamam* (baths), and around what is now the Silverworks Gallery of the Byzantine Museum is the *serai* (residence) that once housed Ali, his harem, and his ornately decorated audience chambers. Though it's hard to imagine in the serenity of today's site, Ali Pasha held most of his tortures and executions at the plane tree near the *serai*, running the gory gamut from skinning to impaling to suspending on hooks hung from the tree's branches. **Katsandonis,** a famed fighter in the War of Independence, is said to have sung patriotic hymns while being brutally hammered to death here, a scene re-enacted frequently

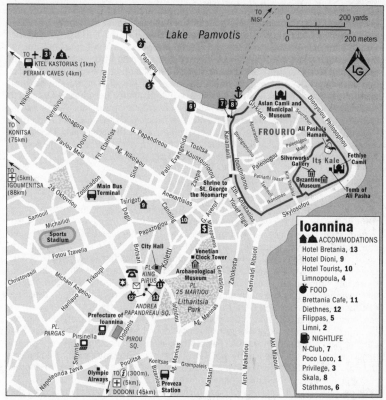

Ioannina

▲▲⌂⌂ ACCOMMODATIONS
Hotel Bretania, 13
Hotel Dioni, 9
Hotel Tourist, 10
Limnopoula, 4

🍎 FOOD
Brettania Cafe, 11
Diethnes, 12
Filippas, 5
Limni, 2

🎵 NIGHTLIFE
N-Club, 7
Poco Loco, 1
Privilege, 3
Skala, 8
Stathmos, 6

in Greek folk shadow-puppet theater. Though a **circular tower** is all that is left from the original Byzantine fortification, the **Byzantine Museum** has a small collection from the period that includes intricate wooden sanctuary doors, stone carvings, calligraphic manuscripts, and post-Byzantine icons. Helpful plaques in the first part of the museum chronicle the history of Epirus and Ioannina in English. (☎27 761. Open M 12:30-7pm and Tu-Su 8am-7pm. €3, students free.) The **Fethiye Camii** (Victory Mosque) to the right of the museum is the third mosque in its location, a space once occupied by a 13th-century church. The current mosque was rebuilt in 1795 by Ali Pasha himself. In front of the mosque, weeds and rubble obscure the **Tomb of Ali Pasha,** a sarcophagus that contains his headless body; his head and neck are buried in Istanbul. The gilded cage that originally decorated the tomb was looted by Nazis in 1943, and it recently was replaced with a green iron approximation. Ioannina is the silversmith capital of Greece, and at the impressive **Silverworks Gallery** you'll find snuffboxes, tea services, and belt buckles to prove it. An etching beside the desk depicts the Frourio as it looked in its glory days. (☎25 989. Site and museum open 8am-7pm. Show your Byzantine Museum ticket for admission.)

MUNICIPAL MUSEUM. The smaller of the Frourio's walled inner areas is a little farther to the left of the Itş Kale—follow signs to the museum housed in the lovely **Aslan Pasha Camii,** whose rusting piles of cannon balls attest to the citadel's once-powerful status. On the left as you enter is the long, rectangular former *medrasa* (school for Qur'anic study). In front of it, the tombstones engraved in Arabic are the remains of an **Ottoman cemetery.** The small building behind the mosque is Aslan Pasha's mausoleum. In 1618, following the 1611 rebellion, the Turks destroyed the former church and replaced it with an elegant mosque. The Municipal Museum, in the former mosque, displays a beautiful *mimbar*, the pulpit from which the Imam recites readings from the Qur'an. The small but fascinating collection focuses on Ioannina's diverse ethnic past, and is divided into Jewish, Greek, and Muslim exhibits. The sword that belonged to War of Independence hero Karaiskaki and a golden dress worn by Lady Vasilikis, Ali Pasha's wife, are particularly impressive. (☎ 26 356. Open daily Sept.-Nov. 8am-3pm; May-Oct. 7am-8pm. €4, EU students €2.) Across from the Municipal Museum, down a set of stairs, is the private collection of **Fotis Rapakousis,** displaying Greek weapons from the 15th century through the Balkan Wars. (Open M-F. Show your Municipal Museum ticket for admission.)

OTHER SIGHTS

NISI. Cheap silver shops, a whitewashed village, and deteriorating monasteries cover this peaceful island. A 10min. ferry ride from the harbor and a world away from the noise and hectic rush of the city, Nisi offers a unique experience since outside vehicles are not allowed on the island. It was here, surrounded by reeds and marsh, that Ali Pasha met his death after seriously falling out of the Sultan's favor. Attempting to hide from the certain punishment that awaited him, Ali fled to the second story of the island's **Saint Pantaleimon monastery.** He soon was found there, and subsequently killed by shots fired up through the floor—the floorboards are now displayed in the museum, complete with reconstructed bullet holes. The victors hung Ali's severed head for public viewing before transporting it back to the Sultan in Istanbul. Though this event obviously marked the end of Ali's regime, Ioannina's claim to fame still rests on his now-detached shoulders. The monastery currently houses the two-room **Ali Pasha Museum,** displaying Ali Pasha's enormous bronze hookah, which he happily puffs in almost every portrait. A large painting of the Sultan ceremoniously receiving the head of his fearsome ex-governor adorns the opposite wall, a constant reminder of who was ultimately victorious. (☎ 81 791. Open daily 9am-9pm. €2 requested.) Signs point the way to St. Pantaleimon and the other four monasteries. A short walk from the museum, the **frescoes** of St. Nicholas Philanthropinos, painted by Katelanou in 1542, depict saints, the life of Jesus, and seven ancient sages, including Plato, Aristotle, and Plutarch, who were said to have foretold the coming of Christ. If the monastery is locked, ask at the house next door for a tour. On sunny days, the light sifted through the stained glass windows of the church bathes the walls and frescoes in gold. At the nearby *krifto scholio* (secret school), the forbidden Greek language was kept alive during Ottoman reign. There is a crypt in the monastery of **Saint John Prodromos** that leads to a secret exit and path to the lake. (☎ 25 885. The 10min. ferries to Nisi from Ioannina's waterfront run every 30min. 6:30am-midnight; in winter every hr. 7am-10pm. €1.50.)

▶ NIGHTLIFE

You don't have to look far to find nightlife in this youthful and happening city. Most of Ioannina's late-night action takes place on the waterfront along the base of the Frourio walls: cafes and discos are along the waterfront on Papagou, and bars sit in the south where Garivaldi meets Ethnikis. To reach a string of relaxed after-hours cafes, walk past the Diethnes sweets shop away from the Frourio walls to Soutsi and Mavili or the beginning of Dodonis. The streets teem with locals sitting at music cafes, talking and enjoying the breezy waterfront area. More options are on the other side of the peninsula; head back to Diethnes and walk along the perimeter of the walls for 400m or take Karamanli, which begins soon after the Ferris wheel, to Eth. Antistasios. Bars and clubs await across from the park.

N-Club, Garivaldi 1 (☎28 028), at the main gate to the Frourio. Fiber-optic cables illuminate this super-modern club, which plays an unusual mix of house, techno, Greek, and reggae music. Beer €3. Mixed drinks €7. Open 10pm-6am.

Skala (☎37 676), behind N-Club. Locals come to this low-key hangout to listen to pop and Greek tunes before hitting the clubs. Beer €3. Mixed drinks €6. Open 9pm-3am.

Privilege (☎69324 25 258). Follow the signs after Poco Loco, walking away from the Frourio. Ioannina's biggest disco has gold-lit columns outside, with private booths and a pool-enclosed bar inside. You must be well-dressed (no shorts) and be over 20 with a photo ID. Cover €5. Beer €5. Open M-Th and Su midnight-3:30am, F-Sa midnight-6am.

Playhouse, Sp. Lambrou and Sakelariou 21 (☎77 731). Rent out games like Candyland and Monopoly (€1 per hr.) as you have a beer (€3). Open 10am-2am.

▓ DAYTRIPS FROM IOANNINA

▓ DODONI Δωδώνη

Buses to Dodoni run from Ioannina's smaller station (30min.; M and F 7am, 4:30pm; €2). Ask to be let off at the theater. You also can take a taxi there (at least €20) and take the bus (passes by daily around 4:45pm) back. If you're stranded, call a taxi (☎26510 46 777), but expect to pay a €2-3 surcharge. ☎26510 82 287. Open 8am-7pm. €2, students and seniors €1, EU students free.

Ancient Dodoni, the site of mainland Greece's oldest oracle, lies at the base of a mountain 23km southwest of Ioannina. An oracle of Zeus and his consort Dione Naia, Dodoni's sacred oak tree was thought to be a portal of the divine wisdom of the king of the gods. From the earliest recorded ceremony as far back as 2000BC, such worthy figures as Odysseus and Achilles sought advice under its leafy shade until the site was all but demolished by the Romans in 167 BC. At its height, Dodoni was the second greatest oracle in the ancient world, surpassed only by Delphi. Unlike Delphi, this oracle was consulted mostly on personal rather than political matters. Unlike the complicated hexameters that served as answers at Delphi, Dodoni's replies were either "yes" or "no," expressed through the doves nestling in the tree, the rustling of its branches, or nature's sounds heard reverberating in the many cauldrons surrounding the oracle. According to Herodotus, an Egyptian priestess who was kidnapped by Phoenician sea traders transformed herself into a dove to escape captivity. She settled at Dodoni and convinced Zeus to establish his oracle at the serene spot. A clan of priests called the **Hellopes, Helloi,** or **Selloi** guarded the heavenly site, but eventually they were replaced by three priestesses called **Doves.** The **Naia festival,** an Olympic-like series of pan-Hellenic athletic and dramatic contests, was held here every four years in Zeus's honor.

The enormous **amphitheater** near the entrance to the site was built in the early 3rd century BC. The original design seated 17,000 before the Romans replaced the lowest rows with a retaining wall and improved the still-visible drainage system to accommodate their blood sports. Every seat in the vast complex has an amazing view of the stage, and it is easy to picture the drama and violence that once occurred here. The acoustics are so good that whispers made on stage can be heard clearly even by those in the nosebleed seats. Sometimes the theater is used in the summers for music and dance performances. Beyond the amphitheater are the ruins of the oracle itself, where a new sacred oak recently has been planted. Little remains today of the original building that housed the tree and its hordes of pilgrims. A 5th-century BC temple and the 350 BC **bouleuterion** and **prytaneion,** now almost totally vanished, once surrounded the oracle. Following the Aetolian sack in 219 BC, a larger Ionic temple to Zeus was built in 167 BC. Later, in the AD 5th century, the site was home to some of the largest early Christian basilicas.

AGIOS GEORGIOS AQUEDUCT

Take the bus to Preveza (1hr., 8 per day 6am-8pm, €6) and ask the driver to let you off at Agios Georgios. Once you get off, cross the highway and take the road leading downhill for about 1km. To return, go back up the road to take the bus back to Ioannina (1hr., 10 per day 6am-7:30pm, €6).

The location of the remains of Nikopolis's (p. 251) Roman **aqueduct,** high in the mountains, is gorgeous, but the well-preserved structure crossing the Louros rapids has a beauty of its own. Construction of the aqueduct at such an altitude was a major feat of contemporary engineering. Over 50 years later, the aqueduct was connected to the city's **nymphaion fountain.** Although the site has no signs or explanations, the area is serene and beautiful, and it's still fascinating to watch the stream flow under the ancient construction.

◪ PERAMA CAVES

Take local bus #16 or 8 from the park behind the city center (15min., every 20min. 7am-10pm, €0.80). At Perama, follow the multiple signs to the cave. Turn left at the blue sign in the middle of Spileou. ☎81 521. Open daily in summer 8:30am-6pm; in winter 9am-5pm. €7, students €3, under 7 free. Tours every 15min.

A 500-step stairway leads through the spectrally lit, glimmering Perama Caves, which are among the largest in the Balkans. The path leads from narrow passageways to immense **caverns** filled with eerily hanging rock formations. The huge cavities were discovered accidently by two locals who were seeking shelter from Nazi bombs during WWII. Subsequent excavations have uncovered bears' teeth and bones in the nearly two-million-year-old stalagmites and stalactites. Certain formations are named after landmarks they vaguely resemble, such as the "Tower of Pisa," the "Egyptian Sphinx," and "The Statue of Liberty." The 45min. Greek and English guided tours give general facts about the caves and their creation. You might be tempted to take pictures in the second chamber, one of the most impressive in the world, but flash photography is strictly forbidden because the heat from the light allows mold to grow. Still, the yellow lighting provided is sufficient to take some snapshots. Hovering around a comfortable 17°C/62°F inside, the cave offers natural relief during the scorching Greek afternoons. The exit puts you 600m away from the entrance, but luckily the walk back yields some beautiful vantage points from which to see Ioannina, the lake, and Nisi.

METSOVO Μέτσοβο   ☎26560

On the western slope of the Katara Pass lies the alpine town of Metsovo. Built into the side of a mountain, the town itself is a piece of art, maintained in near-perfect condition by the fortune left by Metsovite-turned-Swiss-banker Baron Tositsas. The self-proclaimed "Vlach capital" contains some of the last speakers of that Latin-based language, which is currently on the verge of extinction. Its position in the North Pindos mountains makes it a gold mine of exquisite hikes. The intricate local costumes and rugs, along with the festivals and traditional weddings that seem to be one continuous celebration in mid- and late July, display Metsovite culture in full form. Surprisingly, Wi-Fi is available everywhere in this secluded town.

⌁ TRANSPORTATION. From the main plateia, **buses** go to Ioannina (1½hr.; M-Sa 4 per day 6:30am-4:30pm, Su 5:30pm; €4.20) and Trikala (2hr., 8:30am, €5) via Kalambaka (1½hr., €4). The bus to Thessaloniki (5½hr., 5 per day 7am-10:30pm,

€20) passes by on the main highway, but won't stop unless you flag it down. The *periptero* by the central plateia bus stop, across from the statue of a friendly bear, has schedules. **Taxis** (☎ 41 393) wait in the plateia and can be called 24hr.

■ ▋ **ORIENTATION AND PRACTICAL INFORMATION.** Navigating through Metsovo is easy: all roads in Metsovo lead to the **main plateia.** Walking behind the town square's park will lead you to **Hotel Filoxenia** and Yiannis. The bus drops off in front of a sign for **Hotel Egnatia information** (not the hotel but a small souvenir shop bearing the same name). With your back to the sign and the park in front of you, there are two roads to your left. The closer road heads uphill toward Ioannina and Trikala after passing the Tositsas Museum. The road farther to your left when standing at the bus stop leads to John Xaralabapoulos's Rooms and Hotel Olympic. Past the parking lot and to your right are most of the town's restaurants and another section of the plateia, both blocked by the park.

It is helpful to stop by Hotel Filoxenia to speak with British-educated Yiannis at the beginning of your stay. Filling the role of a tourist office, he has prepared binders filled with information about hiking paths, maps, museum hours, and just about anything you would ever want to know about the town. The **town hall,** on the second floor of the large white building that houses the Eurobank, is located where the road to Ioannina meets the plateia. If you walk around to the building's back, you will find a staff that can provide you with brochures about the area, info about hiking trails, and free maps. (☎ 41 207. Open 7am-2:30pm.) The road that wraps around the plateia and the public park goes past the **National Bank** (☎ 41 296; open M-F 8am-2pm) and **Agricultural Bank** (☎ 41 160; open M-Th 8am-2:30pm and F 8am-2pm), both of which have **24hr. ATMs.** There is a 24hr. **hospital** (☎ 41 112) at the top of the town, along the road to Ioannina. To reach the municipal **police** (☎ 41 233; open 24hr.) and the **OTE,** across the street (☎ 42 199; open M-F 8am-2pm), take the slightly downhill street to the right of Kria Folia, a restaurant at the northwestern corner of the smaller section of the plateia. The second road to the right runs downhill to the Agios Nikolaos monastery and to **Tsigas's Super Game Club,** which has **Internet** access. (☎ 41 696. €2 per hr. Beer €1.50. Open 9am-2am.) The **post office,** which has **Poste Restante,** is on the road toward Ioannina and Trikala. (☎ 41 245. Open M-F 7:30am-2pm.) **Postal Code:** 44200.

▐ **ACCOMMODATIONS.** Room prices spike outrageously during Metsovo's two high seasons (mid-July to Sept. and Dec.-Mar.). During these times, the town is best visited as a daytrip. In low season, however, the rooms are more reasonably priced. You can find **domatia** by veering left before the OTE; most offer simple rooms for about €25-30. Hands down the most welcoming option in town is ▨**Hotel Filoxenia ❷,** whose name (meaning "hospitality") says it all. British-educated proprietor Yiannis is a one-stop source for all things Metsovo, even if you don't decide to stay at his cozy ski-lodge-like hotel. Full of wisdom, humor, and experience traversing the mountainous area, he has helpful information, arranges hikes in the nearby Valia Skalda National Park, and stores gear. The rooms have TV, bath, and a mountainside balcony. Find Filoxenia behind the town square's park. (☎ 41 021. Breakfast €4. Singles €25-30; doubles €35-45; triples 50.) **John Xaralabapoulos's Rooms ❷,** which all come with TV and phone, are large, comfortable, and have an understated charm. A handpainted sign reading "Domatia-Rooms" marks the entrance, just past the basketball court. (☎ 42 086. Singles €25-30; doubles €32-40; triples €36-45.) **Hotel Olympic ❸,** behind John Xaralabapoulos's ·Rooms, has wood-paneled rooms with soft double bed, bath, TV, and phone. (☎ 41 337. Breakfast €7. Singles €30-40; doubles €35-45; triples €40-50. MC/V.)

▐ **FOOD.** Many of the restaurants in Metsovo cater to large groups of tourists as well as to locals. In general, it's best to avoid the tourist traps around the central plateia. **Metsovo Yefsis ❷** (Tastes of Metsovo), beneath the National Bank, serves large portions of local dishes at low prices. Believe it or not, while running Hotel Filoxenia to perfection, Yiannis also manages to cook up a storm at his restaurant. Try the meatballs with leeks (€6). (☎42 009. Vegetarian options available. Call in advance for Kosher/Halal options. Open daily 6pm-1am.) **Galaxias ❷**, in an ivy-covered mansion, serves a number of homemade local specialties such as veal with Metsovo village pasta (€7). With your back to the entrance of the town hall, take a left and walk past the small park; you'll see the huge sign reading "Galaxy." Though the mansion is appealing, the sunny, green-garden eating area has a more relaxed, summertime feel. (☎41 202; www.metsovo.com/galaxyhotel. Entrees €5-9. Open 11am-11pm. MC/V.) **To Koutouki Tou Nikola ❷** is found, as its name implies, in Nikola's basement, on the street toward the post office. With your back to the Hotel Egnatia bus stop, you will see the large sign if you look left. It serves trout from Lake Metsovo, delectable soups (boiled goat meat soup with potatoes and carrots; €5) and the town's acclaimed vegetable pies. (☎41 732. Open 11am-1am.) **Kryfi Folia ❷**, in the plateia one shop down from the Agricultural Bank, is a local favorite. This grill master offers meat like *kokoretsi* (lamb intestines; €6.50) and *kontosoufli* (pork and lamb souvlaki; €6). (☎41 628. Open 11am-midnight.)

⊙ SIGHTS. Thanks to the Baron Tositsas and his nephew, Evangelos Averof-Tositsas, Metsovo has far more sights than you'd expect in a 4000-person town. Off the main plateia, the spacious **Evangelos Averof Gallery** exhibits 19th- and 20th-century Greek paintings, including Averof-Tositsas's private collection. Follow the road after the two banks; it's on your right after the bend around the park. (☎41 210. Open mid-July to mid-Sept. M and W-Sa 10am-6:30pm; mid-Sept. to mid-July 10am-4:30pm. €3, students €2.) Between the National and Agricultural Banks, is the **▨Workshop of George Boubas,** who handcrafts traditional costumes and silver jewelry. George guarantees that all his goods are made with non-fading natural dyes, so souvenirs bought here promise to be of good quality. (☎42 580. Open 8am-1:30pm and 3:30-9:30pm. AmEx/MC/V.) The **Tositsas Museum,** 50m up the hill in a mansion to the left of the main road opposite Krini Club, honors the generosity of the town's benefactors. Also known as the folk art museum, it displays traditional costumes, silverware, and wooden carvings, along with a timeline of Metsovo's history. (☎41 084. Open daily mid-July to mid-Sept. 8:30am-1pm and 4-6pm; mid-Sept. to mid-July 8:30am-1pm and 5-7pm. €3. Visitors are only admitted in small groups; wait at the door for the guide who appears every 30min.) The **Agios Nikolaos Monastery** is a 30min. walk from the plateia down the hillside; signs point the way. Built in the 14th century, the monastery was originally one of the most important in the area, though it soon fell into disuse. It was restored in 1700 before being abandoned once more. While it was officially empty, itinerant shepherds used its crumbling chapel as a refuge. The smoke from their fires completely covered frescoes that had been painted in 1702, perfectly preserving them until they were rediscovered in 1950 by Averof-Tositsas. Today, you can see the formerly covered icons and the famous moss-covered bell tower overlooking the picturesque valley below the town. The family-run church has no official hours, but it is open for viewing as long as there is light outside. If it is locked, knock on the door. After visiting the church, walk through the vineyard to the main road. Stay to the left, and 300m after passing the less than romantic sewage station, you'll see a path on your right and signs that lead you the a lovely windmill. From here, it's possible to see the small **Church of the Panagia.** Though the nun that runs the church doesn't allow visitors in, you can walk through the perfectly kept gardens of the church.

For info about **Valia Kalda National Park** (Vlach for "warm valley") and other outdoor activities in Metsovo, contact the town hall (☎41 207) or Yiannis of Hotel Filoxenia (p. 259). Valia Kalda is home to 80 species of birds and a number of endangered animals such as the brown bear, the wild cat, and the wild goat. Its drastic landscape and gushing rivers are rich enough to occupy any outdoors enthusiast for weeks. The town hall gives out an excellent free topographical map.

The village hosts a major *yiorti* (celebration) each year on July 26, which used to be the Vlach courting day; all women and most men dress in traditional bright costumes for the modern festivities, splashing the entire town with color. At some point between July 20 and July 26, depending on the weather, the residents embark on an annual hike up the park to celebrate in honor of the Greek gods. Baron himself was a believer in the Olympian pantheon, and as part of the donation deal, he proclaimed the yearly visit obligatory. Reserve rooms at least three weeks in advance if you will be there for the festival.

Metsovo does not offer much in the way of nightlife, but if you're itching to go out, drop by **Krini Club,** one block up from the post office on the road to Ioannina. The club caters to older Metsovites, but is also a second home to Metsovo's youth—though they don't show up until after midnight. While Krini Club never gets too crazy, it has the best people-watching opportunities in town. (☎41 184. Beer €3. Mixed drinks €6. Open M-Th and Su 6pm-3am, F-Sa 5pm-6am.)

 The 🏔 **Hellenic Mountaineering Club (EOS),** based in Ioannina, supplies information and leads weekend trips throughout the region. (☎26510 22 138. Open M-Sa 7-9pm.) The **Paddler Kayaking and Rafting School** (☎26550 23 777 or 26550 23 101), with offices in Konitsa and Megalo Papingo, gives lessons and oversees outings to local rivers. A major local outfitter is **Alpine Zone,** Josef Eligia 16 (☎23 222; www.alpinesone.gr), located off Averof in Ioannina, specializing in rafting equipment and outings. For more information, contact Marios at Pension Monodendri (☎26530 71 300) or Nikos at Koulis Restaurant (☎26530 41 115), in Monodendri and Papingo respectively. The best time to see alpine flowers is between April and June. Colored foliage flares brilliantly in the dry autumns. The best season for rafting is April through May, when the full rivers start to warm up.

ZAGOROHORIA Ζαγοροχώρια

Between the Albanian border and the North Pindos mountain range, a string of 46 hamlets *(horia)* quietly coexist, showing few signs of interference from modern-day society. A trip to Zagorohoria immerses visitors in the blissful relaxation of simple village life. The tiny, picturesque towns are a tapestry of cobblestoned roads and slate-tiled rooftops that give the area a magical and serene atmosphere. Also home to Vikos Gorge, the deepest canyon in the world, Zagorohoria provides plenty of opportunities for nature enthusiasts to hike around rough-riding rivers, stark peaks, and dark caves. These natural treasures, in addition to the surrounding Vikos-Aoös National Park, entice all who venture out here with picture-perfect scenery and unbeatable sites. While hiking and trekking are the major tourist attractions of the area, the romantic draw of traveling back in time and exploring the traditional villages is enough of a reason to lose yourself in this region.

MONODENDRI Μονοδένδρι ☎26530

Many a traveler has passed dreamily through Monodendri's cobbled maze, illuminated only by twinkling stars and the summertime multitudes of fireflies. Though hikers bearing cameras and sunscreen are now as common as goats and sheep in this tiny village of 150, their presence has not changed Monodendri's character. The area's natural and architectural beauty, location at the top of Vikos Gorge, and proximity to Ioannina make it an unrivaled base for hikers. The must-see natural

NORTHERN GREECE

overlook, ⬛**Oxia Point**, is a very easy 1½hr. walk from the village and has breathtaking views of the entire **Vikos Gorge** (p. 262). The view is best accessed by following a red-blazed trail that begins behind the Monodendri Hotel. As the harsh winters often leave the markers unclear, ask Marios at the hotel to show you the footpath. The view also is accessible by car; Oxia Point lies at the end of the main road 6km past the town. Another equally easy hike (20min.) goes beyond the abandoned **Monastery of Agia Paraskevi**, which is 1km from Monodendri's lower plateia; many signs point the way. The monastery houses an operating icon-painter's workshop. A small terrace has stunning views of the beginning of the gorge trail, and an edgeless, meter-wide path is cut straight into the sheer rock wall. The treacherous path leads to a small cave once used by monks to hide from raiders. Signs from the plateia point along the slightly difficult trail to **Megali Spilia** (30min.), another nearby cave where Zagorohorians used to hide from marauders.

Opposite the bus stop, ⬛**Monodendri Hotel** ❸ has cozy rooms with colorful rugs and a delicious breakfast. The owner's English-speaking son, Marios, is full of info about trekking in the area and picks up passengers from Vikos Village (€50) or Megalo Papingo (€40) after their hikes. Marios's wealth of knowledge and patience with visitors has been aiding *Let's Go* readers, even those not staying the night, for the past decade. (☎71 300; www.monodendrihotel.com. Breakfast €5. Bagged lunch for the trail €3.50. Reception 8am-11pm. Singles €35; doubles €45; triples €60. MC/V.) **Arhondiko Zarkada Hotel** ❸, on the left as you walk up from the bus station, has a pool as well as large, comfortable rooms with modern bath, TV, phone, and gorgeous stone balcony. (☎71 305. Breakfast €6.50. Singles €35; doubles €40; triples €35. AmEx/MC/V.) On the lower road, **Arktouros Hotel** ❸ has simple, comfortable rooms with TV, bath, safe, and minibar. (☎71 455. Singles €35; doubles €55.) A few tavernas are scattered along the main road. The friendliest is ⬛**Katerina's** ❷, on the porch of Monodendri Hotel, where Marios's mother, Mrs. Daskalopoulou, prepares the food. The dessert pies, especially the milk pie (€4), are to die for. Everything on the menu is prepared with love; even the Greek salad (€7) tastes distinctively better here than anywhere else.

The bus stop, all the hotels, and most of the restaurants are on Monodendri's one paved road. **Buses** go to Ioannina (1hr.; M and Th 7:30am, 2:45pm; €3). **Taxis** can take you to Ioannina or Konitsa (€35). Monodendri's lower plateia is accessible by a footpath that descends to the right from the bus stop; follow the path downhill and turn left at the fork. The plateia is home to a cafe, a **phone**, a **mail box**, and signposts for all the trailheads; it also serves as the starting point for all the lookouts and hikes in Vikos Gorge. There is no bank; the closest are in Kalpaki and Konitsa. Monodendri Hotel **exchanges currency** for guests of the establishment and *Let's Go* readers. The nearest **hospital** is in Ioannina. Both the town kiosk, across from Arhondiko Zarkada Hotel, and Monodendri Hotel have good trail maps (around €7.50). **Postal Code:** 44007.

VIKOS GORGE Φαράγγι Βίκου

Vikos Gorge, whose walls are 900m deep and only 110m apart, is the steepest on earth. In spring time, the river that has taken millions of years to form the gorge rushes along the 15km stretch of canyon floor. By summer, all that is left is the occasional puddle hidden among white boulders in the riverbed. Vikos Gorge is splashed with a faded mix of colors that change as the sunlight moves over them. Rusted iron deposits in the gorge's rock leave an orange-pink tint that drips over the gray walls, complemented as the seasons pass with the brilliant hues of spring wildflowers, summer butterflies, autumn foliage, and views of the green waters running below Vikos Village. When night falls, listen for the shrill chirping of crickets and watch fireflies dance in the trees, blending into the star-studded sky.

People have walked through the gorge's deep ravine since the 12th century BC, when early settlers took shelter in its craggy caves. Today, hikers follow its path, which stretches from the village of Kipi in the south to Megalo Papingo at its northernmost tip, and winds its way through the center of the Zagorohoria. The well-marked **trail** through the gorge is the **O3** domestic trail section of the Greek National E4 route, running from the Aoös River near Konitsa all the way to Kipi. Before you go, be sure to get a map (€7.50), sold at the *periptero* on the main road through Monodendri, the Monodendri Hotel (p. 262), and No Limits (p. 264) in Papingo. If you get confused, just look for the red diamonds on white, square backgrounds with "O3" stenciled on them, which consistently mark the path. Most hikers enter the gorge from **Monodendri,** but it also can be accessed from **Kipi,** the **Papingo** villages, and **Vikos Village.** It is a 5hr. walk from Vikos Village to Monodendri and 6hr. from the Papingos to Monodendri.

To reach the gorge from Monodendri, take the marked path from the lower plateia. After about 700m (40min.) along the steep, winding descent, you'll reach a fork in the path. Go left to enter the canyon's dry riverbed of smooth rocks, and head toward the far-off villages of the Papingos and Vikos. After about 4km (1½hr.), the right fork will bring you to the village of Kipi, with its trademark stone bridges. To descend into the gorge, take the left fork as it climbs above the left bank of the riverbed. The path is fairly level and pleasant for some time, continuing through a shady woodland along the riverbank. On the way, you'll pass open groves mowed clean by grazing horses. About 9km (4-5hr.) from Monodendri, you'll reach the crossroads that lead up to Vikos Village. The trail suddenly becomes a meticulously cobblestoned path, which, after about 20m, makes a 90-degree turn up and to the left toward Vikos (300m; about 45min.). If you're Papingo-bound, maintain the course that descends to the right, hugging the riverbanks into the grassy pasture. This area is a popular camping site among backpackers looking to avoid steep room rates. About halfway through the grassy clearing, a frenzy of red arrows on the boulders on the stream's opposite bank marks the ford and the continuation of O3 to Papingo. Another hour out of the gorge brings you to the Megalo Papingo-Mikro Papingo split. From here, it's 30min. to either village.

Hikers entering from the Papingo villages should follow signs from the plateias. Stone stairways lead you most of the way. The trailhead in **Vikos Village** is slightly outside town, but clearly marked signs and willing villagers are available for help. This intermediate-level trail (1½hr.) descends to **Voidhomatis springs,** the radiant source of the Vikos river. In Vikos Village, home to fewer than 30 people, there are two tavernas and one hotel; the only rooms in the tiny village are at **Sotiris Karpouzis ❹.** (☎411 76. Reception open until 1am. €45 for up to three people.) One of the tavernas is in the hotel. The obliging owner of the second taverna, **Foris** (☎42 170), in the plateia, provides rides (€30) to Monodendri.

THE PAPINGOS Τα Πάπινγκα ☎ 26530

Many travelers reach the two enchanting Papingo villages, Megalo (Μεγάλο; large) and Mikro (Μικρό; small), located north of the Vikos Gorge, after a long hike. Aside from the trailheads, the villages look as if they haven't been touched in the last millenium. Recently, however, the Papingos have become a vacation destination for wealthy Greeks from Thessaloniki and Ioannina. Despite the boom in tourism, the villages still maintain the tranquility that characterizes their neighboring hamlets and serve as the starting point for some astonishingly beautiful hikes.

◪ TRANSPORTATION. Buses go to Ioannina (1½hr.; M and Th 6am, 3pm; €4.10). A more dependable alternative is to hike the 3hr. trail to Klidonia, where you can catch buses on the frequent Konitsa-Ioannina route (1hr., 8 per day 5am-8pm, €4).

⚙️🔌 ORIENTATION AND PRACTICAL INFORMATION. The large, austere stone church and its **bell tower** stand at the entrance to Megalo Papingo. From here, a cobblestoned thoroughfare snakes around the town, first ascending to the top and then looping down again; it contains most of the villages' pensions and restaurants. The road to Mikro Papingo is marked to the right of the church, and the **trailhead** for Vikos Gorge is 20m down this road at the end of a well-marked dirt lane on the right. Don't follow the old, yellow sign 50m down the road—contrary to appearances, it does not actually lead to the Vikos trail. Megalo Papingo has a **phone** by the church and a **mailbox** by Lakis Cafe. Mikro Papingo has a phone at the town entrance, near the WWF center; its mailbox is by the trail signpost. Another entrance for Vikos Gorge is located here along with the trailheads for **Drakolimni, Mount Astrakas,** and the **EOS refuge.** For details about hiking, rafting, and paragliding, ask for Nikos at **No Limits,** an office that provides outdoor information, on your right about 10m up the cobblestoned road. (☎26550 23 777. Open 10am-7pm.)

🏠🍴 ACCOMMODATIONS AND FOOD. The recent increase in tourism has raised lodging prices in the chic Papingos. If **pensions** and **domatia** are full or prices are at high-season levels, backpackers may want to hike up to the EOS Refuge by Mt. Astrakas. Though it is illegal, many hikers also choose to freelance camp. Popular locations include the Vikos Village crossroads in the gorge (p. 262), a small clearing halfway down the road from Megalo to Mikro Papingo on the left, and other areas surrounding the gorge. The beautifully furnished rooms at 🅜**Pension Koulis ❸** in Megalo Papingo, with fireplace, TV, and bath, may remind you of an Alpine ski lodge. Facing the town from where the cobblestoned road starts, take the first left after the church. The pension is on the corner of the next crossroads to the left. (☎41 115. Breakfast included. Reception 24hr. Singles €35; doubles €50; triples €65. MC/V.) In Mikro Papingo, go up the main road and take the left fork to find 🅜**Hotel Dias ❸.** The elegant rooms come with sleek and modern showers that will make you forget you're on a budget. (☎41 257. Breakfast included. Reception 8am-11pm. Singles €35; doubles €60; triples €75; quads €90.) **Georgios Reppas's ❹** homey rooms include quilted beds, TV, shared bath, and an amazing sense of tranquility. Look for his house immediately opposite the church in Megalo Papingo. (☎41 711. Breakfast included. Singles €40; doubles €47; triples €50.)

Just outside town on the road to Mikro Papingo is 🅜**Tsoumanis Estiatorio ❷.** The owners, brothers Costa and Spiros, serve lamb from their father's flock and vegetables from their gardens. It is hard to decide whether to concentrate on the colorful plate in front of you or the gorge's surreal beauty, visible from your table. (☎42 108. Entrees €5-9. Open 11am-1am.) **Restaurant Papingo ❸,** to the right of the bell tower, near Pension Koulis, is a popular choice among visitors, serving the standard Greek fare plus some options for the mostly German and English visitors. Though more tourist-oriented than Tsoumanis, the food is tasty and the portions are generous, making it a good place to satiate your hunger after a day of strenuous hiking. (☎42 443. Entrees €8-13. Open noon-2am.)

📷 DAYTRIPS FROM THE PAPINGOS. If you're looking to experience more of the Zagorahorian villages, having a car might be necessary. For those with this option, the opportunities to soak in Greek culture, beauty, and history are endless. Any exploratory trip to the villages should include a visit to the Zagori Information Center in the town of Aspraggeli. As you turn right off the main road from Ioaninna going towards Monodendri, you will pass a gas station on your right; the information center is 500m past it on the right in the white stone building. The friendly staff and the light-up map with historical information are extremely helpful in deciding where to go. (☎22 241. Open daily 9am-6pm)

The town of **Vradeto,** at 1340m, is the highest of all Zagorahorian villages. From here the magnificent Vikos Gorge hike of **Beloi** (1hr.) is accessible. This vantage point is known by the locals to rival Oxia for the best view of Vikos Gorge. In addition to the hike, Vradeto is home to the **Vradeto Steps,** which until 1973 were the only way to access the village. Starting at the bottom of the picturesque steps, in the town of **Kapesovo,** the old 3km path to quaint Vradeto takes less than 2hr.

Also of interest are the towns of **Dilofo** and **Koukouli.** Dilofo is home to the largest house in all of Zagorohoria. Secret Koukouli offers visitors access to many ancient bridges, and is home to Roy and Effi Hounsell, the only English couple living in the 46 hamlets. If you plan on staying in the area overnight, **Roy and Effi's Place ❹,** just above the main town square, is a must. The peaceful, well-kept gardens and rooms fill up quickly, but if you're lucky you'll still get a chance to meet this hilarious and informative couple, who have been living here since 1980. (☎ 71 743. Simple breakfast included. Singles and doubles €50.)

◙ ⛰ SIGHTS AND HIKING. Mikro Papingo hosts the Zagorohoria regional **World Wildlife Federation (WWF).** The office, at the entrance to town in the former elementary school, has a few exhibits about local wildlife, history, and culture. Follow the main road that goes through the village; the building will be on your left at the first fork. (☎ 41 071. Open M-Th 10am-5:30pm, F-Su 11am-6pm. Free.)

The most spectacular Zagorohoria hikes begin in Mikro Papingo. Visitors can climb **Mount Astraka** (2436m). The mountain's 407m deep cave, **Provatrina,** is filled with water. Many footpaths go up to Mt. Astraka; most take about 4hr. and are appropriate for intermediate-level hikers. Another option is to climb to the pristine **⛰Drakolimni** (Dragon Lake). This alpine pool (elevation 2000m) is filled with green-and-black and orange-spotted newts that hang motionless on the wind-whipped grasses. It is well worth the strenuous 4½hr. climb up—the pool's water reflects the sky like a mirror and the air is crystal-clear. Both hikes can be paired with a stay in the **EOS refuge** (elevation 1900m; ☎ 69732 23 100; see below), on a ridge nearby. For those who prefer easier hikes, the fun and family-friendly **Papingo Natural Pools** are a great option. When the road curves right before ascending to Mikro Papingo from Megalo on the main road, you'll see a small bridge and a parking lot. Opposite the parking lot, the white-rock trail begins. As you climb, the natural pools become warmer and cleaner. Snakes and tadpoles are known to inhabit the lower pools, so watch out before taking a dip.

Those who can't get to the Papingos because of limited buses should consider hiking in from the Klidonia bus stop on the Ioannina-Konitsa line (1hr., 8 per day 5am-8pm, €4). From the bus stop, follow the Konitsa-bound bus along the highway to the town's main road on the right opposite a gas station. Ask at the gas station or any of the homes along the road to be pointed to the 5km **Klidonia-Papingo Trail** (Κλειδωνιά-Πάπιγκο). This easy walk, which takes around 1½hr., passes through green hills full of sheep and goats tended by local shepherds. Before you reach the bridge of Aristi, you will see a stop at which there is a footpath for Klidonia. A more difficult but also more scenic option to get to the Papingos is to take the trail up the mountain through the ghost town of **Ano Klidonia** (Upper Klidonia). From the trailhead, at a church visible above town, a path highlighted by red blazes leads up the mountainside. If you get off track, just follow the electric line that runs along the trail. The first shoulder (2km, 1hr.) is of intermediate difficulty, and ascends 900m to yield awe-inspiring views of the Aoös River flood plain and a small abandoned church. Follow the dirt path to the church of Profitis Ilias, where the red-blazed trail begins again. From here you have a sweeping view of Mt. Astrakas on the left and Vikos Gorge on the right. After about one more hour on a fairly level path, take the dirt lane to the west for the route's final kilometer.

NORTHERN GREECE

To get to the refuge from Mikro Papingo, start walking on the trail leading to Drakolimni and Mt. Astrakas; signs reading "To the Refuge" ("Πρός Καταφύγιο") will guide you. This intermediate-level trail climbs past four **springs:** a chapel-topped faucet (Ag. Pandeleimon; 10min.), another faucet (Antalki; 1hr.), a frog-filled trough (Trafos; 2hr.), and a small, cold spring (Krouna; 2½hr.). The path is well marked with O3 triangles and red blazes. Occasionally the trail spiderwebs, but usually all options are valid; keep an eye out for blazes. After the last spring, the trail is exposed and the refuge is visible on its ridge. Another 30min. brings you to the 60-bed **EOS refuge ❶**, 3km from Mikro Papingo. (☎26 553 or 69732 23 100. €10 per person, members of any mountain club €8.) A path (3km, 1¼hr.) from the same starting point descends into the blossom-dotted valley, then climbs a meadow on the opposite ridge. This path passes **Xeroloutsa**, a shallow, life-alter-ingly beautiful Alpine lake, and ends at Drakolimni. In the summer, the meadow's grasses are home to sheep and their shepherds, who are friendly and happy to ges-ture directions to the few visitors who make it up here. Give the flocks a wide berth, as the sheep dogs are very protective and have been known to bite. From the refuge, multi-day treks deep into the Pindos are possible, and hikers usually plan to end in the luxury of one of the valley villages.

MACEDONIA Μακεδονία

Macedonia earned itself a place in history when its native son Alexander forged a massive empire stretching to Egypt and India by 323 BC. A few centuries later, the region served as the geographical entry point for Saint Paul, who brought Chris-tianity to Europe. The historical boundaries of Greek Macedonia under the Byzan-tine Empire were much greater than the modern province's current territory; pieces of the historical region of Macedonia lie within Albania, Bulgaria, and FYROM. In recent decades, Macedonia has become the focal point of tensions between northern Greece and the Balkan states as Greeks have demanded exclu-sive use of the name "Macedonia" and even the return of formerly Hellenic lands. Despite its identity struggle, Macedonia is one of Greece's most multidimensional provinces. Offering a range of attractions—excellent archaeological sites, peace-ful beaches, and beautiful and burgeoning urban areas—Macedonia keeps its visi-tors intrigued with endless surprises and historical flavor.

THESSALONIKI Θεσσαλονίκη ☎2310

Thessaloniki (also called "Salonica") is one of the most historically diverse, cos-mopolitan cities in Greece, second in size only to Athens. With its charming squares, old churches and mosques, and ubiquitous ruins, Thessaloniki dazzles travelers as an evolving monument to European history. Kassandros, King of Macedonia, combined 26 smaller polities into a metropolis in 315 BC that defined ancient urban sprawl. Along with the rest of Macedonia, the city fell to the Romans in 164 BC and soon became capital of the Roman Macedonian province. After the division of the Roman Empire, Thessaloniki flourished as the second-most impor-tant city of the Byzantine Empire, leading to the construction of monumental churches throughout the city and sturdy protective walls surrounding it. Con-quered by the Ottomans in 1430, it served as a place of refuge for many Sephardic Jews expelled from Spain during the Inquisition. The city became part of the mod-ern Greek state in 1913 but soon was devastated by the Great Fire in August 1917, which destroyed much of the city's infrastructure. During WWII, the occupying Nazis murdered 55,000 out of Thessaloniki's 59,000 Jews; today the city's Jewish community numbers just over 1000. Over the last half century, Thessaloniki has risen from unstable conditions to become the major political center of the greater Balkan region, as well as the arts and culture capital of Greece. The cosmopolitan atmosphere and fashion-savvy population give this harbor city a youthful energy that complements its rich and glorious past.

✈ INTERCITY TRANSPORTATION

Flights: Macedonia Airport (☎02319 85 000 or 02314 73 212), 16km east of town. Take bus #78 (€0.60), which runs every 30min. from both the KTEL bus station and Pl. Aristotelous, or by taxi (€15). There's an **EOT** branch (☎9 85 215) at the airport. For tickets, head to **Olympic Airways**, Kountouriotou 3, at the entrance to the port. (☎3 68 311, reservations 3 68 666. Open M-F 8am-4pm; reservations M-F 8am-5pm.) **Aegean Airlines**, 1 Nikis, is on the corner of Venizelou Ave., one block east from the port's passengers terminal. (☎2 39 225. Open M-F 8am-3pm, Sa 8am-2pm.) Flights go to: **Athens** (55min., 24 per day 7am-10:30pm, €80); **Chios** (50min.; Tu 6:50am, W 4:40pm, Th 7:15am, Sa 3:15pm; €60); **Corfu** (55min.; Tu 5:40, W 2:05pm, Th 4:40pm, Su 4pm and 5:30pm; €65); **Hania** (1½hr.; M 2:15pm, W-Th and Sa 10:40am; €130); **Ioannina** (35min.; M 10:45am, Tu 2:10pm, F and Su 11:05am; €55); **Iraklion** (1½hr., daily, €115); **Larnaca, Cyprus** (2hr., daily, €110); **Limnos** (50min.; M and W-Th 6:15am, F-Sa 7am, 7:15pm; €66); **Mytilini, Lesvos** (1½hr., 6:15pm, €93); **Rhodes** (2hr.; M-W 6:15am, F-Sa 7am, 5:30pm; €129); **Samos** (1½hr.; Tu 6:15am, F-Su 7am; €75). Times can change; double-check before booking flights.

Ferries: Buy tickets at **Karacharisis Travel and Shipping Agency,** Kountouriotou 8, 1 block to your left from the main entrance to the port. (☎5 13 005. Open M-F 8:30am-8:30pm, Sa 8:30am-2:30pm.) Three ferry lines run during high season. The Chios line to **Chios** (20hr., €34.20) via **Limnos** (8½hr., €22.10) and **Mytilini** (14hr., €34.40) leaves Sunday night at 1am. The Iraklion, Crete line to **Iraklion** (21-24hr., €38) via **Skiathos** (5½hr., €19), **Paros** (10-12hr., €37.50), **Tynos** (13hr., €37), and **Santorini** (17-18hr., €41) departs Tuesday at 2:30pm. The Naxos line to **Naxos** (14hr., €39) via **Syros** (12hr., €38) and **Mykonos** (13½hr., €41.50) leaves Thursday at 7pm. Buy **Flying Cat** tickets at Karacharisis. Fast boats go to **Skiathos** (3½hr., 1:45pm, €37) via **Skopelos** (2½hr., €37) and **Alonnisos** (3hr., €37). They usually leave at least once per day, but schedules change weekly.

Trains: Main terminal (☎5 17 517), on Monastiriou in the western part of the city. Take any bus down Egnatia (€0.60). Tickets are sold at the **International Trains booth** at the train station. (☎5 99 033. Open daily 7am-9pm.) International trains go to: **Istanbul, Turkey** (14hr., 7:17am, €14), **Skopje, FYROM** (4hr.; 9am, 6pm; €11), and **Sofia, Bulgaria** (7hr., midnight, €50). Both regular domestic trains and high-speed intercity (IC) trains serve most destinations. Trains go to: **Alexandroupoli** (regular: 7hr., 3 per day 7:50am-10:25pm, €10; IC: 5hr., 4 per day 7:05am-1:45am, €25); **Athens** (regular: 7hr., 6 per day 8am-11:45pm, €14; IC: 5hr., 6 per day 7:05am-2:15am, €33); **Drama** (regular: 3hr., 3 per day 7:55am-10:30pm, €6; IC: 2hr., 3 per day 7:20am-1:50am, €16); **Komotini** (regular: 5hr., 3 per day 7:50am-10:30pm, €8.20; IC: 4hr., 3 per day 7:15am-1:45am, €20); **Larisa** (regular: 2hr., 8 per day 7:40am-11:45pm, €5; IC: 1hr., 6 per day 7:05am-2:15am, €12); **Xanthi** (regular: 4½hr., 3 per day 7:50am-10:35pm, €7; IC: 3½hr., 4 per day 6:43am-1:50am, €19). The **Travel Office** (☎5 98 110) has updated schedules and prices in English.

BY BUS

KTEL buses connect Thessaloniki to most major Greek cities; except for buses to the Halkidiki prefecture, all leave from the dome-shaped bus station 3km west of the city center. (☎5 95 408. Call for updated departure times.) Bus #1 is a shuttle between the bus station and the train station (every 10min., €0.50). Bus #78 connects the bus sta-

NORTHERN GREECE

Eptapyrgio Fortress

Eptapyrgiou
Bizaniou
Lahana
Pembti
Eptapyrgiou
Dimitriou
Delta
Thasou
Odis Foka
Triti
N. Plastira
Vermiou
Kastorias

Navarinou
Athdiakou
Filippou Diak
Alamanas
Arahthou
Zappa
Anthon
Eptapyrgiou
Navroumidi
Kap. Elenis
Erasmou
Kp. Ikonn
Mousko
Trigonion Tower

Vakhou
Olimou
Anazonou
Athan. Diak
Aghiou Pavlos
ACROPOLIS
Dragatsaniou
Klathmonos
Epitapyrgiou
Penandrou
Potideas
Xenokratous
Kendavron
Ag. Dimitrios Hospital

Eleftheriou
Ipokratous
Platonos
Riga Fereou
Meg. Alexandrou
Aravissou
Filippou
Ferron
Gherm. Karavangeli
Gheorghiou Papadop

Androniikos Tower
OLD CITY
Ikarou
Ormisia Wall

Manuel Paleologus Tower
Eptapyrgiou
Agnostou
Eptohpglou
Dimadou
Iguomenou

Mousson
Akropoleos
Moreas
Kodrou

Ag. Nikolaos Orphanos

VARNAS SQ.
Nigdis
Tranou
Paraskeva
Zarifi
Soulini
Makri St
Aristidou

Ferron
Eleth Venizelou
M. Romandi
Metara
Papagou
Odysseos
Elpidos

Evdoxou
Efseviou

Vlatadon Monastery
Ossios David

Mouson
Theofilou
Mousson Solou
Arghiroupolou
Olympiados
Kassandrou
Athinas

Turkey

Filippou
Enou
Iraklias
Pileos
Danais
Theofilou
Olimbiados
Ag. Vlahava
Gizi
Eschilou
Euripidou
Kourtsa

Akrita
Kilous
O. Poliorkitou
Iassonos
Ag. N Antipatrou
Ag. Nikolaou
Sofokleous
Seleftou
Iasonidou

Profitis Ilia
Kamenariou
Aladja Imaret

Sahtouri
Al. Papadopoulou
Raktivan
F. Dragoumi
Epaminonda
Pastor
Maed Amyntis
Ag. Dimitriou
Ag. Dimitriou

Panagia Acheiropoietos

Ag. Ekaterini
Olimbiados
Kassandrou
Ardon
Sandrou
T. Papageorgiou
BIT BAZAAR
Roman Agora
Ag. Sofias
Amynta
Platonos
Stratinou

Bey Hamami

Sofokleous
Alexandrou Papanastasiou
Makedonomachon
Antalghiron
Makedonias
Alexandrou Papadopoulou
Zenji
Klavdianou
Str. Doumbiotou
Stouri
EL Venizelou
PL. DIIKITIRIOU
Filippou
Iustinianou
Ioustinou
PL. DIKASTIRIOU

Karkassou
Zalogou
Stourniara
Kap. Agra
Kavouki
Ifestioniou
Fiota
Soutsou
Monasterote Synagogue
Hamza Bey Camii
Panayia Chalkeon
PUBLIC MARKET
Solomou
OSE Office

L. Katsoni
Piston
Panagias
Faneromenis
Borou
Arkadioupoleos
Ag. Dimitriou
Gladstonos
Papazoli
Kristalli
K. Palama
Antigonidon
Amvrosiou
Sintou
I. Dragoumi
Bedesten
Venizelou
Egnatia
Yehudi Hamami
Alpha Bank

Ikoniou Prokopiou
Apollioniados
Ag. Nestoros
Ag. Apostoli (Holy Apostles)
Olympou
Kattaki
Seleftidon
Valaoritou
Katholikon Paikou
Ermou
V. Irakliou
Tsimiski

TO PELLA (38km)
Papathanasiou
Dim. Golanaki
Kolonian
Dragoumanou
Dountoulat
D. Par. Tantalou
Vachou
Prorithtos
Zefitron
Mavili
L. Sofou
Fragkon
Verias
Edessis
Jewish Museum
Canada
PL. ARISTOTELO

PL. GALOPOULOU
Margaropoulou
Michailidou
Afroditis
Monastiriou
Enotikou
Danaidon
Tantalidou
Orfanidou
L. Sofou
Fragkon
Musical Instruments Museum
DUK
City Bus Terminals
Aegean Airlines

PL. DIMOKRATIAS (VARDARI)
Dodekanisou
Fragkon
Diamandi
LADADIKA
Loudia
PL. ELEFTHERIAS

Train Station
26 Oktovriou
Politechniou
Olymbiou
Salaminas
Vaiou
Doxis
Olympic Airways Office
Karachrisis Travel and Shipping Agency

TO DOME (3 km), ANCIENT VIRGNA (95km)
Giannitson Frintou
Sandaroxa
Kazantzaki
Hapsa
Karatasou
Kountounotou

Stavrou Voutira
Anagennlseos

TO 15 16

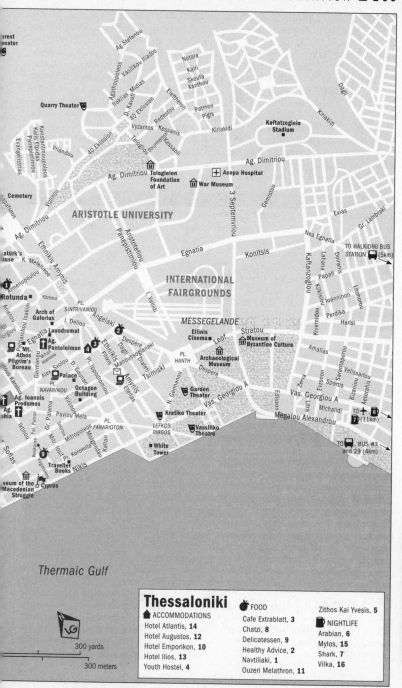

Forest
Theater

Ag. Stefanou

Notara
Kairi
Skoufa
Xanthou

Agathopoleos
Vasilikou Iliados
Iraklias
D. Kavali Midias
Eleftheron
Patmou
Pigis

Quarry Theater

Konstantinoupoleos
Kalis Elpidas
Panepistimiou
Evangelistrias

40 Eklission
Vyzantos
Kessanis
Teloglou Soumela Kessani
Kiriakidi

Dagli
Kiriakidi

Kaftatzogleio
Stadium

Vriandou
Yizinou

Ag. Dimitriou
Teloigleion
Foundation
of Art

Acopa Hospital

Ag. Dimitriou

War Museum

Gemistou

Cemetery

Ag. Dimitriou

Ethnikis Amynis
K. Melenikou

ARISTOTLE UNIVERSITY

Aristoteliou
Panepistimiou

3 Septemvriou

Evias

Gr. Lambraki

Egnatia

Konitsis

Nea Egnatia

Kaftanzoglou
Lahana
Papafi
Doiranis

Ioannou
Kilkisiou
Ioanninon
Lithohorou

TO HALKIDIKI BUS
STATION (5km)

Ataürk's
House

Armenopoulou
Kitreaus

PL.
SINTRIVANIOU
Angelaki

INTERNATIONAL
FAIRGROUNDS

Kivernidou
Perdika
Harisi

Rotunda

Arch of
Galerius
I. Deliou

I. Velidi

MESSEGELANDE

Ellinis
Cinema

Leof.

Stratou
Museum of
Byzantine Culture

Amalias

Egnatia
Germanou
Ag.
Panteleimon

Despere
Dagli
Manoussogianaki
Dialexi

Mt.
Athos
Pilgrim's
Bureau

Ag.
Ioannou

PL.
HANTH

Archaeological
Museum

Zena
Evzonon
Sarantaporou
Velissariou

Palace
Alex. Sivolou
D. Gounari

PL.
NAVARINOU
Octagon
Building

Ethnikis
Amynis
Etenas

Despere

Bizaniou
Spartis
Aetorahis

Ag. Ioannis
Prodomos

Vitonos
Pavlou Mela

N. Germanou

Garden
Theater

Vas. Georgiou A

Eddison
Litra
Michalidi

Vas. Georgiou A

TO
(11km)

Ag.
hia

Gr. Palama
Pat. Paton
Sinina

PL.
FANARIOTON

Megalou Alexandrou

Kostoura
Mtz. Iosif
Pt. Koromila
Kaftari

Mitropoleos
Morgentau

LEFKOS
PIRGOS

Kratiko Theater

Vassiliko
Theatre

White
Tower

TO BUS #3
and 29 (4km)

Sofias
Vogesaou
Traveller
Books
Nikis

seum of the
Macedonian
Struggle

Cyprus

Thermaic Gulf

300 yards

300 meters

Thessaloniki

▲ ACCOMMODATIONS
Hotel Atlantis, 14
Hotel Augustos, 12
Hotel Emporikon, 10
Hotel Ilios, 13
Youth Hostel, 4

🍎 FOOD
Cafe Extrablatt, 3
Chatzi, 8
Delicatessen, 9
Healthy Advice, 2
Navtiliaki, 1
Ouzeri Melathron, 11

Zithos Kai Yvesis, 5

🍸 NIGHTLIFE
Arabian, 6
Mylos, 15
Shark, 7
Vilka, 16

tion to the airport, passing through the waterfront corridor (every 30min., €0.60). International buses leave from the main train station (☎5 99 100) on Monastiriou in the city's western part; take any bus down Egnatia to get there (€0.50). Buses go to: **Istanbul, Turkey** (12hr., Tu-Su 2:30am, €38) and **Sofia, Bulgaria** (6hr., 5 per day 7:30am-10pm, €19). The dome holds offices for each of the KTEL district booths.

Domestic buses to the Halkidiki prefecture leave from the new **Halkidiki Station** (☎3 16 575), in the eastern outskirts of the city. Allow at least 1½hr. to get there. Take bus #31 eastbound down Egnatia from the bus terminal. When bus #31 reaches its final stop, get off, and take the #36 KTEL Halkidiki bus to the station. Your initial bus ticket will allow you to get on the #36 bus for no extra charge. Buses go to: **Armenistis** (2½hr., 4 per day 8:45am-6:30pm, €10); **Ierissos** (1½hr., 6 per day 6:15am-5:45pm, €8); **Kalithea** (1½hr., 13 per day 5:40am-9pm, €6.50); **Nea Marmaras** (2½hr., 3 per day 9:15am-5:15pm, €9.50); **Ouranoupolis** (2hr., 3 per day 6:15am-6:30pm, €9.10); **Sarti** (3hr., 6 per day 7:30am-7pm, €13.40).

DESTINATION	TIME	FREQUENCY	PRICE	TELEPHONE
Alexandroupoli	5hr.	8 per day 7:30am-11pm	€24	☎5 95 439
Athens	6hr.	11 per day 7:00am-11:45pm	€34	☎5 95 413
Corinth	7½hr.	11:30pm	€37	☎5 95 405
Drama	2hr.	Every hr. 7am-7:30pm	€11.50	☎5 95 420
Edessa	1½hr.	Every hr. 6am-9pm	€5.70	☎5 95 435
Florina	3hr.	6 per day 7:30am-7pm	€11.30	☎5 95 418
Grevena	2hr.	5 per day 8:30am-8pm	€12	☎5 95 485
Igoumenitsa	8hr.	8pm	€30	☎5 95 416
Ioannina	6½hr.	6 per day 7:30am-9:30pm	€27.10	☎5 95 442
Karditsa	3hr.	5 per day 8am-8:30pm	€15	☎5 95 440
Kastoria	3hr.	7 per day 7:30am-9pm	€15	☎5 95 440
Katerini	50min.	Every 30min. 6:30am-10:30pm	€5	☎5 95 428
Kavala	2½hr.	Every hr. 6am-10pm	€10.90	☎5 95 422
Komotini	4hr.	7 per day 8:30am-11:30pm	€16.80	☎5 95 419
Kozani	1½hr.	Every hr. 6am-10pm	€10.30	☎5 95 484
Lamia	4hr.	9am, 3:15pm	€21.10	☎5 95 416
Larisa	2hr.	Every hr. 7am-9:45pm	€10.90	☎5 95 430
Metsovo	4½hr.	6 per day 7:30am-9:30pm	€23	☎5 95 442
Parga	9hr.	10am, 9:30pm	€33	☎5 95 406
Patras	7½hr.	4 per day 8:15am-9pm	€33	☎5 95 425
Ancient Pella	1hr.	Every 40min. 6:30am-10:30pm	€2.50	☎5 95 435
Pirgos	10½hr.	M-Th and Sa-Su 10:30am, F 3:30pm	€44	☎5 95 409
Preveza	8hr.	10am	€30	☎5 95 406
Serres	1½hr.	Every 30min. 6am-10pm	€9	☎5 23 210
Trikala	3hr.	6 per day 8am-9pm	€15	☎5 95 405
Veria	1hr.	Every hr. 5:40am- 7:15pm	€5.50	☎5 95 432
Xanthi	3hr.	9 per day 8am-11:30pm	€14	☎5 95 423

⊏ LOCAL TRANSPORTATION

Thessaloniki and its suburbs are connected by an extensive public transportation network. **Local buses** (€0.50 at newsstands, €0.60 on the bus) run throughout the city. An office opposite the train station provides schedules. Maps posted at many of the bus stops show the city routes. The **depot** most frequently visited by travelers is at the train station and is the starting point for bus **#1**, which runs to the KTEL dome, bus **#8**, which goes to the White Tower stop, and bus **#73**. At the small depot at Pl. Eleftherias by the harbor you can catch buses **#5, 6,** and **33,** which navigate the waterfront on Tsimiski and Mitropoleos, and bus **#24,** which goes to the Old City. Buses **#10, 11,** and **31** run down Egnatia. Taxis (☎5 51 525) run down Egnatia, Tsimiski, and Mitropoleos; stands are at Ag. Sophia and the intersection of Mitropoleos and Aristotelous. Rides within the city should not exceed €4, though ordering a taxi by phone adds €1.50 to the fare. **SurfoMania,** Proxenou Koromila 48, has motorbikes and backpacking equipment. (☎2 31 351. Open M, W, Sa 9am-3pm, Tu and Th-F 9am-9pm.)

ORIENTATION

Thessaloniki stretches along the waterfront of the Thermaic Gulf's northern shore from the iconic **White Tower** in the east to the **harbor** in the west. Its rough grid layout—established by French city planner Ernest Hebrard after the Great Fire of 1917—makes it nearly impossible to get lost. The most important arteries run parallel to the water. Closest to shore is **Nikis,** which runs from the harbor to the White Tower and is home to the city's main cafes. Next are **Mitropoleos,** whose traffic runs from the harbor to the tower, and **Tsimiski,** with traffic running the other direction. At the White Tower end, Tsimiski terminates in **Plateia Hanth.** The plateia is a common reference point and a bus stop. Next comes store-lined **Ermou,** named after the god of merchants (Hermes). Farthest from shore is **Egnatia,** a six-lane avenue; the Arch of Galerius stands at its intersection with D. Gounari. Farther inland from Egnatia are **Agios Dimitriou** and the **Old City.** Intersecting all these streets and leading from the water into town are, in order from harbor to tower, **Ionos Dragoumi, Eleftherios Venizelou, Aristotelous, Agias Sophias,** and **Ethnikis Aminis.** Aristotelous, a wide pavilion where breezes sweep unobstructed from the ocean, is the city's center, with a bevy of restaurants, businesses, and banks. The roads north of Ag. Dimitriou grow increasingly tiny and steep toward the Old City's ancient walls, panoramic views, and cheap tavernas. The area between Tsimiski and the Arch of Galerius, **Plateia Navarinou,** with the ruins of Galerius's palace, is a meeting ground for young locals. The older crowd converses in the tavernas of **Ladadika,** at the harbor end of Tsimiski and Mitropoleos.

PRACTICAL INFORMATION

TOURIST AND FINANCIAL SERVICES

Tourist Offices:

EOT (☎9 85 215). At the airport. Open daily 9am-9pm.

GNTO (☎5 00 310), in the port's passenger terminal. Provides free maps and info about sights, buses, and events in Thessaloniki. Open M-F 9am-9pm, Sa-Su 8am-2pm.

Permits for Mount Athos: Visit the **Holy Executive of the Holy Mount Athos Pilgrims' Bureau,** Egnatia 109, 1st fl. (☎2 52 578; fax 2 22 424). Take bus #10 from the train station, bus #31 from the intercity bus station, or any bus along Egnatia, and ask for #109 or the Mt. Athos office (by the Arch of Galerius). All men need permits to visit Mt. Athos. Passports required; pick up permit in person. Women are not allowed to visit the mountain. English spoken. Open M-F 9am-2pm, Sa 10am-noon.

Consulates: See **Consular Services in Greece** (p. 9).

Banks: Banks with **currency exchange** and **24hr. ATMs** line Tsimiski, including **Citi Bank,** Tsimiski 21 (☎3 73 300). Open M-Th 8am-2:30pm, F 8am-2pm. No bank accepts Bulgarian or Albanian currencies. Travelers coming from these countries must head to the **exchange booths** at El. Venizelou's intersection with Ermou.

LOCAL SERVICES

Bookstores:

Molchos Books, Tsimiski 10 (☎2 75 271), has an excellent selection of English, classical, religious, political and art history books along with dictionaries and international newspapers. Open M, W, Sa 9am-3pm; Tu and Th-F 9am-2pm and 5-9pm.

Malliaris, D. Gounari 39 (☎2 77 113), has a large selection of English travel and leisure reading, computer equipment, magazines, and newspapers. Open M-F 9am-9pm, Sa 9am-4pm.

Newsstand, Ag. Sophias 37 (☎2 87 072), offers a wide selection of international newspapers and magazines. Open daily 7am-10pm.

Traveller Books, Proxenou Koromila 41 (☎2 75 215), 1 block inland from Nikis east of Aristotelous. Has English travel guides, including ■ **Let's Go** titles. Open M-Sa 9:30am-3pm, Tu and Th-F also 5-9pm.

Laundromat: Bianca, Panagias Recsias 3 (☎2 09 602). Wash and dry €8. Open M, W, Sa 8am-3pm, Tu, Th-F, Su 8am-8:30pm.

EMERGENCY AND COMMUNICATIONS

Tourist Police: Dodekanisou 4, 5th fl. (☎5 54 871), carries free maps and brochures. Open daily 8am-10pm. For the **local police,** call ☎5 53 800. There are also police booths at the train station.

Hospital: At both **Acepa Hospital,** Kiriakidi 1 (☎9 93 111), and **Hippokratio Public Hospital,** Costantinos Polius 49 (☎8 92 000), some doctors speak English. On weekends and at night call ☎1434 to find which hospital has emergency care.

Telephones: OTE, Karolou Diehl 33 (☎2 41 999), at the corner of Ermou and Karolou Diehl, 1 block east of Aristotelous. Near the Ag. Sophia church between Ag. Sophia and Aristotelous. Open M and W 8:30am-2pm; Tu and Th-F 8:30am-2pm and 5:30-8:30pm. Another location (☎5 51 599) by the intersection of 26 Oktovriou 1 and Pl. Dimokratias, at the west end of Egnatia near the city court. Open M-F 8:30am-2pm.

Internet Access: Behind the shopping complex housing the American Consulate, **E-Global,** Vas. Irakliou 40 (☎2 52 780; www.e-global.gr), is 1 block to the right. €2.20 per hr. €1 minimum. Open 24hr. Another location at Egnatia 17 (☎9 68 404), 1 block east of the Arch of Galerius, has 51 terminals. **Meganet,** Pl. Navarinou 5 (☎2 50 331; www.meganet.gr), overlooks a charming fountain of a boy relieving himself and Galerius's Palace. Noon-midnight €2 per hr., midnight-noon €1 per hr. Open 24hr. **Bits and Bytes,** Vas. Irakliou 43 (☎2 57 812). With 250 computers, it's a gamer's paradise. Noon-midnight €2 per hr., midnight-noon €1 per hr. Open 24hr.

Post Office: Aristotelous 26 (☎2 68 954), just below Egnatia. Open M-F 7:30am-8pm, Sa 7:30am-2pm, Su 9am-1:30pm. A **branch office** (☎2 27 604), on the corner of Eth. Aminis and Manosi near the White Tower, is in charge of parcels. Open M-F 7am-8pm. Both offer **Poste Restante;** to make certain your mail gets to the Aristotelous branch specify *Kentriko* (Center). **Postal Code:** 54101.

ACCOMMODATIONS

Welcome to the big city—don't expect to find comfort and cleanliness at a low price. Thessaloniki's cheaper hotels (doubles around €35) are along the western end of **Egnatia,** between **Plateia Dimokratias** and **Aristotelous.** Most are a bit gritty, ranging from ramshackle sleaze to mere cheerlessness, but all are easy to locate, with neon signs that would make any Las Vegas resident feel at home. Egnatia is loud at all hours; rooms on the street have balconies, while quieter back rooms may have just a window. Some mid-level hotels (doubles €40) are farther away from the noise, set a few blocks behind Egnatia on **Dragoumi** around **Plateia**

Dikastiriou. For more luxurious options, head toward the waterfront area two blocks west of Aristotelous. The closer you get to the water, the more you will pay.

Hotel Olympic, Egnatia 25 (☎5 66 870). Modern, simple, and newly renovated rooms have A/C, TV, phone, fridge, and bath. English-speaking staff is eager to give you advice about Thessaloniki. Breakfast €5. Reception 24hr. Singles €40; doubles €50. €10 discount for *Let's Go* readers all year except Sept. ❸

Hotel Emporikon, Sygrou 14 (☎5 14 431), on Sygrou and Egnatia, about halfway between Aristotelous and Dimokratias Sq. Rooms with bright balconies have a 1970s feel. A little quieter than the others that line Egnatia, the hotel has tiled shared baths and hallway fridges. Singles €25; doubles €35, with bath €40; triples €45. ❷

Hotel Augustos, El. Svoronou 4 (☎5 22 550; www.augustos.gr). Follow Egnatia down to Dimokratias Sq. and take a sharp right onto Karaoli. El. Svoronou is your 1st right; turn and the hotel will be on your left. Rooms have wooden floors and high ceilings. Doubles and triples with baths also have A/C and TV. Reception 24hr. Singles €25, with bath €30; doubles €34/40; triples with bath €55. ❷

Hotel Atlantis, Egnatia 14 (☎5 40 131). Standard rooms have sink, balcony, fridge, and high ceiling; those on the 1st fl. are newly renovated. English-speaking management is warm and hospitable. Rooms and shared baths are well-maintained. Breakfast €4. Reception 24hr. Singles €25, with bath €40; doubles €25/40; triples €30/45. ❷

Hotel Ilios, Egnatia 27 (☎5 12 620), on the western Egnatia budget strip, offers modern rooms with A/C, TV, phone, fridge, and bath. Singles €38; doubles €55; triples €67. ❸

Thessaloniki Youth Hostel, Alex. Svolou 44 (☎2 25 946). Take bus #8, 10, 11, or 31 west down Egnatia. Get off at the Arch of Galerius (Kamara stop), and walk down Gounari toward the water. Alex. Svolou is your 2nd left. The hostel's balconies often are filled with backpackers talking long into the hot nights, but you get what you pay for. 45 beds in 7 rooms. 5-night max stay. Reception 9am-noon and 7-11pm. July 15-Sept. 15 €15 per person; Sept. 16-July 14 €13. ❶

☐ FOOD

Thessaloniki has eight main dining districts. Just behind the port is upscale **Ladadika,** whose restaurants wine and dine older patrons. The restaurants at the corner of **Dragoumi** and **Eleftherios Venizelou** attract a more youthful crowd. Between **Egnatia** and **Aristotelous,** alleyways house *ouzeria,* where roaming musicians squeeze their way through tightly packed tables. A **public market,** with everything from fresh meat to Italian leather sandals, operates daily in the alleys between Egnatia and Aristotelous. Continuing eastward, **Plateia Athonos** is a student favorite, while **Plateia Navarinou** acts as a porch for the tables of well-priced *ouzeria* that overlook Galerius's Palace. Behind the **Rotunda** or before the **White Tower,** find some ostentatiously positioned (and priced) but nevertheless tasty *ouzeria.* The **Old City** brims with tavernas and restaurants that have sweeping views of the gulf. Thessaloniki's restaurants have a delightful custom of giving patrons watermelon or sweets *gratis* (free) after a meal. The local syrup-drenched cake, *revani,* a gift of the many refugees from Asia Minor, is especially good.

☒ Ouzeri Melathron, Karypi 21-34 (☎2 75 016). From Egnatia, walk past the Ottoman Bedesten on El. Venizelou and make a right into the cobblestoned passageway; take the 1st left. The witty, 4 ft. long menus at this secluded gem feature chicken, lamb, snails, octopus, and a variety of cheese dishes. Entrees €4.30-13. Free round of drinks with ISIC. Open daily 1pm-1am. MC/V. ❷

☒ Healthy Advice, Alex. Svolou 54 (☎2 83 255). Svolou runs parallel to Egnatia, close to the water. The friendly, multilingual staff at this Canadian-run joint serves creative Western style sandwiches and salads (€4-6) using the freshest ingredients. Open daily 11:30am-2am. ❶

▨ **Delicatessen,** Kouskoura 7 (☎ 2 36 367). Hands down the most locally popular place to eat souvlaki (€2), and for good reason; after tasting it here, you won't want to eat the Greek staple anywhere else. Open daily 11:30am-3am. ❶

▨ **Chatzi,** El. Venizelou 50 (☎2 79 058; www.chatzis.gr). This bakery has been acting as Thessaloniki's Willy Wonka since 1908 and now has 4 locations. Offers everything from the banal to the bizarre, including adaptations of traditional desserts like nuts *kataifi* (€3), *galaktoboureko,* a cream-filled delight (€2.20), and delicious baklava (€2). Open daily 6:30am-1am. ❶

Navtiliaki, Pl. Ag. Georgiou 8 (☎2 47 583), just behind the Rotunda. This *ouzeri,* known for its excellent seafood, also has meat and vegetarian options in a relaxing, tree-lined setting. Octopus in vinegar €6.80. Eggplant with feta and tomato sauce €3.50. Entrees €8-10. Open daily 12:30pm-1am. Bar open until 2am. ❷

Zithos Kai Yvesis (☎2 68 746), by the intersection of El. Venizelou and Filipou. With your back to Egnatia, walk past the intersection and look for a sign reading "Venizelou 72." The restaurant serves various appetizers and Greek food (€3) including *vlachiko* (pig's intestine stuffed with meat and cheese; €3). Open daily 6pm-2am. ❶

Cafe Extrablatt, Alex. Svolou 46 (☎2 56 900), by the youth hostel. This cheerful, family-run restaurant blends German and Greek cuisine, with crepes, pasta, sausage and mushroom dishes, and over 40 beers. Entrees €7-17. Open daily 11am-1am. ❸

◎ SIGHTS

▨**ARCH OF GALERIUS.** At D. Gounari and Egnatia stands the striking Arch of Galerius, known to locals as *"Kamara"* ("Arch"). Caesar Galerius erected the arch to commemorate his victory over the Persian Shah Narses in AD 297, covering it with relief sculptures detailing his triumphs. According to legend, Christians, who suffered greatly under Galerius's persecutions, rubbed out his face in every panel. Many of the lower panels have faded, but one still can make out the Persians, with their distinctive headgear, and some elephants in the upper panels. In AD 299, Galerius built a huge royal complex around the arch and made Thessaloniki his capital. The structure still plays a role in modern society, serving as the main meeting spot for youth and adults alike.

ROMAN AGORA. The 2nd-century odeon and covered market still stand at the top of Aristotelous. The agora's lower square once held eight **caryatids,** which since have been sent to the Louvre. Known in Ladino, the language of the Sephardic Jews, as *"las Incantadas"* ("the enchanted women"), they were thought to have been magically petrified. The site has undergone major renovations recently, and although they're often overtaken by children playing soccer, the agora and market are the best places in the city to feel the influential Roman presence in Thessaloniki. *(From Egnatia, go inland up Aristotelous; the site is at the end. Open daily 8am-8pm. Free.)*

WHITE TOWER. The White Tower looms over the eastern part of the seafront like an oversized chess piece, a symbol of the city and an easy rendezvous point. Originally part of the 15th-century Ottoman seawall, the tower became the Ottoman death row where Janissaries, members of an elite corps of Ottoman soldiers, carried out notoriously gruesome executions. Blood so often was seen seeping from the tower's stone walls that locals began calling it the "Bloody" or "Red" Tower. One prisoner, Nathan Gueledi, whitewashed the tower in 1890 in exchange for his release, thus inaugurating its current name. A walk to the top of the tower no longer means inevitable death, but instead offers a chance to see a marvelous view of the city and its shoreline. *(At the eastern end of Nikis. Take bus #3, 5, 6, 33, or 39. ☎2 67 832. Open Tu-Su 8:30am-3pm. €2, students free.)*

THE ROTUNDA. The enormous rotunda, now **Agios Georgios,** was erected by Galerius at the end of the AD 3rd century. It was originally a temple to Jupiter, the patron god of the eastern half of the tetrarchy, the Roman Empire's administrative system. In the 5th century, well after Christianity had become the empire's official religion, the rotunda became a church filled with mosaics of saints martyred at the hands of Galerius and Diocletian. Under the Ottomans, the rotunda sojourned as a mosque from 1590 to 1912. An estimated 36 million *tesserae* (small sea pebbles) were assembled to represent gilded facades, birds, and saints, though today they are barely visible. Only those highest in the dome have survived, so bring binoculars. Despite the current construction, the interior is vast and impressive. *(☎9 68 860. From the arch, turn up D. Gounari. Open Tu-F 8am-7pm, Sa-Su 8:30am-3pm. Free.)*

THE PALACE OF GALERIUS. A tiny section of the once 150 sq. km royal complex is open for viewing in Pl. Navarino, two blocks south of the arch. The southeastern section of the mighty palace, which used to extend from the rotunda to the sea, was unearthed in excavations in the 1950s and 60s. The weathered, geometric mosaic floors and partially preserved octagonal hall, believed to have housed Galerius's throne, are particularly notable. *(Open daily 8am-5:30pm. Free.)*

EPTAPYRGIO. Meaning "seven towers," this Byzantine and Ottoman fortress, once part of the Old City's outer wall, was a high-security prison until 1989. Today, it houses a small exhibit about the jail's history and is more of a morbid monument to the penal system than a historical site. *(☎9 68 843. Open Tu-Su 8am-5pm. Free.)*

OLD WALLS. From Egnatia, walk east with the water on your right to Eth. Aminis, the main street before Aristotle University. Take a left and head up the hill until you reach the cemetery; take a left and then your first right up the hill. Once you curve around a corner, the Ottoman era wall will be on your left with the 15th-century **Trigonion Tower** and acropolis in the distance. The walls, rising over 10m, surround the Old City with winding alleyways, typical Byzantine architecture, and panoramic views that will keep your camera busy.

OTHER SIGHTS. The Ottomans ruled Thessaloniki for almost 500 years and left an indelible imprint on its landscape: Turkish buildings and baths still pepper the streets. **Bey Hamami,** built in 1444, was the first bathhouse of its kind in Thessaloniki and was in use until 1968. Its labyrinthine interior has a cool antechamber that leads to a tepid room and the immense domed sauna beyond. Today these decorated domes and colorful marble-tiled floors house various modern art exhibitions. *(On Egnatia, east of Aristotelous. Open M 1pm-7pm, Tu-Su 8am-7pm. Free.)* Built by a bey's daughter from 1467-68 as a *mesçid* (a hall of worship minus the minaret), **Hazma Bey Cami** gained both a minaret and official mosque status in the late 16th century. Although it was an active mosque for Thessaloniki's growing Muslim population for over three centuries and was the largest mosque in Greece, today it is being renovated and is closed to the public. *(On Egnatia, just past El. Venizelou.)* A late 15th-century covered marketplace and craftsmen's workshop, the Ottoman **Bedesten** is said to have emitted delicious perfumes of musk and amber. Inscriptions carved into the domes in French, Greek, South Slavic, and Turkish evoke the varied ethnicities of Thessaloniki in its cosmopolitan heyday. Currently under heavy construction, the marketplace soon will house merchants selling fabrics, fish, meat, and various machine supplies. *(On El. Venizelou, 1 block south of Egnatia.)*

🏛 MUSEUMS

▨**ARCHAEOLOGICAL MUSEUM.** This fantastic collection includes some of the area's most prized artifacts. The treasures from Vergina's royal Macedonian tombs, once the highlight of Thessaloniki's collection, were returned to Vergina (p. 278) in 1998, but the museum still displays plenty of jewels. At the permanent exhibit on Macedonian gold, visitors are led through detailed descriptions of the gold extraction and manipulation process in Macedonia compared to modern techniques. The **Derveni krater** from the late 4th century BC is the most important piece in the collection. This ornate vessel, made of an alloy of tin and bronze, depicts Ariadne and Dionysus's wedding. Initially used as a means of mixing water and wine, the Derveni krater later was used as a depository urn for funerary ashes. It is the only intact bronze vessel with relief decorations preserved from the time period. Sculptures of a famously erotic Aphrodite and parts of an enormous statue of Athena share space with a grand mosaic depicting Dionysus with Ariadne, Apollo stalking Daphne, and Ganymede in Zeus's eagle talons. *(At the eastern end of Tsimiski. Take Bus #12 or 39.* ☎ *8 30 538. Open M 1-7:30pm; Tu-Su 8:00am-7:00pm; reduced hours in winter.* €6, *students and seniors* €3, *EU students and children free.)*

■**MUSEUM OF BYZANTINE CULTURE.** This museum exhibits the largest collection of early Christian wall paintings outside of the Vatican and illuminates Byzantine life. The huge museum, in keeping with Thessaloniki's position as the second-most important city in the Byzantine Empire, tells a far-ranging, secular tale, leading visitors through the rise to the fall of the empire. Through well-organized displays on daily life, economics, engineering, and imperial dynasties, visitors learn that the Byzantine Empire was more than the oft-depicted monocultural theocracy. The painted funerary art and AD 10th-century metal vessels that held holy myrrh from the graves of Thessaloniki's protector saints are particular highlights. *(Stratou Ave. 2. Behind the Archaeological Museum, across from 3 Septemvriou. Take bus #12 or 39.* ☎ *8 68 570; www.mbp.gr. Open M 10:30am-5pm, Tu-Su 8:30am-3pm; reduced hours in winter. Wheelchair-accessible.* €6, *students and seniors* €3, *EU students and children free. Guided tours (around* €15) *available by request.)*

■**JEWISH MUSEUM OF THESSALONIKI.** A sign at the entrance to the museum proclaims, "Thessaloniki: The Metropolis of Sephardism." Inside, exhibits tell the tragic story of that metropolis's height and demise. Waves of Jewish refugees fleeing 15th-century Reconquista Spain were invited by the Ottoman Sultan to settle in his lands. The museum's ground floor uses pictures, gravestones, and folk artifacts to show the subsequent 500-year history of Thessaloniki's Jewish community, once the largest in Europe. At its height, the Jewish population comprised more than half of the city, had over 30 synagogues, and led many of Thessaloniki's industries. The second floor features an extensive timeline, telling the story of the Jews' migration to Palestine in the 1920s and 30s after Thessaloniki's 1917 fire and of pressure from Greek nationalism. The last room commemorates the Holocaust, during which 96.5% of the city's Jewish members were murdered in concentration camps. The role of Thessaloniki Jews in momentous uprisings against the Nazis during the Holocaust is also highlighted, noting that many sang the Greek national anthem as they were being put to their deaths. *(Agiou Mina 13.* ☎ *2 50 406; www.jct.gr. Groups should call in advance. Open Tu-F and Su 11am-2pm, W-Th also 5-8pm. Free.)*

MUSEUM OF ANCIENT, BYZANTINE, AND POST-BYZANTINE MUSICAL INSTRUMENTS. Three floors of this upscale museum display replicas of contraptions used to please the ears, tracing their evolution from 2800 BC to the early 20th century. Detailed descriptions of how musical instruments were produced are placed side-by-side with the current techniques of instrument production. *(Katouni 12-14, at the western end of Tsimiski near the Ladadika district.* ☎ *5 55 265. Open M and W-Su 10am-2pm and 5-7pm. Free.)*

MUSEUM OF THE MACEDONIAN STRUGGLE. Once the Greek consulate to Turkish Thessaloniki (1892-1912), this house now contains memorabilia from the wars that made Macedonia officially Greek, focusing on the **Balkan Wars** (1912-1913). The exhibits include personal artifacts of rebel leader **Pavlou Melas,** along with captured war booty. The models and reproduced photographs shed light on the scope of this nationalistic struggle and its role as one of the triggers of WWII. Although a bit disorganized at times, the museum provides English pamphlets with facts about the collection and a historical overview of the Macedonian War. *(Koromila 23, 1 block from the water, halfway between the White Tower and Pl. Aristotelous. Take bus #3, 5, 6, 12, or 39. ☎2 29 778. Open Tu-F 9am-2pm, Sa 10am-2pm. Free.)*

ATATÜRK'S HOUSE. The three-story house that was the birthplace and childhood home of the founder and first president of the Turkish Republic now displays relics from his life. Pictures of the famed figure with various world leaders adorn the walls, and many items of clothing are also in view. Aside from these artifacts, however, the house is surprisingly banal. Display signs are in Turkish and Greek only. *(Apostolou Pavlou 17. Ring the bell, then present your passport next door at the Turkish Consulate, Ag. Dimitriou 151. Open M-F 10am-5pm. Free.)*

TELOGLION FOUNDATION OF ART. The large museum of Teloglion is part of the Aristotle University complex. Excellent rotating exhibits focus on topics from archaeology to modern art. *(Agiou Dimitriou 159A. ☎9 91 610; www.auth.gr/teloglion. Open Tu-F 10am-2pm, Sa-Su 11am-6pm. Free.)*

WAR MUSEUM. Located behind the hospital in Aristotle University, this haven for gun lovers and war buffs features military paraphernalia used from the War of Independence through the Civil War. Also on display are some Ottoman military artifacts and weapons captured from Greece's enemies. *(G. Labraki 4. ☎2 66 195. Open Tu-F 9am-2pm, Sa-Su 10am-2pm. Free.)*

♫ ENTERTAINMENT

Summer visitors looking for *rembetika* music should spend a weekend night at **Iyoklima,** a popular bar-cafe-club on tiny Axiou, south of Nikis near the port, or **Palios Stathmos,** Voutira 2 (☎5 21 892). **Alpha Odeon,** Tsimiski 43 (☎2 90 100), in the same mall as the US Embassy, is an indoor **movie theater** that shows a variety of American films (€8) and draws students from the nearby Aristotle University. When skies are clear, head outside to catch a film under the stars. American movies with Greek subtitles play at the waterfront **Natali Cinema,** Vas. Olgas 3 (☎8 29 457), 5min. past the White Tower, or at **Ellinis** (☎2 92 304), at Pl. Hanth, across from the Archaeological Museum. (Films show shortly after 9pm and at 11:10pm. €6.) You can't miss the posters plastered all over town for the theater, music, and dance performances at venues like the **Dhasos "Forest" Theater** (☎2 18 092), uptown in the forest near the acropolis, adjacent to the zoo. Other excellent, informal venues include **Kipos "Garden" Theater** (☎2 56 775) in Pl. Hanth, **Damari "Quarry" Theater** (☎2 06 930) in an old quarry in the Saranda Ekklesias district, **Moni Lazariston** (☎6 52 020) in the old Catholic monastery, and **Kratiko** and **Vassiliko Theaters** (☎2 23 785 for both) near the White Tower. The **International Fairgrounds,** across from the Archaeological and Byzantine museums, holds festivals throughout the year. The **International Trade Fair and Song Festival** (Sept.), the **Dimitria Festival** (Oct.; celebrates the city's patron saint with a number of theater productions, films, and dance performances), the internationally revered **Thessaloniki Film Festival** (Nov.; www.filmfestival.gr), and the new **Documentary Festival** (Mar.) all take place at the fairgrounds. Thessaloniki's **Wine Festival,** at which different wineries offer tastings, is celebrated at Nea Elvetia park in September.

◧ NIGHTLIFE

There are four main hubs for late-night fun in Thessaloniki. The **Ladadika** district, which served as the city's red-light strip until the 1980s, is now a sea of dance clubs. The bustling **waterfront** is filled with cafes and clubs. Dance-til-you-drop, open-air discos cluster around the **airport** and feature live modern or traditional Greek music. (Cover €15; includes 1 drink. €8-9 taxi ride from the center.) The **"Bit Bazaar"** area, encompassing 13 all-night wine bars, is popular with a low-key student crowd. To get into many of the chicer establishments, you'll have to dress trendily and, if you're not one yourself, have an attractive woman on your arm. Though the clubs boom until dawn, the summer nightlife isn't much by Salonican standards—most partyers head to the mega-beach clubs of **Kalithea** on Kassandra, Halkidiki (p. 299). Beginning in the warmer months, three **☒pirate boats** transform themselves into floating clubs. One of the boats blasts reggae, another Greek and alternative music, and the third combines disco with Latin beats. The 30min. trips depart from behind the White Tower and continue on past sunrise. (Beer €5, mixed drinks €8). The following clubs are popular year-round, but call in advance for special events during low season.

Vilka, Andreou Georgiou 21 (☎5 15 006). Located in an old factory, this huge complex offers a variety of bars and international-scale clubbing venues. Regularly playing modern Greek *bouzouki,* Vilka's stage also features local rock legends. Entrance can be difficult during popular events. Open daily midnight-8am.

Shark, Themistokli Sofouli and Argonavton 2 (☎4 16 855), in Kalamaria around the gulf. As the night progresses, this glamorous bar-restaurant clears out its tables, turns up the music, and becomes a full-fledged club. Waterfront views of the city's skyline from the balcony (open only in summer) thrill the dancing masses, comprised mostly of young, trendy professionals. Mixed drinks €10. Open daily 9pm-4am.

Night Club Arabian (☎4 71 135), along the highway toward the airport 13km from the city. Arabian supplies standard Greek fare and a relaxed atmosphere to an older crowd in a pseudo-Middle Eastern venue, complete with belly dancers and Arabic music. Cover €10. Open daily 11:20pm-5am.

Mylos, Andreou Georgiou 56 (☎5 16 945), in the far west of the city. Take bus #31 or a taxi (€4). Once a mill, the building now features periodic art exhibits, a restaurant, and bars. The Turkish dessert *ek mek* (pastry made with milk, cake, and pudding and covered with syrup) is served nowhere else in the city. Open daily midnight-4am.

▶ DAYTRIPS FROM THESSALONIKI

▨ ANCIENT VERGINA Βέργινα

Buses (☎23105 95 432) run from Thessaloniki to Veria (1hr., every hr. 8:12am-7:15pm, €6.10). From Veria take the bus to Vergina (20min., 11 per day 6:50am-8pm, €1.30). Ask to be let off at the Vergina archaeological sites. Buses run from Vergina back to Veria (20min., 10 per day 7:20am-8:20pm, €1.30) but are less reliable. Site open M noon-7pm, Tu-Su 8am-7pm; in winter Tu-Su 8am-7pm. Admission to Vergina's sights including tombs, theater, palace, and museum €8; students and seniors €4; EU students free.

Unearthing the ruins of Vergina, once the capital of ancient Macedonia, was an archaeological watershed. Among the finds were Greek inscriptions on Macedonian tombstones that bore Greek names, proving that the ancient Macedonians were in fact a Greek tribe. Scholars believe that the objects found in the tombs could have belonged only to the royal Macedonian family of Philip II, father of Alexander the Great (p. 53). This assumption was verified by the fact that the tombs date to 350-325 BC, the years of Philip's rule. The excavations began in 1856, when Macedonia was still under the Ottoman Empire. A French archaeologist uncovered a Macedonian tomb and other stones, but it was not until over 60 years later that the site underwent heavy excavation. In 1937 a professor from the University of Thessaloniki held classes at the site, and the university was given excavation rights during WWII. The most impressive treasures, however, including the royal tombs and the acropolis, were not found until the late 1970s.

MUSEUM. At once morbid and dazzlingly beautiful, Vergina's museum is the highlight of the site. Museum visitors enter the ⊠**Great Tumulus,** the largest burial mound in Greece at over 12m tall and 110m in diameter. It was built in the early 4th century BC and housed the graves of Vergina's common citizens in addition to the massive royal tombs. The dark museum utilizes a system of small, powerful lights on the ceiling to highlight the artifacts found in the Great Tumulus including Attic vases, clay and ivory figurines, gold jewelry, and carved funerary *stelae* (inscribed columns) of commoners' graves. Four of the **royal tombs** lie in their original locations, and each has an anterior Ionic or Doric colonnade decorated with mythological scenes. The large room behind the colonnade contains the deceased's remains and items intended to accompany him or her into the afterlife. The first tomb in the museum unfortunately was looted in antiquity. The next tomb, nicknamed the **Tomb of Persephone,** lies at the edge of the Tumulus along with a heroon, or shrine. Excavators discovered well-preserved **frescoes,** possibly the work of master artist **Nikomachus,** the most intact of which depicts Persephone being abducted by Hades. The following two tombs are among Greece's most spectacular archaeological finds. The **Tomb of the Prince** probably belongs to Alexander IV, son of Alexander the Great. Born shortly after his father's death, the prince was murdered at the age of 13 by Cassander, one of his father's generals. The silver hydra containing his bones and his spectacular gold myrtle wreath are on display, along with other artifacts. The most impressive of the tombs is that of Philip II, the conqueror who paved the way for his son Alexander's expansions. **Philip's tomb** holds a number of treasures, including a magnificent gold chest that held his remains, a gold wreath that sat on his head when he was placed on the funerary pyre, and fragments of his chryselephantine—gold and ivory—couch. Though the wood has rotted away, the ivory faces, arms, and legs of the couch's diorama, depicting Philip hunting with a young Alexander, still remain.

RUINS. The ruins currently are closed for renovation. To get to the **Palace of Palatitsa,** turn right as you exit the museum and make a left at the intersection. A shortcut through the bus parking lot followed by an uphill walk will get you to the ruins in about 10min. On the walk up to Palatitsa lies the **Macedonian Tomb,** believed to be that of Philip II's mother, **Queen Evridiki.** A downhill path leads to the **ancient theater** where Philip II was assassinated in 336 BC while celebrating the marriage of his daughter. Legend has it that he was punished for committing hubris by declaring himself a god.

ANCIENT PELLA Πέλλα

Ancient Pella is on the main Thessaloniki-Edessa highway, 38km west of Thessaloniki. Take the bus (1hr., every 40min. 6:30am-10:30pm, €2.40) and make sure you're let off at "Ancient Pella," not "New Pella." The site is to the right of where the bus stops, and the museum is on the other side of the street. Buses from Thessaloniki or to Edessa (every 30min.) stop across from the cafe by the archaeological site. Site and museum €6; students €3; seniors, EU students, and under 18 free.

Pella was the center of the world for over a century. When King Archelaus chose to move the capital of his Macedonian state here in 400 BC, the site, situated on what was then the shore of the Theramaic Gulf, fostered eastern trade and developed a rapport with southern Greece. In the 4th century BC, as Philip II became a powerful leader, Pella prospered and grew to be a major city. The splendid new palace was home to intellectual and artistic talents from throughout the Hellenic world; Aristotle was born in Pella in 356 BC. Alexander the Great, Philip's son, inherited the kingdom after his father's assassination in 336 BC. As he conquered eastward to present-day India, Pella remained the capital. But inheritance struggles and the division of Macedonian lands following Alexander's death in 323 BC weakened the empire, and recession of the sea soon made Pella an inconvenient port. The city's glory days ended in 168 BC when it was ransacked by Roman general Aemilius Paulus, who carried away most of the city's riches. A massive earthquake put the nail in Ancient Pella's coffin years later in the 1st century BC.

The Pella **ruins** take only an hour to see, as most of the archaeological site is being excavated by students from the University of Thessaloniki. At the heart of the site are the remains of the **agora**, the commercial center of the ancient city, with the three wells from which much of the pottery in the museum was collected. To the left, the **House of Dionysus** and the **House of the Abduction of Helen** both have well-preserved mosaic floors with beautifully executed scenes. The **House of Plaster** displays a splendid rectangular Ionic colonnade. North of the houses and the agora are the **acropolis** and **palace,** which are off-limits to visitors. Built in 10 stages, the palace is a blend of architectural styles. Expanded by Philip, it fell with the rest of Pella at the hands of Aemilius Paulus. Visitors can witness Macedonian urban planning expertise and concern for hygiene through the exposed extensive underground water and drainage system.

Directly across the highway, the **museum** houses gold-leaf jewelry, terra cotta figurines, and a white marble bust of Alexander the Great. Exquisite mosaics show Dionysus riding a panther, a lion hunt, a female centaur preparing libations in the cave of the nymphs and Dionysus, and a winged griffin devouring a deer (highlighted by grisly splashes of blood). The mosaics, composed of *tesserae* outlined with thin lead strips, are the earliest-known mosaics to mimic a three-dimensional look. The molds that once cast ceramic figures and bowls depict a series of Homeric and erotic scenes and mythological stories. (*Museum ☎ 23820 31 160. Open Apr.-Oct. M noon-7:30pm, Tu-Su 8am-7:30pm; Nov.-Mar. Tu-Su 8:30am-3pm.*)

VERIA Βέροια ☎ 23310

For most, Veria is only a transit point en route to the archaeological allure of Vergina. But in their haste to see Macedonian ruins, travelers miss a city built around the remains of a completely different period of Greek history. With over 70 churches to accommodate a population of less than 40,000, Veria pays allegiance to the importance of Orthodoxy under the Ottoman Empire and provides an interesting view on the cultural remnants of the *Tourkokratia* (Turkish rule). Veria's enchanting Old City, small and relatively untouristed, also has a Jewish quarter which acts as a living testament to Macedonia's Jewish Golden Age. Despite Veria's astonishing number of churches, all but one is closed to the public. The **Resurrection of Christ,** Mitropoleos 3, is near the intersection with El. Venizelou. This 14th-century, one-room church is adorned with stunning frescoes by Verian iconographer George Kallierges. (Open Tu-Su 8:30am-3pm. Free.) At the beginning of Mavromihali, on Pl. Orologiou, is **Apostle Paul's altar,** a marble, mosaic-decorated monument on the site at which the saint is believed to have preached. Veria's **Byzantine Museum,** Thomaidou 26, is down the road that divides the plateia and the altar. The small but beautiful collection of wooden iconographic art from the 9th to 15th centuries is all local—Veria used to be home to a prosperous icon-making industry. (☎ 23310 25 847. Open daily 8:30am-3pm. €2, students free.)

Accommodations in Veria are expensive. **Hotel Veroi ❸,** Raktivan 10, just off Pl. Orologiou, has baths, TV, and phones; some rooms have A/C and fridges. (☎ 23310 22 866. Singles €32, with A/C €35; doubles €48; triples €60.) At **Byzantino Restaurant ❷,** 8 Pl. Orologiou, you can choose from traditional dishes lovingly prepared by the owner's mother and eat in a cozy, stone-covered interior. (☎ 23310 72 243. Veal €6. Open daily noon-midnight.)

The train station (☎23310 24 444), 3km from the town center, is best reached by taxi (€4). **Trains** go to Edessa (35min., every hr. 6:20am-11:15pm, €1.30) and Thessaloniki (1hr., every hr. 5:35am-11:10pm, €2.10). Veria's bus station, Iras 17, is near Pl. Antoniou. **Buses** head to Athens (7hr., 3 per day 8am-8pm, €30), Thessaloniki (1hr., every hr. 5:30am-9pm, €5), and Vergina (20min., 11 per day 6:50am-8pm, €1.10). **Taxis**, available 24hr., sit in Pl. Antoniou. Veria has **no tourist office** but maps of town are posted at the municipal bus stops along most of El. Venizelou and Mitropoleos. The **Bank of Attica**, El. Venizelou 21, one block down from Pl. Antoniou, has an **ATM**. (☎23310 66 820. Open M-Th 8am-2:30pm.) **Karagrapoulos Konstantinos Pharmacy,** El. Venizelou 28, is opposite the Bank of Attica and sells herbal medicines along with normal drugstore ware. (☎233102 23 34. Open M, W, Sa 8am-2:30pm, Tu, Th-F 8am-1:30pm and 5-8:30pm.) **Internet access** is available at **Para Pente Cafe,** Elias 6, one block from Pl. Antoniou off El. Venizelou. (☎23310 24 300. €2 per hr. Open 10am-2pm.) Veria's **post office** is at 72 Mitropoleos. (☎23310 22 333. Open M-F 8am-2pm.) **Postal Code:** 59100.

KAVALA Καβάλα   ☎2510

The gateway to eastern Macedonia and one of Greece's major port cities, Kavala exudes charm that far surpasses its commercial importance. Originally built by Thassian colonists in the 7th century BC, it was named "Neapoli" ("new city") to signify its centrality in the islanders' mainland expansion. The city was renamed "Christopolis" ("city of Christ") during the Byzantine period, as it was the place where the apostle Paul first set foot in Europe. Kavala was given its current name under the Ottoman Empire, which conquered the city in the 14th century. On the eastern hill of the city, the Byzantine district of Panagia shadows the modern city and the port with its meandering cobblestone streets, kastro, and Ottoman imaret. The palm-lined port and Rapsani beach draw travelers seeking a relaxing atmosphere with a more modern pace than on nearby islands.

▐ TRANSPORTATION

Flights: The **M. Alexandrou airport** (☎25910 53 273) is 32km outside the city. Take the bus to Chrissoupolis (every 30min. 6am-9pm, €3) and then a taxi (€3). You also can take a taxi (€25) directly from the city center. **Olympic Airways,** Eth. Antistassis 8 (☎2 23 622), west of the Thassos ferry dock on the waterfront corner with M. Chrisostomou, has daily flights to **Athens** (1hr.; 7am, 9:40pm; €75-100). Open M-F 8am-4pm.

Ferries: Ferries leave from the east end of the port in front of several restaurants and ticket ferry booths. Call or visit the tourist information office for updated information. Every Su at 1pm a ferry goes to **Pireus** (32hr., €40) via **Limnos** (4½hr., €16), **Lesvos** (11hr., €27), **Chios** (15hr., €32), **Samos** (19hr., €39), and **Ikarike** (23hr., €36.40). Student tickets half-price. **Saos,** K. Dimitriou (☎8 35 671), sells tickets to **Samothraki** (3½hr., 3 per week, €16). Buy tickets to **Thassos** (1hr.; 10 per day 8am-10pm; €3, students and children €1.50) at the white ticket kiosks on the Thassos dock.

Flying Dolphins: Leave for **Thassos** (40min., 4 per day, €9) from the eastern dock.

Buses: The station (☎8 37 176) is at the corner of Filikis Eterias and M. Chrisostomou, between the waterfront and the post office. Buses go to: **Athens** (9½hr., 3 per day 9:15am-8:30pm, €49.80); **Drama** (1hr., every 30min. 6am-9:15pm, €3.60) via **Philippi** (20min., €1.70); **Thessaloniki** (2½hr., 15 per day 5:30am-8:40pm, €12.90); **Xanthi** (1½hr., 17 per day 4:45am-8:40pm, €5). To get to **Alexandroupoli** (2hr., 7 per day 9:30am-2am, €12), go to Seven-Eleven, M. Chrisostomou 4 (☎8 37 176), directly opposite the main entrance of the bus station, where you'll find schedules, tickets, and the bus itself. Open daily 9am-midnight.

Taxis: ☎2 32 001 or ☎2 22 424. Just behind the port behind Pl. Eleftherias on the corner of Venizelou and Averof. 24hr.

✦🛈 ORIENTATION AND PRACTICAL INFORMATION

Kavala's most historically interesting area is the **Panagia District.** Located on a peninsula jutting into the Aegean northeast of the port, it is hemmed in by ancient walls under the turrets of the Byzantine fortress. The entrance is on **Poulidou** at the end of **Eleftherios Venizelou,** which runs parallel to the waterfront two blocks inland. The next parallel street seaward is hotel-lined **Erithrou Stavrou,** followed by **Ethnikis Antistasis,** which skirts the waves from the dock to beyond the Archaeological Museum and municipal park. A detailed **map** of Kavala can be found next to the small port police kiosk at the Thassos ferry dock.

Tourist Information Office (☎2 31 011). The large, windowed kiosk off El. Venizelou at Pl. Eleftherias is an English-language oasis of information with helpful staff. Maps (€3) and free brochures, ferry schedules, bus schedules, and accommodations information are available. A ticket window on the side of the kiosk allows you to purchase tickets to the many performances in town. One computer with **Internet** access (€2 per hr.) also is available. Open M-Sa 8am-9:30pm.

Banks: Alpha Bank, El. Venizelou 28 (☎2 29 084). On the corner of Mitropoleos and El. Venizelou, across from the public park. **Exchanges currency.** Open M-Th 8am-2:30pm. Pl. Eleftherias, on El. Venizelou by the tourist office, directly behind the port, is surrounded by banks with **ATMs.** Most open M-Th 8am-2:30pm, F 8am-2pm.

English-Language Bookstore: Papadogiannis, Omonias 46 (☎2 25 885). At the northern side of Pl. Eleftherias. Has a good selection of European and American newspapers and magazines, as well as some books in English. Open daily 8am-9:30pm.

Police: Omonias 119 (☎6 22 273), 4 blocks north of the port. Follow Averof to the OTE, then bear left. 24hr. **Tourist police** (☎6 22 246) on the 3rd fl. of the police building. Open May-Nov. 8am-3pm.

Hospital: Stavrou 113 (☎2 92 000), 4 blocks inland past Panagia. 24hr.

Telephones: OTE (☎5 61 160). In Pl. 28 Oktovriou, near El. Venizelou. Open M and W 7:30am-3pm, Tu and Th-F 7:30am-2:30pm and 6-8:30pm, Sa 8:30am-2:30pm.

Internet Access: Funtazia, El. Venizelou 43 (☎8 36 660), has fast DSL connections and laptop access. €1 per hr. Open daily 9am-3am. **Cyber Club,** El. Venizelou 56 (☎8 31 295), has over 60 high-speed terminals and laptop access. €1 per hr. Frappés €1.50. Beer €2. Open 24hr.

Post Office: The main branch (☎8 33 330) at Kavalas and Stavrou, one block north of the bus station, **exchanges currency.** Open M-F 7:30am-8pm. **Postal Code:** 65110.

⌂ ACCOMMODATIONS AND CAMPING

Domatia are scarce and hotels aren't cheap in Kavala, making it difficult to find a good place to crash. Camping in Kavala's natural setting is a popular option. A few indoor budget accommodations also exist.

🏠 **George Alvanos Rented Rooms,** Anthemiou 35 (☎2 21 781). Enter the Panagia District on Poulidou at the imaret. Turn left at the fork in the street, then take a left up the stairs of Navarinou. Make a sharp left on Anathemiou; it's on your left. This centuries-old house has beautifully furnished, wood-floored, spotless rooms with fridge. Shared kitchen and baths. Reserve at least 1 week in advance. Singles €20; doubles €30. ❷

🏠 **Batis Beach Campground** (☎2 45 918). The beach is 4km outside of Kavala. Blue bus #8 (€1) leaves from in front of the post office, at M. Chrisostomou and Erithrou Stavrou (every 20min. 6am-8pm). Mini-mart and outdoor cinema. €1 to swim in the pool. €5 per person, €4 per small tent, €7 per large tent. MC/V. ❶

Hotel Acropolis, El. Venizelou 29 (☎2 23 543). From the bus station, walk 2 blocks away from the water and turn right on El. Venizelou; it's 1 block on your right. Large, bare but clean rooms have high ceiling, sink, twin beds, and TV. Ask for one of the 3 rooms with amazing view and spacious balcony. Singles €35, with bath €38; doubles €45/56; triples €60/97. ❸

Oceanis Hotel, Erithrou Stavrou 32 (☎2 21 981), at the intersection with Dagli. Colorful, carpeted, spacious rooms are fully equipped with TV, A/C, phone, large balcony, fridge, and sparkling bath. The bar and swimming pool on the roof provide exquisite views of the bay. Breakfast €9. Reception 24hr. Reserve 1 month in advance. Singles €50; doubles €70; triples €80. MC/V. ❹

🄵🄵 FOOD AND NIGHTLIFE

Tavernas line Poulidou in Panagia and the area near the waterfront. ◪**Mikros Mylos Bakery ❶,** Dagli 8, is on the corner of El. Venizelou and Dagli, one block inland from Hotel Oceanis. The endless selection of freshly baked pastries and breads, chocolate truffles, and homemade jams (€7) will satiate any sweet tooth. *Kurabies,* a local specialty (€3 per box), are not to be missed at Mikros. (☎2 28 132. Open daily 6:30am-10pm.) **Al Xalidi ❷,** Theodorou Poulidou 45, is a cozy, brick-lined taverna overlooking the cobblestoned road that allows diners to sip wine from Limnos while enjoying the peaceful surroundings of the Old City. (☎2 33 325. Appetizers €3-4. Entrees €5-7. Open daily noon-1am.) **Oraya Mytilini ❷,** across from the white bus station at the northeast end of port, has colorful tablecloths and a cozy atmosphere. It serves delicious seafood entrees (€4-8) like the "fruit of the sea" dish (rice with mussels, small shrimp, and octopus) and has a terrific view of the port. (☎2 24 749. Entrees €5-9. Open daily 10am-midnight.)

Nightlife options abound throughout the city, especially near Karaoli Dimitrou Sq. and the waterfront street of Athnikis Antistassis. Many tourists head to the beaches of **Palio** or **Aspri Amos,** a cab ride away (€7), but if you prefer to stay in Kavala, check out **Aqua** (☎69463 53 802), on the western corner of Falirou Park or **Omilos** (☎69489 48 552), a restored tobacco factory on the water. Both pick up after midnight and play a mix of Greek and international music.

🄶 SIGHTS

Once home to the Thassian colony of Neapoli, the **Old Town** is now known as the Panagia District. This spiderweb of steep streets and Ottoman-style houses unfolds atop the promontory beside the port.

BYZANTINE KASTRO (CASTLE). The current citadel was constructed in 1425 by the Venetians and later was renovated and enlarged by the Turks. Underneath it are the remains of Byzantine walls dating from the 5th century BC. Known by the locals as "Srourio," the kastro is divided into two fields separated by a tower and wall. A small **amphitheater** and three fortification towers are located in the outer field, while the inner field contains an early Byzantine cistern, an arsenal and food storehouse, and a guardhouse. In later periods the cistern was used as a prison. The amphitheater hosts occasional musical and cultural performances. In the Eleftheria Festival in late June, students celebrate Kavala's liberation from the Ottomans by performing dances at the castle. In July, the international festival of Cosmopolis highlights various cultures through dance, theatre, and photography exhibitions from all corners of the world. (*Follow the signs from Panagia's entrance on Poulidou. Open daily 8am-9pm. €1.50, students €1.*)

OTTOMAN IMARET. This beautiful example of Islamic architecture was built in 1817 by native Kavalian Mehmet Ali, Pasha of Egypt. The imaret—a type of hospice funded by wealthy Muslims to fulfill the Islamic principle of charity—was originally a seminary, poor house, and boarding school. While its current status as a protected hotel doesn't let tourists peek at the historical monument, if you win the lottery you may want to look into staying there. *(On the right as you enter Panagia at Poulidou 38, where the street forks and ascends to the kastro.)*

MEHMET ALI'S HOUSE. Ali's house sits at the very tip of the promontory. The founder of the last Egyptian dynasty, Ali was born here in 1769. He was recognized as the Pasha of Egypt in 1807 and given the island of Thassos as a gift. Another present from the Greeks of Egypt, a bronze statue of Ali mounted on a horse, still stands there. From the house, there are splendid views of the sea and of Kavala. In front you can see green Thassos, an oil rig, and the uninhabited islet of Thassopoula to the left. Though it is currently undergoing massive renovations, the house is still worth a look. *(Continue from Poulidou 3 blocks from the imaret, to where the cliff comes to an end.)*

KAMARES AQUEDUCT. Kamares aqueduct, erected in 1550 under Sultan Süleyman the Magnificent, connects the Old City with the New City and completes the circuit of Panagia. This colossal construction initially doubled as a defensive wall: the Ottoman city's guards would patrol on its top, while water from nearby springs flowed through it. *(To trace the aqueduct's path, take a right off Poulidou onto M. Ali. Take a left onto Navarinou and another left on Issidorou, which edges the western base of the kastro. Follow Issidorou and make a right at the end of the road.)*

OTHER SIGHTS. The **Archaeological Museum** nicely complements any trip to Amphibolis or to the sights of Thassos. Many of its artifacts were plundered by the Bulgarians during WWII, but the museum was reorganized and restored in 1952. The gold jewelry and wreaths, elaborate Hellenistic funeral painting, and the reconstruction of a Macedonian burial chamber are worth checking out. *(In the park on the waterfront, between Ethnikis Antistasis and Erithrou Stavrou, by Farilou Park. ☎ 2 22 335. Open Tu-Su 8am-3:30pm. €2, students €1, EU students free.)* Kavala's **Municipal Folk Museum** houses Kavala's municipal archives and a small but interesting collection. Of particular note are works by Thassian sculptor Polygnotos Vagis, an internationally acclaimed artist of the 1930s whose pieces blend archaic Greek styles with modern influences like Chagall and Matisse. The exhibit also includes local jewelry, games, and artifacts representing aspects of everyday life. *(Filippou 4. On the corner of Mitropoleos and Filippou. ☎ 2 22 706. Open M-F 8am-2pm, Sa 9am-1pm. Free.)*

Kavala has a number of tobacco-related sights, including the **tobacco warehouse,** two blocks from El. Venizelou on the far side of Pl. Kapnergati. Follow Averof, which runs inland from the port, up five blocks. Though it is currently undergoing renovations to accommodate the new municipal center that will share the building, the warehouse was once part of Kavala's booming tobacco industry. Built in the first decade of the 20th century, it has a beautiful pink facade and delicate stone masonry. In the same square, there is a monument to the tobacco workers.

There are 46km of **beaches** west of Kavala. The easiest way to get to the water is by intercity bus. **Rapsani,** in the western part of Kavala, at the end of Eth. Antistasis, has been improved in recent years and currently attracts the most sunbathers. The sandy beach of **Kalamitsa,** 2km past Rapsani, has tavernas, showers, and three bars, and it is slightly less touristy than Rapsani. **Batis** is next, 1km down the shoreline, followed by pebble-covered **Tosca,** renowned for its clean water. The city's main resort beaches, with hot summer nightlife and long strips of sand, are **Palio,** 10km southwest of Kavala, **Nea Iraklitsa,** another 2km, and **Nea Peramos,** 16km from Kavala. *(Buses leave from the post office near the bus station every 20-30min. Take blue bus #8 to all the beaches before Batis (20 per day 6am-8pm). To get to the farther* *beaches, take the green bus (30 per day 6am-10pm; Palio €1, Nea Iraklitsa €1.10, Nea Peramos €1.50). Bus times are flexible. Ask at the bus station for hours. Alternatively, taxis to the beaches range from €3 to Kalamitsa to €10 to Nea Peramos.)*

⚡ DAYTRIP FROM KAVALA

▨ PHILIPPI Φίλιπποι

Take the bus from Kavala to Drama (every 30min. 6am-9:15pm, €1.60). Make sure to specify that you want the archaeological site of Philippi. The bus drops you off at the western section of the site, where the museum is. ☎5 16 470. Site open daily 8am-7pm. €3, students and seniors €2, EU students free. The museum has been undergoing renovations for the last decade.

About 15km north of Kavala, the city of **Philippi** lies in splendid ruin. Originally built on the site of a Neolithic settlement in 360 BC, conquering Philippi was the final step in securing Thassian mainland expansion. With the establishment of Krenides, the islanders, who previously had expanded into mainland Greece by building Neapoli (present-day Kavala), achieved complete control of the Daton region. Rich in precious metals and agriculturally fertile, the area's Pangaion Mountains attracted many to this Macedonian stronghold. Just four years later, **Philip II** of Macedon conquered the city and renamed it after himself. The Macedonians controlled the city until the Roman conquest in 148 BC, and it was here that the Roman Republic later met its demise. The **Battle of Philippi** between the combined armies of Brutus and Cassius and those of Octavian and Mark Antony was fought at the outskirts of the city in 42 BC. The defeat of the former, who had conspired in the death of Julius Caesar, opened the path to an empire for Octavian, later called "Augustus Caesar," who would become Roman Emperor in 28 BC.

A new phase in the city's history began in AD 49 with the visit of **Saint Paul.** In the Bible's book of Acts, Philippi is referred to as "a leading city of the district of Macedonia and a Roman colony," as well as the place where Paul baptized Lydia, the first European Christian. In the mid-4th century, the first Christian church in Europe was built here, and in the 5th and 6th centuries, the city prospered as a religious center, inspiring people from across Europe to make the pilgrimage. After Ottoman conquest, Philippi was left to decay.

The site, which can be appreciated even by non-history buffs, contains the remains of 20 buildings of interest and a museum. The Kavala-Drama highway divides Philippi, leaving the central Roman ruins—the forum, the agora, the Via Egnatia (the important trade route which passed though the city), and the baths— on your left as you exit the bus from Kavala. Across the street, in the western section, lie the Classical and Roman theaters, the museum, and the prison that held St. Paul. In the far northwestern corner is the city's acropolis, built between the 5th and 4th centuries BC and reconstructed during Byzantine control.

LITOCHORO Λιτόχωρο ☎23520

Though Litochoro generally is viewed only as the gateway to Mt. Olympus, its charming small-town atmosphere and proximity to the archaeological site at Dion make it far more than a mere transportation hub. The town's twisting cobblestone paths lead down the mountainside to the plateia known as *kentro* (center), where locals relax in the shadows of Olympus. Litochoro is also, of course, a well of information about the mountain and its trails. Though it's possible to ascend the mountain from its western side, beginning in Kokkinopilos village, this treeless route can't match the lush canyon trails that originate in Litochoro.

⌐ ♬ TRANSPORTATION AND PRACTICAL INFORMATION. Buses (☎81 271) depart from Litochoro's KTEL station, Ag. Nikolaou 20, opposite the tourist office. They go to: Athens (5hr., 3 per day 9:30am-midnight, €28); Larisa (2hr., 8 per day 6am-8:30pm, €5); Plaka (15min., every hr. 10:15am-7:15pm, €1.40); Katerini (30min., €2). To reach Thessaloniki, switch buses at Katerini (1½hr., 16 per day 6:15am-9:50pm, €8).

Agiou Nikolaou, Litochoro's main street, runs east-west leading up to a fountain at **Plateia Agiou Nikolaou,** the central plateia. The **tourist office,** down Ag. Nikolaou near the police station, by the park, provides information in English, free maps of the town, and a €5 map of the mountain. (☎83 100. Open July-Nov. daily 8am-2pm and 3-9pm.) There's a **National Bank** with a **24hr. ATM** in Pl. Ag. Nikolaou. (☎81 025. Open M-F 8am-2pm.) The **police station,** Ag. Nikolaou 20, is just below the plateia, on the left as you walk downhill. (☎81 100 or 81 111. Open 24hr.) The **health center** (☎22 222) is about 5km outside of town by the beach and has 24hr. **emergency** facilities. The **OTE,** Ag. Nikolaou 14, sits across from the tourist booth farther down the main street. (☎84 099. Open 7:20am-2pm.) **Internet** access is available at many of the trendy cafe-bars toward the lower end of town. At **Cafe Artio,** Ag. Nikolaou 82, across from Hotel Park, patrons check email (€3 per hr.), sip frappés (€2.50), play pool (€4 per hr.), and listen to loud pop. (☎21 051. Open 9am-2am.) The **post office** is at 38 Nikolaou. (☎81 265. Open M-F 7:30am-2pm.) **Postal Code:** 60200.

┌ ┮ ACCOMMODATIONS AND CAMPING. Accommodations prices in Litochoro are fairly constant, and any price discrepancies can be eliminated with negotiating. Lodging is more expensive during Litochoro's famous Olympus Marathon that starts and finishes every year in late June. The town is liveliest during this time of year and makes for a worthwhile experience, but remember to make reservations well in advance. Though the cheapest options are the out-of-town campgrounds, there are some affordable indoor options. At **Hotel Park ❷,** Ag. Nikolaou 23, down Ag. Nikolaou from the plateia and past the long park, garish mosaic hallways lead into large rooms with air-conditioning, bath, TV, fridge, phone, and large balcony. (☎81 252. Breakfast €5. Reception 24hr. Singles €25; doubles €35; triples €45.) **Papanikolau ❸,** Niko. Espik. Kitaus 1, behind the plateia on a road that veers off to the left, has tidy, well-maintained, and recently renovated rooms. The sound of chirping birds and the smell of fresh bread that wafts from the breakfast room evoke Litochoro's small-town charm. Rooms have kitchenette, TV, fridge, glassed-in veranda, and air-conditioning. (☎81 236. Breakfast €2.50. Doubles €35; triples €45. Reservations recommended 1 day in advance.) The beach, 5km from town, is chock-full of campgrounds. **Olympus Zeus ❹** rents bungalows that resemble small houses with fridge, bath, and phone. Less crowded than nearby Olympus Beach, this mix between a campsite and a resort has two restaurants, a bar, and a beach volleyball net. (☎22 115; www.olympios-zeus.gr. Singles €40; doubles €50; triples €60; quads €70.) The complex has a **campground ❶** as well. (€6 per person, €3.60 per tent, €3 per car.) **Olympus Beach ❸** has very simple bungalows for one to four people with small bath, bed, and fridge, for a €40 flat rate. The area is like its own small town, with a supermarket, nightclub, 24hr. bar, and beach. (☎22 112; www.olympos-beach.gr.) The owners also offer a nice **campsite ❶** adjacent to the bungalows. (Reception 24hr. €6 per person, €6 per tent, €3 per car. AmEx/MC/V.) Avoid camping on the northern side of the road between the town and the highway, as these areas are army training grounds.

◖ FOOD. For a final feast before heading for the hills, try **Gastrodromio En Olympo ❸,** just off the plateia by the church. Enjoy a remarkable view of the mountain and choose from a menu featuring an array of meat dishes including rabbit, wild boar, and lamb, along with excellent traditional meals. The wine menu is equally varied, with 308 options. (☎21 300; www.gastrodomio.gr. Entrees €8-13.50. Open 10am-midnight. MC/V.) **Ta Mezedakia ❷,** Vas. Ithakisiou 3, specializes in "little appetizers," as its name suggests. On the street that forks right at the police station, the restaurant serves tasty Greek classics in an outdoor seating area. (☎84 574. Entrees €6-10. Open 5pm-midnight.) Those wisely seeking water and trail snacks for the arduous hike up Olympus should stay away from the expensive supermarkets just above the plateia. Instead try **Arvanitides,** Perikliko Torba 14, at the end of short, winding Odos Ermi, which branches off Ag. Nikolaou opposite the Demotic School below the tourist office. (☎21 195. Open 8am-9pm.)

▓ NIGHTLIFE. If you want to party, start your evening in the **bars** around the bottom of Ag. Nikolaou, just below the park. The action moves over to Plaka by midnight and continues toward the beach as the night goes on. **Abbia,** Ag. Nikolaou 100, 5min. past the tourist office, plays bass-heavy pop and Greek music for a young clientele. (☎23 520. Mixed drinks €7. Open 9am-5am.) **Bolero,** Ag. Nikolaou 98, just above Abbia, is a rock bar that caters to a more alternative scene, bringing in a diverse crowd with its hip decor. (☎82 702. Mixed drinks €5. Open 8am-4am.) On the road to Plaka, on the left side of Olympus Beach facing the water, **Caprice** provides the full gamut of nightlife experiences. It has an eating area, dance floor, cafe, bar, and beach access. Special events include grill night and full-moon parties. (☎22 506. Beer €4. Mixed drinks €6. Open 10am-5am). The wealthiest and trendiest Litochorians get down at **White Shark,** a glass-walled disco on a cliff above the sea. (☎22 930. Open 10am-5am.) Partying in Plaka can get expensive: a taxi from Litochoro costs around €6, cover is around €8, and the price of drinks can add up quickly. Fueling up on *retsina* and ouzo at one of the tiki-torch-lit *psistarias* (grills) before hitting the clubs is a cheaper experience-enhancer.

▓ DAYTRIP FROM LITOCHORO: ANCIENT DION (Δίον). ▓**Dion,** at the foot of Mt. Olympus and the ancient Baphyras River, is one of Greece's biggest and most fascinating archaeological sites. In Hellenistic times, Macedonian kings traveled great distances to the city to make sacrifices to Zeus. "Dion," in fact, is derived from a form of Zeus's name. At the **Greek theater,** Alexander the Great made sacrifices to seal the oaths of his assembled armies on the eve of the 334 BC campaign that led him to the far stretches of India. The city was also home to a number of cults worshipping various gods—temples to Artemis, Demeter, Zeus, and, later, Egyptian goddess Isis all cropped up here. In the **Villa of Dionysus,** a large, remarkably intact 2300-year-old mosaic is on display. Dion later fell to the Romans, who built elaborate **public baths.** The baths featured *a hypcaust,* an underground steam system powered by open fires. Destroyed by a combination of earthquakes, fires, and the Visigoths in the AD 4th century, the city (or what remained of it) was preserved by subsequent mudslides. Underneath the wreckage, Christian basilicas lived in harmony with temples of the empire's old religions. Thessaloniki University has been excavating Dion since the 1930s and has uncovered some spectacular artifacts. Almost every winter, however, some of the site, only 5m above sea level, fills with water, and most excavations have to begin anew in the spring. The three-story **museum,** just a 5min. walk into town, displays many of the treasures that have been recovered, such as the recently discovered statue of Zeus. The museum also displays a 1st-century BC **hydravlis,** a forerunner to the pipe organ, the first of its kind found in Greece and the oldest in the world. English explanations make the displays easily accessible. *(A taxi to Dion from Litochoro costs about €10. The walk to Dion takes about 3hr., but it's pleasant, with a constant view of Mt. Olympus. ☎ 23510 53 206. Site open daily 12:30-7:30pm. Museum open Tu-Su 8am-7:30pm. €3, students and seniors €1.50, EU students free.)*

MOUNT OLYMPUS Ολύμπος Όρος ☎ 23520

Mt. Olympus, the highest mountain in Greece, mesmerized the ancients so much that they believed it to be the dwelling place of their immortal pantheon. The sharp peaks saw no successful mortal ascent until 1913, when Christos Kakalos, a Litochorian shepherd, guided two Swiss photographers up to Mytikas's zenith. The group took the first photos of Mt. Olympus, and rumor tells that Kakalos became so famous that he never paid for a meal again. Since its initial conquest, Olympus has been harnessed by a network of well-maintained trails that makes the summit accessible to just about anyone with a head for heights, a taste for adventure, and about two days; the climb is strenuous but not technically difficult. The mountain and its surrounding region became Greece's first national park in 1938. More than 1700 plant species and 23 different types of flowers grow only on the mountain, and its tea leaves are well known throughout the country.

AT A GLANCE

CLIMATE: The mountain and its surrounding region are said to contain all the climates of Europe, from Litochoro's Mediterranean weather to the summit's snowy tundra.

FEATURES: The **Plateau of the Muses** (p. 291), **Mavrologos Gorge** (p. 291), and **Kazania,** "the cauldron" (p. 292).

HIGHLIGHTS: Drinking from the spring at the **Chapel of Agios Spileo** (p. 291), tackling **Kaka Skala,** "the evil staircase" (p. 292), writing your name in the book underneath the Greek flag at the summit of **Mytikas** (p. 292).

GATEWAYS: Litochoro

CAMPING: Camp at any of the refuges listed under **Accommodations.**

■ ORIENTATION

As you ascend, you'll pass leafy, green woodlands and shadowy pine forests before emerging above the treeline to views of the summit and the surrounding bslue sea. Mt. Olympus has eight peaks: Ag. Andonios (2817m), Kalogeros (2701m), Mytikas ("The Needle"; 2918m), Profitis Ilias (2803m), Skala (2866m), Skolio (2911m), Stefani ("The Throne of Zeus"; 2907m), and Toumba (2801m).

■ PRACTICAL INFORMATION

WHEN TO GO. Each winter, well over 7m of snow buries Mt. Olympus, and even in late July, snowfields linger in the ravines. Unless you're handy with an ice pick and crampoons, you'll want to climb between May and October. Mytikas, the tallest peak, is not accessible without special equipment until June, and returns to the domain of professionals around September. **Weather** conditions can change rapidly near the summits; even in mid-summer, be prepared for anything from chilly clouds and rain to unrelenting sun.

Road Conditions: Trails are well-marked and well-maintained but straying from them can be dangerous; most of the rescue team's calls are from lost climbers. Do not climb alone—even if you are traveling alone, try to find someone to hike with at a refuge. Also beware of belladonna berries, small, grape-like black fruit that grow on purple flowers. They are poisonous and just touching them, much less eating them, can cause unconsciousness. Though the climb is not recommended for those at risk of altitude sickness, the hike itself is accessible to people of any (or no) hiking experience.

Mount Olympus

TO PLAKA (4.6km)

Enipeas River

Litochoro

Mantrinies Shoulder

Stavros Refuge (Refuge D, 940m)

Diastavrosi

Mavrologos Gorge

Barba Meadow

Petrostrounga (9561ft)

Strangos (6266ft)

Ithakisiolis Shelter

Falls of Enipeas

Ag. Dionysios

E4

Enipeas River

Kardara (2998ft)

Koromilies (3717ft)

Maltas (4491ft)

Livathaki (7053m)

Rachi Achriani (6597ft)

CAVES
Waterholes ⊙
Roads
Trails

Mandres (7432ft)

Strangos Spring

Skourta (8120ft)

Enipeas Spring

Prionia

Taverna ⊙

Pelekoudia (6529ft)

Simeoforos (7317ft)

Draghasia (7351ft)

Paghos (8779ft)

Frangou Aloni (8782ft)

SEO Trail

Plateau of the Muses

Kakalos Refuge (Refuge C, 8694ft)

Zonaria Trail

Zoletas Refuge (Spilios Agapitos Refuge, Refuge A, 2100m)

MT. OLYMPUS NATIONAL PARK

Kalogeros (8861ft)

Skolio Ridge

G. Apostolidis (SEO Refuge) (9055ft)

Proftis Ilias (9396ft)

Louki Trail

Mytikas (9572m)

Skala (9402ft)

Toumba (9189m)

Stefani (9537m)

Koka Skala Trail

E4

Ag. Antonis (9242ft)

Kakavrakas (8580ft)

Skolio (9610m)

Megala Kazania

Shelter

Ski Lift

Pirgos Girva (7709ft)

Army Refuge Refuge B

Vrisopoules (5905ft)

TO KOKINOPOLOS (15km)

0   2 miles

0   2 kilometers

Refuges: EOS refuge Zolotas "Spilios Agapitos" (☎81 800). Has the most reliable resources for all aspects of hiking—updates on weather and trail conditions, advice on itineraries and routes, and reservations for any of the Greek Alpine Club (EOS) refuges. The staff has years of experience and is happy to give information over the phone in English. As the refuge is 2100m up the mountain, it's best to call from Litochoro before embarking on the climb. Open for calls 6am-10pm. The EOS office (☎82 444) is the small stone building in the parking lot below Litochoro off Ithakisiou. The parking lot is just below Gastrodromio En Olympo and the plateia. It's worth stopping by even if the office is closed—many of the members of the Mt. Olympus search-and-rescue team hang out there, and are glad to help hikers. Open M-F 9:30am-12:30pm and 6-8pm, Sa-Su 9am-noon. The SEO office (Association of Greek Mountain Climbers; ☎83 262), behind Hotel Mirto, is more of a clubhouse than an official resource.

Gear: If you are climbing between June and September, you'll need equipment: sturdy ankle-high shoes, sunscreen, a head covering, some snacks, at least 2L of water, light walking clothes, a wool or synthetic fleece sweater or jacket (the summit is 8-15°C/46-59°F in the summer), and an extra shirt and waterproof windbreaker. You also might want to purchase a light, portable emergency kit. Some hikers swear by trekking poles for maintaining balance and climbing steep terrain, but you will have to bring your own as there is no place to buy or rent them on the mountain. To avoid carrying unnecessary weight, take a small day pack and leave your luggage in Litochoro; the EOS office stores bags for free.

Guides: You can buy a colorful bilingual fold-out map with contour lines and all the major trails at most local shops, kiosks, and bookstores for €4-5. A Road Editions map, produced with data from the Greek Army Geographical Service, is the best and most expensive map (€8).

⛰ ACCOMMODATIONS

Reaching Mytikas in one day is only recommended for experienced hikers up for an 8km, 6-8hr. ascent and a strenuous 4-6hr. hike back down. For those who want to savor the summit trails or are concerned about the possibility of altitude sickness from leaping from the Aegean to 3000m and back in one day, an overnight stay in one of the refuges is a good idea. They provide beds, blankets, meals, and water, but no sheets or towels. Three refuges are near the summits, and all of them, particularly Zolotas, tend to fill up on weekends between June and October. Call at least one week in advance for reservations. At the refuges, breakfasts tend to run €3, soups and salads €2.50-3.50, and pasta and meat dishes €3-5. Bring a flashlight to navigate your way to the bathroom after the generator is shut down. The refuges' managers are prepared to embark on emergency rescues if need be.

Zolotas Refuge, (☎81 800; elev. 2100m), also called "Spilios Agapitos" or "Refuge A." Named after owner Constantine Zolotas, it's about 800m below Skala and Mytikas peaks and can be reached by a very easy walk on the E4 trail. The 110 beds, telephone, and very cold showers make this refuge the largest and cushiest, though also the most crowded—reservations are recommended. Curfew 10pm. Open mid-May to Oct. 6am-10pm. €10, with any Greek mountain club membership €8. You also can set up a tent nearby and use the refuge's facilities for €5. ❶

Kakalos (elev. 2650m), called "Refuge C." Much closer to the summit than Zolotas, on the other side of the mountain in the Plateau of Muses. Accessible by a trail of intermediate difficulty, it has 18 beds. Make reservations through Zolotas. Meals served 6am-9pm. Reception 24hr. €10, with any Greek mountain club membership €8. Open June-Sept. 15 F-Su only to groups (though stranded hikers are not turned away). ❶

G. Apostolidis (elev. 2760m), better known as "SEO Refuge," 15min. from Kakalos, beneath Stefani and Profitis Ilias. Has extraordinary sunrise views. Sleeps 100 and can accommodate extras and late-comers in its glass-walled porch or living room. Make reservations through the Thessaloniki SEO, which runs the refuge. (☎ 23102 44 710. Open M-F 8am-10pm; leave a message for reservations.) Meals served 9am-9:30pm. Reception 24hr. June-Sept. €10, with any Greek mountain club membership €8. ❶

🔧 HIKING

There are three ways to tackle Olympus; all originate in **Litochoro** (elev. 500m). Two of the trails involve heading straight to the trailheads, while the third takes you to the trailhead along a more scenic route. **Prionia** is about a 1hr. drive (taxi €20-25) or an easy 5hr. walk from Litochoro. There are no buses to **Diastavrosi** so you must walk (4hr.), drive (40min.), or take a taxi (€11) from Litochoro. To hike to Prionia via a trail along the **Enipeas Gorge,** begin in Litochoro and, after an easy 4½hr. hike along a river, arrive at the Prionia trailhead.

PRIONIA

The most popular and easiest route begins at Prionia (elev. 1100m). At the trail-head, you'll find drinking-water taps, toilets, and a small restaurant. From here, a 3hr., 4km walk takes you to the **Zolotas refuge.** The well-marked trail is part of the European **E4** path from Spain to Greece. There's one last chance for water before the refuge, about 45min. from **Prionia.** After another 15min. you will be able to see the refuge, but it will be another 2hr. before you reach it. As you approach the treeline, you'll be encouraged by bright clumps of wildflowers.

DIASTAVROSI

The second trailhead is at **Diastavrosi** (also called **Gortsia;** elev. 1300m), 14km away, leading up to Kakalos and the SEO refuges. This longer (11km) includes a stunning ridge walk with views of the Aegean, the Macedonian plain, and Thessaloniki's smog. On cloudless days you may also be able to spy Mt. Athos and Thassos. As you climb higher, the difference in altitude is noticeable as the amount of vegetation dwindles. The well-marked trail reaches the SEO and Kakalos refuges in about 6-8hr. Begin at Diastavrosi's parking lot—to reach it, turn right off the gravel road halfway between Litochoro and Prionia. Then take the uphill path on the left, and follow the red blazes, striped plastic strips on trees, and signs of the mule caravan that uses this route. In about 1hr., you'll pass through the **Barba Meadow,** which has a water tap. An hour later, you'll reach a cement water tank with an unhelpful painted map off to the left. Go straight here, not left, and the path leads up to **Petrostrounga** (elev. 1800m), about 3hr. from the trailhead. Four hours from the trailhead you'll begin approaching the treeline, reaching **Skourta Hill** in another 30min. or so. Here the trees will turn into small grassy fields. The beautiful **Lemos Ridge** leads you gently toward the peaks. About 5½hr. from the beginning of the hike you'll hit the **Plateau of the Muses** (Οροπέδιο Μουσόν; or-eh-PEH-thio moos-ON), a sweeping expanse of green under the Stefani, Toumba, and Profitis Ilias peaks. Take the clearly marked fork left for the **Kakalos refuge** (elev. 2650m) or right for the **SEO refuge** (elev. 2760m). A trail also goes up to the top of Profitis Ilias, where you'll see a tiny stone **church,** built in 1925. You usually can find water in two places along the Diastavrosi trail: at the turn-off between Barba and Spilla (1½hr. from the trailhead, marked on the trail), and at Stragos spring. It's best not to depend on the springs, though, as they run dry in very warm weather.

ENIPEAS GORGE

After spending the night at the Zolotas refuge, ascend to the summit the next day and head to the SEO and Kakalos refuges. Hikers can stay another night there and walk down the next day to Diastavrosi (5-6hr.), or pass the refuges and arrive at Diastavrosi in late afternoon. All the trails to the refuges are simple to follow, and most are marked with red and yellow blazes. The low-key, beautiful trail from Litochoro to Prionia runs along an E4 trail by the Enipeas River through the **Mavrologos Gorge,** whose name means "black mountain," since the trees are so dense that you can't see the sun. The parts of the trail that go up through Enipeas Gorge are not difficult in themselves, but they add about 5hr. to the ascent from Prionia, making it a total climb of 8-9hr. Gorgeous stretches punctuate the 18km climb, but it's a long hike with many ups and downs on multiple bridges, so be sure to bring water. To find the trailhead, walk uphill from Litochoro's main plateia past the Hotel Aphrodite, and follow signs to **Mili** (Μύλοι), past the town cemetery, to the Restaurant Mili. There is drinking water at the trailhead. Continue past the restaurant to the left. When you reach the concrete walkway, make a right and walk along it for a short distance. At the fork, follow the yellow diamond markers reading "E4" up the left side of the Mavrologos Gorge. Keep following yellow diamonds, red blazes, spray-painted numbers, and orange and white plastic strips tied on trees, crossing over the river at the new bridges. Parts of the trail have views down into the gorge. When the trail descends to the river, you will see several lovely, clear green pools; though they couldn't be more tempting, swimming is forbidden. After 3hr. you'll reach the tiny **Chapel of Agios Spileo,** built at the source of a small spring inside a gaping cave. About 20min. farther, after a bridge crossing, follow the dirt road for 60m before turning left up the hill to see the charred shell of the **Monastery of Agios Dionysios,** which was a refuge for Greek partisans during WWII until it was bombed by the Nazis. According to locals, when Ag. Dionysiou built the church in the 15th century, he was aided by a bear. After a short dispute that followed the church's completion, however, the saint petrified the bear, which still can be seen standing across the ridge from the church. You can fill your water bottle here and leave a small donation for the restoration of the large and beautifully situated monastery. Follow the outside wall of the monastery to a fork in the road and continue straight. You'll reach another fork after 15min. Take the left branch to go to the **Falls of Perivoli** and the right branch to reach Prionia after another hour. There are free camping zones between Ag. Dionysios and the Prionia trail.

MYTIKAS

From the refuges, the next step is conquering the top. Once you get there and meet the gods, make sure to write your name in the book underneath the Greek flag at the summit. There are only two trails, both classified as intermediate, to the top: **Louki,** "steep gorge," and **Kaka Skala,** "the evil staircase." Despite its ominous name, Skala is the easier of the two, though both have sheer drops and require some scrambling. Slightly longer, and a detour for hikers ascending from Kakalos or the SEO refuge, Kaka Skala climbs the ridge behind Zolotas on a broad but steep path to the Skala peak (2861m). From Zolotas, walk uphill. After about 45min. (1.2km), you'll find a map at a fork in the road. The left option takes you along the E4 trail to Skala and Skolio peaks; the right is the **Zonaria** trail, which leads to the Louki trail fork and the SEO and Kakalos refuge paths. If you're going via Skala, 50m beyond the signpost you'll find an unmarked fork. Take the right leg and continue ascending for about 1hr. (1km) along exposed terrain until you reach Skala peak. From here hikers can turn up to the Skolio peak (2904m) for a sweeping view of Mytikas and Profitis Ilias, or grab handholds on the mostly vertical "path" plummeting down to the sharp saddle point between Skala and Mytikas and then back up "The Needle." Those distracted by rocks loosed from climbers above should glance to their left—the 500m drop into **Kazania** ("The Cauldron"), named for the clouds of mist that steam up from it, will brush away all extraneous concerns. The climb, which is covered with snow most of the year, takes about 3hr.

The Louki trail should be used only for ascent; only serious climbers should attempt it for the descent. Louki branches off Zonaria about halfway (45min., 700m) between its endpoint on the Skala trail and SEO path respectively. After balancing along the precipitous Zonaria trail, hikers must turn straight up Louki's red-blazed gorge. During a pause in the shower of dust from climbers above, those with particularly good grips can peruse the plaques commemorating their unlucky predecessors, whose final handholds were not as secure as you hope your next one will be. Though 50 people have died trying to meet Zeus, most of the fatalities were caused by attempting ridiculous stunts like taking a picture while making a 50m jump (true story); the trail itself is quite safe. After 300m you will arrive at the top. A little closer to the SEO side of the Zonaria path, a slightly more dangerous trail goes up to Stefani peak, marked by a bent, rusted signpost. Past this is the SEO path, a 20min. walk to the SEO refuge and Plateau of the Muses. The bowl-shaped slopes are known as the **"Throne of Zeus,"** as the chief god is said to rest his enormous cranium on the Stefani (crown) peak above. Approaching the peaks from the Plateau of the Muses, it's about 1½hr. up to Mytikas via Louki, or 4hr. by the Skala route.

SKOLIO

If you decide to resist tempting the gods by climbing to Mytikas, you can take the 20min. hike from Skala to Skolio, the second-highest peak (2911m; 7m shorter than Mytikas). From here, you'll have the best view of Olympus's sheer western face. It takes about 2½hr. to reach the Skolio summit from the Zolotas refuge. From Skolio, a 1hr. walk south along the ridge takes you to the Agios Antonis summit and a path descending back to Zolotas.

EDESSA Εδεσσα ☎ 23810

Edessa, the capital of the prefecture of the same name, retains a small-town feel despite its previous position as an industrial powerhouse. Nicknamed the "Manchester of Macedonia" when its factories boomed in the 1920s and 30s, Edessa now embraces its natural surroundings. Spreading along the edge of a cliff, it yields views of Classical ruins and plains that stretch to Thessaloniki. Edessa's urban space charms travelers with its small rivers that race along side streets and under bridges to finally leap off the cliffs in three captivating waterfalls.

🖃 TRANSPORTATION. From the train station (☎ 23 510), at the end of 18 Oktovriou, **trains** run to: Athens (regular: 7hr., 10am, €23; intercity: 6hr., 1:04pm, €29) via Plati (50min., €3); Florina (2hr., 4 per day 8am-9:40pm, €5); Kozani (2hr., daily 8am, €5); Thessaloniki (regular: 1½hr., 9 per day 6am-10pm, €4.50; intercity: 1¼hr., 9 per day 4:59-9:36pm, €6) via Naoussa (35min., €2) and Veria (40min., €2.10). Edessa's main bus station, Pavlou Mela 13 (☎ 23 511), is at the corner of Fillipou near the center of town. **Buses** go to Athens (8hr., 3 per day 8am-8pm, €37) via Litochoro (2½hr., €10.30) and Larisa (3hr., €14), Thessaloniki (1½hr., every hr. 6am-9pm, €6.70), and Veria (1hr., 6 per day 8am-4pm, €3.90). Buses leave from a stop outside the pastry shop called Ta Souvrakia for Florina (1½hr., 6 per day 8:45am-9:15pm, €10), Kastoria (2hr.; 9:30am, 1:15pm; €10.20), and Kozani (2½hr., 6 per day 10am-8:15pm, €11). With your back to the main bus station, take a right on Filippou and look for the pastry shop three stores down. Schedules are posted inside the main bus station; tickets are sold on the bus. **Taxis** (☎ 23 392) congregate on Dimokratias, near the National Bank in Pl. Megalou Alexandrou.

🖪 🗷 ORIENTATION AND PRACTICAL INFORMATION. With your back to the ticket counter at the bus station, **Pavlou Mela** is in front of you. The street that intersects Pavlou Mela immediately to your right is **Fillipou;** traveling two blocks to your left will lead you to the cliffside. If you make a right onto Fillipou, **Plateia Timenidon** and the town center will be four blocks down the road. From the bus station, make a right onto Pavlou Mela and follow the street until it meets **Egnatia;** here is the drop-off for buses stopping on the way from Kastoria or Florina to Thessaloniki. Egnatia forks right; the branch closer to the hotels is the continuation of Egnatia, and the one closer to the park is **Dimokratias.** Facing the hotels, a left on Egnatia leads to the hospital and to Thessaloniki. On your right, Dimokratias goes past cafe-lined **Plateia Megalou Alexandrou** to an intersection by the stadium, marked by a park full of bars and cafes. The street on the right is **25 Martiou,** the left **18 Oktovriou,** and the sharp right **Filellinon.** 25 Martiou goes to a series of right-branching side streets for the waterfalls, 18 Oktovriou heads to the train station, and Filellinon leads to the old district of **Varosi** and back to Pl. Timenidon. The four rivers that run through the town can be very useful landmarks.

Street maps are posted at many of the city's major intersections. The **tourist information office,** in the waterfall park behind the Public Waterfall Center Restaurant, provides free maps and brochures with information in English about sights, hotels, and transportation. The patient, outgoing employees are knowledgeable about Edessa and the surrounding area. (☎20 300. Open daily 10am-8pm.) The **National Bank,** Arch. Panteleimonos 2, is located behind the taxi station in an old renovated house. (☎23 322. Open M-F 7:30am-1pm.) For **laundry,** try **Kiknos,** Egnatia 37. From the Egnatia/Dimokratias fork in front of the hotels, follow Egnatia in the direction of the hospital. Kiknos will be 200m down on your left. (☎22 872. €8 per load. Open M-F 8am-9pm, Sa 8am-3pm.) To find the 24hr. **police station,** Iroön Polytechniou 13 (☎23 333), follow Dimokratias toward the waterfalls and turn left on Iroön Polytechniou; the station is at the intersection with Arhelaou. The local **pharmacy,** Egnatia 36, is across the street from Kiknos. (☎22 232. Open M-F 8am-3pm and 5-9pm.) The large **hospital** (☎27 441) is just outside town on Egnatia. The **OTE,** Nepma 11, is a blue and white building facing the clock tower on Ag. Dimitriou. (☎27 441. Open M-F 7am-3pm.) **Net Station,** Evripidou 6, next door to Emporiki Bank, has 40 terminals for **Internet** access. (☎29 629; www.edessa-net.com. €2 per hr. Coffee €1.50. Beer €2.) Edessa's **post office,** Pavlou Mela 10, one block up from the bus station on Mela, offers **Poste Restante** and **exchanges currency.** (Open M-F 7:30am-2:30pm.) **Postal Code:** 58200.

⊞⊡ ACCOMMODATIONS AND FOOD. There are a few good deals among Edessa's handful of hotels. **⊞Hotel Alfa ❸,** Egnatia 28, is three blocks uphill along Pavlou Mela and directly in front of the Kastoria-Thessaloniki stop. The rooms in this family-run establishment are painted with pastel colors and have bath, TV, air-conditioning, fridge, and phone. Non-smoking rooms and free Internet access are available. (☎22 221. www.hotel-alfa.gr. English spoken. Breakfast €7.50. Reception 24hr. Singles €35; doubles €50; triples €65. MC/V.) A more luxurious option, **Hotel Xenia ❹,** Fillipou 35, offers well-furnished, carpeted rooms with air-conditioning, bath, TV, fridge, a pool (open to the public for €2-3 per person), and spectacular cliffside views. The pool area turns into a popular club at night with a mixed-aged crowd. (☎29 706; www.xeniaedessa.gr. Breakfast included. Laptop Internet access in each room €1 per hr. Reception 24hr. Singles €60; doubles €85; triples €110; quads €150.) **Hotel Elena ❸,** Dimitriou Rizou 4, is near Varosi just off Pl. Timenidon; walk down Fillipou four blocks from the bus station. Simple white-tiled rooms have air-conditioning, TV, and a nice-sized balcony. (☎23 218. Breakfast €5. Reception 24hr. Singles €35; doubles €45; triples €55.)

Edessa suffers no shortage of **fast food**—cheese pies, rotisserie chickens, and gyros crop up on every street. Inexpensive restaurants are easy to find near the waterfall park and along Dimokratias. The most popular one in town is the **⊞Public**

Waterfall Center Restaurant ❷, at the top of the falls. The sounds of rushing water and a stunning view of the plains accompany every meal at this giant tri-level complex. It serves local specialties like delicious *tsombleki* (potato, eggplant, and stewed veal casserole; €7) and has a large selection of domestic wines. (☎27 810. Entrees €5-8. Open 8am-1am. AmEx/MC/V.) From Hotel Alfa, **Taverna Arxontiko ❷,** Egnatia 60, is a short walk down Egnatia in the direction of the Thessaloniki highway. *Bouzouki* music and dance enhance the authentic Greek dishes for a complete taverna experience. (☎24 221. Pork kebab €5. Open daily 6pm-2am.)

🎞🎭 **ENTERTAINMENT AND NIGHTLIFE.** From July 1 to the end of August, open-air **movies** (€5) are shown just below the aquarium every night at 9pm. Most are American and European films with Greek subtitles.

🎭**Cafe High Rock** has, hands down, the best view in town. Located on M. Alexandrou 2, in the southwestern corner of town on—surprise, surprise—a high rock on the cliff, the terrace seats seem like they're floating. Scrumptious desserts include the traditional *revani* (€2.50), chocolate profiterole topped with cream (€3), and 18 different kinds of ice cream. (☎26 793. Coffee €2. Beer €2.50. Entrees €5-7. Open daily 9am-2am.) You'll find dinner, drinks, and dancing at **Kanavourgeio** and the adjacent club, **One,** at the bottom of the glass elevators inside the huge, old mill. The name, Kanavourgeio, is derived from the Greek word *kanabis,* and refers to the building's past use as a hemp factory. The tableside machinery inside, now elegantly integrated into the wooden decor, once twisted fibers from the bountiful plant into thick ship's rope. One's DJs blast American music straight into space every Friday, Saturday, and Sunday night from mid-June to early September. (☎20 070. Entrees €3.50-8. Cover €5; includes 1 drink. Open daily 8pm-6am.) **Paradise,** inside Hotel Xenia, has a pool and an amazing view from its spot at the tip of the cliff. The eclectic crowd makes for a foreigner-friendly environment. (Beer €3. Mixed drinks €5-5.50. Open 24hr.) The other local club of choice, **Vanilla,** is beneath the cliff, 2km past the hospital on the left-hand side of the Thessaloniki-Pella highway. The already treacherous path down the cliff has the potential to be terrifying in the dark; a short taxi ride (€4) is probably a better transportation choice. Greek and American music plays in the well-decorated interior. (Beer €5. Open Th-Sa midnight-6am.) In the town center, nightlife centers on **Sterna,** a pedestrian street starting from the tree-covered park off Dimokratias. There, cafe-bars draw masses of people to sip coffee and chat late into the night.

◪ **SIGHTS.** Edessa's best sights revolve around the 🏞 **katarrakton** (waterfall), formed by an 11th-century earthquake. The descending concrete stairs let you survey the waterfalls and the agricultural plain below while catching a little spray on your face. A small cave with stalactites and stalagmites is beneath the rushing water. *(Walk down Dimokratias past the stadium where it becomes 25 Martiou and watch for the signs—they'll tell you when to turn right. Open daily 10am-8pm. €0.50.)* At the base of the waterfall, there is another, more expensive option for those seeking an adventure. For €25, you can ride a horse up a path alongside the waterfalls. The marble column ruins of an ancient city sit near a convent on the right-hand side of the valley. The cliff side once was home to various mills and textile factories, all operated by water power. The companies, however, couldn't adjust to modern forms of production and closed in the late 1950s. They stood as deteriorating monuments to Edessa's industrial past until a recent European grant helped redesign and renovate the area, creating an open-air **Water Museum.** The museum, still under construction, now features pre-industrial mills and tanneries, the wool mill, and the cannabis factory. Water still runs through the chutes alongside each mill, and plans are in the works to reopen the flour mill as an educational museum. The tourist office has a free brochure showing the mill locations. The sesame mill has been converted into an ▊aquarium, displaying indigenous amphibians, reptiles, and freshwater fish. The recent death of the passionate town embryologist put the aquarium's existence into jeopardy. Luckily, Mr. Tasos inspired the next generation to carry on his work, and now younger Dimitri inspires visitors just as Mr. Tasos once did. Plans are in the works to create two distinct exhibitions, one an aquarium, the other a living reptile house. *(Aquarium pen M and W-Su 10am-2pm and 5-9pm. €21.50, students €10.75.)* To reach the *kanavourgeio,* follow the steps down along the waterfalls or take one of the two great ▊glass elevators. Descending about 13 stories along the cliffs, they provide sweeping views.

The old town was built on the site of an ancient acropolis and containing several small churches dating back to the 14th century. Varosi retained an active Christian population even during Ottoman occupation and once was surrounded by ancient city walls that held up for eight months of Turkish bombardment. When the Turks finally entered the city in 1389, they tore down the walls as a symbol of their victory. Though the fortifications are long gone, examples of traditional architecture abound: upper stories miraculously protrude out on creaky old wooden beams over stone bases. The quarter's location near the "safe escape" of the lowlands made it a popular spot for WWII resistance fighters, who used the web of connected backyards to evade the Germans. Much of the area, however, was burned in the subsequent fighting. The **Museum of Traditional and Folk Life,** which displays clothing, plates, and jewelry from the region, is located in one of the old buildings on the side of the drop. It's one block down from the intersection of Arch. Panteleimonos and M. Alexandriou and two blocks from High Rock. Ring the bell if the door is locked. *(☎28 787. Open Tu-Su 10am-6pm, though hours vary. €21.50.)*

Below the town, about 3km to the southwest, are the ruins of the **ancient city** of Edessa. Though little remains of the 4th-century BC city, a few columns still stand along the main avenue. Before the discoveries at Vergina, this ancient town was a candidate for the lost capital of the Macedonian Empire; some proud Edessians still cling to the now-debunked theory. The fastest way to the ruins begins at the landing between the two glass elevators. Walk to the right on the sandy path over the little mound to find a winding path. Follow it downhill and go straight; you'll reach the city in 15min. The **clock tower,** built in 1895, occupies a modern block at Pl. Megalou Alexandrou. To see Edessa's rivers united, follow any of the tributaries upstream until you hit the **Byzantine bridge** in Park Kioupri. The footbridge arches over the River Edessias that soon after splits into three rivers, eventually feeding the three different waterfalls in the city.

KASTORIA Καστοριά ☎24670

Kastoria takes its name from the beaver *(kastori)* whose fur brought prosperity to the town in the 17th century. There are more than 50 Byzantine churches throughout the hilly landscape, some overlooking the scenic Lake Kastoria. The **Byzantine Museum** has a large exhibit of icons and manuscripts. *(☎26 7781. Open Tu-Su 8:30am-3pm. Free.)* On the first weekend in August, the **Nestorio River Party** brings thousands of campers to the banks of the Aliakmonas River, 25km from Kastoria, for four days of live music and revelry. *(☎31 204; www.cultureguide.gr. Camping €10 per day, €25 for 4 days.)*

Kastoria lacks budget accommodations. Luxurious ▊**Hotel Kastoria ❹,** Nikis 122, rents spacious rooms, some with lake views, satellite TV, phone, air-conditioning, and bath. *(☎29 453; www.hotelkastoria.com. Breakfast €10. Reception 24hr. Singles €40; doubles €55; triples €100. AmEx/MC/V.)* There are many restaurants and cafes by the lake on Nikis and near the park on M. Alexandrou. **Mamm ❷,** Ptolemeon 6, serves tasty meat dishes. From the taxis, follow 3 Septemvriou and take the first left. *(☎27 333. Sandwiches €4. Entrees €5-7. Open M-Sa 9am-2am.)*

Aristotelis International Airport (☎42 515), 13km from the city, has flights to Athens (1hr., daily 2pm, €95). The bus station, Ath. Diakou 14 (☎83 455), is two blocks ahead on the right. **Buses** go to: Amyntaio (1¼hr.; 2, 5:15pm; €5.10); Athens (9½hr., 3 per day 7am-8:30pm, €41.30) via Kozani (1¼hr., €7); Ioannina (3½hr.; 9am, 3:30pm; €16.30); Thessaloniki (3hr., 7 per day 6am-6:30pm, €15.10). **Taxis** (☎82 100) line up 24hr. by the park at Ath. Diakou and M. Alexandrou. The **tourist office,** a kiosk in the public park, has maps (€2.50) and info but sporadic hours. (☎22 292. Open M-F 8am-3pm, Sa-Su 8am-2pm.) An **Agricultural Bank** with an **ATM** is in Pl. Davaki. (☎22 562. Open M-F 7:30am-2pm.) Walk one block inland on Averof and turn right to find the 24hr. **police station,** Grammou 25 (☎21 517), on the left. The 24hr. **hospital** (☎55 600) is 2km out of town on the road from Mavriozisa.

PRESPA Πρέσπα ☎23850

Territorially shared by Greece, Albania, and FYROM, the cold waters of the Prespa Lakes and their surrounding untouched, verdant terrain seduce the bird-watchers and nature lovers who venture to this remote region. The lakes, Megali (large) and Mikri (small), are separated only by a marshy isthmus, home to a gigantic Dalmatian pelican nesting area. The region's rolling green mountains, huge lakes, and small fishing and farming villages are hard to reach today, but more than a millenium ago, this region temporarily served as the capital of the Balkan world. The lakes' shoreline is studded with beautiful ancient chapels, the earliest dating from AD 908, that act as reminders of the time when exiled Byzantine bureaucrats whiled away their days on the shores of the Prespa Lakes.

▤ TRANSPORTATION. Buses leave from the village square in Ag. Germanos to Florina (1hr.; M, W, and F 8am, 4pm). Call the bus station in Florina (☎22 430) to request stops at Laimos, Plati, or Lefkono. There are only two **Taxi** drivers in the Prespa area. English-speaking Yurgos (☎51 207) will take you around the villages for a hefty fee; non-English speaking Christos (☎69778 93 630) offers more reasonable prices. Trips to Kastoria or Florina are quite expensive (€30) no matter whom you call. Since the villages are far away and difficult to reach given the spotty public transportation, it is best to rent a car in Florina or Kastoria.

▦⁊ ORIENTATION AND PRACTICAL INFORMATION. Visitors to Prespa pass over a mountain to find **Mikri Prespa** pooled below them. Don't be fooled by the diminutive term "Mikri"—this lake is huge. Farther along the road to the Prespas, **Laimos,** the regional center, is before **Agios Germanos,** which is at the eastern end of the road. Before the isthmus that divides the two lakes, the regional road forks; you can continue south toward **Trigono,** or cross the isthmus to reach the town of **Psarades,** on the southern shore of **Megali Prespa.** When crossing the isthmus from Laimos, Megali Prespa is on the right and Mikri on the left. At the end of the isthmus is the small channel of **Koula,** a **beach** (on the Megali side) of the same name, and the regional army post. Following the road left takes you to a floating causeway which passes through marshes, reeds, and the murky waters of the lake. On the other end is **Agios Achillios,** an 11-house island village in Mikri Prespa.

The official **Prespa Information Center,** run by the Society for the Protection of Prespa and the World Wildlife Federation (WWF), is located on the road between Ag. Germanos and Laimos. You will see a sign and a small waterfall before reaching the well-organized center that provides free information about the area's wildlife and history and sells a topographical map with marked hiking trails. (☎51 452. Open 9:30am-7pm.) There are no banks or ATMs in Prespa, but the grocer in Psarades is willing to **exchange currency.** Laimos houses both the **mayor's office,** which has information on the area (☎52 100; open M-F 8am-3pm), and the **OTE** (☎52 178;

open M-F 8am-3pm). The **post office** (☎51 249; open M-F 8am-2pm) is in Ag. Germanos's main square, next door to the 24hr. **police** station (☎51 202). A small, one-doctor clinic (☎46 372) is located in Lefkona and operates 24hr. **Postal Code:** 53077.

▮▯ ACCOMMODATIONS AND FOOD. Inland, Ag. Germanos and Psarades offer the cheapest accommodations, but the best value for your money is found on the Mikri Prespa island of Ag. Achillios, on the right immediately after you cross the causeway. ◪**Agios Achillios Hotel** ❸, the one hotel on this stunning island, offers a ski-lodge experience, complete with fireplace, wooden floors and ceilings, and Slavic folk art on every wall. The included breakfast of sweet cherry juice, eggs, homemade yogurt and honey, toast, and coffee make this option a great value. (☎46 601. Singles €30; doubles €48, triples €62.) In Psarades, local **domatia** (€25-30) combine budget rates with serene lake views and an end-of-the-earth sense of isolation. **Tasos's Domatia** ❷, on the right at the end of the lakefront road, has four quiet, cozy rooms with bath and a view of the inlet. Listen to a frog chorus at night and wake up to waterfowl that may rouse even the heaviest sleeper around 5am. (☎69782 64 775. Singles €24; doubles and triples €28.) **Arhondiko** ❸, one block from Tasos on the continuation of the single road, has elegant, tiny rooms with balcony, TV, and bath. The owner's daughter is a painter and made the artwork that adorns the inn. (☎46 260. Singles €30; doubles €39; triples €47.)

Psarades has a handful of tavernas that serve fresh fish from the lakes. ◪**Syntrofia** ❷, at the end of the waterfront, serves tasty food in a remote setting. The death of owners Lazarus and Georgia Christianopoulos threatened the continuation of this delicious dive, but their children have kept the taverna up, serving fresh fried and grilled fish. (☎46 107. Grilled trout €5. Open 9am-11:30pm.)

◪ SIGHTS. Villages are separated by about 10km, so traveling requires a car or bike. Mikri Prespa, with a maximum depth of only 10m, lies almost entirely in Greece and offers a chance to watch the different species of birds in the area. Its islet hosts the 24-person village of ◪**Agios Achillios.** This tiny town once was part of the mainland, but a slight rise in water levels left it attached to the shore only by an 800m floating causeway. Ag. Achillios contains the ruins of the **basilica** of the same name. Built in AD 980, it was sponsored by the Bulgarian Tsar Samuel II to honor St. Achillios, the Bishop of Larisa, whose bones Samuel brought to the small islet. Difficult as it is to believe now, the Prespa region was briefly the center of the Balkan world, when Samuel used the region as his capital. Its dominance ended when Byzantine Emperor Basil II, nicknamed "Bulgarian Killer," crushed his defiant northern neighbor. The 26 churches scattered throughout the Prespa region are reminders of this remarkable history. Other sights of note are the 11th-century **Church of Saint Germanos** in **Agios Germanos,** featuring beautifully painted, dark-hued **frescoes.** A rickety metal staircase will take you to the top of the adjacent **bell tower.** The tower, with its gigantic steel bell, offers a stunning view of Ag. Germanos and the isthmus between Mikri and Megali Prespa. The 19th-century church of **Agia Paraskevi,** north of Laimos, is adorned with stained-glass windows that filter sun rays through the building. On the southern shore of Megali Prespa, a unique breed of dwarf cows wanders the cobblestones and pebble shores of ◪**Psarades.** Also found on Ag. Achillios, these quadrupeds were bred to adapt to the swamps of the area; legend tells that larger cows used to sink and drown in the swamps. The dwarf cows can be seen feeding at the water's edge, partially submerged in the lake. As the Prespas have over 260 species of avian inhabitants, the isthmus between the lakes has observation areas for birdwatching; bring binoculars and a camera. At sunrise and sunset you will see a remarkable number of birds crossing the isthmus. For the best view of the pelican breeding grounds, climb up the small hill in front of the causeway before you cross onto Ag. Achillios island. Boat trips, arranged at the small dock in Psarades, lead excursions along the southern shoreline of Megali Prespa, with stops at lakeside Byzantine rock paintings, ascetic caves, and monasteries. (☎69782 64 775. About €30 per hr. for 4-5 people.)

HALKIDIKI Χαλκιδική

The three fingers of Halkidiki peninsula—Mt. Athos (Agion Oros), Sithonia, and Kassandra—point southeast into the Aegean, boasting spectacular scenery and amazing beaches. Central and Eastern Europeans and urban Thessalonians spread their bodies out on Sithonia and Kassandra to sunbathe with the backdrop of Agion Oros, "The Holy Mountain," which continues its thousand-year tradition of Orthodox asceticism. Visits to Mt. Athos are strictly regulated, and reservations for pilgrimages should be made a few months in advance (p. 303). Visitors to Sithonia and Kassandra will find no barriers of entry, other than the Halkidiki public transportation system. Frequent buses run between the Halkidiki station in Thessaloniki (☎3 16 575) and the three peninsulas, but bus service does not run from finger to finger; you have to return to Thessaloniki. Kassandra is the most developed; some of the largest nightclubs in Greece are located there in Kalithea. Sithonia, still heavily forested and rural in atmosphere, has managed to resist most of the deleterious effects of tourism and offers visitors plenty of relatively unchartered territory perfect for relaxing and exploring.

SITHONIA PENINSULA Σιθωνιά

Tranquility persists on the isolated beaches of Sithonia, the middle peninsula sandwiched between nightclub-infested Kassandra and hermetic Mt. Athos. Despite more and more tourist shops and services, much of the land is exhilaratingly untouched and accessible to the budget traveler. Terrific camping sites dot the coves off the single road that loops around the coast, providing an affordable window to the supreme nature of the peninsula. Don't let the shoddy internal transportation deter you from discovering Sithonia's treasures.

NEOS MARMARAS Νέος Μαρμαράς ☎23750

Neos Marmaras was one of the many Sithonian villages founded on land taken from Mt. Athos's estates to provide for Greek refugees after the population exchange with Turkey. Vacationers flock for the gorgeous sunsets and surrounding beaches. The town, which is a single strip with restaurants and hotels on one side and water on the other, makes a great hub for exploring the peninsula. At wave-side **Ploton,** 300m from Dionysios on the waterfront, heavy wooden doors open into a raging party of alcohol and smoke. (☎71 704. Beer €6. Mixed drinks €5-8. Open daily 10pm-4am.) Next door at **Molos,** Greeks and foreigners mingle and watch the surf. (☎71 331. Beer €5. Mixed drinks €4.50-8. Open daily 10pm-4am.) The big disco, **Villa** (☎72 900), 2km away, is on the road that goes around the peninsula. Accessible by taxi (€3.50), this local lair blares Greek music.

Vacancies are scarce on summer weekends. Along the waterfront, signs with maps of the village list **domatia;** most singles run around €30, you'll have to haggle to find anything below €20. Past the main church, **Alcano Grill ❷,** a delicious gyro and fast-food joint, offers cheap rooms to rent with unbelievable views of the harbor. Alcano rooms are the best option in town, with TV, air-conditioning, fridge, bath, and panoramic view from an expansive balcony. (☎71 046. Singles €25; doubles €40; triples €50.) **House Filippos ❷,** 20m down from Moto Rental on the main drag, is slightly removed from the waterfront's swarms of tourists.

NORTHERN GREECE

The large rooms have slate floors, TV, air-conditioning, bath, and a huge balcony with hammocks. Each room comes with a full kitchen. (☎71 963. Singles €25; doubles €40; triples €50.) For something cheaper and closer to Sithonia's breathtaking wilderness, try one of the numerous campsites. ◧**Marmaras ❶**, a 20 min. walk from the town in nearby Paradissos, has pine trees, a private sand beach, and an amphitheater-like setting that gives every tent its own level and view of the beach and environs. Tents, provided by the campsite, come with tables, mosquito nets, and mattresses. (☎71 901. Laundry €5. €6 per person, €7 for site and tent, €2 per car. Electricity €3.) As for food, a local favorite, ◧**Ladi ke Rigani ❶**, 20m from the Bank of Greece toward the first bus stop, offers the best meat dishes in Neos Marmaras. (☎71 234. Souvlaki and most dishes under €3. Open daily 11am-2am.) For Greek classics, head to **Dionysios ❷**, in the first plateia, near the small kiosk where the second bus stop is located. Though some of the food caters to tourists seeking international standards, Dionysios spices up many dishes with local flavors and techniques. (☎71 201. Entrees €5-9. Open daily 8:30am-3am. AmEx/MC/V.) Don't pass up a visit to ◧**Nora Natura ❶**, at the second bus stop opposite the Bank of Greece, for natural local products including spices, olive oils, olives, soaps, and halva. Try free samples of their *raki*, honey, and *Loukoumi*, or Greek Delights. (☎71 046. Open daily 9am-1am.) Neos Marmaras's nightlife centers on the strip of bars between the two plateias and a pair of discos on the beach.

Buses (☎23710 22 309 or 23710 22 909) run to Thessaloniki (2½hr., 3 per day 8:15am-6:30pm, €11) via nearby small towns, including Nea Moudania (1hr., €6). The bus coming from Thessaloniki continues to Sarti (1hr., 3 per day noon-8pm, €4). Taxis (☎71 500) sit by the beach and by Dionysios. Because Sithonia's public transportation can be frustrating, renting a moped or car is probably the best way to see the peninsula. Try **Moto Rental**, two doors up from Filippos. (☎72 224. €15 per day. Open daily 9am-10pm). The **first bus stop** is where the road running along the shoreline begins. From here, the bus turns left and goes toward the sea. The **second stop** is at Dionysios restaurant. Immediately ahead is the **taxi stand,** followed by the docks, and the police station and National Bank on the opposite side of the street; this is the **first plateia.** The road then angles left, following the shore, and descends until it arrives at the **second plateia,** which has a *periptero*, a map listing accommodations, and the **third bus stop.** The **fourth bus stop,** the last in Neo Marmaras, is 300m along the same road by the soccer stadium. For help getting oriented, go to English-speaking **Antica,** with one location next to the National Bank and another next to Alcano Grill. This traditional jewelry and gift shop offers detailed maps of the peninsula and books with hiking routes throughout Halkidiki. (☎23710 21 120. Open daily 9am-11pm.) The staff at **Meli Tours,** behind the church, recommends rooms, books excursions, and offers and an all-day boat tour of Mt. Athos (€40) each Wednesday. (☎72 113. Open daily 8am-11pm.) The **National Bank,** with a **24hr. ATM** and **currency exchange,** is just after the police station on the main street in the middle of the first plateia. (☎72 794. Open M-Th 8am-2:30pm, F 8am-2pm.) The **police station** is three doors up from the National Bank, opposite Dionysios. (☎71 111. Open daily 7am-5pm.) There is no hospital in Neos Marmaras, but the town doctor, Serhan Chehade, sees patients and has 24hr. service in case of emergencies. His office, **Halkidiki Health Services,** is next to the National Bank. (☎72 233. Office hours daily 8am-9pm.) **Internet** access is available at **Stadium,** in front of the church and two stores down from Meli Tours. (☎71 097. €2 per hr. Pool tables €6 per hr. Open daily 9am-1:30am.) The **post office,** in the second plateia across the street from the city map, accepts **Poste Restante.** (☎71 334. Open M-F 7:30am-2pm.) **Postal Code:** 63081.

RURAL SITHONIA ☎23750

Explore more of Sithonia by renting a moped or taking the **bus** that goes around the peninsula. Swim to a small island off the long, white beach of **Kalogrias,** or head to **Linerake** on the eastern coast for turquoise, shallow water and a lush landscape. **Kavotripias,** also on the east coast, is a secret paradise of heavenly beaches with mermaids and other figures carved out of the rocks. For water sports head to **Lago-mendra,** a beach 10km before Neos Marmaras coming from Thessaloniki. Another worthwhile trip is to the interior of Sithonia, specifically up the mountain to the traditional village of **Parthenon.** Continue over the mountain to the eastern side, passing through forests and olive orchards and you'll end up near the famous ▨**Camping Armenistis ❶,** which is also accessible from Thessaloniki by bus (3hr.; 11:15am, 2:45, 6:30pm; €11). King among campgrounds, it has every amenity imaginable (including laundry, supermarket, cafe, bar, creperia, and movie screenings) at an isolated site lined with golden sands, crystal water, and coves. This nomad village hosts numerous music festivals every summer that feature local rock bands. Check the website for events. (☎91 487; www.armenistis.com.gr. Free movie screenings W and Sa at 9pm. Reception 8am-midnight. €5.50 per tent, €6.50 per RV. Mobile homes available to rent €75. Electricity €3. MC/V.)

MOUNT ATHOS PENINSULA

OURANOUPOLIS Ουρανούπολις ☎23770

The last secular settlement on monastic Athos, Ouranoupolis is at the top of Halkidiki's easternmost finger, 148km southeast of Thessaloniki. This gateway to the cradle of Orthodoxy lies just beyond a trans-peninsular depression dug by Xerxes as a canal for his invading fleet. There isn't much to see in Ouranoupolis beyond the beaches, and even nicer beaches are plentiful on the other peninsulas, particularly Sithonia; if you're not visiting Athos's monasteries, Ouranoupolis is probably not worth the trip. Tickets for the **cruise** around Athos, which traces the western side of the peninsula, can be purchased from the offices near the tower. (☎71 370. Daily 10:30am and 1:30pm, €16.) Also interesting are the mostly uninhabited **offshore isles,** many of which are recovering from recent devastating fires.

Many people spend the night in Ouranopolis in order to head to Mt. Athos in the morning. There are several reasonably affordable choices. Dozens of private houses offer **domatia** (around €25-30), but make sure to see the room before committing to anything, as some can be run-down and even unpleasant. **Camping Oura-noupoli ❶** lies on a beach 1.5km outside of town along the highway (taxi €2.50) and has showers, a supermarket, and a restaurant. Call in advance to make sure it is open. (☎71 171. Laundry €5. €5 per person, €7 per tent.) The rooms in **Hotel Athos ❷,** which is one street back from the waterfront, are small but elegant, with a nice view of the beach. (☎71 368. Singles €25; doubles €32; triples €40.) Those looking for a last supper before entering Mt. Athos—or a triumphant reward after the monks' spartan cuisine—should avoid the pushy waiters from the row of tavernas on the waterfront. Most of these eateries are tourist traps, serving mediocre food at high prices. Instead, try **Kentpikon ❷,** on the main road that leads to the tower, next to the police station. The friendly, English-speaking waitress serves reasonably priced, tasty dishes, and her adorable, elderly mother is always there to welcome guests. (☎71 204. Entrees €5-9. Open daily 9am-10pm.)

Facing town with your back to the tower, both the main taverna strip and the Athos **ferry office** are on your left. **Ferries** (€5) run only to Mt. Athos. (☎21 041. Call to reserve tickets and receive information. Open daily 8:30am-7pm.) The **bus stop** is in front of the tower in the parking lot. Updated times are posted by the restau-

ATHOS BY SEA

he monasteries of Mt. Athos are some of the most breathtaking sights in all of Greece. However, he gender restrictions and red ape surrounding the holy peninsula prevent many travelers from isiting. But even if it's not possible for you to live the monastic ife for a night, seeing the monasteries by boat is not only a stunningly beautiful daytrip, but also a great way to appreciate the holy peninsula preserved since Byzantine times.

An all-day boat tour from Sithonia visits both the eastern and western coasts of Mt. Athos, stopping in Ouranoupolis for lunch. Meli Tours in Neos Marmaras offers this package deal for €40. A bus picks you up outside the Meli Tours office at 8:15am and drives the scenic route to the port of Ormos Panagias on the eastern coast of Sithonia.

From there, a boat takes you around the Mt. Athos peninsula. Alternatively, you can jump aboard at Ormos Panagias, and he trip will cost you only €25.) You'll be back in Neos Marmaras by 5pm with enough time to enjoy a few hours of daylight before experiencing one of the region's famous sunsets.

☎ 23750 72 113. Meli Tours open daily 9am-11pm. Tour not offered daily, so call in advance for times and reservations.

rant behind the tower. Buses synchronized with the ferry from Athos go to Athens (7hr., 2:15pm, €30) and Thessaloniki (3hr., 6 per day 5:30am-5:30pm, €10). On the Thessaloniki-Ouranoupolis bus, ask the driver to let you off at the beach resort of **Tripiti**, 10km from Ouranoupolis. From there you can take a ferry (10am, noon, 3pm; €4) to **Amouliani**, a small village on an island known to the locals as the "donkey's island." From Amouliani's small port, renting a boat or hiking along the water are the best ways to explore the nearby untouched coves. The town of Ouranoupolis centers around the distinctive, medieval **Fosfori Tower,** by the sea. This beautiful tower has the best views in town, and the museum inside, still a work in progress, represents Mt. Athos's history with Greek and English labels and displays small models of the different monasteries. (☎ 71 389. Open daily 8am-3pm. €2.) The road out of town extends parallel to the waterfront. To reach the **Holy Executive of the Holy Mount Athos Pilgrims' Bureau,** which issues permits for Athos, walk down the path that runs between the waterfront tavernas behind the tower; when you reach the end of the path, take a right and walk up the street for two blocks. Arrive well ahead of your ferry time since lines tend to be long. (☎ 71 422. Open daily 7:30am-2:30pm.) On a right side street two blocks down is an **Agricultural Bank** with a **24hr. ATM.** (Open M and Th 9am-2:30pm, F 9am-2pm.) Three blocks down, **Mamounia Internet Cafe** (☎ 71 577) offers **Internet** access and Wi-Fi on three computers. (€3 per hr. Open daily 10am-2am.)

MOUNT ATHOS Αγιον Ορος
☎ 23770

The monasteries on Mt. Athos have been the paradigm of Orthodox asceticism for over a millennium. Originally settled by five Hellenic cities, Athos, along with the rest of Greece, was conquered first by the Macedonian Empire and then by the Romans. The then-secular settlements thrived under Byzantine control until pirate attacks in the 7th century left the peninsula uninhabited. Athos's current status as a religious community began in AD 963 when Agios Athanasios Athonitis, a friend of the Byzantine emperor, created the first communal monastery on the peninsula; this monastery, known as **Megistes Lavra**, still stands today. For much of the Byzantine and Ottoman periods, Mt. Athos formed the bedrock of Greek Orthodoxy, most notably speaking out against a unification with Western Christendom in the 15th century. Today, the Holy Community of Mount Athos is a semi-autonomous state comprised

OBTAINING A PERMIT. Men who wish to see Mt. Athos must secure a permit in advance; call the **Holy Executive of the Holy Mount Athos Pilgrims' Bureau,** Egnatia 109 (☎23102 52 578; fax 22 424; open M-F 9am-2pm, Sa 10am-noon), in Thessaloniki (p. 266). You must call six months in advance if you want to visit the community during Easter week or if you are not of the Orthodox faith. Even if you forget to reserve a spot far in advance, it is worth calling to see if there is an opening, since the quota sometimes is not filled. You are more likely to get a short-term permit if you are flexible as to the exact day you want to visit Mt. Athos. One hundred daily permits are reserved for Orthodox applicants, including a significant number set aside for Greeks living out of the country, but there are only 10 available for non-Orthodox men. Mail (don't fax) a copy of your passport to the office at Egnatia 109, Thessaloniki 546 38. Call two weeks ahead of your visit to confirm the reservation, and visit the office with your passport to pick up the permit. Though this process can be frustrating, the bureau will deny entry to anyone who fails to complete it. Passes cost €40 for foreigners and €20 for students under age 27 with ISIC. You must strictly observe the date of arrival on your permit—if you arrive a day late, you will be turned away. You will not be admitted without your **passport.** The regular permit is valid for a **4-day stay.** Official extensions are rarely granted—to request one you must go to the peninsula's capital Karyes—but unofficial extensions are easier to come by, as monks often allow considerate, interested visitors to stay longer. If heading to Mt. Athos from Ouranoupolis, **bring your permit and passport** to the Athos office (☎71 422; open 7:30am-2pm) by 7:30am on the day your visit begins. With your back to the entrance of the tower, take a right at the end of the waterfront strip, and walk two blocks uphill. At the office, you will receive your entrance pass, called the "Diamonitirion," complete with the blue seal of the monastic community; you must present this before boarding the ferry to Mt. Athos. Arrive early, as lines are long. Visitors taking the 9:45am ferry must be in Ouranoupolis no later than 9am; if you miss the boat, you will not be able to visit Athos. Taking the first bus leaving from Halkidiki bus station at 5:15am will allow time to pick up your pass and make the boat connection.

of 20 Orthodox monasteries, many *skites* (hamlets), some 1800 monks, and at least as many full-time workers. The verdant peninsula's only non-green surface, the jagged limestone peak of Mt. Athos itself, soars 2027m above the waves. Eagles and jackals roam the area, and natural springs deliver a wealth of water into the sea. The monks sequester themselves against the background of this lush sanctuary, shunning material pleasures to pursue a spiritual life. Emperor Constantine's edict of 1060 **forbids women and female domestic animals from setting foot on the peninsula,** with the exception of the female hens that provide the monks' eggs. Though this rule officially is considered to have come about out of respect for the Virgin Mary, it likely was enacted to end the scandalous relationships between the monks and Vlach shepherdesses who had settled on the mountain. Long pants are mandatory on Mt. Athos and swimming is forbidden.

HISTORY. Named after a Thracian giant buried by Poseidon beneath the mountain, Athos predates Christianity. The Christian tradition began here when, according to legend, the **Virgin Mary** came to the mountain. After Jesus's death, when the apostles divided up areas to visit to preach the "good news," Mary asked for a region as well and was given Iberia in Asia Minor. On her way there, however, the archangel Gabriel directed her to Athos. Before Mary's time, many had tried to tame the rowdy peninsula, from Alexander the Great to Xerxes. Though the peninsula, then known as **"Akte,"** had been a notorious center of paganism, Orthodox Christians believe that the moment Mary's foot graced its soil, the false idols disintegrated in realization of their own worthlessness.

Legend claims that the first monastic settlements were founded by Constantine the Great and his mother, Helen, but monkish habitation was not recorded before the 10th century. Over the following centuries, Athos flourished periodically—at one point it contained 40 settlements and 40,000 monks—but its low points ached with natural disasters, pirate invasions, internal squabbling, and a lack of attraction to monastic ideals. Mt. Athos retained some degree of autonomy during the Turkish occupation by surrendering promptly to the Ottomans, accepting their rule, and sending heavy taxes to Istanbul. During the centuries preceding the Greek liberation of 1821, Mt. Athos was supported and populated by Serbs, Bulgarians, Romanians, and Russians, who still have affiliations with particular monasteries. At the height of imperial Russia's expansionist policies at the end of the 19th century, some 3000 Russian monks inhabited **Agios Panteleimonos.** After WWI, the Treaty of Lausanne made Mt. Athos an official part of Greece while still allowing it to retain much autonomy; a body of monks, elected from each of the 20 monasteries, was set up to legislate and to govern the peninsula. Dwindling vocations through the 1950s threatened the stability of Mt. Athos, and it soon became a prime target for real estate developers; the end of its 1000-year tradition of monastic asceticism seemed imminent. Fortunately, Athos has been rejuvenated in recent years by hundreds of young men, many from Australia and Cyprus, inspired to take vows of Orthodox monasticism.

Starting in the 14th century, financial difficulties brought on the practice of **idiorrythimico,** which allowed monks to keep their own money and eat and pray individually. Today, all the monasteries follow the **cenobitic** system: they are run like communes, with shared money and duties. Athos retains an unsurpassed wealth of Paleologian and late Byzantine art, manuscripts, treasure, and architecture. Each monastery houses *lipsana*, remains of dead saints that only Orthodox men are supposed to be allowed to see. Especially impressive are the **Hand of Mary Magdalene,** which is said to remain (skin intact) in **Simonos Petra,** and the **belt of the Theotokos,** also known as **"Agia Zoni"** ("the holy girdle"), the only relic of the Virgin Mary, in **Vatopediou.** Several monasteries possess fragments of the **True Cross.** The **Gifts of the Magi,** presented to Jesus at his birth, are said to be housed in **Agios Pavlou;** five of the 28 pieces are displayed for nightly veneration.

▐ ▐ TRANSPORTATION AND PRACTICAL INFORMATION

With **permit** in hand, arrive at the western port of **Ouranoupolis** the night before your entry date to Athos. Given the unpredictable nature of Greece's public transportation, arriving in Ouranoupolis that morning if you plan to take the 9:45am ferry is risky. **Buses** run to Ouranoupolis from Athens (7hr., 11pm, €30) and from Thessaloniki's Halkidiki station (2½hr., 3 per day 5:15am-5pm, €10). From Ouranoupolis, the scheduled **boats** go to Dafni (2hr.; 9:45am, noon, 12:10pm; €5). A ferry called Agia Anna, which runs twice daily, continues from Dafni to the skiti community of **Kafsokalivia** at the peninsula's tip, stopping briefly at the monasteries of Simonos Petras, Grigoriou, and Dionysiou, and returning to Dafni before going back to Ouranopoulis. Schedules for Agia Anna change frequently and tickets are bought on board; ask at the boat ticket booth for updated information (Ouranoupolis-Dafni €5, round-trip €10). To reach the peninsula's eastern monasteries, take the **bus,** synchronized with the ferry arrivals, from Dafni to Karyes (30min., €2.50). Get off the boat quickly, as the two buses fill up in a matter of seconds. You also can hike (p. 307) or take the minivan **taxis** (☎23 267) between monasteries. When the buses

www.letsgo.com

LET'S GO
NEW ZEALAND

YOU'D rather be traveling

LET'S GO
FRANCE
2008

LET'S GO
MEXICO

READY. SET. LET'S GO

arrive in Karyes, about 10 minivans wait to take visitors to their respective monasteries. Ask the drivers which minivans go where. The cost of the ride is divided among passengers, so travel with a group to save money. You should not pay more than €7, unless you are going to Megistis Lavra (€10-15).

Because Athos's hikes can be long, arduous, and often are unmarked, a topographical map of the peninsula will be invaluable. Pick up a green **Mount Athos Tourist Map** (€7.50) or buy a **guidebook** with a map (€4-10) in Ouranoupolis or Karyes. If you stay overnight in Ouranoupolis, consider leaving your pack at your hotel or domatia in order to avoid hiking with unnecessary weight. Those arriving on the early bus will be able to leave their packs at the hotel in Karyes or at any monastery. **Karyes,** the capital of Mt. Athos, has an **OTE** next to the Athonite Holy Council Building and a **hotel ❹** (€45 for up to 3 people). To find the **post office**, continue straight ahead after disembarking from the bus and make a left after the large scaffolded church. (☎23 212. Open M-F 8am-2:30pm.) In Dafni you also can find a **convenience store**, a **police station**, and a **cafe. Postal Codes:** Karyes 63086, Dafni 63087.

⊙ SIGHTS

MONASTERIES. On the southeastern tip of the peninsula, **Megistis Lavras** (☎23 754) is the oldest, largest, and wealthiest of the 20 monasteries on Mt. Athos. Its monks are known to be stern and conservative. Though it is one of the more frequently visited monasteries, it's also the most isolated: to get there you will need to get a ride (€10-20 per person depending on the number of visitors) from Karyes, or embark on a long, tiring hike from either Iviron (6hr) or Agia Anna (4hr). With thickly forested hills to the north and the ocean to the south, picturesque **Karakalou** (☎23 225) has the beautiful **brotherly kiss icon** depicting Peter and Paul. Karakalou's rules for non-Orthodox visitors are particularly strict. **Philotheou** (☎23 256), Greek for "God-loving," is one of Mt. Athos's most stunningly located monasteries, on a plateau over the northern coast. The abbey is surrounded by orchards, gardens, and lush chestnut forests. Philotheou, founded by monks from Megistis Lavra in 1015, is one of the stricter monasteries: non-Orthodox guests must eat after the others and are not allowed to enter the church, though many do. Beautifully situated near a meadow overlooking the northeastern coast, **Iviron** (☎23 643; reservations noon-2pm), founded by Georgian monks in 980, was the second monastery on Mt. Athos; it is currently among the most popular and friendly. Father Jeremiah, a

LOCAL LEGEND

PROTECTIVE PANAGIA

Eviron monastery is home to the important Orthodox icon of the Panagia Portaitissa—a traditional depiction of the Virgin Mary holding Jesus with the faces of both mother and child almost entirely blacked out.

One night, a monk by the name of Gabriel had a dream in which Mary came to him and told him to go to the shore. He followed her directions, and at the shore he found the icon. He immediately brought it to the nearby church at the entrance to Eviron monastery.

The monks at Eviron prayed to Mary and promised her that they would protect the icon. In order to do so, they brought it to a secure backroom within the monastery and guarded it. When the monks awoke the next day, the icon was gone; it mysteriously had returned to the church. Shocked, the monks brought it back to the room where it was kept the night before. Despite their efforts to keep it hidden, the same thing happened that night.

After several days, Mary spoke to the monks and told them to stop trying to protect her icon; she was in fact protecting them from harm. They obediently left the icon at the entrance of the monastery to guard against evil, and it remains there to this day.

monk originally from Australia, answers all historical and spiritual questions clearly and patiently. Iviron is home to one of the most important icons in the Orthodox Christian world: the **Panagia Portaiatissa,** a depiction of Mary believed to have performed many miracles. **Pandokratoros** (☎23 880) and nearby **Stavronikita** (☎23 255; reservations noon-2pm) are on the northern coast, close to Karyes and about 5km north of Iviron, accessible by bus. Home to a small community of friendly monks, Pandokratoros was the last monastery to become communal in 1992, and is one of the few that imposes no special restrictions on its non-Orthodox visitors. Stavronikita is the smallest and "youngest" monastery, completed in 1536; it's also one of the friendliest, most peaceful, and most popular; book months in advance. Don't miss the wonderful **mosaic of Saint Nicholas,** known as *Sterdas* ("the one with the oysters"), as it supposedly was found at sea with an oyster stuck to the saint's head. Moated and turreted like a medieval castle, **Vatopediou** (☎23 219; reservations 9am-1pm) lies on the northern coast in a secluded bay and is now populated largely by Greek-Cypriot monks. Though tradition claims it was founded by Constantine the Great, the monastery more likely was erected by three brothers from Andrianoupolis in the late 10th century. Historically favored by emperors and princes, Vatopediou is the most visited monastery on Athos, including recent visits by former U.S. president George H.W. Bush and England's Prince Harry; call at least two months ahead for a reservation. On the edge of a sheer cliff on the southern coast, the breathtaking complex of **Simonos Petra** (☎23 254; reservations 1-3pm) only has room for 10 guests. The extremely kind and hospitable monks invite travelers to relax in the roomy guest quarters, which extend out on a balcony overlooking the cliff to the sea. Under constant renovation, this monastery frequently is booked; you'll need to call at least two months in advance to get a bed. In a secluded bay just southeast of Simonos Petra, **Grigoriou** (☎23 668) is one of the more liberal monasteries. Though the guest-houses are under construction, visitors are treated to large amounts of complimentary *raki*. An hour and a half from Grigoriou, **Dionysiou** (☎23 687), one of Athos's biggest monasteries, rests on a rocky bluff over the Aegean. The monks here are welcoming, English is prevalent, and guest quarters are luxurious. Most rooms are singles, and showers (rare on Athos) with hot water (still rarer) are available. One hour southward along a shoreline path, **Agios Pavlou** (☎23 741; reservations 10:30am-1:30pm) serves as the starting point for visitors hoping to make it to the top of Mt. Athos. A new path makes it possible to spend the night at Ag. Pavlou. The recently renovated **Xeropotamou** (☎23 251; reservations 12:30pm-2:30pm) houses an American monk and, only a 40min. hike from Dafni, is the easiest monastery to access.

SLAVIC MONASTERIES. In addition to the Greek monasteries, Slavs, not to be outdone, inhabit several abbeys. The great migration of Slavs to the peninsula began in the 19th century with the emergence of the Pan-Slavic movement in the Balkans. Both political and religious ambitions converged to give the Slavs and Russians a piece of the monastic action. At one time, there were nearly equal numbers of Greek and Slavic monks on the mountain. However, political turmoil—notably the 1917 Russian Revolution—cut off the supply of funds and novices at the source, ending the Russian government's official role in the area. Today three Slavic monasteries remain: onion-domed Russian **Agios Panteleiomonos** (guest quarters closed for construction), Bulgarian **Zografou** (☎23 247), and Serbian **Hiliandariou** (☎23 797). All Slavic monasteries welcome visitors, but are challenging to reach by foot.

SKITES AND HERMITAGES. Only a handful of Athos's monks still choose to live as ascetic hermits, eschewing material comforts and the "fast-paced" mainstream-monastic lifestyle in favor of caves and huts on the peak's harsh slopes. Monks who have given their lives to meditation and the contemplation of God in isolation inhabit the huts, cells, and tiny churches that dot the southernmost end of the island, between Megistis Lavras and Ag. Pavlou. These small communities are known as *"skites,"* and each is affiliated with one of the larger monasteries. Many hermits will allow you to stay with them, but you must bring your own food and sleeping bag and be careful not to disturb their meditations. The barren southeastern slope of Athos, called **"Karoulia"** after the pulleys the monks use to bring food to their caves, is home to some of the most extreme ascetics and some of the biggest *skites*. **Agia Anna** (☎23 320), at the foot of Mt. Athos, is a *skiti* run by a brotherhood of nine warm, welcoming monks who offer pilgrims rooms and meals.

◤ HIKING

Hikes through Mt. Athos's winding mountain paths, high above emerald coves and speckled by fluorescent blue and yellow butterflies, rival any in Greece. All paths are marked with footprints and occasional signs in Greek. The trail from Megistis Lavras to Agia Anna is one of the wildest and most scenic among the Holy Mountain's family of trekking superlatives. The lack of auto accessibility and the breathtaking bluffs plunging into the blue Aegean beside rocky peninsulas make this region a favorite among the most reclusive hermits. The 8hr. hike can be shortened to 6hr. by stopping at Kafsokalivia (☎23 319) and taking the ferry to Agia Anna or by using the new path that starts from Ag. Pavlou. Other popular hikes include the ascent of Athos's peak, a hot, dry 8hr. trek from Agia Anna (☎23 320). A 6hr. climb will take you to the Church of the Panagia, which has mattresses for overnight stays and a small well to refill your water bottle, just 2hr. from the summit. An easier trail (2hr.) that traverses the Athos mountainside runs from Iviron monastery to Koutloumousiou (☎23 226), near Karyes. Catch a ride from Karyes back to Iviron or continue to another monastery in the vicinity. For any hike, it is advisable to take along a copy of the green Mount Athos Road Editions Map (available in stores in Karyes and Ouranoupolis; €7.50) or another Athos guide. Paths can be narrow and poorly marked, and those on the map might have been swallowed by brush. Stop frequently to verify directions and never hike alone; starting at one of the more popular monasteries will ensure company. Be sure to bring lots of water and bear in mind the lay of the peninsula: western shore hikers will enjoy Athos's shadow until 11am, while the eastern shore is perfect for late afternoon rambles. Make sure to be back from your excursion by sunset, or you will be locked out of a meal and bed. The light monastic fare is insufficient for a long hike, so try to bring some nourishment of your own. If you tell the monks in your monastery that you are going to miss a meal, they might give you a modest amount of bread and vegetables. Alternatively, you can hop into a monk-driven minibus for a bumpy ride back to Karyes. Buses gather at most monasteries at about 8:30am, after the morning meal, to transport people back to Dafni via Karyes. From Karyes, ask around for another bus traveling in your direction or ask the minivan driver to let you off at your monastery of choice. Keep in mind that any special request, especially with fewer people in tow, will cost you extra. At no point, however, should you pay more than €20.

THRACE Θράκη

The province that forms present-day Thrace, in the northeastern pocket of Greece, historically has been home to a people not considered ethnically Greek. In Roman times, Indo-European, non-Hellenic Thracians inhabited the mountainous region until they were subdued by Roman conquest in AD 46. The region then became an imperial trading card, passed from the Byzantine Empire to the Bulgarian Empire, back to the Byzantine Empire, and finally to the Ottoman Empire where it remained for 530 years. Only at the close of WWI in 1919, 90 years after Greece achieved independence, was the region completely returned to Greece. Thrace's mixed population of Greeks, Thracian Muslims, Bulgarians, and Albanians and the equally eclectic food, architecture, and traditions allow visitors to live and breathe a part of Greece's complex and rich history.

XANTHI Ξάνθη   ☎ 25410

Old and new come together at Xanthi, Thrace's most bustling and multicultural city. The vivid landscape, framed by the Rhodopi Mountains to the northwest and the Nestos river to the west, provides a captivating backdrop to the lively streets lined with clusters of multiethnic, multi-generational socializing. Just a few steps from the hectic, modern part of the city, you can get lost among the cobbled streets of Xanthi's Old Town. Winding alleys thread through neighborhoods of Ottoman houses and elegant old mansions, the bounty of a tobacco industry that still buoys much of the town's economy. The student population from the University of Thrace adds a youthful spirit to Xanthi's storied history.

▐ TRANSPORTATION. Xanthi's train station, at the end of Kondili, is about 2km southeast of the central plateia. Head down Karaoli, go right at the rotary and, when the street forks, veer left onto Kapnergaton. Kapnergaton turns into Kondili; there are signs 100m past the stadium and the tennis courts. You also can take a taxi (☎ 22 581; €3) to the central plateia. **Trains** go to: Athens (regular: 12hr.; 2:40am, 2:15pm; €23.90. Regular intercity: 9hr., 10:30pm, €50. Express: 8hr.; 2:58, 8:10pm; €63); Istanbul, Turkey (9½hr., 10:40am, €27); Komotini (30min., 7 per day 3:05am-10pm, €2.40); Thessaloniki (regular: 4½hr., 3 per day 2:40am-5:50pm, €7; express: 3½hr., 4 per day 7:50am-10:30pm, €13). Tickets are sold at the train station and the **OSE Pilot Travel Office,** Thermopylon 2. (☎ 74 018. Open M-F 8:30am-2pm and 5-9pm.) Though trains are the best way to get to and from Xanthi, the bus station is at Dimokritou 6. (☎ 22 684. Open 5am-11pm.) **Buses** run to: Athens (10hr.; 9:30am, 7pm; €50); Avdira and Myrodato beaches (30min., 6 per day 6am-8pm, €2); Drama (2hr., 4 per day 8am-6:30pm, €4); Kavala (1hr., every hr. 6am-10pm, €4.60); Komotini (45min., 14 per day 6:30am-8:30pm, €4); Lagos (30min., 9 per day 7am-7pm, €2.30); Mangana beach (30min., 7 per day 6am-10pm, €2); Thessaloniki (3½hr., 9 per day 6am-7pm, €16). **Taxis** (☎ 72 801 or 72 802) wait outside Pl. Kendriki (corner of Vogdou) and Pl. Baltadzi and run 24hr.

◪ ▨ ORIENTATION AND PRACTICAL INFORMATION. Thrace's western-most city, Xanthi is about 50km northeast of Kavala. The central plateia, **Plateia Kendrikí,** is filled with coffee-drinking locals taking advantage of the outdoor seating. It has an **information center** to the left of the clock tower. From the bus station, go out the door at the back of the seating area and take a left on **Dimokritou** in front of you. At the traffic circle, veer right as Dimokritou becomes **Karaoli** and leads into Pl. Kendrikí. Another main street, **28 Oktovriou,** runs parallel to Karaoli and also leads into the central plateia. **Vassilis Konstantinou,** the main artery in the Old Town, starts from the central plateia and heads directly north to the edge of town.

Xanthi's **town hall,** 6 Mavromihali, is housed in a beautiful 19th-century mansion on the upper end of Vas. Konstantino and provides free city maps. (☎ 23 641. Open M-F 9am-7pm.) The **National Bank of Greece,** Konitsis 13, north of the main plateia, has a **24hr. ATM** and **currency exchange.** Take the first right off Konstantinou as you head toward the Old Town. (☎ 45 844. Open M-Th 8am-2:30pm, F 8am-2pm.) **Laundry** can be done at **Alfa,** next to Hotel Orfeas. (☎ 25 723. Open daily 8am-3pm.) The 24hr. **police,** Neston 2 (☎ 22 654 or 22 684), is north of Karaoli near the bus station.

Two blocks southeast of Pl. Baltadzi is the 24hr. **hospital** (☎72 131). The **OTE** is left of the central plateia as you face the large courthouse across from the church. (☎56 199. Open daily 7:30am-1pm.) **Internet** access can be found at **X-net**, Meletsidou 3, at the entrance to the Old Town, opposite a cluster of tavernas. (☎84 463. €2.20 per hr. during the day, €1.70 at night. Coffee €2. Beer €2. Open 24hr.) The **post office,** Miltiadou 7, is just beyond the clock tower. (☎21 166. Open M-F 7:30am-2pm.) **Postal Code:** 67100.

⚑🏠 ACCOMMODATIONS AND FOOD. Neither tourists nor budget hotels have discovered Xanthi. The coastline resorts of **Mangana beach, Myrodato beach,** and **Lagos** have **campsites** and are served by daily buses to Xanthi. In town, your best bet is modern **Hotel Orfeas ❸,** Karaoli 40, whose carpeted rooms have air-conditioning, TV, and balcony. The friendly staff members speak English. (☎20 121 or 20 122. Breakfast included. Singles €38; doubles €55; triples €65.) For a cheaper but less satisfying stay, try **Hotel Paris ❷,** Dimokritou 12, which offers clean but very small rooms with air-conditioning. (☎20 531. Breakfast €4. Singles €23; doubles €27; triples €32.) The **Hotel Democritus ❹,** 28 Oktovriou 41, just below the central plateia, is a more comfortable option. The spacious rooms have TV, air-conditioning, minibar, phone, and large balcony. (☎25 111. English spoken. Internet access available. Breakfast included. Singles €55; doubles €65; triples €78.)

A Turkish flavor pervades much of Xanthi's cuisine, with specialties like syrupy *kariokes* and *soutzouk-lokum,* known as "Turkish Delight." A **covered market,** off 40 Ekklision just south of the main plateia, has bustling stalls full of fruit, vegetables, and meat. (Open daily until 3pm; the most impressive day is Saturday.) For a cheap and lively option go north on Konstantinou from the central plateia and try **⛲Derelismo Golden ❶,** Konstantinou 5. While the menu is only in Greek, pictures of the food and the friendly staff will help you on your journey to deliciousness. (☎28 222. Souvlaki €2. Fresh vegetable plate €3. Open daily noon-midnight.) Just north of the plateia, on the side street that leads to the National Bank, **Fanarakia Taverna ❷,** Stavrou 18, serves local classics in a courtyard. *Terlou terlou* (fried chicken and pork; €5.80) or minced meat rolls (€4.20) are among the restaurant's specials. (☎84 540. Open daily noon-midnight.) **Klimataria ❷,** under the shadow of the clock tower in the main plateia, features a number of local dishes. Outdoor tables are available in the square. (☎22 408. Appetizers €2-3. Entrees €4-7.)

◐ ♫ SIGHTS AND ENTERTAINMENT. Xanthi's museums include the **Folklore Museum,** Antica 9, which houses traditional dresses and jewelry. (Open W-F 8:30am-2:30pm, Sa-Su 10:30am-3pm. Free.) Down the alley from the Folklore Museum, the **Christos Pavlides Painting Gallery,** Orfeos Pindarou Corner 24, has a bustling restoration workshop and paintings by local artists including, of course, the 20th-century painter Christos Pavlides. (☎76 363. Open M-F 10:30am-1:30pm and 6:30-8:30pm. Free.) Take a 30min. cab ride (€11) from the central square to the hills above Xanthi to visit the **Panagia Archangeliotissa** convent, where beautiful frescoes adorn the walls. The magnificent pictures depict Paul's missions to the area in the AD first century. (Open daily 7am-7pm.) The **Panagia Kalamou,** another convent known for its archaeological collection, is higher up on the mountain and offers the best Xanthi lookout point. (Open daily 8am-1pm and 4-8pm.)

Most of Xanthi's nightlife centers on the area west of Sophias at the edge of the University of Thrace's campus, commonly called "the beach" by students. Small and intimate **Dili Dili,** Xristidi 2, is filled with students into the early morning hours. (☎69447 05 005. Open daily 10:30am-4am.) To groove to American jams, go to **Kyverneio,** Sophias 7a, which has a large bar and leather couches. It is the last cafe before the Old Town. (☎77 577. Open M-Th 9am-2am, F-Sa 9am-late, Su 9am-2am.) **Baiser,** Vassilissis Sofias 5, is a sophisticated, modern bar that keeps the energy flowing with strong frappés. At night, it's packed with students showing off the latest Greek fashions. (☎73 948. Open daily 9:30am-late.)

KOMOTINI Κομοτηνή   ☎ 25310

Forty kilometers east of Xanthi, Komotini dazzles visitors with the youthful charm it gleans from the students who make up 24% of its population. The influence of the city's Turkish population is visible in the architecture of the Old Town, where minarets poke up from whitewashed apartments and church cupolas. A frappé at one of the chic cafes surrounding the main square followed by a visit to the Turkish style bazaar will provide a taste of the multi-faceted gem that is Komotini.

▐ TRANSPORTATION. The **OSE office** (☎22 650) is on Panayi Tzaldari 51. (Open M-F 8am-3pm.) Komotini's train station, in the southwestern corner of the city, is a 20min. walk from the city center. Standing on Orfeos facing the main plateia, go right and keep walking. At the railroad tracks, turn right on Kyprillou; it's seven blocks to the station. **Trains** go to: Athens (regular: 12hr.; 2:50pm, 11:55pm; €23.30. Express: 8½hr.; 6:55am, 1:54, 8:37pm; €50); Istanbul, Turkey (10hr., 11:15am, €25); Thessaloniki (regular: 5hr., 3 per day 10:50am-2:10am, €9; express: 3½hr., 3 per day 7:45am-10pm, €14.70). The bus station, G. Mameli 1 (☎22 912), is on the corner of Tsounta. **Buses** go to: Alexandroupoli (1hr., 14 per day 6am-8:10pm, €5); Athens (10hr.; 8:30am, 6:30pm; €55); Kavala (1½hr., 8 per day 5:30am-8pm, €8.20); Thessaloniki (4hr., 8 per day 5:30am-8pm, €19.90); Xanthi (1hr., 11 per day 6:30am-8:30pm, €4). **Taxis** (☎37 777) are available 24hr. by the OTE south of Pl. Eirinis or in front of Hotel Olympus on Orfeos St.

▛▞ ORIENTATION AND PRACTICAL INFORMATION. To get to the city center, turn right from the bus station and left at the first intersection; follow Ainou to the central **Plateia Eirinis. Orfeos** runs east-west directly north of it; **Zoidou** is a few blocks south. Across Orfeos, a maze of markets, and mosques, marks the Turkish area. The ▨**Turkish bazaar** centers on **Ermou.** Going east on Orfeos away from Pl. Eirinis, you will find **Plateia Vizinou** with a white obelisk and wooded urban park.

Maps and tourist pamphlets are available at the **information office** in the municipal Nomarhio office, Dimokratias 1, at the other side of the park. (☎34 124. Open
M-F 7am-2:30pm.) The **National Bank,** Thisauis 1, north of Pl. Eirinis at the east end
of Orfeos, has a **24hr. ATM** and **currency exchange.** (☎54 901. Open M-Th 8am-
2:30pm, F 8am-2pm.) There is a **Bank of Greece,** Ag. Georgiou 1, at the eastern end
of Pl. Eirinis. (☎34 045. Open M-Th 7:45am-3:15pm, F 7:45am-2:45pm.) The **OTE** is
at Parasiou 2, on a side street south of Pl. Eirinis across from Hotel Orpheus. (☎56
171. Open M-Sa 7am-2:30pm, Tu-W 7am-2:30pm and 5:30pm-8:30pm.) **Laundry** can
be done at **Laundry Express,** Zoidou 35. (☎21 511. Open daily 8am-2:30pm and 6-
9:30pm. €10 per load.) Facing the white obelisk, go 500m north on Aghiadou to the
police station, Aghiadou 8 (☎83 205). The **hospital,** Sismanoglou 45 (☎22 222 or 24
601), is in the southeastern part of town; follow Georgiou east out of Pl. Eirinis.
Find **Internet** access at **The Web,** A. Souzou 8. (☎70 111. €2.10 per hr., €1.70 after
midnight. Open 24hr.) Past the OTE is the **post office,** Parasiou 4. (☎22 344. Open
M-F 7:30am-2pm.) **Postal Code:** 69100.

ⲛ ACCOMMODATIONS. Like Xanthi, Komotini has few budget accommodations. ⲛ**Olympos Hotel ❹,** Orfeos 35, in a converted mansion, offers bright, carpeted
rooms with TV, phone, fridge, hairdryer, and air-conditioning. (☎37 690; Breakfast
€4. Singles €40; doubles €50; triples €62. MC/V.) **Hotel Hellas ❷,** Dimokritou 31, is
just north of the Archaeological Museum. With Pl. Eirinis on your left, follow
Orfeos as it becomes Makedonias and pass its first intersection with Dimokritou;
the hotel is on your right when Makedonias intersects with Dimokritou a second
time. Simple rooms with shared baths sit off hallways adorned with artwork created by the manager's wife. The hotel is in the couple's apartment, giving the entire
establishment a homey feel. The staff, though, does not speak English. (☎22 055.
Singles €25; doubles €33.) **Hotel Orpheus ❹,** Parasiou 1, south of Pl. Eirinis opposite the OTE, has cheerful rooms with TV, fridge, air-conditioning, and balcony.
(☎37 180; fax 28 271. Breakfast €4. Singles €37; doubles €47; triples €55. AmEx/
MC/V.) **EOT's campsite ❶,** about a 30min. taxi ride (€8) out of town near Fanari, is
a great option for anyone looking to save money. (☎25350 31 217. Electricity,
drinking water, bath, and shower available. €4.50 per person; €7.50 per car.)

ⲛ FOOD. Dining options center on Pl. Eirinis. Excellent local fare abounds
among the winding streets of the bazaar. Sweet shops display the colorful cubes
and rolls of Turkish Delights and back alleys boast both Greek and Turkish eateries. ⲛ**To Kouti ❷,** Orfeos 45, one block away from the square and left of Hotel
Olympos, serves specialities like *kotopoulo especial* (spicy Spanish chicken; €6)
and *lukaniko especial* (local sausage topped with cheese; €6). The delicious food
at this traditional Greek taverna matches its romantic ambience. (☎25 774.
Entrees €4-10.) For a Turkish taste, try out **Restauran ❶,** Bakkalbasi 4; its homemade authentic *kofte* (minced meat patties and rice; €2) and Turkish salad
(€1.50) are popular with locals. (☎36 088. Open daily 6:30am-4:30pm.) Another
favorite, **Taverna Petrino ❸,** Kiklis 8, is just two blocks from Orfeos. A delightful
escape from both the summer sun and the traffic of Ermou, Petrino offers a variety
of chicken, fish, and pork dishes served by a courteous English-speaking waitstaff.
Don't miss the octopus with ouzo (€5), the house specialty. (☎73 650. Entrees
€4.50-7. Open daily during high season 11:30am-3am; low season location is
around the corner at Serron 25.) **Restaurant Ydroxos ❷,** Papaflessa 2, on a side
street connecting Orfeos to Pl. Eirinis, has tasty local dishes and a wide selection of homemade salads. Seating is available either under the vine-covered
canopy looking over the bustling square or in the air-conditioned interior.
Ydroxos has an English menu and serves a delicious pudding dessert on the
house. (☎33 786. Thracian pork dish with green and red peppers €5.) In the

square, sit at a balcony table at **Oinopion ❸**, Pl. Eirinis 67, to survey the plateia while enjoying the breeze. The tasty menu includes meat dishes such as the famous Oinopion chicken (€5.50). (☎36 082; www.oinopion.gr. Entrees €4-12.) Head to the square to experience the non-stop nightlife, where cafe bars invite you in with loud music. For a calmer scene featuring Greek and international music at a volume low enough to allow conversations, have a drink at **Cafe Radiofono**, Pl. Eirinis 18. (☎69730 87 150. Beer €3; mixed drinks €5.)

🎇🎆 **SIGHTS AND NIGHTLIFE.** To reach Komotini's **Archaeological Museum**, Simeonidi 4, follow Zoidou westward and bear right at the park onto the cement footpath. Arranged with helpful English explanations, the museum's exhibits focus on artifacts found in Thrace dating from the Neolithic to Byzantine periods. The museum also features Early Neolithic Thracian wall-paintings from the 11th century BC as well as artifacts from a barren Roman fortress at Nestos whose oft-raided walls protected the Via Egnatia and port of Neapolis. Highlights include the spectacular golden bust of Roman Emperor Septimius Severus from Plotinopolis, the 5th-century BC Panathenaic amphora depicting Athena holding a shield, and the 4th-century BC Mask of Dionysus from Maroneia. (☎25310 215 17. Open daily 8am-3pm. Free.) A 30min. taxi ride from Komotini brings you to the beach of Maroneia, which has a few archaeological sites including a well-preserved amphitheater. Head to the square to experience Komotini's non-stop nightlife, where cafe bars invite you in with loud music. For a calmer scene featuring Greek and international music, have a drink at Cafe Radiofono, Pl. Eirinis 18. (☎697 3087 150. Beer €3; mixed drinks €5.)

ALEXANDROUPOLI Αλεξανδρούπολη ☎25510

Travelers often rush through Alexandroupoli on their way to Turkey, the Northeast Aegean Islands, or the hinterlands of Thrace, overlooking the charms of one of the province's most bustling and enchanting port cities. The long-standing military presence in Alexandroupoli has stripped this city of the Muslim influence found in other Thracian cities. Despite its comparative lack of diversity, Alexandroupoli's upscale waterfront cafes along with its cobblestone streets and homey seafood tavernas make it a charming place to get stranded.

📰 **TRANSPORTATION.** Dimokritos Airport (☎45 198), 6km east of town and only reachable by taxi (€4), has flights to: Athens (1hr., 2-3 per day, €75-85), Sitia (2hr., 3 per week, €92), and Thessaloniki (1hr., 3 per week, €65). Buy tickets at **Sever Travel** on Dikastarion and Karaiskaki. Walking inland from the lighthouse it is the first intersection on your left. (☎22 555.) The train station is at M. Alexandrou 1, 400m east of the lighthouse, in front of Pl. Eleftherias. (☎26 395.) **Trains** to: Athens (regular: 14hr., 4 per day 3:22pm-12:29am, €24.80; intercity: 9hr., 5 per day 6:40am-8:30pm, €51.50); Istanbul, Turkey (9hr., noon, €23.30); Komotini (regular: 1hr., 4 per day 1am-4:17pm, €1.90; intercity: 50min., 4 per day 6:45am-9:05pm, €4.70); Thessaloniki (regular: 6hr., 4 per day 1am-4:17pm, €9.70; intercity: 4½hr., 4 per day 6:45am-9:05pm, €16.20); Xanthi (regular: 1½hr., 4 per day 1am-4:17pm, €2.50. Intercity: 1½hr., 4 per day 6:45am-9:05pm, €7). The bus station, El. Venizelou 36 (☎26 479), is off of Maiou, 500m inland from the docks and sends **buses** to: Athens (11hr., 6:30pm, €58); Didimotiho (1½hr., every hr. 4:15am-8:45pm, €7) via Feres (30min., €2) and Soufli (1hr., €4.20); Kipi (45min., 5 per day 6:50am-7:30pm, €3); Komotini (1hr., every hr. 6:10am-8:10pm, €5.20); Thessaloniki (regular: 5hr., 8 per day 5:15am-10pm. Express: 4½hr.; 9:30am, 5pm; €25.80) via Xanthi (1½hr., 8 per day, €8) and Kavala (2hr., 8 per day, €12.80).

There are two main ferry lines. **Saos** lies a few doors up from the waterfront at Kyprou 15. (☎26 721. Open M and W 8:30am-9pm, Tu and Th-F 7:30am-3pm and 5-9pm, Sa 8am-9:30pm, Su 8am-5:30pm.) **Ferries** run to Samothraki (3½hr.), Limnos (5hr.), and Lesvos (12hr.). **Flying Dolphins,** which run June 20 through September 20, zip to Samaothraki (1hr.). Times and prices of ferries from Saos change constantly, so call ahead on the day you want to travel. **Kikon Tours,** El. Venizelou 68, sends one weekly ferry that leaves on Monday at 8:30am. (☎25 455. Open M-F 9am-2:30pm and 6:30-9:30pm, Sa 8:30am-2:30pm.) The ferry stops at: Chios (12hr., €28); Kalimnos (22hr., €39); Kos (20hr., €39); Lesvos (10hr., €21); Limnos (4hr., €15); Rhodes (24hr., €44); Samos (16hr., €34). **Taxis** (☎33 500) are available 24hr. on Megalou Alexandrou. Fares inside the city cost up to €4.

◪◪ ORIENTATION AND PRACTICAL INFORMATION. Everything a traveler could need is within 10min. of the waterfront center, which is marked by a lighthouse. Standing at the lighthouse facing inland, **Megalou Alexandrou** stretches left toward a row of cafes and right toward the train station. Halfway between the lighthouse and the train station, **Kyprou** leads inland to small **Plateia Kyprou.** The three main streets running parallel to Alexandrou (**Dimokratias, Eleftheriou Venizelou,** and **Paleologou**) are about three blocks inland, linked by narrow cobblestone streets. The **tourist police,** Karaiskaki 6, are two blocks inland from the water, just before the lighthouse. (☎37 411. Open M-Th 8am-2pm.) They share a building with the 24hr. **police** (☎37 424). Dimokratias is one long string of banks with **24hr. ATMs,** including the **National Bank of Greece,** Dimokratias 240. (☎64 612. Open M-Th 8am-2pm, F 8am-1:30pm.) There is a 24hr. **hospital** (☎74 000) in the suburb of Hilli. **Net Gaming Network,** Xarilaou Trikoupi 2, has **Internet** access. Head west along Dimokratias until the road splits; take the left fork onto Trikoupi. (☎29 751; www.gnet.gr. €2-3 per hr. Open 24hr.) More Internet can be found behind the large military academy building. The **post office,** M. Alexandrou 42, is on the water 20m west of the lighthouse. (☎23 122. Open M-F 7:30am-2pm.) **Postal Code:** 68100.

▐ ACCOMMODATIONS. Like most of its neighbors, Alexandroupoli has pricey lodgings. The best options are the ones closest to the train and bus stations. During the summer it is recommended that you call ahead. **Hotel Lido ❸,** Paleologou 15, behind the bus station, has a variety of simple rooms. Some face the sea, others have a pleasant city view. Rooms with bath are more expensive; the others share a common bathroom with a squat-style toilet. (☎28 808. Singles €30, with bath €35; doubles €36/42; triples €45.) Walk down M. Alexandrou toward Dimokratias to find **Hotel Marianna ❹,** Malogaron 11. George, the friendly and knowledgeable owner, offers charming, well-kept rooms and advice about exploring the area. (☎81 455. Singles €45; doubles €55; triples €68.) **Hotel Vergina ❸,** Karaoli 74, directly across the street from the train station at the point where M. Alexandrou becomes Karaoli, has 10 clean, well-furnished rooms with bath, TV, air-conditioning and phones. Three of the rooms have a beautiful sea view. (☎23 025. Singles €35; doubles €50; triples €70.) **Camping Alexandroupolis ❶** is 1km west of the town center on the water. (☎28 735. €4.80 per person; €3.40 per tent; €2 per car.)

◖ FOOD. Fast food and cheap cafes line the waterfront and the area around Dimokratias and M. Alexandrou, while a number of good seafood restaurants put tables out along the shore. ▓**Masa Soura ❷,** M. Alexandrou 36, is a 5min. walk from the post office, along the coast away from the large dock. It's known locally for having fresh traditional fish dishes. The *mussels saganaki* (mussels in red sauce; €6.50) served with a cold *ouzo plomari* (€4) are especially tasty. (☎360 52. Entrees €5-10. Open daily 11:30am-3am.) Seaside **Taverna Mylos ❷,** M. Alexandrou 2, across from the post office (look for the windmill), serves delicious fresh sea-

food brought in every morning by Samothrakian fisherman. Ask for the celebrated crab salad served in a
giant shell (€5), or plunge into the impressive ouzo
and *tsipouro* selection. (☎ 35 519. Entrees €2-8.
Open daily until midnight.) Locals flock to **Kokoras
❷**, M. Alexandrou 4, 5min. east of the lighthouse on
the waterfront, for freshly grilled meats at affordable
prices. (☎ 82 647. Entrees €1-6. Open daily 10am-
1am.) Popular and modern **Theofilos ❶**, on the corner
of Kyprou and M. Alexandrou, has an amazing variety
of cheese and meat pastries (€0.60-2.70) and 30
homemade ice cream flavors (€1.50). Sit on the second-floor balcony and watch the fishermen coming
up from the harbor. (☎ 33 882. Open daily 5am-1am.)

◨ ▣ **SIGHTS AND NIGHTLIFE.** Alexandroupoli's
▨**Ecclesiastic Art Museum** is inside the Cathedral of
Agios Nikolaos, one block inland and one block east of
the bus station. The museum features a 19th-century
gilded Bulgarian Gospel and wooden icons alongside
a workshop that demonstrates the process of painting an icon. Ask Nectarius, the English-speaking
priest, to give you a tour. (☎ 81 281. Open Tu-Sa 11am-
1:30pm. Suggested donation €1.) The walls of the
beautiful 19th-century Cathedral of **Agios Nikolaos**
house unique artifacts like the Byzantine Virgin **Trifo-
tissa,** a 13th-century icon of Mary and the baby Jesus
from Aenos. Mary's eyes are prominent in the depiction, and as a result, the icon was worshipped for protection against bad eyesight. The altar is adorned
with magnificent stained glass windows. (Services
are held daily 7-9am and 6:40-7pm.) At night, cafes
and trendy bars along the shore on M. Alexandrou
play a mix of Mediterranean and American music all
night. **So Simple...,** M. Alexandrou in front of Masa
Soura and on the waterfront, is the main dance club
in the area. (€5 beers; €10 mixed drinks.)

DADIA Δαδιά   ☎ 25540

The **Dadia Forest Reserve** lies 40km northeast of Alexandroupoli. It covers over 18,000 acres of wooded
hills near the Turkish border and extends into the
Evros prefecture at the southeastern edge of the
Rodophi mountain range. The forest serves as the
home and breeding ground for hundreds of endangered raptors. Of the 38 European species of these
huge hunters, 36 have been spotted in Dadia, and it is
the only place in Europe where the four European
vulture species (black, bearded, Griffon, and Egyptian) coexist. A well-maintained and marked network
of hiking trails runs throughout the reserve. Different
colored markers indicate the way along the rugged
ridges that break up the golden, untouristed Thracian

plain. From the Ecotourist Center, a main trail leads up a hill to a wooden platform, where you can watch raptors and vultures swoop down onto their prey. Follow the orange path uphill for about 1hr. From the platform, trails extend in all directions, with most leading back to the Ecotourist Center. To head back down, take the trail marked with yellow blazes for about 45min. The red trail (2hr.) takes you to the ruins of a Byzantine castle, built by Emperor Justinian on the peak of the Giberna mountain, while the blue trail (1½hr.) traverses the mountain side and returns to the Ecotourist Center. The Ecotourist Center houses a modest museum that offers interesting information about the flora and fauna found in the Dadia forest. The village of **Dadia** is small, charming, and definitely worth a short visit if you are exploring the surrounding area. Official documents from the Ottoman empire call the town Cimkebir—"village of the great pine"—and the modern name, Dadia, comes from the same thematic root, meaning "pine wood torch." The local **monastery,** which lies 4km outside of the village, was built in 1727, then rebuilt in 1950 after being destroyed in the Balkan wars. In addition, 14 other churches serve the 600 villagers. The town hosts a number of local festivals such as the **Courbani Fair** on January 18, which celebrates an old custom meant to bring good fortune for the crops and animals. On this day, the men of the village slaughter male goats and cook the meat all night in huge cauldrons by the chapel; in the morning, the food is distributed among the houses of the village. To scare off the Christmas spirit known as "Kalikantzari" on **Epiphany,** villagers carry icons out of the church and cling to them as they run through the village chanting, "Lord have mercy."

A **small hotel ❸,** with bird names instead of room numbers, shares a building with the Ecotourist Center. The wooden-floored rooms with air-conditioning, TV, and bath are connected by a veranda that overlooks a picturesque courtyard. (☎25540 32 209. Reserve in advance. Singles €30; doubles €40; triples €50.)

To get to Dadia, take the bus from Alexandroupoli to Didimotiho and get off at Soufli (1hr., every hr. 4:15am-8:45pm, €5). From Soufli, catch the bus to the village of Dadia (20min., 3 per day 8am-2pm). The reserve is approximately 1km from the center of Dadia; follow the signs to the Ecotourist Center. If you miss the last bus back, take a taxi (☎22 888) to Soufli for about €12.

SARONIC GULF ISLANDS
Τα Νησιά του Σαρωνικού

The Saronic Gulf hosts a mix of city chaos and laid-back island flavor. The intrepid will uncover a gold mine of historical and natural sights, though at a steep price. Since the islands are a popular summer getaway for Athenians, room prices skyrocket as availability drops, especially on the weekends. Mid-week and low-season travelers with time to explore will encounter surprising diversity here; despite their geographic proximity, each island retains a distinct character. Aegina's throngs of beer-swilling beachgoers live in a different world than Poros's urbane upper crust, and Spetses's motorbiking hipsters are much farther from Hydra's mule-mounted artists than the 1hr. ferry between them would suggest.

SUGGESTED ITINERARIES: SARONIC GULF ISLANDS

FOUR DAYS Set off on a salty excursion to **Aegina Town** (p. 316), where you can snack on more varieties of pistachio nuts than you ever dreamed of. The ferry you catch to **Hydra** (p. 325) the next day very likely will be the last motorized transport you use for a while—anything more advanced than a donkey is strictly forbidden at this popular honeymoon destination. Finally, spend 2 days on **Spetses** (p. 329), with its ring of ivory beaches.

AEGINA Αίγινα

Athenians make haste to the whitewashed shores of Aegina, where the big city's bustle is transported on summer weekends. Relations with the mainland once were more strained than they are today, as the little island repeatedly betrayed its Athenian neighbor. Aegina first sided against their Hellenic brethren in 491 BC when Xerxes's army laid siege to Athens, kicking off the Persian Wars. Though returning humbly to the Greek side in 480 BC and even winning the praise of the Delphic Oracle for having the swiftest navy on the seas, Aegina turned against Athens in Sparta's 459 BC insurgence against the mainland. Defeated in battle, the island found itself displaced by Athenian colonists, putting an end to Aeginian dominance at the Panhellenic games. Aegina soon sank into geopolitical obscurity, only emerging over two millennia later, in 1827, as the temporary capital of then partially liberated Greece. Travelers to Aegina will find that its attractions are as rich as its legacy, including gorgeous beaches, wild nightlife, and the well-preserved remains of the Temple of Aphaia.

AEGINA TOWN   ☎22970

As soon as your ferry docks in Aegina Town, you'll know that you've entered "the pistachio capital of the world." With preserved, jellied, flavored, red, flaked, shelled, and regular varieties, there are as many ways to eat pistachios here as there are package tour boats from the mainland; fortunately, the tasty nuts are the stronger influence. Those looking for a carefree beachside romp will do well to stay in town. For a more substantive experience, rent a moped and delve deeper into the forested, church-crowned terrain.

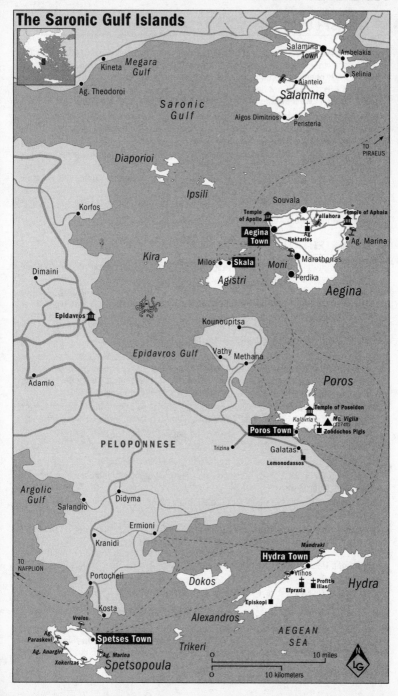

The Saronic Gulf Islands

Kineta

Megara Gulf

Ag. Theodoroi

Saronic Gulf

Salamina Town

Ambelakia

Selinia

Aianteio

Salamina

Aigos Dimitrios

Peristeria

TO PIRAEUS

Diaporioi

Korfos

Ipsili

Souvala

Temple of Apollo

Paliahora

Temple of Aphaia

Aegina Town

Ag. Nektarios

Ag. Marina

Kira

Milos

Skala

Moni

Marathonas

Dimaini

Agistri

Perdika

Aegina

Epidavros

Kounoupitsa

Epidavros Gulf

Vathy

Methana

Adamio

Poros

Temple of Poseidon

Kalavria

Mt. Viglia
(1174ft)

Poros Town

Zoödochos Pigis

Trizina

Galatas

PELOPONNESE

Lemonodassos

Argolic Gulf

Salandio

Didyma

Ermioni

Kranidi

Mandraki

Hydra Town

Vlihos

TO NAFPLION

Profitis Ilias

Efpraxia

Portocheli

Dokos

Episkopi

Hydra

Kosta

Alexandros

Vrelos

AEGEAN SEA

Ag. Paraskevi

Spetses Town

Ag. Anargiri

Ag. Marina

Trikeri

Xokerizas

Spetsopoula

0   10 miles

0   10 kilometers

SARONIC GULF

▐ TRANSPORTATION

Ferries: Kiosks on the docks sell tickets to neighboring islands; check the windows for the latest schedules. **Aegean** (☎25 800; open 6:30am-8pm) and **Hellenic Seaways** (☎27 462; open 6am-9pm) cover most destinations. Ferries to: **Agistri** (20min., 3-4 per day, €3); **Hydra** (2hr., daily, €9); **Piraeus** (1½hr., 11 per day, €7.90); **Poros** (1hr., 4 per day, €7) via **Methana** (45min., 3 per day, €5); **Spetses** (3hr., daily, €12).

Hydrofoils: Hellas Flying Dolphins (☎27 462) has a ticket stand on the quay and goes to **Piraeus** (35min., every hr., €12). In the summer, **Aegean** dolphins also serve **Angistri** (10min., 2 per day, €4.50).

Buses: ☎22 787. In Ethnegarcias Park, at the corner of the waterfront; schedules are taped to the kiosk. Buses run to **Agia Marina** via the **Temple of Aphaia** (30min., 9 per day 7am-8:30pm, €1.70), **Perdika** (15min., 9 per day 6:40am-7:45pm, €1) via **Marathonas,** and **Souvalda** (25min., 8 per day 7am-8pm, €1.30).

Taxis: ☎22 635. The station is to the left of the quay on the waterfront. Marathonas €3.

Mopeds: Mopeds from Aegina's many rental agencies run €7-20 per day.

▐▐ ORIENTATION AND PRACTICAL INFORMATION

The central quay is expensive, but tavernas and hotels get cheaper toward either end of the waterfront street, which is, when facing inland, **Kazatzaki** to the left and **Toti Chatzi** to the right. At a central point, it goes by **Dimokratias.** Running parallel and one block inland, **Pan Irioti** is lined with small shops, markets, tavernas, and the occasional moped rental shop. **Aphaias** runs on a tangent curve to Pan Irioti, and both are bisected perpendicularly by **Aiakou,** which takes you back to the waterfront and is home to upscale shops, bars, and an Internet cafe.

Budget Travel: Karagiannis Travel, Kanari 2 (☎25 664), 1 block inland opposite the ticket kiosks. Ask the congenial staff for info about the island, free maps, free **luggage storage,** flight tickets, and help with accommodations. Bike rentals €6 per day; mopeds from €12; cars from €30. Open daily 8:30am-8pm, later during high season.

Bank: National Bank (☎26 930), to the right of the waterfront quay, past the port police. **Currency exchange** and **24hr. ATM.** Open M-Th 8am-2:30pm, F 8am-2pm.

Police: ☎22 100. Available 24hr. The **tourist police,** Leonardou Lada 11 (☎27 777), are in the same building. Open daily 8am-8pm.

Pharmacy: 3 are along Aiakou. One is always on call for emergencies.

Medical Center: ☎22 222. 1.5km along the waterfront to the left of the ferries when facing inland. Open 24hr.

Telephones: OTE, Paleas Choras 6 (☎22 399, assistance 131), up Aiakou to the right. Open M-Th 7:30am-1:30pm, F 7:30am-1pm.

Internet Access: Surf and Play, 42 Aphaias (☎29 096; www.surfnplay.gr.). Coin-operated computers, Dr. Seuss-inspired walls, and Wi-Fi. €2 per hr., min. €0.50. **e-Global** (☎29 135), 1 block inland, across from the basketball courts to the far right of the waterfront. Has Wi-Fi and dozens of computers. €2.50 per hr. Open daily 9am-4am.

Post Office: Kanari 6 (☎22 398), in Pl. Ethnegersias, behind the bus station. **Poste Restante** and Western Union available. Open M-F 7:30am-2pm. **Postal Code:** 18010.

▐ ACCOMMODATIONS

Rooms here are cheaper than those on any of the other Saronic Gulf islands, with high season doubles going for around €30-45. Unlike on most islands, heading inland does not afford better deals; the cheapest **domatia** can be found on either extreme of the waterfront. Arriving midweek to avoid the weekend Athenian flood will give you some bargaining power.

Pension Giakas, Agios Nikolaos 8 (☎25 664), in the green-doored building behind the inland church. Spacious studios have kitchenette alcove, bath, A/C and TV; ask at Karagiannis Travel. Note that 1st fl. rooms have street side windows that are subject to rounds of ding-dong-ditch by the neighborhood kiddies. Singles €25-40; doubles €30-45. ❷

Hotel Plaza, Kazatzaki 4 (☎/fax 25 600), at the far left end of the waterfront when facing inland. Pretty, modestly furnished, shell-pink rooms come with bath, A/C, fridge, and balcony overlooking the water in this nautically-themed hotel. Reception 24hr. Singles from €30; prices negotiable. ❸

Hotel Avra (☎22 303), 2 doors down from Hotel Plaza. Rooms have A/C, TV, fridge, new bath, and narrow balcony overlooking narrow streets; the dried flowers are a nice touch. Singles €30; doubles €50. ❸

Hotel Pavlou, Aeginitou 21 (☎22 795), behind the church on the far right of the quay, facing inland. Classy rooms have A/C, TV, fan, balcony, fridge, bath, and some peacock feathers to spice things up. Cheaper rates for multi-night stays. The family also runs the slightly cheaper Hotel Athina a few blocks inland. Singles €40; doubles €45-55. ❹

▐ FOOD

Tavernas line P. Irioti along the right side of the harbor, though it can be hard to distinguish between the authentic and the tourist-centric. For a combination of the two, head to the strip of *ouzeria* at the far left of the harbor, past the bus stop. In general, the farther you stray from the ferry dock, the better the food will be. Tavernas around the fish market on Dimokratious (to the right when facing inland) are also a good bet.

Lekkas, Kazntzaki 14 (☎22 527), on the waterfront just past the bus station. Pick among your homemade favorites. The tender special pork (€6.50) is served on sand-top tables. Entrees €4-7. Open daily 9am-late. ❷

Anli (☎26 438). Head up Aikaou and take the first left for 2 blocks. In Anli's courtyard diners can escape the foot traffic while tasting the variety of spaghetti. Entrees €3.80-8. Open daily 9am-3pm and 8pm-3am. ❷

Yacht Club Panagakis, Dimokratious 20 (☎26 654). Tire-sized crepes come with fillings that range from chocolate and walnuts to turkey and mayo. Long drinks €5-7. Crepes €4.50-10. Open daily 7am-late. ❷

▐ NIGHTLIFE

Check out open-air **Cinema Anesis**, featuring nightly showings of Greek and American new releases; pick up a schedule at the ticket office a few blocks inland on Aiakou. (☎26 331. Tickets €7.50. 9 and 11pm showings.)

Inn on the Beach (☎25 116; www.innonthebeach.gr), past the church on the waterfront. Sparkles with harbor lights and palm trees. A chic crowd circulates the bar and private tables, sipping creamy frozen drinks (€10) amid the loud dance tracks. Open daily 11am-3am.

Ellinikon, Toti Chatzi 10 (☎69361 11 213; www.ellinikon.net), down the street from Inn on the Beach. Aegina's main and oldest dance club is a Gordian knot of writhing limbs and swiveling hips that threatens to spill over the street and into the sea. Come W nights for Greek night. Mixed drinks €9. Cover €10, includes 1 drink. Open daily midnight-dawn. AmEx/MC/V.)

◉ SIGHTS

Aegina Town's archaeological fame teeters on the last half-column of the **Temple of Apollo.** The 8m Doric column dates to 460 BC and stands on Kolonna Hill, ancient Aegina's acropolis, to the far left of the waterfront when facing inland; turn left past the playground. Excavation of the site, home to 10 consecutive early Bronze Age communities, is ongoing. Today Byzantine-era cisterns and the foundations of prehistoric homes sit in stony silence alongside the monolithic column. Fortunately, the on-site **archaeological museum** speaks for them, detailing the growth of the town and its fortifications from 2500-1400 BC. Highlights include a magnificent early-Classical sphinx (460 BC), artifacts from the Temple of Aphaia, and an extensive collection of Neolithic pottery. (☎22 248. Museum and site open Tu-Su 8:30am-3pm. €3, students with ID €2.)

The underground church of **Faneromeni,** a 15min. walk inland south of the town, contains a rare icon of the Virgin Mary. Locals say that the night before construction was to begin on a site above Faneromeni, the architect in charge had a vision instructing him to dig instead of build. Doing just that, he unearthed the icon. Call the monastery Moni Kimisis Theotokou to set up an appointment. (☎62 000. Free. Modest dress required.) The **Church Omorfi Elissia,** 2km out of town, is accessible by appointment with the archaeology museum and boasts a number of well-preserved frescoes. (☎22 637. Free. Modest dress required.)

Aeginian citizens gather for theater, songs, fireworks, and feasting during the yearly **Aegina Festival** in mid-August. At the chlorinated splendor of **Faros Waterpark,** 1km to the right of the waterfront, facing inland, you can find a network of pools and slides. (☎22 540. Entrance €3. Open daily 10:30am-7:30pm.)

▶ DAYTRIPS FROM AEGINA TOWN

MARATHONAS. Smaller than Aegina Town and less crowded than Ag. Marina, the peopled beach of **Marathonas** arcs along the island's western coast. Warm waters lap the sandy shore, forming a shallow crescent with views of the Peloponnese. *(7km south of Aegina Town. Buses run from Aegina Town to Marathonas (15min., 9 per day, €1). You also can catch a taxi on the main road, €3 from Aegina Town.)* The seaside tables at family-owned **O Tassos ❷,** just before the church on the main road, let you wriggle your toes in the sand (or dip them in the water) as you eat. Homemade pastries, epic portions, and fresh vegetables from the family farm have earned this taverna well-deserved renown. (☎24 040. Entrees €5.50-7. Open 9am-midnight.)

AGIOS NEKTARIOS AND PALIOHORA. The compound of the massive, marble and bronze church at Agios Nektarios is the second-largest place of worship in the Balkans. As of yet unfinished, the church allows visitors to admire the three-tiered interior and glorious gold-foiled wall paintings.

The turn-off just after Agios Nektarios leads 1km up to ▨**Paliohora,** the "town of 300 churches" and a former refuge from pirate invasions. Built in 1462, the town was destroyed by the Turkish invaders under Barbossa, later regaining its glory only to be abandoned in the 1750s. The only remnants are the 33 churches sprinkled on the hillside. Narrow footpaths interconnect the churches, and many of the small, whitewashed buildings are left open; some churches house icons amid open-roofed rubble. Bring water, as there is nowhere to buy it in the vicinity. (*A 15min. bus ride from Aegina Town; ask to be let off here. Free. Modest dress required.*)

EASTERN AEGINA ☎ 22970

If interior Aegina's beauty starts to seem a little too, well, natural, head to the crowded shores of **Agia Marina,** where sunburned tourists, indistinguishable tavernas, and a buzzing nightlife melt into the pebble beaches. The well-preserved Doric **Temple of Aphaia,** 2km above town, is the main draw to this side of the island for archaeology buffs and the casual admirer alike. Legend tells that this is where the nymph Aphaia, daughter of Zeus and Karme, was rendered invisible in a narrow escape from King Minos's unwelcome advances. Built in the 5th century BC, her temple still boasts a spectacular set of double-tiered columns that provided inspiration for the Parthenon; more details can be found in the on-site **museum.** Evening visitors may be joined by peacocks from the surrounding hills. To get there, take the Agia Marina bus from Aegina Town and ask the driver to stop at the temple, or take the 30min. hike up the steep, gravel shortcut. (☎32 398. Museum open Tu-Su 8am-2:15pm; temple open daily 8am-2:15pm. Museum and temple €4, students €2.) Facing the bus station, continue 300m to the left to reach the trendy "snack bar" **Crystal,** where music, billiards, mixed drinks, and swimming are available both night and day. Make like the predatory fish at ⬛**Barracuda,** where patrons watch swimmers from the balcony overhanging the beach while enjoying lemon and brown sugar *caipirinhias* (€8). Look for the brown door in the taverna-lined plateia in the middle of the waterfront. (☎32 095. Open 11am-2am.) Weekend nights, the dance clubs rev things up for partying Athenians. Before Crystal, signs point inland to the fortress exterior of **Zorba's Castle,** a trendy disco open on weekend nights. (Open daily 1am-late.) Escape the humidity at dance club **Manos,** across from Crystal, where patrons bump and grind away in air-conditioned comfort. (Open F-Sa 9:30pm-late. Open daily mid-July to Aug.)

For those who decide to stay in the shadow of Aphaia, a number of pensions and pricier hotels can be found one block in from the waterfront. You'll find yourself lingering in the newly converted ⬛**Hotel Erato Backpackers ❶,** 100m to the left of the bus stop when facing inland. Once a snazzy hotel, this backpacker paradise comes equipped with free Internet, the cheapest beer on the island (€1.50), a swimming pool, €5 community dinners with wine, and clean, private rooms with TV, fridge, air-conditioning, bath, and balcony. (☎32 322; www.aeginahostel.com. Simple breakfast included. Rooms €15 per person.) To the right of the bus station facing inland, **Hotel Myrmidon ❷** is another budget option, offering rooms with air-conditioning, TV, bath, balcony, and fridge. Beat the heat under the footbridge that runs over the courtyard swimming pool. (☎32 691. www.hotel-myrmidon.gr. Singles €20-25; doubles €28; triples €40. 20% discount for *Let's Go* readers.) Pricey waterfront restaurants crammed with tourists crowd between the gyro and fast-food shops along Aphaias, though a few better options can be found slightly out of town. Facing inland, head 1km to the left past Crystal to reach the gourmet ⬛**O Kostas ❷.** A huge variety of *mezedes* such as *escargot* (€6) and lamb *fricasse* (€7.50) are served with local wine out of the barrel (€5 per liter) on the leafy, barrel-lined terrace. (☎32 424. Open daily 11am-midnight. AmEx/MC/V.) **Restaurant Paradise ❷,** on the waterfront, offers diners a variety of *schnitzel* (€7.50-9) on tables under a cool canopy of trees. (☎32 008. Entrees €5-9. Open daily 10am-late.) On the right side of the waterfront when facing inland, the water views at **O Faros ❷** go well with the large selection of Greek favorites. (☎32 011. Entrees €4.80-10. Open 9:30am-midnight. AmEx/MC/V.)

Buses run from Aegina Town to Agia Marina (40min., 9 per day 7am-8:30pm, €1.70); for nearby sites, tell the driver your destination. You can buy bus tickets in Agia Marina at the **kiosk** in the plateia where the bus lets you off.

AGISTRI ISLAND   ☎22970

Historically a nudist getaway, the tiny, forested island of Agistri off the Aegina coast has seen a recent influx of wealthy Athenians building weekend homes on its lush shores. Head there mid-week to catch the gloriously empty beaches and lower room rates. With only four tiny towns nestled in pine-covered pockets, it is not hard to make it around the island. A completely undeveloped stretch of coast can be found on the opposite side of the island at **Dragonera.** Locals praise the beaches of **Skala,** 3km west of Milos along the waterfront road, where swimmers can choose among sand, pebbled, crowded, and deserted coastline. The Skala waterfront is home to an endless bounty of tavernas and domatia.

Facing inland, head 1km to the left past the church to reach **Studios Anemoni ❷** where white, tiled rooms come with bath, air-conditioning, kitchenette, fan, and balcony. (☎69443 35 098. Singles €25-30; doubles €30-35.) In the same area and only 30m above the water, the simple whitewashed rooms at **Rosy's Little Village ❹** are frequent host to writing and yoga groups. Though the doubles are pricey, the family rooms are a steal for five. (☎91 610; www.rosyslittlevillage.com. Free mountainbike and sunbed use. Doubles €49-60; quints €87.) A little uphill, the locally appraised **Taverna Alkyoni ❷** has a number of tables overlooking the cliffs under a pine forest. (☎91 378. Entrees €6-8. Open noon-1:30pm and 8-11:30pm.)

The water taxi **Agistri Express** services Skala and Milos ports daily. (☎69374 59 221. 25min.; M-F 6 per day 7:30am-8pm, Sa-Su 1-2 per day; €3.50 one-way, €6.50 round-trip.) Buy tickets on board and check the dock for schedules. In summer, **Aegean** has **Flying Dolphins** to Milos port (15min., 2 per day, €4.50). Consider renting a scooter for the day from **Moto Rent Kostas.** (☎91 021. Bikes €6. Scooters €15 per day. Open daily 9am-9pm.) You also can hire a **taxi** (☎91 455 or 69776 18 040).

POROS Πόρος

The land of lemon trees, Poros is two islands connected by a short causeway: larger Kalavria to the north, with thick patches of woods and dark-watered beaches, and smaller Sferia to the south, geared almost entirely toward tourists. The name "Poros" ("Passage") refers to the narrow strait, formed in 273 BC by a volcanic eruption, that separates the island pair from the Peloponnese. In the 6th century BC, the Kalavrian League met in Poros to ward off hostile navies, later ordering the construction of the Temple of Poseidon. When the island came under siege again, the great orator Demosthenes chose to commit suicide near the temple's columns rather than face capture by the Macedonians. Poros was sparsely populated until Greek refugees arrived from Turkey in the 1920s. Today, the island is hardly lacking for people—tourists have descended on its beaches, enjoying the many opportunities to soak up the sun.

POROS TOWN   ☎22980

Beach shops and tavernas sprawl outward from the ferry dock in one long, tourist-snagging tentacle. While the waterfront offers an endless variety of places to spend money, actual sights and entertainment options are limited. Up the hill, however, a few quiet spots provide lovely panoramas of Kalavrita's remaining wilderness. Across the straight from Poros Town, the grittier and more economical Galatas (Γαλατας) provides welcome relief for outdoors enthusiasts. Surrounded by thousands of lemon trees, the small working village serves as a good base from which to uncover the nearby natural and ancient sights.

Poros

▣ TRANSPORTATION. Ferries go to: Aegina (1hr., 3-5 per day, €7.30); Hydra (1hr., daily, €6); Piraeus (2½hr., 3-5 per day, €11.60) via Methana (30min., €3); Spetses (2½hr., daily, €10). Buy tickets at **Family Tours** (☎23 743), across from the ferry dock. **Marinos Tours** (☎23 423; open 7am-9pm), 150m to the right of Family Tours facing inland, sells tickets for **Flying Dolphins**, which go to: Ermioni (1hr., 3 per day, €11.50); Hydra (30min., 6-7 per day, €9.50); Piraeus (1¼hr., 5 per day, €20); Portoheli (1½hr., 2 per day, €15); Spetses (1hr., 5-6 per day, €15.50). The bus station is across from the car ferry dock, to the right of the water taxis. **Buses** leave from the main plateia (every 30min. 7am-midnight, €1) and run to Zoödochos Pigis Monastery via Askeli beach, and to Russian Bay via Neorion. Buses leave Galatas for Athens (M-F 3 per day); Methana (45min., 2 per day); Nafplion (2 per day); Trizina (20min., 3 per day, €1.20). Water taxis run every 15min. all day from the main docks to Galatas (2min.; €0.70, after midnight €1.50). **Taxis** (☎23 003) wait to the right of the ferry landing facing inland. Head to the left from the ferry dock behind Saronic Gulf Tours to **Moto Stelios** for all your moped (€15) and bicycle (€5) rental needs. (☎23 026. Open daily 9am-9pm.)

▰ ▨ ORIENTATION AND PRACTICAL INFORMATION. Ferries and hydrofoils dock in the center of the waterfront, which traces the edge of the small island. The main plateia is to the right-facing inland. **Galatas,** across the strait, has food and lodgings. The often unmanned **tourist kiosk** houses an entertaining, if somewhat unhelpful, touchscreen computer with information on the island. Across from the ferry docks, **Family Tours** offers accommodations help, excursion booking, ferry tickets, **car rental** (from €44 per day), currency exchange, free luggage storage, and the occasional free map. (☎23 743. Open daily 9am-10pm.)

The **National Bank,** on the waterfront to the left of the docks, has a **24hr. ATM,** traveler's check exchange (€20 commission), and cash advances on all credit cards. (☎22 822. Open M-Th 8am-2:30pm, F 8am-2pm.) **Suzi's Launderette Service** is left of the dock in an alley next to International Press. (☎69472 11 776. Wash and dry €10. 2hr. service. Pickup and delivery available. Open M-Sa 9am-2pm and 5-9pm.) To reach the **police** (☎22 256), continue uphill and to the right when facing inland from Nikos Pension. From the main plateia head up the stairs, turning right at the church and going downhill for 250m. The **tourist police** (☎22 462) are in the same building. There is a **pharmacy** (☎25 523) across from the ferry dock. **Galatas clinic** (☎42 222) is open 24hr. **Emergencies** are handled at the **Naval School;** contact the tourist police. The **OTE** is on the waterfront to the left of the National Bank. (☎22 199. Open M-F 7:30am-3pm.) Many waterfront cafes have two or three computers with **Internet** access, usually at exorbitant rates. Join the virtual brawl at **Fight Club,** on the far right side of the waterfront facing inland. Cheap rates, several computers, and Wi-Fi make this the best deal in town. (☎26 400. €2 per hr. Open daily 11am-3am.) **International Press,** left of ferry dock, also has Internet access. (€1 per 15min. Open 9am-11pm.) The **post office** is one block in from the water under the pink Hotel Seven Brothers. Specify Poros Trinzinias for **Poste Restante.** (☎22 275. Open M-F 7:30am-2pm.) **Postal Code:** 18020.

🌃🏠 ACCOMMODATIONS AND FOOD. Accommodations on Poros are generally high-end with a price tag to match. Several domatia and simple hotels cluster by the waterfront of Galatas, where those traveling on a budget or without reservations may have better luck. Across from the water taxi landing in Galatas, **Saronis Hotel ❸** has bright rooms with air-conditioning, TV, fan, bath, and balcony overlooking the water. (☎42 356. Singles €35; doubles €40.) **Nikos Douros ❸** rents clean, simple rooms with air-conditioning, fridge, and bath; be sure to ask for an upstairs room with windows. Facing inland, head left from the ferry dock, turn right after the supermarket, and then right onto Dimosthenous. (☎22 633. Singles €30; doubles €50. Prices negotiable.) Catch a view of the port from the small, pink rooms in pricey **Hotel Seven Brothers ❹,** to the right of the ferry dock and inland past Alpha Bank. In a beautiful salmon-toned building, rooms are equipped with balcony, bath, TV, air-conditioning, and a coffeemaker. (☎23 412; www.7brothers.gr. Singles €55; doubles €65.)

Roasting octopi lure passersby into the indistinguishable tavernas that line the waterfront. Several **grocery stores** and **produce markets** cluster along the waterfront on either side of the dock; the best prices are at the large supermarkets up to the left, past the book market. Follow the alleyway to the right of the cinema and continue uphill about 50m to find **🏠Taverna Karavolos ❷.** Maria and her family whip up specialty snails (€5) and tenderly rendered Greek favorites. (☎26 158. Entrees €6-8. Open daily 7:30pm-1am.) Across the water at Galatas, **Babi's Taverna ❷** (Ο Μπαμπης) is just to the right of the water-taxi landing. Diners can watch the car ferries shuttle between the shores while eating. (☎43 629. Entrees €4.50-10. Open morning-midnight.) **Colona ❶,** just down the waterfront to the right of the dock, meets your fast-food needs in a nicer-than-average atmosphere. (☎22 366. Pork gyro €1.50. Open 10am-6am. Free delivery.)

🅖 SIGHTS. The **Archaeological Museum,** in the middle of the waterfront, has a small collection of tombstone shards and miniature ceramic works taken from other islands. (☎23 276. Open M-Tu and Th-Su 8:30am-3pm. €2, students free.) For a view of the harbor, climb the stairs next to the library and follow the signs to the **clock tower.** Join the hordes of camera-toting tourists in time for sunset.

The 18th-century **Zoödochos Pigis Monastery** ("Virgin of the Life-Giving Spring") is sequestered in an overgrown glade 6km from Poros Town. Greek naval leaders Miaoulis, Jobazis, and Apostolis met here to plan for the uprising of 1821. A tiny church across the street features colorful frescoes and icons; right outside its doors, a small fountain is supplied by the **life-giving spring.** Monks have been drinking these blessed curative waters since 200 BC, so fill up your water bottle and let the invigoration begin. Buses run to the monastery from the stop in the main port. (20min., every hr. 7am-midnight, €1.) The monastery is open daily in summer (dawn-1:30pm and 4:30pm-dusk). Modest dress is required and provided.

The 6th-century BC **Temple of Poseidon** is only accessible by private transportation; bear left at the fork in the road before the monastery and continue for about 15km down the road. A one-way taxi costs about €10. The ruins may be best appreciated by history buffs, but the view will inspire all. (Open daily 9am-4pm.)

🎭🎶 ENTERTAINMENT AND NIGHTLIFE. Come nightfall, most tourists linger over conversation and *retsina*, though a young crowd heads out to the clubs on the far right end of the waterfront. Check billings at the ticket office of **Cine Diana,** to the left of the ferry docks, where you can catch one of the nightly open-air showings of new American releases. (Shows 9, 11pm. €7, children €6.) Start the night with a mixed drink (€4-5) or an alcoholic crepe (€4.50-6) at **Creperie,** to the right of the ferry docks on the waterfront. (☎26 073. Open 9am-6am.) Young locals mingle over frappés at **Centro Cafe Bar** before heading farther down the strip. (☎26 745. Draft beer €2.50. Mixed drinks €7. Open 9pm-3am.) Another 100m down to the right, European tourists pack onto the waterside patio or get a workout dancing indoors at tropical-themed **Malibu.** (☎22 491. Mixed drinks €4-6. Open daily Apr.-Oct. 9:30pm-4am.) After most bars have winded down, you can find the music pounding and trendsters sipping drinks (€5) at **Maskes Music Club,** about 100m past the church at the far right of the waterfront. The ship-themed bar has mirrored wall panels and medieval armor that gleam in the technicolor lights. (☎69723 98 513. Open Apr.-Sept. daily 11pm-6am; Oct.-May F-Sa 11pm-6am.)

🔲🔺 **BEACHES AND OUTDOOR ACTIVITIES.** The bus runs hourly to **Russian Bay.** Along the way it passes **Neorion,** with a sand beach, tavernas, and a water sports center, and **Love Beach,** a secluded local favorite with blue-green waters. When Greeks were denied education during the Turkish occupation, the island by the beach was home to a secret school. Ironically, it's now a popular spot for students to sunbathe while cutting class. On the way to the monastery in the other direction, the bus passes **Askeli,** which has tavernas and water sports. In Galatas, follow the road heading left (facing inland) to reach the lemon grove of **Lemonodassos** ("Lemon Forest"). Follow the signs through the trees for about 1km to 🔲**Kardassi Taverna ❷** for a glass of fresh, tangy 🔲**lemonade** and a view of 38,000 lemon trees. (☎43 300. Open daily 7am-late.) In **Artemis,** 12km farther down the road, the ruins of a temple to the goddess of the same name are visible underwater.

Trizina, the mythical birthplace of the hero **Theseus,** is 15km from Galatas in the other direction. Take a bus (20min., M-F 2 per day, €1.20) or a taxi (about €7) from Galatas. From Trizina, the sanctuary-like 🔲**Devil's Bridge,** so named for the cloven-hoof footprint found in one of the rocks at the gorge's base, is just a 25min. hike outside of town. The shady, lush area is a pleasant change of scenery from the rest of the island's scrubby growth, and the rushing water and cool mountain pools take the edge off the heat. Head uphill from the bus stop in the center of town and go right, following the paved road past olive trees and fragrant citrus groves. At the fork in the road, follow the dirt path heading left and uphill to the ancient **Tower of Diateichisma.** Just past the Tower, take the right fork and continue uphill, staying on the worn path as it leads down into the gorge. Many sections of the path require climbing more than hiking, so be prepared to use both hands to clamber up and down the steep trail. Wear closed-toed shoes, as parts of the path are slick with run-off from the pools.

HYDRA Ύδρα

The steep streets of Hydra (EE-dthrah) accommodate only pedestrians, donkeys, and three garbage trucks, leaving the island blessedly free of mopeds but difficult to explore. Chosen in honor of the plentiful drinking water that once poured forth from the island's rocks, Hydra's name long since has become ironic. An ancient fire rendered the soil fallow, the island barren, and the inhabitants completely dependent on the sea. Foreign exports flourished, and the impressive Venetian-built mansions of the merchants of Hydra's past dot the hills behind the harbor. During Ottoman rule, the Hydriots exchanged the services of 30 young men to the Turkish navy every year for the island's freedom. Hydriot youth thus learned the art of naval battle, a perk when, in 1821, Admiral Miaoulis and the Hydriot elite dedicated their fleet to the Greek revolution. Pride in this military courage persists today; the main thoroughfare is named for Miaoulis. In the 1920s, Pavlos Koundouriotis, grandson of one of the many Hydriot leaders in the War of Independence, took the national helm as President of Greece.

HYDRA TOWN Ύδρα   ☎ 22980

Hydra Town's slippery, cobbled streets stretch like tendrils from the deep blues of the sea into the island's dusty hills. Art students and honeymooning couples mill around the crowded jumble of jewelry shops and cafes down by the port. Away from this frenzy of foot traffic, donkeys and wheelbarrow-pushing fruit vendors share quiet, narrow alleys. As gorgeous as the summers are, the pink-blossomed springs and salt-winded falls give the town a low season like no other.

⌷ TRANSPORTATION

Ferries: Upstairs in the building across the street from the ferry dock, **Hellenic Seaways** sells ferry tickets. To: **Aegina** (2¼hr., 6 per week, €9.20); **Methana** (1½hr., 7 per week, €7.70); **Piraeus** (3¼hr., daily, €13) via **Poros** (1hr., €6); **Spetses** (1hr., daily, €6.80).

Flying Dolphins: Saitis Tours across from the water taxi landing (open daily 9:30am-9:30pm) sells tickets to: **Piraeus** (1½hr., 8 per day, €22); **Poros** (30min., 5 per day, €8.40); **Portoheli** (45min., 4 per day, €11.50); **Spetses** (30min., 6 per day, €11).

Water Taxis: ☎ 53 690. By the mule stand in the southeastern corner of the harbor, to the right of the docks. Each boat's price is divided among up to 8 passengers, so try to find a fuller one. Service to: **Agios Georgios** (Bisti; €40); **Agios Nikolaos** (€50); **Kamini** (€9); **Mandraki beach** (€12); **Metohi** (€30); **Palamidas** (€17); **Vlihos** (€12). A water taxi makes a **daytrip** around the island with beach stops (€120).

✳ ❼ ORIENTATION AND PRACTICAL INFORMATION

Hydra Town's buildings form an amphitheater around the famously picturesque harbor, with the opening facing north. Yachts and fishing boats bob in the center, while water taxis, ferries, and Flying Dolphins dock on the left edge of the harbor. **Tombazi** starts just across the street and runs inland from Alpha Bank past the Internet cafe and several restaurants. **Miaouli** heads into town from the center of the harbor. **Votsi**, on the right side of the harbor just past the clock tower, goes inland past the OTE, police, and medical center. Although street names exist, don't be surprised if locals have never heard of them.

Banks: National Bank (☎52 578), on the waterfront. Has a **24hr. ATM.** Open M-Th 8am-2:30pm, F 8am-2pm. **Alpha Bank,** on the corner where Tombazi meets the waterfront. Offers **currency exchange.** Open M-Th 8am-2:30pm, F 8am-2pm.

Laundromat: ☎ 53 807. Inland from the tourist police. Open M-F 8am-1pm and 5-8pm.

Tourist Police: ☎ 52 205. Follow Votsi inland and bear left at the fork. Look for the coat of arms opposite the OTE. Open 24hr.

Pharmacy: ☎ 53 260. On the inland face of the square past the tourist police. Open M-F 8:30am-2pm and 5-9pm. Internet available.

Hospital: ☎ 53 150. On Votsi, past the tourist police. Look for a brown door with grates set in a stone wall. In an **emergency,** call the 24hr. nurse (☎ 53 150).

Telephones: OTE (☎ 52 399), facing the tourist police. Open M-F 8am-1:30pm.

Internet Access: Flamingo Cafe (☎ 53 485), 20m up Tombazi. €5 per hr., min. €3. Open daily 8:30am-2am.

Post Office: ☎ 52 262. 1 block inland between Miaouli and Votsi. Open M-F 7:30am-2pm. **Postal Code:** 18040.

▛ ACCOMMODATIONS

Hydra has the most expensive accommodations in the Saronic Gulf and some of the most expensive in Greece. Singles are almost nonexistent and doubles are at least €50-60 in high season. Without reservations, weekend accommodations are almost impossible to get; call ahead or arrive on a Thursday. Limiting your stay to weeknights will afford lower room rates and a quieter atmosphere.

Pension Glaros (☎53 679). Walk inland by Alpha Bank, taking the first left down an impossibly narrow alley; look for the sign above the mini-mart. Singles €30-55. ❸

Pension Antonios (☎/fax 53 227), on Spilios Charamis across from Christina's. Walk 200m inland on Tombazi. The cafe-style patio brims with flowers and stacks of magazines. Doubles €60. ❹

Hotel Amarillis (☎53 611; www.amarillishydra.gr). Walk inland on Tombazi and bear right at the fork. This welcoming, family-run hotel has brilliant blue rooms with fridge, TV, A/C, and bath. Singles €45-50; doubles €55-60; triples €60-70. MC/V. ❹

FOOD

Lovebirds play endless rounds of backgammon at the waterfront cafes, where average food comes at prices that reflect the rent. Just a few blocks inland, though, a number of excellent tavernas offer superior fare at reasonable prices.

O Barba Dima's (☎52 967), a short walk up Tombazi, bearing right at Hotel Amarillis. Locals and Greek tourists crowd into this tiny, orange taverna to savor Greek specialties. Entrees €4-8.50. Open for dinner. AmEx/MC/V. ❷

Douskos (☎52 886), in a courtyard 200m inland on Tombazi. Diners linger over a wide range of Greek dishes, enjoying the nightly *bouzouki* performances. Entrees €4-9. Open daily 8am-1am. MC/V. ❷

Christina's Taverna (☎53 615), on Spilios Charamis to the right of Douskos, across from Pension Antonios. Most diners don't bother with the menu, ordering whatever Christina has in the kitchen before heading up to the rooftop terrace. Entrees €6-8.50. Open daily 11:30am-3pm and 6:30pm-midnight. ❷

Anemoni (☎53 136). Bear left uphill from the OTE. Makes unusually large Greek pastries (€1.50-2), fresh ice cream (€2 for 2 hefty scoops), and chocolatey little mouse-shaped cakes. Open daily 8am-11pm. ❶

SIGHTS

LAZAROS KOUNDOURIOTIS HISTORICAL MANSION. The works of Hydriot painter Periklis Byzantios, who taught at the **Fine Arts School** in the **Tombazis Mansion** on the right side of the harbor facing inland, and those of his son, Constantinos, are displayed permanently in the basement of the Lazaros Koundouriotis Historical Mansion. Architecturally unchanged since 1750, the mansion today preserves the 1st floor rooms as Koundouriotis once lived in them. The 2nd floor showcases an extensive array of traditional Hydriot costumes and has brilliant views of the town. (☎52 421. *Head inland on Votsi to the square and take the staircase to the right; follow the small blue signs nearly to the top. Open daily Apr.-Oct. 10am-2pm and 5:30-8:30pm. €4, students €2, children under 11 free.*)

ORTHODOX HYDRA. The white courtyard of the **Church of the Assumption of the Virgin Mary,** beneath the clock tower that dominates the port, offers sanctuary from the busy harbor. The small church is certainly worth a trip, if only for a peek at its gilded ceiling and a few blessed moments of quiet. Built as a convent in 1648, it housed 18 nuns before becoming a monastery in 1770. It is now dedicated to the *kimisis*, the Ascension of Mary. The courtyard surrounds the tomb of Koundouriotis, his statue, and another of Miaoulis. Upstairs is the **Ecclesiastical Museum,** with brightly colored and beautifully preserved 18th-

THE LOCAL STORY

THE UNMOTORIZED LIFE

With noiseless streets untouched by traffic, Hydra's claim to fame proves more of an inconvenience for its residents. The island owns the only three cars allowed on its gleaming streets: two for garbage pickup, and the third for construction needs. Otherwise the heavy lifting is completed by the donkeys, or more commonly, wheelbarrow-pushing homeowners. With many houses only accessible via the steep network of staircases, all groceries and goods are transported by foot, and those building new homes on the hillside must pay to have donkeys transport construction materials.

Unlike most pedestrian-only areas, which once accommodated cars, Hydra never allowed vehicles on the island. In a larger attempt to keep modernization from stripping the island of its allure, Hydra has a number of similar, if somewhat less obvious, restrictions. Residents are forbidden from putting up satellite dishes, installing air-conditioner condensers, or building pools that are visible from the front of the house. The reward for such vigilance, of course, is the ambiance that draws its visitors, convincing some of them to stay on permanently.

and 19th-century scenes from the life of Christ. (☎54 071. Open Tu-Su 10am-5pm. €2. Modest dress required.) An arduous hike will take you to the **Monastery of Profitis Ilias** and the **Convent of Efpraxia**, both on the lower peak overlooking the harbor. Wear sturdy shoes and don't forget to bring water. If they are available, monks may show you around. Inquire about donkey rides at the harbor. (Take Miaouli up from the waterfront; signs point the way as you get higher. Open daily. Modest dress required.)

HISTORICAL ARCHIVES MUSEUM. The museum, established in the early 1900s, houses old Hydriot costumes, census records, naval treasures, relics of the revolution, and an extensive library. The heart of Admiral Andreas Miaoulis is preserved here in an urn of silver and gold. (☎52 355. To the left of the ferry building. Open daily 9am-4:30pm. €3, students €1.50.)

FESTIVALS. Hydra's celebration of Orthodox **Easter** is reputedly one of the best in Greece. Throngs of visitors crowd Kamini beach on Good Friday, where men of the church, in traditional attire like that in the museum, carry the flower-covered *epitaphios* (funeral bier) into the sea. If you're in Hydra Town during the **Miaoulia** (the last weekend in June), join the rest of the island in celebrating the feats of Admiral Andreas Miaoulis at an explosive mock battle held in the harbor. Hydra also hosts two major **boat races,** which mark the beginning and end of the tourist season. One is on March 25 celebrating the day of Greek independence from the Turks, and the other is on October 28, the famed "Ohi Day" when Greeks refused Mussolini's request to set up military installations during WWII.

NIGHTLIFE

Known internationally as a honeymoon destination, Hydra is more an island for lovers than swingers. A chill nightlife kicks up around 1am at **Amalour,** a short walk up Tombazi. Just about everyone old enough to order a beer (€3) kicks off their night to the ethnic and Latin rhythms that shake the shadowed orange walls. (☎69774 61 357. Mixed drinks €7-8. Open daily 8:30pm-late.) A young crowd ransacks **The Pirate Bar,** where DJs spin international tunes in the sword-adorned bar. (☎52 711; www.pirate.gr. Beer €4. Mixed drinks €6-8. Cafe open daily Apr.-Sept. 9am; bar open daily 9pm-6am.) A small and trendy handful ducks into **Nautilus** farther down the waterfront to the right. (☎53 563. Beer €5. Open daily 9pm-late.) At **Saronicos,** around the corner on the waterfront heading away from the church, a fun mix of traditional Greek and American hits keep things lively. (Beer €3. Mixed drinks €6. Cafe open daily noon-9pm; club open daily 9pm-late.)

BEACHES

Many of the "beaches" by Hydra Town are actually industrial-looking cement slabs with a few aluminum ladders descending into the sea. Landings and stairs are cut into the rocks across the harbor from the ferry dock, providing access to a popular swimming area with cool, crystalline, instantly deep waters. The first landing on the right is open to the public, but the next few are lined with cliffside cafes. A 15min. walk to the left when facing the water along the coast takes you past the high-walled artists' colony of **Kamini.** Just beyond it is a tiny, pebbly beach where the drop to the sea is less severe and the water is reasonably shallow. Walking another 20min. brings you to slightly more populous **Vlihos,** guarded by a regiment of Hawaiian-style beach umbrellas. Lively, overcrowded **Mandraki,** a coarse sand beach surrounded by the fortress-like Hotel Mira Mare, is in the opposite direction from town (30min. hike or 10min. water taxi ride). If you have time and money, take a water taxi to the far side of the island, where you can find a quiet beach of your own; agree on a pickup time before getting out. Just 20min. away by boat, the locally adored **Ag. Georgios** (or **Bisti**) beach sparkles with clear water surrounded by verdant foliage, making the water appear turquoise.

> **THE REAL DEAL.** In low season, the Saronic Gulf Islands can be a pleasant escape from the big city, and a quick, reasonable getaway for the budget traveler. During the high season from June to September, however, prices skyrocket, making the islands painfully packed and expensive. Although long ferry rides to farther islands may seem daunting, the cheaper prices and local ambience will be worth the extra hours on the boat. If your schedule is tight, head to **Spetses,** where prices are more negotiable and the beaches are cleaner, quieter, and far less crowded than those on neighboring Saronic Islands.

SPETSES Σπέτσες

Pine trees and a gentle landscape distinguish Spetses from its rockier neighbors. The southernmost of the Saronic islands, Spetses is spared from the heaviest of the Athenian traffic, though weekends still find the main port city packed. Years ago, visitors were welcomed to the island by the sweet, magical scent of vegetation combined with an abundance of honey—hence the name "Spetses," derived from the Venetian term *spezzie* (aromatic or spiced). Spetsians were renowned for their crucial role in the War of Independence, when they dedicated their entire fleet to the cause. Today the ports of Spetses make way for the boatloads of tourists that come to worship the sun on the ivory beaches that ring the island.

SPETSES TOWN   ☎ 22980

In the 1830s, 20,000 Greeks crowded into Spetses's tiny houses, sending the town sprawling up the hillsides. Due to pirate raids and Turkish invasions throughout the tumultuous 19th century, however, residents gradually moved onto the mainland, contributing to Athens's population boom. Today, the 3500 islanders stick around Spetses Town, as close to the water as possible. The 14km of winding coast alternates between pebble beaches and a procession of cafes and bars, turning the town into a 'round-the-clock beach club. Jet setters dock in Spetses's

LET'S HEAR IT FOR THE GIRL

n Greece's famously male-dominated society, the actions of
women have long gone overlooked
or underrated. A rare exception to
his rule is Laskarina Bouboulina,
a woman who has earned a place,
albeit an unofficial one, in the his-
orical account of Greece's struggles against the Turks.

Intelligent, wealthy, and
nationalistic, Bouboulina personally funded a defensive army,
ricked the Turks into permitting
he construction of her heavily
armed battleship, and bravely
commanded legions during the
ebellion. She was the first to
aise a Greek flag on Spetses in
821, beginning the official rebel-
ion against the Turkish occupiers,
and she led an entire fleet of
ships in the blockade and even-
ual victory at Nafplion.

Despite her invaluable contribu-
ions to the Greek struggle for
ndependence, however, the Greek
government did not initially honor
her; rather, in 1825 it stripped her
of any rewards given earlier in grat-
tude for her efforts. Although she
has come to hold a cherished
place in Greek history, to this day
her official title remains the slightly
derogatory "Lady Captain."

In an interesting twist of 19th-
century international intrigue, it
was actually the Russian monarchy that accorded this heroine her
due respect. In 1816, before
Bouboulina's involvement with the
Greek struggle for independence,

Old Harbor, where the nightlife is exported away from the residential town center.

⊡ TRANSPORTATION. Ferries depart daily to Aegina (3hr., €11); Methana (2½hr., €9.60); Piraeus (4hr., €13) via Hydra (1hr., €5.10); Poros (2hr., €6.80). The **Hellenic Seaways** office across from the water taxi landing sells tickets and posts schedules. (☎73 141. Open daily 8am-10pm.) **Alasia Travel** (☎74 098; open daily 8am-9pm), on the waterfront, sells tickets for **Flying Dolphins** to: Hydra (30min., daily, €11.50); Piraeus (2hr., daily, €30); Poros (1hr., daily, €15); Portoheli (15min., daily, €5). **Water taxis** (☎72 072) dock right offshore on the ferry dock and go to: Ag. Marina (€25); Anargiri (€48); Costa (€16); Costoula (€20); daytrip around the island (€63); Emilianos (€33); Hinitsa (€30); Old Harbor (€13); Paraskevi (€48); Porto Heli (€40); Zogeria (€33). Prices are per boat; rates increase 50% from midnight to 6am. **Buses** leave from either end of the port to various destinations. From Ag. Mamas beach 400m to the left when facing inland at the dock, buses service Ag. Anargiri beach via Ag. Marina and Ag. Paraskevi (30min., 7 per day, €2); request a stop for Xilokeriza. Buses leaving from the plateia on the other side of the waterfront go to Anargirios College and Vrellos beach (30-90min., 16 per day, €1.20-1.50). **Taxis** wait to the left of the ferry dock. A number of rental agencies can be found along the waterfront; head across the street from Ag. Mamas beach to **Honda Center** for mopeds. (☎72 335. €15 per day; €20 for 24hr. Open daily 9am-6pm.) **Rent-a-Bike** (☎74 143) is on the street parallel to the harbor. (Bikes €6 per day. Open daily 10am-2:30pm and 5:30-10pm.)

▓▌ ORIENTATION AND PRACTICAL INFORMATION. The waterfront road runs from the left of the ferry dock (facing inland) to the **Old Harbor,** past **Agios Mamas** beach. To the right of the ferry dock, restaurants and cafes line the way up to **Plateia Bouboulina,** with a large playground. The first street inland paral-lel to the water, running to the left, has shops, pharmacies, and tavernas. The Old Harbor, home to bars and tavernas, is a 20min. well-lit walk, €13 water taxi, or €10 carriage ride from the town center; carriages wait by the ferry docks.

Several **travel agencies** lie around the corner on the left side of the boat landing. The Kentros brothers at **Mimoza Travel** (☎75 170) can help find accommodations, book Euroseas catamarans, and provide info about the island. The **Alpha Bank** across from the ferry dock offers **currency exchange,** a **24hr. ATM,** trav-eler's check exchange, and cash advances on debit cards. (☎75 343. Open M-Th 8am-2:30pm and F 8am-2pm.) The **police** are 150m before the Spetses Museum; follow signs to the museum. (☎73 100.

Open 24hr.) The **tourist police** (☎73 100) are to the right of the ferry dock, by the National Bank, and share a building with the **OTE**. A number of **pharmacies** line the street running parallel to the water. The **first aid station** is open 24hr. for **emergencies**. (☎72 472. Call the police to reach a doctor.) When facing inland, head to the right from the ferry dock to reach **1800 Cafe**, which has some of the only **Internet** access in town. (☎29 497. €5 per hr., min. €2.50. Open daily 9am-late.) The **post office** is left of the dock on the road parallel to the waterfront. (☎72 228. Open M-F 7:30am-2pm.) **Postal Code:** 18050.

⌐ ACCOMMODATIONS. Accommodations are expensive and practically unavailable on weekends; don't be surprised to get a well-meaning shrug from **domatia** owners if you come without reservations. For cheap rooms, head left toward the Spetses Museum. To find **Pension Theano ❸,** follow the signs for the Spetses Museum; it's across from the museum, to the right when facing inland. Spacious, bright rooms have air-conditioning, TV, bath, and fridge. Angela and her husband wait at the docks when they have vacancies; if you call ahead, Angela will come to lead you through the unnamed streets. (☎73 064. Singles €30; doubles €50.) Gorgeous, blue-curtained rooms can be found at **Villa Christina Hotel ❸,** around the corner from the movie theater, inland from the ferry dock. Well-appointed rooms with stone floors include TV, air-conditioning, and bath, all surrounding a courtyard covered in magenta bougainvillea. (☎72 218. Breakfast €5. Singles €36-48; doubles €45-60; triples €54-72.) **Hotel Klimis ❹,** on the waterfront, left of the ferry docks, is a short walk from the beach. Wood-ceilinged rooms come with TV, air-conditioning, bath, and balcony so close to the water you can almost feel the spray. (☎72 334. Breakfast €4.20-6.80. Singles €40-55; doubles €55-70.)

◻ FOOD. A number of fast-food joints, souvlaki stands, and grocery stores can be found inland from the ferry dock. For fresh seafood and the scoop on town gossip, locals head to **⬛Bouboulina's ❷,** past Alasia Travel on the waterfront. Across from the fish market, it has first crack at the catch of the day. Char-grilled octopus (€9.50) comes fresh out of the sea each morning. (☎73 033. Seafood entrees €6-8.50. Open daily 11am-1am.) **O Roussos ❷,** on the waterfront just before Ag. Mamas beach, has a similar menu but with a more touristy feel. The *dolmades* (grape leaves) are rendered divine with a drizzle of lemon juice. (☎72 212. Grilled entrees €6-10. Open daily 12:30pm-midnight. MC/V.) **Quarter Pizza ❷,** in the plateia off the road running parallel to the water, is crowded with teens eating gourmet

the Turkish government tried to arrest her and claim her family fortune. Instead of despairing, the clever Bouboulina went to the Russian government for help, reminding them that her late husband had contributed his fleet to Russia during the earlier Turkish-Russian wars. Tsar Alexander I agreed to protect her and her inheritance, arranging a successful meeting with the Sultan's mother to plead for her security.

The Russian government's respect for Bouboulina's actions grew during the course of the Greek War of Independence. After her unceremonious murder due to an inter-family feud, the Russian government posthumously deemed Bouboulina an admiral. The title stuck, and now even in Greece, Bouboulina is popularly known as "the only female admiral in Greek history." The Greek government, however, still never officially elevated her to this military status.

To learn more about Bouboulina, head to ⬛**Bouboulina's Museum.** Tours of her house provide a fascinating torrent of information about her life and belongings. Ticket proceeds go toward the house's restoration.

☎22980 72 416. Open Apr.-Oct. daily for guided tours. €5, students €3, children €1.

pies. The pizzas (€4.60-10), cooked on a wood-fire stove, are available for takeout or delivery. (☎73 036. Beer €2.40. Pasta €4-7. Open daily 11am-midnight.)

◪ SIGHTS. One block inland from the tourist police, **Bouboulina's Museum** houses weapons, revolutionary artifacts, personal items, and documents belonging to the Lady Captain in her second husband's mansion. (☎72 416. Open daily Apr.-Oct. for guided tours. 6-13 per day 9:45am-8:15pm; check the boards in front of the museum for times. €5, students €3, children €1.) Tucked into a residential area in the left of town, the **Spetses Museum** can be found by heading inland from Ag. Mamas beach by the Honda Center; stick to the larger road running left and inland. Enshrined in a 19th-century mansion once owned by Spetses's first governor, Hadziyannis Mexis, the collection includes the Spetses revolutionary flag, various firearms, ancient maps and coinage, religious artifacts, and the cremated remains of Laskarina Bouboulina. (☎72 994. Open Tu-Su 8:30am-2:30pm. €3, students €2, EU students free.) The **Monastery of Agios Nikolaos** stands above the Old Harbor, opposite a square of traditional mosaics. A plaque to the left of the entrance commemorates Napoleon's nephew, Paul Marie Bonaparte, who was preserved in a barrel of rum after he died in the War of Independence. The barrel was stored in a monastic cell here from 1827 to 1832. (Modest dress required.)

▮▮ ENTERTAINMENT AND NIGHTLIFE. Spetses hosts many festivals, the best of which is the **Armada,** a mid-September celebration that reenacts Spetses's victory over the Turkish fleet in the War of Independence. Islanders set off fireworks from a reconstruction of an Ottoman-style ship. The ship sinks soon after, marking the start of festivities. Greeks, particularly Athenians, flood Spetses for the rowdy, memorable event; book accommodations early if you plan to join in. New American releases find an audience in the open-air **Cinema Titania,** about 100m inland from Bouboulina's Museum. (☎72 434. Showings at 9, 11pm. €7.)

Spetses's appeal for restless youth lies mainly in its boisterous bar scene, with a number of waterfront nightspots clustering 20min. away in the Old Harbor. Start things off just left of the ferry docks at ▮**Socrates's,** where British youngsters down beers (€3) while watching sports. The raunchy yet amusing truisms hanging over the bar get funnier with each drink. (☎74 043. Mixed drinks €3. Happy hour 10pm-midnight. Open 7:30pm-2am.) Play a game of billiards (€8 per hr.) at **Delfinia Cafe,** across from Ag. Mamas beach. (☎75 051. Mixed drinks €6. Coffee €2.50. Open daily 10am-1am.) You'll have to fight your way through the crowds to the bar at **Brachera**—it gets so crowded after 1am that dancing is reduced to a rhythmic wiggle. (☎73 581. Mixed drinks €9. Open daily 10pm-late.) Continue onward to the left to reach the blasting dance music of **Club Stavento.** Guest DJs whip the crowd of up to 2000 into a frenzy in the mod white room, but many choose to enjoy the excellent harbor view from the patio entrance. (☎75 245. Cover €8; includes 1 drink. Mixed drinks €8-10. Open daily 11pm-4am, later on F-Sa.)

◪ BEACHES. If you rent a moped, you can see all the beaches on a 24km jaunt around the island, though the bus runs to many of them as well. Sandy **Agii Anargiri,** across the island from Spetses Town, is the most popular beach, with a taverna and a host of water sports. **Agia Paraskevi,** about 1km to the right when facing the sea, is one of the most picturesque in the Saronic Gulf, with pine trees and a quiet shore. Midway along the bus route between Anargiri and Spetses Town is amazingly peaceful ▮**Xilokeriza.** Pure white, smooth stones contrast with the bay's still, brightly colored waters. Hunks of watermelon from the nearby snack bar are big enough for two and make a perfect after-swim snack. Although it's easiest to take a moped there, the bus to Ag. Anargiri passes by the dusty road to the beach (10-15min. walk uphill); check with the driver about return times before you hop off.

EVIA AND THE SPORADES

Stretching out into the azure depths of the Aegean, Evia and the Sporades contain a mixture of natural, cultural, and archaeological treasures, topped off with a healthy dose of hedonism. Evia, Greece's
second-largest island, nudges the coast of Central Greece, stretching
from Karystos in the south, through bustling Halkida, to the therapeutic springs of the northern villages. Beyond Evia, the Sporades arc across the
sea to the north. Vibrant Skiathos has the liveliest reputation, flaunting its beach-
ringed shores for summer travelers. Skopelos is known as one of the greenest
islands in all of Greece, with Byzantine monuments and narrow streets sprinkled
among the lush vegetation. Little Alonnisos harbors pristine wilderness crossed by
hiking trails, while Skyros has remained true to its old ways despite the demands
of modern-day tourism. These islands have beckoned visitors to bask on their sun-
lit shores and hike their shaded forests since Greece's earliest days.

 SUGGESTED ITINERARIES: EVIA AND THE SPORADES

THREE DAYS Use busy **Halkida** (p. 333)
as a hub for exploring Evia. Soothe any
burns incurred by a lazy afternoon on the
famous beaches of **Eretria** (p. 338) by
immersing yourself in the legendarily therapeutic hot springs of **Aedipsos** (p. 336).

ONE WEEK After a few days in **Evia's** (p.
333) towns, head for **Skopelos** (p. 348)
and hike the green hills, where some say
a dragon met a brutal end. Finish by trekking through the gorgeous wilderness of
Alonnisos (p. 352), an island in the
National Marine Park.

EVIA Εύβοια

With warm waters, forested highlands, archaeological treasures, charming villages, and therapeutic baths, Evia offers enough variety to satisfy any pleasure-
seeker. Its capital, Halkida, serves as a portal from the mainland into Evia. A new
suspension bridge allows visitors to traverse the Channel of Evripos with ease,
and ferries connect the island to Aedipsos, Marmari, and Karystos. Because of
Evia's proximity to Athens, floods of Greek vacationers arrive during the summer,
but the island effortlessly absorbs and delights the masses.

HALKIDA Χαλκίδα   ☎22210

Sprawling Halkida, also known as "Chalkis" or "*Chalkida*," is the capital of Evia
as well as its key transportation hub, connecting the island to the mainland. Bustling streets, lively plazas, and packs of young people give the city a vibrant energy.
Its archaeological artifacts, nearby beaches, and urban vibe make Halkida the natural starting point for exploring the more remote parts of the island.

EVIA & THE SPORADES

C TRANSPORTATION. To get to the main part of Halkida from the **train station** (☎22 386), walk out to the right, cross the Old Bridge, and take a left along the waterfront; El. Venizelou intersects five blocks down. **Trains** go to Athens (1¼hr., every hr. 5:50am-11:34pm, €5.10). Halkida's hangar-like **bus terminal,** Stiron 1 (☎22 640), is a 30min. walk from the waterfront's hotels and restaurants. It's easiest to take a taxi (€3) to the waterfront. If you decide to walk, go to the right from the front of the station. At the large intersection, take the middle road, Arethousis. After nearly 20 blocks, take a right on El. Venizelou and follow it until it hits the waterfront. **Buses** go to: Aedipsos (2½hr.; 12:30, 2:30pm; €9.50); Athens (1½hr.; 2 per hr. 5am-9pm, service reduced Sa-Su; €5.90); Karystos (3½hr.; 5:30am, 1, 5:45pm; €3.10); Kimi (1½hr., 7 per day 7:05am-8:15pm, €7.30); Limni (2hr.; 8:15am, 12:30, 5:15pm; €6.80). **Taxis** (☎89 300) run 24hr. from the Old Bridge, Pl. Agios Nikolaos, El. Venizelou, and just outside the bus station.

◼ ☷ ORIENTATION AND PRACTICAL INFORMATION. Halkida's main thoroughfare is **Eleftheriou Venizelou,** which runs perpendicular to the water and ends just before **Voudouri** (the waterfront promenade), which is lined by hotels, restaurants, and bars. **Agios Goviou** runs off El. Venizelou to the left, behind and parallel to Voudouri and toward the Old Bridge; **Farmakidou** does the same, but to the right. **Avanton,** the primary shopping street, runs behind **Plateia Agios Nikolaos** (a park located midway along Voudouri) parallel to the water. The **Erippon Bridge,** or **Old Bridge,** connects Halkida to the mainland at the end of the waterfront. Halkida also is joined to the mainland via the new **suspension bridge,** the connection for most ground transportation, on the city's southern edge.

Halkida has no tourist office, so your best bet is to ask for a map at the hotels on the waterfront. You also can consult the city map posted outside the train station. The **port authority,** across the Old Bridge on Kostantinos Karamanlis, in the white building with blue shutters, dispenses limited info about the city. (☎28 888. Open daily 24hr.) The **National Bank,** El. Venizelou 9, two blocks from the water, has a **24hr. ATM** and **currency exchange.** (Open M-Th 8am-2:30pm, F 8am-2pm.) Pl. Agios Nikolaos borders the waterfront and is home to the **public library** at the corner of Ant. Antoniou and M. Kakara. (Open M-F 7:30am-2:30pm, Sa 8:30am-2pm.) The **tourist police,** Arethousis 153, are 25min. from the bottom of El. Venizelou. (☎77 777. Open M-F 8am-2pm.) The 24hr. **police** (☎83 333) are in the same building. A **pharmacy** can be found at El. Venizelou 24. (Open M and W 8am-2pm, Tu and Th-F 8am-1:30pm and 6-9pm.) To get to the **hospital,** 48 Gazepi (☎21 901), head up El. Venizelou away from the water and turn left onto Papanastasiou. Take the first right onto Kriezotou, then a left at the butcher shop; the hospital is 400m up the hill on the right. There is also a smaller emergency building (☎166) by the museum. The **OTE** (☎22 599) is at the intersection of El. Venizelou and Papanastasiou. **Phones** are directly outside the store and on the Evia side of the Old Bridge. For cheap, fast **Internet** access, go to **Surf on Net** between Hotel Kentrikon and John's Hotel on Ag. Goviou. (☎24 867; www.surfonnet.gr. 6am-9pm €2.50 per hr., 9pm-6am €1. Open 24hr.) To reach the **post office,** Karamourtzouniis 11, walk on El. Venizelou and take the second left from the waterfront. **Poste Restante** and Western Union are available. (☎22 211. Open M-F 7:30am-8pm.) **Postal Code:** 34100.

▐ ACCOMMODATIONS. Most hotels are of the €75-per-night variety, catering to business travelers or Athenian families. If you bargain, you might be able to get rates as low as €40 for a single without bath, but don't expect anything lower, especially in the summer. Near the Old Bridge, **John's Hotel ❹,** Ag. Goviou 9, has rooms with plush carpeting, bath, air-conditioning, phone, and balcony. Enjoy breakfast (€5) in the attractive dining area. (☎24 996. Singles €50; doubles €65;

triples €80. AmEx/MC/V.) **Hotel Kentrikon ❹,** Ag. Goviou 5, by John's Hotel, has inviting rooms with TV, phone, and a shared fridge; some have air-conditioning and private bath. The friendly staff will help you make sense of the city. (☎22 375. Breakfast included. Singles €50; doubles €60; triples €75. Cash only.) To find **Hotel Hara ❹,** Karoni 21, bear right after crossing the Old Bridge, then take the stairs across from the fun-park. Simple, unadorned rooms come with air-conditioning, TV, and tiled bath. (☎76 305. Breakfast included. Singles €50; doubles €70; triples €80. Prices drop after Sept. MC/V.)

⬚ **FOOD.** Several bakeries hide on streets near Ag. Nikolaos, and fast-food joints are bunched at the base of El. Venizelou and by the Old Bridge on the waterfront. Small supermarkets, like **Dia Discount,** Favierou 14, cluster around Papanastasiou off of El. Venizelou. (☎78 960. Open M-F 8:30am-9pm, Sa 8am-8pm.) One of the few inexpensive sit-down tavernas in town, **The Old Bridge ❷,** Voudouri 2, is located on the corner of the waterfront. Its entrees (€5-8) and souvlaki (€1.80) lack frills but are the best values around. (☎77 053. Open daily 10:30am-5am.) Deliciously named pizzas like "The Inferno" and "The Erotica" (tomato, cheese, salami, pepper; €8) emerge from the oven at **Il Posto Ristorante ❸,** a smart Italian eatery offering an impressive selection of pastas (€7-10) on the waterfront. (☎73 841. Open daily noon-1:30am. MC/V.) After dinner, take a stroll to **Cookie Land ❶,** Avanton 59, away from the Old Bridge. The shelves of freshly baked cookies, cakes, and confections (€8.50-10.80 per kg) are delicious enough to erase any pangs of calorie remorse.

◫⬚ **SIGHTS AND NIGHTLIFE.** Palm-lined **Voudouri,** Halkida's waterfront promenade, makes for a splendid evening stroll. Hike up to the **Fortress of Cara-baba,** on the other side of the Old Bridge, for a great view of the city, ocean, and surrounding hills. From Halkida, cross the Old Bridge and head right. Once you reach the fun-park, take the stairs on the left, which lead all the way up the hill to the fortress. Built by Turks in 1688 to protect Halkida from Greek and Venetian marauders, the fortress is extremely well-preserved. You can picnic, climb on the walls, and check out the lookout posts where Turks once guarded the city. (Open daily 8am-10pm. Free.) The **Archaeological Museum,** El. Venizelou 13, is full of finds from the Neolithic, Classical, and Roman eras. It has an impressive display of statues, pottery, and shimmering gold laurels—some pieces date as far back as 11,000 BC. (☎76 131. Open Tu-Su 8:30am-3pm. €2, under 18 free.) The **Church of Agios Nikolaos,** at the far end of Pl. Nikolaos from the waterfront, has high vaulted ceilings that hover above walls covered in intricate iconography. (☎76 649. Open daily 7am-1pm and 4:30-8pm. Modest dress required.) For a picnic or afternoon stroll, visit **Park Farou,** near the lighthouse, at the northern tip of the city by the beaches.

To take a dip or soak in rays, catch the bus to **Eretria,** known for its beautiful beaches. The locals flock to the clean **Souvala, Kourenti,** and **Papathanasiou** beaches, a 15min. walk from the Old Bridge. Walk just past the rocky outcropping at the end of the waterfront to reach Souvala. For Kourenti, follow Avanton four blocks after it becomes G. Chaina, then turn left onto Delagrammatika and walk to the end. Walk across the parking lot and along Eth. Symfiliosis to reach Papathanasiou. For a beach closer to the center of town, head across the Old Bridge and walk to the right on Archien. Makariou until you see the sunbathers on your right; you can see the beach from the waterfront.

After dark, follow the glow of cell phones to the waterfront, where you can observe the teenage scene from the safety of one the many bars that line the boardwalk. (Beer €4-5.50. Mixed drinks €6-8.) **Cafe Abotis** (☎22 562), just south of the Hotel Paliria, and **Jam,** Voudouri 10 (☎22 156), near the Old Bridge, are two popular venues that blast pop music to their outdoor patios and are packed past midnight. (Both open 8:30am-late.) If you feel like burning off those Cookie Land calories, hop a cab (€4) to the suspension bridge and work it out on the dance floor of **Gaz** or **Mist** (mixed drinks €3-6; cover €10).

AEDIPSOS Λουτρά Αιδηψού ☎22260

For thousands of years, the health-afflicted and pleasure-seeking alike have come to submerge in Aedipsos's hot springs. Greek mythology attributes the existence of the springs to a gift of health and strength from Athena to Hercules; affirmation of the waters' healing power can be found in texts by Plutarch and Aristotle. Today, the springs still flow, luring travelers from around the globe to this quaint, seaside town. Let your troubles melt away as you experience Aedipsos's laid-back atmosphere, palm-lined promenade, and serene sunsets.

▐ TRANSPORTATION. Buses leave from the bus station, Thermopotamou 7 (☎22 250), for Athens (3hr.; 7:45am, 1:30, 5:30pm; €11.80) via Arkitsa and Halkida (3hr.; 5:45am, 4pm; €9.20). Alternatively, get to the mainland by catching a **ferry** to Arkitsa (45min.; M-Th 14 per day 5:30am-9:30pm, F-Sa 15-16 per day, Su 18 per day, service reduced in low season; €2.30) from the ferry terminal on 28 Oktovriou. (☎23 330; www.edipsouferries.gr.) **Taxis** (☎23 280) wait outside the ferry terminal.

◪ ▞ ORIENTATION AND PRACTICAL INFORMATION. Aedipsos's longest street is **28 Oktovriou,** which runs all the way along the waterfront. The bus station, uphill from the waterfront, is on the wide tree-lined **Thermopotamou.** After two blocks, Thermopotamou intersects 28 Oktovriou. The first horizontal street inland from 28 Oktovriou is **Ermou,** where most of the town's hotels are located. Moving east from Thermopotamou, the vertical streets are **Omirou, Alexandrou, Autokratoron,** and the prominent **25 Martiou.**

Tourists can find helpful information at **City Hall,** 25 Martiou (☎23 270). The **National Bank** can be reached by walking right onto 28 Oktovriou when exiting the ferry landing, then turning left onto Omirou, one street after Thermopotamou; it **exchanges currency** and has a **24hr. ATM.** (Open M-Th 8am-2:30pm, F 8am-2pm.) Find the **police** (☎23 333) on 28 Oktovriou, just across from the boat dock; follow the side alley next to the ice cream shop, then go up the stairs. A **pharmacy,** Omirou 12, is near the National Bank. (☎24 000. Open M and W 8am-1:30pm, Tu and Th-F 8am-1:30pm and 5:30-9pm.) Follow 28 Oktovriou to the turn in the road where it becomes Posidonos, and turn left onto 25 Martiou to reach the **post office** on the left. (☎22 252. Open M-F 7:30am-2pm.) **Postal Code:** 34300.

EVIA & THE SPORADES

⌐ ⌐ ACCOMMODATIONS AND FOOD. There are a few reasonably priced accommodations in Aedipsos; many can be found on Ermou and its side streets. The best deal is ◼**Hotel Areti ❷**, Omirou 11, which welcomes guests with a lovely lobby and simple but clean rooms with air-conditioning, fridge, bath, and tiled floor. (☎22 473. Singles €20; doubles €30. Cash only.) **Hotel Istiaia ❸**, 28 Oktovriou 2, at the corner of 25 Martiou, is another excellent choice. The hospitable management offers attractive rooms with air-conditioning, TV, fridge, bath, and balcony, many with views of the water. (☎22 049. Breakfast €7. Singles €37; doubles €50, with view €65. MC/V.) To get to **Hotel Katerina ❸**, Ermou 39, exit the ferry landing from the left end of the parking lot with the water at your back, then make a left onto Ermou. The immaculate rooms have bath, air-conditioning, TV, fridge, balcony, and phone. (☎22 610. Singles €30; doubles €40. Cash only.)

Eateries and cafes border the waterfront, but most serve only drinks before 8pm. **To Steki ❸**, 28 Oktovriou 14, by the Omirou intersection, is recognizable by its blue canopy. It serves fresh seafood and traditional Greek fare to a steady crowd (☎69406 05 508. Fish dishes €8-12. Open daily 9am-2am. Cash only.) **Casa Romania ❷**, 28 Oktovriou, near the boat dock, serves mouth-watering pizzas. (☎60 234. Full pizzas €8-9. Open daily 11am-1am.) After a dip in the hot springs, cool off with an ice-cream cone (€1.40) at **Dodoni ❶**, next to Casa Romania. (☎60 226. Open daily 8am-2am.) There is a **5' Supermarket** on Ermou, near the intersection with Thermopotamou. (☎60 130. Open M-F 8am-10pm, Sa 8am-8pm.)

◙ SIGHTS. Since antiquity, Aedipsos's main appeal has been its **hot springs.** While the springs often are recommended by doctors to those suffering from arthritis, respiratory difficulties, and other ailments, even the perfectly healthy can come to relax and rejuvenate. If you'd rather not empty out your wallet for a day of hydrotherapy treatments (€17-83) at the Thermae Sylla Spa in the Wellness Hotel, you easily can experience the springs for next to nothing. Heading right on 28 Oktovriou from the ferry terminal, follow the road along the waterfront as it turns into Posidonos. After you pass the Wellness Hotel, look for the stairs heading to the beaches on your right. The largest concentration of hot springs emptying into the sea is here at ◼**Thermatiki beach.** (€1.60 entrance fee. Open daily 8am-6pm.) You can feel the warmth from the springs for free on the beaches on either side of Thermatiki, and directly in front of the Wellness Center, where hot spring water gushes over a sequence of flat rocks into the sea.

LIMNI Λίμνη ☎22270

A 2hr. bus ride north from Halkida brings you to the wooded cove of Limni, where friendly villagers are curious about the rare outsider who stumbles upon their homes. Fortunately for those looking to experience the unadulterated essence of Greece, this tranquil fishing village has remained a secret. The splendid scenery is as stunning as the dazzling sunsets and serene, star-filled nights. The relaxed pace of life is a breath of fresh air after the noisy chaos of Halkida. Limni's **Folklore Museum,** Anagnosti Goviou 7, to the right of the plateia facing inland, is a great source of information about the town. It houses an extensive collection of historic items from Limni households, including a mosaic floor and formal dining room. Ring the bell and ask the knowledgeable curator for a map of Limni that provides a history of the town. (☎31 335. Open M-Sa 9am-1pm, Su 10:30am-1pm. €2.)

If you want a truly authentic taste of Limni, stay in one of the numerous **domatia** lining Posidonos and Ag. Christodolou. Stop in to ask for rates or call ☎22210 31 640. (Singles typically €35-50; doubles €40-70.) For an unparalleled experience, stay in the ⬛**Graegos Domatia ❹**, run by Margaritis and Antje Papageorgiou. English-speaking, warm, and generous, they offer four spectacular rooms that have all the amenities of studio apartments, including satellite TV, a fully supplied kitchen, and air-conditioning. (☎31 117. Prices range €50-70. Cash only.) The **Plaza Hotel ❸,** to the left of the main plateia, is the only conventional hotel in town; it has comfortable rooms with beautifully tiled floors, TV, air-conditioning, phone, bath, and wooden furniture. (☎31 235. Singles €30; doubles €60.) Locals start the day with a visit to the town **bakery,** uphill to the right of the church. (☎31 001. Full loaf €1.20. Open daily 5:30am-2pm.) They also shop at **Poussos Supermarket,** on Posidonos. (☎31 239. Open M-Sa 8:30am-2:30pm; T and Th-F also 6-9pm.) Stop by ⬛**To Neon ❶**, next to the National Bank, for a scoop of vanilla ice cream with honey swirls (€1) or your choice of sweet Greek confections. (☎31 262.) From 10pm to midnight, the waterfront restaurants serving nightly specials pick up steam. A few blocks down Posidonos from the center of town, local favorite ⬛**Picantico ❷** serves delicious grilled chicken with lemon (€6) on tables right at the water's edge. (☎31 300. Open daily 6pm-2am. Entrees €6-9. Cash only.) **Avra ❷,** a block away from Picantico, is another solid bet for a traditional Greek meal and friendly service. (☎31 479. Entrees €5-8. Open mid-Feb. to mid-Dec. daily 9am-11pm. MC/V.) **Remetzo,** to the left of the plateia, serves cold drinks (€1.30-5) all day and into the night (☎32 510. Open daily 6am-3am or later.)

Buses in Limni stop at the main intersection; ask before you get off when the next one comes, or inquire at To Neon. Bus service in Limni can change on short notice; usually there is a daily bus to Halkida (2hr.; 6am, 10:30, 2pm, 4:45; €7). Though buses run to Aedipsos Springs (30min., 2:30pm, €9), the road occasionally is closed to buses due to treacherous conditions from yearly rain seasons. A **taxi** (€20) will help you make the 30km trip to northern Evia, and can be found up the road to Aedipsos and Athens. (☎32 000. Available 8am-1pm and 5-8:30pm.) Limni's main intersection includes all three of its major streets. Facing the water on **Ag. Goviou, Posidonos** runs left along the waterfront and **Os. Christodolou** extends to the right. **Plateia Eleftherios Antistasis,** the main plateia, is to your right. Despite its small size, Limni has a complete range of services. The **National Bank of Greece,** at the main intersection, has a **24hr. ATM.** (☎31 140. Open M-F 8am-2:30pm.) There is a **laundry service** 50m up the road to Halkida; walk up Ag. Goviou and take a left at the church. (☎31 991. €10-15 per load. Open M-Sa 8:30am-3pm and 6-11pm.) **"@" Internet Cafe,** halfway down Posidonos from the main intersection, offers **Internet** access. (☎31 275. Open daily 11am-1:30pm and 5:30pm-late. €1.50 for 30min., €2.50 per hr.) There are numerous **pharmacies** along Ag. Goviou and Posidonos; the largest is located at the main intersection, across from the National Bank. (☎31 113. Open daily 8am-2pm and 5:30-9pm.) To get to the **post office,** walk a few blocks down Os. Christodolou; it's up a side street on the right. (☎31 216. Open M-F 7:30am-2pm.) **Postal code:** 34005.

ERETRIA Ερέτρια ☎22290

Formerly one of ancient Evia's most important cities, modern Eretria still draws crowds of vacationing Athenians and beach-bound tourists. Walk a few blocks away from the bustling waterfront, though, and you'll notice vacant lots and shuttered hotels, clear signs that the city has fallen on hard times. The expensive hotels and unremarkable restaurants make Eretria unappealing for an extended stay; instead, consider taking a brief daytrip from nearby Halkida to see the picturesque harbor and archaeological ruins.

☐ TRANSPORTATION. Buses stop in Eretria (30min., 1-2 per hr. 6:30am-8:40pm, €1.50) on their way from Halkida to Amarinthos, Karystos, and Kimi. Tickets are sold at the cafe that doubles as the bus station (☎61 602). Consult the bus schedule posted outside for details about trips out of Eretria. Buses stop on Filosofou Menedimou, three blocks inland from the waterfront area. The booth directly opposite the dock in the main port (☎62 492) sells tickets for **ferries** to Skala Oropos (20min., 2 per hr. 5:45am-10:45pm, €1.40), where you can catch a bus to Athens (35min., every hr. 5:40am-8:45pm, €3.30). **Taxis** (☎62 500) wait across from the ferry port and respond to calls 24hr.

☐ ORIENTATION AND PRACTICAL INFORMATION. From the bus stop, walk past the National Bank until you reach Archaiou Theatrou, the palm-lined main street. A 10min. walk to the left is the Archaeological Museum; 5min. to the right is a traffic circle and then the waterfront. At the traffic circle, Amarisias Artemidos runs perpendicularly to the right, and Archaiou Theatrou continues straight ahead, passing the most popular waterfront bars, restaurants, and hotels.

The **National Bank,** on the first corner toward Archaiou Theatrou from the bus station, has a **24hr. ATM** and **exchanges currency.** (☎62 203. Open M-Th 8:45am-1:45pm, F 8:45am-1:30pm.) The **pharmacy** is across the street from the bank. (☎62 775. Open daily 8:30am-2pm and 5-10pm.) The **OTE,** Archaiou Theatrou 17, is in the building just before the traffic circle on the right. (☎60 399. Open M-F 7:30am-2pm.) Find **Internet** access at **Relo@d NetCafe,** 50m down Amarisias Artemidos from the traffic circle. (☎61 181. Open 24hr. €2.50 per hr.) To reach the **post office,** start toward Archaiou Theatrou from the bus station and take the first right, then turn left after one block. (☎62 333. Open M-F 7:30am-2pm.) **Postal Code:** 34008.

☐☐ ACCOMMODATIONS AND FOOD. If you want to spend the night in Eretria, but not in one of the fancy resorts, you have only one option: **Pension Diamanto ❸,** on Archaiou Theatrou, past the traffic circle and on the left. If no one is at reception, visit the small cigarette store next door. The pastel-colored rooms have TV, air-conditioning, fridge, and bath; most have balcony with waterfront view. (☎62 214. Singles and doubles €30-55. Discounts for extended stays.)

There are plenty of fast-food options around the traffic circle, and several waterfront tavernas prepare traditional dishes at reasonable prices. **Remetzo ❷,** Archaiou Theatrou 42, just before Pension Diamanto, serves grilled meats (€6-10), fresh seafood (calamari €6), and heaping salads (€3-5). Their delicious bread (included in the €1 per person cover charge) is more of a bruschetta, toasted and topped with fresh tomatoes, olives, and olive oil. (☎61 446. Open daily 11am-1am. MC/V.) Nearby **Astra ❷,** with tables just inches from the water, is a reliable alternative for fresh seafood and taverna fare. (☎64 111. Grilled octopus €8. Entrees €5-8. Open daily 11am-midnight.) Those interested in stocking up on cheap snacks can head to **Atlantik Supermarket,** on the corner across the street from and to the right of the bus station. (☎60 010. Open M-Sa 8am-9pm, Su 8am-2pm.)

☐☐ SIGHTS AND BEACHES. The courtyard of the **Archaeological Museum,** at the inland end of Archaiou Theatrou, is packed with marble statues, friezes, and pillars. In the modest interior, one room displays ancient tools, statues, and figurines found throughout the city, and another is filled with larger sculptures. The exhibits are in Greek and French, but you can buy an English guidebook (€6). Museum admission also lets you into the **House of the Mosaics,** a 10min. walk from the museum; trade your passport for the keys at the front desk. Coming out of the museum, head to the main road and bear right for three blocks, turning left at the intersection of Antioxou Theodikou. You'll see a sign marking the fenced-in enclosure, which contains the ruins of a grave site, flanked by glass-fronted buildings that cover the mosaics themselves. The 4th-century BC mosaics are incredibly well-preserved and are among the oldest in existence. Flicking the square switches will illuminate the floors. (☎22210 62 602. Museum and mosaics open Tu-Su 8:30am-3pm. €2, students and children free.) On the other side of the main road from the museum is a large excavated portion of **ancient Eretria,** where visitors can peer at the poorly preserved ancient **theater** and the ruined foundations of the city's residential section. Unfortunately, the site is often locked behind a fence to protect the remains, but there is a clear view of the ruins from the road.

The best and most heavily populated **beaches** are along Archaiou Theatrou, past the tavernas and cafes. To escape the crowds, continue along as the waterfront bends to the left—the sandy beach stretches out for another 1.5km. Alternatively, walk 5min. along Filosofou Menedimou from the bus stop away from Archaiou Theatrou to reach a similar beach that extends toward Halkida.

■ **NIGHTLIFE.** Bars along Archaiou Theatrou and Amarisias Artemidos begin to fill up after dark. Almost all have waterfront locations and tasteful decor, perfect for an after-dinner drink. **Teatro,** about halfway down the strip on Archaiou Theatriou, decorated with lanterns hanging over red-and-white sofas, and nautically themed **Helios** (☎62 604), across from Pension Diamanto, are the most popular. Both have harborside seating areas and dance floors across the street. (Both open daily 9am-late. Beer €2-4. Mixed drinks €5-7.)

KARYSTOS Κάρυστος ☎22240

Unimaginative architecture and a grid-like street plan obscure a city that is vibrant, fun, and more alive than ever. Located between imposing Mount Ohi and the sparkling waters of Marmari bay, Karystos hums with a mysteriously enchanting atmosphere enhanced by the gregarious hospitality of its residents. Thrills are more likely to come from visiting hole-in-the-wall restaurants than from partying on the beach (although you can do that too); come in with the right expectations and you likely will be pleasantly surprised.

■ **TRANSPORTATION AND PRACTICAL INFORMATION.** The bus station (☎26 303) is on I. Kotsika, which runs along the right side of the city hall. Take the **bus** to Marmari (20min.; M-Th 4-5 per day, F-Sa 5 per day; €1.50), where you can catch the **ferry** to Rafina (1hr.; M-Th 5-6 per day, F 7 per day, Sa 8 per day, Su 9 per day; €6). Buses from Karystos also go to Athens (4hr.; M-Sa 8am, Su 1:45pm; €7); Halkida (3hr.; M-F 5:30am, 1:45pm; Sa 6am; Su 1:45pm; €9); Nea Stira port (1hr.; M-F 5:30, 8am, 1:45pm; Sa 6, 8am; Su 1:45pm; €2.50) via Stira (45min., €2.20). **Taxis** (☎26 500) wait in the plateia 6am-2am. If you need after-hours service, get a driver's cell phone number.

For comprehensive travel advice, head to ■**South Evia Tours,** on the left side of the central plateia with your back to the sea, through the Kosmos book store. Nikos and his sister Popi can help with everything from **car rentals** (€30-45 per day), to planning local excursions, to booking accommodations. They'll also provide you with a free regional map. Locals often say, "If you have a question, Nikos and Popi know the answer"—so don't hesitate to ask. (☎26 200. Open daily 9am-midnight.) The **Alpha Bank,** off the main plateia on Sachtouri, **exchanges currency** and has a **24hr. ATM.** (☎22 989. Open M-Th 8am-2:30pm, F 8am-2pm.) To find the 24hr. **police** (☎22 262), turn into the small alley just past the bank and climb the stairs at the end of the block on the left. A **pharmacy** is at the head of the central plateia. (☎23 505. Open M, Th, Sa 8am-1:30pm, Tu-W, F, Su 8am-1:30pm and 5-8:30pm.) The **OTE,** El. Amerikis 73, is to the right off I. Kotsika one block above the central plateia. (☎22 399. Open M-Th 7:30am-2pm, F 7:30am-1:30pm.) The only

Internet access in town is available on the three computers at **Polychoros,** just past Hotel Galaxy along the beachfront. (☎24 421. €4 per hr. Open daily 11am-late.) The **post office** is on Th. Kotsika, one street over from I. Kotsika, just above El. Amerikis. (☎22 229. Open M-F 7:30am-2pm.) **Postal Code:** 34001.

▐▐ ACCOMMODATIONS AND FOOD. Hotels in Karystos start at €35 for singles and €45 for doubles during the summer, but South Evia Tours can help you find cheaper **domatia** (€25-35). Follow the waterfront toward the *bourtzi*, turn left one block past the Archaeological Museum, and take the first right to find █**Rooms to Let ❷,** Sachtouri 42. Converted from a charming yellow home, the bright, well-decorated rooms surround a gorgeous courtyard garden. They come with TV, air-conditioning, fridge, bath, and small kitchen. (☎22 071. Laundry available. Singles, doubles, and triples €25-35. For the lowest price, ask for the room with an outside bath.) **Hotel Als ❸,** in a convenient location on the corner of Th. Kotsika and the waterfront, rents 32 spacious, tiled rooms that include TV, air-conditioning, and bath; some have a balcony with a sea view. (☎22 202. Singles €30-40; doubles €40-50; triples €50-55. Discounts for longer stays.) Opposite the beginning of Kremala beach at the corner of Kriezotou and Odysseos, **Hotel Galaxy ❸** is run by a hospitable English-speaking couple and has rooms with smooth earth-colored tiling, TV, air-conditioning, bath, and balcony. Breakfast is included and served in the large, wood-panelled lobby downstairs. (☎22 600. Singles €35-40; doubles €45-55; triples €54-66. Students can call ahead for lower rates. MC/V.)

The restaurants that line the waterfront have everything from fresh seafood to burgers and fries. Don't miss local favorite █**Cavo Doro ❷,** in the alleyway left of the central plateia facing inland, just past the back entrance to South Evia Tours. Dinners can last for hours as the wonderful English-speaking staff introduces you to other travelers. For an appetizer, try the delicious peppers stuffed with mozzarella (€3) or the grilled mushrooms (€3). (☎22 326. Entrees €4-6. Open daily 8am-4:30pm and 7pm-1am.) Popular **Marinos ❷** (Μαρίνος), Kriezotou 98, is on the waterfront to the right as you face the water. It has a variety of seafood entrees like octopus with vinegar (€9) and excellent locally grown meat. (☎24 126. Karystos beef €7. Entrees €6-8. Open daily 11am-midnight. MC/V.)

◙ SIGHTS. In the 11th century, the peep-holes in the back of the **bourtzi,** on the left side of the waterfront, were used to pour boiling oil on attackers. Today patrons invade the fort in August, crowding in to watch student productions; inquire at South Evia Tours about schedules. To learn about the natural environment of the area, check out the **Karystos Environmental Information Center,** 3km out of town toward Halkida. Hands-on exhibits, educational videos, and informational boards in English and Greek make it an excellent place to visit. It opens occasionally to the general public, but the most reliable way to get inside is to organize a group trip through Nikos at South Evia Tours. The **Archaeological Museum,** Kriezotou 58, is housed in the same building as the public library, just past the *bourtzi*. The modest exhibits include a small collection of marble statues and inscribed tablets, along with artifacts from the *drakospita* ("dragon houses") of Stira and Mt. Ohi. (☎25 661. Open Tu-Su 8:30am-3pm. €2, seniors €1, students free. Su free.) Located north of Karystos in the Old Town (accessible by taxi) are the **Montofoli Estate's** wine cellar and rolling vineyards. Built over the ancient site of the church of St. Marcus, the grounds occasionally hold concerts. Guided tours of the estate occur from July to September every Wednesday and Saturday at 7pm. Inquire at South Evia Tours or call ☎25 951 for more info.

▐ NIGHTLIFE. Start your evening at one of the bars that line Karystos's moonlit beaches. The scene especially heats up in the summer, when seasonal bars and clubs open their doors to partygoers. **Kohili Beach Bar** (Κοχυλι), on Psili beach, past the *bourtzi* and Hotel Karystion, serves beer (€3.50-5) and mixed drinks (€5) throughout the day and night. Locals rave about its epic parties on Friday and Saturday nights in the summer. (☎24 350. Open daily 10am-late.) **Archipelagos** (Αρχιπελαγος), on Kremala beach at the right edge of the waterfront facing the sea, taps into the island atmosphere with wooden bars, ferns, hanging lanterns, and seating by the sand. A DJ spins nightly, and there is live music once a week. (☎25 040. Beer €3. Mixed drinks €5-6.50. Open daily 8am-4am.) For a more relaxed scene, try **Ostria Bar** (Οστρια), about a block past Hotel Galaxy coming from the plateia. Funky instrumental, house, and pop music fills the blue, black-lit interior. (☎25 678. Beer €3. Mixed drinks €5-7. Open May-Oct. 24hr.) Across the street from Archipelagos is **Aeriko**, the latest addition to the beach bar scene. Its high ceilings and airy indoor-outdoor design attract a slightly more refined crowd. (Beer €3. Mixed drinks €7. Open daily 10am-late.) Even after the beach has shut down for the night, the party at **Alea**, on the right side of the central plateia facing inland, stays in full swing. Still, expect more socializing than dancing. (☎69329 30 736. Beer €3. Mixed drinks €7.50. Open daily 9am-late.)

� **DAYTRIPS FROM KARYSTOS.** The widely varied terrain of the Karystos region offers an abundance of spectacular daytrips and hikes for outdoor enthusiasts. The 4hr. hike up **Mount Ohi** (elev. 1398m) is awe-inspiring, with arresting vistas of southern Evia and the sea. Though May or early June have optimal climate and conditions for hiking, the mountain path is well-marked and safe year-round. Before hiking, talk to Nikos at South Evia Tours, who can advise you about trails and conditions. Better yet, join one of his inexpensive guided group hikes up the mountain (€20 per person, 6 or 7 times per summer). If you decide to hike on your own, be cautious around rocky parts of the trails and in windy weather, and hike with a partner if you can. To get to the trailhead, take a car or taxi (€5) to the village of **Mili,** or walk the 3km distance yourself by following Aiolou, one block east of the plateia, out of town. A set of mysterious monolithic **columns** appears on the side of the trail about 45min. into the hike, where they were abandoned at the site of an ancient Roman marble quarry. The haunting ruins of the ◪**Dragon House** *(drakospita)* sit on the summit, which you will reach after another 3¼hr. of walking. Believed to date back to Neolithic times, the ruins represent a major ancient achievement—each stone, weighing several tons, was transported up the mountainside. The building may have served as a temple dedicated to Zeus and Hera, and local legend holds that it was inhabited by a dragon who terrorized the region. You can spend the night at the **Mount Ohi Refuge ❶** (elev. 1050m), about 3hr. from the bottom and 1hr. from **Profitis Ilias Peak** at the top, and catch the heavenly sunrise from the summit the next morning. (Refuge also accessible by four-wheel-drive. Contact Nikos at South Evia Tours for access. €9 per person.)

Running from the back of Mt. Ohi to **Kallianou** (41km north of Karystos) and the sea, the **Dimosari Gorge** is a stunning example of natural architecture. Clear, cold water cascades down its length, shaded by the lush forest. The 3½-4hr. trail through the gorge is best accessed by car or taxi. A taxi to Petro Kanolo (a good starting point) and a return trip to Karystos costs around €70. For true mountaineers, a combined ◪**Mount Ohi-Dimosari Gorge hike,** from Mili to Profitis Ilias Peak and down the northern side of Mt. Ohi through the gorge to Kallianou, can be completed in 8½-10hr. It makes more sense, though, to break the trek up into two days, spending the night at the Mt. Ohi Refuge. **Klimataria Taverna ❷,** at the Mt. Ohi end of the gorge, is a convenient place to stop for a bite. Its owners also rent **rooms ❶** (€13) above the taverna. (☎71 300. Open daily noon-midnight.)

On the slopes above Karystos is the majestic **Castello Rosso** (a.k.a. *Kokkino Kastro;* Red Castle), named for the blood spilled there in the many battles for control of it. From Mili, it's a 20min. hike up the hill on the left and across the stone bridge. Other interesting sites in the region include the **Roman aqueduct,** past the Red Castle, and the **stone church** and **cave** at **Agia Triada,** accessible by a 2hr. hike from Nikasi, where the bus (€1.30) can drop you off.

For a taste of the open sea, day cruises are available throughout the Evoikos Gulf, to the Petali Islands, and to the other Cyclades. The trip to the **Petali Islands** stops at private islands with villas built by Picasso and former Greek King Constantinos. The tour (€30-35), which can be booked through South Evia Tours, leaves from the waterfront at 10am and returns at 5pm.

SPORADES Σποράδες

SKIATHOS Σκιάθος

The most popular tourist destination in the Sporades, Skiathos offers everything from gorgeous beaches and majestic forests to serene boat cruises and vibrant nightlife. The waterfront is a busy mix of tavernas, tourist agencies, and rental shops, while side streets reveal an abundance of trinket stores and creperies. It's tempting to write off Skiathos as a tourist trap, but don't judge it until you've visited—go with the flow and let the island do what it does best: provide countless ways to have fun.

SKIATHOS TOWN   ☎ 24270

Arriving in Skiathos Town can be overwhelming. Crowds of shouting hawkers greet ferries at the landing, advertising domatia and waving flyers. Cafes and tavernas line every street, intermingling with tacky beach shops and expensive boutiques. Welcoming bars full of talkative travelers, warm taverna owners who invite you to dine with them, and an almost palpable spunky spirit quickly draw you into the lively and constant buzz.

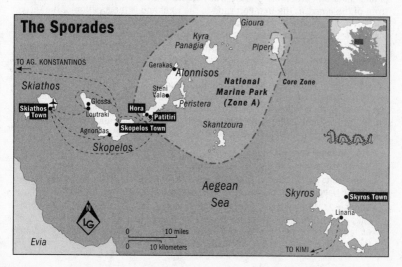

The Sporades

⌐ TRANSPORTATION

Flights: Olympic Airways (☎22 229), at the airport. Open M-F 8am-4pm. Taxis (€3) take you from the harbor to the airport. 1 flight per day goes to **Athens** (50min.).

Ferries: ☎22 209. On the corner of Papadiamantis, opposite the ferry landing. To: **Agios Konstantinos** (3hr.; Th 2:15pm, F 3:55pm, Su 7:55pm; €18); **Alonnisos** (1¾hr., 6 per week, €9); **Glossa** (30min.; daily 10:35am, Tu 11:10pm, F-Sa 2:10pm; €3.30); **Skopelos** (1hr., 2 per day, €5.30); **Volos** (2½hr., 3 per day, €15).

Flying Dolphins: ☎22 018. Buy tickets in the ferry ticket office. To: **Agios Konstantinos** (1¼hr., daily 8:25am, 5:40pm, €27); **Alonnisos** (40min., 5 per day 11:30am-9:45pm, €8.60); **Glossa** (15min., 3-4 per day 11:30am-9:45pm, €8); **Skopelos** (25min., 5 per day 11:30am-9:45pm, €10.30); **Volos** (1¼hr., 3 per day 7:30am-7:10pm, €25).

Charter Boats: From the Old Port. Circuits go around the island (€15) and stop at **Lalaria** and **Castro** beaches. Boats also run to **Tsougria** (€8) and **Skopelos** and **Alonnisos** (€20), among others. Ask the boatmen along the Old Port for more info.

Buses: Facing inland, turn right and follow the waterfront; when the road splits, continue left and walk 1 block to the **bus stop** on the corner. A bus schedule is available at the information kiosk. The bus to **Koukounaries beach** makes stops at southern beaches (30min.; every 15-20min. 7:15am-1am; €1.50, after midnight €1.75). Heading outbound, sit on the driver's side for the best view. When returning, stop #4, on the **acropolis** hill, is at the Old Port near most hotels and domatia.

Taxis: ☎24 461. Line up along the waterfront 24hr.

Car and Moped Rental: Companies like **Avis** (☎21 458) and **Heliotropio** (☎22 430) are located along the waterfront and include insurance in rental prices. Mopeds €15-20 per day. Cars from €35 per day.

✦ ⊘ ORIENTATION AND PRACTICAL INFORMATION

Skiathos's waterfront is more or less an L shape: the **bourtzi**, the small tree-covered peninsula at its corner, divides the Old Port from the New Port. Facing inland in front of the *bourtzi*, the **New Port** runs to the right and is the location of the ferry dock, rental agencies, tavernas, cafes, and tourist shops. The **Old Port** is perpendicular to the New Port and to the left of the *bourtzi*. **Papadiamantis**, Skiathos Town's mostly pedestrian thoroughfare, overflows with cafe-bars, souvenir shops, and clothing stores; it intersects the main waterfront across from the ferry dock. Farther inland, **Evangelistra** intersects Papadiamantis and connects it to **Polytechniou**, or "Bar Street," which runs parallel to Papadiamantis on the left. On the far right of the waterfront facing inland, the road splits. The branch that continues left passes the bus stop, then follows the island's southern coast to **Koukounaries beach.** The branch to the right leads to the **club strip.** Most of the shops and hotels along the waterfront and Papadiamantis give out a free map called "Skymap."

Bank: National Bank (☎22 400), midway up Papadiamantis. **Exchanges currency** and has an **ATM.** Open M-Th 8am-2:30pm, F 8am-2pm.

Laundromat: Miele Laundry. From Papadiamantis, turn right onto the side street opposite the National Bank. Wash €7. Dry €3. Open daily 8am-10pm.

Police: ☎21 111. Upstairs, on the left of Papadiamantis, just past where the road forks around a public water spout. Open 24hr. **Tourist police** (☎23 172), in a small white building on the right side of Papadiamantis, opposite the police. Open daily May-Oct. 8am-9pm; Nov.-Apr. 7am-2:30pm.

Pharmacies: Several pharmacies line Papadiamantis. 1 is across from the National Bank (☎ 24 515). Open daily 9am-2pm and 5pm-midnight.

Hospital: ☎ 22 040. On the acropolis hill behind Skiathos Town. Open 24hr.

Telephones: OTE (☎ 22 399). On Papadiamantis, past the post office. Open M-Th 7:30am-1:30pm, F 7:30am-1pm.

Internet Access: Internet Zone Cafe, Evangelistra 28 (☎ 22 767), to the right off Papadiamantis and across from Sef. €2 per hr. Open daily 10:30am-1am. **Sixth Element,** G. Panora 15 (☎ 24 032), next to the laundromat. €4 per hr. Open daily 9am-12:30am.

Post Office: ☎ 22 011. On the right at the intersection of Papadiamantis and Evangelistra. Offers **Poste Restante.** Open M-F 7:30am-2pm. **Postal Code:** 37002.

🏠 ACCOMMODATIONS AND CAMPING

Domatia are generally the best deal in town; let the dock hawks that meet the ferry compete for you and be sure to bargain. Doubles run €20-30 in spring and fall; €25-50 in summer. The **Rooms to Let Office** in the port's wooden kiosk has lists of available rooms. (☎ 22 990. Open daily 9am-10:30pm.) In August, if you haven't already made reservations, forget about finding a room, much less a cheap one—forgo sleep and party the night away.

Australia Hotel (☎ 22 488). Turn right onto Evangelistra off Papadiamantis; it's in the 1st alley to the left. Tucked away from the bustle of town, Australia has 22 rooms with A/C, TV, bath, fridge, and balcony. Ring the bell outside for service. Singles €20-45; doubles €25-60; triples €45-70. Discounts for extended stays. ❷

Aiolus Pension (☎ 21 402). Turn right off Papadiamantis onto the diagonal street before the tourist police. Go straight past the intersection; it's on the left after the Rent a Moto shop. This slightly out-of-the-way pension's clean, well-furnished rooms have fridge, TV, A/C, and bath. Doubles €30-65; triples €40-75. Discounts for extended stays. ❸

Pension Lazou (☎ 22 324), on the hill overlooking the Old Port. Walk along the Old Port as it bends to the left, and climb the stairs at the very end. Has 12 uniquely furnished rooms with A/C, fridge, and bath. Some overlook the waterfront, but the best view is from the rooftop deck. Quiet hours 3-6pm and 11pm-9am. Call before arrival. Doubles €30-55; triples €45-65. Singles available in low season. ❸

Camping Koukounaries (☎ 49 250), on the bus route to Koukounaries, just before stop #23. Close to Koukounaries and Mandraki beach. Mini-mart on site. €7 per person, €3 per tent, €3 per car. Tent rental €5.50. ❶

🍴 FOOD

Skiathan restaurants accommodate a wide range of tastes and budgets. Greek tavernas abound, but Italian restaurants and other ethnic cuisines are also available. Not surprisingly, exotic food tends to be pricey; back-alley souvlaki stands and tiny tavernas off the main strip feed locals and broke backpackers.

🍽 Hellinikon, 25th Martiou 10 (☎ 23 225), around the corner from Piccolo. Hellinikon, which has been under the same ownership for 17 years, has a menu of meticulously prepared dishes like house specialty lamb *kleftiko* (€7.50). Nightly live *bouzouki* music from a father-son duo enlivens the romantic outdoor seating area. Entrees €7.50-10. Open daily 6pm-late. AmEx/MC/V. ❸

🍽 Giorgios Grill House, Moraifidi 4 (☎ 21 008). Walk up the steps past Rock and Roll Bar; it's the 2nd restaurant in the strip along the water. This gem, frequented by locals and tourists alike, serves exquisitely seasoned grilled meats for low prices.

GIVING BACK

DOG'S BEST FRIEND

raveling in Greece, you've probably noticed the stray-dog popula-
ion that roams almost every
city's streets. The people of Skia-
hos, however, decided to take
 action about this pervasive prob-
em, founding the Skiathos Dog
Shelter to benefit both the island
and the dogs.

Accepting canines of all
breeds and in all sorts of condi-
ions, the committed staff at the
shelter works year-round to provide medical treatment and hous-
ng for the strays. They search
both in Greece and abroad for
permanent owners, and with the
help of British, Danish, and German programs, the shelter has
been vastly successful. According
o Helen Bozas, the manager, in
2003 they were able to find
homes for 320 pups. Still, the
influx is constant, and, in its busiest months, the shelter can
receive up to 14 dogs per day.

Volunteers—both locals and
travelers—are eagerly welcomed
o come in and play with the dogs
or take them on walks. If you
show up with treats from the
supermarket, you'll be greeted
with affectionate, slobbery kisses
from the pups, of course).

*he Skiathos Dog Shelter is about
1km up the hill on the road that
ntersects the main drag at bus
stop #18. ☎24270 49 214;
www.skiathosdogshelter.com.
Arrive between 9am and 2pm to
walk the dogs.*

Chicken on spit €5.50. Grilled meats €5.50-8.50. Open daily 1pm-midnight. AmEx/MC/V. ❷

Sef (☎24 092). Turn right onto Evangelistras from Papadiamantis; it's on your left after a few blocks. Friendly staff and a diverse array of traditional dishes have made Sef popular with locals. Entrees €7-9. Open daily 7:30am-midnight. AmEx/MC/V. ❷

Piccolo Grill House (☎22 780). From the Old Port waterfront, take the stairs on the right across from the cannon and flag, walk past the church, and turn right. Set in a romantic plateia, Piccolo serves tasty meals in a charming atmosphere, putting a Greek spin on Italian classics. Pastas €7-9. Pizzas €8-10. Open daily May-Oct. 6:30pm-12:30am. ❷

"No Name" Fast Food, on Simionos, a block past the left fork on Papadiamantis. Name or not, this is the best spot for a quick, cheap meal. Gyros, burgers, and chicken pitas €2 each. Open daily 11am-midnight. ❶

👁 SIGHTS

Author Alexandros Papadiamantis's tiny 140-year-old house, set back off Papadiamantis about 1½ blocks inland, now serves as the **Papadiamantis Museum.** The exhibit honors the 19th-century realist, one of Greece's best-loved prose writers. Information and short stories are available in English. (Open Tu-Su 9:30am-1:30pm and 5-8:30pm. €1.) Ten kilometers from Skiathos Town on the northern coast of the island, accessible by private vehicle or by boat, are the unimpressive ruins of the island's **kastro.** The 16th-century walled castle once served as a refuge from marauding pirates. You can reach the neighboring **Monastery of the Panagia Eikonistra** or **Kounistra** by hiking or driving. From bus stop #18, they are about 4km along the road, near the top of the large hill. Follow the signs to the monastery. Panagia Eikonistra marks the spot where an old monk is said to have discovered a **miracle-working icon** of the Virgin Mary hanging from a tree, emitting light. Today the icon is in the **Cathedral of the Three Hierarchs,** up the steps from the Old Port, and is escorted back to the monastery every November 20 during the **Presentation of the Virgin.** People visit the monastery for oil from the church's lamp, which is said to have healing power. The **Convent of Evangelista,** 4km north of Skiathos Town on the slopes of Karaflitzanaka, is where the first Greek national flag (a white cross on a blue background) was raised in 1807.

🏖 BEACHES

The most notable sights on the island are its many gorgeous beaches. The best of them, along the southern

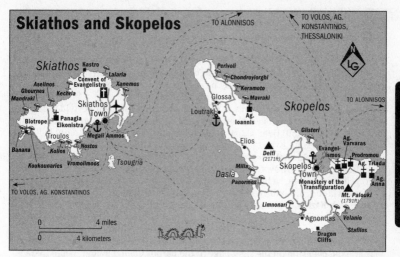

Skiathos and Skopelos

TO ALONNISOS

TO VOLOS, AG.
KONSTANTINOS,
THESSALONIKI

Skiathos
Kastro
Lalaria
Aselinos
Convent of
Evangelistra
Xanemos
Ghournes
Kechria
Mandraki
Skiathos
Town
Biotrope
Panagia
Eikonistra
Troulos
Nostos
Banana
Kolios
Koukounaries
Vromolimnos
Megali Ammos
Tsougria

Perivoli
Chondroyiorghi
Keramoto
Glossa
Mavraki
Loutraki
Ag.
Ioannis
Glisteri
Elios
Ag.
Varvaras
Delfi
(2171ft)
Evangel-
ismos
Prodromou
Milia
Dasia
Panormos
Skopelos
Town
Ag. Triada
Monastery of the
Transfiguration
Ag.
Anna
Limnonari
Mt. Palouki
(1791ft)
Agnondas
Velanio
Stafilos
Dragon
Cliffs

Skopelos

TO ALONNISOS

TO VOLOS, AG. KONSTANTINOS

0   4 miles
0   4 kilometers

coast, are accessible by bus and are always crowded. Those looking for a more varied experience can consider taking a charter boat from the Old Port for a day-long excursion around the island (€15) or to the other Sporades (€20). The cruise around Skiathos stops at the island's kastro and at the small but picturesque **Lalaria** beach, reachable only by boat. A single paved road runs along the southern coast of the island, between Skiathos Town and the most famous beach, **Koukounaries.** The bus makes many stops along the road; a list of the stops is available at the bus station in Skiathos and at Koukounaries (stop #26). Soft sand curves between blue waters and the deep pines of the **Biotrope,** a protected forest area. Koukounaries is the island's most popular and activity-centric beach—expect crowds in July and August. The full slate of water sports includes kayaking (€6 per hr.), water skiing (€20 per 10min.), parasailing (€35 for 1 person, €50 for 2), banana boating (€8 per 10min.), and wind surfing (€15 per hr.). Showers, bathrooms, chairs with umbrellas (€8 per day), and bars pepper the beach. For the best sunset views on the island, head to **Banana** and **Little Banana** (stop #26) up the hill across from the bus stop; signs lead the way. To get to predominately nude Little Banana from Banana, walk down the path to the right just before you reach the main beach. From stop #13 headed toward #14, follow the road on the left to **Vromolimnos.** Here, the staff at **Porto Paradiso ❶** serves mixed drinks (€4-6.50) and milkshakes (€5-6) to cool off the crowds. (☎49 257. Sandwiches €3.50-4.50. Open daily 10am-10pm.) The bus also stops at other beaches, including **Megali Ammos** (stop #5), **Nostos** (stop #12), and **Kolios** (stop #14), though these beaches tend to be crowded. From the later stops, a 30min. walk through a pine forest brings you to the northern beaches, where winds are stronger and beach umbrellas less prominent. **Mandraki,** one of the better options, is up a sandy road from stop #23. To steer clear of the bus route altogether, a 45min. walk north of town past the airport will get you to **Xanemos,** frequented primarily by locals.

🎵 🎧 ENTERTAINMENT AND NIGHTLIFE

Open-air **Cinema Attikon,** on Papadiamantis just before the bank and on the right, plays recent Hollywood releases in English with Greek subtitles. (☎22 352. Shows 9, 11:30pm. €7.) During the summer, there are concerts at the *bourtzi*. Ask at the information kiosk in the harbor for schedules.

The strip on the far right of the waterfront is made up of nightclubs, and great bars lie just above the Old Port and at the beginning of Polytechniou. At the bars, expect to pay €3-5 for beer, €5-7 for mixed drinks, and sometimes a €3-5 cover on busy Saturday nights. In general, you'll find a heavy concentration of friendly Scandinavians and Brits, with relatively few Americans. Pillows serve as chairs on the hill outside lively **Rock and Roll Bar,** in the Old Port up the stairs across from the cannon and flag pole. Patrons enjoy mixed and frozen drinks (€6-9) to hits from the 1970s, 80s, and 90s. (☎22 944. Half-priced drinks 7-9pm. Beer €4-5. Open May-Oct. 16 daily 7pm-3am.) **Kentavros,** off Papadiamantis to the right beyond the Papadiamantis Museum, has been playing everything from British pop to world soul since 1978. (☎22 980. Beer €2.50-4. Mixed drinks €5-6.50. Open daily 9:30pm-3:30am.) Turn left on Evangelistra from Papadiamantis to reach the Polytechniou bars. The tiny ◪**Admiral Benbow Inn,** run by the wonderful Yorkshire-born Elaine and Mick Lyons, overflows with cozy, quirky personality. Take a peek at "Knocking on Heaven's Door," a bathroom door covered with musicians' obituaries. (☎22 311; www.admiral-benbow.co.uk. Open daily 8:30pm-3am.) The nearby wild English pub **Kazbar,** with darts and foosball, plays live music beginning at 11pm. (☎21 781. Beer €3-4.50. Mixed drinks €4-5. Open daily 8pm-late.)

From October to May, Skiathos Town is a ghost town. By July however, it's hard to imagine anything being closed. Partiers stay out until dawn at the disco-bars that line the **club strip** on the right edge of the harbor, facing inland. While there is no cover, beer costs about €5-6, mixed drinks €8, and soft drinks €4. Popular **Kahlua** is the big fish in the club strip's large, diverse pond, flaunting multiple red-lit bars and playing an eclectic mix of international pop music. (☎69456 61 199. Open daily 10pm-late.) In the land of ubiquitous techno syncopation, the hip hop and R&B classics at white-and-red **Remezzo,** near the start of the strip, are a rare treat. (☎24 024. Happy hour 11:30pm-1:30am. Open daily 9:30pm-late.) **BBC,** with a cavernous dance floor and luminescent diamond-shaped tables, plays mainstream hip hop and R&B. (Open 10pm-late.) Following the illuminated steps just past Pink Cadillac will bring you to **Apeva Live,** the only non-disco on the strip. This upscale club features live Greek music. (Drinks €10. Music begins nightly at midnight.) The **Harley Davidson** bar at the end of the strip caters to motorcycle enthusiasts and anyone who likes bikers. (☎24 556. Open daily 10am-3am.)

SKOPELOS Σκόπελος

Tourist-friendly Skopelos sits between the whirlwind of Skiathos and the largely untouched wilderness of Alonnisos, incorporating the best elements of both. Hikes and moped rides through shady forests lead to numerous monasteries, bright beaches, and white cliffs that drop into a sparkling blue sea. By night, the town's waterfront strip closes to traffic, crowds swarm the streets, and a number of low-key bars and a few quality clubs maintain a party atmosphere.

SKOPELOS TOWN   ☎24240

Skopelos Town is built on the steep hills above the harbor. The many moped rental shops, cafes, and tavernas near the waterfront contrast with the narrow streets that twist among whitewashed buildings, beautiful churches, and cafes.

▐ TRANSPORTATION

In good weather, ferries and Flying Dolphins dock at the landing on the left side of the harbor facing inland or at the ferry dock in the center of the waterfront. When it's windy, they go to **Agnondas,** 8km south of town. If you find that you have landed in Agnondas, wait for the bus, which will take you to Skopelos Town (€1). In Skopelos Town, buy tickets for ferries and Flying Dolphins at the **ticket office** (☎22 767), across from the central ferry landing.

Ferries: To: **Alonnisos** (30min., 1-2 per day, €5), **Skiathos** (1hr., 3 per day, €6.20), and **Volos** (3½hr., 2 per day, €17). Buy tickets at Lemonis Travel to **Agios Konstantinos** (4hr., Th-F and Su, €32) and **Thessaloniki** (5½hr.; M, W-Th, Sa; €19.40).

Flying Dolphins: To: **Agios Konstantinos** (2hr.; M-F and Su 7:25am, 4:20pm; Sa 7:25, 10:35am; €32); **Alonnisos** (20min.; M-F and Su 5 per day 11:45am-10:05pm, Sa 10:35am-10:05pm; €8); **Glossa** (30min., 4 per day 6:30am-4:45pm, €8.40); **Skiathos** (45min., 6 per day 6:30am-6:45pm, €10.30); **Thessaloniki** (2½hr.; M-F and Su 9:30pm, Sa 3:35pm; €35.30); **Volos** (2hr.; M 4 per day 6:30am-4:45pm, Tu-Su 3 per day 6:30am-4:45pm; €28.20).

Buses: The bus stop is left of the ferry dock facing inland. 13 **buses** per day go to: **Agnondas** (€1.20); **Milia** (€2.30); **Panormos** (€1.70); **Stafilos** (€1.20). 8 per day to **Glossa** and **Loutraki** (both €3.20). Check the schedules at the Skopelos Town stop and be sure to note return times.

Taxis: ☎69448 43 738. Available 7am-2am next to the bus stop. Call 24hr.

Car and Moped Rental: Motor Tours (☎22 986), to the left of the port facing inland. Rents mopeds (€10-14 per day) and cars (from €30 per day) and has the best prices. Return vehicle during store hours. Open Apr.-Oct. 8:30am-10pm.

✦🛈 ORIENTATION AND PRACTICAL INFORMATION

Tourist agencies, tavernas, and cafes line the waterfront. **Platanos,** a small plateia packed with souvlaki and gyro joints, is opposite the dock, with the small monument to the right and playground to the left. **Galatsaniou** darts upward about 200m to the right of the dock facing inland, between Nostos and Aktaion restaurants.

Budget Travel: Thalpos Travel Agency (☎22 947), 5m to the right of Galatsaniou on the waterfront. The staff provides maps and can help with everything from transportation to catching octopi. Open May-Oct. M-Sa 9am-2pm, Nov.-Apr. available by phone. **Lemonis Travel** (☎24270 22 363), to the right along the waterfront facing inland. Organizes ferry service to Agios Konstantinos and Thessaloniki. Open daily 8:30am-10:30pm.

Bank: National Bank (☎22 691), on the right side of the waterfront facing inland. Has a **24hr. ATM** and **exchanges currency.** Open M-F 8am-2pm.

Landromat: Self Service Laundry (☎23 123), off the back right corner of Pl. Platanos. Cold wash €9, warm wash €12. Dry €6. Open daily 9am-1:30pm and 5:30-8pm.

Police: ☎22 295. Above the National Bank. Available 24hr.

Pharmacy: ☎22 252. In Pl. Platanos, across from the laundromat. Open daily 9am-2pm and 5:30-11pm.

Medical Services: ☎22 222. Follow the left-hand road inland from Pl. Platanos past Ag. Ioannis to the end, then go right at the signs. Open M-F 9am-2pm. M-F 24hr. for **emergencies.**

Telephones: OTE (☎22 139), 100m from the water on Galatsaniou. Open M-F 7:30am-2pm.

Internet Access: An Internet cafe (☎23 093) is on the road running through the back of Platanos. Coming from the waterfront, turn left at the back left corner of the plateia; it's across from Metro nightclub. €3 per hr. Beer €2. Open daily 9am-midnight.

Post Office: ☎22 203. Look for the yellow postbox, 50m past the Internet cafe on the same road. Open M-F 7:30am-2pm. **Postal Code:** 37003.

GREEK FRIES

A charming bit of cultural cross-fertilization manifests itself in french fries, or *tighanites patates* as they're called in Greece. The much-loved companion to American fast food has taken up two opposing positions in Greek cuisine.

At most souvlaki joints, the french fry is not esteemed enough to be served in its own cardboard container; instead, it is stuffed inside the pita souvlaki or gyro itself. This may come as a shock to American palates weaned on the separation of sandwich and fries. However, it cuts back on both the time it takes to devour your snack and the grease left on your fingers.

At the other end of the culinary spectrum is the gourmet french fry, which single-handedly outclasses anything America has to offer in the fry department. Only served in the most expensive restaurants, these finely crafted chunks of potato burst with flavor and crispiness. Though most Americans take for granted the pairing of french fries with a certain red condiment, Greeks certainly do not. At classy establishments, even the most well-meaning request for ketchup will be met with a look of the utmost shock and derision. Consider yourself warned.

ACCOMMODATIONS

The **Rooms and Apartments Association of Skopelos** can provide a list of **domatia.** It's in the stone building next to the town hall. (☎ 24 567. Open daily 9:30am-2pm.) Dock hawks greeting ferries may offer reasonable rooms (singles €15-30; doubles €20-40); bargaining is expected. **☒ Pension Sotos ❷,** inside the inconspicuous door on the corner of Galatsaniou on the waterfront, has a fantastic location at a diamond-in-the-rough price. The renovated, 150-year-old house has 12 exposed-beam rooms with fan, coffeemaker, and bath; some have air-conditioning, TV, fridge, and balcony. A common kitchen, quiet courtyard, roof terrace, and book exchange are bonuses. (☎ 22 549. Singles €18-24; doubles €25-35; triples €55; quads €60. Discounts for extended stays.) To find **Hotel Regina ❷,** take the second alley on the left past the back right corner of Pl. Platanos. Kind owner Viki offers simple, cozy rooms with air-conditioning, TV, ceiling fan, bath, and fridge; some have seaviews. (☎ 22 138. English speakers should call Viki's son Iannis at ☎ 69788 64 092. Breakfast included. Singles €25-40; doubles €35-70; triples €85.) Follow the waterfront to the left (facing inland) past the park to reach **Hotel Akti ❷.** Pretty, tiled rooms have TV, fridge, bath, and balcony with a waterfront view. (☎ 23 229. Singles €25-35; doubles €30-40; triples €35-55.)

FOOD

Also known as "Souvlaki Square," Pl. Platanos abounds with quick bites. For slower-paced dining, head to one of the tavernas along the waterfront. **Taverna O Molos ❷,** down the waterfront to the far right facing inland, is beloved by locals for its impeccable traditional dishes and its location right on the edge of the harbor. (☎ 22 551. Entrees €6-8.50. Lamb *kleftiko* €7.50. Open daily noon-1am.) Follow the waterfront to the left, just past the park, to reach **Limni ❷,** whose traditional Greek cuisine is particularly good. (☎ 24 781. Salads and appetizers €2.50-5. Entrees €5-8. Open daily 6pm-2am.) **Cafe Barramares ❶,** to the right of the boat dock facing inland, dishes out delicious, filling *tiropita* (€3), crepes to go (from €3.50), ice cream sundaes (€3.50-7), and an array of enticing desserts. The luxurious sofas and flat-screen TVs in the outdoor seating area may dangerously encourage your calorie intake. (☎ 22 960; www.skopelosweb.gr/barramares. Open daily 8:30am-2:30am.) **Alpha-Pi Supermarket** has groceries. Take a left from the back left corner of the plateia; it's on the right. (☎ 23 533. Open daily 8am-midnight.)

SIGHTS

While the island's main attractions are its beaches and hikes, Skopelos Town also has an abundance of **churches.** They do not have regular visiting hours, but a good number probably will be open after dinner. Around the harbor to the far right, beautiful white-washed **Panagia ston Pirgo** balances on the rocks. From there, the stairs below the church lead up along the border of the city. The ascent passes tiny, simple **Evangelismos** and 11th-century **Athanasios,** the town's oldest church, just below the kastro. Off to the left is **Genesis tou Christou,** a large, cruciform church with a round cupola and clock tower. Continuing up the side of the city, you will see the **kastro,** originally built by King Philip of Macedon in the 4th century BC. Today it is the site of a traditional taverna that features live Greek music. On the uphill side of the kastro, if you wind your way into town and head for the top of the hill, you will hit **Spiridon.** Slightly farther into the city lies **Papameletiou,** a cruciform basilica built in 1662 with a red-tile roof and small clock tower. **Agios Nikolaos,** just up Galatsaniou on the left, exhibits brightly colored icons and a marble statue of the Virgin. In **Mikhail-Sinnadon,** a stone basilica contains a remarkable *iconostasis.* The **Folklore Museum,** 100m past the OTE, takes up three stories of an 18th-century house and displays artifacts donated by townspeople. While the collection is poorly labeled, it is well presented and definitely worth a look. (☎23 494. Open daily 8am-3pm and 6:30-11pm. €2, under 13 free.)

NIGHTLIFE

A 10min. walk up the stairs by Platanos Jazz Club on the far right of the waterfront, keeping close to the coast, leads to **Anatoli.** If you stop by this *ouzeri* for a drink just before midnight, you might catch Giorgos Xintaris, one of the world's last great *rembetika* singers, singing old songs with a group of friends. (☎22 851. Appetizers €2-5. Beer €3. Mixed drinks €3-7. Open daily 8pm-2:30am.) At **Platanos Jazz Club,** on the far right of the harbor facing inland, relax with jazz, blues, and a drink under a hulking tree. (☎23 661. Beer €3. Mixed drinks €6.50. Open daily 8:30am-2:30am.) **The Blue Bar,** two blocks up Galatsaniou in an alley on the right, plays folk, rock, and blues music to accompany its impressive collection of malt whiskey. (☎23 731. Beer €3. Mixed drinks €6. Open daily 9:30pm-2:30am.) Skopelos's **dance clubs** cluster midway up the street off the back left corner of Pl. Platanos. **Metro,** with a DJ, two bars, and flashing lights, is where most locals head to party the night away. (Cover €5; includes 1 drink. Beer €5. Mixed drinks €6. Open May-Oct. daily 11pm-3:30am, Nov.-Apr. F-Sa 11pm-3:30am.)

BEACHES

Traveling Skopelos's road by bus or car gives you access to lovely southern beaches. Headed out from Skopelos Town, the first beach is dazzlingly beautiful **Stafilos.** This crowded beach is by the hillside where archaeologists discovered the tomb of the ancient Cretan general of the same name. Nearby **Velanio,** over the hill to the left as you face the sea, is less packed. Named for the trickling spring that was a gushing fountain in Roman times, today Velanio is advertised as the only nude beach on Skopelos, though actually most swimmers wear suits. Past the small town of **Agnondas,** a paved road leads about 1km downhill to the secluded beach of **Limnonari,** which more than justifies the walk; ask the bus driver to let you off at the top of the road. Silvery **Milia,** accessible by bus, is the island's longest beach, with water sports and rough surf on windy days. Closer to Loutraki, dirt paths lead to the northern beaches of **Spilia, Mavraki, Keramoto,** and **Chondroyiorgi.**

EVIA & THE
SPORADES

🚶 HIKING

Because of Skopelos's predominantly dirt roads, it is best to explore the island on moped or foot. A 35km asphalt road runs from the Skopelos bus station through **Stafilos** (4km), **Agnondas** (8km), **Panormos** (18km), **Elios** (24km), **Loutraki** (30km), and **Glossa** (32km). Thalpos Travel and various souvenir shops carry *Skopelos Trails* (€12), a great guide to the island's hikes. According to local lore, a fierce dragon once went on a fiery rampage, eating almost everyone on Skopelos, until Ag. Rigine killed it and became the island's protector. The **Dragon Cliffs** *(Drakon-doschisma)*, where the creature was hurled to its death, are now a quiet overlook with a sea view and an altar portraying the dragon's grisly demise. The beginning of the 10min. walk is best reached by moped or bus. It's just off the highway between Stafilos and Agnondas; about 2km after Stafilos, follow the small dirt road that disappears into the woods on the left.

Two paved roads leave the town from the bus depot on the left end of the waterfront facing inland. To reach a set of monasteries, follow the road out of the harbor to the left—signs mark the way to **Mount Palouki**. Small **Evangelismos** was built in the 17th century as part of the Monastery of Xiropotamos of Athos, but today is inhabited by three nuns. Take the left-hand fork up the hot, winding mountain road for the 1hr., 2km hike; if you start early in the morning, you can avoid the heat and the bugs. (Open daily 8am-1pm and 5-8pm. Ring the bell to be let in.) Up the right fork, a 45min. walk leads you to the **Monastery of the Transfiguration** *(Metamorphosis)*. Its chapel, set in a flowered courtyard, dates from the 16th century. Another hour up the hill along the road takes you to two monasteries on ridges overlooking the sea. The first, the **Monastery of Agias Varvaras**, was built as a fortress in 1648. Nearby **Prodromou** contains several wall paintings along with icons dating back to the 14th and 15th centuries. Prodromou, whose astounding setting surveys the entire coast, is now a cloister dedicated to St. John the Baptist. The dirt path that begins behind the building leads to the smaller monasteries of **Agia Triada** and **Agia Taxiarches.** Farther up the road, a trail leads to beautiful **Agia Anna.** For a 4hr. round-trip hike from **Glossa,** take the dirt track across the island to the **Monastery of Agios Ioannis,** which clings spectacularly to a boulder above the ocean. From the main road east of Glossa, turn left on the first dirt road to Steki Taverna. At the road's end, a path drops to the sea; stone steps that have been cut in the escarpment lead to the monastery.

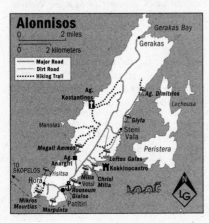

ALONNISOS
Αλόννησος

The only inhabited island within Greece's National Marine Park, Alonnisos is a pleasant starting point for those exploring the marine sanctuary and a refreshing small-town respite after Skiathos. Carpeted with well-marked trails that stretch through the forested hills to the coastal cliffs, it's a veritable paradise for hikers. To the northeast, the small island of Gioura claims to have been the home of Polyphemus, the Cyclops whose eye was gouged out by Odysseus's sizzling lance. Though many islands claim this distinction, Gioura's rocky landscape best fits Homer's description of Polyphemus's cavern, complete with herds of the now-endangered brown goats with black crosses on their backs.

PATITIRI Πατητήρι ☎24240

All boats dock at Patitiri, the island's main town. Impressive rock formations bookend the small harbor and its waterfront, which is lined by cafes and travel agencies. The town's relaxed atmosphere is conducive to enjoyable evenings by the water. Patitiri has little else to offer, but serves as an excellent home base for exploring the rest of the island.

▐ TRANSPORTATION

Ferries: To: **Agios Konstantinos** (4½hr., 6 per week, €31.20); **Kimi** (5hr.; W 8:25pm, Su 7:15am; €10); **Skiathos** (2hr., 10 per week, €7.40) via **Skopelos** (30min., €4.40); **Thessaloniki** (7½hr., W-Th and Sa 1 per day, €23.20); **Volos** (5¼hr., M 2:15pm, €15).

Flying Dolphins: To: **Agios Konstantinos** (2hr.; 6:45am, 4:15pm; €31.30); **Glossa** (25min., 4 per day 6am-5pm, €12.30); **Skiathos** (40min., 5 per day 6am-5pm, €15); **Skopelos** (15min., 6 per day 6am-5pm, €8); **Volos** (2hr., 3 per day 6am-5pm, €30). Reduced schedules in winter; call in advance. Boats going to **Agios Konstantinos** dock to the far left of the harbor.

Buses: Leave from where Ikion Dolophon hits the waterfront. Run to **Hora,** also called "Old Town" (10min.; every hr. 9am-3:20pm, 2 per hr. 7pm-midnight; €1), and **Steni Vala** (30min.; 9:20am, 2:35, 5:50pm; €1.10).

Taxis: ☎65 751. Available along the waterfront until 2am. Call 24hr.

Water taxis: Go to beaches on the eastern coast. Leave the dock between 10-11am and return from the northernmost beach, **Ag. Dimitrios**, at 5:30pm (round-trip €10).

Rentals: Motorbikes can be rented at shops on Pelasgon and Ikion Dolophon. **Dimitri's Place** (☎65 059), in the 1st alley on the left off Pelasgon. €10-15 per day.

▐▐ ORIENTATION AND PRACTICAL INFORMATION

From the docks, **Pelasgon** on the left and **Ikion Dolophon** on the right run inland.

Budget Travel: Alonnisos Travel (☎65 188), on the waterfront. Sells ferry tickets, **exchanges currency,** and books excursions. Open daily 8am-11pm. Flying Dolphin tickets can be bought just to the left of Ikion Dolophon on the waterfront.

Bank: National Bank (☎65 777), on Ikion Dolophon on the left from the water. Has a **24hr. ATM.** Open M-Th 8am-2:30pm, F 8am-2pm.

Laundry: Lena's Laundry (☎65 689). 50m up Pelasgon on the left. Open M-Sa 8:30am-2pm and 5-9pm. Wash and dry up to 5kg, €12.

Police: ☎65 205. Up Ikion Dolophon, past the fire station. Open daily 6am-10pm.

Pharmacy: ☎65 540. Before the Internet cafe. Open daily 8:30am-2pm and 5-10pm.

Hospital: ☎65 208. Opposite the police. Open daily 9am-1pm, 24hr. for emergencies.

Internet Access: Play Cafe (☎66 119), on Ikion Dolophon. Has an inflexible pay-before-use system, but it's the only Internet cafe in town. €4 per hr., min. €1. Open daily 10am-2pm and 5-11pm.

Post office: ☎65 560. A short walk up Ikion Dolophon on the right. Open M-F 7:30am-2pm. **Postal Code:** 37005.

ACCOMMODATIONS AND CAMPING

The **Rooms to Let Office,** to the right of Ikos Travel, can help find rooms in any of the towns on Alonnisos. (☎66 188. Open daily 10am-midnight.) Most of Patitiri's accommodations offer only doubles, triples, or studios, leaving solo travelers with little choice but to upgrade their digs. Domatia hawkers meet the ferry, but beware of prices that seem too good to be true—they often are. Always ask to see the room before finalizing a deal. **Pleiades ❷** is up several flights of steps from the first alley on the right off Pelasgon, overlooking the harbor. The tastefully decorated rooms come with TV, air-conditioning, fridge, and bath with shower curtain; some have balcony. The attached outdoor cafe often serves free coffee for guests. (☎65 235. Doubles €25-50.) To reach **Panorama ❸,** head down the first alley on the left up Ikion Dolophon, walk up the stairs to the top of the hill, and turn into the blue-fenced courtyard. The bright rooms come with TV, air-conditioning, fridge, bath, and a bougainvillea-covered common balcony with a port view. (☎65 240. Doubles €30-55; triples €35-60; 2-bedroom suite with kitchen €70-90.) Find lovely **Ilias Studios ❷** with TV, air-conditioning, bath, balcony, and kitchen about 200m down Pelasgon on the left, opposite I'm Motorbikes. (☎65 451. Doubles €25-50; studios €55-60.) Inquire at Boutique Mary, 100m from the waterfront on Pelasgon, about the simple, comfortable rooms with bath at next-door **Dimakis Pension ❸.** (☎65 294. Doubles €30-35.) One kilometer uphill on the first alley on the left of Pelasgon (look for signs) is the eminently punny **Camping Rocks ❶.** The sites, 50m from swimming rocks, have showers. (☎65 410. €5 per person, €2.50 per tent.)

FOOD

Away from the chaos of the harbor, find **To Kamaki ❷** on Ikion Dolophon past the National Bank. This little *ouzeri* serves delicious home-cooked seafood dishes like mussels *saganaki* (€6.50) at reasonable prices. (☎65 245. Open daily noon-1:30am. MC/V.) **Tzitziphia ❷,** at the corner of Pelasgon on the waterfront, busily caters to locals and tourists looking for quality Greek fare. (☎65 255. Veal *stamnas* with onions €7. Entrees €6-9. €0.50 cover. Open daily noon-12:30am. Group rates available.) For cheap souvlaki and gyros (€2), stop by **To Steki ❶,** near the corner of Pelasgon on the left. (☎66 292. Open daily 6pm-midnight.) Buy fresh produce at the store simply called **Fruits and Vegetables,** past the first alley on the left off Ikion Dolophon. (☎65 020. Open daily 8am-2pm and 5-9:30pm.)

SIGHTS AND NIGHTLIFE

The **History and Folklore Museum** of Alonnisos, up the stairs to the far left of the waterfront facing inland, displays a wide variety of cultural artifacts. Exhibits include weapons used in the Balkan Wars and WWII, historical maps, and an excellent trade series on everything from winemaking to pack-saddle construction. (Open daily 11am-7pm. €3, includes 1 soft drink.)

In the evening, people gather to sip cold drinks (€5) just above the beach and away from the docks at **Kactos Bar,** on the far left of the waterfront. (☎66 054. Beer €2.50. Open daily 7pm-3am.) **Club Enigma,** a short walk on Pelasgon, and **B&B Club,** on Ikion Dolophon, entertain crowds with international pop. (Beer €3-5. Mixed drinks €6-8. Both open F-Sa 10pm-late.)

BEACHES

The closest beach to Patitiri is family-friendly **Rousoum Gialos,** a 5-10min. walk east of the main town. Walk up Ikion Dolophon past the medical center and police station, following the signs. Most of the island's best beaches are accessible from the main road, which runs along the spine of the island from Patitiri to the port of Gherakas in the far north. A 1hr. walk on this road from Patitiri takes you to **Votsi,** the island's other major settlement. Local children dive off the 15-20m cliffs near Votsi beach, just outside the village. The road then passes separate turn-offs for the pine-enclosed beaches of **Milia** and shallower, sandier **Chrisi Milia.** Alonnisos's residents will tell you that **Agiou Dimitriou,** at the end of the coastal road, is the island's most beautiful beach. The clean, pebbled **Marpunta** beach has a strong claim to this title as well; reach it by continuing 1km past Camping Rocks and turning down the path to the left just before you reach the resort entrance. Along the coast from Chrisi Milia is the beach and archaeological site of **Kokkinocastro,** where swimmers occasionally find ancient coins. Nearby **Leftos Galas** has a sandy beach with two tavernas. Buses stop at the tiny fishing village of **Steni Vala,** 12km north of Patitiri (30min., 3 per day, €1.10). Not surprisingly, the **fish tavernas** here are fantastic. **Glyfa beach** is along the shore, a 5min. walk north of the village.

◪ HIKING

Only the southern end of the island is inhabited, leaving mountain wilderness to the north. Trails are marked at regular intervals and range from paved roads to steep, rocky paths. Blue maps, scattered throughout the island, mark trailheads and show routes, indicated by numerical yellow signs. Still, the purchase of a trail map (€3-5) or *Alonnisos on Foot* (€9), a walking and swimming guide, is recommended. The numbers below refer to those of the marked trails. The **Megalo Nero-Agii Anargiri-Megali Ammos-Raches-Votsi trail** (#5, 2½hr.) takes you along the southeastern side of Alonnisos to the secluded monastery of Ag. Anargiri and the beach of Megali Ammos. The trailhead is on the main road near Votsi. Head out Ikion Dolophon from Patitiri to get to the main road, then follow the signs to Votsi and Steni Vala. From Megali Ammos, two 1½hr. trails (#7 and 8) lead north to **Megalo Chorafi.** East of the main road, Megalo Chorafi is the hub for hikes to **Agalou Laka beach** (#14, 45min.) and the church of **Agios Kostantinos** (#6, 2hr.). From Ag. Kostantinos, the trails lead north to the church of **Agios Georgios** (#12, 1hr.) and **Melegakia** (#13, 1½hr.) in the more rugged part of the island. Hikes #12 and 13 both bring you back to the main road. From **Steni Vala,** hike #10 (1hr.) takes you past **Agios Petros beach** to **Isomata** and then to the main road. From Isomata, hike #9 (45min.) winds its way down to **Leftos beach.** Far north, past Ag. Georgios, in Kastanorema, a dirt road leads to the #11 trailhead (1hr.), to **Agios Dimitrios beach.**

◪ DAYTRIPS FROM PATITIRI

▣HORA Χώρα

Buses run from Patitiri (10min.; every hr. 9am-3:20pm, 2 per hr. 7pm-midnight; €1). Schedules are posted at each bus stop. Round-trip taxi €10.

Set high on a hill to ward off pirates, Hora, also called "Old Town" or "Paleo Alonnisos," welcomes visitors looking for the charm that Patitiri lacks. When settlers first came to Alonnisos, they performed a goat sacrifice, cutting the animal into pieces, and placed the pieces of meat at potential building locations. Over subsequent days, if the meat had kept, they concluded that the spot was prime for building, sheltered from the sun, pests, and other elements. With its quiet, crooked alleys that open suddenly onto incredible vistas of the island and wind their way into the dusty hills, Hora is evidence of the success of this system. Tiny 12th-century **Christ Church,** on the left fork from the bus stop, is run by Father Gregorias, the village priest and a legend in the area.

Four easy hiking trails lead from the center of Hora. A short walk along the main road headed toward Patitiri will bring you to the trail to **Vrisitsa** (#3, 1km, 30min.). This miniature beach lies in a secluded cove that seems to smile up at you as you descend to its sandy shore. The trail to **Mikros Mourtias** (#1, 1.5km, 45min.) winds down the hill through the surrounding green trees, offering a fantastic view as it heads to the water. Beginning at the bus stop, walk through town, past the church, and up the stairs to a street lined with cafes. Turn left just before the street ends and walk down the steps of a narrow side street to the trailhead. Mikros Mourtias is a small, quiet beach with perfectly shaped skipping stones. A steeper climb to **Kalovoulos** (#2, 1.5km, 45min.) will bring you to one of the highest points on the island. To reach the path, continue on the main road past the bus stop; it will be on the left. As you start back on the main road to Patitiri, the trail **Patitiri** (#4, 1.5km, 35min.) is a pleasant stroll that connects the Old and New Towns.

If you choose to stay in Hora, bright and spacious **Hiliadromia ❹**, above the gift shop behind the church, has beautiful wood-accented rooms with stone floors, tiled bath, air-conditioning, TV, fridge, and a fantastic balcony view. (☎65 814. Doubles €50-75; studios with kitchen €55-80.) Hora is home to a variety of quaint cafes and tavernas, some on beautiful overlooks. **To Aloni ❷**, at the base of an old windmill to the right of the bus stop, serves Greek food on tables with views of the island's western coast. (☎65 550. Moussaka €5.50. Entrees €6-7.50. Open daily 11am-12:30am.) The oddly named **Rocks ❷**, in the upper part of town, can be reached by climbing the stairs next to Hiliadromia. Greek standbys, including a terrific grilled vegetable plate (€5), are served in its cobblestoned outdoor seating area. (☎65 424. Entrees €6-9. Open daily 6pm-12:30am.)

NATIONAL MARINE PARK

The park islands are accessible by specially licensed boats. Most trips, sold along the Patitiri harborfront, are all-inclusive daytrips; a typical trip departs from the Patitiri dock around 10am, makes stops on 2 or more islands, visits the monastery on Kyra Panagia, and returns around 6pm. Ikos Travel, across from the dock, can assist with arrangements and info. (☎65 620. Open daily 9am-2pm and 4-11pm.) Special hiking and stargazing trips are available in May-June and Sept. €35-40.

Surrounding Alonnisos are the 25 ecologically protected islets of the National Marine Park. The largest are Peristera, Skantzoura, Piperi, Kyra Panagia, Jura, and Psatnoura. Psatnoura, Kyra Panagia, and Skantzoura are owned by nearby Mt. Athos (p. 302) and are used in part for grazing goats. Visiting Jura and Piperi is forbidden in an effort to protect their rare species, including the Mediterranean monk seal. Unless you're an MOm official (p. 78), forget about seeing the seals, but you can watch a documentary and grab a "Save the Seals" poster from the gallery in MOm's headquarters across from the dock in Patitiri. (☎66 350, Athens headquarters 21052 22 888; www.mom.gr. Open June-Oct. daily 10am-midnight.)

SKYROS Σκύρος

Skyros is dominated by two forces—modern tourism and local tradition—that are as diametrically opposed as the terrain found on each side of the island. But while the barren landscape of the south and the green hills of the north will always be separate, the two modes of Skyrian life are beginning to coexist. Preserving the island's folkways has been recognized as an important priority and is a draw for travelers weary of tourist-infested islands. The trend promises to continue, as there is no longer a ferry link to Skyros from the other Sporades. Most visitors here are in the market for more than just a beach-and-bar tour.

SKYROS TOWN ☎22220

Skyros Town—or Horio ("the village") to locals—stands out in bright white contrast to the greens, yellows, and browns of the hills that surround it. Beyond the tavernas, cafes, and bars are the features that give the island its distinctive, almost other-worldly charm. The characteristically small Skyrian houses were built between the 11th and 12th centuries. They owe their compact size to an effort to build the village so that all the homes would be out of view of marauding pirates. Among this maze of whitewashed houses, old men sew sandals by porchlight late into the evening and women embroider patterns they learned from those pesky pirates. During the three-week-long Carnival, just before Lent, the town erupts into a truly wild festival.

TRANSPORTATION. The airport (☎91 625), 20km from Skyros Town, has **flights** to Athens (35min., 2 per week, €33) and Thessaloniki (45min., 3 per week, €57). Take a cab (€11) to get there. No ferries or hydrofoils run to the other Spo-rades, making Skyros a difficult destination to reach on an island-hopping tour. The ferry to Skyros arrives in Linaria, the tiny western port; a **bus** to Skyros Town (the first stop) picks up when ferries arrive (15min., 5 per day, €1) and leaves Sky-ros Town 1hr. before ferry departures. The best way to get to Skyros is to take the bus from Terminal B in Athens to Kimi, Evia (3½hr., 2 per day, €10), then the **ferry** (☎22 020) from Kimi (1¾hr., 2 per day, €8.30). Ask for the bus that goes to the ferry dock, as the bus going to the town of Kimi will bring you to a station that is 5km from the dock. If you land in Kimi proper, take a **taxi** or walk down the long road, following signs for the port. Another bus runs to Molos (10min., 6 per day, €1). Buses stop in Skyros Town at the base of Agoras, the town's backbone road. Schedules change often, so call for times; current schedules are posted at the bus stop. **Taxis** (☎91 666) wait by the central plateia or the bus stop, and usually are available only in the morning. **Pegasus Rent A Car** runs out of Skyros Travel, and rents cars (€40-65 per day) with 24hr. pick-up and delivery. For **moped rentals** (€10-15 per day), look for the sign that points right off Agoras, after Skyros Travel.

ORIENTATION AND PRACTICAL INFORMATION. Agoras runs uphill from the bus stop, passing shops, pharmacies, bars, and restaurants along its way through Skyros Town. Maze-like streets extend outward along the hillsides, and buildings are numbered counterintuitively. Few streets are named, so when venturing off Agoras, pick out landmarks. At the far end of town, looking out across the sea, is **Plateia Rupert Brooke**, dedicated to British poet Brooke and to "immortal poetry." You can reach Pl. Rupert Brooke by walking up Agoras through town until it forks left at Kalypso Bar, then heading left along the wall and walking up until you reach a sign pointing to "Mouseio/ Museum." Veer right and follow the stairs built into the narrow street to the plateia. At Pl. Rupert Brooke, the stairs to the right pass the Archaeo-logical Museum on a 15min. descent to the beach; another set straight ahead leads to the Faltaits Museum.

Skyros Travel, past the central plateia on the left of Agoras walking away from the bus station, sells

Olympic Airways tickets, rents cars, organizes bus and boat excursions, and helps find rooms. Their port office in Linaria opens when ferries arrive. (☎91 600; www.skyrostravel.com. Open daily 9am-2pm and 7-10pm.) You can buy ferry tickets at the **Skyros Shipping Company,** past the plateia on the right, before Skyros Travel. (☎92 164. Open daily 9am-1pm and 7-11pm.) The **National Bank,** past the central plateia on the left, has a **24hr. ATM.** (☎91 802. Open M-Th 8am-2:30pm.) The **police** station is beyond Nefeli opposite the gas station. (☎91 274. Open 24hr., but the small staff may be away on another call.) A **pharmacy** is across from the bank (☎91 617; open M-F 8:30am-1pm and 6:30-10pm) and on the right past Skyros Travel (☎91 111; open daily 9am-2pm and 6pm-1am). The **hospital** (☎92 222) is just out of town behind Hotel Nefeli. To find **Internet** access, walk past the plateia on Agoras until you see **Planet** on the right. (☎92 802. €3 per hr. Open daily 9am-3:30pm and 6pm-12:30am.) To get to the **OTE,** turn right at Skyros Travel, walk to the end of the road, and take another right. (☎91 399. Open M-F 7:30am-1:30pm.) The **post office** is on the far side of the plateia from Agoras and offers **Poste Restante.** (☎91 208. Open M-F 7:30am-2pm.) **Postal Code:** 34007.

ACCOMMODATIONS AND FOOD. Coming to Skyros and staying in a hotel is like coming to Greece to swim in a pool. For the real experience you've got to stay in a **domatio,** such as one of those offered by the old women at the bus stop. Thick-walled, one-room Skyrian houses are treasure troves, brimming with ceramics, Italian linens, icons, embroidery, metalwork, and fine china bought from pirates who looted the Mediterranean. Expect to pay €15-45 for a room; always bargain, and look carefully for landmarks and house numbers, as it's easy to lose your way in the maze of streets. If you don't feel like searching for a room, try **Hotel Elena ❸,** on the first right off of Agoras heading uphill from the bus stop. The clean and comfortable rooms have tiled bath, air-conditioning, TV, and fridge; some have balcony. (☎91 738. Singles €30-40; doubles €35-55; triples €55-65.)

Skyros's excellent food perfectly satiates after-swim hunger. Look for the light-green chairs outside splendid **O Pappou Kai Ego ❷** (Grandpa and Me), on the right immediately after the sharp bend in Agoras. Known in town as "Pappou's," this restaurant serves a delicious "chicken o Pappous" floating in cream sauce over rice (€7.50), a tender nanny goat au lemon (€7), and flaming meatballs with ouzo that are just really cool to see brought to the table. (☎93 200. Entrees €5-9.50. Open daily 7pm-1am. AmEx/MC/V.) Unassuming **To Metopo ❷,** on the left heading into town from the bus stop, is a hangout for Skyrian men looking for a good meal and conversation. (☎93 515. Entrees €6-8. Open daily 1-4:30pm and 7pm-1am.) Past the central plateia on the right, **O Pantelis ❶** (Ο Παντελης) prepares tasty souvlaki with potatoes (€1) and gyros. (☎92 225. Open daily 6pm-2am.)

SIGHTS AND NIGHTLIFE. Don't miss the **Faltaits Museum,** just past Pl. Rupert Brooke. The wonderfully varied private collection of Skyrian ethnologist Manos Faltaits is housed in the frozen-in-time ancestral home of the Faltaits family, one of the first large homes to be built after fears of pirate raids had subsided. The museum collection encompasses folklore items, book collections, traditional costumes, sculptures, and paintings. The vibrant mix of ancient and modern exhibits, at once respectful and daring, preserves the essence of Skyrian culture. Tours (available in English) take you step-by-step through the collection, offering invaluable insight into the collection and even into the nature of the town itself. Conferences and cultural activities are held here throughout the year, including a **theater and dance festival** in late July and August; ask the staff for dates and times. (☎91 232. Open daily 10am-2pm and 6-9pm. Admission and basic tour €2, comprehensive historical tour €5.) Down the stairs to the right of Pl. Rupert Brooke is the **Archaeological Museum,** with a modest collection of pottery, tools, clay figurines, and jewelry. (☎91 327. Open Tu-Su 8:30am-3pm. €2, seniors €1, students free.) Both museums have rooms decorated like traditional Skyrian homes, but if you decide to venture out onto the village's labyrinthine streets, it's perfectly acceptable to knock on a door or two and ask to see the real thing. At the top of the hill on the way to Pl. Rupert Brooke before descending to the plateia, a sign points the way up steps to the **Monastery of Agios Georgios** and the **castle.** Both are closed, but the climb yields a nice view of Molos and the sea coast. Closer to the beaten path, on Agoras after going left at Kalypso, is the "upper village," a stronghold of island tradition. Jewelry, sandals, and other Skyrian items are crafted and sold in its several shops. The museum shop, **Argo,** also can be found here, near Kalypso on the left. (☎92 707. Open daily 9:30am-1:30pm and 6:30-10:30pm.) The shop's proprietor, Niko Sikkes, also leads walking tours of the island.

The central plateia is the heart of nighttime action, surrounded by crowded bars that keep the music loud and the drinks strong. **Kata Lathos,** across from the central plateia on Agoras, has a young, fun atmosphere, with a friendly English-speaking staff and a rooftop patio. (☎91 671. Beer €2.50-3. Mixed drinks €4.50-5.50. Open daily 9am-3pm and 6pm-3am.) To the left of Kata Lathos is the equally popular **Iroön.** (Open daily 8am-late.) **Kalypso Bar,** at the top of Agoras past Pappou's, has a calmer scene, as people gather to chat and sip a nightcap after a tasty Skyrian meal. (☎92 160. Beer €2.50. Mixed drinks €5-6. Open May-Oct.)

🄲 BEACHES. Standing in Skyros's pirate-proof streets, it's easy to forget how close you are to the water. A pleasant, sandy beach stretches below the town, through the villages of **Magazia** and **Molos,** and continues around the point. Head down the stairs after the Archaeological Museum and follow the road leading to the left. The local nude beach, ironically named **Tou Papa to Homa** ("The Sands of the Priest"), remains clean and uncrowded, just south of the local beach. Walk 10-12min. to the right along the seaside road at the bottom of the steps to reach a narrow, slippery dirt path lined with spiky plants. It leads downhill along a wire fence—be careful, as the last 4m is especially steep. From here, you'll have a beautiful view of the **Southern Mountain,** famous in local literature for its hourly color changes in the slanting island light. Locals recommend **Pefkos,** tucked into a cove up the coast from Linaria and accessible by taxi. Barren beaches and **Rupert Brooke's grave,** on the southern portion of the island, are accessible only by dusty paths or boat. Buses from Linaria to Skyros Town will stop at the beaches of **Aherounis,** on the western coast, and small **Mialos,** on the east, if you ask the driver in advance. Boats explore the former pirate grottoes at **Spillies,** on the southeastern coast, and **Sarakino Island,** one of the largest pirate centers in the Aegean. If you keep your eyes peeled, you may see one of the rare, wild **Skyrian ponies.**

CYCLADES
Κυκλάδες

Sun-drenched white houses, winding stone streets, and trellis-covered tavernas define the Cycladic islands as a whole, but subtle quirks make each island distinct. Orange and black sands coat the shoreline of Santorini, rocky cliffs shape arid Sifnos, and celebrated archaeological sites testify to the mythical and historical legends surrounding Delos. Naxos and Paros offer travelers peaceful mountains and villages, Milos's coast is spectacularly unusual with its caverns and deeply colored sand, and notorious party spots Ios and Mykonos uncork some of wildest nightlife on earth. The Little Cyclades and islands like Serifos, closest to Athens, are blissfully under-touristed, populated only by locals and a smattering of Greek vacationers. Visitors to any island, however, can be sure to encounter large quantities of unadulterated local flavor, surrounded by the ever-present cerulean sea.

SUGGESTED ITINERARIES: CYCLADES

FIVE DAYS Start your trip with a healthy dose of hedonism on **Mykonos** (p. 370), where the drinks are strong and the beaches are nude. Afterwards, a couple of days trekking through the delightful churches and villages hidden in **Naxos's** (p. 383) vast olive groves will clear your head. As you stretch out on **Santorini** (p. 416), thank an ancient volcanic blast for covering the island's beaches with distinctive black sand.

TWO WEEKS From **Tinos's** (p. 365) busy harbor, set sail for **Mykonos** (p. 370), whose delights are literally intoxicating. Take a daytrip to sacred **Delos** (p. 378) before exploring **Naxos's** caves and ruins. When you're ready to get back to the party, go to **Ios** (p. 409), where you'll be surrounded by as much alcohol as water. Soak up the sun on **Santorini's** beaches (p. 416), then head to ancient **Akrotiri's** (p. 422) lava-preserved streets.

ANDROS Άνδρος

The second-largest Cycladic island, Andros is a weekend destination for Greece's wealthy ship captains, many of whose families originated here. In an attempt to keep their hideaway unspoiled, the residents have restricted hydrofoil access to the island. Once you make it onto Andros, you'll understand why: the drive from the ferry landing at Gavrio to Andros Town yields magnificent panoramas of the island's beloved beaches. Towns are spread through Andros's mountain ranges, and narrow roads weave around their peaks and valleys down to the coast below. Stone walls outline green and purple fields, and the island's sandy beaches glow in solitude beneath the sun, each more breathtaking than the last. Though Athenians crowd in on the weekends, Andros generally remains a serene escape for international tourists who delight in untrammeled ground and quiet nights.

BATSI Μπατσί ☎ 22820

Climbing its way up the mountainside above an expansive sandy beach, Batsi is the tourist capital of Andros, with the liveliest nightlife and a wide variety of food

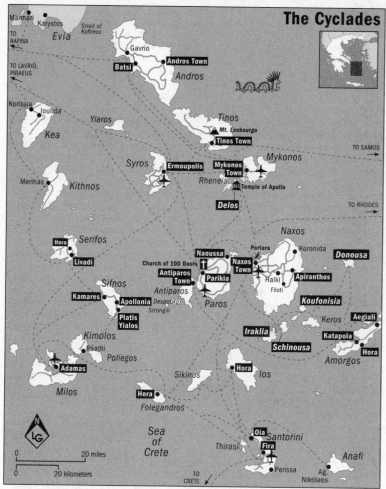

The Cyclades

and accommodation options. Visitors stroll the waterfront by night, pausing for a drink at a *kafeneion* or dancing away the hours in a club.

🖪📶 **TRANSPORTATION AND PRACTICAL INFORMATION.** All ferries to the island arrive in Gavrio, where a bus immediately picks up passengers going to Batsi and Andros Town. If you miss the bus, a taxi will take you to Batsi for €6. From Gavrio, **ferries** sail to Mykonos (2½hr., 4-5 per day, €9.50), Rafina (2hr., 4-6 per day, €9.10), and Tinos (2hr., 4-5 per day, €7.20). The bus stops by the town's long sandy beach in front of Dino's Bikes and in the small central plateia, where the bus schedules are posted. **Buses** (☎22 316) pass through Batsi on their way to Andros Town (45min.; M-F 8 per day 7:30am-9:45pm, Sa-Su 6 per day 10am-9:45pm; €3) and Gavrio (15min., 5-7 per day 9am-8:15pm, €1.50). **Taxis** (☎41 081), available 24hr., line up just before the main plateia. Check schedules and prices in Batsi at **Colours Travel,** on the right side of the plateia facing inland. The agency provides a free tourist info booklet and map, books ferry tickets, **rents cars** (€25-60 per day), and gives helpful advice about hiking on Andros. (☎41 252. Open daily 9am-3pm and 6-11pm.) **Taxi boats** dock at the end of Batsi's wharf and go to Golden beach (round-trip €13). Head to **Dino's Rent a Bike,** on the waterfront road with the huge sign, where the friendly staff will help you learn to ride a **moped** before you rent one. (☎41 003. Mopeds from €16. Helmet and insurance included. Open daily 9am-1:30pm and 5:30-10pm.)

If you want to book tickets and accommodations or search for tours while in Gavrio, **Hellas Ferries,** across from the ferry dock, can meet your needs. (Open daily 8am-11pm.) Heading up the hill past the plateia, the **National Bank** has a **24hr. ATM** and offers **currency exchange.** (☎41 400. Open M-F 8:30am-1pm.) To reach **Psitos Laundry,** walk up the stairs past Taverna Stamatis and Villa Lyra until you come to a paved road; it's 10m on the left. (☎41 246. Wash and dry €3 per kg. Open daily 9am-2pm and 6-10pm.) In an **emergency,** call the **police** (☎41 204) or the **medical center** in Andros Town (☎22 222 or 23 333). To the left of the beach, behind a playground, is a small **medical office;** signs point the way. (☎41 326. Doctor available 9am-1pm.) A **pharmacy** is all the way up the hill, past the National Bank. (☎41 541. Open M-Sa 9am-1:30pm and 6:30-8:30pm.) There is no Internet access in Batsi. **Apomero Cafe,** which has **Internet** access, is a 5min. walk from the Gavrio port, on an uphill road to the right. (☎71 681. €3.50 per hr. Open daily 10am-3pm and 5pm-3am.) The **post office** is between Andros Travel and Dino's Rent a Bike. (☎41 443. Open M-F 7:30am-2:30pm.) **Postal Code:** 84503.

ACCOMMODATIONS AND FOOD. Accommodations generally are easier to find in Batsi than elsewhere on the island, as the plentiful **domatia** here tend to be nicer than hotels for a comparable or lesser price. Expect to pay €20-30 per person per night (lower if you bargain well). Walk to the end of the waterfront with the water on your right to find ⚑ **Villa Lyra ❷,** the best accommodation value in town. Panayiotis Barous, the friendly owner, most likely will be at the souvenir shop he runs, next to the National Bank. The pleasant, inexpensive rooms include TV, air-conditioning, fridge, kitchen, bath, and balcony. (☎41 432. Singles €20-30; doubles and triples €25-40. MC/V.) **Villa Aegeo ❹** is up four flights of stairs to the right of Batsi Gold; past the tree, look for the small sign on the side of the building. The airy rooms have TV, air-conditioning, bath, fridge, kitchenette, and balcony. Singles may not be available during high season. Call ahead for someone to meet you at the bus stop. (☎41 327. Singles €40; doubles €55; triples €65.) **Hotel Chryssi Akti ❹** is easy to spot, directly across from the beach. Guests relax by the pool or laze around in plush, spotless rooms complete with TV, fridge, air-conditioning, bath, and waterfront view. (☎41 236; www.hotel-chryssiakti.gr. Breakfast €4.50. Singles €45-60; doubles €55-73; triples €65-87; quads €77-115. MC/V.) If you're not attached to staying in Batsi itself, you can camp at **Andros Camping ❶,** 300m from Gavrio (follow the directional arrows). This remote campground has a pool, clean bathrooms with showers, common kitchen, mini-mart, and laundry. (☎71 444. Open Apr.-Oct. €5 per person, €3.50 per tent. Tent rental €10-15.)

To find ⚑ **Restaurant Sirocco ❷,** climb to the top of the stairs that begin on the left of the Chinese restaurant; two palm trees mark the bottom. Congenial owner Louie, who worked in Manhattan for 11 years, prepares unbelievably delicious meals out of his grandparents' former home. The Chef's Special (€11) is a divine steak filet covered with edam cheese, onions, and a burnt crust of mayonnaise, with a side of tangy tabasco sauce. Don't miss the bread (€1.50)—it's homemade. (☎41 023. Entrees €6-11. Open daily 6:30pm-midnight.) **Villy's Place ❶,** in the plateia across from the bus stop, is a perfect spot to grab a sandwich (from €2.50) to bring to the beach. (☎41 025. June-Aug. Open

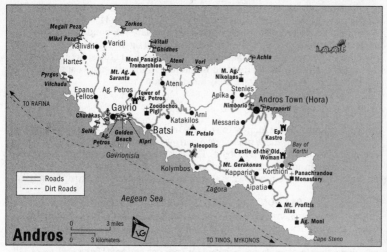

Andros

Roads
Dirt Roads

0   3 miles
0   3 kilometers

Aegean Sea

TO RAFINA

TO TINOS, MYKONOS

TO TINOS, MYKONOS

CYCLADES

24hr.) A **fruit market** is under Capriccio Music Bar on the right side of the waterfront facing inland. (☎42 333. Open daily 8am-10:30pm.)

◐◑ SIGHTS AND BEACHES. With its many ruins and first-rate beaches, Andros is best explored by moped or car. Near the back corner of the wharf's plateia, a gradual outdoor stairway leads upward through two stone walls and along the flowing waters of the town's **natural spring.** The trees, vines, and flowers lining the walls, along with the dim lighting, make this a lovely, romantic area for an evening stroll. The bus from Batsi can drop you off at the ancient capital of **Paleopolis,** where you can explore the remains of an ancient theater, stadium, and small stone houses. A 1hr. hike or faster taxi ride (€6) north of Gavrio will bring you to the stone **Tower of Agios Petros,** which provides superb views of the harbor below. If you crawl inside the bottom of the tower, built in the 4th century BC, you can gaze up at its interior where the floors have long since collapsed. The tower's original purpose remains unclear, but most believe that it once served as a *friktoria*—a building used to send torch signals. A bus from Gavrio (€3) runs twice per day to the **Bay of Korthi,** the site of a charming village and Andros's finest swimming. Korthi is also home to the 30 watermills that run alongside the **Dipotamata** (Twin River) as well as the remnants of the impressive **Castle of the Old Woman,** which once protected its inhabitants from attacking forces.

The bar at **Golden beach** (beer €2.50-4), accessible by water taxi (round-trip €13), taxi (round-trip €8, arrange a pick-up time), or foot (45min.), is a popular spot for daytime partying. The beach also offers a number of water sports. **Kipri,** 400m back on the road toward Batsi, is more low-key. Following the road toward Gavrio, you'll find **Agios Petros,** another secluded stretch of sand. You also can access the peaceful beach of **Vitali,** which sits in a small protected cove 26km north of Gavrio, by private vehicle. If you continue along the river bank in the back left corner of the beach for 200m, you'll find a cave with beautiful stalagmites.

☙ NIGHTLIFE. In the evening, the plateia along Batsi's wharf becomes the center of activity. At **Skala Music Cafe,** next to the taxi stand, an indoor bar serves a two-tiered seating area covered in greenery. (☎41 656. Mixed drinks €9. Beer €6. Open daily 9am-4am.) Up the stairs just past the plateia, **Capriccio Music Bar's**

classy outdoor patio is a great spot to people-watch while having a drink. The party moves to the indoor dance floor around midnight. (☎41 770. Happy hour 7-9pm. Beer €4. Mixed drinks €9. Open daily 9am-late.) Around 1am, follow the locals to the clubs in the back of the plateia, behind the red glow of Cafe Avra, to see how Andros really parties. **Nameless** creates an upbeat atmosphere with a large dance floor, friendly bartenders, and loud mix of mainstream beats. (☎41 698. Beer €6. Mixed drinks €7. Open daily midnight-late.)

ANDROS TOWN ☎22820

Known by locals as Hora, Andros Town is the most gorgeous settlement on the island. A wide, cobbled main street runs along a narrow peninsula, with cafes giving way to colorful homes and rocky outcroppings. Expanses of sandy beach lie directly on either side of the peninsula. Because the accommodations may be prohibitively expensive for budget travelers, Andros Town is also an ideal destination for a daytrip from Batsi.

⌗ TRANSPORTATION AND PRACTICAL INFORMATION. The **bus** leaving Andros Town for Gavrio (1hr., 5-7 per day 8:15am-7:30pm, €3) via Batsi (45min., €2.50) runs out of a depot by the main plateia where **taxis** (☎22 171) wait. A schedule is posted in the outdoor waiting area. **Riva,** on the left by Faros Studios, all the way down the street, **rents mopeds** from €15 per day and **boats** from €80. (☎24 412. Open daily 8am-10pm.)

From the main plateia near the bus station, a pedestrian-only **main street** runs past cafes, boutiques, and banks, ending in **Plateia Kairis.** A 5min. walk past the arch at the far end of Pl. Kairis brings you to the outer edge of town, marked by a large plateia, a statue, and a close-up view of the medieval fortress. **Andros Island Travel,** across from the bank, can book tickets, find rooms, and plan excursions. (☎29 220. Open M-Sa 8:30am-9pm, Su 9:30am-9pm.) You can buy **ferry tickets** at the **Blue Star** office, on the left before Pl. Kairis. (☎22 257. Open daily 9am-2pm and 7-9pm.) **Alpha Bank,** G. Ebirikos 49, with a **24hr. ATM** and **currency exchange,** is down the street on the right as you turn right and walk toward the water. (☎23 900. Open M-Th 8am-2:30pm, F 8am-2pm.) The **police station,** G. Ebirikos 2, is on the inland end of the main street to the left. (☎22 300. Open 24hr.) One of several **pharmacies** along the main street sits right across from the main plateia at G. Ebirikos 29. (☎23 203. Open daily 8am-3pm and 6-11pm.) In **medical emergencies,** dial ☎22 222, or visit the **health center** in the back right corner of the main plateia facing away from G. Ebirikos. The **OTE** is across from the plateia. (☎22 099. Open M-F 7:30am-2:30pm.) **E-waves Internet Cafe,** on the left side of the main street before Pl. Kairis, has **Internet** access upstairs from its cafe-bar. (☎29 129. €3 per hr. Open daily 9am-2am.) The **post office,** G. Ebirikos 14, is inland from the plateia on the main street. (☎22 260. Open M-F 7:30am-2pm.) **Postal Code:** 84500.

⌂ ACCOMMODATIONS AND FOOD. If you visit in high season be prepared to spend big, though accommodations still aren't cheap the rest of the year; **domatia** are the best options (rooms €35-50, in low season €25-35). The **tourist information kiosk** in the main plateia has a list of names and numbers. (☎25 162. Open 8am-11pm.) **Karaoulanis Rooms ❸** is down the street opposite Alpha Bank and down the stairs on the right (look for the arrow), on the left corner of Nimborio beach facing inland. It rents spacious rooms and studios with kitchen, bath, air-conditioning, and TV. Ask Yannis at Riva for more info. (☎69744 60 330. www.androsrooms.gr. Doubles €30-70; studios €50-120.) **Hotel Niki ❹** (Νικη), just before Pl. Kairis next to the Navy Story Cafe, has six nicely decorated rooms with TV, air-conditioning, fridge, bath, and balcony. (☎/fax 29 155. Doubles €65-90; triples €90-110.)

On the way to Pl. Kairis, a number of small family-owned cafes and restaurants serve *mezedes*, milkshakes, and pizza. For a delicious traditional meal, try ▨**Parea ❷** (Παρεα), in the corner of Pl. Kairis, overlooking Paraporti beach. The house specialty is *furtalia* (€3), a delicious omelette-like dish that incorporates zucchini and sausage. (☎23 721. Cover €1. Entrees €5-7. Open daily noon-1am. MC/V.) **Ononas ❸**, on the edge of Nimborio beach across from Karaoulannis Rooms, serves fresh seafood (fried squid €9) and imaginative appetizers like zucchini flowers stuffed with local cheese (€4). (☎23 577. Entrees €7-9. Open daily noon-4pm and 7:30pm-12:30am.) For savory and sweet crepes, head to **Sofrano Kreperi ❶** (Σοφρανο) on the left, across from Alpha Bank. (☎24 152. Crepes from €2.70. Open daily 7am-3pm and 6pm-2am.)

◨◪ **SIGHTS AND BEACHES.** Andros Town's museums go above and beyond the usual offerings of small island towns. The **Archaeological Museum,** a large white building on the left as you enter Pl. Kairis, displays huge *pithoi* (storage jars) from the Geometric-era village of Zagora. The collection includes a marvelous marble statue of Hermes, whose discovery prompted King Otto's father Ludwig to make a special trip to Greece. (☎23 664. Open Tu-Su 8:30am-3pm. €3, students and seniors €2, EU students free.) Turn down the lane to the left upon exiting, and travel down four small sets of stairs (following the arrows on the left wall) to find the permanent wing of the **Museum of Contemporary Art.** Its exhibits display selections of modern art by Greek and foreign artists, including works by 20th-century Greek sculptor Michael Tombros. The weird noises emanating from downstairs are part of an **electromagnetic art** installation, which uses electromagnets to strike metal rods against plastic string, creating a fun-to-watch musical experiment. The museum's new wing is located two sets of steps farther down on the right, and houses three levels of contemporary art that circulates every summer. (☎22 444. Open June-Sept. M and W-Sa 10am-2pm and 6-8pm; Tu and Su 10am-2pm; Oct.-May M and Sa-Su 10am-2pm. €6, students €3, seniors and children under 12 free.) Follow the main road past Pl. Kairis, turn left at the dead end, and continue down Michael S. Polemi to the end to reach the **Maritime Museum of Andros.** It houses models, paintings, and photographs of 19th- and 20th-century sailing vessels. (Open daily 8am-10pm. €2, seniors and under 12 free.) Past the museum is a plateia where the larger-than-life **Alfanis Nautis Statue,** honoring lost soldiers, gazes out at the humble ruins of a **Venetian castle.**

Facing Hora from the sea, **Paraporti beach** is to the left and **Nimborio beach** is to the right. To reach Paraporti's expansive sands, take the steps down from Pl. Kairis past Heaven Rock Cafe. Nimborio, the more popular and more developed beach, is most easily accessed via the street that leads down to the water across from Alpha Bank. **Achla,** north of town, is considered one of Europe's most beautiful beaches, but is accessible only by moped or fishing boat. Just north of Achla lies **Vori,** where you can swim among shipwrecks; locals warn to be careful of sharp metal in the wreckage. Those yearning to see more secluded spots—the many rivers, waterfalls, and monasteries of the island's interior—should inquire at Andros Travel. A beautiful hiking trail originates in **Apika,** 6km north of Andros Town, and leads past **Sariza Springs** to the village of **Stenies.** This small town is home to the largest **waterwheel** in the Balkans and is the site of an old spaghetti factory that was burned down accidentally in 1916 by a Greek priest.

TINOS Τήνος

Marked by towering Mount Exobourgo, Tinos island consists of a tourist-oriented harbor town and a number of remote villages that seem untouched by commercialism. Despite a bustling nightlife, Tinos's main attraction remains the Panagia Evangelistria Church, the largest contemporary shrine of the Greek Orthodox religion. The cool, often unruly breezes that envelop the island explain why the ancient Greeks believed Tinos to be the home of Aeolus, the god of wind.

TINOS TOWN   ☎ 22830

Tinos Town made history when, on August 15, 1940, an Italian submarine torpedoed the Greek cruiser *Elli* as it docked at the town's harbor for the observance of the Feast of the Assumption of the Virgin Mary. Mussolini declared war two months later. Although Tinos since has faded from the international political map, it now plays a dual role as a mecca for both pilgrims and tourists.

⌐ TRANSPORTATION. Ferry schedules vary, so check at the **port authority booth** (☎ 22 220) in the central port or at one of the many **Blue Star ticket offices** (☎ 24 241) along the waterfront. The largest one is directly across from the buses. **Ferries** run to: Andros (2hr.; M-Th 9:15am, 2:30pm; F-Sa 11:30am, 2:30pm; Su 2:30pm; €7.20); Mykonos (30min.; M-Sa 4 per day 9:30am-9pm, Su 2 per day; €4.50); Paros (1hr.; M, W-Th, Sa 9:30am, 5:30pm; Tu, F, Su 9:30am; €10); Piraeus (5½hr., 3pm, €23.20); Rafina (4hr., 2 per day, €15); Syros (20min., 3pm, €5). The **Hellas Ferries office** next door has schedules and tickets for **Flying Dolphins** to Mykonos (15min.; M and W-Su 10:40am; €8), Piraeus (3hr.: M-W 10:40am, 9:15pm; Th 9:15pm: €38.20), and Syros (20min.; M and W-Su 10:40am; €8). There are three ferry ports in Tinos (see below), so ask from where you're leaving when buying tickets. From the central port, **buses** run to: Agios Fokas (5min., 4 per day 11am-5:30pm, €1); Kalloni (45min.; 6:45am, 12:15, 3:45pm; €2.20); Kionia (7min., 11 per day 8am-7:30pm, €1) Skalados (20min.; M 6:45am, 1pm; €1.60); Steni (30min., 6 per day 6:45am-6pm, €1.30); Porto (7 per day 8am-7pm, €1); Pyrgos (45min., 4 per day 6:30am-6pm, €3). A schedule is posted at the KTEL ticket agency across from the central port, next to a Blue Star ticket office. (☎ 22 440. Open daily 8am-9:30pm.) **Taxis** are one block past the waterfront base of Evangelistrias, with the water on your right. (☎ 22 470. Available 6am-1:30am.) For **car and moped rental**, try **Vidalis,** which also has free maps, at one of its several waterfront locations. (☎ 23 400. Mopeds €16-20. Cars €30-45. Open daily 9am-9pm.)

▰▰ ORIENTATION AND PRACTICAL INFORMATION. The town's central port, across from the bus depot, is the docking point for many ferries. Catamarans and hydrofoils dock at the port to the left, facing inland. The newest port, farther to the left around the waterfront, past a playground, is equally trafficked. Activity centers on wide **Megalochares** (you can see the church at the top) and parallel, pedestrian **Evangelistrias** (known as "Bazaar") to the right, facing inland. Among the restaurants near the base of Megalochares, an alley leads away from the central port, through a small plateia with a dolphin statue, to a handful of restaurants and Tinos's cafes and clubs. Many domatia are off Evangelistrias and **Zanaki Alavanou,** on the right of the waterfront. A map of Tinos is to the left of the central port, and most ferry offices give out free paper maps of the town and island.

The English-speaking staff at **Windmills Travel,** Kionion 2, behind the playground by the far left port, can arrange accommodations and rental cars (from €40). They also offer bus tours of the island (€12), excursions to Delos and Mykonos (10am-7pm, €20), and day-long tours (€45) around the island. (☎ 23 398. Open 9am-3pm and 6-9pm.) Banks with **currency exchange** and **24hr. ATMs** line the waterfront, including a **National Bank,** opposite the bus depot (☎ 22 328; open M-Th 8am-2pm, F 8am-1:30pm), and an **Alpha Bank** (☎ 23 608; open M-Th 8am-2:30pm, F 8am-2pm), by the post office. The **police** (☎ 22 100) share a building with the **tourist police** (☎ 23 670; open daily 8am-10pm), 5min. out of town on the road to Kionia, and can be

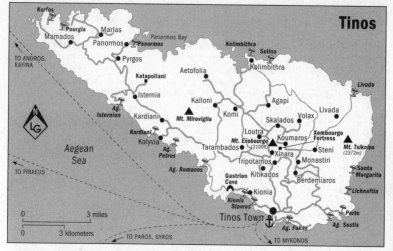

Tinos

reached by phone 24hr. There is a **pharmacy** just to the right of the base of Evange-listrias, next to a Hellas Ferries ticket office. (☎22 272. Open M-F 8am-2pm and 6-9:30pm.) There is a **medical center** (☎22 210) by Tinos Camping. The **OTE** is up Meg-alochares on the right. (☎22 499. Open M-F 7:45am-1:30pm.) The **Sybosion Cafe,** Evangelistrias 13, on the left up the stairs above a photo shop, has **Internet** access on three high-speed computers. (☎24 368. €5 per hr., min. €3. Open daily 8:30am-midnight.) The **post office,** on the right end of the waterfront, also sells phone cards. (☎22 247. Open M-F 7:30am-2pm.) **Postal Code:** 84200.

▐▘▐▘ ACCOMMODATIONS AND CAMPING. Tinos has plenty of accommoda-tions, but rooms fill up around Easter and on weekends in July and August. Family-run ▨**Nikoleta Rooms to Let ❷,** Kapodistriou 11, is on the second right off the traffic circle uphill from thev post office. Bright rooms just 100m from Agios Fokas beach include TV, air-conditioning, fridge, and balcony. Though only some rooms have bath and kitchenette, the common kitchen, garden courtyard, and laundry facilities are available. If the rooms are full, Nikoleta will be happy to help you find alternate lodging nearby. (☎24 719 or 69374 56 488. Singles €20-25; doubles €25-30; triples €35-45; quads €45-50. Reservations are recommended.) **Hermes Rooms to Let ❹,** Evangelistrias 33, midway up the road to the left with blue balconies and shutters, rents cozy rooms with a central kitchen and common baths. They also have apart-ments on Marcos Psaros with have more amenities. (☎69475 34 225. Doubles €40; triples €60.) To the left of Windmills Travel, turn left at the top of the stairs, then right at the street to find **Faros ❸,** Foskolou 2. The six rooms include bath, TV, and air-conditioning, and the common balconies have harbor views. (☎23 530, mobile 69328 00 525. Singles €35; doubles €50; triples €80. Call ahead for lower prices.) Off the traffic circle past the post office, signs point the way to **Tinos Camping ❶,** whose grounds have a kitchen, laundry, showers, cafe, and bar. Watch out for the chickens and ducks—and their droppings. (☎22 344. €7 per person, €4 per tent. Tent rental €7. 2- to 5-person bungalows €30-35, €45-47 with bath. 10% discount for stays over 4 days, 20% for 15 days or more.)

▐ FOOD. Turning into the alleyway just to the right of Mesklies and following it past the plateia with the dolphin statue, you will find **Palaia Pallada ❷** (Παλαια

Παλλαδα), on the right. The taverna, with an attractive ivy-shaded seating area, has earned its top-notch reputation by serving carefully prepared authentic favorites like grilled lamb (€7), vegetable dishes (€3-6), and pasta (€5-8). (☎23 516. Open daily noon-midnight. MC/V.) **Agkyra ❷**, an *ouzeri* located behind the playground, is popular with the locals for its fresh fish (€40-60 per kg) and traditional grilled meats (€7-10). Look for the blue tables flanked by two large trees. (☎23 016. Open daily 11am-4pm and 8am-midnight.) In the middle of the line of tavernas that starts at the base of Megalochares, **Mesklies ❸** is known for its delicious, albeit pricey, pizza (€14-17; takeout €7.50-13) and Greek salads. (☎22 151. Open daily 7am-midnight. MC/V.) For a cheaper bite to eat, head to **Sikoutris ❶** (Συκ-ουτρης), around the corner from Palaia Pallada and down the alley to the right. This souvlaki stand has cheap beer (€1.50-3) and gyros (€1.90) that are a hit with the late night crowd. (☎24 855. Open daily 5pm-3am.) **Champion Supermarket** is on the corner before the post office. (Open M-Sa 8am-9:30pm, Su 9am-2pm.)

◉ SIGHTS. In 1822 a Tiniot nun, Sister Pelagia, had a vision in which the Virgin Mary told her about an icon buried in a field. A year later, the prophesied icon was unearthed, and the imposing **Panagia Evangelistria** was built to house it. The marble church draws daily visits from those who consider it evidence of the Virgin's divine power. The relic is said to have healing powers and is credited with ridding Tinos of cholera, saving a sinking ship, and giving a blind man sight. Gifts of gold, diamonds, jewels, and countless *tamata*—plaques praising Mary's healing powers—cover the chapel. The famous **icon** sits up the red-carpeted flight of steps. More devout pilgrims will approach on hands and knees, some beginning at the red carpet at the base of the church, others as soon as they get off the boat at the port, continuing all the way up the hill. The **Well of Sanctification** is a natural spring that appeared when the icon was found. Today it flows from one of many faucets in the church between two sets of marble entrance stairs to the chapel; visitors can scoop up a bottle of it to drink or to carry as a talisman. To the right is the **mausoleum** of the Greek warship *Elli*, sunk by an Italian torpedo in 1940. (Open daily 6:30am-8:30pm. Modest dress required. Free.)

Tinos's small **Archaeological Museum**, Megalochares 35, uphill from the OTE, displays an ancient sundial, sculptures from the sanctuary of Poseidon and Amphitrite at Kionia, a 5th-century BC relief from a cemetery at Xombourgo, and a 7th-century BC relief showing Athena bursting from Zeus's head. (☎29 063. Tu-Su 8:30am-3pm. €2, students and seniors €1, EU students and children free.) Tinos is strewn with over 1000 large medieval birdhouses called **dovecotes.** They are made of intricate white lattices and are full of nesting birds, and are the island's symbol. The largest and most impressive collection of dovecotes can be found in the village of **Tarambados,** 6km from Tinos Town, accessible by bus. To explore the poorly preserved ruins of the 4th-century BC **Temple of Poseidon and Amphitrite,** near the beach, drive left along the waterfront road.

◪ BEACHES. Sun-worshippers take a page out of the religious pilgrims' book and prostrate themselves before Tinos's beautiful beaches. Facing inland at the center of town, **Agios Fokas** is on the other side of the peninsula to the right, with pebbly sand lining a shallow bay. Picturesque **Kolimbithra** is in a small cove 12km north of Tinos Town. To get there, catch the Kalloni bus at the central port and ask to be let off at Kolimbithra beach. The stretch of sand on the island's northern coast lies seductively below a few small tavernas. In the unlikely event that the beach gets crowded, walk uphill facing the sea to the right and around the peninsula to remote **Selina.** If you find yourself in the Pyrgos or Panormos bay region, continue past the harborside village of **Panormos** and down to the lovely beach. The beach of

Kionia, 3.5km from the center of town, is narrow and pebbly but still attracts a healthy crowd thanks to the frequent buses and multitude of nearby tavernas.

🎵 **NIGHTLIFE.** At night the cafes lining the street between the plateia with the dolphin statue and the playground become happening bars. **Caffe Theugatos** channels a vague atmosphere of ancient Greece, with an indoor, high-ceilinged colonnade past its sizable outdoor patio. (☎24 078. Beer €3. Mixed drinks €8. Open daily 9am-2am.) Colorful hanging bobbles and stashes of pirate booty adorn the popular **Koursaros Music Bar** (a.k.a. **Corsaire**), 10m seaward from Mesklies, on the corner. (☎23 963. Beer €2.50. Mixed drinks €5-6. Open daily 8am-4am.) Walk across the dolphin plateia past Koursaros to reach **Gur-Sas,** which morphs from cafe to bar to club as the night goes on. The touches of Arabian architecture add an exotic flair. (☎22 214. Beer €3. Mixed drinks €7-8. Open daily 8:30am-4am.) To reach Tinos's row of nightclubs, head past Sikoutris up the alleyway and turn right onto Taxiarchon. **Sibylla,** Taxiarchon 17, has a marble dance floor and a DJ who mixes Greek and Euro dance music. (Beer €4. Mixed drinks €6. Open daily 10pm-3am.) Next door, at **Volto** (Βολτο), Taxiarchon 24, clubbers dance under flashing laser lights. (Beer €4. Mixed drinks €7. Open daily 10:30pm-late.) For an unbeatable view and American and international pop music, take a taxi (€2) to **Kactus Bar,** at the base of a windmill above Tinos Town. (Beer €5-6. Mixed drinks €8. Open 10pm-7am.) Those still raring to go when the bars shut down can grab a taxi (€2) to **Paradise,** a thatched-roof "after-club." (Open 3am-9am.)

🥾 **HIKING.** The villages that ring **Mount Exobourgo** (Εξόβουργο Όρος), 14km north of Tinos Town, and the site of the Venetian Fortress **Xombourgo,** on the northeastern side of the mountain. After withstanding 11 assaults, the 13th-century capital fell to the Ottomans in 1715, becoming their last territorial gain. For a panoramic view of the entire island, drive up to the foot of the fortress itself. If you're feeling energetic, climb the mountain from the eastern foothill on a trail lined with wildflowers and brilliant orange moss. On a clear day, the peak offers a magnificent view extending as far as Santorini. At the gated entrance to Xombourgo, head left into the plateia to the little gate where the trail to the top starts. At a fork, the road detours to a church. Go straight to get to the fort. Strong winds buffet Exobourgo, causing the fort to close occasionally; stay low to avoid getting blown off balance. The hike from Tinos Town to Mt. Exobourgo takes 3-4hr.

Alternatively, the trip from Tinos Town to **Loutra** and back takes 3-4hr. and traverses much of the island's interior. Other routes, marked by wooden signposts, don't cut through all the villages. For all of them, bring food, water, comfortable shoes, and a hiking partner. Stick to the trail and be prepared for extremely high winds. Travel agents in Tinos Town have more info on the particular trails. To ascend to the villages of **Kitikados** and **Xinara,** begin by heading left behind the Panagia Evangelistria Church to unmarked **Agios Nikolaos.** Follow this road straight up and to the left, where the asphalt gives way to a broad cobblestone path that takes you past two white chapels within 45min. Past the second white chapel is a small stone bridge with an arch. Cross the bridge if you want to stop in Kitikados; if not, stay on the main trail until you reach the asphalt road where you will turn left. Continue across the road and follow the path to the right of the windmill when you see a small trail marked with a wooden sign. Once you pass the windmill, there is another trail marker on your right. Written in Greek, it points to the climb up to Mt. Exobourgo. Xinara is ahead and **Tripotamos** is behind you. You can ascend Exobourgo from here or continue 1½hr. through quiet Xinara.

To get to the village of Loutra (2hr.), follow the road through town to the church plateia and then head left to the narrow trail. This path begins your descent to the village; turn right when you hit asphalt. Continue on the paved road past Loutra to Skalados; turn right to find a nice hillside taverna. From the taverna, head up and right on a street with steps to another asphalt road. Walk to the right about 15min. until you see the blue sign pointing toward **Volax.** It's worth stopping here to meander through the narrow, low-arched streets and peek into the many basket-weaving workshops in town. Retrace your steps to the blue Volax sign and turn left onto the road. Once it has passed through Koumaros, the road turns into a stone-staired trail that will take you up the northeastern side of Mt. Exobourgo. At the foot of **Sacred Heart,** an impressive Catholic monastery, go diagonally through the plateia to the little gate on the left. The **Xombourgo fortress** is only a 20min. walk up.

▶ **DAYTRIP FROM TINOS TOWN: PYRGOS.** Surrounded by arid, intricately terraced mountainsides, Pyrgos gleams white in the midday sun. It is a center for many of the island's renowned marble sculptors, whose work is highlighted in two museums. The influence of marble seems to crop up everywhere: in streets, monuments, and in the buildings themselves. Pyrgos has evaded the crush of the island's tourists, and an unmistakable small-town charm emanates from its narrow, winding streets. Pyrgos has a variety of ways for visitors to learn more about its central occupation. The two **museums** next to the bus stop are nice introductions, displaying the works of local sculptors. The traditional building on the right houses the busts and drawings of Yannoulis Halepas (1851-1938), the town's most famous sculptor. His story is a tragic one: his mental illness led his mother to destroy all his work, believing that his creativity caused him to go mad; it was only after her death that he entered the most productive period of his life. (Museums open daily 11am-2pm and 5:30-9pm. Admission pass for both €5.) Pyrgos has been home to a **School of Fine Arts** since 1955. Walk up the stairs to the left of the graveyard to check it out; if it's closed, you still can look in the windows to see a staggering number of sculptures lining the walls. For a more hands-on experience, walk up the hill from the bus stop to reach the studio of **Michalis Saltamanikas,** who attended the School of Fine Arts. Visitors are welcome in his roomy workshop, and he's happy to demonstrate—and sell—his work. (☎31 554. Open M-Sa during the work day. Sculptures range from €20 to thousands.)

Throughout the day, locals and tourists gather for casual drinks in the cafes that line the main plateia. For an excellent lunch or dinner, try **Ta Muronia ❷,** on your left as you enter the plateia. It serves spaghetti with local sausage (€4.50) along with traditional favorites. (☎31 229. Entrees €4.50-9. Open daily noon-late.) **Taverna Eirinis ❷,** across from the bus stop, makes *furtalia* (omelette with vegetables and local sausage; €7.50)—the island specialty. (☎31 165. Entrees €5-8. Open daily 10am-2am.) Next to Taverna Eirinis, **Sodaria Cafe ❶** attracts visitors with a sweet tooth, selling homemade cookies for €10.60-14 per kg. (☎31 160. Open in summer 9am-late, in winter 9am-noon and 5-11pm.)

The **bus** from Tinos Town (45min., 4 per day 6:30am-6pm, €3) stops on the southwestern edge of Pyrgos, across from a monument to the town's war heroes. To reach the main plateia, walk up the road past the two museums; when it runs into a wall, walk to the right. Walking across to the far end of the plateia and up the steps will bring you to the (marble, of course) church of **Ag. Nikolaos,** which towers over the village. A 50m walk to the left of the church brings you to an array of sculpted memorials in the town's graveyard.

MYKONOS Μύκονος

Mykonos is known around the world as the party center of the Greek isles. Having come a long way since ancient times, when it was a mere stopping point on the way to

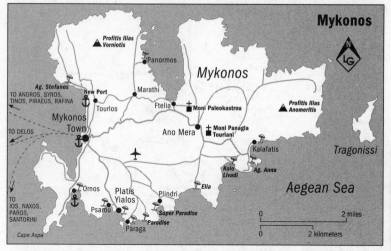

sacred Delos, Mykonos is now one of the most heavily trafficked and lusted-after tourist destinations in Greece. The island's beautiful sand beckons to hedonists of every age, and whitewashed, narrow streets are lined with shops, restaurants, nd every travel service imaginable. At sunset, the unparalleled island-wide party revs into high gear. Mykonos's gay scene, which reached its prime in the 1970s, remains alive and kicking as the island continues to be accepting in a way that most of Greece is not.

MYKONOS TOWN

☎ 22890

Mykonos Town owes its labyrinthine streets, now closed to motor traffic in the afternoon and evening, to Mediterranean pirates. The city's maze was planned expressly to disconcert and disorient marauders and now has a similar effect on tourists. Despite the massive influx of visitors, the town has resisted large hotel complexes, allowing historical churches, traditional fishing boats, basket-laden donkeys, and friendly pelicans to take center stage.

▐ TRANSPORTATION

Flights: Olympic Airways (☎22 490) flies to **Athens** (30min., 4-5 per day, €88) and **Thessaloniki** (1¼hr., 2 per week, €99). **Aegean Airlines** (☎21099 88 300) also goes to **Athens** (30min., 4 per day, €51-100) and **Thessaloniki** (1¼hr., 3 per day, €140-227). Take a taxi (€6) to the airport.

Ferries: Most boats dock at the **Old Port** to the left of the waterfront, facing inland, but occasionally they arrive at or depart from the **New Port** near Ag. Stefanos beach, 3km away. Buy tickets at the **Blue Star Ferries** ticket office (☎28 240) on the waterfront. To: **Andros** (2¼hr., M-F 2-3 per day, €9.50-11.40); **Naxos** (3hr., F 9:20pm, €9.50); **Piraeus** (6hr., 2:15pm, €25.50); **Paros** (3hr., €8.40); **Rafina** (4½hr.; M-W and Su 3 per day, F 4 per day; €17-20.40); **Syros** (2½hr., 2:15pm, €7.50); **Tinos** (35min.; M-W and Su 4 per day 1:15-4pm, Th and Sa 3 per day, F 4 per day 10:30am-2:15pm; €4.50). To get to **Santorini,** you must connect through Paros.

Flying Dolphins: Buy tickets at **Delia Travel** (☎22 322) on the waterfront. To: **Ios** (2½hr., 2:30pm, €26); **Naxos** (1hr., 1-2 per day, €16); **Paros** (1hr.; M-Tu and Th-Su 11:15am,

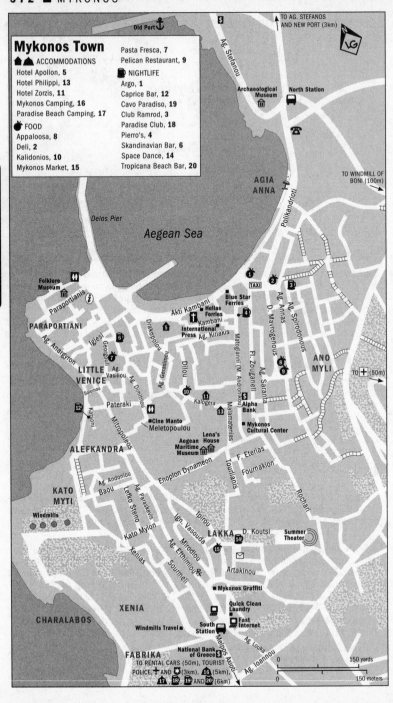

CYCLADES

Mykonos Town

■▲ ACCOMMODATIONS
Hotel Apollon, **5**
Hotel Philippi, **13**
Hotel Zorzis, **11**
Mykonos Camping, **16**
Paradise Beach Camping, **17**

🍎 FOOD
Appaloosa, **8**
Deli, **2**
Kalidonios, **10**
Mykonos Market, **15**

Pasta Fresca, **7**
Pelican Restaurant, **9**

🍸 NIGHTLIFE
Argo, **1**
Caprice Bar, **12**
Cavo Paradiso, **19**
Club Ramrod, **3**
Paradise Club, **18**
Pierro's, **4**
Skandinavian Bar, **6**
Space Dance, **14**
Tropicana Beach Bar, **20**

Old Port ⚓

TO AG. STEFANOS
AND NEW PORT (3km)

Archaeological
Museum

North Station

TO WINDMILL OF
BONI (100m)

AGIA
ANNA

Ag. Stefanou

Polikandrioti

Aegean Sea

Delos Pier

Folklore
Museum

Paraportianis

PARAPORTIANI

Ag. Anargyron

Iglesi

Georgouli

Ag. Vasiliou

LITTLE
VENICE

Solomou

Kasoni

Pateraki

ALEFKANDRA

KATO
MYTI

Windmills

CHARALABOS

FABRIKA

Drakopoulou

Ag. Gerasimou

Diliou

Ag. Dimitriou

Ag. Kiriakis

Akti Kambani

Blue Star
Ferries

Hellas
Ferries

Kambani
International
Press

TAXI

D. Mavrogenous

Ag. Annas

Ag. Spiridonous

ANO
MYLI

TO ⊹ (50m)

Matogianni (M. Andronikou)

Fl. Zouganeli

Ag. Saranta

Kalogera

Alpha
Bank

Malamatenias

Mykonos
Cultural Center

Cine Manto
Meletopoulou

Lena's
House

Aegean
Maritime
Museum

F. Eterias

Fournakion

Enoplon Dynameon

Toulianis

Rocharí

Mitropoleos

Baou

Ag. Andoniou

Lefko Steno

Ag. Paraskevis

Ipirou

Ign. Vasouda

Mirodiou

Ag. Efthimiou

LAKKA

D. Koutsi

Summer
Theater

Kato Mylon

Xenias

Sourmeli

Artakinou

Mykonos Graffiti

XENIA

Quick Clean
Laundry

Fast
Internet

Windmills Travel

South
Station

National Bank
of Greece

Meltos Axioti

Ag. Louka

Ag. Ioannou

TO RENTAL CARS (50m), TOURIST
POLICE, ⊹ AND (3km), 16 (5km)
17 18 19 AND 20 (6km)

150 yards

150 meters

2:30pm; W 2:30pm; €14); **Piraeus** (4hr., 2 per day, €42); **Santorini** (3hr., 2:30pm, €28); **Syros** (1hr., 2 per day, €12.30); **Tinos** (30min., 1-2 per day, €8).

Buses: KTEL (☎ 23 360) has 2 stations. Unless noted, buses are €1.20 during the day and €1.50 after midnight. **North Station,** on the paved road from the ferry dock to the center of town, sends buses to **Agios Stefanos beach** (every 30min.), **Elia** (8 per day 11am-7:30pm) via **Ano Mera,** and **Kalafatis** (7 per day 7am-10pm) via **Ano Mera. South Station,** at the opposite edge of town, near Fast Internet, serves: **Agios Ioannis** (7:30am, every hr. 9:30am-5:30pm, 2 per hr. 6pm-1:30am); **Ornos beach** (7:30am, every hr. 9:30am-5:30pm, 2 per hr. 6pm-1:30am); **Paradise beach** (7:45, 9am, 2 per hr. 10am-7:30pm, every hr. 8pm-6am); **Paraga** (every hr. 9am-2am); **Plati Yialos beach** (7:50, 9am, 2 per hr. 10am-12:30am, 1, 2am). Schedules are posted at the stations and change according to season.

Taxis: ☎ 22 400. Wait at Taxi Sq., along the water. Allow plenty of time; there usually aren't enough taxis to meet demand, especially late at night.

Rentals: Agencies around the bus stops. Bargaining expected. **Mopeds** €15-25 per day.

✈ 🛈 ORIENTATION AND PRACTICAL INFORMATION

Facing inland from the **Old Port,** the road leading to the right along the water takes you past **North Station** and the beach to **Taxi Square** and the waterfront. This same road heading away from Mykonos Town leads to **Agios Stefanos beach** and the **New Port,** 3km away. On the right side of the waterfront is a pier from which excursion boats head to Delos. Past the pier is a series of white-washed churches, a lovely part of town called **"Little Venice,"** and the famous windmill-lined hill. Although plenty of action centers on the waterfront, most of the real shopping, fine dining, and partying occurs among the narrow, winding back streets. Some of the important streets are **Matogianni,** which leads inland from the water, **Enoplon Dynameon,** which catches the bottom of Matogianni, and **Mitropoleos,** which intersects E. Dynameon on its way from Little Venice to **Lakka** and **South Station.** Pick out landmarks for yourself along the way, as navigating Mykonos's maze of streets is not an easy task. The road heading uphill from South Station goes to the **airport,** campsites, and **Paradise beach.** The town's essentials—post office, Internet, markets, and so forth—mostly lie near Lakka and South Station.

Tourist Office: Windmills Travel (☎ 26 555; www.windmillstravel.com), on Xenias, around the corner from South Station. Has maps and helps with everything from last-minute accommodations to scuba diving (2 dives €99) and snorkeling (€25) excursions. The staff also has tips and resources for gay travelers. Open daily 8am-10pm.

Banks: National Bank, Melpos Axioti 6 (☎ 23 163), up the hill from South Station, and **Alpha Bank,** Matogianni 41 (☎ 23 909), at the corner of Kalogera, **exchange currency** and have **24hr. ATMs.** Both open M-Th 8am-2:30pm, F 8am-2pm.

Bookstore: International Press, Kambani 5 (☎ 23 316), in a small plateia opposite Pierro's; follow signs from the waterfront. Sells eclectic books, magazines, and newspapers in several languages including English. Open daily noon-1am.

Laundromat: Quick Clean (☎ 27 323), just below South Station on the right, up 1 flight of stairs. Wash and dry €10. Open daily 8am-midnight.

Police: ☎ 22 716. By the airport. Open 24hr. The **tourist police** (☎ 22 482), with helpful English-speaking staff, are also by the airport. Open daily 8am-9pm.

Pharmacies: Ag. Efthimiou 57 (☎ 24 188). Downhill from South Station. Open M-Sa 9am-2pm and 5-11pm.

Medical Center: ☎ 23 994. On the higher road leading from the port to South Station. Open for **emergencies** 24hr.

Telephones: OTE (☎ 22 699). At the left end of the waterfront in a big white building, uphill and to the right of the dock. Open M-F 7am-2:40pm.

Internet Access: Fast Internet (☎ 28 842), next to Quick Clean Laundry near South Station. Has cheap rates and a room full of flat-screen monitors. €2.40 per hr., min. €2. Open daily 9am-1:30am. **Mykonos Internet World,** Ag. Louka 8 (☎ 79 194), across the street from Fast Internet and up a flight of stairs. Has international phone calls and laptop connections. €3 per hr., min. €1.50. Open daily 9am-1am.

Post Office: ☎ 22 238. Down the street to the right after South Station, across from Space. Exchanges currency. Open M-F 7:30am-2pm. **Postal Code:** 84600.

🏠 🏠 ACCOMMODATIONS AND CAMPING

Mykonos is one of the most expensive of the Greek islands, and rooms are predictably pricey. Most budget travelers find their niche at the island's campsites, whose options far surpass the standard plot of grass. The regular bus service to town is relatively cheap and fast. Plus, most of the early (and late) partying happens near Paradise Beach and is within easy walking distance of both campsites. The information offices by the dock are numbered according to accommodation type: "1" for **hotels** (☎ 24 540; 9am-4pm), "2" for **rooms to let** (☎ 24 860; 9am-11pm), and "3" for **camping** (☎ 23 567; 9am-midnight). Signs on the streets advertise **domatia,** but the rooms farther from town, available through the information office, tend to have better amenities for lower prices. In high season, domatia doubles range €40-80.

Hotel Philippi, Kalogera 25 (☎ 22 294), across from Zorzis. The rooms in this light-blue shuttered hotel have bath, fridge, TV, phone, hair dryer, A/C, and balcony. Despite the hotel's location in the center of town, the gorgeous garden courtyard and rooftop sitting area create a wonderfully peaceful atmosphere. Open Apr.-Oct. Singles €55-85; doubles €70-110; triples €84-132. AmEx/MC/V. ❹

Hotel Apollon (☎ 22 223), with a sign on the waterfront, offers rooms in an enchanting antique-laden house with a cheerful owner. Rooms are simple and cheaper than others in town during the summer. Singles and doubles €50-65, with bath €80-90. ❹

Hotel Zorzis, Kalogera 30 (☎ 22 167), down the street from Hotel Philippi and Hotel Terra Maria. The 10 rooms have TV, A/C, and bath and are full of carefully selected art deco pieces. Owner Jonathan is a great source for information about the "real Mykonos," having lived here for much of his life. Singles €60-120; doubles €60-150; 2-bedroom suites €130-230. Call ahead for better rates. ❹

🏕 **Paradise Beach Camping** (☎ 22 852; www.paradisemykonos.com). Take the bus from South Station (15min., 2 per hr., €1.20). Free pickup at the port or airport. This popular campsite on Paradise beach has clean showers and bathrooms, bars, and a restaurant. Just don't come here (or Mykonos, for that matter) expecting any peace and quiet. Hotel rooms available with A/C and bath. Internet €4.50 per hr. Breakfast included. Free luggage storage; bring your own lock. €5-10 per person; €2.50-4 per small tent, €4.50-7 per large tent. 3-person tent rental with beds €8-18. 1- to 2-person cabin €15-50. Singles €40-90; doubles €50-110; triples €70-135. Apartments also available. ❶

🏕 **Mykonos Camping** (☎ 25 915; www.mycamp.gr), just above Paraga beach and a 10min. walk over the rocks from Paradise beach. Provides a slightly more subdued camping experience in a picturesque location on the sea cliffs. Free pickup and drop-off at the port and airport. Has clean showers and bathrooms, a mini-mart, beachside cafe-bar, and restaurant. Internet €1 per 10min. €4.70-10 per person; €2.60-5 per tent. Tent rental with beds €10-17.50. Dorms €15. 2-person bungalow €12.50-22.50. ❶

FOOD

Food is expensive on Mykonos, with no middle ground between gourmet meals and gyros. The produce stands around South Station and **Mykonos Market,** between the post office and South Station, are good for cheap meals. (☎24 897. Open daily 8am-12:30am.) Creperies and souvlaki joints crowd almost every street, but as is the case with many restaurants in Mykonos, quality and price don't always go hand in hand. Still, as long as you're willing to shell out the big bucks, there are plenty of solid establishments to choose from. Try browsing the streets near Little Venice for a romantic stroll as you choose a place to eat.

Kalidonios, Dilou 1 (☎27 606), at the end of Dilou, off Kalogera. Kalidonios's focus on staying true to a high quality is refreshing in a town with so many tourist traps. It serves a broad range of Greek and Mediterranean dishes made from scratch in a cozy, colorful interior. Customers recommend the lamb *exohiko* (€16.50), a hearty pastry filled with lamb, vegetables, and feta. Entrees €8-15. Open daily noon-12:30am. MC/V. ❸

Appaloosa, D. Mavrogenous 11 (☎27 086), 3 blocks from Taxi Sq. Known as one of the classier restaurants in town, it serves large, creative salads (€8-12), pastas (€7-14), and a few Mexican entrees. The €2 cover includes bread with a delicious homemade olive *pâté*. Open daily 8pm-1am. MC/V. ❸

Pelican Restaurant (☎26 226), past Appaloosa coming from Taxi Sq., under a canopy of vines and flowers. The Greek entrees, such as seafood (€11-25) and lamb with yogurt (€11.50), are worth savoring. Open daily noon-1:30am. AmEx/MC/V. ❸

Pasta Fresca (☎22 563), on Georgouli, near the Skandinavian Bar. The streetside take-out window is a good place to grab a quick meal. The gyros (€2) and chicken pitas (€2) are some of the best and cheapest that you'll find in Mykonos. Open daily 4pm-late. ❶

Deli (☎22 967), on the upper left side of Taxi Sq., with the orange seats and patio. The spaghetti bolognese (€6) and pizza (€3) are better here than at other similarly priced restaurants. Open daily 11am-2am. ❶

SIGHTS

Losing yourself in its colorful alleyways is one of Mykonos Town's cheapest and most exhilarating experiences. A stroll to the **kastro** area—behind the Delos ferry pier, at the far left of the port when facing the water—will take you to the **Paraportiani,** a cluster of white churches. This is also a prime spot to encoun-

THE LOCAL STORY

PETROS: PELICAN OF MYSTERY

Every summer, tourist-paparazzi swarm Mykonos Town, attempting to get a photo of the area's biggest celebrity in action—taking a stroll by the windmills, perhaps, or enjoying a seafood dinner in Little Venice.

The town superstar is a pelican named "Petros." In his standard pose, the white-and-pink bird can be hard to pick out against the town's white buildings—at least until he blinks his beady black eyes and extends his heavy wings and long, slender neck. Though he is constantly surrounded by his admirers, Petros's main concern is scoring free fish; if you feed him, be prepared to be followed and "asked" for more.

But Petros's obsessive fish habit, typical of most pelicans, may be hiding the fact that he's not really Petros after all. The first pelican known as "Petros" lived here for over 30 years after being stranded by a storm in the 1950s and adopted by locals. Since his death, any pelican in Mykonos gets the royal treatment; there are currently two to three regulars.

Petros (or possibly the Petroses) has been sighted all over the northwestern city. To catch a glimpse, wander around the whitewashed churches of the Paraportiani and the surrounding tavernas. Just look for a crowd of tourists wielding cameras.

ter one of the island's famed local ▓**pelicans,** who wait outside the tavernas in the square hoping for a tasty treat. They're great fun to see up close, and usually are surrounded by a crowd of fawning tourists with cameras. From there, walk through **Little Venice,** where the Aegean's sapphire waters lap at the legs of cafe tables and chairs. The line of **windmills** along the waterfront is a fabulous sunset vantage point.

The **Folklore Museum** is divided among three of the island's most historically significant buildings. The main museum in the **House of Kastro,** just above the Delos pier, has displays on traditional Mykonian household items. (☎22 591. Open Apr.-Oct. M-Sa 5:30-8:30pm, Su 6:30-8:30pm. Free.) The **Windmill of Boni,** on the road that leads uphill from North Station, hosts a wine festival each September to celebrate the town's agricultural history. (Open Apr.-Oct. daily 4-8pm.) **Lena's House,** the third building, next to the Aegean Maritime Museum, is an 18th-century upper-middle class home preserved exactly as its owner left it. (☎28 764. Open Apr.-Oct. M-Sa 6:30-9:30pm, Su 7-9pm. Free.) The **Aegean Maritime Museum** is around the corner from the inland end of Matogianni on E. Dynameon. The beautifully manicured garden contains gigantic nautical instruments, including the largest lighthouse in the Aegean. (☎22 700. Open Apr.-Oct. daily 10:30am-1pm and 6:30-9pm. €3, students and seniors €1.50, children free.) The **Archaeological Museum** is on the paved road between the dock and the center of town. It displays a large collection of pottery found throughout the island, including a renowned 7th-century BC *amphora* with scenes depicting the fall of Troy. (☎22 325. Open Tu-Su 8:30am-3pm. €2, students and seniors €1, EU students and under 18 free.) The **Cultural Center of Mykonos,** on Matogianni, hosts rotating exhibits that feature the work of up-and-coming Greek artists. (☎27 791. Open daily 11am-2pm and 7pm-1am. Free.)

▓ NIGHTLIFE

At night, the young and beautiful descend upon Mykonos Town to mingle with mere mortals at cafes, nightclubs, and a handful of pubs. The most popular bars, packed from 11pm until morning, are in Little Venice and Taxi Sq. The scene doesn't really pick up steam until after 2am, when the partying begins in earnest. Around 3 or 4am, the scene shifts to the world-class nightclubs around Paradise Beach, where the dancing continues well past dawn. Mykonos's club scene is one of the most vibrant in Greece, regularly attracting big-name DJs and entertainers, and it's a singular experience that's worth the exorbitant cover fees. If you get tired of crazy parties, head to **Cine Manto,** in Pl. Lymni, which shows English-language films. (☎27 190. Shows 9, 11:30pm. €7.)

▓ **Cavo Paradiso** (☎27 205; www.cavoparadiso.gr), on the cliff over Paradise beach. "Cavo" is considered one of the world's premier dance clubs. Rumor has it that even internationally renowned DJs will settle for a lower salary to spin at the open-air venue. For proof that it's the holy grail of nighttime destinations in Mykonos, just ask the crowd that sometimes waits hours to get in. The debauchery centers on a glowing pool and continues well past sunrise. It's an amazing experience that shouldn't be missed, despite the high entrance fee. Cover €15-50. Open daily 3am-11am.

▓ **Paradise Club** (☎28 766, www.paradiseclub-mykonos.com), on Paradise Beach. Anywhere from 3000 to 5000 people at a time crowd into this open-air venue to dance to famous guest DJs like Erick Morillo and Boy George. Add the pool, beachside tables, and sea breezes, and Paradise is easily one of the top clubs in Mykonos. Cover €15-40. Open daily 1am-morning.

▓ **Caprice Bar,** in Little Venice. Crowds cluster around the candlelit bar, and jump and sing exuberantly with the loud, funky music at this popular post-beach hangout. Gathering steam earlier than most other establishments on the island, it's a great place to watch the sun set and kick off the night. Beer €7. Mixed drinks €12. Open daily 6:30pm-4am.

Skandinavian Bar (☎22 669), near the waterfront. This 2-building complex includes a disco, 2 bars, and a cafe-like seating area. Though large enough for its massive crowds, it still has a casual, intimate atmosphere. Beer and shots €4-6. Mixed drinks from €8. Open daily 8pm-late.

Space Dance (☎24 674; www.spacemykonos.com), by the post office. This is the night-club your mother feared when you told her you were going to Mykonos. Scantily clad dancers strut on elevated platforms, while spectacular light shows and pounding beats saturate the 2-story, notoriously crazy complex. When things get too hot, sweaty partiers cool off in the posh outdoor bar and lounge. Cover €10 women, €20 men, couples €25; includes 1 drink. Beer €6. Mixed drinks €8. Open daily midnight-morning.

Pierro's, in Pl. Kiriaki on Matogianni. The oldest gay bar in Mykonos is still the place to go for a good time. Spontaneous glitter parties and an annual summer theme event (e.g., jungle) keep the crowd on their toes. The owner also runs the calmer **Manto Cafe**, for those who need a breather from the party. Drag shows nightly at 1:30am. Beer €5. Mixed drinks €9-10. Open daily 10pm-5am.

Argo (☎28 766), in Taxi Sq. on the waterfront, on the 2nd fl. One of the best clubs on its end of town, Argo draws partiers with a cozy balcony overlooking the harbor and a sleek black dance floor that rocks with the strains of salsa, Latin, and R&B. Beer €6. Mixed drinks €12. Open daily 10:30pm-late.

Club Ramrod (☎24 301), at the far end of Taxi Sq. from the waterfront, on the 2nd fl. As the not-so-subtle name makes clear, this is one of the most popular gay clubs in Mykonos, especially late at night. Lasers and disco balls illuminate the colorful dance floor as house and pop blare in the background. Drag show nightly at 2am. Beer €4. Mixed drinks €8. Open daily 9pm-5am.

◪ BEACHES

Mykonos has a beach to please everyone. Although all the island's beaches are nude, the degree of nudity depends on where you go. The small beach in Mykonos Town is nice for a quick swim, but the best beaches are out of town, accessible by bus or water taxi from **Ornos** or **Platis Yialos** (€1-3). Chairs and umbrellas (€4) line gorgeous but always crowded **Paradise** in front of the beachside bars and clubs. Widely known as the party beach, it blasts music and serves drinks all day; the revelry kicks into full gear between 5pm and sundown, when bars give away free drinks and T-shirts to get the beachgoers onto the dance floor. **Tropicana Beach Bar**, on Paradise beach, is where international youth go to make spring break last all summer. The most popular place to party your liver away by day, the crowd reaches its peak around late afternoon or early evening, and chugs on into the night. Just don't try to pull any funny business: locals report that the owner, a former heavyweight wrestler, isn't afraid to take discipline into his own hands. (☎26 990. Open daily 8:30am-late.) Water sports (tubing €15, jet-skiing €30-50, water-skiing €30, wakeboarding €30) are available in the afternoon. Nearby **Paraga** beach is accessible by the same bus. Farther away from Mykonos Town, **Elia** is quieter but still has a slew of water sports (jet-skiing €35, wakeboarding €13, paddle boats €15). Nearby **Kalo Livadi**, with similar activities,

 BREAKING NEW GROUND. Although every beach seems like it's already been claimed by the sun-chair-and-umbrella racketeers out to get your €5, don't hesitate to unroll your towel (and plant your own umbrella) amidst the umbrella jungle and sunbathe for free. The chair rentals don't own the sand, and savvy travelers can put their extra money towards their next souvlaki instead.

CYCLADES

is more family-oriented but is only accessible by a few buses per day from South Station. Otherwise, ask the bus to Elia to drop you at the top of the road to Kalo Livadi and walk the 2km down to the beach. **Agios Stefanos** has a magnificent view of the harbor and a small sandy beach perfect for relaxing and working on your tan. Fashionable, trendy **Psarou** stays crowded with vacationing Athenians, as waitresses in bikinis serve drinks from the pricey beachside cafes and restaurants. **Platis Yialos** offers a variety of water sports, and **Ornos** has a lifeguard on duty; both are geared toward families. (Chairs and umbrellas are €8 for 2 of each.) **Panormos,** on the northern coast, 15km from town and accessible only by private vehicle, is remote and private, a relief for those trying to escape the crowds. Windsurfing and sailing are also available (€15-40). **Super Paradise,** accessible by water taxi or private vehicle, 8km from town, is a pebbly beach in a gorgeous setting, lined with bars and covered with umbrellas (2 for €8). The beachgoers' tendency to display much more nudity than the other beaches attracts pleasure-seekers of all ages and sexual orientations.

⚡ DAYTRIP FROM MYKONOS

DELOS Δήλος

Excursion boats leave from the dock (30min., Tu-Su 4 per day 9am-1pm, round-trip €12.50). Buy tickets at either Hellas or Blue Star Ferries on the waterfront. An additional boat heads out from Mykonos's southern beaches 10-10:45am (€10). Most trips let you explore for only 3hr., but each boat line has several return trips, allowing for flexibility. Each company also offers guided tours (€30, including admission). A cheaper option is to buy a guidebook with a map (€5-15) in town or at the entrance to the site. Tinos, Naxos, Paros, and other islands run joint trips to Mykonos and Delos but allow less time to explore. Open Tu-Su 8:30am-3pm. €5, students and EU seniors €3, EU students free.

With its impressive ruins, continuing excavations, and fascinating museum, Delos—the sacred center of the Cyclades—is a must-see. The tiny island is home to the most important **Temple of Apollo,** built to commemorate the birthplace of the god and his twin sister, Artemis. A site of religious pilgrimage in the ancient world, today Delos is essentially a giant, island-wide museum.

HISTORY. According to mythology, after **Zeus,** the philandering king of the gods, impregnated the mortal **Leto** with Artemis and Apollo, he sent her away from Olympus in an attempt to shield her from the wrath of his jealous wife, **Hera.** Leto, desperately seeking a place to give birth, wandered the Aegean, but was refused by island after island, each afraid of Hera's fury. At last the exhausted Leto came upon a floating island shrouded in mist, but it too cowered under Hera's threats. Leto swore by the river Styx—the most sacred of all oaths—that if she were allowed to give birth on the island, it would no longer have to float and that her future son Apollo would bring fame and riches to its shores. Upon hearing this vow, the reassured island stopped drifting and welcomed her. Unhappy and vengeful, Hera made the goddess of childbirth, **Eilythia,** prolong Leto's labor for nine days in revenge. When the infants finally arrived, the mist disappeared and the island basked in light. The island's name thus changed from "Adelos" ("invisible") to "Delos" ("visible"). True to Leto's vow, Delos soon became the seat of her son's worship. Attracting a multitude of pilgrims, Apollo's sanctuary grew to be one of the most important religious and cultural centers in ancient Greece.

Although Delos was colonized by the Ionians in the 10th century BC, its status as a center of worship arose only in the 8th century BC. After it emerged untouched from the **Persian Wars** (p. 52), Delos became the focal point of the **Delian League** (p. 52). During these years, the Athenians ordered at least two "purifications" of the island in Apollo's honor. The second, in 426 BC, decreed that no one should give birth or die on its grounds—an order worshippers took retroactively, exhuming graves and moving bodies to a "purification pit" on nearby **Rheneia.** After Sparta defeated Athens in the **Peloponnesian War** (p. 52), Delos enjoyed independence and wealth. This prosperity soured, however, during the Roman occupation in the 2nd century BC, when Delos became the slave-trading center of Greece. By the end of the AD 2nd century, after successive sackings, the island was left nearly deserted. Today its only residents are legions of lizards and members of the French School of Archaeology, which has been excavating here since 1873.

SIGHTS. Occupying almost 2.5 sq. km, the **archaeological site** includes the Temple of Apollo, the agora, Mt. Kythnos, and the theater quarter. While it would take days to explore the ruins completely, you can see the highlights in 3hr. Most visitors follow a similar route when they dvisembark the ferry; reverse it for more privacy. There are frequent chances to explore off the beaten path; keep an eye out for footpaths off the main trails. Bring a hat, good shoes, and a water bottle. The cafeteria beside the museum is exorbitantly priced, so it's wise to pack some snacks.

The path beyond the admission booth points toward the **Agora of the Competaliasts,** where Roman guilds built their shop-shrines. Continue in the same direction and turn left onto the Sacred Road. Two parallel **stoas,** the more impressive of which (on the left) was built by Phillip of Macedon in 210 BC and dedicated to Apollo, adorn the walk. Bear right and follow this road to the **Sanctuary of Apollo,** a collection of temples built in the god's honor. The sanctuary complex begins when you reach the **Propylaea.** The biggest and most important of the temples is on the right. The famous **Temple of Apollo,** or Temple of the Delians, was completed at the end of the 4th century BC. Its immense, partially hollow hexagonal pedestal once supported an 8m marble statue of the god. Following the direction of the Sacred Road north, 50m past its end, will lead you to the **Terrace of the Lions,** where replicas of the ancient marble felines overlook the Sacred Lake. Five of the original lions are still whole and are protected from the elements inside the museum, along with the partial remains of three others. The body of the ninth, pirated by Venetians, guards the entrance to the Arsenal in Venice.

Past the lions, the **House of the Lake,** with a well-preserved mosaic decorating its atrium, and the desecrated **Sacred Lake,** drained in 1925 to protect against malaria, are both at the bottom of a hill populated with Roman houses. Today, the round shape of the former lake appears as a leafy oasis with a lone palm tree at its center. On the lake's south side is the **Roman agora.**

From the **Archaeological Museum** (free with admission to the site), you can hike to the summit of **Mount Kythnos** (elev. 112m). Wear sturdy, comfortable shoes; though the trail is not too difficult, it can be steep and some of the rocks dislodge easily. Ascending the mountain coming from the direction of the Temple of Apollo, you will pass temples dedicated to Egyptian gods. The elegant bust in the perfectly preserved **Temple of Isis** depicts the sun goddess. The building blocks of the nearby **Grotto of Heracles** reflect Mycenaean architecture (though some experts suggest they're knock-offs). Coming down the mountain, bear left to reach the **House of the Dolphins** and **House of the Masks,** which contain intricate mosaics of dolphins, as well as the most famous mosaic on Delos, *Dionysus Riding a Panther.* Continue to the **ancient theater,** which has a sophisticated cistern (as cisterns go) called **"Dexamene,"** with nine arched compartments. As you weave down the rough path back toward the entrance, you'll see the **House of the Trident,** graced by a mosaic of a dolphin twisted around a trident; the **House of Dionysus,** containing another mosaic of Dionysus and a panther; and the **House of Cleopatra.** The famous statue of Cleopatra and Dioscourides is sheltered in the site's museum.

SYROS Σύρος

Syros, called the "Queen of the Cyclades" for its commercial success and architectural beauty, first rose to power as a Phoenician seaport. Later, the 13th-century Venetians turned it into a thriving trading capital. Steamships and the rise of Piraeus as the modern national port ended Syros's glory days; however, over the last 20 years, the shipbuilding industry has helped it regain its economic footing. Now, Syros is home to almost half of the Cyclades's permanent residents. Visitors are treated to an uncommonly bustling island lifestyle built along the waterfront and the medieval settlement of Ano Syros, high on one of Syros's two peaks.

ERMOUPOLIS Ερμούπολις ☎ 22810

Busy Ermoupolis, the Cyclades's capital and largest city, is named in honor of winged messenger Hermes, god of commerce, communication, and travel. True to its name, the port hosts both shipping magnates and tourists on the go. Neoclassical mansions, most of which now house government agencies, line quieter streets farther inland. Greek, Italian, and Bavarian influences combine in the pastel colors and wrought-iron balconies that hint at the island's opulent past. In the background two church-topped hills vie for supremacy: Catholic church Agios Giorgos caps Venetian settlement Ano Syros to the left, while Greek Orthodox church Anastasis tops the mountain to the right.

▐ TRANSPORTATION

Flights: 7 flights per week go to **Athens** (25min., €80). Take a bus or taxi to the **airport**, southeast of Ermoupolis (☎87 025).

Ferries: To: **Crete** (10hr., 2 per week, €16); **Ios** (5hr., 5 per week, €9); **Mykonos** (1hr., 3-4 per day, €8.10); **Naxos** (1½hr., 3-5 per day, €8.50); **Paros** (1hr., 3-5 per day, €7.50); **Piraeus** (4½hr., 4-5 per day, €25); **Santorini** (6hr., 8 per week, €18); **Tinos** (45min., 2-4 per day, €4). Most boats depart from the right side of the harbor. **Flying Dolphins** go twice daily to **Mykonos** (1hr., €16), **Piraeus** (2hr., €42), and **Tinos** (30min., €11). Schedules vary by season; check with a travel agency.

Buses: ☎82 575. Green **KTEL** buses leave from the depot near the ferry dock. Most buses follow a single loop around the island, departing counterclockwise on the hour (6:30am-midnight) and clockwise on the half-hour (7:30am-12:30am). To: **Azolimnos** (45min., €1.30); **Finikas** (25min., €1.50); **Galissas** (15min., €1.30); **Komito** (30min., €1.50); **Megas Yialos** (35min., €1.50); **Posidonia** (€1.50). Another bus leaves 3 times per day to: **Episkopio** (€1.20); **Manna** (€1.30); **Parakopi** (€1.30); **Kini** (€1.30). 3-5 shuttle buses per day go to **Ano Syros** (€1.20), and a mini-bus goes 14 times per day to **Dili** and **Vrontado** (both €0.70).

Taxis: ☎86 222. Line up 24hr. in Pl. Miaouli.

Rentals: Rental agencies line the waterfront. **Enjoy Your Holidays Rent a Car,** Akti Paeidou 8 (☎87 070), by the central port. Cars €30. Open daily 8am-11pm. **Sigalas Rentals** (☎81 805), in front of the Diogenis Hotel. Mopeds €10; helmet included. Cars from €30. International license required for car rental. Open daily 8:30am-9pm.

▐ ▐ ORIENTATION AND PRACTICAL INFORMATION

Facing inland from the dock, head right and walk down the waterfront for 3min. to **Eleftheriou Venizelou,** the main street, beginning at the winged **statue of Hermes.** El. Venizelou runs inland to **Plateia Miaouli,** a large marble plaza marked by the Neoclassical town hall. Hotels and domatia can be found all along the waterfront and the surrounding streets. Generally, the farther you walk from the port, the nicer your surroundings.

A labeled map of Ermoupolis and a listing of domatia are posted on two large signs at the bus depot.

Tourist Office: ☎85 385. In 2 booths on the waterfront. 1 is across from the ferry terminal; the other 100m toward El. Venizelou. Provide info on Syros's hotels and domatia, as well as free maps. Open daily 9:30am-12:30pm and 3:30-8:30pm.

Budget Travel: Team Work (☎83 400), past the ferry terminal on the waterfront toward the shipyard. Free luggage storage. Open daily 9am-10pm. **Vassilikos Tours** (☎84 444), on the port across from the bus depot. Open daily 8am-midnight. Both provide ferry, hydrofoil, and flight schedules, prices, and tickets.

Bank: National Bank (☎85 350). Walk to the end of the 1st large street on the right off El. Venizelou from the waterfront; it's around the corner on the left. **Exchanges currency** and has a **24hr. ATM.** Open M-Th 8am-2:30pm, F 8am-2pm.

Police: ☎96 100. Behind the theater off the upper-right corner of Pl. Miaouli. Take the right inland street from the far-right corner of Pl. Miaouli, go right at the fork, and continue 200m to the station. Open 24hr.

Pharmacies: Akti Ethnikis Antistasis 42 (☎82 220), on the waterfront 100m past the statue of Hermes. Others are scattered throughout the city. Most open M and W 8am-2pm, Tu and Th-Su 8am-2pm and 6-9pm. A few are open 24hr.

Hospital: ☎96 500. At the left end of the waterfront (facing inland) at Pl. Iroön past the roundabout, a 20min. walk from Pl. Miaouli. Open 24hr.

Telephones: OTE (☎95 508). At the right of Pl. Miaouli. Open M, W, Sa 7:20am-3pm; Tu and Th-F 7:20am-8pm.

Internet Access: Net Cafe (☎79 119), in Pl. Miaouli, to the left of the town hall's staircase. €4 per hr., min. €2. Open daily 8am-midnight.

Post Office: ☎82 590. Down the street from the National Bank. Offers **currency exchange.** Open M-F 7:30am-2pm. **Postal Code:** 84100.

◤ ACCOMMODATIONS

Cheaper accommodations are farther from the waterfront, or outside the city, and the waterfront **domatia** fill up in advance during peak travel season. Domatia owners with available rooms greet incoming ferries at the dock. A large map with info about hotels is at the ferry dock, and the helpful tourist information office has comprehensive listings of the area's accommodations.

Hotel Almi (☎82 812), on the left side of Kithnou across from the bus depot. Look for the dark wooden doors. Pink rooms with wrought-iron beds have a Neoclassical feel but with modern conveniences. TV, bath, and fridge in each room and a common rooftop patio overlooking the sea. Doubles €35-50. ❸

Villa Votsalo, Parou 21 (☎87 334; www.votsalo-syros.com). Walk inland on Hiou (before El. Venizelou from the port); Parou is the 1st left. In a cozy, traditional house, bright rooms are equipped with TV, phone, A/C, and bath. You can see the entire harbor from the rooftop veranda, and the front door is conveniently around the corner from the bustling street market. Doubles €30-55; triples €65-80. ❸

Evdokia Rooms, Persefonis 20 (☎42 756). Walking along the waterfront toward El. Venizelou, turn left on Dodekanissou after Gavriotis Travel and continue climbing uphill for 250m. Turn left on Persefonis in a charming and quiet residential area; Evdokia Rooms is the pink building on the corner. Homey rooms have small chandelier, A/C, TV, and fridge. Call ahead to be met at the port. Doubles €30-45; triples 45-60. ❸

🍴 FOOD

The pedestrian market street Hiou is lined with bakeries and fruit and seafood stalls where curious tourists and busy locals get their daily necessities. Up from the market street is a **mini-mart**. (☎81 008. Open M-F 8am-9pm, Sa 8am-4pm.)

🍽 **To Archontariki,** Em. Roidi 8 (☎86 771), between the OTE on Pl. Miaouli and the waterfront. Gourmands flock here for its legendary cuisine. Veal with thyme and honey in plum sauce €10. Open daily 10am-late. AmEx/MC/V. ❸

La Dolce Vita, Nikolaou Filini 3 (☎86 199), up the street behind the Hermes bust. Serves Italian fare to the tones of Frank Sinatra and other classics on a romantically lit street. Pasta €6-20. Meat dishes €12-25. Open daily 6pm-2am. MC/V. ❹

Kechayia Sweet Shop (☎88 076), on the waterfront corner of El. Venizelou. Makes *chalvathopita* (almond paste, nuts, and chocolate; €1.50), *loukoumi* (flavored gelatin rolled in sugar; €2), and other fabulous local specialties. Open daily 8am-2am. ❶

👁 SIGHTS

For a cultural interlude, visit 🎭**Theater Apollon** in Pl. Vardaka. With plush red-velvet four-tiered balconies and a captivating ceiling mural depicting Mozart, Rossini, and Dante, this playhouse is a museum by day and stage by night. Greek shows, from ancient tragedy to Italian opera to modern comedy, are performed at 9pm multiple times each week—call or stop by the theater for a current schedule. (☎85 192. Tickets €10-30. Discounts for students and seniors.) The **Church of the Assumption** (Kimisis Theotokou) is on Ag. Proiou at the end of the alley opposite the bus station. It displays a painting finished in 1562 by a 20-year-old Domenikos Theotokopoulos, before he was known as El Greco. The church's interior literally sparkles with its gleaming marble columns, crystal chandeliers, and gilded mirrors. (Open Sept.-May 7:30am-12:30pm and 4:30-5:30pm, Apr.-Aug. 7am-1pm and 5-9pm. Free.) Ascend the steps (30min.) at the far left of Pl. Miaouli or take the bus (€1.20) from the waterfront to **Ano Syros,** a medieval Venetian settlement. Facing inland, two hills topped by churches loom over the city; the higher one to the left is Ano Syros. Continue uphill past chalky, crowded houses to the lofty Church of Ag. Giorgios for a panorama of Ermoupolis and the coast below. The town hall's **Archaeological Museum** has a small collection of Cycladic and early Roman art. (☎88 487. Open Tu-Su 8:30am-3pm. Free. No cameras.)

🌃 NIGHTLIFE

The waterfront and Pl. Miaouli buzz with cafes, restaurants, dance clubs, and bars. Most of the popular waterfront locales open as cafes in the morning, turn into bars by night, and host DJs and dancing after midnight. **Kimbara's** stylish, waterfront bar crowd, dances to funky beats played by the in-house DJ. Head past El. Venizelou on the waterfront coming from the dock. (Beer €4.50. Mixed drinks €7. Open daily 8am-3am.) Unpretentiously hip **Plaza**, next to Kimbara, lures young Syriots with portside seating and a steady stream of international rock. (☎85 337; www.plazacafe.gr. Beer €2.50. Mixed drinks €6-8. Open daily 7:30am-late.) Cavernous **Arxaion**, toward the port on the waterfront from El. Venizelou, is trendily futuristic, with modern Greek music, disco balls, and an expansive dance floor. (Beer €3-5. Mixed drinks €6-7. Open daily 9am-4am.)

BEACHES

The closest access to the ocean is at sedate **Agios Nikolaos,** though it's more a broad seaside platform for sunbathers and ladders than a beach. To get there, walk up El. Venizelou through Pl. Miaouli to the right of the library. Head right and pass through Pl. Vardakas up to the right of the Church of Agios Nikolaos. Continue until you see an archway and a stone stairway leading down to the beach. At **Galissas,** family vacationers crowd onto the main beach. You can fight for your eight inches of sand, or climb past the chapel of Agia Pakou on the left side (facing the water) to discover a nudist's paradise in tiny, sheltered **Armeos.** From Ermoupolis, buses go to Galissas (34 per day, €1.30), alternating between a direct 15min. route and a 45min. route that stops in other villages first. Taking the scenic route to Galissas allows you to see the rest of Syros's southern beaches. **Finikas** and **Komito** are popular for water sports like windsurfing. **Megas Yialos's** many small coves provide for solitude, and **Azolimnos** is known for its large, metal waterslide. The shallow waters and relaxed atmosphere at the beach resort of **Vari** attract families and package-tour groups. North of Galissas is the quiet fishing village of **Kini,** ideal for watching a romantic sunset. If you happen to be there on June 29, the Church of Agios Petros invites you and every other living thing within earshot to an all-night festival with revelry, *bouzouki*, and plenty of *kakavia* (fish soup).

NAXOS Νάξος

The gleaming marble Portara, the lone remaining arch of a temple to Apollo, beckons visitors to Naxos from its unguarded peninsula. Naxos once was revered as the home of hedonistic Dionysus. Centuries later, Venetians safeguarded their profits by making Naxos the capital of their mercantile empire. Today, visitors can take buses or rented cars from the eateries and shops of Naxos Town to small, placid villages such as Halki and Apiranthos, dotted with old Venetian towers and early Christian churches. Mopeds are invaluable for navigating Naxos's terrain, where marble quarries and pristine beaches are secluded alongside vast vineyards and quiet olive groves. Hiking is another option; maps of trails and walking paths are available at the information center and various travel agencies in town.

NAXOS TOWN ☎22850

A dense collection of labyrinthine streets, bustling tavernas, and tiny museums radiates to the sea in Naxos Town. Despite its claim as the urban center of Naxos, the town retains an old island charm. Among the tightly packed buildings of Old Naxos, stone archways curve over streets, and trellises of flowers are draped over the whitewashed buildings and Venetian ruins.

◰ TRANSPORTATION

Flights: Olympic Airways (☎ 23 292) has a desk in **Naxos Tours** (☎ 22 095; www.naxos-tours.gr), on the left end of the waterfront. Flights go to **Athens** (€62).

Ferries: All **ferries** from Naxos leave from Naxos Town. 2 docks are at the left end of town, one for large ferries, the other for smaller ferries and daily cruises. For updated schedules and prices, consult www.greekferries.gr. To: **Amorgos** (4½hr., €11); **Crete** (7hr., 1 per week, €20.90); **Donousa** (4hr., €7.50) via **Iraklia** (1hr., €6); **Ios** (1hr., €9.10); **Koufonisia** (3hr., 1 per week, €7.50); **Mykonos** (3hr., €8.20); **Paros** (1hr., 4 per day, €7.50); **Piraeus** (6hr., 4 per day, €27.70); **Rhodes** (13hr., 1 per week, €24.40); **Santorini** (3hr., 3 per day, €12.30); **Schinousa** (2hr., 1 per week, €6.50); **Syros** (2½hr., €8.80); **Thessaloniki** (14hr., €36.70); **Tinos** (4hr., €20.50). **Flying Dolphins** and **Flying Cats** to: **Astypalea, Crete, Ios, Mykonos, Paros, Piraeus,** and **Santorini.**

Buses: ☎ 22 291. Tickets for all buses €1.20-5. Current schedules are available at the station (across from the largest dock) and at tourist offices. Buses to **Apollonas** (2hr., 2 per day 9:30am-1:30pm) and **Filoti** (30min., 4 per day 9:30am-3pm) often are packed. Buses also run to: **Apiranthos** (1hr., 5 per day 9:30am-3pm); **Engares** (Tu and Th 2 per day); **Halki** (30min., 5 per day 9:30am-3pm); **Koronos** (2 per day); **Melanes** (3 per day 9am-3pm); **Plaka beach** (15min., every hr. 8am-midnight) via **Agios Prokopios beach** and **Agia Anna beach; Pyrgaki beach** (1hr., 3 per day) via **Tripodes.**

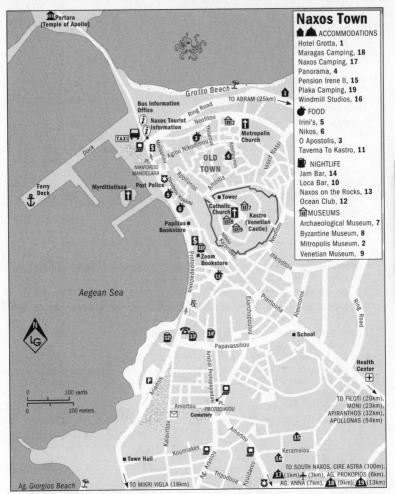

Naxos Town

🏠▲ ACCOMMODATIONS
Hotel Grotta, **1**
Maragas Camping, **18**
Naxos Camping, **17**
Panorama, **4**
Pension Irene II, **15**
Plaka Camping, **19**
Windmill Studios, **16**

🍎 FOOD
Irini's, **5**
Nikos, **6**
O Apostolis, **3**
Taverna To Kastro, **11**

■ NIGHTLIFE
Jam Bar, **14**
Loca Bar, **10**
Naxos on the Rocks, **13**
Ocean Club, **12**

🏛 MUSEUMS
Archaeological Museum, **7**
Byzantine Museum, **8**
Mitropolis Museum, **2**
Venetian Museum, **9**

Portara (Temple of Apollo)

Grotto Beach
TO ABRAM (25km)

Bus Information Office
Naxos Tourist Information
TAXI

Ring Road
Neofitou
Agiou Nikodimou
Thiseous
Metropolis Church

PL. NIKIFOROU MANDELARA

OLD TOWN

Apollonos
Amiritis
Iossif Nassi

Ferry Dock
Myrditiotissa
Port Police

Dock

■ Tower
Catholic Church
Kastro (Venetian Castle)

Papillus Bookstore

$
Zoom Bookstore

Protopapadakis

Nikou Kozandi
Neofitou
Ifikraditou

Aegean Sea

Rx

Exachopoulou
Prantouna
Alexinoros
Ring Road

N
LG

Papavassiliou

■ School

0   100 yards
0   100 meters

P

PL. PROTODIKIOU

Amortou
Cemetery

Aristidi Protopapadaki

Amortou

Health Center

TO FILOTI (20km),
MONI (23km),
APIRANTHOS (32km),
APOLLONAS (54km)

■ Town Hall

Kalavritou
Koumiakes
Ag. Arsiniou
Tripodoua
Kyriakou

Kerameiou

TO MIKRI VIGLA (18km)

Ag. Giorgios Beach

TO SOUTH NAXOS, CIRE ASTRA (300m),
17 (1km), ✈ (3km), AG. PROKOPIOS (6km),
AG. ANNA (7km), **18** (9km), **19** (13km)

Taxis: ☎ 22 444. On the waterfront, next to the bus depot.

Rentals: Auto Tour (☎ 25 480; www.naxosrentacar.com), around the corner from the tourist office on the waterfront; take the 1st left off Pl. Protodikiou. Rentals €25-40 per day, including 24hr. roadside assistance. Open daily 8:30am-9:30pm. **New Car Rental** (☎ 23 595). Rents cars, mopeds, and 4-wheel go-cart-type vehicles.

◼⭐🛈 ORIENTATION AND PRACTICAL INFORMATION

The waterfront along **Protopapadakis** to the right of the harbor is lined with cafes, tavernas, and clubs. After 500m the road forks inland; after another 70m, turn right to find the roundabout of **Plateia Protodikiou**, the central square. The **Old Town** is to the left as you walk toward Protodikiou, accessible via any of the alleyways running inland.

Tourist Office (☎ 25 201 or 24 358), 300m from the dock, by the bus depot. Accommodations assistance, bus and ferry schedules, car rental, **currency exchange,** international telephone, **luggage storage** (€1.50 per day), safety deposit (€1.50), and **laundry** (€9). English-speaking staff has useful information and advice. Open daily 8am-11pm.

Budget Travel: Zas Travel (☎23 330) has 1 location 2 doors down from the tourist center, and another 50m away from the port; both are on the waterfront. Sells ferry and plane tickets and offers information about daytrip cruises and tours of the island. **Internet** access (€4 per hr.) available at the port location. Open daily 8:30am-midnight.

Bank: National Bank (☎23 053) is one of many banks on the waterfront offering **currency exchange** and an **ATM.** Open M-Th 8am-2:30pm, F 8am-2pm.

Bookstore: Papillus (☎23 039), in an alley to the left of the first inland street before Vrakas jewelry, with blue signs reading "gold-silver, used books." Charming owner buys at half the original price and sells for €1-6. Open M-Sa 10am-2pm and 6-11pm, Su 6-11pm. **Zoom** (☎23 675), to the right of the National Bank. Has international magazines, stationery and stamps, photocopying (€0.15 per page), and **Internet** access (€3 per hr.). Open daily 8:30am-11pm.

Police: ☎22 100 or 23 280. On Amortou, the main road heading toward Ag. Giorgios beach from Pl. Protodikiou, 1km out of town. Open 24hr.

Port Police: ☎22 300. On Protopapadakis, across from the small port dock.

Pharmacy: ☎23 183. On the waterfront, right before the OTE. Open M and Th-F 8:30am-2pm and 6-9pm, W 6-9pm.

Medical Services: ☎23 333 or 23 550. Turn inland at the fork in the road past the OTE, at the right end of the waterfront; it is 500m farther on the left. Helicopter to Athens available for **emergencies.** Open 24hr.

Telephones: OTE (☎29 110), left of the fork in the road to the right of the waterfront. Open M-F 8am-2pm.

Internet Access: Heavens Cafe Bar (☎22 747), 20m beyond the police station on the road leading toward Ag. Giorgios Beach. €3 per hr. Free Wi-Fi. Belgian waffles with fresh fruit €5. Scrumptious veggie and cheese crepes €4-5. Open daily 8am-2am. **Matrix Cyber Cafe** (☎25 627), just before the police station on the road leading toward Ag. Giorgios Beach away from Pl. Protodikiou. Offers printing and digital photo service. €3 per hr. Open daily 9am-2am.

Post Office: ☎02 221. Walk down the waterfront with the water on your right, and continue beyond the main street that turns left. Pass a long playground on the right and the post office will be on your left, up 1 fl. Open M-F 7:30am-2pm. **Postal Code:** 84300.

ACCOMMODATIONS

The waterfront tourist information center next to the bus depot can help find accommodations. Naxos has three beach camping options, whose representatives wait eagerly at the dock. All the sites have mini-marts, restaurants, Internet access, moped rentals, and laundry facilities. Prices are similar at each campsite (€4-8 per person; tent rental €2-3). By far the closest to town (2km away) and the most convenient for bar hoppers, **Naxos Camping ❶** is 150m from Ag. Giorgios beach and has a swimming pool. Bamboo walls divide camping areas. (☎23 500. 10% discount for *Let's Go* readers.) For well-maintained facilities 6km inland from Naxos Town, try **Plaka Camping ❶** next to Plaka beach. (☎42 700. Cabins and rooms €40-60.) **Maragas Camping ❶** is on Ag. Anna about 7km from town. (☎42 552 or 42 599. Doubles €18-30. Studios and apartments €60-70.)

Windmill Studios (☎24 594; www.windmillnaxos.com). Take the 1st left after the police station heading away from Pl. Protodikiou toward Ag. Giorgios, then the 1st right. The accommodating owner, George, is among the island's most attentive proprietors. The spotless, spacious rooms have A/C, TV, bath, and kitchen facilities; some have balcony.

Free port shuttle. Singles €18-25; doubles €20-55; triples €25-60. 20% discounts available at New Car Rentals, 100m away on the main street, until June 10. ❷

■ **Pension Irene II** (☎23 169; www.irenepension-naxos.com). On the road heading toward Ag. Giorgios, take the 1st left after the police station and walk 100m. In 2006, this hotel was renovated to include private verandas, a lobby computer for guests' use, and pristine apartments and studios that can accommodate up to 6 guests with A/C, TV, and bath. A 2nd location, the original Pension Irene, is 10min away. Guests at either location can use the pool at Pension Irene II. Free port shuttle. Laundry €8. Singles €20; doubles €20-30; triples €25-35; 5-person apartments with kitchenette €40-50. ❷

■ **Hotel Grotta** (☎22 215; www.hotelgrotta.gr). Follow Ring Rd. along the water and take the dirt path at the sign on the left; the hotel is at the top of the hill. The translucent curtains in the placid dining area beckon guests to this bright, airy haven that overlooks the Portara and the Aegean. Rooms have either sea or mountain view and fridge, A/C, TV, and veranda. Indoor pool and jacuzzi. Free port shuttle. Breakfast included. Laundry €8. Doubles €45-85; triples €55-104. MC/V. ❹

Panorama (☎22 330; www.panoramanaxos.gr). Take a left on the street labeled "Old Market," then another left, following signs to "Panorama" and "Chateau Zevgoli." The unparalleled city and sea view make up for the steep climb toward this hidden gem with a rooftop lounge. The friendly owner, Kiki, painted and refurbished the 16-room hotel in 2007. Some rooms include A/C, others fans. All come with fridge, bath, and TV. Breakfast €5. High-season singles €45, low-season €35; doubles €55/45; triples €71/58; 4-person suite €85/60. ❹

☐ FOOD

Naxos brims with cafes and outdoor *ouzeria*, where chefs cook up fresh seafood and traditional dishes. Dozens of mini-marts offer tasty options for eating on the fly with ubiquitous vendors selling fruit, homemade bread, and local honey.

■ **Taverna To Kastro** (☎22 005), before the entrance to the kastro; turn left away from the waterfront after Rendez-Vous Cafe and follow signs for the castle and museums. At this hilltop taverna, the view is as spectacular as the menu. For 29 years, the chef, Sulis, has been serving local specialties such as baked feta (€4.50) and grilled calamari (€7.50). Excellent service. Open daily 6:30pm-late. ❷

■ **Nikos Restaurant** (☎23 153), along the waterfront and close to the ferry port, above Commercial Bank. For 3 decades, fisherman owner Nikos Katsayannis has been

ON THE MENU

A DRINK TO REMEMBER

The island of Naxos is one of only three places in the world where fragrant citron trees grow. Two families in Halki, making maybe the best possible use of the rare plant, have been using its juices for over 100 years to produce a unique alcohol called "Citron." Today, 5th-generation members of the Vallindras family use the same recipe their relatives developed in 1896. Workers collect the thick leaves from October through February, when they have the best aroma. The plants are then put into the original family press, which, within hours, extracts a clear liquid. Manufacturers then mix in natural coloring to distinguish flavors and strength: the green is sweetest, the yellow is strongest, and the clear is in between.

The after-dinner drink is widely available throughout Naxos, but impossible to find anywhere else. The Vallindras distillery used to export all over the world, but a shortage of trees has forced the distilleries to limit production until replacement trees have grown to maturity. Until then, Citron is available only in Naxos.

The Vallindras distillery in Halki offers free tours, brochures, and samples. ☎22850 31 220. Open daily. Representatives of the Promponas distillery also provide info and samples at their store in Naxos Town, across from Myroditssa. ☎22850 22 258.

serving some of the island's most succulent seafood to locals and dignitaries, including the President of Cyprus. While the outdoor tables beneath the hanging line of drying octopi are ever-popular with patrons and gawking passersby, the indoor seating area overlooking the bay is a great spot to enjoy dinner at sunset. Octopus and onion €9.70. Vegetarian plate €3.50. Snapper dinner for 2 with veggies and fries €22. Lamb Naxos with potatoes, carrots, herbs and cheese €7. Open Apr.-Oct. daily 10am-midnight. ❸

O Apostolis (☎26 777), on the old market street, at the foot of the Old Town. From the ferry quay, make the 1st left after the bus depot, walk 100m, and look for a restaurant sign on a street to the right. At this crowded outdoor spot that sits amid whitewashed walls and overhanging flowers, sampling the grilled shrimp (€10) or whole grilled fish (€12) won't break your piggy bank. Open daily noon-2am. AmEx/MC/V. ❸

Irini's (☎26 780), the 2nd taverna along the waterfront after Zas Travel. A cluster of blue- and white-checked tablecloths under a leaf-covered terrace, nestled in between the waterfront park area and the pedestrian path. The friendly waitstaff serves flavorful local fare and appetizers including the particularly tasty cheese croquettes (€5.50). Fresh green peppers stuffed with sour cream and feta €5.50. Grilled chicken with mushrooms €7.50. Open Mar.-Oct. daily noon-late. MC/V. ❷.

🔄 SIGHTS

Naxos Town is crowned by the **kastro**, with small museums and churches within. Descendents of the Della Rocca Barozzi family, former Italian aristocrats, still inhabit a section of the castle; they have designated part of it as a 🔲**Venetian museum**. In his enchanting stone basement, the dignified and hospitable owner hosts frequent **Sunset Concerts** of classical music and traditional Greek dancing. (☎22 387. Open daily 10am-3pm and 7-10pm. 30min. tours in English, French, and German throughout the day. €3, students and seniors €2; with tour €5. Sunset Concert tickets, which often sell out, are available at reception; €15-20. Complimentary soft drinks and wine M-W and F-Su.) The 🔲**Archaeological Museum,** located in the former Collège Français where Nikos Kazantzakis (p. 70) studied, boasts the world's largest exhibit of early Cycladic marble figurines. (Open Tu-Su 8:30am-3pm. €3, students €2.) The impressive **Catholic Church** is just around the corner. (Open daily 10am-7pm. Tours start at 5pm. Free. Modest dress required.) The **Mitropolis Museum,** next to the Orthodox Church, has elevated glass walkways that lead you over the reconstructed buildings of a 13th-century BC settlement. (☎24 151. Open Tu-Su 8:30am-3pm. Free.) The **Byzantine Museum** is a two-room collection of artifacts from the AD 8th-10th centuries found on Naxos and other Cycladic islands. (Open M-Sa 8am-2pm. Free.)

From the waterfront, you can gaze at the chapel of **Myrditiotissa,** floating above the harbor on its manmade islet, and the marble **Portara** archway, on its own peninsula. Climb up to it to view the ambitious beginnings of an unfinished **temple** dedicated to Apollo, begun on the orders of the tyrant Lydamis in the 6th century BC.

🎵 🎭 ENTERTAINMENT AND NIGHTLIFE

Starting around 11pm, beat-heavy music leads partiers to waterfront clubs, and extended Happy hours lure them into lively bars. For an alternative to the club scene, try the island's outdoor theater, **Cine Astra.** A 15min. walk from the waterfront, on the road to Agia Anna from Pl. Protodikiou, the theater shows English movies with Greek subtitles at 9 and 11pm. (☎25 381. Open May-Oct. daily. €7.)

🔲 **Ocean Club** (☎26 766), at the right end of the harbor, facing the water. Either sip a yummy mixed drink under pink crystal chandeliers on the waterfront patio or sashay indoors to join hip-gyraters on the dance floor of this mod spot. Mixed drinks €5-8. Open M-Th and Su 11pm-late, F-Sa 11pm-morning.

■ **Loca Bar** (☎24 885), at the center of the waterfront, upstairs. Behind the bright green-and-yellow awning, the DJ spins up an irresistible mix of pop, reggae, and house music in a lounge that draws in waterfront strollers. The Singapore Sling, a gin and cherry cocktail specialty, is not to be missed (€6). Open M-Sa 10pm-late, Su 10am-5pm.

Naxos On the Rocks (☎29 224; www.naxosontherocks.com), behind the OTE. Delivers pulsating music that will carry you into the next morning's sunrise with nightly themes such as karaoke and Caribbean. Part of the club functions as a hookah bar.

Jam Bar (☎69420 19 426). Take the 1st left after Klik Cafe, behind the OTE. Drink creative concoctions such as the Naxos Butterfly (€4) in the cool, dim interior or in the outdoor area, a small island of seats sectioned off by low pink walls and large, spherical lights. Shots €2-2.50. Open M-Th and Su 7pm-3:30am, F-Sa 7pm-late.

BEACHES

Beachgoers seeking solitude head away from Naxos Town, but the closest waters are equally beautiful. Buses (€1.20) run regularly from the bus stop to **Agios Prokopios**, **Agia Anna**, and **Plaka** (a beach popular with nude bathers), while **Agios Giorgios** is a short walk from anywhere in town. Clear, sparkling water laps up onto the shores of all these pristine spots, where a wide variety of sporting activities are available. **Naxos Surf** (☎29 170), **Flisvos Sport Club** on Ag. Giorgios (☎24 308), and **Plaka Watersports** at Plaka and Ag. Anna (☎41 264) offer windsurfing, kayaking, and mountain biking equipment and lessons. Desert meets sea at the more secluded beaches of **Mikri Vigla, Abram, Aliko, Moutsouna,** and **Pyrgaki,** where scrub pines, prickly pear, and century plants grow on the dunes. All are accessible by bus from Naxos Town. **Nude** bathers gather on a small portion of the southern protuberance of **Kastraki beach. Walking tours** of the island (€22) are available. Contact Iris Neubauer for information about a 3hr. horseback tour. (☎69488 09 142. €40.)

DAYTRIPS FROM NAXOS TOWN

■ APIRANTHOS

Buses run the 32km from Naxos Town (1hr., 5 per day 9:30am-3pm).

Venturing into Apiranthos may feel like a trip back in time. Old men lead bucket-laden donkeys through crowded streets, and the townspeople speak a unique dialect—a gift of the political refugees who fled here from Crete in the late 18th century. A blue marble road leads into the modest plateia that is Apiranthos's center; beyond the row of tavernas overlooking the valley lie Venetian ruins and 400-year-old homes. The one-room **archaeology museum** exhibits early 3rd-century statues and pottery. (Open daily 8am-3pm. Free.) A €1 ticket grants admission to the **folk art museum** (in the main square; open 10am-1:30pm), the **natural history museum** (to the right of the bus stop; open 10:30am-2:30pm), and the **geological museum** (just beyond the natural history museum; open 10am-1:30pm). Apiranthos is also a good base for exploring central Naxos's **olive groves.** At the start of the main road, steps veer downward and to the right toward marked walking paths. The small size and proximity to Naxos Town make the quiet village an ideal destination for a leisurely half-day trip. For lunch, try **Taverna O Platanos ❷**, a simple terrace restaurant with generous helpings of traditionally prepared local produce. (☎61 460. Beer €2.30. Pork souvlaki €7.70. Open daily 10am-midnight.)

POWER IN NUMBERS

The smaller Cyclades are launching a full-charged campaign to demonstrate that bigger isn't always better. The Isolario Project, begun in 2003 by Media Dell'Arte, a collection of Greek artists and academics, has launched an annual series of festivals among the less populated Cycladic islands.

These festivals, taking place in Folegandros, Donousa, and Sikinos, celebrate the diversity of art and history that defines these smaller but no less significant outposts of Greek culture. The Isolario Project hopes to highlight the diversity of the Cyclades beyond the well-worn island-hopping routes.

The island festivities begin in Folegandros—the project's birthplace—in early July with a program ranging from nighttime astronomy observations to documentary films.

The Donousa Festivities open in late July, featuring exhibitions on the island's history as well as local theater. The revelry wraps up on all three islands at the end of August.

Keep an eye out for the summer's new program posted around the islands to catch the free cultural and art exhibitions.

☎ 21099 69 493; www.mediadel-larte.gr.

CENTRAL NAXOS AND THE TRAGEA

A bus runs the 17km from Naxos Town to Halki (30min., 5 per day 9:30am-2:30pm), from which hikers can access Mino, Filoti, and Pangia Drosiani. Passengers can ask to be let off between stops; the path to Mt. Zeus is en route.

Ancient ruins, medieval churches, and quaint, untouched towns are scattered within the **Tragea,** central Naxos's enormous, picturesque olive grove. By far the best way to see the inner island is by private transport; the sights are primarily along one main road but are often several kilometers from the closest bus stop. An ambitious but feasible bike ride can take you to the major sights.

Colorful buildings and Venetian towers make up **Halki,** the village east of Naxos Town. The surrounding area is known as "Little Mystras" because of its many 6th- to 14th-century churches. In town, store owners hawk homemade linen, jam, and olive oil, while market vendors and the main taverna offer local produce. Halki boasts the Vallindras family's **citron** distillery, one of only two in the world. Recently uncovered frescoes from the 11th and 13th centuries are displayed at Halki's Medieval **Panagia Prottheroni.** The church, adjacent to the bus stop, is often closed, but if you can find the Reverend Vasllis Scordas, he'll open the doors.

Panagia Drosiani, a well-preserved, early Christian edifice with a beautiful miniature dome and 7th-century frescoes, is just north of Halki on the road to **Moni.** The road south brings travelers to **Filoti,** another sleepy cluster of houses, tavernas, and small churches on a lush, steep hill. A 1hr. hike extends from Filoti to the mouth of the **Cave of Zeus,** a damp, dark grotto where an eagle gave the king of the gods his thunderbolts. Forty-five minutes from the cave is **Mount Zeus** (1008m), the tallest peak in Naxos, which usually takes visitors about 2hr. to climb.

The stretch of road northeast of Naxos Town toward **Melanes, Kinidaros,** and **Keramoti** is dotted with intriguing sights. A half-finished but distinguishable 6th-century BC **kouros** lies on its back in a wild garden in **Flerio** (7km east of Melanes), where narrow dirt paths lead to a modest statue garden and a small cafe. On the road back to Naxos Town through Moni, Halki, and Filoti, you will pass the **Timios Stavros** (Holy Cross), a 17th-century nunnery, and the **Temple of Demeter,** which experts currently are restoring.

APOLLONAS AND NORTHERN NAXOS

Buses run from Naxos Town to Apollonas (2hr., 3 per day 9:30am-1:30pm).

Countryside views make the trip to and from Apollonas a peaceful, pleasant way to spend an afternoon. You'll

Zakary "Juggs" Hale
68 S N. Wheeling Ave
Muncie, IN 47383

pass the secluded beach at **Amiti,** down the road from Galini. Farther on is the monastery of **Faneromenis.** One of the more famous **kouroi** of Naxos is just a short walk from the harbor. This *kouros* is nearly 11m tall. From the Apollonas bus stop, walk back along the main road uphill to the fork in the road. Take a sharp right and walk up until you see the stairs at the sign reading "Προς Κούρο" ("toward the *kouros*").

LITTLE CYCLADES

Good things can come in small packages, and nothing proves it better than the Little Cyclades. These tiny isles bridging Naxos and Amorgos are a tranquil and rustic interlude between their larger, increasingly crowded neighbors. In their towns, goats often outnumber people, and star-studded nights center on a single town cafe, drawing an eclectic mix of alternative campers and Greek tourists seeking to find the road less traveled.

KOUFONISIA Κουφονήσια ☎ 22850

The smallest and most popular of the inhabited Little Cyclades, Koufonisia is surrounded by beaches on the southeastern side of the island, called "Ano Koufonisia." The name, meaning "hollow," refers to the caves perforating the island's coastline. Small clothing boutiques, cafes, and a lone ATM line Koufonisia's two main streets, which spring to life in the early evening. Recent spurts in the popularity of Koufonisia's picture-perfect beaches has driven up the price of rooms in the past few years. Despite rising prices, the island's town has preserved a simplicity of setting which continues to lure those in search of complete relaxation.

⌨ ⚡ TRANSPORTATION AND PRACTICAL INFORMATION. Ferry tickets are sold at **Prasinos Tours**, on the main road parallel to the beach, a few buildings past the blue-domed church; a schedule is updated on a board outside its door. (☎71 438. Open daily 8am-2pm and 5-11pm.) **Ferries** go to: Aegiali (2¼hr., 3 per week, €6.50); Iraklia (45min., 1-2 per day, €4.50); Katapola (3hr., 1-2 per day, €6.50) via Donousa (1½hr., 3 per week, €5); Naxos (2¼hr., 1-2 per day, €7) via Schinousa (30min., €4); Paros (3½hr., 4 per week, €15.50); Piraeus (7hr., 3 per week, €29).

Head straight off the ferry dock and hug the beach to find accommodations. Koufonisia's commercial center consists of two main streets. The shorter one runs inland from just past the port to the left of the mini-mart; the longer one springs from its left side, about 100m inland and parallel to the beach. The 24hr. **police** (☎71 375) are on the road leading inland from the port, past Kalamia Music Cafe. Next door is the **medical center.** (☎71 370, doctor 69738 18 612. Open M, W, F 9am-2pm and 6-8pm; Tu and Th 9am-2pm. 24hr. **emergency** service.) The **OTE** is on the main road inland, across from Pension Melissa. (☎22 392. Open 8am-2pm and 5-10pm.) **Internet** access is available at **Kohili** and **Kalamia Music Cafe** (see below). The **post office,** in a boutique next to the Keros Hotel, has **currency exchange** and a **24hr. ATM.** (☎74 214. Open 10:30am-1:30pm and 6-11:30pm.) **Postal Code:** 84300.

▌ ACCOMMODATIONS. Many homes with rooms to let sit on the main road (doubles €50-60; in low season €20-30), but the rising popularity of Koufonisia's beaches has meant rising prices, making camping the best budget option for lone travelers. ◾ **Akrogiali Rooms ❸,** along the road past the beach, has brightly decorated rooms with bath, fridge, TV, air-conditioning, hot pot, stocked dishes, and an intimate, blue balcony with unbeatable beach views. (☎71 685. Doubles €30-60; triples €35-75.) **Maria Prasinou ❷,** the first hotel on the road past the beach, has a quaint cafe over the water where beachgoers pass their nights. The rooms have bath and beautiful harbor views. (☎71 436. Doubles €25-60; triples €35-70. V.) **Sofia Soultania ❷**, next to Maria Prasinou, rents large rooms with TV, bath, and semi-private balcony. (☎71 437. Doubles €45-60; triples €60-75.) **Harakorou Camping ❶**, with few amenities, is in a beautiful location a 15min. walk left from the wharf when facing inland. (☎71 683. €6 per person.)

◧◪ FOOD AND NIGHTLIFE. For tasty, cheap gyros (€2.50) or souvlaki (€1.50), swing by the enormously popular ◪**Strofi ❶**, behind a green window just around the corner from the church on the main road. (☎11 818. Open 6:30pm-12:30am.) **Kohili ❶**, on the main road past Strofi, has croissants (€1.30), coffee (€1.30-3.50), great views of the harbor, and instrumental tunes wafting from the cafe across the street. (☎74 279. Free Internet access for customers. Open daily 9am-1am.) **Kalamia Music Cafe ❶**, 150m along the inland road, by the public phones, provides drinks (frappés €2.50), sweets (€3-6), breakfast (yogurt with honey €4), and an eclectic blend of world music for a crowd of chic, hipster customers. (☎71 741. Free Internet and Wi-Fi available. Mixed drinks €7-8. Open daily 8am-4am.) People crowd into the purple-draped interior of **Emplo** for late-night dancing. Walk uphill to the left of the port and listen for Greek music. (Beer €3. Mixed drinks €6. Open daily 10pm-late.)

◪ BEACHES. You will find more stunning, white-sand ◪**beaches** on little Koufonisia than on most of the other Cyclades combined. The crystal blue stretches spool out in a continuous ribbon along the southern coast. **Ammos** is closest to Hora, just to the right of the ferry dock facing inland; you can spot nearby fishing boats here while spirited locals play soccer on the fine, white sand. Continuing 10min. down the road behind the sand past clusters of domatia leads you to pristine, popular **Finikas**. Quieter **Fanos** waits on the other side of the ridge. The farther you walk, the fewer people (and clothes) you'll see. A 30min. walk along the main inland road takes you to **Pori**, hands down the most gorgeous beach on the island. The brilliant blue, glassy water and fine, white sand are magnificent even by Greek island standards (though blustery winds can whip up the sand to harangue lounging beachgoers). If the sand begins to burn, head for the shaded rocks behind the beach where cave-lined coves and cliffs provide amazing vistas. Regular boats make trips to Pori from the dock at Hora (10min., 4 per day, round-trip €4.50). A daily boat (20min., 5 per day, round-trip €4.50) can take you on a scenic coastal ride to **Kato Koufonisia,** an oasis removed from commercial bustle.

DONOUSA Δονούσα ☎22850

Donousa, with its intimate mainland town and beachside gardens, gives visitors a potent dose of local culture. Although the most remote of the little Cyclades, Donousa is worth the trip, as it shelters a paradisiacal atmosphere removed from the well-trodden, Greek island-hopping routes. Isolated, golden-sand beaches abound beyond the town's clusters of restaurants, tavernas, and pensions, offering those in search of private relaxation ideal stretches upon which to lie out their beach towels. The small town **beach,** with volleyball courts and shallow splashing amid fishing boats, also serves as a thoroughfare between the village and the pensions across the cove. **Kedros beach,** a nicer piece of sandy shore with brilliant waters, stretches out over the ridge. Follow the road perpendicular to the town beach up the hill and turn right at the island's main road. Passing the heliport in the distance on your right, take the dirt path straight ahead at the first bend in the road to descend to the tent-lined sand. Following the rough dirt track on the opposite side of Kedros beach up the coastal hills for 20min. leads to the secluded cove of **Vathi Limenari.** Continuing on this track along the coast 20min. more leads to the expansive and even more pristine **Livadi beach. Skatzohoros,** just to the left of the dock facing inland, is the only nightlife option in town. Almost every evening, patrons sit and talk in the low light under tropical umbrellas, gazing contentedly out to sea. (☎51 880. Beer €3-4. Mixed drinks €5-6. Open June-Sept. daily 9am-4am.)

The few **domatia** in town lie at the other end of the beach and across the cove from the main port; doubles are usually €20-50. Rooms fill up quickly in July and August, but owners are happy to direct visitors to a neighbor with vacant rooms. **Camping** is permitted only on Kedros beach, up the concrete road that begins at the beach and around the bend. Several tavernas are visible from the dock, all serving similar Greek food (entrees €3.50-7). 📷**Corona Borealis ❶,** nestled under the shady canopy of beachside palms at the center of the town beach, is the perfect spot to rejuvenate with one of the 18 exotic iced teas (€3.50) without getting too far from the surf. Playing an eclectic mix that ranges from 90s rock hits to Cuban salsa, this beachside restaurant has a fresh, tempting menu and spontaneous dance parties. (Grilled chicken wrap with corn, peppers, mushrooms, and parmesan €3. Cuttlefish with anise €5. Open 10am-late.) **Meltemi ❷,** just to the right of the bakery when facing inland at the dock, serves simple dishes and has spectacular sunset views. (☎52 241. Moussaka €6. Open June-Oct. daily 9am-4pm and 6pm-late.) Join the daily raid on the delicious goods at the **bakery ❶,** above the now-defunct tourist office facing the dock. (☎51 567. Bread €1.50 per kg. Pastries €1.20-1.80. Open daily 8am-2pm and 5-10pm.) Bear right on the road leading into town from the dock to find the small **mini-mart.** (☎57 582. Open daily 8:30am-1pm and 4:30-9pm.)

The ferry ticket office is at **Sigalas Travel** in the Iliovasilema restaurant. (☎51 570. Open daily 7am-1pm and 5:30-10pm.) **Ferries** go to: Amorgos (1½hr., 6 per week, €6); Iraklia (1½hr., 3 per week, €7); Koufonisia (1¾hr., 3 per week, €5); Naxos (1½hr., 6 per week, €7); Paros (2hr., 3 per week, €12.50); Piraeus (8hr., 3 per week, €29). A **24hr. ATM** is located at the dock, below the bakery. The **medical center** is on the road inland from the dock, on the second floor of the building behind the church. (☎51 506. Open M-F 10:30am-2pm. Call 24hr. in emergencies.) To reach the island's **public phone,** walk 200m up the hill behind To Kima. Below the medical center is the **post office.** (☎29 107. Open M-F 8am-2pm.) **Postal code:** 84300.

SCHINOUSA Σχοινούσα ☎22850

Isolated beaches line the coast of untouched, rural Schinousa, all but guaranteeing a peaceful communion with nature. The island is best enjoyed on foot; explore its rustic, donkey-patrolled interior and get to know its 250 affable inhabitants.

🌐🛈 TRANSPORTATION AND PRACTICAL INFORMATION. All boats dock at tiny **Mersini,** with the village, **Hora,** a 10-15min. walk uphill. **Ferries** go to: Aegiali, Amorgos (3hr., 3 per week, €7.50); Donousa (1½hr., 3 per week, €7); Iraklia (15min., 1-2 per day, €4); Katapola, Amorgos (3hr., 1-2 per day, €10.50) via Koufonisia (30min., €3); Naxos (1½hr., 1-2 per day, €7.50); Paros (2hr., 2-3 per week, €10); Piraeus (7hr., 3 per week, €29).

Nearly everything you'll need can be found on the main road, a 5min. walk from end to end. On the right coming from the port is **Panorama,** a hotel and restaurant that doubles as the **ferry ticket agent** for Blue Star lines and the **post office.** (☎71 160. Open daily 10am-late and before the first ferry of the day.) Past Panorama near the end of the main road is **Giorgos Grispos Travel Agency,** where you can access Western Union and buy **ferry tickets.** (☎29 329. Open Tu, Th, Sa-Su 8am-1pm, 4-4:45pm, and 7-9pm; M, W, F 9am-1pm and 7-9pm.) A **24hr. ATM** is on the main road, on the right after Panorama. Maps of Schinousa (€1) and **phone cards** are available at the mini-marts lining the main road; the bakery sells a useful map (€4) of the Little Cyclades. Two public **card phones** are down at the port and in Hora's plateia. Turning left off the main road at the ATM takes you to the **medical center** (☎71 385), on the right in a clearly marked white building; 24hr. emergency care is available (☎69792 21 735). **Postal Code:** 84300.

🏠 ACCOMMODATIONS. Nearly every restaurant or general store in town offers several rooms to rent and free port transfer. Centrally located **Anesis ❸,** on the right after the ATM, has large, clean rooms with fridge, bath, and panoramic balcony views that look over Tsigouri beach to Iraklia. (☎71 180. Doubles €30-50; triples €45-60.) The hospitable namesake of **Anna Rooms ❸,** on the left past the medical center, rents rooms with common balcony, bath, TV, air-conditioning, and kitchen. (☎71 161. Doubles €30-55; triples €35-60.) **Iliovasilema Hotel ❸,** down the road on the left and run by Anna's daughter, has modern rooms with phone and balcony and a cafe-terrace overlooking the harbor, hills, and ocean. (☎71 948. Doubles €30-45; triples €35-50.) **Agnantema ❸,** 50m past Anna Rooms, has rooms with bath, fridge, kitchenette, air-conditioning, phone, and TV, overlooking a rocky terrace with a gazebo. (☎71 987. Breakfast €5. Doubles €30-50; 4-person studios €80. Reserve in advance during high season.) To find **Grispos Villas ❹,** follow the signs in Hora to Tsigouri beach on the main road and proceed 500m down the dirt road. Grispos's rooms, in a pleasant beachside location, include air-conditioning, TV, fridge, and breakfast. (Doubles €40-70. AmEx/MC/V.)

🍴 FOOD. Loza Pizzeria ❷, filled with traditional music and tasty food, is in the main plateia. (☎74 005. Long *peiridi* pizza €6-8. Baklava €1.30. Open daily 10am-12:30am.) Turning right down a small alley after Panorama reveals **Margarita Restaurant ❷,** an oasis of trendy 20-somethings running an open-air restaurant with great views and serving food with a modern twist on traditional Greek dishes. (☎74 278. Zucchini and feta souffle €4.50. Calamari €8.50. Open daily 9:30am-1am.) At **Panorama ❷,** balcony seating provides a sweeping view of the sea accompanied by light fare and sweets. (☎71 160. Sweet crepes €3.50-6.50. Greek salad €4. Open daily June-Sept. 9am-midnight. V.) On the left of the main road you'll find **To Emporio ❶,** a bakery and mini-mart. (☎71 987. Open daily 6:30am-11pm.)

🏖 BEACHES. The island's pothole-ridden dirt roads are virtually car-free, making it easy to explore the island on foot. Grab a bottle of water and wander until an alluring cove catches your eye. **Tsigouri,** 450m down the first road on the right heading into town from the port, is easily accessible and more developed than the other beaches, with a view of neighboring Iraklia. **Livadi,** a thin stretch of sand cradled by a small bay, is a 15min. walk down the right fork of the road through Hora. Follow the dusty road 2km past the bakery, across the fields, and through the tiny village of Messaria to **Psili Ammos.** This secluded, rocky beach on the far side of the island is sheltered from the heavy surf. Tsigouri beach is Schinousa's only nightlife locale; **Ostria Cafe,** an outdoor bar and restaurant there, is pleasant and low-key. (☎71 174. Beer €2.50-3. Mixed drinks €4-5. Open daily May-Sept. 10am-10pm.)

IRAKLIA Ιράκλια   ☎ 22850

People come to Iraklia to escape the bustle of modern life and immerse themselves in the friendly, small-town atmosphere of this coastal community. You won't have too much company on its peaceful beaches, and a cave with circuitous underground passages contributes to the hideaway feel of this tiny island.

🚌🚢 TRANSPORTATION AND PRACTICAL INFORMATION. Ferries head to: Amorgos (2½hr., 1-2 per day, €12); Donousa (1½hr., 1-2 per day, €7); Koufonisia (45min., 1-2 per day, €4); Naxos (1½hr., 1-2 per day, €6); Paros (3-4 per week, €12.50); Piraeus (6hr., 3-4 per week, €24); Schinousa (15min., 1-2 per day, €4). Schedules are posted around the harbor. **Maria Prasinos** at Villa Panorama (see below) rents cars and mopeds. (☎71 991. Cars €45 per day. Mopeds €15 per day.)

    Agios Giorgios is the island's port and its largest settlement; turn right off the dock past the beach to reach the center of town. This main road splits at multi-story **Perigali,** the local mini-mart where you can buy a map. (☎71 145. Open daily 8am-11pm.) A small ravine runs through the center of town; two roads run alongside it and merge at the top. The **medical center** is past Perigali on the right branch. (☎71 388 or 69774 68 649. Open M, W, F 9:30am-1:30pm. 24hr. emergency service.) All-purpose **Melissa,** 50m farther along the right-hand road, is a general store, ferry ticketer, domatia (see below), and **post office.** (☎71 539. Open daily 6am-11pm.) One of the island's three **phones** is just outside; the second is in Panagia, and the third in restaurant Maistrali up the left fork in the road. **Postal Code:** 84300.

🛏🍴 ACCOMMODATIONS AND FOOD. If you call ahead, your hosts most likely will pick you up at the port. **Anna's Place ❸** is up the hill on the first left off the left fork of the main road. Friendly Anna greets her guests with orange juice, while her comfortable rooms have fridge, bath, and balconies overlooking the port; the studios are palatial. (☎71 145. Doubles €30-60; 3-person studios €40-70.) Turn right on the road after Anna's and then left on the gravel road to find **Villa Panorama ❷**, whose luxurious rooms have fridge, TV, bath, ceiling fan, and personal patio. Enjoy spectacular and expansive views of Agios Giorgios and Livadi beach. (☎71 991. Doubles €20-40.) **Alexandra ❷,** at the top of Agios Giorgios on the left just beyond Anna's, has four small, breezy rooms with bath and fridge, a shared kitchen, and an airy common courtyard and veranda. (☎71 482. Doubles €20-40.) **Maria's ❷,** across the road, rents homey rooms with kitchenette, bath, and a shared balcony. (☎71 485. Doubles €25-50.)

    Ten minutes down the road to Livadi, situated in an isolated spot before the beach along the water, you'll find an enticing variety of creative Greek dishes and international music at alterative 🌊**Makuba ❷**. An open veranda right on the water gives top-notch views to lounging diners who can sip on mixed drinks well into the night. Inquire about the possibility of free camping. (☎29 034. *Raki*-marinated pork with rice and vegetables €7.50. Open May-Sept. daily 10am-late.) **O Pevkos ❷,** up the left fork of the road past Perigali, prepares fresh fish caught by the owner and tasty Greek salads with local feta. You also can buy raw fish (€10-20 per kg) to prepare at home. (☎72 021. Prepared fish €20-40 per kg. Open daily 8am-midnight.) **Maistrali ❷,** up the hill across from O Pevkos, serves meals all day on a casual, beach-themed deck. It also sells postcards, foreign papers, and books, has an international telephone, Internet access (€3 per hr.), and exchanges currency. (☎71 807. Omelettes €2-3.50. Grilled meat €4-7. Open daily 8am-late. MC/V.)

🏖🎉 SIGHTS AND NIGHTLIFE. The shallow, clear waters of **Livadi beach** epitomize Iraklia's appeal: they draw only small crowds, even on hot summer days. If you wade out, you can look at the ruins of the **Venetian Castle** overhead. The water taxi "Anemos" (Tu, Th, Su departs 11am, returns 4pm; round-trip €8) will take you to **Karvounlakos, Alimia, Schinousa,** or beaches on Iraklia; buy tickets at Perigali. To get a sense of what Greece was like 40 years ago, continue past Livadi to the town of **Panagia** (45min. from Ag. Giorgios), where you'll find a church, some cows, and not much else. The taverna **To Steki ❷,** with rooftop seating overlooking hills and the sea, also serves as a general store, bakery, and the island's only gas station—fill up from a canister. (☎71 579. Open daily 7am-2am.)

For a more raucous hangout try **Bar Aki,** the island's only club, down the dirt road from Maistrali. (☎71 487. Beer €3. Mixed drinks €6. Open daily 10pm-late.)

◪ OUTDOOR ACTIVITIES. The ▨**Agios Ioannis Cave,** with tiny waterways, dramatic depths, and a seemingly endless series of chambers, will fascinate adventurous travelers. There is a map of the path on the back of the Iraklia map available in Perigali. Bring a flashlight, candles, matches, and a walking stick if possible and get ready to get filthy. The steep 1hr. **hike** begins past the church in Panagia, where the blue sign points away from the village. After 20min. along the stone-walled dirt path, you'll reach a gate at the bottom of a dip in the land. Pass through and follow the stone wall on your right until it meets another one. Begin a descent down **Mount Pappas** until you encounter a small ravine; at this point, look right to the large, shady tree, indicated on the map. From here, the trail is extremely unclear, and there are a number of goat paths leading off in different directions. Follow the orientations indicated by the map to find the correct path; it's a 10min. walk to the tiny, bright-white cave entrance. Crawling through the small entrance brings you into the caves. You'll need your flashlight right away; leave lighted candles along the way a la Hansel and Gretel to mark your path back. An icon of St. John, who is celebrated in an August festival at the cave, is to the left as you enter. There are said to be 15 rooms inside the cave; the final chamber is so deep that there is no oxygen inside. Be careful—the rocks are slippery and daylight vanishes quickly.

PAROS Πάρος

Pieces of Paros are sprinkled throughout the Western world in the form of its famed translucent marble. Many of antiquity's most celebrated statues and buildings—the Venus de Milo, the Nike of Samothrace, and parts of Napoleon's mausoleum in Paris—took their materials from this locale. Seemingly bottomless Parian quarries still export regularly. The island comes alive in summer, when the golden beaches and lovely mountains teem with travelers. Though the main port of Parikia is less congested than other Cycladic cities, it's just as festive: parties at the beach clubs in Parikia and Naoussa stretch into the wee hours of the morning.

PARIKIA Παροικία   ☎22840

Behind Parikia's commercial facade, flower-lined streets wind through archways, past whitewashed houses, and by dozens of ancient, intimate churches. Wander through the agora to find trendy clothing, colorful jewelry, homemade goods, and many outdoor cafes. While the town's small, pebbly beaches are overpowered by souvenir shops and touristy tavernas, this transportation hub is a lively and convenient base for reaching more remote island locations.

▐ TRANSPORTATION

Flights: Olympic Airways does not have an office in Paros, but you can find schedules at the **Polos Tours** counter. To: **Athens** (M-F 3 per day, Sa 2 per day; €61). From Paros Airport, take the public bus to Parikia (20min.) or Naoussa (35 min.).

Ferries: To: **Amorgos** (3hr., 3 per week, €15.50); **Andros** (3 per week, €14.30); **Astypalea** (4½hr., 4 per week, €22.50); **Crete** (10½hr., 4 per week, €23.50); **Folegandros** (5 hr., 3 per week, €9); **Ikaria** (5hr., 4 per week, €14.30); **Ios** (3hr., 5 per week, €12.50); **Kalymnos** (9hr., 1 per week, €22.70); **Mykonos** (1½hr., 5 per week, €6.80); **Naxos** (1hr., 2 per day, €7); **Piraeus** (5hr., 2 per day, €28.50); **Rhodes** (16hr., 1 per week, €28.70); **Samos** (8hr., 5 per week, €17.70); **Santorini** (3hr., 1 per week, €16.50); **Sikinos** (4hr., 5 per week, €7); **Syros** (1hr., 5 per week, €8.50); **Thessaloniki** (19hr., 2 per week, €37.50); **Tinos** (2½hr., 4 per week, €9). Ferry schedules fluctuate often; for current info, ask at Polos Tours.

Buses: ☎ 21 395 or 21 133. The **bus station** is on the water, to the right of the windmill as you exit the ferry gate. The free local bus (every 30min. 7am-2:30pm) has 8 stops along Parikia's perimeter, including one right outside the gate of the bus station. For all other buses, prices range €1.20-2.40; since times and frequencies change constantly, consult the timetable posted at the bus stop or request a printed schedule at the booth. On weekdays, buses usually run every hr. to **Naoussa** (15min.) via **Kolimbithres.** 11 per day to: **Agia Irini** (10min.); **Parasporas** (5min.); **Pounda** (15min.). 8 per day to: **Marmara** (35min.); **Piso Livadi** (20min.) via **Lefkes; Prodromos** (30min.). 7 per day to: **Ageria** (25min.); **Aliki** (20min.); **Aspro Chorio** (1hr.) via **Naoussa; Chrisi Akti** (1hr.); **Piso Livadi** (45min.); **Pounda beach** (50min.); **Valley of the Butterflies** (12min.).

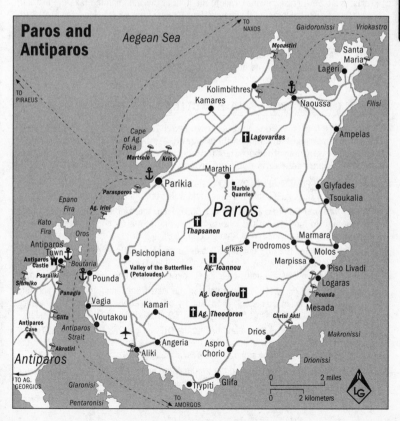

Paros and Antiparos

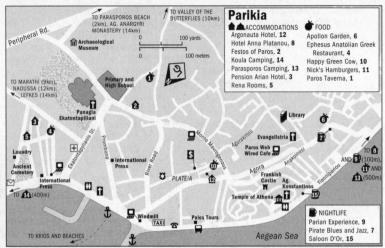

Parikia

▲▲■ACCOMMODATIONS
Argonauta Hotel, 12
Hotel Anna Platanou, 8
Festos of Paros, 2
Koula Camping, 14
Parasporos Camping, 13
Pension Arian Hotel, 3
Rena Rooms, 5

● FOOD
Apollon Garden, 6
Ephesus Anatolian Greek
  Restaurant, 4
Happy Green Cow, 10
Nick's Hamburgers, 11
Paros Taverna, 1

■ NIGHTLIFE
Parian Experience, 9
Pirate Blues and Jazz, 7
Saloon D'Or, 15

Taxis: ☎21 500. Facing inland, walk to the right of the windmill and take the first left; taxis line up at the corner of the plateia. Prices range from €8 (to Naoussa) to €18 (to Agnat). Surcharge of €0.32 per piece of luggage weighing more than 10kg; €1 extra for rides after midnight. Available 8am-3am.

Cars and Motorcyles: Rental shops line the waterfront. **Iria Rent-a-Car** (☎22 132) rents cars for €20-40 per day, as does **Cyclades Rent-A-Car** (☎21 057). A valid driver's license from your home country is sufficient to rent.

■✦◗ ORIENTATION AND PRACTICAL INFORMATION

Cheap hotels, tourist offices, and the town beach lie to the left of the ferry dock. The plateia is straight ahead, past the windmill. To the right, a whitewashed labyrinth of streets brims with shops, restaurants, and cafes. The island's party district is to the far right of the ferry dock and around the bend.

Budget Travel: Polos Tours (☎22 092 or 093; www.polostours.gr), by the OTE. Turn right from the ferry dock gate, cross the street, and walk 50m. Has transportation schedules.

Banks: National Bank (☎22 012 or 21 663). From the windmill, head inland to the plateia and to the right. In the fortress-like building at the far corner. **24hr. ATM** and **currency exchange.** Open M-Th 8am-2:30pm, F 8am-2pm.

Luggage Storage: The luggage deposit behind the windmill and near the bus station holds bags for up to one day. €2 per bag. Open 9am-1am. For unlimited storage time, **Hotel Kontes** (☎21 096) holds bags for €2 per piece, per day, even for non-patrons.

Laundromat: Top (☎21 491). Head right on the waterfront facing the water, and turn right after the ancient cemetery. Drop laundry off with attendant at the convenience shop down the street. Wash €6; wash and dry €9. 10% discount for *Let's Go* readers.

Police: ☎23 333. Across the plateia behind the OTE, on the 2nd fl. Open 24hr. **Tourist police** ☎21 673. Share a building with the town police; tourist police are behind the door opposite the entrance stairs. Open M-F 7am-2:30pm.

Hospital: ☎22 500. 100m beyond the windmill, the large white building called "Health Care Center of Paros" sits behind a small church and faces the waterfront. Open M-F 8am-2:30am. **Emergency** care available 24hr.

Telephones: OTE (☎22 799). 1 block to the right of the windmill (facing inland). Open M-F 8am-3pm.

Internet Access: Many restaurants offer access at no charge; look for the "@" symbol. The city offers "ParosWi-Fi," with slow but free service; the strongest signal is at the windmill. **Marina Internet Cafe** (☎24 885) is on the waterfront, by the ancient cemetery. €1 per 15min., €3 per hr. The cafe has a selection of imported foods and beers, including Japanese, Bavarian, and Irish brews. Open daily 8am-midnight. **Paros Web Wired Cafe** (☎22 003 or 23 957), in Agora on Market St. €2 per 30min., €14 for 5hr.

Post Office: ☎21 236. On the left side of the waterfront facing inland. Open M-F 7:30am-2pm. **Postal Code:** 84400.

▚ ACCOMMODATIONS

Hotels, pensions, and **domatia** in Parikia are as numerous as the dock hawks who gather at the ferry gates to advertise low prices. Negotiating rates can save you money, and always insist on seeing rooms before handing over cash. Nickel pinchers and nature lovers find some of the best bargains at campsites such as **Parasporos Camping ❶** near Delphini beach. (☎22 268. €2 per tent. Tent rental €4.) Another option is **Koula Camping ❶**, whose guests receive a 50% discount at Cine Paros. (☎22 081; www.campingkoula.gr. €6 per person. Tent rental €3. Tiny cabin as a single €7, as a double €12. MC.)

▨ **Rena Rooms** (☎22 220; www.cycladesnet.gr/rena). Turn left from the dock and take a right after the cemetery or call ahead for a port shuttle. Owners George and Rena provide detailed information about the island, a welcoming atmosphere, and bright, clean rooms with fridge, ceiling fan, bath, and balcony. White walls and blue shutters lend a comfortable, cottage-like feel. Free luggage storage. A/C and TV €5. Singles €15-35; doubles €20-40; triples €30-55. Discount if paid in cash. 20% discount for *Let's Go* readers. MC/V. ❶

▨ **Pension Arian Hotel** (☎21 490; www.cycladesnet.gr/arian). From the main waterfront road, go right at the ancient cemetery, 50m beyond Rena Rooms, or call ahead for a shuttle. Immaculate guest rooms overlook a picturesque, lantern-lit garden courtyard. Daily breakfast (€6) includes delicious homemade marmalade from the owner's mother, apricots and plums, and fresh-squeezed orange juice. The attentive proprietress provides flower-adorned beds, in-room Wi-Fi upon request, and a generous dose of hospitality that compels her guests to return again. A/C, TV, fridge, and balcony. Singles €20-40; doubles €30-65. ❷

ON THE MENU

SHAKE IT UP, BABY

Though the exact origins of the frappé are unclear, some reports suggest that the drink was introduced at the 1957 Thessaloniki International Fair, when a Nestle® employee arrived to introduce a new shake-and-drink chocolate milk product. When he couldn't find any hot water for his coffee, he shoveled a couple of scoops of his dry espresso into the chocolate milk container, added a dash of cold water, and shook it up, discovering a tasty new drink in the process.

Whether the story of the frappé's invention is fact or fiction, a gander along Parikia's cafe-laden waterfront proves one incontestable truth: the omnipresence of the frappé makes Greece the capital of cold caffeination. In Paros, the chef at Apollon **Garden Restaurant** (☎22840 21 875) puts her own Parikian spin on this refreshing fave. Use this recipe to shake up your very own frothy batch in a cinch:

1. 2 tablespoons Nescafe® spray-dried instant mix
2. 2 tablespoons sugar
3. 2 cups cold water
4. 2 tablespoons milk

Place all ingredients in a glass, a jar, a shaker, or anything you can put a top over. Shake like crazy for about 30 seconds. Pour the contents into another glass, add ice, and enjoy!

Sofia Pension (☎22 085; www.pensionsofia.com). Turn left from the ferry gate, walk along the main waterfront, then turn left at Katerina Restaurant. Proprietors Sofia and Manolis have created an island haven, from the front-yard garden accented with fountains to the canary on the front terrace. Upstairs rooms have balcony with a view of the Aegean. A/C, TV, and bath. Doubles €35-65; triples and quads €50-75. ❸

Argonauta Hotel (☎21 440; www.argonauta.gr). Across the street from the ferry port, at the entrance of Market Street. A spacious rooftop terrace, private balconies, in-room Wi-Fi access, soothing pastel walls, and proximity to the town's center make this slightly pricier option worth it. Singles €43-60; doubles €52-71; triples €63-85. ❹

Hotel Anna Platanou (☎21 751; www.annaplatanou.gr). A 15min. walk from the port and 5min. from Parikia's clubs. Turn right from the windmill and take a left onto the road adjacent to a light blue church and kiosk; the hotel is directly behind a parking lot. The bright, airy interior and the owner's welcoming spirit more than make up for the trek through Old Town to find this peaceful hideaway. All rooms have A/C, TV, fridge, and balcony; some balconies are sheltered by apricot trees. Doubles €25-65. ❷

Festos of Paros (☎21 635 or 24 192). From the port, turn left at the yellow school building, and the blue fence entrance is on the left. An English-speaking couple runs this no-frills hostel. The doubles and triples, which surround a small courtyard, have few windows, but the sheets, rugs, and bath facilities are spotless. Breakfast included. Pets welcome. Doubles €30-55. ❸

◖ FOOD

▨ **Happy Green Cow** (☎24 691), off the plateia in the narrow walkway behind the National Bank. Offers vegetarian and chicken dishes in an atmosphere that fuses traditional Greek ornamentation with the psychedelic 1960s. Colorful walls, hanging lamps, crystal chandeliers, and mellow music make this restaurant a popular venue. The creative dishes have equally creative names, including the "Cow's Orgasm" (pastry with cheese and peppers; €14). Open Apr.-Nov. daily 7pm-midnight. ❸

▨ **Paros Taverna** (☎24 397), 100m beyond the Church of Our Lady of 100 Doors, near a large parking lot. Locals swear by this family-run spot in which Mama and Papa Bizas serve up a thrifty carnivore's feast: pork souvlaki (€6.50), grilled lamb chops (€7), and beef burgers (€6.50). A grapevine-covered terrace, large portions, and a decent selection of veggie options add to the appeal. Open June-Sept. daily 1pm-1am. ❷

▨ **Ephessus Anatolian Greek Restaurant** (☎21 491), behind the hospital. Menus are available, and there are pre-made dishes on display such as grilled lamb kebab with all the pan drippings and stuffed tomatoes. For €19.50, 2 can enjoy a meal that includes a *tzatziki* starter and a heaping helping of the daily entree special. The simple ambience is as homestyle as the ordering process; the restaurant feels like an extension of the chef's dining room. Open daily 12:30-11:30pm. ❸

▨ **Apollon Garden Restaurant** (☎21 875). Take Agora away from Market Street and watch for the signs. The Spartan-born owner, former manager of a Toronto steakhouse, has hosted celebs and dignitaries from Sean Connery to the King of Sweden. Amid opera music and lush plant life, Apollon's rotating menu features selections such as the filet of pork with dried fruits, figs, plums, apricots and wine (€16.50). Village pie with zucchini and feta cheese €5.50. Open May-Oct. daily 6pm-1am. AmEx/MC/V. ❸

Nick's Hamburgers (☎21 434). Walk right from the port; the restaurant is tucked away in Ventouris Square on your left. Signs boasting "Pure 100% Beef" tempt meat cravers toward this American-diner-style burger joint, which features 14 types of burgers. Cheeseburger €2.20. Hot dog €2.20. Fish and chips €5.80. "Nickfeast" (2 burgers, chips, and salad) €5.50. Open Apr.-Oct. daily 11am-2am. ❶

SIGHTS

PANAGIA EKATONTAPILIANI. According to local legend, St. Helen commissioned the construction of Parikia's largest church, the **Church of Our Lady of 100 Doors,** in the AD 4th century. On a mission in AD 326, the mother of Emperor Constantine stopped to pray at the site, vowing to build a church on the spot if her quest for the Holy Cross was successful—as the lore goes, it was. The main structure of the complex is the mammoth **Church of the Assumption,** where Orthodox Christians make pilgrimage every August 15th in honor of The Feast of Panagia, or Ekaton-tapiliani. The **Church of Agios Nikolaos** (the oldest of the three) and the **baptistry** flank this centerpiece to the north and south, respectively. The white cloister at the entrance of the complex was built in the 17th century as a monastery, but now hosts church offices, an **Ecclesiastic Museum,** and housing for the Paros/Naxos High Priest's infrequent visits. In the museum's small, uncelebrated galleries are Byzantine religious icons and texts. *(Church open daily 7am-10pm. Services M-Sa 7pm, Su 7am. Museum open daily 9am-10pm. €1.50. Modest dress required.)*

OTHER SIGHTS. The **Archaeological Museum** haphazardly displays masterpieces alongside curiosities in a courtyard and three small rooms. The museum claims fame for its glorious *amphorae* (commemorative vases), its 5th-century wingless Nike, and its archaic statue of Gorgon, discovered only a few meters away from its display case. A slab of the marble Parian Chronicle, a history of Greece up to 264 BC, also is housed here. *(Heading away from the water, take a left after Panagia Ekatontapiliani; the museum is at the end of the road. ☎21 231. Open Tu-Su 8:30am-2:45pm. €2, students €1, EU students free.)* A ramble through the Old Town will lead you past the lone remaining wall of the Venetian **Frankish Castle,** where you can see sections of marble and columns removed from the 5th-century BC Ionic Temple of Athena.

♫ 🎭 ENTERTAINMENT AND NIGHTLIFE

For an alternative to club hopping, try **Cine Paros,** across the street from Sofia Hotel in the town center. American films with Greek subtitles begin at 9:30pm nightly (€7); guests at Koula Camping receive a 50% discount.

The waterfront comes alive after dark. Throngs assemble on the sidewalk and the beach, and pedestrians stroll the beach road at all hours of the night. At midnight, the tourist traffic forms a stream flowing toward the clubs at the edge of town. **Pirate Blues and Jazz,** in V. Gravari square on Agora, is a tiny bubble of New Orleans jazz culture in the sprawl of Old Town Parikia. Black and white photographs of John Coltrane, Ella Fitzgerald, and the Cotton Club dot the walls of this intimate, low-ceilinged establishment. (☎21 114. Mixed drinks €8. Open daily 8pm-3:30am.) Follow the crowds to the far end of the harbor where **The Dubliner, Salsa Club, Scandi Bar,** and the **Paros Rock Cafe** all share one roof, connected by a spacious central courtyard. This sweaty, pulsating party complex, which calls itself **The Parian Experience,** attempts to cater to every type of tourist with its different themes. (Beer €3-5. Mixed drinks €5-6. Cover €3, includes 1 drink.) At **Saloon D'Or,** about 100m before the blue church, upbeat rhythms compel loungers off the cushion-clad couches and onto the funky, checkered dance floor. (☎22 176. Beer €2-3. Mixed drinks €7. Open Apr.-Oct. daily 8pm-4am).

🏖 BEACHES

Almost every beach on Paros can be reached in under an hour's drive. **Parasporos** is 2km to the south (from Parikia, a 5min. ride on one of 11 daily buses, €1.20).

Krios, across the harbor from Parikia, is accessible by **water taxi** (every 30min. 10am-6pm, round-trip €2.30). To explore Paros on horseback, call **Horse Riding Koukou.** (☎51 818. €35 for 1½hr., €50 for 2½hr.) For water adventures, take a scuba lesson offered by **Eurodivers Club.** (☎92 071 or 69323 36 464; www.eurodivers.gr. 3hr. of instruction and diving for the uncertified €65; 2hr. dive for the certified €55.) Alternatively, kiteboard with **Paros Kite** (☎92 229; www.paroskite-procenter.com. €350 for 12hr. of lessons. 10% discount for online bookings.)

▶ DAYTRIPS FROM PARIKIA

Just 10km south of town is the shady **Valley of the Butterflies,** or Petaloudes, where the rare (and tongue-twisting) Panaxiaquadripunctaria moths return to the place of their birth to breed, lured back by their strong sense of smell. Petaloudes is one of the few surviving sanctuaries for the moths. June provides only a smattering of the bright black-and-yellow moths, while the height of mating season (late July to late Aug.) sometimes draws millions in a miraculous display. Since the moths do not eat for their entire mating season, they can't expend energy by posing for photographs. Be considerate by not clapping, talking loudly, or shaking the bushes. *(Take the bus from Parikia to Aliki (12min., 7 per day, €1.20) and ask to be dropped off at Petaloudes. Follow the signs road for 2km. ☎91 211. Open daily June 15-Sept. 20 9am-8pm. €2.)*

Five kilometers from Parikia in the center of the island, **Marathi** is home to Paros's idle marble quarries. Still considered to be among the finest in the world, Parian marble is translucent up to 3mm thick, with one-third the opacity of most other marble. A visit to the quarries is a serious undertaking; bring a flashlight and strong shoes and don't go alone. *(Buses run to Marathi approximately 8 times per day. From the bus stop, signs will direct you to the quarries.)* Blink and you might miss **Lefkes,** a tiny town 5km from Marathi. Because so many Parians moved inland to escape plundering coastal pirates, it was the largest village on the island until the 20th century. Beautiful architecture and quaint, untouristed streets make Lefkes an attractive daytrip location. *(From Parikia bus station, take one of 11 daily buses. 20min., €1.20.)*

NAOUSSA Νάουσσα ☎22840

Naoussa is Paros's second port, a natural harbor cradled by long, sandy beaches in the shape of crab claws. Persian, Greek, Roman, Venetian, Ottoman, and Russian fleets have anchored here over the years, leaving subtle marks on the sophisticated town. Naoussa is colorful and festive, overflowing with unique shops, inviting coffeehouses, and trendy nightclubs, but budget travelers should be wary: the upscale environment is pricey.

◧▶ TRANSPORTATION AND PRACTICAL INFORMATION. Naoussa is on two of Paros's bus lines, and **buses** connect it to Parikia (20 min., M-F every hr. 9am-midnight, €1.20). Since departure times change frequently, check the schedule at the bus booth in Parikia and in Naoussa. The main bus stop—a booth where a bus timetable is posted—sits inland along a road with a stream; to get to the port, walk 300m toward the bridge. From Naoussa, **water taxis** also go to the beaches. The white booth with the Greek flag on the waterfront sells round-trip tickets to: Kolimbithres (12min., 12 per day, €4), Lageri (20min., 5 per day, €4.50), and Monastiri (15min., 5 per day, €4). **Taxis** (☎53 490) are available 24hr. by the bridge.

Naoussa can be hard to navigate, but the central bridge is a useful landmark. On the bridge steps that lead away from the port toward the taxi stand, a main road leads out of town toward the beaches of **Kolimbithres** and **Monastiri.** Buses also go to the nude beach at **Lageri.** From the bridge and taxi stand, facing away from the water, two roads head inland, one on the right with a stream down the middle and

CYCLADES

one on the left without a stream. Naoussa's **tourist office,** near the taxi stand by the bridge, has info about the town and accommodations. (☎52 158. Open daily June-Sept. 10am-3pm and 6-10:30pm.) On the road without a stream leading inland, an **Alpha Bank** is on the left. (☎28 233. Open M-Th 8am-2:30pm, F 8am-2pm.) For the 24hr. **police,** call ☎51 202. The **pharmacy** is on the left on the road inland without a stream. (☎51 550. Open daily 8:30am-2pm and 5-11pm.) A **medical center** is in the park just before the church when heading inland on the same road as the pharmacy. (☎51 216. Doctor available 8:30am-2:30pm.) In **medical emergencies,** call the clinic in Parikia at ☎22 500. Behind the tourist office, relax to the sounds of jazz greats such as Ella Fitzgerald while surfing the Internet at **Jam Internet Cafe.** (☎52 203. €2.50 per hr. Open daily 10am-midnight.) The **post office** is 300m up the main street; go right at the bakery and fork in the road. It's just beyond the Santa Maria turn-off. (☎51 495. Open M-F 7:30am-2pm.) **Postal Code:** 84401.

⌂ ACCOMMODATIONS. Though Naoussa has many places to sleep, prices skyrocket in summer when package-tour groups book hotels months in advance. **Domatia** cost about €35-55 for doubles and €40-60 for triples. **Pension Anna ❷** sits around the corner from the taxi stand, the first left off the road out of town. It has spacious rooms with air-conditioning, TV, fridge, and shared balcony. (☎51 328. Doubles €25-55.) A number of upscale pensions with spectacular views of the harbor lie to the right of the waterfront as you face away from the water. Around the corner to the right and 100m up the hill is **Sakis Rooms ❸,** which provides weary travelers with luxurious lodgings in a welcoming atmosphere. Amenities include bath, TV, air-conditioning, fridge, and balcony overlooking the sea. (☎52 171; www.sakisrooms.com. Doubles €35-60; 5-person apartments €50-120. 20% discount for single occupancy of double room.) **Camping Naoussa ❶** is on the road to Kolimbithres. Call for the free port shuttle. (☎51 595. €6 per person. €3-6 tent rental, depending on the season.)

⬚ FOOD. Naoussan kitchens cook famously delicious seafood; the local specialty is the fish plate *gouna*. Behind the church on the commerce road 300m from the bridge, family-run **Diamantis ❷** features meat-heavy Greek fare. Sit on the tree-studded terrace just below the sidewalk and feast on lamb diamantis stuffed with feta, tomatoes, peppers, and onions (€9.60) and other dishes. (☎52 129. Open daily Apr.-Nov. 7pm-1am. AmEx/MC/V.) On the waterfront, **Bitzendaakhe Fish Taverna ❷** earns praise from the locals for the freshest sole filet (€8.50) and swordfish (€10) in town. (☎51 205. Open daily 7pm-midnight.) Next door on the waterfront, **Mouragio ❷** is a simple taverna with an affordable seafood selection and attentive service. (☎51 405. Fried cod €5.50. Open daily Apr.-Nov. 9am-midnight.)

◫◧ ENTERTAINMENT AND NIGHTLIFE. The **Aqua Paros water park** (☎69792 27 768), at Kolimbithres, is a pricey option for waterslide aficionados. On the first Sunday in July, eat, drink, and be merry as you cruise Naoussa's harbor and watch traditional dancing at the **Wine and Fish Festival;** call the tourist office for details.

Posh **clubs** with cavernous dance floors dominate Naoussa's high-season nightlife. If you're in Naoussa in low season before many of the clubs have opened, check out **Insomnia,** a two-level cafe and bar to the left of the bridge. Atop the balcony overlooking sea and sunset, try the club's trademark mixed drink, "The Insomia," a blend of peach, strawberry, and rum in a sugar-rimmed glass. (☎53 388. Beer €5. Mixed drinks €8-10. Opens at 8am as a cafe.) Around the corner at the farthest end of the waterfront port, the DJ at **Shark** delivers a mix of pop and world rhythms. (☎69792 27 760. Mixed drinks €10-12. Open daily 9pm-4am.) The nearby **Sofrano,** a cafe music bar with bright red walls, rocks the sea front with everything from 1960s funk to old-school Aretha Franklin. (☎51 385. Open daily noon-late.)

PISO LIVADI

☎22840

The quiet town of Piso Livadi, 11km from Lefkes, includes a handful of cafes and hotels clustered together on a pristine bay. While it feels removed from the hubbub of the two major port cities, Piso Livadi is close to Paros's nicest beaches, **Logaras** and **Chrisi Akti,** and is accessible by public transportation. **Perantinos Travel & Tourism,** to the left of the bus stop facing the water, provides information about accommodations and ferries. (☎41 736; fax 41 135. Open daily June and Sept. 9am-2pm and 6-8pm, July-Aug. 9am-10pm.) The family owners of Perantinos also run the **Londos Hotel ❸,** on the first right 50m up the road toward Parikia. Its clean rooms come with fridge, bath, and balcony. (☎41 218. A/C and breakfast each €5. Doubles Aug. €40; July €35; June and Sept. €20-25.) **Anna's Studios ❹,** near the end of the wharf, offers spacious balconies directly overlooking the water. Clean doubles and triples include fridge; studio apartments with full kitchen also available. (☎41 320 or 21051 24 342; www.annasinn.com. Doubles €40-65.)

ANTIPAROS Αντ4παρος

☎22840

Literally meaning "opposite Paros," Antiparos is so close to its neighbor that, according to local lore, travelers once signaled the ferryman on Paros by opening the door of a chapel on Antiparos. Most travelers visit the small, undeveloped island as a daytrip to see the caves, while others find it restorative to find a place to stay on the tiny island, which is as peaceful as it is welcoming. Most of the island's 1000 or so inhabitants live in town, where the ferry docks and most accommodations are found.

TRANSPORTATION AND PRACTICAL INFORMATION. Take a direct **ferry** from Parikia (35min, 6 per day 9:30am-7:30 pm, €3) or a **bus** to Pounda (15min., 11 per day, €1.20), then take a boat to Antiparos (10min., 30 per day, €1). The island has two bus routes. One heads for the caves (6 per day 10am-2pm, round-trip €5); another travels to Soros via St. George (3 per day 10am-2pm). During high season, departure frequency may increase, so call Oliaros Tours for current information.

Waterfront **Oliaros Tours** helps with accommodations and sells maps (€0.50). It also has boat and bus schedules, **Internet** access (€4 per hr.), **currency exchange,** and information about cruises and vehicle rentals. (☎61 231, low season 61 189. Open daily 9am-10:30pm.) Since the **National Bank,** on the left up the road to the plateia, is open only April to October, it may be wise to get cash in Parikia. (☎61 294. Open M-F 9am-1pm.) The **laundromat** is behind the windmill, to the left of the port facing inland. (Wash, dry, and soap €8. Open daily 8am-9:30pm.) Reach the 24hr. **police** at ☎61 202. To find the **medical clinic,** walk 200m inland on the main street and take a left before the post office. The number of the doctor on duty is posted. The **post office** is on the left side of the street leading from the water to the plateia. (☎61 223. Open M-F 7:30am-1pm.) **Postal Code:** 84007.

ACCOMMODATIONS AND CAMPING. The **Mantalena Hotel ❸,** to the right of the dock when facing inland, has large rooms with bath, fridge, air-conditioning, TV, and balcony. A family-owned establishment for 37 years, the pristine hotel has two large communal verandas. (☎61 206. Doubles €35-60; triples €42-72. AmEx/MC/V.) About 150m up the main street into town, turn left to find **Galini Hotel ❸.** Clean, spacious rooms with bath, air-conditioning, fridge, and private patio with a sea view sit above a restaurant owned by the family that oversees the hotel. (☎61 420. Doubles €30-50.) A few steps beyond Galini Hotel at the end of the same street, find a retreat on **Lilly's Island ❹.** Though this hotel, with well-manicured gardens and a pool, is on the pricey side, sharing a studio or two-bedroom apartment can make it affordable for a group of up to five travelers. (☎61 411; www.lillysisland.com. Breakfast included. Doubles €70.) **Camping Antiparos ❶** is 800m northwest of town, on the way to Ag. Yiannis Theologos beach. Camping areas are separated by bamboo walls. The beachside has its own mini-mart and restaurant. (☎61 221. May 1-July 14 €4 per person, €2 per tent; €3 tent rental. July 15-Sept. 30 €6 per person, €4 per tent; €4 tent rental.)

◆◆ **FOOD AND ENTERTAINMENT.** At the end of a small break in the buildings 100m up the main road on the left, **Taverna Klimataria ❶**, sheltered by hanging branches and low yellow walls, serves traditional dishes. (☎61 298. Most entrees under €6. Open June-Aug. 24hr., Sept.-May daily 4pm-late.) In the last building before the church on the right of the waterfront dock, **O Statheros ❷** dishes out fresh, hefty portions of seafood under a canopy of hanging octopi. (☎61 172. Fried squid with mint €5.50. Open daily noon-midnight.) **Amargyros ❷** provides a similarly seafood-oriented menu in a more formal environment. (☎61 204. Octopus stew €7. Goat with tomato sauce €6. Open daily Apr.-Oct. 7am-midnight. MC/V.)

Bars, clubs, and late-night eateries can be found around the main plateia. Pass the first sign for Taverna Klimataria on the left of the main road to find **Cafe Yam ❸**, an outdoor restaurant and cocktail bar. Live Brazilian music and colorful plants fill the large, trendy terrace. (☎61 055. Mixed drinks €6.50. Most entrees €8-13. Open daily July 11-Sept. 15 8:30pm-3am.) Try **The Doors** for an intimate bar in a tiny space covered with Jim Morrison memorabilia. (Beer €2-4. Mixed drinks €4-5. Open daily 9pm-late.) **The Stones** is a spacious bar with a dance floor and a patio for people-watching. (Beer €2-4. Mixed drinks €4-5. Open daily 7pm-late.)

◆◆ **SIGHTS AND BEACHES.** The dank stalactite **caves** at the southern end of the island are Antiparos's main attraction. Buses run from Antiparos Town's port every hour from morning through early afternoon (20min., €5 round-trip). The bus trip and cave tour together take 1½hr. Names of ancient visitors are written on the walls with their years of entry. Unfortunately, some of the stalactites were broken off by Russian naval officers in the 18th century and "borrowed" on behalf of a St. Petersburg museum, while still more were destroyed by the Italians during WWII. Despite all this defilement, the caves, which plunge 100m into the earth, are dramatic and impressive; the stalactites stretch to over 7m in length, and the cavernous interior feels like a surreal, otherworldly landscape. (Open daily 10am-3pm; low season 10am-2pm.) Go through the stone archway to the immediate right of the plateia to reach the meager ruins of the 15th-century **Castle of Antiparos**, a village built by the Italian Loredano to defend his holdings from rampant piracy. Though new buildings exist in place of the first ones, which had 3m thick walls, they retain Loredano's original layout. **Psaraliki**, a 5min. walk south of town, is a pleasant beach, as is **Glifa**, a 15min. ride to the east on the bus toward the caves (every hr., €1). **Blue Island Divers** runs scuba diving lessons and tours. (☎61 493 or 69737 30 162; www.blueisland-divers.gr. €50 for 1 dive, €80 for 2.)

AMORGOS Αμοργός

King Minos of Crete was said to rule a kingdom on Amorgos in ancient times, a legend supported by the 1985 discovery of artifacts atop Mt. Moudoulia. Today, much of Amorgos resembles its most enduring sight, the Hozoviotissa Monastery, which burrows into the cliffs below Hora. The steep cliffs and clear waters were captured 20 years ago in the film *The Big Blue (Le Grand Bleu)*, and Amorgos's stunning natural beauty has not changed much since the movie's filming. Though tourism has boomed recently, Amorgos's small size and tight-knit local community have preserved the tranquility and local feel of its port towns. Ferry connections generally stop at Amorgos's two ports in succession—Aegiali in the northeast and larger Katapola in the southwest.

KATAPOLA Κατάπολα ☎ 22850

Whitewashed houses with blue trim, narrow streets climbing up the coastal hillside, and an overhanging Venetian castle make up Katapola, Amorgos's central port. Free from the commercial bustle and tourist hoards of many other Cycladic port towns, the town retains a serene, communal atmosphere even as more visitors have come to the island. The small streets hardly extend beyond the waterfront where the town's main activity is centered; a short walk will bring you to deserted beaches and Minoan ruins.

⌷ TRANSPORTATION. Ferries from both ports of Amorgos go to: Astypalea (3hr., 4 per week, €15); Donousa (1½hr., 6 per week, €7); Iraklia (2hr., 6 per week, €12); Koufonisia (1½hr., 1 per day, €7.50); Naxos (3-6hr., 1-2 per day, €14); Paros (4hr., 1-4 per day, €15); Piraeus (8½hr., 1-3 per day, €29); Schinousa (1¾hr., 6 per week, €10.50); Syros (5hr., 6 per week, €14.50). **Speedboats** go to Naxos (1½hr., 7 per week, €20). The bus station is to the left of the dock facing inland, 200m past the ferry landings. **Buses** connect villages in the summer, running to: Aegiali (45min., 12 per day, €2); Agia Anna (25min., 6-8 per day 10am-6pm, €1) via Hozoviotissa Monastery (20min., €1.20); Hora (15min., 11-15 per day 7:45am-midnight, €1.20); various beaches (9 per day 10am-6pm, €1.20). **Taxis** are available 24hr. (☎69447 43 090 or 69320 00 455).

⌷ ORIENTATION AND PRACTICAL INFORMATION. The town surrounds the ferry dock in a horseshoe, with restaurants, bars, and accommodations on either side. The port is at the center; most tourist services are between the ferry dock and the road to Hora.

Across from the large ferry dock is **Synodinos Tours,** which **exchanges currency,** has maps, and sells ferry tickets. (☎71 201. Open daily May-Oct. 8:30am-10pm and 1hr. before all boat departures; Nov.-Apr. 10am-1:30pm and 5-8:30pm and 1hr. before all boat departures.) **Agricultural Bank,** opposite the ferries, has a **24hr. ATM.** (☎71 872. Open M-Th 8am-2:30pm, F 8am-2pm.) The **laundromat** is past the docks on the way to the beach; take the first right after Pension Amorgos. (☎71 723. Wash and dry €10. Open M-Sa 8:30am-4:30pm and 6:30-9:30pm, Su 10am-2:30pm.) The **police** (☎71 210) are in Hora, but the **port police** (☎71 259; open 24hr.) are across from the ferry dock. The nearest **pharmacy** is in Hora. The **medical center** is at the far left end of the waterfront, in the white building behind the three statues. (☎71 805, emergencies ☎71 805 or 69772 99 674. Open M-F 9am-2:30pm.) **Minoa Hotel,** in the central plateia, has **Internet** access. (☎71 480. €5 per hr., min. €2.50. Open daily 8am-midnight.) The **post office** is located in a small boutique next to the Minoa Hotel, at the back left of the main plateia. (☎71 884. Open M-Tu, Th, Sa 10am-1pm and 7-10pm; W and F 10am-1pm.) **Postal Code:** 84008.

⌷ ACCOMMODATIONS AND FOOD. Katapola is a small town with few hotels and many **domatia.** At the far end of the beach from the port, **Titika Rooms ❷** surrounds a flowery, stone-lined garden; look for the green shutters. A free port shuttle takes you to the pleasant, if cluttered, rooms with bath, fridge, TV, air-conditioning, balcony, mosquito netting, and hair dryer. (☎71 660. Doubles €25-45; triples €30-55.) To reach **Big Blue Pension ❷** from the ferry dock, turn right after the plateia and follow signs uphill, or take the free port shuttle. The pension has spacious rooms, blue windows and doors, and open patios where guests can enjoy harbor views. Flower-studded walkways complement the rooms' bath, fridge, air-conditioning, and TV. (☎71 094. Doubles €25-50; triples €35-60.) **Pension Amorgos**

❸, across from the small ferry dock, rents modern, airy rooms with beguiling white-stucco and arched entries directly on the water, and has a rooftop veranda. (☎71 013. Doubles €30-40; triples/quads €60-70.)

Savor authentic Italian dishes like baked spaghetti (€6) at **Erato ❷,** the last cafe at the end of the wharf. (☎74 102. Pizza €6-8.50. Open noon-midnight.) **Aigaion Cafe ❶,** in the center of the main plateia, serves fruit juice (€3), crepes (€4-7), omelettes (€2.50-4), and mixed drinks (€5.50-6) to locals who lounge and chat into the nights. Inside the funky interior, people play board games and listen to pop music. (☎71 549. Open daily Apr.-Oct. 8am-3:30am; Nov.-Mar. 9am-midnight.) **Mourayio ❷,** across from the dock, has authentic meals in a simple outdoor seating area. Inside, you can get a sneak preview of your meal in coolers full of fresh fish. (☎71 011. Boiled octopus €7. Fried cod €5.50. Moussaka €5. Open 1pm-late.)

🖼🏖 **SIGHTS AND BEACHES.** Follow the signs uphill and out of town past the church to begin the 2km hike to the ancient town of **Minoa,** inhabited between the 10th and 4th centuries BC. Look for the base of the temple among the otherwise unimpressive ruins. The barely distinguishable acropolis once stood on the plateau above the temple. Thorough signs explain the site's history and the former location of the city's main buildings.

Agios Pavlos's shallow turquoise lagoon is exquisite and is only a short walk downhill from the bus stop. Adventurous swimmers can make the 150m crossing to **Nikouria Island,** or take a boat (€3.50), which leaves for the island every hour, for even more seclusion. Take a bus toward Aegiali and ask to be let off at Agios Pavlos (6 per day, €1.20). Various nude beaches provide sand and sun outside of town, opposite the dock. Smooth-stoned **Plakes** and the sandier **Agios Panteleimonas** are quiet, yet easily accessible by foot or boat—taxi boats leave from the left of the dock (every hr. 10am-5pm, round-trip €2.50).

🏔 **DAYTRIP FROM KATAPOLA: HOZOVIOTISSA MONASTERY.** A trip to Amorgos is incomplete without a visit to otherworldly 🏛**Hozoviotissa Monastery.** The 11th-century Byzantine edifice was built into a cliff face—one of the most exhilarating spectacles in all of Greece and an inspiration to the great 20th-century Swiss architect Le Corbusier, among others. Legend tells that attempts to build the monastery on the shore were thwarted; when the workers discovered their tools mysteriously hanging from the cliff, they figured it was an omen and started construction in the seemingly impossible location. If you complete the hike (up 350 stone steps), the monks will treat you to cold water, sweet ginger-flavored liquor, and *loukoumi.* Inside, visitors must lean to the left when climbing the narrow staircase to avoid the cliff face—it protrudes into the building's cave-like interior, which is never more than 5m deep. At the top, a multilingual monk will greet you to provide a short history and answer questions. To see more of the building, come in November when the entire island celebrates the **Feast of Panagia Hozoviotissa** at the monastery. If you miss the bus back, take the stone stairway (10m uphill from the fork in the road leading away from the monastery). A 20min. climb up the stairs will lead you to Hora. The road from the monastery also takes you to the crystal waters of **Agia Anna** and its two small, rock coves; from the bus stop, one is at the end of the path through the clearing, the other at the bottom of the central steps. Catch a bus (20min., 6 per day 10am-6pm, €1.20) from Katapola to the monastery. (☎71 274. Open daily 8am-1pm and 5-7pm. Modest dress required. Free.)

HORA Χώρα ☎22850

Also known as Amorgos Town, the island's small, untouristed capital lies 6km uphill from the harbor at the top of the mountains. An example of Byzantine village planning, Hora's winding streets were constructed to deter and confuse raiding pirates. They now allow visitors to meander along the narrow, cafe-lined walk to **Plateia Loza,** at the far end of town. Sights include a 14th-century Venetian **fortress,** a row of 10 defunct windmills on the mountain ledge above town, numerous Byzantine churches, and the first secondary school in Greece, built in 1821. The remnants of Amorgos's Minoan civilization are visible in the statues and relief carvings at the **Archaeological Museum,** across from Zygos Cafe and downhill from the large church at Pl. Loza. The museum displays unsigned inscriptions and sculptures from Minoa in a small courtyard and indoor area. (☎29 279. Open Tu-Su 8:30am-3pm. Free.) Rugged mountains and a placid coast run alongside the road from Hora to Aegiali. The clearly marked, sunny 4hr. **hike** begins behind Hora and stretches up the mountains to Potamos. Forty minutes into the hike, you'll find the crumbling Byzantine church of **Christososmas** (The Body of Christ) hewn out of a small cave that was once a hermit dwelling. The trail ascends past a series of monasteries before descending to views of miniature **Nikouria Island.** Deserted **Agios Mammas** church is the last significant marker before Potamos appears. From Potamos, hikers can walk 15min. to catch the bus in Aegiali to return to Hora (€2).

If you decide to spend the night in Hora, you can strike a deal with the **domatia** owners who meet your boat, or look for "rooms to let" signs along side streets. **Maria Economidou ❹** has modern, classy rooms. They all come with balcony, kitchenette, and impeccable bath. (☎71 111. Doubles €45; 2-person apartments €50-70.) The reception for **Pension Ilias ❷** is along the road from Hora to the monastery, while the rooms are one street uphill. Rooms have bath, TV, air-conditioning, hot pot, fridge, and a common balcony with views of the valley below; the apartments include full kitchen. (☎71 277. Doubles €25-55; apartments €50-80.) Both establishments will pick you up at the port if you call ahead. **Zygos ❶,** on the cafe-lined alley below Pl. Loza, serves homemade *syko* (candied fruits; €2.80), coffee (€1.50-3), and mixed drinks (€5) on a vine-roofed patio. Leisurely patrons play board games to international music in the comfortable interior. (☎71 350. Open daily 8am-3:30am.) **Liotrivi ❷,** near the bakery on the road to the monastery, puts delicious twists on Greek standards—*kalogiros* (eggplant with veal, feta, gouda, and tomato) and *exohiko* (lamb and vegetables in pastry shell) are the creative house specialities. (☎71 700. Entrees €5-7. Open daily May-Oct. 12:30pm-midnight.) The relaxed cafe downstairs at **Bayoko,** by the bus station, caters to people-watchers and music aficionados, with live jazz performances three times a week. Upstairs, at one of Hora's only clubs, nightly DJs spin Greek dance hits over the small dance floor from 9pm until dawn. (Beer €3-4. Mixed drinks €6. Ouzo €1.50.)

The **police** are in the main plateia with the big church, by Cafe Loza. (☎71 210. Open daily 8am-2pm.) A **24hr. ATM** is located at the bus stop. The **pharmacy** is opposite the bus stop. (☎74 166. Open M-F 10am-2pm and 6-9pm.) The **medical center** sits below the bus stop on the main road into Hora from Katapola. (☎71 207. Open M-F 9am-2:30pm.) Hora is home to the island's **OTE** (☎71 399; open M-F 8am-2pm), on the right 250m past Pl. Loza's major church, and the main **post office** (☎71 250; open M-F 7:30am-2pm), in a corner beyond Pl. Loza.

AEGIALI Αιγιάλη ☎22850

Aegiali, the island's other port, is as close as Amorgos comes to feeling touristy. As a result, the locals seem a little warier of travelers here than on other parts of the island. With a beach and many accommodations, leisurely Aegiali serves best as a base for exploring the beaches along the island's northern edge.

A number of pensions occupy the hillside inland of the waterfront. **Capetan Nikos ❸,** uphill and to the right before the medical center, has rooms with fridge, bath, TV, and air-conditioning managed by laid-back, helpful owner Nikos. Colorful paintings adorn the walls and the common balcony offers a grand view of the harbor. (☎73 026. Doubles €35-65.) Next door, **Poseidon Pension ❸** rents neat, trim rooms with kitchenette, bath, and outdoor seating. (☎73 453. Doubles €30-50; 3- to 4-person studios from €60.) **Camping Aegiali ❶** is just outside town, on the road to Tholaria. You can walk 10min. from the port to the campsite or take advantage of the free port transfer if you call ahead. The site has laundry and cooking facilities, a restaurant, bar, and impeccable showers. (☎73 500. Check-out 3pm. €5.50 per person, €4 per tent. Tent rental €6.) On the opposite end of the beach, past the end of the paved walkway, mellow out at cafe-club-restaurant ⬛**Disco The Que ❶**. They're too chill to have menus, but hipster waiters can tell you which snacks (€3) and meals (€5-7) to munch on during the day and which beers (€2.50) and mixed drinks (€5) to down at night. Music ranges from reggae and psychedelic rock to trance and jazz. (☎73 212. Open daily 10am-late.) **To Steki ❶,** at the edge of the beach past the bus stop, serves standard Greek fare in a simple, inviting outdoor setting popular with locals. (☎73 136. Octopus salad €5.20. Fish €4-6. Pasta €3-5. Open daily 5pm-midnight. MC/V.)

For **ferry** and **high-speed boat** schedules, see the listings for Katapola (p. 406). **Buses** go to Aegiali-Hora-Katapola (45min., 12 per day, €2.40), Lagada (10 per day, €1.20), and Tholaria (10 per day, €1.20). **Taxis** (☎69321 03 077) can be reached 24hr. Most tourist facilities are along the waterfront or just uphill. Facing inland, clubs are to the left along the beach and cafes are to the right. **Amorgos Travel,** on the 2nd floor of the building opposite the bus stop on the waterfront, provides information on accommodations and tours of the island. (☎73 401. Open daily 9am-2pm and 6-9pm.) **Nautilus Travel,** a block inland from the bus stop, sells ferry tickets. (☎73 032. Open daily 10am-10pm.) Facing the port, **Tomas MotoCar** rents cars. (☎73 444. Cars €25-40. Open daily 9am-9pm.) There is no bank in Aegiali. The **police** (☎73 320) are located in Langada; the 24hr. **port police** (☎73 620) are on the road inland to the bakery. A **pharmacy** is up the road by the Island Market. (☎73 173. Open M-F 9:30am-3pm and 6-10pm.) The **medical center** is 100m uphill past the pharmacy near the road to Potamos. (☎73 222. Open M, W, F 9:30am-2pm.) **Phones** are next door to the pharmacy. The **post office** is across from the pharmacy in the mini-mart. (☎73 001. Open daily 8am-11pm.) **Postal Code:** 84008.

IOS Ἴος

This drink-till-you-drop party island is rivaled only by Mykonos when it comes to nocturnal Dionysian rites. Daytime activity centers on the coast, as beachgoers settle down with a drink by the pool or sea to soak up the sun's energy and prepare for the long night ahead. Ios's hoteliers and restaurateurs have been making a successful effort to bring families to enjoy its more peaceful side, which emerges as visitors move farther away from the carousing, hedonistic center. And despite the island's knack for revelry, only three of its 36 beaches have been developed for tourism, so there are plenty of places to stretch out and soothe that hangover.

HORA (IOS TOWN) Χώρα ☎ 22860

If you're not drunk when you arrive, you will be when you leave. In Hora, shots go down and clothes come off faster than you can say "Opa!" Though it is an eerie, unpopulated oasis of calm during the day, the town stirs to life in the evening hours as revelers gear up for another round of drunken festivities. You'll see everything your mother warned you against—wine swilled from the bottle at 3pm, all-day drinking games, partiers dancing in the streets and on bars, people swimming less than 30min. after they've eaten, and so much more. Those in search of quieter pleasures stay in Gialos (the port), while the party animals crowd into Hora.

▐ TRANSPORTATION

Ferries: To: **Anafi** (3hr., 3-4 per week, €9); **Folegandros** (1½hr., 1-2 per day, €5); **Naxos** (1¾hr., 1-3 per day, €9); **Paros** (3hr., 1-3 per day, €10); **Piraeus** (8hr., 2-3 per day, €35); **Santorini** (1½hr., 3-5 per day, €7); **Sifnos** (3hr., 2 per week, €11.50); **Sikinos** (30min., 1-3 per day, €4); **Syros** (4hr., 3-4 per week, €15).

Flying Dolphins: To: **Iraklion, Crete** (2½hr., 3 per week, €37); **Mykonos** (2hr., daily, €26.60); **Naxos** (45min., daily, €20.70); **Paros** (1½hr., daily, €19.40); **Santorini** (45min., daily, €16).

Rentals: Jacob's Moto Rent (☎91 700), by the bus stop at the port and right before entering Mylopotas beach. Motorbikes €15-25. Cars €35-80. **Ios Rent-A-Car** (☎92 300), located in Acteon Travel in the port. Cars €35-60. MC/V.

✦ ▐ ORIENTATION AND PRACTICAL INFORMATION

Ios Town's action is based in three locations, each 20min. apart along the island's paved road. **Gialos,** the port, is at one end; **Hora,** the village, sits above on a hill; frenzied **Mylopotas beach** is 3km farther. During the day, the winding streets behind the church are filled with boutique clothing shops and postcard pushers. As the sun sets, they become the hub of nighttime activity. Buses shuttle between port, village, and beach (every 10-20min. 7:20am-12:30am, €1.20). People generally walk the downhill 3km between Hora and Mylopotas and 10min. downhill path from Hora to Gialos after midnight, but weary partiers also can take one of the three island **taxis** (☎69326 80 896) to and from Gialos.

Budget Travel: Acteon Travel (☎91 343; www.acteon.gr), adjacent to the bus stop in the port. Has 2 branches in Hora and 1 at Mylopotas beach. Sells **ferry tickets,** offers assistance with accommodations, **exchanges currency,** has **Internet** access (€1 per 15min.), and rents vehicles. Main port office open daily 8am-11pm; Hora branch open daily 10am-2pm and 5-10pm.

Banks: National Bank (☎91 565), by the main church in Hora. Has a **24hr. ATM.** Open M-Th 8am-2:30pm, F 8am-2pm.

Laundromat: Sweet Irish Dream Laundry (☎91 584), by the club with the same name, on the main road from the port. Wash and dry €8. Open 9:30am-9pm.

Police: ☎91 222. On the road to Kolitsani beach, past the OTE. Open 24hr.

Pharmacy: ☎91 562. In Hora, next to Acteon Travel. Open daily 8am-midnight.

Medical Center: ☎28 611 or 91 227. At the port, 100m from the dock. Specializes in drunken mishaps. Open M-F 8:30am-2:30pm and 6-8pm for **emergencies** only. In Hora, you can reach a **doctor** (Yiannis) 24hr. at ☎91 137 or 69324 20 200. His office is on the main road next to Fun Pub; open for emergencies 24hr.

Internet Access: All over the port and village. Most charge €4 per hr. **Acteon Travel,** at the port. Open daily 8am-11pm. **Francesco's,** in the village. **Far Out Beach Club,** on Mylopotas beach.

Post Office: ☎91 235. On the main road coming from the port, take a right after Sweet Irish Dream. Receives **Poste Restante.** Open M-F 7:20am-2pm. **Postal Code:** 84001.

ACCOMMODATIONS AND CAMPING

Affordable accommodations can be found in both the frenetic village and beach or in the quiet port. Each area has its own personality, so weigh your interests before making your choice. A tent, bungalow, or room on Mylopotas beach lets you roll hazily from blanket to beach with a herd of other tanned, recovering partiers, cutting out the daytime bus ride in between.

Far Out Beach Club and Camping (☎92 302; www.faroutclub.com), at the end of Mylopotas beach. A non-stop, hopping beachside complex and the hub of activity at Mylopotas beach. Far Out has rooms for every budget, from tents to hotel studios, at rock-bottom prices. Restaurant, bar, mini-mart, volleyball court, swimming pools, bungee jumping, free new movies (shown every evening), showers, laundry, Internet access, live music, scuba diving, and nightly Happy hour (5-8pm, 2-for-1 mixed drinks €5). Check-out noon. Open Apr.-Oct. €4-9 per tent, tent rental €1; cabins €5-12; bungalows €8-18; hotel rooms €12-35 per person. ❶

Francesco's (☎91 223; www.francescos.net), in the village. With your back to the bank, take the steps up from the left corner of the plateia, then take the 1st left. Owned by friendly Francesco and run by his warm family, this hostel is right out of a hip back-packer's dream, with new people to meet, a lounge and bar area perfect for catching the stunning sunset, and cheap dorms to crash in. Reception 9am-2pm and 6-10pm. Check-out 11am. A/C extra in low season. Breakfast €2-4.50, served 9am-2pm. Dorms €11-18; 2-4-person rooms €15-28 per person. ❶

Purple Pig Stars Camping (☎91 302), off the main road entering Mylopotas beach from Hora. Offers outdoor sleeping, camping, and bungalows. The site also has a pool, weekly barbeques, restaurant, bar, international live music, laundry, currency exchange, film viewings, travel agency, and safe deposit boxes. ❶

Hotel George and Irene (☎91 074, www.irene.gr), 3 blocks up from the village's main road. Away from the noise, but still near the action, rooms have balcony, TV, A/C, bath, and safety box. Internet €4 per hr. Laundry €3 per kg. Free transport to and from the port. Doubles €30-75. AmEx/MC/V. ❸

Camping Ios (☎92 035), on the far right of the harbor from the port in Gialos. Has immaculate grounds and a large pool. Common kitchen, safes, restaurant, bar and mini-mart are all available and just a 10min. walk from Hora. Take the footpath across from the bus station. Laundry €3 per 5kg. Check-out noon. Open June-Sept. €8 per person, tent and sleeping bag included. ❶

FOOD

Most eating on Ios coincides with heavy drinking, peaking in the middle of the night at gyro and crepe joints. There are a few better restaurants, though, among the ubiquitous bars and discos, at the port, and on the beach. **Caio Market** (☎91 035) is opposite the bus stop in Hora and provides basic goods 24 hr., and a **supermarket** is in the main plateia.

Ali Baba's (☎91 558), by the Ios gym. Coming down from the main plateia, take a right after you reach the fast-food restaurants. Continue down to the bottom of the road and take a left. Sweat through the delicious, spicy, and impressively authentic Thai menu in

A PUZZLING DEMISE

The biggest mystery for most of Ios's drunken revelers is probably what exactly happened the night before. However, the island's locals and dedicated classicists pride themselves on the island's long tradition of mythic lore.

The course of Homer's life is shrouded in mystery; however, it is undisputed that Plakotos, Ios is the blind poet's burial place. Not knowing his birthplace, Homer approached the oracle at Delphi to gain insight. The oracle ominously answered, "The isle of Ios is your mother's country, and it shall receive you dead; but beware of the riddles of young children."

Weakened by old age, Homer returned to his mother's birthplace, Ios. There he was approached by a group of boys returning from fishing. In accordance with the oracle's prediction, the mischievous children presented him with the following riddle: "What we have caught we leave behind us. What we have not caught we carry with us."

Mystified that the prophecy had been realized and overwhelmed with despondent passion, Homer threw himself off the cliffs. Although epic acolytes may never know the cause of Homer's death, they will never have to suffer the same fate because of the children's riddle. The lousy answer that brought low the most celebrated storyteller of all time: lice.

the enclosed garden and finish your meal with a complementary jello shot. Internet €4 per hr., free for diners. Pad thai €9. Open daily 6pm-1am. ❷

■ **Old Byron's** (☎69781 92 212). Look for the sign by the pharmacy pointing up 3 blocks to this intimate bistro in a shady side street. It puts a creative twist on Greek staples, with dishes like shrimp in phyllo with yogurt and chili dip. Reservations recommended for dinner. Entrees €9-15. Open M-Sa 6-11:30pm, Su noon-11:30pm. MC/V. ❸

Pomodoro (☎91 387), uphill behind Disco 69. This relatively new, sleek addition to Ios' eating scene serves up Italian-Mediterranean cuisine from a perch on Hora's central hill. On the rooftop deck with panoramic views of the island or in the breezy, high-ceilinged downstairs dining area, diners escape the buzz of bars and shops. Traditional wood-fired pizzas €6.50-10.50. Grilled squid with chili jam €6.50. Open daily 6pm-1am. ❷

Polydoros (☎91 132), on Koumbara beach. Walk (1.75km) or take the bus (5min., 1 per hr.) on the road along the harbor's beach. The beloved hangout of many of Ios's residents, who will stand for nothing less than the freshest ingredients. Shrimp *saganaki* with feta €8.50. Open 1pm-midnight. ❷

👁 🏖 SIGHTS AND BEACHES

Pay a visit to the Ios **Archaeological Museum,** in the town hall across from the bus stop, to view artifacts from Ios's long and rich history of habitation, particularly from the ruins of Skarkos. Watch for a tablet that mentions Homerium, an ancient month named in honor of the poet. Check out the second floor to see the latest of a rotating summer exhibition of art from contemporary Greek artists in various media. (Open Tu-Su 8:30am-3pm. €2, Under 18 and students free.) According to legend, Homer died and was buried on Ios; the supposed site of **Homer's tomb** has been worn to rubble, but the spot in Plakatos, on the island's northern tip, still draws a few dedicated tourists. To repent for the previous night's excess, walk toward the windmills to the path at the top of the hill, which leads to the solitary **monastery.** An **Open Theater Festival Program** is held every summer above the windmills on the island—inquire at a travel agency for more info.

During the day, crowds lounge on the **beaches. Mylopotas,** a 20min. walk downhill from Hora, has music blasting, and all parties flock to the debaucherous **Far Out Beach Club** (p. 411) to lounge by the pool, try watersports in the bay, and start drinking early. The long, wide stretch of sand also has beach soccer and volleyball areas. **Koumbara,** 1.75km down the road that follows Gialos beach, draws a much smaller crowd to its large cove, which is a popular place for windsurfing. For those who want quiet and beauty of the natural variety, buses (25min.; 2 per day 11am, 5pm; €6) go to the more secluded ◨**Manganari,** the island's nicest stretch of sand. Gialos (the port beach), Mylopotas, and Manganari all offer watersports, from tubing (€9-25) to windsurfing (€15-55). Continuing uphill from the OTE, look for the path on the left that leads to the secluded beach and crystal pool of water at the little bay of **Kolitsani** (a 15min. walk from Hora). Nude **Psathi,** on the eastern coast, is accessible by moped and bus (daily 11am, 4pm).

▓ NIGHTLIFE

Most of Ios's extraordinary number of bars are packed into the old village, making it easy to hit all the hot spots in one night. The largest and loudest discos line the main road. Many start their night at rooftop and hostel bars, like those at **Francesco's** and **Far Out,** swilling liquor from the bottle in the main plateia or by the pool at sunset, hitting the village between midnight and 1am, then migrating to the discos before sunrise.

Blue Note (☎92 488), off the main plateia, past the fast-food joints, and around the corner to the left. The jolly owner Francesco (also the owner of the popular backpackers' hostel) most likely will be armed with a full bottle of Jager, giving out free shots to fuel the night's revelry. Open 10:30pm-4:30am.

Rehab, tucked away downhill from the village's main plateia. Barhoppers are handed a playing card upon entry; if you can find your match, you'll be treated to a complimentary bucket of mixed drink to share. In the meantime, techno mixes blast to encourage revelers to reveal their hands. Mixed drinks €4-6. Beer €3. Open 9pm-4:30am.

Red Bull (☎91 019), in the main plateia in the village. If flashing lights and glitzy club decor aren't your thing, this small, wood-trimmed bar, which plays loud 90s music and pop hits, will give you wings. Beer €3. Open 9pm-4:30am.

Disco 69 (☎91 064; www.disco69club.com), on the main bar street on the right. Blares mainstream dance music; when the cavernous dance floor gets too crowded with grinding bodies, people hop onto the bar and carry on. Free shot with all drinks. Cover €6 midnight-4am. Beer €5. Open 10pm-4am.

The Slammer Bar (☎91 019), in the left inland corner of the main plateia. If you ask, the bartender will whack your helmeted head with a blunt object before you down a tequila slammer (tequila, Tía María, and Sprite; €3), which gets you equally hammered. Open daily 10pm-4:30am.

Sweet Irish Dream, in a large building on the main road leading from the port. Most save this nighttime reverie for their last stop, pausing to dance on the tables before nodding off in the dark interior, then squinting out into the bright, early morning sun. Cover €5 2:30am-4:30am. Beer €3. Open 11am-4:30am.

FOLEGANDROS Φολέγανδρος

According to legend, King Minos's son made the first footprints on this island and gave it his name. For many years, few followed in the mythic leader's footsteps; Folegandros's rocky cliffs and inaccessible port secluded it from the outside. Unlike Mykonos and Santorini, Folegandros still remains off the beaten island-hopping path, making it an oasis of calm compared with its more rowdy Cycladic neighbors. Its dry, steep hills are terraced with low, snaking stone walls worn by centuries of fierce wind—the only tumultuous presence on this serene island.

HORA Χώρα ☎22860

The capital of Folegandros, cliffside Hora sparkles with whitewashed churches, blue shutters, and fuchsia bougainvillea vines. Hospitable villagers and easy accessibility from the port by bus make it the ideal base on the island.

🖪🔃 TRANSPORTATION AND PRACTICAL INFORMATION. Irregular **ferries** run to: Ios (1½hr., 1-2 per day, €5.50); Kithnos (5hr., 3 per week, €16); Milos (2hr., 3 per week, €7); Naxos (3hr., 1-3 per day, €9.60); Paros (4hr., 1-3 per day, €7.70); Piraeus (10hr., 1-3 per day, €32); Santorini (1½hr., 1-2 per day, €6.90); Serifos (4hr., 2 per week, €10); Sifnos (3hr., 1-3 per day, €4.30); Sikinos (40min., 1-2 per day, €4.30). After disembarking the ferry, you can board the bus from the port, Kararostassi, to Hora. **Buses** (10min.) head to the port before each ferry, then return with new arrivals (16 per day 7:20am-midnight, €1.20). A **taxi** is available at ☎41 048. **Moped rental** (€15) is available at the tourist information office.

The **tourist information** office **exchanges currency,** runs boat tours around the island (€15-25), **stores luggage,** sells maps (€6), and provides info on accommodations. (☎41 158. Open 9am-3:30pm, 6pm-midnight.) Continue down the main road and turn left after Pl. Pounta to find **Maraki Travel,** which **rents cars** (€40 per day), provides **Internet** access (€4 per hr., min. €1.50.), and sells ferry tickets. (☎41 273. Open daily 10am-1pm, 5-9pm.) The only **ATM** on the island is in Pl. Kontarini, the main square. Make a right after Folegandros Snack Bar; it's in the far corner of the plateia. Past Maraki Travel, head straight past the next two tree-filled plateias and bear right after passing Kritikos. A sharp right before the market leads to the **police** (☎41 249). The **pharmacy** (☎41 540) is on the road to the port, after the post office. The **medical center** (☎41 222) is on Pl. Pounta as you enter town from the main road. (Open M-F 9am-2pm. In an **emergency** call ☎69386 10 095.) The **post office** is on the left as you enter town. (☎41 299. Open M-F 9am-2pm.) **Postal Code:** 84011.

🏠🏕 ACCOMMODATIONS AND CAMPING. A recent spike in Folegandros's popularity has created a shortage of space and a rise in prices, so reserve ahead of time in high season. Most accommodations are pricey, and camping is the only real budget option. By the tourist office, near the center of town, **Hotel Polikandia** ❸ has rooms with fridge, bath, fan, safe, phone, and breezy balcony surrounding a lovely flagstone garden and a pool. A limited number of deluxe rooms include kitchenette and bathtub with hydromassage. (☎41 322. Breakfast €5. Singles €30-65; doubles €45-105; triples €45-115.) At **Rent Rooms Lambrini** ❹, across from the police station, the tastefully decorated apartments have balcony, TV, fan, fridge and coffeemaker. Inquire at Asyngrito Taverna in Plateia Maraki. (☎41 266. Doubles €50.) **Rent Rooms Evyenia** ❸, across from Hotel Polikandia, has comfortable rooms with fridge and bath. (☎41 006. Doubles €30-65; 4- to 5-person rooms €40-108.) Its owners also run **Hotel Aegeo** ❹, on the other side of the plateia, a slightly more upscale alternative with fridge, air-conditioning, TV, balcony, and free port shuttle service. Inquire at Rent Rooms Evyenia. (☎41 468. Doubles €40-85.) To find **Livadi Camping** ❶, set back from the beach on the road from the port to Hora, take a left at the sign, walking behind the beach for about 1km, or call for a port shuttle. Spare but clean facilities are close to a secluded beach and include a restaurant. (☎41 478. €5 per person, €2 per tent.)

🍴 FOOD. At **🔲Folegandros Snack Bar** ❶, across from Maraki Travel, owner Michailidia makes what could be the best cappuccino outside of Italy. He provides a wide array of fresh meals and snacks, including crepes (€4.50) and fruit juices (€3-3.50), along with music, games, books, maps, Wi-Fi (€1 per 10min.), and info about the island. (☎41 226. Open daily May-Oct. 7am-midnight.) **🔲Kriti-**

kos ❷ is to the left after Pl. Pounta then straight through two more plateias. It serves fresh meat straight from the owner's herd. Garlic toast drizzled in olive oil and fresh sugar-dusted cake are included to start and finish your meal. (☎41 219. Grilled lamb €6.90. Open daily noon-1am.) **Pounta ❶,** on your left just as you enter Pl. Pounta, the first square from the port road, serves charming, healthful options in a beautiful stone garden. (☎41 063. Yogurt, honey, and fruit €5. Risotto €4. Open daily 8am-3pm and 6:30pm-midnight.) **Piatsa ❶,** sprawled across the raised center of bleached Pl. Kontarini, makes delicious traditional Greek meals. The *matzata* (homemade pasta with pork or chicken; €8.50) is an island speciality. (☎41 274. Open daily 10am-midnight. MC/V.)

🔆🏠 **SIGHTS AND NIGHTLIFE.** The **Church of Panagia,** above the town on Pale-okastro Hill, is an unbeatable place to watch the sunset or photograph white-washed domes against the mountains and sea. From Pl. Pounta, take a sharp right and hike up the zigzagging path past a tranquil three-level cemetery. The torso of a marble Roman statue sits in the masonry of the crumbling stone wall. (Open in summer daily 7-9pm; in winter for religious festivals only.) Walking into town from Pl. Pounta, take your first right up the stairs through the narrow archway labeled "Kastro." You'll find yourself in a triangular fortification of houses, built under Venetian rule in the years following the Fourth Crusade of 1204. On your left after the church of **Agia Anargyron,** walk through the tiny corridor that centuries of townspeople used as a hideout to evade Romans, Franks, Venetians, and Turks. When plundering conquerors and raiding pirates invaded the town, 150 to 200 large families dwelled in this small cliff-top enclosure, each family in its own *monospito* (one-roomed house). Continuing straight through the rows of these houses, you will come to the church of **Our Lady Pantanassa** at the end of the road. From the balcony outside its door, you can catch one of the best views of the island's terraced coastline. To the left is the edge of Hora and the hills leading to Ano Meria; to the right is a panoramic vista looking toward Milos, Kimolos, and Sifnos, all three of which you can see on a clear day. Weekly boat cruises around the island can take visitors to various secluded beaches as well as the mouth of **Chryssospilia** (Golden Cave), once a refuge for islanders during pirate invasions. Although entry to the cave is forbidden due to archaeological investigation of Minoan settlement, local lore insists that there is a secret tunnel connecting this uncharted cave to Panagia. (Cruises May-Sept. M, W, F-Sa 11am, returns 5pm; €25. Includes lunch. Buy tickets at the tourist office.) From July to mid-August, visitors partake in the annual **Folegandros Festivities,** a series of almost nightly exhibitions, concerts, screenings, and performances by Greek artists. The festivities are orga-nized by the Isolario project, which aims to create a cultural and collaborative net-work between the small islands of the Aegean. Find the festivities' scheduled program in Maraki Travel or posted in the main plateia.

In the summer, when the island's permanent population of 650 triples with the influx of tourists, weddings fill the town's plateias with roasting goats and local music. **Greco,** at the bus stop for Ano Meria, is a cafe-bar adorned with artistic lighting and Botticelli-esque murals. (☎41 456. Mixed drinks €6-8. Open daily Apr.-Oct. 11am-2:30pm and 7pm-late.)

🥾 **HIKING.** The hike from Hora to **Agali** takes about 1hr.; it's another 30min. to **Agios Nikolaos beach.** Start from Hora, following the elevated road to Ano Meria. After 20-30min., take one of two dirt paths leading left and down to the glassy, aquamarine beaches and the countryside. Across from one of several small churches, you'll see the trail that snakes down to Agali. It traverses rocky terraces and passes olive trees down the main track into town (stay to the left). There you'll find a few tavernas, domatia, and several tents. A rocky trail past the first tavernas

CYCLADES

on the right leads to Ag. Nikolaos beach. Between the two beaches are intimate, stony coves and beaches made for cool, quiet dips. The low-key beach stop is a popular site for cheery families, and the coves fill quickly with splashing children by mid-afternoon. Alternatively, the bus from Agali (5min., 7 per day 10am-7:30pm, €2) leaves you at a stop 5min. from the sea and sand by foot.

⚡ DAYTRIP FROM HORA: ANO MERIA Άνο Μεριά. Ano Meria has many footpaths leading to secluded **beaches,** including **⬛Livadaki.** This pebbled cove with pristine, turquoise waters is nestled at the mouth of a ravine. Catch the first bus to have the beach completely to yourself, and note the passing time by swimming out to the stone sun dials built into the rocky cove wall. The winding, sometimes rocky trails—the only way to reach the beaches—take a little over 1hr. each and lead hikers on a rustic walk through the terraced countryside to the rugged cliffs along the coast. To find the trails, walk away from the bus stop along the main road until you see signs pointing to the different beaches. The tourist office's daylong boat tours around the island stop at several beaches; inquire upon arrival. For a window into rural island life, stop by the **Folklore Museum** in Ano Meria. On an island whose history is empty of epoch-defining events, the olive presses, looms, and fishing nets detail the perpetual struggle against infertile soil and stormy harbors. Take the bus to Ano Meria and ask the driver to let you off at the museum. (Guidebook €5. Open daily July-Aug. 5-8:30pm. Free.) Those planning an extended stay in Folegandros or who want to aquaint themselves with island culture during July or August should look into **The Cycladic School.** It leads six- to 12-day courses at the local primary school that focus on different combinations of drawing, painting, theater, music, sailing, diving, history, and philosophy. A day at the school includes a lecture, practice, and excursions around the island (p. 83).

SANTORINI Σαντορίνη

Whitewashed towns balanced on plunging cliffs, scorching black-sand beaches, and sharply stratified geological rock formations make Santorini's landscape nearly as dramatic as the volcanic cataclysm that created it. This eruptive past—and stark beauty—has led some to believe that Santorini is the lost continent of Atlantis. The island, also called "Thira," was an outpost of Minoan society from 2000 BC until around the turn of the 17th century BC, when an earthquake destroyed the wealthy maritime settlement of Akrotiri. All hope of recovery vanished when a massive volcanic eruption spread lava and pumice across the island around 1625 BC. The destruction of Santorini heralded the fall of Minoan prominence; the volcanic eruption may have led to a tidal wave that leveled the ancient Minoan palaces on Crete. Natural disaster continues to threaten the safety of Santorini's residents: as recently as 1956, an earthquake caused serious damage to the island. Yet the volcanoes greatly enriched the island's soil, bestowing upon Santorini a greener landscape than that of its mostly barren Cycladic neighbors. Beauty this stunning couldn't be kept secret for long, and armies of tourists pour into Santorini from across the world in parades of weddings and honeymoons. Due to its popularity and the cost of importing water and produce, however, the prices on the island are as steep as the cliffs of the caldera.

FIRA Φήρα ☎22860

Atop a hill and far from the black-sand beaches, Fira's congested assemblage of glitzy shops, whizzing mopeds, and hyperactive crowds can be overwhelming. Tourist traffic has made it easy to find a hamburger or wiener schnitzel, and groups of hotels fearlessly peer over steep cliffs, almost daring the seismically active island to send them tumbling into the sea. Even kitsch and overcrowding, however, can't negate the pleasure of wandering the cobbled streets and arriving at the caldera on the western edge of town in time to watch the sunset.

TRANSPORTATION

Boats dock at one of three ports on the island: Athinios, Fira, or Oia. Most ferries arrive in Athinios and buses meet every boat to take passengers to Fira (25min., €1.70). Be aware that even if your ferry ticket says "Fira," you may be landing in the town of Athinios. Fira's port is down a 588-step footpath from the town; you can walk, or take a cable car (every 20min. 6:30am-11pm; €4, children €2, luggage €2), or hire a donkey (€4). All these methods of transportation are fun and scenic. Santorini's **buses** run frequently and can take you anywhere you want to go, but their convenience leads to overcrowding. Arrive at the station 10min. early to make your bus. Estimated journey lengths are based on ideal circumstances; busy buses often move much more slowly.

Flights: Olympic Airways (☎22 493) flies to **Athens** (50min., 4-5 per day, €85-120) and **Thessaloniki** (1¼hr., 3-4 per week, €125). To reach the office from the bus depot, turn left, then right, then walk 150m. Open M-Sa 8am-5pm, Su and holidays 8:30am-3:30pm. **Aegean Airlines** (☎28 500) also has flights to **Athens** (6-7 per day, €100) and **Thessaloniki** (1-2 per day, €125). Aegean shares an office with Hertz car rental, 200m past Pl. Theotokopoulou on 25 Martiou, on the way to the Youth Hostel. Open M-F 9am-1pm and 6-8pm.

Ferries: Run to: **Anafi** (1½hr., 8 per week, €6.90); **Folegandros** (1½hr., 6 per week, €6.90); **Ios** (1hr., 1-3 per day, €7); **Iraklion, Crete** (4hr., 4 per week, €15.10); **Naxos** (3hr., 1-2 per day, €15.50); **Paros** (4hr., 1-4 per day, €16.50); **Piraeus** (10hr., 2-3 per day, €32.50); **Sifnos** (7hr., 2 per week, €12.50); **Sikinos** (4½hr., 8 per week, €6.70); **Syros** (8hr., 6 per week, €23); **Thessaloniki** (18hr., 2 per week, €42).

Flying Dolphins: Run to **Iraklion, Crete** (2hr., 7 per week, €38), **Mykonos** (3hr., daily, €28-32), and other locations.

Buses: ☎25 404. To: **Akrotiri** (30min., €1.60); **Athinios** (25min., 7-8 per day, €1.70); **Kamari** (20min., 32 per day 7:30am-midnight, €1.20); **Monolithos** (30min., 12 per day 7:10am-8pm, €1.20) via the **airport; Oia** (30min., 25 per day 6:50am-11pm, €1.20); **Perissa** (30min., 32 per day 7am-midnight, €1.90).

Taxis: ☎22 555. In Pl. Theotokopoulou by the bus station. Available 24hr.

Rentals: Marcos Rental (☎23 877), 50m uphill past the plateia. Mopeds €15-20 per day. ATVs €20-30 per day. Helmets included. Open daily 8:30am-8pm.

ORIENTATION AND PRACTICAL INFORMATION

From the bus station, walk uphill and to the right to **Plateia Theotokopoulou,** which is full of travel agencies, banks, and cafes. At the fork, the street on the right is **25 Martiou,** the main cobblestoned road. It leads from the plateia toward Oia and is

CYCLADES

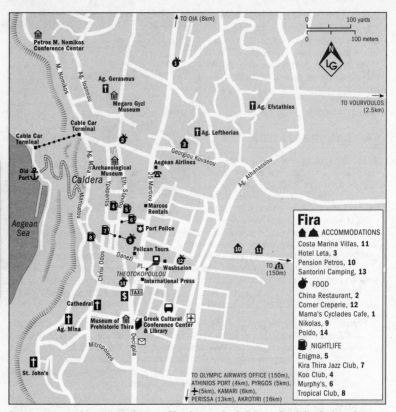

Fira

▲▲ ACCOMMODATIONS

Costa Marina Villas, **11**
Hotel Leta, **3**
Pension Petros, **10**
Santorini Camping, **13**

🍎 FOOD

China Restaurant, **2**
Corner Creperie, **12**
Mama's Cyclades Cafe, **1**
Nikolas, **9**
Poldo, **14**

🍸 NIGHTLIFE

Enigma, **5**
Kira Thira Jazz Club, **7**
Koo Club, **4**
Murphy's, **6**
Tropical Club, **8**

home to several accommodations. Head onto the left branch of the fork and turn onto any westbound street to find many of the best bars, stores, and discos. Farther west is the **caldera** (basin), bordered by **Ypapantis,** where pricey restaurants, hotels, and galleries bask in the stunning vista.

Budget Travel: Pelican Tours (☎22 220; www.pelican.gr), in the plateia, next to the port police. Sells ferry tickets and organizes boat trips to the volcano, hot springs, and Thirasia. Open 8am-11:30pm. AmEx/MC/V.

Bank: National Bank (☎22 370), on a road off 25 Martiou to the left before the plateia. **Exchanges currency. 24hr. ATM.** Open M-Th 8am-2:30pm, F 8am-2pm.

Bookstore: International Press (☎25 301), in the plateia, has magazines and a selection of popular books. Paperbacks €13-14. Open daily 7:30am-midnight.

Library: The Greek Cultural Conference Center and Library (☎24 960), off 25 Martiou, on the corner before the post office. Has a few shelves of English books and free **Internet** access in the basement. Open M, W, F 9am-3pm and 5-8pm; Tu and Th 9am-4pm; Sa 10:30am-2pm.

Laundromat: ☎23 113. Down the hill from the main plateia. Wash and dry €8. Open daily Apr.-Oct. 9am-5pm. Pickup available 24hr. from the adjoining Pelican Hotel.

Medical Center: ☎23 333. Turn left out of bus station and take another left. Open M-F 8:30am-2:30pm. Open 24hr. in **emergencies.**

Telephones: OTE (☎22 121). 200m uphill past the plateia on 25 Martiou. Open M-F 7:30am-3:10pm.

Internet Access: PC World (☎25 551), in the main plateia 2 doors down from the international bookstore. €2.50 per hr. Wi-Fi €4 per hr. Open daily June-Sept. 9am-1am, Oct.-May 9am-10pm.

Post Office: ☎22 238. 50m downhill from the plateia. Open daily M-F 7:30am-2pm. **Postal Code:** 84700.

ACCOMMODATIONS AND CAMPING

In summer, pensions and hotels fill up quickly and prices skyrocket. The cheapest options on the island are the youth hostels on Perissa beach and in Oia and camping in Fira. You can find cheaper places in Karterados, 2km south of Fira, or in the small inland towns along the main bus routes—try Messaria, Pyrgos, or Emborio. Hostels and many pensions will pick you up at the port if you reserve ahead.

Costa Marina Villas (☎28 923; www.pelican.gr), 2 doors down from Pension Petros. In a quiet space away from the road, Costa Marina has spacious rooms with wrought-iron beds, A/C, fridge, bath, phone, and safe; some have kitchen. Breakfast €6. Singles €38-68; doubles €52-84; triples €65-104. MC/V. ❹

Pension Petros (☎22 573; www.astirthira.com). With International Press to your right, follow the traffic downhill to the right, off the plateia; turn left and then right at the end of the street and continue for 50m. Owner Petros shares stories and bottles of wine with travelers. Cozy rooms have patio, bath, TV, fridge, and A/C. Free port shuttle. Singles €25-50; doubles €30-55; triples €45-70. ❷

Hotel Leta (☎22 540), 200m from the plateia. Walking up the main road, follow signs across from the laundromat. This colorful building provides a quiet escape from the crowds, as well as a pool and a scenic view of the sea. Rooms have A/C, TV, bath, and fridge. Free transport to and from the port. Doubles €40-65; triples €50-80. ❹

Santorini Camping (☎22 944; www.santorinicamping.gr). Follow the blue signs away from the plateia (300m). This shady campsite is the most festive spot in town and among the most affordable. The grounds have a pool, bar and billiards, cafe, and mini-mart. Free transport to and from the port. Internet access €2 per 30min., €3 per hr. 24hr. hot showers. Washing machine €4 (soap included). Quiet hours 11:30pm-7am. Check-out noon. Open May.-Oct. €5.50-9 per person, €2.50-4 per child; €3.50 per tent; 2-person bungalow €17-40. Prices vary by season. MC/V. ❶

FOOD

Inexpensive restaurants are hard to find in Fira, but the few that exist are crammed between shops on the tiny streets between the caldera and the plateia. The caldera is lined with fine dining options that impose a hefty fee for their priceless views. Generic but convenient snack shops and gyro joints dot the plateia as budget alternatives for the hungry.

Mama's Cyclades Cafe (☎23 032). Head north on the road to Oia; it's on the right. Mama is chatty and endearingly loud. Homemade preserves and syrup perfect this eatery's cozy morning feel. If you come for lunch or dinner, prepare to be stuffed to the gills as your new Greek Mama makes sure her "babies" eat enough. Blueberry pancakes with hash browns, toast, and jam €5. Open daily 8am-1am. ❷

Poldo (☎24 004), up the street from the National Bank. This classic souvlaki counter offers outstanding gyros (small €1.80, large €4), falafel, and soy burgers (€3.50 each). Open daily noon-late. ❶

Nikolas (☎ 24 550), on Eth. Stavrou, next to the Town Club. In stark contrast to the tourist restaurants overlooking the caldera, Nikolas's atmosphere is undeniably local and down-to-earth, complete with a daily rotating menu in Greek. Beef with noodles €8. Tzatziki €3. Open M-Sa noon-3:30pm and 6-11pm, Su 6-11pm. ❷

Corner Creperie (☎ 25 512). Walking from the bus stop, turn right down the hill after the main plateia. This palm-lined restaurant serves delicious crepes (€5-8) and breakfast foods. Waffles €5.50-7. Eggs, bacon, and juice €5.80. Open daily 8am-late. ❷

China Restaurant (☎ 24 760), to the left after the OTE; walk 50m up the street. This alternative to standard Greek fare is in a rooftop garden complete with hanging lanterns and prices far lower than the nearby caldera restaurants. Broccoli beef €9.90. Chicken in lemon sauce €8.90. Open noon-midnight. MC/V. ❸

🅖 SIGHTS

Walk to the main road from the bus station to reach the **Museum of Prehistoric Thira.** The sleekly designed collection charts Santorini's pre-eruption civilization through frescoes, fossils, marble vessels, reconstructions of the ancient city, and thorough explanatory signs. (☎ 23 217. Open Tu-Su 8:30am-7:30pm. €3, students and EU seniors €2, EU students free. Ticket also valid at Archaeological Museum.) The **Petros M. Nomikos Conference Center,** past the cable car station, houses an exhibition center that currently displays life-size reproductions of Ancient Thira's and Akrotiri's magnificent **wall paintings;** the prized originals are in the National Archaeological Museum in Athens (p. 116) and the Museum of Prehistoric Thira. The brightly colored and intricately detailed murals provide important insights into the history and culture of Santorini's ancient Minoans, as well as the island's former plant and animal life. Look for the detailed model boat in the first room past the entrance. (☎ 23 016. Open daily May-Oct. 10am-9pm. €3, students and seniors €1.50, children under 18 free; audio tour €3.) Fira's **Archaeological Museum,** just steps away from the cable cars, displays Geometric vases, red-and-black figure pottery, marble *kouros* sculptures, and well-preserved figurines. (☎ 22 217. Open Tu-Su 8:30am-3pm. €3, students and EU seniors €2, EU students free.) The **Megaro Gyzi Museum,** uphill off the main road below the clock tower, documents Santorini's history with Venetian maps, old photographs, and paintings. (☎ 23 077. Open May-Sept. 20 M-Sa 10:30am-1:30pm and 5-8pm, Su 10:30am-4:30pm; Sept. 20-Oct. daily 10am-4pm. €3, students €1.50, children under 11 free.)

🅑 🄺 BEACHES AND OUTDOOR ACTIVITIES

Fira is a convenient base for exploring the surrounding beaches. The closest, though least spectacular, is **Vourvoulos,** about a 1hr. walk north of town. The rocky area is one of the more secluded of Santorini's famed black-sand beaches, though the craggy coastline is probably the least conducive to sunbathing. The festive beach towns of **Perivolos** and **Perissa** lie along an expansive 9km stretch of black sand on the southeastern coast, welcoming a more casual crowd of beach bums to its cheap bars and laid-back rooms for rent. Buses leave Fira for Perissa and Perivolos every 30min. (20min., €1.90). Right by the beach, cheery **Youth Hostel Anna** ❶ in Perissa greets budget travelers with Internet access (€3 per hr.), a book exchange, and helpful reception. From the bus stop, take the road along the beach, turning left at the main intersection. The hostel is 500m farther on the right. (☎ 82 182. Dorms €12-15; quads €15.) The island's black sand is hot, so bring sandals.

The little islands along Santorini's caldera rim cater to curious visitors tired of viewing the volcanic strata from afar. The most popular boat excursion goes to the **active volcano** (entrance fee €2), with a 30min. guided hike up the black rocks

WATER, WATER, EVERYWHERE. Nor any drop to drink. It is an unfortunate irony that Santorini, though surrounded by the Aegean and the Sea of Crete, suffers from a major water shortage. Santorini's residents are quick to turn off their faucets, flush every other time they use the toilet, and head to the kiosk or mini-mart for bottled water to drink or cook. Travelers should follow suit, **conserving water** at every opportunity and not drinking from the tap.

to see the crater. Most boats make a stop afterward in the nearby ochre-tinted waters of Palea Kameni or Nea Kameni, warmed by hot sulfur springs, though you have to brave a 50m chilly swim through choppy waters to get there. A longer excursion goes to the island of **Thirasia,** providing about 2hr. to wander through the tiny towns and taverna-lined streets. Built along Thirasia's upper ridge, the sleepy, whitewashed villages of **Manolas** and **Potamos** have gorgeous views of Santorini's western coast. Tour groups dock at **Korfos** or **Reeva.** From Korfos, you'll have to pant up 300 steps or hail a donkey (€4) to get to the villages; Reeva has a paved road. All travel agencies sell boat tours of the caldera, ranging from 3hr. excursions on the volcano (€18) to full-day cruises including dinner and sunset views in Oia (€38-42); no single travel agency offers every option. Ask around to find the right tour to suit your interests.

ENTERTAINMENT AND NIGHTLIFE

Those who want to catch the summer's latest blockbusters can go to the **open-air cinema** in Kamari, where American films (with Greek subtitles) and live concerts take place twice a week; pick up programs at roadside stands in Fira and Kamari. (☎31 074. www.cinekamari.gr. Shows July-Aug. M and W 9:30pm and midnight.) Fira's nightlife is one of the hippest scenes in Greece. Clubs gear up around midnight; most line Eth. Stavrou, between the caldera and 25 Martiou. Beer is €3-4; mixed drinks run €5-8. Covers range from €5-15.

Murphy's (☎22 248; www.murphys-bar.com), next to Enigma. Claims to be the 1st Irish pub in Greece. The long, thin room, plastered with international flags, outdated license plates, and satellite TVs tuned into international rugby and soccer games, is packed with dancing patrons. The bartender rings a bell to the beat and hands out free shots with your 1st beer (€5). Mixed drinks €7.50. Happy hour 3:30-5:30pm and 9:30-10:30pm. Cover €5 after 10pm. Open Mar.-Oct. 11:30am-4am.

Tropical Club (☎23 089), high on the caldera, on the road down to the Old Port. Signature drinks (€8) are as tasty as they are creative; try a "sunset coffee" like the Bob Marley frappé (dark rum, Kahlua, iced coffee, and cream). Arrive by 8pm for balcony seating. At night, a DJ spinning American music transforms the cafe into a choice location to bust a move off Fira's congested main strip. Beer €4. Open daily noon-4am.

Koo Club (☎22 025; www.kooclub.gr). Duck off Fira's debaucherous nighttime streets into Koo's luxurious, palm-tree-lined garden, or enjoy the music at a higher decibel level indoors. Cover €10. Beer €6. Mixed drinks €10. Open Apr.-Sept. 10pm-late.

Kira Thira Jazz Club (☎22 770), across from Nikolas Taverna, on a side street parallel to the main road out of town. Bar hoppers sip the special house sangria (€5) while jazz, blues, and world music set a mellow mood to offset the frenetic pace outside. Periodic live jazz. Beer €3.50-5. Mixed drinks €8. Open daily 9:30pm-3:30am.

Enigma (☎22 466; www.enigmaclub.gr). Settle into one of the comfy chairs in Enigma's blue interior or open-air courtyard to join a scene of Fira's chic nighttime crowd. Cover €10-15. Beer €5. Mixed drinks €10. Open Apr.-Sept. Su-Th 11pm-4am, F-Sa 11pm-6am.

▶ DAYTRIPS FROM FIRA

AKROTIRI. The volcanic eruption that rocked Santorini in the 17th century BC blanketed Akrotiri with lava. Despite destroying the island, the disaster gave Akrotiri a Pompeii-like immortality, preserving the maritime city more completely than almost any other Minoan site. In 1967 its paved streets were uncovered by Professor Spiridon Marinatos, who was killed by a fall at the site in 1974. Only an estimated 5% of the massive city has been excavated, but the sprawling remains attest to the sophistication of Minoan society, with multi-storied houses and extensive sanitary, sewage, and drainage systems. Each house had at least one room decorated with wall paintings; the originals are at the National Archaeological Museum in Athens (p. 113) as well as in the Museum of Prehistoric Thira. The wall paintings are the earliest large-scale examples of this art form in Europe, and they provide valuable information about daily Minoan life. Since no skeletons were found in the city, scholars theorize that everyone escaped before the eruption devastated the area. Once inside, visitors walk on wooden ramps through the streets and squares of the ancient town. Helpful, multilingual signs guide you through the excavation and point out the locations of the wall paintings. Due to current construction and renovations, the area has been shut down until further notice. Check with tourist agencies in Fira to see if the site has reopened and to confirm hours. (☎81 366. Take the bus (15 per day 9am-10pm, €1.60) from Fira.)

Visitors who want to stay in the modern village of Akrotiri, 1km from the archaeological site, can continue on the road from Fira through town to **Carlos Pension ❸** on the right. The rooms with bath have a balcony with views of the southern part of the island and the sea. (☎81 370. Check-out 11am. Doubles €35-55; triples €45-65.) To enjoy a meal as the ocean laps at your feet, follow the signs down the road perpendicular to the archaeological site to reach **Dolphins Fish Restaurant ❸**. Diners sit under shady umbrellas on sun-drenched piers extending onto the water. (☎81 151. Fish €12-15. Open daily 11am-midnight. AmEx/MC/V.) Away from the ancient site, past the Dolphins Fish Restaurant is the magnificent **Red beach,** a 15min. walk from the Ancient Akrotiri bus stop. Though Santorini is renowned for its black beaches, this stretch's remote location, ruddy, smooth sand, and craggy, brick-red cliffs set it apart. However, the narrow, red beach itself is crammed with umbrellas and beach chairs (paddle boat rental €7, canoe €45).

PYRGOS AND ANCIENT THIRA. Once a Venetian fortress, the lofty town of Pyrgos is enclosed by medieval walls. The blue-domed churches dotting this hilltop settlement are a visible legacy of Ottoman occupation. One of these colorful sanctuaries, near the top of town, houses the **Museum of Icons and Liturgical Objects.** To find the museum in the maze of alleyways leading up the hill, follow the signs for adjacent Kafe Kasteli and Franco's. (☎31 812. Open Tu-Su 10am-4pm. Free.) If you continue up past the church, you'll see a small set of steps on the left that leads to rooftop, panoramic views. A 45min. hike up the mountain leads to **Profitis Ilias Monastery.** Built in 1711, it graciously shares its site with a radar station installed by the Greek military, who thought that the station would be safe from attack alongside this antique monastery. The original monastery is open only for formal liturgies; a visit requires strictly enforced modest dress that fully covers arms and legs. (Open M and W 4-5pm, Sa 4:30-8:30pm. Free.) A small, newer church sits in the shadow of its imposing predecessor's looming bell towers, with a small, well-kept garden and chapel providing shelter from the mountaintops' gusty breezes. The unmarked entrance can be found by walking along the left side of the final path; a friendly, multilingual monk greets the few visitors upon entry and answers questions. (Open daily 10am-1pm. Free.) On July 20, the monastery hosts the **Festival of Profitis Ilias,** a primarily religious ceremony involving eating, drinking, and dancing.

From Profitis Ilias, the ruins of **Ancient Thira** are a 1½hr. ▨**hike** away. *(Open Tu-Su 8:30am-2:30pm. Free.)* This challenging trek gives hikers the opportunity to unleash their inner mountain goat as they scramble over the rocky, exposed face of the mountain that separates Kamari and Perissa, revealing fantastic views of the entire island. The winding mountainside path, discreetly descending to the left of the monastery before the radar station, is made up of slippery gravel and craggy rocks, so wear shoes with good traction. Hikers should also keep their eyes peeled for stacks of rocks, red spots, and views of more well-trodden stretches of the path below to navigate the poorly marked first third of the trail. The ruins of the ancient theater, church, and forum of the island's former capital are still visible, replete with carved dolphins and ruined columns overlooking surrounding islands and sea. *(Take the bus (15min., €1.30) from Fira to Perissa, Athinios, or Akrotiri. Ask the driver to let you off at Pyrgos, from where you can hike to the site. Or take a bus to Kamari or Perissa (20min., 32 per day, €1.90). Climb the mountain beside the water to reach the ruins.)*

MONOLITHOS. Small **Monolithos Beach** is comparatively umbrella-free and easily accessible due to its proximity to the airport (5 buses per day, €1). A 15min. walk north along the coastal road affords even greater privacy for beach connoisseurs. The black sand is finer here than at many of Santorini's other beaches, though this means the winds can whip up dark-hued sandstorms. If you're hungry, stop by fish taverna **Skaramagas ❷,** which dishes out seafood caught by the owners. (☎31 750. Calamari €7.50. Greek salad €4.50. Open Apr.-Oct. daily 8am-11:30pm.)

OIA Οία ☎22860

Dazzling sunsets have made the cliffside town of Oia (EE-ah) famous; the little stucco buildings on the cliffs make it breathtaking. In the aftermath of the 1956 earthquake that leveled the town and much of the northwestern tip of the island, inhabitants carved whitewashed houses into the sheer faces of the cliffside. The budget traveler, however, will not survive long in this spectacular setting. Window-shopping pedestrians and hand-holding honeymooners rule the narrow cobblestoned streets at the town's many upscale boutiques, glitzy art galleries, and craft shops. If browsing isn't your bag, hightail it to the cliffs and secure a prime sunset view before camera-armed crowds fill the Western perches of town.

◨▨ **TRANSPORTATION AND PRACTICAL INFORMATION. Ferries** dock at Oia before continuing to Fira or Athinios, and **buses** run from Fira (25min., 23 per day 6:50am-11pm, €1). From the bus stop, face away from the road to Fira, walk to the back left corner of the bus turnaround area, and zigzag to the first alley to the left; follow it uphill to the main plateia.

Karvounis Tours, on the main street near the plateia, sells ferry and airline tickets, **exchanges currency,** and even plans traditional Greek weddings. (☎71 292. Open daily Apr.-Oct. 10:30am-2:30pm and 6:30-10:30pm.) There is a **24hr. ATM** next to Karvounis Tours. ▨**Atlantis Books,** along the main road across from the mayor's office, stocks more than just standard beach reads. Sift through Tolstoy, Shakespeare, and the Yellow Submarine, creatively displayed on hand-built shelves in a variety of languages; some used books and exchange available. Readers who can't bear to leave can contact the owners about working summers in exchange for free room and board. (☎72 346; www.atlantisbooks.org. Open 10am-1am.)

◪◩ **ACCOMMODATIONS AND FOOD.** Most **domatia** proprietors expect extended stays, so prices rise with shorter durations. The Karvounis family of Karvounis Tours also runs ▨**Youth Hostel Oia ❶,** which has a courtyard, impeccable rooms with bath, and a bar open for breakfast and evening drinks. This picturesque white-and-blue hostel makes painfully expensive Oia bearable. Get more

THE BIG SPLURGE

A DINNER WORTHY OF THE GODS

You might be overwhelmed by the various caldera boat cruise options in Fira and Oia. While wading through the many hawkers, consider shelling out extra cash for the "Sunset and Dinner with the Gods." Avoiding the jostling crowds at Oia's western edge, this boat cruise affords passengers a serene and uncontested view of the famous twilight hours from within Santorini's caldera.

At the delicious, traditional Greek dinner with wine, diners can sate their appetites before the fiery sunset. Cocktails and a romantic sail into the sunset bring passengers toward the horizon, giving them front-row seats for the sun's spectacular daily performance.

As dusk sets in and drinks are finished, passengers are returned to a cliffside restaurant in Kamari, Karterados, or Fira, where they can continue their nighttime revelry with the satisfaction of having enjoyed the best view of the Santorini sunset.

Get tickets for the "Sunset and Dinner with the Gods" boat cruise at Kamari Tours (☎22860 31 390) off the main road in Fira near the cathedral, or at the bus station in Oia. Tickets cost €32 per person, including wine, dinner, and a mixed drink. Book early in the day, as the cruise sells out in the afternoon.

bang for your buck during Happy hour (8-9pm) on the roof patio, with cheap drinks and a view of the spectacular sunset. Book online for advance reservations. To get there from the bus station, face the caldera and walk down the top right pathway. Signs will point you to another right turn, and the hostel's daytime back entrance will be on your left. (☎71 465. www.santorinihostel.gr. Breakfast included. Laundry €8 per 5kg. Internet €2 per hr. Check-in 8am-10pm. Open May 1-Oct. 15. Single-sex dorms €14-16.) **Lauda ❹**, perched on the cliffs 100m toward Fira past the plateia, offers traditional but luxurious stucco houses with built-in beds, bath, fridge, and rooftop jacuzzi, complete with views of the caldera. (☎71 204. Doubles €50-70; apartments for up to 4 with A/C and kitchen €70-120.)

Dining here will cost significantly more than in Fira, though some restaurants serve exceptional food at affordable prices. A good budget option that goes beyond souvlaki is ✇**Edwin's ❷**, across the street from the Oia parking lot and on the road to Ammoudi beach. The large, mouth-watering pizzas (€6.50-10) can feed two. (☎71 971. Delivery available. Stuffed mushrooms €3.80. Open daily 1pm-late.) **Restaurant Lotza ❸**, about 100m past the plateia, serves delicious, well-seasoned dishes like *yiourtlou* (minced meat, pita bread, vegetables, and yogurt; €12) in an upscale atmosphere with an unsurpassed view of the caldera. (☎71 357. Open daily Apr.-Oct. 9:30am-midnight.) **Petros ❸** is at the southern end of the town's main road; facing the caldera, turn left in the plateia and walk 300m. Cooks fry up fresh seafood in front of customers. It overlooks the sparkling sea providing clean and simple outdoor seating without the pretensions of many of its swankier cliffside neighbors. (☎71 263. Entrees €6-14. Open daily Apr.-Oct. 6pm-midnight. AmEx/MC/V.) Up the street at **Thalami Taverna ❷**, relatives of Petros serve more standard dishes in a slightly more sophisticated atmosphere. (☎71 009. Octopus €9. Stuffed peppers €6. Open daily noon-midnight. MC/V.) If you can afford to splurge, there is no better place to do it than **1800 ❺**, the town's classiest bistro, with flowering terraces and soft, classical music wafting through the eating area. In a 19th-century mansion, 50m north of the main church and furnished with antique pieces from the original house, this self-titled "slow-food" restaurant has a rotating menu of creative dishes with international influences. (☎71 485; www.1800.gr. Entrees €19-36. Open daily 7pm-midnight. AmEx/MC/V.)

◙◪ **SIGHTS AND BEACHES.** Follow the signs from the plateia to the **Thira Maritime Museum,** which charts the island's rich nautical tradition with model ships, anchors, cannons, antique navigational equipment, maps, and other sea paraphernalia. (☎71 156. Open M and W-Su 10am-2pm and 5-8pm. €3, students €1.50.) A 20min. trip down the 236 stone stairs at the end of the main road leads to rocky **Ammoudi Beach,** where boats are moored in a startlingly deep swimming lagoon. There is no sand and no obvious beach, but the path to the left leads to swimming holes filled with blue water and volcanic rocks; swimmers should prepare themselves for a refreshing shock when jumping into the caldera's pools. Weary bathers unwilling to walk up the cliffside for dinner can get a plate of fresh fish at one of the three **tavernas** at the bottom of the stairs overlooking the tiny harbor. In the evening you can hire a donkey (€4) to get back up the steep slope.

MILOS Μήλος

Milos's shoreline curves in and out, stretching into some of the most celebrated beaches in the Cyclades. Shaped over centuries by mineral deposits and volcanoes and accented by pale, cerulean waters, the coast is sublimely dramatic. Venturing past the cavernous rock formations toward the island's center leads to the small towns of Plaka and Trypiti, where travelers can explore winding roads, catacombs, and Orthodox churches.

ADAMAS Αδαμάς ☎22870

Adamas is not the most picturesque of Milos's towns. Its inviting eateries, wide array of accommodations, and centralized bus system, however, make the buzzing port a good base for exploring the island's outlying beaches and villages.

◪ TRANSPORTATION

Flights: Olympic Airways (☎22 380, Milos airport 22 381). Take the stairs up to your left after the National Bank. Daily flights to **Athens** (€35-55) fill up quickly, especially during high season; book far in advance. Open M-F 9am-3pm.

Ferries: From Milos, ferries follow an ever-changing but (luckily) posted schedule. Sail daily to: **Piraeus** (7hr., €20), **Serifos** (2hr., €7), and **Sifnos** (1hr., €6.30). 8 per week go to **Kithnos** (2hr., €11), and 3 per week travel the **Iraklion-Kassos-Karpathos-Halki-Rhodes** route. 2 per week to **Kimolos** (30min., €4). A ferry to **Folegandros-Sikinos-Ios-Naxos-Pyros-Syros** (€7.10, though farther destinations will be more expensive) and **Santorini** (€17) departs almost daily.

Flying Dolphins: Twice as fast and twice as expensive as ferries. 15 per week travel the **Sifnos-Serifos-Kithnos-Piraeus** line. €20-35.

Buses: ☎51 062. Buses leave almost every hr. from the Agricultural Bank on the waterfront to **Plaka (Horio), Pollonia,** and **Trypiti** (€1.20-2.90). They also run to **Hivado-limni** (both the beach and nearby Milos Camping), **Paleohori,** and **Provatas** (every hr. 9am-2am, €2-3). Check schedules in the bus station and travel offices; the tourist office has English schedules.

Taxis: ☎22 219 in Adamas, 21 306 in Triovassalos. Line up by the waterfront 24hr. The chart at the bus station lists prices. Available by phone 24hr.

Moped and Car Rental: Milos Rent a Car (☎22 120), across from the port, part of Sophia's Tourist Office. Bikes €10-20 per day. Cars €25-50 per day. 23+. Must have had a license for over 1 year to rent cars. **Milos Camping** and most hotels also rent vehicles for competitive prices.

✈ 🔋 ORIENTATION AND PRACTICAL INFORMATION

From the ferry dock, follow the waterfront to the right to reach the center of town.

Tourist Office: ☎22 445; www.milos-island.gr, across from the dock. Has brochures, maps, ferry and bus timetables in English, and a complete list of the island's rooms and hotels. Agents can provide useful information about daytrip excursions including diving, kayaking, and boat trips. Free luggage storage. Open daily 10am-4pm and 6-11:30pm.

Tourist Agencies: Sophia's Tourist Office (☎24 052). With your back to the boat, it is to the right of the official agency. Has a friendly and knowledgeable staff. **Brau Kat Travel** (☎23 000), about 100m from the port, up the 1st flight of stairs inland. The incredibly attentive workers offer advice about island tours and accommodations. **Milos Travel** (☎22 000) and **RIVA Travel** (☎24 024) are located farther down the waterfront. All 4 agencies sell ferry tickets and help with bus schedules.

Banks: National Bank (☎22 332), with a **24hr. ATM,** near the post office along the waterfront. **Agricultural Bank** (☎22 330), in the central plateia. Both open M-F 8am-2pm. Both banks **exchange currency.**

Laundromat: ☎22 228. Take the 1st left after the waterfront up a narrow street; after taking a sharp right at the "Corali" sign, take the next left and it will be at the end of the street on the left. €9 per 5kg.

Police: ☎21 378. In Plaka. Open 24hr. **Tourist police** ☎22 445.

Pharmacy: ☎21 405. On your right on the main road, past the Agricultural Bank and the supermarket. Open M-Sa 9am-2pm and 6-10pm, Su 11am-2pm.

Medical Services: ☎22 700 or 22 701. In Plaka. Open 24hr.

OTE: ☎21 214. In Plaka, before the bus station.

Internet Access: Internet Info (☎28 011), on the main road past the Agriculture Bank. €6 per hr. Open daily 11am-1:30pm and 6pm-midnight.

Post Office: ☎22 345. On your right, past Internet Info, part of a newsstand. Offers **Poste Restante** and express mail services. Open M-F 8am-2pm. Larger post office is in Plaka. **Postal Code:** 84801.

▛ ACCOMMODATIONS AND CAMPING

Rooms fill up quickly at the cushier hotels, but a smattering of inexpensive **domatia,** where availability is often plentiful and bargaining fruitful, lies 200m behind the waterfront. Many establishments also offer well-priced studio apartments, which are a good option for groups.

▨ **Semiramis Hotel** (☎22 117; www.hotelsemiramis.gr). Follow the main road past the bus station and turn on the narrow road that forks to the left, 25m after the supermarket. A free minibus runs from the dock. The exceptionally generous and friendly owner offers spacious, clean rooms that are convenient and have fan, sink, and shared bath. Breakfast (€3.50) is available 8:30-11am in a leafy, trellised backyard. Sister hotel **Dionysus,** 50m farther along the main road, offers pricier accommodations with a few more amenities. Doubles €25-50; triples €30-60. Traveler's checks accepted. MC/V. ❷

▨ **Portiana Hotel** (☎22 940). At the far end of the ferry port. Butter-colored walls, translucent window swags, and a terrace that overlooks the bay make this conveniently located hotel a good, if slightly pricey, bet. Rooms have A/C, fridge, TV, private terrace, some with sea view. Breakfast included. Doubles €75-120; triples €85-120. ❹

Anezina and Iliopetra (☎24 009; www.anezinahotel.com), set back from the waterfront about 50m. These sister hotels offer colorful rooms with A/C and fridge, though they also come with a hefty high-season price. Doubles €30-80; triples €35-100; studio apartments with kitchens €50-120. MC/V. ❸

Camping Milos (☎31 410), located at Hivadolimni beach, 7km from port. Buses go to and from the port after the public buses stop running. A pristine, turquoise pool and open-air caf-eteria, both overlooking Hivadolimni beach from a steep cliff, lend this newly renovated campsite an air of elegance and luxury. At dusk, a poolside bar and dance floor opens. Com-munal kitchen, laundry, and mini-mart on site. Tent, bike, and car rentals available. €5 per person, €4 per tent. Bungalow for 2 with fridge and bath €50-70. ❶

FOOD

At dusk, the dozens of waterfront tavernas on Adamas's shoreline fill up with lively diners and the glow of hanging lanterns. Most offer traditional Greek menus.

Navayio (☎23 392), 100m down the road from the Agricultural Bank along the sea. This outdoor taverna serves excellent swordfish fillet (€11.50). Open 1-11pm. ❸

O Kinigos (☎22 349), 50m from the main dock. Clear pots with floating rose petals and teal-colored chairs distinguish this traditional eatery from its plainer neighbors. Mous-saka €5. Open daily 9am-midnight. ❷

Artemis Bakery, on the corner at the fork in the road across from the bus station. Arte-mis is ideal for picnics or breakfast, with an unusually wide selection of freshly baked goods that includes bagels, foccacia, and brownies (€2-6). Open daily 11am-6pm. ❶

Pitsounakia (☎21 739), opposite the Agricultural Bank. The souvlaki (€3) here is a tasty, fast option; those who want to linger can eat in the garden seating area. Open daily 11 am-1am. ❶

SIGHTS AND BEACHES

A few meters beyond Adamas's narrow strip of activity is the icon-filled **Ecclesias-tical Museum.** (Open daily 9:15am-1:15pm and 6:15-10:15pm. Free.) While perusing the exhibit, you might overhear music from the adjacent **Church of the Holy Trinity.**

Years of volcanic eruptions, mineral deposits, and aquatic erosion have carved each beach on Milos into a small natural wonder. The island's unique, impressive coast is comprised of dark, multicolored sand, cavernous rock for-mations, and steep, jutting cliffs. Swimmers wade between the rocks at the canyon of **Papafragas,** near the Filokipi bus station, and look at years of graffitied engravings. Beachgoers can lie near the enormous orange- and red-striped sedimentary rocks at **Provotas,** tiptoe across a smooth, glacier-like stretch at **Paleohori,** stake out a spot at crowded **Hivadolimni,** or explore the deep, secluded cave hideouts at a local favorite, **Kleftiko,** known to locals as "pirates' hideaway." If you're having trouble choosing which beaches to visit, you can check out pictures of each on postcards at every kiosk and tourist office. Boat and kayak excursions will take you to hard-to-reach spots like **Tsi-grados,** a glittering beach only accessible by private transport on tricky roads. Buses travel to the major shores every one to two hours for €1.20. The tourist office or any tourist agency can help arrange all-day **boat tours,** which usually cost about €20 per person and include a lunch stop in Kimolos. **Sea Kayak Milos** (☎21 365) plans kayak trips (€35-55) and **Milos Diving** (☎41 296; www.milosdiv-ing.gr) provides a range of diving excursions.

NIGHTLIFE

Nightlife in Adamas is less than wild, but the few bars are chic and popular. **La Costa's** white chairs and cafe tables surround an enormous blue historic ship, complete with sails and rigging. With your back to the sea, go left past the tourist agency and around the curve of the beach cove adjacent to Adamas. You really can't miss the giant boat. (☎24 008. Mixed drinks €7-9. Open 9pm-3am.) The white chairs, balcony, and seaside view make **Aragosta Cafe,** both above and beside Milos Travel, exude a laid-back sense of cool. Late-night dancing takes place at the upstairs cafe. (Piña colada €10. Cafe open 8am-3am, club open 8pm-3am. MC/V.) Next door is **Vipera Lebetina,** a dance club draped with sheer, blue curtains and metal decorations. The DJs spin mainstream foreign music until they switch to Greek tracks late into the night. (Open daily 9pm-2am.)

▶ DAYTRIPS FROM ADAMAS

PLAKA Πλάκα AND TRYPITI Τρυπητή

Buses from Adamas run to Plaka and Trypiti (15min., every hr., €1.20).

The path adjacent to the bus stop in Plaka leads to the large, yellow **Archaeological Museum.** It houses artifacts unearthed at Fylakopi, including the 14th-century BC painted statuette known as the "Lady of Fylakopi." (☎21 620. Open Tu-Su 8:30am-3pm. €3, seniors €2.) For a 360° view of the island, climb upward for 15min. from the bus station to the **Panagia Thalassitra Monastery** at the top of the old castle, in the town of **Plaka,** 6km from Adamas. Opposite Plaka's police station, follow the signs downhill through twisting streets to the terrace of the **Church of Panagia Korfiatissa,** which opens directly onto the lush countryside and the bordering sea. Next door in a 200-year-old house is the **Folk Museum.** It captures the lives of Miloans from the 17th century to present-day, displaying life-sized figures in local customary dress. (☎21 292. Open Tu-Sa 10am-2pm and 6-9pm, Su 10am-2pm. €2, students and children €1.)

A 3min. walk from the Archaeological Museum leads to the tiny town of **Trypiti.** From Trypiti, a paved road winds down past several sights, including the spot where the **Venus de Milo,** since moved to the Louvre in Paris, once stood, and a well-preserved Roman **theater** with a riveting ocean view; ask at the tourist office about performances there. At the end of the road and down a set of stairs, you will see signs for the **catacombs,** an early Christian burial site hewn into the cliff face. Virtually no painting or artifacts remain, but the well-lit cavern is eerily fascinating. Of the five chambers, only one is open to the public. (☎21 625. Open Tu-Su 8am-7pm. €2, students €1. Su free.) You also can see part of a Dorian stone wall built between 1100 and 800 BC. At the ruins of **Fylakopi,** 3km from the fishing village of **Pollonia** toward Adamas, British excavations unearthed 3500-year-old **frescoes,** now displayed in the National Museum in Athens. Other treasures from the site are exhibited in Plaka's archaeological museum (see above).

KIMOLOS Κίμωλος

Ferries go from Adamas to Kimolos 1-2 times per week; smaller boats, which also transport mopeds and cars, make the journey from Pollonia 3 times per day at 7:15, 11am, and 2:15pm, weather permitting (€2.50).

Kimolos, with its secluded beaches and rarely explored roads, is a lovely distraction. Boats drop visitors off in the sleepy port of **Psathi,** where a few cafes serve frappés on the beach and the family-run taverna, ▣**To Kima ❶,** makes tasty traditional dishes. (☎51 001. Zucchini pie €4.20. Fava beans €3. Chicken souvlaki €8. Open M-Sa noon-midnight.) An uphill, paved road directly across from the dock leads to stony **Aliki beach,** where pleasant and quiet **Sardis Domatia ❸** sits, a bit set back from the water. Recently renovated rooms have fridge, air-conditioning, bath, and coffeemaker. (☎51 458. Taverna attached. Doubles and quads €35-75.) Farther along is the town of **Hora,** where travelers head to the kastro or embark on hikes through the mountains. If you haven't rented a moped, traveling around the island is difficult, but the island's single **taxi** (☎ 51 552) is available to take you wherever you please. Watertaxis, such as **Delphini Sea Taxi** (☎ 51 437), are also available to take you back and forth from hard-to-reach beaches.

SIFNOS Σίφνος

Ships to Sifnos drop visitors at Kamares, a charming, tiny collection of eateries and pottery shops that overflow with celebrated Sifniot *keramika* (ceramics). Though the port has an abundance of appealing accommodations and a pleasant strip of beach, most travelers head straight to Apollonia or to the small villages nestled on cove-like shores. While days in Sifnos are quiet and sleepy, nights often bring lively local festivals; each of the island's 365 churches hosts an annual celebration for the entire community on its patron saint's name day.

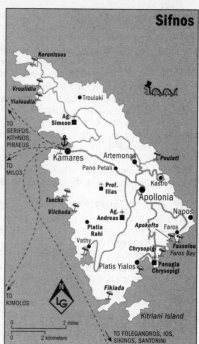

KAMARES Καμάρες ☎ 22840

Kamares is a modest, attractive port. Hovering yachts, sailboats, and ferries almost overwhelm the thin strip of beach, which teems with tavernas and information offices. Peaceful and mellow, the town is filled with vacationing families who sun themselves on the shallow shore.

▐ TRANSPORTATION. Most **ferries** from Sifnos travel in short routes with multiple stops. To: Folegandros (2 per week, €9.50); Ios (2 per week, €12); Kimolos (7 per week, €9); Milos (7 per week, €8.10); Piraeus (7 per week, €21); Santorini (2 per week, €13.80); Serifos (7 per week, €7.50); Sikinos (2 per week, €11.20). High-speed **catamarans** go to: Kithnos (1 per week, €11); Milos (2 per week, €9.80); Piraeus (2 per week, €21); Serifos (2 per week, €10). The main bus stop is in front of the tourist office near the ferry landing. Four **buses** leave daily for Apollonia (10min., every hr. 7:30am-8:30pm, €2), where you can change buses to get to Artemonas, Faros, Herronisos, Kastro, Platis Vathy, and Yialos; consult the schedule in the tourist office for more details. A number of **taxis** are available 24hr. on the island. You can call the drivers' cell phones (☎ 69446 96 409 or 69444 44 904) directly. **Niki Rent a Car**, 200m down the main road from the dock, has some of the best rates. (☎ 33 993 or 69456 56 147. Bikes €12-22. Cars €25-65. Prices vary with season, increasing from mid-June to Aug. AmEx/MC/V.)

▐▌ ORIENTATION AND PRACTICAL INFORMATION. Just opposite the ferry dock, the extremely helpful Anglophones in the **information office** help visitors find

CYCLADES

rooms, store luggage (€0.50 per piece), and decipher boat and bus schedules. (☎31 977. Maps €1.30-3. Open in high season daily 9am-midnight; in low season before and after ferry arrivals.) Along the waterfront as you walk from the dock to town, the English-speaking staff at **Aegean Thesaurus Travel Agency** happily provides the same services as the tourist office; they also sell tickets for ferries and Flying Dolphins. (☎33 151. Open in high season daily 9:30am-10pm; in low season before and after ferries arrive.) **The Bookshop,** a few stores down on the main strip, sells maps with hiking trails (€1.50), international newspapers, magazines, and fiction and also offers a used book exchange. (☎33 521. Open daily 8am-1am.) In an **emergency,** call the **police** (☎31 210) in Apollonia. The **pharmacy** (☎33 541) is about 200m away from ferry port on the main road. A **doctor** is on call 24hr. at the **medical clinic.** (☎31 315. Open M-F 10am-1pm, Tu and Th also 5-7pm.) **Yamas Internet Cafe,** 100m beyond the ferry port along the main raod, has movie showings on the top terrace, as well as **Internet** access. (€5 per hr. Mixed drinks €7.) Mailboxes are scattered throughout the town, but the nearest **post office** is in Apollonia. **Postal Code:** 84003.

⌂⌂ ACCOMMODATIONS AND CAMPING. During high season, it may be difficult to find a budget hotel room. **Domatia** are good options in terms of availability, price, and quality, and Kamares is full of them; the tourist office has an exhaustive list. Walk 150m on the main road along the ferry port, turn right at the mini-market, and go up the stairs to find **Podotas Group Hotel and Apartments ❹.** Sizable, simply adorned studios have TV, air-conditioning, and balcony. Some have a kitchenette, and all come with stellar service by attentive owners George and Margarita Podotas. Sister property wth similar prices in Apollonia. (☎32 329. Doubles €45-59; triples €49-62.) Turn right 10m uphill from Niki's Car Rental on the main road, and the second building of its kind on your left is **Hotel Kiki ❹.** The spotless rooms with bath, TV, air-conditioning, fridge, and balcony overlook Kamares and the harbor. (☎32 329. Doubles €45-59; triples €49-62.) **Meltemi Rooms ❷,** behind Hotel Kiki, has clean rooms with air-conditioning and bath. (☎31 653. Doubles €20-50; triples €30-60; quads with kitchen €50-90.) To re-experience sleep-away camp, pitch a tent at ▨**Maki's Camping ❶,** where a friendly, conscientious staff creates a family atmosphere and volunteers information about the island. From the port, turn left toward Niki Rent a Car where a road descends to the left and leads to the site, 200m opposite the beach. The campgrounds include a taverna, mini-mart, laundry (€5 per load), common kitchen, and showers. Private rooms are also available. (☎32 366; www.makiscamping.gr. €6 per person, €17 per tent; doubles €20-30.) A more secluded campsite, **Platis Gialos Camping ❶** is a 30min. bus ride from Kamares then a 10min. walk down a rocky road away from the beach; follow the signs. (☎71 286. €4 per person; tent rental €3.)

◖▣ FOOD AND NIGHTLIFE. Sifniot specialty *revithada* (chickpea soup; €2.50-5.50) can be found most everywhere that serves Greek cuisine. ▨**Ristorante Italiano de Claudio ❷,** up the main street toward Apollonia, serves memorable pizza (€7.50-11) and *rigatoni delicati* (pasta with chicken, asparagus, and cream sauce; €9). (Open 6pm-1am. AmEx/MC/V.) Across the street, **O Kapetan Andreas ❷,** a lantern-lit restaurant on the beach, specializes in seafood. (☎32 356. Fish soup €3. Open daily noon-midnight.)

Young locals spend late nights at trendy **Cafe Folie,** a cafe-bar about 150m along the beach, past Camping Maki. Turquoise cushions and orange lanterns decorate a wide outdoor terrace that extends out onto the ocean. (☎31 183. Mixed drinks €7-9. Open daily 9am-3am.) The **Old Captain Bar,** midway along the waterfront strip, serves milkshakes (€5) and a variety of rum punches (€8) under thatched umbrellas on the sand. The unofficial pirate theme keeps the bar festive and amusing. (☎31 990. Open daily 10am-3am.)

APOLLONIA Απολλώνια ☎ 22840

The streets of Apollonia, the island's capital and heart, meander about the hilltop, but each leads back to the main, paved road, from which buses carry beachgoers to nearby shore-side villages. Memorable restaurants and quaint houses carpet the small village, and the narrow lanes contain almost all the island's nightlife.

🔁🗐 TRANSPORTATION AND PRACTICAL INFORMATION. All the essentials a traveler needs can be found in the main plateia, where the bus from Kamares makes its first stop. **Buses** to Artemonas and Kamares (10min., €1) wait in front of the post office; those to villages and beaches like Kastro (€1.20) and Platis Yialos (€2) stop around the corner on the mountain road next to the Hotel Anthousa. Buses run to these destinations at least once every hour. The schedules by the plateia stop outside the travel agency have exact times.

Aegean Thesaurus, near the post office, has **currency exchange,** accommodations assistance, bus and ferry schedules, a **24hr. ATM,** and useful island information packs for €2.50. (☎ 33 151. Open daily 10am-10pm.) **Alpha Bank** is up the main road from the bus stop, on your left before Hotel Anthousa. It has a **24hr. ATM.** (☎ 31 317. Open M-Th 8am-2:30pm, F 8am-2pm.) To get to the **police station,** walk up the main road from the plateia. Turn left at the fork in the road with the signposts. A bit farther up, it is the building on the right with the large Greek flag in front. (☎ 31 210. Open daily 9am-1pm.) There is a **pharmacy** next to the post office. (☎ 33 541. Open daily 9am-2:30pm and 5pm-10pm.) The **medical center** (☎ 31 315) is across from the police station. An **OTE** is 50m down the road back to Kamares on the right (☎ 31 215. Open daily 7:30am-2:30pm.) The **Billiard Cafe,** on the road out of Apollonia to the right, has **Internet** access. (€6 per hr. Open daily 10:30am-midnight.) The **post office** is in the main plateia. (☎ 31 329. Open M-F 7:30am-2pm.) **Postal Code:** 84003.

🗐 ACCOMMODATIONS. Summer vacancies are rare in Apollonia, and it's best to make reservations far in advance if you're traveling in July or August. **Hotel Anthousa ❸,** on the mountain road to Artemonas, is above the pastry shop around the corner from the main plateia. From its clean rooms with air-conditioning, TV, fridge, bath, and phone, you can see both the deep ravine over which the hotel sits and the sea. The video arcade is an added perk for those who need their fix of push-button animation. (☎ 31 431. Laundry €12. Singles €35-45; doubles €45-55. MC/V.) To find the **Sifnos Hotel ❸,** head up the paved road from the plateia. At the fork in the road, the hotel is on the corner on your right, above a bakery. The hotel's spacious, inviting rooms include air-conditioning, TV, fridge, bath, and phone. (☎ 31 624. Singles €30-45; doubles €40-65. MC/V.) **Hotel Sofia ❹** is just off the plateia; head up the wide paved road from the plateia until you see it on your left, above the supermarket. Rooms have TV, air-conditioning, and bath. (☎ 31 238. Doubles €42-55.) **Nikoleta Rooms ❹,** across from the Eko gas station, rents quiet and clean doubles with TV, air-conditioning, kitchenette, phone, bath, and balcony, some with a peaceful view of the sea. (☎ 31 538. Doubles €40-60.)

🗐🗐 FOOD AND NIGHTLIFE. On the main street, **To Troulaki ❷** serves tantalizingly fresh traditional Sifnos fare. (☎ 32 362. Baked lamb €7. Open daily 9am-9pm.) The restaurant at the **Sifnos Hotel ❷** serves *revithada* (€5) only on Sunday, but you can get *imam baldi* (eggplant with onions and tomato; €4.50), another favorite, any day of the week. (☎ 31 624. Open 8am-1am. MC/V.) The strong coffee brewed at **Vegera ❶,** on your left just before the police station and clinic, makes their crepes (€3.50-5) and rich, gooey caramel cake taste even sweeter by comparison. The expansive balcony that looks over Sifnos's gentle mountains provides a lovely setting in which to savor your dessert. (☎ 33 385. Open daily 9am-3am.)

CYCLADES

Stroll up the hill toward Kastro on the road away from Hotel Anthousa to find the cafes and clubs that define Sifniot nightlife. Live Greek music plays every night until sunrise at the multi-tiered local hangout **Aloni,** on the road to the police station before Vegera, about 75m toward Artemonas on the left. The **Camel Club,** up the road toward Platis Yialos past the Eko gas station, blares international tunes and exudes a vague Middle Eastern theme. (Open daily 9pm-4am or later.)

◤ **DAYTRIPS FROM APOLLONIA.** Buses travel to enchantingly remote villages throughout the island—maps are available at bookstores and tourist agencies for €2-3.50. To see fascinating architecture and a slice of history, catch the bus to **Artemonas,** 1.5km from Apollonia, where Greek aristocrats from Alexandria built mansions. In **Kastro,** 2km east of Apollonia, a cluster of whitewashed houses are balanced on a mountain with a sweeping panorama of the steep drop to the sea below. You can take the bus or walk to Kastro along the road from Apollonia; it's mostly downhill with a stone path shortcut 300m from the bus stop. The quiet village has little activity, but the architectural remains, including remnants of homes from the Geometric period, a wall from the Classical period, and Venetian ruins, give a broad overview of the island's past. The tiny **Archaeological Museum,** at the center of the town, houses a handful of clay figurines of goddesses from the Mycenaean period and the head of an archaic *kouros.* (Open Tu-Su 8am-3pm. Free.) There are no hotels in Kastro, but if you ask around, you will be able to find **domatia.** Visible from the path around the town's periphery and accessible by a marked footpath, a stone cliff juts into the ocean. On it is the tiny **Epta Martires Church** (Seven Martyrs), as well as a popular spot for those daring enough to go **cliff diving.** Another footpath leads to the sparkling cove at **Poulati,** which is a great place for snorkeling.

Buses run hourly to **Platis Yialos,** a busy, beautiful beach town 12km from Apollonia. For a meal while you're there, **Kalimera ❷** serves French and Greek dishes and sugary desserts. (☎71 365. Entrees €6.85-13.50. Open 9am-midnight.) **Faros,** the bus stop before Yialos, is a series of round shores connected by footpaths. Since there is plenty to do in the area and the public transportation is infrequent, you may want to make this stop a full daytrip. Numerous little tavernas blend together at busy **Fasolou** and **Apokofto** beaches nearby. A mountainous footpath leads to the striking **Panagia Chrysopigi Monastery.** To reach it, as well as the adjacent Chrysopigi beach, take the 30min. hike from Faros or walk 10min. from Platis Yialos. A bridge connects the 17th-century monastery's rocky islet to the mainland. Forty days after Easter, locals celebrate the two-day **Festival of Analipsos.**

SERIFOS Σέριφος

Stony Serifos's rocky terrain comes straight out of mythology. After Perseus decapitated the petrifying, snake-haired Medusa, he took her head back to King Polydectes of Serifos, who had sent him on the mission. When he found out the monarch was just trying to get him out of the way so he could put the moves on Perseus's mother, Danae, irate Perseus flashed Medusa's head at Polydectes, turning his royal court (and the island) to stone. Whether or not you believe in Gorgons, it's hard not to appreciate the rock cliffs that rise high above the water. Sitting by the chapel and crumbling kastro in Hora, hikers can see almost all of the small island's rugged, legendary landscape.

LIVADI Λιβάδι   ☎ 22810

Livadi is a pleasant spot to make a base for exploration. Uncrowded, traditional restaurants and busy bars keep visitors happily entertained. Hora, a small town nestled high above the port, is accessible by a steep hike or bus.

⊟ ⋈ TRANSPORTATION AND PRACTICAL INFORMATION. Almost all the island's services are located on the waterfront. From Serifos, **ferries** travel at least once a day to: Kimolos (€8); Kithnos (€7.20); Milos (€7); Piraeus (€16); Sifnos (€6). Your ferry may stop at another island before getting to the one you want. **Flying Dolphins** go daily to Milos, Piraeus, and Sifnos (1-2 times per day on an ever-changing schedule). The bus stop is on the left, directly across from the 2nd newsstand on the way from the ferry landing to town. **Buses** run from Livadi to Hora (14 per day 8am-10:30pm, €1); a return bus follows the same schedule with a 15min. delay. Another bus heads to Koutalas and Megalo Livadi (Tu, Th and Sa-Su). Buses also go to the monastery daily, waiting 30min. before rumbling back to Livadi. For exact departure times, consult the schedule at the bus stop. To contact one of the island's four **taxi** drivers, call one of their cell phones. (☎69738 01 051, 69444 73 044, 69449 08 637, or 69324 31 114.)

Krinas Travel, the first left as you walk from the dock, rents cars (€44-68 per day) and mopeds (€16-22) at the best prices on the island. (☎51 500. Open M-Sa 9:30am-10pm, Su 9:30am-8pm). **Apiliotis Travel,** on the waterfront just before the butcher shop, sells hydrofoil and ferry tickets and has English schedules. (☎51 155. Open before and after ferry arrivals.) **Alpha Bank,** on the waterfront up the second flight of stairs on your left, has a **24hr. ATM.** (☎51 780. Open M-F 8am-2:30pm.) For 24hr. **police,** dial ☎51 300. To get to the **pharmacy,** take a left after the first supermarket from the dock, walk past the bakery, take a right, and continue about 30m. (☎51 205. Open daily 9am-2pm and 6-8pm.) The **medical center** can be reached at ☎51 202. On the way to Hora, behind Apilotis Travel, is an **OTE** (☎51 399). **Vitamin C** has **Internet** access. (☎79 352. €3 per hr. Open 9am-2am.) The **post office** is across the street. (☎51 239. Open M-F 7:30am-noon.) **Postal Code:** 84005.

⋈ ⊡ ACCOMMODATIONS AND FOOD. Though small, Livadi has a wide range of rooming options. Turn left at the first set of stairs from the ferry port, then go right and walk 100m to find **Hotel Naias ❷.** Simple, balcony-flanked rooms have air-conditioning and TV—some with seaview. (☎51 479. Breakfast €5. Singles €20-40; doubles €50-60. Haggle for better prices. Open Apr.-Oct.) To reach **Alexandros-Vassilias ❹,** on Livadakia beach, take an immediate left when you get off the boat. Bear left and walk uphill for about 500m. When you come to a fork, take the left branch, and you will find this bustling, friendly establishment with an attached taverna. Its 4-person studios with kitchens are perfect for families. (☎91 119. Doubles €65-75; triples €90-100; 4-person studios €115.) Sand and thatched beach umbrellas bump up against the charming facade of **Hotel Albatross ❸,** a few doors down from Maistrali. (☎51 148. Singles €30-50; 4-bed suites €55-70; without A/C prices reduced.) The ◪**Coralli Campgrounds ❶,** popular with backpackers, is 20m from Livadakia beach and 700m left of the port. Call for the free minibus or continue along the beach from Alexandros-Vassilias. The stone-floored bungalows have TV, air-conditioning, fridge, and bath, and the grounds have a mini-mart, laundry, pool, cafeteria, common refrigerators, and kitchen sinks. (☎51 500; www.coralli.gr. €6 per person, children under 11 €3. Doubles €65; triples €72; quads €85; 6-person room €95.)

Restaurants and cafes spring from hotels and line the waterfront. For an inexpensive but amazingly filling meal, head to **Stamadis ❷** at the right end of the waterfront. (☎51 729. Stuffed zucchini €5. Fresh fish €7-10. Open daily noon-1am.) **Frutopoleio O Petros ❶,** next to Apiliotis Travel, sells delicious fresh fruit, including apricots (€7 per kg) and oranges (€1 per kg). The restaurant at **Hotel Anna ❷,** where daily fish specials "depend on our local fisherman," serves Greek and Italian dishes. (☎51 666. Traditional Greek noodles with prawns €15. Open daily 1pm-1am.) **Vitamin C ❷,** near the Hotel Serifos Beach, offers pizza (€10-11) and mixed drinks (€4-6) with which to wash it down. (☎79 352. Open 9am-2am.)

CYCLADES

◢◣ BEACHES AND NIGHTLIFE. Serifos's secluded beaches stretch along the island, with sand unblemished even by footprints. To reach **Psili Amos,** walk all the way along the beach to the right of Linadi, then follow the road over the headland. Stay on the road after it becomes paved. The walk is steep in places and takes at least 45min. To reach unnamed beaches, head north along Serifos's paved and dirt roads. For those without a vehicle or swift-footed mule, a bus travels once daily to **Mega Livadi** and **Koutalas.**

Karnayia, on the waterfront, blasts classic tunes from the 1970s and 80s. (Mixed drinks €7-9. Open daily 9am-3am.) **Hook,** a rooftop dance club next to Vitamin C, plays a mix of American Top 40 and Greek hits. (Drinks €5-8. Open daily 11pm-late.) The terrace of the **Yacht Club,** a beachside cafe-bar 50m down the waterfront, past Hotel Serifos Beach, is a popular evening destination for an older crowd. (☎51 888; www.yachtclubserifos.gr. Drinks €5-8. Shots €4. Open 9am-late.)

⚑ DAYTRIPS FROM LIVADI. Venturing out of Livadi to Hora and other remote locales allows for a greater appreciation of Serifos's legendary landscape.

HORA. Whitewashed Hora offers bits of history and culture, a likely relief for the beach-weary traveler. If you climb up the first series of steps on the right, past the 2nd plateia, to the small **chapel** that crowns the town, you will be rewarded with an absolutely amazing view. The crumbling remains of the **kastro** invite you to poke around; follow the signs painted along the numerous steps up. The **Archaeological Museum,** open only during high season, exhibits artifacts from Hora's Roman years. (Open Tu-Su 8:30am-3pm.) If you can't tear yourself away at night, **Apanemia Domatia ❸** is 200m down the stone path to the left of the green supermarket. There is no sign, but maroon shutters distinguish it from the neighboring buildings. Look for the EOT sign next to a doorway. (Doubles €30-40; 4-person apartments €60.) Other domatia in town go for similar prices. The bus from Livadi stops in a small square in front of a well-stocked **supermarket** and a few **tavernas.** *(If you're feeling ambitious and energetic, you can take the steep 5km hike up to Hora. Otherwise, catch the bus for €1, which runs roughly every 45min.)*

NORTHERN SERIFOS. Traditional villages and scattered churches, monasteries, and traces of ruins blanket the northern part of the island. The **Monastery of the Taxiarchs** (☎51 027), 10km beyond Hora toward Galani, was built in 1400. Legend says a Cypriot icon mysteriously appeared in the monastery and returns whenever removed. The monastery also houses an Egyptian lantern, several Russian relics, and a 17th-century stone plate in the floor depicting the Byzantine Double Eagle, which appeared on the empire's flag. Between 1600 and the 1940s, small groups of Orthodox monks lived together in this castle-like edifice. Today, if you arrive by bus, you may meet the lone monk who has lived here on his own for 30 years. Call ahead to arrange a visit. By foot, the trip takes 2hr.; the monastery and town by the port have no facilities, so bring provisions for the hike. *(Serifos's interior is not easily accessible without a car or moped. Taxis will leave and pick up at a set destination; buses run once or twice per day to the monastery and to Galani.)*

KITHNOS Κύθνος

At dusk local teenagers promenade the horseshoe-shaped perimeter of Kithnos's quaint harbor. The inlet is so well-protected by surrounding rocks that, except for the *meltemi* season in August and the few times a day when the ferries arrive, Greeks generally describe it as being *san lathi* (as calm as oil). It's safe to say that the local attitude follows suit—Kithnos's locals are famously laid-back and welcoming, embodying simple small-town life.

MERIHAS Μέριχας ☎ 22810

The main port of the island, Merihas harbors most of the island's tourists in addition to its ferry landing. Merihas is attractive and quiet, but also quite small, and has fewer conveniences and amenities for tourists than many other island towns.

☐ ☐ TRANSPORTATION AND PRACTICAL INFORMATION. Ferries sail to: Folegandros (6hr., 2 per week, €15); Kea (1½hr., 3 per week, €8); Kimolos (3hr., 5 per week, €11.10); Milos (4hr., 2 per day, €10); Piraeus (3hr., 1-2 per day, €12); Santorini (8hr., 2 per week, €19.10); Serifos (1¼hr., 1-2 per day, €8); Sifnos (2½hr., daily, €6.80); Sikinos (7hr., 2 per week, €13.40); Syros (2½hr., 2 per week, €6.70). **Catamarans** dash to: Mykonos (1½hr., 6 per week, €21); Rafina (3½hr., 6 per week, €19.10); Santorini (2 per week); Syros (1hr., 6 per week, €15); Tinos (2hr., 6 per week, €23). Two **buses** stop at the waterfront and go to Driopis (30min., infrequent schedule), Hora (15min., every 1½hr. 7:15am-9:15pm), and Loutra (30min., every 1½hr. 7:30am-9:30pm). All trips cost €1-2; return buses follow a schedule 15min. behind the one listed here. For a **taxi,** call ☎ 6944 74 3791 or 6944 27 1609.

The port town offers an abundance of rooms to let, a few tavernas and businesses, and several waterfront markets. The **tourist office** is by the dock. (☎ 32 250. Open mid-June to Aug. 9:30am-1:30pm and 5:15-9pm.) Heading into town from where the boat arrives, take a left and go up the first flight of stairs. On the left is the helpful **Antonis Travel Agency,** with information on rooms and ferries, and cars and mopeds to rent. (☎ 32 104; fax 32 291. Cars from €30. Mopeds from €12. Open 9:30am to 10 or 11pm.) Reach the **tourist police** at ☎ 31 201. Farther along the waterfront, veering right as if you were going to walk along the beach, a store labeled "Cava" will be on your left; inside, a representative of the **National Bank** will **exchange currency** and traveler's checks. A **24hr. ATM** is located in front of the tourist office. The **pharmacy** is two doors to the left facing Antonis Travel. (Open 8am-2pm and 6-8:30pm.) For medical issues, a **doctor** is available (☎ 31 202, 32 234, or via cell phone at 69775 69 231). The post office is in Hora. **Postal Code:** 84006.

☐ ☐ ACCOMMODATIONS AND FOOD. Accommodations surround the small beach in town. Walking along the port about 200m with the sea on your right, turn left just before the arched mini-bridge to locate a series of **domatia. Kythnos Hotel ❹** is left of Antonis Travel Agency when facing inland. Rooms with air-conditioning, TV, fridge, and veranda are simple but comfortable. (☎ 32 092. Breakfast €5. Doubles €40-55; triples €50-65.) Rooms at **Bouriti ❹** have kitchenette and bath and are great for families. Walk along the beach, turn left after Remezzo, and pass the supermarket; the owners may be behind the supermarket counter. (☎ 32350. Triples €40-50; quads €60-70. Bargain for lower prices.)

Ikos Araps Pizzeria ❶, at the left corner of the harbor, has plastic chairs beneath a white awning. Local school kids grab omelettes (€4.70) before the bus comes, and teenagers with late-night munchies order bowls of macaroni with tomato, meat, and cheese (€6) at the counter inside. (☎ 32 190. Open daily 8am-2:30pm and 7pm-2am.) **Sailors Restaurant ❸,** on the central waterfront, waves flags out in front. Take your pick from its selection of locally caught fresh fish—they're still flopping. Lobster spaghetti (€65 per kg), mixed fish (€17), and Kithnos goat cheese croquettes (€4) are specialties. (☎ 32 056. Open daily 9am-midnight. MC/V.) Two doors down, the friendly staff at **Yialos Restaurant ❸** serves traditional home-cooked food (€4-10) raved about by locals.

☐ ☐ BEACHES AND NIGHTLIFE. The road that leads toward the beaches of Hora and Loutra also passes a turn-off for the small town of ▧**Kolona.** After the turn-off, head left before a white building and follow this path until you reach a long beach. Because it is protected from ocean currents, the right side (facing the ocean) is warm while the left is cool. **Taverna Loukas ❷** sits above the beach, waiting to relieve your hunger with grilled meat dishes and local wine. (Open during beach hours, roughly 10am-8pm.) A road that heads in the other direction from Merihas takes you past little **Driopis** with its **Folk Museum** and **Byzantine Museum.** (Follow the signs from the church in the plateia. Both open 10am-2pm and 7-9pm.) **Akrotiri** is the only place in town with a huge outdoor dance floor. Spectators converge at either of the two bars on the multi-tiered balcony. (☎32 754 or 32 755. Beer €3. Mixed drinks €8. Open daily 6-11pm as a cafe, 11pm-late as a club.) After dinner bring the crew for ice cream (€5) and mixed drinks (€8) at laid-back **Byzantio Club.** (☎32 259. Open daily 9am-late.) Trek uphill at the right of the harbor to find **Agnanti**—you can't miss the colored lights that illuminate the entrance. Ask the DJ to play your favorite song.

KEA Κέα (Τζία)

The lushness of this verdant island is uncharacteristic among the Cyclades; escape the main port to discover Kea's preserved beauty. The crowd, which predominantly consists of Greeks who return regularly, comes to bask in the well-kept secret that is Kea. Oak-covered mountains harbor the twisting streets of Ioulida, the island's capital. *Ammouthitses* (little coves) speckle the island's perimeter.

KORISSIA Κορισσία   ☎22880

The island's main port runs along a short waterfront. While Korissia exudes a friendly, relaxed atmosphere, it still provides all the services under the sun.

⊡ ⁊ TRANSPORTATION AND PRACTICAL INFORMATION. From Kea, **ferries** depart for Lavrio (1¼hr.; M-F 3 per day, Sa-Su 5 per day; €6). **Catamarans** zip passengers to Kithnos or Lavrio once daily. The **Flying Dolphin** ticket office is directly across from the ferry landing. Tickets for normal ferries can be purchased at the ticket office, a few doors to the left and next to Yiannis Rent a Car. Two **buses** (€1.60-3.20) travel to: Ioulida (12min., 5 per day); Katomeria (3 per day); Otzias beach (3 per day); Pisses beach (3 per day); Vourkari (7min., 5 per day). Schedules for times and stops are posted at the main stop in front of the landing dock in Korissia. Buses do not run regularly until mid-June, before which they serve as school buses. **Taxis** line up at the ferry landing; call them individually. (☎69730 12 813, 69373 82 702, or 69773 31 431. €6-7 to Ioulida; €5-6 to Vourkari.) **Yiannis Rent a Car** is on the right before the ticket office, away from the dock. (☎21 898. €35-45 per day. AmEx/MC/V.)

Any questions about the island can be answered at the Flying Dolphin ticket office across from the landing, connected to the **Stegathi Bookshop** (☎21 435; lepoura@pel.forthnet.gr). **Alpha Bank** is one block past the ATM on the left. (☎22 702. Open M-Th 8am-2:30pm, F 8am-2pm.) There is a **24hr. ATM** at the Flying Dolphin ticket office, and another is located on the corner of the harbor, to the right of the Karthea Hotel. **Our Tzia Laundromat** has dry cleaning. To get there, continue from Piraeus Bank along the bay, make a right at the far side of the river, and turn left after 100m. (☎21 154. Open M-Sa 8am-1pm and 6-8pm.) The **tourist police** can be reached at ☎21 100. The station is located a few blocks back from the waterfront. The **pharmacy** is located in Ioulida. (☎22 277; fax 69455 47 567. Open M and W 9am-2pm, Tu and Th-F 9am-2pm and 5:30-8:30pm, Sa 10am-1pm.) The **medical clinic** is also in Ioulida and can be reached at ☎22 200. **Internet** access is available at **Art Cafe** (☎21 181; elio@sound.gr) on the waterfront next to the National Bank ATM (€2 for first 30min., rates decrease for longer increments). **Postal Code:** 84002.

ACCOMMODATIONS AND FOOD. Korissia boasts most of Kea's accommodations, making it a good home-base. **Kostis Rooms ❸** is isolated on a plot of farmland overlooking the port. Atmosphere and beach proximity make up for unadored rooms with TV, fridge, and veranda. (☎21 483. Doubles €30-50. One week min. stay in high season.) The first hotel on the bay's corner is **Hotel Karthea ❹**, in a modern building. Clean but unexciting rooms have bath, air-conditioning, and TV; some have bay views. (☎21 204. Breakfast included. Singles €70; doubles €90.) **Hotel Korissia ❹** is partially hidden from the main road by reeds. It has rooms with TV, air-conditioning, bath, and veranda. Kitchenettes (€5-10 extra) are in some rooms. (☎21 484. Doubles €70; triples €80-90. AmEx/MC/V.) **Camping Kea ❶**, 50m from Pisses beach, is about 30min. by bus from Korissia. It has a mini-market, laundry facilities, and bathrooms. (☎31 302. €5.50 per person, €5.50 per tent.) At the far end of the beach on the left is **Hotel Tzia ❹** (☎21 305), with doubles with bath, TV, and a terrace that opens onto the beach (Rooms €65-75. A/C €5 extra.)

Along the waterfront are various cafes and restaurants. The atmosphere is pleasant, but beware of aggressive stray cats that will stalk your food, perhaps even attempting to jump onto a table. **Akri ❷**, after the supermarkets by the beachside road, serves delicious homemade food like *strapatsiata* (tomato, egg, and cheese casserole; €5.) (☎21 196; fax 69775 74 957. Open noon-midnight.) **Cafe Ezaharoplasteio ❷** (Καφέ Εξαχαροπλαστείο) is perfect for a milkshake (€3) or ice cream and also serves breakfast. (☎21 493. Open 9am-11pm.)

DAYTRIP FROM KORISSIA: IOULIDA. Ioulida, also known as Hora, overlooks steep ravines and oak trees. Paths snake through the closely placed houses and shops. The **Lion of Kea** is a sculpture, surrounded by whitewashed stones, thought to have been carved by Kean men in the 6th century BC to ward off evil nymphs who were harming their wives. It lies 1.5km northeast of Ioulida (about a 10min. walk). Follow the main road leading northeast out of town past Agios Spiridon church and bear left when the road veers right. Continue until you reach a metal gate; down the stairs you'll find the sculpture. Crickets hum from the trees around **Otzias beach,** 15min. by bus from Korissia, famously clean due to changing tides. Shaded by pine trees, **Pisses beach** (30min. from Korissia by bus) has emerald-tinted waters. The narrow streets of Ioulida hide culinary gems like **En Lefki ❶**, a hip cafe serving grilled sandwiches (€1.50) and amazingly delicious *karithopites* (warm walnut pie with ice cream; €3.50) on a wide terrace overlooking both mountains and sea. (☎22 155. Open daily 8am-midnight.)

DODECANESE
Δωδεκάνησα

Dotted along the Turkish coast, the Dodecanese Islands are closer to Asia Minor than to Athens—no small matter in Greece's centuries-long territorial battle with Turkey. Home to Hippocrates, father of medicine, and the exile asylum of St. John, author of the Bible's book of Revelation, the Dodecanese are marked by a history of persistent life in the face of seemingly constant conquests and invasions. Although the islands flourished culturally during the Hellenistic period, the Roman Empire soon took over. A favorite target of religious luminaries, the inhabitants of these islands were among the first to convert to Christianity. During the 14th century, Christian crusaders built heavily fortified castles over many ancient temple grounds as bases for their religious wars. Ottoman rule began in 1523 and persisted until 1912. Due to their proximity to Turkey, the lucky Dodecanese received special concessions from the Sultan and continued to prosper. Under the direction of Mussolini, Italian fascists took over in 1912 and developed the islands primarily for use as naval bases, with several islands seeing heavy bombing during WWII. The Dodecanese ultimately joined the Greek nation in 1948. Eclectic architecture is the most visible legacy of all these comings and goings: Greek and Roman ruins, fortresses built by crusaders, Ottoman mosques, and stark Italian architecture coexist, mixed with bright blue-and-white homes. The islands themselves are just as diverse in landscape as in character. From Rhodes's fertile hills to Nisyros's volcanic terrain, and Kos's buzzing nightlife to Karpathos's secluded beaches, the Dodecanese offer a thorough mix of traditional villages, stunning beaches, ruined temples, and young metropolises.

 SUGGESTED ITINERARIES: DODECANESE

FOUR DAYS On **Rhodes** (p. 438), bypass the main port and head for **Lindos** (p. 450), with its undisturbed, traditional charm. After wandering through its streets, lie before Helios on this island of the Sun. Then move on to **Kos** (p. 469) for more beaches and endless parties.

TEN DAYS After worshiping the sun on **Rhodes,** spend 1 or 2 days on **Karpathos's** (p. 453) magnificent beaches,

among the area's best. Stop back through Rhodes again on your way to the other islands, taking the chance to explore the winding streets of **Rhodes Town** (p. 439) or less touristed **Lindos.** Peer into **Nisyros's** (p. 467) simmering volcano, then prolong the excitement at **Kos's** high-octane parties. Wrap up your trip on **Astypalea** (p. 476), whose small town friendliness and gorgeous surroundings will make you never want to leave.

RHODES Ρόδος

The ancients chalked up Rhodes's bright climate to a case of love at first sight. When the sun god Helios saw the nymph Rhodos swimming, it is said that he was instantly smitten. Her father Poseidon granted Helios Rhodos's hand in marriage and called up a mountain from the sea beneath where the girl swam. As Helios descended to this island, the warmth of his affection dried its lakes and rivers,

DODECANESE

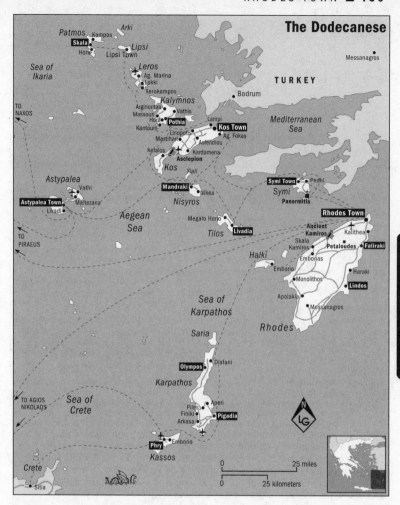

The Dodecanese

turning Rhodes into the Island of Sun. Today, sun worshippers still flock to Rhodes's welcoming shores, making the island the undisputed capital of the Dodecanese. Though touristy resort towns cluster in the north, Rhodes's natural wonders dominate other sections of the island, with sandy beaches stretching along the east coast, jagged cliffs skirting the west, and green mountains dotted with villages filling the interior. Ruins in Kamiros, Ialyssos, and Lindos reveal Rhodes's bygone days as a Hellenic power, while the slumbering medieval fortress towns of Monolithos and Rhodes Town retain their majesty from the days of conquest.

RHODES TOWN   ☎22410

As locals like to say, Rhodes Town always has been a conquered city. First came the Turks, then the Italians, and now tourists flood the streets, coming off any of

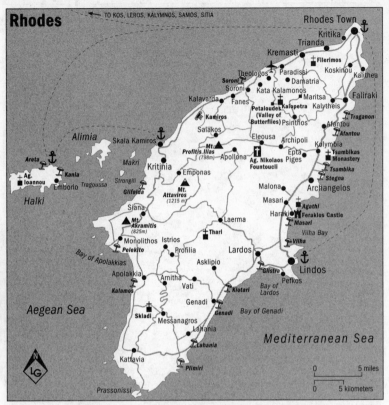

Rhodes

TO KOS, LEROS, KÁLYMNOS, SAMOS, SITIA

Rhodes Town

Kritika

Trianda

Kremasti

Filerimos

Theologos · Paradissi · Koskinou · Kalithea

Soroni · Damatria

Soroni · Kata Kalamonos · Maritsa · Falraki

Kalavarda · Fanes · Kalopetra · Kalytheis

Petaloudes · Psinthos

(Valley of · Afantou

Butterflies) · Traganon

Kamiros · Afantou

Salakos · Archipoli · Kolymbia

Eleousa · Epta · Tsambikas

Skala Kamiros · Mt. · Apollona · Piges · Monastery

Alimia · Profitis Ilias · Ag. Nikolaos · Tsambika

(798m) · Fountoucli · Stegna

Makri · Kritinia · Emponas · Malona · Archangelos

Areta · Mt. · Masari

Kania · Attaviros · Masari · Agathi

Ag. · (1215 m) · Haraki · Feraklos Castle

Ioannou · Strongili · Masari

Emborio · Tragoussa · Glifaida · Laerma · Vilha Bay

Halki · Siana · Vilha

Mt. · Lardos

Akramitis · Thari

(825m) · Istrios

Monolithos · Profilia · Lindos

Pelekito · Asklipio

Apolakkia · Arnitha · Glistra

Kalamos · Vati · Pefkos

Aegean Sea · Genadi · Bay of

Kiotari · Lardos

Skiadi · Genadi · Bay of Genadi

Messanagros

Lahania

Mediterranean Sea

Kattavia · Lahania

Plimiri

Prassonissi

0 _____ 5 miles

0 _____ 5 kilometers

the 11 cruise ships that can be accommodated offshore. Sunburnt masses jostle one another among the souvenir shops on the winding, cobblestoned paths of the Old Town. Clubs, bars, and timeless beaches lie farther to the north in the New Town, where hints of the medieval influence still crop up. A walk along the perimeter of the Old Town reveals the simple beauty of the high stone walls and white streets, and a hike to the ancient acropolis at sunset rewards trekkers with a view of a fire-streaked sky over the stadium.

⬛ TRANSPORTATION

Travel agencies: Many agencies are found scattered around town and clustered by the bus and ferry stations. In the Old Town **Gregory Travels** can exchange currency and book flights and excursions. (☎74 668. Open daily 9am-10pm.) In the New Town **Rhodos Travels** and **Charlampis Travel** offer similar services.

Flights: Diagoras International Airport (☎88 700), 16km out of town, near Paradisi. Accessible by bus (frequently 6:45am-10:40pm, €2) from the west bus station. **Olympic Airways,** Ierou Lohou 91 (☎24 555), 2 blocks inland from the post office. Open M-F 8am-4pm, ticket window closes at 2:30pm. Flights to: **Athens** (5 per day, €76); **Iraklion, Crete** (1-2 per day, €108); **Karpathos** (2 per day, €32); **Kassos** (daily, €38); **Kastellorizo** (daily, €26); **Thessaloniki** (daily, €126). **Aegean Airways** flies to **Athens** (5 per day, €29) and **Thessaloniki** (daily, €132).

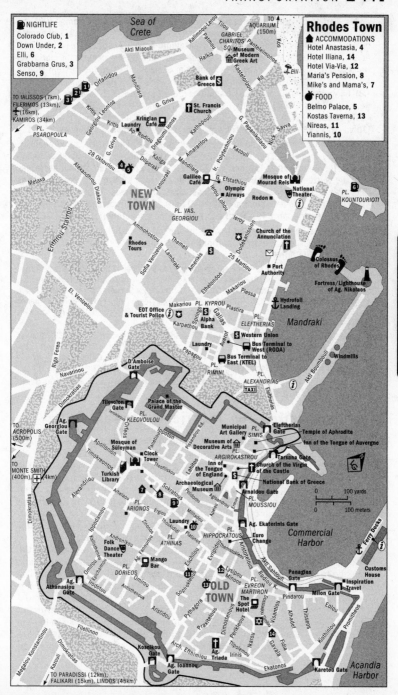

Rhodes Town

NIGHTLIFE
Colorado Club, **1**
Down Under, **2**
Elli, **6**
Grabbarna Grus, **3**
Senso, **9**

ACCOMMODATIONS
Hotel Anastasia, **4**
Hotel Iliana, **14**
Hotel Via-Via, **12**
Maria's Pension, **8**
Mike's and Mama's, **7**

FOOD
Belmo Palace, **5**
Kostas Taverna, **13**
Nireas, **11**
Yiannis, **10**

Sea of Crete

TO AQUARIUM (150m)

GABRIEL CHARITOS SQ.

Museum of Modern Greek Art

Akti Miaouli

Bank of Greece

St. Francis Church

TO IALISSOS (7km), FILERIMOS (13km), (16km), KAMIROS (34km)

Kringlan Café
Laundry

PL. PSAROPOULA

28 Oktovriou

Galileo Café

Mosque of Mourad Reis

National Theater

NEW TOWN

PL. VAS. GEORGIOU

Olympic Airways

Rodon

PL. KOUNTOURIOTI

Rhodes Tours

Church of the Annunciation

Port Authority

Colossus of Rhodes

Fortress/Lighthouse of Ag. Nikolaos

EOT Office & Tourist Police

PL. KYPROU

Alpha Bank

Western Union

Laundry

Bus Terminal to West (RODA)

Bus Terminal to East (KTEL)

PL. ELEFTHERIAS

Mandraki

Hydrofoil Landing

Windmills

D'Amboise Gate

PL. RIMINI

PL. ALEXANDRIAS

TAXI

TO ACROPOLIS (500m)

Tilevolon Gate

Ag. Georgiou Gate

Palace of the Grand Master

PL. KLEOVOULOU

TO MONTE SMITH (400m), (4km)

Mosque of Süleyman

Clock Tower

Turkish Library

Municipal Art Gallery

Eleftherias Gate

Temple of Aphrodite

Inn of the Tongue of Auvergne

PL. SIMIS

Museum of Decorative Arts

PL. ARGIROKASTROU

Tarsana Gate

Church of the Virgin of the Castle

Inn of the Tongue of England

Archaeological Museum

National Bank of Greece

Arnaldou Gate

PL. ARIONOS

PL. MOUSSIOU

Laundry

PL. ATHINAS

Ag. Ekaterinis Gate

Euro Change

Commercial Harbor

Ferry Docks

Folk Dance Theater

PL. DORIEOS

Mango Bar

PL. HIPPOCRATOUS

Panagias Gate

Customs House

Inspiration Travel

Milon Gate

Ag. Athanasiou Gate

OLD TOWN

EVREON MARTIRON

The Spot Hotel

Ag. Triada

Kosnikou Gate

Ag. Ioannou Gate

TO PARADISSI (12km), FALIKARI (15km), LINDOS (45km)

Karetou Gate

Acandia Harbor

DODECANESE

Ferries: Ferries leave from the eastern docks in Commercial Harbor, across from the Milon Gate into the Old Town. Ferry schedules should be confirmed at a travel agency or the Port Authority upon arrival; try **Charlampis Travel,** Australias 1 (☎35 934), across the street from the ferry docks. Some services do not begin until late June. Halki Island can also be reached by boat from Skala Kamiros on the western side of the island. To: **Agios Nikolaos, Crete** (12hr., 2 per week, €25); **Halki** (2½hr., 2 per week, €8); **Kalymnos** (5½hr., daily, €18); **Karpathos** (5hr., 6 per week, €18); **Kassos** (7hr., 6 per week, €22); **Kos** (2½hr., 2 per day, €14); **Leros** (5½hr., daily, €19); **Patmos** (7hr., daily, €22); **Piraeus** (13½hr., 2 per day, €31); **Samos** (10hr., 1 per week, €27); **Sitia, Crete** (10hr., 2 per week, €24.60); **Symi** (1¾ hr., 2 per week, €14); **Tilos** (4hr., 3 per week, €11).

Flying Dolphins: Hydrofoils and catamarans run to all the nearby islands and beaches. Contact any of the travel agencies or inquire on the docks for schedules and ticket information. The **Dodekanisos Express** (☎22410 70 590), a high-speed catamaran, leaves from the western docks of Commercial Harbor and runs to: **Symi** (1½hr., €14); **Kos** (2hr., €28); **Leros** (4½hr., €38); **Kalymnos, Lipsi,** and **Patmos.** All trips leave Rhodes at 8:30am and 3pm and return at 6:30pm. Daily catamaran excursions from Mandraki Port to **Kos** (round-trip €49), **Symi** and **Panormitis Monastery** (round-trip €26).

Buses: Stations lie 1 block apart behind the central plaza. Schedules at the station kiosks or the EOT (see **Practical Information**). Be sure to ask for complete times and listings when you arrive.

East Station is served by **KTEL.** Schedules listed are for M-Sa; contact EOT or ask the station clerk for Su schedules. Service to: **Afantou** (13 per day 6:45am-10pm, €2); **Arkhangelos** (13 per day 6:45am-9:15pm, €2); **Faliraki** (frequently 8:15am-10pm, €2); **Genadi** (7 per day 8am-6:30pm, €5); **Haraki** (10am, 3pm; €3.40); **Kiotari** (7 per day 6:45am-7:30pm, €5); **Kolymbia beach** (10 per day 9am-10pm, €3); **Laerma** (M-F 1pm, €5); **Lindos** (15 per day 6:45am-7:30pm, €4); **Malona; Masari** (4 per day 9am-2:30pm, €3).

West Station is served by **RODA** (☎26 300). To: **Damatria** (3 per day 4:45am-2:10pm, €2); **Kamiros** (9:45, 11:20am, 1:30pm; €4.10); **Paradisi** (6 per day, 10:30am-9:10pm); **Paradisi Airport** (8 per day 6am-10pm, €2); **Pastida** and **Maritsa** (8 per day 5:40am-9:30pm, €2) **Salakos** (3 per day 6:55am-2:40pm, €3.20); **Soroni** (1:15, 8pm, €2); **Tholos** (10 per day 7:30am-11pm, €2.10).

Taxis: ☎69 800. In Pl. Alexandrias; prices posted across from the kiosk. 24hr. Radio taxis (☎64 734) also are available.

ORIENTATION AND PRACTICAL INFORMATION

The city is composed of two districts. The modern **New Town** spans the north and west with ritzy hotels, trendy boutiques, and a happening nightclub scene. The **Old Town** centers on touristy **Sokratous,** a bustling, cobbled street descending from the castle to the commercial harbor. The Old Town streets form a labyrinth of medieval structures that are still in use as houses, tavernas, and souvenir shops. Keep your eyes open for Byzantine influences, and be prepared to get lost in the maze of narrow streets despite your best efforts to follow a map. Unless you're in the market for an "I love Rhodes" magnet, skip the central plazas and wander the outer streets, many of which still evoke an Old World charm and ambience.

Ferries depart from the **Commercial Harbor** outside the Old Town. **Mandraki,** the New Town's waterfront, is where yachts, hydrofoils, and excursion boats dock. Beaches lie to the north, beyond Mandraki and along the city's west coast. The tourist office, bus stations, and a taxi stand are in **Plateia Rimini,** beneath the fortress's turrets, at the junction of the Old and New Towns. From Mandraki, head a block inland with the park on the left. From the Old Town, walk out the D'Amboise Gate in front of the Palace and follow the road as it curves around the park. Or, follow Aristotelous to Ermou until it joins Mandraki. Tourist nightlife in the New Town swarms around **Orfanidou,** dubbed "bar street," while the local scene converges mainly at **Militadou** in the Old Town.

Tourist Office: EOT (☎44 333; www.ando.gr/eot), a few blocks up Papagou from Pl. Rimini, at the corner of Makariou and Papagou. Provides helpful advice for daytrip planning, as well as free maps, brochures in several languages, and complete M-Sa bus schedules. English and Greek information desks. Open M-F 8am-2:45pm.

Banks: Banks and **ATMs** abound throughout both the New and Old Towns. The **Eurochange** booth (☎31 847), at Pl. Hippocratous in the Old Town, has **currency exchange** and cash advances. Open daily 9am-9pm. **National Bank** has an office with an **ATM** in the Old Town at Pl. Moussiou. Open M-Th 8am-2:30pm, F 8am-2pm. The **Commercial Bank of Emboriki** (☎22 123) is just across the way, on Ippoton, and also has an **ATM**. Open M-Th 8am-2:30pm, F 8am-2pm. In the New Town, **Alpha Bank** (☎32 742) offers **currency exchange**, a **24hr. ATM**, and **American Express** services. Open M-F 8am-10pm, Sa 10:15am-2:30pm.

American Express: Rhodos Tours Ltd., Amohostou 23. (☎21 010), Open M-Sa 9am-1:30pm and 5-8:30pm. There is also a Western Union (☎26 400) located behind the central plaza. Open M-F 8:30am-9pm, Sa 8:30am-3pm.

Laundromat: Tornado Laundry (☎37 659), in the New Town on Ap. Rodiou, charges €4 for wash and dry. Open M-F 8:30am-10pm, Su 11am-5pm. One block west of the bus stations, **Express Laundry** (☎22 514) offers the same services. Open daily 8am-11:30pm. In the Old Town, **Laundromat** (☎76 047), 33 Platonos, by Pl. Athina, offers wash and dry for €4.50. Open M-Sa 8am-8pm.

Police: ☎27 653. On Eth. Dodekanisson, one block behind the post office. Open 24hr. **Tourist Police** (☎27 423). Behind the EOT building and up a flight of stairs. Open daily 8am-2pm. In an **emergency** dial ☎100.

Hospital: ☎80 000. On Ag. Apostoli. Open 24 hr. for emergencies. In a **medical emergency** dial ☎166.

Telephones: OTE, Amerikis 91, at the corner of 25 Martiou in the New Town. Open M-F 7:30am-1:30pm. For information dial ☎133.

Internet Access: In the New Town, Kringlan Cafe, 14 Dragoumi Ionos (☎39 090) offers free Wi-Fi on a breezy terrace; enjoy it over cake (€1-2) or a mixed drink (€4-6). Open daily 6:30am-midnight. Computers €3 per hr. Galileo Cafe, Ir. Polytechniou 13 (☎20 610; www.galileocafe.gr), at the corner of G. Efstathiou in the New Town. Offers both computers and Ethernet cables for laptops. €1.20 per 30min. €2 per hr. Mixed drinks €5. Open daily 9am-3am. In the Old Town, Mango Bar, Pl. Dorieos 3 (☎24 877; www.mango.gr) charges €4 per hr. Open M-Sa 10am-1am, Su 10am-midnight. Also offers rooms (singles from €35). Near Pl. Hippocratous, The Spot Hotel, 21 Perikleous (☎34 737) has Wi-Fi. €5 per hr. Open 8am-11pm. Rooms from €35.

Post Office: Main branch (☎30 290) on Mandraki, next to the Bank of Greece, has **Poste Restante.** Open M-F 7:30am-8pm, Sa 7:30am-2pm. **Postal Code:** 85100.

▐ ACCOMMODATIONS

Most **pensions** in the **Old Town** are scattered about the narrow, cobbled paths between Sokratous and Omirou. Prices vary with the season, and you can cut a deal with hostel owners if you plan to stay for a few nights. Even the cheapest accommodations are bright and airy. In the **New Town**, charmless, expensive hotels seem to merge into one sprawling corporate Colossus. Some affordable and even delightful pensions, however, can be found a block or two inland from the waterfront and on the narrow streets of Rodiou, Dilperaki, Kathopouli, and Amarandou.

Hotel Anastasia, 28 Oktovriou 46 (☎28 007; www.anastasia-hotel.com). Just off the street and away from the rowdy hordes, find the peaceful, vine-enclosed garden-bar of this family-run pension. Mihalis Anghelu, the friendly owner, readily shares the lowdown on Rhodes. Nine bright, airy rooms each include at least 2 twin beds, bath, large wardrobe. Be careful not to trip on the pet turtles roaming the garden. Breakfast included. A/C €3 per day. Singles €35; doubles €50. V. ❸

Hotel Iliana, 1 Desiadou Gevala St. (☎30 251). From Pl. Evreon Martiron, follow Dossiadou Simiou past the synagogue; it will be across the street and on the left, up a flight of stairs. Budget's the word at Hotel Iliana with its simple rooms with bath. Singles €10; doubles €15. ❶

Maria's Pension, Lisia 147 (☎22 169), off the main drag of Sokratous. This charming, family-run pension has freshly painted, breezy rooms arranged around a courtyard. Singles €20; doubles €30, with bath €35. ❸

Hotel Via-Via, Pythagora 45 and Lisipou 2 (☎77 027; www.hotel-via-via.com). Lives up to its advertisement as a "Hotel de Charme." Owner Beatrice designs each individually themed room with subtle and refreshing taste. Rooms have TV, A/C, and fridge; some share bathrooms. Singles €30; doubles €57; rooftop double €67. ❸

Mike's Taverna & Mama's Pension, Menekleous 28 (☎25 359), 2 blocks south of the Turkish Library. Gregarious owner Mike says he runs his little pension on the code of music, peace, and love. Comfortable whitewashed rooms, clean shared baths, and a view from the rooftop terrace spanning both the harbor and the Old Town. Music from the nearby bar provides free entertainment all night; bring earplugs to get some shut-eye. Dorms €10; singles €20; doubles €25. ❶

⬢ FOOD

With their quadri-lingual menus and matching tree canopies, many of the restaurants in Rhodes Town have little setting them apart from one another. Traditional Greek fare and fish and chips abound at the more touristed spots, though a few authentic restaurants lay tucked away from the main drags. Cheap, greasy fare abounds on Orfanidou, and crepe stands (€2-5) line the streets of the Old Town. Some of the best dining options in the Old Town are clustered on Pl. Sophokleous; from Pl. Hippocratous, turn onto Pithagora, hang a right on Platanos, then veer left after the mosque to find this hidden street's excellent cuisine.

▧ **Yiannis Taverna,** Platonos 41 (☎36 535), in the Old Town. Go down the street next to Senso nightclub for 50m. Whatever Yiannis lacks in atmosphere is more than made up for in the unparalleled traditional food, which comes in heaping portions. Try the spiced *dolmades* (stuffed grape leaves, €7.50) or treat yourself to the selection of fresh fish. Entrees €5.50-8.50. Open daily 9am-11pm. ❷

Kostas Taverna, (☎26 217) 2 blocks south of Pl. Hippocratous. Peacefully away from the tourist centers. Munch on the fried octopus (€6) or the specialty moussaka (€7) on the roofed terrace in the back. Open daily 9am-midnight. MC/V. ❷

Nireas, Sophokleous 22 (☎21 703). Serves high-quality seafood, prepared according to local recipes. Try the fried calamari (€8). Ordering a fresh fish to share (€30-48 per kg) can be a good way to go for larger groups. Open daily 5pm-2am. AmEx/MC/V. ❸

Belmo Palace, 28 Oktovriou and Ionos Dragouni (☎25 251). Feels more like a family-run diner. Patrons find themselves chatting with hospitable owner Yiannis while munching on pizza (€3.50) and spaghetti (€4). The Greek platter (€8) comes piled with *tzatziki*, stuffed tomatoes, *dolmades*, and fava beans covered with a tasty red sauce. Open daily 10am-11:30pm. AmEx/MC/V. ❷

◉ SIGHTS

OLD TOWN

Plaques scattered throughout the medieval Old Town mark historical sites and museums constructed by the **Knights of Saint John.** In 1309, the Knights conquered the Dodecanese (with the exception of Astypalea, Karpathos, and Kassos), replaced their Hellenistic ruins with towering Gothic edifices, and revived trade with Europe. Strewn among the ruins of these bygone ages, there remains the influence of the **Ottomans,** who ousted the Knights in 1523 AD. Though the Turkish bazaar of old has long since transformed into the kitschy shopping strip of Sokratous, a historic mosque, a library, and Turkish baths pay tribute to the city's Islamic ancestry. Also, accessible through any of the tunnels in the fortress wall, the ▓**parkland** surrounding the fortifications has cannonball-strewn pathways in the peaceful region lying between the fortress's inner and outer walls.

■ **PALACE OF THE GRAND MASTER.** At the top of the hill, a tall, square tower marks the entrance to the Palace of the Grand Master, erected by the Knights as a symbol of Rhodes's recovered military power. With moats, drawbridges, huge watchtowers, and enormous battlements, the 300-room palace stands in the center of the walls that enclose the Old Town. Just outside the old moat, it is bordered by a blossoming city park that stretches for blocks. The palace survived the long Ottoman siege of 1523, though it was converted into a prison by the Turks after their victory. In 1851 an earthquake damaged the building; the natural disaster was followed five years later by the devastating explosion of 300-year-old ammunition in a depot across the street. The citadel was restored to its former glory at the beginning of the 20th century during the Italian occupation under the watchful eye of Mussolini, who planned to use the palace as a summer home. Just after the Italians finished importing a collection of 16th- and 17th-century **mosaic floorwork** from Kos, however, WWII broke out, leaving little time for the dictator to take vacations. (☎ 25 500. €6, students €3, EU students free. Su Free. The mosaics, in addition to Japanese vases and an exhibit on Ancient Rhodes, can be viewed M 8:30am-3pm, Tu-Su 8am-7:30pm. The accompanying museum is closed M.)

PLATEIA ARGIOKASTROU. Dominating one side of the plateia with its halls and courtyards, the former **Hospital of the Knights** has been reborn as an **Archaeological Museum.** Its treasures include the exquisite marble statue from the late 4th century BC, **Aphrodite Bathing,** also called the "Marine Venus." After it fell into the sea during an earthquake, centuries of erosion polished the statue's fluid contours. (☎ 22410 25 500. Open Tu-Su 8:30am-3pm. €3, students €2.) The cobbled **Avenue of the Knights,** or Ippoton, sloping uphill near the museum, was the city's main boulevard 500 years ago and is one of the few major streets free of souvenir shops. The lack of kitsch makes this street one of

THE HIDDEN DEAL

SO FRESH AND SO CLEAN

Closer to Turkey than to the Greek mainland, Rhodes displays a strong and long-lasting Turkish influence on the island. The Turkish baths, built in 1558 and covering over 1000 sq. m, stand in the center of the Old Town at Pl. Arionos. Step inside and be transported from the touristed streets to the sanctum-like interior with domed ceilings.

The traditional Turkish bath is divided by gender and has three main compartments, each progressively warmer than the last. Bathers enter the first room to strip down, the second to wash, and the third to soak in the heat. The marble-lined rooms form a heated maze of basins and running water. Star-shaped openings in the ceiling allow natural light to fall into the cavernous rooms. Hot and cold water taps fill large marble basins—get the temperature just right, then use the provided shallow, metal bowl to scoop water out and onto yourself. Freshen up quickly, or make like a local and linger in the relaxing rooms for the recommended one to two hours.

Renting a locker and basin costs €1.50; an additional massage runs €5. Bring your own towel and a bar of soap, or rent them for €1 apiece.

the most picturesque in the city—untainted by shops or even parked cars. During the Knights' reign, the **inns** of each of their different divisions lined the street. Each division, called a "tongue," maintained its own inn where members would gather to eat, socialize, and converse without pesky language barriers. The **Inn of the Tongue of England** is a 1919 copy of its 1483 predecessor, which was destroyed in one of the Knights' many defensive battles. At the foot of Ippoton, you'll find the **Church of the Virgin of the Castle,** an 11th-century Byzantine church, which has been gradually reworked with Gothic elements up through the 14th century.

PLATEIA SIMIS. Inside Eleftherias Gate to the right and up a flight of stairs, the **Municipal Art Gallery** boasts 13 rooms of lithographs, sculptures, and oil paintings by contemporary, local, and national artists. You can gaze over the entire plateia from its cool, sunny rooms. *(Open Tu-Sa 8am-2pm. €3, students €1.)* In the middle of the plateia, behind the sandstone and stucco ruins of the 3rd-century BC **Temple of Aphrodite** stands the 16th-century **Inn of the Tongue of Auvergne,** with an Aegean-style staircase. Across the street, the **Decorative Arts Collection** offers a glimpse of contemporary Greek artwork. *(Open Tu-Su 8:30am-2:40pm. €2.)*

ORFEOS STREET. Evidence of the city's Ottoman past lines this street, especially toward the top of the hill. A walk down Orfeos will take you by a large **clock tower** and the **Mosque of Süleyman,** originally built after Sultan Süleyman the Magnificent captured Rhodes in 1522 and restored in the early 19th century.

TURKISH HORA. The Hafiz Ahmed Aga Library (Turkish Library), built in 1793 opposite the mosque, houses 830 volumes of handwritten 15th- and 16th-century Persian and Arabic manuscripts of classic literature. Scrolls and paintings are displayed in the museum off the courtyard. *(Open M-Sa 9:30am-4pm.)* While many of the ancient sites are in various stages of decay and restoration, the 500-year-old **Turkish Baths** in Pl. Arionos welcome locals and travelers alike. Lather up in the heated maze of marble rooms and stone basins as locals have done for centuries. *(Open M-F 10am-5pm, Sa 8am-5pm. €1.50.)*

JEWISH QUARTER. Plateia Evreon Martiron (Jewish Martyrs' Square) lies in the heart of the old Jewish Quarter. Sephardic Jews arrived on the island after fleeing the Spanish Inquisition in 1492 and added a distinctive flair to some of the Old Town's medieval architecture. In 1944, almost 2000 Jews were taken from this square to concentration camps. Pl. Evreon Martiron has since been overrun by tourist cafes and shops, though a small, touching memorial in the center pays tribute to the victims of the Holocaust. Although the streets in this area show some wear and tear, they provide a pleasant reprieve from the crazed main plaza. Down Dossiadou Simiou (off Pl. Evreon Martiron and Simiou) is the **Kahal Shalom Synagogue.** Originally constructed in 1577 and restored by five Greek-Jewish families after WWII, the synagogue is the last of the six that once stood in Rhodes. Inside, intricate stone mosaics cover the floor, and a newly opened **museum** offers visitors information on the heritage of Jews in Rhodes. *(☎22 364. Open M-F 10am-3pm. Services F 5pm. Modest dress required.)*

NEW TOWN AND MANDRAKI

Stately Italian architecture permeates the modern business district. The bank, town hall, post office, and National Theater number among the stone buildings inspired by the fascist aesthetic that dominates Eleftherias. Opposite them sits the majestic **Governor's Palace,** with its unique mix of Byzantine, medieval, and Spanish styles, and the **Church of the Annunciation,** built by the Italians in 1925 to replicate a cathedral destroyed in an 1856 explosion. In the Byzantine style, beautifully painted scenes of the life of Christ line the arches and ceilings, and chandeliers hang over the center nave. *(Open daily 7am-noon and 5-7:30pm. Modest dress required.)*

Three inoperable **windmills** stand halfway down the harbor's pier marking the path to the **Fortress of Agios Nikolaos,** which guarded the harbor from 1464 until the end of WWII. The **Mosque of Mourad Reis** is named after the Turkish admiral who died in the 1523 siege of Rhodes. His mausoleum, the domed building inside, served as the Turkish cemetery. Turbans indicate male graves; flowers, female ones. Rhodes Town's small **aquarium,** also a marine research center, exhibits aquatic life from the Aegean. *(At the tip of Cos. ☎27 308. Open daily Apr.-Oct. 9am-8:30pm; Nov.-Mar. 9am-4:30pm. €4.50, students €2.)* A few blocks inland in Gabriel Charitos Sq. you'll find the stately **◩Museum of Modern Greek Art,** home to a three-story collection of 20th-century Greek oil paintings and sculptures. *(☎43 780. Open Tu-Th and Sa 8am-2pm, F 8am-2pm and 5-8pm. €3, students €1.)* Follow signs from the EOT to reach the **Acropolis of Rhodes,** famous for its dazzling sunset vista. The ancient stadium, a popular place for locals to go running, stands below the temple.

COLOSSUS OF RHODES. Few places are known for a sight that no longer exists, but Rhodes, with its absent **Colossus,** is one of them. The towering 33m bronze statue, one of the **Seven Wonders of the Ancient World,** once stood guard over Mandraki harbor. Rhodians, giddy over their defeat of Demetrius Poliorcetes, sold the enemy's abandoned battle equipment and used the funds to build an enormous monument in the shape of the sun-god Helios. Sadly, sunset came quickly for the Colossus—it only stood for about 54 years before breaking in an earthquake around 226 BC. Fearing a curse, Rhodians left the giant hunks of bronze undisturbed until AD 654, when they were carried off by Arab pirates raiding the town. Although it once was thought that the Colossus stood straddling the harbor, calculations now show this to be impossible. More likely, its "lovely light of unfettered freedom" shone in the courtyard of the temple of Helios. Today, the Colossus has left no earthly trace. A pair of bronze deer stand in commemoration on either side of the harbor entrance, marking the spots where the statue's gigantic feet are wistfully imagined to have been planted.

OUTSIDE THE CITY

Excursion boats trace the coast from Rhodes Town to Lindos, providing a great escape to an ancient town less tinged by commercial materialism. The boats stop at the beaches of Kalithea, Faliraki, and Tsambika, among others. Ask around for prices and schedules on the docks until you find the right fit. *(Most leave the city around 8:30am and return in the early afternoon. Tickets from €11.)* Excursion boats also go to nearby islands like Symi and Halki for €25 roundtrip. The PADI certified **Trident Diving School** offers dives to any of the number of coves and wrecks offshore. Pack a lunch. *(☎29 160; www.tridentdivingschool.com. 2-tank dive €70, equipment included.)*

🎵 📷 ENTERTAINMENT AND NIGHTLIFE

In the early evening, check out one of several cultural events before hitting the rowdy bars. **Saint Francis Church** (☎23 605), on Dragoumi Ionos in the New Town, echoes with sublime organ recitals. Recitals every Su 10pm; check the schedule online at www.catholicchurchrhodes.com.) In the winter, the **National Theater,** on Efstathiou Georgiou off Mandraki across from the Church of the Annunciation, stages productions. (☎20 265. Ask for a performance schedule at the EOT.) Nearby **Rodon** shows flicks and subtitled classics in an outdoor, vine-covered amphitheater. In June, it hosts an annual Ecocinema film festival, showing environmentally and anthropologically themed documentaries. Another option is to check with the EOT to see if you can catch a performance at the **Folk Dance Theater.**

After indulging your intellect, let your animal instincts take the helm with a good old-fashioned pub crawl on either side of town. The nightlife has two major centers in the Old Town; a slightly mellower crowd of locals and tourists gathers in the bars on Pl. Arionos. Conversation and drinks can be enjoyed at **Rogmi tou Hronou,** where the stone-walled rooms illuminated by a back-lit drink selection are open from noon-4am. (☎25 202. Live music F nights.) Flashing lights and packed clubs can be found down the street on **Militadou,** one block behind Sokratous. Bars line the street and music pours out of every door, creating a carnival atmosphere. By midnight, the boundaries between bars have disappeared completely, and there's not a bare spot to be found on the cushioned stone benches scattered along the street. A tipsy crowd stands on Sokratous in front of **Senso,** where partygoers drink and mingle until 6am. (☎69451 57488.) Drink prices are comparable everywhere. Quieter bars more suitable for conversation can be found in the plateias between Ag. Fanouriou and Eschilou, where tourists and locals alike linger over mixed drinks and *mezedes*. Nightlife in the New Town has the youthful electricity of any large city. Popular bars and clubs are scattered throughout, but crowds of tourists converge on the "bar street" of **Orfanidou.** On one end of the street, **Colorado Club,** Orfanidou 57, is the king of New Town nightlife, packing partyers into three floors of perpetually crowded rooms. One floor has a live rock band blasting 80s hits, the second offers disco music and an accompanying light show, and the third provides a bump-and-grind venue with a live DJ. (☎75 120; www.coloradoclub.gr. Drinks €2-8. Cover €5. Open daily 10:30pm-6am.) **Down Under,** Orfanidou 37, features crowds bumping to the live DJ. The Aussie staff just might dance on tables to loud pop and hip hop. (☎22410 32 982. Drinks from €4.50. Open daily until 4am.) Just a few doors down, **Grabbarna Grus** offers comfy chairs, a live DJ, and a tiny, elevated "dance floor" (which strangely resembles a table) packed with enthusiastic patrons clamoring for drinks. (☎69394 74 644. Beers €4. Open daily 9pm-5am.) Sick of techno? Head to **Elli** for Greek music and dancing in the basement of the domed building on Pl. Kountourioti. (☎22 545. Drinks €5.50-8.)

◪ DAYTRIPS FROM RHODES TOWN

A few kilometers inland from the coast, the Rhodesian geography changes drastically. Beaches seamlessly rise into mountains, offering opportunities for scenic hikes or quiet contemplation. These quieter spots often are left out of the party package tours, so you are more likely to encounter families and older couples than young revelers. Sturdy shoes and bug repellant are a must for attempting these often steep and wooded trails.

VALLEY OF BUTTERFLIES. In the late summer months, countless Jersey tiger moths migrate to **Petaloudes,** or the Valley of Butterflies. Located 5km inland from Theologos, the valley is where the moths return to spend their final days in the shade of fragrant Styrax trees. During this time the moths fast, living only on water and body fat to conserve energy for rigorous mating sessions; afterward, in a sad state of post-coital affairs, they die of starvation. Although the butterflies can be elusive (particularly in early summer), the hike alongside a bubbling stream and cascading waterfalls makes the valley a worthwhile destination. The best butterfly viewing can be done from mid-July to late August. A **cafe** near the main entrance overlooks one of the larger waterfalls, and provides a break between the upper and lower parts of the forested trail. Butterfly numbers dwindled a few years ago due to visitor harassment but the insects since have returned thanks to security guards and a surveillance cameras. If you have energy left after reaching the top of the 1km trail, continue 300m up to the **Monastery of Kalopetra** to see the restored mosaics and a panoramic view of the island. *(☎22410 81 801. Open Easter-Oct. 8am-7pm. June 15-Sept. 13. €5, low season €3; children under 12 free. Four buses run daily 9:30am-1:30pm from Rhodes Town's west station. The 45min. bus ride is €4* *and drops you off at the main entrance, located in the middle of the ascending path; visitors also can enter near the monastery on top of the mountain, or at the museum below.)*

EPTA PIGES. Eleven kilometers south of Faliraki, just before Kolymbia, a road to the right leads 3km down an unshaded highway and up a steep incline to Epta Piges. The aqueduct, built by Italians to bring water to Kolymbia, now quenches its visitors' thirst for excitement. Hurtling down the 150m pitch-black natural water-slide is the fastest way to reach the picturesque fresh-water pool below. If the destination sounds nicer than the journey, take the path next to the tunnel that is used to return from the pool. A streamside **taverna,** home to a family of peacocks, sits at the mouth of the aqueduct. Get off the Rhodes-Lindos bus at Kolymbia, and follow the sign to Epta Piges, which you'll reach after a 50min. walk. Renting a car or moped is generally a much better way to get there, especially in the midday sun. Continue inland past Epta Piges to visit the 13th- and 15th-century frescoes of the Byzantine **Church of Agios Nikolaos Fountoucli,** 3km past Eleousa.

TSAMBIKAS MONASTERY. A restaurant on the coastal road marks Tsambikas Monastery. A 1km road will lead you to the restaurant; the Byzantine cloister and its panoramic views are 1km farther up a steep, rocky trail. The monastery takes its name from the sparks *(tsambas)* that reportedly were seen coming from atop the hill. Upon climbing up to investigate, locals discovered a Cypriot icon of the Virgin Mary that mysteriously had appeared there, miles from its home. Angry Cypriots ordered that the icon be returned, and the locals obliged—but the icon kept coming back. By its third return, everyone agreed that it belonged in Rhodes. To this day, some women ascend the mountain to pray to the Virgin Mary for fertility. If the prayer works it is said that the baby should be named "Tsambikos" or "Tsambika." One bus runs to long, sandy **Tsambika beach,** 1km south of the turn-off for the monastery. *(Ask at the east bus station in Rhodes Town for times. Buses to Archangelos, Faliraki, and other destinations that pass the turn-off will let you off there.)*

KAMIROS. The smallest of Rhodes's three ancient cities, Kamiros surpasses Rhodes Town in intricacy and preservation. This Hellenistic city was built into a hollow and constructed in an impressive chessboard design. Three levels of settlement developed; the lowest "public" level slopes up like an amphitheater to the highest level, which contains the acropolis. A visit to the precinct of Athena Kamiras on the acropolis gives a clear sense of the city's well-planned layout. The giant cistern on the north side of the temple (circa 5th or 6th century BC) and the colonnade (2nd century BC) are other noteworthy archaeological finds. *(Buses run daily from Rhodes Town's west station to Kamiros at 9:45, 11:15am, and 1:30pm. (€4.) ☎40 037. Open Tu-Sa 8am-7:10pm. €4, students €2.)*

FALIRAKI Φαλιράκι ☎22410

There's little to Faliraki besides bars and beach. A few years ago, the town was packed with raucous European partiers, but due to bad press about its frat-boy image, the tour packages and party-hardy crowds have waned. The main drag of tourist shops and restaurants now is more reminiscent of an abandoned strip mall than the holiday playground it used to be. Beach crowds need not wait for dark to pound one back—most bars are open all day. **Jimmy's Pub,** inland on Hermou, is a British bar with Guinness on tap and soccer and car races on TV. Beachside **Chaplin's** is a popular hangout by day for sunbathers. Come nightfall, many cafes and bars will put up their chairs and make space for dancing as partiers crawl out of the sun and into the disco lights. Across from Jimmy's, **Jamaica Bar** offers beers (€3-4) and mixed drinks (€4-6). A mellower crowd enjoys live football over the specialty "fishbowls"(€12 and up): over-sized drinks meant for sharing. (☎85 221. Open daily 10:30am-3am.) Head a few doors down on the same side of the street to

Breeze Bar, where a booming sound system accompanies dancing on any horizontal surface you can find. (☎69372 28 252. Beers €2.50-5. Open daily 10am-3am.)

Since European tour packages abandoned the town, many pensions and hostels have closed down. **Studio Olga ❷,** across from the beach and behind the taxi stand, offers doubles with air-conditioning, TV, kitchenette, bath, patio, and fridge. Look for the yellow Steve's Studios sign, and walk down the driveway past the first building. (☎85 115. Check-out at noon. Singles €20.) Fast-food joints line Hermou and the Rhodes-Lindos highway with slightly pricier variations on a similar theme. An average meal runs €6-9. For a reprieve from fast food, walk toward the highway on Hermou and go several blocks left on Apollon, past an Internet gaming bar. There you will find **Manolis ❷,** which has earned a reputation for the most authentic *mezedes* (€1.80-8) in Faliraki. (☎86 561. Greek dishes €5-9. Open M-Sa 4pm-midnight, Su 1pm-midnight. MC/V.)

Faliraki is 15km south of Rhodes Town. There are two main bus stops: one on the Rhodes-Lindos highway and one on the waterfront. **Buses** run to Lindos (1hr., 14 per day, €3.30) from the former stop and to Rhodes Town (15min., 16 per day 6:55am-8:40pm, €2) from the latter. Faliraki is also a base for excursion boats to Lindos (round-trip €12) and Symi (round-trip €22). Grab a **taxi** (☎69 800) at the stand next to the waterfront bus stop. (€13 to Rhodes Town, €30 to Lindos.) **Dimitra Travel,** at the corner one block in as you approach the beach from the highway, has **currency exchange,** an international phone, excursion boat tickets, a **24hr. ATM,** phonecards, and car rental. (☎86 140. Motorbikes €15-20 per day. Cars from €25. Open daily 9am-11pm.) Western Union is available at Isis Travel across the Rhodes-Lindos highway. (☎85 060. Open daily 9am-9pm.) **Emporiki Bank** can be found by taking a left on the Rhodes-Lindos highway coming off the beach. Down a block and on the right, it has a **24hr. ATM.** (Open daily M-Th 8am-2:30pm and F 8am-2pm.) Opposite the waterfront bus stop facing the beach, is the **police office.** (☎84 700. Open daily 6am-2am.) The **pharmacy** is on Hermou next to Dimitra travel; look for the green cross. (☎85 998. Open daily 9am-11pm.) Next to the police office is the **first-aid station.** (☎85 555. Open daily 10am-5pm.) A 24hr. **medical center** (☎85 852) is across the street from the pharmacy. For **emergency care,** call ☎80 000. Find **Internet** access at **Yasoo! Cyber Cafe,** on the left as you walk toward the highway from Jamaica Bar. (☎85 507. €2 per hr. Open daily 10am-1am.)

LINDOS Λίνδος ☎22440

Fifty kilometers south of Rhodes town, escape into the undisturbed past of Lindos. The whitewashed houses clustered at the foot of a castle-capped acropolis make Lindos one of the most picturesque towns on the island. People and donkeys stroll the winding alleys and cobbled mosaics tile courtyards and footpaths. Tourist shops cater to the daytime crowds on the roads leading up to the acropolis, but other, less traveled streets remain untouched, offering a glimpse of ancient ambience. Lindos has made recent efforts to become more accessible to visitors, offering improved amenities while retaining its small-town charm. In July and August, room prices rise dramatically as accommodations become scarce. From the ruins of the 4th-century BC Temple of Athena Lindia within the acropolis, Lindos's panoramic views of the aquamarine sea are hard to rival.

▐ TRANSPORTATION. Lindos is a pedestrian-only city—no traffic may pass beyond the town square at the bottom of the hill. The main road to Rhodes Town and Pefkos lies at the top of the hill, where you'll find the KTEL **bus** stop and kiosk. After 3pm buses also make a stop in the town square. Buses to: Faliraki (14 per day 6:50am-7:15pm, €3.30); Kalathos (14 per day 6:30-7:15, €1.20); Kalithea (5 per day 1pm-7:15pm); Kiotari-Genadi (8 per day 7:45am-10:30pm, €2); Kolymbia beach

(4 per day 11am-1pm, €3); Pefkos-Lardos (7 per day 7:40am-8:30pm, €1.20); Rhodes Town (14 per day 6:50am-7:15pm, €4.30). Check at the bus kiosk for changes to the schedule. **Taxis** can be found in the town square or half-way up the street to the main road. Free blue-and-yellow **shuttles** run between the bus station and the Lindos town square down the hill (every 10min. 8am-3pm) and the Lindos beach (approximately every hr. 9am-5pm). **Excursion boats** from Lindos depart at 9am and return at 5pm, hitting Rhodes Town (2½hr., €12) and other pit stops as they travel along the coast. Boats also take daytrips to Symi (€40-45 round-trip) and Turkey (€60, passport required). Renting a **donkey** and guide (€5), the only non-walking option in town, is a traditional way for visitors to ascend the mountain to the acropolis or head down the steep paths to the beach. Pick up a ride at the donkey stand just past the town square.

ORIENTATION AND PRACTICAL INFORMATION. It's best to find your way around Lindos by using landmarks and house numbers; street signs are few and far between, and many streets don't have names at all. From the town plaza, **Acropolis** winds down into town and up to the acropolis; signs point to the beach after 50m. **Apostolou Pavlou** crosses Acropolis just past the **Church of the Assumption of Madonna**. The **tourist information booth,** located in the town plateia, can equip you with a free, albeit undetailed map of Lindos town. It also provides bus and excursion schedules, general info on Lindos and the acropolis, and doubles as a multilingual newsstand. (☎31 900. Open daily 9am-9pm.) A **24hr. ATM** is next to the tourist info booth and to the left. **Island of the Sun Travel,** located on Acropolis about 100m past the church, offers excursion booking, **car rental,** and **currency exchange.** (☎31 264. Open mid-May to Oct. daily 9am-11pm.) Sheila Markiou, an American expat, runs the superb **Lindos Lending Library** with her daughter, offering more than 7000 English, French, German, Greek, and Italian books. While it's only a library for permanent residents, visitors can buy a used book for half off, or sell one of their own. To get there, pass the church on your left, and take the right fork; it is on the left. (☎31 443. Open M-Sa 9am-8pm.) Sheila also runs a **laundry** service out of the store, with the same hours. (Wash and dry €7.50.) **Public toilets** can be found in the plateia. The **police** are at the end of the road, 200m past the pharmacy and on the left. (☎31 223. Open M-F 8am-3pm; 24hr. for emergencies.) The **pharmacy** is just past Yannis Bar, down the right side of Acropolis. (☎31 294. Open daily 9am-9pm.) The **medical clinic** is on the right after taking a right facing the church entrance. (☎31 224. Open daily 9am-3pm.) **Lindos Internet Cafe,** 150 m up the path to the left of the donkey stand, is a comfortable place to check email over a €6 full English breakfast. (☎32 100. Open daily 8:30am-1am. €4 per hr.) **Emporiki Bank** is right above the donkey stand and offers **currency exchange.** (☎31 270. Open M-F 8am-2pm.) The **post office** is uphill from the donkey stand right before the Internet cafe. (☎31 314. Open M-F 7:30am-2pm.) **Postal Code:** 85107.

> **TIP**
> **CHEAP ROOMS, HAPPY OWNERS.** When bargaining for domatia, do not be tempted to comment negatively on the room to bring down the price. Rather, bargain honestly from your wallet's perspective. Owners will be much more accommodating to travelers who admit that "you have a very nice pension, but that is more than I can spend for the evening," than to those who criticize their rooms.

ACCOMMODATIONS. Signs advertising rooms can be found just past the pharmacy: take the first right and head uphill and toward the left. In late July and August many pensions will fill up, so call ahead for reservations. Take the first right past the pharmacy, follow the street as it curves to the left, then turn right at the fork to find **Mrs. Zinovia's Rooms to Let ❷,** #484 on an unnamed street. Spacious rooms with private bath and kitchenette look out on a lemon tree and mosaiced courtyard. (☎31 973. Singles €25-34.) Take the first left off Acropolis to find **Pension Electra ❸**. Clean, airy rooms with attached bath and fridge open onto the sunny courtyard with a terrific view of the sea. (☎31 266. Singles €30; doubles €35.) Next to Pension Electra, **Pension Katholiki ❸**, #65 on an unnamed street, has four whitewashed rooms with lofted beds, bath, and kitchenette. The decorated stone facade in the courtyard that dates from 1640 and the phenomenal rooftop view are added bonuses. (☎31 445. Rooms €40.)

🕽🕽 **FOOD AND NIGHTLIFE.** Many of the tavernas in town serve similar fare at reasonable prices, and some have incredible rooftop views. More restaurants lie along the street on the first left off Acropolis; head farther down the road to the small beach and the number of waterside restaurants at the bottom of the hill. Enjoy the view from the rooftop terrace of **I Love Billy's Bar ❶**. You'll love Billy's because it's cheap (hamburgers €2; beer €2), because it's greasy (eggs with bacon €2.50), and because large projectors show the latest soccer game. (☎31 655. Look for the blue sign off Acropolis. Open daily 8am-1am.) Around the corner from the ancient theater ruins, **Swedco ❶** offers croissants (€1.40) and slices of cake (€2) in a comfy cafe setting. Take the first left past the pharmacy. Avoid the in-cafe charge by getting your food to go. (☎31 233. Open daily 8am-midnight.)

Nightlife action begins at **Yannis Bar** on Acropolis (☎31 245. Drinks €4-7. Open daily 7am-3am.) Continue the festivities down the street at **Four 04.** Hang out at the chill bar over drinks (€4) until 3 or 4am. Head toward the town square on Acropolis to find **Ikon Cafe Bar** for mixed drinks (€5) and conversation.

🅖 **SIGHTS.** Lindos's ancient **acropolis** stands on sheer cliffs 115m above town, caged by scaffolding and the walls of a crusader fortress. The site was excavated by the Danish Archaeological School between 1902 and 1912. The dig yielded everything from Neolithic tools to a plaque inscribed by a priest of Athena in 99 BC, listing the dignitaries who supposedly visited Athena's temple—Hercules, Helen of Troy, Menelaus, Alexander the Great, and the King of Persia. Just before the final staircase, you'll find a carving of an ancient trireme, or warship with three sets of oars on each side, supposedly by Pythokreitos (famous for his Nike of Samothrace). Lined with staircases, the daunting 13th-century **crusader castle** marks the site's entrance. The arcade, built around 200 BC at the height of Rhodes's glory, originally consisted of 42 Doric columns laid out in the shape of the Greek letter Π. The large stone blocks arranged against the back wall were bases for bronze statues that have long since been melted down. The remains of the Doric-style **Temple of Athena Lindia** come into view at the top of the rocky incline. Erected in the 4th century BC, the temple was cut off completely from the outside, accesible only through one of the five entrances found on one wall. Today the temple is undergoing renovations, though the spectacular panoramic view still can be appreciated from its steps. At the foot of the acropolis lie the remains of the **ancient amphitheater.** Ask for the helpful pamphlet at the acropolis ticket window. (☎31 258. Open in summer M 12:30pm-7pm, Tu-Su 8am-7pm; in winter Tu-Su 8:30am-2:40pm. €6, students €3.) Walk 100m in from the town square to find the **Church of the Assumption of Madonna**, featuring an intricately patterned mosaic floor, paneled ceilings, and a **museum.** (Open M-Sa 9am-3pm and 4:30-6pm, Su 9am-3pm. Museum €1.50. Modest dress required.) The Churches of Greece also offers a **walking tour** of the monasteries near Lindos. Meet at 10am behind the church, next to the door labeled #99. Walks are personalized for each group and can include swimming or lunch breaks. (Offered every M-Sa. Voluntary donation.)

KARPATHOS Κάρπαθος

Ancient mythology claims that the island of Karpathos was the home of the Titans, a clan of giants who spawned the Olympian gods. Though one look at its austere mountain landscape makes the legend believable, today the island's winding coastline finds better use as a quiet getaway for beach-goers and hikers. Tourism has been a major boon to the Karpathian economy over the last 50 years, as travelers are drawn to the island's stunning pale-green coastline by the tantalizing offer of a slower pace of life. While the industry has changed the island, Karpathians' tie to their homeland remains strong. Though countless islanders fled to the United States after WWII when the Italian occupation ruined the economy, many Greek-Americans now return for summers to run family-owned restaurants and shops. In the north, cultural traditions have been preserved in the villages, and the hypnotically beautiful coves and beaches that stretch along the southeast make Karpathos an ideal stop for beach bunnies, mountain men, and anyone looking to kick back and relax with Mother Nature.

PIGADIA Πηγάδια ☎ 22450

A bustling ferry center, Pigadia is host to its fair share of outdoor cafes, nightlife hotspots, and spectacular views. In the winter it lies dormant, only coming to life in the summer when thousands of Greek-Americans descend to reopen the shops and tavernas for the onslaught of mostly European visitors. Despite the large resort hotels and tourist shops, Pigadia retains a refreshing authenticity in both its food and lifestyle. The touristy kitsch that has infected other islands is less pervasive here, perhaps due to the Greek-Americans' nostalgia for the utopian Karpathos of generations past.

TRANSPORTATION. Flights leave from Karpathos Airport to: Athens (45min., daily, €73); Kassos (15min., daily, €25); Rhodes (30min., 1-3 per day, €32); Sitia (1hr., daily). **Ferries** go to: A. Nikolaos (2 per week, €20.10); Kassos (1½hr., 3 per week, €7.40); Piraeus (21hr., 23 per week, €32.90); Milos (2 per week, €33.40); Rhodes (5hr., 3 per week, €18); Thira (2 per week, €26.20). Chrisovalandou Lines runs daily excursions to Olympos (1½hr.; leaves 8:30am, returns 6pm; €22 includes bus ride into the town) and offers other beach packages (3 beaches in one day; €25 including lunch). Schedules change seasonally so check with Possi Travel (☎ 22 235) when you arrive. All **buses** leave from the main station, on the 3rd street parallel to the water, across the street from the supermarket and the minigolf course. Although there is another bus stop across from the taxi stand on Dimokratias, getting on at the origin is a better bet unless you are sure of the schedule. Buses only run on a regular schedule during the high season from mid-May to October; check the kiosk (☎ 22 338) at the main station for the timetable. Buses go to most villages on the southern part of the island (€1-3). Tickets sold on board. No service Sunday or local holidays. Buses to: Amopi (20min.; 10:15am, 3pm); Aperi and Apelia (1¼hr.; M, W, F 9:30am); Aperi, Volada, Othos, and Piles (40min.; 6:50, 11am, 1:30pm); Arkasa, Finiki, and Lefkos (1hr.; M, W, F 9:30am, 1:30, 6:30pm); Menetes, Arkasa, and Finiki (45min., M-F 2pm). **Taxis** (☎ 22 705) run 24hr., though cabs might not be at the stand between 2-7am. Arrange the night before for an early-morning ride, either by phone or in person. Taxi prices are posted on a tree outside the stand (€8-18 to nearby villages; €15 to the airport). There are several rental agencies on the same road as the bus stand. Facing inland from the bus stand, walk right for two blocks, and **Moto Carpathos** is on the right. (☎ 22 382; www.motocarpathos.gr. Motorbikes €14-16 per day, including insurance. 21+. Ask about the seven-day discount. Open daily 8:30am-2pm and 6-10pm.) Closer to the waterfront, **Circle Rent A Car** is located about 200m west of Hotel Blue Sky. (☎ 22 690. Cars €30-35 per day. 10% discount for rentals of more than two days. Open 8:30am-1pm and 5-8:30pm.)

■ 7 ORIENTATION AND PRACTICAL INFORMATION. Three main roads run parallel to each other and the waterfront; the first runs along the water and is lined with open-air tavernas and clubs. The second extends above and one block inland from the dock, featuring many shops, cafes, and rental locations. The police, post office, main bus station, and some domatia lie along the third. The taxi stand and a bus stop are on **Dimokratias**, a main street which runs perpendicular to the others.

For budget travel, **Possi Travel and Holidays,** on the waterfront, sells ferry and plane tickets, books excursions, **exchanges currency,** and has bus and ferry schedules. Western Union is available. The friendly, English-speaking staff is ready and willing to help with any logistical problem. (☎22 235; fax 22 252. Open M-Sa 8am-1pm and 5:30-8:30pm.) The **National Bank**, opposite Possi Travel, has **currency exchange** and a **24hr. ATM.** (☎22 409. Open M-Th 8am-2:30pm, F 8am-2pm.) **ATE Bank,** by the police station, one block east of the supermarket also has a 24hr. ATM. (Open M-Th 8am-2:30pm, F 8am-2pm.) Find the **police** station on the first left past the hospital, up a block and on the left. (☎22 222. Open 24hr.) The **hospital** is on the 2nd road parallel to the waterfront on your left. (☎22 228. English spoken. Open 24hr.) The **OTE** can be found past the post office. (☎22 399. Open M-F 7:30am-2pm.) For **Internet,** look no further than **Cafe Galileo** on the left after a short walk past the National Bank. Features DSL connections, camera card readers, printing, scanning, a full bar (drinks €2-6), and sandwiches (€3-4). At night, enjoy the hopping bar atmosphere over backgammon and beers. (☎23 606. €3 per hr. Open daily 10am-2:30pm and 6pm-late.) Other access can be found at **Internet Cafe Potpourri,** one block west of Galileo, at a three-way intersection opposite Olympic Airways. Connect on DSL lines over crepes (€3.50) and Greek coffee. (☎29 073. €3 per hr. Open daily 8am-1am.) To reach the **post office** follow the signs to the left from the intersection of Dimokratias and the second street inland. (☎22 219. Open M-F 7:30am-2pm.) **Postal Code:** 85700.

■ ■ ACCOMMODATIONS AND FOOD. **Christina's Rooms ❷** are palatial, with amenities fit for a king. From the water, walk up Dimokratias, take a left, and look for the sign on a pink and yellow house. Rooms include bath, balcony, air-conditioning, TV, and fridge; several rooms have kitchens. Ask about the top-floor single with exclusive roof access. (☎22 045. Singles €20; doubles €25-30; triples €30.) To find **Hotel Blue Sky ❷,** head right from Dimokratias on the second major street; it's on the first corner on the left. Gigantic suites boast a sitting room, kitchen, bath, TV, fridge, coffee maker, large closet, and wrap-around balcony with a view of the sea. The 1970s furniture and the silk flowers in the rooms give off a grandmotherly vibe, and Maria, the owner, might not let you leave the building without a juicebox and a pastry. (☎22 356. Singles and doubles €25.) Head one block uphill from the taxi stand and take the left fork to get to **Elias Rooms for Rent ❸.** Climb the stairs until they curve to the right; it's on the left. English-speaking Elias can provide plenty of helpful information about the island. Ask about the traditional *soufa* (lofted) beds. (☎22 446; www.eliasrooms.com. Singles €30; doubles €25-35.)

Countless tavernas line the waterfront, each offering some combination of Greek specialties, a selection of international drinks, and wicker chairs. **The Life of Angels ❷** is two blocks past the National Bank on the second road from the water. Look out for a blue sign in Greek on the right. Owner Zoe and her daughter, Angel, serve traditional Greek fare (€5.50-8) and vegetarian options. Stop by the airy rooftop to enjoy a glass of house wine (€2.50-5) and, after 9pm on Wednesday or Saturday, live Karpathian music. (☎22 984. Open daily 10am-2pm and 5pm-midnight.) Sample an unending selection of traditional Karpathian *mezedes* at **Taverna Orea Karpathos ❷,** located right across from the ferry docks. Small plates designed for sharing run €3-7 and feature everything from local cheese-sprinkled

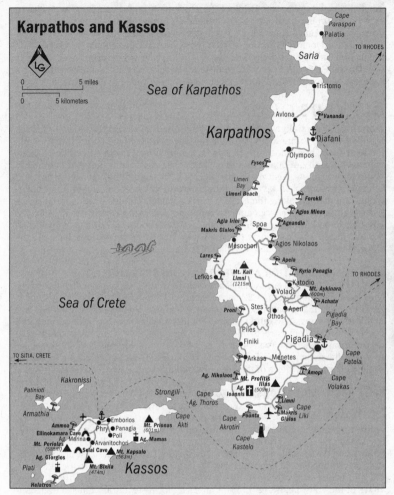

Karpathos and Kassos

makarounes (€6.50) to flavorful grilled squid. (☎22 501. Open daily noon-late.) At the rooftop **Anemoussa ❸**, halfway up the staircase next to Liquid, you can satisfy your craving for Italian, Chinese, or the local fruits of the sea. Sauces are as delicate as the classical music that floats in the air. (☎22 164. Entrees €5-10. Drinks €2.50-4. Open daily 6pm-midnight.) Next door to Orea Karpathos, **Mouragio Cafe ❶** offers patrons the option to enjoy a view of the port over sandwiches (€2-5) and drinks (€2.50-3.50) in a relaxed open-air setting. (Open daily noon-late.)

🎆 **NIGHTLIFE.** In contrast to the club scenes on islands like Kos and Ios, Karpathos offers a mild take on the nightlife scene. Bars and lounges fill up around 11pm where revelers mingle until the clubs open at 1am. Revelers begin their nights at **Anoi,** one block east of Liquid and up a flight of stairs. The stuccoed mosaic walls and cushioned staircase outside provide a chill atmosphere for the conversation-minded traveler. (☎23 960. Drinks €2-6. Open daily 6pm-1am.) Stop by **Galileo** to experience its bar incarnation before heading farther down the same street and downstairs to **Liquid,** a mod lounge that gets going around 10pm. (☎69763 15 529. Drinks €4-6. Open 7:30pm-1am.) Two doors down at **Enigma Club,** the DJ plays all night. Don't miss the Happy hour from 9pm-12:30am where drinks are €4. (☎22 632. Drinks €6-7. Open daily 10:30pm-4am.) Revelry continues at **Oxygen Club** and **Amnesia,** where throngs of young locals and tourists dance to house and hip hop.

OLYMPOS Ολυμπος ☎22450

Isolation defines Olympos's legacy. The inhabitants of two nearby villages founded the city after an earthquake destroyed their homes; they intentionally chose an inaccessible location, high in the mountains, to avoid pirate raids. Today, Olympos is a city of centuries-old customs that continue to fascinate ethnographers and linguists. Visitors weave their way through tightly packed white and blue houses and sit in tavernas among women in traditional embroidered garments and men speaking the archaic Dorian dialect. Though outside interest has led Olympians to preserve and, in some cases, rekindle craft traditions, the younger generation has drifted from its roots to schools and jobs on neighboring islands. Those who stay enjoy the windswept beauty of the terraced hills and the staggering coastlines topped by crumbling windmills.

⌨❼ TRANSPORTATION AND PRACTICAL INFORMATION. From **Diafani,** take a **taxi** or the small **bus,** which leaves shortly after the boat from Pigadia arrives (bus fare is included in the €22 boat ticket). A 2½ hr. **hike** along the valley floor is an alternative if you have the time, energy, and drinking water—it's a long, hot, uphill trip. In town, navigation is fairly simple: a main pathway snakes uphill and connects to small side streets filled with houses. The church and the **post office** are on the corner when the road ends. Many of the town's tavernas and shops can be found on the main road, and meandering through the narrow streets on the crown of the hill promises views of the lines of windmills on the west side of the town.

▮❑ ACCOMMODATIONS AND FOOD. While many visitors make only a day-trip of Olympos, those who stay overnight are rewarded by the peaceful atmosphere and late-night tavernas. Olympos also boasts rooms where luminous, colorful embroidery lines the windows, tables, and the intricately carved, split-level *soufa* beds; it is customary for children to sleep on the raised half of the loft, while dried goods and blankets are stored below. Some of the best accommodations in Olympos are at **Hotel Aphrodite ❸,** located down the stairs to the left of the church, where four rooms, outfitted with bath and balcony, offer breathtaking views of the coast below. (☎51 454. Call ahead for reservations. Singles €30; doubles €40; triples €45.) **Pension Olympos ❷,** on the right about 150m up the pathway, rents rooms with beautiful hand-carved *soufa,* bath, and peaceful balcony with mountain views. (☎51 009. Singles €20; doubles €30-35.)

To find ▨**Milos Tavern ❶,** follow the path past Hotel Aphrodite and down the hill; it's on the left. The building serves both as a functional windmill and as a restaurant complete with brick oven. Try the savory pies (€2) while taking in the full views down both the sea and valley sides of the hill. (☎51 333. Entrees €5-7. Open daily 7am-10pm.) Find the proprietor Nikos Filipakis, originally from Baltimore, at his nearby restaurant, the **Parthenon Cafe ❶,** where the homemade lentil soup (€3.50) and the *makarounes* with goat cheese (€5) are definite winners. (☎51 307. Open 7:30am-late.) The family-run **restaurant ❷** attached to Pension Olympos serves goat with tomato sauce (€8) among other traditional entrees (€4-8), which you can enjoy over beer. (Open 7:30am-late.) Tiny **Sinandes ❶,** across from Parthenon Cafe, offers honey-drenched, fried *loukoumades* (€5), a deliciously sticky dessert. Locals play cards at one of the four tables, though if you're lucky they'll pull out their *zambuna* (bagpipe-like traditional instruments) and serenade you.

◙ **SIGHTS.** Olympos's traditional culture and crafts are the region's main draw; tourists marvel at the local women's black-and-white hand-embroidered garb, and shops selling handmade scarves line the street. Also noteworthy are the locally grown spices, honey, and olive oil. Several working **windmills** overlook the western cliffs where Olympian women grind the flour that they bake into bread in huge, stone ovens. If you brave the tiny ladder inside one of the windmills, you can watch the whirling from behind the scenes. Just past Parthenon Cafe is the lavishly decorated 8th-century church **Kimisi tis Theotokou.** Gold foil blankets its wooden altar and restored 16th-century frescoes of scenes from the life of the Virgin Mary adorn the walls. (Open every morning and evening for services, and occasionally when daytime tours pass through. Ask Papa Yannis for a tour.) From the church, follow the stairs down and to the right and ask a local or tour group leader to point you in the direction of **Papa Yannis's house.** Inside, visitors can see an authentic Olympian *soufa* at its finest, with an overwhelming display of colorful embroidery and ceramic plates covering every inch of wall and chat with Yannis and his wife Irina over juice. (Free.) Check out the footpaths leading both north and south of the town passing through pine forests. **Hikes** range from 5-16km across areas known for their falcon and eagle populations. Ask at the post office or Cafe Parthenon for maps and directions.

SOUTHERN KARPATHOS

West of Pigadia, winding roads climb toward enchanting villages and cloud-covered mountains and snake down to the relaxed west coast. Karpathos is home to a number of blissful beaches, many of which can be found off the Pigadia Airport road. ▨**Amopi,** voted one of the best in the Mediterranean, lives up to its reputation with golden sands that slide into crystal-green waves. Amopi is connected to other beach coves by a trail that skirts the cliff edge. At least three walking routes run from Pigadia to Amopi; each takes about 1½hr. Head away from the ferry docks to the outskirts of Pigadia and take a left at the **7-11 Snack Bar ❶** (☎22450 22 885). A hike along the dusty but beautiful riverbed takes you to the main road. Take a right and walk on the paved road the rest of the way to Amopi or stick to the dirt road to find one of the less crowded but equally beautiful beaches. Those with their own ride may want to visit the deep green-blue waves across from Mira Isle and the long coves between Cape Kastelo and Cape Akrotiri. For those sunning at the water's edge, **Taverna Avra ❶** (☎22450 81 172) offers sandwiches (€4) and mixed drinks (€2-6) such as the "Between the Sheets." Overlooking the small cove behind rows of spunky palm trees **Amopi Cafe Restaurant ❷** (☎22450 81 138) serves a variety of Greek appetizers (€2-5) and special gyros (€5.75) with live music Friday nights from 8:30-midnight. On the other side of the beach at the top of the hill, the funky-shaped ▨**Skala** (☎69796 80 146) mixes a variety of drinks (€4-6) over tablecloths made of collared-shirts. The balcony view and fanciful architecture are unbeatable, as are the open-hearted staff members. A taxi to Amopi costs €8.

The southern city of **Aperi** was the island's capital in medieval times until Arab raids and menacing pirates forced Karpathians to abandon their homes and retreat inland. Now Aperi is home to an icon of the Virgin Mary revered throughout Karpathos. According to legend, a monk discovered the icon while chopping wood and blood began spurting from one of the logs. Each time the icon was moved, it would disappear—only to reappear in an old church in Aperi. A bishop's church, **Koimisis Theotokou,** was built on the spot in 1886. (Open daily 8-11am.)

West of Aperi lies **Piles,** where winding paths retain an old-world charm and quixotic appeal. A walk through the rows of traditional Karpathian houses—picturesque white boxes with decorative railings on the balconies— leads to olive groves and charming tavernas that serve the town's famous honey. Two kilometers west of Piles, the road hits Karpathos's stunning west coast.

The wind-swept remains of five parallel Cyclopean walls mark the town of **Arkasa,** home also to the ruins of an ancient acropolis atop the nearby cape of Paleokastro. Rounding out the town's riches are the mosaic floors of a 5th-century basilica, preserved at the church of **Agia Sophia.** Although few hotels in Arkasa have single rooms and high prices are the norm, some pensions do exist. South of Arkasa, campers can crash in a cove near sandy **Agios Nikolaos.**

North of Arkasa, the tiny fishing port of **Finiki** now consists mostly of tourist establishments. Farther north, the small beach town of **Lefkos** offers a gorgeous stretch of coast to naturalists who shy away from crowded beaches in favor of a quiet, rocky cove. Inland there is forested hiking terrain.

All these mountain villages and coastal towns are accessible by bus from Pigadia. If you find yourself stranded, call a cab (☎22450 22 705) to pick you up; rides run from €8-35. Hairpin turns in the road create a number of stupefyingly beautiful photo ops that can't be captured from a bus window. Renting a car or motorbike in Pigadia will give you maximum beach-going, photo-snapping, engine-revving freedom, but keep in mind that the steep, winding roads lack guardrails.

KASSOS Κάσος

Few landscapes evoke Homeric times better than the bare, rocky sprawl of Kassos, the southernmost island in the Dodecanese. Its wintertime population of 1200 nearly triples in the late summer months. The island offers a disarmingly slow pace of life; locals volunteer introductions and chat in cafes and on the docks. A lack of major sights has allowed the island to keep its small-town feel, though the intrepid traveler will find plenty of monasteries, caves, and other hidden treasures.

PHRY Φρύ ☎22450

Phry's main attractions are the open arms, big hearts, and running mouths of its residents, who warm up quickly to travelers. Proud of their tiny island, locals of this small port town will volunteer advice on the best beaches and how to traverse the rocky, church-filled mountains.

◧ TRANSPORTATION. Flight and ferry times change with the tide; tourist offices on either Karpathos or Kassos can provide schedules and tickets. **Flights** go to Athens (daily, €85); Karpathos (7 per week, €25); Rhodes (9 per week, €38); Sitia, Crete (daily, €42). **Ferries** run to: Agios Nikolaos, Crete (4½hr., 3 per week, €16); Karpathos (1½hr., 3 per week, €5); Piraeus (17hr., 3 per week, €32); Rhodes (7hr., 3 per week, €22); Sitia, Crete (2½hr., 3 per week, €10). **Buses** make a loop from Phry through the surrounding villages (most locations less than €0.80). Check schedules at the tourist agency. **Taxis** are the most common way to get around. (☎69779 04 632. €3-5 between villages.) **Rent A Moto** rents mopeds (€15) and all-terrain vehicles (€40) and is located on the main street behind the tourist agency. (☎41 746. Open daily 9am-1pm and 3-8pm.) Cars also can be rented by inquiring at the tourist agency.

▉▊ ORIENTATION AND PRACTICAL INFORMATION. All of Kassos's tourist services are in Phry. Emmanuel Manousos at **Kassos Maritime and Tourist Agency,**

to the right of the port, by O Milos, provides maps, friendly advice, and timetables. (☎41 323; www.kassos-island.gr.) Ask around to find **Elias Galanakis,** an expat from Zimbabwe who writes the local newspaper. A valuable source of information about accommodations, restaurants, and beaches, Elias is a good ally. (☎41 145.) The **Cooperative Bank of Dodecanese,** just behind O Milos taverna, offers **currency exchange** and cash withdrawal. (☎42 730. Open M-F 9am-1:30pm.) A conspicuous blue **24hr. ATM** sits in Pl. Iroön Kasou, by the ferry docks. The **police station** is a block inland on a narrow street to the left of Anagennissis and just past the post office. (☎41 222. Open 24hr.) The small **hospital** on Kriti, past the bus stop, provides emergency first aid only; serious cases are flown to adjacent islands. (☎41 333. Open M-F 9am-1:30pm.) The **OTE** is a few blocks inland. (☎41 300. Open M-F 8:30am-2pm.) **Internet** access can be found at **ACS,** which, located behind the post office, also offers scanning (€1), photo printing (€1), and Wi-Fi. (☎42 751. €3 per hr. Open 10am-2pm and 5pm-midnight.) The **post office** is off Pl. Iroön Kasou. (Open M-F 7:30am-2pm.) **Postal Code:** 85800.

⌐ ACCOMMODATIONS. Except for mid-July through August when prices rise, Kassos's hotels offer a good deal, many amenities, and have plenty of vacancies. Heading off the ferry docks, the road leading up and toward the left offers a variety of airy accommodations with friendly managements. About 500m down and on the right, the palatial, condo-like rooms at ◪**Evita Village** ❸ have full kitchen, TV, air-conditioning, and canopy beds (☎69727 03 950. Singles €30; doubles €35.) Toward the beginning of the street and on the right, **Euili** ❷ offers pristine rooms with bath, fridge, TV, air-conditioning, and balcony overlooking the sea. (☎41 661. Singles €25; doubles €30.) Past Euili and on the left, beachside **Flisvos** ❸ has simple, whitewashed rooms overlooking the nearby beach cove. (☎41 284. Singles €30; doubles €35.) Closer to the town center, inquire at the tourist agency about **Anagennissis** ❸, located next door; 12 rooms have bath, air-conditioning, fridge, and some have balcony. (☎41 323; www.kassos-island.gr. Breakfast €7.50. Singles €30-45; doubles €40-60. Book online for a discount.) **Anesis** ❸, one street behind the tourist agency, has seven simple rooms with balcony and bath; check in at the supermarket below. (☎41 234. Singles €20; doubles €25.)

◪▣ FOOD AND NIGHTLIFE. Staples of Kassian cuisine include *dourmadakia* (stuffed cabbage), locally churned goat cheese, and *roikio* (flavorful dandelion leaves). Several restaurants are clustered near the church; if the owner of one is tired of cooking for the moment, he may just send you to his buddy next door. Fishermen, large Kassian families, and the occasional daytripping tourist gather at **O Milos** ❷, an open-air spot overlooking the sea next to the port, to smoke, argue politics, and chomp down cuttlefish (€6) and the day's fresh catch. (☎22450 41 825.) Only 10min. out of town, **Taverna Emborios** ❷, down the street leading to the left as you leave the port, offers a beachside vista as well as fish prepared any style (€6) or sold by the kilogram (€45).

Although the nightlife on Kassos isn't a bump-and-grind affair, Kassians do stay out late, chatting in cafes over coffee and drinks until the wee hours of the morning. **Kafe Matheos,** a diner nicknamed "the Plateia," is the undisputed gossip hub and social center of Phry, and it counts the mayor and visiting members of Parliament as patrons. (☎41 320. Drinks €1.50-4. Open 24hr.) A more lively atmosphere can be found at tiny night club **Perigiali** (☎41 767), across the street from O Milos.

◪▨ SIGHTS AND THE OUTDOORS. A 10min. boat trip away, on a neighboring island, waits glistening ◪**Armathia beach.** This calm, sheltered stretch of soft sand remains untarnished by tourism and pollution. Locals hail Armathia as the finest beach in Greece—a true oasis, with turquoise waters as clear as the Caribbean and

DODECANESE

as warm as the south of Crete. George Manousos begins running the small boat in mid-July. (☎41 047. €15 round-trip; set your own departure and pickup times.)

Leisurely excursions by foot or private transportation to the residential villages above Phry give insight into the island's agriculturally centered life. Head uphill from Phry and make a left at the gas station to get to the tiny village of **Panagia.** Notable for the showy homes left behind by Kassian sea captains of yore and the **Virgin Mary of Giorgi** church, Panagia celebrates a yearly festival on August 15th commemorating the Virgin with food and dance. For another interesting outing, try searching for the elusive cave of **Selai,** about 1.5km west, down the footpath beyond the cave **Ellinokamara.** To get to Ellinokamara, follow the road past the airport through the village of Agia Marina. Stay to your right whenever the road forks, until you reach a dirt road. After a 15min. walk you'll see a small wooden gate on your left leading up the mountain; hike up between the stone walls until you see the entrance to the cave appear over the wall on your right. A taxi ride there (€3.50) will drop you off at the marina; follow the footpath up to the monastery.

The interior of the unpeopled monastery of **Agios Giorgios** at Hadies is filled with impressive, gold-painted icons and commands magnificent views of the gorgeous **Helatros beach** below. The older families of Phry still have cells at the monastery, which they inhabit for the festival of St. George.

From **Poli,** a 4km, 40min. hike along an uphill asphalt road to **Agios Mamas Monastery** brings you to scenic views of the southeastern coast from atop a dangerously sharp cliff face. The boulders visible from the monastery are reputed to be the hulls of three ships, turned to stone by vengeful monks.

SYMI Σύμη

Pastel houses bloom like wildflowers on the cliffs overlooking Symi's main port, which has welcomed the incoming boats of sailors, fishermen, and sponge divers for thousands of years. Each of the colonial homes has unique artistic flourishes and individual charms. In the 18th century, the island saw its golden years when the *belles artes* thrived under the protection of the ruling Ottoman Empire. While today many travelers only stop here en route from Rhodes to Kos, the island still beckons families and older travelers looking to escape the decadence of the other islands. Panormitis Monastery, on the southern side of the island, remains one of the holiest places in Greek Orthodoxy and an important point of pilgrimage.

SYMI TOWN   ☎22460

Symi Town, the heart of the island's activity and where all public boats arrive, is divided into two sections: Yialos, the harbor area; and Horio, the residential village on the hillside up a flight of 383 steps. Ferries disembark in the main Yialos harbor, though past the clock tower another smaller cove houses the shipyard. Another small village, Pedhi, sits in the valley below Horio, south of Yialos. The town was constructed in the Middle Ages as a fortification against pirate raids; trekking your way up to Horio under the hot Symian sun may give you an appreciation for this defense tactic. Luckily, there is an hourly bus.

▚ TRANSPORTATION

Ferries: Ferry tickets can be purchased at any of the travel agencies or at the ANES office by the waterfront. 3-4 per week to **Kos** (€10) and **Rhodes** (€7). 2 per week to **Astypalea** (€26), **Nisyros** (€10), and **Tilos** (€7). Schedules vary with the season; check with the travel agencies for the most updated times.

Hydrofoils: Hydrofoil to **Rhodes** (1hr., 2-3 per day, €14). The **Catamaran Dodekanisos Express** departs W and Su 9:30am to: **Kalymnos** (€28); **Kos** (€20); **Leros** (twice daily, €36); **Patmos.**

Excursion Boats: The boats **Poseidon** and **Triton** (☎20 215) offer day-long round-trip tours (€35; lunch included) around the island, stopping at Panormitis Monastery and a number of coves and beaches. Find them at the docks by the footbridge, on the same side as the pharmacy.

Buses: The green **Symi Bus** stops at Pl. Ikonomou 2 blocks to the left when facing the pharmacy. Every 30min.-1hr. 8:10am-11:10pm to **Horio** (5min., €0.70) and **Pedhi** (10min., €0.70).

Taxis: Next to the bus stop on the eastern waterfront. The island's taxis must be reached by mobile phone; check the local newspaper for new taxi numbers. (☎69452 52 308, 69746 23 492, 69465 68 731, 69441 05 596, or 69452 73 842).

Rentals: Glaros, to the left of the police station. (☎71 926. Cars €35 and up; motorbikes €10. Open daily 8:30am-10pm.)

⊞ ☷ ORIENTATION AND PRACTICAL INFORMATION

The steps leading up to Horio connect to Yialos in two places: behind the pharmacy and next to Kalodoukas Holidays. To reach Pedhi, a 30-40min. walk from Yialos, climb up to Horio and take the main road going down the other side.

Budget Travel: Kalodoukas Holidays (☎71 077), behind Vapori Bar, to the right of the steps to Horio, sells hydrofoil tickets, exchanges currency, and arranges mountain walks. Open daily 9am-1pm and 5-9pm. V. **Symi Tours** (☎71 689), 1 block inland as the waterfront road curves, sells tickets for the Dodekanisos Express. Open M-Sa 9am-1pm and 5-8pm; Su 9am-1pm. Two doors down, **ANES** (☎71 444) sells ferry tickets. Open M-Sa 9am-2pm and 6-9pm; also open 1hr. before boat departures.

Banks: National Bank (☎72 249), on the waterfront directly across from the footbridge, has a **24hr. ATM** and offers currency exchange. Farther up toward the clock tower, **Alpha Bank** (☎71 085) additionally cashes travelers checks with a €2 per check fee. Both open M-Th 8am-2:30pm, F 8am-2pm.

Police: ☎71 111. On the 2nd fl. of the white building near the clocktower. Open 24hr.

Medical Services: ☎71 290. To the back left of the church in Yialos, opposite Hotel Kokona. Open M-F 8:30am-2pm; call 24hr. for emergencies. The doctor in Horio can be reached at ☎71 316. Serious medical concerns often taken to Rhodes.

Telephones: OTE (☎71 212), inland on the back left side of the town square in Yialos.

Pharmacy: ☎69747 29 450, on the waterside one block from the bus stop. Open M-Sa 9am-1:30pm and 5:30-9pm.

Internet Access: Directly across from the footbridge on the clock-side of the harbor, **Evoi Euav** (☎72 525) offers free Wi-Fi. €4 per hr. Open daily 8am-late. Up the hill in Horoi, **Glaros Cafe** (☎69757 86 010) offers computers and high-speed connections. €3 per hr. Open daily 8am-6pm. **Roloi** (☎71 597), on the street around the corner from Vapori Bar, has computers and doubles as a recording studio. €2 per hr. Open daily 9am-3am.

Post Office: ☎71 315. In the same building as the police, up the flight of stairs on the left. Open M-F 7:30am-2pm. Also offers Western Union services. **Postal Code:** 85600.

⌐ ACCOMMODATIONS

Accommodations get pricier as you head up the hill and the view improves, though there are some economical pensions in Yialos one street in from the waterfront. ▨**Pension Egli ❷**, behind the pharmacy and up a flight of stairs, has spacious, bright rooms complete with stylish furniture. Affordable for one, and a steal for more, the rooms are conveniently located right along the stairs to Horio, and only 100m from the Yialos town center. (☎71 392. Singles €25.) Past the post office on the stairs to the left of the police station **Hotel Anastasia** ❸ offers well-ventilated, clean rooms with balcony, bath, and a great view. (☎71 364. Singles €35.) **Hotel Kokona ❸**, to the left of the church tower, has breezy rooms with bath and private balcony. (☎71 549. Singles €35; doubles €45.) Located directly in front of the church, the bright, airy rooms at **Hotel Albatross ❸** have bath and flowing curtains overlooking the sea. (☎71 707. Doubles €39.) Up the hill in Horio right before the restaurant Milos, **Hotel Fiona** offers spacious doubles with green furniture, bath, balcony, and a breathtaking view. (☎72 088. Breakfast included. Doubles €50.)

🏠🍴 FOOD AND NIGHTLIFE

Like many island waterfronts, Symi's is lined with indistinguishable restaurants catering to tourists. More authentic options at reasonable prices are clustered at the far end of the waterfront past the shipyard, and up in Horio's heights. Symian cuisine is renowned throughout the Dodecanese for its seafood, particularly its delightful small shrimp. At the end of the road, inland from Symi Tours, the owner at **Meraklis Taverna ❷** will likely greet you with a glass of ouzo. Family-run for over 25 years, Meraklis serves mouthwatering Greek specialties (€5-10) and fish (€8-14) cooked to perfection. (☎71 003. Open daily 11am-midnight.) One of the oldest and most respected tavernas in Horio, **Georgios's Taverna ❸**, at the top of the stairs, serves traditional Greek dishes. (☎71 984. Prawns €9. Entrees €6-9. Open daily 9am-4pm and 7pm-midnight.) To find **Milos Restaurant ❸**, take a left on the street just before Georgios's; it's one block in on the left. The 18th-century converted windmill offers a variety of *mezedes* (€6.50-9) on an outdoor terrace. (☎71 871. Entrees €7-12. Open daily 7:30-11pm.) At dockside **Tholos ❷**, at the far end of the small harbor to the right of the dock, try the famed small Symi shrimp (€10) or the stuffed vegetables (€6) while enjoying the seabreeze. (☎72 033. Open daily noon-3:30pm and 7-11:30pm.)

Symian nightlife keeps it low-key as locals and tourists relax with drinks at one of the several cafe-bars in town. **Jean and Tonic Pub,** in Horio, up the hill from Georgios's on your right, draws an older crowd to the artfully converted 500-year-old building. Cheery owner Jean mingles and drinks with customers under the pomegranate tree. (☎71 819. Happy hour 9-10pm. Open daily 9pm-6am.) Cosmopolitan **Vapori Bar** stacks recent foreign-language newspapers on its blue wicker chairs where a young crowd gathers to drink the specialty mojitos (€9) and dance in the street. (☎72 082. Mixed drinks €8-9. Open daily 8am-late. Happy hour 6:30-8:30pm.) Across the street, **Harani Bar** serves up exotic drinks such as the apricot and banana "Yellow Bird" on a relaxed, outdoor terrace. (☎71 422. Mixed drinks €7. Happy hour 6:30-8:30pm. Open daily 4pm-late.) Those looking for a quiet spot for conversation and a selection of over 90 mixed drinks (€5-8) can bask in the red interior of **Evoi Euav.** (☎72 525. Happy hour 5:30-6:30pm. Open daily 8am-late.)

🏖️☀️ BEACHES AND SIGHTS

A number of excellent coves and beaches are accessible by water taxi; look for signs by the small boats in the Yialos harbor. Irini Konstantinos runs excursion boats to all the major beaches; boats leave at 10 and 11am and pick up from the beach at 4, 5, and 6pm. (☎69448 01 003.) **Agia Marina** is a small, charming island within swimming distance of the shore (€8 by water taxi). **Agios Georgios,** reached only by excursion or taxi-boat, has deep, glassy waters set against a stunning 300m vertical cliff (€9.50). **Agios Nikolaos,** a 30min. walk or €8 round-trip boat ride from Yialos, is a beautiful half-sand, half-pebble beach. In the southeast, explore **Nanou's** expansive bay (€9.50) or the narrow, pebbly strip of **Marathounda** (€11). Tiny **Nos** is a 10min. walk along the waterfront from Yialos, past the shipyard.

Signs lead through the maze of streets to a handful of ruins. Little remains within the walls of the dismantled 15th-century **Castle of the Knights of Saint John,** which was used for ammunition storage during WWII, aside from the **Church of the Virgin of the Castle.** If that isn't enough to fill your old ruins quota, follow the signs to **Pontikokastro,** a semi-excavated prehistoric mound near the windmills.

The **Naval Museum,** in a yellow building past the footbridge, provides a look at model ships and boating tools from Greece's history. (Open daily 11am-2:30pm and 7-9pm. €1.50 includes museum booklet.) At the top of the road to Horio, signs point toward the quaint **Archaeological and Folkloric Museum,** which displays unearthed sculptures, ancient relics, and everyday objects owned by 19th- and early 20th-century Symiots. (☎71 114. Open Tu-Su 8am-2:30pm. €2, students free.)

▓ DAYTRIP FROM SYMI

PANORMITIS MONASTERY

Daily bus service runs between Symi Town and Panormitis. (30min., 8:30am departure, 11:30am and 1:30pm return. €2.50.) Weekly tour boats running from Yialos include Panormitis on day-long trips around the island; daily tour boats from Rhodes stop here as well for at least 1hr. on the way to Symi Town. A taxi costs over €20; consider roughing the rigorous 32km hike by foot, though ask around about a 20km shortcut through the mountains. Daily services open to the public, 7am and 7pm. Open daily 7am-2pm and 4-7pm. Modest dress required. ☎72 414. Entry ticket for both museums €1.50, students and under 12 free.

Panormitis Monastery, on the southern part of the island, is the second most important monastery in the Dodecanese, after the Monastery of St. John in Patmos. Dedicated to the Archangel Michael, protectorate of sailors and travelers, Panormitis attracts nearly 4,000 sailors to the islands for the saint's feast day on November 8. Throughout the year, visitors come to the monastery to pay homage, and couples, hoping for childbearing luck, come offering votives. Though the monastery's founding date remains a mystery even to the monks, its most recent renovation was in the 1700s. The wooden altar screen, carved from a walnut tree over the course of a hundred years, adorns one side of the church. The museums contain ecclesiastical relics, folk exhibits, and a pair of carved ivory tusks over 5ft. tall. The monastery allows visitors to spend the night in one of the simple rooms in their annexes. Free in the winter when there are plenty of vacancies, a room with five beds costs €32 per day in the summer and should be booked in advance.

TILOS Τήλος

With its untouched streets and peaceful beaches, Tilos slips under the radar of most pleasure-seekers. The 300 permanent residents and 3000 goats that call this island home have managed to fend off the stock-and-trade tourism of larger islands, leaving the serene, natural beauty that was praised by poet Irinna in 350 BC. Most who come find themselves returning to the peaceful paths, sights, and cafes that make Tilos a near-perfect stop for those in search of relaxation. Follow a goat path to a secluded red-sand beach and spend the day next to the breathtaking cliff shores, and you may see why.

GIVING BACK

LET FLY, TILOS!

Above the sage bushes and bleating goats, over 10% of the world's population of Eleonora's Falcons make their nests on Tilos Island. The falcon is one of over 150 bird species that can be found on Tilos's mountainous coasts, drawing bird-watchers and hikers to the island.

An increase in visitor traffic prompted the formation of the Tilos Park Association (TPA), which monitors seal, turtle, falcon, and orchid populations on Tilos and its 16 uninhabited islets. Founded in 2004 by Konstantinos Mentzelopoulos, the Livadia-based TPA has mounted an aggressive campaign to ensure the protection of Tilos's natural treasures.

With the support of over one third of the island's residents, the TPA organizes regular seminars on conservation and operates an information booth in Livadia.

Volunteers can help with clean-up efforts on the beaches and paths, species monitoring, building a new nature appreciation trail, or island surveillance for illegal activities. The TPA also welcomes volunteers in their clean-up campaigns or to complete ecology field work for academic credit.

Contact Konstantinos Mentzelopoulos. ☎22460 70 880; www.tilospark.org.

LIVADIA Λιβάδια ☎22460

Tilos's small port village nestles between mountains and sea; its handful of unnamed streets stretches along the length of a smooth-pebbled beach and winds up into the surrounding hills. Though crowded in August, Livadia slumbers for most of the year, with many of its shops and restaurants closed during the winter. Visitors in early summer or September and October will enjoy a quiet, friendly welcome and glorious solitude amid the warm waves.

▣ TRANSPORTATION

Travelers will find frequent access to Tilos by catamaran from Rhodes Town, and ferries run between Tilos and its neighbors a few times a week. Schedules change with the season, so be sure to check with a travel agency.

Ferries: To: **Astypalea** (7hr., 3 per week, €11); **Kalymnos** (4½hr., 3 per week, €11); **Kos** (3hr., 3 per week, €8); **Nisyros** (2hr., 3 per week, €7); **Piraeus** (16hr., 1 per week, €44); **Rhodes** (2½hr., 3 per week, €12); **Symi** (2hr., 2 per week, €7). Confirm times at Stefanakis Travel Service.

Hydrofoils: High-speed **catamaran** tickets can be purchased at the **Sea Star** office on the waterfront 1 block from the church. (☎44 000. Open M-F 8:30am-2:30pm, Sa-Su 10am-2pm.) To: **Symi** (1hr., every W) and **Rhodes** (1½hr., 6 per week, €19).

Excursion Boats: From mid-Apr. to Oct. **Stelios** (☎69391 06 527) runs an excursion cruise Tu-Th to the island's many beaches for a cookout and swimming (€20-30 includes lunch; min. 10 people). He also runs a charter trip every Su; trips leave between 10 and 10:30am and return between 4 and 5pm. Look for his waterfront "office," under the tree just past the church, to sign up.

Buses: The **bus stop** is in the center of the town square, in front of a cafe and supermarket. Buses run 3 times per day (5 times in high season) to **Agios Antonio, Eristos beach,** and **Megalo Horio** (9:45am-2:45pm, €0.60-1). An **excursion bus** runs to the **Monastery of Saint Pandeleimon.** (Every Su 11am, stays for 1hr.; €4 round-trip.) The schedule changes with the season. Check return times with the driver.

Taxis: The island's 2 individual taxis can be reached 24hr.; call **Nikos Logothetis Taxi** (☎69449 81 727) or **Taxi Maik** (☎44 066).

Rentals: At the port, **Tilos Travel** rents **cars** (€35-50 per day) and **motorbikes** (€15-20 per day) with insurance. **Bicycles** (€5-8 per day) are also available. Across from Michali's Taverna, find **Drive Rent A Car** (☎44 173), which rents motorbikes (€15 per day) and cars (€30-35 per day) with insurance. Open M-Sa 10am-10pm.

⚡ 🔢 ORIENTATION AND PRACTICAL INFORMATION

The main road begins at the port, curves through town, and heads back to the waterfront; the far end is lined with tavernas and small beachfront hotels. Continuing up the mountain, you'll pass **Mikro Horio** on the way to **Megalo Horio.**

Budget Travel: ☒**Tilos Travel** (☎44 294; www.tilostravel.co.uk), at the ferry dock, sells walking maps (€4), exchanges currency, rents rooms and vehicles, offers a free book exchange, and keeps scrapbooks about Tilos. Open daily 9am-2pm and 6-8pm. At the corner, **Stefanakis Travel Service** (☎44 310) sells ferry tickets, provides accommodations advice, and rents cars (€35 per day). Open daily 8am-1pm and 5:30-10pm.

Bank: The **Cooperative Bank of the Dodecanese** (☎70 704; www.bankdodecanese.gr), located just past the mini-mart, handles **currency exchange** and operates a **24hr ATM.** Open Apr.-Oct. M-F 9am-2pm; Nov.-Mar. M-F 10am-2pm.

Police: ☎44 222. The white-and-blue building opposite Stefanakis. Open 24hr.

Medical Services: ☎69448 87 869. Behind the church. Doubles as the **pharmacy.** Open M-F 11am-1pm; emergency phone answered 24hr.

Internet Access: Balthazar (☎44 388) above the mini-Market offers Wi-Fi and computers with high-speed Internet access. €2 per hr. Open daily 10am-late.

Post Office: ☎44 350. In the square. Open M-F 9am-1:30pm. **Postal Code:** 85002.

🏠 ACCOMMODATIONS

With such infrequent ferry service to Tilos, pension and hotel owners expect to rent rooms for several days at a time—often with better rates for longer stays. Rates spike during the high season, though basic rooms at low prices can be found farther up the mountain road. Luxury hotels on the water's edge give way to more basic apartments farther inland.

☒ **Milios** (☎44 204), up in Megalo Horio. Nestled in an Eden-like garden, has spacious rooms with bath, balcony, unbelievable view, and in some rooms, attached kitchen. Charismatic owner Niko offers the low-down on getting around Tilos. Doubles €20-45, depending on kitchen facility. ❷

Sevas Studios (☎44 237), a 5min. walk up the hill past the bus stop. Ask for Antonis at the supermarket on the corner before making the trek. Take in the ocean view from the spacious, bright rooms where comfortable doubles have TV, bath, and fridge. Singles €20; doubles €30. ❷

Georgia's Rooms to Let (☎44 261). Take a right after the church—the rooms are just past the intersection on the right. Comfortable doubles have bath, and balcony overlooking a perfectly manicured garden. Doubles €30. ❸

Blue Sky Apartments (☎44 294, or ask at Tilos Travel). Attached to Tilos Travel, Blue Sky features sunny two-level rooms with fantastic harbor views. Fully-furnished rooms feel like apartments and feature chic decor, private kitchen, bath, balcony, and a lofted bedroom. Singles €30-55; doubles €35-60. ❸

🍴 FOOD

A number of tavernas line the waterfront from the police station on, offering similar Tilian grilled fare.

☒ **Grill House and Creperie** (☎44 148), closer to the square, just up the hill from the police station. The favored local hangout formerly known as Nick Time Pita Time offers a taste for every palate and pocketbook, from pot roasted goat stew (€8.50) to volcanic, calzone-like covered pitas (€4.50) and gyros (€1.80) the size of rolled newspapers. Free delivery 5pm-midnight to Livadia, Megalo Horio, and Eristos beach. ❶

Michali's Taverna (☎44 359), up the street to the right of the church. Mihali whips up traditional dishes served on an outdoor patio frequented by cats. Entrees €5-8. Open daily 1-3pm and 7-11pm. ❷

Sophia's (☎44 340), just past the church and on the water. A mother-and-son establishment that dishes up a delightfully bubbly clay pot of moussaka (€5.70) and daily vegetarian favorites. Entrees €4-7. Open daily 8am-3pm and 5:30pm-late. ❷

Pavlos (☎44 011), on the beach. Find your souvlaki and french fry fix here where the gyro pita (€2.50) can fill any sunbather—just remember to wait 30min. before hopping back in the water. Open daily 10am-midnight. ❶

🔘 SIGHTS

The 15th-century village of **Mikro Horio** sits 3km up the road from Livadia. Abandoned in 1960 as residents gave up the farming life and opened businesses on the waterfront, the town has only two functional buildings: the summer dance bar and the Agia Zoni chapel. Four kilometers farther, in **Megalo Horio**, lie the remains of the **fortress** built by the ever-present Knights of St. John. Neolithic tools and midget elephant fossils dating from roughly 5000 to 2300 BC were unearthed in the **Cave of Harkadio** in 1971. Paleontology buffs and circus fans curious to see the findings can check out the recovered bones, which have been laid to rest in the nearby **museum**. (Open daily 9am-1pm. Free.) Pick up the hiking path at the top of the staircase behind Restaurant Castro to reach the pebbled beach of **Agios Andonis**. The idyllic seaside village dotted with closet-sized chapels lies along the road to **Plaka beach** farther west. Continuing to the south will take you to the 15th-century **Monastery of Agios Pandeleimon** atop a rock, towering over cyprus trees and trickling streams. Inside the pebbled yard stands a 200-year-old cyprus tree and a mosaiced icon of Jonas, the 15-century founder of the monastery.

Perhaps the best way to experience Tilos is to explore its wild sage patches and goat-filled grottoes on foot. Walking maps can be found at Tilos Travel or at the supermarket, along with advice on how to find beaches accessible only from hiking routes. Several routes, varying in difficulty, steepness, and the rockiness of terrain, all take about 1hr. from Livadia. More routes can be found by taking the bus to their starting points. Trekkers of all levels can hire **licensed guides** Iain and Lyn from **Tilos Trails.** (☎44 128. About €20.)

🔘 NIGHTLIFE

Livadia residents keep it quiet at home, exporting the party over the mountain to the abandoned **Mikro Horio.** From late June to the end of September, the capital city gets converted into a town-wide disco, with lights strung in crumbling houses and dancing in the streets and on the rooftops. Take one of the free shuttles from the town square to get your groove on in this spooky, Greek-pop filled landscape. (☎69320 86 094. Open daily 11pm-late.) For those with conversation in mind, climb the stairs next to the mini market to get to **Balthazar,** where a mixed crowd gathers to drink, talk, and play cards. Enjoy a mixed drink (€4.50-5) overlooking the water on the outdoor terrace, or try the specialty ice cream desserts, decorated with everything from sprinkles to sparklers. (☎44 388. Internet €2 per hr. Open daily 10am-late.) **Cafe Ino,** on the waterfront, offers young locals a choice from their 114-listing mixed drink menu (€6) on a yellow-toned, outdoor terrace. (☎44 002. Open daily 7pm-late.) Farther down the beachfront, **Micro Kafe** offers special house wine served with plates of *mezedes* in a converted stone-house bar. (☎69320 86 094. 1L of wine with 10 *mezedes* €16. Open daily 11am-late.)

NISYROS Νίσυρος

Visitors are drawn to this obsidian and pumice island to walk among the sulfur crystals and steam of the five separate craters that make up Nisyros's active volcano. Daytripping tourists move in cycles from the dock to the volcano to the waterfront tavernas, leaving the rest of the island a peaceful place to unwind. Quiet villages are made up of winding streets and the whitewashed, cubic architecture typical of the Dodecanese. Relics dating back to the Classical and Byzantine Eras are sprinkled throughout the island, interspersed with the unusual sand and stone beaches tinted black with volcanic rock.

MANDRAKI Μανδράκι ☎22420

Mandraki's leisurely rhythm of life seems immune to the bubbling sulphur pit only 5km away and the volcano-minded tourists who arrive en masse on daytrips from Kos. Beyond the harbor, winding stone streets give way to the hill-top monastery, the nearby black-stone beach, and gorgeous views of neighboring islands.

▐ TRANSPORTATION

Ferries: Several ferry lines connect Nisyros to neighboring islands on a regular basis. Tickets can be bought at one of the agencies or last minute on the docks. **Kentris Travel** (☎31 227), located on the main road past the town hall, sells tickets and has schedules. Open daily 9am-1pm and 5-9pm. **Blue Star Ferries** has service to: **Astypalea** (4hr., €9.50); **Kalymnos** (3hr., €7); **Kos** (1½hr., 3 per week, €7.50); **Piraeus** (14hr., every Su, €44); **Rhodes** (4hr., 1 per week, €12); **Tilos** (1½hr., 1 per week, €6.50). **ANES** serves: **Symi** (2 per week, €9.82) and **Kos** (2 per week).

High-speed boats: Hydrofoil tickets are available at **Diakomihalis Travel** (☎31 459); follow the main road 250m to the right, past the bank. M-F and Sa to **Kos Town** (1½hr., €10). F and Su to: **Halki** (2½hr., €12); **Rhodes** (5hr., €12); **Tilos** (1hr., €8). Service to Halki, Rhodes, and Tilos is only on F in the winter. Check with Diakomihalis for an updated schedule.

Excursion Boats: Enetikon Travel sends daily commercial boats at 7am and 3:30pm to **Kardamena, Kos** (1hr., €7) and **Kos Town** (2hr., €12.50). Diakomihalis Travel also has boats at 3:30pm that go to **Kardamena** (1hr., €7.50) and **Kos Town** (daily, €12).

Buses: A municipal bus makes rounds through the villages, leaving from the Mandraki harbor 6 times per day. To: **Emporios** (20min.); **Loutra** (4min.); **Nikea** (25min.); **Pali** (10min.); **White beach** (10min.). Daily excursion buses also head to the volcano when the boats from Kos arrive, usually 10am-noon. €7 round-trip, includes volcano entry. Purchase tickets at the Enetikon dockside stand or in their office.

Taxis: Both of the island's taxis must be reached by cell phone. Both **Babis's** (☎31 460 or ☎69456 39 723) and **Irini** (☎69799 69 810) are based in Mandraki. To White beach (€5) and the volcano (€25 round-trip, with a 25min. stop at the crater).

Rentals: Yannis (☎31 750), across from the bank, rents **motorbikes** from €10 per day. Rentals are also available at **Manos K.** (☎31 029) on the dockside. Cars €25-40, motorbikes €10, insurance included. Open 9am-12:30pm and 4-7:30pm. **Diakomihalis Travel** charges €25-35 per day, minimal insurance included. Must be 21+ with at least 1 year driving experience.

DODECANESE

ORIENTATION AND PRACTICAL INFORMATION

The main road in Mandraki starts at the ferry docks and follows the waterfront (to the right as you face inland) until it forks at the bank. To the right, the road continues along the waterfront, at the end leading down a striped path to a small stony beach. To the left, the road takes you inland to **Plateia Ilikiomeni** (Old Woman Square), a cobbled plateia nearly overwhelmed by the ficus tree in its center and filled with cafes and tavernas. Cross through the square and take a left to find the stairs leading up to the cliff-side monastery.

Budget Travel: Enetikon Travel (☎31 180), on the right side of the road leading into town from the docks, helps with tickets, hotel reservations, book exchange, and bus and boat tours. Friendly, multilingual staff, also offers walking maps of the island. Open daily 9:30am-1:30pm and 6:30-9pm. Head past the bank to **Diakomihalis** (☎31 015) to buy ferry, plane, bus, and excursion boat tickets or rent a car, exchange money, or receive helpful information. Open daily 9am-1pm and 6-9pm. MC/V.

Banks: The **Cooperative Bank of the Dodecanese** (☎48 900), the only bank on the island, is on the waterfront road; turn right from the dock. **Currency exchange** available M-F 9am-2pm. A **24hr. ATM** is located right off the ferry docks.

Emergency: ☎31 217 for an ambulance. The surgeon is located right before Pl. Ilikiomeni. Major medical emergencies are taken to nearby Kos for treatment.

Internet Access: Proveza (☎31 618), far down the waterfront next to Kleanthis. Offers several computers with high-speed access and Wi-Fi. €2.50 per hr. Open daily 10am-3pm and 5pm-midnight.

Police: ☎31 201. In a white building near the dock. Phone answered 24hr.

Post Office: ☎31 249. Down the left fork past the bank; offers Western Union services. Open M-F 7:30am-3pm. **Postal Code:** 85303.

ACCOMMODATIONS AND FOOD

Rooms almost always are available, except during the August 15 Festival of the Panagia, when reservations should be made. The ⬛**Three Brothers Hotel ❸**, to the left as you leave the ferry dock, is one of Mandraki's best. Spacious, whitewashed rooms lit by paper lantern come with bath, fridge, and balcony. The breezy lounge overlooking the harbor is a great place to meet other guests or to hang out with the charismatic brothers themselves. Studios with full kitchens, air-conditioning, and TV also available. (☎31 344. Singles €23-30; doubles €40; studios €35-60.) **Hotel Porfyris ❷**, down the left fork from the bank, offers sterile, spacious rooms with bath, balcony, and pool facilities. (☎31 376. Singles €25; doubles €40.) **Volcano Studios ❷**, on the main road along the waterfront above the Volcano Cafe, rents simple rooms with fridge and bath; some have a balcony overlooking the water. (☎31 340. Singles and doubles €20.) At **Hotel Romantzo,** behind the Three Brothers, dimly lit rooms with bath and fridge open onto the upstairs terrace, with amazing views. (☎/fax 31 340; www.nisyros-romantzo.gr. High season doubles €45, with breakfast €55; triples €55/70. Low season doubles €25/35.)

Restaurants with similar menus and prices line the waterfront, and smaller cafes cluster in the plateia. Mandraki's best seafood may be at **Restaurant Kleanthis ❷**, far down along the waterfront, which prepares appetizing *mezedes*, shellfish entrees, and a variety of Nisyrian dishes. The *pithia* (chickpea fritters; €3) are a local specialty. (☎31 484. Fried octopus €5.50. Open daily noon-5pm and 8pm-late.) At **Restaurant Irini ❶**, in the plateia, a hot spot for local gossip, pass through the kitchen and take a peek at that night's grilled special or try the specialty lamb (€6) or vegetable starters (€3.50). Irini's newly opened cafe next door offers desserts. The traditional Greek favorites range €4-6, and include a variety of vegetarian dishes. (☎31 365. Open daily 9am-late.) One block in from the waterfront before the bank, **Cafe Nisyros** (☎31 460) serves heaping portions of tasty chicken souvlaki (€7). Patrons at **Cafe Fikos ❶,** next door, can lounge under the ficus while enjoying a cold *soumada* (€2), a sweet Nisyrian almond drink. (Open daily 11am-3pm and 6pm-late.)

🎇 DAYTRIPS FROM MANDRAKI

🎇 MANDRAKI VOLCANO. Test your balance on the rock edge or plunge into the blinding white, sulphorous depths of Mandraki's enormous **Stefanos Crater.** Steam hisses from the chalk-white earth, and yellow sulfur crystals grow on the rims of numerous, bubbling pits. Tread lightly in the crater, as the soft, clay-like earth may sink or open up. No special safety precautions are needed, though a bottle of water and a pair of sturdy shoes will help—the ground is boiling hot and the trail into the crater is steep and sandy. The volcano has been inactive since its 1872 eruption, though geologists have determined that it is responsible for a number of earthquakes. A 10min. walk along the trail behind the snack bar leads to nearby **Polyvotis and Alexandros craters,** virtually unvisited but no less spectacular. Shoes with some traction are advisable for those wanting to venture into the craters, as the paths are sandy and steep. Bringing a bottle of water is also a good idea, as the crater provides no shade and the snack bar is a long way back up the trail. Two different routes lead from the volcano back to Mandraki; ask for a walking map at Enetikon Travel. Both walks afford impressive views of the mountains and sea; neither is difficult, and each takes about 2½hr. to complete. *(Entrance €1.50. Municipal bus from Mandraki drops off in the nearby town Emborios, from which the crater is a 4km hike. Excursion buses to the crater itself leave regularly from the harbor; €7 includes admission.)*

MONASTERY OF OUR LADY SPILLANI. Beyond the plateia and between two houses, a twisted stone staircase leads up the cliff past tiny cells carved into the rock face, once used to house anti-Turkish artillery. The quaint, whitewashed 17th-century church at the top grants sweeping views of the sea below. Among the many silver-framed idols and hanging incense-burners lies a portrait of St. Nikolaos, recently discovered by an altar boy on the rear face of an icon that had been covered with an old cloth for over two centuries. The **church** at the bottom of the staircase will house a collection of precious votives until the church museum reopens. *(Monastery open daily 9am-3pm. Donations welcome. Modest dress required.)*

BEACHES. The black pebble beach of **Hohlaki** is a short walk from the end of the waterfront road along a beautifully striped coastal footpath. **White,** on the road to Pali just past Loutra, is also almost entirely black despite its name. Dust from nearby pumice quarries once gave the pebbly beach a pale top layer, but now that the quarries are inactive, the beach's natural dark color has returned. Sandy, picturesque **Lies,** 3km east of Pali, is the island's optimal tanning spot, just over the hill and within walking distance from the locally favored **Pachy Amos.** If there is sufficient demand, Enetikon Travel runs boats (€8 round-trip) to the beaches of **Yali,** a small island nearby with pumice stone quarries.

KOS Κως

Antiquity best knew Kos as the sacred land of Asclepius, god of healing, and the birthplace of Hippocrates, father of ancient medicine. The endless stretches of beach and booming nightlife have made the tourist industry explode in cities such as Kos Town and Kardamena, where strings of bars line the streets. However, travelers wary of parties or looking for a day off can relax amid the beautiful cliffs and fields dotted by blue-roofed chapels and ruins.

KOS TOWN   ☎ 22420

Radiating from the jumbled ruins at the heart of the city, Kos Town's beaches and pubs remain the city's main attractions. A young crowd arrives each summer to explore the beaches and unkempt ruins by day before hitting up the bustling bar scene by night. Visitors can experience Kos Town's cocktail of liquor, lights, and lovin' at the seemingly endless row of bars and clubs that line the beachside streets in the north part of the city. While tourist kitsch has permeated the city, the fortress and nearby Asclepion maintain their original beauty and merit a visit.

⌐ TRANSPORTATION

Flights: Olympic Airways, Vas. Pavlou 22 (☎ 51 567, reservations 28 331), has flights to **Athens** (from €104). Open M-F 8am-2:30pm. Flights can be booked faster and more conveniently at many of the travel agencies.

Ferries: Schedules differ among companies and with the season; check schedules and prices at a travel agency. A Blue Star office (☎ 28 914) sits on the waterfront between Ioannidi and Vas. Pavlou. To: **Astypalea** (4hr., 1 per week, €15); **Kalymnos** (1hr., 3 per week, €6); **Katapota** (7hr., 2 per week, €22.50); **Leros** (3hr., 1-2 per day, €12); **Nisyros** (1½hr., 1 per week, €7.50); **Patmos** (4hr., 1-2 per day, €15); **Piraeus** (11-15hr., daily, €44); **Rhodes** (4hr., daily, €14); **Symi** (3hr., every W, €18); **Syros** (5hr., 3 per week, €33). Boats also run to **Bodrum, Turkey** every morning (20min.; round-trip €20, including port tax).

Flying Dolphins to: **Kalymnos** (45min., daily, €11); **Leros** (30min., daily, €16); **Lipsi** (2hr., daily, €16); **Patmos** (2½hr., daily, €22.40); **Pythagorio, Samos** (5hr., daily, €25).**Dodecanisos Express** to: **Kalymnos** (40min., daily, €11.50); **Leros** (1¾hr., daily, €16.40); **Lipsi** (2hr., daily, €16.40); **Patmos** (2½hr., daily, €22.40); **Rhodes** (2hr., daily, €27.50); **Symi** (1½hr., daily, €20).

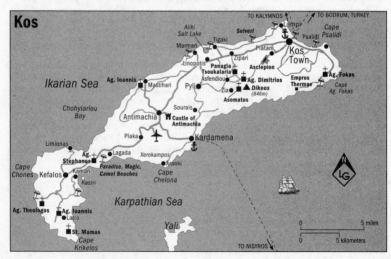

Intercity Buses: ☎ 22 292. Leave from the intersection of Kleopatras and Pissandrou. Buses run M-Sa with reduced service Su to: **Antimachia** (40min., 4 per day 9:10am-9pm, €2); **Asfendiou-Zia** (40min., 3 per day 7am-1pm, €1.60); **Kardamena** (45min., 6 per day 9:10am-9pm, €2.60); **Kefalos-Paradise** (1hr., 6 per day 9:10am-9pm, €3.60); **Marmari** (35min., 12 per day 9am-11pm, €1.60); **Mastihari** (45min., 7 per day 9:10am-9pm, €2.40); **Pyli** (30min., 4 per day 7am-3pm, €1.60); **Tigaki** (30min., 12 per day 9am-11pm, €1.60). Schedules change monthly and are posted by the bus stop and at the EOT; buy tickets on board, or get a 20% discount by purchasing beforehand at the bus kiosk.

Local Buses: A. Koundourioti 7 (☎ 26 276), on the water. Fares run €0.70-1.20. To: **Agios Fokas** (#1 and 5, 20min., every 20min. 6:45am-10:30pm); **Ika-Abavris-Ag. Nektarios** (#6, 11 per day, 7:50am-9:15pm); **Lampi** (#2, 10min., every 40min. 6:30am-11pm); **Messaria** (#4, 10min., 15 per day 8am-10pm); **Paradisi-Kako Prinari** (#7, 9:45am-9:45pm); **Platani** (#4, 5min., 15 per day 8am-10:45pm); **Thermae** (#5, 20min., 9 per day 9:45am-5:45pm).

Trains: Blue mini-trains go from the EOT to **Asclepion** (15min., Tu-Su on the hr. 10am-5pm, €4 round-trip). **Citywide tours** on a green mini-train leave every 30min. 10am-5pm from the waterfront train stop (€4).

Taxis: Radio Taxi (☎ 22 777) has a kiosk and 24hr. cabs near the inland end of the Avenue of Palms, just after A. Koundourioti splits. To the airport €25. 24hr. min. €5.

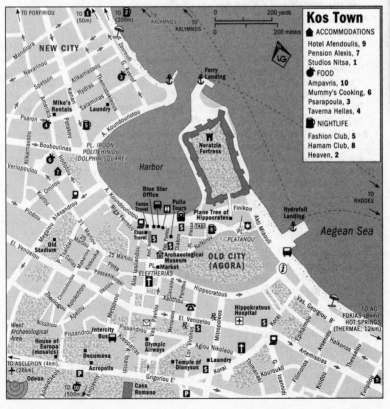

Kos Town

Rentals: Mike's (☎21 729), 20 Amerikis. Mopeds €9-15 per day. Bikes €2-4 per day. Open M-Sa 9am-2pm and 5:30-8pm, Su 10am-1pm and 6-8pm.

◼◼ ◼ ORIENTATION AND PRACTICAL INFORMATION

The coastal road (**Zouroudi** in the northwest; **Akti Koundourioti** curving around the harbor; and both **Akti Miaouli** and **Vasileos Georgiou B'** to the southeast, past the castle) are lined with standard theme bars and souvenir stands. On **Vasileos Pavlou**, just off A. Koundourioti, is a practical group of travel agencies, banks, and 24hr. ATMs. The town centers on **Plateia Eleftherias**, just a bit farther inland, where you'll find the **Archaeological Museum**, a large market, and some nondescript cafes. A plethora of pubs pack together on the cobblestoned streets branching off **Nafklirou (Bar Street)** in the **Old City**, where the rollicking night kicks off in Kos Town. Nafklirou borders the ancient **agora**, and culminates at the gigantic **Plane Tree of Hippocrates** and the well-preserved **Castle of the Knights of Saint John.** Heading south on Vas. Pavlou takes you to **Grigoriou E'** with the **odeon, Altar of Dionysus,** and **House of Europa.** The club scene winds up in Pl. Plessa, circles Pl. Iroön Politechniou, and continues along the beachside bars of **Zouroudi.**

Tourist Office: ◼EOT, Vas. Georgiou B' 1 (☎24 460; www.hippocrates.gr). Free maps, bus and ferry schedules, hotel review booklets, and information on upcoming events and opportunities on the island. Open M-F 7:30am-3pm.

Budget Travel: Many travel services line the waterfront and side streets, though some do not cover all the ferry lines. **Fanos Travel,** 11 Akti Kountouriotou (☎20 035), on the waterfront, 1 block west of the city bus stop. Sells ferry and air tickets and offers car rental (€30 and up), motorbike rental, **currency exchange,** excursion booking, and **Internet.** Open 8am-10pm. **Exas Travel Service,** 4 Ioannidi (☎29 900; www.exas.gr). The staff provides schedules for all lines and books tickets for **GA Ferries, Catamaran Dodecanisos Express,** and other air and sea lines. Open daily 9am-10pm. MC/V. **Pulia Tours,** Vas. Pavlou 3 (☎/fax 26 388), also offers ferry schedules and can book tickets and arrange excursions to Turkey. Open daily 7am-11pm.

Banks: Banks line A. Koundouriotou between And. Ioannidi and Pl. Plessa, many offering **24hr. ATMs. Alpha Bank,** Koundourioti 5 (☎27 487), between Vas. Pavlou and Al. Diakou. Offers American Express and **currency exchange.** Open M-Th 8am-2:30pm, F 8am-2pm. After banking hours, you can exchange currency at virtually any travel agency along the waterfront.

Laundry: Easy Laundry (☎29 172), on Themistokleous. Wash and dry €6. Discounts for those working in Kos Town. Open daily 9am-8pm. Happy Wash Laundry Service (☎23 424), on Mitropoleos. Wash and dry €6. Will iron for an additional fee. Open M-F 9am-9pm, Sa 9am-6pm.

Emergency: ☎22 100. For an **ambulance** call the hospital at ☎22 300.

Police: A. Miaouli 2 (☎22 100 or 22 222). In the big, white building next to the castle. Some English spoken. Open 24hr. **Tourist police:** ☎22 444. Upstairs in the same building. Open daily 7am-2pm.

Pharmacy: On almost every major street. One is at the corner by the hospital at El. Venizelou 2 (☎26 426). Open M, W, F 8am-1:30pm and 5-9pm.

Medical Services: Hippocratous 34 (☎22 300). Some English spoken. Open 24hr.

Telephones: OTE (☎23 499), at Lor. Vironos and Xanthou. Open M-F 7:30am-3pm.

Internet Access: Expect to pay at least €2 per hr. **Del Mare Internet Cafe,** Meg. Alexandrou 4A (☎24 244; www.cybercafe.gr). Fast connections in a food-friendly environment. €1 per 30min. Open daily 9am-1am. **E-Global Internet Cafe** (☎27 911), on the corner of Artemissias and Korai. €2 per hr. Open 24hr. **De Haven Cafe** (☎26 898), on the waterfront. €3 per hr. Open daily 10am-midnight.

Post Office: ☎22 250. On Vas. Pavlou. From El. Venizelou, walk 1 block inland. Open M-F 7:30am-2pm. Western Union available. **Postal Code:** 85300.

ACCOMMODATIONS

Most budget options are on the right side of town when facing inland along G. Averof. Kos's dock hawks are notoriously aggressive and in most cases should be avoided; if you do choose to haggle, ask for a business card, and insist on seeing the room before you hand over any dough. Those interested in **camping** should inquire at the EOT for information on open campsites.

▧ **Pension Alexis,** 9 Irodotou (☎28 798). From the port, head inland on Meg. Alexandrou and take the 1st right onto Irodotou. Kind Sonia and her son Yannis offer transportation advice, maps, and insiders' tips on Kos. Spacious, breezy doubles share a recently remodeled bathroom with massage-like water pressure. Some rooms have bath and all offer access to the wraparound balcony, views of the fort, and a fan. If all rooms are full, Sonia will help arrange other accommodations or finagle a price break at her brother Alexis's elegant Hotel Afendoulis. Breakfast €5. Laundry €5. A/C €3. Singles €25; doubles €30-33; triples €39-45; quads €48-50. ❷

Hotel Afendoulis, Evripilou 1 (☎25 321). From Vas. Georgiou B', take a right on Evripilou. Owner Alexis's mantra is "everybody must be happy," and it is rare that guests leave his hotel any other way. Alexis will pick you up from the port and join you for breakfast and a tour of the island. Doubles have A/C, bath, TV, fridge, and balcony. Internet from a sunny, indoor terrace is a bonus. Breakfast €5. Laundry €5. Singles €25-35; doubles €30-45; triples €40-55; quads €54-65; basement €25-30. ❷

Studios Nitsa, Averof 47 (☎25 810). Take Averof inland from A. Koundourioti. Large studios each come loaded with fridge, kitchenette, bath, TV, A/C and balcony overlooking the street. Only 50m from the beach and close to the nightlife, this is a good choice for those planning to paint the town. Singles from €20; doubles €25-40. ❷

FOOD

The major fruit and vegetable **market** in Pl. Eleftherias, across from the Archaeological Museum, caters to tourists and is more expensive than it looks; the many **mini-marts** sell fruit at cheaper prices. Fast-food stalls and cafes line the roads one block in from the waterfront.

▧ **Taverna Hellas,** Psaron 7 (☎30 322), down the street from Pension Alexis at Amerikis. Owner Dimitris teams up with Mike from Mike's Rentals to serve up heaping portions of steaming plates. Vegetarian options available. Entrees €4.50-8. Open daily 10am-3pm and 5pm-midnight. ❷

Mummy's Cooking (☎28 525), 1 block down Bouboulinas from the Dolphin Roundabout. A pleasant mix of locals and tourists stream in to enjoy the homemade food that comes piled ridiculously high. Mummy's hospitable son Ilias will happily decode Greek menu items and provide suggestions. Entrees €5-8. Open M-Sa 7am-midnight. ❷

Ampavris (☎25 696), a 6min. walk up Ampavris. Homemade Greek dishes are authentic and cheap. The menu itself takes an educational spin, featuring pictures and bios of the complete pantheon. Entrees €4.50-7. Open daily 6pm-midnight. ❷

Psarapoula, G. Averof 17 (☎21 909), inland from the far end of the port. Run by matronly Poula and her family, this local favorite has a wide range of seafood and Greek specialties. Seafood entrees €7-14. Open daily 1pm-late. ❸

DODECANESE

SIGHTS

The magnificent ■**Neratzia Fortress,** built by the Knights of St. John in the 14th century, greets ships as they glide into the harbor. It is only accessible via a bridge from the Plane Tree of Hippocrates; the bridge once stretched across an outer moat filled with seawater and could draw back to cut the castle off entirely from the mainland. A second construction phase in the late 15th century added the distinctive stout towers and elaborate double walls. Unlike the ruins to the city's south, the fortress remains incredibly well-preserved and is one of the best examples of medieval architecture in all of Greece. Make like the knights and patrol the tops of the exterior walls for unbeatable views from the former lookouts and weaponry holes. (☎27 927. Open Tu-Su 8am-7:30pm; last entrance at 7pm. €3, students €2, EU students and under 19 free.)

Fall head over heals for the world's largest collection of headless marble statues at the **Archaeological Museum** in Pl. Eleftherias. An imposing 4th-century depiction of Hippocrates graces the northwestern room, and a Roman mosaic depicting Asclepius's arrival on Kos can be found in the central courtyard. (☎28 326. Open Tu-Su 8am-7:30pm. €3, students €2, EU students and budding archaeologists free.)

Off Pl. Platanou, the **Plane Tree of Hippocrates,** allegedly planted by the great physician 2400 years ago, has grown to an enormous 12m in diameter. While it is alluring to envision Hippocrates teaching and writing beneath its noble foliage, the tree is actually only 500 years old. The west archaeological area's **House of Europa** contains well preserved floor mosaics, one depicting Europa's abduction by Zeus in the sneaky guise of a bull. Across the street, wander along the semi-circle of seats at the 3rd-century **odeon** (Roman theater). One block east on the same side of the street, the **Casa Romana** villa is undergoing restorations. Among Kos's **Roman ruins** stands a desolate pair of Corinthian columns and the scattered remains of what was once a lively **agora** in the 4th century BC. In the heart of the Old City, the uninspiring field of broken masonry is little more than a jumble of stones amid unruly weeds. Other poorly tended ruins include the **Temple of Dionysus** on Grigoriou E'.

ENTERTAINMENT AND NIGHTLIFE

On Vas. Georgiou, Orfeas (☎25 713) is an open-air cinema showing films during the high season. Ask at the EOT or call the cinema for the schedule. Young crowds are drawn to the exuberant nightlife in Kos Town, which satisfies every taste from the luxurious lounges to the disco-pumping nightclubs and standard pubs. By 11pm, the masses converge around **Nafklirou** in the Old City and between Averof and Zouroudi in the New City. Clubs and bars produce an endless supply of live entertainment, themed nights, and half-liter sized drinks to keep up the fun; expect to pay €3-6 for a beer and €6-8 for mixed drinks. Sly greeters standing outside the bars wait to lure revellers in.

Fashion Club, Kanari 2 (☎22 592), by Pl. Iroön Politechniou. This red and chrome cavern hosts Kos's wildest nights, attracting trendy locals and tourists looking for a posh scene. The outdoor green-lit bar sits under the building-sized projection of the Fashion Network, and funky wax-drip candelabras inside create an intimate atmosphere. 3 bars, 2 dance floors, and a 1700-person capacity make Fashion Club Kos's biggest and most ostentatious nightclub. Happy hour until midnight. Mixed drinks €5. Indoor club cover nightly €10-15; includes 1 drink. Open nightly 11pm-4am; cafe opens 7pm.

Heaven (☎23 874). Follow Zouroudi north past the end of the string of bars, it is on the left. Guest DJs let loose in the sleek club room, and patrons also dance to the Greek pop next door. Luxurious, canopy-covered sofas with an ocean view provide an excellent spot to sip a drink. Beers €4-5. Mixed drinks €7. Open M-Th and Su 10am-4am, F-Sa 10am-dawn. Clubs open at midnight.

Heart Rock (☎69442 11 395; www.heartrock.gr), on Nafklirou. Blasting rock tunes keep up with the dancing bodies all night. Mixed drinks €6. Open daily 8pm-5am.

Hamam Club, Nafklirou 1 (☎24 938), inland from the Pl. Diagoras taxi station in the Old City. A crowd lounges outside listening to the nightly covers of popular tunes until the club opens at midnight, when Greek and American hits echo in the former Turkish bath. Happy hour 9pm-midnight.

🔳 DAYTRIPS FROM KOS TOWN

🔳 THE ASCLEPION

About 4km southwest of Kos Town. Take a 15min. ride on the blue mini-train to get there in summer. By bike or moped follow the sign west off the main road and go straight. ☎28 763. Open Tu-Su in winter 8am-2:30pm; in summer 8am-7:30pm. €4, students €2.

Nestled majestically in a cyprus forest on the mountainside, the Asclepion was an ancient sanctuary devoted to Asclepius, god of healing. In the 5th century BC, **Hippocrates** founded the world's first medical school and hospital here and forever changed the course of science. Combining early priests' techniques with his own, Hippocrates made Kos ancient Greece's leading medical center. Present-day doctors still travel here to take the Hippocratic oath and to pay homage.

Most of the ruins date from the 2nd and 3rd centuries BC. The complex was built on three levels, called *andirons*, which were carved into a hill overlooking Kos Town, the Aegean, and the coast of Turkey. Trees dot each level, providing much-needed shade and creating pleasant areas to gaze at the view. The lowest *andiron* holds a complex of 3rd-century Roman baths, complete with a *natatio* (swimming pool), *tepidarium* (lukewarm pool), and *caldarium* (sauna). It once was home to the medical school and the anatomy and pathology museums. Elegant 2nd-century columns remain standing on the second level, which once contained temples to Asclepius and Apollo. The 60-step climb to the third *andiron* leads to the remnants of the main **Temple of Asclepius** and a paramount view of the site, the town below, and Asia Minor across the sea. Although the temple is remarkably preserved, much of its structure is gone, recycled by the Knights of St. John in building Kos Castle. The spectacular view and what remains of the once-grand layout, however, still are very impressive. Reenactments of the Hippocratic oath are performed once a week in the summer; ask at the EOT for the schedule.

OTHER DAYTRIPS

NORTHERN KOS. Piping hot water streams into the semi-circle of rocks at **Empros Thermae,** where Greeks once soaked away dermatological ailments. Bathers today lounge in the beachside springs while waves splash over the rock barrier, providing titillating currents of hot and cold. Crowds usually thin by evening, allowing for a more peaceful soak. *(Southeast of Kos Town, along the coastal road; catch one of the regular buses at the town center (€1). When the bus drops you off, descend the steep cliff path to get to the beach. From there it is a short walk to the springs. Open 24hr. Free.)*

Along the western coast, a small road suitable for biking extends parallel to the main road, giving ample opportunity to take a bike tour of the gorgeous island's less-visited areas. Sandy **Lampi beach** lies just a few kilometers northwest of Kos Town. About 8km from town, the beautiful **Selveri beach** has clear sand, shallow waters, and a panoramic view of the Turkish coast.

CENTRAL KOS. The resort beaches of **Tigaki** and **Marmari,** both under 20km from Kos Town, are quite developed. Between the two, however, the vast **Aliki Lake** supports a variety of wildlife, from flamingoes that wade in the flats to loggerhead turtles in the surrounding brush. Until 10 years ago, the lake was used for salt production, when sea water channeled into the lake would be left to evaporate until salt collection took place in the summer. Head south and up the winding cliff paths to the freshwater springs of **Pyli,** which afford gorgeous views of the plain and sea below. Farther west, the small port area of **Mastihari** offers little more than a modest taverna and pension scene. **Antimachia,** on the main road farther south, houses a well-preserved traditional home and windmill. (€1.50 for both. Open daily 8:30am-6pm.) Locals flock here for the **Honey Festival** in the second half of August, when the village buzzes with Greek dancing and travelers collecting free honey. Around the bend of the airport, the road enters the carpeted pine forest of ▨ **Plaka Valley.** Here, flocks of full-feathered peacocks idly parade around, providing a truly stunning show. Some travelers choose to avoid **Kardamena** to the east, a slightly smaller version of Kos Town, with all of the tourist industry but less of the charm. *(From Kos Town, head southwest along the minor coastal road.)*

SOUTHERN KOS. Hills, ravines, and the occasional pasture roll across Southern Kos, surrounded by the island's most worthy and populated **beaches.** A few ancient columns mark **Kefalos,** Kos's ancient capital, whose colorless town can be bypassed for its surrounding beaches. Head northeast on the coastal road to get to **Camel, Paradise,** and **Magic** beaches, where you can sunbathe and windsurf against the breathtaking view of the southern peninsula. Farthest east, the beach of **Agios Stephanos** lies next to well-preserved ruins of a mosaiced basilica. Visitors can lie in the shade of olive trees among crumbling walls or swim to a nearby rocky islet, crowned with a small blue-and-white church. North of Kefalos, the small natural port of **Limionas** shelters a few boats and has a cliffside taverna. South from the ancient capital lies the deserted, pebbly beach of **Agios Theologos,** whose foamy green waves batter the shore. *(A moped allows unobstructed exploration. The bus (1hr., 6 per day 9:10am-9pm, €3.60) will let you off at any of the beaches.)*

ASTYPALEA Αστυπάλια

Nicknamed "Banquet of the Gods" by the ancient Greeks due to its high-quality fish, bountiful flowers, and overflowing honey, Astypalea draws summer crowds of city-weary Greeks ready for astounding mountaintop views and a taste of a quieter life. Surrounded by unpredictable seas, the butterfly-shaped island is an unusual stop for foreign travelers, though local tourism spikes in late July and August. Those who brave the ferry schedules and find their way here will discover pristine beaches, peaceful mountain hikes, outstanding ruins, and warm locals proud of their island's past and present.

ASTYPALEA TOWN ☎22430

Although development has begun to crawl into the neighboring villages of Livadi and Maltezana, Astypalea Town is still the heart of the island. The town is composed of two main areas: Pera Gialos, by the port, and Chora, the section atop the steep hill. White houses cluster in a cubist array around the main road that connects the two areas as it snakes steeply uphill. Daunting staircases line the small side streets, providing rather strenuous shortcuts from the winding main road.

 TRANSPORTATION. Flights leave from **Astypalea Airport,** 9km east of Chora, to Athens (45min., 5 per week, €58) and Rhodes (1½hr., 3 per week, €51) via Kos (1hr., €51) and Leros (20min., €47). All flights are on Olympic Airlines; contact

Astypalea Tours (☎61 571) for schedules and tickets. The island is serviced by two **ferry** ports, one in Pera Gialos and another in the north by Ag. Marina; ask which port when you buy your ticket. **Blue Star Ferries** sails to: Donousa (5hr., 3 per week, €16); Egiali (4 per week, €15); Kalymnos (2½hr., 1 per week, €11); Kos (4hr., 1 per week, €15); Naxos (6hr., 4 per week, €23); Nisyros (5hr., 1 per week, €10); Paros (8hr., 4 per week, €28); Piraeus (12hr., 5 per week, €33.50); Rhodes (9-11hr., 1 per week, €28.50); Tilos (6hr., 1 per week, €14). The **Blue Star Ferry office** under Hotel Paradisos on the waterfront sells tickets and has the most updated ferry schedules. (☎61 224. Open daily 9am-2pm and 6-9:30pm.) Another ship goes to Kalymnos (3 hr., 3 per week, €10.50), contact Astypalea Tours for tickets. No hydrofoils or Flying Dolphins serve the island. **Buses** run four times per day from 9:35am-6:35pm to: Analipsi (25min., €1.50); Chora (5min.); Livadi (30min., €1); and Maltezana (30min., €1). Buses leave from the station in Pera Gialos where the road turns inland at the start of the beach. Another bus stop is up in Chora where the road crosses the line of windmills. In high season, the frequency increases; check with the tourist office for schedules. The chalkboard near the bus stops lists specific times. The island's two **taxis** are reachable by cell phone. (☎69757 06 365 and 69720 84 135. Available 24hr.) Rent **cars** and **motorbikes** at **Vergouli Rent a Car,** right behind the museum on the main road. (☎61 351. Cars from €25 per day; insurance included. 23+. Motorbikes from €9 per day. Open daily 8am-2pm and 5-9pm.)

■ ☑ ORIENTATION AND PRACTICAL INFORMATION. As Astypalea's settled areas are relatively small, getting around its unnamed streets is surprisingly easy. The main road starts at the port and continues to the right through the center of **Pera Gialos,** then turns left to head uphill to **Chora.** Once in Chora's main plaza, follow the road uphill to the left to reach the **castle,** or take the road right to the giant **windmills** and toward **Livadi.**

A small **tourist office** is located in the fourth windmill from the castle. The friendly, English-speaking staff offers ferry and bus schedules, accommodations listings, and information about the island. (☎61 412; www.astypalaia.com. Open M-Sa 10am-2pm and 6-9pm.) **Astypalea Tours,** up the hill on the main road just past the museum, sells airline and ferry tickets and can help decode schedules. (☎61 571. Open daily 9am-2pm and 6:30-9pm.) **Emporiki Bank** is located next to the police station and offers **currency exchange** and a **24hr. ATM.** (☎61 402. Open M-Th 8am-2:30pm, F 8am-2pm.) You can find the **police** on the second floor of the white building with a Greek flag on the waterfront. (☎61 207. Open 24hr.) The **port police** are in the same building. The **hospital** is in the main plaza in Chora. (☎61 222. In an **emergency,** call ☎69720 35 050.) Midway up the main road between Pera Gialos and Chora is the **pharmacy.** (☎61 444. Open M and W 9am-1:30pm, Tu and Th-F 9am-1:30pm and 6-8:30pm, Sa 10am-12:30pm. The **post office** is on the main road just before the central plaza in Chora. Western Union available. (☎61 223. Open M-F 9:30am-2pm.) **Postal Code:** 85900

Ⅰ ☐ ACCOMMODATIONS AND FOOD. Options for accommodations abound in Astypalea; pensions cluster around the port, on the hill facing the castle, and in nearby towns. Finding a room in the low-season is easy, though come mid-July through August rooms and tavernas fill up quickly. Many pensions higher up the hill offer spectacular views with a price tag to match; stick to the port to find more budget options. On the side of the small beach in Pera Gialos, **Avra Studios ❸** has spacious rooms with kitchenette, bath, TV, air-conditioning, and a balcony overlooking the sea. (☎61 363. Rooms flat rate from €30-35.) When getting off at the port, follow the main road to find **Hotel Astynea ❷.** Rooms with soaring ceilings include bath, fridge, TV, air-conditioning, and balcony. (☎61 040. Singles €20; doubles €20-30. V.) **Camping Astypalea ❶** is 2.5km east of town. Take the bus toward

DODECANESE

ON THE MENU

DINING DODECANESE

For the culinarily inclined, island-hopping can afford more than beautiful vistas and blue seas. Despite being close neighbors, the Dodecanse islands, which snake up the eastern edge of the Aegean, each have their own flavorful versions of national favorites. Tavernas prepare variations on traditional Greek meals, spiced up with local ingredients. Here are a few specialties that should not be missed:

Tilos goat: Due to the lack of grass and leafy plants on the desert-like island, the goats maintain an unusual diet of underground shoots, making their meat especially tender and flavorful. Common entrees include stuffed goat baked in the oven and various goat meat stews.

Nisyros soumada: The volcanic island of Nisyros was once a major supplier of almonds. Though its trading days have slowed, today Nisyros is famous for its non-alcoholic almond drink, *soumada*. When made with honey, preserved baby tomatoes, and capers, the usually bitter drink can taste quite sweet.

Symi shrimp: Symi's locally caught shrimp usually are cooked in olive oil and traditional spices. The especially tiny shrimp have tender shells and are too small to dissect, so enjoy them whole. One particularly delicious dish is

Maltezana (15min., €1) or follow the signs from the port. (☎ 61 900. €6-7 per person, €2 per tent. No dogs.) Camping anywhere else is illegal.

Most restaurants are near the waterfront or in Chora's plateia. For a break from purely traditional fare, take the right-forking road with your back to the castle to find ◪**Aiolos ❶.** This pizzeria puts a Greek spin on the crispy-crusted Italian classic. Owner George whips up a mean Aegean topped with shrimp, mussels, and gouda (€4.40), and offers maps and advice about the island. (☎ 61 359. Pizzas €2.70-4.40. Open daily 6pm-1am. Free delivery.) **To Akrogiali ❷,** on the far end of the beach in Pera Gialos, serves fresh fish and standard Greek dishes. Take a seat at one of the tables on the beach to enjoy the gigantic shrimp with feta (€8) or the delightful pot of mousaka (€6.50) and the sea view. (☎ 61 863. Open daily 4pm-2am.) At **Meltemi ❶,** in Chora's central plateia, locals gather day and night for snacks (€2.50-5), coffee, and drinks. (☎ 61 479. Beer €2. Open daily 10am-late.)

◪◪ **SIGHTS AND BEACHES.** Overlooking the sea, the 15th-century ◪ **Castro of Chora** was built by the Knights of St. John to protect against pirate attacks. Nearly the entire population of Astypalea once lived within its walls, when the island survived by collaborating with pirate protectorates. The castro nearly was leveled in a 1953 earthquake, and restoration efforts began relatively recently. The breathtaking views from the castro's peepholes and rooftops (accessible by ladder) make the long hike up worth it. Two whitewashed churches, **Megali Panagia** on the road to the right and the **Portiaitissa,** lie within its walls. Another monastery, the **Panagia Flevariotsa,** is an hour east of Chora and can be reached by car or taxi. A striking row of defunct **windmills** lines the main road near Chora's central plateia. In Pera Gialos, the tiny **Archaeological Museum** on the main road to Chora houses artifacts unearthed around the island. (Open M-F noon-1pm. Free.)

The beach at **Livadi,** only a few minutes' walk down the hill from Chora, becomes quite crowded over the summer. A 20min. hike southwest along the coast takes you to **Tzanaki beach,** a beautiful, uncrowded stretch. Four kilometers farther along a dirt path, the pebbly beach at **Agios Konstantinos** is one of Astypalea's best. Tranquil, secluded beaches like **Kaminiakia** and **Vatses** are southwest past Tzanaki, but are difficult to find without private transportation and good directions. From there, the hidden cave of **Vatses** is accessible by boat. Northeast of Astypalea Town, the main road leads toward the other "wing" of the butterfly-shaped island, passing the campsite and several sandy beaches. Another cave, **Spilia Negrou,** is in the northwestern section of this part of the island. Both of Astypalea's famous caves are dark and potentially dangerous to those unfamiliar with their geography. Knowledgeable guides, however, are available; the tourist office can help put you in contact with one. Wear sturdy shoes and bring a flashlight. In the far northeast of the island, the monastery of **Agios Ioannis** overlooks a small waterfall—perhaps the most charming sight on the island.

Astypalea's locals recently have begun a concerted effort to facilitate exploration of the island's lesser developed areas. A **rock climbing** area recently opened near Livadi, featuring planned climbs geared toward every level of difficulty. The site is free, but climbers should plan on bringing their own gear; at press time an equipment rental system was in the works. If scaling a mountain seems a bit much, you can follow one of the newly marked **hiking trails** that start from the climbing area. Four different routes, between 1½-4hr. and of varying difficulty, wind down the mountain. Friendly, helpful **George Giannoulis** (☎61 359; giannoulisg@mycosmos.gr), one of the organizers of this endeavor, is the ultimate source for information about Astypalea's outdoor opportunities.

KALYMNOS Κάλυμνος

Once famous for the sponges deemed "Kalymnian gold" harvested from the depths of the sea, today, Kalymnos draws travelers to its natural caves and sprawling beaches. Only a short ferry ride from Kos Town, Kalymnos has remained free of kitsch but still can satisfy any traveler's need for adventure, nightlife, and relaxation. The interior's rugged mountains cascade into wide beaches and blue-green water, delighting both divers and rock climbers. Though more heavily visited than its western neighbor Astypalea, Kalymnos retains its small island charm with all the conveniences of a tourist destination. In summer, Kalymnos hosts festivals for rock climbing and diving and the finals tournament in Greek volleyball.

POTHIA Πόθια   ☎22430

Locals proudly will tell you that Kalymniots are the only "real" Greek islanders; they retain a vibrant culture, live there year-round, and are able to host travelers hospitably without losing their unique island character. A bustling port town, Pothia maintains the goods and services of a happening metropolis without spoiling its thriving local culture. Fast, fashionable youth nonchalantly speed by on motorbikes, but for the most part, life in Pothia is slow; except for in July and August, most local bars close by 1am.

shrimp and feta cheese *saganaki*, prepared in the traditional two-handled *saganaki* frying pan.

Kos honey: Beehives—termed "honey boxes"—dot the Kos countryside, providing the island's famous honey. The honey is later spiced with everything from orange to thyme and used in desserts such as *loukoumades* (honey puffs) and *halva*. The annual honey festival in Antimachia pays homage to the tradition and provides a sampling of all the varieties.

Kassos cabbage: The *dourmadaika* (stuffed cabbage) comes filled with potato and meat and is spiced with *roikio* (locally picked dandelion leaves). The cabbage also can be stuffed with minced meat and rice in a particularly delicious variation of the traditional Greek *dolmades*.

Retsina: Top your meal off with a bottle of *retsina*, the favored wine of the Dodecanese. Produced in Greece for nearly 3000 years, this white or rose wine is not made anywhere else in the world. After brewing, it is run over pine needles, leaving it with a strong taste of forest and smoke. The strong taste is too much to handle for many tourists; some choose to dilute the drink with soda. *Retsina* is less likely to offend your palate if you enjoy it at room temperature—served cold, the resinous taste is quite intense—with a traditional Dodecanese meal.

▐▀ TRANSPORTATION

Flights: Leave from Argos airport, 3km east of Pothia. To: Athens (30min., 8 per week, €69). Inquire at Magos Tours for tickets.

Ferries: To: **Agathonisi** (6hr., 4 per week, €9.50); **Alexandroupoli** (20hr., 1 per week, €38.50); **Arki** (5hr., 4 per week, €8.50); **Astypalea** (3hr., 4 per week, €10.50); **Chios** (7½hr., 1 per week, €20); **Kos Town** (1hr., 6 per week, €6); **Leros** (1½hr., 6 per week, €9); **Limnos** (16hr., 1 per week, €34.50); **Lipsi** (2¾hr., 4 per week 7am, €9); **Mytilini** (10hr., 1 per week, €29.50); **Patmos** (4hr., 6 per week, €10); **Piraeus** (9 hr., 4 per week, € 42); **Rhodes** (5hr., 8 per week, €18); **Samos** (4hr., 5 per week, €18).

High-speed boats: **Flying Dolphins** go to: **Kos** (30min., 7 per week, €12); **Leros** (40min., 7 per week, €15); **Lipsi** (1hr., 7 per week, €15); **Patmos** (1¾hr., 7 per week, €20); **Samos** (2hr., 7 per week, €25.50). The **Catamaran Dodecanisos Express** runs to: **Kos** (40min., Tu-Su 3:30pm, €10.20); **Leros** (1hr., 6 per week, €15.40); **Lipsi** (2hr., 4 per week, €15.10); **Patmos** (1½hr., 4 per week, €20.10); **Rhodes** (3hr., daily 3:30pm, €35); **Symi** (2½hr.; W, F, Su 3:30pm; €28.50).

Excursion Boats: Round-trip boats to the beaches on **Pserimos** (€3-6) and **Vlichadi** (€8) leave 9-10am from the harbor and return 5-6pm. Also go to **Bodrum, Turkey** (€30; bus tour in Bodrum included); **Leros** (€27); **Lipsi** (€27); **Patmos** (€36). Inquire at **Magos Tours** (☎ 28 777) for more information.

Buses: Leave from just past the town hall in the harbor center to: **Argos** (#4, 3 per day 7:25am-4:45pm, €1); **Elies** (#2; 15 per day 7:30am-10pm, €0.30); **Emporios** (50min.; 9am, 3pm; €2); **Hora** (#2; 15 per day 7:30am-10pm, €0.30); **Kantouni** (#2; 20min., 15 per day 7:30am-10pm, €1); **Limani** (#3; 12 per day 7:15am-7:30pm); **Massouri** (#1; 25min., 10 per day 6:50am-9:30pm, €1.50); **Platy Gialos** (#4; 4 per day 8:45am-7:10pm, €1.50); **Vlihadia** (#4; 8 per day 6:50am-8pm, €1.50); **Vathi** (#5; 30min., 4 per day 6:30am-5pm, €2).

Taxis: ☎ 50 300. In Pl. Kyprou. Available 24hr. €7.50 to the Airport.

Rentals: Similarly priced options line the waterfront and side streets. Rent **mopeds** at **Kostas Moto Rentals** (☎ 50 110), behind the port authority under the church. €10-12 per day; insurance included. Open daily 9am-1pm and 2-9pm. **Spiros Kipreos** (☎ 51 770), around Club Miami and upstairs. Rents **cars** (from €30) and **motorbikes** (€10 and up). 21+. MC/V.

✦ ▐ ORIENTATION AND PRACTICAL INFORMATION

Ferries arrive at the far left end of the port (facing inland). The road from the dock bends around the waterfront and past the square at the far end, where the large, cream-colored municipal building, church, and Nautical Museum stand. Passing the municipal building to the right, the road continues along the coast to **Vathi**. Turning left just past the municipal building leads inland up the shop-lined **Eleftherias** to **Plateia Kyprou**, where you'll find the taxi stand and pay phones. Continue on Eleftherias to reach **Horio, Myrties,** and **Massouri**.

Tourist Office: Tourist ▣**kiosk** (☎ 50 879; www.kalymnos-isl.gr), at the end of the ferry docks. The friendly, English-speaking staff provides free maps and boundless information on upcoming events, museums, and island-wide sites. Run by the **Municipal Tourist Organization** (☎ 59 056), they can also help arrange accommodations and bargain with hostels. Open daily 8:30am-8:30pm.

Budget Travel: Magos Tours (☎ 28 777), on the main road next to Ciao Cafe, before the road curves to the right; look for the Blue Star Ferries sign. Sells airplane, ferry, hydrofoil, catamaran, and excursion tickets for all the islands. Open daily 9am-4pm and 5-

10pm. **Kapellas Travel** (☎29 265), next to the pharmacy, also sells ferry and flight tickets. Open daily 9am-1:30pm and 5:30-9pm.

Banks: Several banks line Patriachou Maximou. **National Bank** (☎51 501) on the waterfront. Has a **24hr. ATM** and **currency exchange.** Open M-Th 8am-2:30pm, F 8am-2pm. **Emporiki Bank** (☎29 475), 1 block inland on the same street. Also has **currency exchange** and an **ATM.** Open M-Th 8am-2:30pm, F 8am-2pm.

Pharmacy: ☎28 468. Just behind Emporiki Bank. Offers homeopathic and allopathic cures. More pharmacies line Eleftherias. Open daily 8:30am-1:30pm and 5:30-9pm.

Police: ☎22 100. Go up Eleftherias and take the left fork at the taxi stand. In a blue and yellow building on the right. Open 24hr.

Hospital: ☎23 025. On the main road to Hora, 3km from Pothia. Open 24hr. Dial ☎50 499 for an **ambulance.**

Internet: Neon Internet C@fe (☎59 120) has 2 locations, though the waterfront one serves more as a late-night hangout. Head 2 blocks up from the bus stop on the street that runs parallel to the coastal road to get to the computer-filled alternative. Pool tables and €3 per hr. Internet make this a popular stop for teenagers. Open daily 9am-1am. **Heaven Internet** (☎50 444), closer to the ferry docks. Offers Wi-Fi and high-speed access. €3 per hr. Photo printing €2 per photo. Open daily 9am-1am.

Post Office: ☎28 340. Up Eleftherias, 200m past the police station on the right. Western Union available. Open M-F 7:30am-2pm. **Postal Code:** 85200.

ACCOMMODATIONS AND FOOD

Most of Pothia's accommodations are around the waterfront and offer similar prices; other pensions in neighboring towns and beaches offer more amenities at the same price. **Hotel Therme ❸,** above Cafe Kaiki on the waterfront, has spacious rooms with fridge, TV, bath, and balcony overlooking the harbor. (☎29 425. Singles and doubles €35.) **Pension Niki ❷** offers peach-colored rooms with TV, fridge, air-conditioning, bath, and a huge shared terrace. Niki's daughter Maria waits at the docks; if you don't see her, head inland at the National Bank and follow the road as it curves to the right. Follow the sign, which points down the side street. (☎48 135. Singles €20.) On the waterfront, **Greek House ❷** has simply decorated rooms that share a common kitchenette; all have fridge, air-conditioning, and bath. Though the treehouse-like stairs may be daunting, the view from the terrace at the top is worth the climb. If the Greek House is full, owner Papadi will help you find another room. (☎29 559. Singles €20; doubles €25.) **Camping,** though uncommon, is legal on all the island's beaches.

A number of tavernas and pizzerias line the waterfront, offering familiar Greek foods at similar prices. **Thraka ❷,** on the waterfront near Hotel Therme, prides itself on having souvlaki-shack prices with the quality and atmosphere of a good taverna. The huge meat platters come heaped with rice, salad, *tzatziki*, and fries. (☎28 888. Gyros €1.80. Entrees €5-10. Open daily 9am-3pm and 5:30pm-late.) The octopus balls (€4.50) hit the spot at **Orea Kalymnos ❷,** on the waterfront just past the town hall. (☎69488 30 028. Entrees €2.50-6. Open daily 1pm-midnight.)

SIGHTS AND BEACHES

The **Nautical Museum,** on the second floor of the gray building behind the municipal building, explains the life and work of the island's sponge divers. (☎51 361. Open M-F 7:30am-1pm. €1.50.) The **Museum of Kalymnos,** housed in the former mansion of sponge barons Catherine and Nikolaos Vouvalis, reconstructs their luxurious lifestyle in the three rooms open for display. Follow the signs heading up Eleftherias just before Pl. Kyprou. (☎23 113. Open Tu-Su 8:30am-2pm. Free.)

DODECANESE

The sandy **beach** to the left of the port police has clear water but a rather industrial backdrop. From the port police, take the road to the left to reach the beach at **Therma,** only 1km out of town, where a pleasant, crowded beach also hosts the **scuba diving center.** With over 12km of continuous approved diving area, Kalymnos has the largest site in Greece; in summer the boat Pegasus offers diving excursions off Therma beach. (☎69441 80 746; www.kalymnosdiving.com.) A short walk around the bend leads to a quiet swimming spot. **Vlihadia beach,** 5km from Pothia and west of Therma, is perhaps the best beach on the island, with crystal-clear waters and fewer patrons than neighboring locales. The **Sea World Museum** at the port in Vlihadia contains meticulously collected sponge diving memorabilia and various underwater finds. (☎50 662. Open daily 9am-8pm. €2.) Each year at the end of August, divers from around the world arrive for the **Annual International Kalymnos Diving Festival** (☎59 056) to try out new gear, visit the trade show, watch demonstrations of the old diving techniques used to harvest sponges, and enjoy nightly parties.

Grass, wildflowers, mandarins, limes, and grapes cover the **Vathis Valley** (5.5km northeast of Pothia), which begins at **Rina** village. There's no beach here, but you can swim from the pier. Within swimming range on the northern side of the inlet is **Daskalio,** a stalagmite cave that you can explore on foot.

🎵 🎭 ENTERTAINMENT AND NIGHTLIFE

In the words of one local cab driver, people in Pothia have a "program": they eat from 8 to 10pm, drink coffee at the harbor until midnight, and then head up to the clubs in Massouri until sunrise. Others finish the night in Pothia, chatting in one of the cafes or lounges on the waterfront. The harborside **Club Miami,** a young hangout, provides a place for conversation at the tables stretching nearly to the water's edge. Splurge on the Miami Special (€5), a mysterious and intoxicating concoction. (☎22 423. Mixed drinks €4. Open daily 7am-2am.) Next door, at the equally popular **Neon Internet C@fe,** the drinks are slightly less pricey. (☎28 343. Beer €2.50. Mixed drinks €3-4. Open daily 9:30am-late.) At **Blue Note,** to the left of Hotel Olympiada when facing inland, locals mingle beneath palm trees bathed in aquamarine light. Outside, the wood and steel tables are just removed enough to allow for conversation. Head inside to try your luck on the dance floor, open in winter. (☎50 888. Drinks €3.50-5. Open daily 8am-late.)

WESTERN COAST OF KALYMNOS ☎22430

The road north from Pothia is lined with villages. The first of these, **Hora,** was Kalymnos's capital until the threat of piracy made seaside living too dangerous. Churches line Hora's streets, including the **Church of Christ Jerusalem,** built by Byzantine emperor Arcadius after he survived a storm at sea. The half-domed stone blocks with carved inscriptions are from a 4th-century BC temple to Apollo that stood on the same site. The beachside footpath leads to a quiet cove with strange and wonderful rock formations—beware of sea urchins nestled in the rocks. Farther north, between Masouri and Armeos, the cliff faces give way to gargantuan caves, making for some of the best **rock climbing** on the planet. Nearly 20 climbing areas feature over 500 routes of varying levels of difficulty, ranging from level 4c to 9a. Maps of all the caves and detailed books cataloging all the climbs and their relative difficulties can be found in bookstores and supermarkets. (☎59 445 or the tourist kiosk for more info.) The **Municipal Athletic Organization** (☎51 601; www.kalymnos-isl.gr/climb) also has useful info. Numerous **hiking routes** cover the island and its surrounding islets, providing the opportunity to walk through the mountains, along the coast, through gorges and orchards—or all of the above. Ask at the tourist kiosk for routes; maps can be purchased at a supermarket (€5-6).

The village of **Kantouni,** home to a popular if slightly unremarkable **beach** south of Panormos, is accessible by bus from Pothia. From the bus stop, follow the beach and clamber over the rocks for about 10min. to reach the relatively empty black sand beach of **Plati Yialos.** A number of accommodations dot the cliffs above Plati Yialos. Take the cliffside road up 50m to reach **San Marcos ❷.** Spacious suites come with kitchenette, air-conditioning, bath, and terrace-like balcony. (☎47 654. Singles €20; doubles €35-45.) Dine to the reggae beats at the open-air **Domus Restaurant and Bar ❷,** farther up the Kantouni beach. Beach-weary travelers play backgammon on the bohemian patio. (☎47 760. Mixed drinks €4-5. Restaurant open daily 6:30pm-midnight; bar open daily 11am-late.) Popularly known as Cantena, **Rock & Blues ❷** next door has played just that since 1978. Grab a meal (€6-10) in the evening, and stick around for the international tunes played all night. (Mixed drinks €5. Happy hour 8-9pm. Open daily 10am-4am.) **Cafe Del Mar,** where the bus stops, offers blue-toned lounge chairs in a breezy spot by the ocean. (☎48 018. Cafe open daily 10am-late.)

Those looking for after-hours fun should head to **Massouri,** where the single paved road houses a line of bars and lounges. The ever-lively Massouri **beach**

PEACE AND QUIET FOR POCKET CHANGE. Tired of loud, crazy Massouri? For €2-3, hop on a boat to vehicle-free, tranquil **Telendos,** an islet less than 1km away. Pristine pebble and sand beaches with nary a motorbike within an earshot will revive even the most party-weary. A few pensions and tavernas line the waterfront. Boats leave from Myrties every 10-15min. 6am-midnight. Call ☎69448 79 073 or 69490 28 564 to contact the boat captains.

stretches down the steep cliff below main street and is well-populated with sun-bathers, volleyball players, and watersporting locals. In the evening grab the last bus from Pothia (9:30pm) or a cab (€7.50) to check out the cafe bars at their live-liest. A number of accommodations hug the cliff above the main street; head 200m past the bus stop, and make a left up the stairs a little past Igloo Cafe. Take the first left off the stairs and follow the path to its end at **Tina ❷,** where tiled, spacious rooms have kitchenette, air-conditioning, and enormous balcony with a view of the sea. Find American expat owner Kelly at her restaurant on the main street below. (Singles €20; doubles €25-35. Rooms for up to 4 available. €5 extra per bed.) Climb up from the beach or down from the street to the tiki-inspired **Stavedo Beach Cafe ❷,** (☎47 696; www.stavedo.com), that prides itself on being the only bar that can serve meals and rent watersporting equipment. Breezes and percussion jazz make for a relaxed atmosphere. (Beer €3. Sandwiches from €2.50. Canoes €7; windsurf boards €15. 2-for-1 Happy hour 8-10pm. Open daily 10am-late.) Facing the bus stop, walk up the main street to the right to get to **Ambiance Cafe Bar,** which sets the mood with a circular bar and huge windows overlooking the sea. (☎47 882. Mixed drinks €4-4.50. Open daily 6pm-midnight.)

PATMOS Πάτμος

The land of the foretelling of the Apocalypse, Patmos retains a strong religious culture even as cruise ships unload tourists at the monasteries and pebbled beaches. Ancient Patmians worshipped the huntress goddess Artemis, said to have raised the island from the sea. With St. John's exile to the island in AD 95 and his subsequent writing of the book of Revelation in a cave overlooking the town, the island became a central point of Christianity. Patmos was dubbed "The Jerusalem of the Aegean," and in 1088 the Monastery of St. John was built on a hill overlooking the entire island. Locals claim that the island's religious core is most apparent during the week of Easter but maintain that a sacred feel permeates the island year-round. The narrow, well-balanced island offers a mix of tourist amenities and tranquil escapes; almost everyone will find something praiseworthy about Patmos.

SKALA Σκάλα ☎22470

Built along a graceful arc of coastline, the colorful port town of Skala is mirrored by a virtual city of yachts docked in the water. Town life stretches across the long, waterfront strip, where bakeries, *ouzeria*, and tavernas lay nestled between night-and-day cafes. With its central location and easy access to most amenities, Skala is the most convenient place to stay on the island. A 10min. bus or moped ride connects you with most major villages and sights, and a short walk brings you to the beach on the other side of the island.

▪ TRANSPORTATION

Ferries: Tickets can be purchased at offices near the plateia; Blue Star tickets available at Apollon Travel. Ferries go to: **Aki** (4 per week, €4); **Kalymnos** (3hr., daily, €10.50); **Kos** (4hr., daily, €11.50); **Leros** (1hr., daily, €6.40); **Lipsi** (1½hr., 1 per week, €4.80); **Naxos** (1 per week, €14.40); **Panormissi** (4 per week, €6.50); **Paros** (1 per week, €16.60); **Piraeus** (10-12hr., 1 per week, €32); **Rhodes** (8hr., 2 daily, €22.10); **Samos** (3hr., 6 per week, €6).

Flying Dolphins: 1 per week to **Agathonissi** (1hr., €13). 8 per week to: **Kalymnos** (1½hr., €20.10); **Kos** (2hr., €22.40); **Leros** (50min., €12.40); **Lipsi** (20min., €9.40); **Rhodes** (5hr., €43.10); **Samos** (2½hr., €14.50); **Symi** (4½hr., €40.80).

Excursion boats: To **Fourni, Ikaria, Samos, Lipsi, Leros,** and **Psili Ammos,** among several other destinations; some boats offer round-the-island tours of Patmos. Check schedules and prices at the docks or call ☎69767 96 469.

Buses: Next to the Welcome Cafe at the ferry docks. To: **Chora** (10min., 9 per day 7:40am-7:30pm, €1.30), **Grikos** (20min., 7 per day 9:15am-7:30pm, €1.30), and **Kampos** (20min., 4 per day 8:15am-6:30pm, €1.30). Purchase tickets on board.

Taxis: ☎31 225. On the waterfront across from the post office. Available 24hr. €1 surcharge after midnight; €4.50 to Chora.

Rentals: Many car and motorbike rental agencies line the waterfront street. Rates spike in July and Aug.; some agencies recommend reserving a car ahead of time for the summer season. Walk down the main street toward the OTE to find **Aris Rent a Car and Moto** (☎32 542), on the left side of the street. Cars from €25 per day. Mopeds €8.50-15 per day. Open daily 8am-8pm. **Rent A Car Patmos** (☎32 203). On the 2nd fl. of the building just inland of the post office. Cars €25-35 per day, depending on the season. Open daily 8am-8pm. MC. **Motor Rent Express** (☎32 088), next door to Rent a Car Patmos. Has 1-person motorbikes (from €6) as well as larger mopeds (€10-15 per day). Open daily 8am-8pm.

◼▪ ORIENTATION AND PRACTICAL INFORMATION

Skala's amenities are huddled around the port and extend along the waterfront road almost all the way to Meloi Beach. Excursion boats dock opposite the line of cafes and restaurants, while larger vessels dock near the Welcome Cafe, across from the Orthodox Information Center. The street heading inland from the main plateia is lined with cafes and tourist shops and leads to the OTE, ending at rocky **Holhaka Beach.** Facing the ferry docks, head left to **Meloi Beach** (15min. by foot) or right up to the monasteries of Hora (4km).

Tourist Office: Across from the taxi stand; rarely staffed. Instead, head across from the Welcome Cafe to the new ▩**Orthodox Culture and Informational Center** (☎32 709). The extremely friendly staff provides brochures, timetables, and advice on the island's hidden treasures. The center also offers interactive multimedia on Patmos's religious heritage. Open daily 9am-1pm and 5-9pm.

Budget Travel: All over the waterfront, though each only offers info for the ferry lines it works with. **Apollon Travel** (☎31 324) sells hydrofoil, ferry, and airplane tickets, helps with accommodations and rentals, and **exchanges currency.** Open daily 8am-9pm. **G.A. Ferries** (☎31 217), off the street leading to OTE. Open 9am-1pm and 5-9pm.

Banks: National Bank (☎34 050), in the far end of the plateia. Has **currency exchange** and a **24hr. ATM.** Open M-Th 8am-2:30pm, F 8am-2pm. **Emporiki Bank** (☎34 140), farther down the waterfront toward Meloialso. Offers **currency exchange, 24hr. ATM,** and cashes traveler's checks (€6 per transaction; banknotes €3). Open M-Th 8am-2:30pm and F 8am-2pm.

Luggage Storage: Welcome Cafe (☎31 583), next to the dock. Open 24hr.

Laundry: **Meltani** (☎33 170). Wash and dry €10. Open 8:30am-7pm.

Showers: Internet Place (☎69737 45 253). Soap, shampoo, and towel rental €5. Internet €5 per hr. Open 8am-1pm and 5-9pm.

Police: ☎31 303. In the large Italian building on the corner of the main plateia. Upstairs from the post office. Open 24hr.

Pharmacy: A number of pharmacies surround the plateia. 1 can be found a block in from the water north of the plateia. (☎31 500. Open M, Tu, Th-F 9am-2pm and 5:30-9pm; W and Sa 9am-2pm and 7-9pm; Su 11:30am-1pm and 7-9pm.)

Medical Center: ☎31 211. 2km down the main road to Hora, across from Apokalipsi Monastery. Open daily 8am-2pm; 24hr. for emergency care. In an **emergency,** call the police or the pharmacy who will contact the doctor on call.

Telephones: OTE (☎31 399). Follow the road past Dodoni Internet Place. Open M-F 8am-1pm. The Welcome Cafe at the ferry dock has an international phone.

Internet Access: Igloo Cafe (☎33 188), across from Welcome Cafe. €4.50 per hr., min. €2. Open 7am-1am. **Dodoni Internet Place** (☎32 202). Facing National Bank, head 1 block inland on the left street. Several computers, 1 with a webcam. Internet €5 per hr., min. €2. Pastries €1.50-2.30. Open 8am-midnight.

Post Office: ☎31 316. Open M-F 8am-2pm. **Postal Code:** 85500.

🏠🏠 ACCOMMODATIONS AND CAMPING

Domatia will run €20-25 for singles and €30-35 for doubles. Leaving the docks, head about 400m to the right along the waterfront; a number of pensions and hotels are clustered a couple blocks inland. Beachside pensions lie by Hohlaka beach, 200m beyond the OTE, heading inland from the port.

Stefanos Studios (☎32 415), directly behind restaurant Remezzo. New studio rooms come with kitchenette, bath, A/C, and balcony overlooking the harbor. Find Stefanos at the campsite; he also will gladly pick up from the port. The lush garden offers zucchini, eggplants, and pomegranates for guests to enjoy. Doubles €25-40. ❷

Pension Sydney's (☎31 689). Take a left 1 block past the electric company and head 150m uphill; it is on the left. Comfortable, whitewashed rooms have bath and a balcony overlooking the mountains. The gracious owner Dimitrios shares drinking water, house wine, and advice on the island's many restaurants. Singles €20. ❷

Katina's Rooms for Rent (☎31 327). Go inland at Celine's Music Club and curve right with the street; take the 1st right and follow the street to the end. If she has vacancies,

Katina is usually at the docks with her car. Large, whitewashed rooms have kitchenette, bath, TV, and fresh flowers. Singles €20-25, doubles €25-35. ❷

■ **Stefanos Flower Camping at Meloi** (☎31 821), 1.5km northeast of Skala. Follow the waterfront road along the port and all the way over the hill, taking the left fork to Meloi; or skip the walk and ask Stefanos for a ride. Jungle-like rows of tall grass divide the campsite into lots, providing ample privacy and a neighborhood feel to the sprawling maze. On-site restaurant (cheeseburgers €3; grilled platters €6), book exchange, shared kitchen, clean showers, and hospitable managers. Scooter rental €8-10 per day. Parking €1.50. Mopeds €1. Sites €6-7-per person, tents €2 each. Restaurant open daily 9am-12:30am. Campsite open Apr.-Oct. ❶

🍴 FOOD

Patmos island offers exquisite melt-in-your-mouth seafood, with a culinary reputation to match. Side-street tavernas with penciled-in prices often offer the freshest seafood at the lowest prices. Don't be daunted by the per-kilogram price for fish: a typical serving is about 250g.

■ **Chiliomodi** (☎34 080), past Koukoumavla on the opposite side of the side street; look for the Greek sign. This small restaurant has earned a stellar reputation among locals for its fresh fish lightly cooked in olive oil, lemon juice, and spices. The assorted grilled fish platter (€7.50) comes heaped with 4 whole fish, pleasing discerning palates and ravenous appetites alike. The complimentary fruit plate makes for a sweet afterthought. Open 7pm-late. ❷

To Kyma (☎31 192), next to Meloi beach, on Aspiris Bay. The 2km walk from town makes for a pleasant evening stroll. Follow the waterfront road around the port and up the hill; when you start descending, take the right fork and continue another 200m to the bay. Fresh fish hot off the charcoals (€30-45 per kg) and seating inches from the water. From the campground, the walk only takes 5min. Open daily 6:30pm-1am. ❸

Remezzo (☎31 553), at the foot of the hill on the road to Meloi. The chef artistically prepares the house specialty, chicken with prunes and orange sauce (€9.50). Complimentary Patmian almond cake from a generations-old recipe will leave you with a sweet taste in your mouth. Open daily noon-2am. ❸

Loukas Taverna (☎32 515), across from the OTE. Serves up a variety of standard Greek favorites on a comfortable outdoor terrace. Entrees €5-7. Open noon-midnight. ❷

🎵 NIGHTLIFE

While Patmos's monastic pilgrims tend to be a high-minded set, the local youth know how to get their earthly pleasures. Waterside cafes stay open late as locals and travelers linger on the beaches studded with lights. The clubs in Skala can all be reached by foot, and most turn up the music by 11pm.

■ **Koukoumavla** (☎32 325; www.patmos-island.com/koukoumavla). Facing inland from the Welcome Cafe, head to the left and take the 1st right up a side street; it is on the left. The free-spirited owner sells the handmade books and purses on display in this funky cafe, while her Italian husband whips up mixed drinks (€4-7) at the hand-painted bar. Patrons can grab a seat in bohemia or head outside to the family-friendly "Elfland," a shady garden of colorfully painted furniture and toys. Large pressed sandwiches €2-4.50. Open daily 11am-2am.

Isalos Bar (☎69390 09 807), down a side street behind the post office. Blacklights and tealight candelabras cast mysterious shadows on the stone walls and arches of Skala's most popular club. Patrons dance on 2fl. of orange-streaked shadows to the melodic jazz and Greek pop that plays all night. Mixed drinks €5-7. Open daily 11pm-late.

Konsolato (☎32 060), on the waterfront across from the flashing red beacon. Locals and tourists alike gather after 1am to dance to the live DJ in the Chinese lantern-motifed bar. During the frequent *sfinakia* (shots) tradition, people line up at the bar and go bottoms-up in unison. Mixed drinks €7. Open 11pm-late.

▓ DAYTRIPS FROM SKALA

RURAL PATMOS. Unvisited coves and breathtaking vistas await those who long to get away from the tourists on Skala's streetside strip of beach. Locals hail **Psili Ammos** as the best beach on the island, though without private transport it is the most difficult to reach. Take the southern road past Chora until signs for the beach appear; from there the beach is a 20min. hike over the hill. The untouched stretch of sand with gorgeous views of the peninsula more than makes up for the effort. From Skala, the closest beach is **Hohlaka,** at the end of the road with the Skala OTE. Beachgoers can catch epic sunsets melting into the water, though the windy, rocky beach does not make for great swimming. **Meloi,** an easy walk over the hill from Skala, has large trees that envelop the sandy beach—a prime barbecue spot. Follow the signs on the port-side road to Meloi to get to **Aspiris Bay,** which commands fantastic views of virgin coast. A bit farther north, the more developed beaches of **Agriolivadi** and **Kampos** offer a number of tavernas and are a pleasant option for those traveling by bus. Over the hill from Kampos, **Vagia Beach**—rocky, secluded, and serene—seems a world apart with lush cliffs overhanging glassy, blue water. Go east along the road to Livadia and follow the path down to find an appealing, **unmarked beach** set against a small bluff. A bit farther east, cliff-lined **Livadia Beach** has spectacular views of the islets just offshore. While bus service extends only to Kambos, you can reach more secluded beaches by hiking or biking. Strong winds batter **Lambi Beach,** which is famed for its multicolored pebbles, now rare from years of being collected by locals for their homes' floor mosaics.

HORA Χώρα ☎22470

The reverent solace of the monastery atop the hill diffuses through the sloped and crooked streets of Hora, while the intricate maze of white houses defies even the most adept cartographers. The town's cobbled paths reveal sprawling gardens behind grand doors and rusty-hinged gates.

The turreted, 15m walls and imposing gateway built into the **Monastery of Saint John the Theologian** to combat piracy make it look more like a fortress than a place of worship. Founded in 1088 by Ag. Christodoulos as a memorial to St. John, the monastery once laid claim to all of Patmos and several neighboring islands. Around the main courtyard's holy well, the walls are covered with glimmering, intricate mosaics and 17th-century **frescoes,** including one portraying St. John's duel of faith with Kinopas, a priest of Apollo. The excellent ▓**treasury museum** preserves 33 original pages from the Gospel of St. Mark, making it the second-largest collection in the world—though only one page is displayed. Two floors of glass cases with detailed English placards guard 12th-century icons, ornate ceremonial jewels, renowned works of 11th-century Cretan art, and a 7th-century Book of Job. Look for Helkomenos, an icon painted by **El Greco,** near the end of the exhibit. (☎20 800. Monastery and treasury open M, W, F-Sa 8am-1:30pm, Tu, Th, Su 8am-1:30pm and 4-6pm. Monastery free. Treasury €6, students €3. Modest dress required; shawls provided. Ask at the gift shop about the daily 3pm services.)

The monastery holds 10 chapels within its walls. The **Chapel of the Virgin Mary** is covered with gold-laden 12th-century frescoes, hidden behind the wall until they were exposed by 1956 tremors. The small door on the left before the exit allows visitors to view several famous skulls and the casket containing Ag. Christodoulos's corpse. Up the right side of the hill from the bus stop, follow the white signs to the **Convent of Zoodochos Pege,** where a new museum hosts a number of religious icons and artifacts. The church has a number of beautiful frescoes, including one of the Panagia which, seen from the right, appears to have three eyes. Legend has it that the icon disappeared in 1956 to help cure a sick Patmos woman, returning three days later with an additional eye. (☎31 256. Chapel and museum open M-Sa 10am-noon. Chapel free, museum €3. Modest dress required.)

A short hike 2km down the road leads to the **Apocalypsis Monastery,** built on the site where St. John stayed while on Patmos. Head downstairs to the **Sacred Grotto of the Revelation,** adjacent to the **Church of Saint Anne,** where the Apocalypse was revealed to St. John. The power of God is said to have caused the cracks in the walls of the cave as St. John, stricken to the ground in shock, received the book of Revelation. (☎31 234. Open M, W, and F-Sa 8am-1:30pm; Tu, Th, and Su 8am-1:30pm and 4-6pm. Modest dress required.)

If the monasteries have filled your religious quota but left your stomach empty, try popular **Vagelis Restaurant ❷,** in the central plateia. The cooks whip up a mean eggplant salad (€4) and *rebetiko* (rolled roast pork; €10). Follow the signs branching off the road to the monastery. (☎31 967. Open daily 11am-2pm and 6-11pm; high season 7pm-1am.)

Hora is 4km from Skala, a trip you can tackle by **bus** (10min., 10 per day, €1.30), taxi (€4.50), or foot. The hike down along the easily found foot and donkey paths affords unparalleled views of the entire island. Buses to Grikou also depart from the hilltop bus stop (15min., 5 per day, €1.30).

NORTHEAST AEGEAN ISLANDS

Flung toward the outskirts of Greece closer to Istanbul than to Athens, the islands of the Northeast Aegean remain sheltered from the cultural creep of globalization. With limited transportation to even their Dodecanese neighbors, the islands go about life in the Aegean at their own pace with their own rules. Deck chairs and resorts are rarities in this part of Greece, where vast wilderness, local hospitality, and undisturbed beaches are commonplace. The strength of the cultural authenticity here is palpable, a traveler's welcome and reward.

 SUGGESTED ITINERARIES: NORTHEAST AEGEAN ISLANDS

THREE DAYS Enjoy the enlightened atmosphere of Sappho's home, **Lesvos** (p. 507), before visiting the castle-topped port city of **Limnos,** for tranquil beaches and glorious sunsets.

TEN DAYS After embarking on the lush hikes on **Thassos** (p. 525), nicknamed the "Green Island," discover the dazzling

beauty hidden in **Limnos's** (p. 519) barren wilderness. Explore the many diverse towns in **Lesvos** (p. 507), with an extended stay in storybook village **Molyvos** (p. 513). Take a daytrip to the **Petrified Forest** (p. 518), 1 of only 2 in the world, before moving to the less-traveled villages and beaches on **Chios** (p. 500).

SAMOS Σάμος

Those who take the time to explore Samos will find the allure of the lush mountainsides sloping into crystal seas. Once the home of Pythagoras and Aristarchus (who discovered that the Earth revolved around the sun 1800 years before Copernicus), Samos retains a proud Greek culture. Despite its proximity to Turkey and having been under the sultanate's rule, Samos saw little influx of Turkish culture. Though the island is a popular stepping stone en route to Turkey, travelers who approach Samos as a destination are rewarded by the ruins, nightlife, luminous beaches, and lovely hikes leading to hidden waterfalls and caves.

SAMOS TOWN (VATHY) Βαθύ   ☎ 22730

Though larger than Samos's second port, Pythagorio, Vathy receives fewer tourists. Tavernas unfurl along a graceful parabola of coastline. Behind them, narrow streets and stairways stretch up the hillside toward the residential area. Public gardens, a children's playground, hole-in-the-wall restaurants, and excellent bars give Vathy a lived-in quality too often absent from port towns. The entire town is referred to as either "Vathy" or "Samos Town," and both options are correct.

▐ TRANSPORTATION

Flights: Olympic Airways (☎ 61 219). Walk a few blocks up Kanari from the Archaeological Museum; it's on your left. To: **Athens** (1hr., 4 per day, €60-120); **Chios** (20min., 3

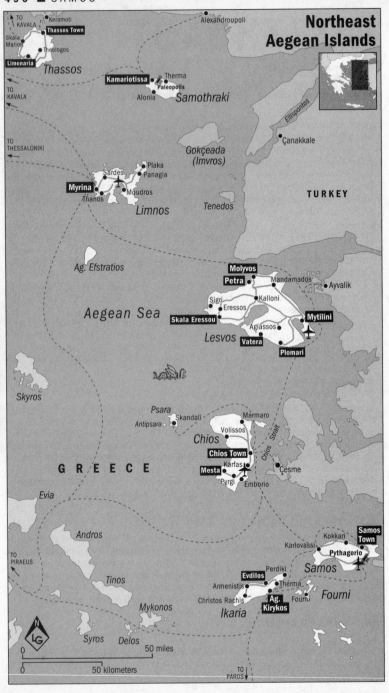

Northeast Aegean Islands

TO KAVALA
Keramoti
Thassos Town
Skala Marion
Theologos
Limenaria
Thassos

TO KAVALA

TO THESSALONIKI

Alexandroupoli

Kamariotissa
Therma
Paleopolis
Alonia
Samothraki

Ellispontos

Çanakkale

Gokçeada (Imvros)

Plaka
Panagia
Sardes
Myrina
Thanos
Moudros
Limnos

Tenedos

TURKEY

Ag. Efstratios

Aegean Sea

Molyvos
Petra
Mandamados
Ayvalik
Sigri
Kalloni
Eressos
Skala Eressou
Agiassos
Mytilini
Lesvos
Vatera
Plomari

Skyros

Psara
Skandali
Antipsara
Marmaro
Volissos
Chios
Chios Town
Karfas
Mesta
Pyrgi
Emborio
Çeşme

Chios Strait

GREECE

Evia

Andros

Kokkari
Samos Town
Karlovassi
Pythagorio
Samos

TO PIRAEUS

Tinos

Perdiki
Evdilos
Armenistis
Therma
Christos Rachis
Ag. Kirykos
Fourni
Fourni

Mykonos

Ikaria

Syros
Delos

50 miles

50 kilometers

TO PAROS

NORTHEAST AEGEAN

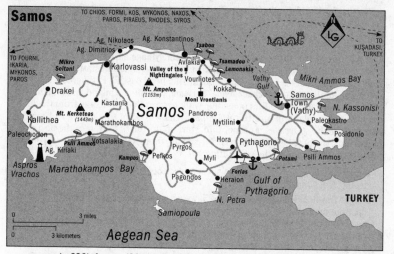

per week, €30); **Lesvos** (30min., 3 per week, €30); **Limnos** (25min., 3 per week, €36); **Rhodes** (40min., 2 per week, €36); **Thessaloniki** (1hr., 3 per week, €50). Open M-F 8:15am-3:30pm. **Aegean Airways** flies to **Athens** (1hr., 2-3 per day, €30-120); tickets available at travel agencies. The **airport** (☎61 219), near Pythagorio, is only accessible by taxi (€17 from Skala) or infrequent bus service to the airport crossing (4 per day, €1.90). Consider taking a bus to Pythagorio (€1.90), followed by a taxi (€3-4).

Ferries: To: **Agios Kirykos, Ikaria** (3hr., 1-3 per day, €9); **Chios** (3½hr., 2-3 per week, €13); **Evdilos, Ikaria** (3hr., 5 per week, €11); **Fourni** (2hr., Tu-Su 1-2 per day, €7.50); **Kalymnos** (3hr., 4 per week, €13); **Kos** (every Sa, €15); **Lipsi** (2hr., 4 per week, €10); **Mykonos** (6hr., 6 per week, €20-25); **Paros** (8hr., 3 per week, €18); **Piraeus** (16hr., 1-4 per day, €34.50); **Rhodes** (10hr., every Sa, €33); **Syros** (8½hr., 5 per week, €24); **Thimena** (2hr., 5 per week, €7).

Flying Dolphins: Leave from the port at Pythagorio, heading daily to: **Chios** (2½hr., 3 per week, €20); **Kalymnos** (2hr., €26); **Kos** (5hr., €25.50); **Leros** (1½hr., €20.10); **Lipsi** (1¼hr., €14.50); **Patmos** (1hr., €14.50). **Hydrofoils** from Vathy service **Fourni** (1½hr., 2 per week, €15).

Excursion boats: Daily to **Kuşadasi, Turkey** (1½hr.; 8:30am, 5pm; €45 round-trip, plus €10 Turkish port tax). You can add a bus ride and tour of nearby **Ephesus** for €23 more, including entrance fees. Turkish entrance **visas** (US$20) must be purchased at the border by citizens of Australia, Ireland, the UK, and the US planning to stay for over 1 day. Canadians must pay CDN$45 for a visa; euro equivalents accepted.

Buses: The **KTEL** office (☎27 262) is 1 block in from the waterfront on Lekati, past Pl. Pythagoras. To: **Airport Crossing** (25min., 4 per day); **Heraion** (30min., 4 per day); **Hora** (30min., 6 per day); **Karlovassi** (50min., 6 per day); **Kokkari** (20min., 6 per day); **Mytilini** (20min., 4 per day); **Pythagorio** (30min., 10 per day). Most fares €1-3. Reduced service Sa. No service Su, though major sites may be served during the summer; ask at the office. Bus tour around the island stopping at major sights including the the Valley of Nightingales (Th-F 8:30am, €27).

Rentals: **Autounion** (☎27 513), on the waterfront by the docks. Cars €25 per day; motorbikes €10 per day; bikes €5. Open 8:30am-3:30pm and 5:30-9:30pm. In a kiosk next to ITSA Travels, find **Pegasus** (☎24 470). Cars €30 per day; motorbikes €12 per day. Open 8am-11pm.

Taxis: ☎28 404. Available 24hr. in Pl. Pythagoras. To: airport €17; Pythagorio €12.

⚓ ❼ ORIENTATION AND PRACTICAL INFORMATION

The waterfront is home to most services. **Plateia Pythagoras,** identifiable by its four large palm trees, consists of cafes, a taxi stand, and a giant lion statue. It is located 250m to the right of the port when facing inland; head past Pl. Pythagoras until you see signs pointing to the **Archaeological Museum,** two blocks inland and adjacent to the **Municipal Gardens.** To find pensions, walk toward Pl. Pythagoras from the ferry dock and turn inland before Hotel Aeolis. Signs will point to a number of nearby pensions on the staircases. For nightlife, start up the hill to the left of the port (facing inland); the best bars and clubs are 400m up, though dancing venues are on the far side of the harbor by the post office.

Tourist Office: ☎28 530. On a side street 1 block before Pl. Pythagoras. Open mid-July to Aug. M-F 10am-1pm.

Budget Travel: ◪**ITSA Travel** (☎23 605; www.itsatravelsamos.com), on the waterfront opposite the port. The English-speaking staff helps locate accommodations, has ferry and Flying Dolphin tickets, offers free maps, recommends sights and restaurants, plans excursions to Turkey, and offers free luggage storage. Open daily 6am-10pm and when boats arrive. AmEx/MC/V. **Rhenia Tours** (☎88 800), farther along the waterfront. Sells airplane and ferry tickets, offers Western Union, and rents cars (€41 per day). Open 8am-9:30pm. **By Ship Travel** (☎25 065), next to ITSA, has boat schedules and **car rental** (€30 per day). All agencies listed **exchange currency.**

Bank: National Bank, on the waterfront just beyond Pl. Pythagoras, has a **24hr. ATM.** Open M-Th 8am-2:30pm, F 8am-2pm.

Police: ☎22 100. After Pl. Pythagoras on the far right of the waterfront when facing inland. The **tourist police** (☎87 344) are in the same office. Open 24hr.

Hospital: ☎83 100. Facing inland, 10min. to the left of the ferry dock. Open 24hr.

Telephones: OTE (☎22 299). On Kanari behind the church. Open M-F 7:30am-1:30pm.

Internet Access: Nethouse (☎22 986), on the waterfront right before the post office. Offers cheap Internet (€2 per hr., min. €0.50.) and a huge DVD selection in English and Greek (€1.50 for 5 days). Open M-Sa 8am-2:30pm and 5-10:30pm. Pythagoras Hotel (☎28 601), 600m up the hill from the port, by the hospital. €3 per hr.

Post Office: ☎28 820. On the waterfront, just before the military post and police. Open M-F 7:30am-2pm. Western Union available. **Postal Code:** 83100.

⌂ ACCOMMODATIONS

Recent crackdowns on unlicensed pensions have forced many budget accommodations to shut down or operate illegally. Consult ITSA Travels for a good deal if you're having trouble finding a room.

◪**Pythagoras Hotel,** Kalistratou 12 (☎28 601), across from the hospital. Rooms are clean, airy, and the cheapest in town. The location by the beach and several nightlife spots, the snack bar, Internet access (€3 per hr.), and baths make this hotel a backpacker's heaven. The shared terrace overlooking the water and rooms that open onto the wraparound balcony make for a community feel. Singles €20; doubles €28-45. ❷

Hotel Artemis (☎27 792), on the waterfront next to Pl. Pythagoras. Offers spacious doubles with bath, fridge, TV, and A/C, smack in the middle of town. The bright indoor terrace is a popular spot to sit and chat with other guests. Singles €20; doubles €25. ❷

Pension Trova, Kalomiris 26 (☎27 759). Head along the waterfront and go inland when you see the sign for Hotel Aeolis; take a left before the stairs and follow the signs. Clean rooms have fan and shared bath; some with balcony. For larger groups, Maria rents a fully equipped house by the bus station; usually for longer stays, in the low season you might be able to rent it for a few nights. Singles €20; doubles €20-25; house €50. ❷

Medousa Hotel, Sofouli 25 (☎23 501), on the waterfront halfway between the port and Pl. Pythagoras. The most convenient accommodations in town, with no hill-climbing involved. An elevator goes up to well-appointed rooms that have bath, A/C, fridge, and a view of the harbor. Ask at Dodoni cafe downstairs. Singles €25; doubles €35. ❷

◖ FOOD

On side streets just a block inland from the water, a number of hole-in-the-wall tavernas serve up unbeatable homemade dishes, while the waterfront tavernas are noted by locals for their delicious renditions of national favorites. Samian cuisine is notable for its sweet regional wine, the Muscat of Samos, which, depending on your taste, is either sickeningly saccharine or the nectar of the gods. A large **supermarket** sits behind the Archaeological Museum.

▧ **Restaurant Christos** (☎24 792), in Pl. Nikolaos to the left of Pl. Pythagoras facing inland. Daily offerings of newly invented specials. A case displays the day's selection, including restaurant favorites such as feta-stuffed peppers (€3.50) or fresh lamb with dill and lemon (€7). Entrees €5-7. Open daily 11am-late. ❷

Taverna Aprovado (☎80 552), 1 block behind the main drag, inland from Hotel Aeolis. Serves up authentic dishes with huge portions at low prices—not to mention the ▧**free shot of ouzo** that comes with every meal. Entrees €5-8. Open noon-1am. MC. ❷

Taverna Artemis (☎23 639), facing inland from the docks, follow the waterfront road to the left. Locals gather to munch on the *briam* (mixed vegetables in tomato sauce; €4) and traditional Greek favorites. Entrees €4-7. Open 6:30am-2am. ❷

Gregory's Taverna (☎22 718). Facing Olympic Airlines, head up the street to the right for 200m. Hailed by locals for its fresh meat. Entrees €5-7. ❷

◖ NIGHTLIFE

The nightclub scene centers on two waterfront poles on opposite sides of the harbor. Facing inland from the ferry docks, a number of bars 400m to the left have dance floors and waterfront terraces. Music-blasting discos are 500m in the opposite direction, where sound-proof doors keep the neighborhood deceivingly quiet.

THE BIG SPLURGE

ANOTHER KIND OF TURKEY DAY

A world away—but only a 1hr. boat ride—from Samos Town, the Turkish coastal city of Kusadasi offers a glimpse of a culture unseen in Samos. A day spent roaming the bazaars dotted with mosques and hamams offers the rare opportunity to visit a land so close and yet so different.

The Kusadasi coast is a patchwork of housing developments in the works. The male-dominated bazaars sprawl in countless shops and winding alleyways. With no observed siesta, shoppers can bargain for "genuine fake" versions of anything all afternoon. Carpet merchants offer glasses of apple tea to those who watch their silk spinning and rug knotting demonstrations. The ruined fortress on Pigeon Island now hosts a number of cafes overhanging the Aegean coast.

Many day trippers to Kusadasi also visit the ruined Roman city of Ephesus, 30min. north. Streets flanked by columns lead to the breathtaking amphitheater overlooking the forested valley.

Turkey is accessible from Samos Town (Vathy) via excursion boat (1½hr.; 8:30am, 5pm; €45, plus a €10 Turkish port tax). A bus tour of Ephesus can be added for an additional €23, including site entrance fee. For stays over 1 day, a US$20 visa can be purchased upon entrance. Contact ITSA Travel for tickets.

Mble, 400m uphill to the left of the ferry docks. Under blue lighting, sip a mixed drink (€7) on the packed terrace balcony overhanging the water, where a spotlight gives the water an eerie, fish-attracting glow. Open 9:30am-morning.

Stelios Beach Bar (☎87 263), farther up the street past Hotel Pythagoras, to the left and downstairs on the beach. Patrons lounge in this tiki-inspired bar, enjoying the spontaneous fire shows from the bar. Free sunbeds. Mixed drinks €5. Open 9am-late.

Escape Music Bar, next to Mble. Outdoor terrace overlooking the necklace of harbor lights. The dance floor indoors picks up after 2am, where Greek and American hits keep the young, local crowd on their toes all night. Mixed drinks €7. Open 8pm-4am.

Xantres Club (☎69490 78 611), on the far side of the waterfront by the post office. Soundproof walls conceal the booming Greek pop. Locals gather after 3am to dance in the blacklight to the sounds of the nightly DJ. Mixed drinks €7. Open 11:30pm-7am.)

👁 SIGHTS

The excellent, informative **Archaeological Museum,** behind the Municipal Gardens, contains more proof of the Heraion's bygone splendor than do the crumbled remains of the site itself. The museum's two buildings house treasures from the ancient Heraion (the temple of Hera) and other local digs, explained in detail by English labels. The first building holds Laconian ivory carvings and some statues, most notably the colossal 5m **kouroi** from 560 BC. Pieces of this magnificent figure were found built into existing walls and cisterns; its grey-white banded marble was a distinctive regional signature of ancient Samian sculptors. The purpose and meaning of the sculptures remains unclear, though the *kouroi* are thought to have been votives to Hera from wealthy families. The same building houses the well-preserved Genelos group, a rather ostentatious offering to Hera depicting the aristocratic donors, the Genelos family, themselves. The group once graced the Heraion's Sacred Way, and of the original series of six life-sized sculptures, four have survived. In the second building, an exhibit on Hera worship displays a collection of the various pieces of pottery, jewelry, and small sculptures dedicated to the goddess. The last room, upstairs on the right, includes a case of fascinatingly nightmarish, gryphon-engraved cauldron handles known as **protomes.** (☎27 469. Open Tu-Su 8:30am-3pm. €3, students and seniors €2, EU students free.)

🏛 DAYTRIPS FROM SAMOS TOWN

ANCIENT PYTHAGORIO Πυθαγόρειο

A bus from Vathy (30min., 10 per day, €1.90) arrives at Pythagorio, now a modern beach town built on much of the ancient ruins, 14km south of Vathy.

The ancient city of Pythagorio, once the island's capital, thrived as a commercial and political center during the late 6th century BC under Polykrates the Tyrant. The writings of historian Herodotus recount how Polykrates undertook the three most daring engineering projects in the Hellenic world—two in Pythagorio. The first, the **Tunnel of Eupalinus,** lies 1500m up the hill to the north of town. This 1.3km underground aqueduct diverted water from a spring on the hill to the city below. Tunnel construction began at two different sites and, despite a miscalculation, the two sides were connected. Climbing down the steep staircase leads to the 200m passageway that is now open to the public. The rock-hewn path runs along the top of a deep trench that falls off on the right, though grating and lights make the tunnel passable. Claustrophobes should note that ceilings are low and the tunnel is narrow. The 20min. walk to the tunnel passes a number of other minor sites on the hill, including an **ancient theater** now refurbished with a wooden stage. Taking the right fork uphill at the theatre leads to the monastery at **Panagia Spyliani,** where benches offer incredible views of the island outside the whitewashed chapel. *(From the bus stop facing inland, take the first left and head uphill to the excursion bus stop, then follow the signs to the left. Open Tu-Su 8:45am-2:30pm. €4, students €2, EU students free.)*

Polykrates's second feat, the 40m deep **harbor mole,** is still in use today as a breakwater, supporting the modern pier. Blocks, columns, wall fragments, and entablatures are strewn throughout the town of Pythagorio in fenced-off plots of weeds. The sandstone-colored ruins of the **Castle of Lykurgus,** constructed during the War of Independence, rise up on the waterfront between the stretches of houses and the sea. The **Church of the Transfiguration,** a pale-blue variant of classic Orthodox architecture, and the remains of a **basilica** are also nearby.

HERAION Ιραίον

A bus from Vathy (30min., 4 per day, €1.70) drops off in Heraion Town. The temple is 1km back on the road from Vathy. ☎95 277. Open Tu-Su 8:30am-3pm. €3, students €2. As transportation back is infrequent, bring cash for a taxi (€16).

Polykrates's third engineering feat is the Heraion, or **Temple of Hera,** where the faithful once brought their offerings down the *kouros*-lined **Iera Odos** (Sacred Way) leading from Pythagorio to the temple steps. Samian devotees had worshipped Hera for seven centuries by the time Polykrates began enlarging the temple in the 6th century BC. Fire damage in 525 BC left only one of the original 134 columns standing; though only minimally reconstructed after the fire, the 118m by 58m temple retained its historic prestige. In 80 BC Cicero convinced Roman authorities to turn the building into a kind of museum for earlier votive offerings. The site became a place of unlimited asylum under the Romans, attracting vagabonds and miscreants. The temple fell into decay after the collapse of the Roman Empire, and the Byzantines eventually erected a church on the site. Today the most interesting finds from the remains are stored in the Archaeological Museum in Samos Town, though the temple still merits a short visit. From the Sacred Way, a walk along the beach brings you back to the temple. If you can't enter through the beachside back gate, look for the path leading inland to the main road and the entrance, farther along the beach past two houses. Come prepared with a jug of libations, lest you suffer Hera's wrath in the form of heat stroke.

NORTHERN AND WESTERN SAMOS

Rent a car to check out the mountainside villages, or hire a taxi for the day (€25).

The northern coast of Samos has many crowded, sandy **beaches** and a few less-frequented pebble beaches tucked into coves. Most of the coast is easily accessible from the coastal road to **Karlovassi.** On a peninsula 10km west of Samos Town, you'll find the village of **Kokkari,** where both **Lemonakia beach** and nearby **Avlakia,** 1km west of Kokkari, are hailed by locals for clear water and white-pebble shores. Buses to Karlovassi (6 per day) also service Kokkari, though check with the driver for return times. Farther west, head inland from the village of **Agios Konstantinos** to **Manolates,** a traditional village famed for its terra cotta pottery. The drive southeast to Pythagorio runs through lush foliage with views of the ocean. From Manolates, hike through the renowned **Valley of the Nightingales** where sweet songs and untouched rainforests greet nature enthusiasts.

The village of **Vourliotes,** 5km south of Avlakia, was a favorite of renowned Greek actress Melina Mercury. Several kilometers above the town, the 16th-century monastery **Moni Vrontianis** watches over the populace below. From the redroofed hamlet of **Marathokambos,** go a few kilometers west to find the spacious, sandy beaches of **Votsalakia** and **Psili Ammos.**

A short drive west of Karlovassi leads to the **waterfalls of Potami.** A 15min. hike brings you to the lake where the waterfall collects in three pools. You can hike to other waterfalls, 2km west of **Paleo,** in the island's northwestern corner.

FOURNI Φούρνι ☎ 22750

The lobster-shaped archipelago of Fourni continues the mountainous ridge that forms larger neighbors Samos and Ikaria. With 2700 residents involved in maritime activity, the islands are known for spectacular seafood cuisine and a relaxed pace of life. Quiet streets lead to pristine beaches under windmill-studded hills. Locals chat until late in the outdoor tavernas lining the waterfront, providing the rare opportunity to experience an authentic island community.

█🛈 TRANSPORTATION AND PRACTICAL INFORMATION. To give Fourni residents access to the outside world, the government sponsors ferry lines to and from the island, allowing for cheap, daily access. As boats may only run to the island once a day, expect to spend at least one night. Several of the island's monasteries and archaeological sites are nestled in the mountaintops and can be difficult to access. At the mouth of the inland road on the waterfront, **GA Ferries** sells tickets for all the ferry lines. (☎ 51 481. Open 10am-2pm and 8-10:30pm.) Fourni is accessible from Agios Kirykos by **ferry** (1½hr., daily, €5); inquire at Icariada Travel. A ferry from Samos Town stops at Karlovassi, Agios Kirykos, and Thimena en route to Fourni (3hr., 3 per week, €7.70), alternating days with a smaller private boat (3hr., 4 per week, €7.50.); consult ITSA Travels. In high season, hydrofoils from Pythagorios make daytrips to Fourni (2hr., 1-2 per week, €30) via Patmos and Lipsi. From Fourni, Thimena is accessible via ferry (20 min., 4 per week, €3), though ask around at the dock if you can't find a ride. Daily **boat excursions** to Keramidou Beach (€10 round-trip), Chrysomilia (€10 round-trip), cruise tours around Fourni (€16), and long-distance daytrip cruises to several islands including Lipsi, Leros, Patmos, and Kalymnos (€45) are arranged at the tourist office.

The sleepy waterfront strip has one main road that leads inland 150m to the main square passing many of the town's facilities on the way, including the **Internet** cafe. The **tourist office** is halfway up the road on the left where the friendly, English-speaking staff offers free maps of the island, advice on beaches and sights, accommodations help, and boat excursions to beaches. (☎ 51 546. Open daily 10am-3pm and 7:30-10:30pm.) The island offers no car rental, though **scooters** are available for €12 per day. The island **coast guard** (☎ 51 207) doubles as the police.

█🖿 ACCOMMODATIONS AND FOOD. Facing inland, follow the waterfront road to the right where **Studios Nektaria ❶** has wood-paneled rooms with fan and bath. Friendly Dimitris offers advice on the island. Ask about the rooftop room with a terrace overlooking the harbor. (☎ 51 365. Singles €15; doubles €15-35.) More rooms can be found at **Amurianu ❷,** to the left off the inland road. Two-room suites come with kitchenette, bath, balcony, and enough space for four to sleep; inquire at the tourist office. (☎ 51 408. Rooms €25-30, high season €50.)

Waterfront tavernas and cafes offer spectacular seafood cuisine at similar prices. Head inland to the back of the main square to find local hangout **I Kali Kardia ❷.** Traditional meals such as *gardoupa* (cow liver; €8) and *kleftiko* (pork with vegetables; €8) are served along with seafood. (☎ 51 217. Open 7:30am-1am.)

🮥 BEACHES. A bus route is in the making, but travelers may find it best to travel by boat to the different beaches on the island or hike along the mountain road. It's a 5min. walk to the left of Fourni Town when facing inland to the sandy beach of

Psili Ammos. Here, enjoy views of the offshore island Thimena and of the construction project that soon will make a port here. The coastal road south of the port leads to the untouched beaches of **Kambi** and **Ag. Ioannis** set against hills. Northeast of Fourni Town, the popular beach of **Chrysomilia** is serviced regularly by boats, allowing for a daytrip to its taverna-lined shores. Halfway up the road to Chrysomilia, the local favorite **Kamari** is accessible by car or a 40min. hike across the island.

IKARIA Ικαρία

Ikaria is named after the reckless young Icarus, who plunged to a watery demise after flying too close to the sun; a legendary rock marks the spot of his fall. Ikaria's history matches the rebellious attitude of its namesake: during the Balkan Wars a revolutionary movement led to the formation of a short-lived Ikarian republic. With an agricultural economy and no major tourist industry, the island remains one of the poorest in the region. The Communist Party (KKE) enjoys huge popularity on the island; anti-EU banners make a jarring addition to the peaceful landscape. Ikaria's coastline is speckled by serene, untouristed beaches, some with natural hot springs. Looming above the sea is an enormous chain of green alpine mountains. Besides providing dramatic vistas, the mountainous terrain makes transportation around the island difficult. Visitors patient with the island's often inexplicable schedule, though, are rewarded with an unspoiled slice of Greece.

AGIOS KIRYKOS Άγιος Κήρυκος ☎ 22750

Ikaria's port town is little more than a shaded plateia stretching along giant steps that lead to the sea. After 6pm, locals begin to hang out by the pier and sip frappés. With the KKE headquarters and a prevalent macho youth culture, the town plays by its own rules and keeps a baffling schedule; even at midnight you'll see small children playing energetically in front of the cafes as their parents chat and gossip.

> **TIP** **ON YOUR OWN.** Ikaria has an unquestionable sense of authenticity that. Precisely because the island doesn't cater to tourists, however, getting around can be frustrating and difficult on a budget. Be prepared either to **rent a vehicle** and tackle the long, winding mountain roads on your own or to spend a wad of cash on **taxis** if you can find a driver willing to take you where you want to go.

 TRANSPORTATION. The **airport** (☎ 32 197) is on the island's northeastern tip, near Faros Beach, and has flights to Athens (50min., 1 per day Tu-Su, €44) and Iraklion, Crete (2 per week, €100); contact **Icariada Travel,** in the plateia where the English-speaking staff also provides ferry schedules and free luggage storage. (☎ 23 322. Open daily 9am-2:30pm and 5:30-9:30pm.) **Ferries** run between the southern port of Agios Kirykos and the northern Evdilos, depending on the company. Plan ahead as bus service between the two cities is practically nonexistent and a taxi ride (€27) may be in order. Ferries run to: Fourni (1hr., daily, €5.30); Mykonos (3 per week, €14.10); Naxos (3 per week, €12.50); Paros (4hr., 2 per week, €14.40); Piraeus (10hr., daily, €29); Samos Town (3hr., daily, €9); Syros (3 per week, €14.50). **Flying Dolphins** go in the summer to Fourni (30min., 4 per week, €10) and make a circuit of Patmos; Lipsi; Leros; Kalymnos; and Pythagorio, Samos (2hr., 3 per week, €15). **Bus service** on the island is fickle, if it exists at all; buses may run in one direction one day and the other the next. If you do happen to be relying on public transport, expect to spend the night or call a cab to get home. Buses leave from the waterside parking lot in front of the tourist office and go from Agios Kirykos to Evdilos (1½hr.) and continue to Armenistis (2hr., 1-2 per day, €6). A fairly regular **green bus** runs to Therma every hour from 9am-2pm and 5-9pm from in front of Alpha Bank. (5min., €1.20.) **Taxis** congregate in front of Alpha Bank in the plateia and can be reached by mobile. (☎69726 40 154, 69778 41 327, or 69723 98 568; a complete list can be found in the tourist office.) Next to Alpha Bank, **Glaros Car Rental** has cars from €24 a day. (☎23 637. Open 9am-2pm.)

🛈 PRACTICAL INFORMATION. The town's main pier is marked by a copper sculpture of Icarus plummeting to the ground. Coming off the ferry, walk up the pier onto the main waterfront road, then turn right to reach the town plateia, which is the center for all tourist services and most of the town's daily life. The first white building on the left walking into the plateia houses the **tourist office,** where free maps and island guides are available, as well as any bus and ferry schedules that exist. (☎24 047. Open 9am-2pm and 5-9pm.) Given the simple road network, some travelers are able to find their way back by hitchhiking should they find themselves stranded, although Let's Go does not recommend hitchhiking. On the waterfront at the far end from the ferry docks, **Alpha Bank** has **currency exchange** and a **24hr. ATM,** and cashes travelers checks with no fee. (☎22 264. Open M-Th 8am-2:30pm, F 8am-2pm.) Up the road inland from the plateia, **ATE Bank** has a **24hr. ATM.** (☎22 987. Open M-Th 8am-2:30pm, F 8am-2pm.) The **police** (☎22 222), up the stairs to the left of Alpha Bank, are open 24hr. One block inland on the side street next to Cafe Remezzo, you'll find the **pharmacy** (☎22 212. Open 9am-1pm.) The local **hospital** (☎32 330) is two streets inland from the pier. About 100m up the street are the **OTE** (☎22 499; open M-F 7:30am-3pm) and the **post office** (☎22 413; open M-F 7:30am-2pm). **Postal Code:** 83300.

🏠🍴 ACCOMMODATIONS AND FOOD. Ikaria does not have a large selection of **domatia.** A few are clustered by the waterfront and above Alpha Bank. Inquire at the tourist office if you are having trouble finding a room. To reach 🏠**Akti Hotel ❷,** climb the stairs on the right side of Alpha Bank and take your first right. Guests often sit on the cliffside patio, gazing at the harbor and chatting until late. The Greek-American owner Marsha knows the island inside-out and can direct you to the hot springs, nearby sandy beaches, and the best places to stop for a drink. Remodeled rooms come with air-conditioning, TV, fan, hair dryer, well-appointed bath, Wi-Fi, and a door leading onto the patio. (☎23 905; www.pensionakti.gr. Singles €20-25; doubles €25-50.) Next to Akti Pension is 🏠**Hotel O'Karras ❷,** where airy, well-decorated rooms provide a refuge from the sun. Small rooms come with bath and balcony directly overhanging the main row of cafes. (☎22 494. Doubles €25.) **Pension Ikaria ❸,** one block inland from the plateia in the same building as Ston Tsouri, has tasteful rooms. The faux-candle lights and old-school pulse phones make for added charm, as do the fridge, TV, fan, bath, and balcony overlooking the cafes. (☎22 108. Doubles €30.)

For a waterfront dotted with several bakeries and cafes, Agios Kirykos suffers from a lack of tavernas that serve full meals. Head inland toward the post office and **Klimataria ❷** will be on the right. The goat with potatoes (€7) is one of several Greek dishes that give the restaurant its favored reputation among locals. (☎22 686. Entrees €5-7. Open daily 10am-midnight.) **Ston Tsouri ❷** (Στον Τσουρη), in the plateia, has an *Odyssey*-length menu but rotates what's available daily. Local cheeses and Ikarian wines make watching the stunning sunsets from the tables a multi-sensory experience. (☎22 473. Greek entrees €7-8. Open daily noon-late.)

🏖️🎶 BEACHES AND NIGHTLIFE. Incredible beaches sprinkled with boulders and white pebbles unfold between the coastal road and the glassy sea. There are two natural **hot springs** in the ocean. You can bathe in the spring water at **Therma** (Θέρμα), 2km north of Agios Kirykos on the way to the airport. The green bus runs between the two beaches approximately every hour from 9am-2pm and 5-9pm (€1.20). You also can walk down the path by the police station. Unlike Agios Kirykos, Therma has a number of bathhouses where spring water is piped into private stalls. The water is radioactive and is used to treat ailments from rheumatism to neurological difficulties. The best is on the far right of the beach when facing the ocean and is open 8-10am and 5-8pm. Where the bus lets out, another bathhouse has several stalls but runs €4 for a stay. (Open 6-11:30am.) For those without health problems, the natural hot spring off the beach across the street is free and always open. Farther north, by the airport, the small town of **Faros** offers a number of unremarkable but pleasant beaches. Because of the fickle buses, you may need a taxi from Agios Kirykos.

All the town's nightlife is within a 20min. walk along the coastal road heading left from the ferry dock, facing inland. Ikaria's little light pollution leaves the stars strikingly visible, setting the scene for a lovely nighttime stroll above the sea. By 2am young locals gather at **5 Minutes Til** (Παρα Πεντε) for some liquid courage and DJ-spun dance hits to get them revved up for the evening. Its location near the docks and periodic free shots make it a favorite. (Mixed drinks €5-7. Open daily 5pm-late.) The next stop, **■Camelot Club,** mixes it up Medieval style as techno beats fill the castle-themed club. Stone archways and monstrous wooden chandeliers overhang dancers that would put Lancelot and Guinevere to shame. In the winter it becomes a disco. (☎24 065. Open 6pm-late.) Pressing on up the road, **Wha Wha's** classic rock tunes spill over the three open-air terraces leading down to the beach. (Drinks €2-5. Open 11pm-late.)

EVDILOS Εύδηλος ☎22750

The winding, mountainous road to Evdilos passes craggy rock faces under soaring windmills and skirts village-dotted valleys on its way to the northern coast. Side roads branch off to stretches of sandy beach and up into mountaintop villages, but the road sees little traffic; not many islanders travel between the two ports. The red-roofed houses of Evdilos circle the serene stretch of pebbled harbor, where locals gather in waterfront cafes or take a swim in the crystalline waters. Because the town receives hydrofoils and has a central location, it serves as a convenient base to explore the many beaches and villages on the northern face of the island.

🖻🔃 TRANSPORTATION AND PRACTICAL INFORMATION. Buses are difficult to catch and service is spotty, but regular transport to Armenistis is supposed to exist. **Taxis** are a pricier but far more reliable option; call an hour in advance, as cabs are in Agios Kirykos. (☎69726 40 154. To Agios Kirykos €27; Armenistis €9.)

The waterfront curves up from Alpha Bank, past the lower square, and around to a number of travel agencies on the far side of the docks. A stone pathway leads up and to the right when facing inland, heading 150m to the upper plateia where a few more tavernas and pensions cluster. The English-speaking staff at **Nas** (☎31 947), on the far right side of the waterfront facing inland, offers ferry and air tickets, accommodations booking, tours, and **currency exchange.** There is a **24hr. ATM** at the end of the harbor, outside **Alpha Bank.** (Open M-Th 8am-2:30pm, F 8am-2pm.) Take the stairs to the right of Nas Travel to reach the **pharmacy** (☎31 394). Follow the road between Nefko and Art Cafe toward Kampos to find the **police** (☎31 222). In an **emergency,** call the **health center** (☎33 030). The **post office** is just past the police on the same road. (☎31 225. Open M-F 7:30am-1:30pm.) **Postal Code:** 83302.

🖪🗒 ACCOMMODATIONS AND FOOD. With few options for domatia in the area, consider booking in advance or ask at the travel agencies. Head up the street that passes between Nefko and Art Cafe to reach **Spanos ❷**, where bright rooms come with TV, fan, bath, and access to the balcony. Inquire in the store across the street. (☎69321 53 668. Rooms €20-25.) Soaring ceilings and private balconies jutting out over the waves make the rooms at **Apostolos Stenos's Rooms to Rent ❸** a lovely spot to watch the sunset. Rooms come with bath and shared kitchen and outdoor terrace downstairs. From the upper plateia, veer to the right around the large building on the square. Follow the road with white painted circles on it for 20m; the pension is on the right just before the road comes to the edge of the coast. (☎31 365. Singles €30-35; doubles €30-40. Open June-Aug.)

The usual assortment of small tavernas and *kafeneia* fills the plateia. On the corner of the plateia, **To Nefko ❷** is a favorite among locals for *mezedes*, such as the eggplant or chicken salads (€3.50) served on tables in the main square. (☎33 027. Entrees €5-6. Open Sept.-July 7:30pm-late, Aug. 1pm.-late.) The staff at **Stou Tsakoniti ❷**, in the old stone building near the pizza shop, serves a variety of *mezedes* and homemade yogurts at reasonable prices. (Open 6am-late.) On the waterfront and to the right facing inland, **To Koralli ❷** has a variety of seafood, including the octopus with potatoes (€7) and Greek dishes. (☎31 924. Entrees €6.50-9.) **Ta Kimata ❶**, on the waterfront, caters to late-night ferry arrivals with an array of sweets (€1.50), and the only ice cream in town. (☎31 952. Open 24hr.)

The waterfront nightlife centers around the two bars in town. Locals gather in the modern lounge of **Art Cafe** to sip coffee (€2) and drinks (€5). A rowdier crowd gathers around the nightly DJ at **Sto Peripou** to dance to the international music as late as the landlord allows. (☎31 974. Mixed drinks €4-5. Sangria €4.)

▶ **DAYTRIPS FROM EVDILOS.** One of the most popular resorts in Ikaria, **Armenistis** (Αρμενιστής), 15km west of Evdilos, boasts the beaches of **Livadi** and **Mesachti** to the west, along with a few restaurants and bars. Though it is a challenge to reach, Armenistis has more tourist facilities than Evdilos and is close to some of the best beaches and hiking routes on the island. Idle stone fountains hidden under the canopy of shady green leaves mark the entry to the town of **Christos Rachis** (Χριστός Ράχες), a classic traditional Ikarian village (7km south of Armenistis). To avoid the midday glare, the residents have adopted a strange nocturnal schedule; the best time to visit is between 11pm and dawn, when locals run their errands. Ikaria's best-organized hiking trails originate from here and are marked by little orange footprints. Pick up the very handy *Round of Rahes on Foot* (€4.50) at any local supermarket. Trails lead to the region's major beaches as well as several monasteries and hidden sights accessible only by foot.

The asphalt ends 5km west of Armenistis, leaving a dirt road that runs to **Nas,** one of the Aegean's undiscovered treasures. The sandy beach, flanked by huge rock walls, mediates between an aggressive sea and a serene river, ending in a freshwater pool. A 25min. hike south takes you to the small waterfall that forms its beginning. To reach the falls, head inland past the pool. The hike is best accomplished by hugging the river, so you may get your feet wet. Toward the end of the walk, you will see a cavernous rock enclosure on top of the eastern ledge, a favorite haunt for local goats. The waterfall is just a few minutes past this point.

CHIOS Χίος

Radiating from the centrally located glitz of Chios Town, tree-speckled hills harbor the natural charms and wonders of the island. Traditional villages and sandy shores in the north give way to orange and lemon orchards that encircle Genoese mansions in the south. The local economy hinges on the production of mastic, an evergreen resin used since antiquity in medicines, chewing gum, and cosmetics. Trails lead through mastic groves and fields of native tulips, while the island's caves, medieval villages, and monasteries can be discovered by bus or car. Though visitors descend en masse, the island retains an effortless character in which traditional artistry and natural wonders are allowed to resonate in all their splendor.

CHIOS TOWN ☎ 22710

Chios's port town has an electric pulse that doesn't pause for the wayward tourist. The waterfront showcases hip cafes where trendy young locals lounge, talking and drinking frappés all afternoon. Inland, quiet shop-lined streets are dotted with museums and shops. Farther north, the quiet residential section slumbers under the shadow of the castle, disturbed only by the occasional blare of a moped.

▊ TRANSPORTATION

Flights: Olympic Airways has flights to: **Athens** (1hr., 2-5 per day, €65-83); **Limnos** (1¾hr., 2 per week, €36); **Mytilini, Lesvos** (30min., 2 per week, €40); **Rhodes** (1¾hr., 2 per week, €41); **Samos** (35min., €28); **Thessaloniki** (1-2hr., 4 per week, €60). **Aegean Air** also flies to Athens (1hr., 2 per day, €50-84); contact Travel Shop (☎20 160) for rates and schedules.

Ferries: Go to: **Agios Kirykos, Ikaria** (6hr., every Tu, €12); **Alexandroupoli** (12½hr., 1 per week, €13.50); **Çesme, Turkey** (45min., daily, round-trip €30); **Kavala** (14½hr., 2 per week, €35); **Lesvos** (3hr., 2 per day, €14); **Limnos** (9½hr., 2 per week, €22); **Piraeus** (9hr., 2 per day, €26-33); **Samos** (3½hr., 3 per week, €13); **Thessaloniki** (19hr., every Th, €31). Citizens of Australia, Canada, Ireland, the UK, and the US will have to buy a visa (US$20) if staying more than 1 day in Turkey.

High-speed Ferries: To: **Lesvos** (1½hr., daily, €19) and **Piraeus** (5hr., daily, €33).

Excursion Boats: Daily trips leave from Chios to **Çesme** and **Izmir, Turkey** (€30-40 round-trip, plus €10 Turkish port tax); ask at Sunrise Tours or **Kanaris Tours** (☎42 490). Open daily 6am-10pm. Kanaris offers daily excursions to Inousses Island (€20).

Buses: Service is split between local blue buses and long-distance green buses; both stations are between the harbor and the Municipal Gardens.

Blue bus station (☎22 079), just up from the plateia on Dimokratias. Buses travel short distances from Chios Town. Routes connect **Karfas, Kontari, Megas Limionas, Thimiana,** and smaller towns along the way (14 per day 6:35am-8:30pm, from €1.15). Tickets available at the station, or on board for a small fee. Reduced service Sa-Su.

Green bus station (☎27 507), on the waterfront near the ferry docks. Open 24hr. Offers bathrooms, lockers, bus tickets, and is a popular backgammon-player hangout. Tickets can be bought at the station or onboard to: **Agia Fotia Beach** (5 per day); **Armolia** (5 per day); **Emporios** (3 per day); **Kalamoti** (5 per day); **Kardamila** (6 per day); **Kataraktis** (6 per day); **Komi** (4 per day);

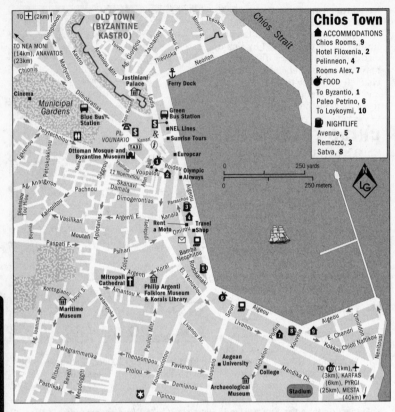

Chios Town

▲ ACCOMMODATIONS
Chios Rooms, 9
Hotel Filoxenia, 2
Pelinneon, 4
Rooms Alex, 7
🍴 FOOD
To Byzantio, 1
Paleo Petrino, 6
To Loykoymi, 10
🌙 NIGHTLIFE
Avenue, 5
Remezzo, 3
Satva, 8

Lagada (6 per day); **Lithi** (3 per day); **Mesta** (5 per day); **Nagos** (2 per day); **Nenita** (7 per day); **Pyrgi** (7 per day); **Volissos** (3 per day M, W, and F). Tickets from €1.70.

Taxis: ☎69756 07 513. Gather 24hr. across Pl. Vounakio from the Municipal Gardens. To: Emporios Beach (€27), Karfas (€6.5), Mesta (€27), and Nea Moni (€12-15). €1-2 surcharge after midnight.

Rental: Europcar (☎21 666), 1 block south of Sunrise Tours on the waterfront. Cars €30 per day. Open daily 8am-1pm and 4-10pm. **Rent a Moto** (☎25 113), just off the waterfront. Scooters €14-20. Open daily 7am-10pm. AmEx/V.

✳🛈 ORIENTATION AND PRACTICAL INFORMATION

Facing inland from the ferry docks, a right on **Kanari** takes you past the tourist office to **Plateia Vounakio,** the social center of town. Many cafes and services, including taxi and bus stands, can be found right before reaching the **Municipal Gardens.** Left of Vounakio lies **Aplotarias,** the market street, with several grocery stores and bakeries. Between the ferry dock and the Municipal Gardens, fortress walls hug the predominantly residential **Old Town.**

Tourist Office: Kanari 18 (☎44 344). Walk toward the plateia on Kanari, and look for the "i" sign on your left. English-speaking staff has maps, brochures, and bus, ferry, and airplane schedules as well as advice on museum and hiking routes. Open May-Sept. M-F 7:30am-3pm and 6:30-9:30pm, Sa-Su 10am-1pm; Oct.-Apr. M-F 7:30am-2pm. **Sunrise Tours,** Kanari 28 (☎93 586), just off the waterfront on Kanari. Books air tickets, boat tickets, excursions to Turkey, accommodations, and bus tours around the island (€15-20). Open M-Sa 9am-10pm. AmEx/MC/V. **Travel Shop,** Aigeou 56 (☎20 160), on the middle of the waterfront under the conspicuous Olympic Airways sign. Offers air and ferry tickets. Open daily 8:30am-8:30pm. MC/V. **NEL Lines,** Aigeou 16 (☎23 971), near where Kanari meets the waterfront road. Open daily 8am-10pm.

Bank: National Bank, Kanari 8 (☎22 831), next to the OTE in the plateia. **Exchanges currency,** has a **24hr. ATM.** Open M-Th 8am-2:30pm, F 8am-2pm.

Pharmacy: Several are near Pl. Vounakio. One is on Kanari across from the Tourist Office. ☎23 131. Open M and W 8am-2pm, Tu and Th-F 8am-2pm and 5:15-8:30pm.

Hospital: El. Venizelou 2 (☎44 306, first aid station 44 302). 3km north of Chios before Vrondados.

Telephones: OTE, Tzon Kenety 1 (☎28 199), up the block from the tourist office. Open M-F 7:30am-3pm.

Internet access: A number of cafes with fast connections can be found on the waterfront road. **Fantasy,** Aigeou 60 (☎23 896). €2 per hr., min. €1. Open daily 10am-2am. **In Spot,** farther south on the waterfront, has 24hr. access. €2.40 per hr.

Tourist Police: ☎81 539. On Kountouriotou.

Post Office: 2 Omirou (☎25 668). On the corner of Omirou and Rodokanaki, 1 block inland. Offers Western Union. Open M-F 7:30am-2pm. **Postal Code:** 82100.

ACCOMMODATIONS

Most accommodations are on the far end of the waterfront from the ferry dock. In high season, a tourist agency can help you find a room, but consider heading to nearby **Karfas** if Chios Town gets too crowded. Artful decor and excellent harbor views make ▨ **Chios Rooms ❷,** Aigeou 110, a great place to stay. The converted mansion boasts rooms with TV and narrow, shared bathrooms. The New Zealand-born owner can give you advice about the island and transportation. (☎20 198; www.chiosrooms.gr. Singles €25; doubles €35, with bath €40; triples with bath €45.) One block behind Satva, **Rooms Alex ❸,** Livanou 29, has six small rooms with fridge, air-conditioning, TV, and bath, that connect to a rooftop garden. Owner Alex can give you info on transportation and accommodations anywhere on the island. (☎26 054. Doubles €30.) At **Hotel Filoxenia ❹,** Voupalou 8, just off the waterfront on Voupalou, guests are just steps away from both bus stations, the main shopping streets, the municipal gardens, and the waterfront. Rooms come with air-conditioning, fridge, bath, and balcony. (☎22 813. Singles €38; doubles €50.) **Pelinneon ❹,** Aigeou 54, is on the water where Paraschou goes inland. Rooms come with air-conditioning, TV, fridge, bath, and views of nothing but sky and water. The location couldn't be better, but it means that the rooms can get noisy. Inquire at Rent a Car George Psoras. (☎43 755. Doubles €50.)

FOOD

Awash with cafes and gyro stands, Chios comes up short on the taverna scene. Several can be found around **Pl. Vounakio** and far down the left side of the waterfront when facing inland. *Ouzeri* **Paleo Petrino ❷,** Aigeou 80, on the waterfront between Goody's and Il Fungo, serves traditional dishes such as the eggplant dip (€3.90) and has a large selection of local ouzos. The stone facade adds a high-class touch to the outdoor tables. (☎29 797. Entrees €4.50-6.50. Open daily noon-2am.)

Escape the waterfront's fashion parade at **To Byzantio ❶**, 9 Afon Ralli, around the corner from the mosque. Diners choose their meals from the counter at this friendly cafe. Homemade spicy vinegar sits on each table, ready to add a potent kick. (☎41 035. Most entrees around €5. Open M-Sa 7am-11pm.) About a 15min. walk from the city center, **To Loykoymi ❷** has quiet garden seating and grilled platters. Facing inland, walk along the waterfront to the far left, past the statue, staying with the road as it curves. (☎24 959. Entrees €4.50-7.50. Open daily 9pm-late.)

👁 SIGHTS

Chios Town has several museums, with the more worthwhile exhibits located in the southern part of town. The best collection resides at the sprawling, 1200 sq. m ▧ **Archaeological Museum** where an extensive array of Neolithic, Archaic, and Classical artifacts have detailed English placards. Don't miss the display of golden lily-form wreaths. (☎44 239. Open Sept.-June Tu-Su 8:30am-2:45pm; July-Aug. daily 8am-7:30pm. €2, students €1, EU students free.) Founded by shipping enthusiasts, the reconverted mansion of the **Chios Maritime Museum** has a wealth of intricate models and shipping artifacts. Borrow one of the English-language guides, where interesting tidbits are mixed with technical jargon for each display. Models range from the *U.S.S. Constitution* to Chinese trading vessels. Be sure to catch the WWII memorial next to the museum. (☎44 140; www.nauticalmuseum.com. Open M-Sa 10am-2pm. Free.) The **Philip Argenti Folklore Museum,** Korai 3, within the **Korais Library,** next to the Mitropoli cathedral, examines the phenomenal Chian embroidery and clothing through traditionally dressed mannequins. Also on display are a number of European-style portraits of the Argenti family from the 18th century onward, complete with the family pedigree. (☎44 246; www.chiosnet.gr/koraes. Open M-Th 8am-2pm, F 8am-2pm and 5-7:30pm, Sa 8am-noon. €2, students free.) To the right facing inland at Pl. Vounakio, follow Tzon Kenenti toward the waterfront to enter the **Byzantine kastro,** reconstructed by the Genoese. Enclosing the empty, winding streets of the Old Town, the walls make the neighborhood itself seem like a museum. The castle also houses the tiny **Justiniani Museum,** where a dozen 14th-century frescoed wall paintings of various prophets and a golden cut out of the archangel Michael are kept. (☎22 819. Open Tu-Su 8:30am-3pm. €2, students free.) The mid-19th-century **Ottoman Mosque,** in Pl. Vounakio across from the gardens, houses the paltry collection of the **Byzantine Museum of Chios;** both mosque and museum are closed indefinitely for renovations.

In July and August, the Prefecture of Chios finances **free guided tours** of the island's monuments. Visitors must provide their own transportation to the various sites, where a guide will wait at a set meeting point. (Open M-F, tours start 10am and noon). For more information, contact the tourist office or **Ena Chios Development Corp** (☎44 830; www.enachios.gr).

🎵 📷 ENTERTAINMENT AND NIGHTLIFE

From mid-July through mid-September the **open-air cinema** in the public gardens shows nightly movies. The tourist office carries a booklet with the season's schedule; posters for that week's movies are also on display outside the cinema. Showings are at 7 and 9pm, and tickets (€5) can be bought at the cinema.

Waterfront bars overflow with chic clientele by 10pm and packs of wandering trendsters take over the sidewalks later on. Chios's scene revolves around the bars and clubs on the water. Head to the crowds and Heineken umbrellas of **Remezzo,** 52 Aigeou, where the young and beautiful don their tightest clothing and coolest attitude in the standing-room only interior. (☎42 848. Beer €3.50. Mixed drinks €6. Open daily 8am-3:30am.) Puff on a hookah on one of the outdoor couches at the orientally themed **Satva,** Aigeou 110, across from Chios Rooms. (☎21 290. Mixed drinks €6-8. Hookah €10 for the evening, tobacco €5. Open daily 8am-4am.) Down the waterfront from the ferry dock, red lights signal go at the street-themed **Avenue,** Aigeou 70. (☎24 907. Drinks €5-6. Open daily 8am-3:30am or later.) For billiards (€8 per hr.) and a beer, head to **Fantasy,** which also has Internet.

▣ DAYTRIPS FROM CHIOS TOWN

▨ MESTA Μεστά
Green buses run from Chios Town to Mesta M-F 5 times per day (€3.10).

One of the most fascinating villages in southern Chios, Mesta got its name from the Greek word *mesto*, meaning "a very well-thought-out idea." The town was founded in 1038, when representatives from four neighboring towns put their heads together to solve the perennial pirate problem. Their solution was to build a town where the houses were connected to one another, forming a fortification wall like that of a castle. Each house had a ladder leading to the roof where residents could flee should their initial line of defense fail, as well as an incomplete staircase leading down from the roof, from which residents could ward off their would-be raiders. In dire situations, the residents could run along the rooftops to the central tower, now incorporated into the church. Today, Mesta looks almost exactly as it might have during the Byzantine era; due to archaeological decree, all new houses must be built in the original style with delightful stonework, rounded arches, and painted wooden doors. It's easy to get lost in the narrow, cobbled streets, but most wind up back at the central plateia, the nucleus of village life and home to the town's two tavernas. Pick your meal from that day's fresh selection at **Mesaionas Cafe,** which also offers intriguing Chian cheeses (€2.50-5) and sour cherry juices for €1.60. (☎76 050. Open daily 6am-late. MC/V.)

While its quaint Byzantine design is an attraction in itself, Mesta houses two beautiful **churches** that are well worth a look. In the main plateia, **The Great Taxiarchi,** once termed "The Manger," was constructed 160 years ago and is the third-largest church in Greece. The impressive pale blue interior is filled with silver votives and chandeliers, all gifts from the devoted. From there, church keeper Georgina gladly will take you to the **Older Taxiarchi.** Dating from 1412, this church contains an enormous walnut *iconostasis,* carved over the course of 35 years in the early 18th century. Repaired in 1833 after a fire, the altar retains its glory; the church keeper can narrate the Biblical scenes depicted in the intricate carvings as well as the symbolism of its many features. (☎76 044. Great Taxiarchi open daily 11am-3pm and 4-6pm. Older Taxiarchi open by request. Modest dress required.)

From Mesta, a 40min. hike along the well-marked trail leads to the similarly walled town of **Olympi** and makes for a pleasant evening stroll.

▨ PYRGI Πυργί
Take the Pyrgi bus from Chios (7 per day, €2.40). Pyrgi and Mesta are on the same route; ask at the Chios bus station for info on how to time your visits to catch the bus en route.

The villages in the southern half of the island, called Mastichohoria, cultivate the lentisk trees that produce Chios's famous resin. High in the hills, 25km from Chios Town, the village of Pyrgi greets visitors with its buildings' intricate black-and-white geometric facades. In the afternoon, old men congregate in the central plateia by the church to gossip over ouzo; their wives pass the time chatting in the rustic narrow alleyways that separate their tiny homes. Pyrgi is also home to the 12th-century **Agioi Apostoloi** church, a replica of the Nea Moni, in a small alley off the plateia. Thirteenth-century frescoes cover the interior of the church.

NORTHEAST AEGEAN

NEA MONI Νέα Μόνι AND ANAVATOS Ανάβατος

ENA guides lead free tours from the entrance of the monastery every Th at 10am and noon. A taxi ride will cost €12-15.

On the eastern half of the island, several sites recall the Ottoman Turks' invasion of the island in 1822. Pine-covered mountains 16km west of Chios Town cradle **Nea Moni** (New Monastery). Built in the 11th century, the monastery was inspired by the appearance of an icon of the Virgin Mary, and is one of the world's most important Byzantine monuments. Though an 1881 earthquake destroyed much of the complex, most structures have been restored. The 11th-century floor mosaics have been indefinitely covered to prevent further erosion. The artists who created them were also responsible for those of Hagia Sophia in Istanbul. A few meters before the entrance to the complex, an arched crypt contains the grisly skulls and bones of monks and villagers massacred by the Turks. The skeletons are the remains of the 600 priests and 3500 women and children who sought refuge from the attacks. An adjoining chapel just inside the entrance houses a **memorial** to the tragedy. An on-site **museum** displays church garments and religious items. Unfortunately, the church is undergoing renovations so check with the tourist office for the current status. (Open Nov.-Mar. daily 10am-6pm. €2, Su free.)

For a haunting experience, head to **Anavatos,** an abandoned village built into the hillside, 15km west of Nea Moni. The village's women and children threw themselves from these cliffs in resistance to the Turkish invasion; today, the ruins, the pines below, and a statuette of an angel pay tribute to their sacrifice. A walk through the fortifications provides amazing views of the hills. The church near the right of the site's entrance has a folk-art rendition of the tragic event.

NORTHERN CHIOS

Vrondados and Daskalopetra are 9km accessible by blue buses from Pl. Vournakio in Chios Town.

The pleasant shores of **Vrondados** and **Daskalopetra** are 9km north of Chios Town. A 2min. walk inland from the shore of Daskalopetra takes you to the **Sanctuary of Cybele.** Statues dating from the site's glory days are now in the Archaeological Museum in Chios Town, but you still can see the **Stone of Homer,** where the poet is rumored to have held lectures. A circle of stone seats surrounds the rock, which affords a magnificent view of the sea. After Daskalopetra, the main roads wind northwest along the coast past Marmaron to **Nagos,** a rocky beach (perhaps once a popular spot to go to when cutting Homer's class). High in the hills near the center of the island, the village of **Volissos** is crowned by a Byzantine fort.

SOUTHERN CHIOS ☎ 22710

Karfas, 7km south of Chios Town, is home to the sandiest, most tourist-covered beach on the island. Many take up temporary residence here, close to both the beach and Chios Town's amenities. Karfas's main beach offers water sports and activities. Farther south, beige cliffs collide against the black stones and tranquil blue water at spectacularly beautiful ⬛ **Emporios Beach,** on the island's southern tip. One part of the beach is up the only road to the right when facing the water. A smaller, less crowded shore is up the stairs to the right from the first beach. When you've had enough sunshine, descend into the **Cave of Olympi** and spelunk to your heart's content. Though known for centuries, the cave only was opened in 1985. Its Jurassic-era stalagmites and stalactites are still growing, thanks to the mineral-rich waters that continue to drip in the interior. (Open Tu-Su 10am-8pm. Free.) The cave is inaccessible by public bus. If you have private transportation, take the main road from Olympi southwest toward the coast. On Thursdays at 9am, Kanaris Tours runs a bus tour (€20) that visits Armolia, Pyrgi, the Cave of Olympi, Mesta, and Emporios Beach. One kilometer southwest of the cave, the beach of **Agia Dynami** is praised by locals for its beautiful sunsets.

Though the south is dominated by pricey beachfront resorts, a few economical options do exist. Facing the water from the bus stand, follow the road that leads uphill to the right from the waterfront about 500m to ■ **Markos's Place ❷**. Small, whitewashed rooms surround communal terraces on the relaxed, 8000 sq. m compound that is a regular host to painting and yoga conferences. Friendly Markos prepares breakfast buffets when there is sufficient demand. (☎31 990. Breakfast €6.50. Singles €25; doubles €35. Min. 2-night stay.) Follow the inland road from the bus stop as it curves to the right and runs parallel to the waterfront to find **Ocean Blue Rooms ❸**. Rooms with air-conditioning, TV, bath, and balcony provide shady refuge from the sun. (☎33 014. Doubles €30.) Up the inland road from the bus stop and down the left fork, **Family Studios ❹** has spacious, white-on-white rooms with bath, fridge, and kitchenette. (☎31 125. Doubles €40.)

The staff at the **tourist office,** across the street from the bus stop, keeps a list of accommodations in town and can help you find a room. Blue **buses** run from Pl. Vournakio in Chios Town (14 per day, 6:35am-8:30pm, €1.15).

LESVOS Λέσβος

Ouzeria, olive groves, and mountain roads harmonize with the sandy stretches and petrified trunks on Lesvos in an irresistible siren song. Lesvos defies categorization, offering a taste of everything smaller islands have to offer, from nightlife and a rich collection of museums to hiking and castle-crowned cities. Lesvos's cultural riches match those of its terrain: countless great minds have called this island home, including 7th-century BC poet Sappho and artist Theophilos Hadzimichali. Lesvos remains a major producer of ouzo and olive oil, with distilleries dotting the countryside. The island almost lost its workforce in a 428 BC threat from the Athenian assembly to execute the island's adult male population. Fortunately, that threat was unfulfilled and Lesvos continues to enchant visitors with its varied landscapes, unique town atmospheres, and extensive cultural offerings.

NORTHEAST AEGEAN

MYTILINI Μυτιλήνη ☎ 22510

Each morning, the capital's harbor yawns into a modern, working city marked by glitzy shops, local markets, and waterfront *kafeneia*. The ruined castle looks on from the peninsula to the north, once an islet separated by the channel Euripos. Most visitors to Mytilini come on business or en route to the rest of Lesvos, leaving the city as a playground for trendy students. The commercial beat only goes so far, though, and exploration farther inland and north reveals a much calmer Mytilini.

▐ TRANSPORTATION

Flights: The **airport** (☎ 61 590) is 6km south of Mytilini. Take a green bus from the intercity bus station, or a taxi (€5-6). **Olympic Airways,** Kavetsou 44 (☎ 28 659; open 8am-3pm), has another office at the airport, as does **Aegean Airlines** (☎ 61 120). Tickets for both Olympic and Aegean flights can be purchased at almost any travel agency in town. To: **Athens** (1hr., 6 per day 8am-6:10pm, €50-150); **Chios** (25min., 2 per week, €31); **Limnos** (35min., 5 per week, €41); **Rhodes** (1hr., 5 per week, €58); **Samos** (45min., 2 per week, €41); **Thessaloniki** (daily, €87-98).

Ferries: To: Chios (3hr., daily, €14); Kavala (11hr., 2 per week, €30); Limnos (5hr., 3 per week, €17); Piraeus (12hr., daily, €35-41); Thessaloniki (13hr., 1 per week, €35).

Excursion Boats: Take daytrips to **Ayvalik, Turkey** (1½hr., daily, €35) and **Dikeli, Turkey** (3 per week 8:30am, €20).

Intercity Buses: Intercity bus station (☎ 22570 28 873), at the corner of Ilia Iliou and Smyrnis. Buses crisscross the island with Mytilini as the home base. Schedules for the island's buses are available here and at most information or tourist agencies throughout Lesvos. Buses go to: **Agiassos** (25min., 4 per day); **Eressos** (2 per day); **Gera** (7 per day) via **Kalloni; Mandamados** (1hr., 4 per day); **Molyvos** (2hr., 5 per day, €5) via **Kalloni** and **Petra; Plomari** (30min., 5 per day, €3.10); **Polichnitos** (1½hr., 3-4 per day) via **Vatera; Sigri** (3½hr., 1 per day) via **Kalloni.** Buses run July-Aug. 9am-7pm; Sept.-June 9am-3:30pm. Reduced service Sa-Su. €2-7, depending on distance.

Local Buses: ☎ 22570 28 873, in Sappho Sq. on the waterfront. Pick up a schedule from the knowledgeable staff in the kiosk. To: **Agia Marina** (45min., every hr. 6:50am-8:40pm) via **Varia** (€1.15), **Agios Rafael** (every 30min. 6am-9:40pm, €1.15) via **Thermi** (€1), and the **airport** (8 per day, 7:10am-7pm).

Taxis: ☎ 23 500. Line up behind the tourist office and on the corner of Ermou and Vournazon. To: airport (€8), Molyvos (€45), Varia (€3.50), and Vatera (€45).

Rentals: Payless (☎ 81 100), in Sappho Sq. Cars €35-45. Open daily 7am-10pm.

▐ ▌ ORIENTATION AND PRACTICAL INFORMATION

Mytilini's harbor opens to the south, and cafes, bars, and hotels line the waterfront street **Pavlou Koundourioti.** On the center of the waterfront, **Sappho Square** is home to many tourist amenities and serves as the central day and nighttime hangout. The **old market** stretches along **Ermou,** home to pharmacies, boutiques, and bakeries. Ermou becomes **Kavetsou** at its southern end, where it intersects **Vournazon** one block inland on the harbor's western side.

Tourist Office: (☎ 28 812), in Sappho Sq. The friendly staff offers free maps, info about the island, accommodations advice, updated listings for nearby concerts and festivals; also showcases an amusing collection of mannequins dressed in traditional Lesvian gear. Open M-F 7:30am-3pm.

Budget Travel: ▨ **Zoumboulis Travel** (☎ 37 755; www.zoumboulistours.gr.), on the right side of the waterfront facing inland. The friendly staff has flight, ferry, and excursion tick-

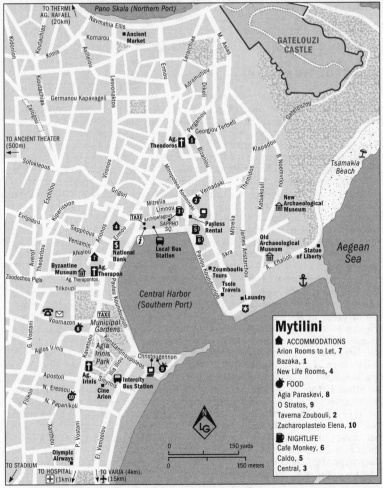

ets, plans trips to Turkey, and serves as a de facto tourist office with maps and advice on the island. Open daily 7am-10pm. **Tsolos Travel** (☎48 030), farther down on the waterfront. Offers flight and ferry tickets and car rental. Open M-F 8am-9pm, Sa 8am-2pm and 5-9pm, Su 9am-2pm and 5-9pm. AmEx/MC/V.

Bank: National Bank, 28 Kounodourioti, on the left side of the harbor facing inland. Has a **24hr. ATM.** Open M-Th 8am-2:30pm, F 8am-2pm.

Laundromat: ☎27 065. On Aristarchou by the ferry docks. Wash and dry €10. Open M and W 8am-2pm; Tu and Th-F 8am-2pm and 5:30-8pm.

Tourist Police: ☎22 776. Across the street from the laundromat.

Hospital: ☎57 700, southwest of town on P. Vostani and Navmachias Elis. 24hr. **Ambulance** ☎166.

Telephones: OTE, Vournazon 8 (☎27 399). Open M-F 8am-8:30pm.

Internet Access: Sponda (☎41 007), 1 block behind the waterfront on the right side of the harbor facing inland. €1.80 per hr. Billiards €7 per hr. **InSpot** (☎45 760), across the harbor. €2.40 per hr. Open 24hr.

Post Office: 2 Vournazon (☎28 823). Open M-F 7:30am-2pm. **Postal Code:** 81100.

ACCOMMODATIONS

The hotels on the waterfront are elegant but pricey; head to Ermou to find plentiful **domatia.** If you are met at the ferry, be sure to negotiate, and keep in mind that longer stays often result in lower rates. Doubles run €30-35 before July 15 and €35-55 in late summer. **Bazaka ❸**, around the corner from Agia Theodoros, has clean rooms with TV, fridge, bath, and a balcony terrace. The inland location allows some relief from buzzing mopeds, while it is still within easy walking distance from both the castle and nightlife scene. (☎26 360. Doubles €35. 2-night min.) One block north of Agios Therapon, gold-toned walls frame beautiful, hand-painted murals at **Arion Rooms to Let ❹**, on Alkaiou and Arionos 4. Small rooms with lustrous hardwood floors have TV, fridge, and bath. (☎42 650. Doubles €40.) **New Life Rooms ❸**, in a beautiful Art Nouveau building on Ermou, has a handful of simple rooms with fridge and bath. (☎23 400. Singles €30-35; doubles €40-50.)

FOOD

From Ermou, head right on Mitropoleos Komninaki and then left on Vernardaki to find ▧**Taverna Zoubouli ❷**, Vernardaki 2. At Zoubouli, one of the oldest tavernas in Mytilini, canaries and hookahs surround the outdoor tables. The list of house specials like the *tabakas* (veal stewed with tomato, feta, and yogurt; €5.50) and the pork stuffed with orange and cheese makes navigating the large menu easier. Travelers may enjoy one of the 25 available flavors of tobacco. (☎21 251. Entrees €4.50-7. Hookah €5 per hr. Open daily noon-2am.) Walking seaward on the southwestern quay brings you to Mytilini's best fish tavernas. Octopi hang to dry in front of tables right by the water at **O Stratos ❷**, which offers an ocean's worth of fish in a large, shaded seating area. (☎21 739. Entrees €5-8. Fish €30-40 per kilo. Open daily 11am-1am.) Catch the day's NASCAR racing at **Agia Paraskevi ❶**, on Vournazon past the intersection with Kavetsou, home to the best souvlaki in town. (☎46 666. Entrees €1.50-8. Open daily 6am-2:30am. Free delivery.) For a sugar high that will last all day, head to **Zacharoplasteio Elena ❶**, which sells tantalizing almond confections and specializes in the wedding treat *yemata*. (☎27 133. Open daily 8am-9:30pm.)

ENTERTAINMENT AND NIGHTLIFE

Cine Arion, on Smyrnis across from the intercity bus station, plays mostly American films nightly on the theater's two screens. (☎44 456. Weekly schedules at the ticket window. Showings start 7:30-10:15pm. €6-7.)

Mytilini's nightlife centers on Sappho Sq., where a number of all-day cafes turn up the lights and music come nightfall. Facing inland on the right, **Cafe Monkey** serves deliciously creamy coffees (€3.50) and mixed drinks (€7) under outdoor mist fans and distinctive tear-drop lights. (☎37 717. Mixed drinks €5-6. Open daily 7am-3am.) International music and a waterfall of mist characterize **Central,** on the corner of the square. Patrons lounge at the breezy bar, playing backgammon and chatting. (☎47 995. Drinks €5-6. Open daily 6am-4am.) The more modern **Caldo** is another popular stop on the nightlife circuit. (Drinks €6-8. Open daily 7am-3am.)

◉ SIGHTS

ARCHAEOLOGICAL MUSEUMS. Two museums share Mytilini's collection of archaeological relics. Tickets are good for both on the same day. The well-designed ◪**new Archaeological Museum,** 8 Noemvriou, contains the permanent exhibit "Lesvos from the Hellenistic to Roman Times," displaying finds ranging from 2nd-century BC cooking utensils to AD 3rd-century Roman sculptures and busts. The undisputed highlights are the restored mosaic floors from ancient villas at Ag. Kyriaki, displayed in their original layout under glass tiles, allowing you to walk on top. Most exhibits have English signs and the museum is wheelchair-accessible. (☎40 223. Open Tu-Su 8am-3pm. €3, students €2, EU students and under 18 free.) The **old Archaeological Museum,** Argiri Eftalioti 7, up the hill behind the main port, has a less-inspiring roundup of Lesvian artifacts from prehistoric to Roman times. Each exhibit, however, is accompanied signs that use both mythological and historical elements to explain the significance of these fragments of ages past. The collection focuses on earthenware jars and small figurines found during the excavations at Thermi. The smaller building hiding behind the museum contains administrative and legal tablets written in the rare Aeolian dialect, now known to scholars primarily through Sappho's writings. (☎28 032. Open Tu-Su 8:30am-3pm.)

GATELOUZI CASTLE. The sprawling Gatelouzi Castle extends over a pine-covered hill near the museums, above the northern port. Though the original building was erected in AD 483-565 by Emperor Justinian, the castle bears the name of Franceso Gatelouzi, who received the entire island of Lesvos as a dowry in 1354. Centuries of Genoese, Ottomans, and Greeks have maintained the castle walls and underground tunnels that once hid women and children in times of war. The castle, one of the largest in the Mediterranean, was built in several stages by its various captors, with the lower part an entirely Turkish addition after their 1462 capture of the castle. Because locals took stones from the castle to rebuild fallen structures after WWII, little more than rubble remains of its interior. The path along the walls, though, affords panoramic views of the city and both harbors. (☎27 970. Open Tu-Su 8am-2:30pm. €2, students €1.)

RELIGIOUS AND BYZANTINE SIGHTS. The late 19th-century **Church of Agios Therapon,** on the western side of the harbor and one block inland on Ermou, is impressive for its enormous size, 4.5m wide chandelier, and cherished icons. (☎22 561. Open M-F 7am-1pm and 4-9pm, Sa-Su 7am-1pm and 6-9pm. Free. Modest dress required.) Across the square, the **Byzantine Museum,** on Pl. Ag. Therapon, contains Christian iconography from the 13th through 19th centuries along with other ecumenical treasures. (☎28 916. Open M-Sa 9am-1pm. €2, students free.) Inland and north of the harbor (one block off Ermou) is the **Church of Agios Theodoros,** the oldest in Mytilini, which houses the bones and skull of its patron saint.

OTHER RUINS. The highest point on the northern side of Mytilini is the 3rd-century BC **ancient theater,** from the Hellenistic period, where 15,000 spectators attended performances and enjoyed near-perfect acoustics. The effect was so impressive that it inspired Pompeii to build Rome's first stone theater. The nearby **Roman Aqueduct** also merits a visit.

▶ DAYTRIPS FROM MYTILINI

VARIA (Βαριά). Only 4km south of Mytilini along El. Venizelou, the tiny, unassuming village of Varia surprises wayfarers with the ◪**Musée Tériade.** It has an excellent collection of oil paintings, etchings, and Picasso, Miró, Léger, Chagall, and Matisse

THE IDIOT'S GUIDE TO DRINKING OUZO

When you go out for your first meal in Greece, don't be surprised, shocked, or flattered if your waiter rushes out before your entree arrives to present you with a shot glass full of opaque liquor and the simple command, "Drink!" He's just assuming that you, like almost every Greek, want to cleanse your palate and ease your mind with some ouzo.

There's an art to enjoying the anise-flavored national drink, however, which is important to know if you don't want to reveal yourself as a neophyte. First, don't take that shot like a frat boy. Good ouzo is around 40% alcohol by volume, and it just isn't made to be chugged. It's invariably served with a glass of water for the purpose of mixing; that's what turned your shot milky-white. The key is to keep adding water as you drink to avoid dehydration and other ill effects.

Second, snack on some *mezedes* while you take your ouzo. Munching on a salad, some cheese or vegetables will temper the alcohol and prolong the experience. That's the point, after all: Greece's obsession with ouzo is not really focused on getting plastered on something that tastes like licorice. Instead, it's about drinking lazily, relaxing in a *kafeneion*, and chatting with friends for the entire afternoon until the sun sets and dinner begins.

lithographs with captions in English, French, and Greek. Tériade, a native of Lesvos (born Stratis Eleftheriadis), was a leading 20th-century publisher of graphic art in Paris. (☎ 22510 23 372. Open Tu-Su 9am-2pm and 5-8pm. Free.) On the same street just before the Musée Tériade, the **Theophilos Museum** exhibits 86 paintings by self-taught Greek artist Theophilos Hadzimichali. His vivid natural and patriotic works are internationally recognized and can be found in homes across the islands. (Local buses to Varia leave Mytilini every hr. (20min., €1.15). Tell the driver you're going to the museums, as they are a little past Varia town. ☎ 22510 41 644. Open Tu-Su 10am-4pm. €2, students and under 18 free.)

 THE REAL DEAL. Despite an extensive and organized public bus system, many of Lesvos's treasures remain accessible only via taxi or private transportation. Taking out a car is far cheaper than the taxi fare and allows for complete freedom to explore the far-flung villages and monasteries, as well as access to many of the museums and parks only serviced once daily by public transport.

AGIOS RAFAEL. Twenty kilometers into the hills above Mytilini is the Monastery of Agios Rafael. The saint was active in working modern-day miracles, making his chapel and grave a major place of pilgrimage. The door on the bottom level of the church marked "Αγιασμα" leads to a source of holy water. (Local buses from Mytilini leave every 30min. 6am-9:40pm, €1.15.)

AGIA PARASKEVI. The town of Agia Paraskevi has a small plateia lined with cafes. Heading into town, 4km north of the Shell station, the new ◖**Museum of Industrial Olive Oil Production in Lesvos** houses the machinery and presses of the olive oil trade in its converted oil factory. The outdoor annex exhibits the social and economic factors that influenced the industry. (Drive 35km toward Kalloni from Mytilini. ☎ 22530 32 300. €3, students free. Open M and W-Su 10am-5pm.)

VATERA. With calm waters and 8km of wide, unbroken sands, Vatera is Lesvos's premier **beach.** Surprisingly untouristed, the sandy stretch is accesible by road for its entire length. Locals lounge under the spectacular display of stars at the cafes and restaurants that dot the coast. The ruins of the **Temple of Dionysus** sit to the right of the beach when facing the water, at the cape of **Agios Fokas.** Some of the column remnants are from 300 BC, while others date to AD 100, when early Christian temples were built over the site. The ruins aren't hugely impressive, but the sunsets from the beach on the other side of the point are truly awesome. Though long by foot, the journey makes for a pleasant bike ride: follow the road along the beach and veer left after the bridge. On the opposite side of the intersection, **Zouros ❶** serves masterful meat dishes such as the veal with tomatoes and fries (€5.50) on a beachside patio popular with locals. (☎22520 61 259. Entrees €4.50-5.50. Open daily 8am-midnight.) *(To get to Vatera, 58km from Mytilini, you can take the bus (1½hr., 3-4 per day, €4.20). It enters on the main road, runs the length of the beachside road, and drops off and picks up anywhere along the beach. A taxi ride is about €45. If you have private transportation, you also can visit Vatera as a daytrip from Plomari or Polichnitos.)*

PLOMARI. The vibrant, traditional flavor of this tiny fishing village is unlike any other on Lesvos. Home to several ouzo distilleries and surrounded by olive groves, Plomari's faded, crumbling buildings glow with the luster of small-town life. Originally a Turkish region, Plomari first was home to Greeks in 1841 after a fire in nearby Megalochorio drove residents southward. The village's warmth now attracts an influx of tourists, some of whom breeze through on their way west to Vatera, others of whom stay to explore Plomari's cultural heritage. Lesvos is renowned for its ouzo production, and Plomari in particular is known for its local brews. The **Barbayanni Ouzo Factory,** about 2km east on the road to Agios Isodoros, is the production site for one of Greece's oldest and most beloved privately owned ouzo companies, still controlled by the founding family. You can take a peek at 19th-century distillation devices in the adjacent **Ouzo Museum** in addition to observing the fascinating production process in the current factory. (☎22520 32 741; www.barbayanni-ouzo.com. Ask at the factory for a free tour of the museum. Open Tu-Su 10am-2pm.) To reach small, rocky **Ammoudeli beach,** follow the waterfront road out of town to the right from the bus stop, facing the water. Continuing straight past the beach brings you to **Agios Nikolaos,** a church that sparkles with icons spanning 400 years. About 3km east of town past the ouzo factory, the sandy, golden expanse of **Agios Isodoros beach** draws a large, bronzed following. Plomari also serves as a central point for the web of **"Olive Trails"** that span the grove-covered countryside; hiking maps are available in town. *(Plomari is a 40km bus ride from Mytilini (1½hr., €3.30). The bus stops in Plomari's main plateia, next to the taxi stand.)*

MOLYVOS Μόλυβος ☎22530

Hilly and cobbled, the town of Molyvos (a.k.a. Mithymna) is a quintessential storybook village, winding up from the sea toward a towering castle. Home to an illustrious school of fine arts, a marketplace, and several high-end tavernas, the city caters to upscale tourism. However, budget travelers and hotel-dwellers alike will enjoy the serene atmosphere and access to the area's beaches.

TRANSPORTATION

The bus stop is right before town, 10m from the fork that leads to Eftalou. **Buses** run between Anaxos and Eftalou (15 per day 9:30am-8:15pm, €1.20) via Petra and Molyvos. Ask at the tourist office for schedules. The intercity bus runs to Mytilini (1½hr., 5 per day, €5.90). To the immediate right of the National Bank, **Kosmos Rentals** rents **mopeds** (€14-24 per day) and **cars** (from €35). Prices include full insurance, tax, and unlimited mileage. (☎71 710. Open daily 8am-1pm and 5-9pm.) **Taxis** (☎71 480) stop at the intersection on the main road heading into town from the bus stop; a ride to Eftalou or Petra costs €5.

ORIENTATION AND PRACTICAL INFORMATION

Molyvos has three primary roads that run along different levels of the hill. The **main road** leads from the bus station past the tourist office and runs downhill 600m to the harbor. On your left as you enter town, another road leads down to the beach where a number of bars and restaurants border the shore. The third cobbled road veers right and goes through the agora past shops and restaurants.

Tourist Office: (☎71 347; www.mithymna.gr), on the main road 30m from the bus stop. The friendly, English-speaking staff provides free maps of the town, updated bus schedules, accommodations advice, and sights recommendations. They also can help coordinate where and when to make connections to get around the island by bus. Open May-Sept. daily 10am-3pm and 4-8:30pm.

Budget Travel: Com Travel (☎72 161; www.comtravel.gr), on the harbor where the downhill road levels out. The English-speaking staff sells flight and ferry tickets and plans excursions. Open M-W and F-Su 9am-10pm, Th 9am-4pm and 6-10pm. MC/V.

Bank: National Bank (☎71 210), next door to Com Travel. Has a **24hr. ATM.** Open M-Th 8am-2:30pm, F 8am-2pm.

Bookstore: Estravagario Books (☎71 824), past the post office on the right side. Offers English books and Greek-language guides. Open daily 9am-2:30pm and 5-11pm.

Laundromat: ☎71 622. Follow the main road to Eftalou; it is just before the taverna on the corner. Wash and dry €9. Smaller loads €2.60 per kg. Open daily Sept.-June 9am-3pm and 5:30-11pm; July-Aug. 9am-midnight.

Tourist Police: ☎22510 71 222. Go up the hill past the post office, down the street across from the bakery, then another 400m.

Pharmacy: ☎71 903. Along the 1st uphill road, before the turn to Nassos Guest House. Open M-Sa 9am-2pm and 5-10pm.

Medical Services: ☎71 333. Go uphill past the post office. Open daily 9am-1:30pm.

Internet Access: Central Cafe (☎72 255), down the coastal road just before the harbor. €3 per hr. Open daily 6am-midnight.

Post Office: ☎71 246. Heading to the harbor, follow the uphill road 300m past the tourist office. Western Union and traveler's check exchange available. €3 per check. Open M-F 7:30am-2pm. **Postal Code:** 81108.

ACCOMMODATIONS

Signs for **domatia** dot the road to Eftalou is lined with more expensive studios and hotels; the tourist office will gladly help you find a bed that meets your budget.

Nassos Guest House (☎22510 71 432; www.nassosguesthouse.com), on the road up the hill into town; head right at the first steep switchback and look for the Nassos sign. Homey, inviting, and thoughtfully decorated rooms have a community feel with the common kitchen, balcony, and bath. Your host, Tom, will answer any Lesvos-oriented questions. The book exchange, Internet and laundry facilities, and private balconies with views of the water below add to the appeal. Washing machine €3. Open in the summer only. Reservations recommended in Aug. Singles €20; doubles €25-40. ❷

Marianthis House (☎71 447). Take the road to Eftalou and turn left at the taverna. Peaceful doubles with fridge, TV, and bath overlook the garden. Upstairs studios come with sleeping room for 3 and kitchenette. Doubles €25; studios €30. ❷

Mpaliaka Mirsini (☎71 414), just before the tourist office. Close to town without the noise. Spacious rooms have fridge, TV, A/C, and kitchenette. Doubles €35-40. ❷

Sea Melody (☎71 158), farther downhill and across the street from Com Travel. Pretty, peach-colored rooms with shell motifs come with fridge, TV, bath, A/C, and a lovely view of the water. Inquire at the mini-mart across the street. Doubles €40. ❹

Camping Mithimna (☎22510 71 169; www.molivos-camping.com), 1.5km out of town on the road to Eftalou. This spacious campground has common picnic areas and sparse foliage separating tent sites. Late arrivals can set up shop and pay rent in the morning, though those without tents should call in advance. €4.50-5.50 per person; €3 per small tent, €3.50 per large tent. ❶

FOOD

Harbor restaurants line the waterfront but may stretch the pocketbook; head farther inland for smaller tavernas that serve excellent food at reasonable prices.

Taverna Traditional (☎ 72 241). Take the road past the tourist office up toward the post
office, taking the 2nd steep switchback to the right. This tiny, family-run taverna serves
homemade Greek favorites on a rooftop terrace overlooking the town. Entrees €4-7.
Open daily 8am-2pm and 5pm-late. ❷

Taverna O Gatos (☎ 22510 71 661; www.gatos-restaurant.gr.), midway up the hill
before the post office. Has served traditional fare for over 20 years, including lamb with
feta and tomatoes (€7.90). The sea breeze and sunset from the rooftop tables garnish
the down-home dishes. Entrees €6.70-8.50. Open daily 10am-late. MC. ❷

The Captain's Table (☎ 71 241). The fisherman who supplies this Aussie-owned restaurant is reputedly one of the island's best. The captain's platter for 1 (€12) or 2 (€23)
lets you taste the full range of his talents. Enjoy complimentary olives and sweet cinna-
mony bites. Open daily 5:30pm-late. MC/V. ❸

Friends Gyros Stand (☎ 22510 71 567), on the main road. Among standard options,
several meatless pitas are stuffed with cucumbers, french fries, green peppers, feta,
and other tasty ingredients. Pitas €1.40-1.60. Open daily noon-late. Free delivery. ❶

SIGHTS

The dominant feature of Molyvos's skyline is the **kastro,** the medieval castle whose
view is worth the climb. The castle, once an important transfer point for trade in
olives and oil, was repaired by Gatelouzi in 1373 and later buttressed by the Turks.
Though it's currently closed for renovations, when reopened the former theater of
war will host theatrical events; ask at the tourist information office for details.

ENTERTAINMENT AND NIGHTLIFE

In the summer, spend an evening under the stars at open-air **Cinema Arion,** just past
the bus stop heading into town. Posters for that week's English-language showings
are outside the cinema. (☎ 69776 26 976. €6.20. Showings start 9:30pm.)

Molyvos keeps a relaxed after-hours atmosphere, many locals preferring to
lounge over drinks rather than grind the night away. The **Cafe Bazaar,** on the right
side of the hill heading down to the harbor, has an array of international snacks
and the best strawberry daiquiris (€6.50) on the island. (Open daily 11am-2:30pm
and 4pm-4am.) On summer nights, head across the street to the **nightclub** of the
same name, where soul, funk, and jazz bounce off the blue floor-lights in the cave-
like hall. (Open daily midnight-noon.) At **Conga's Beach Club,** accessible from both
the beachfront and main roads, you can while away entire days in a haze of beach,
bongos, and booze. Beachside tables and tropical decor, complete with hammocks
and lanterns, entertain the young crowd. (☎ 72 181. Beer €3. Mixed drinks €7.
July-Aug. cover €5. Happy hour 7-11pm. Open daily 10am-3:30am.) Those in
search of a quiet after-dinner hangout and a game of billiards can head to **Nuevo,** on
the beachside road, across the street and inland from the Olive Press Hotel. (Open
daily 5pm-midnight. Mixed drinks €5. Beer €3. Billiards €6 per hr.)

BEACHES

A narrow, pebbly beach extends to the south toward Petra and is accessible from
the first road to the left as you enter Molyvos. Beach umbrellas abound, and showers and changing rooms are free. More inviting shores can be found at **Eftalou,**

whose beautiful black-pebble beaches stretch in several coves along the road; the farther ones are more protected from the wind and are frequented by nude bathers. The bus from Molyvos drops off in the middle of the main beach. Walk about 300m to the end of road to the left facing inland and follow the signs to find Eftalou's spa-like **thermal baths,** one of the few with coed pools. The 44-46.5°C, slightly radioactive waters are amazingly relaxing and reportedly effective against an entire host of ailments. The knowledgeable, multilingual staff gives advice on proper soaking procedures and can answer all questions concerning the baths' health benefits. (☎71 245. €3.50 for 45min. in the pool, €5 for 20min. in a private bathtub; includes free locker storage. Towel rental €1. Children 6 and under free.)

PETRA Πέτρα ☎22530

Named for the monolithic 27m rock in the town center, quiet Petra extends along a sunny, beach-lined plain 5km south of Molyvos. The beaches and cobbled, vine-roofed streets make it a popular daytrip or an alternative place to stay in the area. Head up Theodokou past the post office and climb the 114 rock-hewn steps to the **Church of the Holy Mary with the Sweet Smile,** which grants stunning views of the village and the sea. An intricately carved pale gray roof arches over the icons and chandeliers, with the eye of God gazing down from the center, frontmost dome. (Open daily 8:30am-9pm. Modest dress required.) The **Vareltzidaina House Museum,** an opulent mansion one block inland from Ermou to the right of the square facing inland, is also a worthwhile stop. (Open daily 8am-2:30pm.) Facing Nirvana Travel and continuing to the right, the **Diavasis Fitness Center** offers Tae Kwon Do and Greek dancing lessons. (One-day membership €4. Open M-F 4:30-8pm.)

Rooms in Petra are slightly cheaper than in Molyvos but are more expensive than in neighboring Anaxos. Facing inland, head to the right past Nirvana Travel to reach **Toyla ❸,** where spacious studios within a stone's throw from the beach come with air-conditioning, TV, kitchenette, gleaming bath, and balcony. (☎41 122. Doubles €30.) The beachfront hosts the usual slate of indistinguishable tavernas. If you're looking for a less run-of-the-mill dinner, follow Theodokou past the steps leading to the church and continue to your left at the fork in the road. The long walk along cobbled streets leads to **O Rigas ❷,** the oldest taverna in town, serving *papoutsakia* (eggplant stuffed with meat) and other home-cooked Greek fare. (☎41 405. Entrees €4-7. Open daily 7pm-late.) The town's many delectable products are brought together at the **Agricultural Cooperative of Petra,** at the fork before town off the main road across from the playground. Here you'll find local ouzos, olive oils, and cheeses. (☎41 208. Open daily 8am-2pm and 5:30-9:30pm. MC/V.)

Parallel to the water, **Ermou** is lined with bakeries and shops. To the right on the water facing inland is **Nirvana Travel,** which has ferry and flight tickets, bus schedules, **currency exchange,** and excursion bookings by boat and jeep. It also can help with diving trips, accommodations, and **car rentals.** (☎41 991; www.nirvanatravel.gr. Open M-Sa 9:30am-2pm and 6:30-10pm. MC/V.) A **24hr. ATM** is by the OTE on the main road. Next to Nirvana Travel is a **pharmacy** (☎41 394). The **OTE** is to the left of the plateia on the road to Molyvos. 1960s tunes and **Internet** access are available at **Cafe To Kyma** on the far left of the waterfront when facing inland. (Wi-Fi available. €3 per hr. Open daily 8am-1am.) The **post office,** which **exchanges currency,** is straight inland from the central plateia, on Theodokou. (Open M-F 7:30am-2pm.) Local **buses** go to Molyvos in the summer (15 per day 9:40am-8:25pm, €1.20) and stop 200m down the beach. Taxis (☎71 480) are just a phone call away.

SKALA ERESSOU Σκάλα Ερεσού ☎22530

The birthplace of poet Sappho, Skala Eressou welcomes families, archaeologists, and lesbian couples alike to share in its golden, sandy embrace. The beach, deemed one of the world's best, lies between two mountainous peaks, affording sunset vistas from the cafe-bars on the shore. A preponderance of rainbow flags fill storefronts, and many of the town's services are gay-friendly.

TRANSPORTATION AND PRACTICAL INFORMATION. A **bus** runs between Skala Eressou and Mytilini via Eressos (3hr., daily 11am and 1:15pm, €8). The bus stops in a large parking lot on the main road two blocks from the waterfront. There are only two taxis in the area, and trips must be arranged in advance through Sappho Travel; a taxi to Sigri costs about €25, and it's €70 to the airport.

Facing inland, the main road hits the waterfront a few meters to the left of a short **footbridge** (facing inland), which divides the town. Restaurants and cafes line the waterfront to the left, bars to the right, and many accommodations can be found one block inland. Joanna and the incredibly helpful, English-speaking team at ◪**Sappho Travel**, one block from the bus stop, provide info about the town, book ferry and flight tickets, help with accommodations, and **exchange currency.** They also arrange boat trips (€35), sunset women-only cruises (€20), and local walks (☎52 130; www.sapphotravel.com. Open M-Sa 9am-2:30pm and 6-10pm, Su 11am-2pm and 6-9pm.) Though there is no bank in Skala Eressou, a **24hr. ATM** can be found outside Sappho Travel. Opposite the church and around the corner, you'll find a **laundry** service. (☎52 255. Wash and dry €10. Open M-Sa 11am-1pm.) The nearest **police** are in Eressos (☎53 222). The 24hr. **medical clinic** can be found on a side street; head right when facing Sappho Travel (☎53 947 and 69370 27 349.) In case of **emergency,** call the **health center** (☎56 440, 56 442, or 56 444), in Antissa, 11km from Skala Eressou. Free Wi-Fi **Internet** access is widely available in cafes lining the water; bring your laptop and chill at **Aqua** over breakfast. (☎52 048. Breakfast €4.50-8. Open daily 9am-late.) **Internet Eressos** is on the waterfront to the right facing inland, before Zorba the Buddha. (☎52 082. €1 per 10min. Open daily 10:30am-3pm and 7pm-midnight; closed Th mornings.) The **post office** is in Eressos. (☎53 227. Open M-F 8am-2pm.) **Postal Code:** 81105.

ACCOMMODATIONS. Many options for accommodations can be found close to the waterfront, from pricey hotels to budget, women-only pensions. While most of the town's facilities are gay-friendly, this is not necessarily true across the board. Ask at Sappho Travel if you have trouble finding a room. Facing Sappho Travel, make a left and follow signs for Krinelos on the right to reach **Maria Pantermou ❶**. The husband-wife team offers simple doubles with air-conditioning, fridge, bath, and access to the wraparound balcony. (☎53 267. Singles €15; doubles €20-35.) The good-humored couple who runs **Pension Krinelos ❸**, just behind Maria Pantermou, offers affordable, homestyle lodgings. Clean rooms come with bath, air-conditioning, and fridge and open onto the shared terrace, lending the place a community feel. (☎53 376. Doubles €30, with kitchenette €45.) A 7min. inland walk from the church leads to the women-only **Hotel Antiopi ❷**, where simple rooms come with bath and wall murals. The community feel is buffeted by the shared patio, upstairs terrace overlooking the fields, and the rooftop jacuzzi. Hospitable owner Teresa brings in groups of writers, artists, and birdwatchers. (☎53 311; www.antiopihotel.com. Breakfast included. Singles €25-30; doubles €35-60.) Turn right past the bus stop and walk 50m to find the women-only **Hotel Mascot ❸**. The 10 rooms come with air-conditioning and fridge and include breakfast in a common nook that encourages guests to mingle. Reservations are booked through Sappho Travel. (☎52 130. Doubles €30-50.) Unorganized **camping** is permitted on the beach, though the police have been known to clear out campsites.

FOOD. Food in Skala Eressou is generally very good and the town is a vegetarian paradise—at least by Greek standards. To the left of the bridge and on the waterfront when facing inland, **Ouzeri Soulatso ❷** is the most traditional Greek taverna in town. Diners are treated to a deep-sea harvest of fresh fish and a variety of ouzos; head up to the storefront case to pick your meal. (☎ 52 078. Grilled entrees €4-8. Open daily noon-midnight.) Heading in the opposite direction on the waterfront, the locally acclaimed **Samadhi Restaurant ❷** offers pineapple-encrusted chicken bombay (€9) and other international treats. (Entrees €6.50-9.50. Open daily 6-11pm.) Past Soulatso, family-run **Eressos Palace ❷** offers huge portions of fresh food at deliciously low prices. The fisherman's souvlaki (€5.50) is made with a variety of skewered and grilled fish, and a number of vegetarian dishes are available as well. (☎ 53 858. Entrees €4-8. Open daily 8am-2am.)

■■ **ENTERTAINMENT AND NIGHTLIFE.** Behind the main plateia, open-air **Cine Sappho** has nightly 9:30pm showings of English-language movies in the summer. Every September, Skala Eressou hosts the week-long **Women's Festival.** Around 400 participants come to enjoy the theatrical, artistic, and sporting activities, as well as the series of workshops, massage therapies, and parties.

The nightlife scene, dominated by chill lounges that spill onto the sand, is (unsurprisingly) lesbian-friendly. The close proximity to the water makes for easy swimming access on hot summer evenings. In keeping with town decree, all bars turn off the music at 2am, though patrons are welcome to stay and chat until dawn. Facing inland on the bridge, follow the waterfront to the right to reach most of the bar lounges, including the lime green ■**Parasol.** Umbrellas adorn this tropical cocktail bar, where patrons throw back the patented vodka-and-melon Wooloomooloo Wonders. (☎ 53 287. Mixed drinks €6-7.50. Homemade pizzas €9. Open daily 9:30am-late.) Farther down the waterfront away from town, international music accompanies ouzo and tapas (€3) at **Zorba the Buddha.** (☎ 53 777. Mixed drinks €7. Open 10am-3am.) In the main plateia, **The Tenth Muse** offers savory pancakes (€5-6) by day, and becomes a popular bar by night. (☎ 53 287; www.the-tenthmusecafe.com. Beer €2.50-4. Mixed drinks €5.50-6.50. Open daily 8am-4am.)

◙ **SIGHTS.** The 5th-century mosaics once housed in the early-Christian basilica of **Agios Andreas,** three blocks north of the beach, are now in Mytilini's new Archaeological Museum (p. 116). Though the church was named after the apostle Ag. Andreas, a Cretan archbishop of the same name happened to die nearby a couple centuries later. His grave, the **Tomb of Agios Andreas,** was incorporated into the site, though it only contains half of his remains; the other portion was claimed by Crete. The **river,** just west of Skala's center, is home to many rare and exotic birds. Peak **birdwatching** season is from April to May. Heading back toward Sigri 2.5km after the fork, you'll reach the turn-off up to **Ipsilou Monastery.** Dating back to AD 800, the monastery sits on the Ordymnos volcanic dome and commands an amazing view of northwestern Lesvos's rugged, desolate hills. One of the priests will walk you through the excellent **museum,** across from the chapel. It houses 17th- and 18th-century artifacts and religious vestments, as well as a number of 16th-century writings and icons. (Open daily 7:30am-10pm. Modest dress required. Free.)

▶ **DAYTRIPS FROM SKALA ERESSOU.** In the small fishing village of **Sigri,** several small tavernas cluster near the plateia. Sandy and calm, Sigri's **beach** is protected from the northern winds by the town's 18th-century **Turkish castle.** Less-frequented beaches lie farther down the coastal, unpaved road to Eressos.

A **petrified forest,** 18 km from Sigri, is one of only two such forests in the world (the other is in the southwestern United States). The remains of the fossilized trunks scattered throughout the parched hillside are around 20 million years old, and some remnants are over 20m in length. The trees were preserved in exquisite and colorful detail during an ancient volcanic meltdown that almost instantaneously blanketed the original forest. Elements in the lava slowly replaced the plants' organic matter in the eons-long calcification process. A 1.5km walking trail brings visitors to the site, and the forest itself takes at least 1hr. to appreciate fully. Make sure to bring water and a hat. (☎54 434; www.petrifiedforest.gr. Open daily May 15-Oct. 14 8am-8pm; Oct. 15-May 14 8am-4pm. €2, children under 15 free.) In Sigri, the ▧Natural History Museum of the Lesvos Petrified Forest has an international display of plant fossils dating back to the Paleozoic Era. The museum, well-designed enough to turn anyone into an aspiring geologist, includes interactive displays on volcano formation, tectonic motion, and the geological history of the Aegean. (☎54 434; www.petrifiedforest.gr. Open daily 8am-10pm. €5, students €2.50). The easiest way to reach the site and museum is by private vehicle, as public buses from Skala Eressou to Sigri run only once per day in high season (€8). An unpaved coastal road connects Skala Eressou to Sigri directly. A taxi from Skala Eressou to the village of Sigri costs about €25. Bus service does exist between Mytilini and Sigri (3hr., 1 per day 1:15pm, €7.40). A network of **hiking trails** connects Eressos to the petrified forest and Sigri, as well as a number of geoparks in the area; pick up a detailed map of the trails from a travel agency or the museum.

On the road from Eressos to Molyvos, a number of small, cobbled villages offer a taste of traditional Greek life. Three broad trees shade the wide plateia of **Andisa** village, 12km north of Eressos, where locals sip frappés and purchase melons from local vendors. **Restaurant Perdinon ❷**, on the main square, is popular for its juices (€1.50) and homemade cakes. (☎56 106. Entrees €4-6.) Nine kilometers farther north, the winding streets of **Vatousa** lead to a **Painting Gallery.** (☎51 185. Free.)

LIMNOS Λήμνος

The lively island of Limnos reveals varied treasures, from well-preserved wetlands and archaeological sites to silent sand dunes and a pack of migrating flamingoes. Peacefully remote and unflinchingly quiet, this far-flung island's majestic sunsets, sparkling beaches, and bustling local communities make it a favorite getaway.

MYRINA Μύρινα ☎22540

Fanning out behind the castle-crowned peninsula, the glittering city of Myrina spans two calm beaches that reflect the city's relaxed lifestyle. Residents and visitors stroll the cobbled streets windowshopping, sip frappés on the waterfront until late, or scale the heights of the Venetian castle to catch a dazzling sunset behind distant Mt. Athos. Largely untouristed, the island retains a strong small-town feel and is perfect for those in search of an escape.

▐ **TRANSPORTATION.** The airport is 20km out of town and served only by taxis (€20). The **Olympic Airways** office, next to the post office, sells plane tickets. **Flights** go to: Athens (50min., 2 per day, €75); Chios (2hr., 5 per week, €36); Lesvos (35min., 5 per week, €30); Rhodes (5 per week, €60); Thessaloniki (5 per week, €60). **NEL, SAOS** and **G.A. Ferries** serve Limnos; ferries dock on either end of the horseshoe-shaped port, so be sure to ask where to wait. **Ferries** run to: Kavala (5hr., daily, €16); Lavrio, near Athens (10hr., 3 per week, €27.70); Mytilini, Lesvos (5½hr., 3 per week, €19); Piraeus (25hr., 1 per week, €35); Samos (13hr., 1 per week, €30); Samothraki (2½hr., 4 per week, €13); Thessaloniki (4 per week, €35). **Pravlis Travel** sells ferry tickets for GA and NEL and has an office one block inland behind the little port. (☎22 471. Open M-F 9am-2:30pm and 6-9:30pm, Sa 9am-2pm, Su 6-9:30pm.) The **SAOS kiosk** (☎29 571) is across from the ferry dock. The bus station is in Pl. El. Venizelou, the second plateia along Karatza in the far-left corner

SPINNING A CURE

In 1916, the small village of Varos, in the center of Limnos by the present-day airport, was struck by a horrible plague. As the disease quickly decimated the population, one woman in the village had a vision. In it, Agios Charalambos, one of the Greek Orthodox Church's saints, directed her to spin thread from locally produced cotton and wrap it around the village's borders to ward off the plague. The next morning, the woman shared her vision with her weakening townspeople. Eager to try anything that might eradicate the epidemic, a large group congregated to join her in immediately setting upon the task of spinning large amounts of thread. They surrounded Varos with the seemingly never-ending strand, and sure enough, the plague disappeared from the village.

Today, Varos's residents commemorate this story during Lent. The village women re-enact the frenetic spinning session, making 13 balls of thread from local cotton. The thread is then taken to the small Church of Saint Charalambos, where the villagers pray to the saint, thanking him profusely for saving their village. After the service, the townspeople, continuing the re-enactment of the original wrapping, symbolically bind the village with the thread, draping it around the village's borders for an entire day.

between a tourist agency and a coffee shop. KTEL **Buses** (☎22970 22 464) run to Kalliopi (3 per day); Karpasi (5 per day); Livadohori (4 per day); Plaka (2 per day), among several small villages around the island. **Car rental** is available at a number of places on the waterfront, including **Holiday Car Rental** across from Petrides Travel. (☎23 280. Cars €25-40.) **Taxis** (☎23 820) are available in the main plateia and charge €25 one-way to the archaeological sights at Poliochni and Hephaestia.

■■ **ORIENTATION AND PRACTICAL INFORMATION.** The city has two main waterfronts on opposite sides of the castle. **Turkikos,** facing Turkey, is the active port, with Myrina's best fish tavernas and a sandy beach at its far end. **Romeikos,** on the northern side of the castle, is a family-friendly waterfront lined with parks, playgrounds, and hip cafes. To find it, head inland up **Karatza,** the town's commercial artery, and take a left when you can spot the sea in between the buildings.

Family-run since 1969, **Petrides Travel,** on Karatza, has everything but ferry tickets, offering flights, car rental (€25-40 per day), and guided excursions. Buses go to sites and beaches (half-day €15, whole day €20), and boats visit Isostatious (€35) and Samothraki (€65). (☎22 039; www.petridestravel.gr. Open daily 8am-4pm and 6pm-midnight.) Karatza leads inland from Pl. 8 Oktovriou to the town's central plateia and contains **Emporiki Bank,** which has a **24hr. ATM** (open M-Th 8am-2:30pm, F 8am-2pm), **taxis** (☎23 820), and **card phones.** One block farther on Karatza, Garofallidi runs to the right; following it will take you to a self-service **laundromat** in the Hotel Astron. (☎24 392. €6.50 per 1-2kg load, €9.20 per 5-6kg. Open daily 8am-2pm and 5-9pm.) Down Garofallidi is a large intersection with the **police station** on the corner. (☎22 200. Open 24hr.) There are several **pharmacies** on Karatza. Follow Garofallidi inland to reach the **hospital.** (☎22 222. Open 24hr.) **Internet** access can be found 24hr. in Turkikos at the mouth of Karatza at **Excite.** (☎25 525. Midnight-8am €1.50, 8am-midnight €2.50.) The **post office** is one block inland on Garofallidi. (☎22 462. Open M-F 7:30am-2pm.) **Postal Code:** 81400.

⌂ **ACCOMMODATIONS.** Catering mostly to Greek families, the hotels in town are expensive. A few **domatia** can be found in Turkikos and a few blocks inland behind the archaeological museum. If you have a phone card and some patience, try calling around to compare prices, though you may end up paying top dollar despite your efforts. One of the only budget options in town, **Hotel Aktaion ❷,** on the waterfront next to Hotel Lemnos, has simple rooms with small balcony and fridge. Constant prices throughout the summer and a friendly husband-wife pair make the rooms an amazing deal. (☎22 258. Singles with bath €20; doubles €25, with bath €25-30.) Facing inland at the bus station, continue down Mitropoleos to the left for 300m to **Aithalia ❹.** The friendly management offers new doubles with air-conditioning, TV, kitchenette, and bath; upstairs rooms have balcony. (☎25 448; www.aithalia.gr. Doubles €45.) **Hotel Lemnos ❸,** near the ferry dock in Turkikos, rents clean, standard rooms with air-conditioning, TV, fridge, phone, balcony, and castle views. (☎22 153. Singles €35; doubles €45.)

❏ FOOD. High-quality, reasonably priced food is easy to find in Myrina; both Turkikos and Romeikos are lined with quality tavernas and cafes. *Psiari* (fish) tavernas line the *limanaki* (little port) of Turkiko; facing inland head right, just before the beach begins. Tucked in the corner of the little port, **To Limanaki ❷,** on the far end, lets patrons choose whatever fish their hearts desire from the icy vats near the kitchen. (☎23 744. Fish €35-45 per kg. Open daily 7pm-late.) The sea literally crashes up to the tables at **Taverna Kosmos ❷,** along Romeikos to the left when facing the water. A slew of Greek comfort foods, including moussaka (€5) and beef in tomato with fries (€6.50), dominate the well-rounded menu. (☎22 050. Open daily 10am-2am.) About 50m to the right of the archaeological site facing the water, **Taverna Oi Tzitzifies ❷** (Οι Τζιτζιφιες) is a popular sand-top lunch spot. (☎23 756. Greek salad €4. Auburgines with bechamel €5.50. Entrees €4-8. Open daily 1pm-midnight.) Facing inland at Romeikos, head to the left to join the coffee-sipping crowd at beachfront ⛵**Jacob's Frappe ❶,** where 20 varieties of the slow-roasted favorite are churned out night and day. Ever caffeinated, it becomes a hopping club by night. (Coffee €3-4. Mojitos €6. Open daily 9am-4am.)

⛿ SIGHTS. The ⛵ **kastro,** piercing the skyline and dividing the waterfronts, is home to several dozen deer. Enjoy the stunning sunset view and the ruins of the 7th-century BC fortress, reworked by Venetians in the 13th century. Signs from the harbor point to the rocky trail leading to the entrance. The best time to visit is just before sunset, allowing at least an hour of dusk to explore the walls and crumbling buildings. (Always open. Always free.) At the far end of Romeikos, to the left when facing inland, the well-curated **archaeological museum** has a collection of artifacts with informative English and Greek explanations printed on canvas drapes. Finds from the ancient settlements of Hephaestus, Poliochni, and the Kabeiron include a series of terra cotta siren sculptures and an impressive skeleton of a sacrificed bull calf. (☎22 990. Open Tu-Su 8:30am-3pm. €2, students free.)

Continue 100m along the waterfront past the museum to the archaeological area, **Prehistoric Myrina.** Catwalk-like paths lead visitors over the well-preserved foundations of a 4th-millennium BC proto-urban settlement that was rebuilt repeatedly after recurring earthquakes. The stone building that sits at the site's entrance continuously plays an amusing and informative video with English subtitles, using computer simulations to show what the village looked like in its heyday. (☎22 257. Open Tu-Su 9am-3pm. Free.)

⛵ DAYTRIPS FROM MYRINA. Though most of the island's attractions are best reached by car or moped, a couple of travel agencies such as Petrides arrange **bus excursions** around Limnos. Taxis go from Myrina to all sites for €25 each way but will expect to be paid for waiting time while you explore; negotiate a total price with the driver before departing. Limnos has a number of notable **archaeological sites,** all on the opposite side of the island from Myrina. **Poliochni,** on the eastern coast, is the oldest proto-urban settlement discovered in all of Europe, dating from the late Neolithic period (5000-4000 BC). One of the most complex fortified cities of its time, it is credited with being the site of Europe's first parliament. **Ancient Hephaestia,** on the northeastern coast of the island, was the location of a sanctuary to Hephaestus, god of fire and metallurgy, whose divine forge was supposedly on the island. Going on to follow his divine example, ancient Limnians took up the trade and set up their metalworking shops on the island's volcanic soil. Farther up the coast is the **Kaveiron,** an 8th-century BC sanctuary once used by a secret cult to worship the Kaveiroi, Hephaestus's children. Ceremonies were held to honor the birth of humanity and the rebirth of nature. Near the sanctuary is the cave, where Philoctetes, a Greek archer in the Trojan Wars, lived after he was bitten by a snake and abandoned by his companions. During full moons, islanders and visitors still gather on the nearby beach to celebrate with food, drink, guitars, and good spirits.

Limnos has a number of ecological sights, including the longest **sand dunes** in Europe (near Gomati beach, on the northern coast), the **waterfalls** near Kaspakas, and the **hot springs** at Therma. The baths built over the hot spring offer a variety of massages and facials, with a 20min. soak running €12. If things aren't hot enough, try Aphrodite's pool (€35 for 20min.), built for two. (☎62 062. Open daily 10am-2pm and 5-9pm.) During winter and spring, the western salt plain of Lake Aliki hosts migrating **flamingoes** that descend on the island in a blur of pink. After working up an appetite, head to **Taverna Mandela ❷** (☎61 899), in Sares.

Most of Limnos's sandy **beaches** are near Myrina. The most popular beach on the island is shallow **Riha Nera,** just north of Romeikos. **Avlonas,** on the way to Kaspakas, is large and uncrowded, with two islets of its own. Go along the steep mountain road to find **Agios Yiannis** nearby. On the road to Kontias is **Nevgatis,** an easily accessible beach with 2km of unbroken sands.

SAMOTHRAKI Σαμοθράκη

Samothraki (also called "Samothrace") was once a place of pilgrimage for Thracian settlers who belonged to a cult that worshipped the great Anatolian gods. Modern-day Samothraki, too, inspires a cult-like devotion: many Greeks on and off the island attest to its undeniable magnetic energy. Remote and dominated by wilderness, Samothraki attracts those who prefer hiking boots to high heels. The laidback crowd emits a *joie de vivre* that can be a refreshing change from the run-of-the-mill summer glitz of other islands.

KAMARIOTISSA Καμαριώτισσα   ☎25510

This transportation hub is an excellent starting point for exploring and surveying Samothraki's many charms. Kamariotissa's serene attitude is apparent even amid the plethora of tourist agencies along the waterfront and occasional traffic from arriving and departing buses and boats. Relative to the surrounding wilderness, Kamariotissa feels like an urban center.

☞ TRANSPORTATION. Ferries dock on the southern edge of town and run to: Alexandroupoli (2½hr., 1-2 per day, €11); Kavala (3½hr., 2 per week, €16); Lesvos (7hr., Sa 5:15pm, €28); Limnos (3½hr.; M-Tu 6:15pm, Sa 5:15pm; €15). **Flying Dolphins** run to Alexandroupoli from mid-June to mid-September (1hr., 1-2 per day, €18). For tickets and schedules, ask the port police or **Saos Tours.** (☎23 512. Open daily 10am-1pm and 6-9pm.) **Buses** stop on the waterfront across from Saos Tours and go to Hora (7 per day, 8am-7:40pm, €1), Profitis Ilias (5 per day, 6:30am-8pm, €1.50) via Alonia and Lakoma, and Therma (4 per day, 7:10am- 5:15pm, €2). Schedules and prices fluctuate often, especially during the low season; consult the bus drivers and stands for more information. **Taxis** (☎41 733) wait on the waterfront 24hr. The best way to get around the island is by car or moped, either of which you can rent from **Kyrkos Rentals,** located on the waterfront where you disembark from the ferry. (☎ 41 620. Mopeds and bikes €15 per day including helmet and insurance; cars €30-50 per day. Domatia singles and doubles €30-50 depending on season. Open daily 8am-midnight, depending on ferry schedule.)

■ 🖪 ORIENTATION AND PRACTICAL INFORMATION. Everything in Kamariotissa is located on one street along the waterfront. This road runs out of town to the northeast, and the road to Hora runs east out of town just past the bus stop (at the stop sign). The **National Bank** with a **24hr. ATM** and **currency exchange** is just near the point of disembarkment along the main road. (☎ 41 750. Open M-Th 8am-2:30pm, F 8am-2pm.) A Greek flag marks the 24hr. **port police** (☎ 41 305), whose station is five shops down from the bank. The **pharmacy** is 10m east of the only stop sign in the village on the road to Hora. (☎ 41 698. Open daily 9am-2pm, M-F also 6-9pm.) The town's pharmacies rotate 24hr. duty; check the schedule posted on the door of any one for more information. **Cafe Aktaion,** on the waterfront across from the ferry docks, entertains the video game generation with 20 computer stations with **Internet** access, two pool tables, and a foosball table. (☎ 41 056. €3 per hr. Pool tables €5 per hr. Open daily 8am-2am.) The **police station** (☎ 41 203; open 24hr.), **medical clinic** (☎ 41 217; open 24hr.), and **OTE** (☎ 41 299) are in Hora. The **post office** (☎ 41 244) is at the end of the main port road; facing the ferries, go left for about 100m. **Postal Code:** 68002.

🖪 🖪 ACCOMMODATIONS AND CAMPING. Many travelers breeze through Kamariotissa on their way to Therma and the campsites. Some camp illegally in the surrounding area, but there's no reason to avoid the established campsites. **Domatia** signs abound along the waterfront road and prices for a single range €25-35. **Kaviros Hotel ❸** in Therma (to the left of the grocery store) has rooms with air-conditioning, TV, fridge, and bath. (☎ 98 277. Singles and doubles €30-40 depending on season.) **Brisko Rooms ❸** has quiet accommodations off its flower-lined terrace. To get there, turn left out of Cafe Aktaion and take the next left inland. Only some of the rooms have an ocean view, but all rooms come with air-conditioning, TV, fridge, bath, and balcony. (☎ 41 328. Singles €30; doubles €35; triples €45.) **Hotel Kyma ❸,** on the waterfront on the outskirts of Kamariotissa, at the beginning of the road to Therma, has clean, simple rooms close to a stone beach. Rooms have small private bath, fridge, and air-conditioning. (☎ 41 263. Doubles €50; triples €65. Low-season prices reduced.) **🖪Camping Platia ❶,** 15km from Kamariotissa and 2km beyond Therma on the coast, has showers, baths, a mini-mart, and phones. This excellent choice is bounded by wilderness on one side and a spectacular view of the Aegean on the other. (☎ 98 244. €3 per person, 12 and under €2; €3 per tent.) **Camping Varades ❶,** 5km from Therma on the coastal road, has similar amenities to Camping Platia as well as a cafe, but it also has more concrete than greenery. (☎ 98 291. €3 per person, under 15 €2; €3 per tent.)

🖪 FOOD. Waterfront tavernas in Kamariotissa specialize in fresh seafood. You can't go wrong with the fresh fish at **Sinatisi ❷,** a few doors down from the National Bank. (☎ 41 308. Entrees €5-10. Open daily 8am-5pm and 8pm-late.) At **Klimataria ❷,** adjacent to hotel Kyma, enticing home-cooked dishes await your selection behind a glass counter in the kitchen. Pork roasted with potatoes, yogurt, eggs, and cheese (€6) and "goat in oven" (€6) are two of the specialties. (☎ 41 535. Open daily noon-5pm and 7pm-1am.) **Cafe Moka ❶,** on the waterfront, will satiate any sweet tooth with its 20 flavors of homemade ice cream and a variety of pastries and cakes. (☎ 41 093. Greek coffee €2. Strawberry milkshake €3.50. Ice cream €1.50 per scoop. Open daily 6am-midnight.)

NORTHEAST
AEGEAN

■ ■ **ENTERTAINMENT AND NIGHTLIFE.** ■**Cafe Therma** at the entrance to the nearby village of Therma is a favorite for locals and wandering types. Tables overlook the sea while guests sit in the shade of old sycamore trees. Flanked by two creeks trickling down from the peak of Fengari, this understated cafe offers drinks, *mezedes* (€4), and an air of tranquility. Live music is played at night and it is common for people to break out their guitars or bongo drums. (☎938 325. Open 24hr.) Kamariotissa's tavernas often stay open late, bringing young crowds to their dance floors. **Cafe-Bar Diva,** on the waterfront, plays up-to-date MTV-style hits during the day and popular Greek music at night. (☎41 060. Mixed drinks €2-6. Open daily 8am-late.) **Rebel,** a dance club to the right of the docks on the waterfront, plays mostly Greek music until mid-summer, when it changes to American hits to fit the more touristy audience. (☎41 554. Open June-Sept. midnight-8am.)

■ **BEACHES.** The island's only sand beach is the soft arc of **Pahia Ammo** on the southern coast, whose radiant blue water could have splashed off a postcard. The best way to get to Pahia Ammo is to rent a car or moped, as buses are infrequent. Stony black beaches ring the rest of the island. Ask a bus driver to drop you off anywhere along the coast, then hunt down an isolated stretch of shore. At the end of the line along the northern coast is popular **Kypos,** whose main attraction is a cave that looks out at the rocky beach. Three white **buses** per day go to Kypos. Schedules change frequently; ask bus drivers in Kamariotissa for schedules.

■ **DAYTRIPS FROM KAMARIOTISSA**

The verdant island of Kamariotissa holds a wealth of trails leading to cascading waterfalls, mountain vistas, and the summit of the steep mountain Fengari. Trails are generally unmarked; the best way to explore them is to rent a vehicle in Kamariotissa and head to the coast or interior. Hiring a local tour guide, available for a negotiable fee at some of the trailheads, is also a good idea, as trekkers who attempt to ascend alone can get lost or injured in the wild terrain. Ask locals from the villages that dot the mountain's flanks for directions to trailheads.

THERMA. The most convenient hub for outdoor activities is the small town of Therma, about 13km from Kamariotissa. Its houses, spread out on the mountainside, are framed by two streams. Tavernas and domatia dominate the village, making it a quiet, down-to-earth, and attractive alternative to Kamariotissa. A multitude of local mini-marts and equipment stores can outfit your camping trip.

Thermal water bursts from the refreshing **thermal springs** at a scorching 92°C and is cooled down to 42°C for public use. Public baths are nude, with men and women separated. To take a dip in your own private hot spring, walk right at the parking lot before Cafe Therma up a wide dirt path for 100m. Take the first downhill path at your right, which has been paved with rocks, and walk into the white house that is not far from the initial dirt path. *(Buses from Kamariotissa stop at the base of town next to the thermal springs. Entrance to private and public baths €2.)*

The trail to the summit of **Fengari** (4hr.) is also accessible from Therma. Walk up the main road in town and ask the friendly owners of the domatia on your left for the best way up. The trailhead is hidden near Hotel Orfeos. Enchanting ■**Fonias waterfall,** 17km from Kamariotissa and 5km past Therma, will revive any tired soul slowed by the scorching Aegean sun. Follow the main road that goes around the island away from Kamoriotissa for 5km; you'll reach a large parking lot from which the well-marked path will lead you to the first of seven waterfalls in about an hour. The easy 2km hike meanders alongside a gurgling stream and beneath twisted trees. Watch your step; the trail can be slippery since it ends at a waterfall. The first three waterfalls don't require superb hiking skills or a guide, but if you are interested in continuing on, it is best to hire or ask a local to go with you. For a less visited option, try the waterfalls near Therma. While the hike is easy, trails are unmarked, so ask the workers at Cafe Therma for information about hiring a local guide. *(To get to the hidden waterfalls, take the left fork through town from the bus stop. Take the first right after a mini-mart and follow this road past tavernas and a bakery. When the road ends, turn left and follow the unpaved road; when it meets an asphalt-paved road, turn right. The road ends again at Taverna Yefiris; turn right and head up the shaded road. The dirt trail follows the stream on the right side of the road; head right or left 20m before the Marina Hotel.)*

PALEOPOLIS. Paleopolis and its ▨**Sanctuary of the Great Gods** lie 6km east of Kamariotissa and are Samothraki's premier archaeological attractions. Before the island's 4th-century BC Aeolian colonization, pre-Olympian gods ruled over Samothraki: the Great Mother goddess Axieros and her cronies Axiokersa, Axiokersos, and Kasmilos. Members of the secret cult that worshipped these gods were among the island's earliest inhabitants, possibly dating back to the 7th century BC. Since disclosing initiation secrets was punishable by death, very little is known today about their rituals. Purification rites took place in the Anaktoron, at the lowest part of the temple complex, and the Hieron, a courtyard whose re-erected columns now form the site's central attraction.

It is reported that Philip II of Macedon, Alexander the Great's father, first met Olympias, a princess from Epirus and Alexander's mother, at their initiation into this cult. The enormous cylindrical **Arsinoëin Rotunda,** given to Samothraki by Queen Arsinoë II of Egypt (288-270 BC), demonstrates the continued patronage of the site by Alexander's successors, the Ptolemys. The sacrificial site's walls (now in the museum) are decorated with rosettes and ox heads. In the center, the **Doric Hieron,** containing pits for sacrifices, an altar for libations, and seats for the audience, was the place of initiation where the candidates were purified.

The **Winged Victory** (or **Nike**) **of Samothrace,** the statue that is the pride of the island, stood upon a marble base here before it took a mid-19th-century trip to Paris, where it currently perches in the Louvre. The remains of an **ancient theater** sit on the overlooking hillside. Above the sanctuary are the remains of the ancient town of Samothraki where the apostle Paul stopped in AD 49-50 on his way from Asia Minor to Phillipi. It is believed that the AD first-century **Christian Basilica,** whose ruins lie at the eastern edge of the ancient harbor, was built in commemoration of Paul's visit. *(Take the bus to Therma and ask to be let off at the ruins. Site open Tu-Sa 8:30am-8:30pm. €3 students €2, EU students free.)*

Beside the ruins, the **Paleopolis Museum** houses many of the site's artifacts such as libation vessels and figurines. Of particular note are the giant entablatures from the Arsinoëin Rotunda and the Hieron, a bust of the blind Samothrakian prophet Tiresias, and a galling cast of the missing-in-action Nike. Other highlights include the beautiful winged and draped Akroterial statue of victory from the Hieron, an inscription from the Anaktoron in Greek and Latin forbidding the uninitiated from entering the inner sanctum (AD 200), and the erotic scenes depicted on a first-century BC pot. *(☎41 474. Open Tu-Su 8:30am-3pm. Museum admission included in Sanctuary of the Great Gods entrance fee.)*

THASSOS Θάσος

Just 20km off the coast of Kavala (p. 281) lies Thassos, a green jewel which has run into an inordinate amount of trouble over the centuries. According to legend, Thassos's origins are wrapped in misfortune: After Europa's devoted brother finally gave up chasing his sister—who had met the all-too-common fate of being abducted by a lusty Zeus—he built the first settlements on this remote island.

Despite Europa's brother's scorn for Zeus's actions, Thassos soon fell victim to a less mythic type of lust. As an ancient exporter of gold, silver, and its famous wine, Thassos attracted the unwelcome attention of Phoenician, Athenian, and Roman conquerors. Those Thassians who were not killed or sold into slavery during the conquests were forced to hide, fleeing to mountain villages or caves. This "Green Island" sweetened its lot with a thriving beekeeping culture, producing jam and honey that was renowned through the ancient world. Since then, the island's greenery has been threatened by a new foe: massive forest fires. The forests are slowly coming back, though, and the northeastern regions around Thassos Town which escaped the fires are especially beautiful. In recent years, Thassos has escaped its historic woes to become a tourist-oriented island, attracting throngs of Northern Europeans who seek a quiet place in the sun. Its cool, shaded mountains and isolated southern coast are a hiker's paradise.

THASSOS TOWN   ☎ 25930

The island's capital and tourist center is built atop the foundations of the ancient city, and ruins crowd the Old Port area. Also known as Limenas (from *limani*, meaning "harbor"—not to be confused with nearby Limenaria), Thassos Town sees the highest concentration of tourists on the island. Despite the massive amount of visitors, Thassos lacks the fast pace of many other Greek islands.

▊ TRANSPORTATION

Ferries: The arrival and departure point for ferries from Kavala is not in Thassos Town, but in the village of **Skala Prinos,** 18km west. From there, ferries go to **Kavala** (1½hr.; 10 per day 6am-8:30pm, €2.50-3.50; cars €15) and **Keramoti** (30min., 20 per day 5:45am-9pm, €2). Bus schedules between Skala Prinos and Thassos Town are synchronized with the ferries, so it is easy to continue to Thassos Town by hopping on a nearby bus. In Thassos Town both the port police and the ticket booth (located at opposite sides of the new harbor) post schedules.

Flying Dolphins: Hydrofoils zip to **Kavala** from Thassos Town (45min.; 4 per day 8:10am-3:45pm; €9, children €4.40), and from Limenaria, on Thassos's southern coast (45min.; 8:20am, 3pm; €11). Schedules are posted at the port police and ticket booth, and docked boats indicate departure times with signs above their doors. You can buy tickets either prior to boarding or onboard.

Buses: When you arrive in Skala Prinos from Kavala, walk left to find buses for Thassos Town and Limenaria, whose departure times correspond with the arrival of the ferries from Kavala. The **Thassos Town** bus station (☎22 162) is located across from the hydrofoil landing on the waterfront. Open daily 7:30am-8:15pm. To: **Aliki beach** (1hr., 3 per day 10:45am-4:15pm, €3); **Limenaria** (1hr., 9 per day 6:20am-6:20pm, €3.30) via **Skala Prinos** (25min., €2); **Panagia** (15min., every hr. 6:45am-6pm, €1); **Skala Potamia** (30min., 12 per day 8:10am-6pm, €1.30); **Theologos** (1½hr., 6 per day 9am-4:15pm, €4.30). A bus laps around the island and back to Thassos Town (3hr., 5 per day 6:20am-4:15pm, €8). Ask at the **Indispensable Holiday Services** tourist office or bus office for paper schedules in English.

Taxis: ☎23 391. Near the ports.

Water Taxis: ☎22 734. Run once daily from Thassos Town to **Golden beach** (€3) and **Makryamos** (€3). Schedules change often—call the tourist office for departure times.

Rentals: Cars and mopeds can be rented all over Thassos Town. **Budget,** on Theagenus (☎23 150; fax 22 421), rents cars (€30-50 per day for first 100km; includes $300 damage waiver). Open daily 9am-1:30pm and 5-9pm.

✈ ❓ ORIENTATION AND PRACTICAL INFORMATION

A small crossroads near the bus station and the National Bank connects the water-front road leading to **Agousti Theologiti Cafe** and **18 Oktovriou,** a jungle of souvenir shops that runs parallel to the water one block inland. With your back to the water, the **Old Port,** the ancient **agora,** and the nearest beach are on the left. The small central plateia is about two blocks farther inland.

Tourist Offices: Thassos Tours (☎22 546), under the yellow sign on the waterfront. Helps with accommodations and island tours and rents motorbikes (€12) and cars (€30-50). International license required. Open daily 8:30am-midnight. **Indispensable Holiday Services** (☎22 041), on 18 Oktovriou behind the row of tavernas. Exchanges currency and has maps. Karyn, who speaks English, is extremely helpful and informative. Open M-Sa 9am-1:30pm and 6-9pm.

Bank: The Commercial Bank (☎22 703), next to Indispensable Holiday Services, exchanges currency. **Agricultural Bank** (☎22 970) is across the road. Both have **ATMs** and are open M-Th 8am-2:30pm, F 8am-1:30pm.

Police: ☎22 500. On the waterfront by the port police.

Pharmacy: ☎23 210. In the central plateia, 3 blocks inland from the waterfront. Open daily 8am-10pm.

Medical Services: Health Center (☎71 100 or 71 498), Prinos. Open 24hr. Although there are 6-7 doctors, there is no **hospital** on Thassos; the nearest is in Kavala.

Telephones: OTE (☎22 399), on 18 Oktovriou, 1 block inland from Thassos Tours. Open M-F 7:30am-3:10pm.

Internet Access: Millennium Net (☎58 089). From the tourist office, turn left and continue walking past Hotel Xenia. 6 computers. €2 per hr. Beer €2. Coffee €1.50. Also try **Corner Net Cafe** (☎58 086), 2 blocks in from the police station down the street from Lena Hotel. €3 per hr. Open daily 10am-2am. Wi-Fi available for the same price.

Post Office: ☎22 114. Across the street from Corner Net Cafe. Open M-F 7:30am-2pm. **Postal Code:** 64004.

⌂ ACCOMMODATIONS

The streets behind 18 Oktovriou are crammed with signs advertising **domatia;** most cost €20-25 for a single. They usually offer a clean room and include a Greek break-fast of salad, feta cheese, and pastries. The best value in Thassos Town is ▓**Hotel Lena ❷,** located next to the post office on M. Alexandrou, four blocks inland from the beach. Amy, the American owner, is personable and courteous, and the recently renovated building has 22 large rooms with air-conditioning, TV, bath, balcony, and a shared fridge. Reserve rooms a week in advance during high season. (☎22 933. Breakfast included. English spoken. Open May-Oct. Rooms €25. 10% discount for *Let's Go* readers.) **Hotel Athanassia ❷** seems more like domatia than a hotel. Walk down the waterfront with your back to the Old Port and make a left immediately after the Hotel Xenia. The hotel is on the right at the end of a narrow lane, swallowed by grapevines and plane trees. Away from the touristy area, this is one of the quieter options in town. There are spacious rooms, some with bath. (☎22 545. Singles and doubles €25; triples €30.) **Studio Amy ❷** caters to the self-sufficient traveler, with kitchen facilities in each of the eight rooms and a shared barbecue, fridge, and garden. This studio complex, which belongs to the same owner as Hotel Lena, is on the main road going to Prinos across the street from the Elin gas station. Send a fax 10 days in advance to reserve during the summer. (☎22 933; fax 23 873. English spoken. Doubles €25.)

NORTHEAST AEGEAN

FOOD

The waterfront is packed with restaurants designed to cater to a wide range of European tastes and tavernas where fresh fish and octopus appetizers dominate. The promenade is extremely tourist-oriented; multilingual menus offer "full English breakfasts" along with plates of schnitzel, pizza, and pasta. The best of these international options is **Restaurant Thassian ❷**, along the waterfront to the right of the bus stop, founded by an English woman named Katherine who walks around meeting every customer. The European and Greek dishes are cooked to perfection and served with complimentary ice cream, cake, and coffee. (☎22 403. Entrees €5-10.) **Restaurant Syrtaki ❸**, 150m past the Old Port at the end of the waterfront road, is famous for its *mezedes* (€10 per person). With an ocean view, tables on the beach under a shaded canopy, and live Greek folk music Wednesday, Saturday, and Sunday nights, food is just one of the many draws. (☎23 353. Entrees €4-11. Open daily noon-midnight. AmEx/MC/V.) Established in 1952, **Simi Restaurant ❷**, in the Old Port, was the first restaurant in town and is still one of the most popular. Though you might be forgotten by waiters in this laid-back atmosphere, the fish and shellfish are irresistible. (☎22 517. Reservations required for parties of more than 5. Entrees €6-10. Open daily 10am-12:30am. MC/V.)

SIGHTS AND ENTERTAINMENT

Maps of the **Old Town** are available at Indispensable Holiday Services. Just behind the Old Port are the ruins of the ancient **agora.** (Open daily 8am-7pm.) From here, or from the promontory beyond the Old Port, trails lead to the 4th-century BC **theater** (closed). Past the theater, a lit trail leads to the **acropolis**, home to a **Genoese fortress.** The trail continues to the **Temple of Athena** and the rock-carved **Altar to Pan**, above which is the scenic peak and a **secret stairway** down. Marble **Cyclopean walls** that once encircled the city are well-preserved here. Continuing down the walls is the **Gate of Parmenon**, with an eerie **Evil Eye** rock facing downhill. Even the archaeologically disinclined will enjoy a trip to the ▓**Gate of Silenos,** which is an ancient main gate graced with a full-length, excited centaur. Follow Scolis several blocks out of the town center. Beyond Silenos, the walls continue past the **Gate of Hercules** and **Gate of Zeus and Hera,** which both have reliefs.

Beach lovers might have a hard time choosing among Thassos's beautiful sands. To the south, ▓**Aliki's** twin coves shelter bleached white rock and crevices ideal for snorkeling. Between Panagia and Potamia, the popular **Chrisi Ammoudia,** better known as the **"golden beach,"** stretches endlessly. Take the bus or a water taxi to this favorite, known for its long sandy beaches. Don't be discouraged by the swarms of tourists; more isolated spots can be found along the clear turquoise water in both directions from Limenaria—just rent a bike or head out on foot and pick a cove. Ask at the bus station to find out which bus heads past a particular beach. You can find superb **hiking** in the relatively untouched interior, as many unmarked trails snake into the mountainous inland.

▓**Cafe Karnagio** is on a cliff at the end of the waterfront walkway, past the old harbor and away from the racket of motorbikes. Thoughtful night owls can sip ouzo from a seat on the wooden roof with one of the best views in town. (☎23 170. Beer €2. Open daily 9am-2am.) Locals and tourists flock to a number of music bars and dance clubs that blend together in a haze of alcohol and bass. **The Grand Cafe,** on K. Dmitriadi one block inland from 18 Oktovriou, is a quiet coffee shop during the day and a club blaring house, Greek, techno, and pop music at night. (Mixed drinks €8. Open daily 11am-6am.) The younger locals gravitate to the **Just in Time Club,** across the road from the Grand Cafe. This American-owned club plays progressive and hip-hop music. (Mixed drinks €6. Open daily 9:30am-4am.)

LIMENARIA Λιμενάρια ☎25930

Thriving Limenaria is on a curve of stony beach at the island's southern tip. Smaller and more relaxed than its bustling counterpart, Limenaria is a haven of calm waves and lazy sunsets. Unfortunately, the town is no longer a secret—a resort feel prevails as the island is invaded by sun-craving Europeans every summer. Subsequently, the village is turning into one big tourist attraction which closes down from October to April; hotels are high in both quality and price.

Hotels and rented rooms abound in Limenaria, with many hotels stationed on the waterfront and **domatia** scattered throughout town. ▓**Hotel Molos** ❷ has bright, pleasant rooms with TV, bath, and balcony overlooking the water. Walk down Eth. Antistasis and turn right at the waterfront; Molos is 50m down. (☎51 389. Breakfast €3, lunch €6, dinner €8, all meals €10. Singles €20-30; doubles €30-40; triples €35-45. MC/V.) **Hotel Asterias** ❸, on the waterfront about 60m down from Molos, has sunny air-conditioned rooms with kitchen, fridge, and pale blue walls. (☎52 497. Breakfast included. Reception open 8am-1am. English spoken. Singles €35; doubles €45; triples €50. AmEx/MC/V.) **Avgoustos Rented Rooms** ❷ offers domatia with bath, Spanish-style balcony, and air-conditioning. Walk down Eth. Antistasis, turn right, and follow the waterfront road until it bends inland; go another block. (☎52 310. Open late June to early Sept. Doubles €33.) The entire waterfront fuses into one tacky mega-restaurant, comprised of the town's numerous tavernas and snack bars. To get to **Il Mare** ❷, walk down to the waterfront on Eth. Antistasis. Homemade delicacies such as the lamb *kleftiko* (broiled in oven with feta cheese; €7) are cooked by the owner and served on romantic tables along the water. (☎53 170. Entrees €4-8. Open daily 11am-1am. AmEx/MC/V.) Down the waterfront 200m is **Restaurant Maranos Flisvos** ❷, with a large wine cask teetering precariously over the entrance. It offers a calm, easygoing environment with the sounds of classic *rembetika* and a variety of fish choices. (☎51 239. Entrees €4-8. Open daily 8am-2am. AmEx/MC/V.) Come nightfall, the waterfront restaurants function as one long bar. **Istos Cafe-Bar, Nile Bar, Larry's Bar,** and **Cristina's** blare a jumbled audio mess of Greek and American favorites. (Beer €3. Mixed drinks €5-6.)

The road leading out of town, Eth. Antistasis, runs perpendicularly away from the shore to an intersection with Polytechniou, one block inland. From the main intersection of Eth. Antistasis and Polytechniou, **buses** go to: Thassos Town (45min., 8 per day 6:30am-6:30pm, €3.30) via Skala Prinos (20min., €2); Theologos (15min., 8 per day 7:20am-7:20pm, €1.30); around the island (stops in Limenaria twice a day 7:30am, 3:50pm; 1 day of unlimited rides €8). For car rental, go behind the Agricultural Bank ATM to **Speedy Rent-a-Car.** (☎52 700. Cars €15-25. Open daily 9am-1:30pm and 5-10pm.) On the waterfront 150m right of Hotel Molos is **Blue City Tours,** which arranges excursions and has information on buses, ferries, and flights to Kavala. (☎51 695. English spoken. Open daily 8:30am-1:30pm and 6-8:30pm.) A few meters past the OTE, **Agricultural Bank** has an **ATM.** (☎52 683. Open M-Th 8am-2:30pm, F 8am-2pm.) The **police** are at the inland waterfront, before the National Bank. (☎51 111. Open 24hr.) The **OTE** is on Antistasis. (☎51 399. Open M-F 7:30am-3:10pm.) The **post office** is on the inland waterfront, close to the police station. (☎51 296. Open M-F 7:30am-2pm.) **Postal Code:** 64002.

NORTHEAST AEGEAN

IONIAN ISLANDS
Νησιά Του Ιόνιου

 Just west of mainland Greece, the Ionian Islands entice travelers with their lush, green vegetation that rolls gently to the edge of the shimmering turquoise waters. The unusual architecture and colors in the villages hint at a different history than much of the rest of Greece—these islands were not conquered by Ottomans, but instead bear the marks of Venetian, British, French, and Russian occupants. Each of these civilizations has left its own cultural fingerprint. Today, the islands are a favorite among Western Europeans and adventurous travelers seeking the unconventional. Multicultural for millennia, each of the Ionian Islands maintains a unique identity while sharing an unparalleled beauty.

 SUGGESTED ITINERARIES: IONIAN ISLANDS

FOUR DAYS Lounge by **Kephalonia's** (p. 553) sky-blue water, then push past the crowds on **Zakynthos** (p. 561) to appreciate the Venetian arches, isolated beaches, and brilliantly green foliage.

ONE WEEK Start in **Corfu** (p. 530), checking out beaches and cultural sights during the day, then heading to the Pink Palace Hotel in **Agios Gordios** (p. 542) at night for some general carousing. Help protect sea turtles on **Zakynthos** (p. 561) and swim through **Kephalonia's** underground lakes. After seeing why Odysseus was so determined to get back to **Ithaka** (p. 549), test your windsurfing skills in **Vasiliki, Lefkada** (p. 547).

CORFU Κέρκυρα

Homer first sang Corfu's praise by writing of its "honeyed fig," "unctuous olive," "boisterous waves," and friendly inhabitants, who helped Odysseus in a desperate time of need. In 743 BC, Corfu was colonized by Corinth, a close ally of Sparta. When the island broke into conflict with its mother city a few centuries later, it joined with Athens, sparking the Peloponnesian War. From the Franks to the Venetians to the British to today's tourist masses, Corfu (Κέρκυρα, KEHR-kee-rah) has captivated all who come to its shores. There's a reason why this place continues to be desired by so many: from archaeology to debauchery, Corfu has it all. Budding archaeologists will find ruins galore, those tired of clothes can strip down at any number of nude beaches, and people seeking a laid-back village experience will stumble upon it without even having to look. Corfu's natural and manmade treasures justify the Homeric fuss even today.

CORFU TOWN   ☎ 26610

Encouraging you to get lost in the most positive sense of the word, Corfu Town, unapologetically Italian in feel, teems with delicious distractions day and night. Laundry lines tied to ornate iron balconies, fragrant yellow roses, Venetian buildings, and green-shuttered alleyways exhibit the genuine flavors that make this town a lively center of Mediterranean culture.

Ionian Islands

TO ANCONA, BRINDISI, BARI
VENICE, TRIESTE

ALBANIA

Sidari
Ag.
Stefanos
Kassiopi
Mt.
Pantokrator
Koulara
Kalami
Gimari
Paleokastritsa
Barbati
Ipsos
Nissaki
Corfu Town
Glyfada
Pelekas
Kanoni
Corfu
Ag.
Gordios
Benitses
Messonghi
Baukaris
Igoumenitsa
Lefkimi
Kavos

Ioannina

GREECE

TO BRINDISI, ITALY

Parga

Paxi
Gaios

Antipaxi

Arta

Preveza

*Ionian
Sea*

Lefkada Town
Ag. Nikitas
Ag. Nikolaos
Lefkada
Nidri

Porto Katsiki
Vasiliki
Agiofili

Fiskardo
Frikes
Stavros
Kioni
Ithaka
Myrtos
Dexa
Gidaki
Vathy
Piso
Aetos
Filiatro
Agia
Efimia
Antisamos
Sami
Kephalonia
Lixouri
Argostoli
Poros
Xi
Lassi
Ormous
Lourda
Pesada
Skala

Astakos

TO PATRAS

Agios Nikolaos
Volimes
Smuggler's
Wreck
Alykes
Tsilivi
Planos
Kyllini
Zakynthos Town
Porto Roma
Zakynthos
Lagana
Vasilikos
Keri
Gerakas

0   30 miles
0   30 kilometers

N

IONIAN ISLANDS

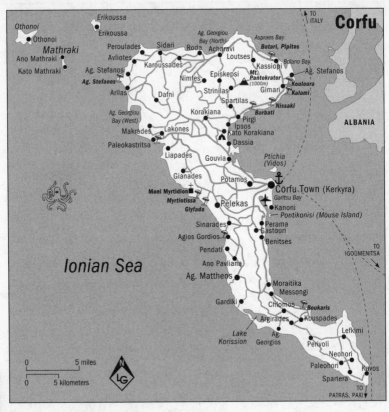

⊡ TRANSPORTATION

Flights: Olympic Airways, Iak. Polila 11 (☎38 694, reservations 38 695). From the post office, walk 1 block on Rizopaston Voulefton toward the Old City and turn right. Open M-F 7:30am-7:30pm. Flights go to **Athens** (1hr., 2-3 per day, €120-150) and **Thessaloniki** (1hr.; Tu, F, Su 11:40pm; €70-100). In summer, almost 50 charter flights per day fly through Corfu's airport; book 2-3 days in advance. A 5min. taxi ride (agree on about €10 beforehand) is the quickest way to the **airport** (☎33 811). You can get dropped off 1km away if you take blue bus #11 to Pelekas (tell the driver).

Ferries: Get tickets at least 1 day in advance during high season; when traveling to Italy, find out if the port tax (€7-10) is included in the cost of a ticket. Prices vary according to season, ferry line, and class. Try **Fragline** or **HML** for **Brindisi** and **Strindzis Lines** for **Venice. International Tours,** El. Venizelou 32 (☎39 007), and **Ionian Cruises,** El. Venizelou 38 (☎31 649), are both located across the street from the Old Port on El. Venizelou. Ferries to: **Bari, Italy** (10hr.; 4 per week M-F 8:30am-10:45pm; €49); **Brindisi, Italy** (8hr., Tu-Su 1-2 per day, €35); **Igoumenitsa** (1½hr.; every hr. 6:30am-10pm; €6.50, students €3.20 except July-Aug.); **Patras** (8hr., 5 per week, €30); **Paxi** (1-3 per day, €15.10); **Venice, Italy** (24hr., daily, €65).

Buses: Green KTEL buses (☎30 627) go between I. Theotoki and the New Fortress (accessible from I. Theotoki or Xen. Stratigou). **Blue municipal buses** (☎31 595) leave from San Rocco. For a schedule with return times and prices for both types, ask at the white info kiosk at the station. Open daily 8am-10pm. The tourist info office in the green kiosk in San Rocco has English timetables for all buses.

Green buses: To: **Agios Gordios** (45min.; M-Sa 6 per day 8:15am-8pm, Su 3 per day 9:30am-5:30pm; €1.90); **Agios Stefanos** (1½hr.; M-Sa 4 per day 5:15am-4pm, Su 9:30am; €3.50); **Barbati** (45min.; M-Sa 5 per day 9am-4:30pm, Su 9:30am; €1.90); **Cavos** (1½hr.; M-Sa 10 per day 5am-8pm, Su 3 per day 5am-3:30pm; €3.80); **Glyfada** (45min.; M-F 8 per day 6:45am-8pm, Sa 7 per day 9am-8pm, Su 3 per day 10am-5:30pm; €1.90); **Ipsos** and **Pirgi** (30-45min.; M-F 10 per day 6:45am-4:30pm, Sa 6 per day 9am-4:30pm, Su 9:30am; €1.40); **Kassiopi** (1hr.; M-Sa 6 per day 5:45am-4:30pm, Su 9:30am; €3); **Messonghi** (45min.; M-Sa 5-6 per day 8:45am-3:30pm; Su 9:30am, 3:30pm; €1.90); **Paleokastritsa** (45min.; M-Sa 6 per day 9am-6pm, Su 4 per day 10:30am-6pm; €2); **Sidari** (1hr.; M-Sa 8 per day 5:15am-8pm, Su 9:30am; €2.90). Buy tickets onboard. **KTEL** also runs to **Athens** (8hr.; 8:45am, 1:15, 7:30pm; €37.70) and **Thessaloniki** (8hr.; 7:45am, 7:30pm; €40); prices include ferry. Buy tickets at the green bus station.

Blue buses: To: **Achilleon #10** (30min.; M-Sa 6 per day 7am-8pm, Su 4 per day 9am-8pm; €1); **Agios Ioannis** and **Aqualand #8** (30min.; M-F 13 per day 6:15am-10pm, Sa 12 per day 7:10am-9pm, Su 6 per day 8am-9pm; €1); **Benitses** (30min., 13 per day 6:45am-10pm, €1); **Kanoni** and **Mouse Island #2** (30min.; M-F 2 per hr. 6:30am-10pm, Sa every hr. 6:30am-9:30pm, Su every hr. 9:30am-9:30pm; €1); **Pelekas #11** (30min.; M-F 7 per day 7am-8:30pm, Sa 6 per day 2:15-8:30pm, Su 8 per day 10am-8:30pm; €1). Buy tickets at the kiosk.

Taxis: ☎ 33 811 or 31 595. At the New and Old Ports, the Spianada, Pl. San Rocco, and Pl. G. Theotoki. Ask for the price before you get in—they vary a great deal, especially for short distances. From 1-6am, fares are doubled. Taxis respond to calls 24hr.

Car Rental: Europcar, Venizelou 30 (☎ 46 931; www.europcar.com.gr) and **InterCorfu Rent a Car,** Venizelou 46 (☎ 41 709), on the water at the New Port. Small cars from €45-60 per day; price varies by season. Ask if 20% tax, 3rd-party insurance, and over 200km are included.

Moped Rental: Travelers should note that many roads, especially those far from Corfu Town, are not well paved and can present serious risk to moped drivers; stick to the main roads, which have fewer potholes. If you decide to rent, there are various places along the waterfront, especially near the New Port. **Easy Rider,** 3rd Parodos El. Venizelou (☎ 43 026), is across from the customs house on the corner of Xen. Stratigou. Mopeds from €25 per day (helmet included). Rental fee should include 3rd-party liability and property damage insurance. Open daily 9am-9pm.

■✴ 🔓 ORIENTATION AND PRACTICAL INFORMATION

Befuddling alleys and ubiquitous waters may add to Corfu Town's charm, but they also can cause stress for anyone with a plane or ferry to catch. Most visitors arrive in the **New Port,** which is next to the **Old Port** in front of a large square on the town's northern coast. The **New Fortress,** the conspicuous edifice by the ports, is a good reference point. From the customs house at the New Port, it's about 1km to the center of town, **Plateia San Rocco;** locals will say and understand "Saroco" for short. To get there from the New Port, cross the intersection at the light, turn right, and walk uphill on **Avramiou,** which eventually turns into **Ioanni Theotoki.** The long driveway of the **KTEL (green) bus terminal** will be on your left as you pass, and the **blue bus terminal** is in the square. The **Old Town** can be reached by walking along the waterfront toward the Old Port. If you follow the waterfront with the water on your left past the Old Port square, circling the Old Town, you will see the **palace** on your left and a long park known as the **Spianada,** the town's social center, straight in front of you. Two streets encircle the Spianada: **Eleftherias** (which becomes **Kapodistriou**) is farther inland; **Polytechniou** curves around the outside. While picturesque, a walk around the Old Town can confuse even the best navigators. To avoid getting lost, use the prominent and central National Bank at the entrance of the Old Town as a reference point; the pedestrian walkway in front of the bank leads to San Rocco's main feeder street, **G. Theotoki.**

Tourist Office: Tourist Information (☎20 733), on Pl. San Rocco in a green kiosk. Friendly, English-speaking staff helps with any questions. Open daily 9am-2pm and 6pm-9pm. The **EOT** (☎37 520) has a help desk and plans for an additional office.

Banks: Banks with **24hr. ATMs** line the larger streets and the waterfront by the ports. **National Bank,** Alexandras 30 (☎47 728), is on the corner of Alexandras and Rizopaston Voulefton across from the post office. Open M-Th 8am-2:30pm, F 8:30am-1:30pm.

Beyond Tourism: The Pink Palace (p. 542) hires hotel and club staff and DJs. Mail a letter of introduction, resume, and photo in advance. Usually a minimum 2-month commitment is required, but friendly owner Dr. George is open to negotiating.

Bookstore: Xenoglosso, Markora 45 (☎23 923). From the police station, walking away from San Rocco, turn left onto Markora. The wonderful collection includes classic novels, books about Greece, and language materials. Limited selection in English. Open M, W, Sa 8am-2pm, Tu and Th-F 8:30am-2pm and 5-8:30pm.

Laundromat: "New Port" Laundry, Sp. Mouriki 2 (☎38 457), on the road perpendicular to the waterfront, opposite port customs. Wash and dry €10. Open M-F 8:30am-3pm and 5:30-9pm, Sa 5:30-8:30pm.

Police: ☎39 294. Heading toward the New Port, turn right off I. Theotoki along Pl. San Rocco onto the short street that intersects Markora. Open 24hr. In an **emergency,** dial ☎100. The **tourist police** (☎30 265 or 39 503) are located on the 4th fl. of the police building. Open daily 7am-2pm. **Port Police** ☎32 655.

Hospital: Corfu General Hospital (☎88 200 or 45 811), on I. Andreadi. The tourist office or tourist police can help find an English-speaking doctor. For an **ambulance,** call ☎166.

Internet Access: Netoikos Cafe, Kaloheretou 12-14 (☎47 479), behind Ag. Spiridon church. €3 per hr. Open M-Sa 10am-midnight, Su 6pm-midnight. **Eden** (☎26 900), in San Rocco by the info kiosk. Has 10 terminals. €3 per hr. Open daily 8am-midnight.

Post Office: ☎25 544. On the corner of Alexandras and R. Voulefton. **Poste Restante** and **currency exchange** available. Open M-F 7:30am-8pm. **Postal Code:** 49100.

ACCOMMODATIONS

There's no getting around the fact that Corfu Town is expensive; tourist packages drive up prices for the low budget traveler. Relatively cheap accommodations do exist, though, especially in low season. Travelers looking for bargains may have some luck with the **Association of Owners of Private Rooms and Apartments in Corfu,** Iak. Polila 24, which has a complete list of rooms in Corfu and the phone numbers of the landlords who lease them. (☎26 133. Open M-F 9am-3pm and 5-8pm.) If you are traveling in high season, call several weeks in advance to ensure availability. Otherwise, towns and campgrounds just outside the city can be worthwhile alternatives. Prices are flexible and depend on the duration of your stay, the time of year, and the vacancy of the hotel or domatia. Since competition is fierce, don't hesitate to ask for a lower fee.

Hotel Astron, Donzelot 15 (☎39 505), past Spilia with the water on your left. The old wooden furniture in the rooms is the only part of the hotel not recently renovated. Rooms have TV and A/C. Plans for additional improvements such as a pool and Wi-Fi are in the works. Prices inflate to the listed high by Aug. Expect to pay more for a sea view. Singles €45-60; doubles €55-85; triples €80-95. ❹

Hotel Atlantis, Xen. Sratigou Ave 48 (☎35 560), 1 block from the New Port toward the Old Town, on the waterfront. Simple, red-carpeted rooms have TV, A/C, phone, balcony, and bath. Reception 24hr. Singles €60-75; doubles €70-100; triples €84-120. ❹

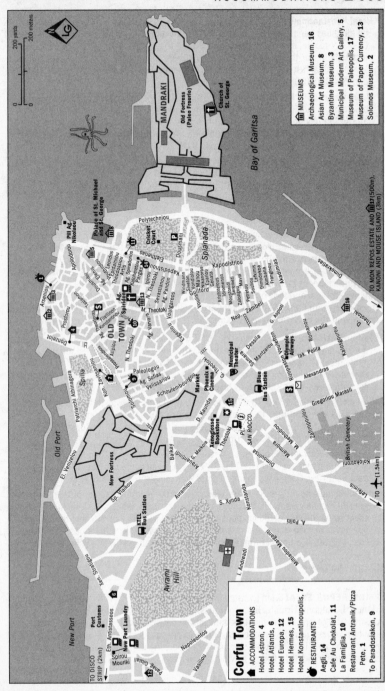

Corfu Town

MANDRAKI

Old Fortress
(Paleo Frourio)

Church of
St. George

Bay of Garitsa

TO MON REPOS ESTATE AND 🏛17(500m),
KANONI AND MOUSE ISLAND (3km)

Palace of St. Michael
and St. George

Polytechniou

Cricket
Court

PII Ag.
Nikolaou

Splanada

Kapodistriou

Dousmani

Eleftherias

Leonidos
Theodambou
Filissou

Ag. Spiridonos

Agiou
Theodora

Kapodistriou

Kapodistriou

Arseniou

Prosfou

Donzelot

Spilia

Old Port

Patriarch Athinagora

Paleologou
Ag. Sofias
Velissariou

Schoulembourgou

Market

Phoenix
Cinema

Xenoglosso
Bookstore

PL.
SAN ROCCO

Municipal
Theater

Blue
Bus Station

New Fortress

Bakay

Avuaniti

Sp. Vlaikou

KTEL
Bus Station

Arkamiou

S. Xynda

Konstanda

A. Politi

Avrami
Hill

I. Andreadi

Mitadou Margariti

Napoleontos

Vasiliou

TO DISCO
STRIP (2km)

Eth. Antistasseos

Spirou
Mouriki

New Port Laundry

Panag. Gitsiali

New Port

Port
Customs

Xen Stratigou

TO
(1.5km)
Lefkimis

Dimokratias

M. Methodiou

Mamora

Alexandras

Gregoriou Marasli

British Cemetery

Kolokotroni

Zafiropoulou

Olympic
Airways

Iak. Polila

Vraila

Romanou

Kolokairou

G. Aspiou

Dessila

Dimokratias

Akadimias

Dimokratias

Nao. Zambeli

Theotoki

🏛16

ACCOMMODATIONS
- Hotel Astron, 4
- Hotel Atlantis, 6
- Hotel Europa, 12
- Hotel Hermes, 15
- Hotel Konstantinoupolis, 7

RESTAURANTS
- Aegli, 14
- Cafe Au Chokolat, 11
- La Famiglia, 10
- Restaurant Antranik/Pizza
  Pete, 1
- To Paradosiakon, 9

🏛 **MUSEUMS**
- Archaeological Museum, 16
- Asian Art Museum, 8
- Byzantine Museum, 3
- Municipal Modern Art Gallery, 5
- Museum of Paleopolis, 17
- Museum of Paper Currency, 13
- Solomos Museum, 2

200 yards
200 meters

N

Hotel Konstantinoupolis, K. Zavitsianou 11 (☎48 716), at the Old Port. This beautiful building has been greeting guests since 1862 with its traditional long Venetian shutters. Airy rooms, some with balcony and an amazing view, have TV, A/C, and a perfect location in the middle of the large square at Spilia. Call in advance in high season. Breakfast €7. Laundry services available. Reception 24hr. Singles €60-80; doubles €80-100; triples €90-120. ❹

Hotel Hermes, G. Markora 14 (☎39 268), around the bend from the police station, by the noisy public market. Complete with an old-fashioned push-button phone operator in the reception area, this hotel has an undeniably retro style. Spacious, clean rooms include fridge and fan. Breakfast €5. Reception 24hr. Singles €30, with bath €35; doubles €38/50; triples €45. MC/V. ❸

Hotel Europa, P. Gitsiali 10 (☎39 304). Europa rents simple, small rooms with decent views, though the location is not particularly convenient or well lit. Breakfast €6. Reception 24hr. Singles €25, with bath €35-40; doubles €40-50; triples €50-65. ❷

▐ FOOD

The main restaurant areas are by the Spianada and the Old Port. Lots of similar tavernas are scattered throughout the Old Town's maze of alleyways. Homemade wines and beers are available all over the island: light white *kakotrygis*, richer white *moscato*, dry *petrokorintho* red, and dark *skopelitiko*. Light yellow *tsitsibira* (ginger beer) is another specialty. A daily **open-air market** sells inexpensive fruit, vegetables, and fish on Dessila, off G. Theotoki and below the new fortress. (Open daily 6am-2pm.) **Supermarkets** are located on I. Theotoki, in Pl. San Rocco, and beyond the bus station on Alexandras. (Open M-F 8am-9pm, Sa 8am-8pm.)

▌To Paradosiakon, Odos Solomou 20 (☎37 578), at the corner of Ag. Sofias. Look for the salmon pink walls. Highly recommended by locals, this small restaurant, whose name means "tradition," makes amazing, freshly cooked food. The chef cooks whatever she buys in the market each day, giving the classic meals a sense of spontaneity. Entrees €4-8.50. Open daily Mar.-Nov. 10am-midnight. ❷

▌La Famiglia, Arlioti 16 (☎30 270), tucked away in an alleyway in the area known to locals as Kantouni Bizi. This romantic Italian restaurant with top-notch service and dishes feels like a fancy restaurant without the fancy prices. All the pasta dishes are exceptional. Entrees €7.50-10. Open daily noon-1am. ❸

Restaurant Antranik/Pizza Pete, Arseniou 21 (☎22 301), a 2min. walk past Hotel Astron. Offers large pizzas (€7-11), 20 types of homemade ice cream (€6-8), and a waterfront view. Open daily spring-summer 9am-midnight. AmEx/MC/V. ❷

Aegli, Kapodistriou 23 (☎31 949). Claims to be the oldest restaurant in town, and its years of experience show in the excellent service and somewhat fancy ambience. Tables either sit on the side of the restaurant in a snug walkway or look out onto the beautiful Spianada. *Kleftiko* (lamb in a clay dish with tomatoes, onions, potatoes, and melted feta; €12.50) is a Corfiot favorite. Open 10am-11:30pm. AmEx/MC/V. ❸

▥ MUSEUMS

▌MON REPOS ESTATE. In a grandiose effort to please his Corfiot wife, Sir Frederic Adams, the second British High Commissioner of the Ionian Islands, mandated the construction of one of the most elegant and expansive estates in Greece. However, only two years after they moved in, the Adamses relocated to Madras, India. The grounds changed hands many times until they became the summer home of Greece's ex-royal family in 1864. Today, a walk through the estate gives a glimpse of Corfu's gorgeous terrain (including the 2000 trees Adams received as a housewarming gift from the British Empire) and passes by excavation sites. Look for the intriguing **Museum of Paleopolis,** which exhibits an eclectic collection of period rooms from the palace, along with archaeological finds from excavations around Corfu. Each display, including an ancient version of a cosmetics kit and a collection of 510 silver Corinthian and Corycian coins, is labeled with full explanations in English and Greek. Those tired of perusing ancient artifacts can enjoy the air-conditioned multimedia exhibit that gives a thorough summary of local history. *(To reach the palace, head up the path to the right just inside the main gate. ☎ 41 369. Estate open daily 8am-7pm. Free. Museum open Tu-Su 8:30am-3pm. Longer hours in the summer. €3, EU students €2.)* From the palace, with the water on your left, follow the forested path overlooking the sea to the tiny, pebbly **Kardaki beach.** Corfiot poet Lorenzos Mavilis wrote that anyone who drinks from its spring will remain on the island forever. To the right of the palace as you face the museum entrance, a path leads to two Doric temples: the last remains of the **Temple of Hera** (the Heraion), and the more impressive **Kardaki Temple,** thought to have been dedicated to either Poseidon, Apollo, or Asclepius. *(Take the #2 bus toward Mouse Island and tell the driver you want to be dropped off at Mon Repos. 10min., €0.60.)*

■ PALACE OF SAINT MICHAEL AND SAINT GEORGE. This palace was built by Adams's predecessor, British Lord High Commissioner Sir Thomas Maitland, during the British occupation of the Ionnian Islands (1814-1864). Presiding over the Spianada, it combines Neoclassical and mythology-based sculpture with Asian artifacts. The building originally was intended to house the High Commissioner, the Ionian parliament, and the ceremonies of the orders of St. Michael and St. George. Later used by the ex-royal family as a ceremonial palace, it was renovated to hold the EU summit meeting in 1994. Glance around at the intricate ceilings, heavy mahogany doors, and the impressive Throne Room. The palace also contains the **Museum of Asian Art,** which displays 10,550 artifacts from three formerly private collections as well as individual donations. The well-organized collection, with such treasures as Samurai weapons and a set of six-fold screens, includes objects from Afghanistan, Cambodia, China, India, Japan, Nepal, Pakistan, and Tibet. *(☎ 30 443. Open Tu-Su 8am-7:30pm. €3, students and seniors €2, EU students free.)* The **Municipal Modern Art Gallery (Dimotiko Pinakothiki),** beside the palace, has a small display of Corfiot paintings and various rotating exhibits. *(☎ 48 690. Open Tu-F 9am-5pm, but hours of special exhibits vary. €1.50, students and seniors €1.)*

BYZANTINE MUSEUM. This impressive collection of religious artifacts is housed in the small, late 15th-century **Church of the Most Holy Virgin Antivouniotissa,** which still operates as a church on the December 26 and August 23 feasts of the Virgin. Gold communion cups, 15th- through 19th-century priestly vestments, and iron-covered gospel books are some of the highlights of the permanent exhibit in the room next to the church. The collection of **Cretan School** icons is also worth seeing, if only to observe the painted "wallpaper" (a red floral pattern that adorns much of the church) and wood ceiling carvings. The museum displays 90 icons including the famed 16th-century icon of Mary Magdalene calling Jesus "Rabouni" ("my teacher"), as described in the Gospel of John. The many different styles and influences in the collection are attributed to the influx of Cretan artists who stopped in Corfu on their way to Venice after the 1646 fall of Rethymno. *(Past the Old Port with the waterfront on your left; there are signs on Arseniou. ☎ 38 313. Open Tu-Su 8:30am-7pm. €2, students and seniors €1, EU students free. Modest dress required. Combined ticket for the Old Fortress, Byzantine Museum, Archaeological Museum, and Museum of Asian Art €8, students and seniors €4; available at any of the sights.)*

ARCHAEOLOGICAL MUSEUM. Ancient coins, bronze laurel leaves, and detailed statuettes will catch any visitor's attention, but the highlight of this large collec-

IONIAN ISLANDS

tion is hands-down the frightening **Gorgon Pediment** (590-580 BC) from Corfu's Doric Temple of Artemis. The oldest surviving pediment in Greece, it shows Medusa with her offspring, Pegasus and Chrysaor. According to myth, the creatures were born at the moment when Perseus cut off their mother's snake-covered head, though in the pediment she appears full of life. *(Armeni Vraila 1, down the steps leading to the Spianada, past Hotel Corfu Palace. ☎ 30 680. Open Tu-Su 8:30am-7pm. €3, students and seniors €2, children and EU students free.)*

OTHER MUSEUMS. Located in the house where Dionysios Solomos spent the last 20 years of his life, the **Solomos Museum** pays tribute to the beloved national poet. The first to use Demotic Greek in poetry, Solomos was part of the vibrant artistic community that once made the Old City its headquarters. His *Hymn to Freedom* provided the lyrics of Greece's national anthem. Beyond a myriad of photographs and photocopies, the museum holds pieces of the tree that inspired the poet. *(Look for the sign in an alleyway on Arseniou just west of the Byzantine Museum, toward the New Port. ☎ 30 674. Open M-F 9:30am-2pm. €1, students free.)* If the coins in the archaeological museums weren't enough, feed your love for money even more at the **Museum of Paper Currency** in the Ionian Bank Building, down N. Theotoki from the Spianada. The proud owner of the first bank note printed in Greece, the museum displays examples of all Greek currency ever circulated. *(☎ 41 552. Open M-F 10am-2pm. Free.)*

👁 SIGHTS

After invading Vandals and Goths destroyed ancient Corfu (Paleopolis) in the AD 5th and 6th centuries, residents built a more defensible city between the twin peaks of the Old Fortress. Wary of Ottoman raids, the Venetians strengthened the existing structure, constructed the New Fortress, and built thick walls around the growing city. A series of underground tunnels, now closed, connected the Old Fortress to the new one and all parts of Corfu Town. The tunnels later provided refuge for Corfiots after the first WWII air raids in 1940.

OLD FORTRESS (PALEO FROURIO). Linked to the Spianada by a 60m iron bridge that spans the 10th-century moat, the Old Fortress is a symbol of Corfu's history. The Byzantines, Venetians, and British all fortified the two hilltops, and ruins from each period remain. Most visitors find themselves drawn to the red **bell tower** near the summit and the **Church of Saint George**, which for years was closed to the public but now is open most days from 9am-6pm. Amazing panoramic views of the city and the sea await the determined who climb to the top of the tower. In the summer, Greek rock stars perform on the vast plateau next to the church (ask at the tourist information kiosk for a concert schedule). Explanations in English are sparse, so consider buying a guidebook (€4-6) from the museum. *(Just east of the Spianada. ☎ 38 313. Open daily 8am-7pm. €2, students and seniors €1, EU students free.)*

NEW FORTRESS. The result of the Venetians' second attempt to protect their city, the 350-year-old walls of the New Fortress once were considered the archetype of military architecture. Currently, the massive edifice hosts a small rotating art exhibit, a playground, and the occasional stray dog. Despite its somewhat paltry offerings, the fortress's location above the docks yields sweeping views of the town. Concerts and theatrical events take place here during the summer. *(At the top of Solomou; look for signs as you walk along Velissariou from the Old Port. ☎ 45 000. Open daily 9am-9pm. €2, EU students free.)*

CHURCH OF AGIOS SPIRIDON. Housing the embalmed body of the island's patron saint, Ag. Spiridon, this church, built in 1596, is an important Orthodox pilgrimage point. The biblical scenes on the 18th-century Baroque ceiling and the Renaissance-style icons draw tourists as well. Inside, a silver casket holds the remains of the 3rd-century saint, whose spirit is believed to wander the streets performing good deeds for the island's residents and visitors. In fact, four times per year, the casket is paraded through the city to purify the streets of evil spirits. Rumor has it that if the priest opens the gold cover of Spiridon's casket during your visit, you can catch a glimpse of his blackened face. Some tourists kiss the permanently exposed feet for good luck. *(Take Ag. Spiridon off the Spianada; it's on the left. Open daily 6am-9pm. Modest dress required.)*

KANONI AND MOUSE ISLAND. Praised in traditional songs about Corfu, Mouse Island (Pontikonisi) is located near the beautiful bay at Kanoni, the ancient capital of the island. Enjoy the jaw-dropping view at the now-famous Cafe Kanoni, serving patrons since 1864. *(Coffee €1.50. Snacks €3.50-6.50. Open daily in summer 8am-5pm.)* Then walk down to the water, where the tiny Vlacherna Monastery of the Virgin Mary juts into the water. Summer tourists can take frequent, small water taxis to Mouse Island. There, the only building you will find among the rich flora is the one-room 13th-century Byzantine Church of the Pantocrator, surrounded by cypresses. *(Take the #2 bus or a taxi to Kanoni, €10-12. Water taxis to Mouse Island 10am-9pm, €2.50.)*

♫ 🞲 ENTERTAINMENT AND NIGHTLIFE

The **Phoenix cinema,** G. Theotoki 42, two blocks from San Rocco after Dessila on the left, plays movies in English regularly. Look for placards on G. Theotoki. (☎ 28 310. Tickets €7.) The **municipal theater** (☎ 33 598), between Dessila and Mantzarou, has occasional drama, dance, and music performances, publicized on bulletin boards all over town.

STARING CONTEST. Greek men are notorious for casting intense, longing gazes at women in clubs and cafes. The penetrating glares can intimidate those unfamiliar with the culture, but they are usually a harmless, if annoyingly ubiquitous, part of the bar scene. In Greek slang, the men who cast these predatory looks are known as *kamaki,* the Greek word for "harpoon." Unless a woman is looking to be hooked, she should feel free to swim away.

Less than 2km west of the New Port, the disco strip, known as **Emboriko Center,** is the undisputed center of nightlife in Corfu Town in July and August. The best way to get to the strip, located on Eth. Antistasios, is by taxi (€4-7, more after midnight). Beer is generally €3-5.50, and mixed drinks are €7-10. Crowds of locals and tourists intermingle in the bars and cafes, each of which offers its own take on the ideal evening out. Most clubs here close down for low season and, when they reopen, frequently change names and/or ownership; ask the locals about the status of various clubs before heading out. **Crystal,** at the end of the strip (open daily midnight-7am), and **Prime,** in the center of the strip (open daily 10pm-5am), are your best bets for an international dance-off: Corfiots and mostly European tourists come for the relatively cheap alcohol (beer €3.50) and loud music. Popular **Envy,** where Corfiots go to lose the foreign masses, blasts Greek music. (Open daily 11pm-4am.) **Ekarti,** despite its snobbish reputation, wins as Corfu's bona fide hot spot. The club for Greeks who know how to party and are willing to shell out plenty of euro for it, Ekarti often has no cover but doesn't serve mixed drinks for under €7. (Open daily 10pm-4:30am.)

These clubs are only open in high season; earlier in the summer you can take a taxi (€7-9) or bus #7 to **Gouvia's** small club scene. **Whispers Bar** fills with groups of friends, talking and listening to the music ranging from the latest club hits to 1960s classics (beer €3-5). In Corfu Town itself, the elegant little cafes that line the Spianada are open year-round and usually lively until about 1am. On the palace side of the park, sip one of many sinfully rich frappés (€3) at **Cafe au Chokolat,** Eleftherias 36. This young hangout has some pretty fancy hot and cold chocolate drinks as well, including the cholesterol-boosting cold white-chocolate-and-hazelnut shake (€3.50). (☎80 019. Open 9am-1am.)

❄ FESTIVALS

Carnival season, beginning in February or March (depending on the date of Orthodox Easter), is largely secular in Corfu. The most entertaining traditions include "The Gossip," two Thursdays before the final Sunday of Carnival. In something like a street theater performance, women call out the latest gossip from windows across alleys in the center of the Old Town. On the last Sunday, the festival culminates with the burning of King Carnival, when the effigy "King" is tried and sentenced to death by fire for his hand in all the year's misfortunes. Corfu's animated **Easter** celebrations are reflected in the ornate Palm Sunday procession of the embalmed body of Ag. Spiridon, Corfu's saint. On Holy Saturday (the day before Easter), for good luck, Corfiots throw pots full of water out their windows at 11am; kids can be seen walking the streets, happily waiting to be drenched. In August, Corfu once again is filled with festivities, this time celebrating the **Barcarola** festival on top of docked boats in the harbor. In recent years the municipality has struggled to raise the funds necessary for this celebration; they have decided to throw one colossal Bacarola every two or three years.

▶ DAYTRIP FROM CORFU TOWN

ACHILLION PALACE

In Gastouri. Take bus #10 from Methodiou, 200m west of Pl. San Rocco (20min.; M-Sa 6 per day 7:20am-8pm, Su 4 per day 9am-8pm; €1). ☎56 210. Open daily 8am-7pm. €7; groups €4; EU students, ISIC holders, and children €2.

From housing an estranged empress to providing the filming location for the 1981 James Bond flick *For Your Eyes Only*, the Achillion Palace continually has intrigued visitors with its exquisite architecture, ornate designs, and flourishing gardens. Built in 1889, the magnificent property first belonged to the Austrian Empress Elizabeth, whose turbulent familial affairs brought her to this secluded estate. Having developed a penchant for Classical literature, she named her palace after the nearly invincible hero Achilles. The empress spent her summers here until she was assassinated by an Italian anarchist in 1898. The palace then changed hands a number of times. First sold to German Kaiser Wilhelm II, it served as a military hospital for French troops during WWI, then became a Nazi headquarters in WWII. In 1962, it became home to the first Greek casino. Today, the palace houses a museum with ornate rooms and beautiful grounds. The most impressive parts of the palace are in its roof gardens, including two sculptures of Achilles. The first is a white stone Achilles dying on his side, grabbing the spear that has penetrated his heel. The second Achilles, a high, imposing statue overlooking the island, stands at the back of the roof garden.

WESTERN CORFU

Western Corfu's wide expanses of golden sand, hidden crystal coves, majestic cliffs, and rock formations serve as a backdrop for the glimmering cerulean sea. While it sees its share of tour buses, the area doesn't suffer from the same degree of over-development that mars the east and north.

PELEKAS Πέλεκας   ☎ 26610

Removed from the mass tourism of the beach resorts, the village of ◪**Pelekas** sits at the top of a hill that towers over the island, providing views of breathtaking landscapes and famously beautiful sunsets. Its relaxed mentality, friendly people, and proximity to Corfu's nicest beaches make this town an essential stop on the island. A 5min. walk uphill from the center of the village takes you to the natural "balcony" known as **"Kaiser's throne";** according to locals, Wilhelm II would spend hours on end in silence on this hilltop, staring at the beauty that spread out below him. Indeed, sunset views from this spot, rivaled only by those from Mt. Pantokrator, are arguably the best on the island, and a visit at any point during the day will let you admire all of Corfu's glory at once.

Staying in Pelekas is overwhelmingly peaceful—the village is not touristdrowned (although it certainly deserves the attention), and its people extend genuine Greek hospitality to visitors. Rooms to let are plentiful and well priced, but call ahead in high season to secure a spot. ◪**Pension Tellis and Brigitte ❷,** down the hill from the bus stop on the left side of the street, has the friendliest hosts in town, who do their best to make each visitor feel at home. The comfy rooms are in a little yellow house covered with bougainvillea and gigantic sunflowers. Balconies have superb views of the surrounding countryside. (☎94 326. Singles €20; doubles €30-40; triples €40-50.) **Jimmy's Pension ❷,** right under Jimmy's restaurant, has fantastic rooms with air-conditioning, TV, fridge, large bath, and high ceilings that make the already large rooms seem even more spacious. (☎94 284. Reception in restaurant 8am-midnight. Singles €25-30; doubles €30-40; triples €40-50. AmEx/MC/V.) On the road to the beach, next to the fork for Glyfada, **Pension Paradise ❸** rents rooms with mountain view, large bath, TV, fridge, and fully equipped kitchen. (☎94 530. Doubles €35; triples €50. Reception 9am-10pm.)

Pelekas has a disproportionately large number of restaurants and tavernas that offer dinner with a spectacular view. On top of a 300-year-old olive orchard is Pelakas's gastronomical all-star, ◪**Taverna Pink Panther ❷,** which serves Greek and Italian food. Take a left at the fork above the bus station, and continue for 300m downhill. Each member of the owner's family takes part in the delicious enterprise, making and serving creamy cake (€2 per slice), large pizzas (from €7), and plentiful drinks. (☎94 361. Open daily 8am-3am.) As you walk up the main hill toward Glyfada, **Jimmy's ❷** serves Greek specialties and many vegetarian options, including the traditional *tsigareli* (seasonal green vegetables in spicy tomato sauce). Wooden floors and furniture lend a comfortable feel to the simple but excellent food. (☎94 284. Entrees €7-10. Open daily 8am-midnight.)

Take **bus #11** from San Rocco in Corfu Town (20min., 7 per day 7am-8:30pm, €1). A free shuttle bus (8 per day 10am-10pm) connects the town, the main sandy **beach,** and the nearby beach of Glyfada. The same bus will take you to the more isolated beach of **Myrtiotissa** (p. 541). From the drop-off point, it's a 20min. walk to the water. Signs with bus times are posted all over town.

GLYFADA Γλυφάδα   ☎ 26610

With the most famous beaches on Corfu, Glyfada attracts more tourists than Pelekas, but its seemingly endless shore accommodates the throngs admirably. Cliffs bracket both of Glyfada's **beaches,** where crashing waves make swimming a bit unpredictable. Those not sunbathing can partake in many activities—the beaches have parasailing (singles €34; doubles €50), waterskiing (€47 per 30min.), and jetskiing (€80 per hr. or €200 per day), and rent motorboats (from €70 per day), kayaks, inner tubes, and paddle boats. Though this is the ultimate laid-back vacation spot, relatively expensive accommodations might persuade you to stay in nearby Pelekas and take daily excursions here. In July and August, tan-centric mornings turn into dance-and-drink-fueled afternoons at **Aloha Bar** on the beach. (Open daily until 9pm.) North of Glyfada, accessible via a dirt path off the main Pelekas road, lies **Myrtiotissa beach.** Extolled by author and Corfu resident Lawrence Durrell as the most beautiful beach in the world, Myrtiotissa is divided in two by a large rock formation. The south side is an unofficial nude beach while the north is more family-oriented. A short walk up the road is the monastery **Moni Myrtidion,** which takes its name from an icon of the Virgin found in myrtle bushes over 700 years ago. (Open 7am-7pm. Modest dress required.) **Green KTEL buses** leave from Corfu Town (30min., 4 per day 9am-4pm, €2), and a free bus that leaves from the parking lot by the beach connects Pelekas to Glyfada (10min., 8 per day 10am-10pm).

PALEOKASTRITSA Παλαιοκαστρίτσα ☎26610

Paleokastritsa **beach** rests among six small coves and sea caves, and locals claim its waters are Corfu's coldest and most beautiful. It is worthwhile to head up the mountain overlooking Paleokastritsa; walking along the main road can be tiring, but there are some great views before reaching the top. From lookout points along the road, you can see most of the six coves. On the beach, vendors sell their goods to tourists, many of whom apparently travel with their dogs. Hiring or renting a motorboat (30min., €10), paddle boat (€11 per hr.), or kayak (singles €4 per hr.; doubles €7) will enable you to reach the caves where many tourists take a dip and snorkel. According to legend, Phoenician princess Nausicaä found the shipwrecked Odysseus washed ashore in one of these caves. Hop on a taxi boat from the main beach (☎69799 78 619; open 9:30am-6pm) to tour three picturesque caves and travel to incredible off-white beaches, only accessible from the water. Organize pickup time at your leisure. Prices are negotiable, but the standard cave tour (available in English) ranges €8-10 per person. Projecting out from a hill over the sea, bright white **Panagia Theotokos Monastery** (open 7:30am-4pm), founded in 1228, boasts a museum with a collection of Byzantine icons and engraved Bibles. Sunlight reflects off the whitewashed courtyard walls and highlights the colors in the lovely little garden, which offers startlingly beautiful views of the expansive shoreline. Come as early as possible—by mid-morning it's a mess of tour buses. **Green KTEL buses** arrive from Corfu Town (45min., 6 per day 9am-6pm, €2).

AGIOS GORDIOS Άγος Γόρδιος ☎26610

Fourteen kilometers west of Corfu Town, Agios Gordios is highlighted by impressive rock formations and a lovely, surprisingly wide **beach.** The main road, running perpendicular to the sand, has a short stretch of touristy restaurants, mini-marts, and some of the best and cheapest souvenir shops on the island. But in reality, most visitors to Agios Gordios couldn't tell you where those shops are; the majority never make it beyond the premises of the town's infamous **Pink Palace Hotel ❷,** a favorite with American and Canadian backpackers in search of instant (and constant) gratification. After taking a mandatory shot of free pink ouzo with you, the staff will lead you through the list of events. From then on, it's up to you how to sin away the day. The Palace's impressive list of amenities makes it a self-contained party resort: there's laundry service (€9), Internet access (€2 per 35min.), a jacuzzi, basketball and volleyball courts, a nightclub, four-wheel-drive rental (€15-30 per day depending on horsepower), a kayak safari (€10), a "booze cruise" with clothing-optional cliff-diving (€15), and various water sports. Saturday nights bring a weekly dance-and-drink-fest, when some faux-Greek traditions heighten the fun: hundreds of pink toga-wrapped partiers down countless shots of ouzo as Dr. George, the hostel's owner, and his male workers break plates on willing guests' heads in a spirit of revelry that would make Dionysus proud. Nights at the Palace are not for the faint of heart, or the weak of liver. The drunken debauchery can be too much for many, but the resident spiritual guide and guru, Dylan, provides a much-needed escape. Along with great conversations, he offers massages (€10), and free daily yoga or meditation. Lock up your valuables in the safety deposit box at the front desk before taking part in any of the daily events. (☎53 103; www.thepinkpalace.com. Breakfast and dinner included. Check-out 9am. Dorms, open only in high season, from €18; rooms with A/C, phone, balcony, and bath €25-30. AmEx/MC/V with surcharge.)

To get to the Palace from Corfu Town, take the green bus to Agios Gordios; it leaves from the New Port. (45min.; M-Sa 5 per day 8:15am-8pm, Su 3 per day 9:30am-5:30pm; €1.50). Dr. George sends staff to meet incoming ferries at the port, and buses arranged by the Palace run to and from Athens, stopping in Patras. (€49. Breakfast, dinner, and pickup/drop-off at the Corfu Town ferry included.)

For a relaxing daytrip from Agios Gordios, walk to the adjacent town of **Sinerades.** Here, locals sit on their ivy-lined porches, interact with passers-by, and provide a real Greek experience. It might be worth stopping by just to have dinner at **Grill Room Sinerades ❶**, the only restaurant in town. The flavorful food attracts an eclectic crowd. (☎54 510. Entrees €3-6. Open daily 7pm-1:30am.)

EASTERN CORFU ☎ 26610

The eastern coast of Corfu is the most developed and least aesthetically pleasing part of the island. The first 20km north of Corfu Town are thoroughly Anglicized by throngs of rowdy expats, and the beaches are thin strips that edge a busy, clamorous coastal road; avoid them unless you're looking for sweaty crowds and overpriced junk. Everything—beach, restaurants, hotels, and nightlife—is consolidated into one strip. It's slightly cheaper than beautiful Corfu Town and close enough to enable frequent trips, so it's easy to make this area your base for exploring the island if you can stand the neon lights, plasticky shops, and third-rate restaurants that stretch as far as the eye can see. **Gouvia** and **Dassia**, the first two resorts north of Corfu Town, thrive off package tours. The nightlife in Dassia is the most pleasant, aside from that in Corfu Town. Along the beach past the pricey Elia Beach Hotel, you'll find cafe and lively bar **Edem.** Wild nights here involve spinning people on a chair hanging from the ceiling or lighting the bar on fire. (☎93 013. Beer €4. Mixed drinks €8. Open daily 10am-3am.) A bit farther north, visitors to the notorious town of **Ipsos** have unlimited access to souvenir stands, fast-food joints, and C-class hotels that line the flat stretch of road from

TOP 10 SIGNS YOU'VE BEEN IN GREECE FOR A WHILE

While backpacking around Greece and mingling with locals, you're sure to absorb some native behaviors. Here are some telltale signs that it's all Greek to you—and you get it.

1. You find yourself considering traffic signs to be mere "caution advisories."

2. Every time you meet an old woman you expect her to offer you a room to rent.

3. You find yourself calling every food store, no matter how diminutive or limited its offerings, a supermarket.

4. You've taken to calling both friends and hated enemies *"malaka."*

5. You believe that the olive (and its by-products) is a key ingredient to healthy living, rather than an optional salad/martini additive.

6. You refer to the time period since 1600 as "recent times."

7. You refuse to call Istanbul anything but "Constantinoupoli."

8. You think that the food pyramid must be some sort of conical meat dish composed of souvlaki.

9. You've started taking sides in regard to the Peloponnesian War of the 5th century BC.

10. You've resolved to name your first-born child Panos.

across the mountain. Guests guzzle the day away at tacky bars like the depressingly named **Alcoholics Anonymous,** only to collapse a few hours later onto the yellow sand like beached whales. The scene is almost identical at night, as clubs offer gimmicks like free shots and foam parties to anyone willing to drop a few euro. **Pirgi,** a quieter extension of Ipsos, has much of the same €2-per-pint atmosphere.

Your best bet may be to settle down at a campground like **Karda Beach Camping ❶,** between Dassia and Ipsos on the main road. The site's proximity to the bus station makes Corfu Town and the rest of the island easily accessible. (☎93 595; www.kardacamp.gr. Playground, mini-mart, showers, pool. Sites €3.50, €6 per person, €5 per tent; 4- to 5-person tent rental €24; apartment-style bungalows €39. Electricity €4.) **KTEL green buses** serve Ipsos and Pirgi (30min.; M-F 10 per day 6:45am-4:30pm, Sa 6 per day 9am-4:30pm, Su 9:30am; €1.40). **Blue buses** head to Dassia via Gouvia (every 30min. 7-9am and 7-10:30pm, €1).

NORTHERN CORFU ☎26630

Past Pirgi, the road winds below steep cliffs. ■ **Mount Pantokrator,** a bare rock jutting out of the forested hills, towers 1km above, while dramatic vistas of dark, wooded Albania are visible across the straits. Roman emperors Tiberius and Nero both vacationed here, though tourism has erased most traces of the ancient world on the northern coast. This area is not Corfu's most attractive, but the mountain road and a couple of lovely small beaches make it worth a short visit.

The wide, sandy beach of **Agios Stefanos** is set into a gulf of high sandstone cliffs. With only two or three tavernas, the beach is less developed than the island's resorts, though watersports still are available (single canoe €9, double €12; parasailing €33). The trip there is a treat in itself: the coastal road curves inland past fern-filled hillsides of figs, olives, and cypresses and then passes through a picturesque mountain village. Though this area usually is visited as a daytrip, the few who decide to stay will find hotels and domatia for around €35-40. **Buses** run from Corfu Town to Kassiopi (1½hr.; M-F 4 per day 5:15am-4pm, Sa 3 per day 5:30am-2pm; €3) and Sidari (M-F 4 per day 9:30am-4pm, Sa-Su 6 per day 9:30am-4pm; €1). There is no bank or ATM in town, so bring enough cash for your stay.

The sheer slopes of northeastern Corfu cradle several fine **beaches,** including **Barbati,** 10km north of Ipsos, nearby **Nissaki,** and the twin beaches **Kalami** and **Kouloura.** The town of Kalami, with its spacious, flat-stoned beach, is a welcome respite from the masses that pack the eastern coast, but recent thefts have left locals bitter and suspicious of the visiting tourist population. This attitude is more apparent in super-secluded Kouloura than in Kalami; Kalami has recovered well, but the friendliness that once characterized Kouloura is all but gone. Kalami attracts visitors who come to see the home of author Lawrence Durrell, "set like a dice on a rock" in the southern end of town. Durrell's former abode is now the pleasant **Taverna White House ❸,** which serves typical Greek fare and overlooks the sea. (Entrees €10-13.) **Kalami Beach Taverna ❸,** right on the shore, has vegetarian options, fish cooked less than an hour after being caught by the owner's brother, and a nice view of the marina. (Entrees €7-13. Fish dishes €11-28.) Kouloura and Kalami are a brief walk from the main road north of Gimari village. Head down from the bus stop on the main road; soon you'll see a yellow sign on the right marking the shortcut path to Kalami. If you're going to Kouloura, continue down the road until you reach a fork with signs for Kouloura and Kalami; turn right down this road. Blue "To the Beach" signs on the left mark the path down to Kouloura, while signs on the right side of the road point you toward Kalami.

Mount Pantokrator offers breathtaking views of all of Corfu. To get to the top, start at **Spartillas,** a village 7km north of and inland from Pirgi along the bus route. Follow the road used each summer by villagers on their way to the annual festival at Pantokrator Monastery. There is no footpath, but hikers can embark on a nice 4-5hr. walk to the top by taking the same dirt road as the cars. The windy road leads you through small clusters of houses and green orchards; if you look toward the west in the early evening, you may see one of the famous Corfiot sunsets that paint the entire sky a dazzling gold. As you make your way up to Pantokrator, try to make a stop in a small town called **Strinilas**, on the way if you're starting from Spartillas. Don't pass up the opportunity to eat at ■ **A La Palaia ❷**. With an astonishing view of perfect sunsets, this traditional, family-fun restaurant is as authentic as it gets. All the fruits and vegetables are grown organically in their gardens, and all the meat is raised locally. (☎72 622. Entrees €6-9. Open 11:30am-11pm.) At the top of the mountain, you'll find **Cafe Pantokrator ❶** at the entrance to the church. This cafe serves small snacks and drinks, but frequently is closed. (Coffee €1.50. Egg salad sandwich €4.50. Open daily 9:15am-9pm.)

LEFKADA Λευκάδα

Thucydides reported that Lefkada was part of the mainland until 427 BC, when the inhabitants dug a canal to make their home an island. A bridge now connects Lefkada to the mainland, just 50m away. The obvious effect is that Lefkada feels much less like an island escape and more touristy, especially near the continental connection. That said, no amount of souvenir shops in busy summer tourist centers can diminish Lefkada's miles of white-sand beaches and stunning mountainous terrain. With a little effort, you can skirt the heavily trafficked port towns and major roads to find the island's unspoiled secrets and natural beauty.

LEFKADA TOWN ☎ 26450

The waterfront and pedestrian streets near the main plateia of Lefkada Town are the centers of the town's social scene, offering locals and travelers plenty of shops, restaurants, and opportunities to interact with the most conspicuous of tourists. Meandering into the tiny alleys off the harborside road and the shopper-friendly pedestrian central corridor will reveal Lefkada Town's quiet allure hidden under its bustling surface. Picturesque houses in the old Venetian style are newer than they look, built after extensive damage from earthquakes in 1867 and 1948, but nonetheless they feel authentic among the meandering pathways.

⌷ TRANSPORTATION. Ferries leaving from Nidri and Vasiliki link Lefkada with Ithaka and Kephalonia. The bus station (☎22 364) is past the port and along the water on the left. **Buses** cross the canal to Athens (5½hr., 4 per day 7am-5:15pm, €29) and Thessaloniki (M-F and Su 9:45am, €35.40). Local buses run to: Agios Nikitas (20min.; 6:40am, 2:15pm; €1.20), Nidri (45min., M-F 15 per day 5:15am-7:30pm, €1.40), and Vasiliki (1hr., M-F 4 per day 6:45am-7:30pm, €3). Pick up a recent schedule at the station for additional routes and return times; service is reduced on Sundays and expanded in high season. **Taxis** (☎21 001) line up by the start of Str. Mela and by the bus station. **Eurocar** (☎23 581), on Panagou, two blocks to the right of Hotel Nirikos, rents **mopeds** (€10 per day). There are many rental shops along the road, so feel free to bargain.

◪ 🛈 ORIENTATION AND PRACTICAL INFORMATION. Legend has it that the Venetians designed Lefkada Town in the shape of a fish bone. The main road, **Stratigou Ioanou Mela** (a.k.a. **Goulielmou Derpfield**) runs from the right end of the waterfront, facing inland, through town. Str. Mela and the winding streets branching off from it are pedestrian- and bike-only (although drivers have been known to challenge this) until they hit the **plateia,** packed with cafes and the occasional traveling music act. **8th Merarhias,** which becomes the waterfront road to the left of the start of Str. Mela as you face inland, envelops the downtown area and leads out to Vasiliki. As it sweeps around the inland perimeter of town, it becomes **Agelou Sikelianou, Petrou Filippa Panagou,** and **Dimitriou Golemi** in progression.

There is no tourist office, but ask at the travel agencies on Str. Mela for info about ferries, tours, or sights. **Fos Travel** sits two blocks down Str. Mela from the water on the left. It lists accommodations, car/bike rentals, boat hire, and excursions. (☎ 24 975. MC/V.) A **National Bank** (open M-Th 8am-2:30pm, F 8am-2pm) with a **24hr. ATM** is on Str. Mela. Facing the bus station, walk left and follow the road as it leads away from the water to find the **tourist police** in front of the **police** station on your left. (☎ 29 370. Tourist police provide general info and help with accommodations. Open daily 8am-2pm.) Several **pharmacies** sit on Str. Mela near the bank. For the **OTE,** turn right off Str. Mela onto Skiardesi, before the National Bank; turn left when it ends at I. Marinou. (Open M-F 7:30am-1:30pm.) **Internet C@fe Lefkada,** on Ch. Koutroumpi, has **Internet** access. (☎ 21 507. €2.50 per hr. Coffee €1-1.50. Open M-Sa 8am-6am, Su 10am-2am.) Past the bus station with the water on your left, look for **Cafezinho,** Golemi 14, which also has Internet access. (☎ 22 965. €2 per hr. Coffee €1.50-2.) The **post office** is on Str. Mela about 150m past the National Bank. (☎ 24 225. Open M-F 7:30am-2pm.) **Postal Code:** 31100.

⌂ ACCOMMODATIONS. Most hotel rooms in Lefkada Town cost upwards of €40 in high season, so budget travelers should consider staying elsewhere. As always, signs list domatia that can be negotiated, especially during low season. Travel agencies suggest **Ligia,** a domatia-packed village 5km outside of town. Frequent buses to and from Nidri and Vasiliki pass through Ligia (10min., €1). If you do stay in Lefkada Town, there are reasonably priced domatia a few blocks from the harbor, to the right of Str. Mela facing inland. One relatively affordable option is **Hotel Nikiros ❸,** at the beginning of Str. Mela on the waterfront. Plain rooms each come with modern bath, TV, and air-conditioning. Request a room with a balcony overlooking the water for the same price. Nikiros houses a delightful cafe and restaurant. (☎ 24 132. Breakfast €5. Singles €30-35; doubles €40-45. AmEx/MC/V.) **Hotel Santa Maura ❸,** two blocks from the water on Str. Mela, has decently sized rooms in a 19th-century building. Rooms come with bath, air-conditioning, TV, and balcony. (☎ 21 308. Singles €30 and up; doubles €40 and up. Reservations recommended, especially in high season.) Directly across the street is **Pirofani Pension ❹.** Rooms upstairs are spacious with matching furniture, TV, air-conditioning, fridge, bath, balcony, and plentiful sunlight. (☎ 25 844. Singles €35-67; doubles €45-75.)

◘ FOOD. Dining options in Lefkada Town, especially along Str. Mela, are pricey and tourist-oriented; you'll have to work a little to find authenticity. Walking up Str. Mela, you'll see a yellow sign across from the tower clock Ag. Nikolaos that leads to **Lighthouse Tavern ❷.** This small restaurant is known for its peaceful, vine-shaded garden seating area, complete with chirping pet birds. Enjoy moussaka (€7) under the old-fashioned hanging lanterns outside. (☎ 25 117. Entrees €6-12. Open daily 5pm-midnight.) One of the oldest local favorites is family-owned **Taverna Regantos ❸,** 75m down Dimarmou Verrioti, the first right from the plateia as you approach from the waterfront. As you dine on well-priced seafood, ask for a translation of the quotes and song lyrics painted on the walls. (☎ 22 855. Salads €2-4. Swordfish dish €10. Most fish €15-35 per kg. Open daily 7am-3am.) **To Petrano ❶,** just before the plateia on Str. Mela, offers many crepes (€2.50-6) that can be topped with a wide variety of confections and ice cream (€1.20 per scoop). Slushies (€1.50) are good for beating the heat. (Open daily 10am-1am, July-Aug. 24hr.)

◙◪ **SIGHTS AND BEACHES.** The **Archaeological Museum** is located 1km down the waterfront road. Take a left as you exit Str. Mela and follow the road with the water on your right for 1km; it's the big white building on the right. This wonderful museum houses a collection of artifacts from ancient Lefkas, as well as finds from ancient graves at Nidri. Panels provide explanations and interesting information on Lefkas's history and culture in English. The museum also documents the work of 19th-century archaeologist Wilhelm Dorpfeld, who was convinced that Lefkada, not Ithaka, was Odysseus's mythic home. Focal points include 6th-century BC terra cotta figurines of dancing nymphs and a sarcophagus with its original skeleton and burial goods still inside. (☎23 675. Open Tu-Su 9am-1:30pm. Free.) In late August, Lefkada hosts the annual **Folklore Festival,** bringing dance troupes from around the world to perform in the streets. (Free.)

While Lefkada Town has no sandy beaches, the northwestern coast has kilometers of white pebbles and clear water. Catch a bus (3 per day, €1.20) to the best stretch of beaches along the island's west coast, starting at **Agios Nikitas** and continuing to serene **Faneromenis Monastery,** which treats visitors to stunning views. (Free. Modest dress required.)

◧ **NIGHTLIFE.** As the sun sets, the party gets started at the small cafe-clubs located to the right of Str. Mela (facing inland). At **Cafe Excess** (☎24 704) and **Coconut Groove,** Ag. Sikelianou 4 (☎23 341), stylish rooms swell with sweaty locals dancing to pounding rock tunes. (Cafe Excess open daily 8am-3am; upstairs club open Th-Sa after 10pm. Coconut Groove open in high season daily 10pm-4am, in low season F-Sa 10am-4pm; upstairs cafeteria open daily.) Two-story **Capital** has a swimming pool and blasts pop hits to make for (in)famous all-night parties. Walk with the water on your right past the large white museum building; it's on the left, about 1km from town. Taxis cost roughly €4. (☎25 138. Beer €3. Mixed drinks €6-7. Cover in Aug. €7. Open daily mid-July to mid-Aug.; Sa mid-Aug. to mid-July.)

VASILIKI Βασιλική ☎26450

Vasiliki's position between mountains creates distinct wind patterns that make it one of the world's premier windsurfing towns. The long beach gives a sweeping view of multicolored sails, as boats run to coves nearby. Not far from the waterfront stone road of the town are beaches unique for their sheer, pale stone cliffs.

◪⟁ **TRANSPORTATION AND PRACTICAL INFORMATION.** Almost everything in Vasiliki lies either along the waterfront or on the main road running perpendicular to the harbor. Walk 5min. with the water on your left; the road continues straight inland as the waterfront part curves to the left. The bakery at the end of the main road's commercial stretch doubles as the town's bus stop. Four **buses** per day (7:15am-8:45pm) run to and from Lefkada Town (1hr., €2.90) and Nidri (30min., €1.70). A **ferry** leaves at least once daily from Fiskardo (1hr., €6.40). **GM Rentals,** on the main road, rents mopeds (€10 per day) and cars (€25-50 per day). Renting either one is a good idea if you want to avoid overly touristed beach towns. There are plenty of rental places in town, so feel free to bargain. (☎31 650. Open daily 8:30am-11pm. Often closed 2:30-5pm.)

Twenty meters from the water up the main road is **Samba Tours,** which provides ferry and bus information, boat excursions, car rental, plane tickets, photocopying, faxing, safety deposit boxes, **currency exchange,** accommodations advice, and **Internet** access. They also sell local olive oil and eggs. (☎31 555. Internet €4 per hr. Open daily 9am-2:30pm and 5-11pm; July-Aug. 9am-11pm.) There are no banks in Vasiliki, only **ATMs.** One is on the left of the waterfront as you face inland, next to the elementary school. A self-service **laundromat** is at the right end of the waterfront, facing inland. (☎69723 42 072. Wash and dry €4.50. Open 24hr.) The 24hr. **police station** is inland around the left side of Hotel Vasiliki Bay. (☎31 218. Main office open daily 8am-2pm.) For medical **emergencies,** contact the **health center** (☎31 065) on the main road; go straight through the intersection with the bakery/bus stop. To reach the **post office,** walk toward the port from the bus station. It is after the crossroads, on the left side of the main road. (Open M-F 7:30am-2pm.) **Postal Code:** 31082.

☎☎ ACCOMMODATIONS AND CAMPING. Rooms for rent are plentiful along the waterfront, the main road past the bakery, and the side streets branching off them. With a little work you should be able to find **domatia** for €20 per person or less in low season, €30 in high season. The friendly brothers who own the mini-mart opposite the ferry dock, to the right side of the waterfront when facing inland, let spacious rooms with bath and balcony at **Hotel Dimitrius ❷.** (☎31 221. Singles €20-45; doubles €25-50.) To find **Hotel Vasiliki Bay ❷,** walk past the main road, fork to the right continuing along the harbor, then take the next right. The hotel is another 200m on the left. Rustic green furniture, large bath, fridge, balcony, TV, and air-conditioning make these rooms a great deal. (☎31 077. Singles €25; doubles €30; triples €40.) **Vasiliki Beach Camping ❶,** popular among the windsurfing crowd, is a clean, affordable campsite only 80m from the beach. The bar, laundry, showers, nearby supermarket, and waterfront location will make travelers glad they opted for sea-breeze ventilated tents. (☎31 308. €6-7.50 per person; €5-6 per small tent; €6-7 per large tent; €3.50-5 per car.)

☐ FOOD. Nearly all restaurants in Vasiliki are on a short stretch of the waterfront and are indistinguishable in quality and price. If you can sift through the ordinary, though, you can find a quality inexpensive meal. **Miramare ❷,** toward the far right side of the waterfront facing inland, offers the best views of the harbor and bay area from its own pier. The extensive menu includes pasta (€5.50-7), pizza made in a round brick-oven (€9-11.50), and various meat options. (☎31 336. MC/V.) **The Pirate Place ❸,** on the main road from the bus station, is a local favorite. The love of all things buccaneer is apparent in this handsome stone building establishment. (☎31 837. Salads €3-11. Entrees €6-16. Open 6pm-midnight.) For a meal right near the beach, check out **Kuare Akite ❷,** next to Remozzo bar about 400m from the edge of town. Though they offer a variety of salads (€3-6) and local rabbit *stifado* (€8), the specialty is definitely the selection of fish (€35-55 per kg). Enjoy any of the options on the large outdoor patio, shaded and framed by plants. (☎31 119. Open May-Sept. 11am-midnight. MC/V.)

◙ SIGHTS. Boat tours to several of the island's beaches leave from Vasiliki. Hours and prices fluctuate so be sure to check the daily schedule information. During high season, tours head to Lefkada's best beach, breathtaking ◙**Porto Katsiki** (Port of the Goat), at the base of towering white cliffs (40-50min.; round-trip leaves 11am and returns 5pm, €10). Porto Katsiki is also accessible by car or moped: drive to the end of the main road, turn left, and keep an eye out for signs. The drive takes about 1hr. and is followed by a difficult 30min. walk. The boat ride to Porto Katsiki also passes a **lighthouse** built on the site of the **Temple of Lefkas Apollo,** on the southernmost tip of the island. The ancient poet **Sappho,** rejected by her beloved Phaon, is said to have leapt to her death from these 70m high cliffs. Boat excursions will take you to the best views of Sappho's jumping point.

▨ NIGHTLIFE. Nightlife options in Vasiliki are slim pickings, but **Zeus's Bar,** on the waterfront, has a slew of shots and mixed drinks to soothe the sting of a sunburn or a thunderbolt. Don't question the god's determination: the trance, techno, rock, and pop play all night until the two dance floors are empty. (☎31 560. Beer

€2.50-4. Shots €3. Drinks €6-7. Open daily 10am-5am.) **Abraxa's Tunnel Bar,** down the main street away from the water and marked by a Guinness sign, plays classic rock after 11pm. The oldest nighttime hangout in town, Abraxa also hosts Saturday night disco parties and the occasional midweek reggae and latin nights. (Beer €2.50-4. Mixed drinks €5. Open 8:30pm-3am.)

LICENSE TO CHILL. Getting around islands on public transportation can be difficult. Renting a car is a great option for those 20 years of age and older. A moped is cheaper, but new laws, which most rental shops follow, mandate that those renting must have a Class A or equivalent license for all bikes 50cc and over. So, when island hopping, don't forget to bring your license!

ITHAKA Ιθάκη

What Homer called a "wine-dark" sea of legend appears instead a clear and beckoning blue as it meets the steeply rising green hills of Ithaka upon white beaches. Panoramic vistas of the Adriatic are as ubiquitous as the motor scooters that transport locals to villages, where the atmosphere is far more relaxed and quiet than that found on nearby Kephalonia or Lefkada. Massive ferries, the island's only

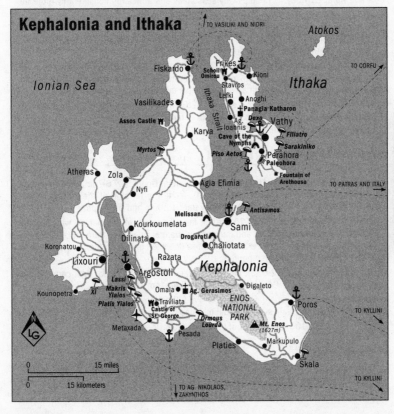

physical connection to the outside world, dwarf Ithaka's small port towns. Traverse Odysseus's legendary home to see the pebbled beaches, rocky hillsides, and terraced olive groves that drew him back here through countless obstacles.

VATHY Βαθύ ☎ 26740

The clear waters of the bay are the focus of Ithaka's capital, which unfolds along the curving perimeter of the cove. Slightly inland, the red-roofed, pastel-colored houses separated by narrow streets and stone stairways compete for views of the sloping Ithakan landscape. The charming stone plateia and old-fashioned street lamps are the deliberate touches of a town aware of the romantic stirrings it evokes in visitors, Greek and foreign alike.

◧ TRANSPORTATION

Ferries: Vathy's **ferry docks** are on the far right of the waterfront, about a 4min. walk to the right of the town plateia. Ferries depart from Frikes, on the northern tip of Ithaka, to **Lefkada** (2½hr., 11am, €6.40) via **Kephalonia.** Departures from Piso Aetos go to **Astakos** (3:20pm, €8), **Kephalonia** (45min.; 3:20, 4pm; €2.50), and **Patras** (4pm, €14.50) or from Vathy to **Kephalonia** (1hr.; 7am, 4pm; €5.10) and **Patras** (3¾hr.; 7am, 4pm; €14.50). Schedules vary seasonally and ferries run considerably more frequently in July and Aug.; check with the staff at Delas Tours or Polyctor Tours.

Taxis: (☎ 33 030). Taxis line up by the water, in front of the plateia. Call ahead, as there are not many on the island. It is even better to arrange in advance with the drivers in person; find them sitting at outdoor tables in the plateia next to their cars. €30 per hr.

Car Rental: AGS Rent a Car (☎ 32 702). On the waterfront 2 blocks to the right of the plateia. June-Aug. from €30-35, includes insurance; Apr.-May and Sept.-Oct. from €25. Open daily 8:30am-9pm. Call ahead to reserve automatic transmission vehicles.

Scooter Rental: Rent a Scooter (☎ 32 840). On a side street off the waterfront, directly across from the port police and to the right before the plateia. Rents from €10 per day. Open daily 9am-2:30pm and 5-9pm.

▚ PRACTICAL INFORMATION

Tours: Delas Tours (☎ 32 104), in the main plateia. Open daily 6-7am, 9am-2pm, and 5:30-9:30pm. **Polyctor Tours** (☎ 33 120), along the far side of the plateia as you approach from the port police. Open daily 9am-1:30pm and 5:30-9pm.

Banks: National Bank (☎ 32 720), in the far right corner of the plateia, with Polyctor Tours on your left. **24hr. ATM** and **currency exchange.** Open M-Th 8am-2:30pm, F 8am-2pm. **ATE** and **Alpha Bank** (☎ 33 690), a few doors left of Net, on the plateia, have the same services and the same hours.

Laundry: Polifimos (☎ 32 032), behind the National Bank, in the far right corner of the plateia. Wash and dry €4 per kg. Open M-Sa 8am-1pm and 6-9pm.

Police: ☎ 32 205, in emergencies ☎ 100. From the plateia, turn right on the first street after Drakouli, and walk straight uphill for three blocks. It will be on the right side.

Pharmacy: ☎ 33 105, to the right of the post office. Open daily 8:30am-2pm, 5-10pm.

Medical Services: ☎ 32 222. Turn right after Drakouli and walk uphill about 150m past the police station.

Telephones: OTE (☎ 32 299), on the waterfront, just before Hotel Mentor when coming from the plateia with the water on your left. Open M-F 7:20am-3pm. Hours vary depending on the season.

Internet Access: Net (☎33 450), on the left side of the plateia facing inland. 2 fl. of computers, touch-screen gaming, and a full bar. €4 per hr. Mixed drinks €4. Open daily 8am-2:30pm and 6pm-midnight. **Nirito Cafe** (☎32 437). €4 per hr. Coffee €2. Baklava €2.50. Open daily 7am-2am.

Post Office: ☎32 386, in the plateia near Delas Tours. Open M-Th 8am-2:30pm, F 8am-2pm. **Postal Code:** 28300.

ACCOMMODATIONS

Cheap **domatia** are definitely the way to go over tempting but pricey hotel rooms. Numerous signs around town indicate homes with rooms to let.

Aktaion Domatia (☎32 387), across from the ferry dock on the far right side of the waterfront (facing inland). A comfortable, convenient option offers rooms with bath, TV, A/C, fridge, and pleasant view of the bay. Many vehicles going to Vathy pass by here, so light sleepers should ask for one of the rooms on the inside. Singles €30; doubles €56. Negotiate for discounts in low season. ❷

Ms. Martha (☎32 352). Bear left in front of the National Bank, past Niko's Taverna, then turn right at the T intersection, walk 1 more block, and turn left; the rooms are a few houses down. Old-fashioned rooms have bath, kitchenette, fan, and access to a white marble balcony with a great harbor view. Prices are negotiable depending on season and length of stay. Singles €20-25; doubles €30-55. Reduced prices in winter. ❷

Ms. Vaso's Rooms (☎32 119). Follow the road from the ferry dropoff ramp with the water to the left, until you reach a wide corner in the road. Follow the side street next to the building with a sign that says "Laguda" and walk up the stairs. The front porch has a gorgeous view of Vathy and the bay. Small rooms feature wooden wall and ceiling paneling, A/C, fridge, and all but one have a bath. From €25. ❷

Hotel Mentor (☎32 433; www.hotelmentor.gr.). Facing inland, it's on the far left of the waterfront with a large sign. The biggest hotel on the island, Mentor has an outdoor shaded lounge with a great view of the bay, as well as basic but spacious rooms with bath, balcony, A/C, and TV. Some have harbor views—request these rooms early, as they fill up quickly. Breakfast included. Check-out noon. Singles €50-80; doubles €72-105. Discounts in low season. ❹

FOOD

Seemingly endless tavernas and seafood restaurants line the waterfront. In addition to the tavernas, two **supermarkets** are in town. To get to one of them, walk from the plateia with the water on your left a few blocks until a sign points to the right down a side street; the market will be on the left.

Kantouni (☎32 918). In a menu featuring many locally grown foods, one specialty is the *pastitsada*—veal with carrots and tomato sauce served with spaghetti. Lobster pasta €75 per kg. Mixed vegetable plate €5.50. ❸

Niko's Taverna (☎32 039), across the street and down the road from the National Bank. All types of meat are offered minced, roasted, and grilled. Don't fret, herbivores: there are many vegetarian options, too. Specialties include moussaka (€6), calamari (€6), and veal *stifado* (€8). Try local red and white wines with dinner. Salads €3. Cover €1. Open Apr.-Nov. 7pm-2am. MC/V. ❷

Sirene's (☎33 001). Across the street and to the right of Trexantiri. Offers an Ithakan omelette (€5.50) and basic Greek fare featuring locally grown vegetables. Recently added to the menu are entrees such as the lamb with potatoes (€11.50) cooked in the traditional *tserepa* style—within clay pots. Entrees €7-10. Open 7-11:30pm. MC/V. ❷

Drakouli (☎ 33 435), on the left end of the waterfront facing inland. Outside this mansion-turned-cafe, tables are arranged near a palm-lined garden and a fenced lake fed by the bay across the street. Inside find casually displayed antiques and wood-paneled floors. These touches of class are as sweet as the ice cream (€2 per scoop) or the signature sundae (€7) that combines several flavors. Sandwiches €2-3.50. Beer €2.50-4. Coffee €2-3.20. Open daily 9am-midnight. ❶

◙ **SIGHTS.** Though small, Ithaka has so much historical tradition that each little village has something worth seeing. In Vathy, most everything is located near the central plateia. Turn right after Dragoumi cafe and take the first left to find the **Vathy Archaeological Museum,** two blocks down on the right. The tiny collection displays finds from ongoing excavations at the Sanctuary of Apollo at Aetos—a site containing the ruins of a city dating back to 700 BC—as well as ceramics and artifacts from the Dark Age. Animal-shaped ritual vases from the 6th or 7th century BC and ivory and amber jewelry from the Geometric period are highlights. (☎ 32 200. Open Tu-Su 8:30am-3pm. Free.) Turn right onto the footpath near Alpha Bank to find the **Folklore and Nautical Museum.** The peach-colored museum houses a large collection of nautical memorabilia as well as artifacts from Ithaka's colonial period. Art and literature buffs will appreciate the early 19th-century illustrations of Homer's characters on the second floor. (☎ 33 398. Open M-Sa 10am-2pm. €1.)

◨◪ **BEACHES AND THE OUTDOORS.** The most popular beaches in Vathy are slightly out of the way, but their beauty justifies the effort to reach them. Because most tourists are disinclined to hike the winding, hilly roads, you may find yourself pleasantly alone. Jaw-dropping ◪**Filiatro** and **Sarakiniko,** 3.5km and 2.5km away from Vathy, respectively, are surrounded by steep hills that drop down toward the water, ending in majestic, almost vertical arrays of pale rock. To get to these beaches, walk with the water to your left from the Vathy plateia, turn right after Hotel Mentor, and head toward the mountain to the left of town as you face inland. Take the uphill road; the road to Filiatro will turn left off the main road. It's a 50min. walk in total to this beach, but the views from high above are well worth it. The road to Sarakiniko ends at a small harbor, with the beach 100m to the right, requiring a jaunt over some rocks. There is a small **cafe** ❷ at Filiatro that often loudly plays popular Greek music during summer afternoons; its food selection is limited, so you may want to bring your own lunch. (Calamari €6. Small fish €6. Beer €2. Coffee €2.50. Open daily 10:30am-8pm; July-Aug. open much later.) The closest beach to Vathy is family-oriented **Dexa,** with a long, pebbled shore and plenty of shady olive trees. To get there from Vathy, follow the main road out of town (with the water on your right) up and over the hill for 30min. To spend a languid afternoon on the shores of **Gidaki,** a deserted island, you'll need to take a boat (round-trip €7-8), which runs twice a day during high season.

Two kilometers outside of Vathy is the **Cave of the Nymphs,** where water *naiads* (nymphs) were worshipped and, according to legend, where Odysseus hid the treasure the Phoenicians gave him. Archaeologists had been excavating the cave, but now the site appears to have been abandoned. Check with taxi drivers and tour operators before going. If it is closed, you still can walk around the site and view the two separate entrances (one for the gods and one for mere mortals). To get to the cave, walk around the harbor with the water on your right on the road to Piso Aetos and Stavros, then follow the signs along the road winding up the mountain for about 1.5-2km. After a scenic hike with views of Vathy, you'll find the entrance up a flight of steps to the right, just before the paved road ends.

◪ **DAYTRIPS FROM VATHY.** Trying to get to most of the sights on this small island without a taxi or car may make you feel like Odysseus on his beleaguered journey home. If you plan to see many sights, the cheapest option is to rent a motorbike or car, or hire a taxi by the hour (€30 per hr., bargain for better rates). The island's sole **bus,** which doubles as a school bus, runs north from Vathy to **Frikes** (30-40min.) Taxis to Frikes cost about €25. Domatia (€25-40) information is available at the snack bar on the supermarket end of the short harborside road. The bus goes on to exceptionally beautiful ▨**Kioni** (1hr.; taxi €30), a small village whose crystal blue harbors and white-pebble beaches make it a favorite of locals and tourists. In high season, the bus generally runs twice per day, at 5:30am and 2pm, both returning immediately. Around 3km south of Frikes, **Stavros** sits high in the mountains. Its naturally shaded town square has signs indicating directions to all the local sites. Domatia are available locally—look for the signs. The **Archaeological Museum** houses a collection of excavated items from Pilicata Hill, an archaeological site on Ithaka. Keep an eye out for signs; it's 700m past the town's church, off a side street on the right-hand side. (Usually open Tu-Su 8am-2pm. Small donation expected.) A site that locals call *"Scholi Omirou"* **("Homer's School"),** where Odysseus's Palace is said to have stood, is down the road from the museum. Follow signs from the town square, past the museum turn-off and to the left when the road forks. Until very recently, the location, and even the existence, of this palace was little more than a rumor. In the last decade, however, after a resurgence of interest in the area, archaeologists have dated Mycenaean ruins, intact architectural structures, Hellenistic towers, and even an untouched Roman grave. On the hike up, notice the mountainside *melanithros*, or natural springs. (Free. Taxi from Vathy €20.)

Near the village of **Agios Ioannis,** on the island's western side, are several stunning pebble beaches with views of Kephalonia alongside some of the island's ritziest real estate. A taxi to Ag. Ioannis from the Vathy plateia costs €20. The **Monastery of Panagia Katharon,** dedicated to the Virgin Kathariotissa (patroness of the island), is more than 600m up on Ithaka's highest mountain, ▨**Mount Neritos;** take a moped or taxi (round-trip €25) toward Anoghi and follow the signs. This monastery, open from sunrise to sunset, has operated as a church since the 1500s. It holds an icon of the Virgin Mary painted by St. Luke that is said to work miracles. Women must cover their legs in the sanctuary, and all visitors must observe the monks' rule to close the front door in order to keep wandering goats off the premises. Bring a camera—on a clear day, your snapshots may match the common postcard images depicting the view from this mountain. In Anoghi, the island's former capital, on the road to Stavros that passes around Mount Neritos, the modest church of **Agia Panagia** has occupied the town square for over 300 years. Inside the church are delicately worn frescoes; outside is a bell tower and a relic of a tank used to fight the Germans in WWII.

For a great view and a taste of modern Greek culture, make your way to **Perahora,** a small village uphill on the mountainside 4km above Vathy. A wine festival invites visitors here at the end of July each year. Be sure to visit the ruins of **Paleohora,** the island's capital until it was abandoned in the early 16th century. To find them, follow the signs in Perahora to the community center until you reach a footpath that leads through olive groves. When the path diverges, take the upper branch to the ruins. Here lies an abandoned Byzantine church with the remains of frescoes on the inner walls, as well as ancient foundations scattered around. In the village, you can marvel at the intricately designed icon screen of the Church of the Dormition of the Virgin. The road leading to Perahora is on the far right of the waterfront as you face inland (opposite the road to Stavros)—follow the signs uphill. A taxi from Vathy costs €7.

KEPHALONIA Κεφαλονιά

Massive mountains, subterranean lakes and rivers, caves, dense forests, and more than 250km of coastline make Kephalonia a nature-lover's paradise. Though it is the largest of the Ionians, Kephalonia lacks convenient buses. A car or moped is necessary to appreciate its beauty, with spectacular sights often kilometers from

A MODERN ODYSSEY FOR ANCIENT ITHAKA

For years, geographic discrepancies between the Ithaka described in Homer's epic and the modern island of the same name have been the source of confusion among academics.

Researcher Robert Bittlestone, with the help of James Diggle and John Underhill, thinks he has found the former land of King Odysseus, not on the island of Ithaka, but on the Paliki peninsula of Kephalonia. Bittlestone is convinced that recent plate tectonic movement of the plate of Africa moving north into the plate of the European continent has pushed the Paliki peninsula upward, destroying a channel that separated the land from the main mass of Kephalonia. The process of land-filling that merged the alleged two islands was aided by debris falling down into the gap from the mountains that flank the isthmus on either side. Studies of the land showing it to be loose sediment strengthen this theory which, if correct, would explain certain passages in the Odyssey that identify ancient Ithaka as the "westernmost of all Ionian islands." It also would make clear why Odysseus led the "Kephalonians" in battle.

While the theory remains contentious, roaming the island of Kephalonia—rather than Ithaka—may bring you closer to the ancient king than you had thought.

the port towns. With your own transportation, you'll uncover villages on lush hillsides, pebble beaches framed magnificently by austere cliffs, and rocky hills that that welcome brilliant sunsets.

ARGOSTOLI Αργοστόλι

☎26710

The capital of and by far the largest town on Kephalonia, Argostoli is a lively city with yellow and orange buildings that dot the hills. Other parts of the island may be more picturesque, but Argostoli offers urban convenience and access to the rest of Kephalonia.

⌐ TRANSPORTATION

Flights: Olympic Airways (☎28 808). Office located at the airport in the nearby town of Minies. 2 flights per day to **Athens** (€75) during high season. 3 flights per week to: **Corfu** (€35); **Preveza** (€30); **Thessaloniki** (€80); **Zakynthos** (€28).

Ferries: Kephalonia has multiple ports for different destinations. Buses connect Argostoli to other ports, including **Sami** (p. 558), where ferries leave for **Corfu, Ithaka,** and **Patras,** as well as for **Italy** in July-Aug. Prices and times are seasonal; inquire at a travel agency. From Argostoli boats go to **Kyllini** on the Peloponnese (daily, 30min., €12.30) and **Lixouri, Kephalonia** (20min., every 30min. until 10:30pm, €1.60). From Poros, on the southeastern coast, ferries leave for **Kyllini** (1 per day, €8). Ferries leave from Pesada, on the southern coast of Kephalonia and go to **Ag. Nikolaos** (2 per day, €4) on the northern end of Zakynthos. Buses do not go from the port of Pesada to Argostoli, so you'll have to take a taxi (€16-20). Multiple ferry companies operate out of Argostoli, so check with the tourist office for updated times and prices.

Buses: ☎22 281. The station is on the southern end of the waterfront, in a light pink building all the way to the left facing inland. Brochures with schedules, prices, and return times available. Open daily 7am-8pm. Buses head to: **Agios Gerasimos/Omala** (30min.; 10am, 12:30, 2:15pm; €1.50); **Fiskardo** (1½hr.; 10:30am, 2pm; €5); **Poros** (1½hr.; 10:30am, 1, 2:15pm; €4.50); **Sami** (40min., 5 per day 7:30am-3:45pm, €4); **Skala** (10:15am, 2:15pm; €4.50). Buses meet the ferry and continue to **Athens** (3 per day, €26). Local service reduced Sa-Su.

Taxis: ☎28 505 or 22 700. Plenty line up in the plateia. Available 24hr.

Rentals: There are many rentals along the waterfront. **Sunbird,** Antoni Tristi 127 (☎23 723), to the left of the

IONIAN ISLANDS

Port Authority facing inland. Rents cars (from €40) and mopeds (from €15). Open daily 8:30am-2pm and 5-9pm. Discounts for longer rentals.

✳ 🛈 ORIENTATION AND PRACTICAL INFORMATION

The town's cafe-packed and hotel-lined main plateia is two blocks from the water. Walk from the water on **21 Maiou,** across from the Port Authority and GNTO/EOT. To the left of the plateia, facing inland, **Lithostrotou** is a pedestrian area with high-end stores and dozens of leather, postcard, and jewelry shops. Many museums and galleries are between the plateia and Lithostrotou.

Tourist Office: ☎22 248. Beside the Port Authority near the ferry docks. Helpful staff provides free maps and information about sights and beaches, and some assistance with accommodations and restaurants. Information in English, French, German, Greek, and Italian. Open July.-Aug. daily 8am-2:30pm.

Bank: National Bank (☎25 191), between Hotel Olga and Hotel Tourist along the harbor. **Currency exchange** and **24hr. ATM.** Open M-Th 8am-2:30pm, F 8am-2pm. Other banks and ATMs line the waterfront.

Laundromat: Laundry Express, Lassis 46b. Walk inland on Vyronos for 9 blocks, turning left onto Lassis. The laundromat is 2 blocks farther on your right. Self-service.

Police: ☎22 200. On I. Metaxa across from the tourist office. Open 24hr.

Tourist Police: ☎22 815. In the police station. Open daily 7am-10pm.

Telephones: OTE (☎28 599). On Gerassimou Livada, to the left of the Archaeological Museum walking toward the plateia. Open M-Th 7:30am-1:30pm, F 7:30am-1pm.

Internet Access: B.B.'s Club (☎26 669), in the bottom right corner of the plateia facing inland. "B.B.'s" stands for both "Bad Boys" and the full "Bar and Billiards." €2.50 per hr., min. €1. Coffee €2. Open 9am-2am.

Post Office: ☎23 173. 2 blocks up from the water on Lithostrotou, at the intersection of Kerkyras. Open M-F 7:30am-4pm. **Postal Code:** 28100.

▐ ACCOMMODATIONS

Rooms in bustling Argostoli are in high demand. In high season, private rooms are often the cheapest option, though many are relatively far from the center of town. Bargain, but don't expect to find a room for much less than €35. In low season, the prices of domatia and hotels are fairly similar. If you plan to stay in a hotel, call ahead. Otherwise, renting a car or moped allows you to stay in **domatia** and still have access to the beach. The tourist office maintains a list of available domatia.

St. Gerassimos, 6 Ag. Gerassimou Str. (☎28 697). Turn left past Hotel Olga on the waterfront road with the water on your right; the hotel will be on the right. Family-run establishment offers 7 rooms from June-Sept., each with TV, balcony, A/C, and bath. A larger room is available for a family—call ahead to reserve. Rooms €20-45. ❷

Hotel Tourist, Ant. Tritsi 109 (☎22 510; htourist@hol.gr), along the waterfront past the fruit market with the water on your right. Has 22 rooms comfortably equipped with TV, A/C, and fridge. Some rooms have a deck with a great view of the harbor. Breakfast €6. Low season singles €40; doubles €55. July singles €50; doubles €60. Aug. singles €60; doubles €80. ❹

Hotel Allegro, Andrea Xoida 2 (☎22 268). Take a left on the street just before Alpha Bank; the hotel is on the right. Allegro offers 16 rooms with convenient access to the waterfront and plateia. Singles €30; doubles €40; triple with bath €60. Rooms with bath roughly €10 extra. A/C €5-10 extra. ❸

Hotel Mirabel, Central Square 281 (☎25 381; www.mirabel.gr), in the near left corner of the main square, facing inland. Small but fully equipped rooms have A/C, TV, and ample closet space. The breakfast area and garden are pleasant. Breakfast included. Singles €50; doubles €65. Book early. ❹

▐ FOOD

Food may be cheaper on the waterfront, but try to avoid the generic restaurants that line Ant. Tristi; selection and quality are generally better in the plateia. Those visiting on Saturday mornings can check out the well-organized **farmers' market** for fresh fruits and vegetables; fruit shops, bakeries, and supermarkets line the water between the bus station and port. **Polatos,** Ant. Tristi 32, across from Alpha Bank, has a large selection of fresh fruits at the lowest prices. (Open daily 5am-10:30pm.)

▨ Captain's Table Restaurant, I. Metaxa and 21 Maiou on the waterfront or Rizospaston 3 in the plateia. Be on your best behavior, since after enjoying the vegetarian, grilled meat, or fresh seafood dishes, you'll want an invitation to return for another meal with the captain. Salads €3-10.50. Greek classics and vegetarian selections €5.20-9. Fresh fish from €11. ❷

La Gondola, 21 Maiou. Amply cushioned, but often packed, outdoor seating. They serve Greek dishes, but people come for divine Italian dishes like *risotto sabbia d'oro* (€8.80) with pumpkin and shrimp. Pizza €8.60-10. Pasta €5.60-10.20. Greek entrees €7-8.30. Wine from €8.50. Open 7pm-1am. MC/V. ❷

Kohenoor (☎26 789), at the intersection of Str. Metaxa and Lavraga, 1 block toward the water from the plateia. The sign simply reading "Indian Restaurant" is more than enough to distinguish it from Argostoli's limited options. Inside you'll find tasty curries at reasonable prices. Specialties include chicken *tikka masala* (€9) and *vindaloo* lamb (€10). Appetizers €4-5. Open daily 6:30pm-midnight. V. ❸

SIGHTS

Argostoli's **Archaeological Museum** is in a beautiful building a few blocks south of the plateia, across from the Municipal Theater on R. Vergoti. Pottery and jewelry from excavations around the island and Melissani Lake are displayed with explanations in Greek and English. Vintage photographs of an 1899 excavation at Sami are on display, as are some of the 3rd-century BC tombstones found there, complete with remarkably well-preserved names of the dead. Make sure to stop by the 2nd-century BC **mosaic** from the temple of Poseidon. (☎28 300. Open Tu-Su 8:30am-3pm. €3, seniors and students €2, children and EU students free.) The **Historical and Folk Museum,** two blocks from the Archaeological Museum, on the road to the left of the theater, contains an impressive display of 19th-century objects. Of particular interest are the 20th-century photos of Argostoli, including shots of damage from the devastating 1953 earthquake, and religious items and tiles that survived the quake. (☎28 835. Open M-Sa 9am-2pm. €4, students €3, children under 12 free.) The **Focas-Cosmetatos Foundation,** one block to the left of the plateia facing inland, has a large collection of 18th- and 19th-century furniture, coins, and paintings, as well as photos from the period of the 1953 disaster. The Foundation recently finished a botanical garden to showcase and preserve the plants of the Ionian Islands and the Mediterranean basin. Admission to the Foundation also gets you into the garden outside of town—ask for directions. (☎26 595. Open M-Sa 9:30am-1pm and Tu-Sa 7-10pm. €3, under 14 free.)

DAYTRIPS FROM ARGOSTOLI

Renting a moped or car allows you to roam between sights and beaches, unrestrained by inconvenient bus schedules. You also can get to ✴**Myrtos beach** (p. 561) on the western coast, considered to be one of Europe's most stunning shores.

CASTLE OF ST. GEORGE. This Venetian castle is 7km southeast of Argostoli, overlooking the village of Travliata. From its 18th-century battlements, you can admire the panorama that once inspired Lord Byron. Its underground tunnels once connected the castle to Argostoli and were used as a getaway system through WWII. *(By moped, head toward Skala and bear left when the road splits, or take either the Poros or Skala buses.* ☎68 395. *Open daily 8am-8pm. Free.)*

LIXOURI. In the center of the western peninsula, Lixouri is a large and vibrant town, yet less touristed than the capital. If you wish to spend the day here, you can rent a **moped** at several places in town and explore the charming villages in the area. You also can take one of the local **buses,** including the one that runs twice a day to **Xi,** a red-sand beach surrounded by cliffs. The town itself, with its small cafes and bakeries, is a wonderful place to settle and unwind. For a change of scenery, a small beach is at the far left of the waterfront, facing inland; it's a 5min. walk along a lovely tree-lined promenade. *(Boat from Argostoli 30min., every 30min., €1.60. Buy tickets on board. 15min., returns immediately; 9:15am, 2:45pm; €1.)*

SOUTHERN COAST BEACHES. A few beaches and noteworthy towns dot the area south of Argostoli. Closer to the capital city than white-sanded **Ormous Lourda, Makris Yialos** and **Platis Yialos** share breathtaking shorelines below an enormous cliff. You can sit above the sands and listen to the crashing waves or join the tanning population on the lounge chairs below. *(Take the Lassi bus; 5min., 10 per day 9am-6:30pm, €1. You also can walk from the central plateia. Facing inland, take the road to the left side of the plateia and follow the signs. The beaches are about 3km away.)*

EAST OF ARGOSTOLI. The **Monastery of Agios Gerasimos,** 13km from Argostoli, was built around the underground cove where Ag. Gerasimos spent his last days on earth. Today, a small ladder toward the back of the church allows guests access to that cove. When a large enough crowd forms at the monastery, the monks open the silver casket that holds his preserved body. On the night of August 16, nearby **Omala** hosts a festival and vigil in the saint's church; for two days, Omala's residents honor him by drinking their fill of wine. The villages of **Fragata** and **Marcupulo** also have festivities. *(Ask at the tourist office for info on the festival. Buses run from Argostoli to Ag. Gerasimos/Omala; 10am, 12:30, 2:15pm; €1.50.)* **Skala** is yet another village with a never-ending beach; this one is pebble and sand. The small town offers bathers crystal clear water 37km from Argostoli and history buffs the remains of a 2nd-century Roman villa. Almost all of its structure is gone, but the mosaic floors are remarkably well-preserved. *(Look for the signs as you walk down the road from the bus stop toward the water. Open Tu-Su 8:30am-3pm. If it's closed, a view is still available from the sides. Free.)* The ruins of an ancient temple are 2km in the other direction. *(Walk with the water on your right side and follow the signs.)* There's no shortage of dining choices along the beach, many serving fresh, inexpensive seafood.

SAMI Σάμη ☎ 26740

As you stroll through Sami, stunning views in all directions make it difficult to decide which is more lovely: the tempestuous blue waves crashing on the white-sand beach or the lush, village-dotted hills cradling the town. Sami's main advantages are its central location as a small port and its proximity to the natural wonders of Melissani Lake, Drogarati cave, and Antisamos beach. In the late 1990s, Nicolas Cage starred as an Italian military officer occupying Kephalonia during WWII in *Captain Corelli's Mandolin*. The picturesque Venetian buildings seen in the film, however, were actually created by skilled set-makers; in reality, the 1953 earthquake wiped out most of Sami, leaving modern architecture in its wake.

TRANSPORTATION. From Sami, **ferries** sail to Patras (2½hr.; 8:30am, 5pm; €14.50) and Vathy (1hr., 11:30pm, €6.40). In July and August, international ferries go to Brindisi, Italy (daily, €45). **Buses** leave the station on the left end of the waterfront, facing inland, for Argostoli (45min., 4 per day, €4) and Fiskardo (1½hr., €4). There are no buses on Sundays. Expensive **taxis** (☎ 22 308) line up on the waterfront facing the plateia.

ORIENTATION AND PRACTICAL INFORMATION. Poseidonos, the waterfront street lined with cafes, intersects the main plateia. White-pebble beaches lie both to the left and right of the town center. Ferries land on the left side of the town plateia facing inland. From the bus station, facing the water, turn left to reach the plateia. You may be able to see the top of the blue-and-white Hotel Kyma, which sits on **I. Metaxa,** Sami's main road; this road runs parallel to the water one block inland. The plateia lies between the road and the waterfront. Following the inland road with the water on your right leads to Argostoli.

The staff at **Blue Sea Travel,** next to the bus station, sells ferry tickets and offers general information. (☎ 23 007; www.samistar.com. Open daily 8am-11pm.) A **Tourist Information** office is open on the left of the waterfront, in the far left corner facing inland. (23 280. Open daily 9am-9pm.) Sami has several **banks; Emporiki Trapeza,** on the waterfront to the right of the plateia as you face inland, has **currency exchange** and a **24hr. ATM.** (Open M-Th 8am-2:30pm, F 8am-2pm.) The 24hr. **police** station, I. Metaxa 14 (☎22 100), is located on the main road toward Argostoli, near the post office, three blocks from the plateia. **Pharmacies** are on the main road to Argostoli. Take a right onto the road from the plateia facing inland, and one will be on your left at I. Metaxa 37. The **OTE** is one block past the post office. (Open M-F.) For **Internet** access, try **Melissini Restaurant,** next to the campground. Walk along the waterfront road with the water on your right, then down the path along the beach. (€5 per hr. Pool €3 from 9am-7pm. Open 8:30am-11pm). The **post office** is on the road to Argostoli, two blocks off the right corner of the plateia at the fork in the road. (Open M-F 7:30am-2pm.) **Postal Code:** 28080.

▚▞ ACCOMMODATIONS AND CAMPING. Because Sami is a convenient base for travel within Kephalonia, rooms are in high demand and get relatively expensive in the summer. The street leading to the nearby village of **Karavomilos,** toward Melissani Lake, is lined with **domatia.** The rooms above **Riviera Restaurant ❸** along the harbor, one block from the bus station, have kitchen, bath, and air-conditioning for a low price. The rooms are accessible by a white marble staircase to the side of the restaurant. Check in at Hotel Kastro, located on a side street off the waterfront road to the right of the plateia facing inland. (☎22 282. Singles €35-60.) If you are dying to stay in town, **Hotel Kyma ❷,** is a good option. (☎22 064. Singles €20-30; doubles €30-60; triples €39-50.) **Hotel Melissani ❹,** two blocks inland from the Port Authority, on the far left of the waterfront (follow the signs), has 15 rooms with balcony, fridge, TV, and bath. The top-floor room has a private rooftop patio, though there is also a roof patio for all guests. (☎22 464. Breakfast €7.50. Singles €40-55; doubles €42-65; triples €54.60-78.) **Karavomilos Beach Camping ❶,** a 15min. walk from town with the water on your right, is in a huge field. The site is clean, with hot showers, electricity, laundry, Internet access, and a minimart. (☎22 480; www.camping-karavomilos.gr. Office open 8:30am-noon and 4:30pm-midnight. €6-7.50 per person; sleeping bag rental €0.50; €3.50-4 per small tent, €4.50-5.50 per large tent. Electricity €3.80.)

◖ FOOD. Taka Taka Mam ❶ serves standard Greek fare by the ocean at a great bargain. Some of its plates run up to €8, but travelers can keep it cheap with the gyro and grill staples. (☎22 816. Gyros €1.80. Souvlaki €1.40. Beer €2-2.50.) **Mermaid Restaurant ❷,** Taka's waterfront neighbor, is less tacky than other harborside options and has many vegetarian options (☎22 202. Salads €3-5. Fresh okra €4.50. Vegetarian moussaka of Cythera €6. Other entrees €6.50-15.) **Pizza Tereza ❷,** toward the far right end of the waterfront cafes (facing inland), provides a little taste of Italy with vegetarian options available. (Sizable pizzas €5.70-9. Open daily 9am-midnight.) At night, young locals drive around the main square blasting Greek pop; at the few bars along the harbor, you can enjoy drinks all night long.

◪◩ SIGHTS AND BEACHES. Sami's two popular caves are a short drive from town. Stalactite- and stalagmite-filled **Melissani,** 2km from Sami, is part of the huge, underground Lake Karavomilos. Its deep blue waters run deeper than 15m and flow from as far as Argostoli. Finding it is simple, though the walk will take 30-45min.; go along the beach with the water to your right until you come to a small ocean-fed pond with a waterwheel on the far side. Turn left after the restaurant by the pond, walk inland to the road about 30m, and turn right; you'll see signs down this street. The boat tour of the cave lasts 10-15min., and the knowledgeable boatmen explain the history and pose for photos. Because the cave has an open roof measuring 50m by 30m, you'll want to go when the sun is high in the sky. (☎22 997. Open daily 9am-sunset. €6 entrance.) **Drogarati,** 4km from Sami, is a large cavern full of spectacular stalactites and stalagmites over 150 million years old. To find it, walk inland on the road to Argostoli and follow the signs (45min.) or take the bus to Argostoli and ask to be let off at Drogarati; you'll be dropped off at the fork, a 5min. walk from the caves. (☎22 950. Open until dark. €4.) **Agia Efimia,** 9km north of Sami, is a pretty harbor town, popular with the yachting crowd, that definitely deserves a visit. Buses (15min., 2 per day, €3.50) run from Sami to Agia Efimia. Ask the Fiskardo bus driver to let you off there (15min., €3.50).

Isolated and alluring ■**Antisamos** beach is a must if you get to this side of Kephalonia. The long, white-pebble beach is enclosed by rolling green hills, home to the island's colorful butterflies and many wandering goats. You can take a taxi to Antisamos (€9) or you can hike there (1¼hr.) by following the waterfront left from the plateia as you face inland; take the road next to the Port Authority. Since the hike is uphill, fairly long, and challenging, bring plenty of water and wear good shoes.

FISKARDO Φισκάρδο ☎ 26740

The road north ends at must-see Fiskardo, one of the few Kephalonian villages unaffected by the 1953 earthquake. That stroke of luck has left it a rare example of the island's 18th- and 19th-century architecture. The crescent-shaped waterfront is tinged with the pastel hues of the modest buildings surrounding it. At night a romantic aura pervades the town, which twinkles with the dim lights of boats resting in the water. A splendid walk through the woods or a swim from the rocks takes you to the forested bit of land across the harbor, home to a lighthouse and a ruined 15th-century Venetian fortress. The port, meanwhile, is home to a great number of yachts and boats clustered closely together on the docks. Fiskardo's white-pebble beach is only 500m from town, on the road to Argostoli, in a quiet cove with flat rocks for sunbathing.

■ **TRANSPORTATION AND PRACTICAL INFORMATION. Ferries** go to Nidri, Lefkada (2hr., 1-5 per day, €6.40) and Vasiliki (1hr., €6.40). In July and August, the same boats also run to Frikes, Ithaka (€3.40). **Buses** for Argostoli leave from the parking lot next to the church, uphill from the town. Two buses per day run to Argostoli (1½hr.; 6:30am, 4:30pm; €5) and Sami (1½hr.; 6:30am, 4:30pm; €4). **Nautilus Travel Agency,** at the right end of the waterfront, answers transportation and lodgings questions and provides **currency exchange.** (☎41 440. Open daily 9am-10pm.) In high season, you can rent motorboats from **Regina,** before Nicholas Taverna when walking from town and by the ferry docks. Rentals start at €40 per day plus fuel at current per-liter price. (☎69389 84 647. Open daily 9am-6pm.)

■ **ACCOMMODATIONS AND FOOD.** Rooms are not cheap in Fiskardo, even in the scattered **domatia.** Early in summer, simple doubles are not often found below €40. For the best view in the village, stay at ■**Tavern Inn ❹,** whose rooms have bath, fan, and balcony. Looking out over the rocks and crashing waves, guests can see the famed lighthouse and nearby Ithaka. To find the Inn, walk with the water on your left for 100m out of the town center. (Rooms €42-58.) The well-maintained rooms at **Anatoli ❸,** next to Elli's Restaurant and Cafe on the right side of the harbor, have air-conditioning, TV, and common kitchen. (☎41 204. Check-in at Elli's. Rooms €30-65.) Some cheap rooms are just outside of town. **Tassia Restaurant ❸,** on the waterfront, 2.5km inland in Antipata, offers apartments for four with two rooms, bath, and kitchen, as well as studio rooms in town for up to two. (☎41 205. Apartments €60-90; studios €30-45.)

Pink-and-blue **Lagoudera ❷** is just off the waterfront next to the post office. The pleasant outdoor reed-roofed terrace accented by lanterns and plants make for a great dining atmosphere a at reasonable price. (☎41 275. Entrees €6-11.) At **Nicho-**

las Taverna ❸, located 200m to the right of the port facing inland, couples can enjoy a romantic dinner by the water. Gregarious Nicholas attests to his family-run taverna's status as a dining institution by putting newspaper and magazine clippings about himself at the front of his menus. On Fridays, get your groove on with Greek dancing. (☎41 307. Salads €4-7. Fish €46-70 per kg. Entrees €7-15. Open 8:30am-1am. MC/V.) Wasting your money and your appetite on pre-packaged ice cream is pointless when you can try the authentic variety at **Dodoni ❷,** next to Nautilus Tours. (€1.70 per scoop. Other desserts from €3. Coffee €2.50-3.50.)

◑◐ SIGHTS AND BEACHES. Venturing away from the waterfront proves quite rewarding. To reach the old-fashioned lighthouse, walk all the way around the waterfront with the sea on your right to Nicholas Taverna. A short and shaded path picks up where the road ends. Ruins of an old fortress are nearby. If you need to cool off and aren't in the mood for a trek, a smaller, though heavily trafficked, pebble beach offers first-rate views of neighboring Ithaka. With the water on your left, head along the waterfront road for about 10min.; the beach is just past the Roman graves. Off the road from Argostoli and Sami to Fiskardo is one of Europe's most breathtaking beaches, **◪Myrtos.** The snowy white pebbles and clear, blue water are stunning enough, but the beach's location, pressed against the cliffs, makes it divine (4km from main road turn-off). Ten kilometers up the road from the Myrtos turn-off is the equally incredible Venetian **Castle of Assos,** on a steep, wooded peninsula connected to the island by a narrow isthmus. Completed in the early part of the 17th century, much of the castle is well preserved. Fiskardo buses stop at the Assos turn-off; it's a 4km walk to the small, peaceful village (also worth a visit) and another few kilometers to the castle.

ZAKYNTHOS Ζάκυνθος

The varied landscapes of Zakynthos are filled with an exceptional palette of colors—white cliffs rise from aquamarine water, sun-bleached wheat fields wave in the shadow of evergreens, and magenta flowers frame the twisting streets. Away from Zakynthos Town and its neighboring touristed beaches, you'll encounter Zakynthos's true beauty. Pale, pebbled beaches are easily accessible from the island's eastern coastal towns. Boats carry tourists around the coast to the sparsely populated western side of the island, where dramatically steep cliffs form enticing caves and hidden coves. A large population of endangered loggerhead sea turtles takes refuge off the island's southern shores. Those who venture away from the shops selling oversized, plush sea turtles quickly will come to understand why the Venetians called Zakynthos the "flower of the east."

ZAKYNTHOS TOWN ☎26950

Beyond the heavily-kiosked sidewalk of the waterfront road, arcaded streets and delicate Old World buildings welcome visitors to Zakynthos Town. After an earthquake destroyed the city in 1953, locals recreated the Venetian architecture in areas such as Pl. Solomou, creating pleasant, if not authentic, areas for locals and travelers alike to stroll and rest. Though buzzing crowds of tourists and street vendors make for a hectic scene early in the day, walking through the streets or by the waterfront at sunset is a peaceful pleasure. Zakynthos Town is a convenient base for daytrips to see the island, as many companies offer boat tours that leave from the town's docks. If the call of the wild burns in your veins, buses from the town provide access to more remote beaches.

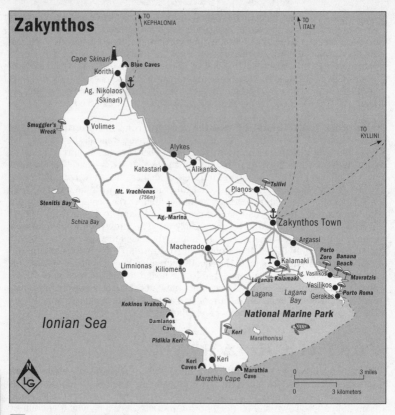

Zakynthos

TO KEPHALONIA

TO ITALY

TO KYLLINI

Cape Skinari
Korithi
Blue Caves
Ag. Nikolaos (Skinari)
Smuggler's Wreck
Volimes
Alykes
Katastari
Alikanas
Tsilivi
Mt. Vrachionas (756m)
Planos
Stenitis Bay
Schiza Bay
Ag. Marina
Zakynthos Town
Argassi
Macherado
Porto Zoro
Banana Beach
Kalamaki
Limnionas
Kiliomeno
Ag. Vasilikos
Mavratzis
Laganas Kalamaki
Vasilikos
Porto Roma
Lagana
Lagana Bay
Gerakas
Kokinos Vrahos
National Marine Park
Damianos Cave
Ionian Sea
Pidikla Keri
Keri
Marathonissi
Keri Caves
Keri
Marathia Cape
Marathia Cave

0   3 miles
0   3 kilometers

◰ TRANSPORTATION

Flights: The **airport** (☎28 611) is 3km south of town. Flights to: **Athens** (45min., 1-2 per day, €76-10); **Corfu** (3 per week, €52); **Kephalonia** (3 per week, €32); **Thessaloniki** (3 per week, €96). The **Olympic Airways** office recently moved to the airport. Purchase plane tickets from tour companies along the waterfront road 9am-2pm.

Ferries: Ferries for **Kyllini** in the Peloponnese (1½hr., 5-6 per day 5:30am-7:15pm, €6.50) depart from the southern dock, on the left side of the waterfront as you face inland. Tickets for Kyllini ferries can be bought at **Praktoreio Ploion** (☎26278 22 083), next to Hertz on Lomvardou past the police station with the water on your right. Open daily 8:30am-8:30pm. **Agios Nikolaos (Skinari),** about 30km north of Zakynthos Town, has ferries to **Pesada, Kephalonia** (1½hr., 1-2 per day, €4). Zakynthian buses do not run to Ag. Nikolaos, and a taxi will run €40. Returning to Kyllini and heading to Kephalonia by ferry is another alternative. For more information, call the **port police** (☎28 117 or 28 118).

Buses: Filita 42 (☎22 255), behind the Praktoreio Ploion. From Pl. Solomou, walk 6 blocks south with the water on your left and 1 block inland. Schedules change monthly; check the info window. To: **Athens** (6hr., 5 per day 5am-6:45pm, €22.10 including ferry); **Patras** (3hr.; 7:30am, 2:30pm, 6:45pm; €6.50 including ferry); and **Thessaloniki** (10hr., M-Th and Su 7:30am, €42 including ferry). **Local buses** run to: **Alykes** (M-F 4 per day 6:50am-4:45pm, Sa-Su 4 per day 7:40am-4:30pm; €1.50); **Argassi** (M-F 10 per day 6:45am-11:30pm, Sa-

Su 7 per day 9am-11:30pm; €1.20); **Lagana** (M-Sa 15 per day 7:15am-11:30pm, Su 8 per day 7:15am-8:10pm; €1.20); **Kalamaki** (M-Sa 12 per day 7:15am-11:30pm, Su 8 per day 7:15am-8:10pm; €1.20); **Tsilivi** (M-Sa 12 per day 6:40am-11pm, Su 6 per day 7am-7pm; €1.20); **Vasilikos** (M-F 4 per day 6:45am-5:30pm; Sa-Su 10am, 3pm; €1.50).

Taxis: ☎ 48 400. Line up on Venizelou street, a left off the waterfront road just before Pl. Solomou with the water on the right. You also can flag one down on the waterfront road in front of Solomou. Available 24hr. For rides in the early morning, make arrangements the day before.

Rentals: Hertz, Lomvardou 38 (☎ 45 706). Cars from €50 per day; includes unlimited km, insurance, and tax. Open daily 8am-2pm and 5:30-9pm. **EuroSky Rentals,** A. Makri 6 (☎ 26 278; www.eurosky.gr), 2 blocks inland on A. Makri, by Pl. Solomou. Mopeds €15 per day. Cars from €30. Open daily 9am-2pm and 6-9pm.

✦❼ ORIENTATION AND PRACTICAL INFORMATION

The waterfront runs between **Plateia Solomou** and **Agios Dionysios church.** Each end has a dock: Kyllini ferries dock at the left end facing inland, by Ag. Dionysios; all other boats, including daily cruises, dock at either end. The waterfront street, **Lomvardou,** is lined with restaurants, gift shops, ferry agencies, and car and moped rentals. The next street inland is **Filita,** with the bus station and fast-food stands; Filita becomes **Klavdianou** toward Pl. Solomou. Behind it are **Foskolou, Alexandrou Roma,** and **Tertseti,** all of which either change names or end between **Martinegou** and Ag. Dionysios. Just inland from Pl. Solomou is **Plateia Agiou Markou,** a major gathering spot for both locals and tourists, separated by a pedestrian-only street called **Dimokratias Square.** Al. Roma becomes a pedestrian shopping area between **Tzoulati** and Pl. Ag. Markou.

Bank: National Bank (☎ 26 808), on Pl. Solomou. **Exchanges currency** and has a **24hr. ATM.** Open daily M-F 8am-2:30pm. Other ATMs sit along Lomvardou and around Pl. Solomou.

Police: ☎ 24 480. **Emergency** ☎ 100. At the intersection of Lomvardou and Fra. Tzoulati. Open 24hr. The **tourist police** (☎ 24 482) are in the same building. Enter through the door to the side of Fra. Tzoulati, take a right, and they are at the end of the hallway. Open daily 7:30am-2:30pm.

Hospital: ☎ 59 100. Uphill and 600m inland from the city center. Walk down Lomvardou to Ag. Eleftheriou. Follow this road inland to Kokkini, where the road goes right, becoming Ag. Spiridona. Follow the signs from the waterfront. Open 24hr.

Internet Access: Connect Internet, 88 Lomvardou (☎ 44 622). €3 per hr., min. €2. Ask about becoming a member for a lower hourly rate. Coffee €2-3.50. Beer €3.50. Juice €4. Sandwiches €1.50-2.50. Open daily 9am-1am.

Post Office: ☎ 42 418. On Tertseti, the 4th street inland from the waterfront, near Xenou. **Exchanges currency.** Open M-F 7:30am-3:30pm. **Postal Code:** 29100.

▐ ACCOMMODATIONS

Rooms in Zakynthos Town fill up in July and August and tend to be expensive year-round. Large waterfront hotels charge around €90 for a double in high season; reasonably priced hotels with lower-quality service crowd the blocks to the very right of the waterfront, facing inland, after the port. One option is to stay in Argassi, 3km away, where you can find domatia and hotels on the main street. If you do want to stay in town, put on your poker face and bargain.

Hotel Diana (☎ 28 547; www.dianahotels.gr) in Pl. St. Markou, adjacent to the Catholic church. Offers location and luxury for predictably high prices, although it's a relative bargain during low season. Elegant rooms have A/C, bath, and TV. Breakfast included. Singles €45-60; doubles €55-85. MC/V. ●

Athina Marouda Rooms for Rent, Tzoulati and Koutouzi (☎45 194), 3 blocks inland from the police. Simple rooms with sparse furnishings are accessed by narrow, twisting staircases and hallways. The central location, common kitchen, and shared bath keep people strapped for cash nicely satisfied. Singles €15; doubles €25. ❶

Hotel Yria, Kapodistrou 4 (☎44 682; http://zakynthos-net.gr/yria), 3 blocks past Pl. Solomou to the far right of the waterfront facing inland. Carpeted rooms have A/C, TV, phone, bath, fridge, and small balcony. Look for the hotel's rooftop sign as you walk with the water on your right. Singles €45-60; doubles €55-70; triples €65-90. ❹

Hotel Aegli (☎28 317), on Lomvardou, 2 blocks south from Pl. Solomou with the water on your left. Unassuming lobby close to Zakynthos Town's most heavily trafficked stretch of road. Bright, colorful, well-maintained if not quite modern rooms with TV, balcony, fridge, A/C, and large bath. Singles €30-45; doubles €40-60; triples €50-70. ❸

🄵 FOOD

Along the waterfront road, numerous restaurants inhabit nearly every block. On Al. Roma, toward Pl. Ag. Markou, cafes and fast-food joints line up one after another. The **Veropoulos Supermarket,** on Lomvardou, 50m to the right of the police station, facing inland, sells a wide variety of fruit, vegetables, cereal, and snacks. In the sweltering summer, swing by for the freezing-cold air-conditioning even if you're not hungry. (Open M-F 8am-9pm, Sa 8am-8pm.)

Village Inn, Lomvardou 20 (☎26 991). This interesting bar/takeout/sit-down restaurant features no lodging, and, despite its name, feels like a blues joint. Over 20 years in their water front spot and a large menu that features a kids section and vegetarian options (mixed vegetables €8). Eat out front or inside by the garden area. Live music Th. Lamb in lemon sauce with oregano €9. Moussaka €7. Open daily 8am-midnight. ❷

Nikos Restaurant (44 277), on the far left end of the waterfront road, in Ammos Square by Ag. Dionysis church. Features outdoor seating in the small park that separates it from the waterfront. Come for the local fish and seafood, or the very affordable Greek cuisine (from €5.50). Local favorite pork steak €6.50. Salads €2.90-4.50. Beer €2-2.50. Entrees €5.50-15. Open daily 10am-2am. ❸

Venetsiana, in Pl. Ag. Markou. The oldest restaurant in the plateia exudes an Italian air out to its umbrella-shaded seating. House specialty beef *stamnas* €8.50. Other similarly enticing dishes include fresh pizza. Entrees €6-15.90. Open daily 8am-1am. ❸

Molos, 26 Lomvardou (☎23 939). This takeout paradise serves delicious Greek dishes in a convenient location near the pickup points for many boat tours. *Pastitsio* €5. Club sandwich plate €5. Homemade rabbit dish €7. Open daily 10am-midnight. ❷

🄶 SIGHTS

🄴ECCLESIASTICAL MUSEUM. The Ecclesiastical Museum features beautifully sculpted crosses, Ag. Dionysios's vestments, and his handwritten documents. Engraved Bibles from the 13th through 17th centuries were protected from repeated pirate attacks on the Monastery of Strofades, where the saint lived. Letters written in Latin between late 16th-century religious leaders are remarkably well-preserved, and magnificent paintings line the stairs to the second floor. *(Behind the Church of Agios Dionysios. ☎44 126. Open daily 8am-10pm. €2, under 18 free.)*

CHURCH OF AGIOS DIONYSIOS. The intricate designs throughout the church, named in honor of the island's patron saint, make its colorful frescoes pale in comparison. In a room enclosed by silver walls, a silver chest holds some of the saint's relics. At night, only the *iconostasis* is lit up, making it visible from the street. *(In front of the Ecclesiastical Museum. Open daily 8am-10:30pm. Modest dress required.)*

BYZANTINE MUSEUM. The Byzantine Museum houses two floors of icons from the Ionian School, a distinctive local hybrid of Byzantine and Renaissance art styles. Two 17th-century *iconostases* on the first floor are extravagantly detailed, and a 16th-century *iconostasis* from St. Andreas's monastery fills an entire second-floor room. Check out the Renaissance-style room with the magnificent *Virgin and Child with Angels* from the Church of Panagia Phaneromeni (late 18th century). Many of these artifacts were rescued by locals who risked their lives to pluck them from the dusty rubble of area churches after the 1953 earthquake, as documented in poignant photos. *(In Pl. Solomou facing the water. ☎ 42 714. Open Tu-Su 8:30am-3pm. €3, seniors and students €2, EU students free.)*

MUSEUM OF DIONYSIOS SOLOMOS. Solomos, born in Zakynthos and buried inside the museum, is Greece's national poet; the first verses of his "Hymn to Liberty" became the Greek National Anthem. The exhibit includes everything from the dust from Solomos's first grave to inkpots used by the poet to hand-written manuscripts of his most famous poetry. It also highlights the lives of other famous Greeks, exhibiting even the piano of composer Paul Karren. There is little explanation provided, but tours in English and Greek can be arranged with the museum staff for a small donation. *(In Pl. Ag. Markou. Open daily 9am-2pm. Info booklet €3. €3, seniors and students €2, under 12 free.)*

STRANIS HILL. A hearty walk gets you to **Stranis Hill,** 1km above town. Along with a ruined Venetian castle, Solomos's home, where the famous "Free Besieged" was written, stands on this hill. The views of Zakynthos are particularly dazzling at night. *(Take Tertseti, which becomes N. Koluva, to the edge of town, or head inland from Pl. Ag. Markou; take a right onto Therianou, a left onto Filikon, and follow the signs uphill to Bohalis. Turn left at the junction and go a bit farther.)*

▶ DAYTRIPS FROM ZAKYNTHOS TOWN

You can see all of Zakynthos, including the otherwise inaccessible **western cliffs,** by boat. Shop around for a cruise on Lomvardou. The tours that highlight most of the island's sites usually run €16-25. Most tours leave in the morning, usually around 9am, return around 5:30 or 6pm, and prefer that reservations be made the day before. Don't buy from hawkers around gift shops—while their ticket prices are usually about the same as the agencies', they do not offer refunds and give little explanation after

THE HIDDEN DEAL

HARDLY A HACKNEY

Walking the streets of Zakynthos Town in the late afternoon or at night, you'll hear the clip-clop of horses as they pull carriages around the town. While many travelers brush off carriage rides as a tourist gimmick, drawing in parents eager to please enchanted children or boyfriends hoping to facilitate a romantic moment, Zakynthos's equestrian offerings deserve consideration.

Despite intense inflation over the past few years, these rides have remained reasonably priced. For €20, a friendly driver will take you on a ride through the streets, showing you Zakynthos Town from many different angles. This price is per carriage—not per person—so bring some friends or that special someone. As with most things in Greece, try to bargain in low season.

Instead of walking around the city during a raging hot afternoon or having a taxi cart you around, gently roll along the old Venetian city's streets. Without being at the mercy of a Greek taxi cab driver's taste in music, the soft patter of hooves allows for plenty of opportunities to whisper sweet nothings to your significant other.

Drivers line up along the waterfront road by Pl. Solomou. Rides are offered 4-10pm, but run to midnight in July and August.

they take your money. Cruises go to many of the island's most spectacular sights, including the **Blue Caves** on the northeastern shore past Ag. Nikolaos. The azure sea reflects off the ceilings of the stalactite-filled caverns, creating a blue glow throughout. For a more intimate experience, skip the huge ships and take a small fishing boat from Ag. Nikolaos (€5 for a glass-bottomed boat). If you go swimming by the caves, watch out for jellyfish. Southwest of the Blue Caves is the **Smuggler's Wreck,** a large boat skeleton that has made the beach one of the most photographed in the world ever since its unintentional landing in 1980. Most cruises stop for 30-60min. on the beach. To avoid noontime crowds, try to go in the mid-afternoon. Other cruises from Zakynthos Town visit **Marathonissi**, which is also called Turtle Island because of its proximity to loggerhead turtle nesting grounds and its turtle-like shape. Inquire at the tourist police or at one of the agencies in town. Renting a **moped** will let you explore with far less hassle—there are rental agencies all along Lomvardou and the streets slightly inland (€10-15). If you decide to go solo, buy a road map (€1-5) and ask for directions; the island is developing rapidly, and new roads may not appear on old maps.

> **!** Sunbathers should note that they share Zakynthos's beaches with a resident population of **endangered sea turtles;** a simple stroll through the sand potentially could destroy hundreds of turtle eggs. Zakynthos is making efforts to protect the turtles and their nests, encouraging waterfront properties to take certain precautions and indicating which beaches have nests. Gerakas, Kalamaki, and Laganas have turtle populations; ask at tour companies which other beaches are turtle territory.

The bustling beach town of **Argassi** is 2km south of Zakynthos Town. Buses run to the village daily (M-F 10 per day 6:45am-11:30pm, Sa-Su 7 per day 9am-11:30pm; €1.20) but it's an easy 30-40min. walk on the main road out of town with the water on your left. Argassi, like nearby Laganas, differs immensely from Zakynthos Town; it is a resort town built to cater to tourists, where as Zakynthos town is an authentic Greek city. Argassi is filled with restaurants and clubs designed in the typical style-over-substance manner—an artificially appealing show to attract tourist dollars. Bars host nightly parties with themes like Toga Night; one spot, Avalon, is a re-creation of a medieval castle. Moped and car rental agencies, many restaurants, and a children's go-cart racetrack are just a few of Argassi's amenities.

Wide, sandy **Tsilivi beach,** 5km up Zakynthos Town's waterfront road with the water on your right, is not the place to go if you're trying to flee the tourist masses. Lined with chairs, the beach is crowded with sun-seeking foreigners and people playing adventure sports. Tsilivi is nearly as close as Argassi, but the mountainous terrain and the higher number of oblivious tour bus drivers make reaching Tsilivi on foot more challenging. Local buses run daily from Zakynthos Town (M-Sa 12 per day 6:40am-11pm, Su 6 per day 7am-7pm; €1.20). Follow the signs down the main road leading to the beach from the bus stop.

> **SANDY BED? YES PLEASE** If you want to spend days exploring Zakynthos's many beaches without being tied to a particular town, grab your sleeping bag and head to **Zante Camping ❶**, 1km past Planos on Ampula beach. Its quiet location, amid beautiful flora and sands devoid of tourist footprints, makes it a wonderful place to get acquainted with the island. To get there, catch the Tsilivi bus from Zakynthos Town. (☎61 710. €5, children free; €5 per tent, €3 per car. Electricity free.)

For those dying to escape the crowds, nearly untouched beaches carpet the peninsula that stretches out 6km from Zakynthos Town. Farthest south, 2km past Vasilikos, are the serene sands and crystal-clear water of **Porto Roma.** A few minutes north, though, **Mavratzis** ensures that the hedonistic carousal is never too far away. Its adventure sports and party resort draw a young, international crowd.

Porto Zoro and **Banana Beach** can't be beat for quiet afternoons of sipping piña coladas and lounging under the sun. Buses leave Zakynthos Town for Vasilikos (M-F 4 per day 6:45am-5:30pm, Sa-Su 10am, 3pm; €1.50). Rent a bike in Zakynthos Town and take an early morning ride to Porto Roma. Try **Rent A Bicycle;** make a left at road just before Pl. Solomou walking with water on right; the shop is on the left one block down. (☎69471 80 928. €4 per hr., €10 per day.) Then spend the day heading back to town, stopping at each beach along the way, or spend the night in one of the many domatia by the beaches. Travelers should note that some spots on the western coast of the peninsula are protected areas that must be vacated in the evenings, when sea turtles come ashore to nest. Soft, white-sand beaches fringe **Alykes,** 8km from Zakynthos Town. Buses run from Zakynthos Town (M-F 4 per day 6:50am-4:45pm, Sa-Su 4 per day 7:40am-4:30pm; €1.50).

AGIOS NIKOLAOS (SKINARI) Αγιος Νικόλαος ☎26950

At the extreme northern tip of Zakynthos, a typically Ionian drive away from the bustle of tourist-centric beach towns, is tiny Agios Nikolaos. This village, about the length of a city block, is the port of Cape Skinari. (Confusingly, Agios Nikolaos is sometimes referred to as Skinari.) You can buy tickets on the waterfront for a fishing boat tour of the **Blue Caves** (45min., starting 9-9:30am, €5; €7 in glass-bottomed boat) and the ▨**Smuggler's Wreck** (2hr., starting 11-11:30am, €15), accessible only by water. These tours are considerably shorter than those from Zakynthos Town. During high season, boats leave every 5-15min. from the dock.

Domatia with similar amenities can be found on the road 200m before and after the town. **Hotel La Grotta ❷,** the only hotel in Skinari, is in the middle of the village and to the right of the port facing inland. Spacious rooms come with air-conditioning, balcony, and shower. Proprietors are willing to bargain. They also can help arrange car rentals. (☎31 224. Rooms €20-40. MC/V.) **La Grotta Restaurant ❷** offers a variety of salads, from the typical Greek to the "La Grotta Special." The barbecue burger (€6) is surprisingly zesty. (Salads €4.50-6.50. Open daily 8am-11pm.)

Ferries to Pesada, Kephalonia depart from here. Bus service is nonexistent, so incoming ferry passengers need to arrange their own transportation to Zakynthos Town. You might require a **taxi** (€40), as Skinari has no rental agencies.

IONIAN ISLANDS

CRETE Κρήτη

On an island barely 250km long, palm-tree forests collide with mountain ravines; sheltered, white-sand coves lie alongside slopes of olive groves; and windmill-strewn plains are minutes from limestone caverns. Crete's diversity is as cultural as it is environmental. Isolating mountain ranges have preserved rural lifestyles that seem completely removed from the cities and tourist towns along the coast. Its location as the southernmost point in Europe invited influence from the Egyptians and Phoenicians along with the Turks, Venetians, and Germans, the marks of which can be seen in everything from ancient ruins to WWII memorials strewn across the island. Fusing together Eastern, African, Mediterranean, and European influences, the laid-back sensibility of this island is distinctly Cretan.

 SUGGESTED ITINERARIES: CRETE

FIVE DAYS Explore western Crete, basing your trip in bustling **Hania** (p. 569). Hike the **Samaria Gorge** (p. 577), the longest in Europe, before sunning yourself on **Plakias's** (p. 586) sleepy hidden coves and breezy beaches. Some bus hopping will take you through the beach caves and former hippie mecca at **Matala** (p. 599) and to under-visited **Phaistos** (p. 600), where you can see what remains of the Minoans.

TWO WEEKS After seeing **Hania's** Venetian arsenal, climbing past the wild goats of the Samaria Gorge, and ascending to the ancient palaces of **Phaistos,** relax on **Paleohora's** (p. 579) white-sand beaches, taking a daytrip to idyllic **Elafonisi** (p. 581). Then quench your thirst with water from **Zaros's** (p. 598) famous springs. Spend 1 day in **Iraklion** (p. 589), then rent a car and circle the quiet, mountain-ringed villages of the **Lasithi Plateau** (p. 612). Continue your eastward journey to **Sitia** (p. 617), from which you can take daytrips to the palm-tree forest of **Vai** (p. 619) and the ironically life-filled **Valley of Death** gorge (p. 619).

The seeds of civilization (as well as the first olives) were planted in Crete, with records of life on the island dating back to 6000 BC. Its ruins predate Hellenic culture, attesting to the advancement of Minoan society. Disasters—earthquakes, a tidal wave from an enormous volcanic eruption on Santorini, and Mycenaean invasions—plagued 3rd millennium BC Minoan society until the civilization was wiped out entirely. Power struggles ensued for the next 3000 years as empires strove to claim this hotly contested island as their own. Dorians occupied the island in the 8th century BC, followed 1000 years later by Romans. Next, Crete fell under rickety Byzantine rule before Arabs conquered the island in AD 827, only to lose it again to the Byzantines. In 1204, the Byzantines again ceded the island; this time to Frankish crusaders. When it finally was sold to the Venetian Empire, Crete became a thriving commercial hub dominated by Venetian nobles and local merchants. In 1646 the island fell to the Turks, who ruled the resentful islanders until the Cretans finally won independence in 1898, 70 years after most of Greece. After the Balkan Wars, Crete joined the Greek state. A strong guerilla resistance combated the German occupation here during WWII, leaving the islanders with a justifiable sense of pride about their revolutionary and indomitable nature.

Though Crete is divided into four prefectures—Hania, Iraklion, Lasithi, and Rethymno—the territorial divisions do not affect its unified feel. According to a Greek saying, a Cretan's first loyalty is to his island, his second to his country.

Crete's sense of identity, however, also expresses itself in an overwhelming hospitality, as natives strive to show visitors why their island is so exceptional. Don't be surprised to be invited in to share watermelon or a bottle of *raki* with your pension hosts on a hot day. Locals are eager to share their insider knowledge of secluded beaches and gorgeous hikes with interested visitors. Yet Crete's spirit is almost impossible to capture or define, as its best qualities—the relaxed pace of life, rebellious streak, and seemingly infinite diversity—are only minute samples of the island's rich offerings.

GETTING THERE. Olympic Airways (☎21096 66 666) and **Aegean/Cronus Airlines** (☎21099 88 300) run frequent, cheap, and fast domestic flights from Athens to Iraklion, Hania, and Sitia. Consult the **Transportation** section of your destination for more information on flights. Many travelers take the 14hr. **ferry** from Piraeus to Crete, landing in Iraklion, Hania, Sitia, or occasionally Rethymno or Agios Nikolaos. Boats run frequently during the summer, but often irregularly. All prices listed are for deck-class accommodations; bring a sleeping bag to snooze on the deck or lounge.

HANIA PREFECTURE

Gorgeous beaches, steep, rocky gorges, and pine-covered hills dot the western tip of Crete. Tourists flock to these natural wonders in droves, but somehow Hania manages to maintain some semblance of its distinct character. By day, the region's small villages and pristine beaches call nature lovers to experience untapped wilderness and local hospitality. By night, the capital city welcomes party animals seeking hedonistic revelry.

HANIA Χανιά ☎28210

The island's second-largest city, Hania takes on its annual surge of summer tourists with a refined ease typical of this port town's open atmosphere. The gritty outer streets give way to charming pedestrian boulevards full of stylish shops and cafes by the Old Venetian Harbor. Visitors meander through maze-like cobblestoned alleys, listening to traditional Cretan music from cafes or waiting for the setting sun to silhouette the lighthouse and nearby Venetian and Ottoman domes.

■ TRANSPORTATION

Flights: Olympic Airways, Tzanakaki 88 (☎53 760), across from the municipal gardens. Tickets sold daily 8:15am-3:30pm. Flights to **Athens** (4-5 per day, €55-90) and **Thessaloniki** (1½hr., 3 per week, €115).

Ferries: If you're arriving by ferry, you'll dock in the nearby port of **Souda.** Take the bus from the dock, which stops on Zymvrakakidon by Pl. 1866 (15min., €1). **ANEK Office,** Pl. Market 2 (☎27 500). From Hania's port town, **Souda,** ferries go to **Piraeus** (9½hr.; 9, 11:30pm, €30). Open daily 7:30am-9pm. Catch the bus to Souda in front of the municipal market where El. Venizelou meets Chatzimichali Giannari (25min., every 20min. 6am-10:40pm, €1).

Buses: The **bus station** (☎93 052) fills the block of Kidonias, Zymvrakakidon, Smyrnis, and Kelaidi. Buses to: **Elafonisi** (2½hr., 9am, €9.50); **Hora Sfakion** (2hr., 3-4 per day 8:30am-2pm, €6.50); **Iraklion** (2½hr., 20 per day 5:30am-9pm, €11.50); **Kastelli,** also called Kissamos (1hr., 14 per day 6:30am-9pm, €4); **Paleohora** (2hr., 4 per day

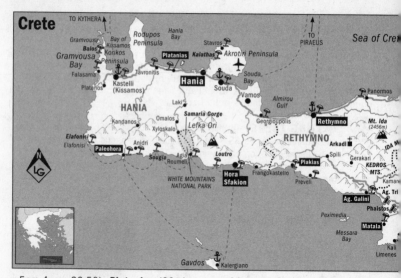

5am-4pm, €6.50); **Platanias** (20min., every 30min. 6:30am-11pm, €1.60); **Rethymno** (1hr., 20 per day 5:30am-9pm, €6); **Samaria Gorge (Omalos)** (1hr., 4 per day 10:10am-6:15pm, €5.90); **Sougia** (2hr., 1-2 per day 5am and 1:45pm, €6.10).

Taxis: ☎98 700. In Pl. Machis Tis Kritis and on Pl. 1866's eastern side. Available 24hr.

Car and Moped Rental: Agencies are on Halidon. Mopeds €18-25 per day; cars €25-50. Some rentals only allow for 100km; driving more may cost €0.06-0.20 per km.

■★ ■ ORIENTATION AND PRACTICAL INFORMATION

To get to the city center from the bus station, turn right onto **Kidonias,** walk one block, then turn left onto **Zymvrakakidon,** which runs along one side of a long park called **Plateia 1866.** At the far end of Pl. 1866, the road becomes **Halidon** and leads to the **Old Venetian Harbor,** full of outdoor restaurants, pensions, and narrow alleyways. **Skalidi** intersects Zymvrakakidon where it becomes Halidon; to the right,

> **CAR COUNTRY.** Though bus service between major hubs in Crete like Hania, Iraklion, and Rethymno is surprisingly prompt, frequent, and cheap, it will only get you as far as the next trampled tourist destination. To really mine the island's gems, consider renting your own wheels.

Skalidi becomes **Chatzimichali Giannari.** One hundred meters farther, Chatzimichali Giannari splits into **Tzanakaki** and **Eleftheriou Venizelou.** Hania's business district is across from the **Municipal Market** near the fork in Chatzimichali Giannari. Sunbathers can head west of the harbor along the waterfront to find a popular long, thin stretch of sand at **Nea Hora.** The top of **Promahonas Hill,** on Baladinou just off of Halidon, yields an overview of Hania.

> **Tourist Office:** Kidonias 29 (☎36 155; www.chania.gr), in the city hall. Provides free maps of the city and information on buses, museums, monasteries, Samaria Gorge hikes, and boats on the southern coast. Open M-F 8:30am-2:30pm with self-service until 8pm, Sa 9am-2pm.

CRETE

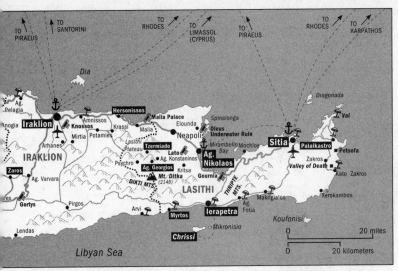

Bank: National Bank (☎38 934), on the corner of El. Venizelou and Tzanakaki. Open M-Th 8am-2:30pm, F 8am-2pm. **24hr. ATM.**

Luggage Storage: At the bus station. €1.50 per bag for 24hr. Open daily 6am-9pm.

Bookstores: NewsStand, Skalidi 8 (☎95 888), sells guidebooks, newspapers, and a large selection of Dutch, English, French, German, and Italian magazines. Open daily 8am-11:30pm. The American and Irish owners of the consignment shop **To Pazari,** Daskalogianni 46, buy and sell used books in English, French, and German, as well as an eclectic mix of second-hand clothes, jewelry, appliances, and music. Open M and W 8:30am-2pm, Tu and Th-F 8:30am-1:30pm and 6-9pm, Sa 8:30am-3pm.

Public Toilets: In Pl. 1866 near the bus stop and at the corner of El. Venizelou and A. Papandreou near the Municipal Market.

Police: (☎25 811), 250m down Apokronou on the left. Open daily 8am-2pm. The **tourist police** (☎25 931) are in the tourist office. Open daily 10am-2pm.

Hospital: ☎22 000. Located in Mournies, 6km south of Hania. Open 24hr.

Telephones: OTE, Tzanakaki 5 (☎11 888). Open M and W 7:45am-1:45pm, Tu and Th-F 7:45am-8pm.

Internet Access: Triple W Internet Cafe (☎93 478), on Baladinou, just off Halidon. Prints, burns CDs, faxes, scans, has webcams, and uploads digital photos. Internet €2 per hr. Coffee and mixed drinks €1.80-6. Sandwiches and snacks €2-6. Open 24hr. **Cosmos 2½** (☎74 499), in Pl. Venizelou at the end of Halidon in the Old Harbor, provides full computer services and Wi-Fi. €2 per hr. Drinks €1-4. Open daily 9am-2am.

Post Office: Tzanakaki 3 (☎28 445). Western Union available. Open M-F 7:30am-8pm, Sa 7:30am-2pm. **Postal Code:** 73100.

■ ACCOMMODATIONS AND CAMPING

Inexpensive rooms are hard to come by, especially since some of the cheapest pensions recently have been shut down. The New Town pensions have dazzling views of the harbor but are near noisy night spots. Reasonable prices, though, can be found in the Old Town. Reception desks usually open between 8-10am, so call ahead if you plan to arrive early.

CRETE

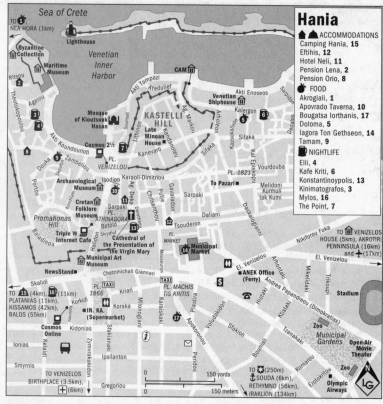

Hania

▲▲ ACCOMMODATIONS
Camping Hania, 15
Eftihis, 12
Hotel Neli, 11
Pension Lena, 2
Pension Orio, 8
🍴 FOOD
Akrogiali, 1
Apovrado Taverna, 10
Bougatsa Iorthanis, 17
Doloma, 5
Iagora Ton Gethseon, 14
Tamam, 9
🍸 NIGHTLIFE
Elli, 4
Kafe Kriti, 6
Konstantinoypolis, 13
Kinimatografos, 3
Mylos, 16
The Point, 7

Pension Lena, Ritsou 5 (☎86 860). Turning off Theotokopoulou on the way to the Byzantine Collection reveals a street lined with multicolored buildings and potted plants that provide a homey atmosphere. With TV, A/C, bath, hot pot, and a random assortment of dishes and books in every room, as well as a communal roof deck, these feel more like studios than hostel rooms. Singles €25; doubles €35; triples €45. ❷

Pension Orio, Zambeliou 77 (☎94 357). Located in the heart of the twisting cobblestone roads that make up the Old Harbor, Pension Orio serves a bountiful included breakfast that lures even the wariest travelers up its steep, spiral stairwell to snuggle into one its chintzy bedrooms. Singles €25-30; doubles €35-40; triples €40. ❷

Eftihis, Tsouderon 21 (☎46 829). Turning right off Halidon onto Skrydlof will lead you to a street of trendy shops, where you'll find the most affordable rooms in the city. Simple and fairly clean with balcony and A/C, these rooms provide a convenient home base in the center of the Old Harbor. The friendly owners say to call any time for a reservation. Singles €15; doubles €20; triples €30. ❶

Hotel Neli, Isodion 21-23 (☎55 533; www.nelistudios.com). You can feel like a Venetian doge standing on your own wrought-iron balcony overlooking narrow cobblestoned streets at this classy pension in the Old Harbor. Spacious and elegant rooms, with kitchenette, fridge, bath, TV, and A/C, are blocks away from the center of the city at Pl. El. Venizelou. Singles €30; doubles €38-45; triples €40-50; quads €50-60. ❸

Camping Hania, Ag. Apostoli (☎31 138). Take Skalidi west out of town and continue as it becomes Kisamou. 4km down the road, take a right at the sign. Alternatively, take the bus to Kallimaki (15min., every 15min., €1) from Pl. 1866 and get off once you see the signs. Sequestered within walls among a number of hotels and apartments, this site has laundry (€4.50), a pool, a restaurant, and a mini-mart. Proximity to the beach (450m) is another plus. €6 per person, €4 per tent. Tent rental €10. ❶

◘ FOOD

You can build a fantasy meal from the snacks at the open-air **Municipal Market** in cleverly named Pl. Market. The smells of cheeses (€7-8.30 per wheel), meats (€4-9.50 per kg), fish (€3-10 per kg), spices, and baked goods waft from the stalls, which sell everything from sea sponges to sunglasses. (Open daily 8am-2:30pm, Tu and Th-F also 6-9pm.) Inside, **Iagora Ton Gethseon** ❷ provides freshly cooked seafood. (Most fish dishes €4.50-9. Open daily 10am-4pm.) For other cheap options, try the well-stocked and convenient **IN.KA. Supermarket,** in Pl. 1866, on the right coming from Halidon. (☎90 558. Open M-F 8am-9pm, Sa 8am-6pm.)

▩ **Bougatsa Iorthanis,** Apokronou 24 (☎88 855). This local favorite serves 1 dish and 1 dish only: *bougatsa* (€2.40), a scrumptious *mizithra* cheese pastry available with or without sugar. Open M-F and Su 6am-2pm, Sa 6am-1pm. ❶

Tamam, Zambeliou 49 (☎96 080). Served in a former Turkish bath complex, traditional Greek meal options abound, and the wine list is even longer than the menu. Many vegetarian alternatives. Complimentary *raki* and honey cake to finish your meal. Pork with cheese in white sauce €7. Wine €6-28. Open daily 1pm-12:30am. ❷

Doloma, Kalergon 5. If you want to escape the tourist-saturated, waterfront cafes and hunker down for a quiet, traditional Greek meal, sneak behind the Venetian shiphouse to order a Greek salad (€3.50) or moussaka (€6) with locals. Complimentary baklava for dessert. Open daily noon-11pm. ❷

Akrogiali, Akti Papanikoli 19 (☎73 110), on the waterfront in Nea Hora, a 12min. walk westward along the water past the Maritime Museum. This beachfront restaurant caters to seafood lovers. Order from a variety of freshly caught local fish (€6-12) and, if you're feeling more adventurous, try the urchin (€9). Open M-Sa 6pm-1am, Su 11am-1am. ❸

Apovrado Taverna (☎58 151). Sarpaki and Isodion. Candlelit tables spill out onto Athinagora under fuchsia bougainvilleas and the shadow of the city's cathedral. In this quiet, romantic setting, you can sample Anna's rabbit onion stew (€8) or aubergine with cheese and tomato (€5.50). Open daily 10am-midnight. ❷

◎ SIGHTS

VENETIAN INNER HARBOR. The **Venetian lighthouse** marks the entrance to Hania's stunning architectural relic, the Venetian Inner Harbor, which retains its original breakwater and arsenal. The Egyptians restored the lighthouse in the style of a minaret during their occupation of Crete in the late 1830s, leaving only the base as part of the Venetian original. On the western side of the main harbor, the **Maritime Museum** describes the tumultuous 6000 years of Crete's naval and merchant history in maps and models, also housing an extensive seashell collection. The second floor houses a large exhibition on Crete's remarkable expulsion of the Nazis in 1941. (☎91 875. *Open daily Apr.-Oct. 9am-4pm; Nov.-Mar. 9am-2pm. €3, students €2.*) The **Venetian shiphouse,** at the end of the harbor where Arholeon meets Akti Enoseos, provides lasting evidence of Venetian influences in Hania. Recently restored, the shiphouse occasionally presents art exhibitions. (*Contact tourist office*

TOP 10 GORGE-OUS HIKES IN CRETE

The mountainous terrain of Crete includes over 30 gorges, most of which are open for a leisurely stroll or daring exploration.

1. Europe's longest (at 18km) gorge at **Samaria** (p. 577) is a must-hike for any self-respecting outdoor adventurer.

2. Don't be intimated by the name. **The Valley of Death** (p. 519), or Death Gorge, is a spectacular 6.5km to the beach full of thriving flora.

3. Scrambling down the ruins of a Venetian bridge will lead you through the grounds of **Gouverneto** to a view of the Cretan sea from overlooking cliffs.

4. If you're in the mood for a bungee jump, **Aredana Gorge** can satisfy your thirst for adventure.

5. Veteran gorge-walkers recommend the **Agia Irini** for those who prefer relative isolation.

6. Drink from Crete's sweetest and highest altitude spring, **Livios,** on your trek to up **Gigilos.**

7. Shaded **Imbros Gorge** provides a walk through WWII history.

8. Pilgrims and explorers alike trek to Agios Nikolaos church, via the **Zaros Gorge** (p. 598).

9. Drink in the ocean view from the mountaintop town of **Anidri** before climbing through the gorge to the beach.

10. Although not technically a gorge, the walk to **Balos** (p. 576) sets a stunning backdrop for the idyllic lagoon to come.

for current schedule.) Turning left on the waterfront from Arholeon you will come to **CMA,** the Center for Mediterranean Architecture, which hosts symposia, conferences, and exhibits open to the public on issues ranging from water management to modern Greek art. (☎27 184. *Call for availability and schedule of current exhibit.)* At the corner of Kandanoleu and Kanevaro, just north of Kanevaro on **Kastelli Hill,** lie reminders of Hania's Bronze Age prosperity, including the **Late Minoan House** (1450 BC) and other fenced-off and unmarked monuments.

MUNICIPAL GARDENS. Enjoy the floral shade of the Municipal Gardens *(Dimotikos Kypos)*, to the left as you walk down Tzanakaki from the city center. Once the property of a *muezzin* (Islamic prayer caller), the garden is now home to an open-air **movie theater** that screens international films (☎41 427; *shows 8:45, 10:45pm; €7),* two tiny zoos that boast an amusing combination of goats and peacocks, and the city's clock tower. In July and August, annual cultural festivals take place, celebrating local and national Greek artists with weekly concerts and performances all over the city—consult the tourist office for details.

ARCHAEOLOGICAL MUSEUM. The Archaeological Museum, on Halidon about 40m past the cathedral, features a broad collection of Cretan artifacts, from early Minoan to Hellenistic times. The building's high-ceilinged halls are lined with clay shards, gold jewelry, Roman floor mosaics, and other artifacts from the Hania area dating from Neolithic to Roman times. A modern room to the right of the entrance displays a bronze cup with a rare inscription in Linear A, the Minoans' mysterious, undeciphered script. The ancient coin collection includes gold tokens once placed in the mouths of the dead to pay Charon, the ferryman of the River Styx, to ferry souls to the underworld. (☎90 334. *Open M 1-7:30pm, Tu-Su 8am-7:30pm. €2, students €1, EU students free.)* You can buy a joint ticket at the Archaeological Museum that admits you to the Byzantine Collection on Theotokopoulou as well. Housed within a former Venetian monastery, which later was converted into a mosque during Turkish occupation, the collection provides a classic example of Venetian architecture in addition to charting the history of Hania from early Christian times to Ottoman rule in wall paintings, mosaics, coins, and icons. (☎96 046. *Open Tu-Su 8:30am-3pm. €2, students and seniors €1, EU students free; joint ticket €3.)*

OTHER MUSEUMS. For a more creative look at the area's history, walk next door from the Archaeological Museum to the **Cretan House Folklore Museum.** Recreating traditional Cretan life through a collection of tools and homemade presentations of scenes from everyday village life, this small, two-story museum bursts at the seams with crafts and practices from traditional Crete, including an embroidery workshop. (☎90 816. *Open daily 9am-3pm and 6-9pm. €2.*) Near the intersection with Skalidi, the **Municipal Art Gallery,** Halidon 98-102, shows rotating exhibits of modern Greek art, which usually last one to three months. (☎92 294. *Open M-F 10am-2pm and 7-10pm, Sa 10am-2pm. €2; students €1; seniors, artists with ID, military personnel, and children under 17 free. W free.*) Those eager to learn more about former prime minister Eleftherios Venizelos (p. 57) can visit the **Venizelos House,** the former residence of Greece's most celebrated political leader, preserved and augmented with documents, photos, and articles. (*Pl. Venizelou, in Halepa, 5km outside the Old Harbor. Follow the scenic coastline east from the Old Harbor for 45min. until it meets with El. Venizelou and Pl. Venizelou, or catch a bus (7min., every 10min., €0.80) in front of the Municipal Market.* ☎56 008. *Open M-F 11:30am-1:30pm and 7-9pm, Sa-Su 7-9pm. Free.*)

NIGHTLIFE

Hania offers several entertainment options. For traditional music and local company, head to **Kafe Kriti,** Kalergon 2, on the eastern side of the harbor. Live Greek and Cretan music plays nightly at 8:30pm; ask the owner, an instructor of traditional dance, to teach you some moves. (☎58 661. *Beer €3. Bottle of raki €5. Open daily 6pm-3am.*) **Konstantinoypolis,** at Dorotheaou and Skydlof, is a typical outdoor Greek cafe by day and a hookah bar by night, with live, traditional Greek music. Removed from the bustle of the waterfront, this late-night cafe allows for mellow people-watching, as the musicians and owner sit at tables outdoors to gossip with customers all night. (*Hookah €10-12. Beer €3-5. Open daily 9am-4am*). **The Point,** Sourmeli 2, also on the Old Harbor, is an oasis for those maxed out on techno and *bouzouki.* The eclectic music, from 1960s hits to hip hop, and balconies with harbor views draw both locals and tourists. (☎57 556; www.pointchania.com. *Mixed drinks €6. Open daily 9pm-late. AmEx/MC/V.*) Techno music pours from **Kinimatografos,** a waterfront club with a serious strobe light. (☎99 293. *Beer €5. Mixed drinks €7-8. Open daily 10am-dawn.*) Next door, **Elli** cranks 1970s American rock up loud enough to be heard over Kinimatografos's thumping bass. (☎72 130. *Beer €3. Mixed drinks €6.*) **Mylos,** a dance club for beach-party devotees, is an €11 taxi away in Platanias (see below).

> **TIP** **THE MIDNIGHT HOUR.** If you're feeling antsy to get your party on in Hania, follow the example of locals and start by having a long, late dinner and a glass of wine or *raki* at a cafe along the harbor. Clubs and bars don't really get pumping until 12-1am; otherwise, you might find yourself nursing a drink with the bartenders and bouncers who man Sourmeli Street in the earlier evening.

DAYTRIPS FROM HANIA

PLATANIAS Πλατανιάς
Patanias is accessible from Hania by bus (30min., every 30min., €1.60). To get back to Hania, either take a cab (€11) or party until the 6:30am bus arrives the next morning.

Platanias's beaches seem to have 1000 tourists for every local. The area's fame springs from a large rock island, **Agios Theodori,** better known in legend as the sea monster whom Perseus turned to stone with the aid of Medusa's severed head. Today, the pumping beats of swanky rock club **Mylos** have the opposite effect, driving packed crowds of mostly European tourists to bump and gyrate. White canvas sheets decorate the ceiling of the converted bread mill, massive amplifiers hang from braided rope, and the DJ spins tunes from a crow's nest above the dance floor. The massive, oval-shaped bar and neon-blue fishtanks draw nightly partygoers from midnight until morning. Take the last bus from Hania, get off at the bus stop at Platanias Center, and walk away from Hania. After about 200m, a huge sign will alert you to the right-hand turn-off that leads past a large parking lot to Mylos and the **beach.** (☎60 449. Wine €6. Beer €7. Mixed drinks €8. M-Th and Su cover €8, F-Sa €10; includes 1 drink. Open daily June-Sept. midnight-8am.)

AKROTIRI PENINSULA

The Akrotiri Peninsula is best navigated by car, which will allow you to visit all of the sights in 1 day. You will need 2 days using the bus due to erratic schedules. From Hania, a bus goes to Stavros (1hr., 6 per day 6:45am-8pm, €1.50); get off at the end of the line in front of Cristiana's Restaurant.

Just northeast of Hania is the sparsely populated peninsula of Akrotiri, home to herds of goats, rows of olive trees, several monasteries, and sheltered coves. Since WWII, it's also been inhabited by American soldiers who live in the US military base there and coexist, sometimes uneasily, with Hania's natives. At **Kalathas,** a small white-sand beach 11km from Hania, sunbeds with umbrellas go for €4 per day. Enjoy the soothing Mediterranean sun from the shore, or swim out to the craggy little island to explore tide pools. Kalathas lies on the route of the bus to **Stavros,** another sheltered inlet with crystal-clear waters and sunbeds for daily rental (€5 for 2 chairs). With a handful of cafes, a calm cove, and a mining hill, you may recognize the scenery from the movie *Zorba the Greek.* Take the bus (1hr., 6 per day 6:45am-8pm, €1.50) and get off at the end of the line in front of **Cristiana's Restaurant.** Just past the Hania airport, 16.5km from the city, is the monastery of **Agia Triada.** Built in 1606 near ruins of a Minoan temple, Agia Triada has produced traditional olive oil since 1632. Take the bus (30min., 2-3 per day, €2) and enjoy a peaceful walk through the grounds and small **museum,** with a collection of mostly 19th-century pieces. You can bottle the experience in the form of the famous olive oil. (☎63 310. Open M-Sa 9am-7pm, Su 10am-7pm. €2.) Follow the road up into the hills, complete with wild goats, unmarked ruins, and narcissus flowers, 4km to ■**Gouverneto.** This austere monastery requires modest dress, so leave your shorts and sleeveless shirts at home. (☎63 319. Open M-Tu and Th 9am-noon and 5-7pm, Sa-Su 5-11am and 5-8pm. Free.) From the monastery, the stone path leading down to the sea passes **St. John's Cave** (1km, about 15min.) and numerous Venetian ruins. Legend has it that St. John was attacked by a bear while drinking from the cave's fountains. Before any harm was done, a miracle turned the animal to stone, saving the monk and preserving the outline of the beast in the shape of the cave's stalagmite patterns. Following the path farther leads you through the ruins of a bridge complex and into the rocky gorge below, eventually presenting a spectacular vista from bluffs and Venetian ruins overlooking the Cretan Sea (5km, 1hr.). It's worth the long, rocky walk, but remember to bring sunblock and a water bottle.

Cristiana's Restaurant ❸, one of the few restaurants in Stavros, Cristiana's is set under a large wooden roof on stone floors, with a view of the water. (☎39 152. Greek salad €3.50. Shrimp with bacon €12. Open daily 7:30am-11pm.) Get refreshments under a lush grape arbor 100m inland at **Zorba's Original Tavern ❷.** (☎39 402. Souvlaki €5.20. Open daily 8:30am-midnight.)

BALOS

You can reach Balos by car or boat. To drive there, take Skalidi west out of Hania toward Kissamos. You will hit Kissamos after about 40km of beautiful countryside. Pass the town and in about 3km look for a sign for a phone on the side of the road. Make a right at the phone (you also will see signs for Kaliviani), and make an immediate left by the sign for the Balos Hotel. After about 1km, you will pass through a tiny town. Just outside of it, make a right at the small sign for Balos. After 5km on this road, you will pass a white chapel; the parking lot lies 3km beyond the church. When you arrive at the parking lot, take the small marked path and hike 30min. to the lagoon.

Nestled away on the northwestern tip of Crete, Balos's heavenly ▣**blue lagoon** is Crete's uncontested best beach, where sand, sea, and sky melt into one. Almost entirely enclosed by bright-white sand, the lagoon's knee-deep, warm water drifts seamlessly into the deeper, brilliant blue water closer to shore. For those more inclined to hike than lounge on the beach, take one of the **boat cruises** that leave from Kissamos port, 3km outside of town along the main road heading away from Hania. The boat stops at nearby **Gramvousa,** an island with a 16th-century Venetian fortress and a cave that supposedly led the Minoans to Scandinavia in ancient times. The steep walk up to the fortress yields a breathtaking view of the sheer cliffs of Crete and the sparkling water below.

SAMARIA GORGE Φαράγγι της Σαμαριάς   ☎28250

The most popular excursion on Crete is the spectacular 5-6hr. hike down the ▣**Samaria Gorge,** a formidable 18km pass through the **White Mountains National Park.** (Open May-Oct. 6am-6pm. €5, under 15 and student groups free. Keep your ticket, as you must return it when you exit.) The gorge is the longest in Europe, and was sculpted over 14 million years by rainwater. The rocky trail can trip you up, but if you take a look around you'll see epiphytes (plants that don't need soil to grow) peeking out from sheer rock walls, wildflowers bordering the path, elusive *kri-kri* (wild goats) clambering around, and endangered gryphon vultures and golden eagles soaring overhead. People have lived in and around the gorge for centuries, as the 1379 church of **Saint Maria of Egypt** attests.

The town of **Xyloskalo** boasts no more than the ticket booth, a cafeteria, a shop, and the last toilets you'll see for hours. From the trailhead, follow a noisy but nearly dry river with turquoise waterfalls and pass between stunningly steep cliff walls as high as 600m and as narrow as 3.5m. Much of the hike is shaded by clumps of pines and by the walls of the gorge itself. For the first 6km, the trail continues the steady, seemingly never-ending descent into the gorge. After 1km more, hikers reach the former village of **Samaria,** inhabited in prehistoric times and part of the national park since 1962. The trail continues past Samaria on a rocky riverbed through the narrowest part of the gorge. You'll end up in the small beach town of **Agia Roumeli** on the southern coast; from there, experienced hikers can embark on a 10hr. trail to **Hora Sfakion** (p. 578) along one of the most outstanding coastlines in Greece. Another option is to take a path from Xyloskalo that ascends **Mount Gigilos** to the west, passing Linoseli, a crisp spring frequented by Zeus in myth. If you're only interested in the gorge's final, dramatic tail, you can start at Agia Roumeli; the path begins behind Hotel Livikon at the rear of the village. This 1½hr. climb to the north takes you through the gorge's narrowest pass: the **Iron Gates.**

If you go early, the soft morning light lends the park a surreal, lunar feel. It's always smart to bring water, trail snacks, and supportive shoes with good treads. One small water bottle will suffice; potable water sources line the trail. There are enforced rules concerning littering, so make sure to dispose of your trash in one of the bins along the trail. The gorge is dry and dusty in summer, and worn stones on the path are very slippery. If you get tired, look for **donkey taxis** that wait to pick up weary travelers at sporadic rest stations. Be sure to bring enough **cash** to get to the gorge and home again; there are **no banks** on either end.

If you want to spend the night in Omalos, **Gigilos Hotel ❶**, on the main road, is a good place to rest up before the hike. (☎28210 67 181. Singles €15-20; doubles €20-25; triples €30-35.) The town of Agia Roumeli, at the end of the gorge, caters to tired, hungry hikers. Though it has little more than restaurants, souvenir shops, and lodgings, its peaceful beach is a well-deserved reward for a hard day's hike. **Hotel Agia Roumeli ❷** is a good place to crash, with air-conditioning and a balcony. (☎91 241. Singles €25-30; doubles €40; triples €45.) **Kri-Kri ❸,** on the left on the street from the gorge, has somewhat cramped rooms with air-conditioning, fridge, and a small balcony. (☎91 089. Doubles and triples €30-45. AmEx/MC/V.)

For gorge info, call the **Hania Forest Service** (☎28210 97 317) or consult the Hania, Rethymno, or Iraklion tourist offices. Though it's possible to reach the gorge from many tourist towns, Hania is the closest and allows for the most flexibility. **Buses** from Hania go to Omalos and Xyloskalo, the town at the trailhead (1½hr., 3 per day, €5.90). Early buses (7:30, 8:30am, July-Aug. also 6:15am) can get you to Xyloskalo in time for a day hike. From Rethymno, take the 7am bus through Hania to Omalos (€9). Earlier risers can take the 5:30am bus from Iraklion through Rethymno to Hania (€11) to catch a connecting bus to Omalos. The last bus (to Hania or Rethymno €6.50; to Iraklion €11.50) from Hora Sfakion leaves at 7:15pm. **Ferries** run from Agia Roumeli to Hora Sfakion (1¼hr., 3-4 per day, €7.50) via Loutro (45min.), and to Paleohora (1½hr.; Apr.-Oct. daily, Nov.-Mar. 3 per week; €11) via Sougia (45min., €6.30). Buy tickets at the ferry office (☎28250 91 251), a block from Kri-Kri. Call in advance for ferry times. The last ferry arrives at 7pm.

HORA SFAKION Χώρα Σφακίων   ☎28250

The tiny port town of Hora Sfakion, often called simply Sfakion, serves as the southern coast's transportation hub. Its quiet streets and arbor-covered tavernas are a common resting spot after the Samaria Gorge hike, and its location makes it a convenient base for daytrips to the area's smaller gorges and lovely beaches. Walk 8km (2hr.) through the historic footsteps of former British and Cretan evacuees during World War II to the coastal town of Komitades, where you can catch the daily bus back to Hora Sfakion. Ask to be dropped off at Imbros Gorge by one of the buses to Hania (€2.50). At Aredana Gorge, after strapping on your hiking boots, you can cross the vertigo-inducing Bailey Bridge to visit the abandoned traditional Cretan village of Aredana. Descend the challenging, worn muletrack to trek the gorge to its outlet at Marmara beach (2½hr.), from which you can walk 2km along to the coast to Loutro and catch a ferry (15min., 3-4 per day, €4) back to Sfakion. For more information about the hikes and bus availability visit www.west-crete.com or www.horasfakia.com.

Hotel owners in Hora Sfakion know that their town is a convenient rest stop for hikers, and they charge accordingly. Sequestered behind a thick arbor and shaded stone archways, grotto-like ◙**Hotel Xenia ❸**, on the harbor road at the far end from the ferry landing, has refreshing, spacious rooms with air-conditioning, fridge, TV, phone, and a balcony on the shoreline. (☎91 490. Check-out noon. Doubles €35; triples from €40.) Following the right fork of the harbor road uphill past the bakery leads to **Stavris ❷,** where the friendly owners offer clean rooms with bath and balcony with a great view of the western coastline. (☎91 220. A/C €4. Singles €20-22; doubles €22-25; triples €25-32.) The air-conditioned rooms with balcony at **Hotel Samaria ❷,** one of the first buildings on the harbor road, let you cool down without spending a fortune. (☎91 261. Singles €25; doubles €30; triples €40. MC/V.) Catch a bite to eat and a charming seaside view at one of the many tavernas which line the harbor road. **Lefka Ori ❷,** near the end of the harbor road next to Hotel Xenia, serves simple, hearty food and Sfakion specialities. (☎28240 91 209. Grilled octopus €7.20. Stuffed tomatoes €4. Open 8am-late.)

The town consists of one main harborfront road, which opens off a plateia 50m uphill from the ferry dock. Four **buses** (☎28210 91 288) per day go to Hania (2hr., last bus 7:15pm, €6.50), dropping off passengers bound for Iraklion (3hr., €11.50) and

Rethymno (2hr., €6.50) at Vrises. Buses leave Vrises for Rethymno and Iraklion every hour. Don't worry if your ferry is late—the buses wait for the boats to arrive. **Ferries** from Hora Sfakion go to Agia Roumeli (1¼hr., 3-4 per day, €7.50). From April to October, most routes stop in Loutro. To get to Loutro in the winter, go by foot or boat taxi. Schedules can change, so you may want to check with the ticket office (☎91 221). **Boats** also run three days a week to Gavdos, a sparsely populated island that is the southernmost point in Europe (1½hr., F-Su 11am, €12). Daily **fishing boats** to Sweetwater beach, named for the fresh, spring water that bubbles up through the limestone below, leave at 10:10am and return at 5:30pm (€3.50). **Taxis** (☎91 269) pick up at the ferry dock. In the plateia you'll find **Sfakia Tours,** where you can **rent cars.** (☎91 272. Cars €40-55 per day. Open daily 8am-10pm.) The **police station** (☎91 205) lies about 1km up the road away from the harbor in the village. Next to Sfakia Tours is the **post office.** (☎91 244. Open M-F 7:30am-2pm.) **Postal Code:** 73011.

PALEOHORA Παλαιοχώρα ☎28230

Paleohora, 77km south of Hania, is a peninsular retreat flanked by a rocky harbor, smooth beaches, and splendid mountains. Small enough to do without street names, Paleohora welcomes beachgoers, monastery-lovers, hikers, and archaeologists alike with friendly smiles and warm meals.

⌷ TRANSPORTATION. The bus station (☎41 914) is on El. Venizelou on the edge of town. **Buses** go to Hania (2hr., 3-5 per day, €6.50) and Samaria (2hr., 6:15am, €5.50). **Ferries** leave the port for Agia Roumeli (2hr., 1 per day, €11) via Sougia (1hr., €7). Ferries then go from Agia Roumeli to Hora Skafion (1hr., 4 per day, €5) via Loutro (30min.). One boat per day departs Paleohora for Elafonisi at 10am and returns at 4pm (1hr., €7). A boat goes to Gavdos three times per week (3½hr.; M, Th, Sa 8:30am, returns 2:30pm; €15). Constantly changing ferry schedules make planning ahead difficult, so consult a local travel agency for the most current times. For a taxi, contact the **Paleohora Taxi Office.** (☎41 128. Open daily 8am-11:30pm.) You can rent a **car** (€20-45), **moped** (€15-20), or **bicycle** (€3-10) at any of Paleohora's travel agencies.

⌷⌷ ORIENTATION AND PRACTICAL INFORMATION. The town's restaurants and bars cluster around the main thoroughfare, **Eleftheriou Venizelou,** which runs down the center of the peninsula from north to south. Heading north on El. Venizelou takes you to Hania; going south brings you to the ruins of an old castle. El. Venizelou crosses **Kentekaki,** which leads west to the beach and east to the harbor. Turning left on Kentekaki then right on the harbor road will lead you to **tourist information,** two blocks before the port. For cheap car rentals and information about boats and tickets, visit the friendly people at **Notos Rentals,** to the left as you walk up El. Venizelou from the bus station. (☎42 110; www.notoscar.com. Open daily 8am-10pm.) The talented staff also does **laundry, exchanges currency,** and offers **Internet** access. (Wash and dry €8. Internet €1 per 30min. Open daily 8am-10pm.) **Syia Travel,** on Kentekaki past the pharmacy, is helpful for ferry information and tickets, as well as for basic information about the region. (☎41 198. Open daily 9am-2pm and 5-10pm.) **Bank of Hania,** with its **24hr. ATM,** is three blocks up El. Venizelou on your left. (☎83 060. Open M-F 8am-2:30pm.) The **port police** (☎41 214) are four blocks farther down the main street on the right. Turn right toward the beach one block after the OTE and walk two more blocks to the **police station** (☎41 111). Taking a right toward the beach behind the OTE will lead you to the **public health center.** (☎41 211. Open M-F 9am-1pm.) The **OTE** is two blocks beyond the Bank of Hania. (☎41 200. Open M-F 7:30am-3pm.) To find the **post office,** turn right on Kentekaki toward the beach, then turn right again on the beach road and walk 100m. (☎41 206. Open M-F 7:30am-2pm.) **Postal Code:** 73001.

THIRD EYE RESTAURANT

The owner of family-run Third Eye Vegetarian Restaurant, Eftichios Botonakis, is the proud proprietor of the only vegetarian restaurant in Crete.

A Paleohora native, Botonakis has been witness to the various reincarnations of the small beach town—from rural fishing village under a dictatorship to hippie mecca to what is now a popular tourist package destination. Rooted in the ideals of the days when Paleohora was "a hippie resort," Botonakis strives to apply a metaphysical "third eye" when running his restaurant, understanding food, and living his life in alternative ways.

On the presence (or lack thereof) of vegetarians in Greece: "The Greeks love their meat."

On vegetarianism in Crete: "100 years ago, the most traditional Cretan food was almost all vegetarian. People ate meat, but it was once, maybe twice a week. Vegetarian meals like stuffed tomatoes and peppers or potato and vegetable stews were the most typical dishes—and they had no meat."

On Paleohora's countercultural heyday: "My family moved down from the mountains around Paleohora in the 1960s to look for a better life. Back then, the town was all just sand and beach. From 1974—after the university revolution that ended the Greek dictatorship—to around 1982, Paleohora was somewhat of a

⌂⌂ ACCOMMODATIONS AND CAMPING. Most accommodations are located on the side streets off El. Venizelou. Small hotels line the road closest to the harbor, while cheaper rooms can be found in the Old Town past the harbor on the far side of Kentekaki. Just off the beach road, **The Third Eye ❶** provides the best deal in Paleohora with a balcony, air-conditioning, fridge, and common kitchen at a range of prices. (☎41 234. Singles €15-35; doubles €25-35; apartment €40-50.) At **Dream Rooms ❷**, a white building in the middle of the harbor road, your dreams will come true if you've been hoping for a fan, bath, and a common fridge. Some rooms have a balcony looking out on the harbor and surrounding mountains. (☎41 112. Singles €25; doubles €30; triples €35.) **Villa Anna ❹** is a good choice for groups or families. Facing the castle ruins on the main street, turn right before the tourist office, take the second right, and walk toward the beach; the Villa is on the right after two streets. Large apartments with private bath, a lush garden, and a playground are a great alternative to Paleohora's homogenous hotels. (☎46 428. 1-bedroom apartment for 2-3 people €40-50; 2-bedroom for 4-5 €60.) Turn right off Venizelos walking south from the bus stop and walk two blocks to reach **Anonymous Homestay ❷**. In addition to its spacious rooms with bath, air-conditioning, and a common kitchen, there is an intimate backyard garden where you can relax away from the hubbub of the harbor and beach. (☎41 509; www.anonymoushomestay.com. Singles €20; doubles €25.) **Camping Paleohora ❶** is a 15min. walk to the east of town. The campsite has its own **restaurant** and a beautiful pebble beach. Walk away from town on El. Venizelou, turn right just after the bus station, take the second left on the last paved road before the beach, and follow the signs 1km to the site. (☎41 120. Open Apr.-Oct. €4 per person, €3 per child, under 4 free; €3-4 per tent, €3 per car. Tent rental €6 tent rental. Electricity €3.)

◖ FOOD. At sunset the main street closes to vehicles, and restaurants set up rows of tables, converting the street into one long dining area. Off the main street, the **◪Third Eye Vegetarian Restaurant ❶** offers over 50 Asian, Greek, and European dishes, all created from organic ingredients grown on the proprietors' family farm. Every night they prepare 20 dishes and 14 salads for diners, accompanied twice a week by live music— from Indian to traditional Greek—in the outdoor garden. To get there, take Kentekaki in the direction of the beach and look for the signs directing you left. (☎41 234. Entrees under €5. Open Apr.-Oct. daily 9am-11pm.) Stop by the intimate **◪Restaurant Small Garden ❷** and try something from the daily changing menu of non-Greek, creative fusions. Turn right at the OTE coming from the bus stop and go one block. (☎ 42 281. Entrees €8. Open daily 2:30-11pm.) To reach **Niki's Pizzeria ❷,** walk toward the beach past Syia Travel and take the second left; the garden seating area is on the right. Niki's tasty pizzas (€4-6) are cooked in an outdoor, igloo-shaped brick oven and feature a variety of toppings, from pepperoni to calamari. (☎ 41 532. Open daily 11am-2pm and 6pm-1am.)

📺 🎭 **ENTERTAINMENT AND NIGHTLIFE.** The local **cinema** shows American films at 10pm. (€6, children €5.) **Skala,** the main bar in town situated opposite the port, caters to a mellow, lounging crowd outdoors while spinning pop beats inside on the dance floor. Stay all night and you can grab an early breakfast before catching your morning ferry at the port. (Beer €3.50-4.50. Mixed drinks €5-7. Breakfast €1.50-7. Open 24hr.) **Club Paleohora,** across from Camping Paleohora, is the town's popular disco. Follow the directions to the campsite or take the minibus (every 20-40min. 11pm-4am, free) that transports clients from the port to the disco. (☎ 41 225. Beer €3. Mixed drinks €4. Cover F-Sa €5; includes 1 drink. Open May-June 15 and Oct. F-Sa 11pm-5am; June 16-Sept. daily 11pm-5am.)

📷 **DAYTRIPS FROM PALEOHORA. Elafonisi** is a beach across from a small uninhabited island at the southwestern corner of Crete. Visitors wade across the shallow 100m inlet that divides the mainland from the lovely island. Walking away from the mainland along the island brings you to increasingly umbrella-free, pristine beaches of fine-grained sand and translucent waters speckled with small islands. Back on the mainland side are restrooms and a **taverna ❶** with plastic beer crates for seats. (Sandwiches €2.50-3.50. Burgers €3.50. Drinks €1.50-3. Open daily 8am-10pm.) A 300m walk up the dusty road will get you a table overlooking the beach at **Panorama ❷.** (☎ 28220 61 548. Chicken with lemon €6. Open Apr.-Oct. daily 8am-11pm.) Panorama also has **rooms ❸** for those who miss boat back. (Doubles €30-40.) Walk 6km up the road from Elafonisi to reach the cliffside monastery **Chrysoskalitissa,** built from and supported by the cliffs and operated by an order of nuns. The cream-colored monastery will appear on your left when you come to a small church on the left side of the road; continue walking along the main road into the village and take a sharp left toward the monastery at the sign. (Open daily sunrise-sunset. Free. Modest dress required.)

Escape the crowds of Paleohora's beach at nearby **Anidri beach.** Hikers should take the road out of town past Camping Paleohora and continue 5min. until the

hippie resort. People came to explore and see the world. Every day, you could look out on the beach and it would be covered with 100 tents, 25 campfires, and everyone with guitars singing songs. Nudism was much bigger then than it is now. It was a totally different mentality."

On his adoption of "the third eye": "I got the idea for the name for my restaurant when I went to a Third Eye restaurant in Nepal 20 years ago. But the third eye is really a new way to see food—and health—and a philosophy.

"The Greeks have a saying: A laugh starts in the stomach but then goes to the mind. That idea is behind one of the reasons I started this restaurant with my family. Many Greeks have started putting meat into traditional vegetarian dishes to make more profit, but the third eye, something that I think comes more from Asia and different mentalities, is all about trying to welcome everyone—that's why our vegetarian food has a lot of different cultural influences."

Take Kentekaki in the direction of the beach and look for the signs directing you left. ☎ 28230 41 234. Entrees under €5. Open daily Apr.-Oct. 8:30am-3pm and 6-11pm.

road forks. The low road to the right—the easy way—takes you along the coast to the beach (45min.). The high road to the left—the exciting way—brings you through the mountains and up to the village of Anidri. On the latter route, take a right just before the cafe (1hr.) and onto a road with a sign pointing to a church, the gorge, and the beach. Follow this road to its end and make another right. You'll reach a stone road with a sign pointing back to the cafe; turn left and go down to the dry riverbed. Follow the occasional sign and stone marker through the small gorge to the beach (40min. from town). Your only company on the beautiful path will be roaming goats; wear sturdy shoes and bring water and snacks. The pebble beaches at the bottom, especially the one farthest to your left, are smooth, unblemished strips surrounded by high cliffs. Some bathers choose not to weigh themselves down with bathing suits. Most visitors leave by taking the coastal road, which returns you to the right branch of the fork near Camping Paleohora.

RETHYMNO PREFECTURE

Western Crete has struggled for years to maintain its identity amid surging tourism. Rethymno has met success where its neighbor Iraklion has failed, as each town in the area manages to maintain a sense of individuality. Modest seaside towns fill only short sections of the shore with tavernas, leaving long stretches to the birds, waves, and hikers. The melding of Ottoman, Venetian, and Greek architecture complements the blue waters of the southwestern coast and the rich, dark mountains and deep canyons of the interior.

RETHYMNO Ρέθυμνο   ☎ 28310

Rethymno has a reputation for bizarre power struggles. According to myth, Zeus was born to Rhea in the cave of Idaion Andron outside this regional capital. The titan Cronus, antsy about his infant son's approaching dominion, came up with the obvious solution of eating him. Luckily for Greek mythic history, Rhea tricked Cronus into swallowing a stone instead, and Zeus grew up to be king of the gods. Warlike humans followed Cronus's quest for power, though they more often decided to sack and rebuild cities—visible in Rethymno's skyline of minarets and ruined Venetian fortresses—instead of stirring immediate family struggles. Potent *raki*, Crete's answer to ouzo, may cloud the minds of travelers seeking to understand the changing cycles of history that have marked this city, but it certainly will help them begin to understand the companionable Cretan approach to living.

▶ TRANSPORTATION

For **flights,** go to **Olympic Airways,** Koumoundorou 5, opposite the public gardens. (☎22 257. Open M-F 8am-3:30pm.) Buy **ferry** tickets to Piraeus (daily 8pm, €30) at any travel office. **Buses** run from the **Rethymno-Hania station** (☎29 644), overlooking the water off I. Gavriil, and go to: Agia Galini (1hr., 4-6 per day, €5.30); Arkadi Monastery (1hr., 2-3 per day, €2.40); Hania (1hr., 17 per day 6:15am-10:30pm, €6); Iraklion (1½hr., 18 per day 6:30am-10:15pm, €6.50); Plakias (45min., 5-7 per day, €3.90). **Taxis** (☎22 316) congregate at Pl. Martiron 4, Pl. Iroon, and the Public Gardens and are available 24hr.

◀ ⁇ ORIENTATION AND PRACTICAL INFORMATION

Plateia Martiron is between the **Old City** to the north and the **New City** to the south. To get to the plateia from the bus station, climb the stairs at the back of the station's parking lot onto **Igoumenou Gavriil** and go left; Pl. Martiron is to your left just after the **public gar-**

Rethymno

▲▲ ACCOMMODATIONS
Elizabeth Camping, **10**
Olga's Pension, **7**
Hotel Leo, **6**
Youth Hostel, **8**

● FOOD
Diporto, **5**
Katerina's, **2**
Ovelisterio, **9**
Taverna Kyria Maria, **3**

▌ NIGHTLIFE
Karma Cafe, **1**
Rock Cafe Club, **4**

dens. The **waterfront** lies at the north end of the Old City, with a maze of ancient streets filling the space between the main thoroughfare of I. Gavriil and the water. The Venetian **Fortezza** overlooks the waterfront, and a beach meets the city's eastern edge.

Tourist Office: (☎29 148; www.rethymnon.gr). At the far eastern end of the waterfront on El. Venizelou. Pick up free town maps, bus and ferry schedules, and info on rooms, restaurants, and Rethymno Prefecture. Open 8:30am-8:30pm.

Banks: Numerous banks with **24hr. ATMs** line Koundouriotou to the east of the public gardens. The **National Bank** (☎55 228), on Koundouriotou next to the town hall, **exchanges currency.** Another branch is in the Old City on Tsouderon. Open M-Th 8am-2:30pm, F 8am-2pm.

Bookstores: Ilias Spontidaki, Souliou 43 (☎54 307), buys and sells new and used books. Open daily 9am-11pm. **NewsStand,** in Pl. Iroön (☎25 110), carries a wide selection of English books, travel guides, and foreign magazines and newspapers. Open daily 9am-midnight.

Laundromat: Tombazi 45 (☎29 722). Wash and dry €9. Open daily 8am-2pm and 5-8pm.

Public Toilets: On the corner of the Public Gardens closest to Pl. Martiron.

Police: ☎100. In Pl. Iroön Polytechniou. Open 24hr.

Tourist Police: ☎28 156, in the same building as the tourist information office. Open daily 8am-2:30pm.

Pharmacy: Over 35 pharmacies dot the city, each marked by a green cross and a sign reading "φαρμακείο." Each pharmacy lists which one is open all night that evening.

Hospital: Trandalidou 18 (☎87 100). From I. Gavriil at the bus station, take a right on Kriari and turn left onto Trandalidou. Open 24hr.

Telephones: OTE, Koundouriotou 26 (☎59 500). Open M and W 7:30am-3pm, Tu and Th-F 7:30am-9pm, Sa 9am-3pm.

Internet Access: Game Net Cafe, Koundouriotou 8, in Pl. Martiron. This cafe has the best rates in town at €2.50 per hr., €1.50 after midnight. **Cafe Galero** (☎54 345), at the Rimondi Fountain. €3 per hr. Open daily 7am-3am.

Post Office: Main branch, Moatsou 19 (☎22 303). From the OTE, walk down G. Hatzidaki into the New City. Western Union available M-F 7:30am-8pm. Open M-F 7:30am-8pm. **Postal Code:** 74100.

⚑ ACCOMMODATIONS AND CAMPING

Picturesque streets near the fortress and the Venetian port are lined with ideally located but expensive hotels and domatia. A few, however, offer both low prices and an location in the Old City.

⚑ Youth Hostel, Tombazi 41-43 (☎22 848; www.yhrethymno.com). From the bus station, walk down I. Gavriil and take the 1st left at Pl. Martiron through the Porta Megali; Tombazi is the 2nd right. The gardens and outdoor bar (beer and wine €1.50-2) buzz with backpackers. Outdoor beds available in the summer. Breakfast €2-4. Solar-powered showers during the day. Sheets €1. Internet €3 per hr. Wi-Fi €5 per day. Reception July-Aug. 8am-noon and 5-11pm. Check-out 10am. Dorms €9 per night, €54 per week. ❶

⚑ Olga's Pension, Souliou 57 (☎53 206), off Antistasis. You'll feel like part of the family with owners George, Stella, and Yiannis. Enjoy Stella's delicious cooking either downstairs at Stella's Kitchen (Open M-Sa 8:30am-9pm and Su 9am-1pm) or in the rooftop garden. All rooms have ceiling fan, TV, A/C, and fridge; some have bath or balcony. Breakfast €5. Singles €25-30; doubles €30-35; triples €45. ❷

Hotel Leo, Vafe 2 (☎26 197), off Souliou. Decorated with wood floors, high windows, antique lamps, and white stucco, the rooms in Leo's 650-year-old building boast bath and a quiet atmosphere. Singles €30; doubles €35; triples €40; quads €45. ❸

Elizabeth Camping (☎28 694), 3km east of town on the old road to Iraklion. Take the hotel bus from the Rethymno station and ask the driver to stop at the campsite (every 30min. 7:30am-9:30pm, €0.85). Pitch your tent under a bamboo cover at this warm, family-owned campground and take advantage of your proximity to the wide beach. Campers gather at barbecues (€5-8) on Th and at "Save the Sea Turtles" slide shows every F (free). Taverna open 8:30am-10pm. Laundry €4, with soap €4.50. Parking €3-3.50. Safe available. Open Apr.-Oct. €5-6 per person, €6-7 per tent, €5-6 per caravan. Tent rental €8. 10% discount for stays of 7 days or more. ❶

🍴 FOOD

An **open-air market** on El. Venizelou by the New Town marina opens Thursdays at 7am and closes around 2:30pm, though the selection dwindles by 10am. If you don't mind bruised fruit or need to save a few euro, come at the end for the best deals as the vendors try to shed their remaining products. For affordable nighttime eats, tourists and locals head to **Plateia Titou Petichaki.**

Taverna Kyria Maria, Moskovitou 20 (☎29 078), to the right down the small alley behind the Rimondi fountain. Under a vine-draped grape arbor filled with hanging bird cages, Kyria Maria is one of the best bets in town. Octopus in wine sauce (€9) is their

GET CONNECTED & SAVE WITH THE HI CARD

An HI card gives you access to friendly and affordable accommodations at over 4,000 hostels in over 60 countries, including across Europe. Members also receive complementary travel insurance, members-only airfare deals, and thousands of discounts on everything from tours and dining to shopping, communications and transportation.

Join millions of HI members worldwide who save money and have more fun every time they travel.

 Hostelling International USA

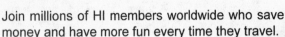

MAP INDEX

MAP LEGEND

⊞ Hospital	✈ Airport	⚓ Monastery	🕯 Lighthouse
℞ Pharmacy	🚌 Bus Station	Ancient Ruins	∧ Cave
🏥 Police	🚂 Train Station	🏛 Museum	⊙ Spring
✉ Post Office	Ⓜ Metro Station	🏛 Temple	Bath
ⓘ Tourist Office	Internet Cafe	Beach	Volcano Crater
🏦 Bank	Restrooms	Hotel/Hostel	Park
Embassy/Consulate	Church	⌂ Camping	Beach
• Site/Point of Interest	Synagogue	Restaurant	Water
☎ Telephone Office	Mosque	Nightlife	Building
Theater	Castle	Ferry Route/Landing	City Wall
Library	Waterfall	Pedestrian Zone	Contour Lines
TAXI Taxi Stand	Mountain Range	Stairs	The Let's Go compass always points NORTH.
	0-999m 1000-1999m >1999m Mountain	Hiking Trail	